FOR REFERENCE

Do Not Take From This Room

CRITICAL SURVEY

OF

LONG FICTION

CRITICAL SURVEY

OF

LONG FICTION

Second Revised Edition

Volume 3

Ralph Ellison - Jamake Highwater

Editor, Second Revised Edition
Carl Rollyson
Baruch College, City University of New York

Editor, First Edition, English and Foreign Language Series
Frank N. Magill

SALEM PRESS, INC.
Pasadena, California   Hackensack, New Jersey

Managing Editor: Christina J. Moose
Research Supervisor: Jeffry Jensen
Acquisitions Editor: Mark Rehn
Photograph Editor: Karrie Hyatt
Manuscript Editors: Lauren M. D'Andrea, Doug Long
Research Assistant: Jun Ohnuki
Production Editor: Cynthia Beres
Layout: William Zimmerman
Graphics: Yasmine Cordoba

Copyright © 2000, by Salem Press, Inc.

Some of the essays in this work, which have been updated, originally appeared in the following Salem Press publications: *Critical Survey of Long Fiction, English Language Series, Revised Edition* (1991), *Critical Survey of Long Fiction, Foreign Language Series* (1984).

Library of Congress Cataloging-in-Publication Data

Critical survey of long fiction / editor, Carl Rollyson ; editor, English and foreign language series, Frank N. Magill.—2nd rev. ed.

p. cm.

"The current reference work both updates and substantially adds to the previous editions of the Critical survey from which it is partially drawn: the Critical survey of long fiction. English language series, revised edition (1991) and the Critical survey of long fiction. Foreign language series (1984)"—Publisher's note.

Includes bibliographical references and index.

ISBN 0-89356-885-6 (v. 3 : alk. paper) — ISBN 0-89356-882-1 (set : alk. paper)

1. Fiction—History and criticism. 2. Fiction—Bio-bibliography—Dictionaries. I. Rollyson, Carl E. (Carl Edmund) II. Magill, Frank Northen, 1907-1997.

PN3451.C75 2000
809.3—dc21   00-020195

First Printing

PRINTED IN THE UNITED STATES OF AMERICA

CONTENTS

CRITICAL SURVEY
OF
LONG FICTION

RALPH ELLISON

Born: Oklahoma City, Oklahoma; March 1, 1914
Died: Harlem, New York; April 16, 1994

PRINCIPAL LONG FICTION

Invisible Man, 1952
Juneteenth, 1999

OTHER LITERARY FORMS

Ralph Ellison's reputation rests primarily on *Invisible Man*, but *Shadow and Act* (1964), a collection of nonfiction prose, established him as a major force in the critical theory of pluralism and in African American aesthetics. Arranged in three thematically unified sections, the essays, most of which appeared originally in journals such as *Antioch Review*, *Partisan Review*, and *The New Republic*, emphasize the importance of folk and popular (especially musical) contributions to the mainstream of American culture. Several of the essays from *Shadow and Act* are recognized as classics, notably "Richard Wright's Blues," "Change the Joke and Slip the Yoke," and "The World and the Jug." In addition, Ellison published several excellent short stories, including "Flying Home" and "Did You Ever Dream Lucky?" A collection of essays, *Going to the Territory*, was published in 1986.

ACHIEVEMENTS

Ellison occupied a central position in the development of African American literature and of contemporary American fiction. Equally comfortable with the influences of Fyodor Dostoevski, Mark Twain, Louis Armstrong, Igor Stravinsky, James Joyce, and Richard Wright, Ellison was the first African American writer to attain recognition as a full-fledged artist rather than as an intriguing exotic. Whereas Caucasian critics had previously, and unjustly, condescended to African American writers such as Langston Hughes, Zora Neale Hurston, and Richard Wright, most granted Ellison the respect given Euro-American contemporaries such as Norman Mailer and Saul Bellow. A 1965 *Book World* poll identifying

Invisible Man as the most distinguished postwar American novel simply verified a consensus already reflected in the recurrence of the metaphor of invisibility in countless works by both Caucasians and African Americans during the 1950's and 1960's.

Within the African American tradition itself, Ellison occupies a similarly prominent position, although his mainstream acceptance generates occasional reservations among some African American critics, particularly those committed to cultural nationalism. A *Black World* poll, reflecting these reservations, identified Wright rather than Ellison as the most important black writer. The discrepancy stems in part from the critical image in the late 1960's of Ellison and James Baldwin as leading figures in an anti-Wright "universalist" movement in African American culture, a movement that some critics viewed as a sellout to Euro-American aesthetics. In the late twentieth century, however, both Euro-American and African American critics recognized Ellison's synthesis of the oral traditions of black culture and the literary traditions of both his black and his white predecessors. The consensus of that time viewed Ellison as clearly more sympathetic than Wright to the African American tradition. As a result, Ellison seems to have joined Wright as a major influence on younger black fiction writers such as James Alan McPherson, Leon Forrest, Toni Morrison, and David Bradley.

Ellison's most profound achievement, his synthesis of modernist aesthetics, American Romanticism, and African American folk culture, embodies the aspirations of democratic pluralists such as Walt Whitman, Mark Twain, and Langston Hughes. His vernacular modernism earned Ellison an international reputation while exerting a major influence on the contemporary mainstream. With a reputation resting almost entirely on his first novel, Ellison's career is among the most intriguing in American literary history.

BIOGRAPHY

Despite Ralph Waldo Ellison's steadfast denial of the autobiographical elements of *Invisible Man* and his insistence on the autonomy of the individual imagination, both the specific details and the general sensibility of his work clearly derive from his experience of growing up in a southern family in Oklahoma City, attending college in Alabama, and residing in New York City during most of his adult life. Ellison's parents, whose decision to name their son after Ralph Waldo Emerson reflects their commitment to literacy and education, moved from South Carolina to the comparatively progressive Oklahoma capital several years before their son's birth. Reflecting on his childhood, which was characterized by economic hardship following his father's death in 1917, Ellison emphasizes the unusual psychological freedom provided by a social structure that allowed him to interact relatively freely with both whites and blacks. Encouraged by his mother Ida, who was active in socialist politics, Ellison developed a frontier sense of a world of limitless possibility rather than the more typically southern vision of an environment filled with dangerous oppressive forces.

During his teenage years, Ellison developed a serious interest in music, both as a trumpet player and as a composer-conductor. Oklahoma City offered access both to formal classical training and to jazz, which was a major element of the city's nightlife. The combination of Euro-American and African American influences appears to have played a major role in shaping Ellison's pluralistic sensibility. After he was graduated from high school in 1933, Ellison accepted a scholarship to the Tuskegee Institute, founded by Booker T. Washington, where he remained for three years, studying music and literature, until financial problems forced him to drop out. Although he originally planned to finish his studies, his subsequent relocation to New York City marked a permanent departure from the South.

Arriving in the North in 1936, Ellison established contacts with African American literary figures, including Langston Hughes and Richard Wright, who encouraged him to develop his knowledge of both the African American literary world and Euro-American modernism, especially that of T. S. Eliot and James

(National Archives)

Joyce. Never as deeply involved with leftist politics as Wright, Ellison nevertheless began developing his literary ideas in reviews and stories published in radical magazines such as *New Masses*. In 1938, Ellison, who had previously supported himself largely as a manual laborer, worked for the Federal Writers' Project, which assigned him to collect urban folklore, providing direct contact with northern folk culture to complement his previous knowledge of southern folkways. Ellison's short fiction began appearing in print in the late 1930's and early 1940's. After a short term as managing editor of *Negro Quarterly* in 1942, he briefly left New York, serving in the merchant marine from 1943 to 1945. Awarded a Rosenwald Fellowship to write a novel, Ellison returned to New York and married Fanny McConnell in 1946.

Invisible Man, which took Ellison nearly seven years to write, was published in 1952, bringing him nearly instantaneous recognition as a major young writer. The novel won the National Book Award in 1953, and its reputation has continued to grow. Starting in 1952, Ellison taught at Bard College, Rutgers University, New York University, and other institutions. In addition, he delivered public lectures, wrote essays, and worked on a second novel. Less inclined to direct political involvement than contemporaries such as Amiri Baraka and James Baldwin, Ellison participated in the Civil Rights movement in a relatively quiet manner. He nevertheless attracted political controversy during the rise of the African American nationalist movements in the mid-1960's. Refusing to endorse any form of cultural or political separatism, Ellison was attacked as an aesthetic European and a political reactionary, especially after accepting appointments to the American Institute of Arts and Letters (1964) and to the National Council on the Arts and Humanities, acts which were interpreted as support for the Johnson Administration's Vietnam policy. During the mid-1970's, however, these attacks abated as nationalist critics such as Larry Neal rosc to Ellison's defense and a new generation of African American writers turned to him for aesthetic inspiration. Retired from full-time teaching, during the 1980's Ellison continued to work on his second novel, *Juneteenth*, which was delayed both by his own perfectionism and by events such as a house fire that destroyed much of the manuscript during the 1960's. The novel was incomplete at the time of his death on April 16, 1994, in New York.

ANALYSIS

A masterwork of American pluralism, Ralph Ellison's *Invisible Man* insists on the integrity of individual vocabulary and racial heritage while encouraging a radically democratic acceptance of diverse experiences. Ellison asserts this vision through the voice of an unnamed first-person narrator who is at once heir to the rich African American oral culture and a self-conscious artist who, like T. S. Eliot and James Joyce, exploits the full potential of his written medium. Intimating the potential cooperation between folk and artistic consciousness, Ellison confronts the pressures which discourage both individual integrity and cultural pluralism.

INVISIBLE MAN

The narrator of *Invisible Man* introduces Ellison's central metaphor for the situation of the individual in Western culture in the first paragraph: "I am invisible, understand, simply because people refuse to see me." As the novel develops, Ellison extends this metaphor: Just as people can be rendered invisible by the willful failure of others to acknowledge their presence, so by taking refuge in the seductive but ultimately specious security of socially acceptable roles they can fail to see *themselves*, fail to define their own identities. Ellison envisions the escape from this dilemma as a multifaceted quest demanding heightened social, psychological, and cultural awareness.

The style of *Invisible Man* reflects both the complexity of the problem and Ellison's pluralistic ideal. Drawing on sources such as the blindness motif from *King Lear* (1605), the underground man motif from Fyodor Dostoevski, and the complex stereotyping of Richard Wright's *Native Son* (1940), Ellison carefully balances the realistic and the symbolic dimensions of *Invisible Man*. In many ways a classic *Künstlerroman*, the main body of the novel traces the protagonist from his childhood in the deep South through a brief stay at college and then to the North, where he confronts the American economic, political, and racial systems. This movement parallels what Robert B. Stepto in *From Behind the Veil* (1979) calls the "narrative of ascent," a constituting pattern of African American culture. With roots in the fugitive slave narratives of the nineteenth century, the narrative of ascent follows its protagonist from physical or psychological bondage in the South through a sequence of symbolic confrontations with social structures to a limited freedom, usually in the North.

This freedom demands from the protagonist a "literacy" that enables him or her to create and understand both written and social experiences in the terms of the dominant Euro-American culture. Merging the narrative of ascent with the *Künstlerroman*, which also culminates with the hero's mastery of literacy (seen in creative terms), *Invisible Man* focuses on writing as an act of both personal and cultural significance. Similarly, Ellison employs what Stepto calls the "narrative of immersion" to stress the realistic sources and implications of his hero's imaginative development. The narrative of immersion returns the "literate" hero or heroine to an understanding of the culture he or she symbolically left behind during the ascent. Incorporating this pattern in *Invisible Man*, Ellison emphasizes the protagonist's links with the African American community and the rich folk traditions that provide him with much of his sensibility and establish his potential as a conscious artist.

The overall structure of *Invisible Man*, however, involves cyclical as well as directional patterns. Framing the main body with a prologue and epilogue set in an underground burrow, Ellison emphasizes the novel's symbolic dimension. Safely removed from direct participation in his social environment, the invisible man reassesses the literacy gained through his ascent, ponders his immersion in the cultural art forms of spirituals, blues, and jazz, and finally attempts to forge a pluralistic vision transforming these constitutive elements. The prologue and epilogue also evoke the heroic patterns and archetypal cycles described by Joseph Campbell in *Hero with a Thousand Faces* (1949). After undergoing tests of his spiritual and physical qualities, the hero of Campbell's "monomyth"—usually a person of mysterious birth who receives aid from a cryptic helper—gains a reward, usually of a symbolic nature involving the union of opposites. Overcoming forces that would seize the reward, the hero returns to transform the life of the community through application of the knowledge connected with the symbolic reward. To some degree, the narratives of ascent and immersion recast this heroic cycle in specifically African American terms: The protagonist first leaves, then returns to his or her community bearing a knowledge of Euro-American society potentially capable of motivating a group ascent. While it emphasizes the cyclic nature of the protagonist's quest, the frame of *Invisible Man* simultaneously subverts the heroic pattern by removing him from his community. The protagonist promises a return, but the implications of the return for the life of the community remain ambiguous.

This ambiguity superficially connects Ellison's novel with the classic American romance that Richard Chase characterizes in *The American Novel and Its Tradition* (1975) as incapable of reconciling symbolic perceptions with social realities. The connection, however, reflects Ellison's awareness of the problem more than his acceptance of the irresolution. Although the invisible man's underground burrow recalls the isolation of the heroes of the American romance, he promises a rebirth that is at once mythic, psychological, and social:

> The hibernation is over. I must shake off my old skin and come up for breath. . . . And I suppose it's damn well time. Even hibernations can be overdone, come to think of it. Perhaps that's my greatest social crime, I've overstayed my hibernation, since there's a possibility that even an invisible man has a socially responsible role to play.

Despite the qualifications typical of Ellison's style, the invisible man clearly intends to return to the social world rather than light out for the territories of symbolic freedom.

The invisible man's ultimate conception of the form of this return develops out of two interrelated progressions, one social and the other psychological. The social pattern, essentially that of the narrative of ascent, closely reflects the historical experience of the African American community as it shifts from rural southern to urban northern settings. Starting in the deep South, the invisible man first experiences invisibility as a result of casual but vicious racial oppression. His unwilling participation in the "battle royal" underscores the psychological and physical humiliation visited upon southern blacks. Ostensibly present to deliver a speech to a white community group, the invisible man is instead forced to engage in a massive free-for-all with other blacks, to scramble for money on an electrified rug, and to confront a naked white dancer who, like the boys, has been rendered invisible by the white men's blindness. Escaping his hometown to attend a black college, the invisible man again experiences humiliation when he violates the unstated rules of the southern system—this time imposed by blacks rather than whites—by showing the college's liberal Northern benefactor, Mr. Norton, the poverty of the black community. As a result, the black college president, Dr. Bledsoe, expels the invisible man. Having experienced invisibility in relation to both blacks and whites and still essentially illiterate in social terms, the invisible man travels north, following the countless southern blacks involved in the "Great Migration."

Arriving in New York, the invisible man first feels a sense of exhilaration resulting from the absence of overt southern pressures. Ellison reveals the emptiness of this freedom, however, stressing the indirect and insidious nature of social power in the North. The invisible man's experience at Liberty Paints, clearly intended as a parable of African American involvement in the American economic system, emphasizes the underlying similarity of northern and southern social structures. On arrival at Liberty Paints, the invisible man is assigned to mix a white paint used for government monuments. Labeled "optic white," the grayish paint turns white only when the invisible man adds a drop of black liquid. The scene suggests the relationship between government and industry, which relies on black labor. More important, however, it points to the underlying source of racial blindness/invisibility: the white need for a black "other" to support a sense of identity. White becomes white only when compared to black.

The symbolic indirection of the scene encourages the reader, like the invisible man, to realize that social oppression in the North operates less directly than that in the South; government buildings replace rednecks at the battle royal. Unable to mix the paint properly, a desirable "failure" intimating his future as a subversive artist, the invisible man discovers that the underlying structure of the economic system differs little from that of slavery. The invisible man's second job at Liberty Paints is to assist Lucius Brockway, an old man who supervises the operations of the basement machinery on which the factory depends. Essentially a slave to the modern owner/master Mr. Sparland, Brockway, like the good darkies of the Plantation Tradition, takes pride in his master and will fight to maintain his own servitude. Brockway's hatred of the invisible man, whom he perceives as a threat to his position, leads to a physical struggle culminating in an explosion caused by neglect of the machinery. Ellison's multifaceted allegory suggests a vicious circle in which blacks uphold an economic system that supports the political system that keeps blacks fighting to protect their neoslavery. The forms alter but the battle royal continues. The image of the final explosion from the basement warns against passive acceptance of the social structure that sows the seeds of its own destruction.

Although the implications of this allegory in some ways parallel the Marxist analysis of capitalist culture, Ellison creates a much more complex political vision when the invisible man moves to Harlem following his release from the hospital after the explosion. The political alternatives available in Harlem range from the Marxism of the "Brotherhood" (loosely based on the American Communist party of the late 1930's) to the black nationalism of Ras the Exhorter (loosely based on Marcus Garvey's Pan-Africanist movement of the 1920's). The Brotherhood promises complete equality for blacks and at first encourages the invisible man to develop the oratorical talent ridiculed at the battle royal. As his effectiveness increases, however, the invisible man finds the Brotherhood demanding that his speeches conform to its "scientific analysis" of the black community's needs. When he fails to fall in line, the leadership of the Brotherhood orders the invisible man to leave Harlem and turn his attention to the "woman question." Without the invisible man's ability to place radical politics in the emotional context of African American culture, the Brotherhood's Harlem branch flounders. Recalled to Harlem, the invisible man witnesses the death of Tod Clifton, a talented coworker driven to despair by his perception that the Brotherhood amounts to little more than a new version of the power structure underlying both Liberty Paints and the battle royal. Clearly a double for the invisible man, Clifton leaves the organization and dies in a suicidal confrontation with a white policeman. Just before Clifton's death, the invisible man sees him selling Sambo dolls, a symbolic comment on the fact that blacks involved in leftist politics in some sense remain stereotyped slaves dancing at the demand of unseen masters.

Separating himself from the Brotherhood after delivering an extremely unscientific funeral sermon, the invisible man finds few political options. Ras's black nationalism exploits the emotions the Brotherhood denies. Ultimately, however, Ras demands that his followers submit to an analogous oversimplification of their human reality. Where the Brotherhood elevates the scientific and rational, Ras focuses entirely on the emotional commitment to blackness. Neither alternative recognizes the complexity of either the political situation or the individual psyche; both reinforce the invisible man's feelings of invisibility by refusing to see basic aspects of his character. As he did in the Liberty Paints scene, Ellison emphasizes the destructive, perhaps apocalyptic, potential of this encompassing blindness. A riot breaks out in Harlem, and the invisible man watches as DuPree, an apolitical Harlem resident recalling a number of African American folk heroes, determines to burn down his own tenement, preferring to start again from scratch rather than even attempt to work for social change within the existing framework. Unable to accept the realistic implications of such an action apart from its symbolic justification, the invisible man, pursued by Ras, who seems intent on destroying the very blackness he praises, tumbles into the underground burrow. Separated from the social structures, which have changed their facade but not their nature, the invisible man begins the arduous process of reconstructing his vision of America while symbolically subverting the social system by stealing electricity to light the 1,369 light bulbs on the walls of the burrow and to power the record players blasting out the pluralistic jazz of Louis Armstrong.

As his frequent allusions to Armstrong indicate, Ellison by no means excludes the positive aspects from his portrayal of the African American social experience. The invisible man reacts strongly to the spirituals he hears at college, the blues story of Trueblood, the singing of Mary Rambro after she takes him in off the streets of Harlem. Similarly, he recognizes the strength wrested from resistance and suffering, a strength asserted by the broken link of chain saved by Brother Tarp.

These figures, however, have relatively little power to alter the encompassing social system. They assume their full significance in relation to the sec-

ond major progression in *Invisible Man*, that focusing on the narrator's psychological development. As he gradually gains an understanding of the social forces that oppress him, the invisible man simultaneously discovers the complexity of his own personality. Throughout the central narrative, he accepts various definitions of himself, mostly from external sources. Ultimately, however, all definitions that demand he repress or deny aspects of himself simply reinforce his sense of invisibility. Only by abandoning limiting definitions altogether, Ellison implies, can the invisible man attain the psychological integrity necessary for any effective social action.

Ellison emphasizes the insufficiency of limiting definitions in the prologue when the invisible man has a dream-vision while listening to an Armstrong record. After descending through four symbolically rich levels of the dream, the invisible man hears a sermon on the "Blackness of Blackness," which recasts the "Whiteness of the Whale" chapter from Herman Melville's *Moby Dick* (1851). The sermon begins with a cascade of apparent contradictions, forcing the invisible man to question his comfortable assumptions concerning the nature of freedom, hatred, and love. No simple resolution emerges from the sermon, other than an insistence on the essentially ambiguous nature of experience. The dream-vision culminates in the protagonist's confrontation with the mulatto sons of an old black woman torn between love and hatred for their father. Although their own heritage merges the "opposites" of white and black, the sons act in accord with social definitions and repudiate their white father, an act that unconsciously but unavoidably repudiates a large part of themselves. The hostile sons, the confused old woman, and the preacher who delivers the sermon embody aspects of the narrator's own complexity. When one of the sons tells the invisible man to stop asking his mother disturbing questions, his words sound a leitmotif for the novel: "Next time you got questions like that ask yourself."

Before he can ask, or even locate, himself, however, the invisible man must directly experience the problems generated by a fragmented sense of self and a reliance on others. Frequently, he accepts external definitions, internalizing the fragmentation dominating his social context. For example, he accepts a letter of introduction from Bledsoe on the assumption that it testifies to his ability. Instead, it creates an image of him as a slightly dangerous rebel. By delivering the letter to potential employers, the invisible man participates directly in his own oppression. Similarly, he accepts a new name from the Brotherhood, again revealing his willingness to simplify himself in an attempt to gain social acceptance from the educational, economic, and political systems. As long as he accepts external definitions, the invisible man lacks the essential element of literacy: an understanding of the relationship between context and self.

His reluctance to reject the external definitions and attain literacy reflects both a tendency to see social experience as more "real" than psychological experience and a fear that the abandonment of definitions will lead to total chaos. The invisible man's meeting with Trueblood, a sharecropper and blues singer who has fathered a child by his own daughter, highlights this fear. Watching Mr. Norton's fascination with Trueblood, the invisible man perceives that even the dominant members of the Euro-American society feel stifled by the restrictions of "respectability." Ellison refuses to abandon all social codes, portraying Trueblood in part as a hustler whose behavior reinforces white stereotypes concerning black immorality. If Trueblood's acceptance of his situation (and of his human complexity) seems in part heroic, it is a heroism grounded in victimization. Nevertheless, the invisible man eventually experiments with repudiation of all strict definitions when, after his disillusionment with the Brotherhood, he adopts the identity of Rinehart, a protean street figure who combines the roles of pimp and preacher, shifting identities with context. After a brief period of exhilaration, the invisible man discovers that "Rinehart's" very fluidity guarantees that he will remain locked within social definitions. Far from increasing his freedom at any moment, his multiplicity forces him to act in whatever role his "audience" casts him. Ellison stresses the serious consequences of this lack of center when the invisible man nearly becomes involved in a knife fight with Brother Maceo, a friend who

sees only the Rinehartian exterior. The persona of "Rinehart," then, helps increase the invisible man's sense of possibility, but lacks the internal coherence necessary for psychological, and perhaps even physical, survival.

Ellison rejects both acceptance of external definitions and abandonment of all definitions as viable means of attaining literacy. Ultimately, he endorses the full recognition and measured acceptance of the experience, historical and personal, that shapes the individual. In addition, he recommends the careful use of masks as a survival strategy in the social world. The crucial problem with this approach, derived in large part from African American folk culture, involves the difficulty of maintaining the distinction between external mask and internal identity. As Bledsoe demonstrates, a protective mask threatens to implicate the wearer in the very system he or she attempts to manipulate.

Before confronting these intricacies, however, the invisible man must accept his African American heritage, the primary imperative of the narrative of immersion. Initially, he attempts to repudiate or to distance himself from the aspects of the heritage associated with stereotyped roles. He shatters and attempts to throw away the "darky bank" he finds in his room at Mary Rambro's. His failure to lose the pieces of the bank reflects Ellison's conviction that the stereotypes, major aspects of the African American social experience, cannot simply be ignored or forgotten. As an element shaping individual consciousness, they must be incorporated into, without being allowed to dominate, the integrated individual identity. Symbolically, in a scene in which the invisible man meets a yam vendor shortly after his arrival in Harlem, Ellison warns that one's racial heritage alone cannot provide a full sense of identity. After first recoiling from yams as a stereotypic southern food, the invisible man eats one, sparking a momentary epiphany of racial pride. When he indulges the feelings and buys another yam, however, he finds it frostbitten at the center.

The invisible man's heritage, placed in proper perspective, provides the crucial hints concerning social literacy and psychological identity that allow him to come provisionally to terms with his environment. Speaking on his deathbed, the invisible man's grandfather offers cryptic advice which lies near the essence of Ellison's overall vision: "Live with your head in the lion's mouth. I want you to overcome 'em with yeses, undermine 'em with grins, agree 'em to death and destruction, let 'em swoller you till they vomit or bust wide open." Similarly, an ostensibly insane veteran echoes the grandfather's advice, adding an explicit endorsement of the Machiavellian potential of masking:

Play the game, but don't believe in it—that much you owe yourself. Even if it lands you in a strait jacket or a padded cell. Play the game, but play it your own way—part of the time at least. Play the game, but raise the ante, my boy. Learn how it operates, learn how *you* operate. . . . that game has been analyzed, put down in books. But down here they've forgotten to take care of the books and that's your opportunity. You're hidden right out in the open—that is, you would be if you only realized it. They wouldn't see you because they don't expect you to know anything.

The vet understands the "game" of Euro-American culture, while the grandfather directly expresses the internally focused wisdom of the African American community.

The invisible man's quest leads him to a synthesis of these forms of literacy in his ultimate pluralistic vision. Although he at first fails to comprehend the subversive potential of his position, the invisible man gradually learns the rules of the game and accepts the necessity of the indirect action recommended by his grandfather. Following his escape into the underground burrow, he contemplates his grandfather's advice from a position of increased experience and self-knowledge. Contemplating his own individual situation in relation to the surrounding society, he concludes that his grandfather "*must* have meant the principle, that we were to affirm the principle on which the country was built but not the men." Extending this affirmation to the psychological level, the invisible man embraces the internal complexity he has previously repressed or denied: "So it is that now I denounce and defend, or feel prepared to de-

fend. I condemn and affirm, say no and say yes, say yes and say no. I denounce because though implicated and partially responsible, I have been hurt to the point of abysmal pain, hurt to the point of invisibility. And I defend because in spite of all I find that I love. In order to get some of it down I *have* to love."

"Getting some of it down," then, emerges as the crucial link between Ellison's social and psychological visions. In order to play a socially responsible role—and to transform the words "social responsibility" from the segregationist catch phrase used by the man at the battle royal into a term responding to Louis Armstrong's artistic call for change—the invisible man forges from his complex experience a pluralistic art that subverts the social lion by taking its principles seriously. The artist becomes a revolutionary wearing a mask. Ellison's revolution seeks to realize a pluralist ideal, a true democracy recognizing the complex experience and human potential of every individual. Far from presenting his protagonist as a member of an intrinsically superior cultural elite, Ellison underscores his shared humanity in the concluding line: "Who knows but that, on the lower frequencies, I speak for you?" Manipulating the aesthetic and social rules of the Euro-American "game," Ellison sticks his head in the lion's mouth, asserting a blackness of blackness fully as ambiguous, as individual, and as rich as the whiteness of Herman Melville's whale.

JUNETEENTH

Forty-seven years after the release of *Invisible Man*, Ellison's second novel was published. Ellison began working on *Juneteenth* in 1954, but his constant revisions delayed its publication. Although it was unfinished at the time of his death, only minor edits and revisions were necessary to publish the book.

Juneteenth is about a black minister, Hickman, who takes in and raises a little boy as black, even though the child looks white. The boy soon runs away to New England and later becomes a race-baiting senator. After he is shot on the Senate floor, he sends for Hickman. Their past is revealed through their ensuing conversation.

The title of the novel, appropriately, refers to a

day of liberation for African Americans. *Juneteenth* historically represents June 19, 1865, the day Union forces announced emancipation of slaves in Texas; that state considers Juneteenth an official holiday. The title applies to the novel's themes of evasion and discovery of identity, which Ellison explored so masterfully in *Invisible Man*.

Craig Werner

OTHER MAJOR WORKS

SHORT FICTION: *Flying Home and Other Stories*, 1996.

NONFICTION: *The Writer's Experience*, 1964 (with Karl Shapiro); *Shadow and Act*, 1964; *Going to the Territory*, 1986; *The Collected Essays of Ralph Ellison*, 1995 (John F. Callahan, editor).

BIBLIOGRAPHY

Applebome, Peter. "From Ellison, a Posthumous Novel, with Additions Still to Come." *The New York Times*, February 11, 1999. This article gives information on the origins of *Juneteenth*, both historical and personal to Ellison.

Benston, Kimberly, ed. *Speaking for You: The Vision of Ralph Ellison*. Washington, D.C.: Howard University Press, 1987. A useful resource of responses to Ellison's fiction and essays. Also includes an extensive bibliography of his writings.

Bloom, Harold, ed. *Ralph Ellison*. New York: Chelsea House, 1986. A good collection of essays on Ellison's writings, with an introduction by Bloom.

Busby, Mark. *Ralph Ellison*. Boston: Twayne, 1991. An excellent introduction to Ellison's life and work.

Nadel, Alan. *Invisible Criticism: Ralph Ellison and the American Canon*. Iowa City: University of Iowa Press, 1988. A look at Ellison's place in the study of American literature.

O'Meally, Robert G. *The Craft of Ralph Ellison*. Cambridge, Mass.: Harvard University Press, 1980. Traces Ellison's development as a writer and includes considerations of his fiction published after *Invisible Man*.

_____, ed. *New Essays on "Invisible Man."* New York: Cambridge University Press, 1988. A collection of essays which includes many responses to questions raised by earlier critics.

Parr, Susan Resneck, and Pancho Savery, eds. *Approaches to Teaching Ellison's "Invisible Man."* New York: Modern Language Association, 1989. Part 1 surveys reference books, critical studies, and background studies. Part 2 provides several different interpretations of the novel by noted critics. Other sections explore the novel in the context of African American, American, and European traditions, ways to teach the novel thematically, and sample study guides.

Trimmer, Joseph F., ed. *A Casebook on Ralph Ellison's "Invisible Man."* New York: Thomas Y. Crowell, 1972. An invaluable aid to students and teachers, this volume is a collection of social and literary background material useful for understanding the traditions that inform *Invisible Man*. Also contains critical essays.

Watts, Jerry Gafio. *Heroism and the Black Intellectual: Ralph Ellison, Politics, and Afro-American Intellectual Life*. Chapel Hill: University of North Carolina Press, 1994. Chapters exploring critic Harold Cruse's influential interpretation of black intellectuals, the biographical background to *Invisible Man*, the relationship between the novel and black music, the responsibilities of the black writer, and a discussion of heroism conceived as an artistic antidote to racism. Includes notes and bibliography.

LOUISE ERDRICH

Born: Little Falls, Minnesota; June 7, 1954

PRINCIPAL LONG FICTION

Love Medicine, 1984 (revised and expanded 1993)
The Beet Queen, 1986
Tracks, 1988
The Crown of Columbus, 1991 (with Michael Dorris)

The Bingo Palace, 1994
Tales of Burning Love, 1996
The Antelope Wife, 1998

OTHER LITERARY FORMS

Jacklight (1984) and *Baptism of Desire* (1989) are books of poetry (along with a few folktales) which present vivid North Dakota vignettes, as well as personal reflections on Louise Erdrich's relationships to her husband and children. Her memoir of her daughter's birth, *The Blue Jay's Dance: A Birth Year*, was published in 1995.

ACHIEVEMENTS

A poet and poetic novelist, Erdrich learned to draw on her Ojibwa (also known as Chippewa) and German-immigrant heritage to create a wide-ranging chronicle of American Indian and white experience in twentieth century North Dakota and Minnesota. She received fellowships from the MacDowell Colony in 1980 and from Dartmouth College and Yaddo Colony in 1981. Since she began to publish her fiction and poetry in the early 1980's, her works have garnered high critical praise, and her novels have been best-sellers as well. *Love Medicine*, Erdrich's first novel, won the National Book Critics Circle Award in 1984, and three of the stories gathered in that book were also honored: "The World's Greatest Fishermen" won the five-thousand-dollar first prize in the 1982 Nelson Algren fiction competition, "Scales" appeared in *Best American Short Stories, 1983* (1983), and "Saint Marie" was chosen for *Prize Stories 1985: The O. Henry Awards* (1985). Two of the stories included in the novel *Tracks* also appeared in honorary anthologies: "Fleur" in *Prize Stories 1987: The O. Henry Awards* (1987) and "Snares" in *Best American Short Stories, 1988* (1988). In addition, Erdrich was awarded a National Endowment for the Arts Fellowship in 1982, the Pushcart Prize in 1983, and a Guggenheim Fellowship in 1985-1986.

Erdrich's works often focus on the struggle of Native Americans for personal, familial, and cultural survival. Yet her treatment of white and mixed-blood characters also reveals an empathic understanding of the ways in which people of all races long for closer connection with one another and the land.

BIOGRAPHY

Louise Erdrich, whose grandfather was tribal chair of the Turtle Mountain Band of the Ojibwa Nation, grew up in Wahpeton, a small town in southeastern North Dakota. Her father, Ralph Erdrich, is a German immigrant who taught in Wahpeton at the American Indian boarding school. Her mother, Rita Gourneau Erdrich, is a three-quarters Ojibwa who also worked at the school. Erdrich's mixed religious and cultural background provided a rich foundation for her later poetry and fiction.

Erdrich earned two degrees in creative writing, a B.A. from Dartmouth College in 1976 and an M.A. from The Johns Hopkins University in 1979. In 1981, she married Michael Dorris, a professor of anthropology and head of the Native American studies program at Dartmouth. Erdrich and Dorris devoted much of their married life to ambitious family, literary, and humanitarian goals. Dorris, who was three-eighths Modoc Indian, had previously adopted three Lakota Sioux children; together Erdrich and Dorris had three daughters. Professionally, they collaborated on virtually all the works that either one published—whether fiction, poetry, or nonfiction. Thus, Erdrich has acknowledged Dorris's important contribution to her fiction; similarly, she collaborated with him on his first novel, *A Yellow Raft in Blue Water* (1987), and on his study of fetal alcohol syndrome (FAS), *The Broken Cord* (1989). Erdrich and Dorris donated money and campaigned for legislation to combat FAS, which afflicts the lives of many American Indian children born to alcoholic mothers.

Unfortunately, their private lives became difficult. All of their adopted children were permanently affected by the alcoholism of their mothers and led troubled lives after adolescence. One son attempted to extort money from his parents, and their daughter became estranged. The oldest adopted child, Abel (renamed "Adam" in *The Broken Cord*), was struck by a car and killed in 1991, an event that deeply affected the marriage.

Erdrich and Dorris eventually moved from New

(Michael Dorris)

Hampshire to Minneapolis and later separated after fifteen years of marriage. During subsequent divorce proceedings, Dorris, who had been profoundly depressed since the second year of their marriage, attempted suicide twice. He succeeded on April 11, 1997.

ANALYSIS

In a 1985 essay entitled "Where I Ought to Be: A Writer's Sense of Place," Louise Erdrich states that the essence of her writing emerges from her attachment to her North Dakota locale. The ways in which Erdrich brought this region to literary life have been favorably compared by critics to the methods and style of William Faulkner, who created the mythical Yoknapatawpha County out of his rich sense of rural Mississippi. Like Faulkner, Erdrich created a gallery of diverse characters spanning several generations, using multiple points of view and shifting time frames. Erdrich's fiction further resembles Faulkner's in that the experience of her characters includes a broad spectrum of experience "from the mundane to the miraculous," as one critic put it. Erdrich's stories generally begin with a realistic base of ordinary people, settings, and actions. As her tales develop, however, these people become involved in events and perceptions that strike the reader as quite extraordinary—as exaggerated or heightened in ways that may seem deluded or mystical, grotesque or magical, comic or tragic, or some strange mixture of these. Thus, one critic has described Erdrich as "a sorceress with language" whose lyrical style intensifies some of the most memorable scenes in contemporary American fiction.

LOVE MEDICINE

Erdrich's first novel, *Love Medicine*, spans the years 1934-1984 in presenting members of five Chippewa and mixed-blood families, all struggling in different ways to attain a sense of belonging through love, religion, home, and family. The novel includes fourteen interwoven stories; though the title refers specifically to traditional Ojibwa magic in one story, in a broader sense "love medicine" refers to the different kinds of spiritual power that enable Erdrich's Native American and mixed-blood characters to transcend—however momentarily—the grim circumstances of their lives. Trapped on their shrinking reservation by racism and poverty, plagued by alcoholism, disintegrating families, and violence, some of Erdrich's characters nevertheless discover a form of "love medicine" that helps to sustain them.

The opening story, "The World's Greatest Fishermen," begins with an episode of "love medicine" corrupted and thwarted. Though June Kashpaw was once a woman of striking beauty and feisty spirit, by 1981 she has sunk to the level of picking up men in an oil boomtown. Unfortunately, June fails in her last attempts to attain two goals that other characters will also seek throughout the novel: love and home. Yet though she appears only briefly in this and one other story, June Kashpaw is a central character in the novel, for she embodies the potential power of spirit and love in ways that impress and haunt the other characters.

Part 2 of "The World's Greatest Fishermen" introduces many of the other major characters of *Love Medicine*, as June's relatives gather several months after her death. On the one hand, several characters seem sympathetic because of their closeness to June and their kind treatment of one another. Albertine Johnson, who narrates the story and remembers her Aunt June lovingly, has gone through a wild phase of her own and is now a nursing student. Eli Kashpaw, Albertine's granduncle, who was largely responsible for rearing June, is a tough and sharp-minded old man who has maintained a traditional Chippewa existence as a hunter and fisherman. Lipsha Morrissey, who, though he seems not to know it, is June's illegitimate son, is a sensitive, self-educated young man who acts warmly toward Albertine. In contrast to these characters are others who are flawed or unsympathetic when seen through the eyes of Albertine, who would like to feel that her family is pulling together after June's death. These less sympathetic characters include Zelda and Aurelia (Albertine's gossipy mother and aunt), Nector Kashpaw (Albertine's senile grandfather), and Gordon Kashpaw (the husband whom June left, a hapless drunk). Worst of all is June's legitimate son King, a volatile bully. King's horrifying acts of violence—abusing his wife Lynette, battering his new car, and smashing the pies prepared for the family dinner—leave Albertine in dismay with a family in shambles.

Love Medicine then shifts back in time from 1981, and its thirteen remaining stories proceed in chronological order from 1934 to 1984. "Saint Marie" concerns a mixed-blood girl, Marie Lazarre, who in 1934 enters Sacred Heart Convent and embarks on a violent love-hate relationship with Sister Leopolda. In "Wild Geese," also set in 1934, Nector Kashpaw is infatuated with Lulu Nanapush, but his affections swerve unexpectedly when he encounters Marie Lazarre on the road outside her convent. By 1948, the time of "The Beads," Marie has married Nector, had three children (Aurelia, Zelda, and Gordie), and agreed to rear her niece June. Nector, however, is

drinking and philandering, and June, after almost committing suicide in a children's hanging game, leaves to be brought up by Eli in the woods. "Lulu's Boys," set in 1957, reveals that the amorous Lulu Lamartine (née Nanapush) had married Henry Lamartine but bore eight sons by different fathers. Meanwhile, in "The Plunge of the Brave," also set in 1957, Nector recalls the development of his five-year affair with Lulu and tries to leave his wife Marie for her, but the result is that he accidentally burns Lulu's house to the ground.

The offspring of these Kashpaws and Lamartines also have their problems in later *Love Medicine* stories. In "A Bridge," set in 1973, Albertine runs away from home and becomes the lover of Henry Lamartine, Jr., one of Lulu's sons, a troubled Vietnam veteran. "The Red Convertible," set in 1974, also involves Henry, Jr., as Lyman Lamartine tries unsuccessfully to bring his brother out of the dark personality changes that Vietnam has wrought in him. On a lighter note, "Scales," set in 1980, is a hilarious account of the romance between Dot Adare, an obese clerk at a truck weighing station, and Gerry Nanapush, one of Lulu's sons who is a most unusual convict: enormously fat, amazingly expert at escaping from jail, but totally inept at avoiding capture. "A Crown of Thorns," which overlaps with the time of "The World's Greatest Fishermen" in 1981, traces the harrowing and bizarre decline of Gordie Kashpaw into alcoholism after June's death.

Though in these earlier *Love Medicine* stories the positive powers of love and spirit are more often frustrated than fulfilled, in the last three stories several characters achieve breakthroughs that bring members of the different families together in moving and hopeful ways. In "Love Medicine," set in 1982, Lipsha Morrissey reaches out lovingly to his grandmother Marie and to the ghosts of Nector and June. In "The Good Tears," set in 1983, Lulu undergoes a serious eye operation and is cared for by Marie, who forgives her for being Nector's longtime extramarital lover. Finally, in "Crossing the Water," set in 1984, Lipsha helps his father, Gerry Nanapush, escape to Canada and comes to appreciate the rich heritage of love, spirit, and wiliness that he has inherited from his diverse patchwork of Chippewa relatives—especially from his grandmother Lulu, his great-aunt Marie, and his parents, June and Gerry.

THE BEET QUEEN

In *The Beet Queen*, her second novel, Erdrich shifts her main focus from the American Indian to the European-immigrant side of her background, and she creates in impressive detail the mythical town of Argus (modeled on Wahpeton, where she was reared, but located closer to the Ojibwa reservation) in the years 1932-1972.

The opening scene of *The Beet Queen*, "The Branch," dramatizes two contrasting approaches to life that many characters will enact throughout the novel. On a cold spring day in 1932, two orphans, Mary and Karl Adare, arrive by freight train in Argus. As they seek the way to the butcher shop owned by their Aunt Fritzie and Uncle Pete Kozka, Mary "trudge[s] solidly forward," while Karl stops to embrace a tree that already has its spring blossoms. When they are attacked by a dog, Mary runs ahead, continuing her search for the butcher shop, while Karl runs back to hop the train once again. As the archetypal plodder of the novel, Mary continues to "trudge solidly forward" throughout; she is careful, determined, and self-reliant in pursuit of her goals. On the other hand, Karl is the principal dreamer—impressionable, prone to escapist impulses, and dependent on others to catch him when he falls.

The Adare family history shows how Karl is following a pattern set by his mother, Adelaide, while Mary grows in reaction against this pattern. Like Karl, Adelaide is physically beautiful but self-indulgent and impulsive. Driven to desperation by her hard luck in the early years of the Depression, Adelaide startles a fairground crowd by abandoning her three children (Mary, Karl, and an unnamed newborn son) to fly away with the Great Omar, an airplane stunt pilot.

In Argus, Mary tangles with yet another beautiful, self-centered dreamer: her cousin Sita Kozka, who resents the attention that her parents, Pete and Fritzie, and her best friend, the mixed-blood Celestine James, pay to Mary. Yet Mary prevails and carves a solid niche for herself among Pete, Fritzie, and Celestine,

who, like Mary, believe in a strong work ethic and lack Sita's pretentious airs.

A number of episodes gratify the reader with triumphs for Mary and comeuppances for the less sympathetic characters Karl, Adelaide, and Sita. Mary becomes famous for a miracle at her school (she falls and cracks the ice in the image of Jesus), gains Celestine as a close friend, and in time becomes manager of the Kozka butcher shop. By contrast, Karl becomes a drifter who finds only sordid momentary pleasure in his numerous affairs. Meanwhile, Adelaide marries Omar and settles in Florida, but she becomes moody and subject to violent rages. Similarly, Sita fails in her vainglorious attempts to become a model and to establish a fashionable French restaurant; she escapes her first marriage through divorce and becomes insane and suicidal during her second.

Yet even as Erdrich charts the strange and sometimes grotesque downfalls of her flighty characters, she develops her more sympathetic ones in ways that suggest that the opposite approach to life does not guarantee happiness either. Mary is unsuccessful in her attempt to attract Russell Kashpaw (the half-brother of Celestine), and she develops into an exotically dressed eccentric who is obsessed with predicting the future and controlling others. Like Mary, Celestine James and Wallace Pfef are hardworking and successful in business, but their loneliness drives each of them to an ill-advised affair with Karl, and he causes each of them considerable grief. In addition, the union of Celestine and Karl results in the birth of Dot Adare (who grows up to be the ill-tempered lover of Gerry Nanapush in the *Love Medicine* story "Scales"); since Celestine, Mary, and Wallace all spoil the child, Dot turns out, in Wallace's words, to have "all of her family's worst qualities." As a teenager, Dot herself comes to grief when she is mortified to learn that the well-meaning Wallace has rigged the election for Queen of the Argus Beet Festival so that she, an unpopular and ludicrously unlikely candidate, will win.

Yet in addition to the defeats and disappointments that all the characters bear, Erdrich dramatizes the joy that they derive from life. The compensations of family and friendship—ephemeral and vulnerable as these may be—prove to be significant for all the characters at various times in the story, particularly at the end. The irrepressible vitality of these people, troublesome as they often are to one another, keeps the reader involved and entertained throughout the novel.

TRACKS

Erdrich's third novel, *Tracks*, is concentrated, intense, and mystical. It is the shortest, covers a time span of only twelve years, and alternates between only two first-person narrators. This compression serves the story well, for the human stakes are high. At first, and periodically throughout the novel, the Chippewa characters fear for their very survival, as smallpox, tuberculosis, severe winters, starvation, and feuds with mixed-blood families bring them close to extinction. Later in the novel, government taxes and political chicanery threaten the Chippewas' ownership of family and tribal land. In response, Erdrich's Chippewa characters use all the powers at their command—including the traditional mystical powers of the old ways—to try to survive and maintain their control over the land.

Nanapush, one of the novel's two narrators, is an old Chippewa whom Erdrich names for the trickster rabbit in tribal mythology who repeatedly delivers the people from threatening monsters. In *Tracks*, Erdrich's Nanapush often does credit to his mythological model, Nanabozho, by wielding the trickster rabbit's powers of deliverance, wiliness, and humor. He saves Fleur Pillager, a seventeen-year-old girl who is the last but one of the Pillager clan, from starvation. Later he delivers young Eli Kashpaw from the sufferings of love by advising him how to win Fleur's heart. Also, Nanapush is instrumental in saving the extended family that forms around Fleur, Eli, and himself. This family grows to five when Fleur gives birth to a daughter, Lulu, and Eli's mother, Margaret Kashpaw, becomes Nanapush's bedmate. As these five come close to starvation, Nanapush sends Eli out to hunt an elk; in one of the most extraordinary passages of the novel, Nanapush summons a power vision of Eli hunting that the old man imagines is guiding Eli to the kill. Nanapush also demonstrates the

humor associated with his mythological model in his wry tone as a narrator, his sharp wit in conversation, and the tricks that he plays on his family's mixed-blood antagonists: the Pukwans, Morrisseys, and Lazarres.

Foremost among these antagonists is the novel's other narrator, Pauline Pukwan. A "skinny big-nosed girl with staring eyes," Pauline circulates in Argus from the Kozkas' butcher shop to the Sacred Heart Convent, and on the reservation from the Nanapush-Pillager-Kashpaw group to the Morrissey and Lazarre clans. At first attracted to Fleur by the beauty and sexual power that she herself lacks, Pauline later takes an envious revenge by concocting a love potion that seems to drive Fleur's husband, Eli, and Sophie Morrissey to become lovers. Ironically, though one side of her believes in a Catholic denial of her body, Pauline later gives birth out of wedlock to a girl named Marie, and at the end of her narrative Pauline enters the convent to become Sister Leopolda—the cruel nun who later torments her own daughter, Marie Lazarre, in *Love Medicine*.

Though Erdrich clearly feels passionately about the sufferings visited on her Chippewa characters in *Tracks*, she treats this politically charged material with her usual disciplined restraint. Her dispassionate, deadpan use of first-person narrators (never broken by authorial commentary) matches the understated, stoic attitude that Nanapush adopts toward the numerous waves of hardship and betrayal that the Chippewas must endure.

If in some ways *Tracks* seems to conclude with a feeling of fragmentation and defeat, in other ways it strikes positive notes of solidarity and survival, especially when considered in relation to *Love Medicine* and *The Beet Queen*. Fleur disappears, leaving her husband and daughter, but Nanapush uses his wiliness to become tribal chairman and then to retrieve Lulu from a distant boarding school. At the end, the reader is reminded that Nanapush has addressed his entire narrative to Lulu: The old man hopes that his story will convince Lulu to embrace the memory of Fleur, "the one you will not call mother." Further, the reader familiar with *Love Medicine* will realize how this young girl, who becomes Lulu Lamartine, carries on the supernaturally powerful sexuality of her mother Fleur and the wily talent for survival of Nanapush, the old man who gave her his name and reared her.

THE BINGO PALACE

The Bingo Palace takes place roughly ten years after the end of *Love Medicine* and follows several characters who were introduced in the first three novels. Primary among these is June Kashpaw's luckless son Lipsha Morrissey, back on the reservation after a series of failed jobs. His uncle, shrewd businessman Lyman Lamartine, offers him a job at his bingo parlor as a part-time bartender and night watchman. After his dead mother June appears with bingo tickets that are destined to change his luck significantly, gentle Lipsha not only wins a prize van but also pockets more of Lyman's money by continuing to win. A further complication in their relationship is Shawnee Ray Toose (Miss Little Shell), champion jingle-dress dancer, with whom Lipsha is promptly smitten, even though she has had a son by Lyman.

This loosely structured novel recounts Lipsha's sweet but faltering courtship of Shawnee, who rebuffs both of her suitors; Lyman's schemes to erect a splendid bingo palace on the last bit of Pillager land; and a joint vision quest that is serious for Lyman but comic for Lipsha, whose vision animal turns out to be a skunk that really sprays him. Lipsha has another abortive reunion with his father, escaped convict Gerry Nanapush, and is left stranded in a stolen car in a blizzard until his great-grandmother Fleur Pillager steps in. Erdrich employs techniques of Magical Realism, as the dead speak and the lake monster Misshepeshu continues to strike terror into the hearts of all except the dauntless Fleur.

THE ANTELOPE WIFE

Erdrich's seventh novel, *The Antelope Wife*, shifts to a new set of characters and a new locale, Minnesota. A young cavalry private, Scranton Roy, is sent to quell an American Indian uprising but mistakenly attacks a neutral Ojibwa village. Realizing his error, he manages to rescue a baby whom he then nurses with his own miraculous milk and raises to adulthood. In this way the white Roy family begins a relationship that spans five generations with two Ojibwa families.

The infant's grieving mother marries a man named Showano and bears twin girls. Her twin granddaughters Zosie and Mary Showano figure prominently as the wife and the lover of Scranton Roy's grandson and as the two mothers of Rozina Roy Whiteheart Reads, herself the mother of twin daughters. Rozina wants to leave her husband Richard for a Minneapolis baker, Frank Showano. Although this novel was completed just before Michael Dorris's death, it is uncomfortably prescient in its account of the unhappy marriage between Rozina and her suicidal husband.

This is a novel of repeated family patterns (lost mothers, lost daughters), emphasized by the linking imagery of the archetypal headings that introduce each section. In this subtle and seamless blending of Ojibwa myth with contemporary life, Magical Realism becomes even more pronounced. Frank Showano's brother Klaus is nearly destroyed by his infatuation with a seductive, shape-shifting antelope woman. The windigo, a cannibal hunger spirit, is a very real presence and threat, while some chapters are narrated by a talking dog named Almost Soup. *The Antelope Wife* affirms the vitality of Ojibwa culture on and off the reservation.

If Louise Erdrich had been born two hundred years earlier, she might have become a traditional Ojibwa storyteller, whose tales would have reminded her listeners of their unchanging relationship to the land and to the mythic and legendary characters who inhabited it. Several generations removed from such a stable and undamaged culture, Erdrich nevertheless was able to create a richly neotribal view of people and place. Her novels testify to the profound interrelatedness of her characters—American Indian and white, contemporaries and ancestors—both with one another and with their midwestern homeland.

Terry L. Andrews, updated by Joanne McCarthy

OTHER MAJOR WORKS

POETRY: *Jacklight*, 1984; *Baptism of Desire*, 1989.

NONFICTION: *The Blue Jay's Dance: A Birth Year*, 1995.

CHILDREN'S LITERATURE: *The Birthbark House*, 1999.

BIBLIOGRAPHY

Beidler, Peter G., and Gay Barton. *A Reader's Guide to the Novels of Louise Erdrich.* Columbia: University of Missouri Press, 1999. An informative handbook for students of Erdrich.

Brehm, Victoria. "The Metamorphoses of an Ojibwa *Manido*." *American Literature* 68 (December, 1996): 677-706. This article traces the evolution of the legendary Ojibwa water monster Micipijiu (Misshepeshu), with a fascinating section on the symbolism and significance of the monster in Erdrich's *Love Medicine, Tracks,* and *The Bingo Palace.*

Chavkin, Allan, ed. *The Chippewa Landscape of Louise Erdrich.* Tuscaloosa: University of Alabama Press, 1999. Essays by Allan Chavkin, John Purdy, and Annette Van Dyke, among others. Covers most of Erdrich's oeuvre.

Erdrich, Louise. "Where I Ought to Be: A Writer's Sense of Place." *The New York Times Book Review* 91 (July 28, 1985): 1, 23-24. In this invaluable essay, Erdrich discusses her roots and sense of purpose as a writer. She describes contemporary American society as a nomadic culture that is in danger of losing its humanity and argues that writers should cultivate an exhaustively detailed sense of a specific place, no matter how trivial and vulgar some of the cultural details of that place may seem.

Ferguson, Suzanne. "The Short Stories of Louise Erdrich's Novels." *Studies in Short Fiction* 33 (Fall, 1996): 541-555. Ferguson examines four of Erdrich's prizewinning short stories, "Saint Marie" and "Scales" (later chapters 2 and 11 of *Love Medicine*), and "Fleur" and "Snares" (chapters 2 and 5 of *Tracks*), highlighting the shifts in character, emphasis, and interpretation between their initial publication in short-story form and their later form in the novels.

Smith, Jeanne Rosier. *Writing Tricksters: Mythic Gambols in American Ethnic Literature.* Berkeley: University of California Press, 1997. A thorough examination of ethnic trickster figures as they appear in the work of Maxine Hong Kingston, Louise Erdrich, and Toni Morrison. Chapter 3 explores the trickster characteristics of Old Nanapush, Gerry Nanapush, Lipsha Morrissey, Fleur Pillager, and others.

Stookey, Lorena Laura. *Louise Erdrich: A Critical Companion.* Westport, Conn.: Greenwood Press, 1999. A good study of Erdrich's works. Includes bibliographical references and an index.

F

JAMES T. FARRELL

Born: Chicago, Illinois; Feburary 27, 1904
Died: New York, New York; August 22, 1979

PRINCIPAL LONG FICTION

Young Lonigan: A Boyhood in Chicago Streets, 1932
Gas-House McGinty, 1933
The Young Manhood of Studs Lonigan, 1934
Judgment Day, 1935
Studs Lonigan: A Trilogy, 1935
    (collective title for *Young
    Lonigan*, *The Young Man-
    hood of Studs Lonigan*, and
    Judgment Day)
A World I Never Made, 1936
No Star Is Lost, 1938
Tommy Gallagher's Crusade,
    1939
Father and Son, 1940
Ellen Rogers, 1941
My Days of Anger, 1943
Bernard Clare, 1946
The Road Between, 1949
This Man and This Woman,
    1951
Yet Other Waters, 1952
The Face of Time, 1953
Boarding House Blues, 1961
The Silence of History, 1963
What Time Collects, 1964
When Time Was Born, 1966
Lonely for the Future, 1966
New Year's Eve/1929, 1967
A Brand New Life, 1968
Judith, 1969
Invisible Swords, 1971
The Dunne Family, 1976
The Death of Nora Ryan, 1978

OTHER LITERARY FORMS

James T. Farrell began his career, as so many other novelists have done, by writing short stories, and his more than two hundred tales are an integral part of the vast world he portrays. Most of his stories have been gathered in collections such as *Calico Shoes and Other Stories* (1934) and *$1,000 a Week and Other Stories* (1942), but there are several stories and manuscript works that remain unpublished. His poetry, collected by Farrell himself in a 1965 edition, seems to be the product of early and late speculations—the early poetry probably coming from the period of *Studs Lonigan* and the later poetry seemingly produced during the early 1960's when he was beginning his "second career" with *A Universe of Time*, an unfinished multicycled series of novels, stories, and

(CORBIS/Bettmann)

poems. All the poetry is uneven in quality and, despite some remarkable effects, is not memorable. Farrell also published volumes of literary criticism, cultural criticism, and essays on a wide range of subjects. *The Mowbray Family* (1946), a play written with Hortense Alden Farrell, is a dramatic treatment of the same material that he treats brilliantly in his fiction. The drama, however, lacks the vitality of his novels and seems lifeless alongside a work such as *My Days of Anger.* His letters remain to be collected, and his biography has yet to be completed.

Achievements

Farrell's career encompassed many diverse literary movements and trends. He was active to the end of a long life, publishing his last novel in the year before his death. On the evidence of his three major complete works, the *Studs Lonigan* trilogy, the Danny O'Neill series (or the O'Neill-O'Flaherty series, as Farrell preferred to call it), and the Bernard Carr trilogy, Farrell presented urban America and the people who sprang from it with a brutal candor rarely equaled in American literature.

His youth, spent in Irish-Catholic, lower- and middle-class Chicago, gave him the milieu from which a whole society could be examined and explained. His career began with his conscious decision to quit a steady job and become a writer and survived despite indifference, shock, bad reviews, prejudice, and ignorance. Farrell's social activism led him into and out of Marxist circles, sustained him through attacks by the Marxist critics who accused him of abandoning the cause, and gave him the focus necessary to show Americans an entire society that survived and prospered in spite of its environment.

Farrell never achieved great popularity; his style was deemed too flat and brusque, his language profane, and his methods inartistic. His fiction was considered basically plotless or merely photographic, and he was condemned, especially by the Marxists, for failing to be didactic. In the years following his death, however, the scope of his urban vision has been recognized; Farrell's fictional world has the breadth of conception associated with greatness and has been compared favorably to that of William

Faulkner. Much like Theodore Dreiser, whom he admired, Farrell went his own way when it was extremely unpopular to do so, and his impact on modern fiction remains to be assessed.

Biography

James Thomas Farrell was born on February 27, 1904, in Chicago, where he lived until 1931, except for a short sojourn in New York City during the 1920's. The son of a family of Irish teamsters and domestics, he was the product of a curious dual lifestyle in his youth. One of fifteen children, Farrell was taken, when he was three, to live with his maternal grandparents as the result of his own family's impoverished condition. His grandparents, John and Julia Daly, were of the same poor, hard-working stock as his father and mother, but they were somewhat more financially stable and lived a different, more affluent life. The difference in these two families was important in Farrell's development.

Living with the Dalys, Farrell found himself in a neighborhood of modern brick buildings which were a sharp contrast to the poor, wooden-shack neighborhood where his parents lived with the rest of their children. The personal confusion and divisions of loyalties caused by this unusual arrangement were only a part of Farrell's childhood problems. Living in one household and coming from another made Farrell the center of many family tensions and involved him in most of the family's disagreements.

Farrell entered Corpus Christi Parochial Grammar School in 1911, and through the course of his education was a loner and a dreamer. He became an excellent athlete, taking seven letters in sports at St. Cyril High School. He attended St. Cyril after giving up early plans to attend a seminary to become a priest. He excelled in his studies and was active on the St. Cyril *Oriflamme,* the school's monthly magazine, in addition to being an active member of the high school fraternity, Alpha Eta Beta. He was desperately in need of acceptance, but his classmates sensed that he was different and his social incapacity was another influence on his later life.

After high school, Farrell went to work full-time for the Amalgamated Express Company, where he had worked summers while in school. After nearly two years with the express company, Farrell felt trapped by the routine and, in 1924, enrolled in night classes at De Paul University as a pre-law student. He first encountered political and economic theory there and first read Theodore Dreiser. The financial and mental strain eventually became too much for Farrell, and he left De Paul and the express company in 1925. He then took a job as a gas station attendant for the Sinclair Oil and Refining Company and saved part of his wages for tuition at the University of Chicago.

In eight quarters at the University, completed between 1925 and 1929, Farrell became a voracious reader, enjoyed an intellectual awakening which has been compared to Herman Melville's similar awakening in the 1840's, and discovered that he wanted to become a writer. In 1927, he dropped out of school and hitchhiked to New York City, determined to succeed as a writer. He returned to Chicago in 1928, reentered the University, and began to write, placing critical articles and book reviews in campus publications and in Chicago and New York newspapers. By 1929, he had sold his first story, "Slob," to a little magazine, and his career was launched.

Farrell and Dorothy Patricia Butler were secretly married in 1931. (Farrell was to divorce Dorothy later, marry the actress Hortense Alden, whom he also divorced, and remarry Dorothy in 1955.) Farrell and Dorothy sailed for France immediately after their wedding. In France, Farrell discovered that he had little in common with the American expatriates in Paris and that he had important admirers and supporters such as Samuel Putnam, James Henle, and Ezra Pound. The publication of *Young Lonigan* and *Gas-House McGinty* by the Vanguard Press during this period established Farrell as a writer and confirmed his faith in his vision. He began to publish a great number of short stories, and by the time the Farrells returned to New York in 1932, his conceptions for the entire *Studs Lonigan* trilogy and the first Danny O'Neill novel, *A World I Never Made*, were outlined. He was prepared to become an integral part of American literary history. His contribution to American letters included stormy confrontations with Marxist critics and novelists and a staunch de-

fense of the integrity of art and the artist as opposed to the socialist demands that fiction, and all art, serve the party.

The 1930's were the end of the personal experiences that Farrell used as the material for his major fiction; the *Studs Lonigan* trilogy, the Danny O'Neill series, and the Bernard Carr trilogy are all drawn from the same well. In describing that world, Farrell was determined to "shake the sack of reality" until it was empty. In 1957, he completed his original life plan for twenty-five volumes which were to be "panels of one work" and had begun a second lifework, called *A Universe of Time*, of which he had published seven volumes (*The Silence of History*, *What Time Collects*, *When Time Was Born*, *Lonely for the Future*, *A Brand New Life*, *Judith*, and *Invisible Swords*). Farrell died in New York on August 22, 1979, before this lifework was complete.

ANALYSIS

An understanding of James T. Farrell and his work on the basis of one novel, or even as many as three individual novels, is impossible. Farrell's vision was panoramic, however limited his subject matter may have been, and cannot be understood except in terms of large, homogeneous blocks of fiction. He did not write exclusively of Chicago or of Irish Catholics, but it was on this home "turf" that he most effectively showed the effects of indifference and disintegration on an independent, stubborn, often ignorant, urban subculture. He was at once appalled by and attracted to the spectacle of an entire people being strangled by the city and by their own incapacity to understand their position, and he was most successful when he embodied the society in the life and times of an archetypal individual.

Farrell's three major, complete works total eleven novels; each of the eleven creates another panel in the same essential experience. While the *Studs Lonigan* trilogy, the five novels of the O'Neill-O'Flaherty series, and the Bernard Carr trilogy have different protagonists, they all share a common impulse and reflect Farrell's almost fanatical obsession with time, society, and the individual's response to both. Studs Lonigan, Danny O'Neill, and Bernard Carr are extensions or facets of Farrell's primal character, pitted against a hostile urban environment.

STUDS LONIGAN: A TRILOGY

The *Studs Lonigan* trilogy, arguably Farrell's best and certainly his best-known work, is the story of the development and deterioration not only of the title character, but also of the Depression-era, Irish-Catholic Chicago society from which he springs. In the fifteen-year span of *Young Lonigan*, *The Young Manhood of Studs Lonigan*, and *Judgment Day*, Farrell shows the total physical, moral, and spiritual degeneration of Studs Lonigan.

Studs is doomed from the moment he appears just prior to his graduation from grammar school. His announcement that he is "kissin' the old dump goodbye tonight" is ominously portentous. He drops out of high school, goes to work for his father, a painting contractor, and becomes a member and leading light of the gang that hangs out in Charlie Bathcellar's poolroom. The association with the gang is Studs's life—everything else is "plain crap." Through a swirl of "alky," "gang-shags," "craps," and "can-houses," Studs fights to prove himself to be the "real stuff" and ultimately finds himself a frail, thirty-year-old shell of the vigorous youth he once was. The physical ruin of Studs Lonigan, however, is only the result of larger deficiencies.

Studs is a sensitive, moral being who consciously rejects his innate morality as a weakness. He blindly accepts his Catholic upbringing without believing it. There is never a present for Studs Lonigan—there is only a future and a past. In *Young Lonigan*, the future is the vision of Studs standing triumphantly astride the fireplug at 58th and Prairie proclaiming his ascendancy to the brotherhood of the gang. The past is his rejection of juvenile harassment he suffered as the result of his one moment of ecstasy with Lucy Scanlan in Washington Park. He proclaims himself the "real stuff" and flees from human emotions and the potentialities of those experiences with Lucy.

Studs consistently refuses to allow his emotional sensitivity to mature. The spiritual stagnation which results confines him to dreams of future aggrandizement or of past glories. The future dies, and Studs is left with memories of his degeneracy. His affair with Catherin Banahan awakens new sensibilities in Studs, but he is unable to nurture them, and they die stillborn. His heart attack at the beach, his dehumanizing odyssey through the business offices of Chicago looking for work, his shockingly prurient behavior at the burlesque show, and his final delirium are simply the payment of accounts receivable.

As Studs dies, his world is dying with him. His father's bank has collapsed, the mortgage on his building is due, Studs's fiancée is pregnant, and the gang has generally dispersed. These are not the causes of Studs's failures, however; they are reflections of that failure. Studs is the product and the producer. He is not a blind victim of his environment. He makes conscious choices—all bad. He is bankrupt of all the impulses which could save him. He batters and abuses his body, he strangles his emotions, and he clings to the stultifying spirituality of a provincial Catholicism. As Lucy Scanlan dances through his final delirium and his family abuses his pregnant fiancée, Studs Lonigan's dying body becomes the prevailing metaphor for the empty world it created, abused, and in which it suffered.

THE O'NEILL-O'FLAHERTY SERIES

Danny O'Neill, of the O'Neill-O'Flaherty series, is the product of the same environment, but recognizes that he controls his destiny in spite of overbearing environmental pressures and, by the end of the series, seems on the verge of success. If he succeeds, he does so because he refuses to fall into the trap that Studs builds for himself, and he thus escapes into the larger world that Studs never knows. In the five novels of the series, *A World I Never Made*, *No Star Is Lost*, *Father and Son*, *My Days of Anger*, and *The Face of Time*, Danny not only escapes the strictures of environment but also sloughs off the psychological and spiritual bondage of family and religion and creates his own freedom.

Farrell's most clearly autobiographical work, the O'Neill-O'Flaherty series, portrays Danny's growth from 1909 to 1927—from a five-year-old child to a man breaking from college and Chicago. Unlike the *Studs Lonigan* trilogy, the O'Neill series portrays a larger world and more diverse elements of that world. While the Lonigan trilogy is dependent on the portrayal of its central character for action and meaning, Danny's story introduces more people and more settings and thus illustrates one of the major differences between Studs and Danny. Whereas Studs demands his personal image as a loner but actually depends heavily upon his gang as a prop, Danny begins as an atypical child—the result of his life in a bifurcated family much like Farrell's own—and learns the hypocrisy of the accepted values around him, which prompts him to formulate and depend on his own personal values.

The process by which Danny reaches this understanding is the contorted progress of a hybrid adolescence. Born to Jim and Lizz O'Neill, a poor, working-class Irish couple, he is taken to live with his grandparents, of the lace-curtain Irish variety, because his parents cannot support their already large family. He is accepted wholeheartedly by his grandmother, and he accepts her as a surrogate mother, but he has problems rationalizing his relatively opulent life while his natural siblings are dying of typhoid and neglect. He also refuses, violently, to return to his natural parents, to the poverty in which they live, and to the oppressive Roman Catholicism that his mother practices.

The tensions forged between the two families are the stuff of which Danny is made, but he is also affected by the lonely, drunken promiscuity of his Aunt Peg, the decorous commercialism of his Uncle Al, and the maternal tyranny of his grandmother, Mary O'Flaherty. Danny grows up alone in a world which he has difficulty understanding and which seems to engulf but reject him summarily. He is not a clear member of either of the families that are the heart of the story, he is rejected by Studs Lonigan's gang because of his youth and because he is considered a neighborhood "goof," and he cannot find the love he desperately seeks. Only late in the series does he understand Jim, his father, and come to accept him for what he is—a hardworking, decent, poor, Irish laborer, who loves his children desperately enough to thrust them into a better world than he can make for them.

By the time Danny understands his father, Jim is dying, Danny has discovered the importance of books, he has had a hint of love through a college affair, and he has realized that education may be his key to a broader world. In the course of his intellectual discoveries at the University of Chicago, he has rejected religion and become something of a socialist. He has also discovered that New York City is the hub of the world, and, after quitting his job and dropping out of college in order to pursue his dream, seems on the verge of simultaneously discovering himself and success by migrating to New York.

The O'Neill series, then, comes full circle—from Chicago back to Chicago both actually and metaphorically; the distinction is unimportant. For all his effort to escape what he views as mindless and oppressive, Danny finally seems to understand that his basic character is still that of the poor, hardworking Irishman that, with all its flaws, is at least pitiable rather than repugnant. As Danny prepares to escape from Chicago, he escapes with a fuller appreciation and self-preserving understanding of his heritage and an ability to progress beyond his previous angry rejections. He does not give up his new certainties, particularly in relation to the Church and religion (he has become an avowed atheist), but he displays a tolerance and acceptance of himself and his culture that are the foreground of promised success.

THE BERNARD CARR TRILOGY

Bernard Carr seems to take up the story where Danny leaves it. The trilogy of *Bernard Clare* (Farrell changed the name to Carr in the second novel after a man named Bernard Clare brought libel proceedings against him), *The Road Between*, and *Yet Other Waters*, is Farrell's attempt to represent the lives of a generation of artists in New York during the Depression era and in the circles of politically radical activism.

The trilogy, for the first time in Farrell's fiction, is largely set in New York. Bernard's life in New York, however, is highlighted with periodic flashbacks of Chicago; thus Farrell's integrity of vision is preserved, and Bernard's lower-class origins are discovered. Bernard is the last member of Farrell's Irish-Catholic trinity—he is the embodiment of the whole man whom Studs could not become and Danny might well have become had his story been continued.

Bernard's New York is a world of struggling artists and Communists. In the early New York years, Bernard becomes involved with Communists and then rejects them as being little more than a gang—brutes who demand mindless adherence to the party propaganda, no matter what that adherence does to artistic integrity and vitality. He also recognizes that the dogma of Communism is akin to that of Roman Catholicism—that they are both crutches for weak men.

Bernard's marriage introduces him to family life and the wonder of birth and rearing a child, and it is the spur in his attempt to recover and understand his family and his heritage. During all of these events, Bernard is achieving a limited success from his writing, and by the end of the trilogy he has brought all the pieces together and has found himself, his vocation, and an enlightened ability to see life for what it is and make the most of it.

The Bernard Carr trilogy does not carry the impact of the Lonigan saga, but the diffusion necessary to present Bernard's story precludes the grim concentration necessary to portray Studs and his life. The world expands for Danny and Bernard, and that expansion naturally admits the people, ideas, ideals, and philosophies which are the components of an expanded sensibility.

The dovetailing of the experiences and environments of his three major characters is what ultimately makes Farrell's work live. Their stories make up a tapestry which mirrors the world from which they sprang and rivals it for true pathos and vitality.

Clarence O. Johnson

OTHER MAJOR WORKS

SHORT FICTION: *Calico Shoes and Other Stories*, 1934; *Guillotine Party and Other Stories*, 1935; *Can all This Grandeur Perish? and Other Stories*, 1937; *The Short Stories of James T. Farrell*, 1937; *$1,000 a Week and Other Stories*, 1942; *Fifteen Selected Stories*, 1943; *To Whom It May Concern and Other Stories*, 1944; *When Boyhood Dreams Come True*, 1946; *The Life Adventurous and Other Stories*, 1947; *A Hell of a Good Time*, 1948; *An American Dream Girl and Other Stories*, 1950; *French Girls Are Vicious and Other Stories*, 1955; *An Omnibus of Short Stories*, 1956; *A Dangerous Woman and Other Stories*, 1957; *Saturday Night and Other Stories*, 1958; *Side Street and Other Stories*, 1961; *Sound of a City*, 1962; *Childhood Is Not Forever*, 1969; *Judith and Other Stories*, 1973; *Olive and Mary Anne*, 1977.

PLAY: *The Mowbray Family*, pb. 1946 (with Hortense Alden Farrell).

POETRY: *The Collected Poems of James T. Farrell*, 1965.

NONFICTION: *A Note on Literary Criticism*, 1936; *The League of Frightened Philistines and Other Papers*, 1945; *The Fate of Writing in America*, 1946; *Literature and Morality*, 1947; *The Name Is Fogarty: Private Papers on Public Matters*, 1950; *Reflections at Fifty and Other Essays*, 1954; *My Baseball Diary*, 1957; *It Has Come To Pass*, 1958; *On Irish Themes*, 1982.

BIBLIOGRAPHY

Bogardus, Ralph F., and Fred Hobson. *Literature at the Barricades: The American Writer in the 1930s*. Tuscaloosa: University of Alabama Press, 1982. This three-part work on American writers of the 1930's includes two essays on Farrell. The essay by Donald Pizer shows how *Studs Lonigan* incorporates the attitudes toward character and experience associated with the 1930's. A reprint of a 1939 essay by Farrell himself provides a convincing description of the 1930's writer.

Branch, Edgar M. *James T. Farrell*. New York: Twayne, 1971. After tracing Farrell's "plebeian origin," Branch discusses major works including the *Studs Lonigan* trilogy, the *O'Neill-O'Flaherty* series, and the Bernard Carr trilogy. Essays on other works including the cycle of *A Universe of Time* follow. A chronology, notes, a selected bibliography, and an index complete the work.

_____. *Studs Lonigan's Neighborhood and the Making of James T. Farrell*. Newton, Mass.: Arts End Books, 1996. A look at the Chicago neighborhood of Farrell's youth and the inspiration for the Studs Lonigan series. Includes illustrations, maps, bibliographical references, and an index.

Fried, Lewis F. *Makers of the City*. Amherst: University of Massachusetts Press, 1990. Fried argues that Farrell portrays the city as a liberalizing and democratizing force. Fried does an excellent job of weaving together discussion of Farrell's life, career, and fiction. He also provides a helpful bibliographical essay on other studies of Farrell.

Pizer, Donald. *Twentieth-Century American Literary Naturalism: An Interpretation.* Carbondale: Southern Illinois University Press, 1982. This fine book opens with an essay on Farrell's *Studs Lonigan* trilogy, declared to be "the archetypal thirties novel." Cites techniques such as indirect discourse and stream of consciousness as contributing to the novels' success. Notes, bibliography, and an index are included.

Wald, Alan M. *James T. Farrell: The Revolutionary Socialist Years.* New York: New York University Press, 1978. After a chronology and an introduction, this book follows Farrell's literary career from its emergence in the 1920's through the mid-1970's. Presents Farrell as a prolific and successful revolutionary novelist. Contains a section of illustrations in addition to notes, a bibliography, and an index.

WILLIAM FAULKNER

Born: New Albany, Mississippi; September 25, 1897
Died: Byhalia, Mississippi; July 6, 1962

PRINCIPAL LONG FICTION

Soldiers' Pay, 1926
Mosquitoes, 1927
Sartoris, 1929
The Sound and the Fury, 1929
As I Lay Dying, 1930
Sanctuary, 1931
Light in August, 1932
Pylon, 1935
Absalom, Absalom!, 1936
The Unvanquished, 1938
The Wild Palms, 1939
The Hamlet, 1940

Go Down, Moses, 1942
Intruder in the Dust, 1948
Requiem for a Nun, 1951
A Fable, 1954
The Town, 1957
The Mansion, 1959
The Reivers, 1962
The Wishing Tree, 1964 (fairy tale)
Flags in the Dust, 1973 (original version of *Sartoris*)
Mayday, 1976 (fable)

OTHER LITERARY FORMS

William Faulkner published two volumes of poetry and several volumes of short stories. Most of his best stories appear in *Knight's Gambit* (1949), *Collected Short Stories of William Faulkner* (1950), and the posthumous *Uncollected Stories of William Faulkner* (1979). His early journalistic and prose pieces have been collected and published, as have his interviews and a number of his letters. Also published are several interesting minor works, including a fairy tale, *The Wishing Tree* (1964), and a romantic fable, *Mayday* (1976). New Faulkner material is steadily seeing print, much of it in the annual Faulkner issue of *Mississippi Quarterly.* Scholars are making public more information on Faulkner's screenwriting in Hollywood, where he collaborated on such major successes as *To Have and Have Not* (1945) and *The Big Sleep* (1946). Several of his works have been adapted for television and film; notably successful were film adaptations of *Intruder in the Dust* and *The Reivers.*

ACHIEVEMENTS

When Faulkner received the Nobel Prize in Literature in 1949, he completed an emergence from comparative obscurity that had begun three years before. In 1946, when nearly all of Faulkner's books were out of print, Malcolm Cowley published *The Portable Faulkner.* Cowley's introduction and arrangement made clear "the scope and force and interdependence" of Faulkner's oeuvre up to 1945.

Even in 1945, Faulkner was reasonably well known to the readers of popular magazines, his stories having appeared with F. Scott Fitzgerald's and

Ernest Hemingway's in publications such as the *Saturday Evening Post*, *Scribner's Magazine*, *Harper's Magazine*, and *The American Mercury*. Despite his success in selling short stories and as a Hollywood screenwriter, Faulkner's novels, except for the notorious *Sanctuary*, had little commercial success until after Cowley's volume and the Nobel Prize. The notoriety of *Sanctuary*, widely reviewed as salacious, brought him to the attention of the film industry; it was his screenwriting which sustained him financially during the years of comparative neglect when he produced the series of powerful novels which constitute one of the major achievements of world fiction. His first novel to appear after Cowley's volume, *Intruder in the Dust*, was filmed in Faulkner's hometown, Oxford, Mississippi, and released in 1949.

After the Nobel Prize, honors came steadily. He was made a member of the French Legion of Honor, received two National Book Awards for *A Fable* and *Collected Short Stories of William Faulkner*, and received two Pulitzer Prizes for *A Fable* and *The Reivers*. He traveled around the world for the United States State Department in 1954. During 1957, he was writer-in-residence at the University of Virginia. Recognition and financial security, while gratifying, neither diminished nor increased his output. He continued writing until his death.

Faulkner has achieved the status of a world author. His works have been painstakingly translated into many languages. Perhaps more critical books and articles have been written about him in the late twentieth century than about any other writer with the exception of William Shakespeare. Critics and scholars from all over the world have contributed to the commentary. Faulkner's achievement has been compared favorably with that of Henry James, Honoré de Balzac, and Charles Dickens; many critics regard him as the preeminent novelist of the twentieth century.

BIOGRAPHY

William Cuthbert Faulkner was born in New Albany, Mississippi, on September 25, 1897. His ancestors had emigrated from Scotland in the eighteenth century. Faulkner's great-grandfather, William Clark Falkner, was a colonel in the Civil War; wrote *The White Rose of Memphis* (1881), a popular romance; and provided a model for the patriarch of the Sartoris clan in *The Unvanquished*. Faulkner's family was very important to him. The oldest son of Maud and Murry Falkner, William Cuth-

(The Nobel Foundation)

bert later became the head of the family. He took this responsibility seriously, struggling most of his life to care for those whom, whether by blood or moral commitment, he considered members of his family. In 1924, he changed the spelling of his family name to Faulkner.

Faulkner discovered his storytelling gifts as a child, but his writing career did not really begin until after his brief training for the Royal Air Force in Canada, shortly before the World War I Armistice in 1918. He attended the University of Mississippi for one year, worked at odd jobs, and published a volume of poetry, *The Marble Faun* (1924). He took writing more seriously, with encouragement from Sherwood Anderson, while living in New Orleans in 1925. The influence of Anderson, especially his "The Book of the Grotesque" from *Winesburg, Ohio* (1919), seems to pervade Faulkner's work. During his apprenticeship he spent several months traveling in Europe. Out of his experiences in New Orleans and Europe came a number of journalistic sketches, most dealing with New Orleans, and a group of short stories set in Europe.

The early novels are interesting, but Faulkner began to show his powers as a prose stylist and as a creator of psychologically deep and interesting characters in *Sartoris*, which he had originally written as *Flags in the Dust*. Beginning with *The Sound and the Fury* through *Go Down, Moses*, Faulkner wrote the major novels and stories of his Yoknapatawpha series. Of the ten novels he published in these thirteen years, five are generally considered to be masterpieces: *The Sound and the Fury*, *As I Lay Dying*, *Light in August*, *Absalom, Absalom!*, and *Go Down, Moses*. At least two others, *Sanctuary* and *The Hamlet*, are widely studied and admired. The entire series of novels set in the mythical Yoknapatawpha County, Faulkner's "little postage stamp of native soil," is sometimes considered as a great work in its own right, especially when all of the Snopes trilogy (*The Hamlet*, *The Town*, *The Mansion*) is included with the above named masterpieces. Stories from his two collections of the 1929-1942 period regularly appear in anthologies; "Old Man" and "The Bear," which are parts of *The Wild Palms* and *Go Down, Moses*, are perhaps his best-known novellas.

Faulkner's personal life was difficult and has provoked much critical interest in tracing relationships between his life and his work. The family-arranged and unhappy marriage to Estelle Oldham in 1929 ended in divorce. Both Faulkner and his wife were subject to alcoholism. He carried on a virtually continuous struggle against debt, resentful and unhappy over the necessity of working in Hollywood in order to keep his family solvent. Though Faulkner was a fiercely loyal husband and father, he was also capable of philandering.

Faulkner preferred to work at home in Mississippi. Still, he traveled a great deal, first for education, later to deal with publishers and to work in Hollywood, and finally as a goodwill ambassador for the United States. He met and formed acquaintances with several important contemporaries, notably Nathanael West, Sherwood Anderson, and Howard Hawkes.

Faulkner died of a heart attack on July 6, 1962, after entering the hospital to deal with one of his periodic drinking bouts.

ANALYSIS

When William Faulkner accepted the Nobel Prize in December, 1950, he made a speech which has become a justly famous statement of his perception of the modern world and of his particular place in it. In the address, Faulkner speaks of the modern tragedy of the spirit, the threat of instant physical annihilation, which seems to overshadow "the problems of the human heart in conflict with itself." He argues that all fiction should be universal and spiritually significant, "a pillar" to help humankind "endure and prevail." Literature can be such a pillar if it deals with "the old verities and truths of the heart, the universal truths lacking which any story is ephemeral and doomed—love and honor and pity and pride and compassion and sacrifice."

All of Faulkner's greatest works were written before the first explosion of the atomic bomb, yet in all of them there is an awareness of the threat of annihilation of which the bomb may be only a symptom: a kind of spiritual annihilation. Lewis P. Simpson argues that Faulkner, like the greatest of his contemporaries, dramatizes in most of his novels some version of the central problem of modern man in the West, how to respond to the recognition that man has no certain knowledge of a stable transcendent power which assures the meaning of human history. Panthea Broughton makes this view of Faulkner more concrete: In Faulkner's world, characters struggle to find or make meaning, exposing themselves in various ways to the danger of spiritual self-destruction, of losing their own souls in the effort to find a way of living in a universe which does not provide meaning.

The immense quantity of critical commentary on Faulkner provides several satisfying ways of viewing and ordering the central concerns of his novels. While the way into Faulkner suggested by Simpson and Broughton is only one of many, it seems particularly helpful to the reader who wishes to begin thinking about Faulkner's whole literary career. Broughton demonstrates that the Faulknerian universe is characterized essentially by motion. Human beings need meaning; they need to impose patterns on the motion of life. Out of this need spring human capacities for mature moral freedom as well as for tragic destructiveness. Closely related to this pattern that Broughton sees in Faulkner's stories are his tireless experimentation with form and his characteristic style.

In his essay in *William Faulkner: Three Decades of Criticism* (1960), Conrad Aiken notes the similarities between Faulkner's characteristic style and that of Henry James. The comparison is apt in some ways, for both in their greatest novels seem especially concerned with capturing in the sentence the complexity of experience and of reflection on experience. As Walter Slatoff, in the same volume, and others have shown, Faulkner seems especially drawn to paradox and oxymorons, kinds of verbal juxtaposition particularly suited to conveying the tension between the motion of life and the human need for pattern. Once one notices these aspects of Faulkner's style in a complex novel such as *Absalom, Absalom!*, in which Faulkner's characteristic style finds its ideal subject, much that initially seems obscure becomes clearer.

Faulkner seems to have found most instructive the "loose" forms characteristic of the Victorian panoramic novel as it was developed, for example, by his favorite author, Charles Dickens. Faulkner's novels generally contain juxtapositions of attitudes, narrative lines, voices, modes of representation, and emotional tones. His more radical and probably less successful experiments in this vein include the alternation of chapters from two quite separate stories in *The Wild Palms* and the alternation of fictionalized historical narrative with dramatic acts in *Requiem for a Nun*, a kind of sequel to *Sanctuary*. *Light in August* is his most successful work in this direction. Somewhat less radical and more successful experiments involved the incorporation of previously published stories into "collections" and sustained narratives in such a way as to produce the unity of a novel. Parts of *The Unvanquished*, the Snopes Trilogy, and *A Fable* have led dual lives as stories and as parts of novels. *Go Down, Moses* is probably the most successful experiment in this direction. Faulkner was particularly interested in the juxtaposition of voices. His career as a novelist blossomed when he juxtaposed the voices and, therefore, the points of view of several characters in *The Sound and the Fury* and *As I Lay Dying*. In *Absalom, Absalom!*, the juxtaposition of voices also becomes the placing together of narrative lines, comparable episodes, points of view, modes of narration, attitudes, and emotional tones. This one novel brings together everything of which Faulkner was capable, demonstrating a technical virtuosity which in some ways is the fruit of the entire tradition of the novel. *Absalom, Absalom!* also realizes to some extent a special potential of Faulkner's interest in juxtaposition, the conception of his Yoknapatawpha novels as a saga that displays a unity of its own.

The technique of juxtaposition, like Faulkner's characteristic style, reflects his concern with the problems of living meaningfully within the apparently meaningless flow of time. Because life will not stand still or even move consistently according to patterns of meaning, it becomes necessary to use multiple points of view to avoid the complete falsification of his subject. Juxtaposition, the multileveled and open-ended sentence, and the oxymoronic style heighten the reader's awareness of the fluidity of the "reality" which the text attempts to portray. Faulkner's most tragic characters are those who feel driven to impose so rigid a pattern upon their lives and on the lives of others as to invite destruction from the overwhelming forces of motion and change. These characters experience the heart in conflict with itself as the simultaneous need for living motion and meaningful pattern.

THE SOUND AND THE FURY

The Sound and the Fury is divided into four parts to which an appendix was later added. Faulkner repeated in interviews that the novel began as a short story which grew into the first section. He then found that the point of view he had chosen did not tell the whole story even though it closely approximated the flow of events before a nonjudgmental consciousness. Gradually, Faulkner found himself retelling the story four and, finally, five times. The effect of reading these juxtapositions may be described as similar to that of putting together a puzzle, the whole of which cannot be seen until the last piece is in place. Like several of Faulkner's novels, notably *Absalom, Absalom!*, *The Sound and the Fury* is not fully comprehendible upon a single reading. The first reading provides a general idea of the whole with subsequent readings allowing one to fill in the details and to see ever more deeply into this moving narrative.

The novel concerns the tragic dissolution of the Compson family. The decline dates decisively from the marriage of Candace (Caddy), the only daughter of Jason Compson III and Caroline Bascomb. Caddy's marriage is not the sole cause of the family's decline; rather, it becomes symbolic of a complex of internal and external forces that come to bear on this Mississippi family early in the twentieth century. Caddy becomes pregnant by Dalton Ames, a romantic, heroic, and apparently devoted outsider. Her mother then seeks out Sydney Herbert Head as a respectable husband for her. After the marriage, Herbert finds he has been gulled and divorces Caddy. These events deprive all the Compson men of their center of meaning. Quentin, the oldest son who loves Caddy not as a sister but as a woman, commits suicide. Jason III drinks himself to death, having lost the children upon whom his meaning depended. Jason IV seeks petty and impotent revenge on Caddy's daughter, also named Quentin, because he believes the failure of Caddy's marriage has deprived him of a chance to get ahead. Benjy, the severely retarded youngest brother, suffers the absence of the only real mother he ever had. Control of the family passes to Jason IV, and the family ceases finally to be a place where love is sustained, becoming instead, despite the efforts of the heroic and loving black servant, Dilsey, a battleground of petty scheming, hatred, and revenge.

This general picture emerges from the internal monologues of Benjy, Quentin (male), and Jason IV, from a third-person narrative centering on Dilsey and Jason IV, and from the final appendix. Each of the four main sections is set on a particular day: Benjy's section on his thirty-third birthday, Easter Saturday, 1928; Jason's on Good Friday; and Dilsey's (the fourth section) on Easter Sunday of the same year. Quentin's section is on the day of his suicide, June 2, 1910. As the portrait of the family's decline emerges from these juxtaposed sections, their tragic significance becomes apparent.

Benjamin Compson's internal monologue consists of images, most of which are memories. At the center of his memory and of his stunted life is Caddy, whose "hair was like fire" and who "smelled like trees." Every experience of Benjy, which evokes these images or which resembles any experience he has had with Caddy, automatically triggers his memory. As a result, Benjy lives in a blending together of past and present in which memory and present experience are virtually indistinguishable. The spring of his suffering is that for him the experience of losing Caddy is continuous; the memory of her presence is perfect and the experience of her absence is constant.

This section proceeds by a series of juxtapositions which place Benjy's present, deprived condition starkly beside the richness of his memory. Though the pattern is difficult to see at first, repeated readings show that Faulkner works in this section primarily by pairing certain events: the funeral of Damuddy (Caroline's mother and Benjy's grandmother) and

Caddy's wedding with all the attendant suggestions of meaning; Caddy with her boyfriends on the porch swing and Quentin (female) with her boyfriends; Benjy at the gate waiting for Caddy to come home from school one Christmas and Benjy waiting at the gate on the day Jason IV leaves it open. This last event, part of Jason's spitefulness against Caddy, leads to Benjy's castration after he grabs a school girl to ask about Caddy, though he cannot speak. Among the many pairings, the most pathetic appears at the end of the section. Benjy remembers his family long ago:

> Her hair was like fire, and little points of fire were in her eyes, and I went and Father lifted me into the chair too, and Caddy held me. She smelled like trees.

> *She smelled like trees. In the corner it was dark, but I could see the window. I squatted there, holding the slipper. I couldn't see it, but my hands saw it.*

The contrast between the firelight of the library, with its mirror and the loving people and the now barren and dark library with only one of Caddy's wedding slippers reveals much of the mood, the meaning, and the effectiveness of technique in Benjy's section.

Quentin's section also proceeds largely by the juxtaposition of memory and present experience. Quentin's memories are triggered by present events and he is sometimes unable to distinguish between memory and external reality. He commits suicide at the end of his first year at Harvard. As he carries out his plans to drown himself, he is caught up in various events which repeat aspects of his loss of Caddy, the last being a picnic with some college classmates during which he remembers his abortive attempt to be the brother who avenges a wronged sister. This memory is simultaneous with and is repeated in a fight with Gerald Bland, the kind of womanizer Quentin wishes Dalton Ames was.

Perhaps the major irony of Quentin's suicide is that the state of being which he desires is in many ways like the state in which his youngest brother suffers. Quentin wishes to be free of time, to end all motion. He gives as a motive his fear that grief over the loss of Caddy will attenuate, for when grief is gone,

his sister will have become meaningless and his life utterly empty. Yet his grief, of which every event reminds him, is unbearable. He wishes to keep Caddy as she was and to deny the repetitions which force him to remember her loss. Though he sees such a transcendent state in many images in his world, he can only *imagine* himself in that state, for it is impossible in life. Suicide seems his only alternative. In death, he can at least shirk everything, he can at least escape the *again* which to him is a sadder word than *was*.

Quentin's relationship with Caddy is highly problematic. One fairly simple way of understanding how his sister becomes so important to him that he must commit suicide when she marries is to observe Quentin's and Caddy's relationship with their parents: Jason III does not love Caroline. She believes that he has come to resent the fact that her family is socially inferior. In reality, she is a selfish and stupid woman who is completely inadequate as a mother and wife. Her husband is unable to deal with her. His growing unhappiness and cynicism magnify her weakness. The result is that these children have no real parents, and the responsibility falls on the gifted Caddy. Despite her extraordinary capacity, Caddy is a girl. When she grows into a woman, she must inevitably betray the brothers who depend on her love. Even when she is with them, she cannot love them as an adult would; she cannot teach them to give. Her gifts lead her to another who is also capable of passion, Dalton Ames. This affair exaggerates the meaning of the betrayal by heightening the inadequacy of the family, including Quentin, to meet Caddy's needs. Caddy's sense of her parents' failure is captured in her memory of a picture in a book which made her think of her parents as keeping her from the light. Quentin needs Caddy not only as a mother, a source of pure affection, but also as a center of meaning. She embodies all the forms and traditions to which Quentin clings to escape the despair his father teaches him. Losing her, he loses his life.

Jason's section of the novel is much easier to read, for his interior life is more or less in the present. He neither desires nor even conceives of any transcendent reality; he desires power above all things, even money, though he is well aware that money is, in his world, the superior means to power. He delights in the power to be cruel, to make others fear him, yet he is remarkably impotent. His impotence stems from his inability to imagine in others any motives different from his own. In these respects, his character, as well as the mode in which it is presented, recalls the jealous monk in Robert Browning's "Soliloquy of the Spanish Cloister." Jason's interior monologue is the only one of the three which has all the marks of being spoken. It is as if Jason were two people, one constantly explaining and justifying himself to the other.

Jason tells primarily about his troubles bringing up Caddy's daughter, Quentin. The girl has been left in the care of the family while the divorced Caddy makes her way in the world. Quentin becomes the central instrument of Jason's revenge against Caddy for the failure of her marriage and the disappointment of his hope. Jason is so fixed on his need to exercise cruel power that he is unable to restrain himself sufficiently to keep the situation stable. He drives Quentin out of the family, losing the monthly checks from Caddy which he has been appropriating, the hoard he has collected in part from this theft, and the one person on whom he can effectively take his revenge.

"I've seed de first en de last," says Dilsey. She refers to the beginning and the end of the doom of the Compson family, to Caddy's wedding and Quentin's elopement. Each of these events suggests more meanings than can be detailed here, but the importance of Dilsey's section is that she sees a pattern of human meaning in the events which threaten an end to meaning for so many. Her part in these events has been a heroic struggle to bind the family together with her love and care, a doomed but not a meaningless struggle, for she can still see pattern, order, meaning in all of it. The events of Easter morning, in which Dilsey figures, suggest that at least one source of that power to mean and to love is her community at the African American church service, a community which, in the contemplation of the Christian symbols of transcendence, attains an experience of communion which partakes of the eternal even though it is temporary. Dilsey's church is a model of the family, and her ex-

perience there is not unlike Benjy's experience in Caddy's arms on Father's lap before the library fire. The Compson family has somehow lost this experience. As the appendix suggests, all of the Compsons, except perhaps for Benjy, are damned, for they have all, in various ways, come to see themselves as "dolls stuffed with sawdust."

The Sound and the Fury is in part an exploration of the loss of the Christian world view. Temple and Popeye in *Sanctuary* respond in ways similar to Jason's. Addie in *As I Lay Dying* and Horace Benbow in *Sanctuary* play parts similar to Quentin's. Benbow attempts to prove the truth of the traditional view he has inherited from his family and class, the view that "God is a gentleman" and that Providence takes an active hand in human affairs. He is disastrously and blindly wrong and apparently suffers the loss of his faith. Addie Bundren's attempt to impose order on her world seems even more disastrous because Faulkner centers attention on the suffering she causes her family.

AS I LAY DYING

In *As I Lay Dying*, Addie Bundren wants and fails to find a kind of transcendent communion with some other being. When she realizes the inevitable impermanence of such communion, she plans revenge against the people who have failed her, especially her husband, Anse. She makes him promise that he will bury her with her relations in Jefferson. This simple promise is a subtle revenge because it binds Anse with words for which he has too much respect and it becomes a terrible vengeance when Anse comes to fulfill that promise. Addie believes that a word is "a shape to fill a lack." By this she means that the communion she feels when she is pregnant with her first-born is an essential experience for which words are unnecessary and inadequate. Not only are words inadequate to this experience, but they are also symbols of separation from this experience. At one point Addie reflects, "I would think how words go straight up in a thin line, quick and harmless, and how terribly doing goes along the earth." By making Anse "promise his word," Addie forces her husband to attempt a union of saying and doing, an attempt which sends Addie's entire family on a grotesque and tortured journey along the earth.

Addie imposes a verbal pattern on her family in revenge because pregnancy and passion are temporary. Each pregnancy ends in separation. Her one love affair is with the Reverend Whitfield, whom she describes as "the dark land talking the voiceless speech." When this affair ends in the birth of Jewel, her third son, her despair is complete. The promise she extracts from Anse elicits a catastrophic juggernaut, for she dies at the beginning of a storm which floods the area, making the wagon journey to Jefferson next to impossible.

The novel is presented in a series of monologues similar in depth and intensity to Quentin's in *The Sound and the Fury*. As the narrative emerges from these monologues so do the internal relationships of the family. The reader becomes intensely aware of the feelings and the needs of each family member. Anse is driven not only by his promise but also by the desire to regain the dignity he believes he loses by having no teeth. A sedentary man, he has needed this prod to set him in motion. He eventually returns, not only with teeth and dignity, but with several other new possessions as well, including a new wife. Cash, the oldest son, is the family's repository of technical skill. Almost without questioning, he solves the material problems of the journey. In crossing the flooded river, he breaks his leg, yet he finishes the journey in incredible pain. Darl, the son Addie has rejected, is the most sensitive of her children. He is seemingly capable of a kind of communion that might have fulfilled her, for he seems able to read minds and to know of events he does not see. He opposes the journey at every significant point, understanding that it is Addie's revenge and that it threatens to tear apart the family. Anse finally commits Darl to a mental hospital in order to escape financial responsibility for a barn which Darl ignites in an attempt to burn Addie and end the journey.

Jewel, product of the Whitfield affair, though he is barely articulate, comes to seem the living embodiment of Addie's wordless will to revenge. He saves the coffin from the flood when the wagon overturns in the river and from the fire in the barn. He sacrifices his much prized pony in trade to replace the mules

lost in the river crossing. Dewey Dell, the only daughter, is desperate to reach Jefferson where she believes she can get an abortion. She shares Darl's sensitivity and hates it because it makes her feel naked and vulnerable. She violently assists in the capture of Darl for she is glad to be rid of the kind of communion Addie so deeply desired. Vardaman, the youngest son, suffers loss. Drawn along on the journey by promises of bananas and a view of a toy train, he registers all the family's pain: the loss of a mother, the dislocations of the journey, the humiliation as Addie begins to smell, the shiftless poverty of Anse, the sufferings of the brothers, the vulnerability of Dewey Dell and, finally, the loss of Darl. Because the unity of the family is his identity, he suffers a kind of dismemberment.

This brief glimpse hardly conveys the richness and power of this novel. Still it should make clear that part of the novel's meaning derives from Addie's attempt to impose a rigid pattern upon a significant part of her family's life and the extreme suffering her success brings about.

SANCTUARY

Popeye and Temple in *Sanctuary* are lost children, victims of their moment in history, in that they are without souls. Their culture has failed to give them reasons for doing one thing rather than another. They do not have the natural acquisitiveness of Jason IV and the Snopeses, nor do they have a motive such as revenge to give direction to their lives. Popeye wears the mask of a gangster, though the mask slips occasionally. It is the role itself which gives Popeye substance and makes him appear somewhat like a normal human being. He also has a vague desire which he expresses in his abduction of Temple Drake. He desires to join the human community, to live a meaningful life. Just as he imitates gangsters in order to take possession of some identity, he also imitates the acts of men who reveal themselves to be under the power of a strong motive. He tries to desire and to possess Temple Drake because other men desire her. He fails even to desire her and apparently, as a result of this failure, he gives up his life. He has money, says the narrator, but there is nothing to buy with it.

Temple is perhaps the most fully developed example in early Faulkner of a character who simply flows, who seeks no meanings at all, but merely acts out her impulses. When she is abducted by Popeye, she is freed of the social restraints which have never been made important to her. Nothing in her experience has taught her to internalize social restraints as communal values. She is virtually without values, virtually unable to make moral choices; freed of external restraint, she seeks pointless and ultimately unsatisfying gratification of whatever impulses come to the fore. She becomes capable of killing in order to achieve sexual satisfaction. In her final act in the novel, she pointlessly condemns an innocent man to death as she begins to adopt Popeye's failed strategy, assuming a role to pass the time.

In Temple one sees that the utter surrender to motion is no solution to the search for meaning in Faulkner's world. Neither surrender nor rigid resistance to the flow of events will suffice. Faulkner's heroes, like Dilsey, are generally those who are able to find a balance between what Broughton calls the abstract and the actual, a balance which seems to answer the cry of the heart and to make loving possible. Faulkner's novels suggest that the modern tragedy of a lack of soul, of spiritual annihilation, results from some decisive break in the process by which one generation teaches the next how to love.

LIGHT IN AUGUST

The central juxtaposition in *Light in August* is between Lena Grove and Joe Christmas. Lena Grove, scandalously pregnant and deserted by Lucas Burch, alias Joe Brown, walks the dirt roads of Alabama, Mississippi, and finally Tennessee in tranquil search of a husband. She is a center of peace and faith and fertility, though all around her may be waste and catastrophe. She is like the peaceful center of Herman Melville's Grand Armada on the outer circles of which the stricken whales murder one another. Byron Bunch, who loves her at first sight even though she is nine months pregnant, tells his friend, the Reverend Gail Hightower, that Lena seems to have two persons inside her, one who *knows* that Lucas Burch is a scoundrel who will never marry her, and another who *believes* that God will see to it that her family will be together when the child is born. God somehow keeps

these two persons within Lena from meeting and comparing notes.

When the child is born, there is a family indeed, for Lena seems to attract all the help she needs. Byron is camped outside her door. Gail is there to deliver the child. Joe Christmas's grandparents are present, reliving a past moment which promises them some small redemption. Even Lucas Burch makes a brief appearance before leaving the field open to Byron. Lena's tranquil faith, her trust in the world and its people, and her submission to her natural being make her into a kind of Faulknerian heroine. She is capable of finding meaning for herself in the flow of life, and this meaning attracts and vitalizes others. The images used to describe her are filled with the paradoxes of stillness in motion. This attitude gives her power, not a power that she often consciously uses, but still a real power to draw recluses such as Byron and Gail out of spiritual death and into the flow of living.

While Lena moves peacefully through the book, seeking a husband and bearing a child, Joe Christmas careens through the last days of his life, the culmination of more than thirty years of bigoted education. Joe's life story is the center of a novel which is composed largely of condensed biographies. Of the major characters, only Byron and Lena have relatively obscure pasts. Gail, Joanna Burden, and Joe are presented as the end products of three generations in their respective families. Even Percy Grimm, a relatively minor character, receives a fairly full biography. Each of these lives contrasts starkly with the life of Lena and, eventually, with Lena and Byron's relationship. Gail, Joanna, Joe, and Percy are, in the words of Gail, "lost children among the cold and terrible stars." They are the children of a generation that saw its world crumble and that adopted fanatic versions of Calvinism mixed with an inherited racism in order to resist the flow of history with its threat of meaninglessness. They are products of the failure of love. While Lena, miraculously immunized against lovelessness, is capable of accepting the world and its lawful motion as her home, most of the other major characters resist and reject the world, living in alienation.

Joe's life reveals the sources and meanings of resistance and alienation. The story of his life comes in several blocks. After learning that Joe has murdered Joanna, the reader is plunged deeply into the suffering consciousness of the murderer during the twenty-four hours preceding the crime. Joe is seen as a driven man: He seems to be under the control of the voices which speak inside him, and he is unaware of the loving, caressing voices in his natural environment. This glimpse into his consciousness reveals ambivalent attitudes toward his racial background, a hatred of the feminine, a sense that Joanna has somehow betrayed him by praying over him, and a sense of being an abandoned child who wants to be able to say with conviction, "God loves me, too." The middle section of the novel separates into strands the inner voices that drive Joe to murder which, in his culture, is a suicide.

In an orphanage at age five, Joe accidentally provokes the dietician into speeding his placement with a family. His adoptive father, the Calvinist fanatic Simon McEachern, teaches Joe the skills of resistance to nature. He learns to cultivate a rocklike will and an indomitable body. He learns to relate to people impersonally. He grows up not only without love but also in resistance to love: To be a man is not to love. McEachern derives his hatred of the world from his Calvinist theology, while Joe learns to resist the world in defense of his selfhood. Joe is not a Calvinist; he resists the content of McEachern's teachings by mastering its forms. Inside Joe, the voice perhaps first awakened by a girl who mothered him in the orphanage continues to speak. Joe continues to desire to love, to belong, and ultimately to be free of the voices which drive him.

Of the forms Joe's rebellion against his culture takes, those involving sex and race seem most significant. Joe's desire to love and be loved is revealed and betrayed in his adolescent affair with Bobbie Allen, a local prostitute, a relationship which paradoxically combines intimacy with impersonality. In his adult life, his rebellion often takes the form of asserting his presumed black blood. In doing so, he provokes a ritual reaction which becomes the dominant pattern in his life, the pattern that is worked out in full when he kills Joanna and suffers the consequences.

His affair with Joanna, his life and death in Jefferson, Mississippi, replay the patterns of his life in their full significance, bringing him again to the moment of rebellious protest in which he faces an authority figure in the fullness of his identity and strikes out in murderous self-defense. Joe and Joanna are virtually doubles. They proceed through tortured and perverse phases of sexual relations until they reach a kind of purged state of near normality, a point at which both seem seriously able to contemplate marriage, children, a normal human life. When Joanna enters menopause, however, she is simply unable to accept the natural flow of time. Her "sins" with Joe lose their meaning if they do not lead to marriage, motherhood, and "normal" feminine fulfillment. She reverts to her inherited Calvinism and racism, changing from Joe's double to McEachern's double. Betrayed herself, she betrays Joe, trying to form into a piece of her sick world. Joe responds to this change as he responded to McEachern's attempt to cast him into Hell.

During Joe's flight from the pursuing Jefferson authorities, he comes closer than ever before to the peace, freedom, and love he has desired. In his disorientation and physical suffering, for the first time in his life, he feels unity with the natural world. He partakes of "the peace and unhaste and quiet" that are characteristic of Lena's experience because for the first time he is really free of the compulsive voices of his culture, free to feel at home in his world.

Contrasted to this experience is the story of Joe's first five years as told to Gail by Joe's fanatical grandfather, Doc Hines, and by his grandmother. Doc Hines sees himself as the agent of a Calvinist deity avenging the lust after worldly pleasure symbolized by femininity and the inferior race ("God's abomination upon the earth"). Against these disembodied "voices of the land," Joe emerges as somewhat ambiguously victorious in his death. Joe's death is inevitable. Even though he seems to have found freedom from the internal compulsions which have driven him to self-destruction, he cannot escape the consequences of his actions in the world. He can only accept. The way in which Joe accepts the consequences of his acts suggests for him a kind of heroic status.

Joe's death is inevitable because he has set in motion a deeply embedded social ritual, a fateful machine which cannot stop until it has completed its movement. The community's heritage of Calvinism and racism has produced that ritual machine. In a desperate need to assert control over the flow of history, the culture has embraced the Calvinist denial of all things in this world which might turn one's attention from God.

Among other elements which contribute to the view of Joe as a hero is his effect on Gail. Gail has been on the edges of all the events of these days in Jefferson. He has had several opportunities to mitigate suffering, but he has, on the whole, failed to act. He is afraid to leave his sanctuary in order to help those he could really help. Joe appears at Gail's door, moments before dying, like an avenging god to strike Gail down in a kind of judgment, even as Gail confesses part of his sin. Finally, Joe dies in Gail's house, another sacrifice to the very kinds of rituals and legalisms which Gail has used to buy what he calls peace, the right to sit unmolested in his house dreaming of his grandfather's absurdly heroic death. Gail learns from this experience. He goes on to make, to himself at least, a full confession of his sins. He faces the fact that what he has wanted, a sterile stasis in a dead past moment, was selfish, that this desire has led him to bring about his wife's death, to welcome being ostracized by the town, ultimately to serve his small need at the cost of abandoning those he promised to serve when he became a minister.

The juxtaposition of lives tragically ruined by a heritage of racism and fanatical Calvinism with Lena's life creates an unforgettable and moving work. One of the easily overlooked effects of the whole is the impression it gives of a community whose heart is basically good, which responds, albeit sometimes grudgingly, with sympathy to those in need and with kindness to those in trouble. Lena brings out this side of the community. On the lunatic fringe of the community are those who express the deep compulsions which thrive in the insecurity of modern life. Joe is brought up to evoke this underside of the community which it would like to forget. They are not to forget. The images of horror pass from one generation to the next. The uncertainties of life, especially in a world which seems to have lost the easy comfort of religious consensus, continue to produce personalities such as those of Doc Hines and Percy Grimm, who cannot deal with or bear an indifferent universe. Their rigid imposition of abstraction upon the flow of life forces them ever backward to the legalism of their secret rituals. Society is tragically in the grip of the past despite its great desire to be finally free of these compulsions.

ABSALOM, ABSALOM!

Absalom, Absalom! juxtaposes differing accounts of the same events. In *The Sound and the Fury*, Faulkner thought of himself as trying to tell the whole story and finding that he had to multiply points of view in order to do so. In *Absalom, Absalom!*, as Gary Stonum argues, "the labor of representation is . . . made a part of the text." The story is only partly known; it is a collection of facts, not all of which are certain, which seem to those who know them profoundly and stubbornly meaningful. The various characters who try their formulae for bringing those facts together into a meaningful whole are the historians of the novel. Faulkner has written a novel about writing novels, about giving meaning to the flow of events. *Absalom, Absalom!* dramatizes so effectively the processes and obstacles to creating a satisfying structure for events and offers such an ideal wedding of structure, content, technique, and style, that many critics regard it as Faulkner's greatest achievement. With *The Sound and the Fury* this novel shares characters from the Compson family and a degree of difficulty which may require multiple readings.

The central concern of the narrative is the life of Thomas Sutpen and his family. Sutpen has appeared out of nowhere to build a vast plantation near Jefferson, Mississippi, in the early nineteenth century. Apparently without much wealth, he nevertheless puts together the greatest establishment in the area, marries Ellen Coldfield, a highly respectable though not a wealthy woman, and fathers two children by her. When Sutpen's son, Henry, goes to college, he meets and befriends Charles Bon. Charles and Sutpen's daughter, Judith, fall in love and plan to marry. For no apparent reason, Sutpen forbids the marriage and Henry leaves his home with Charles. During the Civil War, Ellen dies. Near the end of the war, Henry and Charles appear one day at the plantation, Sutpen's Hundred, and Henry kills Charles. After the war, Sutpen becomes engaged to Rosa Coldfield, Ellen's much younger sister, but that engagement is suddenly broken off. A few years later, Sutpen fathers a daughter with Milly Jones, the teenage daughter of his handyman, Wash Jones. When Sutpen refuses to marry Milly, Jones kills him. Then Sutpen's daughter, Judith, and his slave daughter, Clytie, live together and, somewhat mysteriously, care for the descendants of Charles Bon by his "marriage" to an octoroon.

Though not all the known facts, these constitute the outline of the story as it is generally known in Jefferson. The major mysteries stand out in this outline. Why did Sutpen forbid the marriage? Why did Henry side with Charles and then kill him? Why did Rosa agree to marry Sutpen and then refuse? Why did Sutpen get a squatter's daughter pregnant and abandon her, bringing about his own death? Why did Judith take responsibility for Bon's family? These are the questions to which Rosa Coldfield, Jason Compson III and his father General Compson, and Quentin Compson and his Harvard roommate Shreve McCannon address themselves. A rough chapter outline will give an idea of the novel's structure while suggesting how the various accounts interrelate.

The setting in chapters 1 through 5 is day one of time present, early September, 1909, before Quentin Compson leaves for Harvard. (1) Afternoon, Rosa tells Quentin about Sutpen in summary, painting him as a destructive demon of heroic proportions. (2) Evening, Jason III repeats his father's description of how Sutpen built his empire of one hundred square miles and married Ellen. (3) Evening, Jason III gives the public version, with some inside information, of Rosa's relationship with Sutpen, centering on her involvement with the Judith-Charles relationship and her eventual refusal to marry Sutpen. (4) Evening, Jason attempts to explain why Sutpen forbade the marriage and why Henry killed Charles. He argues that

Bon intended to keep his octoroon mistress/wife when he married Judith. Jason offers this explanation as plausible but does not really feel it is adequate. (5) Later that same evening, Rosa tries to explain why she refused to marry Sutpen, giving her own version of how she came to be on the scene and describing the death of Bon and its effect on the family. She ends this part by revealing her belief that the Sutpen mansion contains some secret which she intends to discover that evening.

Chapters 6 through 9 are set in day two of time present, January of 1910; Quentin and Shreve spend an evening in their Harvard dormitory working out their version of the Sutpen story. (6) Quentin has a letter saying that Rosa is dead. The story is recapitulated with more details coming to light and completing the story of the Sutpen line in outline. (7) Quentin and Shreve concentrate on Sutpen's youth, retelling his story up to his death in the light of information Quentin received directly from his grandfather. (8) The boys work out the story of Charles Bon's and Henry Sutpen's relationship, constructing a new answer to the question of why Henry killed Charles. Not only was Charles Henry's half brother, but he also had black blood. (9) Quentin recalls his trip with Rosa to Sutpen's house on the September night and his brief meeting with the returned Henry. They finish Jason III's letter and contemplate the whole story.

The novel's climax comes in chapter 8 when Shreve and Quentin construct their explanation. They "discover" through intense imaginative identification with Henry and Charles a meaning latent in the facts they have gathered. Their discovery implies that Sutpen prevented the marriage and alienated Henry by revealing that Charles and Henry were half brothers. The substance of their discovery is that the first wife whom Sutpen put aside, the mother of Charles, was a mulatto. Sutpen reserves this information as his trump card in case Henry comes to accept an incestuous marriage. Only this revelation could have brought Henry to kill Charles rather than allow him to marry Judith. The means by which the boys arrive at this conclusion reveal much about the meanings of the novel. Not least among these meanings is the revelation of a sickness at the "prime foundation" of the

South, the sickness of a planter society that prevents one from loving one's own children.

There is no way for the boys to *prove* this solution. Their discovery is above all an imaginative act, yet it has the ring of truth. No one who is alive, except Henry, knows what passed between Sutpen and Henry in the conversations which broke off the marriage and led to the murder, and Henry tells no one before his own death. The truth is utterly hidden in the past. The materials which make up this truth are fragmentary, scattered in distance, time, and memory. Only through the most laborious process do Quentin and Shreve gather the facts together from the narratives of their elders and a few documents. Informants such as Rosa and Jason III are Sherwood Anderson grotesques; they have chosen simple truths to which they make all their experiences conform. Rosa's portrait of Sutpen grows almost entirely out of Sutpen's proposal that they produce a child before they marry. Jason III's portrait of Charles Bon is an idealized self-portrait. Even eyewitnesses such as General Compson and Rosa have faulty memories and biased points of view. In the world of this novel, the truth is difficult to know because the facts on which it is based are hard to assemble.

When the facts are assembled, they are even harder to explain. Jason realizes that he has "just the words, the symbols, the shapes themselves." Quentin and Shreve are able to explain, not because they find the facts, but because they use their imaginations so effectively as to find themselves in the tent with Sutpen and Henry in 1865 and in the camp when Charles tells Henry that even though they are brothers, Charles is the "nigger" who is going to marry his sister. Quentin and Shreve have felt Thomas Sutpen's motives, his reasons for opposing the marriage. They have felt Charles's reasons for insisting on the marriage and Henry's victimization as an instrument of his father. They have entered into the heart's blood, the central symbolic image of the novel, the symbol of the old verities which touch the heart and to which the heart holds as truth. Sutpen's honor is embodied in the design that will crumble if he accepts Charles as his son or allows the marriage. The love of sons for fathers and of brothers for sisters becomes a tragic trap within that design. If love, honor, courage, compassion, and pride are found at the center of these inexplicable events, then the boys have discovered "what must be true." As Cass Edmonds says to young Ike McCaslin in *Go Down, Moses*, "what the heart holds to becomes truth, as far as we know truth."

In order for Quentin and Shreve to complete this act of imagination, they must come to understand Sutpen more fully than anyone does. The key to understanding Sutpen comes in chapter 6, when Quentin repeats what he has learned from General Compson, to whom Sutpen has confided much of his life story. Sutpen is the child of an independent mountain family who have fallen on hard times and have become tenant farmers. His ambition springs into being on the day he discovers that in the eyes of the plantation owner's black doorman he is insignificant "white trash." On that day, he determines to right this injustice by becoming a planter himself. He dreams that when he is a planter, he will not turn away the boy messenger from his door. He becomes a planter in Haiti, then abandons everything to go to Mississippi. Having built a second plantation there and begun his dynasty again, he sacrifices his son to cancel the son by the first marriage. As General Compson sees it, Sutpen's great weakness is his innocence. Sutpen is never able to understand how history betrays him. By becoming a planter, Sutpen inevitably adopts the material forms which determine the morality of the planter, and he lacks the imagination to circumvent those forms. In fact, Sutpen is so literal, rigid, and puritanical in his adoption of the design that he becomes a grotesque of a planter. The messenger boy who comes to his door is his own mulatto son, yet Sutpen can only turn away without even so much as an "I know you are my son though I cannot say so publicly."

Sutpen's innocence and the rigidity of his design account for many of the mysteries of his life. As General Compson says, Sutpen seems to think of morality, even of life as a whole, as like a cake; if one includes the ingredients and follows the recipe, only cake can result. Supten's design is so abstract that he is utterly blind to the feelings of others. He fails to anticipate Rosa's probable reaction to the second proposal. He never thinks of how Wash will react to his treatment of Milly. He never expects that Charles Bon will be the boy at his door. When Sutpen tells his story to General Compson, he is seeking the missing ingredient which has twice prevented him from completing his design and his revenge. Sutpen's boyhood experience has cut him off from the truth of the heart. He has, instead, rigidly grasped a single truth and has made it into a falsehood in his Olympian effort to make the world conform to the shape of that truth.

Because of Sutpen's failure, many children stand before doors which they cannot pass. Only an act of sympathetic imagination can get one past the symbolic doors of this novel, but most of the children are so victimized that they are incapable of imaginative sympathy. Even Quentin would not be able to pass his door, the subjects of incest and a sister's honor, without help from Shreve. Without Quentin's passion and knowledge, Shreve would never have seen the door. Their brotherhood is a key "ingredient" in their imaginative power.

Many significant elements of this complex novel must remain untouched in any brief analysis. One other aspect of the novel, however, is of particular interest: In *Absalom, Absalom!*, Faulkner suggests the possibility of seeing the Yoknapatawpha novels as a saga, a unified group of works from which another level of significance emerges. He chooses to end *Absalom, Absalom!* with a map of Yoknapatawpha County. This map locates the events of all the preceding Yoknapatawpha novels and some that were not yet written, though the relevant Snopes stories had appeared in magazines. Reintroducing the Compson family also suggests that Faulkner was thinking of a unity among his novels in addition to the unity of the individual works. It seems especially significant that Shreve McCannon, an outsider, neither a Compson nor a southerner nor an American, makes the final imaginative leap which inspirits Sutpen's story with the heart's truth. In this way, that truth flows out of its narrow regional circumstances to a world which shares in the same heart's blood. With *Absalom, Absalom!*, Faulkner may have seen more clearly than before how his novels could be pillars to help men

"endure and prevail" by reminding them of those "old verities," the central motives which bind humankind and the Yoknapatawpha novels together.

GO DOWN, MOSES

In *Go Down, Moses*, Faulkner juxtaposes two sides of the McCaslin family. This contrast comes to center on Lucas Beauchamp, a black descendant, and Isaac McCaslin, a white descendant of L. Q. C. McCaslin, the founder of the McCaslin plantation. Although the novel divides roughly in two and has the appearance of a collection of stories, it is unified as an explanation of the opening phrases which summarize Isaac's life. Ike is distinguished by his refusals to inherit the family plantation or to own any other land because he believes the earth belongs to no man, by his love for the woods, and by the fact that though he has married and is uncle to half a county, he has no children.

"Was," "The Fire and the Hearth," and "Pantaloon in Black" deal primarily with the black McCaslins. Taken together, these stories dramatize the suffering of basically good people, black and white, as they struggle to make and preserve their marriages and to honor their blood ties despite the barrier of racism.

"Was" tells how Tomey's Turl and Tennie arrange their marriage. Turl and Tennie are slaves on neighboring plantations in the days when such farms were half a day's travel apart. In this comic interlude, remembered from before Isaac's birth, Hubert Beauchamp, owner of the neighboring farm, tries without success to marry his sister, Sophonsiba, to Isaac's father, Buck McCaslin. It becomes clear that the plot to land Buck is a cooperative effort among the slave couple and the Beauchamps. The plot ends with a poker game in which Buck's twin, Uncle Buddy, nearly outmaneuvers Hubert. That Turl is the dealer convinces Hubert to settle for the advantages he has gained rather than chance losing everything to Buddy. Buck escapes for the time being, though he eventually marries Sophonsiba, and Tennie and Turl achieve their marriage. These two marriages generate the two main characters of the novel, Lucas and Isaac. From this point of view the tale is funny and almost heartwarming, but it has a tragic undertone, for Turl, it turns out, is half brother to the twins. Even though Buck and Buddy are reluctant and enlightened slaveholders, they try to prevent their brother's marriage and must be tricked into permitting it.

This barrier of race which separates brothers and threatens marriages is the center of "The Fire and the Hearth." This long story dramatizes two pairs of conflicts. In the present, Lucas Beauchamp discovers a gold piece buried on Roth Edmonds's plantation. The Edmonds have become inheritors of the McCaslin land because of Isaac's repudiation. In his mad search for "the rest of the gold," Lucas becomes a barrier to the marriage of his daughter with George Wilkins, a rival moonshiner. To get rid of Wilkins, Lucas uses the very racist rituals which have caused him suffering; he appeals to Roth's paternalistic dominance of his black tenants. This conflict reminds Lucas of his previous conflict with Roth's father, Zack. In this conflict, Zack and Lucas, who were reared as brothers, nearly kill each other because as a black, Lucas simply cannot believe Zack's statement that though he had the opportunity, he has not cuckolded Lucas.

The second present conflict arises when Lucas's wife, Mollie, decides she will divorce her husband because he has become obsessed with finding gold. When she announces this plan to Roth, Roth remembers his own relationship with Lucas and Mollie, especially that Mollie is the only mother he ever had. His childhood memories prominently include the shame he felt when racism came between him and his "family." Now, when he most needs to, he cannot talk with them heart to heart.

In "Was" and "The Fire and the Hearth," the wall of racism divides lovers, brothers, parents, and children. All suffer because what their hearts yearn for is forbidden by their racial experience. Familial love is blocked by racism. "Pantaloon in Black" completes this picture of tragic suffering with a powerful image of what whites, especially, lose by inherited racist attitudes. Rider and Mannie, tenants on Edmonds land, love passionately. When Mannie dies, Rider cannot contain his grief. He moves magnificently toward a complex love-death. Juxtaposed to this image is the marriage of a local deputy which contains no passion or compassion. They live separate lives, the wife's emotional needs satisfied by card parties and motion pictures. Their brief discussion of Rider's grief and death reveals that because they are unable to see their black brothers as human, they are cut off from imagining their feelings, cut off from sympathy and, finally, cut off from their own humanity.

"The Old People," "The Bear," and "Delta Autumn" tell the story of Isaac: of his education for life in the woods, his consecration to that life, the resulting decision to repudiate his inheritance and the consequence of that decision, including his wife's refusal to bear his children.

Isaac's education begins with Sam Fathers. Sam contains the blood of all three races which share in the founding of America. In him the wilderness ideal of brotherhood is made visible. On the other hand, Sam contains the sins of the American Indians who sold land not theirs to sell and then went on to buy and sell men, including Sam, who was sold as a slave by his own father. Sam is the last of the old people and, therefore, figures in both the origins and the victimizations of the races. When Isaac perceives these meanings in Sam's life, his spontaneous response is, "Let him go!" But this Mosaic wish is futile, Ike is told. There is no simple cage which can be unlocked to free Sam. From that moment, Ike tries to discover some effective way to set some of God's lowly people free.

By means of the stories of the old people, Sam teaches Ike that, in the wilderness, all people are guests on the earth. In the wilderness, the hunt becomes a ritual by which man, in taking the gifts of the land for his sustenance, participates in the immortal life processes of the cosmos. Here even the barriers between life and death lack significance. Opposed to this view is the civilization represented by the divided fields outside the wall of the big woods. In this outer world, land ownership divides the haves and the have-nots. Conceiving of the land as dead matter to be bought and sold leads to conceiving of people as beasts to be bought and sold. Ike comes to see this decline in humanity in his own family history as contained in the ledgers of the plantation commissary.

In part 4 of "The Bear," having seen the death of

Old Ben, the bear which stands for the life of the old wilderness, Ike explains to his older cousin, Cass Edmonds, why he will not accept his inheritance, the McCaslin plantation. Though quite complex, his argument is mainly that if owning land leads directly to the exploitation of God's lowly people, then refusing to own the land may help end such exploitation. He takes on the responsibility of attempting to realize in civilization the values of the wilderness to which he has consecrated himself. Among the reasons for his choice is the pattern he sees in his family history.

His grandfather, L. Q. C. McCaslin, seems almost incomprehensible to Ike because he bought a beautiful slave, fathered a daughter with her, and then fathered a son, Tomey's Turl, with that daughter. To Ike, these acts represent the worst of the violations which arise from arrogant proprietorship. In his grandfather's will, in the subsequent actions of Buck and Buddy in freeing slaves, in the Civil War and in his own education, Ike sees a pattern which leads him to think his family may have a responsibility to help bring an end to these wrongs. By repudiating his inheritance, he hopes humbly to participate in making love possible between the races.

Critics disagree about whether readers are to see Ike as heroic in the tradition of saintliness or as a fool who hides his light under a bushel by refusing to risk the exercise of power in behalf of his beliefs. While Ike does not fall into Sutpen's trap, largely because he conceives of his mission as acting for others rather than for himself, he may choose too passive a means to his end. It may be that Faulkner intended a suspension between these alternatives which would heighten the tragic dimensions of moral choice in the complex welter of human events. It is difficult to fault Ike's motives or his perception of the situation, but when assessing the effectivenes of his actions, one finds roughly equal evidence for and against his choice.

In "Delta Autumn," Ike is a respected teacher. He speaks with a wisdom and authority which command attention, if not full understanding, from his companions and which speak directly to Roth Edmonds's shame at his inability to marry the mulatto woman he loves and to claim his son by her. While Ike has noth-ing of which to be ashamed, his refusal of the land has helped to corrupt the weaker Roth. Ike has known that he would probably never see the amelioration for which he has worked and, more than any of his companions, Ike understands that something sacred, which he can call God, comes into being when people love one another. Nevertheless, he must suffer seeing the sins of his grandfather mirrored by Roth, for Roth's mistress is a descendant of Tomey's Turl. Ike must tell that woman to accept the repudiation of her love, and he must accept her accusation that he knows nothing about love. Whether Ike is a saint or a fool seems endlessly arguable. That he is to some extent aware of this dilemma may be part of the tragic significance of his life. He cannot learn whether his example will contribute to ending the shame of denied love which results from racism and which perpetuates it. He can only believe.

"Go Down, Moses," the last story, reemphasizes the desire for spiritual unity between the races and the apparently insuperable barriers which remain. Mollie Beauchamp's grandson, Samuel Worsham Beauchamp, is executed for murdering a Chicago policeman. Sam is the opposite of Sam Fathers. He is the youngest son, sold into the slavery of making money too fast, which devalues human life. Mollie's grieving chant that Roth Edmonds sold her Benjamin into Egypt echoes the imagined grief of the biblical Jacob whom his sons claim will die if they return from Egypt without their youngest brother. Roth has taken responsibility for this young relation and then has repudiated him. Mollie's accusation is fundamentally correct. The sympathetic but paternalistic white community of Jefferson cannot see this connection and so, despite its good heart, it cannot cross the barrier between races and truly enter into Mollie's grief. Gavin Stevens, the community's representative, feels driven from the scene of grief before the fire on the hearth by the intense passion of Mollie's grieving. Ike's sacrifice has changed nothing yet, but whether it was a bad choice remains hard to decide.

Faulkner wrote many fine novels which cannot be discussed here. The Snopes Trilogy and *The Reivers* are often included among his masterpieces, in part because they reveal especially well Faulkner's great but sometimes overlooked comic gifts.

Faulkner's reputation has grown steadily since his Nobel Prize. Some critics are ready to argue that he is America's greatest novelist. They base their claim on the power of his novels to fascinate a generation of readers, to provoke serious and profound discussion about the modern human condition while engaging significant emotions, and to give the pleasures of all great storytelling, the pleasures of seeing, knowing, believing in and caring for characters like oneself at crucial moments in their lives. The quantity and quality of his work, as well as the worthy unity of purpose which emerges from analysis of his career, tend to confirm the highest estimate of Faulkner's accomplishment.

Terry Heller

OTHER MAJOR WORKS

SHORT FICTION: *These Thirteen*, 1931; *Doctor Martino and Other Stories*, 1934; *The Portable Faulkner*, 1946, 1967; *Knight's Gambit*, 1949; *Collected Short Stories of William Faulkner*, 1950; *Big Woods*, 1955; *Three Famous Short Novels*, 1958; *Uncollected Stories of William Faulkner*, 1979.

SCREENPLAYS: *Today We Live*, 1933; *To Have and Have Not*, 1945; *The Big Sleep*, 1946; *Faulkner's MGM Screenplays*, 1982.

POETRY: *The Marble Faun*, 1924; *A Green Bough*, 1933.

NONFICTION: *New Orleans Sketches*, 1958; *Faulkner in the University*, 1959; *Faulkner at West Point*, 1964; *Essays, Speeches and Public Letters*, 1965; *The Faulkner-Cowley File: Letters and Memories, 1944-1962*, 1966 (Malcolm Cowley, editor); *Lion in the Garden*, 1968; *Selected Letters*, 1977.

MISCELLANEOUS: *The Faulkner Reader*, 1954; *William Faulkner: Early Prose and Poetry*, 1962.

BIBLIOGRAPHY

Blotner, Joseph. *Faulkner: A Biography*. 2 vols. New York: Random House, 1974. Once criticized for being too detailed (the two-volume edition is some two thousand pages) this biography begins before Faulkner's birth with ancestors such as William Clark Falkner, author of *The White Rose of Memphis*, and traces the writer's career from a precocious poet to America's preeminent novelist.

Brodhead, Richard H., ed. *Faulkner: New Perspectives*. Englewood Cliffs, N.J.: Prentice-Hall, 1983. One volume in the Twentieth Century Views series under the general editorship of Maynard Mack, offering nearly a dozen essays by a variety of Faulkner scholars. Among them are Irving Howe's "Faulkner and the Negroes," first published in the early 1950's, and Cleanth Brooks's "Vision of Good and Evil" from Samuel E. Balentine's *The Hidden God* (Oxford, England: Oxford University Press, 1983). Contains a select bibliography.

Cox, Leland H., ed. *William Faulkner: Biographical and Reference Guide*. Detroit, Mich.: Gale Research, 1982.

_____. *William Faulkner: Critical Collection*. Detroit, Mich.: Gale Research, 1982. These companion volumes constitute a handy reference to most of Faulkner's work. The first is a reader's guide which provides a long biographical essay, cross-referenced by many standard sources. Next come fifteen "critical introductions" to the novels and short stories, each with plot summaries and critical commentary particularly useful to the student reader. A three-page chronology of the events of Faulkner's life is attached. The second volume contains a short potpourri, with Faulkner's "Statements," a *Paris Review* interview, and an essay on Mississippi for *Holiday* magazine among them. The bulk of the book is an essay and excerpt collection with contributions by a number of critics including Olga Vickery, Michael Millgate, and Warren Beck. Includes a list of works by Faulkner including Hollywood screenplays.

Gray, Richard. *The Life of William Faulkner: A Critical Biography*. Oxford, England: Blackwell, 1994. A noted Faulkner scholar, Gray closely integrates the life and work. Part 1 suggests a method of approaching Faulkner's life; part 2 concentrates on his apprentice years; part 3 explains his discovery of Yoknapatawpha and the transformation of his region into his fiction; part 4 deals with his treatment of past and present; part 5 addresses his exploration of place; part 6 analyzes his final novels, reflecting on his creation of Yoknapatawpha. Includes family trees, chronology, notes, and a bibliography.

Inge, M. Thomas, ed. *Conversations with William Faulkner.* Jackson: University Press of Mississippi, 1999. Part of the Literary Conversations series, this volume gives insight into Faulkner the person. Includes bibliographical references and index.

Vickery, Olga W. *The Novels of William Faulkner.* Baton Rouge: Louisiana State University Press, 1959. This volume, with its comprehensive treatment of the novels, has established itself as a classic, a *terminus a quo* for later citicism. The chapter on *The Sound and the Fury*, providing an analysis of the relation between theme and structure in the book, remains relevant today despite intensive study of the topic.

Volpe, Edmond L. *A Reader's Guide to William Faulkner.* New York: Noonday Press, 1964. While many books and articles have contributed to clearing up the murkiest spots in Faulkner, the beginning student or general reader will applaud this volume. In addition to analysis of structure, themes, and characters, offers critical discussion of the novels in an appendix providing "chronologies of scenes, paraphrase of scene fragments put in chronological order, and guides to scene shifts."

Williamson, Joel. *William Faulkner and Southern History.* New York: Oxford University Press, 1993. A distinguished historian divides his book into sections on Faulkner's ancestry, his biography, and his writing. Includes notes and genealogy.

JESSIE REDMON FAUSET

Born: South Hill, New Jersey; April 27, 1882
Died: Philadelphia, Pennsylvania; April 30, 1961

PRINCIPAL LONG FICTION

There Is Confusion, 1924
Plum Bun: A Novel Without a Moral, 1929
The Chinaberry Tree: A Novel of American Life, 1931
Comedy, American Style, 1933

OTHER LITERARY FORMS

In addition to the four novels, Jessie Redmon Fauset wrote short stories, poems, nonfictional pieces, and works for children. She also translated the work of some Haitian writers.

ACHIEVEMENTS

Jessie Fauset was one of the most prolific novelists of the Harlem Renaissance of the 1920's, when her works were highly praised for introducing the reading public to a class of African Americans unknown to whites. Perhaps more important than her own works was her publishing and nurturing of other Harlem Renaissance writers as literary editor of *The Crisis*, the journal of the National Association for the Advancement of Colored People (NAACP), from 1919 to 1926. In that capacity, she published works by Langston Hughes, Claude McKay, Nella Larsen, Jean Toomer, and Countée Cullen. In 1920, Fauset also became the managing editor of the short-lived *The Brownies' Book*, writer W. E. B. Du Bois's magazine for children. Her first novel, *There Is Confusion*, was nominated for the Harmon Award in Literature in 1928.

BIOGRAPHY

Jessie Redmon Fauset, the youngest of seven children born to Redmon Fauset, an African Methodist Episcopal minister, and Annie Seamon Fauset, was born in South Hill, New Jersey, on April 27, 1882. She attended the public schools in Philadelphia and graduated as an honor student from the Philadelphia School for Girls. When she sought admission to Bryn Mawr College, rather than admit her, they supported her application to Cornell University. Fauset graduated Phi Beta Kappa from Cornell in 1904. Whether she was the first black woman to attend Cornell or to be elected to Phi Beta Kappa, both of which are often speculated, Fauset "was one of the best educated Americans of her generation."

Denied employment in Philadelphia's integrated schools, Fauset began teaching high school in New York in 1905. After a year there and a year in Baltimore, she moved to the M Street High School (later named Dunbar High School) in Washington, D.C., where she taught for fourteen years. In 1921, a few months after receiving her master's degree from the University of Pennsylvania, Fauset joined the staff of *The Crisis* as literary editor. In 1924 she published her first novel. Fauset left *The Crisis* and returned to teaching in 1926. In 1929, she married a businessman, Herbert Harris, and between 1929 and 1933, she completed three other novels. When her husband died in 1958, Fauset returned to Philadelphia, where she died in 1961.

ANALYSIS

Although she had been writing for *The Crisis* since her undergraduate days, it was not literary aspiration that spurred Fauset to write novels, but rather the 1922 publication of T. S. Stribling's novel about a middle-class mulatto, *Birthright*. Realizing that there was "an audience waiting to hear the truth about" African Americans, Fauset felt that those who were better qualified than whites to present the truth should do so. In presenting such truth, Fauset wrote about characters she knew best: educated African Americans from respectable family backgrounds, whose values and goals were, as she stated, "not so vastly different from other Americans." Fauset used traditional literary forms in her writing, such as the sentimental novel, Greek tragedy, and fairy tales, and was criticized for offering nothing innovative during a time when African American writers were experimenting with cultural forms and themes. In addition, because Fauset's novels focused on women and women's issues, they were dismissed in the 1930's by both white and black male critics. With the burgeoning interest in African American women's literature in the 1970's, female critics began to discover the complexity of Fauset's novels and to note her treatment of gender, class, and race issues. As a result, Fauset's works have become the focus of increased critical attention.

THERE IS CONFUSION

Fauset's first novel, *There Is Confusion*—a tale of two families—is structured by three separate but connected plotlines, the first of which focuses on the Marshalls, a well-to-do family. Joanna, the youngest of the four children, encouraged by her father's thwarted dreams of greatness, wants to become a dancer. The second plotline focuses on Peter Bye, the fourth-generation descendant of a family whose lives are intertwined with their wealthy white former owners. While Peter's grandfather, Isaiah, refuses to accept his relative's offer to serve as their coachman and goes on to found a school for black youths in Philadelphia, Peter's dreams of becoming a surgeon are thwarted because he longs to be recognized by the white Byes and is not. Meriwether, Peter's father, deciding instead that "the world owes [him] a living," does nothing. Influenced by his father's attitude, Peter becomes entangled in the legacy of racial hatred and aspires to nothing. It is only when he becomes attracted to Joanna and is influenced by her goals of greatness that he decides, in order to win her love, to become a doctor.

The third plotline, the story of Maggie Ellersley, the daughter of a washerwoman, involves a conventional marriage. Aspiring to the middle class, Maggie begins working for Joanna's father, where she meets and takes an interest in his son, Philip. The interest appears to be mutual; however, Joanna intervenes and tells Maggie that she should marry someone in her own class. A hurt Maggie does so, then becomes a successful businesswoman when the marriage fails. After a second failed marriage, Maggie goes to France to volunteer during the war and encounters the dying Philip. They marry, and she takes care of him until his death.

Within each plotline Fauset heavy-handedly reveals the obstacles to the achievement of each character's dreams: Joanna's dream of becoming a professional dancer is thwarted by race; Peter's dream (or lack thereof) is influenced by family legacy; Maggie's dream is hindered by class. Yet Fauset also reveals how each character achieves despite the obstacles. Unable to dance in a white theater troupe, Joanna starts her own dance class but is asked to dance the role of the colored American in "The Dance of the Nations" when the white woman chosen for the part lacks the technique. Joanna attains instant success and is eventually asked to perform three roles.

Peter, because of his love for Joanna, becomes a surgeon; however, she has no interest in assuming the conventional roles of wife and mother. Therefore, caught in the web of circumstances characteristic of sentimental novels, and through a series of contrived coincidences, Peter ends up in Europe during the war and meets one of his white relatives. Young Meriwether dies in Peter's arms, but not before extracting the promise that Peter would visit the senior Meriwether. By moving beyond hate, Peter not only receives the long-awaited recognition from the white Byes but also wins Joanna as his wife.

As evidenced by the many hardships that Maggie undergoes, Fauset suggests that Maggie's aspiration—to transcend one's class through marriage—is the most problematic. Maggie achieves her desired middle-class status not through her marriages, but rather through her business acumen. Moreover, by developing a political and racial consciousness and selflessness and traveling to Europe to aid black soldiers, she is reunited with her first love. *There Is Confusion* ends, as do all sentimental novels, on a happy note. While there are many ideas introduced in the novel, critic Carolyn Sylvander states that the theme that dominates is that "surviving the hardships engendered by discrimination places the black person and the race in a position of superiority."

PLUM BUN

Fauset's second novel, *Plum Bun*, is considered by most critics her best. As with *There Is Confusion*, a middle-class African American family is at the novel's center, but unlike *There Is Confusion*, its plot is centered on one protagonist, Angela. In addition, the novel is structured in five parts, using a nursery rhyme as its epigraph and unifying element:

> To market, to market
> To buy a plum bun;
> Home again, home again,
> Market is done.

In the first section, entitled "Home," Fauset's readers are introduced to the Murray family: Junius and Mattie and their two daughters, Angela and Virginia. This section also provides the background information important to the rest of the novel. Angela and Virgina are exposed early on to their mother's fairy-tale view of marriage. Just as importantly, they are exposed to her views on color. Although Junius and Virginia are both brown-skinned, Mattie and Angela are light enough to pass—which they often do "for fun." Junius is not opposed to this as long as no principle is being compromised. The result is, however, that Angela grows up seeing her mother on occasion publicly ignore her dark husband and daughter. When the parents die within two weeks of each other, Angela decides to move to New York in order to further her personal and professional goals. In "Market," Angela becomes the art student Angele Mory and is indoctrinated in the worldly ways of courtship. In section 3, entitled "Plum Bun," Angele meets Roger Fielding, an affluent white man, whom she dates and eventually hopes to marry. Roger does not propose marriage but rather cohabitation. Angele does not agree, and he eventually ends the relationship, but not before Angele has publicly denied Virginia, who has also moved to New York.

In "Home Again," the novel's fourth section, Angele, in search of companionship, admits her love for Anthony Cross, a fellow art student who is also passing. Having resolved never to marry a white woman, Anthony rejects Angele and becomes engaged unknowingly to her sister.

In the final section, "Market Is Done," Angele decides to focus on her art. She wins a scholarship to study in Paris but forfeits it by revealing that she, too, is black when fellow student Rachel Powell is denied money for her passage because of her race. Angele decides to support her own study in Paris. Before she leaves the United States, she returns "home" to Philadelphia and is reunited with a former admirer, Matthew Henson. Knowing that Virginia is really in love with Matthew, and learning that Matthew loves Virginia, Angele does not interfere. Instead she moves to Paris, seemingly destined to be alone; however, Anthony appears that Christmas Eve, sent with Matthew and Virginia's love. Like *There Is Confusion*, *Plum Bun* has a happy ending.

By including the nursery rhyme and fairy-tale motifs within the marriage plot, Fauset explores the choices and compromises women make regarding marriage. The novel "without a moral" indeed has one: Adhering to the traditional conceptions of marriage is problematic when race, class, and gender are factors.

THE CHINABERRY TREE

Fauset's theme of the effects of race, gender, and class as focused within two-parent, multiple-sibling families is abandoned in her third novel. *The Chinaberry Tree* relates the story of two cousins, Laurentine Strange and Melissa Paul, who are both products of illicit relationships.

Laurentine is the product of an illicit romantic relationship between a master, Colonel Halloway, and his former slave, Sarah. Accepting the community's opinion that she has "bad blood," Laurentine isolates herself from the community, and rejection from a suitor reinforces her feelings of inadequacy and propels her to further isolation. Melissa, the product of an adulterous relationship between Judy Strange and the married Sylvester Forten, is sent to Red Brook to live with her relatives. She meets and falls in love with Malory Forten, who, unknown to her, is her half brother. The novel explores both women's responses to being innocent victims of fate.

The Chinaberry Tree is not merely Fauset's attempt to reveal that "negroes are not so vastly different" nor that their lives are elements of a play falling together, as stated in its foreword. It is a subtle illustration of women making choices and accepting the consequences: Both Sal and Judy Strange choose forbidden loves. In spite of their "bad blood," as the daughters are seemingly tainted by their mothers' choices, Laurentine and Melissa are able to find true love at the novel's end. What appears to be another example of Fauset's blind acceptance of the values of nineteenth century sentimental fiction is a subtle commentary on women refusing to adhere to the constrictions placed on their lives.

COMEDY, AMERICAN STYLE

Fauset structured her final novel around the elements of drama, with its chapters entitled "The Plot," "The Characters," "Teresa's Act," "Oliver's Act," "Phebe's Act," and "Curtain." In this, Fauset's darkest work, she returns to the format of the two-parent family. The novel chronicles the life of Olivia Blanchard Cary, a light-skinned African American, who, shaped by two incidents in her childhood, chooses a life of passing. She marries a black doctor, not for love but rather for status, and they have three children. Nonetheless, Olivia's obsession with color consciousness destroys the family. When the oldest child, Teresa, falls in love with the dark-skinned Henry Bates, Olivia intervenes and forces her to marry a French man.

The youngest child, Oliver, suffers the most because of his bronze skin color. Rejected by his mother from birth and often made to play the role of servant or denied in public, he commits suicide. Only Christopher survives intact through his marriage to Phebe Grant. When the novel ends, Olivia has finally achieved her objective: Living alone in France—her husband has divorced her, and her children have abandoned her—she passes as white. In this, her only novel that does not have a happy ending, Fauset's use of satire is quite evident. One critic pointing to Fauset's subversion of the Cinderella motif notes that neither mother nor daughter is happily married, and both are poor. Another critic illustrates the ironic use of the Snow White motif: Olivia pronounces the bitter truth in her pregnancy with Oliver that he would be "the handsomest and most attractive of us all," and by doing so she unwittingly proclaims that black is beautiful.

Paula C. Barnes

BIBLIOGRAPHY

McDowell, Deborah. "Jessie Fauset." In *Modern American Women Writers*, edited by Lea Baechler and A. Walton Litz. New York: Charles Scribner's Sons, 1991. A general discussion of Fauset's role in the Harlem Renaissance as editor and writer, the article provides an analysis of Fauset's four novels to illustrate their "thematic and ironic complexity."

Sato, Hiroko. "Under the Harlem Shadow: A Study of Jessie Fauset and Nella Larsen." In *The Harlem Renaissance Remembered*, edited by Arna Bontemps. New York: Dodd, Mead, 1972. While asserting that Fauset "is not a first rate writer," Sato argues that race is the central concern of the novels' middle-class characters.

Sylvander, Carolyn. *Jessie Redmon Fauset: Black American Writer*. Troy, N.Y.: Whitston, 1981. In this definitive critical biography on Fauset, Sylvander argues that reading Fauset's novels as compared to her life is too simplistic.

Wall, Cheryl. *Women of the Harlem Renaissance*. Bloomington: Indiana University Press, 1995. Wall provides an excellent discussion of all of Fauset's works yet believes Fauset achieved distinction as a journalist and essayist.

EDNA FERBER

Born: Kalamazoo, Michigan; August 15, 1885
Died: New York, New York; April 16, 1968

PRINCIPAL LONG FICTION

Dawn O'Hara: The Girl Who Laughed, 1911
Fanny Herself, 1917
The Girls, 1921
So Big, 1924
Show Boat, 1926
Cimarron, 1930
American Beauty, 1931
Come and Get It, 1935
Saratoga Trunk, 1941
Great Son, 1945
Giant, 1952
Ice Palace, 1958

OTHER LITERARY FORMS

In addition to twelve novels, Ferber wrote eight plays, two novellas, eighty-three short stories, and two autobiographies. Although her novels have perhaps been the most enduring part of her work, her short stories and plays were equally or more important during her lifetime. Almost all her work, except drama, first appeared serially in magazines. In addition, she wrote numerous short articles and commentaries. Twenty-two Emma McChesney stories made Ferber a best-selling writer. These were first published in *The American Magazine* or *Cosmopolitan* between 1911 and 1915 and later were collected in *Roast Beef Medium* (1913), *Personality Plus* (1914), and *Emma McChesney and Co.* (1915). Emma McChesney also was the heroine of *Our Mrs. McChesney* (1915), Ferber's first play written with George V. Hobart. The McChesney character was a significant innovation—the first successful businesswoman depicted in popular American literature. Finally, however, Ferber declined *Cosmopolitan*'s proffered contract for as many McChesney stories as she wished to write at a price she could name. Ferber saw herself, instead, as a novelist and dramatist. Plays written with George S. Kaufman, especially *Dinner at Eight* (1932), *The Royal Family* (1927), and *Stage Door* (1936), enjoyed long Broadway runs and secured her fame as a dramatist. Her autobiographies, *A Peculiar Treasure* (1939, 1960) and *A Kind of Magic* (1963), explain her motivations and detail her writing techniques. The books also are intensely personal and revealing. The second, written after her health began to deteriorate, is rambling and repetitive but essentially completes the story of her active life.

ACHIEVEMENTS

Ferber maintained herself as a best-selling author and a popular celebrity from the appearance of the Emma McChesney stories in 1911 to the publication of *Ice Palace* in 1958. During this period, she was cited several times as America's best woman novelist, and literary notables, such as William Allen Wright, Rudyard Kipling, and James M. Barrie, praised her work. Her reputation, however, abruptly declined in the late 1960's. Resurgence began in the 1980's, fueled mostly by interest in her several social crusades. Advocacy of social and political causes in her fiction significantly influenced public opinion and policy. Ernest Gruening, territorial senator elect of Alaska, for example, cited Ferber's *Ice Palace* as important in winning Alaska's statehood. Explication of regional history and culture in her novels also played a prominent part in raising pride in American culture after World War I. Her short story *Half Portions* received the O. Henry Award in 1919. In 1924, her novel *So Big* won the Pulitzer Prize for fiction. Jerome Kern and Oscar Hammerstein II's classic musical play *Show Boat* (1927), based on Ferber's novel, was the first American musical with a serious plot derived from a literary source. The story also was used in a successful radio serial program and four films; it made so much money that Ferber referred to it as her "oil well." She associated with many prominent theatrical, literary, and political figures, including members of the Algonquin Round Table, the literary circle which met for lunch at New York's Algonquin Hotel. At least twenty-seven films are based on her works.

BIOGRAPHY

Edna Jessica Ferber was the second daughter of a Hungarian Jewish immigrant storekeeper, Jacob Charles Ferber, and Julia Neuman Ferber, daughter of a prosperous, cultured German Jewish family. She was named Edna because the family, hoping for a male child, had already selected the name Edward. When she was born in Kalamazoo, Michigan, her father owned and operated a general store. Soon the business faltered, and they moved in with Julia's parents in Chicago. After moving to Ottumwa, Iowa, then back to Chicago, then to Appleton, Wisconsin, the store still failed to prosper. Jacob Ferber, though intelligent, kindly and cultured, never acquired business skills and soon lost his sight. Thus, Julia assumed management of the business and became the head of the family. With great personal effort and the active assistance of Edna, she stabilized the business, paid off debts, and maintained the family's independence.

Edna described Ottumwa as narrow-minded and sordid. There she experienced anti-Semitism and witnessed a lynching. During her high school years at Appleton, however, she enjoyed pleasant, tolerant, midwestern small-town life. Unable to afford college tuition in 1902, she began her professional writing career as a reporter for the *Appleton Daily Crescent*. Eighteen months later the editor, who had hired her on the strength of her reportorial writing in her high school paper, left, and Ferber was fired. The most credible reason given for her dismissal was her imaginative "embroidering" of news reports. She then became a reporter on the *Milwaukee Journal*. Exhausted by overwork and anemia, she returned home

(Library of Congress)

in 1905 and began writing fiction. High school and about five years of newspaper writing comprised Ferber's entire preparation for her literary career.

After her father's death in 1909, her mother sold the store and took her two daughters to Chicago. There, while her mother and sister earned their living, Edna continued writing. In 1912, after selling some of her work, she moved to New York but remained closely attached to her mother. Thereafter, she and her mother resided in hotels or apartments in New York, Chicago, and elsewhere but considered themselves New Yorkers. Though they did not always actually live together, their lives were closely intertwined. In 1938, Edna built a house for herself in suburban Connecticut, pointedly leaving her mother in a New York apartment. After Julia died, Edna sold her house and returned to a New York apartment. During her last ten years, a painful nervous disorder impaired her writing. Never married, she died of stomach cancer in New York City on April 16, 1968.

ANALYSIS

Ferber was a feminist, a conservationist, a crusader for minorities and immigrants, and a staunch believer in the work ethic and American culture. Strong women characters rising above the limitations of birth and gender dominate her novels; most men in her works are weak, and many desert their women and children. She describes and condemns mistreatment of African Americans, Jews, Latinos, and Native Americans. Results of unrestrained capitalism and wasteful exploitation of natural resources are decried. Her novels celebrate regional culture and history in an effective and pleasing style that clearly reflects her journalistic background. Characterization, however, is less effective and plots tend toward melodrama and coincidence.

All of Ferber's novels were commercial successes, and many remained in print for decades after publication. Her first novels, *Dawn O'Hara: The Girl Who Laughed* and *Fanny Herself*, are strongly autobiographical. They remain interesting because they show Ferber's literary growth. Background material in *Great Son* is sketchy, characters are stereotypic,

and the plot is contrived. At the time of its writing, Ferber was preoccupied writing World War II propaganda. Her final novel, *Ice Palace*, is a political tract of little literary merit; Ferber was ill at the time of its writing.

THE GIRLS

Ferber expected this book to be a best-seller and considered it her best novel. The story recounts six decades of Chicago middle-class history and intergenerational conflict. Charlotte Thrift, forbidden to marry an unsuitable boy, loses him to death in the Civil War. She never marries. Her unmarried niece, Lottie, under her mother's domination, keeps house for her mother and aunt. Lottie finally rebels, joins the Red Cross during World War I, has a brief affair, and returns with her illegitimate daugher, whom she passes off as a French orphan. Charly (Charlotte), Lottie's niece, falls in love with a poet, who is killed in World War I, and moves in with her aunt and great-aunt. All three are strong personalities, while their men are either incompetent boors or scoundrels.

SO BIG

Ferber's first best-seller effectively contrasts humble life in the Halstead Street Market with that of pretentious Chicago society. A genteelly reared orphan, Selina Peake, goes to teach school in a community of Dutch market gardeners, where she must adjust to a brutal existence. Her only intellectual companion is thirteen-year-old Roelf, the artistically talented son of the family with whom she lives. After a year, she marries kindly Pervus DeJong, an unimaginative, unenterprising widower. They have a son, Dirk, nicknamed So Big. After Pervus's death, Selina makes their farm a thriving success. She sacrifices all for So Big, who, after a few years as a struggling architect, shifts to a banking career and high society. In contrast, Selina's first protégé, Roelf, becomes a famous sculptor. At the end So Big finally realizes that his life is empty. Although the novel was critically acclaimed, characterization barely develops beyond stereotypes, and many anecdotes are clichés.

SHOW BOAT

Show Boat describes life aboard late nineteenth and early twentieth century Mississippi River showboats and their cultural significance. Magnolia Hawkes, daughter of Captain Andy and Parthenia Hawkes of the showboat Cotton Blossom, marries Gaylord Ravenal, a charming professional gambler. After Captain Andy's death, Magnolia, Gaylord, and their daughter Kim move to Chicago, where they squander Magnolia's inheritance. Magnolia, deserted by her wastrel husband, becomes a successful singer and raises Kim to become a successful serious actress. Parthenia inherits and successfully operates the showboat. Parthenia, Magnolia, and Kim are all protofeminist career women. Captain Andy, though competent and wise, defers to Parthenia in almost everything. African Americans are presented as patient, upright, and hardworking people. A tragic incident of miscegenation and the injustice of southern law balance the romanticized account of the showboat life, which is charming.

CIMARRON

Cimarron is set in Oklahoma between the 1889 land rush and the 1920's oil boom. Sabra Cravat begins life as a genteel, impoverished southern girl but ends up an assured newspaperwoman and congresswoman. Her husband, Yancey Cravat, a flamboyant lawyer-newspaperman of dubious background, starts grandiose projects, performs heroic acts, and upholds high ideals, but he accomplishes little. Desertion of his family clears the way for Sabra's rise. These characters exemplify the tension between those who "won" Oklahoma and those who "civilized" it. Also, interaction between Native and Euro-Americans is perceptively treated.

AMERICAN BEAUTY

Ferber rhapsodically describes the Connecticut landscape in this novel, in which abuse of land and resources is chronicled. Polish immigrant culture is sympathetically presented, and the indigenous New Englanders are depicted as played-out aristocrats. Judy Oakes and her niece, Tamar Pring, are strong, stubborn women devoted to their aristocratic background and ancestral home. Their hired man, Ondy Olszak, a kindhearted, hard-working, unimaginative Polish immigrant, maintains the farm at just above subsistence level. Tamar seduces and marries Ondy, and their son Orrange combines Ondy's peasant vigor and Tamar's cultural sensibilities. Although Orrange inherits the farm, Ondy's family forces him to sell. Millionaire True Baldwin, who, as an impoverished farm lad, had aspired to marry Judy Oakes, buys it. Fortunately, Baldwin's architect daughter, Candace (Candy) Baldwin, sexually attracted to Orrange, hires him to manage the farm.

COME AND GET IT

Ferber draws heavily on her own background in this story of resource exploitation, unrestrained capitalism, and social contrast. After lumberjack Barney Glasgow fights his way up to a managerial position at the mill, he marries his boss's spinsterish daughter. Timbering and papermaking thrive under his direction, until he is fatally attracted to Lotta Lindaback, granddaughter of his longtime lumberjack pal, Swan Bostrom. Barney's daughter, frustrated by unacknowledged desire for her father, marries a dull young businessman. Bernard, Barney's son, pursues Lotta when Barney restrains his own passion for her. Barney then fights with Bernard and expels him from the house. Immediately afterward, Barney and his family are killed in an explosion. Bernard marries Lotta and builds an industrial empire in steel and paper. Lotta, meanwhile, enters international high society. The Great Depression forces Lotta's return to Wisconsin, where her twins come under the influence of Tom Melendy, an idealistic young man of a mill-hand family. Rejecting their parent's materialism, they return to the simple Bostrom ways.

SARATOGA TRUNK

In this story, Ferber decries the evils of unrestrained capitalism and the decadent snobbery of New Orleans high society. She also promotes women's causes and natural resource conservation. Illegitimate Clio Dulain and Texas cowboy-gambler Clint Maroon join forces to extort money from Clio's aristocratic father. Then they move to Saratoga, New York, where Clio sets out to snare a rich husband. Although she entraps railroad millionaire Van Steed, she drops him for Clint when Clint is injured fighting for Van Steed's railroad, the Saratoga Trunk. Thereafter Clio and Clint become railroad millionaires but idealistically give their wealth to charity. Clio subtlely manipulates Clint in all important matters.

GIANT

Ferber's flamboyant version of Texas history and culture exemplified the Texas mythology and earned violent protests from Texans. Ferber's typical strong female central character, Leslie Lynnton, daughter of a world-famous doctor living in genteel shabbiness, is swept off her feet by a visiting Texas rancher. Transported to his gigantic ranch, she finds her husband ruled by his spinster sister, Luz. Luz dies violently, and, with great skill and wisdom, Leslie guides her man through repeated crises as the great cattle and cotton "empires" are hemmed in by vulgar oil billionaires. The original Texans, Mexican Americans, are shown as deeply wronged, patient, dignified, and noble. Unfortunately, the book's end leaves ongoing problems unsolved.

Ralph L. Langenheim, Jr.

OTHER MAJOR WORKS

SHORT FICTION: *Buttered Side Down*, 1912; *Roast Beef Medium*, 1913; *Personality Plus*, 1914; *Emma McChesney and Co.*, 1915; *Cheerful—By Request*, 1918; *Half Portions*, 1919; *Gigolo*, 1922; *Mother Knows Best*, 1927; *They Brought Their Women*, 1933; *Nobody's in Town*, 1938 (includes *Nobody's in Town* and *Trees Die at the Top*); *One Basket*, 1947.

PLAYS: *Our Mrs. McChesney*, pr., pb. 1915 (with George V. Hobart); *$1200 a Year*, pr., pb. 1920 (with Newman A. Levy); *Minick*, pr., pb. 1924 (with George S. Kaufman); *The Royal Family*, pr. 1927 (with Kaufman); *Dinner at Eight*, pr., pb. 1932 (with Kaufman); *Stage Door*, pr., pb. 1936 (with Kaufman); *The Land Is Bright*, pr., pb. 1941 (with Kaufman); and *Bravo!*, pr. 1948 (with Kaufman).

NONFICTION: *A Peculiar Treasure*, 1939, 1960 (revised with new introduction); *A Kind of Magic*, 1963.

BIBLIOGRAPHY

Gaines, James R. *Wits End, Days and Nights of the Algonquin Round Table*. New York: Harcourt Brace Jovanovich, 1977. An anecdotal history illuminating Ferber's association with the Algonquin group.

Gilbert, Julie Goldsmith. *Ferber: Edna Ferber and Her Circle: A Biography*. New York: Applause, 1999. A good biography of Ferber. Includes an index.

Goldsmith, Julie Gilbert. *Ferber: A Biography*. Garden City, New York: Doubleday, 1978. An intimate biography by her grandniece.

Goldstein, Malcolm. *George S. Kaufman: His Life, His Theatre*. New York: Oxford University Press, 1979. Details Ferber's association with Kaufman.

Kunkel, Thomas. *Genius in Disguise, Harold Ross of the New Yorker*. New York: Random House, 1995. Reveals Ferber's involvement with *The New Yorker*.

Shaughnessy, Mary Rose. *Women and Success in American Society in the Works of Edna Ferber*. New York: Gordon Press, 1977. Discusses Ferber's place in the women's movement.

GABRIEL FIELDING
Alan Gabriel Barnsley

Born: Hexham, Northumberland, England; March 25, 1916

Died: Bellevue, Washington; November 27, 1986

PRINCIPAL LONG FICTION

Brotherly Love, 1954

In the Time of Greenbloom, 1956

Eight Days, 1958

Through Streets Broad and Narrow, 1960

The Birthday King, 1962

Gentlemen in Their Season, 1966

Pretty Doll Houses, 1979

The Women of Guinea Lane, 1986

OTHER LITERARY FORMS

Gabriel Fielding's literary reputation rests primarily on his prose, but his early work was in poetry, published in two collections, *The Frog Prince and Other Poems* (1952) and *XXVIII Poems* (1955), neither of which matches his prose in quality or critical acclaim. He also published two books of short stories—*Collected Short Stories* (1971) and

New Queens for Old: A Novella and Nine Stories (1972)—which are substantial enough in literary quality and theme to form a significant part of Fielding's canon.

ACHIEVEMENTS

By 1963 Fielding had established the reputation which was maintained, but never enhanced, by his later work. Some critics view Fielding as a Catholic writer, comparable with Graham Greene, Evelyn Waugh, and Muriel Spark, concerned with social and moral issues from a specifically Catholic point of view; this aspect of his work was duly recognized when he was awarded the St. Thomas More Association Gold Medal in 1963 and the National Catholic Book Award in 1964. Other critics, however, see him as a writer belonging to the school of European existentialist writers, sharing their philosophic worldview; this second estimate was expressed in the W. H. Smith Literary Award, which Fielding received in 1963.

BIOGRAPHY

Alan Gabriel Barnsley was born in Hexham, Northumberland, England, on March 25, 1916, the fifth of six children of an Anglican vicar. After going to school at St. Edward's, Oxford, he took a B.A. at Trinity College, Dublin, and from there went to St. George's Hospital, London, from which he was graduated with a medical degree in 1941. He immediately started his war service in the Royal Army Medical Corps, continuing his service until demobilization in 1946. After the war, he was in general medical practice in Maidstone, Kent, until 1966, part of his duties being those of Medical Officer for Maidstone Prison, the experience of which contributed significantly to several of his novels. He did not start writing seriously until his middle thirties, and in 1966, when he considered his literary career to be established, he left the medical profession to become, first, Author in Residence and, then, Professor of English at Washington State University, Pullman, a position which he held until retirement. Fielding died in Bellevue, Washington, on November 27, 1986.

ANALYSIS

In the context of British novelists of the twentieth century, Gabriel Fielding presents some characteristics that distinguish his work sharply from that of the mainstream novelist and, at the same time, place him firmly in a tradition that, in fact, goes back to the realistic social novel of Daniel Defoe. Fielding's distinctiveness lies in a steadiness and explicitness of worldview and ethical philosophy which raise his novels well above mere stories or entertainments; his identification with British literary tradition reveals itself in the spell he casts as a storyteller whose characters, plots, and settings have the dramatic quality of those found in the works of Thomas Hardy and Charles Dickens, striking the reader's mind like reality itself and haunting the memory forever. The result of what is, for a British novelist, an unusual combination of philosophic outlook and intensity of fictional realization is an integrated creativity that expresses the writer's unified sensibility of spirit and mind and that evokes within the reader an intense and often uncomfortable urge to reassess his or her own preoccupations and prejudices, yet whose effect is ultimately cathartic.

Fielding's major novels—*In the Time of Greenbloom, The Birthday King*, and *Gentlemen in Their Season*—pursue and explore a theme which is more frequently found in the European novel than the British: that of individual responsibility in an irrational world. Each of the three novels has a different "world" as its setting—a middle-class English county, Nazi Germany, and postwar liberal London—but the dilemmas of decision and action that face the protagonists in each novel are of the same kind. The novels' settings reflect the stages of Fielding's own life: country vicarage and Oxford, wartime military service, and postwar intellectual life in London. In many ways one feels that the novels represent a working-out in fiction of the writer's own perplexities, which were not resolved until his immigration to the United States—to the more primal setting of eastern Washington and the Moscow Mountains, where it is clear that Fielding found a peace and joy of life, and a professional satisfaction, which had eluded him in England.

The autobiographical element of Fielding's work is seen most clearly in the four novels concerning the Blaydon family. The family name itself is a well-known Northumbrian place-name, while the chronicles of John Blaydon—spanning childhood in *Brotherly Love*, adolescence in *In the Time of Greenbloom*, adulthood and medical studies in *Through Streets Broad and Narrow*, and wartime medical service in *The Women of Guinea Lane*—reflect the early progress of Fielding's own life. Of the three Blaydon novels, *In the Time of Greenbloom* is the most striking, in its presentation of a guilt-ridden and domineering adult society bent on finding sin in the young. In the novel, twelve-year-old John Blaydon is wrongly blamed for the death of his friend Victoria Blount, who has been murdered by a hiker in a cave. He is made the scapegoat for an adult crime, and he is ready to acquiesce in the guilt forced on him by the adult world when he is saved by the ministrations of Horab Greenbloom, an eccentric Jewish Oxford undergraduate who applies to John's sense of guilt a bracing dose of Wittgensteinian positivism and Sartrean existentialism. Greenbloom's therapeutic interest is that of one scapegoat for another, and his remedy is to make John see that the empty, abstract categories of the adult moral scheme lead ultimately to personal irresponsibility and inevitable pangs of guilt which must be transferred to the innocent and vulnerable for punishment.

The theme of blame, and the accompanying figure of the scapegoat, had initially been explored in *Brotherly Love*, in which John observes and chronicles the moral demolition of his older brother, David, by his domineering mother. She forces him to become a priest, thereby perverting David's natural creative talents into sordid sexual encounters and alcoholism. In this earlier novel, the adult world is only too successful in transferring its empty notions of duty, faith, sin, and shame to the adolescent, but there is no suggestion of an alternative, redemptive way. *In the Time of Greenbloom* offers hope for redemption in the magus figure of Greenbloom through his resolute opposition to spurious objective abstraction and his insistence that John must make his own moral decisions and not accept those offered by his elders. (In this and in several other respects, Fielding anticipates the concerns and solutions offered in Robertson Davies' *The Deptford Trilogy*.)

The Birthday King

The theme of guilt, blame, and the scapegoat principle is one that preoccupies Fielding in all of his major novels, but nowhere does it achieve more compelling realization than in *The Birthday King*, which elevates and generalizes John's suffering in a northern English county to the agony of a whole race in wartime Nazi Germany. The novel chronicles the rise and fall of Nazi Germany through the lives of two Jewish brothers, Alfried and Ruprecht Waitzmann, who are directors of a large industrial group and thus somewhat protected from liquidation by the Nazis. The contrasting responses of the two brothers to the dictatorship of Adolf Hitler represent the twin facts of Jewishness and of humans as a whole in reaction to mindless oppression. Alfried, as a rather self-indulgently pious man, innocent yet provocative, opts for the untidiness of life, represented by the dirty, smelly goat in the Kommandant's garden. His rejection of the hygienic bureaucracy and simple slogans of the Nazis causes him to be imprisoned and tortured in an attempted "cure" of his wayward individuality, and he thus becomes the scapegoat, despised by his friends more than by the Nazis (for whom he actually lightens the burden of guilt). Ruprecht, on the other hand, represents the alternative path: survival at any cost. He is an opportunist and a schemer, preserving the family business by betraying Alfried and running his factories on forced labor for the Nazi regime.

The novel explores the consequences of the brothers' different choices—sacrifice and survival—each of which has been made with existential authenticity, both in their different ways morally "right." Alfried's response, with its mystical innocence and awkward honesty, is that of the child who rejects the adult world of organized belief and consequent absurd moral simplifications. Ruprecht's response is just as true to his own shrewd, aggressive, and lucky nature in a world in which he sees Germany as one gigantic concentration camp in which the only possible choice is for survival. The kind of choice each brother makes is less important than the fact that each actually makes a conscious choice freely, rather than choosing to join the bored sleepwalkers: the camp Kommandant, his puritanical wife, and the aristocratic remnants of old Germany, such as von Hoffbach and von Boehling, who applaud the new Wagnerian romanticism of the Third Reich while sneering at the inferior social status of the Nazi party upstarts. For Fielding, the only corrective to the mind-numbing boredom represented by Nazi Germany is the exercise of free will in subjective decision.

GENTLEMEN IN THEIR SEASON

Boredom provides the focus of *Gentlemen in Their Season* as well, but Fielding narrows his scope to marriage in the postwar, liberated world. In many ways, this novel is more complex than the earlier and, arguably, better novels in that issues are less clear-cut and the possibility of authentic decision is consequently much reduced. Moreover, the setting and characters, in their familiarity and ordinariness, are uncomfortably close to the reader, who is unable to distance himself from the action as he is in *In the Time of Greenbloom* and *The Birthday King*. The plot of *Gentlemen in Their Season* concerns two middle-aged, middle-class liberal intellectuals, Randall Coles and Bernard Presage, whose marriages, to an assertive humanist and a rather religiose Catholic, respectively, have stagnated to the point of artificiality, which takes the form of clever parties, esoteric intellectualism, mutual criticism, and automatic churchgoing. Each man drifts into a pointless affair, with tragic consequences for a third party, Hotchkiss, whose simple Christian faith in monogamy has already led to his imprisonment for the manslaughter of his wife's lover, who escapes from prison to confront her current lover, Coles, and to force him to practice the morality that he preaches as director of religious programming for the British Broadcasting Corporation (BBC). In impulsive reaction, and horrified at having to make a simple act of faith in front of Hotchkiss, Coles betrays him to the police, who kill him in their attempted arrest.

This novel, probably the blackest, most ironic and comic of all of Fielding's novels, reduces the sleepwalking quality of a whole nation in *The Birthday King* to the level of ordinary, casual, and unthinking behavior of men whose abstract conceptions of what modern marriage should be make them indecisive, vacillating, and morally irresponsible, while they continue to justify their behavior on intellectualized principles remote from the concerns of real life. Hotchkiss, by breaking out of prison and confronting Coles, makes the only authentic decision in the whole course of events, and by consciously being an agent, rather than a victim to whom things lamely happen, he forces action on the part of others and thus, in his self-sacrifice, atones for the sins of his intellectual and social superiors.

The central concern in all of Fielding's major novels is the moral necessity for human action in the fullest sense of deliberate, self-aware decisiveness in a society that is largely content to go along with the crowd, to rationalize behavior in terms of social, political, religious, and intellectual abstractions. The actions that result from such decisiveness may, in fact, lead to the protagonist's becoming the scapegoat for society's somnambulistic and self-justifying atrocities but ultimately awaken the sleepwalkers for a while, dazzling people into self-awareness by their enormity. Although this theme is existential, it is a Catholic existentialism, reconciling the principles most fundamental to Christian faith with the natural, human, subjective conscience, and promoting will as a necessary accompaniment to belief. Adult institutions of class, politics, and church may, and for most do, substitute slogans for principles and apologetics for action, but the blame lies not in the institutions themselves but in society's slavish and easy acquiescence in the precepts which demand least exercise of will.

The starkness of Fielding's theme associates his work most closely with European preoccupations, constantly reminding the reader of figures such as Jean-Paul Sartre, Albert Camus, Hermann Hesse, and Günter Grass. The only British writer who shares these preoccupations is Graham Greene, whose continentalism makes most British critics, who are more comfortable with what might be called the "cardigan-and-post-office" kind of novel, suspicious of the underlying philosophic concerns of his fiction. The poor critical response in Great Britain to Fielding's work arises, one imagines, from a similar fear of philosophic depth.

Despite the philosophic significance of Fielding's novels, they are works of literature, not of philosophy. What elevates Fielding beyond the level of mere "messenger," didacticist, or programmatic writer is the other face of his work: the elevation of narrative over precept, of imagery and language over naked theme. His novels are by no means mere illustrative allegories of readymade themes, but explorations in narrative which lead, perhaps to the surprise of the writer, to inevitable philosophic conclusions. It is the power and richness of plot, character, and language, and the concreteness of setting that put Fielding in the grand tradition of the English novel with Dickens, the Brontës, and Hardy, making his novels compelling and memorable in themselves, not merely as vehicles of Catholic-existentialist thought. The elemental images of purifying water and oppressive earth, the institutional images of the prison, the school, the hospital, and the bureaucratic machinery, together with the evocative associations of proper names ("Badger," "Toad," "Greenbloom," "Hubertus," and "Presage") interweave with one another and with settings rich in symbolism (the cave where Victoria is murdered, the Anglo-Catholic church with its dead image of Christ, the deserted swimming pool where Ruprecht and Carin make love, the camp of forced workers, Alfried's punishment cell, and Hotchkiss's prison cell), creating a text of such richness as to transcend its constituent parts and to enter the reader's consciousness like reality itself. The texture of Fielding's language is that of the best dramatic poetry: Images, allusions, and references, in the vigorous expression of quite ordinary speech, cluster and weave to engender a depth and breadth of experience which triggers unconscious associations supporting the reader's conscious interpretation of plot and character to produce a wholly new, vital, and often disturbing sensibility.

Frederick Bowers

OTHER MAJOR WORKS

SHORT FICTION: *Collected Short Stories*, 1971; *New Queens for Old: A Novella and Nine Stories*, 1972.

POETRY: *The Frog Prince and Other Poems*, 1952; *XXVIII Poems*, 1955.

BIBLIOGRAPHY

Bloom, Harold, ed. *Twentieth Century British Literature*. Vol. 2. New York: Chelsea House, 1986. The entry on Fielding lists his works up to his novel *Pretty Doll Houses*. Reprinted here is an interview with Fielding from 1967, entitled "The Longing for Spring," which provides much useful information on the author and his work up until the mid-1960's.

Borrello, Alfred. *Gabriel Fielding*. New York: Twayne, 1974. Part of Twayne's English Authors series, this is a good introduction to Fielding's life and works. Includes bibliographical references and an index.

Bowers, Frederick. "Gabriel Fielding." In *Contemporary Novelists*, edited by James Vinson. London: St. James Press, 1976. Appraises Fielding in the light of his growing reputation as a major novelist with commentary on three of his novels: *In the Time of Greenbloom, The Birthday King*, and *Gentlemen in Their Season*. An appreciative essay that cites his novels as "good dramatic poetry."

_____. "Gabriel Fielding's *The Birthday King*." *The Queen's Quarterly* 74 (Spring, 1967): 148-158. Explores the themes of guilt, innocence, and personal responsibility in this novel, comparing the work to existentialists Albert Camus and Jean-Paul Sartre.

_____. "The Unity of Fielding's *Greenbloom*." Review of *In the Time of Greenbloom*, by Gabriel Fielding. *Renascence* 18 (Spring, 1966): 147-155. A favorable review, in which Bowers claims that the novel is of "major importance and worth in theme and execution." Comments on the existentialist nature of the novel, comparing it to the philosophy of Søren Kierkegaard, and on the scapegoat theme in this work.

HENRY FIELDING

Born: Sharpham Park, Somersetshire, England;
    April 22, 1707
Died: Lisbon, Portugal; October 8, 1754

PRINCIPAL LONG FICTION

An Apology for the Life of Mrs. Shamela Andrews,
    1741
*The History of the Adventures of Joseph Andrews,
    and of His Friend Mr. Abraham Adams*, 1742
*The History of the Life of the Late Mr. Jonathan
    Wild the Great*, 1743, 1754
The History of Tom Jones, a Foundling, 1749
Amelia, 1751

OTHER LITERARY FORMS

Henry Fielding's literary output, besides his novels, can be categorized in three groups: plays, pamphlets and miscellaneous items, and journals. In addition, the publication of his three-volume *Miscellanies* (1743) by subscription brought together a number of previously published items, as well as new works, including the first version of *The History of the Life of the Late Jonathan Wild the Great*, commonly known as *Jonathan Wild*, and an unfinished prose work, "A Journey from This World to the Next."

Fielding's dramatic works, many presented with great success at either of London's Little Theatre in the Haymarket or the Drury Lane Theatre, include ballad opera, farce, full-length comedy, and adaptations of classical and French drama. Most are overtly political in theme. Because of their contemporary subject matter, few have survived as viable stage presentations, although *The Covent Garden Tragedy* (1732) was presented by The Old Vic in London in 1968. Fielding also wrote a number of prologues, epilogues, and monologues performed in conjunction with other dramatic pieces.

The pamphlets and miscellaneous items which are currently attributed to Fielding, excluding those for which he merely wrote introductions or epilogues, are "The Masquerade" (1728), a poem; *The Military History of Charles XII King of Sweden* (1740),

a translation; "Of True Greatness" (1741), a poem; "The Opposition: A Vision" (1741), a poem; "The Vernoniad" (1741), a poem; "The Female Husband" (1746); "Ovid's Art of Love Paraphrased" (1747); "A True State of the Case of Bosavern Penlez" (1749); "An Enquiry into the Causes of the Late Increase in Robbers" (1751); "Examples of the Interposition of Providence in the Detection and Punishment of Murder" (1752); "A Proposal for Making an Effectual Provision for the Poor" (1753); "A Clear State of the Case of Elizabeth Canning" (1753); and *The Journal of a Voyage to Lisbon*, published posthumously (1755).

Fielding edited and made major contributions to four journals: *The Champion* (November 15, 1739-June 1741; the journal continued publication without Fielding until 1742); *The True Patriot* (November 5, 1745-June 17, 1746); *Jacobite's Journal* (December 5, 1747-November 5, 1748); and *The Covent-Garden Journal* (January 4-November 25, 1752).

ACHIEVEMENTS

Fielding's lasting achievements in prose fiction—in contrast to his passing fame as an essayist, drama-

(Library of Congress)

tist, and judge—result from his development of critical theory and from his aesthetic success in the novels themselves. In the preface to *The History of the Adventures of Joseph Andrews, and of His Friend Mr. Abraham Adams*, more commonly known as *Joseph Andrews*, Fielding establishes a serious critical basis for the novel as a genre and describes in detail the elements of comic realism; in *Joseph Andrews* and *The History of Tom Jones, a Foundling*, popularly known as *Tom Jones*, he provides full realizations of this theory. These novels define the ground rules of form that would be followed, to varying degrees, by Jane Austen, William Makepeace Thackeray, George Eliot, Thomas Hardy, James Joyce, and D. H. Lawrence, and they also speak to countless readers across many generations. Both, in fact, were translated into successful films (*Tom Jones*, 1963; *Joseph Andrews*, 1978).

The historical importance of the preface results from both the seriousness with which it treats the formal qualities of the novel (at the time a fledgling and barely respectable genre) and the precision with which it defines the characteristics of the genre, the "comic epic-poem in prose." Fielding places *Joseph Andrews* in particular and the comic novel in general squarely in the tradition of classical literature and coherently argues its differences from the romance and the burlesque. He also provides analogies between the comic novel and the visual arts. Thus Fielding leads the reader to share his conception that the comic novel is an aesthetically valid form with its roots in classical tradition, and a form peculiarly suited to the attitudes and values of its own age.

With his background in theater and journalism, Fielding could move easily through a wide range of forms and rhetorical techniques in his fiction, from direct parody of Samuel Richardson in *An Apology for the Life of Mrs. Shamela Andrews*, to ironic inversion of the great man's biography in *Jonathan Wild*, to adaptation of classical structure (Vergil's *Aeneid*, c. 29-19 B.C.) in *Amelia*. The two major constants in these works are the attempt to define a good, moral life, built on benevolence and honor, and a concern for finding the best way to present that definition to the reader. Thus the moral and the technique can never be separated in Fielding's works.

Joseph Andrews and *Tom Jones* bring together these two impulses in Fielding's most organically structured, brilliantly characterized, and masterfully narrated works. These novels vividly capture the diversity of experience in the physical world and the underlying benevolence of natural order, embodying them in a rich array of the ridiculous in human behavior. Fielding combines a positive assertion of the strength of goodness and benevolence (demonstrated by the structure and plot of the novels) with the sharp thrusts of the satirist's attack upon the hypocrisy and vanity of individual characters. These elements are held together by the voice of the narrator—witty, urbane, charming—who serves as moral guide through the novels and the world. Thus, beyond the comic merits of each of the individual novels lies a collective sense of universal moral good. The voice of the narrator conveys to the reader the truth of that goodness.

Although the novels were popular in his own day, Fielding's contemporaries thought of him more as playwright-turned-judge than as novelist. This may have been the result of the low esteem in which the novel as a form was held, as well as of Fielding's brilliant successes in these other fields. These varied successes have in common a zest for the exploration of the breadth and variety of life—a joy in living—that finds its most articulate and permanent expression in the major novels.

Today Fielding is universally acknowledged as a major figure in the development of the novel, although there is still niggling about whether he or Richardson is the "father" of the British novel. Ian Watt, for example, claims that Richardson's development of "formal realism" is more significant than Fielding's comic realism. Other critics, notably Martin Battestin, have demonstrated that Fielding's broader, more humane moral vision, embodied in classical structure and expressed through a self-conscious narrator, is the germ from which the richness and variety of the British novel grows. This disagreement ultimately comes down to personal taste, and there will always be Richardson and Fielding partisans to keep the controversy alive. There is no argument, however, that of their type—the novel of comic realism—no fiction has yet surpassed *Joseph Andrews* or *Tom Jones*.

BIOGRAPHY

Henry Fielding was born April 22, 1707, in Sharpham Park, Somersetshire, to Edmund and Sarah Fielding. His father, an adventurer, gambler, and swaggerer, was a sharp contrast to the quiet, conservative, traditional gentry of his mother's family, the Goulds. In 1710, the family moved to Dorset, where Fielding and his younger brother and three sisters (including the future novelist Sarah Fielding) would spend most of their childhood on a small estate and farm given to Mrs. Fielding by her father, Sir Henry Gould.

The death of Fielding's mother in April, 1718, ended this idyllic life. Litigation over the estate created a series of family battles that raged for several decades. In 1719, Fielding was sent to Eton College, partly because the Goulds wanted him influenced as little as possible by his father, who had resumed his "wild" life in London, and partly because he disliked his father's new, Catholic wife. Remaining at Eton until 1724 or 1725, Fielding made many friends, including George Lyttleton and William Pitt. At Eton he began his study of classical literature, a profound influence on his literary career.

Few details are known of Fielding's life during the several years after Eton. He spent a good deal of time with the Goulds in Salisbury, but he also led a hectic, boisterous life in London, spending much time at the theater, where the popular masquerades and burlesques influenced him greatly. His visits to the theater stimulated him to try his own hand at comedy, and in February, 1728, *Love in Several Masques*, based on his own romantic adventures of the previous year, was performed at Drury Lane.

In March, 1728, Fielding enrolled in the Faculty of Letters at the University of Leyden (Netherlands), where he pursued his interest in the classics. In August, 1729, at the age of twenty-two, he returned to London without completing his degree.

It is clear from his literary output in the 1730's that Fielding was intensely involved in theatrical life. From 1730 through 1737 he authored at least nine-teen different dramatic works (as well as presenting revivals and new productions of revised works), most with political themes, at both the Little Theatre in the Haymarket and the Drury Lane. In addition to writing ballad opera, full-length comedies, translations, and parodies, Fielding was also producing, revising the plays of other writers, and managing theater business. He also formed a new, important friendship with the artist William Hogarth.

His theatrical career came to an abrupt halt (although a few more plays appeared in the 1740's) with the passage of the Licensing Act of 1737 which resulted in the closing of many theaters. Fielding's political satire offended Prime Minister Sir Robert Walpole and had been part of the motivation for the government's desire to control and censor the theaters.

In addition to this theatrical activity with its political commentary, Fielding found time from 1733 to 1734 to court and marry Charlotte Cradock of Salisbury. Charlotte's mother died in 1735, leaving the entire estate to the Fieldings and alleviating many of the financial problems caused by the legal disputes over the estate in Dorset. The couple moved from London to East Stour the same year, although Fielding regularly visited London, because he was manager, artistic director, and controller-in-chief of the Little Theatre. The first of their three children, Charlotte, was born April 17, 1736.

Fielding's relentless energy (and desire to add to his income) compelled him to begin a new career in late 1737, whereupon he began to study law at the Middle Temple. He became a barrister on June 20, 1740, and spent the next several years in the Western Circuit. During this service he became friends with Ralph Allen of Bath. He remained active in the practice of justice, as attorney and magistrate, until he left England in 1754.

Fielding continued to involve himself in political controversy, even while studying law. He edited, under pseudonyms, *The Champion*, an opposition newspaper issued three times a week, directed against Prime Minister Walpole (a favorite subject of Fielding's satire). Later he would edit *The True Patriot* in support of the government during the threat of the Jacobite Rising, *Jacobite's Journal*, and *The Covent-Garden Journal*.

From theater to law to journalism—Fielding had already charged through three careers when the first installment of Richardson's *Pamela* appeared on November 6, 1740. Deeply disturbed by the artificiality of the novel's epistolary technique, and appalled by its perversion of moral values, Fielding quickly responded with *An Apology for the Life of Mrs. Shamela Andrews*, often referred to as *Shamela*, an "antidote" to *Pamela*. Although published anonymously, Fielding's authorship was apparent and created ill feelings between the two authors that would last most of their lives.

The success of *Shamela* encouraged Fielding to try his hand at a more sustained satire, which eventually grew into *Joseph Andrews*. In 1743 he published, by subscription, the *Miscellanies*, a collection of previously published works, and two new ones: an unfinished story, "A Journey from This World to the Next," and the first version of *Jonathan Wild*.

Although the mid-1740's brought Fielding fame, success, and money, his personal life was beset with pain. He suffered continually from gout, and Charlotte died in November, 1744. In the following year he became involved in the propaganda battles over the Jacobite Rising. On November 27, 1747, he married his wife's former maid, Mary Daniel, and some sense of peace and order was restored to his private life. They would have five children.

While forming new personal ties and continuing strong involvement in political issues, Fielding was preparing his masterwork, *Tom Jones*. He also took oath as Justice of the Peace for Westminster and Middlesex, London, in 1748, and opened an employment agency and estate brokerage with his brother in 1749. His last novel, *Amelia*, was not well received, disappointing those readers who were expecting another *Tom Jones*.

The early 1750's saw Fielding's health continue to decline, although he remained active in his judgeship, producing a number of pamphlets on various legal questions. In June of 1754, his friends convinced him to sail to Lisbon, Portugal, where the climate might improve his health. He died there on October 8, 1754, and is buried in the British Cemetery outside of Lisbon. *The Journal of a Voyage to Lisbon*, his last work, was published one year after his death.

ANALYSIS

Analysis and criticism of Henry Fielding's fiction have traditionally centered on the moral values in the novels, the aesthetic structure in which they are placed, and the relationship between the two. In this view, Fielding as moralist takes precedence over Fielding as artist, since the aesthetic structure is determined by the moral. Each of the novels is judged by the extent to which it finds the appropriate form for its moral vision. The relative failure of *Amelia*, for example, may be Fielding's lack of faith in his own moral vision. The happy ending, promulgated by the *deus ex machina* of the good magistrate, is hardly consistent with the dire effects of urban moral decay that have been at work upon the Booths throughout the novel. Fielding's own moral development and changes in outlook also need to be considered in this view. The reader must examine the sources of Fielding's moral vision in the latitudinarian sermons of the day, as well as the changes in his attitudes as he examined eighteenth century urban life in greater detail, and as he moved in literature from *Joseph Andrews* to *Amelia*, and in life from the theater to the bench of justice.

As is clear from the preface to *Joseph Andrews*, however, Fielding was equally interested in the aesthetics of his fiction. Indeed, each of the novels, even from the first parody, *Shamela*, conveys not only a moral message but a literary experiment to find the strongest method for expressing that message to the largest reading public. This concern is evident in the basic plot structure, characterization, language, and role of the narrator. Each novel attempts to reach the widest audience possible with its moral thesis. Although each differs in the way in which Fielding attempts this, they all have in common the sense that the *how* of the story is as important as the *what*. The novels are experiments in the methods of moral education—for the reader as well as for the characters.

This concern for the best artistic way to teach a moral lesson was hardly new with Fielding. His classical education and interests, as well as the immediate human response gained from theater audiences during his playwriting days, surely led him to see that fiction must delight as well as instruct. Fielding's novels are both exemplars of this goal (in their emphasis on incidents of plot and broad range of characterization) and serious discussions of the method by which to achieve it (primarily through structure and through narrative commentary).

The direct stimulation for Fielding's career as novelist was the publication of Samuel Richardson's *Pamela*, a novel that disturbed Fielding both by its artistic ineptitude and by its moral vacuousness. Fielding was as concerned with the public reaction to *Pamela* as he was with its author's methods. That the reading public could be so easily misled by *Pamela*'s morals disturbed Fielding deeply, and the success of that novel led him to ponder what better ways were available for reaching the public with his own moral thesis. His response to *Pamela* was both moral (he revealed the true state of Pamela/Shamela's values) and aesthetic (he exposed the artificiality of "writing to the moment").

Sermons and homilies, while effective in church (and certainly sources of Fielding's moral philosophy), were not the stuff of prose fiction; neither was the epistolary presentation of "virtue rewarded" of *Pamela* (nor the "objectively" amoral tone of Daniel Defoe's *Moll Flanders*, 1722). Fielding sought a literary method for combining moral vision and literary pleasure that would be appropriate to the rapidly urbanizing and secular society of the mid-eighteenth century. To find that method he ranged through direct parody, irony, satire, author-narrator intrusion, and moral exemplum. Even those works, such as *Jonathan Wild* and *Amelia*, which are not entirely successful, live because of the vitality of Fielding's experimental methods. In *Joseph Andrews* and *Tom Jones*, he found the way to reach his audience most effectively.

Fielding's informing moral values, embodied in the central characters of the novels (Joseph Andrews, Parson Adams, Tom Jones, Squire Allworthy, Mr. Harrison) can be summarized, as Martin Battestin has ably done, as Charity, Prudence, and Providence.

Fielding held an optimistic faith in the perfectability of humanity and the potential for the betterment of society, based on the essential goodness of human nature. These three values must work together. In the novels, the hero's worth is determined by the way in which he interacts with other people (charity), within the limits of social institutions designed to provide order (prudence). His reward is a life full of God's provision (providence). God's providence has created a world of abundance and plenitude; man's prudence and charity can guarantee its survival and growth. Both Joseph Andrews and Tom Jones learn the proper combination of prudence and charity. They learn to use their innate inclination toward goodness within a social system that insures order. To succeed, however, they must overcome obstacles provided by the characters who, through vanity and hypocrisy, distort God's providence. Thus, Fielding's moral vision, while optimistic, is hardly blind to the realities of the world. *Jonathan Wild*, with its basic rhetorical distinction between "good" and "great," and *Amelia*, with its narrative structured around the ill effects of doing good, most strongly reflect Fielding's doubts about the practicality of his beliefs.

These ideas can be easily schematized, but the scheme belies the human complexity through which they are expressed in the novels. Tom Jones is no paragon of virtue, but he must learn, at great physical pain and spiritual risk, how to combine charity and prudence. Even Squire Allworthy, as Sheldon Sacks emphasized in *Fiction and the Shape of Belief* (1964), is a "fallible" paragon. These ideas do not come from a single source, but are derived from a combination of sources, rooted in Fielding's classical education; the political, religious, and literary movements of his own time; and his own experience as dramatist, journalist, and magistrate.

Fielding's familiarity with the classics, begun at Eton and continued at the University of Leyden, is revealed in many ways: through language (the use of epic simile and epic conventions in *Joseph Andrews*), through plot (the symmetry of design in *Tom Jones*), through theme (the importance of moderation in all the novels), and through structure (the relationship of *Amelia* to Vergil's *Aeneid*). The preface to *Joseph*

Andrews makes explicit how much Fielding saw in common between his own work and classical literature. His belief in the benevolent order of the world, especially illustrated by country living, such as at Squire Allworthy's estate (Paradise Hall), is deeply rooted in the pastoral tradition of classical literature. These classical elements are combined with the beliefs of the latitudinarian homilists of the seventeenth and eighteenth centuries, who stressed the perfectibility of humankind in the world through good deeds (charity) and good heart (benevolence).

While Fielding's thematic concerns may be rooted in classical and Christian thought, his literary technique has sources that are more complex, deriving from his education, his own experience in the theater, and the influence of Richardson's *Pamela*. It is difficult to separate each of these sources, for the novels work them into unified and original statements. Indeed, *Joseph Andrews*, the novel most closely related to classical sources, is also deeply imbued with the sense of latitudinarian thought in its criticism of the clergy, and satire of Richardson in its plot and moral vision.

The London in which Fielding spent most of his life was a world of literary and political ferment, an age of factionalism in the arts, with the Tory wits (Jonathan Swift, Alexander Pope, John Gay, John Arbuthnot) allied against Colley Cibber, the poet laureate and self-proclaimed literary spokesman for the British Isles. Swift's *Gulliver's Travels* (1726) and Gay's *The Beggar's Opera* (1728) had recently appeared; both were influential in forming Fielding's literary methods—the first with its emphasis on sharp political satire, the second with the creation of a new literary form, the ballad opera. The ballad opera set new lyrics, expressing contemporary political and social satire, to well-known music. Fielding was to find his greatest theatrical success in this genre and was to carry it over to his fiction, especially *Jonathan Wild*, with its emphasis on London low life and its excesses of language.

It was a time, also, of great political controversy, with the ongoing conflicts between the Tories and Jacobites about the questions of religion and succession. Prime Minister Walpole's politics of expediency were a ripe subject for satire. Fielding's career as journalist began as a direct response to political issues, and significant portions of *Joseph Andrews* and *Tom Jones*, as well as *Jonathan Wild*, deal with political issues.

These various sources, influences, and beliefs are molded into coherent works of art through Fielding's narrative technique. It is through the role of the narrator that he most clearly and successfully experiments in the methods of teaching a moral lesson. Starting with the voice of direct literary parody in *Shamela* and moving through the varied structures and voices of the other novels, Fielding's art leads in many directions, but it always leads to his ultimate concern for finding the best way to teach the clearest moral lesson. In *Tom Jones* he finds the most appropriate method to demonstrate that the world is a beautiful place if man will live by charity and prudence.

Shamela

The key to understanding how *Shamela* expresses Fielding's concern with both the moral thesis and the aesthetic form of fiction is contained in the introductory letters between Parsons Tickletext and Oliver. Oliver is dismayed at Tickletext's exuberant praise of *Pamela* and at the novel's public reception and popularity. The clergy, in particular, have been citing it as a work worthy to be read with the Scriptures. He contends that the text of *Shamela*, which he encloses, reveals the "true" story of Pamela's adventures and puts them in their proper moral perspective. By reading Oliver's version, Tickletext will correct his own misconceptions; by reading *Shamela* (under the guidance of the prefatory letters), the public will laugh at *Pamela* and perceive the perversity of its moral thesis.

Shamela began, of course, simply as a parody of Richardson's novel, and, in abbreviated form, carries through the narrative of the attempted seduction of the young serving girl by the squire, and her attempts to assert her virtue through chastity or marriage. Fielding makes direct hits at Richardson's weakest points: His two main targets are the epistolary technique of "writing to the moment" and the moral thesis of "virtue rewarded" by pounds and pence (and marriage).

Fielding parodies the epistolary technique by carrying it to its most illogical extreme: Richardson's technical failure is not the choice of epistolary form, but his insistence on its adherence to external reality. Shamela writes her letters at the very same moment she is being attacked in bed by Squire Booby. While feigning sleep she writes: "You see I write in the present tense." The inconsistency of Pamela's shift from letters to journal form when she is abducted is shown through Fielding's retention of the letter form throughout the story, no matter what the obstacles for sending and receiving them. He also compounds the criticism of Richardson by including a number of correspondents besides Shamela (her mother, Henrietta Maria Honora Andrews, Mrs. Jewkes, Parson Williams) and including various complications, such as letters within letters within letters.

Fielding retains the essential characters and key scenes from *Pamela*, such as Mr. B's hiding in the closet before the attempted seduction, Pamela's attempted suicide at the pond, and Parson Williams's interference. For each character and scene Fielding adopts Richardson's penchant for minute descriptive detail and intense character response to the event; he also parodies the method and seriousness of the original by revealing the motives of the characters.

The revealing of motives is also Fielding's primary way of attacking the prurience of Richardson's presentation, as well as the moral thesis behind it. He debunks the punctilio (decorum) of the central character. Shamela's false modesty ("I thought once of making a little fortune by my person. I now intend to make a great one by my virtue") mocks Pamela's pride in her chastity; the main difference between them is Shamela's recognition and acceptance of the mercenary motives behind her behavior and Pamela's blindness to her own motivation. Richardson never examines the reliability of Pamela's motivations, although he describes her thoughts in detail. Fielding allows Shamela to glory in both her ability to dupe the eager Squire Booby and her mercenary motives for doing so. The reader may, as Parson Oliver wants Tickletext to do, easily condemn Shamela for a villain but never for a hypocrite.

Fielding also attacks Richardson's refusal to describe the sexual attributes of his characters or to admit the intensity of their sexual desires, particularly in the case of Pamela herself. Pamela always hints and suggests—and, Fielding claims, wallows in her suggestiveness. Fielding not only describes the sexual aspects directly, but exaggerates and reduces them to a comic level, hardly to be taken sensually or seriously. *Shamela* quickly, fully, and ruthlessly annihilates the moral thesis of "virtue rewarded" through this direct exaggeration. Fielding does not, however, in his role as parodist, suggest an alternative to *Pamela*'s moral thesis; he is content, for the time, with exposing its flaws.

This first foray into fiction served for Fielding as a testing ground for some of the rhetorical techniques he used in later works, especially the emphasis on satiric inversion. These inversions appear in his reversal of sexual roles in *Joseph Andrews*, the reversal of rhetoric in the "good" and "great" in *Jonathan Wild*, and the reversal of goodness of motive and evil of effect in *Amelia*. Fielding's concern to find a rhetorical method for presenting a moral thesis was confined in *Shamela* to the limited aims and goals of parody. He had such success with the method (after all, he had his apprenticeship in the satiric comedy of the theater), that he began his next novel on the same model.

JOSEPH ANDREWS

Like *Shamela*, *Joseph Andrews* began as a parody of *Pamela*. In his second novel, Fielding reverses the gender of the central character and traces Joseph's attempts to retain his chastity and virtue while being pursued by Lady Booby. This method of inversion creates new possibilities, not only for satirizing Richardson's work, but for commenting on the sexual morality of the time in a more positive way than in *Shamela*. The most cursory reading reveals how quickly Fielding grew tired of parody and how *Joseph Andrews* moved beyond its inspiration and its forerunner. Even the choice of direct narration rather than epistolary form indicates Fielding's unwillingness to tie himself to his model.

Most readers agree that the entrance of Parson Adams, Joseph's guide, companion, and partner in misery, turns the novel from simple parody into complex fiction. Adams takes center stage as both comic butt, preserving Joseph's role as hero, and moral guide, preserving Joseph's role as innocent.

Adams's contribution is also part of Fielding's conscious search for the best way to convey his moral thesis. The narrative refers continually to sermons, given in the pulpit or being carried by Adams to be published in London. These sermons are generally ineffectual or contradicted by the behavior of the clergy who pronounce them. Just as experience and the moral example of Adams's life are better teachers for Joseph than sermons—what could be a more effective lesson than the way he is treated by the coach passengers after he is robbed, beaten, and stripped?—so literary example has more power for Fielding and the reader. Adams's constant companion, his copy of Aeschylus, is further testament to Fielding's growing faith in his exemplary power of literature as moral guide. In *Joseph Andrews*, narrative art takes precedence over both parody and sermon.

Fielding's concern for method as well as meaning is given its most formal discussion in the preface. The historical importance of this document results from both the seriousness with which it treats the formal qualities of the novel and the precision with which it defines the characteristics of the genre, the "comic epic-poem in prose." The seriousness is established through the careful logic and organization of the argument and through the parallels drawn between the new genre and classical literature (the lost comic epic supposedly written by Homer) and modern painting (Michelangelo da Caravaggio and William Hogarth).

Fielding differentiates the comic epic-poem in prose from contemporary romances such as *Pamela*. The new form is more extended and comprehensive in action, contains a much larger variety of incidents, and treats a greater variety of characters. Unlike the serious romance, the new form is less solemn in subject matter, treats characters of lower rank, and presents the ludicrous rather than the sublime. The comic, opposed to the burlesque, arises solely from the observation of nature, and has its source in the discovery of the "ridiculous" in human nature. The ridiculous always springs from the affectations of vanity and hypocrisy.

Within the novel itself, the narrator will continue the discussion of literary issues in the introductory chapters to each of the first three of four books: "of writing lives in general," "of divisions in authors," and "in praise of biography." These discussions, although sometimes more facetious than serious, do carry through the direction of the opening sentence of the novel: "Examples work more forcibly on the mind than precepts." Additionally, this narrative commentary allows Fielding to assume the role of reader's companion and guide that he develops more fully in *Tom Jones*.

While the preface takes its cue from classical tradition, it is misleading to assume that *Joseph Andrews* is merely an updating of classical technique and ideas. Even more than *Shamela*, this novel brings together Fielding's dissatisfaction with Richardson's moral thesis and his support of latitudinarian attitudes toward benevolence and charity. Here, too, Fielding begins his definition of the "good" man in modern Christian terms. Joseph redefines the place of chastity and honor in male sexuality; Parson Adams exemplifies the benevolence all people should display; Mrs. Tow-wowse, Trulliber, and Peter Pounce, among others, illustrate the vanity and hypocrisy of the world.

The structure of the novel is episodic, combining the earthly journey and escapades of the hero with suggestions of the Christian pilgrimage in John Bunyan's *The Pilgrim's Progress* (1678-1684). Fielding was still experimenting with form and felt at liberty to digress from his structure with interpolated tales or to depend on coincidence to bring the novel to its conclusion. The immediate moral effect sometimes seems more important than the consistency of rhetorical structure. These are, however, minor lapses in Fielding's progression toward unifying moral thesis and aesthetic structure.

JONATHAN WILD

In *Jonathan Wild*, Fielding seems to have abandoned temporarily the progression from the moral statement of parody and sermon to the aesthetic statement of literary example. *Jonathan Wild* was first published in the year immediately following *Joseph Andrews* (revised in 1754), and there is evidence to indicate that the work was actually written before

Joseph Andrews. This is a reasonable assumption, since *Jonathan Wild* is more didactic in its method and more negative in its moral vision. It looks back toward *Shamela* rather than ahead to *Tom Jones*.

Jonathan Wild is less a novel, even as Fielding discusses the form in the preface to *Joseph Andrews*, than a polemic. Critic Northrop Frye's term, "anatomy," may be the most appropriate label for the work. Like other anatomies—Sir Thomas More's *Utopia* (1516), Swift's *Gulliver's Travels*, and Samuel Johnson's *Rasselas, Prince of Abyssinia*, (1759)—it emphasizes ideas over narrative. It is more moral fable than novel, and more fiction than historical biography, altering history to fit the moral vision.

More important, it was Fielding's experiment in moving the moral lesson of the tale away from the narrative (with its emphasis on incident and character) and into the rhetoric of the narrator (with its emphasis on language). Fielding attempted to use language as the primary carrier of his moral thesis. Although this experiment failed—manipulation of language, alone, would not do—it gave him the confidence to develop the role of the narrative voice in its proper perspective in *Tom Jones*.

Fielding freely adapted the facts of Wild's life, which were well known to the general public. He chose those incidents from Wild's criminal career and punishment that would serve his moral purpose, and he added his own fictional characters, the victims of Wild's "greatness," expecially the Heartfrees. Within the structure of the inverted biography of the "great" man, Fielding satirizes the basic concepts of middle-class society. He differentiates between "greatness" and "goodness," terms often used synonymously in the eighteenth century. The success of the novel depends on the reader's acceptance and understanding of this rhetorical inversion.

"Goodness," characterized by the Heartfrees, reiterates the ideals of behavior emphasized in *Joseph Andrews:* benevolence, honor, honesty, and charity, felt through the heart. "Greatness," personified in Wild, results in cunning and courage, characteristics of the will. The action of the novel revolves around the ironic reversal of these terms. Although Wild's actions speak for themselves, the ironic voice of the narrator constantly directs the reader's response.

Parts of *Jonathan Wild* are brilliantly satiric, but the work as a whole does not speak to modern readers. Fielding abandoned the anatomy form after this experiment, recognizing that the voice of the narrator alone cannot carry the moral thesis of a novel in a convincing way. In *Jonathan Wild*, he carried to an extreme the role of the narrator as moral guide that he experimented with in *Joseph Andrews*. In *Tom Jones*, he found the precise balance: the moral voice of the narrator controlling the reader's reaction through language and the literary examples of plot and character.

TOM JONES

In *Tom Jones*, Fielding moved beyond the limited aims of each of his previous works into a more comprehensive moral and aesthetic vision. No longer bound by the need to attack Richardson nor the attempt to define a specific fictional form, such as the moral fable or the comic epic-poem in prose, Fielding dramatized the positive values of the good man in a carefully structured narrative held together by the guiding voice of the narrator. This narrator unifies, in a consistent pattern, Fielding's concern for both the truthfulness of his moral vision and the best way to reach the widest audience.

The structure of *Tom Jones*, like that of *Joseph Andrews*, is based on the secularization of the spiritual pilgrimage. Tom must journey from his equivocal position as foundling on the country estate of Squire Allworthy (Paradise Hall) to moral independence in the hellish city of London. He must learn to understand and control his life. When he learns this lesson, he will return to the country to enjoy the plenitude of paradise regained that providence allows him. He must temper his natural, impetuous charity with the prudence that comes from recognition of his own role in the larger social structure. In precise terms, he must learn to control his animal appetites in order to win the love of Sophia Western and the approval of Allworthy. This lesson is rewarded not only by his gaining these two goals, but by his gaining the knowledge of his parentage and his rightful place in society. He is no longer a "foundling."

Unlike the episodic journey of *Joseph Andrews*, *Tom Jones* adapts the classical symmetry of the epic in a more conscious and precise way. The novel is divided into eighteen books. Some of the books, such as 1 and 4, cover long periods of time and are presented in summary form, with the narrator clearly present; others cover only a few days or hours, with the narrator conspicuously absent and the presentation primarily scenic. The length of each book is determined by the importance of the subject, not the length of time covered.

The books are arranged in a symmetrical pattern. The first half of the novel takes Tom from his mysterious birth to his adventures in the Inn at Upton; the second half takes him from Upton to London and the discovery of his parentage. Books 1 through 6 are set in Somerset at Squire Allworthy's estate and culminate with Tom's affair with Molly. Books 7 through 12 are set on the road to Upton, at the Inn, and on the road from Upton to London; the two central books detail the adventures at the Inn and Tom's affair with Mrs. Waters. Books 13 through 18 take Tom to London and begin with his affair with Lady Bellaston.

Within this pattern, Fielding demonstrates his moral thesis, the education of a "good man," in a number of ways: through the narrative (Tom's behavior continually lowers his moral worth in society); through characters (the contrasting pairs of Tom and Blifil, Allworthy and Western, Square and Thwackum, Molly and Lady Bellaston); and through the voice of the narrator.

Fielding extends the role of the narrator in *Tom Jones*, as teller of the tale, as moral guide, and as literary commentator and critic. Each of these voices was heard in *Joseph Andrews*, but here they come together in a unique narrative persona. Adopting the role of the stagecoach traveler, the narrator speaks directly to his fellow passengers, the readers. He is free to digress and comment whenever he feels appropriate, and there is, therefore, no need for the long interpolated tales such as appeared in *Joseph Andrews*.

To remind his readers that the purpose of fiction is aesthetic as well as moral, the narrator often comments on literary topics: "Of the Serious in Writing, and for What Purpose it is introduced"; "A wonderful long chapter concerning the Marvelous"; "Containing Instructions very necessary to be perused by

modern Critics." Taken together, these passages provide a guide to Fielding's literary theory as complete as the preface to *Joseph Andrews*.

Although in *Tom Jones* Fielding still schematically associates characters with particular moral values, the range of characters is wider than in his previous novels. Even a minor character, such as Black George, has a life beyond his moral purpose as representative of hypocrisy and self-servingness.

Most important, *Tom Jones* demonstrates Fielding's skill in combining his moral vision with aesthetic form in a way that is most pleasurable to the reader. The reader learns how to live the good Christian life because Tom learns that lesson. Far more effective than parody, sermon, or moral exemplum, the combination of narrative voice and literary example of plot and character is Fielding's greatest legacy to the novel.

Lawrence F. Laban

OTHER MAJOR WORKS

PLAYS: *Love in Several Masques*, pr., pb. 1728; *The Temple Beau*, pr., pb. 1730; *The Author's Farce, and The Pleasures of the Town*, pr., pb. 1730; *Tom Thumb: A Tragedy*, pr., pb. 1730 (revised as *The Tragedy of Tragedies*, pr., pb. 1731); *Rape upon Rape: Or, Justice Caught in His Own Trap*, pr., pb. 1730 (also known as *The Coffee-House Politician*); *The Letter-Writers: Or, A New Way to Keep a Wife at Home*, pr., pb. 1731; *The Welsh Opera: Or, The Grey Mare the Better Horse*, pr., pb. 1731 (revised as *The Grub-Street Opera*, pb. 1731); *The Lottery*, pr., pb. 1732; *The Modern Husband*, pr., pb. 1732 (five acts); *The Old Debauchees*, pr., pb. 1732; *The Covent Garden Tragedy*, pr., pb. 1732; *The Mock Doctor: Or, The Dumb Lady Cur'd*, pr., pb. 1732 (adaptation of Molière's *Le Médecin malgré lui*); *The Miser*, pr., pb. 1733 (adaptation of Molière's *L'Avare*); *Don Quixote in England*, pr., pb. 1734; *The Intriguing Chambermaid*, pr., pb. 1734 (adaptation of Jean-François Regnard's *Le Retour imprévu*); *An Old Man Taught Wisdom: Or, The Virgin Unmask'd*, pr., pb. 1735; *The Universal Gallant: Or, The Different Husbands*, pr., pb. 1735 (five acts); *Pasquin: Or, A Dramatic Satire on the Times*, pr., pb. 1736; *Tumble-Down Dick: Or,*

Phaeton in the Suds, pr., pb. 1736; *Eurydice: Or, The Devil's Henpeck'd*, pr. 1737 (one act); *Eurydice Hiss'd: Or, A Word to the Wise*, pr., pb. 1737; *The Historical Register for the Year 1736*, pr., pb. 1737 (three acts); *Miss Lucy in Town*, pr., pb. 1742 (one act); *The Wedding-Day*, pr., pb. 1743 (five acts; also known as *The Virgin Unmask'd*); *The Fathers: Or, The Good-Natured Man*, pr., pb. 1778 (revised for posthumous production by David Garrick).

NONFICTION: *The Journal of a Voyage to Lisbon*, 1755.

TRANSLATION: *The Military History of Charles XII King of Sweden*, 1740.

MISCELLANEOUS: *Miscellanies*, 1743 (3 volumes).

BIBLIOGRAPHY

Battestin, Martin C. *The Moral Basis of Fielding's Art: A Study of Joseph Andrews*. Middletown, Conn.: Wesleyan University Press, 1959. An important study arguing that in *Joseph Andrews* Fielding presents an allegory of the conflict between vanity and true Christian morality. Like John Bunyan's *The Pilgrim's Progress*, the novel traces the movement from the sinful city to the redemptive countryside. Sees the story of Mr. Wilson not as a digression but as a central expression of the novel's theme.

Battestin, Martin C., with Ruthe R. Battestin. *Henry Fielding: A Life*. London: Routledge, 1989. *The Sunday Times* voted this work one of the four best biographies of the year. Based on fourteen years' research, this detailed biography replaces Wilbur L. Cross's *The History of Henry Fielding* (1918, New York: Russell & Russell, 1945) as the definitive story of Fielding. Includes a useful bibliography of Fielding's writings.

Bloom, Harold, ed. *Henry Fielding*. New York: Chelsea House, 1987. Essays on Fielding's major novels, his anti-Romanticism, and his uses of style, history, and comedy. Includes chronology and bibliography.

_____, ed. *Henry's Fielding's "Tom Jones."* New York: Chelsea House, 1987. Essays on the style and structure of the novel, with an introduction by Bloom succinctly detailing the history of criticism of the novel and Fielding's handling of Squire Western. Includes a chronology and bibliography.

Johnson, Maurice. *Fielding's Art of Fiction: Eleven Essays on "Shamela," "Joseph Andrews," "Tom Jones," and "Amelia."* Philadelphia: University of Pennsylvania Press, 1961. Johnson writes in his introduction, "I want to suggest how, in his fiction, Fielding attempted vigorously and cheerfully to define the good life, within the severe limitations set by Fortune, society, and man's own errant nature" (pages 16-17). These eleven pieces provide a good critical survey of Fielding's fiction.

Mace, Nancy A. *Henry Fielding's Novels and the Classical Tradition*. Newark: University of Delaware Press, 1996. Examines the Classical influence on Fielding.

Pagliaro, Harold E. *Henry Fielding: A Literary Life*. New York: St. Martin's Press, 1998. Part of the Literary Lives series, this is an excellent, updated biography of Fielding. Provides bibliographical references and an index.

Rivero, Albert J., ed. *Critical Essays on Henry Fielding*. New York: G. K. Hall, 1998. A good collection of essays about Fielding's major novels. Includes bibliographical references and an index.

Sacks, Sheldon. *Fiction and the Shape of Belief*. Berkeley: University of California Press, 1964. Posits three categories of fiction: satire, apologue, and novel. Argues that, because Fielding uses characters to demonstrate his moral stance, his works are novels, but that his various digressions, providing more overt moral lessons, are apologues.

Stoler, John A., and Richard D. Fulton. *Henry Fielding: An Annotated Bibliography of Twentieth-Century Criticism, 1900-1977*. New York: Garland, 1980. After listing a number of major Fielding bibliographies and various editions of his works, this bibliography provides a comprehensive, annotated list of secondary works. Arrangement is by title, so students seeking material on a specific work, such as *Tom Jones*, can quickly find what they need.

Watt, Ian. *The Rise of the Novel: Studies in Defoe, Richardson, and Fielding.* Berkeley: University of California Press, 1957. While praising Fielding's "wise assessment of life," Watt believes that Fielding's novelistic techniques reject verisimilitude for the sake of the moral. Hence, Watt sees Fielding's approach as a fictional dead end. Contains some useful observations about Fielding's plots and language.

F. SCOTT FITZGERALD

Born: St. Paul, Minnesota; September 24, 1896
Died: Hollywood, California; December 21, 1940

PRINCIPAL LONG FICTION

This Side of Paradise, 1920
The Beautiful and Damned, 1922
The Great Gatsby, 1925
Tender Is the Night, 1934
The Last Tycoon, 1941

OTHER LITERARY FORMS

Charles Scribner's Sons published nine books by F. Scott Fitzgerald during Fitzgerald's lifetime. In addition to the first four novels, there were four volumes of short stories, *Flappers and Philosophers* (1920), *Tales of the Jazz Age* (1922), *All the Sad Young Men* (1926), and *Taps at Reveille* (1935); and one play, *The Vegetable: Or, From President to Postman* (1923). The story collections published by Charles Scribner's Sons contained fewer than a third of the 165 stories that appeared in major periodicals during his lifetime; now, virtually all of Fitzgerald's stories are available in hardcover collections. Fitzgerald also wrote essays and autobiographical pieces, many of which appeared in the late 1930's in *Esquire* and are now collected, among other places, in *The Crack-Up* (1945). Fitzgerald's Hollywood writing consisted mainly of collaborative efforts on scripts for films such as *Gone with the Wind* (1939) and others, although during his life and since his death there

have been various screen adaptations of his novels and stories. Fitzgerald's notebooks, scrapbooks, and letters have also been published, and the record of his literary achievement is nearly complete.

ACHIEVEMENTS

Curiously, Fitzgerald has appealed to two diverse audiences since the beginning of his career: the popular magazine audience and the elite of the literary establishment. His work appeared regularly in the 1920's and 1930's in such mass circulation magazines as the *Saturday Evening Post, Hearst's, International, Collier's,* and *Redbook.* The readers of these magazines came to ask for Fitzgerald's flapper stories by name, expecting to find in them rich, young, and glamorous heroes and heroines involved in exciting adventures. Popular magazines in the 1920's billed Fitzgerald stories on the cover, often using them inside as lead stories. Long after Fitzgerald lost the knack of writing the kind of popular stories that made him famous as the creator of the flapper in fiction and as the poet laureate of the jazz age, magazine headnotes to his stories identified him as such. Those who recognized the more serious side of his talent, as it was evidenced particularly in his best stories and novels, included Edmund Wilson, George Jean Nathan, H. L. Mencken, Gertrude Stein, Edith Wharton, and T. S. Eliot, who offered criticism as well as praise. Fitzgerald was generous with advice to other writers, most notably to Ring Lardner, Ernest Hemingway, and Thomas Wolfe, but also to struggling unknowns, who wrote to him asking advice and received it.

Many of Fitzgerald's critical opinions went into the public domain when he published essays in *Esquire* in the late 1930's, his dark night of the soul. Regarded by some in Fitzgerald's time as self-pitying, these essays are now often anthologized and widely quoted for the ideas and theories about literature and life that they contain. At the time of his death, Fitzgerald seemed nearly forgotten by his popular readers and greatly neglected by literary critics. After his death and the posthumous publication of his incomplete *The Last Tycoon,* a Fitzgerald revival began. With this revival, Fitzgerald's reputation as a novelist (principally on the strength of *The Great Gatsby* and *Tender Is the Night*), short-story writer, and essayist has been solidly established.

BIOGRAPHY

Francis Scott Key Fitzgerald was born in St. Paul, Minnesota, on September 24, 1896. His mother's side of the family (the McQuillan side) was what Fitzgerald referred to as "straight 1850 potato famine Irish," but by the time of his maternal grandfather's death at the age of forty-four, the McQuillan fortune, earned in the grocery business, was in excess of $300,000. Fitzgerald's father was a poor but well-bred descendant of the old Maryland Scott and Key families. Always an ineffectual businessman, Edward Fitzgerald had met Mary McQuillan when he had come to St. Paul to open a wicker furniture business, which shortly went out of business. In search of a job by which he could support the family, Edward Fitzgerald moved his family from St. Paul to Buffalo, New York, in 1898, then to Syracuse and back to Buffalo. When Fitzgerald was eleven, the family returned to St. Paul and the security of the McQuillan wealth.

With McQuillan money Fitzgerald was sent (for two painfully lonely years) to private school, the Newman School in Hackensack, New Jersey. Discovering there a flair for writing musical comedy, Fitzgerald decided that he would attend Princeton, whose Triangle Club produced a musical comedy each year. At Princeton, Fitzgerald compensated for his feelings of social inferiority by excelling in the thing he did best, writing for the Triangle Club and the *Nassau Literary Magazine*. During a Christmas vacation spent in St. Paul, Fitzgerald met Ginevra King, a wealthy Chicago debutante whose initial acceptance of Fitzgerald was a supreme social triumph; her later rejection of him became one of the most devastating blows of his life. He kept her letters, which he had typed and bound and which ran to over two hundred pages, until his death.

In 1917, Fitzgerald left Princeton without a degree, accepted a commission in the army, and wrote the first draft of what was to become his first novel, *This Side of Paradise*. During the summer of 1918, Fitzgerald met Zelda Sayre while he was stationed

(CORBIS/Bettmann)

near Montgomery, Alabama, and having recently received word of Ginevra King's engagement, he fell in love with Zelda. Zelda, however, although willing to become engaged to Fitzgerald, did not finally agree to marry him until he could demonstrate his ability to support her. Fitzgerald returned to New York, worked for an advertising firm, and revised his novel, including in it details from his courtship with Zelda. When Charles Scribner's Sons agreed in September, 1919, to publish the novel, Fitzgerald was able to claim Zelda, and they were married in April of the following year.

The first two years of their marriage were marked by wild parties, the self-destructive mood of which formed the basis for some of the scenes in Fitzgerald's second novel, *The Beautiful and Damned*. After a trip to Europe, the Fitzgeralds returned first to St. Paul and then to Great Neck, New York, where they lived among the Astors and Vanderbilts while Fitzgerald accumulated material that would figure in *The Great Gatsby*.

In the decade that followed the publication of that novel, the Fitzgeralds lived, among other places, on the French Riviera, which would provide the background for *Tender Is the Night*. Zelda headed toward a mental collapse, a fictionalized version of which appears in the novel; Fitzgerald sank into alcoholism. In 1930, Zelda was institutionalized for treatment of her mental condition. The rest of Fitzgerald's life was spent writing stories and screenplays that would pay for her treatment, both in and out of institutions. In 1937, Fitzgerald went to Hollywood, met Sheila Graham, worked under contract for MGM Studios, and accumulated material for his last novel, while Zelda remained in the East. Fitzgerald died of a heart attack on December 21, 1940, while working on his unfinished novel, *The Last Tycoon*.

ANALYSIS

"The test of a first-rate intelligence," F. Scott Fitzgerald remarked in the late 1930's, "is the ability to hold two opposed ideas in the mind at the same time, and still retain the ability to function." At his best—in *The Great Gatsby*, in parts of *Tender Is the Night*, in the unfinished *The Last Tycoon*, and in parts of his first two novels, *This Side of Paradise* and *The Beautiful and Damned*—Fitzgerald demonstrates the kind of intelligence he describes, an intelligence characterized by the aesthetic principle of "double vision." An understanding of this phrase (coined and first applied to Fitzgerald's art by Malcolm Cowley) is central to any discussion of Fitzgerald's novels. "Double vision" denotes two ways of seeing. It implies the tension involved when Fitzgerald sets things in opposition such that the reader can, on the one hand, sensually experience the event about which Fitzgerald is writing, becoming emotionally immersed in it, and yet at the same time retain the objectivity to stand back and intellectually criticize it. The foundation of double vision is polarity, the setting of extremes against each other; the result in a novel is dramatic tension. By following the changes in Fitzgerald's narrative technique from *This Side of Paradise* to *The Beautiful and Damned* to *The Great Gatsby* and finally into *Tender Is the Night*, one can trace the growth of his double vision, which is, in

effect, to study his development as a literary artist.

The major themes of Fitzgerald's novels derive from the resolution of tension when one idea (usually embodied in a character) triumphs over another. Amory Blaine, the protagonist of Fitzgerald's first novel, *This Side of Paradise*, is a questing hero armed with youth, intelligence, and good looks. Anthony Patch in *The Beautiful and Damned* has a multimillionaire grandfather, a beautiful wife, and youth. Jay Gatsby in *The Great Gatsby* possesses power, newly made money, and good looks. Finally, Dick Diver in *Tender Is the Night* has a medical degree, an overabundance of charm, and a wealthy wife. The common denominators here are the subjects with which Fitzgerald deals in all of his novels: youth, physical beauty, wealth, and potential or "romantic readiness"—all of which are ideals to Fitzgerald. Set against these subjects are their polar opposites: age, ugliness, poverty, squandered potential. Such conflict and resulting tension is, of course, the stuff of which all fiction is made. With Fitzgerald's characters, however, partly because of the themes with which he deals and partly because of his skillful handling of point of view, the choices are rarely as obvious or as clear-cut to the main characters at the time as they may be to a detached observer, or as they may seem in retrospect to have been. Daisy, for example, so enchants Gatsby and the reader who identifies with him that only in retrospect (if at all) or through the detached observer, Nick, does it become clear that she and the other careless, moneyed people in the novel are villains of the highest order. It is Fitzgerald's main gift that he can draw the reader into a web of emotional attachment to a character, as he does to Daisy through Gatsby, while simultaneously allowing him to inspect the complexity of the web, as he does through Nick. That is what Fitzgerald's double vision at its best is finally about.

For the origins of Fitzgerald's double vision, it is helpful to look at several ingredients of his early life, particularly at those facets of it which presented him with the polarities and ambiguities that would later furnish the subjects and themes of his art. "In a house below the average on a block above the average" is the way that Fitzgerald described his boyhood home.

A block above the average, indeed. At the end of the "block" on Summit Avenue in St. Paul lived James J. Hill, the multimillionaire empire builder referred to by Gatsby's father in the last chapter of *The Great Gatsby*. The Fitzgerald family, however, nearly in sight of such wealth, lived moderately on the interest from his mother's inheritance, taking pains not to disturb the capital; Fitzgerald's father, in spite of his idealistic gentility and an ancestral line that linked him to the Maryland Scott and Key families, was unable to hold a good job. One of Fitzgerald's most devastating memories was of his father's loss of a job with Procter and Gamble, which left the older Fitzgerald, then beyond middle age, broken and defeated. When Fitzgerald was sent East to boarding school and then to Princeton, it was with his mother's money, less than a generation earned, and with considerably less of it than stood behind most of his classmates. Early, then, Fitzgerald, a child with sensitivity, intelligence, and good looks—qualities possessed by most of his heroes and heroines—was impressed with the importance of money, at least with the lifestyle of the moneyed class. Yet Fitzgerald's participation in that lifestyle, like that of many of his fictional creations, was limited by something beyond his control: the fixed income of his family. In addition, he watched his father, an idealist unable to compete in a materialistic world, defeated.

With this kind of early life, Fitzgerald was prepared, or more accurately left totally unprepared, for the series of events in his life which formed the basis of much of his later fiction. Two of these stand out: his romantic attachment to Ginevra King, a wealthy Chicago debutante who in his words "ended up by throwing me over with the most supreme boredom and indifference"; and his relationship with Zelda Sayre, who broke their engagement (because Fitzgerald was neither rich enough nor famous enough for her) before finally marrying him after his first novel was accepted for publication by Charles Scribner's Sons. Fitzgerald emphasizes the importance of the Ginevra King episode in particular and of biographical material in general in his essay "One Hundred False Starts": "We have two or three great and moving experiences in our lives. . . . Then we learn our

trade, well or less well, and we tell our two or three stories—each time in a new disguise—maybe ten times, maybe a hundred, as long as people will listen." The subjects and themes from those experiences formed what Fitzgerald called "my material."

Through Ginevra King, Fitzgerald saw the opportunity to be accepted into the wealth that the King family represented. Her father, however, did not conceal his "poor boys shouldn't think of marrying rich girls" attitude, recorded in Fitzgerald's notebooks, and when Fitzgerald was "thrown over" in favor of an acceptable suitor with money and social position, he saw the rejection not only as a personal one but also as evidence that the emergence of an upper caste in American society had rendered the American Dream an empty promise. Curiously though, Fitzgerald's infatuation with wealth and the wealthy, symbolized by the Kings, stayed with him for the rest of his life. As he wrote to his daughter in the late 1930's on the eve of seeing Ginevra King for the first time since she had rejected him nearly twenty years earlier, "She was the first girl I ever loved and I have faithfully avoided seeing her up to this moment to keep that illusion perfect." It was this experience, then, coupled with the near-loss of Zelda and their subsequent, complex relationship that would provide his "material." Fitzgerald also describes an attitude which grows out of these experiences of enchantment and loss and which he identifies variously as his "solid gold bar" or his "stamp": "Taking things hard—from Ginevra to Joe Mank. That's the stamp that goes into my books so that people can read it blind like Braille."

Fitzgerald's achievements rest on three obsessions which characterized him as an artist and as a man. The first of these was "his material." It included the subjects of youth, wealth, and beauty and was an outgrowth of his social background. The second was his "solid gold bar" or his "stamp," which he defined as "taking things hard," an attitude which grew out of his background and was partly rooted in his feelings of social inferiority. The third was his "double vision," an artistic perspective that remained his goal until the end. This double vision matured as he gained objectivity toward his material. With these cornerstones, Fitzgerald constructed a set of novels which document the development of one of the most complex and fascinating literary personalities of modern times, which chronicle a time of unparalleled frivolity and subsequent national despondency in America, and which speak with authenticity about an international wasteland almost beyond reclaiming. "The evidence is in," wrote Stephen Vincent Benét regarding the body of Fitzgerald's work in a review of the incomplete *The Last Tycoon*. "This is not a legend, this is a reputation—and seen in perspective, it may well be one of the most secure reputations of our time."

THIS SIDE OF PARADISE

Writing in 1938 about the subject matter of his first novel, Fitzgerald alludes to its origins in his experience: "In 'This Side of Paradise' I wrote about a love affair that was still bleeding as fresh as the skin wound on a haemophile." The love affair that he refers to is his relationship with Ginevra King, and it is but one of many episodes from Fitzgerald's life—his courtship with Zelda is another—that are loosely tied together in *This Side of Paradise* to form a *Bildungsroman*. Unlike the novel of "selected incident," the *Bildungsroman* is a novel of "saturation"—that is, a novel in which the hero takes on experiences until he reaches a saturation point; by virtue of his coming to this point he reaches a higher level of self-awareness. In *This Side of Paradise*, Amory Blaine, the hero and thinly veiled Fitzgerald persona, reaches this point when, at the end of the novel, he rejects all of the values that have been instilled in him, embraces socialism, and yells to the world, "I know myself . . . but that is all."

The route which Amory follows to arrive at this pinnacle of self-knowledge is more a meandering process of trial and error than it is a systematic journey with a clearly defined purpose. His mother, whom Amory quaintly calls by her first name, Beatrice, and whom he relates to as a peer, instills in Amory an egotism (almost unbearable to his own peers as well as to the reader) and a respect for wealth and social position. These qualities make Amory an object of ridicule when he goes away to an eastern boarding school. His years at St. Regis are

spent in isolation, and there he finally makes the emotional break with his mother that frees the "fundamental Amory" to become, in Fitzgerald's words, a "personage." The landmarks of this becoming process are, for the most part, encounters with individuals who teach Amory about himself: "The Romantic Egotist," as he is referred to in book 1 of the novel, is too solipsistic to go beyond himself even at the end of the novel. After learning from these individuals, Amory either leaves or is left by them. From Clara, a cousin whose beauty and intelligence he admires, he learns that he follows his imagination too freely; he learns from his affair with Rosalind, who almost marries him but refuses because Amory lacks the money to support her, that money determines the direction of love. Through Monsignor Darcy, he learns that the Church of Rome is too confining for him; and from half a dozen of his classmates at Princeton, he discovers the restlessness and rebelliousness that lead him to reject all that he had been brought up to believe, reaching out toward socialism as one of the few gods he has not tried.

The reader will perhaps wonder how Amory, whose path has zigzagged through many experiences, none of which has brought him closely in contact with socialism, has arrived at a point of almost evangelical, anticapitalistic zeal. It is worth noting, however, that, in addition to its interest to literary historians as an example of the *Bildungsroman*, *This Side of Paradise* also has value to social historians as an enlightening account of jazz age manners and morals. One contemporary observer labeled the novel "a gesture of indefinite revolt," a comment intended as a criticism of the novel's lack of focus. The social historian, however, would see the phrase as a key to the novel's value, which view would cast Amory in the role of spokesman for the vague rebelliousness of the "lost generation," a generation, in Amory's words, "grown up to find all gods dead, all wars fought, all faiths in man shaken." As Malcolm Cowley has noted, "More than any other writer of these times, Fitzgerald had the sense of living in history. He tried hard to catch the color of every passing year, its distinctive slang, its dance steps, its songs . . . its favorite quarterbacks, and the sort of clothes and emotions its people wore." John O'Hara, for one, recalls the impact of *This Side of Paradise* on his generation: "A little matter of twenty-five years ago I, along with half a million other men and women between fifteen and thirty, fell in love with a book. . . . I took the book to bed with me, and I still do, which is more than I can say of any girl I knew in 1920." By Fitzgerald's own account, the novel made him something of an "oracle" to his college readers, and largely on the strength of *This Side of Paradise*, Fitzgerald became the unofficial poet laureate of the jazz age.

Yet, for those interested in Fitzgerald's development as a novelist, the value of *This Side of Paradise* goes beyond its worth as a novel of growth or its importance as a social document. In it are contained early versions in rough form of most of the novels that Fitzgerald later wrote. By the time of its completion, Fitzgerald's major subjects were cast and marked with his "stamp": "taking things hard." Amory "takes hard" the breakup with the young, wealthy, and beautiful Isabel, modeled on Ginevra King. Amory "takes hard" his rejection by Rosalind by going on an extended drunk, similar to Fizgerald's response when Zelda refused to marry him until he demonstrated that he could support her. Event after event in the novel shows Fitzgerald, through Amory, "taking hard" the absence of wealth, the loss of youth, and the ephemerality of beauty. Even in the characterization of Amory, who is born moneyed and aristocratic, Fitzgerald seems to be creating his ideal conception of himself, much the way Gatsby later springs from his own platonic conception of himself. With his subject matter, his themes, and his distinctive stamp already formed, Fitzgerald needed only to find a point of view by which he could distance himself, more than he had through Amory, from his material. He had yet, as T. S. Eliot would have phrased it, to find an "objective correlative," which is to say that he had not yet acquired the double vision so evident in *The Great Gatsby*.

THE BEAUTIFUL AND DAMNED

Although *The Beautiful and Damned*, Fitzgerald's second novel, is usually considered his weakest, largely because of its improbable and melodramatic ending, there is evidence in it of Fitzgerald's growth as a writer. Unlike *This Side of Paradise*, which is a subjective rendering through a thinly disguised persona and which includes nearly everything from Fitzgerald's life and work through 1920 (one critic called it "the collected works of F. Scott Fitzgerald"), *The Beautiful and Damned* moved toward the novel of selected incident. Written in the third person, it shows Fitzgerald dealing in a more objective fashion with biographical material that was close to him, in this instance the early married life of the Fitzgeralds. Whereas *This Side of Paradise* was largely a retrospecive, nostalgic recounting of Fitzgerald's recently lost youth, *The Beautiful and Damned* projects imaginatively into the future of a life based on the belief that nothing is worth doing.

In spite of the differences between the two novels, however, particularly in narrative perspective, it is clear that the characters and subjects in *The Beautiful and Damned* are logical extensions, more objectively rendered, of those introduced in *This Side of Paradise*, making the former a sequel, in a sense, to the latter. With slight modifications, Anthony Patch, the hero of *The Beautiful and Damned*, is Amory Blaine grown older and more cynical. Add to Amory a heritage that links him to Anthony Comstock, a mother and father who died in his youth, a multimillionaire grandfather, and half a dozen years, and the result is a reasonable facsimile of Patch. To Amory's Rosalind (a composite of Ginevra King and Zelda), add a few years, a "coast-to-coast reputation for irresponsibility and beauty," and a bit more cleverness, and the result is strikingly similar to Gloria Gilbert, the heroine of *The Beautiful and Damned*, who will, unlike Rosalind, marry the hero.

When Fitzgerald created Rosalind, of course, Zelda had for the time being rejected him. Her reappearance in *The Beautiful and Damned* as the hero's wife reflects Fitzgerald's change in fortune, since he and Zelda had been married for two years when *The Beautiful and Damned* was published. Their life together provided the basis for many of the experiences in the novel, and there is good reason to believe that the mutual self-destructiveness evident on nearly every page of the novel reflects Fitzgerald's fears of what he and Zelda might do to each other and to themselves. In *This Side of Paradise* Amory knows himself, "but that is all." Anthony carries this knowledge two years into the future and cynically applies it to life: He will prove that life is meaningless and that "there's nothing I can do that's worth doing." His task is to demonstrate that it is possible for an American to be gracefully idle. Gloria's goal is to avoid responsibility forever, which was essentially Rosalind's goal in *This Side of Paradise*. The kind of life that Gloria and Anthony desire is dependent on the possession of wealth, of which Anthony has promise through the estate of his grandfather, a virtual guarantee until the social-reformer grandfather happens into one of the Patches' parties and disinherits Anthony.

The novel could logically end there, but it does not. Instead, its long conclusion leads the reader through a maze of melodramatic circumstances and improbabilities. Gloria and Anthony contest the will and, with dwindling funds, sink into despair and self-destructiveness. Gloria auditions for a part in a motion picture and is told that she is too old; Anthony remains drunk, tries unsuccessfully to borrow money from friends, and finally gets into a senseless fight with the film producer who has given Gloria the news that she is too old for the part she wants. On the day of the trial that will determine whether the will is to be broken, Anthony loses his mind and is capable only of babbling incoherently when Gloria brings him the news that they are rich.

The major flaw in the novel is this long, melodramatic ending and the thematic conclusions it presents. On the one hand, Fitzgerald posits the theory that life is meaningless, yet Anthony's life is given meaning by his quest for money, not to mention that the philosophy itself can be practiced only when there is enough money to support it. Certainly Gloria, who is sane and happy at the novel's end, does not seem much impressed by life's meaninglessness, and the reader is left with the feeling that Anthony, when the advantages that his inheritance can offer him are evident, will recover from his "on-cue" flight into insanity. The effect of the ending is to leave the reader with the impression that Fitzgerald had not thought the theme carefully through; or, as Edmund Wilson

hints, that Fitzgerald himself had not taken the ideas in either of his first two novels seriously:

> In college he had supposed that the thing to do was to write biographical novels with a burst of energy toward the close; since his advent into the literary world, he has discovered that another genre has recently come into favor: the kind which makes much of tragedy and what Mencken has called "the meaninglessness of life."

The greater truth suggested by Wilson here is that through 1922 Fitzgerald was writing, in part, what he thought he should write. With the completion of *The Beautiful and Damned*, his apprenticeship was over, and with an artistic leap he moved into his own as an original prose stylist, writing in *The Great Gatsby* what Eliot called "the first step that American fiction has taken since Henry James."

THE GREAT GATSBY

For Amory Blaine in *This Side of Paradise*, there are four golden moments, as many perhaps as there are new and exciting women to meet; for Anthony Patch in *The Beautiful and Damned*, the moment is his meeting with Gloria Gilbert. For Jay Gatsby, the golden moment is the time when "his unutterable vision" meets Daisy's "perishable breath." For Fitzgerald, the artistic golden moment was the creation of *The Great Gatsby*. Critics have marveled that the author of *This Side of Paradise* and *The Beautiful and Damned* could in less than two years after the publication of the latter produce a novel of the stature of *The Great Gatsby*. Clearly, the writer of *This Side of Paradise* did not blossom overnight into the author of *The Great Gatsby*. The process by which Fitzgerald came to create *The Great Gatsby* is a logical one. From the beginning of his career as a novelist, Fitzgerald stayed with the subjects and themes that he knew well and that were close to him: wealth, youth, and beauty. What did change between the creation of *This Side of Paradise* and *The Great Gatsby* was Fitzgerald's perspective on his material and his ability to objectify his attitudes toward it. In 1925, Fitzgerald was more than five years removed from his affair with Ginevra King, which gave him the distance to be Nick Carraway, the novel's "objective" narrator.

Yet he was also near enough in memory that he could recall, even relive, the seductiveness of her world; that is, he was still able to be the romantic hero, Jay Gatsby. In effect, he had reached the pivotal point in his life that allowed him to see clearly through the eyes of both Gatsby and Nick; for the time of the creation of *The Great Gatsby*, he possessed double vision.

The success of the novel depends on Fitzgerald's ability to transfer to the reader the same kind of vision that he himself had: the ability to believe in the possibilities of several opposite ideas at various levels of abstraction. On the most concrete level, the reader must believe that Gatsby will and will not win Daisy, the novel's heroine and symbol of the American ideal. On a more general level, the reader must believe that anyone in America, through hard work and perseverance, can and cannot gain access to the best that America has to offer. Until Daisy's final rejection of Gatsby in the penultimate chapter of the novel, the reader can, indeed, believe in both alternatives because both have been seen, from the perspective of Gatsby (who believes) and from the point of view of Nick (who wants to believe but intellectually cannot).

The central scene in *The Great Gatsby* nicely illustrates how Fitzgerald is able to present his material in such a way as to create dramatic tension through the use of double vision. This scene, which occupies the first part of chapter 5, is built around the reunion of Gatsby and Daisy after a five-year separation. The years, for Gatsby, have been devoted to the obsessive pursuit of wealth, which he wants only because he believes it will win Daisy for him. Daisy, who has married Tom Buchanan, seems to have given little thought to Gatsby since her marriage. The moment of their reunion, then, means everything to Gatsby and very little to Daisy, except as a diversion from the luxurious idling of her daily existence. In this meeting scene, as Gatsby stands nervously talking to Daisy and Nick, Fitzgerald calls the reader's attention to a defunct clock on Nick's mantlepiece. When Gatsby leans against the mantle, the clock teeters on the edge, deciding finally not to fall. The three stare at the floor as if the clock has, in fact, shattered

to pieces in front of them. Gatsby apologizes and Nick replies, "It's an old clock."

On the level of plot, this scene is the dramatic high point of the novel; the first four chapters have been devoted to preparing the reader for it. The image of Daisy's desirability as she is seen through Nick's eyes in chapter 1 has been followed with an image at the chapter's end of Gatsby standing, arms outstretched, toward the green light across the bay at the end of Daisy's dock; the image of the emptiness of the Buchanans' world in chapter 1 has been followed with the image in chapter 2 of the valley of ashes, a huge dumping ground in which lives the mistress of Daisy's husband Tom; the open public gathering of Gatsby's lavish parties in chapter 3 has been set against the mysterious privacy of Gatsby's life. All of these scenes have come to the reader through the central intelligence, Nick, who has learned from Jordan Baker a truth that, at this point, only Gatsby, Jordan, and Nick know: Gatsby wants to turn time backward and renew his relationship with Daisy as if the five years since he has seen her have not gone by. Nick, Daisy's cousin and Gatsby's neighbor, is the natural link that will reconnect Daisy and Gatsby. To the tension inherent in the reunion itself, then, is added the ambivalence of Nick, who, on the one hand, despises Gatsby's gaudiness but admires his romantic readiness; and who is captivated by Daisy's charm but also, by the time of the meeting in chapter 5, contemptuous of her moral emptiness.

On coming into the meeting scene, the reader is interested, first on the level of plot, to see whether Gatsby and Daisy can renew their love of five years before. In addition, he is interested in the reaction of Nick, on whose moral and intellectual judgment he has come to depend. At a deeper level, he is ready for the confrontation of abstract ideas that will occur in the clock scene. The clock itself, a focal point of the room in which Gatsby and Daisy meet, represents the past time that Gatsby wants to repeat in order to recapture Daisy's love for him. That this clock, which has stopped at some past moment, can be suspended on a mantelpiece in front of them affirms the possibility of bringing the past into the present. Yet, the fact that they all envision the clock shattered on the floor suggests that all three are aware of the fragility of this past moment brought into the present. The fact that the clock does not work hints at the underlying flaw in Gatsby's dream of a relationship with Daisy.

The scene is a foreshadowing of what the rest of the novel will present dramatically: the brief and intense renewal of a courtship that takes place behind the closed doors of Gatsby's mansion, a courtship that will end abruptly behind the closed doors of a Plaza Hotel room after a confrontation between Gatsby and Tom convinces Daisy finally to reject Gatsby. The death of Myrtle, Tom's mistress; Gatsby's murder by Myrtle's husband; Daisy and Tom's "vacation" until the confusion dies down; Gatsby's funeral, whose arrangements are handled by Nick—all follow with an unquestionable inevitability in the last two chapters of the novel. Nick alone is left to tell the story of the dreamer whose dreams were corrupted by the "foul dust" that floated in their wake and of the reckless rich who "smashed up things and people and then retreated back into their vast carelessness, or whatever it was that kept them together, and let other people clean up the mess they had made."

At this endpoint, the reader will recall the ominous foreshadowing of the broken clock: Gatsby cannot, as Nick has told him, repeat the past. He cannot have Daisy, because as Nick knows, "poor guys shouldn't think of marrying rich girls." Gatsby cannot have what he imagined to be the best America had to offer, which Nick realizes is *not* Daisy. Yet, the fault does not lie in Gatsby's capacity to dream, only in "the foul dust" which floated in the wake of his dreams—a belief in the money-god, for example—which makes him mistake a counterfeit (Daisy) for the true romantic vision. "No—Gatsby turned out all right at the end," Nick says in a kind of preface to the novel, a statement which keeps Fitzgerald's double vision intact in spite of Gatsby's loss of Daisy and his life. At the highest level of abstraction, the novel suggests that an idealist unwilling to compromise can and cannot survive in a materialistic world, an ambivalent point of view that Fitzgerald held until his death. No longer did he need to write what he thought he should write; he was writing from the vantage point of one who saw that he had endowed the world of Ginevra King with a sanctity it did not deserve. Part of him, like Gatsby, died with the realization. The other part, like Nick, lived on to make sense of what he had lost and to find a better dream.

TENDER IS THE NIGHT

For the nine years that followed the publication of *The Great Gatsby* (sometimes referred to as "the barren years"), Fitzgerald published no novels. During the first five of these years, the Fitzgeralds made four trips to Europe, where they met Ernest Hemingway in 1925 and where they lived for a time on the French Riviera, near Gerald and Sara Murphy, prototypes for Dick and Nicole Diver in Fitzgerald's last complete novel, *Tender Is the Night*. In 1930, Zelda had her first mental breakdown and was hospitalized in Switzerland. Two years later she had a second one. For Fitzgerald, the years from 1930 to 1933 were years during which he was compelled to write short stories for popular magazines, primarily the *Saturday Evening Post*, to enable Zelda to be treated in expensive mental institutions. All of these years were devoted to developing a perspective on his experiences: his feelings about Zelda's affair with a French aviator, Edouard Jozan; his own retaliatory relationship with a young film star, Lois Moran; his attraction to the lifestyle of the Murphys; Zelda's mental illness; his own alcoholism and emotional bankruptcy. He carried the perspective he gained through seventeen complete drafts, fully documented by Matthew J. Bruccoli in *The Composition of Tender Is the Night* (1963), to its completion in his novel.

Partly because it attempts to bring together so many subjects, partly because it deals with so complex a theme as the decline of Western civilization, and partly because of its experimentation with multiple points of view, *Tender Is the Night* is usually regarded as Fitzgerald's most ambitious novel. The story line of the novel is straightforward and has the recognizable Fitzgerald stamp. Its hero, Dick Diver, is a gifted young American in Europe who studies psychiatry with Sigmund Freud, writes a textbook for psychiatrists, marries a wealthy American mental patient, and over a period of years makes her well, while sinking himself into an emotional and physical decline that leads him away from Europe to wander aimlessly in an obscure part of upper New York state. The plot rendered chronologically can be represented as two *v*'s placed point-to-point to form an *X*. The lower *v* is Dick's story, which follows him from a relatively low social and economic position to a high one as a doctor and scientist and back again to the low point of emotional bankruptcy. The story of his wife Nicole can be represented by the upper *v*, since Nicole starts life in America's upper class, falls into mental illness (caused by an incestuous relationship with her father), and then rises again to a height of stability and self-sufficiency.

Fitzgerald, however, does not choose to tell the story in chronological sequence, electing instead to focus first on Dick Diver at the high point of his career, following him through his training in a flashback, and ending the novel with his collapse into anonymity. Nicole's story, secondary to Dick's, is woven into that of Dick's decline, with the implication that she has helped to speed it along. Nor does Fitzgerald select for the novel a single focus of narration, as he does in *The Great Gatsby*. Instead, book 1 of the novel shows Dick in June and July of 1925 at the high point of his life, just before the beginning of his decline, from the viewpoint of Rosemary Hoyt, an innocent eighteen-year-old film star whose innocence Dick will finally betray at his low point by making love to her. Book 2 contains four chronological shifts covering more than a decade, beginning in 1917, and is presented variously from Dick's and then Nicole's perspective. Book 3 brings the story forward one and a half years from the close of book 2 to Dick's departure from the Riviera and Nicole's marriage to Tommy Barban, and it is from the point of view of the survivor, Nicole.

The complicated shifts in viewpoint and chronological sequence are grounded in the complexity of Fitzgerald's purposes. First, he is attempting to document both the external and internal forces which bring about the decline of a gifted individual. In Dick Diver's case, the inward flaw is rooted in an excess of charm and in a self-destructive need to be used, which the reader can best see from Dick's own perspective. From without, Nicole's money weakens his

resistance and serves as a catalyst for the breaking down of his will power, a process more clearly observable in the sections from Nicole's point of view. The value of seeing Dick at a high point early in book 1 through Rosemary's eyes is that it emphasizes how attractive and desirable he could be; by contrast, the fact of his emotional bankruptcy at the end of the novel gains power. Fitzgerald, however, is also attempting to equate Dick's decline with the decline of Western society, a subject that had come to him primarily through his reading of Oswald Spengler's *The Decline of the West* (1918-1922). As Fitzgerald wrote to Maxwell Perkins: "I read him the same summer I was writing *The Great Gatsby* and I don't think I ever quite recovered from him." The moral invalids of the international set, who gather on "the little prayer rug of a beach" in *Tender Is the Night*, are, like the characters in Eliot's wasteland, hopelessly cut off from the regenerative powers of nature. There is evidence that even Nicole, whose strength seems assured at the novel's end, may soon be in danger of being overcome by Barban, whose name hints at the barbarian takeover of Western culture predicted by Spengler.

At first glance, *Tender Is the Night* may appear far removed in theme and narrative technique from *The Great Gatsby*, even farther from the two apprenticeship novels, *This Side of Paradise* and *The Beautiful and Damned*. Yet, it does not represent a radical departure from what would seem a predictable pattern of Fitzgerald's growth as a novelist. In *Tender Is the Night*, as in all of his earlier work, Fitzgerald remains close to biographical material, particularly in his drawing on actual people for fictional characters and parts of composite characters. Dick and Nicole Diver are patterned, in part, on Gerald and Sara Murphy, whose "living well" Fitzgerald admired and to whom he dedicated the novel. The Divers are, of course, also the Fitzgeralds, plagued in the 1930's by mental illness and emotional bankruptcy. Similarly, Rosemary Hoyt, whose innocent and admiring viewpoint sets up the first book of the novel, is patterned after the young actress Lois Moran, and Tommy Barban is a fictional representation of Zelda's aviator, Jozan. Also, in drawing on subjects and themes that had characterized even his earliest work, especially wealth and its corrosive influence, Fitzgerald was extending his past concerns from as far back as *This Side of Paradise* into the present, most notably in Baby Warren in *Tender Is the Night*, who callously "buys" Nicole a doctor. Finally, the multiple viewpoint of the novel is a logical extension of the narrator-observer in *The Great Gatsby*, an attempt to carry objectivity even further than he does in that novel. Only perhaps in his reaching into historical prophecy does Fitzgerald go beyond his earlier concerns. Yet even *The Great Gatsby*, which Nick calls "a story of the West," appears on one level to address the moral decay of society on an international level. What *Tender Is the Night* finally reflects, then, is a novelist who has gained philosophical insight and technical skill and has added them onto the existing foundation of his craftsmanship.

Bryant Mangum

OTHER MAJOR WORKS

SHORT FICTION: *Flappers and Philosophers*, 1920; *Tales of the Jazz Age*, 1922; *All the Sad Young Men*, 1926; *Taps at Reveille*, 1935; *The Stories of F. Scott Fitzgerald*, 1951; *Babylon Revisited and Other Stories*, 1960; *The Pat Hobby Stories*, 1962; *The Apprentice Fiction of F. Scott Fitzgerald, 1907-1917*, 1965; *The Basil and Josephine Stories*, 1973; *Bits of Paradise*, 1974; *The Price Was High: The Last Uncollected Stories of F. Scott Fitzgerald*, 1979.

PLAY: *The Vegetable: Or, from President to Postman*, pb. 1923.

NONFICTION: *The Crack-Up*, 1945; *The Letters of F. Scott Fitzgerald*, 1963; *Letters to His Daughter*, 1965; *Thoughtbook of Francis Scott Fitzgerald*, 1965; *Dear Scott/Dear Max: The Fitzgerald-Perkins Correspondence*, 1971; *As Ever, Scott Fitzgerald*, 1972; *F. Scott Fitzgerald's Ledger*, 1972; *The Notebooks of F. Scott Fitzgerald*, 1978; *F. Scott Fitzgerald on Authorship*, 1996.

MISCELLANEOUS: *Afternoon of an Author: A Selection of Uncollected Stories and Essays*, 1958.

BIBLIOGRAPHY

Berman, Ronald. *"The Great Gatsby" and Fitzgerald's World of Ideas*. Tuscaloosa: University of Alabama Press, 1997. Explores Fitzgerald's political and social views of his era and how he incorporated them into his seminal novel.

Bloom, Harold, ed. *F. Scott Fitzgerald*. New York: Chelsea House, 1985. A short but important collection of critical essays, this book provides an introductory overview of Fitzgerald scholarship, plus readings from a variety of perspectives on his fiction.

Bruccoli, Matthew J., ed. *New Essays on "The Great Gatsby."* Cambridge, England: Cambridge University Press, 1985. This short collection includes an introductory overview of scholarship, plus interpretive essays on Fitzgerald's best-known novel.

_____. *Some Sort of Epic Grandeur*. New York: Harcourt Brace Jovanovich, 1981. In this outstanding biography, a major Fitzgerald scholar argues that Fitzgerald's divided spirit, not his lifestyle, distracted him from writing. Claims that Fitzgerald both loved and hated the privileged class that was the subject of his fiction.

Eble, Kenneth. *F. Scott Fitzgerald*. New York: Twayne, 1963. A clearly written critical biography, this book traces Fitzgerald's development from youth through a "Final Assessment," which surveys scholarship on his texts.

Gale, Robert L. *An F. Scott Fitzgerald Encyclopedia*. Westport, Conn.: Greenwood Press, 1998. Provides everything students should know about Fitzgerald's life and works. Indispensable.

Gross, Dalton, and MaryJean Gross. *Understanding "The Great Gatsby": A Student Casebook to Issues, Sources, and Historical Documents*. Westport, Conn.: Greenwood Press, 1998. Part of the Literature in Context series. An excellent study guide for students of the novel. Includes bibliographical references and an index.

Kuehl, John. *F. Scott Fitzgerald: A Study of the Short Fiction*. Boston: Twayne, 1991. Part 1 discusses Fitzgerald's major stories and story collections; part 2 studies his critical opinions; part 3 includes selections from Fitzgerald critics. Includes chronology and bibliography.

Lee, A. Robert, ed. *Scott Fitzgerald: The Promises of Life*. New York: St. Martin's Press, 1989. Includes essays on Fitzgerald's major novels, his *Saturday Evening Post* stories, his treatment of women characters, and his understanding of ethics and history.

Tate, Mary Jo. *F. Scott Fitzgerald A to Z: The Essential Reference to His Life and Work.* New York: Facts on File, 1998. A comprehensive study of the man and his oeuvre. Provides bibliographical references and an index.

GUSTAVE FLAUBERT

Born: Rouen, France; December 12, 1821
Died: Croisset, France; May 8, 1880

PRINCIPAL LONG FICTION

Madame Bovary, 1857 (English translation, 1886)
Salammbô, 1862 (English translation, 1886)
L'Éducation sentimentale, 1869 (*A Sentimental Education*, 1898)
La Tentation de Saint Antoine, 1874 (*The Temptation of Saint Anthony*, 1895)
Bouvard et Pécuchet, 1881 (*Bouvard and Pécuchet*, 1896)
La Première Éducation sentimentale, 1963 (wr. 1843-1845 *The First Sentimental Education*, 1972)

OTHER LITERARY FORMS

"The novelist's novelist," as Henry James called him, Gustave Flaubert became an undisputed, if controversial, master of prose fiction in a great age of French prose. Celebrated as the founder of the modern novel, especially in its psychological dimensions, Flaubert published no poetry (if one excepts segments of *The Temptation of Saint Anthony*) but did write a great many dramatic scenarios and fragments, as the manuscript collection at the Rouen library illustrates. Among his early plays is the unpublished "Loys XI" (written in 1838), the last play of his youth; like his later plays, this one clearly demonstrates that, although he was devoted to the drama and infused his novels with dramatic elements and ef-

fects, he was not a talented dramatist. Flaubert's *Le Château des cœurs* (pr. 1874; *The Castle of Hearts*, 1904), written in 1863 in collaboration with his lifelong friend Louis Bouilhet, is a *féerie*, a play that highlights and relies upon the marvelous to carry it. The one play of his maturity of which he is sole author, a farcical comedy in four acts called *Le Candidat* (1874; *The Candidate*, 1904), lasted for four performances at the Vaudeville in Paris. Although it was fueled by Flaubert's contempt for the Third Republic and the grasping materialism of its bourgeois industrialists—and thus potentially explosive—the play is full of stereotypes. Edmond de Goncourt characterized it as a particularly painful failure, funereal and glacial.

Flaubert's *Correspondance, 1830-1880* (1887-1893)—especially his frequently unamorous love letters to his mistress, Louise Colet, his epistles to George Sand, Maxime Du Camp, Ivan Turgenev, and his notes to a host of friends and literary figures of the era—makes for extraordinarily fascinating reading. André Gide, one of many twentieth century writers who have expressed their debt to Flaubert's let-

(Library of Congress)

ters, wrote that for five years the *Correspondance* was his bedside book. The letters provide a particularly useful picture of the inner Flaubert, his life, his theories about art, and his vocation as a writer. They help form a theoretical canon that explicates his intentions and works in the way the essays of Jean-Paul Sartre, Albert Camus, or Michel Butor serve to gloss their novels. An accomplished and prolific correspondent, Flaubert appears in his letters in ways he does not overtly appear in his fiction.

Flaubert's travel book, *Par les champs et par les grèves* (1885; *Over Strand and Field*, 1904), written with Maxime Du Camp, is an account of their walking tour of Touraine and Brittany from May to July, 1847. The *Dictionnaire des idées reçues* (1910, 1913; *Dictionary of Accepted Ideas*, 1954), most likely an object of the copying efforts of Bouvard and Pécuchet in the projected second volume of his last and unfinished novel, occupied Flaubert from at least 1850 as a possible anthology of idiocy (*un sottisier*), compendium of foolish conventional opinion, and monument to error.

Apart from his novels, Flaubert's greatest contributions to literature and those upon which a major portion of his fame rests are contained in the volume *Trois Contes* (1877; *Three Tales*, 1903). These three stories, "Un Cœur simple" ("A Simple Heart"), "La Légende de Saint Julien l'Hospitalier" ("The Legend of St. Julian, Hospitaler"), and "Hérodias," reflect many of Flaubert's historical interests, artistic preoccupations, and themes and are major products of his fully mature artistry.

ACHIEVEMENTS

"If all high things have their martyrs," wrote Flaubert's English contemporary, Walter Pater, "Gustave Flaubert might perhaps rank as the martyr of literary style" (*Appreciations*, 1889). Flaubert's great and unquestionable achievement as founder and master of the modern novel lies precisely in his perfection of a literary style that seeks to capture the essential unity of idea and form, a style that seeks, before all, *le mot juste*, a style that, in Pater's (and later T. S. Eliot's) phrase, involves a natural economy "between a relative, somewhere in the world of thought, and its cor-

relative, somewhere in the world of language." This style uses elements of composition functionally and emphasizes the more formal dimensions of the novel; in Flaubert's hands, the novel achieves a beauty of form and a power that relate it to the other arts. Flaubert's influence extends to such of his contemporaries and near-contemporaries as Guy de Maupassant, Pater, and James, to writers such as Gide and Oscar Wilde, and to such contemporary writers as Butor and Sartre. Sartre's study of Flaubert, *L'Idiot de la famille* (1971-1972), stands as a forceful witness to his lengthy engagement with Flaubert's life, meaning, and place in the intellectual life of subsequent generations. No one writing in French can fail to reckon with Flaubert; no one writing in English should fail to do so.

One public distinction accorded Flaubert in his lifetime was one his father had received in 1839 for his work in medicine. On the strength of his writing, especially for *Madame Bovary*, and in part because it attracted the notice of Princess Mathilde and opened the court to him, Flaubert was named Chevalier de la Légion d'Honneur in 1866. In his *Dictionary of Accepted Ideas*, he writes of this title: "Make fun of it, but covet it. When you obtain it, always say it was unsolicited."

The most complete collection of Flaubert's works is the twenty-two volume Conard edition, issued in Paris in 1910-1933. His manuscripts are in many locations but principally in the Bibliothèque Nationale (Paris), the Bibliothèque Historique de la Ville de Paris, the Collection Louvenjoul (Chantilly), and the Bibliothèque Municipale (Rouen).

BIOGRAPHY

Born on December 12, 1821, at the Hôtel-Dieu in Rouen, Gustave Flaubert was the fifth of six children and the fourth son of Dr. Achille Cléophas Flaubert, director of Rouen's hospital and founder of its medical school, and Caroline (Fleuriot) Flaubert, herself the daughter of a physician. Only three of the Flaubert children survived infancy: Achille, the eldest (who later became a physician and replaced his father as master of Rouen's hospital), Gustave, and a sister, Caroline, who was Gustave's junior by two and a half years and who died in childbirth at the age of twenty-one. Flaubert's early and prolonged associations with examining rooms, surgeries, dissecting rooms, and the medical scientists who used them left clear marks upon his thought and fiction. His formal education began at the age of nine at Rouen's Collège Royal; there he came under the strong influence of Pierre-Adolphe Chéruel, a disciple of the historian Jules Michelet. An avid student of history, young Flaubert won several prizes for historical essays in the course of pursuing the *baccalauréat*, which was awarded to him in 1840.

In some sense, Flaubert's own sentimental education began at the age of fourteen, when he met Madame Maurice Schlésinger (Elisa Foucault), the wife of a music editor, during a family summer vacation at Trouville. Elisa, who was then twenty-six, became for him an ideal of the beloved but inaccessible woman, the object of unrequited (and unexpressed) love. With great acuity, Enid Starkie asserts that in this first meeting with Elisa, "Flaubert experienced the illumination which permanently fixed the pattern of his emotional life." The beautiful and elusive Madame Arnoux of *A Sentimental Education* is modeled upon Madame Schlésinger.

Upon his graduation from Rouen's *lycée*, Flaubert traveled to the south of France and to Corsica before taking up intermittent study of the law in Paris, study that ended in 1844 with his first major attack of epilepsy. This attack did not merely render him an invalid for several months; it profoundly altered the course of his life. During this illness, Dr. Flaubert bought a house outside Rouen at Croisset and moved his family there; in this house, facing the Seine, "the Hermit of Croisset" was to write some of the greatest fiction in the French language. The year 1846 marked Flaubert's decision to remain permanently at Croisset: In January, his father died; in March, his sister, Caroline, died giving birth to a daughter; and he and the only household he would ever have, his mother and his infant niece, took up domestic life together at Croisset.

Somewhat later in 1846, another event took place that would alter Flaubert's life: On July 28, he met Louise Colet, who became his mistress from 1846 to

1848 and again from 1851 to 1854. This passionate, often stormy, and finally disastrous relationship occasioned some of Flaubert's most important letters. It is arguable that after the first rupture between them (1848), he again pursued her in 1851 to study at first hand the Romantic obsessions he would dissect in *Madame Bovary*—that is, at best, a partial explanation of his intense attraction to her. His self-enforced rustication, away from Paris, away from Louise, led to an irrevocable break in 1854.

Flaubert was not, however, simply the Hermit, as several writers have portrayed him. Croisset remained his primary residence and his place to engage in serious writing over the years, but he also moved about a great deal. In 1847, he and Maxime Du Camp made their celebrated walking tour of Brittany; early in 1848, Flaubert was an eyewitness to the revolutionary fighting at the Palais-Royal in Paris; from November, 1849, through July, 1851, he journeyed, mainly with Du Camp, throughout the Middle East, Greece, and Italy. With the publication of *Madame Bovary*, Flaubert entered and fully enjoyed Parisian life, dividing his time between Paris and Croisset from 1856 to his death in 1880.

Early in 1857, *Madame Bovary* caused one of the few great public events of Flaubert's life: He was prosecuted on charges of obscenity and blasphemy. The result was the Napoleonic equivalent of a Scotch verdict, with the ruling that the charges were "not proven." After the notoriety of the trial, the remainder of Flaubert's life was spent in comparative quiet, interspersed with some romantic liaisons, some hard financial times through the improvidence of his niece's husband, and, most of all, the work of producing more remarkable fiction. Flaubert was still at work on *Bouvard and Pécuchet* when he died at Croisset of a cerebral hemorrhage on May 8, 1880.

ANALYSIS

Long the subject of a large and still increasing volume of literary criticism and debate, the novels of Gustave Flaubert are susceptible to a variety of approaches. Classified as a realist, his works deprecated by some of his contemporaries as supreme examples of the excesses to which novelistic realism was prone,

Flaubert refused to consider himself an advocate of something he so hated—reality. The psychological realism of *Madame Bovary*, for example, as noted by Charles Baudelaire in an early review, clearly strikes a new note in the development of the novel and is one of Flaubert's major contributions to the genre. This realism is, nevertheless, tempered by some elements of Romanticism, even though Flaubert regarded Romanticism not as an intellectual or artistic doctrine to be prized but as a disease. One objective of the Romantic generation of the 1830's, *épater le bourgeois* (to shock the middle class), surely seems to be at work in Flaubert's fiction; just as surely, the manner of accomplishing this artistic task has little in common with the many Romantic efforts of the age. In one of the earliest studies of Flaubert, Guy de Maupassant hailed Flaubert as an advocate of impersonality in art, and Flaubert's method of composition as well as numerous letters seem to bear out this notion. Conversely, while he could write, for example, that there was nothing of himself, his sentiments, or his life in *Madame Bovary*, he could still exclaim, "Madame Bovary, c'est moi!" (I am Madame Bovary!).

Flaubert's intentions, then, and the circumstances of his life have figured significantly in the interpretation and evaluation of his fiction. One useful way of thinking about his work as a writer and the writing he produced is to consider his life and work spent in the service of art, a demanding art that provided a refuge from the world of ordinary provincial and urban affairs, an art that helped him reorder experience into the image of objective reality without sacrificing all the Romantic traits he had developed in his youth. One primary Romantic element in the novels is the sense of disillusionment attendant upon the recognition that Romantic ideals themselves are untenable. This sense is usually dominant in the endings of Flaubert's novels, endings that are supremely important in adjusting the reader's perspective. Such Romantic aspects of his novels are usually overlooked—understandably so, because the restrained language, seemingly objective tone, and intense scrutiny of personality overshadow other elements. It has been said that Flaubert, a Romantic by nature, became a realist and a classicist by discipline.

MADAME BOVARY

Having turned his hand to writing at an early age, Flaubert was thirty-five when he published his masterpiece, *Madame Bovary*, a novel that has been variously interpreted and characterized. For every just claim that Flaubert undertook this novel to purge himself of the Romantic disease, there are equally cogent claims that the work is a Romantic novel, though different in kind from its predecessors. Emma Bovary is surely the victim of her own Romanticism and, like the legions of Romantic heroes and heroines, is one who longs for absolutes and seeks after something that either does not exist or exists but imperfectly. Her aspirations are completely out of proportion to her capacities and her situation in life. Thus, while *Madame Bovary* may be seen as a literary tour de force that makes superb use of organization and of great virtuosity in the handling of structure and text, it remains essentially a novel that both eschews the received objective of entertainment and sets forth an argumentative analysis of society as that society encourages Emma's folly, blames her for it, and triumphs over it.

The work is divided into three unequal parts that correspond to the three stages of the lives of Emma and her husband Charles. Before turning to the story itself, however, it is essential to look closely at the novel's title: Flaubert called the novel not *Emma Bovary* but *Madame Bovary*. The emphases upon her married name, upon the marriage itself, upon her role as wife (and as mother) are paramount. They are the very things that she will betray and that, in her betrayal, will precipitate her ruin. Moreover, Emma can have no place in the work separate from Charles; one particularly important clue to the nature of the work is the narrative device that opens the novel and then disappears as the objective narrator replaces the first voice that the reader hears. This voice belongs to one of Charles's young classmates at the *lycée*, a classmate who begins casually enough ("We were in class") and who then talks about Charles, his provenance, and his inauspicious beginnings, including having to write the conjugation of *ridiculus sum* twenty times. The idea that Charles is, in fact, ridiculous remains central to the novel, a novel that does not end with Emma's death but with his. Shortly before his death, Charles makes what the narrator considers his one great statement in life; speaking to Rodolphe Boulanger, Emma's first seducer, Charles says: "It is the fault of fate." This statement sums up Charles's inability to understand and to act, the foolishness of his perception of life, and the conventionality of its expression in clichés. The work also ends with the factual statement that the monumental stupidity of another character, Homais, the town chemist, has at last gained proper recognition: Homais has received the Croix de la Légion d'Honneur.

The first of the novel's three segments introduces Charles in a sort of choric prologue to this tragedy of dreams. In what Enid Starkie calls a duet between Charles and Emma, Flaubert presents each of the characters in a series of tableaux that leads the reader through the romance of courtship and the marriage of Charles and Emma, and also to Emma's disillusionment with the unexciting marriage. This section ends, symbolically, with the Bovarys' move from Tostes to Yonville, with the news that Emma is pregnant, and with her burning her now dessicated, tattered wedding bouquet. Each of these occasions, like the rest of the events in the novel, is presented in a detached, declarative, unsentimental manner.

Part 2 consists of another series of tableaux featuring a platonic but potentially passionate relationship between Emma and Léon Dupuis and her carefully plotted seduction by Rodolphe. Indeed, by the time Rodolphe appears, Emma has so languished at Yonville and has so nourished fleshly lusts and acquisitive passions that she is ready for an affair. Having yielded to Rodolphe, she continues to respond to him in an aggressively positive way, especially once Charles's stupidity, matched only by the ignorance of Homais, has led to the crippling of the boy Hippolyte and the consequent diminution of Charles in her eyes and of her, by association, in the eyes of the bourgeoisie of Yonville. Just when she thinks she will finally be free of the tedium of Yonville and the boredom of her marriage to Charles by fleeing with Rodolphe, Rodolphe not only fails to take her away but also flees himself, to avoid what he rightly perceives as her possessive nature: Having captured her, his first thought is how to become free of her.

In the novel's final section, Emma has irretrievably abandoned herself to her Romantic notions of how her life ought to be lived, the high passion of her affair with Léon, the possession of fine things, and the indulgence of her whims; she assumes an inexhaustible supply of funds to support her new style. Predictably, her affair with Léon and her neglect of Charles and their daughter, Berthe, bring her to moral bankruptcy, while her constant borrowing and signing of promissory notes bring her and Charles to financial bankruptcy. In the end, she cannot pay, cannot tap Rodolphe or Léon or anyone with sufficient funds who will not exact her favors in return for the money. Having lived beyond her means in many senses, she chooses an excruciatingly painful death by arsenical poisoning. Charles, the physician, is helpless for a second time when death claims his wife, yet so involved is he with her existence that his interest for readers barely survives hers: His own end is a necessary consequence of hers.

SALAMMBÔ

Flaubert's second novel, *Salammbô*, is unsettling, entirely different from his first; it is arguably the cruelest novel of the nineteenth century. In a letter to the celebrated critic Charles-Augustin Sainte-Beuve, Flaubert said he wanted "to fix a mirage by applying to antiquity the methods of the modern novel." The mirage he fixes is ancient Carthage, in a novel that has been called both Romantic and anti-Romantic and that, like many of his works, contains both elements. *Salammbô* is a work of picturesque barbarity and gratuitous violence; it is an unrelieved, pathological compendium of atrocities that the Marquis de Sade would have enjoyed thoroughly. Neither a "historical novel," a novel of "historical reconstruction" (as Jules Michelet, Augustin Thierry, and other nineteenth century writers defined the genre), nor a psychological novel like his first one, *Salammbô* is a great Parnassian epic that should be judged more as a poem than as a novel. In its last chapters, the nightmarish mirage becomes a surrealistic vision, what Maurice Nadeau calls "a hallucination described in cold blood."

Flaubert achieves these nightmarish effects through his full and objective descriptions of brutality and through his emphasis on the unreality of the landscape, an emphasis achieved through the use of lapidary objects and architecture. These techniques are prime contributions to what Victor Brombert calls an "epic of immobility." The motif of predation, in which birds and animals of prey become recurrent metaphors and evolve into symbols, coalesces with the lapidary metaphors to help create an absolute sense of dehumanization. This sense is never far from the novel's surface and is constantly reinforced by other recurrent elements: the all-pervasive themes of mutilation and self-mutilation, obsessions with disease, the ravages of hunger and thirst, and cannibalism and vampirism. All of these elements and more combine to produce an overwhelming sense of disgust with things as they are.

The story progresses from the colorful opening revels, in which the priestess Salammbô appears on the tower high above the exotic garden in which the mercenaries hold their feast, through Mathô's theft and Salammbô's recovery of the sacred veil of Tanit, to the horrific destruction of Mathô, to the somewhat unexpected but internally logical statement that the story has been told to explain how the priestess came to die for having touched Tanit's veil. Throughout this bizarre tale of the revolt of a mercenary army that the Carthaginians employed in the wars with Rome, there is no character who approaches full humanity. The exaltations of place over person, of the animalistic and supernatural dimensions over ordinary human existence, of solid objects over all, lead the reader less toward any sympathy with the characters than to either impassiveness or revulsion. Salammbô herself is one more beautiful object among many beautiful objects, and, through her death, she achieves oneness with the gorgeous artifacts that surround her. An overblown exotic fantasy of gargantuan proportions, the work may also be read as a parable of waste, futility, decadence, and inhumanity that has direct application not only to the highly stylized Carthaginian world but also to the bourgeois France of Flaubert's own time.

A SENTIMENTAL EDUCATION

In *A Sentimental Education*, an ironic self-portrait of the artist as a young man, Flaubert's life and times are both at the core and on the surface. Frédéric Moreau, like his creator, is part of a generation of young intellectuals in revolt against the bourgeois mediocrity that surrounds them; in sympathy with the bohemian life, they are in love with love and passionately in love with passion. Also like his creator, Frédéric conceives an inordinate passion for an older, married woman, a love that cannot be requited. When Flaubert wrote this second version of *A Sentimental Education*, he had already changed from a youthful, aspiring law student more interested in being an aspiring writer to an accomplished and widely recognized novelist. His first attempt to write the story of his generation, the earlier version of *A Sentimental Education* (written 1843-1845 and published in 1963 as *The First Sentimental Education*), underwent considerable revision; the celebration of Romanticism and the enthusiasms and sufferings of youth in the first version are replaced by irony and detached and sardonic realism in the second. What remains constant is the notion that life has cheated the characters by replacing their illusions with reality. The great exception is Madame Arnoux: Surely there are lapses when the reader is allowed to see or at least divine her limitations, but in general she is depicted as the apotheosis of both internal and external beauty. Frédéric shares some of the nobility that attaches to Madame Arnoux's character simply because his love for her remains the fixed star of his existence. Otherwise, he is little better than the rest of the odd characters who populate the novel and whose counterparts lived in Flaubert's France.

One of the novel's primary themes is selling— and, in some sense, selling out. From Monsieur Arnoux to Monsieur Dambreuse to Husonnet to Deslauriers, the notion of selling one's wares and oneself is a constant, and the theme of prostitution, literal and figurative, permeates the work. Both the demimonde of Rosanette and the fashionable world of Madame Dambreuse share the same principle, or lack of it, of barter and bargaining. Closely related to this theme is that of betrayal, which exists on every level and in every character (again, with the exception of Madame Arnoux). Both themes work together to form the basis of Frédéric's education.

That education is a series of initiations—into bohemia, high society, finance, and politics—in which Frédéric discovers cheapened ideals, infidelity, and lost innocence; in short, he finds that reality is antithetical to his Romantic vision of the world. In more than one sense, Frédéric's education is truly sentimental. At the novel's close, for example, Frédéric and Deslauriers meet and agree that the best time they ever had was a frustrated adolescent visit to a provincial bordello; in this agreement, the replacement of the present with a nostalgic desire to recapture the past, Flaubert demonstrates the extent to which the sentimental Frédéric has not been fully educated, as evidenced by the tenacity with which he grasps at the few Romantic notions left him.

THE TEMPTATION OF SAINT ANTHONY

The transition from *A Sentimental Education* to *The Temptation of Saint Anthony* is an abrupt one, even though the latter was in progress almost as long as the former, possibly longer if one reads "Smarh" (written 1839) and other juvenilia as a prelude to it. Both antedate *Madame Bovary* in Flaubert's consciousness and are filled with the elemental novelistic matter he continually reshaped and refined; both very diverse works seem to have held his attention simultaneously over a long period of time. His tale of Saint Anthony as "Smarh" went through three successive versions (1846-1849, 1856, 1870) before he finally published it as *The Temptation of Saint Anthony* in 1874. When he read the first version to Maxime Du Camp and Louis Bouilhet, they advised him to burn it, because the Romanticism it exemplified was out of fashion. When Flaubert published part of the work in 1856, Charles Baudelaire accorded it enthusiastic praise. It was still, in 1856, a provisional work; Flaubert struggled on with it, intent upon finding the optimum form into which he could pour the myriad ideas, emotions, and suggestions that the legend of Saint Anthony evoked for him.

Like its predecessors, the final version is a "pandemonic prose poem," in Victor Brombert's phrase, that blends dramatic fragments, monologues, proems, and epic conventions. Ostensibly the story of a hermit tempted by the world, the flesh, and the Devil, it is a work of Romantic decadence that explores and exploits such topics as human sexuality, integrity and bad faith, and the credos and desires of Romanticism as those topics relate to the subject of Saint Athanasius's hagiography and to Everyman. It has a particular relevance to Flaubert's own psyche, what Charles Baudelaire called the secret chamber of Flaubert's mind, as tensions between orgy and asceticism, worldly and mystical perspectives, and reality and illusion are played out in the text. A poetic novel of some eroticism, it is firmly imbued with a hatred of the flesh as well as with an unwillingness to part with it. A work that asks fundamental questions about the nature of life, moral choice, and ethical action, it is finally on the side of death. At the bottom of this work, as in much of Flaubert's writing, there exists a disturbing and thoroughly Romantic longing for oblivion; this longing informs and colors Anthony's reactions to most situations and to himself.

The novel is replete with allusions to theological controversies, historic persons and events, and mythological, mystical, and religious lore that strike modern readers, as they struck Flaubert's contemporaries, as bewildering. Enid Starkie is not alone in judging the novel as largely unreadable without fairly large amounts of specialized knowledge. For example, its seven parts or chapters suggest to Michel Butor a pattern based on an analysis of the Seven Deadly Sins, but that scheme does not fit exactly; it is possible that the mystical associations of the number seven are all that Flaubert intended. In any case, the general reader has only limited access to the novel.

BOUVARD AND PÉCUCHET

In his last and unfinished novel, *Bouvard and Pécuchet*, Flaubert continued his analysis of the human condition and the human psyche by rendering a nearly perfect double portrait of human stupidity particularized in his two bourgeois antiheroes. The first meeting of two copy clerks on a deserted boulevard on a hot Parisian afternoon in 1838 marks the beginning of an extraordinary friendship. Bouvard soon receives a small but sufficient legacy, and, after a gap of three years, Pécuchet retires from his work; they are now poised for a lifelong venture in retirement in the country place they had sought for the intervening three years. The rest of their story takes place in Chavignoles, Normandy, where they set up as country gentlemen—without, however, having any clear idea of what that may involve. Their rural adventures uniformly end in disaster and are predicated mainly upon ignorance and the perfect confidence that if one reads the great books of direction, one will succeed. Disregarding the experience of those around them, the citified bunglers draw down ruin upon their garden, farm, produce, and livestock. Their bungling does not end there.

Each new failure drives them further into abstruse research: Instead of becoming apprentices or hiring well-qualified, honest masters, they plunge themselves into a regressive quest after first principles. Their failed attempt at canning, for example, leads them to chemistry, then medicine, archaeology, and the study of evolutionary theory; they come, encyclopedically, a very long way from learning the right way to can vegetables. This pattern of regression away from ordinary life and the daily attention it requires is one they follow throughout the novel. The unbalanced quest for first principles leads them to study history and literature in general; in this quest after the past, they overlook the fact that their present is quickly disintegrating.

Some critics find in the novel's last chapters an increasingly sympathetic presentation of the pair. As their disillusionment—with sex, politics, religion, education, and the law—becomes complete, they seem to emerge as objects of pity as well as of irony. Given the importance Flaubert attached to the endings of his works, it is particularly unfortunate that his last novel remains unfinished. In the face of their abysmal failure, the two old men take up copying, the task they had worked at in Paris; what they copy, the matter of a proposed second volume for the novel, is not fully known, although some hints exist. The copying of words, words of others, and the interjection of their own comments serve as a fitting occupation for Flaubert's characters. Throughout his own career as a writer/copier, Flaubert had consistently

stressed the necessity of the right words, the classical, disciplined finish that frequently captured his own regret, and presumably would capture the regrets of Bouvard and Pécuchet, that, after all, things did not work out well. To the last, even in his bitter exposition of Rousseauism, the Enlightenment, and encyclopedism, he was never free of the regret for lost illusions.

John J. Conlon

OTHER MAJOR WORKS

SHORT FICTION: *Trois Contes*, 1877 (*Three Tales*, 1903); *Novembre*, 1885 (wr. c. 1840; *November*, 1932).

PLAYS: *Le Candidat*, pr., pb. 1874 (*The Candidate*, 1904); *Le Château des cœurs*, pr. 1874 (with Louis Bouilhet; wr. 1863; *The Castle of Hearts*, 1904).

NONFICTION: *Par les champs et par les grèves*, 1885 (with Maxime Du Camp; *Over Strand and Field*, 1904); *Correspondance, 1830-1880*, 1887-1893; *Dictionnaire des idées reçues*, 1910, 1913 (*Dictionary of Accepted Ideas*, 1954); *Notes de voyage*, 1910.

MISCELLANEOUS: *The Complete Works*, 1904 (10 volumes); *Œuvres complètes*, 1910-1933 (22 volumes).

BIBLIOGRAPHY

Addison, Claire. *Where Flaubert Lies: Chronology, Mythology, and History*. Cambridge, England: Cambridge University Press, 1996. An extremely useful guide, with chapters on Flaubert's major fiction, the chronology of his novels, and his major characters. Includes a comprehensive bibliography.

Bart, Benjamin F. *Flaubert*. Syracuse, N.Y.: Syracuse University Press, 1967. Considered by many scholars to be the definitive biography. Draws on much unpublished manuscript material. Bart takes a very psychological approach to his subject.

Bloom, Harold, ed. *Emma Bovary*. New York: Chelsea House, 1994. Part of a series on major literary characters. There is a section of critical extracts by the most distinguished commentators on Emma Bovary, along with essays on her language, the novel's style, and its use of memory. Includes a bibliography.

Buck, Stratton. *Gustave Flaubert*. New York: Twayne, 1966. A short introduction, including a chapter of biography, and chapters on all of Flaubert's major prose works. Includes chronology, notes, and annotated bibliography.

Porter, Laurence M., ed. *Critical Essays on Gustave Flaubert*. Boston: G. K. Hall, 1986. Porter begins with an introduction clearly explaining Flaubert's important and critical receptions. There are essays on every major work of prose, detailed notes, and an unusually thorough annotated bibliography on each of Flaubert's novels.

Ramazani, Vaheed. *The Free Indirect Mode: Flaubert and the Poetics of Irony*. Charlottesville: University Press of Virginia, 1988. A very helpful, detailed study of Flaubert's use of verbal irony, point of view, voice, and language (especially metaphor). Includes notes and bibliography. Recommended for the advanced student.

Williams, Tony, and Mary Orr, eds. *New Approaches in Flaubert Studies*. Lewiston, N.Y.: E. Mellen Press, 1999. Part of the Studies in French Literature series, this is a contemporary study of Flaubert's works. Provides bibliographical references and an index.

(Library of Congress)

Unwiederbringlich, 1892 (*Beyond Recall*, 1964)
Frau Jenny Treibel, 1893 (*Jenny Treibel*, 1976)
Effi Briest, 1895 (English translation, 1914, 1962)
Die Poggenpuhls, 1896
Der Stechlin, 1898 (*The Stechlin*, 1996)

OTHER LITERARY FORMS

In addition to the novels mentioned above, Theodor Fontane's works include numerous poems, novellas, theater reviews, travel journals, autobiographical writings, four volumes of letters, and essays on literature, history, and art. This extremely prolific writer was a journalist for many years before he was able to devote himself mainly to belles lettres.

ACHIEVEMENTS

When considering Fontane's writing, one thinks not only of nineteenth century Prussia, of her landscapes and cityscapes, of her people—particularly the declining gentry, the prosperous upper middle

THEODOR FONTANE

Born: Neuruppin, Prussia; December 30, 1819
Died: Berlin, Germany; September 20, 1898

PRINCIPAL LONG FICTION

Vor dem Sturm, 1878
L'Adultera, 1882
Schach von Wuthenow, 1883 (*A Man of Honor: Schach von Wuthenow*, 1975)
Cécile, 1887
Irrungen, Wirrungen, 1888 (*Trials and Tribulations*, 1917; also as *A Suitable Match*, 1968)
Stine, 1890 (English translation, 1969)

class, the faithful servants—but also of the emerging working class. Beginning with his *Wanderungen durch die Mark Brandenburg* (journeys through Mark Brandenburg, which appeared between 1865 and 1882) and culminating in his major novels, Fontane painted a fascinating social panorama of his age.

BIOGRAPHY

Henri Theodor Fontane was born on December 30, 1819, in Neuruppin, Prussia. Both of his parents were of French descent, part of the French Huguenot colony that had existed in Prussia since the Edict of Potsdam of 1685. Fontane's father was a pharmacist. During the first year of his marriage, he acquired a well-established pharmacy in Neuruppin. He was not, however, a good businessman, and he lost considerable amounts of money at the gambling table. In 1827, the elder Fontane sold his pharmacy in Neuruppin and purchased another in Swinemünde. The Fontane family then moved to Swinemünde, a port town that was much livelier than Neuruppin. For Fontane, Swinemünde was always imbued with a certain poetic quality, and he transmuted it into the setting of a few of his works. He attended the *gymnasium* (academic high school) in Neuruppin for a few years, but eventually he switched to a vocational school in Berlin and, in 1836, was apprenticed to a pharmacy there. During those years, his father's fortunes went from bad to worse, and his parents eventually separated.

His father's financial failures meant that, from a very young age, Fontane had to rely almost exclusively on his own resources in order to make a living. While still an apprentice in the pharmacy in Berlin, he wrote poems and novellas, a few of which were published. In April, 1844, he began his one-year military service. During the summer of the same year, he was given leave in order to accompany a friend on a trip to England. He was fascinated by that country and particularly by the city of London. He resolved to find a way to live in England for several years.

In 1847, Fontane received his license as a "first-class pharmacist," but he never practiced his profession in any consistent manner. He became active in a few literary societies in Berlin and received several assignments as a journalist. In 1850, he married Emilie Rouanet-Kummer, to whom he had been engaged for five years. In 1851, their first son was born, and the struggle for day-to-day survival intensified.

In 1852, Fontane was sent to London for several months, as a correspondent for the *Preussische Zeitung*. After his return, he published *Ein Sommer in London* (1854; a summer in London), a collection of essays that are full of his admiration for British history and society and for the country's wealth. Fontane did not, however, hesitate to criticize the prevailing materialism and social injustice. His summer in London in 1852 and his knowledge of the English language and of British institutions were important factors when the Prussian government chose a press agent to be sent to London to present its views on world affairs to the British press.

In 1855, Fontane was posted to London for more than three years and, for the first time in his life, had a comfortable income. These years in England were very important to his development: They were a fruitful period of learning, of absorbing a foreign culture, and of contrasting it to his own. Toward the end of his assignment in England, Fontane went on a journey to Scotland, treading in the footsteps of Ossian and Sir Walter Scott. Shortly after his return to Berlin, he published a very personal account of his journey to Scotland: *Jenseits des Tweed* (1860; *Across the Tweed*, 1965), which received favorable critical reviews. More important, Fontane's work on *Across the Tweed* led to a number of insights, comparisons, and transmutations which were to find their way into *Wanderungen durch die Mark Brandenburg*, in which his monumental depiction of the landscape, the towns, the people, and the history of Mark Brandenburg was to set the stage for his novels and novellas.

In 1860, Fontane joined the editorial staff of the conservative *Kreuzzeitung*, not out of political conviction but in order to have a regular income. Ten years later, he was finally able to break "the chain on which my daily bread dangles." In 1870, he was appointed theater critic of the prestigious (and liberal) *Vossische Zeitung*, with which he remained associated until 1890.

Except for a brief internment by the French during the Franco-Prussian War (Fontane had served as a war correspondent), the last third of his life was relatively free of anxiety. Most of his time was devoted to writing, and he was increasingly recognized as a major literary voice. In 1894, when most of his major works (but not his two greatest novels) had been published, he was awarded an honorary doctorate by the University of Berlin. He was held in esteem by the adherents of naturalism, though their emerging literary form was quite unlike his own. Fontane died on September 20, 1898, apparently from a stroke. One of the papers found on his desk was a list of those people who were to receive copies of his just-published masterpiece, *The Stechlin*.

ANALYSIS

Theodor Fontane's novels may be divided into three categories, according to their subject matter: first, novels dealing with the conflicts arising from class distinctions, frequently involving a young nobleman and a girl from the lower classes; second, novels about marriage, in all cases involving adultery; and third, vast epic panoramas of Prussian society with diffuse plots, skillfully depicted settings, and carefully nuanced utterances by large numbers of characters. This third category includes Fontane's earliest novel, *Vor dem Sturm*, and his final masterpiece, *The Stechlin*.

A SUITABLE MATCH

Turning to a detailed consideration of the first category, one should look first at *A Suitable Match* and *Stine*. The plot of *A Suitable Match* centers on a love affair between Botho von Rienäcker, an officer of the Prussian nobility, and Lene, a seamstress. Botho is eventually induced by family considerations to marry a rich young woman of his own class. Lene also gets married to an honest man, a Pietist recently returned from America. Fontane uses this simple plot to create realistic yet subtle portraits, not only of the two protagonists but also of the two social strata that they represent.

Particularly notable in the novel is Fontane's treatment of dialogue. The first two chapters take place in and around a nursery and vegetable farm where Lene, her mother, and Mr. and Mrs. Dörr (the owners of the nursery) live. It is early summer, and "Baron Botho" often visits Lene and spends parts of his evenings in Mrs. Dörr's kitchen, drinking apple cider and conversing with his friends. In these conversations, the characters reveal themselves not only as individuals but also as types who share their attitudes and circumstances with many other members of their class. The conversations in Mrs. Dörr's kitchen are juxtaposed with the one among Botho, his uncle, and another young nobleman. They meet in an exclusive Berlin restaurant (whose decor is as carefully described as Mrs. Dörr's kitchen), they drink Chablis, and most of their conversation is concerned with contemporary society and politics. Only at one point does Botho's uncle touch upon the critical issue at hand—when he says that Botho is "practically committed" ("Du bist doch so gut wie gebunden"). This incident is a good example of Fontane's seemingly effortless artistry, because, later on, during a moment of supreme happiness, Lene ties a bunch of flowers with a strand of her own hair. As she gives the flowers to Botho, she uses almost the same words "Now you are tied [committed to me]" ("Nun bist du gebunden"). The irony of the matter is that Botho *is* committed to marry a young noblewoman, and when his mother insists that he honor that commitment, he obeys. When a fellow officer asks Botho for his advice in a similar matter, Botho stoutly defends the existing class distinctions and advises his friend to terminate his relationship with the young bourgeoise in question. A few years later, however—when he decides to burn a packet of letters that Lene had once written to him, as well as the withered bunch of flowers—he realizes that he still is and always will be "tied" to her.

In *A Suitable Match*, existing social conventions are portrayed as of paramount importance. When they conflict with individual happiness, Botho's happiness must be subordinated to them. The fact that life goes on passably well is adumbrated by Mrs. Dörr in the first chapter. This fact is also demonstrated through the Pietist's account of his first meeting with Lene and through the narrator's account of Botho's marriage.

STINE

The conflict between social conventions and personal happiness is accentuated and rendered more poignant by the tragic conclusion of *Stine*. The main plot of this novel concerns a love affair between a young girl of the working class and a young count. Stine and Waldemar (the two young people) meet during a supper party arranged by Stine's sister Pauline but paid for by Pauline's lover, an aging count who is Waldemar's uncle. Pauline's way of life—specifically, her total financial dependence on the Count—constitutes an important secondary action of this novel. Accounts of Pauline's present and past life are skillfully interwoven in the narration, and the reader learns that she is a widow with a dependent child who simply cannot make ends meet without the Count's financial help—without, in fact, selling herself to him. When Stine first speaks to Waldemar alone, she makes it clear to him that she prefers a life of poverty to the kind of life her sister leads. Later, Waldemar offers to marry her and to immigrate to America with her, but she refuses and explains to him that the difference between their social classes would preclude any kind of permanent happiness for them. Thereupon, Waldemar, who has been unable to obtain his uncle's support for this marriage, commits suicide. Thus, Waldemar dies because all the people who surround him (including his beloved) tell him that a Count cannot marry a working-class girl, that class distinctions are insuperable barriers.

The reader is left with the impression that Waldemar is a victor of sorts, that the old caste system will not survive for long. Contemporary social conventions are attacked, not only by Waldemar but also by the Baron (a friend of Waldemar's uncle to whom Waldemar first turns for help), who says that he is always happy to see someone breaking through the *Krimskrams* (nonsense) of class distinctions. Even Waldemar's uncle admits that "the divine order of the world does not completely correspond to the calendar of the state and to the ranking list of society." He goes even further and states that "at the present time" he and his ilk are still the *beati possidentes* (happy proprietors). He says to Waldemar: "Be a proprietor, and you are in the right. . . . Why deprive ourselves of this possession and . . . conjure up a future which may not benefit anyone, and certainly not us?" Statements such as this one, if read in conjunction with the accounts of Pauline's precarious financial situation, add a considerable dimension of social criticism to the novel. It becomes clear to the reader that the opulence of the nobility is based upon the low wages of the working class and on a total absence of a social security system for these people. It is, of course, no accident that *Stine* was written at a time when a comprehensive social security system was being debated in the Prussian parliament. (The social security law was finally passed in 1889.)

JENNY TREIBEL

In *Stine* as well as in *A Suitable Match*, politics is deftly subsumed in the actions and in the characterizations. That is not quite the case in *Jenny Treibel*, the most lighthearted work in the first category of Fontane's novels. Again, the representatives of two social classes interact and mingle socially, but they cannot intermarry. In *Jenny Treibel*, however, the obstacle is not the insurmountable barrier of class distinction but the determination of one of the protagonists, Mrs. Jenny Treibel, a successful social climber. In her youth, she had been poor and idealistic and had had an affair with an equally poor and idealistic high school teacher named Schmidt. She had left him and married an industrialist. When the novel opens, Jenny rules over a substantial villa, over her husband, who is only a *Kommerzienrat* but who has higher political ambitions, and over her somewhat spineless son Leopold, who works in his father's firm. Jenny's older son has already married a suitably rich young woman from Hamburg. The other social circle consists mainly of Mr. Schmidt, his vivacious and intelligent daughter Corinna, and his nephew, Marcell. During a supper party, Corinna flirts with the visiting British businessman, but only in order to attract Leopold's attention. On the way home, she admits to Marcell that she intends to marry Leopold and live a life of luxury, come what may. Marcell is despondent because he loves her and hopes to marry her. Nevertheless, during an outing with both families and some mutual friends, Corinna contrives a sort of engagement to Leopold.

Leaving aside Mr. Treibel's ill-starred political maneuvers, the comedy has two high points, both involving Jenny. In one encounter, she forbids Leopold to marry Corinna, and he refuses to obey her. In the other one, she tries to dissuade Corinna from her endeavor, and the latter refuses to relinquish her "rights" to Leopold. Yet, Jenny wins in the end: Her daughter-in-law conveniently has a sister who will receive a considerable dowry. Jenny invites this young woman to spend a few weeks in her house, and Leopold must at least be polite to her. Meanwhile, he writes letters to Corinna every day, assuring her of his love and steadfastness, but he does not go to see her. Some two weeks later, Marcell receives a tenured appointment as a teacher and is thus able to get married. At this point, Corinna is more than tired of Leopold's letters and more than ready to accept Marcell. The strength of the novel lies in the indulgent irony with which the various characters are depicted and the loving attention paid to details, lifestyles, food and drink, and nuances of speech. The novel's subject matter is aptly summed up by Corinna when she says that she was not allowed to marry Leopold because she did not have a dowry that would have doubled the Treibels' assets. Such subject matter may be trivial, but Fontane's artistry in presenting it makes the novel a first-rate comedy of manners.

Effi Briest

Fontane's first three novels about marriage and adultery (*L'Adultera*, *Cécile*, and *Beyond Recall*) are uneven in artistic quality. They may be regarded as essentially preparatory to his undisputed masterpiece, *Effi Briest*. The plot of this latter work is based on an anecdote, "a story of adultery like a hundred others," and it is quite simple: Effi von Briest, the seventeen-year-old daughter of a family of the lower nobility, marries Geert von Innstetten, a member of the same social class, thirty-eight years of age. He is a civil servant stationed in the remote seaside town of Kessin. Kessin is a dull place: With one or two exceptions, the townspeople do not measure up to Effi's social and educational levels, and the members of the country gentry in the neighboring estates are narrow-minded and bigoted and receive her coolly. Innstetten

tries his best to be attentive to her, but he also has to devote considerable time and effort to his duties and his career. After a year or so, Effi gives birth to a daughter, but even this happy event does not alter the essentially tranquil and boring quality of her life in Kessin. Then Major von Crampas is stationed there, and he brings some life into the town. He organizes amateur theatrical productions in which Effi and other local notables perform. Effi knows that Crampas is a notorious ladies' man, and she sees through him quite easily. Yet, out of boredom, nonchalance, or frivolity, she allows herself to be seduced by him. Her affair with Crampas, with its attendant problems of secrecy and dissembling, does not bring her much joy. She is therefore relieved when Innstetten informs her that he has been promoted and will be transferred to Berlin. The Innstettens move into a suitably elegant apartment in the capital and begin leading the kind of social life that befits members of the upper classes. Effi becomes a society lady and is quite happy. Crampas is forgotten. Then, almost seven years after their arrival, Innstetten accidentally discovers a packet of letters that Crampas had written to Effi. Innstetten challenges Crampas to a duel and kills him. He then banishes Effi from his home. She lives in a small apartment in Berlin, financially supported by her parents but forbidden to go to their home and shunned by all members of high society. After three years of this kind of life, she is finally allowed to see her daughter, but the child has been completely turned against her and only parrots words drilled into her by her father or her governess. Effi is so upset by this encounter with her child that she has a complete nervous breakdown. Severely ill, she is finally allowed to return to her parents' home. There she spends a few months in a trancelike kind of happiness, almost beatific, and finally dies.

Effi's fate, as sketched above, certainly produces a certain amount of empathy in the reader, but the real interest of the novel lies in the more general conflict between the concepts of personal happiness and social conventions. Many of the characters in *Effi Briest* are thwarted in their pursuit of happiness by a complex set of rules and regulations, which are presented by the narrator in such a manner as to question their validity. The novel contains a wealth of well-drawn characters, and they are carefully orchestrated to express this crucial problem. The problem arises early in the novel, when Effi meets the various members of the country gentry around Kessin. They are drawn as a stiff, prissy, and bigoted lot, and the reader is prompted to ask himself how much happier they could be and how much happier they could make an intelligent and lively young woman like Effi if they were a little warmer, more natural, and more forthcoming. Juxtaposed to these dull and hidebound characters is the figure of Roswitha, Effi's faithful servant. She is a simple, humane person who does not hesitate to demonstrate such deeply felt emotions as grief, love, and compassion. While Effi's mother is prompted by her concern for the norms of society to forbid her sinful daughter to enter her parental home, Roswitha stays with her in very humble circumstances and remains her servant and companion until the end.

This and similar criticisms of social conventions may be regarded as inferential; they may be discerned from a close consideration of plot and characterization. There is, however, at least one protagonist who undergoes a development to the point where he overtly and consciously attacks contemporary social conventions. After Innstetten has discovered the incriminating letters, he has a long conversation with a colleague, whom he asks to act as a second in the duel. The colleague tries to dissuade Innstetten from the duel, particularly in view of the fact that Effi's adultery occurred almost seven years earlier, but Innstetten retorts:

> I have thought it all over. A man is not just an individual, he belongs to a whole, and we must always pay attention to the whole, we are absolutely dependent on it. If I could manage to live in isolation, I could ignore the matter . . . but that . . . society-something [*Gesellschafts-Etwas*] which tyrannizes us does not ask about charm or love or statutes of limitations. I have no choice. I must.

At this point in the narration, Innstetten follows the dictates of the "society-something" and proceeds to kill Crampas. His and Crampas's seconds notify the authorities, and everything is in perfect legal order.

On his way back to Berlin, however, Innstetten begins to have his doubts. He remembers the way Crampas looked at him during his dying moments, and he tells himself that he did not kill him out of hatred, which would at least have been a human emotion, but because of a "concept, a made-up story, a comedy almost." Yet he says to himself, "I must now continue the comedy, and must send Effi away and ruin her, and myself along with her." It is this "must," this obedience to human-made codes of behavior, no matter how much one doubts their validity, that brings grief and sometimes catastrophe upon many of Fontane's characters. In Innstetten's case, it takes three years of solitary suffering on his part and a moving letter from Roswitha (who begs him to send Effi her favorite old dog) for him to realize that "culture and honor" and "all this nonsense" are the cause of his and Effi's suffering.

It is the supreme irony of this novel that Effi, shortly before her death, expresses her conviction that her husband, in all of his cruelty, has treated her justly. It should be noted that the opposing views reached by the two protagonists are expressed by them, not by the narrator (who intrudes almost nowhere in the novel). In a brief epilogue that is set one month after Effi's death, her mother expresses doubts whether she and her husband gave Effi the right kind of education and whether Effi might not have been too young to marry. Her husband gives his standard response: "That leads us too far afield." In the final analysis, this evasive answer must be given to the question regarding Fontane's own stand on the problem of personal happiness versus social conventions. He raises many questions; he allows some of his major characters to attack contemporary codes of behavior, but those characters who infringe upon them are punished.

Vor dem Strum

Fontane's "Prussian," or historical, novels and are vast panoramas of the entire Prussian society. One of them takes place in the period of 1812 to 1813 and the other one in the late 1890's. Walter Möller-Seidel has described *Vor dem Strum* as the best historical novel written in Germany in the nineteenth century. Fontane himself described his intentions as follows: ". . . to introduce a large number of characters from Mark Brandenburg from the winter 1812-1813 [and] to depict the manner in which the great feeling which was born then . . . affected various kinds of people." The "great feeling" was the joy and relief that the Prussian people felt at Napoleon's defeat in Russia in 1812 and the anticipation that Prussia would soon be free of French domination and occupation. (Prussia had previously been defeated by the French and forced into an alliance with them against Russia.)

In the novel, as the demoralized remnants of the defeated French army move westward into Prussia, the Prussian king still respects his pact with Napoleon, but the members of the nobility urge him and his government to attack the French and to rid the fatherland of them. This political aspect constitutes one strand of this long (seven-hundred-page) and diffuse novel: Several members of the rural gentry organize a militia and attempt unsuccessfully to drive the French out of Frankfurt an der Oder. Several other strands of the action concern the relationships between two noble houses, their plans for intermarriage, and the disparate destinies of the young people in question. In addition, the novel abounds in vivid depictions of contemporary literary life, of members of the middle and peasant classes, and it even contains a breathtaking account of the battle of Borodino, which is at the same time a moving antiwar text. Obviously, this overabundance of material does not make for a tightly constructed plot, but toward the end of the novel, a unifying tenor does emerge—namely, the renewal of society. It is surely no accident that Lewin von Vitzewitz, the young heir to the manor of Hohen-Vietz, marries Marie, the daughter of a traveling circus artist. Lewin's father welcomes her into his family just as Lewin is about to leave for the war of liberation against the French. The timing of these two events seems to symbolize a juncture between the renewal of the Vitzewitz dynasty and that of the entire country. All in all, the various strands of the action, the vivid descriptions, and the loving care expended on each detail add up to a fascinating panorama of Prussian society at a crucial point in its history.

THE STECHLIN

Turning to *The Stechlin*, Fontane's last work, it may be well to quote from a letter of his in which he described his work to a Berlin publisher: "At the end an old man dies and two young people marry; that is more or less all that happens in five-hundred pages." Fontane's description of his novel is accurate as far as the paucity of the action is concerned, but it is misleading when one considers the abundance of symbolism and political and moral thought that the work contains. For the most part, the novel is set in the village of Stechlin and in the manor house of the same name, which is inhabited by Dubslaw von Stechlin, a retired major in his sixties. The marriage alluded to above is the one between Dubslaw's son Woldemar and Armgard von Barby, the daughter of a retired diplomat living in Berlin. This marriage solves Dubslaw's one major problem: Armgard's dowry will permit Woldemar to repay a mortgage that his father had to take on the manor, and the necessary repairs will be made. As a result, the material base for the continued existence of the Stechlin dynasty in its accustomed style would seem to be assured.

The many questions raised in the novel, however, go far beyond the material base of the Stechlin estate. Throughout the work, there are conversations and discussions about the role of the nobility and about the social contract between various segments of the population, as well as about the individual's relationship to society. The novel encompasses a vast political spectrum, and the reader becomes acquainted with supporters of the three main political parties—namely, the Conservatives, the Progressives, and the Social Democrats. As usual with Fontane, it is difficult to discern his own sympathies, but on the basis of the unequivocally positive characterization accorded to Pastor Lorenzen (the village pastor and Woldemar's mentor), it seems safe to say that the views he expresses are very close to the ones the author reached in his old age. Some of Lorenzen's statements, while a little dated now, bear rereading and rethinking even in the twentieth and twenty-first centuries. Consider, for example, his definition of the modern age:

The main contrast between the modern and the old [ways of life] consists of the fact that human beings are no longer placed in their positions on the basis of their birth. . . . Previously one was a lord of a manor or a weaver of linen for three-hundred years; now every weaver can one day be the lord of a manor.

This statement is as relevant, and as debatable, in our day as it was in Fontane's time. Some of Lorenzen's and Dubslaw's other discussions sound even more relevant to our time, particularly the one about the pollution caused by a chemical plant in their county and Dubslaw's proposal that the workers, instead of working there, should each till half an acre of land, which the state should give them. Lest it appear that *The Stechlin* consists only of dry political or philosophical treatises, it should be pointed out that all of these serious thoughts are presented with light irony, that the interlocutors are depicted with all of their human foibles, and that none of them is presented as a villain. In this way, an air of lightheartedness and serenity pervades the whole work. Upon some reflection, Lorenzen's, Dubslaw's, and Melusine's concerns for their contemporaries emerge as age-old universal concerns—namely, man's care for his fellowman. Thus, in his last work, Fontane's thoughts transcended his previous preoccupation with individual happiness vis-à-vis social conventions to encompass a profound reflection on the question of collective well-being.

Franz P. Haberl

OTHER MAJOR WORKS

NONFICTION: *Ein Sommer in London*, 1854; *Jenseits des Tweed*, 1860 (*Across the Tweed*, 1965); *Wanderungen durch die Mark Brandenburg*, 1865-1882.

MISCELLANEOUS: *Sämtliche Werke*, 1959-1975 (24 volumes).

BIBLIOGRAPHY

Bance, Alan. *Theodor Fontane: The Major Novels*. Cambridge, England: Cambridge University Press, 1982. A discussion of all of Fontane's major fiction, with notes and bibliography. Recommended for advanced students.

Chambers, Helen. *The Changing Image of Theodor Fontane*. Columbia, S.C.: Camden House, 1997. Chapters on reviews and early criticism, with chapters on later work in the 1970's and 1980's and a discussion of Fontane and the realistic novel. Includes notes and bibliography.

Velardi, Carol Hawkes. *Techniques of Compression and Prefiguration in the Beginnings of Theodor Fontane's Novels*. New York: Peter Lang, 1992. A somewhat specialized study, but there is a good introduction for the beginning student and a useful bibliography.

Wansink, Susan. *Female Victims and Oppressors in Novels by Theodor Fontane and François Mauriac*. New York: Peter Lang, 1998. An interesting combination of literary and cultural criticism situating Fontane in his time while also reading the novels as complex studies of the interaction between characters and societal norms. Includes notes and bibliography.

Zweibel, William I. *Theodor Fontane*. New York: Twayne, 1992. The place to start not only for the beginning student of Fontane but for scholars wishing to review current research on the subject. Chapter 1 situates Fontane in his times; other chapters explore antiquarianism and romantic destiny, balladry and psychology, Fontane's treatment of the Prussian state, and his later fiction. Provides chronology, notes, and an annotated bibliography.

FORD MADOX FORD
Ford Madox Hueffer

Born: Merton, England; December 17, 1873
Died: Deauville, France; June 26, 1939

PRINCIPAL LONG FICTION

The Shifting of the Fire, 1892
The Inheritors, 1901 (with Joseph Conrad)
Romance, 1903 (with Conrad)
The Benefactor, 1905

The Fifth Queen, 1906
Privy Seal, 1907
An English Girl, 1907
The Fifth Queen Crowned, 1908
Mr. Apollo, 1908
The "Half Moon," 1909
The Nature of a Crime, 1909 (serial), 1924 (book;
    with Conrad)
A Call, 1910
The Portrait, 1910
The Simple Life Limited, 1911
Ladies Whose Bright Eyes, 1911
The Panel, 1912
The New Humpty-Dumpty, 1912
Mr. Fleight, 1913
The Young Lovell, 1913 (also known as *Ring for
    Nancy*)
The Good Soldier, 1915
The Marsden Case, 1923
Some Do Not . . . , 1924
No More Parades, 1925
A Man Could Stand Up, 1926
The Last Post, 1928
A Little Less Than Gods, 1928
When the Wicked Man, 1931
The Rash Act, 1933
Henry for Hugh, 1934
Vive le Roy, 1936
Parade's End, 1950 (includes *Some Do Not . . .* ,
    No More Parades, *A Man Could Stand Up*, and
    The Last Post)

OTHER LITERARY FORMS

Ford Madox Ford was an extremely prolific author, working in virtually every literary form. His children's stories and fairy tales include *The Brown Owl* (1891); *The Feather* (1892); *The Queen Who Flew* (1894); *Christina's Fairy Book* (1906); and the pantomime *Mister Bosphorus and the Muses* (1923). His volumes of poetry include *The Questions at the Well* (1893, as Fenil Haig); *Poems for Pictures* (1900); *The Face of the Night* (1904); *From Inland and Other Poems* (1907); *High Germany* (1911); *Collected Poems* (1913); *On Heaven, and Poems Written on Active Service* (1918); *A House* (1921);

(Archive Photos)

New Poems (1927); and *Collected Poems* (1936). Ford, who is acknowledged with Joseph Conrad as coauthor of the novels *The Inheritors* and *Romance*, may have had some hand in the composition of a number of Conrad's other works during the decade from 1898 to 1908. Ford's biographical, autobiographical, and critical works include *Ford Madox Brown* (1896); *Rossetti* (1902); *Hans Holbein, the Younger* (1905); *The Pre-Raphaelite Brotherhood* (1907); *Ancient Lights* (1911); *The Critical Attitude* (1911); *Henry James* (1913); *Thus to Revisit* (1921); *Joseph Conrad: A Personal Remembrance* (1924); *The English Novel* (1929); *Return to Yesterday* (1931); *It Was the Nightingale* (1933); and *Mightier Than the Sword* (1938). During the last years of his life, Ford served as professor of comparative literature at Olivet College in Michigan and prepared his final book, a massive critical history of world literature, *The March of Literature* (1938). His history and travel books include *The Cinque Ports* (1900); *Zeppelin Nights* (1916); *Provence* (1935); and *Great Trade Route* (1937). Collections of essays include *The Soul of London* (1905); *The Heart of the Country*

(1906); *The Spirit of the People* (1907); *Women and Men* (1923); *A Mirror to France* (1926); *New York Is Not America* (1927); and *New York Essays* (1927). Several volumes Ford classified simply as propaganda, including *When Blood Is Their Argument* (1915) and *Between St. Dennis and St. George* (1915). Ford also edited *The English Review* and later *The Transatlantic Review* and wrote much ephemeral journalism.

ACHIEVEMENTS

It is generally agreed that Ford's *The Good Soldier* is one of the masterpieces of modernism, a major experimental novel of enormous historical and artistic interest. His tetralogy *Parade's End*, composed of *Some Do Not . . .*, *No More Parades*, *A Man Could Stand Up*, and *The Last Post*, is also a key work in the modernist revolution, more massive than *The Good Soldier*, more sweeping in its treatment of historical change, but less daring in its formal innovations. After these five novels, there is a considerable drop in the quality of Ford's remaining fiction. The historical trilogy concerning Henry VIII (*The Fifth Queen, Privy Seal*, and *The Fifth Queen Crowned*) is cited by some critics as meriting serious reading. Scattered among his many volumes, works such as *A Call* reward the reader with surprisingly high quality, but most of the lesser books are all too obviously potboilers.

Ford was equally at home in the English, French, and German languages, and he contributed to the cosmopolitan and polyglot texture of European modernism. As an editor of influential literary magazines, he recognized and encouraged many writers who have since become famous. His collaboration with Joseph Conrad in the 1890's corresponded with Conrad's most productive artistic period, but whether Conrad's achievements were stimulated by Ford's collaboration or accomplished in spite of Ford's intrusion is still under debate. Ford also exercised a considerable influence on Ezra Pound during Pound's early London years. Later, after World War I, Ford was associated with all the prominent writers of the Parisian Left Bank: James Joyce, Ernest Hemingway, Jean Rhys, and others.

Ford's achievement then, was as a man of letters whose diverse contributions to modern literature—particularly as an editor and as a champion of modernist writers—far transcended his not inconsiderable legacy as a novelist.

BIOGRAPHY

Ford Madox Hermann Hueffer was born in what is now London on December 17, 1873; he was named for his maternal grandfather, the pre-Raphaelite painter Ford Madox Brown (1821-1893). Brown had two daughters: The elder married William Michael Rossetti (brother to the poet Dante Gabriel Rossetti); the younger daughter, Catherine, married the German journalist Francis Hueffer, music critic for the London *Times*, who wrote many books and had a serious scholarly interest in Richard Wagner, Arthur Schopenhauer, and Provençal poetry. Ford was born to this couple and grew up in an intellectual hothouse of painters, musicians, artists, and writers with advanced ideas. His family expected him to be a genius, which led him to acquire, early in his life, a sense of inadequacy and failure. Ford tended later to falsify information in his biography and to have difficulty separating reality from fantasy in his recollections. He attended the coeducational Praetorius School in Folkestone, apparently an institution with very modern ideas of education. One of his schoolmates there was Elsie Martindale, a young woman whom he married against her parents' wishes in 1894. Perhaps this elopement by the impetuous young lovers shows Ford's tendency to play out in reality the conventions of courtly love, a subject of intense study by Ford's father and a preoccupation of the author himself in all his fiction, evident even in his final book, the critical survey *The March of Literature*. Ford and Elsie did not, however, find passionate love a practical way to attain long-term happiness or stability.

In September, 1898, Edward Garnett introduced Ford to Joseph Conrad, now recognized as one of the greatest English-language novelists, even though his native tongue was Polish. Ford, like Conrad, was multilingual, and, at least to some degree, he helped Conrad with the niceties of the English idiom. The two would often write in French, then translate the work into English. By the spring of 1909, however, Ford and Conrad had quarreled and were never again closely associated. They acknowledged that they collaborated on *The Inheritors* and *Romance*, although Ford must have had at least some slight hand in many of Conrad's fictions written between 1898 and 1909. In fairness, the reader should note that Ford, too, must have had his ideas and his style permanently shaped to some degree by his collaboration with the older, more worldly master, Conrad.

Conrad had married an Englishwoman, Jessie George, in 1896, and he lived in a settled and respectable way with her until his death in 1924. At least in part, Conrad's breach with Ford stemmed from Jessie's dislike for what she regarded as Ford's ever more outrageous sexual behavior. In 1903, Ford had an affair with his wife's sister, Mary Martindale. Throughout his fiction, Ford replays similar real-life issues of passion, adultery, and their tawdry consequences. Thomas C. Moser in *The Life in the Fiction of Ford Madox Ford* (1980) maintains that Ford's writing follows a cyclical pattern, with each outburst of creativity triggered by the introduction of a new love into his life: Elsie Martindale, Mary Martindale, Arthur Marwood, Violet Hunt, Brigit Patmore, Jean Rhys, Stella Bowen, and Janice Biala. Moser's thesis is a bit too neat to be completely convincing, but its outline suggests the generally messy personal life that Ford must have been living while writing his voluminous works.

ANALYSIS

From his association with Conrad, his study of Henry James and of the rise of the English novel, and his knowledge of French literature, Ford Madox Ford developed his notion of *literary impressionism*, which is central to an understanding of his masterpiece, *The Good Soldier*. Ford's clearest statement of his theory of literary impressionism is found in *Joseph Conrad: A Personal Remembrance*. Literary impressionism, Ford says, is a revolt against the commonplace nineteenth century novel, or "nuvvle," as he calls it. The impressionist novel should not be a narration or report, but a rendering of impressions. Rather than following a linear plot, giving one event after another as

they occur, the impressionist novel enters the mind of a storyteller and follows his associated ideas in a tangled stream of consciousness, so that vivid image becomes juxtaposed to vivid image, skipping across space and time in a collage of memory and imagination. The impressionist novel takes as its subject an *affair*, some shocking event which has already happened, and proceeds in concentric rings of growing complication as the storyteller cogitates. The focus of the novel is internal rather than external. The reader must focus on the storyteller's mental processes rather than on the events themselves. The impressionist novel is limited to the mind of the storyteller, and so is finally solipsistic. The novel refers to itself, so that the reader can never "get out of" the storyteller's limited mentality and judge whether he is reliable or unreliable, perhaps merely a madman telling a tale which has no connection whatever to reality. Limited and unreliable narration, time-shifts, fragmentation of details torn from the context in which they occur, verbal collages of such fragments in configurations produced by the narrator's association of ideas, defamiliarization of the commonplace—all these are characteristics of Ford's best work.

The traditional nineteenth century English novel depended on the convention of the linear plot. The process of reading from page one to the end of the text was generally assumed to correspond to the passage of time as one event followed another in the story, so that the hero might be born on page one, go to school on page fifty, commit adultery or consider committing adultery on page one hundred, and meet his just reward in the concluding pages of the book. In *The Good Soldier*, Ford Madox Ford rejected this linear structure and substituted for it the "affair": A shocking set of events has already occurred before the book begins, and the narrator weaves back and forth in his memories related to the affair. Gradually, in concentric circles of understanding, the reader learns the complicated situation underlying the superficial first impressions he may have formed. The drama of the story shifts from the events of the tale to the process of the telling; such stories necessarily contrast first appearances with deeper "realities" revealed in the narration.

THE GOOD SOLDIER

The Good Soldier concerns two married couples: Arthur Dowell (the narrator) and his wife Florence (Hurlbird) Dowell and Edward Ashburnham and his wife Leonora (Powys) Ashburnham. The events of the story take place between August, 1904, and August, 1913, a nine-year period throughout most of which the two couples are the best of friends, living the life of the leisured rich at European spas, in elegant, cultivated idleness. There is an elegiac tone to this work, reflecting the autumn sunshine of the Edwardian era and a way of life which would be brutally wiped out with the outbreak of World War I.

The texture of the novel invites the reader to consider the conflict between appearance and reality. For most of the nine-year period of the action, Arthur Dowell believes that his wife is suffering from a heart ailment which confines her travels and requires her to be shut in her room under peculiar circumstances from time to time. He subsequently learns, however, that her heart is sound and that these arrangements are necessary to allow her to commit adultery, first with a young man named Jimmy and later with Edward Ashburnham himself. Dowell imagines Ashburnham to be a model husband, only gradually learning that he has engaged in a series of affairs and that his wife does not speak to him except when required to do so in public. This novel is like a hall of mirrors, and any statement by the narrator must be doubted.

Because readers are accustomed to novels with linear plots, the novel is more easily understood if the plot is rearranged into the customary linear sequence of events. Edward Ashburnham is from an ancient Anglican landholding family who owns the estate Branshaw Teleragh. As the novel opens, he has recently returned from serving as a military officer in India and arrives at the health spa, Bad Nauheim, in Germany, where he meets the Dowells for the first time. Although he appears to be brave, sentimental, and heroic, like the knights in ancient romances, the reader learns that he has been involved in a series of unfortunate affairs with women. His parents arranged his marriage to Leonora Powys, a convent-educated Catholic girl, whose impoverished family had an es-

tate in Ireland. Religious and temperamental differences soon cause their marriage to cool. While riding in a third-class carriage, Edward tries in a blundering way to comfort a servant girl and is arrested for sexual misbehavior in what is called the Kilsyte case. This misadventure leads him for the first time in his life to consider himself capable of bad conduct. His next affair involves a short-lived passion for a Spanish dancer, La Dolciquita, who demands cash for spending a week with him at Antibes. Reckless gambling at the casino, combined with the direct expenses of La Dolciquita's passion, substantially deplete Edward's inherited fortune. His wife, Leonora, makes herself the guardian of his estate and sets out to recover their financial losses. She demands that he take a military post in India for eight years and doles out his spending money carefully while squeezing his tenants and lands back in England for as much profit as possible.

In India, Edward finds his next woman, Mrs. Basil, whose husband, a brother-officer, allows the affair to continue in order to blackmail Edward. Eventually, Mrs. Basil's husband is transferred to Africa so that she can no longer stay with Edward. Edward then makes an alliance with Mrs. Maidan, also the wife of a junior officer. Mrs. Maidan has a heart condition and accompanies the Ashburnhams to Bad Nauheim for treatment. On the day that the Dowells and the Ashburnhams first meet, Leonora Ashburnham has found Mrs. Maidan coming out of Edward's bedroom in the hotel. Enraged, Leonora has slapped her and, in doing so, entangled her bracelet in Mrs. Maidan's hair. Florence Dowell, in the hall, sees them struggling there and comes to help. Leonora lamely explains that she has accidentally caught her bracelet in Mrs. Maidan's hair, and Florence helps them get untangled, as the sobbing Mrs. Maidan runs to her room. That evening, Leonora Ashburnham insists on sitting at the Dowells' dinner table in the hotel so as to prevent any gossip about that day's events in the hallway. Mrs. Maidan soon commits suicide, leaving Edward free to form a liaison with Florence Dowell herself.

Edward's ward, Nancy Rufford, is being educated in the same convent where Leonora went to school.

As Nancy grows to a mature woman, Edward becomes attracted to her, but he is caught in the conflict between love and honor. He desires Nancy, but he is honor-bound not to violate his sacred trust to protect her. After Florence Dowell learns of Edward's affection for Nancy (along with some other distressing developments), she too commits suicide. Edward remains firm, however, and refuses to take advantage of his ward or corrupt her, even when she openly offers herself to him. He arranges for her to be sent to her father in Ceylon. On her voyage there, she cables from Brindisi a cheerful note implying that she feels no sorrow about leaving him. Edward then commits suicide with a penknife, and Nancy goes insane when she hears of his death. His widow, Leonora, marries a rabbitlike neighbor, Rodney Bayham, while Arthur Dowell is left as the proprietor of the Branshaw Teleragh estate, where he nurses the insane Nancy Rufford.

From the exterior, to those who know him only slightly, Edward Ashburnham appears almost superhumanly noble, the ideal of the British country gentleman and good soldier. If the reader believes all that is alleged about him, he is quite the contrary, a raging stallion, recklessly ruining every female he meets. The superficial goodness is merely a veneer masking his corruption. All the other characters, as well, have two sides. Florence Dowell, the respectable wife, has had an affair before her marriage to Arthur with the despicable Jimmy and may have married simply to get back to her lover in Europe. She certainly does not hesitate to become Edward Ashburnham's mistress and commits suicide when she learns in a double-barrelled blow that Edward is attracted to Nancy Rufford and that the man in whose house she committed adultery with Jimmy is now talking with her husband in Bad Nauheim. Leonora is purposeful in trying to manage her husband's estate economically, but she is cruel and unloving. The reader can easily imagine that her husband would be driven to seek other company. Arthur Dowell, the narrator himself, is stupid, lazy, and piggish.

Since the story is told entirely from the point of view of Arthur Dowell, and since his is a limited intelligence, the reader can never entirely trust his narration as reliable. Dowell may assert on one page that a character is noble, yet show the reader in a hundred ways that the character is despicable. The reader is caught in the web of Dowell's mind. Clearly, Dowell sometimes does not tell the "truth"; but since the total work is fiction, the reader is not simply confronted with a conflict between appearance and reality but with the status of competing fictions. Is Edward a noble knight or a despicable roué? The story evaporates into the impressions in Dowell's mind. What Dowell thinks or believes *is* the truth at that moment in the fiction. It could be seriously argued that Edward, Leonora, and Florence have no external "reality" at all, that they are simply the imaginings of the sickly Dowell as he tells or dreams his story. This approach may shock readers of conventional fiction, who are accustomed to reading a novel as if the characters were real people, yet all characters in every fiction are simply projections of the author's creative imagination.

PARADE'S END

Ford's massive tetralogy, *Parade's End*, consists of four separate novels: *Some Do Not . . .; No More Parades; A Man Could Stand Up*; and *The Last Post*. The main theme of these works repeats a major concern of *The Good Soldier*, the destruction of the Tory gentleman. Edward Ashburnham in *The Good Soldier* belongs to the same class as Christopher Tietjens, the protagonist of *Parade's End*. Both are said to have been modeled on Ford's friend Arthur Marwood, who collaborated with Ford in publishing *The English Review*. Ashburnham is the landowner of Branshaw Teleragh, whereas Tietjens's family owns the Groby estate. Both feel an obligation to their dependants and take seriously their stewardship over the land. Both are highly altruistic in certain areas but are tormented by the conflict between their sexual impulses and what is considered proper or honorable behavior. They are Tory gentlemen, landowning, relaxed in manner, Anglican in religion, physically vigorous, classically educated, generous, virile, and possessed of a worldview in which man's place in the universe is clearly defined. Such men are assailed on all sides by women, by modern commercial industry, by Catholics and Jews, by fascists and communists, and finally by the internal contradictions of their own characters. World War I smashed that class of Tory landholding gentlefolk once and for all, in an externalization of that internal battle.

Because the books are a kind of verbal collage, creating a palimpsest of memory and imagination, weaving backward and forward through the minds of characters who are frequently under stress and incapable of reporting events without distorting them, the linear plot of the tetralogy is difficult to summarize. The first novel, *Some Do Not . . .*, opens with Christopher Tietjens traveling in a railway carriage. His destination, unknown to him at the time, is the future world, the wasteland created by World War I and the destruction of the comfortable Tory universe into which he was born. His wife, Sylvia, has a child of whom he is perhaps not the true father, and she has run away with another man to Europe. Christopher meets an attractive young woman named Valentine Wannop. In the course of the tetralogy, Valentine replaces Sylvia as Tietjens's mate. The war, when it breaks out, is a terrifying expression of the conflict already implied in the mind of Christopher. In *No More Parades*, Christopher sees the men on the battlefield harassed by infidelity at home. The combat scenes in the next volume, *A Man Could Stand Up*, include ones in which Christopher is buried in a collapsed trench under fire, fights desperately to free his companions, and then is demoted for having a dirty uniform. At the end of this book, Valentine and Christopher come together in a nightmare party celebrating the end of the war. The final volume in the tetralogy, *The Last Post*, is composed of a series of dramatic monologues in which the reader learns that the estate has passed to other hands and that the Groby elm, signifying the Tietjenses' ownership of the land, has been cut down.

Ezra Pound suggested that Ford's contribution to modern literature could be measured less by reference to any given works than by "the tradition of his intelligence." While most of Ford's many novels have been consigned to oblivion, *The Good Soldier* and *Parade's End* testify to his manifold gifts as a man of letters and as a godfather to the modernists.

Todd K. Bender

OTHER MAJOR WORKS

POETRY: *The Questions at the Well*, 1893 (as Fenil Haig); *Poems for Pictures*, 1900; *The Face of the Night*, 1904; *From Inland and Other Poems*, 1907; *Songs from London*, 1910; *High Germany*, 1911; *Collected Poems*, 1913; *Antwerp*, 1915; *On Heaven, and Poems Written on Active Service*, 1918; *A House*, 1921; *New Poems*, 1927; *Collected Poems*, 1936.

NONFICTION: *Ford Madox Brown*, 1896; *The Cinque Ports*, 1900; *Rossetti*, 1902; *The Soul of London*, 1905; *Hans Holbein, the Younger*, 1905; *The Heart of the Country*, 1906; *The Pre-Raphaelite Brotherhood*, 1907; *The Spirit of the People*, 1907; *Ancient Lights*, 1911 (published in the United States as *Memories and Impressions*, 1911); *The Critical Attitude*, 1911; *Henry James*, 1913; *When Blood Is Their Argument*, 1915; *Between St. Dennis and St. George*, 1915; *Zeppelin Nights*, 1916; *Thus to Revisit*, 1921; *Women and Men*, 1923; *Joseph Conrad: A Personal Remembrance*, 1924; *A Mirror to France*, 1926; *New York Is Not America*, 1927; *New York Essays*, 1927; *No Enemy*, 1929; *The English Novel*, 1929; *Return to Yesterday*, 1931 (autobiography); *It Was the Nightingale*, 1933 (autobiography); *Provence*, 1935; *Great Trade Route*, 1937; *Mightier Than the Sword*, 1938; *The March of Literature*, 1938.

CHILDREN'S LITERATURE: *The Brown Owl*, 1891; *The Feather*, 1892; *The Queen Who Flew*, 1894; *Christina's Fairy Book*, 1906; *Mister Bosphorus and the Muses*, 1923.

BIBLIOGRAPHY

Bender, Todd K. *Literary Impressionism in Jean Rhys, Ford Madox Ford, Joseph Conrad, and Charlotte Brontë*. New York: Garland, 1997. Examines style and technique in the four authors. Includes bibliographical references and an index.

Cassell, Richard A., ed. *Critical Essays on Ford Madox Ford*. Boston: G. K. Hall, 1987. In his introduction, Cassell reviews Ford criticism, which he believes becomes more laudatory and perceptive after 1939. Though there are essays dealing with Ford's romances, poetry, and social criticism, the bulk of the book focuses on *The Good Soldier* and *Parade's End*. Also valuable are contributions by literary figures such as Graham Greene, Ezra Pound, and Conrad Aiken. Well indexed.

_____. *Ford Madox Ford: A Study of His Novels.* Baltimore: The Johns Hopkins University Press, 1961. The first three chapters (biography, aesthetics, literary theory) are followed by close readings not only of the major works (*The Good Soldier, Parade's End*) but also of neglected minor fictional works, particularly *Ladies Whose Bright Eyes, The Rash Act*, and *Henry for Hugh.* Also includes helpful discussions of Joseph Conrad's and Henry James's influence on Ford.

Green, Robert. *Ford Madox Ford: Prose and Politics.* Cambridge, England: Cambridge University Press, 1981. Unlike earlier studies which applied New Criticism to Ford's work, places Ford within his historical context and identifies his political beliefs. Asserts that Ford drew no firm line between fiction and nonfiction, treating such works as *Ancient Lights* and *Henry James* as important in themselves and glossing over Ford's major fiction, *The Good Soldier* and *Parade's End.* Also contains a chronological bibliography of his work as well as an extensive yet selected bibliography of Ford criticism.

Huntley, H. Robert. *The Alien Protagonist of Ford Madox Ford.* Chapel Hill: University of North Carolina Press, 1970. Focuses on the Ford protagonist, typically a man whose alien temperament and ethics produce a conflict with his society. After extensive treatments of neglected novels (*An English Girl, A Call, The Fifth Queen*), concludes with an entire chapter devoted to *The Good Soldier*, which is discussed in terms of Ford's historical theories.

Judd, Alan. *Ford Madox Ford.* Cambridge, Mass.: Harvard University Press, 1991. A very readable, shrewd biography. However, this major university press includes no source notes and only a brief bibliographical note.

Leer, Norman. *The Limited Hero in the Novels of Ford Madox Ford.* East Lansing: Michigan State University Press, 1966. After defining "heroism" in Ford's thought, Leer discusses the early novels and the ineffectual hero before an extended analysis of *The Good Soldier* and *Parade's End.* Leer sees a decline in Ford's post-1929 fiction, but praises Ford's travel books of the same period. A first-rate bibliography of secondary sources is also included.

MacShane, Frank, ed. *Ford Madox Ford: The Critical Heritage.* London: Routledge & Kegan Paul, 1972. An invaluable collection of reviews and responses, gleaned from literary journals, to Ford's fiction and poetry. Includes an 1892 unsigned review of *The Shifting of the Fire*, as well as essays by such literary greats as Theodore Dreiser, Arnold Bennett, Ezra Pound, Conrad Aiken, Christina Rossetti, H. L. Mencken, Graham Greene, and Robert Lowell. There are reviews of individual novels, essays on controversies in which Ford was embroiled, and general studies of Ford's art.

RICHARD FORD

Born: Jackson, Mississippi; February 16, 1944

PRINCIPAL LONG FICTION
A Piece of My Heart, 1976
The Ultimate Good Luck, 1981
The Sportswriter, 1986
Wildlife, 1990
Independence Day, 1995

OTHER LITERARY FORMS
Rock Springs (1987) brings together short stories that previously appeared in *Esquire, Antaeus, The New Yorker, Granta*, and *TriQuarterly.* Richard Ford has written screenplays, including an adaptation of his novel *Wildlife. Women with Men* (1997) is a collection of three novellas set in Montana, Chicago, and Paris that all revolve around the complications of romantic love.

ACHIEVEMENTS
Ford has received increasingly high critical praise ever since *The Sportswriter*, which was generally re-

garded as one of the best novels of 1986. His short-story collection *Rock Springs* received accolades from many of North America's major reviewers. Ford's novels mark a return of the Southern writer and a high point for "neorealist" or minimalist fiction. As such, they combine the symbolic and psychological depth of William Faulkner with the blunt, forceful prose of Ernest Hemingway, two writers whom Ford has acknowledged as being primary influences. Ford's evocation of a transient, displaced America is rendered with a deceptive simplicity that itself acts as counterpoint and comment on the complexity of postmodern American society.

BIOGRAPHY

Richard Ford was the only son of Parker Carrol, a salesman, and Edna (Akin), a housewife. Ford spent his youth in Jackson, Mississippi, but after his father's nonfatal heart attack in 1952, Ford lived part of each year at his grandparents' hotel in Little Rock, Arkansas. As a teenager in Mississippi, Ford had several minor scrapes with the law. His father had another heart attack and died in Ford's arms in 1960.

(AP Photo/Columbia University)

Ford entered college at Michigan State University in 1962 to study hotel management. While there he met his future wife, Kristina Hensley, in 1964. They were married in 1968; Kristina eventually earned a Ph.D. in urban planning. Ford gave up hotel management for English, and was graduated with a B.A. in 1966. He began and abandoned a law degree, then pursued a master of fine arts degree in fiction writing (awarded 1970) at the University of California at Irvine, where he studied under E. L. Doctorow. In 1970 he applied himself to becoming a full-time writer, attempting, without success, to publish short stories. The following year he began work on his first novel, *A Piece of My Heart*.

Ford has received numerous awards and honors, including a Guggenheim Fellowship, two grants from the National Endowment for the Arts, an American Academy of Arts and Letters Award for Literature, and the 1994 Rea Award, which is given annually to a writer who has made a contribution to the short story as an art form. In 1995, Ford's novel *Independence Day* was the first book to win both the Pulitzer Prize and the PEN/Faulkner Award.

Along with his own writing, Ford has edited issues of the literary journals *Ploughshares* (1996) and *Triquarterly* (1998), as well as *The Granta Book of the American Short Story* (1992). He also edited *The Granta Book of the American Long Story* (1998) and *The Essential Tales of Chekhov* (1998). Ford has taught at the University of Michigan, Williams College, and Princeton University. The lives of Ford and his wife reflect the transience that is one of the major themes of his writings; they have moved frequently and had lived in twelve houses by the late 1990's, when they were living in New Orleans.

ANALYSIS

Richard Ford's novels have been called neorealist and minimalist, and, although Ford disavows a connection to the minimalist school of writing, a deceptive simplicity of style does mark his novels. In response to the clutter of contemporary America, Ford has retreated into a spare vision in which each image in his stripped-down prose resounds beyond itself. In the same fashion, the simple relationships of family and friendship that form the nexus of his narratives imply larger complexities. Ford often writes in the first person, and his central protagonists tend to be the marginalized: observers, outsiders, people carried away by circumstances. The mood of his novels is often one of impermanence, and this finds its analogue in the bleak, large, often featureless landscapes of the South and the Midwest that Ford favors. Characters move across these landscapes, through relationships, through livelihoods, with a casualness that demonstrates at once the potential and the rootless condition of twentieth century life.

A PIECE OF MY HEART

In Ford's first novel, *A Piece of My Heart*, two men, Robard Hewes and Sam Newel, arrive on an uncharted island in the Mississippi River peopled only by Mark Lamb, his wife, and their black servent, Landrieu. Hewes arrives to take a short-term job running poachers off the island. He has come to nearby Helena, Arkansas, to take up an old relationship with his cousin, Buena, now married to an industrial-league baseball player named W. W. That relationship is threatened by the possible jealousy of W. W. and the manic sexuality of Buena. Newel, a Southerner now living in Chicago, arrives at the prompting of his lover, Beebe Henley, a stewardess and granddaughter to Mrs. Lamb. One month from completing his requirements for a law degree, Newel is emotionally unbalanced, and Henley suggests a rest on the island. Newel is haunted by memories of his youth, memories that revolve around the grotesque and absurd: a midget film star, a pair of lesbians in a motel room, an electrocution.

The novel oscillates between the story of Hewes and Newel, and these characters are in many ways mirror images or complements of each other; both displaced Southerners, they are driven by contradictory passions. On a symbolic level, Hewes is the body and Newel the mind; together, they are the spiritually troubled and physically corrupt South. The island on which they meet their fates is uncharted and lies between the states of Mississippi and Arkansas; like Joseph Conrad's Congo, it is a metaphoric destination, the human condition, the allegorical South. All the characters on the island are bound by their in-

ability to escape the forces that have isolated them. Thus they go to their fates with sheeplike acceptance, a fact reflected in the game Ford plays with their names: Lamb, H*ewe*s, N*ewe*l. The island becomes, for the two main characters, not an escape or a place of homecoming, but a crucible for the forces that have shaped, and will destroy, both them and the culture they represent.

Having satisfied his lust, Hewes seems bent on escape. He takes Buena to a motel and there recoils from her insistent, and perhaps perverse, sexuality. His rejection prompts her to turn on him and call on her husband for vengeance. Hewes runs back to the island, but, though he escapes W. W., he cannot escape the retarded boy who guards the boat and who himself may be a symbol of the incestuous coupling in which Hewes has been engaging. Newel cannot escape the absurd and the contingent, and he witnesses the comically maladroit death of Lamb while the two are fishing together. Of all the novel's characters, Lamb comes the closest to the cantankerous and colorful Southerners of Faulkner, and his death may mark the passing of the Southern individualist. Newel lies to Mrs. Lamb about Lamb's last words, apparently too embarrassed to repeat their absurd banality.

The novel begins and ends with the image of the retarded boy on the riverbank with the gun in his hand. If this image summarizes Ford's view of the South, the other image patterns of the novel reflect the contingency of American life as a whole. Beebe Henley's job moves her to different corners of the globe almost every day. Newel's luggage disappears. When Hewes and Newel cross the river to the island, Newel sees a deer, swimming across the river, suddenly pulled under the water by a powerful force, never to rise again. Nothing is permanent or reliable; Ford's characters fight their personal battles on uncharted land surrounded by the constant flow of the river that most signifies the South, but that also, in its power and treachery, represents the larger America.

THE ULTIMATE GOOD LUCK

Contingency and displacement become synonymous with violence and deceit in Ford's next novel. In *The Ultimate Good Luck*, Harry Quinn, an alienated Vietnam veteran, is asked by his former lover Rae to help free her brother, Sonny, from a jail in Oaxaca, Mexico, where he is serving a sentence for drug smuggling. Quinn makes arrangements to free Sonny through bribery with the help of a local lawyer, Bernhardt, but matters become complicated. Sonny's superiors believe that Sonny stole some of the drugs he was carrying and hid them before he was arrested. Oaxaca itself is under terrorist siege and is filled with police. Bernhardt's allegiance and motives are inscrutable. Quinn is terrorized by Deats, an "enforcer" working for Sonny's superiors. Unsuspected layers of power unfold, often in conjunction with arbitrary violence.

Indeed, the novel is dominated by images of violence and chance. The contingency that dominated *A Piece of My Heart* here is marked for higher stakes. With a flat, tough prose reminiscent of Dashiell Hammett's, Ford presents a *film noir* world of threat and hidden danger. The novel opens with a scene of violence and casual sexuality: Quinn meets an Italian tourist and takes her to a Mexican boxing match that is especially vicious. This casual encounter is indicative of Quinn's life; in flashback the reader discovers that Quinn first met Rae, by chance, at a dog-racing track; he has pursued jobs, such as game warden, that have brought him close to violence. As the novel unfolds, these chance encounters and acts of violence become less controllable. Quinn sees three American girls vanish during their vacation. He and Rae see a family of tourists killed by a terrorist bomb as they stand in front of an ice-cream store; Sonny is attacked and mutilated in jail; Deats binds Quinn and threatens him with a scorpion. Even Quinn's own body, hardened by war and decorated with tattoos, betrays him in a fit of dysentery. Oaxaca becomes a nightmare landscape of violence and confusion, closer to Quinn's Vietnam experience than "the world." Like the island of the first novel, Oaxaca becomes a crucible of the forces that drive the characters, a metaphoric landscape of their souls.

The plot is resolved by death. Sonny is killed in jail, Bernhardt is gunned down, and Quinn ends his search in a shootout with strangers. Although Quinn takes some pride in his accomplishment, his survival is simply the ultimate good luck, another chance in a series of gambles.

THE SPORTSWRITER

The Sportswriter was Ford's most well received novel, though it may be his least typical. Told in the first person by Frank Bascombe, a thirty-eight-year-old short-story writer turned sportswriter, the novel details Bascombe's adventures over an Easter weekend, beginning with an annual pilgrimage, with his former wife (referred to only as X), to the grave of his first son, who died at age eight of Reye's disease. It was that death that had led to Bascombe's divorce and what he calls his period of "dreaminess," actually a form of detachment or emotional numbness. Over the course of the Easter weekend, Bascombe flies with his lover, Vicki Arcenault, to Detroit, where he interviews a paraplegic former football hero, Herb Wallagher. Cutting the trip short, they return home to Haddam, New Jersey. Bascombe visits the home of Vicki's parents on Easter Sunday, but the visit is interrupted by a call from X: Walter Luckett, a member of the Divorced Men's Club, a casual society to which Bascombe belongs, has committed suicide. Before returning to Haddam, Bascombe fights with Vicki. Bascombe eventually takes a late train into Manhattan to visit his office, something he does not normally do. There a chance encounter with a new female writer sparks what will become an affair. In the epilogue, Bascombe is in Florida, waiting for a young Dartmouth woman to visit. He seems to have overcome grieving for his son, and he may be on the verge of writing fiction once more.

Detached, ironic, and cerebral, Bascombe looks for solace in the mundane and regular: He keeps up the appearances, if not the reality, of a suburban husband and father; he revels in the petty regularities of Haddam; he studies the regularized and "safe" world of professional sports. At these pursuits he is successful, but his adherence to routine and detail itself becomes part of his dreaminess, his detachment. Unable, or unwilling, to extend himself emotionally, he remains aloof from Walter Luckett's grief over a brief homosexual affair, he rejects the vision of the crippled former athlete he interviews, and he ultimately quarrels and breaks with Vicki. His failure to continue writing fiction is an analogue of his inability to connect emotionally, and the novel itself, this fictional memoir, may be a movement back toward a regularized life.

WILDLIFE

Wildlife is told as a memoir. Set in 1960, when Joe, the narrator, is sixteen years old (Ford's own age in 1960), the novel details the breakdown of the marriage of Jerry and Jeanette, Joe's parents. The family had recently moved to Grand Falls, Montana, where Jerry works as a golf professional. When he is fired because of a misunderstanding, Jerry signs on to fight the forest fires that rage in the hills outside the town. That sudden decision sends Jeanette into a short affair with a well-to-do local man named Warren Miller. The bulk of the novel is a re-creation of the events of those three days, told with stark simplicity. Joe, like the child protagonists of Ford's short stories, seems caught in the emotional detachment that was precipitated by the marriage breakdown and forced to re-create the situation with the dispassion that has marked his subsequent life. The result is a hesitant accumulation of detail and dialogue, as the retelling of the events becomes a cathartic event for Joe.

The novel is dominated by the image of fire. There are the fires that burn in the foothills and that capture the father's imagination. It seems they cannot be extinguished; they burn through the winter, ignoring the natural seasons, and they come to stand for the unpredictable and confusing in the human experience. When Jerry leaves to fight these fires, he sets off a metaphorical fire in his wife, a yearning for passion and completeness that she attempts, unsuccessfully, to fulfill with the affair. When Jerry returns and discovers the adultery, he drives to Warren Miller's house and attempts to burn it down with a bottle of gasoline. That fire, like the mother's adultery, burns itself out and leaves behind recriminations and guilt. Ultimately ineffective, both of these fires succeed only in scarring the psychic landscape of the characters who set them.

The most starkly realistic of Ford's novels, and the closest to minimalist in its style, this novel received mixed reviews. Some critics have found in the simplicity of its prose a poetic intensity (particularly in the descriptions of the forest fire and Jerry's attempt to burn down the house); others have found that the stark dialogue threatens to push the novel into banality. In tone and style, *Wildlife* is certainly more reminiscent of Ford's short stories than of his previous novels.

INDEPENDENCE DAY

Independence Day continues the story of Frank Bascombe that Ford began in *The Sportswriter*. Seven years have passed, and Bascombe has turned from sportswriter to real estate agent in Haddam, New Jersey. Set over a few days in the summer of 1988, *Independence Day* revolves around a climactic Fourth of July weekend in which Bascombe attempts to reconnect with his troubled son. The narrative timeline of the novel is not limited to that weekend; it meanders through the time that Bascombe takes preparing for the holiday and includes Bascombe's meditations about the circumstances of his current troubles: his continuing affection for his ex-wife, his girlfriends, his troubled children, and his real estate clients.

The most compelling relationships in the book are between Bascombe and his children. Bascombe wants to be a good father, but because of his divorce from his children's mother, he feels exiled from their daily lives. He is especially worried about Paul, who has been arrested for shoplifting condoms. Paul has grown fat and slovenly, and he still mourns the death of his brother Ralph. Paul has shaved off most of his hair and, because he has fixated on his dog, which was run over by a car almost a decade before, has taken to barking like a dog.

Bascombe attempts to bring himself closer to his son by taking him to the Baseball Hall of Fame for the Fourth of July weekend. Along the way, he hopes, he will "work the miracle only a father can work." The trip is a disaster. Instead of offering reconciliation, the trip confirms Bascombe's fears that the boy is, as his therapists say, ahead of his age intellectually but "emotionally underdeveloped."

Bascombe begins the novel by claiming a sort of happiness, saying that he is in an "existence period" of his life. However, it is a time of falling property values and unease in the suburbs, and he is overcome by an anxious malaise reminiscent of a John Cheever or John Updike character. Haddam, New Jersey, is an upper-middle-class place where little happens. Its solitude is precisely the danger to Bascombe. Left alone with his thoughts, his worry and concern force him to look with a great deal of introspection at every aspect of his world. Unable to commit to his present girlfriend, he does not commit to anything except his desire to return to the past. Bascombe is living in a state where past and present coexist, where memory becomes experience, and where experience is recounted with almost dreamlike qualities.

The novel suggests that one must look beyond the surface of things in order to see with clarity and precision. The contrast between the seemingly secure surface of suburbia and the various awarenesses of mortality that Bascombe encounters hold the long novel together. Bascombe searches for a way to interact emotionally with the world and people around him. This novel is not only a story or a plot—a sequence of events that happen to its characters—but also a search for a way of thinking that might guide an individual through a consistently troubling life.

Paul Budra, updated by Jeffrey Greer

OTHER MAJOR WORKS

SHORT FICTION: *Rock Springs*, 1987; *Women with Men: Three Stories*, 1997.

EDITED TEXTS: *The Granta Book of the American Short Story*, 1992; *The Granta Book of the American Long Story*, 1998; *The Essential Tales of Chekhov*, 1998.

BIBLIOGRAPHY

Ford, Richard. Interview by Kay Bonetti. *Missouri Review* 10 (Fall, 1987): 71-96. An excellent and intensive interview in which Ford, with characteristic candor, discusses his life and writing influences. An essential article.

_____. "The Three Kings: Hemingway, Faulkner, and Fitzgerald." *Esquire* 100 (December, 1983): 577-587. In this article Ford frankly discusses his own formation as a writer and the influences of Ernest Hemingway, William Faulkner, and F. Scott Fitzgerald on his writing and consciousness. An essential article for understanding Ford's literary self-consciousness.

Gold, Victor. "The Far Side of Yoknapatawpha County." *National Review* 28 (November, 1976): 1240-1241. One of the first reviews to acknowledge Ford as a promising novelist, this reading of *A Piece of My Heart* compares him to Faulkner, especially in the use of symbolism and treatment of the South. Although short, this review touches on most of the major symbol patterns in the novel.

Johnson, Charles. "Stuck in the Here and Now." *The New York Times Book Review*, June 18, 1995, 7-8. Available online at http://search.nytimes.com/books/. This review of *Independence Day* offers a challenging reading of Ford's novel and insights into the bitterness that Ford's narrator, Frank Bascombe, feels at the beginning of the novel. This review begins with plot summary and then discusses the importance of Ford's work; although it slights Ford's descriptions of landscape, it offers insight into the way that he creates his characters.

Lee, Don. "About Richard Ford." *Ploughshares* 22 (Fall, 1996): 226-235. This essay begins with a narrative of how Ford learned that he had won the Pulitzer Prize in 1996. Offers a telling anecdote of Ford's final revision of the novel and a brief chronology of Ford's life and writing career, This essay also discusses how Ford came around to fiction writing. A brief analysis of each of Ford's books is juxtaposed with comments by Ford that clarify his intentions.

Manguel, Alberto. "America's Best Novelist." *Saturday Night* 105 (July/August, 1990): 60-61. This review of *Wildlife* examines Ford's decision to recount the complexity of American society in a style that is simple almost to a fault. Though not a long article, it does manage to isolate the distinctive qualities of Ford's prose and argue for his place at the head of his generation of American writers.

Schroth, Raymond A. "America's Moral Landscape in the Fiction of Richard Ford." *The Christian Century* 106 (March, 1989): 227-230. Primarily a discussion of *The Sportswriter*, with some mention of *The Ultimate Good Luck* and *Rock Springs*, this article provides a general discussion of Ford as a distinctively American writer. Schroth's intelligent analysis of *The Sportswriter* leads him to compare Ford with such writers as William Dean Howells and Frank O'Connor. A good introduction to Ford's work.

E. M. FORSTER

Born: London, England; January 1, 1879
Died: Coventry, England; June 7, 1970

PRINCIPAL LONG FICTION

Where Angels Fear to Tread, 1905
The Longest Journey, 1907
A Room with a View, 1908
Howards End, 1910
A Passage to India, 1924
Maurice, 1971 (wr. 1913)

OTHER LITERARY FORMS

In addition to his novels, E. M. Forster wrote short stories, travel books, biographies, essays, and criticism. A number of these works, as well as his novels, have already appeared in the standard Abinger Edition, in progress. *The Celestial Omnibus and Other Stories* (1911) includes his frequently anthologized story "The Road from Colonus" and five other stories written in a fantastic vein that is found much less frequently in his novels. *Aspects of the Novel* (1927) remains one of the most widely read discussions of that genre, while the essays of *Abinger Harvest—A Miscellany* (1936) and *Two Cheers for Democracy* (1951) have also found many receptive readers. In *Marianne Thornton: A Domestic Biography, 1797-1887* (1956) Forster recalls his great-aunt, a woman whose long life plunged him into the social history of a milieu going back to the closing years of the eighteenth century. A useful description of Forster's uncollected writings by George H. Thomson may be found in *As-*

pects of E. M. Forster (1969), a *Festschrift* honoring the author on his ninetieth birthday. In the same volume, Benjamin Britten recounts one more Forster achievement: the libretto he coauthored with Eric Crozier for Britten's opera *Billy Budd* (1951).

ACHIEVEMENTS

Forster will continue to stand a little apart from other major novelists of the twentieth century. Because he made it difficult to decide by which standards his work should be judged, assessing it fairly presents problems. Unlike many of his Bloomsbury friends, he did not rebel against the Victorians or their literary habits; neither did he embrace the literary trends of his own time with any great enthusiasm. He lamented the encroachment of a commercial culture, but he did not war on the modern world. Although he composed a set of lectures on the novel, its plural title, *Aspects of the Novel*, anticipates his refusal to develop therein any single theory of the form

(Archive Photos)

in which he distinguished himself. On the one hand, his work is impossible to pigeonhole; on the other hand, his six novels do not entitle him to a lonely eminence overshadowing his most able contemporaries.

Readers of the novel will not lose sight of Forster, however, because the very ambiguities and inconsistencies which frustrate efforts to find a niche for him continue to intrigue critics. Forster lived long enough to see his reputation fade and then rebound strongly. He had gained critical acclaim while still in his twenties, written a masterpiece in midlife, and published no fiction for nearly two decades before Lionel Trilling's *E. M. Forster* (1943) swung critical attention back to him. Since that time, a formidable body of books and articles dealing with Forster has formed, and many aspects of his work have been studied in great detail. While incapable of putting Forster in a specific place, his critics agree overwhelmingly that he deserves a place of honor among English novelists.

Forster's critics, fortunately, do not hold his unusually protracted silence against him. The author's failure to write a novel in the final forty-six years of his life has been explained in various ways—for example by noting that instead of exercising his talents in succession, husbanding his resources, exhausting one mode before moving to another, Forster put all of himself into the first six novels and then ceased at an age when many novelists are just reaching their prime. Whatever the reason for his early retirement from a literary form successfully practiced by so many older writers, he furnished his critics no occasion to regret the decline of his powers.

Those powers yielded fiction marked by a blend of qualities—intelligence, wit, sensitivity, compassion, and ever-alert moral imagination—that few other writers can match. No doubt, many readers begin *A Passage to India* in the line of duty—for it has attained the rank of "classic"—but they are likely to complete it, and then begin the earlier ones, out of a desire to know better a man who could write so movingly and yet so tough-mindedly about the climate created by racial and religious prejudice. Few such readers are disappointed, for while the earlier novels are less fine, the distance between *Where Angels Fear to Tread* and *A Passage to India* is not nearly so great as that between the apprentice and masterworks of most writers. Even if his final novel is, as one critic puts it, "Forster's sole claim upon posterity," those who delve into his other works will continue to reap rewards in proportion to the attention they bestow on them, for neither wit nor wisdom is ever far away.

The critical consensus is that Forster's most successful mode is comic irony, and his name is often coupled with those of Jane Austen and George Meredith, whose test for comedy—"that it shall awaken thoughtful laughter"—Forster passes with flying colors. Critics invariably hasten to point out that Forster refused to confine himself to this mode; in the midst of deploring these deviations from high comedy, they find in Forster's odd blends of comedy, melodrama, fantasy, lyricism, and tragedy a distinctiveness they would not willingly relinquish.

BIOGRAPHY

Edward Morgan Forster lived a long but rather uneventful life. Born on New Year's Day, 1879, he was reared by his possessive mother and worshipful great-aunt (whose biography he later wrote) after the death of his father from tuberculosis before Forster turned two. Happy, protected, and dominated by women in his early years, he suffered painfully the transition to the masculine, athletically oriented Tonbridge School—later the model for Sawston School in *The Longest Journey*. After a more congenial four years, 1897 to 1901, at King's College, Cambridge, he took a second-class degree. In the next few years, he wrote seriously, traveled in Italy and Greece, tutored the children of a German countess, and also indulged in walking tours of his native land.

His first novel, *Where Angels Fear to Tread*, much of which is set in Italy, received favorable reviews in 1905, and Forster produced three more novels in the next five years, of which *A Room with a View* drew also on his Italian experience, while *The Longest Journey* and *Howards End* both reflect his keen delight in the English countryside. Thereafter, having attained a considerable reputation as a novelist, he slowed his pace. He began, but could not finish, a novel called *Arctic Summer*; completed a novel about homosexuality, his own orientation, which he knew to be unpublishable; and brought out a volume of short stories. Among his many friends he numbered Virginia Woolf, as well as others of the Bloomsbury group, of which, however, he was never more than a fringe member. World War I found him in Egypt as a Red Cross worker. Although he disliked Egypt, his life there led to the writing of two nonfiction books.

Forster had first visited India in 1912, but his second sojourn there as personal secretary to the Maharaja of Dewas gave him the opportunity to observe the political and social life closely enough to inspire him to write another novel. *A Passage to India*, which appeared in 1924, increased his fame and led to an invitation to deliver the Clark Lectures at Trinity College, Cambridge, in 1927, published later that year as *Aspects of the Novel*. Although he continued to write for several more decades, he published no more novels. Forster received a number of honors, culminating in the Order of Merit, presented to him on his ninetieth birthday. He died in June of 1970.

ANALYSIS

E. M. Forster's most systematic exposition of the novelist's art, *Aspects of the Novel*, is no key to his own practice. Written three years after the publication of *A Passage to India*, the work surveys neither his achievement nor intentions. While full of the insights, charm, and homely but colorful metaphors which also distinguish Virginia Woolf's *Common Reader* volumes (1925, 1932), the book is an enthusiast's, rather than a working writer's, view of the novel, as if Forster were already distancing himself from the form which earned him his fame as a writer.

A lecture given twenty years later by Lionel Trilling, who had already published his book on Forster, gives a better sense of Forster's achievement. In "Manners, Morals, and the Novel," later published in *The Liberal Imagination* (1950), Trilling explains the novel as the writer's response to the modern world's besetting sin of snobbery, which he defines as "pride in status without pride in function." Europeans, and perhaps especially the English, familiar with snobbery as a manifestation of class structure, re-

quire less explanation than do Americans of the novel's relation to snobbery. The central tradition of the English novel from Henry Fielding through Jane Austen, Charles Dickens, William Makepeace Thackeray, and George Meredith—and indeed English comedy as far back as Geoffrey Chaucer's *The Canterbury Tales* (1387-1400)—stands as evidence.

In Forster's time, however, that tradition was being modified. For one thing, the greatest English novelists at work during Forster's formative years were a wealthy American expatriate and a retired Polish mariner. No one as sensitive as Forster could escape the influence of Henry James and Joseph Conrad, but these men made curious heirs to Dickens and Thackeray and George Eliot. James, while intensely interested in the textures of society, focused his attention on the relations between the English (and Continental) leisure class and those American travelers that Mark Twain had christened "innocents abroad," thus limiting his social scrutiny, in Forster's opinion, to the narrow perceptions of a few wealthy idlers. Conrad diverged even more sharply from the path of previous English novelists, for he neither understood nor cared to understand any level of English society. A man of his temperament and interest might be imagined as a literary force in the midcentury United States of Nathaniel Hawthorne's *The Scarlet Letter* (1850) and Herman Melville's *Moby Dick* (1851), but not in the England of Thackeray's *Vanity Fair* (1847-1848) and Dickens's *Bleak House* (1852-1853). Nevertheless, Conrad was more in tune with his own literary milieu than Meredith, who at the end of the century reigned as the grand old man of English letters, and Conrad's work, like that of James, diverted the creative energy of many of the new century's novelists into new channels.

Of native English novelists still regarded as substantial, the most active at the time of Forster's entry into the field were Arnold Bennett, H. G. Wells, and John Galsworthy—all men born in the 1860's and all inheritors of the native tradition of the novel, albeit on a somewhat reduced scale. The next generation of novelists, born slightly after Forster in the 1880's, included Woolf, James Joyce, and D. H. Lawrence, all of whom published their initial works after Forster had already written five of his six novels. This latter group obviously belongs to a new literary dispensation. Society and its network of snobbery, though still significant, have receded into the background, and the conflicts of the protagonists are waged at a more personal, intimate, sometimes semiconscious level. Clearly the work of psychologists such as Sigmund Freud and Henry James's brother William influenced these later writers and drove them to develop literary techniques adequate to the task of a more truly psychological novel.

Forster, as has been suggested, stands in the middle. A friend of Virginia Woolf and in her mind, certainly, no part of the decaying tradition she trounced so severely in her essay "Mr. Bennett and Mrs. Brown," Forster nevertheless anticipated few of the technical innovations of the novelists who reached their maturity after World War I. His last novel stands with the post-Freudian achievements. *Howards End*, his most ambitious novel, is in most respects a novel of the old school. It is denser, symbolically richer, than the characteristic work of Bennett, Wells, and Galsworthy, but the same might be said of *Bleak House*, written more than half a century earlier.

Only around the time of Forster's birth did novelists begin to insist on the novel as an art form and write theoretical defenses of it. Meredith delivered a lecture on "The Idea of Comedy and the Uses of the Comic Spirit" (1877), which, though mentioning Miguel de Cervantes and Fielding, has more to say of Artistophanes and Molière; Henry James's essay "The Art of Fiction" appeared in 1884. By the century's end, novelists had achieved respectability, and Conrad could soberly echo Longinus: "Art is long and life is short, and success is very far off."

Such new expressions of the novelist's kinship with poet and playwright did not end the nineteenth century habit of producing loose, baggy narratives in a diversity of modes, punctuated by their author's abrupt changes of direction, interpolated moral essays, and episodes introduced for no better reason than a hunch that readers, who cared nothing for artistic integrity, would enjoy them. Stock literary devices that storytellers had accumulated over the centuries—bizarre coincidences, thoroughly improbable

recognition scenes thrust into "realistic" contexts, the bundling forth of long-lost (often supposedly deceased) personages in the interests of a happy or surprising denouement, all devices that twentieth century novels would shun—still flourished in Forster's youth, and he used many of them unashamedly.

If Forster's moment in literary history partly explains his wavering between Victorian and modern canons, his skeptical, eclectic temperament must also be cited. His astute analyses of the morals and manners of society involved him in comedy, tragedy, romance, and fantasy—the sort of "God's plenty" that the supposedly neoclassical John Dryden admired in Chaucer and Ben Jonson in William Shakespeare. Such men would write any sort of work and take up with any sort of character. Forster was similarly indiscriminate. His veneration for Leo Tolstoy's *War and Peace* (1865-1869), though "such an untidy book," betrays his Englishman's weakness in believing that God's plenty would overcome the artist's scruples.

Of course Forster's novels are not as long as *War and Peace* or the Victorian ones that readers worked their way through in installments spread over many months. Compared to the seamless garments of Woolf or even the longer works of Joyce and William Faulkner (both of whom exhibit an un-English type of variety but also an astonishing coherence), Forster's juxtapositions of sharply contrasting modes invite criticism by readers who take in his works in two or three successive evenings. Thus, while Forster does not belong with Wells and Galsworthy, neither does he quite keep company with the greatest of his slightly younger contemporaries, for he loved too much the variety and freedom that most earlier English novelists permitted themselves.

Nevertheless, his motto for *Howards End*—"Only connect"—applies to his work generally. If he does not always make the artistic connections, his consistent theme is the necessity of making moral connections with fellow humans, of struggling against the class divisions which so many Englishmen, including a number of his fellow novelists, took for granted. In his novels, prudence is invariably on the side of those who, like Henry Wilcox in *Howards End* and Ronnie

Heaslop in *A Passage to India*, resist the breakdown of social barriers; but courage, generosity, friendship, and sympathy are found among Forster's liberal opponents of snobbery. In the world of Forster's novels, the closed class is always sterile and corrupt.

Forster's eclecticism, his versatility, his refusal to ignore the claims either of heart or head make the reading of his novels an ambiguous but rich experience. Never, though, does he seem like a mere exhibitionist. Rather, his openness to life's variety amounts to a perpetual invitation to the participation of alert and open-minded readers. He is far less afraid of a gaucherie than of a missed opportunity to "connect."

WHERE ANGELS FEAR TO TREAD

Forster's shortest and most tightly focused novel is *Where Angels Fear to Tread*. A young man named Philip Herriton is commissioned by his mother and sister Harriet to bring back from Italy the infant son of Lilia Carella, the widow of another of Mrs. Herriton's sons. Within a year after marrying Gino Carella, the aimless son of a small-town dentist, Lilia died giving birth to a son. Aided by Harriet and by Caroline Abbott, who as Lilia's traveling companion had been able to do nothing to ward off the offensive marriage, Philip finds Gino resistant to Mrs. Herriton's pocketbook and ultimately becomes involved in a shabby kidnapping venture engineered by Harriet—a venture that ends with the accidental death of the child. On the way home, Philip finds himself drawn emotionally to Caroline, who reveals that she too has fallen in love with Gino. In the common effort to minister to the pitifully unregenerate Harriet, however, Philip and Caroline become friends.

Thus summarized, the novel bears some resemblance to one by Henry James. Forster enjoys contrasting Anglo-Saxon and Italian mores, and he shares James's fascinated horror over the machinations and intrigues of sophisticated schemers. He may have owed the idea of centering the story on a somewhat detached emissary to James, whose novel *The Ambassadors* (1903) appeared shortly before Forster began work on his own book.

Forster's handling of his material, however, differs substantially from James's. He cannot resist scathing treatment of the characters whose company he expects his readers to keep and with whom they are to sympathize. Harriet, appalled by Italy's uncleanliness, carries a bottle of ammonia in her trunk, but Forster has it "burst over her prayer-book, so that purple patches appeared on all her clothes." Prayer brings out the worst in many of Forster's characters, an exception being Caroline, who is able to pray in the church in Gino's hometown, "where a prayer to God is thought none the worse of because it comes next to a pleasant word to a neighbor." For Philip to develop neighborliness is a struggle. Not only is he much less experienced and resourceful than Strether or any other Jamesian ambassador, he is also decidedly unattractive: callow, priggish, and cowardly. Caroline's assessment of him in the final chapter, though tardily arrived at, is accurate enough: "You're without passion; you look on life as a spectacle, you don't enter it; you only find it funny or beautiful." By the time he hears this, however, Philip has learned what neither his mother nor his sister ever suspects: that the son of an Italian dentist can love his child more than wealth, that he is capable of trust and friendship, that he can be not merely angered but also hurt by a betrayal. Philip has also felt enough by this time to be hurt by Caroline's words.

Though selfish and short-sighted, Gino is without the treachery of a Jamesian Italian such as Giovanelli in *Daisy Miller* (1878). Indeed, Forster makes him morally superior to the Herriton women. Fixing on a domestic vignette of a sort impossible in any well-appointed English household (or in a James novel, for that matter)—Gino bathing his infant son—Forster draws Caroline into helping him and lets Philip come upon them so engaged, "to all intents and purposes, the Virgin and Child, with Donor." Forster's heroes tend to idealize people who are only behaving a little better than expected, but the capacity to idealize is a symptom of their regeneration.

Harriet tricks Philip into the kidnapping; he discovers the ruse only after the baby has died and his own arm has been broken in a carriage accident. He returns to confess the transgression, only to have the grief-stricken Gino cruelly twist his broken arm and then nearly choke him to death before Caroline appears to stop him. In a typically Forsterian piece of symbolism, she persuades Gino and Philip together to drink the milk that had been poured for the child. In a pattern that Forster repeats in later novels, Philip, though excessive in his estimate of Caroline's goodness, is nevertheless "saved" by it. Salvation is at least partly illusion, but such an illusion serves him better than the cynicism that Philip has spent his youth imbibing.

THE LONGEST JOURNEY

Like Philip, Rickie Elliot of *The Longest Journey* is frail and aesthetic. In addition, a deformed foot which he has inherited from his father marks him as different from his Cambridge classmates. At the beginning of the novel, both his father, whom he despised, and his beloved mother are dead; his father's sister, Mrs. Failing, is his closest relative. On her Wiltshire estate lives a young man, Stephen Wonham, an illegitimate half-brother to Rickie. Rude, truculent, undiscriminating in his choice of companions, and more or less a habitual drunkard, Stephen also proves loyal and almost pathetically trusting. The relationship between the two brothers forms the core of the novel.

The title of the book, from Percy Bysshe Shelley's poem *Epipsychidion* (1821), alludes to the folly of denying the rest of the world for the sake of "a mistress or a friend," with whom, in consequence, one must "the dreariest and longest journey go." In the midst of mulling over the poem, Rickie ironically decides to take his journey with Agnes Pembroke, a girl whose first lover, a strapping athlete, has died suddenly of a football injury. Death, it may be noted, always strikes with unexpected suddenness in Forster's novels. The marriage disgusts Rickie's closest friend, Stewart Ansell, and Rickie himself comes soon enough to regret it. Discouraged by Agnes and her elder brother Herbert from pursuing a career as a writer, Rickie takes a teaching post at Sawston School, where Herbert is a master. By a strange coincidence, a maladjusted boy at the school writes a letter to Stephen Wonham, among other total strangers, asking Stephen to "pray for him." Agnes's practical mind senses trouble if Stephen appears at the school, but mercifully the boy withdraws before Stephen can carry out an offer to come visit him. Rickie, while not

fond of Stephen, is willing for him to receive his aunt's property when she dies; not so Agnes. When Mrs. Failing sends the troublesome Stephen packing, he decides to visit Sawston and inform Rickie of their relationship—about which Rickie already knows.

Outside the school, Stephen meets Stewart Ansell, on hand to verify for himself the death of his friend's spirit in his loveless union with the Pembrokes, and, after receiving an insult, knocks him down. Before Stephen can see Rickie, Agnes intercepts him and offers him the money she is sure he wants in return for leaving Sawston and sparing Rickie the embarrassment of acknowledging him. Stunned and stung, the utterly unmercenary Stephen leaves, but Ansell, won over not only by Stephen's fist but also by his principles, breaks into the Sawston dining hall during Sunday dinner and, in front of masters, students, and all, rebukes Rickie for turning away his own brother in the latter's deepest distress. As the assemblage gapes, Ansell reveals what he has correctly intuited: that Stephen is not the son of Rickie's father, as Rickie had supposed, but of his beloved mother. At this news Rickie faints.

Although wildly improbable, the scene has an electric intensity about it. Ansell, with all the clumsy insistence of a true egalitarian and all the insight of a true friend, has, while mistakenly charging Rickie with complicity in Agnes's treachery, stripped away the hypocrisy behind which the couple has hidden. There is about this revelation something of the quality of the recognition scene of a tragedy such as Sophocles' *Oedipus Tyrannus* (c. 429), with Rickie the lame protagonist faced with the consequences of his disastrous marriage and of his unjust assumption about his father, as well as of his denial of his brother.

From the time Rickie listened mutely to his classmates' discussion of whether the cow in the field was "there" if no one was present to perceive her, he has searched unavailingly for reality. He has misinterpreted his love for Agnes as real, watched his son—inevitably deformed like his father and himself—die in infancy, and seen his attempt at a schoolmaster's life tumble. Now he tries, none too successfully, to effect a reconciliation with his brother. He leaves Agnes and the school and tries to rekindle the flame of his short-story writing. When Stephen disappoints him on a visit to Mrs. Failing by breaking a promise not to drink, Rickie concludes that people are not "real." Finding Stephen sprawled drunkenly across the tracks at a railroad crossing, Rickie finds the strength to move him from the path of an oncoming train—but not the strength to save himself.

Rickie's aunt and brother-in-law, incapable of seeing his rescue of Stephen as worthwhile, see him as a failure whose life is mercifully over. Stephen, who is no thinker, is not so sure. In the final chapter, he feels himself to be in some sense the future of England, for he is now the father of a girl who bears the name of his and Rickie's mother. Dimly, he acknowledges that his salvation is from Rickie.

Not only does *The Longest Journey* run to melodrama, but it also incorporates some rather tedious moralizing, both on the part of Mrs. Failing and in an interpolated essay by Forster which forms the whole twenty-eighth chapter (although the chapter is a short one). Probably the greatest burden, however, is the one Stephen Wonham is forced to carry. First of all, he is the disreputable relative who knocks people down and falls down drunk himself. He serves a contrasting and complementary purpose as a kind of spiritual extension of Rickie, particularly after Rickie, recognizing him as his mother's son, begins to invest him with her excellencies, as recollected. In the final chapter, Stephen becomes the consciousness of the novel itself.

Without Stephen, however, Forster's brilliant portrait of Rickie is not only incomplete but also depressing, for Rickie dies, sad to say, murmuring agreement with Mrs. Failing's antihumanist convictions that "we do not live for anything great" and that "people are not important at all." Stephen exists and procreates and retains the idea of greatness to prove Rickie wrong.

A Room with a View

Forster sends his principals off to Italy again in *A Room with a View*. The room in question is one which Lucy Honeychurch and her elder cousin Charlotte Bartlett do not enjoy at the beginning of their stay in a Florentian hotel but which two other travelers, the elderly Mr. Emerson and his son George, are more than willing to exchange for the one that furnishes the ladies with only a disappointing view of the courtyard. Characteristic of Forster's well-bred characters, they lose sight of Emerson's generosity in their horror at the directness and bluntness of his offer, for he has interrupted their conversation at dinner before other guests: "I have a view, I have a view." Having defied the convention that forbids hasty and undue familiarity with a stranger, Mr. Emerson must be certified by an English clergyman, after which the ladies somewhat stiffly accept the view. Mr. Emerson, of course, has throughout the novel a "view" which the cousins, who hate the darkness but blanch at openness, achieve only with difficulty.

Soon an unexpected adventure literally throws Lucy and George Emerson more closely together. While enthusiastically and uncritically buying photographs of Italian masterpieces, Lucy witnesses a stabbing in a public square. She faints; George catches her and, after throwing her blood-spattered photographs into the River Arno, conducts her away gently. Later, Lucy puzzles over the affair and comes to the conclusion that, despite his kind intentions, George Emerson is devoid of "chivalry."

When circumstances throw them together again, George impulsively kisses Lucy. Such behavior drives Lucy and Charlotte to Rome, where they meet Cecil Vyse. He is propriety itself, never once offering to kiss Lucy, and back in England Lucy and Vyse become engaged. By coincidence, Vyse has met the Emersons and introduces them to the neighborhood where Lucy and her mother live. Though well-intentioned, Vyse is one of Forster's snobs. He is also a drab lover, and when Lucy finally tastes one of his unsatisfactory kisses, she is thrown into a panic by the prospect of another meeting with George. They meet again, and George kisses her again, with the result that Lucy deems George impossible and Vyse intolerable and breaks her engagement to the latter with the resolve never to marry anyone.

Clearly Forster is on a different, more wholeheartedly comic, course in this novel, and the denouement fulfills the tradition of romantic comedy, the inevitable marriage of Lucy and George being brought about through the ministrations of a lady who casts off her role as an apparently irredeemable snob—cousin Charlotte. What Forster says of the Honeychurch house, Windy Corner, might almost be said of the novel: "One might laugh at the house, but one never shuddered." Despite the play of Forster's wit throughout the novel and the sympathy he extends to a girl as silly as Lucy, the reader does shudder occasionally. Two murders, the real one Lucy sees and a supposed one, interrupt the proceedings. The latter is a rumor, bruited about by a clergyman named Eager, that Mr. Emerson has murdered his wife. The charge is baseless and seems to have been injected to deepen Emerson's character as a man of sorrows. The real death is even more gratuitous—unless it is meant to validate George Emerson's seriousness and dependability.

Events lead Lucy into a series of lies which she supposes to be little white ones but which threaten general unhappiness, until Mr. Emerson, whom she has led to believe that she still intends to marry Vyse, induces heart's truth and persuades her to marry George. The novel ends with the honeymooners back in Florence speculating on Charlotte's motive in bringing about Lucy's climactic meeting with Mr. Emerson. They conclude that "she fought us on the surface, and yet she hoped."

Mr. Emerson, in two respects at least, echoes the writer of the same name. He is convinced of the importance of discovering Nature, and he is an apostle of self-trust. A good man, he grows tedious after the initial chapter, functioning finally as his son's advocate. George himself never quite comes into focus, and the reader is forced to accept on faith Charlotte's change of heart. The lightest of Forster's novels, *A Room with a View*—had it been lighter yet and avoided the rather heavy-handed symbolism of the "view" and the dark—might not have turned out the weakest of the five novels Forster published in his lifetime.

HOWARDS END

Howards End, Forster's most ambitious novel, recounts the adventures of two sisters, Margaret and Helen Schlegel, after two encounters with people not of their quiet, cultivated London set. At the beginning, while a guest at the country home of the Wilcoxes (a family the Schlegels had met while traveling abroad), Helen has become engaged—at least in her own mind—to one of the Wilcox sons, Paul. Her visit and engagement end awkwardly when her aunt whisks her back to London. The second incident grows out of Helen's inadvertently taking home from the theater the umbrella of a bank clerk named Leonard Bast. Standing "at the extreme verge of gentility," Leonard wishes to approach closer. The idealistic Schlegels appreciate the impulse and strike up an acquaintance. Meanwhile, the Wilcox connection is reestablished when the Wilcoxes rent a flat across from the house where the Schlegels, including younger brother Tibby, live, and Margaret, the oldest Schlegel, comes to know Mrs. Wilcox.

A quiet, even dull woman, Ruth Wilcox is an utterly charitable person who conveys to Margaret "the idea of greatness." Her husband Henry, a prosperous businessman, and the three Wilcox children—young adults like Helen and Tibby—radiate energy, good humor, and physical health but lack wit, grace, and any sense of beauty. Suddenly, a quarter of the way through the novel, Ruth Wilcox dies.

In marrying Henry Wilcox, Margaret proves very nearly as improvident as Lilia Herriton or Rickie Elliot. The two have little in common, and before long a series of fortuitous events shakes their precarious union. As a result of offhand bad advice from Henry, duly passed on by the Schlegel sisters, Leonard Bast loses his job. Leonard makes a pilgrimage to Oniton, one of several Wilcox estates on which Henry and Margaret are living. Unfortunately, Leonard chooses to bring along his unbecoming common-law wife, who turns out to be a former mistress of Henry Wilcox. When Henry angrily turns the Basts away, the conscience-stricken Helen insists on trying to compensate Bast. Like Stephen Wonham, he indignantly refuses her money. The impulsive and emotionally overwrought Helen refuses to abandon him. Later Helen disappears into Germany for a time; on her return Margaret discovers that she has conceived a son by Leonard.

When Margaret relays to her husband Helen's request that she be permitted to stay at the unused Howards End for one night, he indignantly refuses, and Margaret realizes that Henry, the betrayer of his own first wife, is unrepentant in his maintenance of a moral double standard. One tragic scene remains. Leonard appears at Howards End to beg forgiveness for sinning with Helen, Charles Wilcox (Henry's other son) totally misunderstands the intruder's motive and strikes him down with the flat of a sword, and Leonard's weak heart gives way. Charles is convicted of manslaughter, and at the end, Margaret, Helen and her child, and the broken-spirited Henry are living together at Howards End.

The reader will have noted similarities to Forster's first two published novels—the melodrama, the improbable coincidences, the often awkward modulations between comic and tragic tone, and so on. The pattern of events in *Howards End*, on the other hand, is both more richly and less intrusively symbolic. As many critics have observed, this is a novel about England, written in the uneasy pre-World War I years of growing antagonism between Germany and England. Forster permits himself a series of meditations on, paeans of praise to, his native isle in the manner of John of Gaunt's "This blessed plot, this earth, this realm, this England" speech in *Richard II* (1595-1596). At the same time, Forster clearly intimates that England is also the Wilcoxes—insular in their outlook, stolid in their prejudices, merciless in their advocacy of the class structure. The Schlegel sisters spring from a German father and revere German Romantic culture. Chapter 5 of the novel celebrates their (and Forster's) extraordinary sensitivity to Ludwig van Beethoven; it is after a performance of the *Fifth Symphony* that Helen takes Leonard's umbrella.

Margaret also loves England, typified by Howards End, which is no ancient seat of the Wilcoxes but a property which had belonged to Mrs. Wilcox herself, even though she sometimes seems to be amid alien corn there. England, Forster seems to say, needs to unite the best in its Wilcoxes, its providers and healthy consumers of material goods, with the Schlegel principle, expressed in the love of art and civilized discussion. By themselves the Schlegels are ineffectual. They can only watch helplessly as commercial development dooms their London house. After Helen has been carried away by her feeling for

Leonard's plight, she flees to her father's ancestral home but cannot live there. Only at Howards End can she live securely and watch her child grow up.

As a symbol for England and for the possibilities of a balanced life, Howards End might seem to have some deficiencies. It is lacking in beauty and tradition. It has become the seat of a philistine family, for even the saintly Ruth demonstrates no artistic interest more highly developed than a fondness for flowers and for a certain adjacent meadow in the early morning. On her first visit to Howards End, Helen Schlegel sees more of nature's beauties than any of the Wilcoxes, who are preoccupied with croquet, tennis, and "calisthenic exercises on a machine that is tacked on to a greengage-tree," ever perceive.

The agent who renders Howards End truly habitable is an uneducated farm woman who refuses to accept her "place." When Margaret first visits Howards End, where, it is thought, they will *not* make their home, she finds Miss Avery there. The old woman, who for a second mistakes Margaret for the first Mrs. Wilcox, has taken it upon herself to guard the empty house. Her presumptuousness, which in the past has taken the form of wedding gifts to both Henry's daughter and daughter-in-law—gaucheries the Wilcoxes are quick to condemn—extends shortly thereafter to unpacking the Schlegel books and other personal belongings, which have been stored there following the expiration of the lease on the London house. After ranging the Schlegel library in bookcases and arranging the Schlegel furniture to suit herself, the woman declines to accept even polite criticism: "You think that you won't come back to live here, Mrs. Wilcox, but you will."

Thus it is an intuitive country person who joins the half-foreign Schlegel culture to the native Wilcox stock. Miss Avery also sends over a country boy, Tom, after Helen and Margaret, in defiance of Henry, spend a night together at Howards End. "Please, I am the milk," says Tom, speaking more truth than he knows. As in *Where Angels Fear to Tread*, the milk is spiritual as well as physical nourishment. Peopled with such life-affirming folk, Howards End becomes a sustaining place, an embodiment of what English life might yet be if the deepening disorder of 1910 is somehow averted. Finally won over to permitting Helen to reside there—and thus at least tacitly acknowledging his own fornication—Henry decrees that at his death the property will pass to Margaret; Ruth Wilcox herself had wanted to give it to her.

The motto of *Howards End* is "Only connect." In the house, "the prose and passion" of life, the Wilcox and Schlegel principles, are joined through the ministrations of another of Forster's characters willing to defy the class system in the interests of a nobler order.

The central symbol of *Howards End* is hay. Ruth Wilcox is first observed "smelling hay," a product that the naturally fertile estate produces in abundance. The rest of the Wilcoxes, Miss Avery at one point observes maliciously, all suffer from hay fever. Forster uses the hay very much as Walt Whitman, whom he occasionally quotes and from whom he appropriated the title of his final novel, uses the grass: to suggest life, sustenance, hope, democracy. At the end of the novel, the chastened Henry's case of hay fever seems to have subsided when Helen, her baby, and Tom burst in from the meadow, with Helen exclaiming, "It'll be such a crop of hay as never!"

MAURICE

Written a few years after *Howards End, Maurice* did not see print until the year following Forster's death. In a later "terminal note" to this novel of a homosexual, Forster observed a change in the public's reaction to this subject from one of "ignorance and terror" at the time he wrote it to "familiarity and contempt" in his old age, so he continued to withhold the work. Maurice Hall also defies the class system, for his sexual partner is a gamekeeper on a college classmate's estate. Given the rigid penal code of the time, the novel is also about criminality.

Aside from his sexual orientation, Maurice resembles his creator very little, being rather ordinary in intellect, little drawn to the arts, and rather robust physically. Whereas Rickie Elliot had been effeminate, his deformed foot a symbolic impediment to satisfactory heterosexuality, Maurice seems quite "normal" to his friends. His college friend Clive Durham, leaning somewhat to homosexuality in college, ironically changes after an illness and a trip to Greece, and marries. The Durhams are gentlefolk, though somewhat

reduced, and Maurice has gotten on well with them, but Clive's marriage drives a wedge between them. After indulging in, and apparently escaping from, a furtive but passionate affair with Alec Scudder, their gamekeeper, Maurice suffers a blackmail threat from his former lover, but in the end Alec proves true, and instead of emigrating with whatever conscience money he might have extracted, Alec returns to the Durham estate, where, in the boathouse, the two come together again. At the end, Maurice's revelation to the conventionally horrified Clive leaves the latter trying "to devise some method of concealing the truth from Anne"—his wife.

Maurice demonstrates Forster's conviction that the desire for loving human relations is proof against the snobbery of all social classes. Although it could not be printed when it was written, the novel now seems more dated than Forster's other works, perhaps because its style is plain and drab. It obviously suffers from its lack of a contemporary audience, although Forster showed it to Lytton Strachey and received some constructive advice. Significantly, when Oliver Stallybrass, the editor of the Abinger Edition of Forster's works, assembled his favorite quotations from Forster, he could find nothing in *Maurice* worth including.

A PASSAGE TO INDIA

Although Forster committed himself wholeheartedly to friendship, it cannot be called the central theme of any of his novels until *A Passage to India*. The friendship of Rickie Elliot and Stewart Ansell, while vital to the former's development and self-discovery, is subordinated to the theme of brotherhood, in its familial sense, and Rickie can find no basis for friendship with Stephen. The incipient friendship of Margaret Schlegel and Ruth Wilcox is aborted by the latter's death. *A Passage to India*, while treating of brotherhood in its largest sense, is at heart a novel of friendship and its possibilities in the context of a racially and religiously fragmented society.

Beginning with the visit to India of the mother and fiancée of Ronnie Heaslop, the young colonial magistrate, and the complications of their encounters with a few educated natives, the narrative comes to focus on the friendship that as a consequence waxes and wanes between the English schoolmaster Cyril Fielding and the young Muslim Dr. Aziz. Forster dedicated the book to another Anglo-Indian friendship: his own with Syed Ross Masood, who first knew Forster as his tutor in Latin prior to Masood's entrance to Oxford in 1906, and who provided the impetus for Forster's own initial passage to India a few years later. Since Anglo-Indian prejudice was one of the loquacious Masood's favorite subjects, Forster understood it well by the time he came to write the novel. Indeed, his friendship with Masood demonstrated the possibility of such a relationship surviving the strains imposed on it by one partner's determination to pull no punches in discussing it.

Aziz, accused by Ronnie's fiancée Adela Quested of assaulting, or at least offending her (for she remains vague about the matter throughout), in a cave they are exploring, is a less masterful and self-confident figure than Masood, and the reader knows all along that there must be some mistake. Adela has seen how Ronnie's Indian service has exacerbated the weaker aspects of his character, and she has broken off their engagement, but she is not, as Aziz affects to believe, a love-starved female—at least not in the crude sense Aziz intends.

Forster draws an unforgettable picture of the tensions between the colonial rulers and the Indian professional class. The most idealistic Englishmen, it seems, succumb to the prevailing intolerance. It is an effort to consider the natives as human, as when Ronnie, told by his mother, Mrs. Moore, of her meeting with a young doctor, replies: "I know of no young doctor in Chandrapore," though once he learns that his mother has actually been consorting with a Muslim, he identifies him readily enough.

An exception to the rule is Fielding, already over forty when he came to India and a continuing believer in "a globe of men who are trying to reach one another." When Aziz' trial divides the community more openly and dangerously than usual, Fielding supports the young doctor—a move that assures the enmity of the English without guaranteeing the affection of the skeptical Indians. After Adela withdraws her charges against Aziz, the intimacy between the two men reaches its height; almost immediately, however, they quarrel over Aziz' determination to make his tormentor pay damages.

Fielding cannot persuade Aziz to show mercy, but Mrs. Moore can, even though she has left the country before the trial and in fact has died on her return passage. For the sake of the mother of the detested man whom Aziz still believes Adela will marry, he spares the young woman, knowing that the English will interpret this decision as an indication of guilt. With Adela finally gone, Aziz mistakenly assumes that Fielding, now contemplating a visit to England, intends to marry her himself. When the friends meet again two years later, the old frankness and intimacy has been shattered. Although Fielding has married, his bride is the daughter of Mrs. Moore.

The final chapter is a particularly excellent one. As Aziz and Fielding ride horses together, the former vowing that they can be friends but only after the Indians "drive every blasted Englishman into the sea," the horses swerve apart, as if to counter Fielding's objection. Not religion, land, people, even animals want the friendship now. It is difficult to escape the conclusion that under imperial conditions no rapprochement is possible.

Much of the interest in this novel has centered on Mrs. Moore, a rather querulous old woman with a role not much larger than Mrs. Wilcox's in *Howards End*. Although she joins the roster of Forster's admirable characters who defy the taboos that divide people, she refuses to involve herself in the Aziz trial. Nevertheless, the Indians make a legend out of her and invest her with numinous powers. Critics have tended to regard her as a more successful character than Mrs. Wilcox. Part of the explanation may lie in Forster's decision to allow the reader to see her not only at first hand but also through the eyes of the Indians. If their view of Mrs. Moore is partly illusion, the illusion itself—like the more familiar illusions of the English—becomes itself a part of the truth of the situation. It is one of Forster's virtues that he knows and communicates the often conflicting values and attitudes of native Indians.

Nor is the Indian version of Mrs. Moore completely illusory, for in addition to her openness and candor, Mrs. Moore in one respect surpasses all the Europeans, even the gentle Fielding. She loves and respects life, especially unfamiliar life. It is illuminating to contrast her attitude with that of two incidental characters—missionaries who live among the people and never come to the whites' club. They measure up to their calling very well for Forster clergymen, allowing that God has room in his mansions for all people. On the subject of animals they are not so sure; Mr. Sorley, the more liberal of the two, opts for monkeys but stumbles over wasps. Mrs. Moore, more alert to the native birds and animals than she is to many people, is even sympathetic to a wasp ("Pretty dear") that has flown into the house. It is doubtless significant that the wasp is very different from the European type. Long after she is gone, Professor Godbole, Aziz' Hindu friend, remembers her in connection with the wasp. Love of humble forms of life, which the other Westerners in the novel notice only as irritations if at all, is for the Indians of Forster's *A Passage to India* a reliable indication of spirituality.

The sensitivity of Mrs. Moore and the good will of Fielding seem like frail counterweights to the prevailing cynicism and prejudice which stifle the necessarily furtive social initiatives of well-intentioned victims such as Aziz. If these flawed but genuine human beings have little impact on the morally bankrupt society in which they move, they have for more than half a century heartened readers of like aspirations.

Robert P. Ellis

OTHER MAJOR WORKS

SHORT FICTION: *The Celestial Omnibus and Other Stories*, 1911; *The Eternal Moment and Other Stories*, 1928; *The Collected Tales of E. M. Forster*, 1947; *The Life to Come and Other Stories*, 1972; *Arctic Summer and Other Fiction*, 1980.

PLAY: *Billy Budd*, pb. 1951 (libretto; with Eric Crozier).

NONFICTION: *Alexandria: A History and a Guide*, 1922; *Pharos and Pharillon*, 1923; *Aspects of the Novel*, 1927; *Goldsworthy Lowes Dickinson*, 1934; *Abinger Harvest—A Miscellany*, 1936; *Virginia Woolf*, 1942; *Development of English Prose Between 1918 and 1939*, 1945; *Two Cheers for Democracy*, 1951; *The Hill of Devi*, 1953; *Marianne Thornton: A Domestic Biography, 1797-1887*, 1956; *Commonplace Book*, 1978.

BIBLIOGRAPHY

Beauman, Nicola. *E. M. Forster: A Biography*. New York: Knopf, 1994. A well-informed biography drawing on new archival material. Includes a family tree.

Crews, Frederick J. *E. M. Forster: The Perils of Humanism*. Princeton, N.J.: Princeton University Press, 1962. This comprehensive, readable introduction to Forster's novels and short stories argues that, although Forster's mind is anchored in liberalism, he is always aware of the liberal tradition's weaknesses. Claims that "his artistic growth runs parallel to his disappointments with humanism." Although he is agnostic and anti-Christian, Forster's "books are religious in their concern with the meaning of life" and the virtues of private freedom, diversity, personal relationships, sincerity, art, and sensitivity to the natural world and its traditions. Indexed.

Furbank, P. N. *E. M. Forster: A Life*. London: Secker & Warburg, 1978. This major biographical study written by another famous novelist is readable and perceptive in its analyses of the novels, short stories, and criticism. Finds pertinent influences on Forster's writing in his childhood, adolescent, and early adult years. An index is included.

Gransden, K. W. *E. M. Forster*. 1962. 2d ed. New York: Grove Press, 1970. This insightful study summarizes Forster's career, the influences of Samuel Butler, George Meredith, and Jane Austen, and his novels and short fiction. Included is a postscript to the 1970 revised edition which celebrates Forster's tenacious hold on his readers as well as selective primary/secondary bibliographies and an index.

Iago, Mary. *E. M. Forster: A Literary Life*. New York: St. Martin's Press, 1995. A succinct study of Forster's novels and work for the BBC. Helpful notes.

McConkey, James. *The Novels of E. M. Forster.* Hamden, Conn.: Archon Books, 1957. This historically important study looks forward to the 1960's emphasis on textual and philosophical criticism of Forster's writings. Analyzes the author's use of point of view, fantasy, images, symbols, and rhythms and demonstrates that both the transcendent and the physical worlds are always present in Forster. Selective primary and secondary bibliographies and an index conclude the book.

Trilling, Lionel. *E. M. Forster.* Norfolk, Conn.: New Directions, 1943. This is one of the most important, most influential assessments of Forster ever written. Trilling's discussion of Forster and the liberal imagination went far to influence a revival of interest in the work. Considers Forster's novels, short fiction, and criticism to show that his work is to be explained in terms of his emphasis upon the disastrous effects of "the undeveloped heart." An index is included.

(Camera Press Ltd./Archive Photos)

JOHN FOWLES

Born: Leigh-on-Sea, England; March 31, 1926

PRINCIPAL LONG FICTION

The Collector, 1963
The Magus, 1965, 1977
The French Lieutenant's Woman, 1969
Daniel Martin, 1977
Mantissa, 1982
A Maggot, 1985

OTHER LITERARY FORMS

In addition to his novels, John Fowles has written philosophy, essays for scholarly and popular audiences, criticism, poetry, and short fiction. He has also translated several other writers into English. *The Aristos: A Self-Portrait in Ideas*, published in 1964, is his philosophical "self-portrait in ideas." Patterned after writings of Heraclitus, the fifth century B.C.E. Greek philosopher, it reflects Fowles's philosophical stance, outlining many of the views which Fowles expresses more fully and artistical1ly in his fiction. His collected poetry is published in *Poems* (1973); much of it reflects his period of residence in Greece, the major setting for *The Magus*. His longer nonfiction pieces reflect his love for and interest in nature: *Shipwreck* (1974), a text to accompany the photographs of shipwrecks along the English coast near Fowles's home, and *Lyme Regis Camera* (1990), a text to accompany photographs of the town, its inhabitants, and its immediate environs; *Islands* (1978), about the Scilly Islands off the English coast, but more about the nature of islands as a metaphor for literature and the writer; *The Tree* (1980), an extension of the same theme with emphasis on the tree as representative of all nature; and *The Enigma of Stonehenge* (1980), a further extension of nature to encompass the mystery of a sacred place. All these themes are touched on in the varied pieces collected in *Wormholes: Essays and Occasional Writings* (1998). These themes find definition and elaboration in his fiction. Fowles's only collection of short fiction, *The Ebony Tower*, includes a novella from which the title is taken, three short stories, and a translation of a medieval romance with a "Personal Note" that comments on its relation to his fiction. The collection, entitled *Variations* in manuscript, also reflects Fowles's central themes in the longer fiction.

ACHIEVEMENTS

Fowles's place in literary history is difficult to assess. He has established an excellent reputation as a writer of serious fiction, one who will continue to be read. He continues to receive the notice of numerous critics; more than a dozen books have been published about him. Fowles, however, is no "ivory tower" author; he enjoys a wide readership, and several of his novels have been made into motion pictures, including *The Collector*, *The Magus*, and *The French Lieutenant's Woman*. Readers can expect to find in Fowles's works a good story with a passionate love interest, complex characters, a healthy smattering of philosophy, all presented within the context of the plot. Critics can slice away multiple layers to get at the wheels-within-wheels of meaning on existential, historical, philosophical, psychological, and myriad other levels.

Because Fowles rarely tells the same story in the same way, genre is a topic of much discussion among his critics. His fiction reflects not only his experimentation with genre, but also his questioning of authorial voice, the continuum of time, moments out of time, split viewpoint, a story without an ending, a story with a choice of endings, and still another with a revised ending. Despite such experimentation, most of the novels are in many ways quite old-fashioned, reflecting the ancient boy-meets-girl, boy-loses-girl, boy-seeks-to-find-girl-again-and-in-so-doing-finds-himself quest motif that characterizes so much fiction. They are fairly straightforward "good reads" without the dizzying experimentation of a James Joyce to make them virtually inaccessible to all but the most diligent reader. On any level, Fowles is enjoyable, and what reserves him a place among memorable writers is that he is discoverable, again and again.

BIOGRAPHY

John Fowles was born in Leigh-on-Sea, Essex, England, on March 31, 1926, to Robert and Gladys Richards Fowles. During World War II, his family was evacuated to the more remote village of Ippeplen, South Devon, and it was there that Fowles discovered the beauty of the country of Devonshire, his "English Garden of Eden" that figures so prominently in other guises in his fiction. During that same period, he was a student at the exclusive Bedford School, where he studied German and French literature, eventually rising to the stature of head boy, a position of great power over the other boys in the school. It was there that he got his first taste of literature, which he loved, and power, which he despised. The knowledge of both was influential in his own writing.

From Bedford, he went into military service, spending six months at the University of Edinburgh and completing training as a lieutenant in the merchant marine just as the war was ending. Following the war, he continued his education in German and more particularly French literature at New College, Oxford University; he graduated in 1950 with a B.A. with honors. His fiction owes many debts to his study of French literature, particularly his interest in existentialism as espoused by Jean-Paul Sartre and Albert Camus and his knowledge of the Celtic romance, from which stems his expressed belief that all literature has its roots in the theme of the quest.

Upon graduation, Fowles taught English at the University of Poitiers. After a year at Poitiers, he took a job teaching English to Greek boys on the island of Spetsai in the Aegean Sea. The school, the island, the aura of Greece, and the thoughts of the young teacher became the material for *The Magus*, his first novel (although not published first). It was also on Spetsai that he met Elizabeth Whitton, whom he married three years later. For Fowles, Greece was the land of myth, the other world, the place of the quest. Leaving Greece, Fowles suffered the loss of another Eden, but that loss inspired him to write. While writing, he continued to teach in and around London until the publication of *The Collector* in 1963, the success of which enabled him to leave teaching and devote himself full time to writing. The following year he published *The Aristos*, and in 1965 he finally published *The Magus*, twelve years after its conception.

A year later, he and Elizabeth moved to Lyme Regis in Dorset, a small seaside town away from London where they have continued to live. First living on a rundown farm, the Fowleses later moved to an eighteenth century house overlooking Lyme Bay. The dairy, the house, and the town of Lyme figure prominently in his third novel, *The French Lieutenant's Woman*, a work that established his international reputation. Following its success were his *Poems*, *The Ebony Tower*, *Daniel Martin*, the revised version of *The Magus*, *Mantissa*, and *A Maggot*.

Fowles's love of nature is evident in his writing as well as his life, especially in such nonfiction works as *Islands* and *The Tree*. At his home in Lyme Regis, he oversees a large, wild garden overlooking Lyme Bay and fosters the natural development of the flora, passions that have not died since boyhood. One that has died, however, is the collection of living things. Once a collector of butterflies, like his character Frederick Clegg in *The Collector*, Fowles now abhors such activities. Rather, he collects Victorian postcards and antique china, reads voluminously, goes to London infrequently, and shares a very private life with his wife, who is his best critic. It was a life he very much enjoyed until he suffered a mild stroke in early 1988. Although the stroke caused no permanent damage, it left him depressed by the sudden specter of death and by a resulting loss of creative energies. By the mid-1990's most readers who had followed Fowles's career did not expect him to add to his body of work, but he said at the Fowles seminar in Lyme Regis in 1996 that he was again at work.

ANALYSIS

John Fowles's fiction has one theme: the quest of his protagonists for self-knowledge. Such a quest is not easy in the modern world because, as many other modern authors have shown, the contemporary quester is cut off from the traditions and rituals of the past that gave people a purpose and sense of direction. Still, desiring the freedom of individual choice which requires an understanding of self, the Fowlesian protagonist moves through the pattern of the quest as best he can.

Following the tradition of the quest theme found in the medieval romance, which Fowles sees as central to his and all of Western fiction, the quester embarks on the journey in response to a call to adventure. Because the quester is in a state of longing for the adventure, oftentimes not recognized as such by him, he readily responds to the call. The call takes him across a threshold into another world, the land of myth. For Fowles's questers, this other world is always described as a remote, out-of-the-way place, often lush and primeval. In this place the quester meets the usual dragons, which, in modern terms, are presented as a series of challenges that he must overcome if he is to proceed.

Guided by the figure of the wise old man who has gone before him and can show the way, the quester gradually acquires self-knowledge, which brings freedom of choice. For Fowles's heroes, this choice always centers around the acceptance of a woman. If the quester has attained self-knowledge, he is able to choose the woman—that is, to know and experience love, signifying wholeness. Then, he must make the crossing back into the real world and continue to live and choose freely, given the understanding the quest has provided.

What separates the journey of the Fowlesian hero from the journey of the medieval hero is that much of it has become internalized. Where the quester of old did actual battle with dragons, monsters, and mysterious knights, the modern quester is far removed from such obvious obstacles. He cannot see the enemy in front of him, since it is often within him, keeping him frozen in a state of inertia that prevents him from questing. The modern journey, then, can be seen in psychological terms; while the events are externalized, the results are measured by the growth of the protagonist toward wholeness or self-knowledge. Thus, as Joseph Campbell describes in *The Hero with a Thousand Faces* (1949), "The problem is . . . nothing if not that of making it possible for men and women to come to full human maturity through the conditions of contemporary life."

Each of Fowles's protagonist/heroes follows the pattern of the mythic quest. Each journeys to a strange land (the unconscious): the Greek island of Phraxos and Conchis's more secret domain for Nicholas Urfe, the isolated countryside house for Frederick Clegg, the primitive Undercliff of Lyme Regis for Charles Smithson, the hidden manor in the forests of Brittany for David Williams, the lost landscape of his youth and the journey up the Nile for Daniel Martin, the interior space of the mind of Miles Green, and the ancient landscape of Stonehenge plus the mystery of the cave for Bartholomew and Rebecca. Each undergoes a series of trials (the warring aspects of his personality) intended to bring him to a state of self-consciousness. With the exception of Clegg, whose story represents the antiquest, each has the aid of a guide (the mythical wise old man): Conchis for Nicholas, Dr. Grogan for Charles, Breasley for David Williams; Professor Kirnberger, Georg Lukács, a Rembrandt self-portrait, and others for Daniel Martin; the various manifestations of the muse for Miles Green; and Holy Mother Wisdom for Bartholomew and Rebecca. Each has an encounter with a woman (representative of "the other half" needed for wholeness): Alison for Nicholas, Miranda for Frederick, Sarah for Charles, the "Mouse" for David, Jane for Daniel, Erato for Miles, Holy Mother Wisdom for Bartholomew, and Bartholomew for Rebecca. The ability of the quester to calm or assimilate the warring aspects within him, to come to an understanding of himself, and as a result reach out to the experience of love with the woman, represents the degree of growth of each.

Feeling strongly that his fiction must be used as "a method of propagating [his] views of life" to bring a vision of cosmic order out of modern chaos, Fowles sees himself on a journey to accomplish this task. An examination of his fiction reveals the way in which he tackles the task, providing his readers with a description of the journey that they, too, can take.

THE MAGUS

The Magus was Fowles's first novel (although it was published after *The Collector*), and it remains his most popular. Fowles himself was so intrigued by the novel that he spent twelve years writing it, and even after publication, produced a revised version in 1977 because he was dissatisfied with parts of it. While some critics see changes between the original and the revision, there is little substantive difference between the two books beyond the addition of more explicit sexual scenes and the elaboration of several sections; thus the discussion of one suffices for the other.

The story derives from Fowles's period of teaching in Greece, and its protagonist, Nicholas Urfe, is much like Fowles in temperament and situation. As is often the case with Fowles, his fiction describes protagonists of the same age and temperament as himself at the time of his writing; thus an examination of the corpus reveals a maturing hero as well as a maturing author. In this first novel, Nicholas is twenty-five, Oxford-educated, attracted to existentialism, and bored with life. He is the typical Fowlesian protagonist, wellborn and bred, aimless, and ripe for the quest.

Discontented with his teaching job in England, he, like Fowles, jumps at the opportunity to teach in Greece. His subconscious desire is for a "new land, a new race, a new language," which the quest will provide. Just before going, he meets Alison, who is to become the important woman in his life, although it takes many pages and much questing through the labyrinth of self-knowledge on Phraxos for Nicholas to realize this. Alison, as the intuitive female, the feeling side Nicholas needs for wholeness, recognizes the importance of their relationship from the beginning, while Nicholas, representing reason, does not. In discussing the elements of the quest that bring Nicholas to an understanding and acceptance of the feeling side of himself which allows him to experience love, one can chart the pattern of the quest which Fowles presents in variations in all his fiction.

On Phraxos, Nicholas responds to the call to adventure embodied in the voice of a girl, the song of a bird, and some passages of poetry, especially four lines from T. S. Eliot: "We shall not cease from exploration/ And the end of all our exploring/ Will be to arrive where we started/ And know the place for the first time." These lines state the mystery of the journey that awaits him: to quest outside so as to come back to himself with understanding. Put another way, it is the yearning in humankind for the return to the harmony of the Garden of Eden. It is, as well, the thesis of *Four Quartets* (1943), which solves for Eliot the problem of the wasteland. Finally, it is the concept that motivates almost all of Fowles's questers, beginning with Nicholas.

Crossing the threshold beyond the *Salle d'Attente*, or Waiting Room, to the domain of myth at Bournai, Nicholas meets Conchis, his guide through the quest. Under Conchis's tutelage, Nicholas's "discoveries" begin. Nicholas understands that something significant is about to happen, that it is somehow linked to Alison, and that it restores his desire to live. Conchis exposes Nicholas to a series of experiences to teach and test him. Some he describes for Nicholas; others make Nicholas an observer; and still others give him an active, sometimes frightening role. In all, whether he is repulsed, fascinated, or puzzled, Nicholas wants more, allowing himself to be led deeper and deeper into the mysteries. These culminate in the trial scene, during which Nicholas is examined, his personality dissected, his person humiliated. Finally, he is put to the test of his ability to choose. Longing to punish Lily/Julie, the personification of woman Nicholas romantically and unrealistically longs for, he is given the opportunity at the end of the trial to flog her. His understanding that his freedom of choice gives him the power to resist the predictable, to go against the dictates of reason alone and follow the voice of the unconscious, signifies that he has become one of the "elect." Nicholas emerges from the underground chamber reborn into a higher state of consciousness. He must then make the return crossing into the real world.

To begin the return journey, he is given a glimpse of Alison, although he has been led to believe that she has committed suicide. Realizing that she is alive and that she offers him "a mirror that did not lie" in her "constant reality," he understands that the remainder of the quest must be toward a reunion with Alison. Apparently, however, he is not yet worthy of her, being dominated still by the ratiocinative side of himself, that part that seeks to unravel logically the mystery that Conchis presents. Thus, on his return to London he is put through additional tests until one

day, completely unsuspecting of her arrival, he sees Alison again and follows her to Regents Park for their reunion.

Signifying the experience of the Garden of Eden when man and woman existed in wholeness, the park provides an appropriate setting for their reunion. Echoing lines from Eliot, Nicholas has arrived where he started. Now he must prove that he is worthy of Alison, that he can accept the love she once offered freely, but that he must win her just as Orpheus attempted to win Eurydice from the dead. Becoming his own magus, he acts out a drama of his own making, challenging Alison to meet him at Paddington Station, where their journey together will begin. Unlike Orpheus, who was unsuccessful in bringing Eurydice from the dead, Nicholas has the confidence gained in his quest to leave Alison and not look back, knowing that she will be at the train station to meet him. While there is some question among critics as to whether Nicholas and Alison do meet and continue their journey together, Fowles has indicated that "Alison is the woman he will first try to love." Certainly, in either case it is the element of mystery that is important, not whether Nicholas wins this particular woman. The significance is in his yearning for her, demonstrating that he has learned to accept and give love, that he has journeyed toward wholeness.

What makes such a journey significant for the reader is that he or she can partake of the experience as an insider, not as an outsider. This results from the narrative technique Fowles employs. In Fowles's first-person narrative, Nicholas reveals only what he knows at any particular point on his journey; thus the reader sees only what Nicholas sees. Not able to see with any more sophistication than Nicholas the twistings and turnings of Conchis's "godgame," the reader must do exactly what Nicholas does: try to unravel the mystery in its literal sense rather than understand the "mystery" in its sacred sense. Believing every rational explanation Nicholas posits, one learns as he learns. As his own magus, Nicholas leads the reader into the mystery he was led into, not spoiling one's sense of discovery as his was not spoiled, and providing one with the experience of the journey as he experienced it. Of course, behind Nicholas is the master magus Fowles, whose design is to lead each reader to his own essential mysteries. The technique provides an immediacy that allows each reader to take the journey toward his own self-discovery; the novel provides a paradigm by which the mystery of Fowles's other novels can be deciphered.

THE COLLECTOR

The Collector, in sharp contrast to *The Magus*, presents the other side of the coin, sounding a warning. Here the protagonist is the antihero—his captured lady, the heroine. She goes on the journey he is incapable of taking, which, in his incapacity to understand her or himself, he aborts.

Frederick Clegg, the protagonist, shares many similarities with Nicholas of *The Magus*. Each is orphaned, in his twenties, and aimless. Each forms an attachment to a blond, gray-eyed woman, and each goes to a remote land in which the relationship with this woman is explored. Each is given the opportunity to become a quester in that land, and each tells a first-person narrative of the experience. In each, the narrative structure is circular, such that the novel arrives where it started.

The major difference, of course, is that Nicholas journeys toward wholeness; Clegg, while given the same opportunities, does not. The reason for Clegg's failure lies in the fact that he cannot understand the mythic signals; thus, he cannot move beyond his present confused state. The novel begins and ends in psychic darkness; the hero does not grow or develop. Yet, while Clegg remains unchanged, the captive Miranda, trapped as Clegg's prisoner, undergoes a transforming experience that puts her on the path of the quest Clegg is unable to take. The tragedy is not so much Clegg's lack of growth as it is the futility of Miranda's growth in view of the fact that she cannot apply in the real world the lessons learned in her quest. She is incapable even of having any beneficial effect on her captor.

Part of the problem between Miranda and Clegg lies in the differences in their cultural backgrounds. Miranda has the background of a typical Fowlesian quester in terms of education and social standing; Clegg's, however, is atypical in his lower-class roots and lack of education. Part of the thesis of this novel

is the clash between these two as representative of the clash between the "Many" and the "Few," which Fowles describes in detail in *The Aristos*. The novel, presented as a divided narrative told first by Clegg and then by Miranda, depicts in its very structure the division between Miranda and Clegg that cannot be bridged.

The first problem for Clegg as a quester is that he captures the object of his quest, keeping her prisoner in a hidden cellar. In psychological terms, Miranda, the feeling side of Clegg, is kept in the cellar "down there," which disallows the possibility of union. Clegg remains a divided man, living above in the house, with Miranda imprisoned below. Miranda, however, discovers that her "tomb" becomes a "womb" in which she grows in self-consciousness and understanding. Thus, the quest centers on her and the antiquest centers on Clegg.

As a butterfly collector, Clegg sees Miranda as his prize acquisition. He hopes that she will come to love him as he thinks he loves her, but what he really prizes is her beauty, which he has hoped to capture and keep as he would a butterfly's. When she begins to turn ugly in her vitality and lack of conformity to his preconceived notions of her, she falls off the pedestal on which he has placed her, and he then feels no compunction about forcing her to pose for nude photographs.

Clegg's problems are many. On a social level, he identifies too closely with what he sees as the judgment of the middle class against his lower-class background. On a psychological level, he is possessed by images from his past, the negative influences of his aunt, and his upbringing. His sexual fears and feelings of personal inadequacy combine to lock him into his own psychological prison in the same way that he locks Miranda in hers. Trapped in his internal prison, the outward presence of Miranda remains just that, outside of himself, and he cannot benefit from her proximity. She, however, while externally imprisoned by Clegg, is not prevented from making the inward journey toward self-discovery. At the same time, there is within Clegg, although deeply buried, a desire to break away and move onto the mythic path, and Miranda sees that aspect of him, his essential innocence, which has caused him to be attracted to her in the first place. Nevertheless, it is too deeply buried for Miranda to extract, and his power over her becomes his obsession. When he blurts out, "I love you. It's driven me mad," he indicates the problem he faces. Love is madness when it takes the form of possession, and Clegg is possessed by his feelings in the same way that he possesses Miranda. As Miranda asserts her individuality and Clegg becomes repulsed by her, he is able to shift blame for her death to her as a direct consequence of her actions.

While Clegg learns nothing from his experience and uses his narrative to vindicate himself, Miranda uses her narrative to describe her growing understanding and sense of self-discovery, aborted by her illness and subsequent death. After her death, Clegg cleans out the cellar, restoring it to its original state before Miranda's arrival. This circular structure, returning the reader to the empty cellar, echoes the circular structure of *The Magus*, except that Clegg has learned nothing from his experience, and Nicholas has learned everything. It is not that Nicholas is essentially good and Clegg essentially bad; rather, it is that Clegg cannot respond to the good within him, rendered inert by the warring aspects of his personality. Clegg's failure to respond to the elements of the quest is, in some respects, more tragic than Miranda's death, because he must continue his death-in-life existence, moving in ever-decreasing circles, never profiting or growing from the experience of life. In his next conquest, he will not aim so high; this time it will not be for love but for "the interest of the thing."

Reflecting the bleakness of Clegg's situation, the novel is filled with images of darkness. The pattern of *The Collector* is away from the light toward the darkness. Miranda's dying becomes a struggle against "the black and the black and the black" and her last words to Clegg—"the sun"—are a grim reminder of the struggle between them: the age-old struggle of the forces of light against those of darkness. Miranda's movement in the novel is upward toward light, life, and understanding; Clegg's is one of helpless descent toward darkness, evil, and psychic death.

THE FRENCH LIEUTENANT'S WOMAN

With *The French Lieutenant's Woman*, Fowles returns to the theme of the successful quest. Here the quester is Charles Smithson, much like Nicholas in social standing and education. The important differences between the novels are that *The French Lieutenant's Woman* is set in Victorian England and that Charles, in his thirties, a decade older than Nicholas, reflects the older viewpoint of the author. Like Nicholas, his twentieth century counterpart, Charles is representative of his age and class. Also like Nicholas, Charles is somewhat bored with his circumstances, despite the fact that he is finally taking the proper course of marriage to the proper lady, Ernestina. Not nearly so aware of his boredom as is Nicholas, Charles is nevertheless immediately attracted to Sarah upon their first meeting, sensing instantly that she is not like other women. Meeting her again in Ware Commons and its more secret Undercliff, Charles finds in this "other world" the mythic encounter for which he unconsciously yearns. A seeker after fossils, he subconsciously fears his own extinction in the receding waters of the Victorian age, a gentleman left behind in the face of the rising tide of the Industrial Revolution.

Sarah, having recognized her uniqueness in a world of conformity, relishes her position apart from others, particularly in its ability to give her a freedom other women do not possess. As the French lieutenant's woman (a euphemism for whore), she is outside society's bonds. Capitalizing on her position, she has already begun her own quest when she meets Charles; thus, she leads him to his own path for the journey. Ernestina represents the known, the predictable, the respectable; Sarah, the opposite: the unknown, the mysterious, the forbidden. Torn between the two choices, Charles eventually comes to know himself well enough to be able to make the more hazardous choice, the one more fraught with danger, yet far more likely to lead to wholeness.

The feeling and reasoning aspects of Charles's psyche war within him. Seeking advice from Dr. Grogan, he gets the proper scientific viewpoint of Sarah and is prescribed the proper course of action: return to Ernestina. One side of Charles, the rational, longs to do so; the other side, the feeling, cannot. Thus, after much wrestling with the problem, Charles chooses Sarah, breaks his engagement to Ernestina, and returns to Sarah for what he thinks will be the beginning of their beautiful life in exile together—only to find her gone. At this point, Charles's real journey begins. Sarah has brought him to the point of resisting the predictable and recognizing his feeling side; he must now learn to live alone with such newfound knowledge.

Such a choice is not a simple one, and the reader must choose as well, for there are three "endings" in the novel. The first is not really an ending, as it comes in the middle of the book. In it, Charles rejects Sarah, marries Ernestina and lives, as it were, happily ever after. One knows, if only by the number of pages remaining in the book, that this is not really the ending; it is merely Victorian convention, which the author-god Fowles quickly steps in to tell the reader is not the actual ending. Thus, the reader passes through another hundred pages before he comes to another choice of endings, these more realistic.

The first is happy; the second is not. The endings themselves indicate the evolutionary process that Charles, as well as the novel, takes; for if one includes the hypothetical early ending, one moves from the traditional Victorian view to the emancipated view of Charles's and Sarah's union to the final existential view of the cruelty of freedom which denies Charles the happy ending. Fowles wanted his readers to accept the last ending as the right choice, but feared that they would opt for the happy ending; he was pleased when they did not.

In the first ending, the gap between Charles and Sarah is bridged through the intercession of Lalage, the child born of their one sexual encounter. The assertion that "the rock of ages can never be anything but love" offers the reader a placebo that does not effect a cure for the novel's dilemma. Fowles then enters, turns the clock back, and sets the wheels in motion for the next ending. In this one, the author-god Fowles drives off, leaving Sarah and Charles to work out their fate alone in much the same way that Conchis absconds from the "godgame" when Nicholas and Alison are reunited in *The Magus*. In both

cases, Fowles is trying to demonstrate that the freedom of choice resides with the individual, not with the "author." Since Sarah fears marriage for its potential denial of her hard-won freedom and sense of individuality, she cannot accept Charles's offer to marry, nor can he accept hers of friendship in some lesser relationship. Sarah then gives Charles no choice but to leave, and in his leaving he is released from his bonds to the past, experiencing a new freedom: "It was as if he found himself reborn, though with all his adult faculties and memories." Like Nicholas in *The Magus*, the important point is not whether he wins this particular woman but that he has learned to know himself and to love another. This is what sets him apart as an individual, saves him from extinction, and propels him into the modern age.

THE EBONY TOWER

Intending to name his collection of short works *Variations* because of its reflection of various themes and genres presented in his longer fiction, Fowles changed the name to *The Ebony Tower* (after the title novella) when first readers thought the original title too obscure. Anyone familiar with Fowles's themes, however, immediately sees their variations in this collection. The volume contains the title novella, followed by a "Personal Note," followed by Fowles's translation of Marie de France's medieval romance *Eliduc* (c. 1150-1175), followed by three short stories: "Poor Koko," "The Enigma," and "The Cloud." In his "Personal Note," Fowles explains the inclusion of the medieval romance, relating it first to "The Ebony Tower," more generally to all of his fiction, and finally to fiction in general.

The title story describes a quester who inadvertently stumbles into the realm of myth only to find that he cannot rise to the challenge of the quest and is therefore ejected from the mythic landscape. The other three stories are all centered on enigmas or mysteries of modern life. These mysteries arise because "mystery" in the sacred sense no longer appears valid in modern humanity's existence. The movement of the stories is generally downward toward darkness, modern humankind being depicted as less and less able to take the journey of self-discovery because it is trapped in the wasteland of contemporary existence. Thus, the variations in these stories present aspects of the less-than-successful quest.

David Williams of "The Ebony Tower" leaves his comfortable home and lifestyle in England and enters the forests of Brittany, the land of the medieval romance, to face an encounter with Henry Breasley, a famous (and infamous) painter. Because David is a painter himself, he is interested in the journey from an artist's perspective; he does not anticipate the mythic encounter that awaits him in this "other" world. Within this other world, Breasley attacks the "architectonic" nature of David's work in its abstraction, in contrast to Breasley's art, which has been called "mysterious," "archetypal," and "Celtic." In defaming David's art for its rigidity and lack of feeling, Breasley serves as a guide to David. David also finds the essential woman here in the figure of Diana, "The Mouse." The two characters offer him the potential of becoming a quester. The story represents the forsaken opportunity and its aftermath.

David's problem, like that of Nicholas and Charles at the beginning of their quests, is that he is so caught up with the rational that he cannot understand the emotional, in others or in himself. To all that he finds bewildering, he tries to attach a rational explanation. When finally confronted with pure emotion in his meeting with Diana in the Edenic garden, he hesitates, fatally pausing to consider rationally what his course of action should be. In that moment, he loses the possibility of responding to his innermost feelings, failing to unite with the woman who represents his feeling side; as a result, he is evicted from the mythic landscape.

Caught between two women, his wife and Diana, David cannot love either. His situation is in sharp contrast to that of Eliduc, who also encounters two women, and can love both. For Eliduc, love is a connecting force; for David, a dividing force. Thus, when David leaves the Brittany manor, he runs over an object in the road, which turns out to be a weasel. Here the weasel is dead with no hope of being restored to life. In *Eliduc*, love restores the weasel to life.

The rest of the story is David's rationalization of his failure. Like Clegg of *The Collector*, David first recognizes his failure but knows that he will soon forget the "wound" he has suffered and the knowledge of his failure. Already the mythic encounter seems far away. By the time he arrives in Paris, he is able to tell his wife that he has "survived." Had David succeeded in his quest, he would have done far more than survive: He would have lived.

The remaining stories in the collection are connected to the title story by the theme of lost opportunities. In "Poor Koko" the narrator, a writer, is robbed by a young thief who burns his only possession of value, his manuscript on Thomas Love Peacock. The story is the writer's attempt to understand the seemingly meaningless actions of the thief, which he finally comes to realize extend from the breakdown in communication between them. On a larger scale, the clash between the boy and the old man is the clash between generations, between a world in which language is meaningful and one in which it is empty.

In the succeeding story, "The Enigma," a mystery of a different kind is presented: the disappearance of John Marcus Fielding, member of Parliament, and the subsequent investigation by Sergeant Jennings. The first mystery focuses on the reason behind the disappearance of Fielding, whose body is never discovered and whose motive is never revealed. What is hinted at by Isobel Dodgson, the former girlfriend of Fielding's son and the last person to have seen Fielding before he disappeared, is that Fielding absconded from life because it offered no mystery; thus he provided his own by disappearing.

The second and more engaging mystery is seen in the developing relationship between Jennings and Isobel. While theirs is not of the dimensions of the relationship between Charles and Sarah, Nicholas and Alison, or even David and Diana, since they are not on the mythic journey, it is nevertheless interesting because it provides a sense of mystery. In a world that motivates a Fielding to walk out, it will have to suffice.

The last story, "The Cloud," is probably the most mysterious in the literal sense, although it describes a world most lacking in mystery in the sacred or mythic sense. The setting is a picnic with two men,

Peter and Paul, and two women, sisters, Annabel and Catherine. While the setting describes an idyllic day, one senses from the outset that this is not paradise, because the women are lying in the sun, "stretched as if biered," an image of death that pervades the story. Catherine has apparently suffered the loss of a loved one, presumably her husband, and is in deep depression. She seems unable to make the crossing back into the world. Language does not serve as a bridge, and her feelings elicit no depth of response from the others. Thus, by the end of the story, she enters a myth of her own making, which is described in the story she invents for her niece about the princess abandoned by her prince. Catherine remains behind, unbeknown to the others when they leave the woods, and the reader is left with the assumption that she commits suicide, symbolized by the presence of the dark clouds rolling over the scene. Thus, the dark image of the ebony tower in the first story is replaced by the dark cloud in the last, and the reader has come full circle once again.

DANIEL MARTIN

Having described aspects of the failed quest in *The Ebony Tower*, Fowles once again returns to the theme of the successful quest in *Daniel Martin*. This time the quester is a mature man in his forties, as was the author at the time of the novel's composition, and this time Fowles is able to write the happy ending that had eluded him in his other fiction. The first sentence of the novel contains its thesis and the summation of Fowles's philosophy: "WHOLE SIGHT OR ALL THE REST IS DESOLATION." Like the questers in *The Magus* and *The French Lieutenant's Woman*, Daniel Martin must take the mythic journey to learn the meaning of whole sight and to change his world from a place of desolation to one of fulfillment.

While the first sentence of the novel states the thesis, the epigraph states the problem: "The crisis consists precisely in the fact that the old is dying and the new cannot be born; in this interregnum a great variety of morbid symptoms appears." Trapped in the wasteland of contemporary existence, Daniel experiences "morbid symptoms" in his failure to feel deeply and to be connected to a meaningful past. It is

the movement of the novel from the crisis to whole sight that constitutes the quest.

The call to adventure comes with a phone call announcing the impending death of Anthony, an old friend. In going to England to be at his friend's bedside, he returns to the land of his youth and to the time when love was real. That love was with Jane, who later married Anthony, forcing both Daniel and Jane to bury their true feelings for each other. With Anthony's death, Daniel is once again faced with the dilemma of his own happiness and the role that Jane can play in it. At the same time, Daniel is wrestling with the problem of his desire to write a novel; subsequently, as the story unfolds, Daniel's novel unfolds, such that at the completion of the story one also has the completion of Daniel's novel, the demonstrable product of his successful quest.

Moving in and out of time, the novel skips from Daniel's boyhood to his present life in Hollywood with Jenny, a young film actress, to his memories of happy days at Oxford, and to his continuing relationship with Jane in the present. It also has several narrative points of view: Daniel tells certain sections, the omniscient author tells others, and still others are told by Jenny.

Daniel is aided on his journey by several wise old men: among them, Otto Kirnberger, the professor he and Jane meet on their trip up the Nile; and the Hungarian Marxist literary critic Georg Lukács, whose writings explain Daniel's choices as a writer. Daniel also describes several Edenic settings which he calls the experience of the "*bonne vaux*." Remembrance of these experiences at Thorncombe, at Tsankawi, and at Kitchener's Island reinforce his desire to bring them more fully into his life; thus he quests on.

Realizing that the essential element of the quest is his ability to express his love for Jane, he worries that he will be rejected by her. Jane, less certain of her ability to choose her own future, tries to retreat from his declaration of love, telling him that she sees love as a prison. Jane is not yet ready to accept Daniel, but they journey on together, this time to Palmyra, a once beautiful but now desolate and remote outpost. In this wasteland, they experience the renewal of love. The catalyst comes in the form of a sound, "a whimpering, an unhappiness from the very beginning of existence." The sound is that of a litter of forlorn puppies, followed by another sound from their bedraggled mother, who tries to protect her puppies by acting as a decoy to distract the couple. The scene propels Jane out of her own wasteland into an enactment of a private ritual. Burying her wedding ring in the sand, she symbolically severs herself from her restrictive past to connect with the present and Daniel.

On his return to England, Daniel then severs himself from his remaining past by rejecting Jenny, recognizing all the while the importance of compassion in his relations with her and others. Following their last meeting, he enters a nearby church and is confronted with a living picture of all that he has learned: the famous late Rembrandt self-portrait. In this vision of compassion and whole sight, Daniel sees how far he has come and where the path into the future will lead. In Daniel's experience of the happy ending, the reader sees also a beginning. Thus, the last sentence of the novel one reads becomes the first sentence of the novel that Daniel will write. Again the experience is a circle, arriving where it started, with the circle expanding as it does in *The Magus* and in *The French Lieutenant's Woman.*

The movement of Fowles's fiction through *Daniel Martin* suggested the completion of a cycle: from a statement of the thesis in *The Magus*, to a statement of its opposite in *The Collector*, to an examination of the thesis from a different historical perspective in *The French Lieutenant's Woman*, to variations in *The Ebony Tower*, and to arrival at the long-sought happy ending in *Daniel Martin*. One could easily anticipate that the next novel would be very different, and so it was. *Mantissa*, which Fowles defines in a footnote, is a term meaning "an addition of comparatively small importance, especially to a literary effort or discourse." The novel's critical reception was mixed, some critics applauding the obvious departure from Fowles's customary style and others deploring its seeming frivolousness. Fowles contends that it should be taken as "mantissa," a kind of lark on his part. In it, he explores the role of creativity and freedom for the author, expressed through his protagonist Miles Green, as he wakes up to find himself an amnesiac in

a hospital. The action of the novel, although it appears to have numerous characters entering and leaving the hospital, is really taking place in the protagonist's head, with the various characters representing manifestations of the muse Erato. The debate between muse and author gives Fowles the opportunity to turn the essential question of "freedom to choose," which he makes the object of the quest for his protagonists in his novels, into the object of the quest for the author/protagonist in this one. It also gives Fowles the opportunity to poke fun at the literary-critical approaches of the day, especially deconstruction. Finally, it gives Fowles the perfect opportunity to write graphically about sexual encounter, which he claims is one of the reasons he revised *The Magus:* to correct a "past failure of nerve."

A MAGGOT

In his next novel, *A Maggot*, he again chooses a title that requires explanation, his use of the term being in the obsolete sense of "whim or quirk." He goes on to explain in his prologue that he was obsessed with a theme arising out of an image from his unconscious of an unknown party of riders on horseback, and his desire was to capture this "remnant of a lost myth." This same obsession with an image is what led to the writing of *The French Lieutenant's Woman*, the historical novel set in the nineteenth century. In *A Maggot*, the temporal setting is the eighteenth century, and, as in *The French Lieutenant's Woman*, the struggle of a man and a woman to break out of their trapped existence is once again the focus. The man is Bartholomew, the son of a wealthy lord, and the woman is a prostitute named Fanny whose real name is Rebecca Lee. Bartholomew leads Rebecca into the quest, but he disappears, and the remainder of the novel becomes a search for the truth behind the events leading to his disappearance. To conduct this investigation, Bartholomew's father hires the lawyer Henry Ayscough, and the form of the novel shifts from third-person omniscient to first-person depositions, as Ayscough locates and questions everyone connected with the journey leading to the mysterious disappearance of Bartholomew. Everyone has a different view of the event, none of which Ayscough finds convincing. His desire for the truth is based on a belief that there is a rational, logical explanation; yet, despite the thoroughness of his inquiries, he cannot come up with one, finally concluding, without the evidence to prove it, that it must have been a murder.

The crux of the problem lies in his statement to Rebecca, "There are two truths, mistress. One that a person believes is truth; and one that is truth incontestible. We will credit you with the first, but the second is what we seek." Rebecca's belief, that Bartholomew has been transported by a maggot-shaped spaceship to June Eternal and that she has been reborn into a new life, frees her to break out of the trap of her existence by founding what will become the Shaker Movement, which the daughter to whom she gives birth at the end of the novel will take to America. The mystery of Bartholomew's disappearance is never solved, and the reader is left to decide where the truth lies. For Rebecca, the central quester, the truth she experienced in the cave gives her the freedom to choose a new life, which is the object of the quest.

Carol M. Barnum, updated by David W. Cole

OTHER MAJOR WORKS

POETRY: *Poems*, 1973.

NONFICTION: *The Aristos: A Self-Portrait in Ideas*, 1964; *Shipwreck*, 1974; *Islands*, 1978; *The Tree*, 1980; *The Enigma of Stonehenge*, 1980 (with Barry Brukoff); *A Brief History of Lyme*, 1981; *Lyme Regis Camera*, 1990; *Wormholes: Essays and Occasional Writings*, 1998; *Conversations with John Fowles*, 1999 (Dianne L. Vipond, editor).

MISCELLANEOUS: *The Ebony Tower*, 1974 (novella, 3 short stories, and translation of a French medieval romance).

BIBLIOGRAPHY

Acheson, James. *John Fowles*. New York: St. Martin's Press, 1998. An excellent introduction to the life and works of Fowles.

Aubrey, James R. *John Fowles: A Reference Companion*. New York: Greenwood, 1991. An indispensable tool for the student of Fowles. Contains a biography, summary descriptions of Fowles's principal works and their receptions, a perceptive and judicious survey of the principal secondary works treating the Fowles canon, an extensive set of explanatory notes on Fowles's fiction, and a comprehensive bibliography.

Baker, James R., and Dianne Vipond, eds. "John Fowles Issue." *Twentieth Century Literature* 42 (Spring, 1996). A collection of essays on Fowles's work, together with two poems by Fowles and an interview with Fowles conducted by Dianne Vipond.

Barnum, Carol M. *The Fiction of John Fowles: A Myth for Our Time*. Greenwood, Fla.: Penkevill, 1988. Discusses six novels and the short-story collection from the point of view of the quest motif, which unites the seemingly disparate approaches of the fiction under a central theme. Includes notes, index, and a subdivided bibliography.

Foster, Thomas C. *Understanding John Fowles*. Columbia: University of South Carolina Press, 1994. An accessible critical introduction to Fowles's principal works. Contains an annotated bibliography.

Huffaker, Robert. *John Fowles*. Boston: Twayne, 1980. A good overview and introduction to Fowles, including chronology through 1980. Discusses fiction through *Daniel Martin*, focusing on the theme of naturalism. Includes notes, selected bibliography, and index.

Loveday, Simon. *The Romances of John Fowles*. New York: St. Martin's Press, 1985. Includes a chronology through 1983 plus an introductory chapter on the author's life and work. Discusses the fiction through *Daniel Martin*, with a concluding chapter that places Fowles in the romance tradition. Notes, subdivided bibliography, and index.

Palmer, William J., ed. "Special Issue: John Fowles." *Modern Fiction Studies* 31 (Spring, 1985). An excellent collection of essays on the fiction through *Daniel Martin*, plus an interview and a good, selected bibliography, subdivided by individual works, as well as general essays and interviews.

Pifer, Ellen, ed. *Critical Essays on John Fowles*. Boston: G. K. Hall, 1986. A collection of essays previously published elsewhere in journals. A good introduction by the editor is followed by essays organized under two themes: the unity of Fowles's fiction and discussions of individual works. Coverage through *Mantissa*. Includes notes and an index.

Tarbox, Katherine. *The Art of John Fowles*. Athens: University of Georgia Press, 1988. Discusses the novels through *A Maggot* with emphasis on Fowles's dictum to "see whole." Does not include a chapter on *The Ebony Tower*. The last chapter is an interview with the author. Notes, subdivided bibliography, and index.

ANATOLE FRANCE
Jacques-Anatole-François Thibault

Born: Paris, France; April 16, 1844
Died: La Béchellerie, near Tours, France; October 12, 1924

PRINCIPAL LONG FICTION

Le Crime de Sylvestre Bonnard, 1881 (*The Crime of Sylvestre Bonnard*, 1890)

Les Désirs de Jean Servien, 1882 (*The Aspirations of Jean Servien*, 1912)

Thaïs, 1890 (English translation, 1891)

La Rôtisserie de la Reine Pédauque, 1893 (*At the Sign of the Reine Pédauque*, 1912)

Le Lys rouge, 1894 (*The Red Lily*, 1898)

L'Orme du mail, 1897 (*The Elm Tree on the Mall*, 1910)

Le Mannequin d'osier, 1897 (*The Wicker Work Woman*, 1910)

L'Anneau d'améthyste, 1899 (*The Amethyst Ring*, 1919)

Monsieur Bergeret à Paris, 1901 (*Monsieur Bergeret in Paris*, 1922)

L'Histoire contemporaine, 1897-1901, collective title for previous 4 novels; *Contemporary History*)

Histoire comique, 1903 (*A Mummer's Tale*, 1921)

L'Île des pingouins, 1908 (*Penguin Island*, 1914)

Les Dieux ont soif, 1912 (*The Gods Are Athirst*, 1913)

La Révolte des anges, 1914 (*The Revolt of the Angels*, 1914)

OTHER LITERARY FORMS

Of the twenty-five volumes which make up the standard French edition of the complete works of Anatole France, more than fifteen are given over to one form or another of prose fiction: ten novels (thirteen if one counts the tetralogy, *Contemporary History*, as four separate novels), ten collections of short stories, and four volumes of fictionalized autobiography. The remainder of the twenty-five-volume set exhibits a startling variety of literary forms: poetry, theater, biography, history, literary criticism, philosophy, journalism, and polemical writings. France's first publication was a book-length critical study of the French Romantic poet Alfred de Vigny (1868), after which he published two volumes of his own poetry, one containing lyric poems, the other a play in verse, and several long narrative poems. In the 1880's

(Library of Congress)

and 1890's, he wrote a regular weekly column, mostly about books and the literary world, for a prominent Paris newspaper, *Le Temps*. The best of those columns were republished in five volumes under the title *La Vie littéraire* (1888-1892; *On Life and Letters*, 1911-1914). His major venture into the writing of history was *La Vie de Jeanne d'Arc* (1908; *The Life of Joan of Arc*, 1908), published after a quarter of a century of research. That same year, he published his one original prose work for the theater, *La Comédie de celui qui épousa une femme muette* (1903; *The Man Who Married a Dumb Wife*, 1915), a farce based on a well-known medieval fabliau. His major speeches and occasional writings, on such issues of the times as the Dreyfus Affair, socialism, and pacifism, were collected and published in several volumes under the title *Vers les temps meilleurs* (1906, 1949). Philosophical meditations on human nature and civilization can be found in a volume entitled *Le Jardin d'Épicure* (1894; *The Garden of Epicurus*, 1908), consisting of pieces on general subjects originally written for his weekly newspaper column and not included in the volumes of *On Life and Letters*. One may say, in sum, that Anatole France was the complete man of letters, who tried his hand at just about every form of writing practiced in the literary world of his time. It is nevertheless accurate to say that the writing of fiction so dominated his output, throughout his career, that it constituted his true vocation.

ACHIEVEMENTS

The election of Anatole France to the Académie Française in 1896 and his winning of the Nobel Prize in Literature in 1921 were the major public landmarks of the great success and recognition he achieved during his career as a writer, first in his own country and then in the international arena. At the height of his fame, in the early years of the twentieth century, he was widely regarded as France's greatest living author, celebrated for his wit, his wisdom, and his humanitarian vision. The paradoxes of that fame, however, were multiple and heavy with irony: The fame had been an unusually long time in coming (he was nearly fifty years old before he had his first sig-

nificant success with the public), it was based largely on his association with public events rather than on his genuine but esoteric literary talent, and it lasted only briefly. Indeed, the greatest paradox of his fame was its bewilderingly rapid eclipse after his death. His reputation would not regain the luster of his glory years, around the turn of the twentieth century.

France himself lived long enough to be the saddened witness of a major erosion of his fame in a storm of bitter controversy, which made him an object of both worship and hatred but for purely nonliterary reasons. The truth is that the great fame he enjoyed, during a brief period of his life, was of the public sort, only indirectly occasioned by his writings, which, even at their most popular, appealed to a rather narrowly circumscribed audience. One must separate his fame from his achievements as a writer—which is not to say that his achievements were minor, but only that they were literary and aesthetic, hence accessible to relatively few at any time. As a novelist and short-story writer, France made his mark in the fiction of ideas, and as a literary critic, he established, by personal example, the validity of subjective impressionism as a method. Those are the two major achievements of his career in letters, the accomplishments that have affected literary history. To those literary achievements, one should add a more personal achievement: the creation of a highly distinctive, instantly identifiable style of classic purity and elegance, with subtle rhythms and limpid clarity, which perfectly translated the skeptical and gently ironic view he held of the human condition.

BIOGRAPHY

The only child of a well-established Parisian bookdealer, Anatole France, born Jacques-Anatole-François Thibault, was seemingly predestined to the world of books. His father, Noël-François Thibault, ran the sort of bookshop that was also a gathering place of the literati, who would come not only as customers but also as friends. They would sit and talk with the owner, whom they called by the familiar diminutive "France," an abbreviation of François. Once the son was old enough to help in the shop and participate in the daily conversations, he was naturally called "le jeune France," a custom that suggested to young Anatole the pen name he would choose when he began to write. Shy and unassertive by nature and unprepossessing physically, Anatole matured into an unworldly and bookish young man, easily intimidated by the "real" world and much given to periods of solitude and quiet reverie. In his twenties, he did occasional research and editing chores for the publishers of dictionaries and encyclopedias, having definitely decided against following in his father's footsteps as a bookseller. Eventually, he became a reader of manuscripts for a publisher, wrote articles for ephemeral journals, and took a civil servant's position, working in the Senate Library, all the while using his leisure moments to learn the craft of writing. He was thirty-three, and a published but thoroughly obscure and unknown author, when he overcame his timidity long enough to marry, in 1877. The marriage produced one child, a daughter born in 1881, but was otherwise an unhappy relationship for both sides which ended in a bitter divorce in 1893, after a prolonged separation.

France's unhappy domestic life was the backdrop for his long personal struggle to find his own "voice" and establish himself as a writer. By the 1880's, he had abandoned poetry and was experimenting with different modes of prose fiction, trying both the novel and the short-story forms but attracting very little attention from the reading public. Only after he became the regular literary critic for *Le Temps* and had published a genuinely popular work, the novel *Thaïs*, did he feel securely established enough as a writer to give up his post at the Senate Library. Thereafter, all through the 1890's, his books sold well, and he rose rapidly in public esteem, aided in part by a newfound interest in and involvement with politics and public affairs. In particular, the Dreyfus Affair outraged his sense of justice and galvanized him into public action for the first time in his life. He was then a man in his fifties, and he discovered, a bit to his own surprise, a radical social thinker beneath the placid and conservative exterior he had always presented to the world. During the first years of the new century, he became outspokenly anticlerical and socialistic in his views but was soon plunged into disillusionment when he

saw that even victory, as in the Dreyfus Affair, produced little real change in society, and that his own activism served only to make him controversial and the object of vicious attacks, which he found especially painful to endure. This mood of disillusionment drove him to withdraw into himself once more and to give up active involvement in public affairs. His work increasingly concerned the past and took on an unaccustomed satiric edge. The outbreak of World War I tempted him briefly into the public arena once more, to proclaim his pacifist views, but when he was assailed as unpatriotic, he retreated, this time definitively, into the private world of letters. It is perhaps suggestive of the depth of his wounds from the public fray that his literary preoccupations during the final decade of his life were almost exclusively autobiographical. His career as a novelist had effectively ended with the publication of *The Revolt of the Angels* in 1914.

ANALYSIS

The world of books into which Anatole France was born was surely the strongest influence in determining his vocation as a writer, but that influence went far deeper still, for it also determined the kind of writer he would be. Almost all the subjects he chose to write about, in his long career, were derived from or related to books in some way. He was a voracious reader all of his life, and the many books he wrote not only reflect that wide reading but also reveal that what he read was more immediate and more vital to him—more nourishing to his creative imagination, indeed more *real* to him—than the quotidian reality in which he lived. Even when most actively involved in public events, as he was in the years immediately before and immediately after the turn of the century, he tended to approach events as abstractions, dealing with them as intellectual issues, somehow detached from specific occurrences involving specific human beings. This conscious need to convert real events into matter for books can be seen most clearly in the tetralogy that he so pointedly entitled *Contemporary History* and in which he contrived to write about current events as though they were already in the distant past or even the stuff of legend.

Concomitant with his irreducibly bookish view of the world was his almost instinctive taste for storytelling. Whether as reader or as writer, nothing charmed him more than the unfolding of a narrative. Even factual writing—history and biography, for example—he treated as an exercise in storytelling, going so far as to characterize good literary criticism as a kind of novel in which the critic "recounts the adventures of his soul among masterpieces," as he put it in the famous preface to *On Life and Letters*. The art of storytelling was the art he set out to master in his long and difficult apprenticeship, and the storytelling impulse can be identified as the very heart of his vocation as a writer.

To the mind of the man of letters and the instinct of the teller of tales must be added a third characteristic: the outlook of the determined skeptic. France trained himself, from an early age, to question everything and to discern the contradictions and ironies in all forms of human behavior, including his own. He cultivated a perspective of distance and detachment from both people and events, but he learned to temper the bleakness and isolation of such a perspective with feelings of sympathetic recognition of the folly common to all humankind. A subtle blend of pity and irony came to be the hallmark of his view of the affairs of this world, expressed in the tone of gentle mockery with which his celebrated style was impregnated in the works of his maturity. Indeed, all three central characteristics of France—the literary turn of mind, the narrative impulse, and the ironic perspective—can be found in everything he wrote, including the youthful works of poetry, fiction, and literary criticism through which he gradually learned the writer's trade. Those three traits can be seen fully developed for the first time in the novel that won for him his first public recognition, *The Crime of Sylvestre Bonnard*, in 1881.

THE CRIME OF SYLVESTRE BONNARD

Published to the accolades of the Académie Française, *The Crime of Sylvestre Bonnard* provided Anatole France with his first taste of success. The improbable hero of the book is an elderly, unworldly scholar and bibliophile who explains, in his own words, in the form of diary entries, how he came to acquire a coveted medieval manuscript and how he rescued a young girl from poverty and oppression. What holds the reader's interest is not the trivial plot but the character of Sylvestre Bonnard, whose naïve narrative style, in his diary, constantly and unwittingly reveals his own bumbling incompetence in dealing with the practical side of life. The reader quickly recognizes as comical the dramatic earnestness with which the simpleminded scholar narrates the only two "adventures" that have ever intruded into his serene existence. The ironic discrepancy between the excited tone of the narrator and the mundane character of the events he narrates is echoed suggestively in the title, which promises a thriller but delivers nothing more violent than a book lover's crime: Having promised to sell his personal library in order to create a dowry for the damsel in distress he has rescued, Sylvestre Bonnard confesses, at the end of the diary, that he had "criminally" withheld from the sale several items with which he could not bear to part.

Perhaps the greatest skill the author displays in this book is that of artfully concealing the inherent sentimentality of the material. The key device of concealment is mockery: Sylvestre Bonnard's interest in old books and manuscripts is magnified, in both incidents, into a grand and criminal passion by a transparently mock-heroic tone. This device distracts and amuses the reader, preventing inopportune reflections about the "fairy-tale" unreality of the happy ending of each incident. It is also true that the eccentric character of Sylvestre Bonnard is charming and that the novelty of a gentle fantasy, published at the height of the popularity of the naturalistic novel in France, must have struck many readers of the day as a welcome relief. It was for such reasons, no doubt, that the novel enjoyed mild critical acclaim and modest sales in 1881, even as its author, sternly self-critical, recognized its limitations of both form and content and set about immediately trying to do better. What France retained from *The Crime of Sylvestre Bonnard* for future use was the tone of gentle and sympathetic irony about human foibles. In the decade that followed, he experimented with fictionalized autobiography, tales of childhood, and themes borrowed from history or legend, seeking above all a composition that he—and his readers—could recognize as a fully realized work of art. He reached that goal with the publication of *Thaïs* in 1890—his first critical and popular success.

THAÏS

The story of Thaïs, the courtesan of Alexandria, has a bookish source, as does most of France's fiction; he changed the legend of Thaïs, however, by giving the central role in the tale to the monk, Paphnuce, whose ambition for saintliness inspires in him the project of converting the notorious actress and prostitute to Christianity. The well-known plot, in which the saintly monk succumbs to sin even as the notorious sinner seeks salvation in piety, is thus, in France's version, seen almost exclusively from the point of view of the monk. The character of Thaïs is developed hardly at all, while the complex motivations of Paphnuce are analyzed and explored in detail. This imbalance in the point of view, however, does not affect the fundamental irony of the story. Thaïs, though superficially presented, is shown clearly to be a seeker of pagan pleasure and prosperity, who yet was influenced in early youth by piety, having been secretly baptized, and whose growing fear of death and damnation happens to make her receptive to the preachings of Paphnuce at that particular time of her life. Paphnuce, on the other hand, has had a long struggle against his own sensuality in trying to live as a monk, and is unaware that his sudden project of converting Thaïs is really prompted by his unconscious but still unruly sensual yearnings. When the two meet, therefore, each is ignorant of the other's true disposition, and Paphnuce, moreover, is ignorant of his own desires. Their encounter is thus fated to be sterile, for by that time, Thaïs is already on her way to salvation, and Paphnuce is proceeding precipitously in the opposite direction. France exploits the irony of their opposing trajectories by making the occasion of their meeting the longest and most concentrated episode in the book. The effect is structural: The book is designed as a triptych, with the shorter first and last segments employed to introduce the protagonists and then to record the ultimate fate of each, while the middle segment, equal in length to the other two combined, examines and analyzes their encounter from every angle and demonstrates the impossibility of any fruitful contact between them, because by that time each is in an unanticipatedly different frame of mind.

The structure of the book is perhaps what critics and public admired most about *Thaïs*. It has a satisfying aesthetic quality which announced that France had mastered the sense of form necessary for the achievement of a work of art. The book's success must also, however, be attributed to the subtle complexity of the ideas the author was able to distill from what is, after all, little more than a mildly indecorous comic anecdote. *Thaïs* is a profound and suggestive exploration of the hidden links between religious feeling and sexual desire and, beyond that, of the intricate and unexpected interplay between pagan and Christian ideals and thought and between worldliness and asceticism as patterns of human behavior. In this novel, characterization and realistic description count for comparatively little, and in spite of the daring subject matter, there is not a hint of prurience. The best effects are achieved by a tasteful and harmonious blend of elegant style, well-proportioned structure, and subtle ideas, all presented with gentle irony through the eyes of an amused and skeptical observer. *Thaïs* remains a delight for the thoughtful and attentive reader, one of France's finest achievements.

At about the same time as *Thaïs* was being composed, France was also diligently exploring the short-story form. Employing similar material from history or legend, he was striving to find the ideal fusion of form and content that would yield a work of art in that genre also, and in some of the stories of the volume entitled *L'Étui de nacre* (1892; *Tales from a Mother of Pearl Casket*, 1896), notably the famous "Procurator of Judea" and "The Juggler of Our Lady," he succeeded as fully as he had for the novel in *Thaïs*. Thereafter, having earned his artistic spurs in both the novel and the short story, France developed his career in both domains, alternating a novel and a volume of short stories with something approaching regularity over the next twenty years. What is notable in the work of those years is the visible effort he made to avoid the facile repetition of past successes, to explore and experiment with new techniques, and to strive to develop and grow as an artist. During the 1890's, for example, he followed the gemlike stories of *Tales from a Mother of Pearl Casket* with a comic fantasy of a novel called *At the Sign of the Reine Pédauque*, then used a trip to Florence, Italy, as inspiration for a volume of short stories, *Le Puits de Sainte-Claire* (1895; *The Well of Saint Clare*, 1909), and a surprisingly conventional love story, *The Red Lily*, appearing in 1894. Those publications confirmed his newly won stature as a major writer and earned for him election to the Académie Française in 1896.

CONTEMPORARY HISTORY

His next project, *Contemporary History*, began as a series of weekly newspaper articles commenting on current events by means of anecdotes and illustrative tales. Soon he began interconnecting the articles by using the same set of characters in each. The articles could have formed the basis for a volume of short stories, but instead, France conceived the notion of weaving selected articles from one year's output into a novel that would record the main events of that year in a kind of fictionalized history. It was a bold experiment, which eventually ran to four volumes and occasioned some brilliant writing and the creation of one truly memorable character, Monsieur Bergeret, a scholar and teacher of a wittily ironic turn of mind, who usually articulated the author's own skeptical view of public events. Some consider *Contemporary History* to be France's finest work, but while it does make unflaggingly entertaining reading, as well as offer a valuable historical record, it may be too randomly structured and too variable in tone to be artistically satisfying for the sophisticated modern reader. It deserves respect, however, both as an interesting experiment in a new kind of fiction and as the inauguration of a new thematic vein in France's work: the overt exploitation of public events, especially politics, in the writing of fiction. The novels and short stories published between 1900 and 1914 are almost all in this new political vein, sometimes seriously polemical, more often comic and satiric. The most widely read work of that period is the amusing and clever *Penguin Island*, which gives a brief and jaun-

diced view of French history as though it were a history of a society of penguins. The masterpiece of this period, however, and probably the finest of all Anatole France's novels, is his reconstruction of the atmosphere of the French Revolution, called *The Gods Are Athirst*, published in 1912.

THE GODS ARE ATHIRST

France's strong interest in the period of the French Revolution was undoubtedly inspired by his youthful browsing in his father's bookshop, which specialized in that subject. During the 1880's, France began work on a novel about the revolutionary period, but he abandoned it, rearranging some of the completed fragments into short stories that turned up, a few years later, in the collection *Tales from a Mother of Pearl Casket*. By 1910, when he began to work on a new novel of the Revolution, he had been through his own personal "revolution"—involvement in the Dreyfus Affair and public espousal of socialism—only to suffer rapid disillusionment with the way human nature seems inevitably to distort and betray ideals. Something of that disillusionment must have shaped *The Gods Are Athirst*, for it concentrates on the process by which the Reign of Terror developed out of revolutionary zeal for liberty, equality, and fraternity and, by means of the inclusion of a large and varied cast of characters, seeks to depict how daily life was affected by this process. The novel is set in Paris and covers a time span of about two years, from 1792 to 1794.

At the very heart of the novel, France places a struggling young painter, a pupil of Jacques Louis David, whose name is Évariste Gamelin and who, in 1792, is active in the revolutionary committees of his quarter. Gamelin is depicted as a mediocre artist but one who is serious in his devotion both to art and to the humanitarian ideals of the new Republic. His seriousness is a function of his youthful innocence, which is unrelieved by any element of gaiety or humor but which endows him with a capacity for tender feelings of affection or sympathy. Those tender feelings are the noble source of his support for the Revolution, but he gets caught up in complex and emotionally charged events that he is incapable of understanding, and, as a member of a revolutionary tribunal, he unwittingly betrays his own humanitarian principles by voting for the execution of innocent people to satisfy the bloodthirsty mob of spectators. Gamelin thus embodies the book's fundamental and deeply pessimistic theme, which is that even decent individuals and noble ideals will fall victim to the winds of fanaticism. At the ironic end of the novel, Gamelin the terrorist is himself condemned and executed by the Reign of Terror.

Gamelin is surrounded by an array of different types who give magnificent density to the novel's re-creation of the past. Most memorable, perhaps, is Maurice Brotteaux, a neighbor of Gamelin and a former member of the nobility, now earning his living by making puppets to sell in toy shops. Brotteaux is a skeptic and a witty ironist—unmistakably the author's alter ego—who, though not unsympathetic to the Revolution, deplores its decline into fanaticism, consoling himself by reading his ever-present copy of Lucretius's *De rerum natura*. The author's intentional irony in this detail is that the Latin poet's work had the original purpose of explaining nature to his contemporaries without reference to the supernatural, in order thus to liberate his compatriots from their superstitious fear of the gods. As the novel's title suggests, Lucretius's noble project is a futile exercise when the gods thirst for blood. Gamelin's fiancée, the voluptuous Élodie, adds a fascinating psychological element to the novel, for as her lover Gamelin grows more and more savage in his condemnation of his fellow citizens, she is surprised to discover that, her horror of him notwithstanding, her sensual attraction to him intensifies: The more blood there is on his hands, the more uncontrollable her passion becomes.

The novel is masterful in its smooth handling of the welter of significant characters and details, the unobtrusive integration of known historical figures and events into an invented narrative, and the creation of both a sense of inevitable tragedy in the action and the feel of epic grandeur in the composition as a whole. It is an impressively vast canvas the author attempts to encompass here—the greatest and most complex of his career. Although there is, of necessity, much weaving back and forth from setting to setting and from one group of characters to another,

the clarity and focus of the narrative line are never blurred, and the careful structure accentuates for the reader the inexorability of the mounting dramatic tension enveloping more and more of the novel's characters. In the manner of a classical tragedy, the novel closes with the return of uneasy calm after the catastrophe and the indication that the dead will be quickly forgotten and that life will go on as before. The final paragraph shows Élodie taking a new lover and employing the same endearments to him as she had used at the start of her affair with Gamelin.

The Gods Are Athirst does not quite attain the majestic historical sweep that a subject such as the French Revolution might be expected to command, perhaps because the figure at its center, Évariste Gamelin, is deliberately not cast in the heroic mold. Yet it is a fine and powerful novel, and its unforgettable images carry their intended message to issues beyond the events described, revealing something fundamentally important about human conduct in any revolution and, indeed, in any group situation subject to the volatile incitements of mob psychology. This brilliant novel, written when the author was nearly seventy, proved to be the artistic culmination of France's long career. The novel that followed it, *The Revolt of the Angels*, is a merry fantasy of anticlerical bent, amusing to read but making no artistic or intellectual claims to importance. It proved, simply, that this veteran teller of tales still had the skill and magic, at seventy, to hold the attention of the reading public.

THE RED LILY

As a writer of fiction, France has always eluded classification. He showed little interest in the precise observation of daily reality that was the hallmark of his naturalist contemporaries, nor did he strive to win fame with sensational plotting, flamboyant characters, or studies in spicily abnormal psychology. Though allied, at certain times, with the Parnassians and the Symbolists, he never submitted himself fully to their aesthetic discipline in his own art. He followed his own bent, and because he was so steeped in books and erudition, so unsociable and so fond of solitude, and so little driven by ambition, he tended to cut a strange and solitary figure in the literary world. In both manner and matter, he was really quite unlike anyone else then writing. Probably nothing contributed more to his uniqueness as a writer than his absolute addiction to ideas. The originating inspiration for everything he wrote was neither an event nor a character nor a situation nor even a new literary trick to try out, but ever and always an idea, a concept, an abstraction that he wanted to bring to life by means of a story, a play, or a poem. Even his most conventional novel, *The Red Lily*, seems to be only a routine story of frustrated love and jealousy. What truly animates that novel is the daring concept of feminine independence, which entrenched social attitudes and the habits of male possessiveness in love relationships put out of the reach of even the most lucid and intelligent women, even in that haven of enlightened individualism, Florence. Though not a great novel, *The Red Lily* penetratingly probes an idea that was very advanced for the time: the idea that a woman who conceives the ambition to be a person in her own right, rather than an accessory to someone else's life, faces tragically insuperable obstacles. One can identify a seminal idea of that kind at the very center of the concerns of every novel and every short story France wrote. Ideas are his trademark—not surprisingly, because his literary imagination was so completely grounded in books, rather than in life, and because his carefully maintained view of the world was a skepticism so systematic, and so bathed in irony, that it kept reality at a distance and made the life of the mind virtually the only life he knew. Such a writer is not for everyone, but in spite of the low ebb of his reputation since his death, his audience will never entirely vanish as long as there are those who relish the pleasures of the intellect.

Murray Sachs

OTHER MAJOR WORKS

SHORT FICTION: *Nos Enfants*, 1886; *Balthasar*, 1889 (English translation, 1909); *L'Étui de nacre*, 1892 (*Tales from a Mother of Pearl Casket*, 1896); *Le Puits de Sainte-Claire*, 1895 (*The Well of Saint Clare*, 1909); *Clio*, 1900 (English translation, 1922); *Crainquebille, Putois, Riquet, et plusieurs autres récits profitables*, 1904 (*Crainquebille, Putois,*

Riquet, and Other Profitable Tales, 1915); *Les Contes de Jacques Tournebroche*, 1908 (*The Merry Tales of Jacques Tournebroche*, 1910); *The Garden of Epicurus*, 1908; *Les Sept Femmes de la Barbe-Bleue et autres contes merveilleux*, 1909 (*The Seven Wives of Bluebeard*, 1920); *The Wisdom of the Ages and Other Stories*, 1925; *Golden Tales*, 1926.

PLAYS: *Crainquebille*, pb. 1903 (English translation, 1915); *La Comédie de celui qui épousa une femme muette*, pb. 1903 (*The Man Who Married a Dumb Wife*, 1915).

NONFICTION: *Alfred de Vigny*, 1868; *La Vie littéraire*, 1888-1892 (5 volumes; *On Life and Letters*, 1911-1914); *Le Jardin d'Épicure*, 1894 (*The Garden of Epicurus*, 1908); *Vers les temps meilleurs*, 1906, 1949; *La Vie de Jeanne d'Arc*, 1908 (*The Life of Joan of Arc*, 1908); *Le Génie latin*, 1913 (*The Latin Genius*, 1924); *Sur la voie glorieuse*, 1915.

MISCELLANEOUS: *The Complete Works*, 1908-1928 (21 volumes); *Œuvres complètes*, 1925-1935 (25 volumes).

BIBLIOGRAPHY

Brousson, Jean Jacques. *Anatole France Abroad.* New York: Robert M. Bride, 1928. This biography reads more like a novel than a work of scholarship, but it gives a firsthand portrait of France by his secretary.

_____. *Anatole France Himself: A Boswellian Record.* Philadelphia: Lippincott, 1925. The first volume of Brousson's biography. As the subtitle indicates, the book imitates Boswell's life of Dr. Johnson, providing colorful scenes and lively dialogue. A good introduction to the milieu in which France became a writer.

George, W. L. *Anatole France.* New York: Henry Holt, 1915. An early but still valuable introductory study, with chapters on the satirist and critic, the philosopher and theologian, the historian and politician, the craftsman and man.

Jefferson, Carter. *Anatole France: The Politics of Skepticism.* New Brunswick, N.J.: Rutgers University Press, 1965. Jefferson evaluates France in literary terms, noting that earlier studies support or quarrel with his opinions. Nevertheless, his chapter titles suggest an approach not altogether different from his predecessors: "The Conservative," "The Anarchist," "The Crusader," "The Socialist," "The Bolshevik." Includes notes and bibliography.

Tylden-Wright, David. *Anatole France*. New York: Walker and Company, 1967. A lively evocation of the epoch in which France thrived as a writer. Written more for the general reader than the scholar. Contains a bibliography but no notes.

Virtanen, Reino. *Anatole France*. New York: Twayne, 1968. An excellent introductory study, with chapters on France's childhood and youth, his early fiction, his mature work as novelist and critic, and on his legacy. Provides chronology, notes, and annotated bibliography.

(Library of Congress)

HAROLD FREDERIC

Born: Utica, New York; August 19, 1856
Died: Kenley, Surrey, England; October 19, 1898

PRINCIPAL LONG FICTION

Seth's Brother's Wife: A Study of Life in the Greater New York, 1887
In the Valley, 1890
The Lawton Girl, 1890
The Return of the O'Mahony, 1892
The Copperhead, 1893
Mrs. Albert Grundy: Observations in Philistia, 1896
The Damnation of Theron Ware, 1896
March Hares, 1896 (as George Forth)
Gloria Mundi, 1898
The Market Place, 1899

OTHER LITERARY FORMS

Harold Frederic was a journalist by profession so it is no surprise that he wrote a considerable amount of nonfiction. A large portion of his copy for *The New York Times* was essayistic and well researched and developed. Extended pieces also appeared regularly in English and American magazines. Two sizable groups of dispatches were brought out in book format, *The Young Emperor William II of Germany: A Study in Character Development on a Throne* (1891) and *The New Exodus: A Study of Israel in Russia* (1892). The first of these is not a notable work, despite the fact that its subject became one of the crucial figures of the early twentieth century—and despite the fact that, like almost all of Frederic's fiction, it is a character study. The second work, however—a series of reports on pogroms under Czar Alexander III—was so effective that Frederic became *persona non grata* in Russia. One is tempted to add to his list of nonfiction the novel *Mrs. Albert Grundy*, a book that hangs by a narrative thread and is precisely what its subtitle proclaims: *Observations in Philistia*, that is, satirical sketches of the London bourgeoisie.

Also not surprising for a journalist, Frederic tried his hand at short fiction. His output ranges from poorly written juvenile beginnings to very readable stories about Ireland to a number of short novels and short stories about the Civil War. These latter pieces are his best; they are collected in variously arranged editions and attracted the attention of writers such as Stephen Crane. In them, Frederic examines the effect of the war on the people at home in central New York through insightful and striking situations and through a skillful handling of description, dialogue, and point of view.

ACHIEVEMENTS

Writing a preface for a uniform edition for Scribner's 1897 edition of his Civil War stories, *In the Sixties*, Frederic remarks about the upstate New York places and people in his fiction that "no exact counterparts exist for them in real life, and no map of the district has as yet been drawn, even in my own mind." This statement was written at a time when Frederic had left his American fiction behind and turned his attention to English matters; the journalist who desired fame as a serious writer did not wish to be taken for someone who merely transcribed the personal experiences of his youth. Although Frederic's fiction is almost evenly divided between American subject matter on the one hand and English and Irish on the other, the influence of America is felt even in the non-American works, and Frederic's acknowledged masterpiece, *The Damnation of Theron Ware*, is thoroughly American.

Thomas F. O'Donnell has argued that Frederic is upstate New York's greatest writer since James Fenimore Cooper. In his regional novels, Frederic studies politics (*Seth's Brother's Wife*), history (*In the Valley*), socioeconomics (*The Lawton Girl*), and religion (*The Damnation of Theron Ware*), and thus gives a comprehensive view of his part of the world. Just as Gustave Flaubert anchors his sweeping presentation of human passions in *Madame Bovary* (1857) in the Caux, a rural district of Normandy which easily matches the provinciality of the Mohawk Valley, so, too, does Frederic derive the Jamesian solidity of specification so central to the art of the novel from the authoritatively detailed depiction of his native region.

Although his first model was the successful popular French combination of Erckmann-Chatrian, Fred-

eric grew into a major writer because of his keen observation (sharpened by his reportorial work), his Howellsian sympathy with the common man, and above all, his Hawthornian understanding of the truth of the human heart and the complexity of the American Adam. Hence, Frederic is partly a realist, like Flaubert, and partly a romancer, like Nathaniel Hawthorne, but also, like both of these, a writer with universal themes that are embedded in regional actuality. Were it not for his premature death, he might well have duplicated the achievement of his American fiction with his English fiction. As it is, his reputation will stand on his American works.

BIOGRAPHY

Harold Frederic was born on August 19, 1856, in Utica, a small city of then about twenty thousand, situated in the picturesque Mohawk Valley of upstate New York. His family tree reached far back into colonial times to Dutch and German farmers and artisans, and he could proudly point out that all four of his great-grandfathers had fought in the Revolutionary War. When Frederic was only a year and a half old, his father died in a train derailment; his mother, however, was energetic and capable and kept the family above water until she remarried. She was a somewhat severe woman, not given to spoiling her children, and Frederic always remembered the early morning chores he had to do in the family milk and wood businesses before setting out for school. He also remembered the Methodist upbringing he received and the unseemly bickerings among the parishioners of his neighborhood church.

Like many children at the time, Frederic did not receive extensive schooling and was graduated from Utica's Advanced School at the age of fourteen. For the next two years, he worked for local photographers, slowly progressing from errand-boy to retoucher. He then tried his luck in Boston, dabbling in art and working for a photographer, but in 1875, he returned to Utica and changed his career by becoming a proofreader for the town's Republican morning paper, shortly afterward switching to its Democratic afternoon counterpart. By this time, Utica had almost doubled its population and had become a political center of the first order, giving the state a governor in Horatio Seymour and the country two senators in Roscoe Conkling and Francis Kernan (it would later add a vice-president in James Sherman). Frederic became a firm Democrat and took a lively interest in politics. He soon became a reporter for his paper and also began writing fiction; it was sentimental and imitative beginner's work, but enough of it was published to encourage him.

The centennial celebration of the Battle of Oriskany in 1877 proved to be an intellectual milestone in Frederic's life. He helped prepare the occasion, convinced that the battle had been a turning point of the war and not merely a minor skirmish away from the major battlefields. As he listened to Horatio Seymour's call for a greater awareness on the part of the living of their proud and important history, Frederic resolved to write a historical novel that would give the Mohawk Valley its due and its present inhabitants the historical connectedness Seymour demanded. The regionalist Harold Frederic had come into being, even though *In the Valley* was not published until 1890, respectively and affectionately dedicated to the memory of the late governor.

That fall, Frederic married his neighbor Grace Williams. At that point, he was able to support a family because of his financial success at the *Observer*, becoming news editor in 1879 and editor in 1880, a seasoned and successful journalist before he turned twenty-four. During that time, Frederic's Methodism was softened through his friendship with Father Terry, an accomplished Irish Catholic priest with a modern and unorthodox outlook who introduced him to Utica's growing Irish community. For the rest of his life, Frederic would be a champion of the Irish, and he paid literary tribute to Father Terry and his circle of friends a few years later in his finest novel.

In 1882, Frederic took another step ahead in his career in becoming editor of the *Evening Journal* in Albany, the state capital. Barely settled in town, the Democratic editor made his Republican paper bolt the party line, thereby helping Grover Cleveland become governor. Cleveland appreciated the support and took a genuine liking to the young newspaperman. Frederic was even bolder—and quite prophetic— the

following year when he wrote that Cleveland ought to run for President. In early 1884, the paper changed ownership, and Frederic lost his job. Helped by the recommendation of Cleveland's chief lieutenant, he secured a position as foreign correspondent with *The New York Times* and sailed for England with his wife and their two daughters.

Frederic's position with the respected American paper and a letter of introduction from Governor Cleveland soon established him in London. A daring tour of cholera-stricken Southern France made him a celebrity, and Cleveland's accession to the presidency made Frederic a person of importance. He was admitted to a number of London clubs, where he met many of England's political leaders, the men behind Irish home rule, and the foremost intellectuals, artists, and writers of the day. In this milieu, being only a newspaper correspondent was not satisfactory to Frederic; he set about his literary career with great determination and energy, hoping to become financially independent of journalism and famous as well.

From 1887 on, Frederic's novels appeared in rapid succession, and while they brought him considerable contemporary reputation (*The Damnation of Theron Ware* was a sensation on both sides of the Atlantic Ocean), they did not bring him financial independence. That would have been hard to do even if the sales had been bigger, since Frederic enjoyed a comfortable lifestyle and had a growing family to support. In fact, he had to support two families, for in 1890, he met and fell in love with Kate Lyon, a fellow upstate New Yorker, openly established a second household, and subsequently had three children with her. For some time, Harold and Grace Frederic had been drifting apart. While he split his time between his two families, it was Kate's place that became the center of his intellectual and artistic life, and it was there, for example, that he entertained his friend Stephen Crane.

Financial necessities put a great strain on Frederic. Between his continuing journalistic work (which he carried out thoroughly and faithfully and which involved several extended trips to the Continent), his writing (for which he continued to educate himself by reading widely), his club life, and his family life (including return visits to America and to his beloved Mohawk Valley as well as vacations in Ireland), he simply wore himself out. Of imposing physique, he drew upon his strength so recklessly that he suffered a stroke in August, 1898, from which he never recovered. Kate Lyon's resistance to doctors and her trust in a Christian Science healer led to a widely publicized manslaughter trial after Frederic's death on October 19; eventually, the defendants were acquitted. Heavily in debt, Frederic had left his family in such financial trouble that friends took up a collection. Five months later, Grace died of cancer. In 1901, the ashes of Harold and Grace Frederic were brought home to their native valley.

ANALYSIS

Harold Frederic was not one of those writers who burst upon the scene with a *magnum opus* and then fade from view; rather, his writing steadily improved from *Seth's Brother's Wife* to his masterpiece, *The Damnation of Theron Ware*. Ever since the Oriskany Centennial, Frederic's ambition had been the writing of *In the Valley* as the great American historical novel. The preparation for this book was so slow and painstaking that it took years, as well as the experience of writing *Seth's Brother's Wife* first, to complete the Revolutionary War novel. *In the Valley* interprets the Revolutionary War as more of a struggle between the democratic American farmers and the would-be aristocratic American landed gentry than as a conflict between crown and colony. It gives a stirring description of the Battle of Oriskany, but its plot is trite, pitting the sturdy Douw Mauverensen against the slick Philip Cross as political opponents and rivals for the same woman.

In his uniform-edition preface, Frederic states that he firmly controlled everything in *Seth's Brother's Wife* and *In the Valley*, but that in *The Lawton Girl*, "the people took matters into their own hands quite from the start." More than one great novelist has insisted that in truly great fiction, the author does not prescribe to his characters but rather allows them to unfold as they themselves demand, integrating them into the whole. *The Lawton Girl* is a respectable book, despite some plot and character contrivances,

for the longer rope Frederic had learned to give to his characters and for his continuing ability to ground his work in regional authenticity.

Before *The Damnation of Theron Ware* appeared, Frederic had published *The Return of the O'Mahony*, a playful work that expresses his strong interest in Ireland and Irish home rule. Even in this pleasant book, there is, as Austin Briggs and others have noted, the abiding sense of a past that conditions the present, a theme familiar from Nathaniel Hawthorne's *The House of the Seven Gables* (1851). *March Hares* (published under the pseudonym of George Forth), is a comedy of mistaken identities in a make-believe world. These light works were followed by the weightier novels *Gloria Mundi* and *The Market Place*. *Gloria Mundi* is essentially concerned with an investigation of the English aristocracy, which Frederic shows as a hollow, outdated remnant of medieval caste structure. This major theme is accompanied by a variety of probing social observations, at the end of which stands the insight of the new Duke of Glastonbury: "A man is only a man after all. He did not make this world, and he cannot do with it what he likes. . . . There will be many men after me. If one or two of them says of me that I worked hard to do well, and that I left things a trifle better than I found them, then what more can I desire?"

This distillation of Frederic's ultimate philosophy of life is evident as early as Seth Fairchild, but it is not a view shared by Theron Ware or the central figure of *The Market Place*, Joel Stormont Thorpe. Ware has visions of greatness and power; Thorpe is the most ruthless and most successful of financiers and prepares by way of sham philanthropy to go into politics and rule England. Frederic's final assessment of people in this world is therefore a very balanced and realistic one: One would like to have the Seth Fairchilds without the Theron Wares and the Stormont Thorpes, but the wish is not going to make those who want to do with the world what they like desist or disappear. The present will always have to find its own way against the past and will always in turn become the next present's past; so passes the glory of the world, and so also does the world go on and on in continuous struggle between good and evil.

SETH'S BROTHER'S WIFE

Seth's Brother's Wife has all the strengths and weaknesses of a respectable first novel, but only in the late twentieth century did critics begin to take it as something more than a mixture of realistic regionalism and sentimental melodrama. Its very title is confusing, since Seth Fairchild, not Isabel, is the book's main character, since personal integrity rather than amatory complication constitutes the book's principal theme, and since—as the subtitle, *A Study of Life in the Greater New York*, signals—the book's compass reaches well beyond the three people mentioned in the title. Set in the Mohawk Valley region in the early 1880's, *Seth's Brother's Wife* is the familiar story of a young country lad who goes to town, experiences sometimes severe growing pains, but in the end prevails because of his basic personal decency and his values, which, though tested to the breaking point, hold and are therefore rewarded. Frederic called the novel a romance, and one does well to see it in a line of American stories of initiation that begins, if not with Benjamin Franklin's *The Autobiography* (1791), then with Charles Brockden Brown's *Arthur Mervyn* (1799-1800), and reaches Frederic by way of Nathaniel Hawthorne.

One of three brothers, Seth comes from a farming family whose fortunes have been declining. His brother John is editor of the local paper; his other brother, Albert, who is college-educated, is a successful New York City lawyer and comes home to establish residence and a political base for his bid to be a congressman. Albert finds Seth a job with the area's leading daily newspaper; reminiscent of Frederic's own career, Seth eventually becomes editor and is instrumental in the paper's bolting from its traditional political adherence. Seth finds himself opposing his brother, to whom he owes his position in the first place, and supporting his friend Richard Ansdell, a principled reform candidate who has done much for Seth's intellectual and moral growth.

In a powerful sequence of chapters all set during the same night, the ruthless Albert corners the well-meaning but immature Seth. Seth has fallen under the spell of Albert's young, neglected, city-bred wife, Isabel, and although he never fully succumbs to the

temptation, Seth feels the sting of Albert's attack on his political purity: How hypocritical that Seth stand on ethics in politics when he was about to make love to his brother's wife. As Albert leaves to discuss with his henchman, Milton Squires, a scheme of buying the nomination, Seth stumbles out into the darkness conscious of his weakness and foolishness, finds his old love Annie, and proposes to her on the spot in order to save himself from himself.

The nominating convention is ruled by the area's political boss, Abe Beekman. Beekman rebuffs Albert's attempt to buy him off (he is in politics for the fun, not the money) and decides to have Ansdell nominated. When news of Albert's death arrives, Beekman turns into the driving force behind the investigation, and after many melodramatic plot complications—including a suspicion that Seth took revenge on his brother—all ends well: Squires is convicted of murdering Albert to get the buy-off money; Seth is united with Annie; Isabel leaves the uncongenial countryside and goes to Washington where, in a pointed undercutting of the validity of happy endings, she will marry Ansdell.

A plot summary of this action-packed book is inadequate to clarify Frederic's major concerns and accomplishments. The conflict between city and country, which is so essential to Arthur Mervyn's initiation, is developed here with forceful realism and admirable balance. Life on the farm is dispiriting, squalid drudgery amid often incredibly vulgar exemplars of humankind, but it is also the smell of blossoms in the orchard and the rustle of autumn leaves underfoot and the taste of fresh cider. Life in the city means not only new cultural and intellectual dimensions but also the distraction of the beer hall and, down the dark alley, the depths of prostitution. In politics, honesty and expediency are played against each other without a facile conclusion; most important, Beekman is no saint and Ansdall no new founding father.

Frederic manages to make none of the major characters a one-dimensional stereotype: The good ones have enough weakness (even Annie does), and the bad ones (even Isabel) have enough strengths to forbid easy and schematic moralizing. Seth is the case in

point. The youngest, handsomest, and most promising of the brothers, he is also the most sluggish and
the most foolish, almost the proverbial fairy-tale late
bloomer. His temporary infatuation with Isabel
makes him say things about his sweetheart Annie that
are as contemptible as Theron Ware's thoughts and
comments about his wife at a similar juncture, but
unlike Ware, Seth—with some help from John and
Annie and even from Albert—catches himself in
time. His ability—which is lacking in Albert, in
Ware, and in Arthur Mervyn—to realize that he has
been as "weak as water" is his saving grace and the
book's chief moral; there is no bedrock in this world
other than the hard-won decency of one's own character. That may not be the basis of the American
dream, Frederic seems to say, but it is much more
than its sobering simplicity might at first suggest,
and after all, the only way to life in this imperfect
world.

THE DAMNATION OF THERON WARE

Whatever differences of opinion literary critics
have had over the years concerning Frederic's novels,
they have been unanimous in designating *The Damnation of Theron Ware* as his masterpiece, and they
have generally accorded it a high rank in American
literature. The book is so complex, ironic, and ambiguous that no unified critical interpretation has
emerged; among the best readings are those of John
Henry Raleigh, Stanton Garner, and Austin Briggs,
and one cannot afford to overlook Edmund Wilson's
caution that no truly great novel was ever built on the
humiliation of its hero.

The novel opens on the closing session of the annual conference of Central New York's Methodist
Episcopal Church. With leisure and deliberation,
Frederic sketches the decline of Methodism in the
faces of its ministers. Successively, the deterioration
of sterling qualities of devotion, honesty, and simplicity is visible in the faces of the younger generations of ministers, with those of the most recently or-
dained reverends showing almost no trace of them.
This verdict, however, is not confined to the clergy.
For most of the parishioners, true worship has long
since given way to elbowing for social position
within the congregation. It is in this spirit that the

standing-room-only crowd listens to the eagerly
awaited announcement by the bishop of the ministe-
rial assignments for the upcoming period of service.

The well-to-do and socially ambitious Tecumseh
congregation, having housed the conference in style
in its fine and new facilities, is bent upon adding to
its glory by adorning itself with an "attractive and
fashionable preacher." On the basis of the sermons
delivered at the conference, the congregation's
choice is the Reverend Theron Ware, a young minister who has made a study of pulpit oratory, and
whom Frederic describes as a "tall, slender young
man with the broad white brow, thoughtful eyes, and
features moulded into that regularity of strength
which used to characterize the American senatorial
type." Ware and his wife, Alice, are quietly informed
that they are Tecumseh's choice, but to the bitter disappointment of the couple and the uncharitable outrage of the congregation, the district's plum is
awarded to an uncharismatic older pastor. Even here,
it is evident that among Theron's and Alice's personal qualities, the spiritual ones are not strongly developed.

Theron is assigned to Octavius, a town twice as
large as their previous one, Tyre, and much larger
than his first entirely rural post. Like Seth Fairchild,
Theron Ware is a country-bred young man who, because of his better than average intellectual abilities,
leaves the farm to move on to bigger and presumably
better things; like Seth, he—at least initially—neither
glorifies nor condemns his country background, and
again like Seth, he marries the loveliest and most refined country girl around. Their first year in Tyre is
filled with all the radiance of a new life together, until they discover that they are heavily in debt, a discovery which forces them into a joyless attempt at
mere survival for the remainder of their time there,
and from which they are miraculously released by a
gift from Abram Beekman, who had figured so im-
posingly in *Seth's Brother's Wife*.

The Octavius congregation is old-fashioned in a
mean way, believing in "straight-out, flat-footed
hell," no milk on Sundays, and no flowery bonnets in
church. Theron's first meeting with the trustees is a
bitter revelation; the very names of their leaders,

Pierce and Winch, suggest the tortures of the Inquisition. Theron rejects their attempt to reduce his already skimpy salary but sacrifices Alice's bonnet without a fight (though not long afterward, he buys himself a new shining hat). To improve his finances, he decides to write a book on Abraham, the Old Testament patriarch. Cogitating about it on a walk, he by chance witnesses the last rites of the Catholic Church upon an Irish workman who has fallen from a tree to his death. The elaborate Latin ceremony with its sonorous, bell-like invocations deeply impresses Theron, as do the priest, Father Forbes, and the organist, the striking Celia Madden. The workman's fall prefigures Theron's own, but it is some time before Frederic's careful structure becomes evident.

The chance acquaintance leads to other meetings between Theron and Celia and Theron and Forbes, entirely destroying Theron's narrowly preconceived notions of the Irish and of Catholicism. His first visit with the urbane and educated priest turns into an eye-opener for Theron: Forbes dismisses Theron's fundamentalist notions of Abraham with a brief survey of modern scholarship on the subject; he discourses learnedly on "this Christ-myth of ours"; he admits to exercising pastoral functions without troubling himself or his congregation overly about fine points of doctrine. Similarly, Forbes's agnostic friend, Dr. Ledsmar, impresses Theron with his scientific learning and the easy authority of his judgments on art, science, and religion. Celia Madden, finally, captivates Theron's emotional side with her sophisticated looks, her self-assured behavior, and her musical proficiency. In their several ways, the lives of these three are firmly grounded in traditions against which Theron's country background and seminary education appear painfully paltry.

The threesome has opened up a new world for Theron, a world that he fervently desires to comprehend and enter. What he calls his "illumination" (Frederic uses light imagery in many key scenes and gave the English edition the title *Illuminations*) is really intoxication: What for others might be light is for him heady wine against which he proves helpless. In his urge to foist himself upon the three, he attempts the sort of manipulation that has made him a slick preacher, substituting public relations techniques for substance. When he condemns everything his life has been, including his wife, Forbes, Ledsmar, and Celia all turn away from him. Forbes—who, despite his latitudinarianism, would never think of maligning his Church—is shocked by Theron's defamation of his congregation and of his Episcopalian roots. Ledsmar, who among other things conducts inhumane scientific experiments, resents Theron's prying into a possible liaison between Forbes and Celia, abruptly terminates their meeting, and gives Theron's name to an evil-looking lizard in his collection. Celia's case is more complicated; in a memorable scene, she practically seduces Theron with her enchanting personality, her bewitching playing of Frédéric Chopin, and her quasi-Arnoldian Hellenism. At a meeting in the forest, she permits the fawning, craven minister to kiss her lightly, a kiss which she later explains as a good-bye, but one which Theron takes quite the other way. Whatever Theron's considerable shortcomings, Celia does play with fire, and it is fitting that Frederic has her apologize in *The Market Place* for the extravagant ways of her youth.

The more Theron is enamored of Celia, the more he hardens himself against Alice (appropriately, Celia is not only a short form of the name of the patron saint of sacred music but also a classy anagram of "Alice"). Alice in turn has been receiving the innocent, chiefly horticultural attentions of the church's junior trustee. Theron, who rationalizes away his own infidelity, suspects Alice and Gorringe and draws self-justification from the situation. His downward progress is rapid and complete, not only through Celia but also through Sister Soulsby, a professional fund-raiser employed by the trustees to void the church debt. She fixes Theron's strained relations with his congregation but requires of him the casting of an immoral, fraudulent vote with his erstwhile nemesis Pierce.

Theron Ware lacks entirely that which saves Seth Fairchild: the ability to be honest with himself, to admit his weakness, to recognize his complicity with evil, and to be grateful for his wife's love. Celia really dismisses Theron for the wrong reason when she tells him that he is "a bore"; much more to the point is the indictment by her brother Michael, who, on his deathbed, gives Theron the ringing "damnation" speech that warrants the book's American title. It is to Sister Soulsby's credit that she puts the fallen Theron Ware together again, sending him (and Alice) to Seattle to go into the real-estate business. Much has been made of that ending; some critics take it to mean that a chastened Theron will begin a new and—more fitting for him—secular life, whereas others see in his political vision at the very end (he sees himself as a United States senator) the continuation of his failure to understand anything about himself. Perhaps one may tolerate immorality more readily in politicians than in clergymen, and perhaps Frederic does not use irony when he describes Theron's features as senatorial in the beginning, but one must also remember that boss Beekman is a rather decent fellow after all, a man whose outstanding characteristic in *Seth's Brother's Wife* is his ability to size up people and whose counsel to Theron to quit the ministry and go into law instead, Theron unfortunately and condescendingly disregards.

Much, too, has been made of Theron Ware as a Faust figure. This is surely a libel on Johann Wolfgang von Goethe's *Faust* (1790) at least. Critics also go too far when they insist that Theron is a fallen Adam. Theron never quests like Faust, and he is never innocent to begin with; his is a myth several numbers smaller than theirs. Conversely, not enough has been made of the money side of Theron Ware. He lives beyond his means and goes into debt in Tyre; he trades his wife's flowery hat off against a sidewalk repair bill; he glories in visions of Celia's wealth; he plays the big spender in New York after "inadvertently" having brought along the church collection. More than any other myth, Frederic's fable is surely about that aberration in the American makeup which accounts for the "In God We Trust" stamped on the quarter dollar.

As in *Seth's Brother's Wife*, so in *The Damnation of Theron Ware*, Frederic makes no one entirely good and no one entirely bad. For the longest time, he manages to make the reader sympathize with Theron. It is only when Theron turns viciously and deviously against his own wife that he is truly damned.

Frederic produced in *Seth's Brother's Wife* a solid first novel. Its strength lies in its authenticity of place, people, and dialect; its weakness in its insistence on a cloak-and-dagger plot, which at times overshadows the basic theme of growth of character. In *The Damnation of Theron Ware*, Frederic achieves a powerful blending of regional ambience and psychological penetration of character, only slightly marred by an occasional touch of melodrama.

Frank Bergmann

OTHER MAJOR WORKS

SHORT FICTION: *The Copperhead and Other Stories of the North During the American War*, 1894; *Marsena and Other Stories of the Wartime*, 1894; *In the Sixties*, 1897; *The Deserter and Other Stories: A Book of Two Wars*, 1898; *Stories of York State*, 1966 (Thomas F. O'Donnell, editor).

NONFICTION: *The Young Emperor William II of Germany: A Study in Character Development on a Throne*, 1891; *The New Exodus: A Study of Israel in Russia*, 1892.

BIBLIOGRAPHY

Bennett, Bridget. *The Damnation of Harold Frederic: His Lives and Works*. Syracuse, N.Y.: Syracuse University Press, 1997. A scholarly biography with a separate chapter on *The Damnation of Theron Ware*. Includes a chronology, detailed notes, and extensive bibliography.

Briggs, Austin, Jr. *The Novels of Harold Frederic*. Ithaca, N.Y.: Cornell University Press, 1969. A thorough study of Frederic's novels, this book is mostly literary criticism, with a chapter on each of the major novels, a bibliography, and an index. The frontispiece is a pencil sketch of Frederic drawn by Briggs himself.

Garner, Stanton. *Harold Frederic*. Minneapolis: University of Minnesota Press, 1969. This short pamphlet is a good general introduction, touching on biography and major works, but has no room for details. The bibliography is not as thorough as those available in the other works.

Myers, Robert M. *Reluctant Expatriate: The Life of Harold Frederic*. Westport, Conn.: Greenwood

Press, 1995. The preface provides a succinct overview of the state of Frederic's reputation. Includes very useful notes and bibliography.

O'Donnell, Thomas F., and Hoyt C. Franchere. *Harold Frederic*. New York: Twayne, 1961. The first book-length study of Frederic, this book is valuable for its annotated bibliography, a chronology of his life and writings, and an index. After a chapter of biography, proceeds to address each of Frederic's novels in a separate section, including a full chapter on *The Damnation of Theron Ware*.

O'Donnell, Thomas F., Stanton Garner, and Robert H. Woodward, eds. *A Bibliography of Writings by and About Harold Frederic*. Boston: G. K. Hall, 1975. The most complete listing of material on Frederic, this bibliography is the place for all students of Frederic to begin their research. Lists all of his works and articles and books, both popular and scholarly, about his works.

CARLOS FUENTES

Born: Panama City, Panama; November 11, 1928

PRINCIPAL LONG FICTION

La región más transparente, 1958 (*Where the Air Is Clear*, 1960)

Las buenas conciencias, 1959 (*The Good Conscience*, 1961)

La muerte de Artemio Cruz, 1962 (*The Death of Artemio Cruz*, 1964)

Aura, 1962 (novella; English translation, 1965)

Zona sagrada, 1967 (novella; *Holy Place*, 1972)

Cambio de piel, 1967 (*A Change of Skin*, 1968)

Cumpleaños, 1969 (novella)

Terra nostra, 1975 (English translation, 1976)

La cabeza de la hidra, 1978 (*The Hydra Head*, 1978)

Una familia lejana, 1980 (*Distant Relations*, 1982)

Gringo viejo, 1985 (*The Old Gringo*, 1985)

Cristóbal nonato, 1987 (*Christopher Unborn*, 1989)

La Campaña, 1990 (*The Campaign*, 1991; first volume of the trilogy *El tiempo romantico*)

Diana: O, La Cazadora Solitaria, 1994 (*Diana, the Goddess Who Hunts Alone*, 1995)

OTHER LITERARY FORMS

In addition to his work as a novelist, Carlos Fuentes has cultivated short fiction throughout his career. His earliest work was a collection of short stories, *Los días enmascarados* (1954; the masked days); this volume and subsequent collections such as *Cantar de ciegos* (1964; songs of the blind) and *Agua quemada* (1980; *Burnt Water*, 1980) have been critically acclaimed. (*Burnt Water*, Fuentes's first short-story collection to be translated into English, contains stories published in earlier collections as well as in *Agua quemada*.) The subjects of these stories are reminiscent of his novels. They are set in contemporary Mexico and are characterized by social and psychological realism. Several stories feature the interpenetration of the real and the fantastic, so much a part of the author's longer fiction.

Fuentes has also written several plays. In 1970, he published *El tuerto es rey* (the blind man is king) and *Todos los gatos son pardos* (all cats are gray). This latter work dramatizes the author's fascination with the subject of the Conquest of Mexico and portrays Hernán Cortés and other historical figures. *Orquídeas a la luz de la luna* (*Orchids in the Moonlight*), which premiered at Harvard University in 1982, is Fuentes's first play produced in the United States.

ACHIEVEMENTS

Fuentes is known the world over as one of Latin America's premier novelists and intellectuals. He has earned this reputation through involvement in international affairs and prodigious creative activity. Fuentes has produced a broad spectrum of literary works in several genres which convey a sense of Mexican life, past and present. The image of Mexico has been projected by means of extremely varied treatments in his works, from the historical and legendary backgrounds of the Conquest in *Terra nostra* to the analysis of contemporary social reality and the profound aftershocks of the Mexican Revolution in

Carlos Fuentes, with his wife Silvia, receiving the Latin Identity award in 1999.
(AP/Wide World Photos)

was fellow at the Woodrow Wilson Center for Scholars in 1974. From 1975 to 1977, Fuentes served as Mexican ambassador to France. Fuentes has also received the Villa-rrutia Prize, Mexico's most important literary award, for *Terra nostra*. Harvard University awarded Fuentes an honorary doctorate in 1983. His literary production as a whole was recognized with the Alfonso Reyes Award and the National Literature Prize in Mexico. The long list of literary prizes he has received also includes the prestigious Miguel de Cervantes Prize (Spain, 1987), the Rubén Darío Prize (1988), the New York City National Arts Club Medal of Honor (1988), and the Orden of Cultural Independence (Nicaragua, 1988).

The Death of Artemio Cruz. While Fuentes has manifested his concern for the historical and social realities of Mexico, he has also experimented with fantastic fiction in his short stories and the novella *Aura*, and he has evoked the voluptuousness of decadent settings in *Holy Place*. In view of Fuentes's achievements in capturing and imagining the myriad faces of Mexican reality, it is hardly any wonder that his literary production must be analyzed from several critical stances. Fuentes has resisted any narrow categorization of his work with the dictum: "Don't classify me. Read Me!" Fuentes is one of Latin America's most popular novelists, and his works are eagerly awaited by critics. He is considered to be on the same level with such luminaries of Latin American literature as Mario Vargas Llosa and Gabriel García Márquez in his desire to produce the "total novel," which epitomizes the aspirations and experiences of humankind.

Fuentes has been in the forefront of Mexican letters for decades. As a young writer in the 1950's, he was a cofounder of the prestigious *Revista mexicana de literatura* (Mexican literary review). In 1972, he was elected to the Colegio Nacional of Mexico. He

BIOGRAPHY

Even though Carlos Fuentes described himself as a product of "petit bourgeois stock," there is nothing common about him. His father was a diplomat, an attaché to the Mexican legation, when he was born. At the age of four, Fuentes learned English in Washington, D.C., where his father served as counselor of the Mexican Embassy. Oddly enough, the dawning of Fuentes's consciousness of Mexico occurred in the United States. He credits his father with having created a fantasy of his homeland, a "non-existent country invented in order to nourish the imagination of yet another land of fiction, a land of Oz with a green cactus road." As a teenager, Fuentes began to travel on his own. He studied the politics, economics, and society of Spanish America, and he developed a sympathy for socialism which he has fervently maintained ever since. Fuentes's interest in socialism blossomed in Chile, especially after learning about Pablo Neruda, whose poetry had already become the anthem of the working person.

While living in Santiago, Fuentes attended The Grange, the Chilean capital's bilingual British school, where he cultivated an appreciation of classical and modern writers. While enrolled there, he began to think about becoming a writer, he has recalled, in order to "show himself that his Mexican identity was real." He started to read the Spanish masters of the Golden Age, and he contributed short stories, written in Spanish, to school magazines. After a six-month stay in Buenos Aires, where he read the great works of Argentine literature, he finally returned to Mexico. As a young but mature man, imbued from afar with the myths of his homeland, Fuentes was finally struck by the contrasts between Mexico and more urbane centers of civilization where he had lived. The Mexico that has become the background of his fiction is a land which still bears the scars of the Mexican Revolution, where the promises of progress clash head-on with the problems of an impoverished indigenous population, and where tangible reality is forever overshadowed by the persistence of the past.

After he developed an ample body of writing on modern Mexico, Fuentes, a combative essayist and crusader against Hispanic dependency upon foreign interests, trained his sights on the United States. On numerous occasions, he has criticized American military and economic involvement in Latin America, and like many other writers from Latin America, he has suffered accordingly. To prevent him from visiting the United States, the Immigration Service branded Fuentes an "undesirable alien"—a ban eventually lifted in response to aroused public opinion. Fuentes has become a spokesman for the preservation of Mexican—and, by extension, Latin American—cultural diversity, arguing the need for an alternative to the choices offered by the world's two superpowers. He has advocated the coexistence of ancient and modern, indigenous and imported traditions in the Hispanic world as an antidote to powerful foreign influences.

Mexican President Luis Echeverría rewarded Fuentes's interest in improving Mexico's international relations by naming him ambassador to France, 1975 to 1977. Since retiring from his diplomatic post, Fuentes has lived in the United States, where he is in great demand on university campuses and at professional meetings as an eminent scholar and stimulating lecturer.

ANALYSIS

Few confrontations in history have been more dramatic or devastating than that between Hernán Cortés and Montezuma II. When the Conquistador, Cortés, met the Aztec monarch, Montezuma, two calendars, two worldviews, and two psychologies collided. The Aztec's cyclic concept of catastrophism which held that the earth and its creatures must die and be reborn every fifty-two years came into direct conflict with the European vision of a linear time and the notion of progress. The Machiavellian Spaniard was perceived by the Aztecs as a god who had returned to his homeland from the East as prophesied in native mythology. On the other hand, Cortés, with fine irony, depicted Montezuma as a simple and naïve man torn by the workings of superstition, a man whose initiative and aggression against a potential enemy were blocked first by shock and then by curiosity about the mortal who was to become his master.

Remote as they seem, these events from sixteenth century Mexico serve as a background for the works of one of modern Mexico's most prolific and honored writers, Carlos Fuentes. Fuentes claims kinship to both great patriarchs of Mexico's past from a biological and cultural standpoint, and the key to their relationship is the notion of diverse worlds in collision which characterized the Conquest and which the modern Mexican has assimilated in his works. To survey the Mexico of Carlos Fuentes is to come in contact with a land of dizzying contrasts and violent conflicts. Fuentes's Mexico is a timeless realm where the steamy and violent past of indigenous Tenochtitlán is evident in a sleazy and materialistic Mexico City built upon the ruins of ancient temples.

As a theoretician of the modern Latin American novel, Fuentes has advocated such marvelous juxtapositions in fiction. For Fuentes, the novel's continued life depends upon a new concept of reality which accommodates a mythic substratum beneath everyday experience. The reader of Fuentes's novels observes a complex Mexican reality in which the barrier between past and present has eroded.

TERRA NOSTRA

Fuentes's reorganization of time is the principal structural element of his masterpiece, *Terra nostra*. This massive, Byzantine work, an ambitious blend of history and fiction, is indeed nothing less than a compendium of Western civilization, from the Creation to the Apocalypse. In a narrower sense, the focus of the work is Hispanic civilization and the historical background of the epoch of discovery and conquest. In keeping with Fuentes's goals for fiction, the work succeeds in erasing temporal and spatial boundaries and becomes a Mexican *Finnegans Wake* (James Joyce, 1939)—timeless, circular, and meticulously constructed.

In the formal divisions of the work, Fuentes places the reader at the center of a maelstrom of times and places. The novel is divided into three sections, "The Old World," "The New World," and "The Next World." Within "The Old World," time abruptly shifts from twentieth century Paris to sixteenth century Spain. Fuentes intends this descent into the past to resemble an excursion into the wellsprings of Hispanic culture. The reader emerges in the Spain of Philip II, the monarch who built the Escorial. The erection in this novel of the mausoleum by El Señor, the embodiment of the Spanish monarch, is a metaphor of Philip's (and, by extension, Spain's) mad obsession with halting the passage of time. It is here that El Señor holes up and futilely resists change.

The futility of this scheme surfaces in the second part of the novel, which chronicles the discovery and conquest of the New World. The promise of new lands and a new vision of time fire the imagination of the Old World. "The Ancient," an indigenous patriarch reminiscent of Montezuma, captures this vision in his retelling of a tribal legend:

> Between life and death there is no destiny except memory. Memory weaves the destiny of the world. People perish. Suns succeed suns. Cities fall. Power passes from hand to hand. Princes collapse along with the crumbling stone of their palaces abandoned to the fury of fire, tempest and invading jungle. One time ends and another begins. Only memory keeps death alive, and those who must die know it. The end of memory is the end of the world.

This new reckoning of time is an embodiment of perpetual change which threatens the stagnation of the Old World in the novel. El Señor, the defender of temporal paralysis, recoils at the threat in the last part of the novel and ultimately fails to freeze Hispanic tradition within the confines of the sixteenth century. His decree that the New World, with its nonlinear passage of time, does not exist is repudiated in an exuberant celebration of change in the novel's conclusion, when the action returns to Paris in the twentieth century.

In addition to the abrupt shifts in time and space which are employed in a particularly radical form in *Terra nostra*, Fuentes exploits throughout his fiction other modern literary techniques, such as hallucinatory imagery, stream of consciousness, interior monologue, and numerous devices adapted from the cinema, including flashback, crosscutting, fades, and multiple points of view. When one considers that the twentieth century is the "Age of Film," it is not surprising that Fuentes's works display a thoroughgoing affinity with cinema. In particular, *Aura*, *Holy Place*, *Distant Relations*, and *The Death of Artemio Cruz* reveal that Fuentes's vision of modern Mexico is perceived through the camera's eye.

AURA

The theme of *Aura*, one of Fuentes's early novels, is the persistence of the past. Fuentes communicates this theme by means of overlaying, as in cinematographic projections, images of light upon darkness and old identities upon youthful characters. The climax of the story features an astounding and erotic union of personalities as his characters from the twentieth century embody personalities of the nineteenth.

Appropriately enough, the catalyst of this experiment in time is a historian, Felipe Montero. A young man dedicated to preserving the past, Montero's ambition is to sum up the chronicles of the Discoverers and Conquistadors in the New World, but financial need forces him to undertake a more modest project. He agrees to edit and publish the papers of a Mexican general, dead since the turn of the century. Consuelo, the General's widow, orders Felipe to live in the ancestral mansion, and he must even learn to write in the style of the General in order to complete the assignment. Surrounded by relics of the past, then, Felipe is gradually seduced by them. What adds ardor to the historian's undertaking is Felipe's discovery of Aura, Consuelo's young niece and companion. During the course of the novel, Felipe learns that Aura is indeed an "aura" of Consuelo's lost youth, a spiritual emanation of the past who is willed into existence to capture Consuelo's early love for the General.

Through a variety of cinematic techniques such as closeups and montage, Fuentes has the illusion of Aura's presence deceive Montero into believing that she is real. The purpose of this deceit is to render, in a visual way, the author's concept of simultaneity. When Felipe observes how the two women seem to mimic each other at a distance, their separate identities are mirror images of each other. For Fuentes, the two women's divergent personas are surface manifestations of an underlying unity. Fuentes's experiment in cinematic fiction is complete when Felipe stares at Aura's image in photographs from the nineteenth century and discovers his own face superimposed on the image of the General. At the end of the novel, Consuelo has succeeded in uniting past and present in her double identity and in that of Felipe. He now embodies the spirit and flesh of the deceased General.

DISTANT RELATIONS

Fuentes's novel *Distant Relations* carries the cinematic overlaying of past and present one step further than in *Aura*. Fuentes acknowledges his debt to the world of film when he dedicates the novel to the Spanish director Luis Buñuel, with whom he collaborated on a screenplay. In addition to the visual impressions of film in this novel, Fuentes evokes the auditory effect of overdubbing in the recurrent citation of lines from Jules Supervielle's poem "La Chambre Voisine" (the adjoining room). The poem sets the scene for the juxtaposition of several settings, each with its own temporal reality and cast of characters; Fuentes intertwines the various plots that correspond to the different settings so that the barriers of time and space dissolve.

The title refers to the phenomenon of secret correspondences between people and to their need to bridge the distances that alienate them from one an-

other. The distant relations (or, more literally, "distant family") of the title are a French Count, a Mexican archaeologist, and a wealthy Frenchman. Fuentes suggests the relationship of the latter two in his choice of a common family name, Heredia. The choice is most fortuitous because it refers to the Spanish word *herencia* (inheritance) and more significantly to two poets of the nineteenth century, one French, José Maria de Hérédia, and the other Cuban, José Maréa Heredia, who were cousins. It is curious, then, that Fuentes cites verses from the French Hérédia's *Les Trophées* (1893; English translation, 1897) but makes no reference to the work of the Cuban Heredia (who spent several years of his life in Mexico). An apt reference might have been taken from his narrative poem "En el teocalli de Cholula" (upon the temple at Cholula). Heredia's poem, like Fuentes's novel, features a surrealistic clashing of realities which leap across the centuries. The narrator of the poem experiences a vivid hallucination of an Aztec human sacrifice which occurred before the arrival of Cortés. Fuentes engages in this kind of novelistic archaeology in *Distant Relations* when the Count's past and that of the two Heredias come together.

HOLY PLACE

A more explicit fascination with film imagery forms the basis for Fuentes's bizarre novel *Holy Place*. The novel claims that filmmaking creates icons which rival those of classical mythology. One case in point is the charismatic Mexican actress Claudia Nervo. She is depicted as a twentieth century siren who lures men to their doom. Her son, Guillermo (affectionately called "Mito," a name derived from the diminutive Guillermito and which also means "myth"), is neurotically attracted to her as well. More a decadent Des Esseintes from the pages of Joris Karl Huysmans's *À Rebours* (1884, 1903; *Against the Grain*, 1922) than a Ulysses, he surrounds himself with voluptuous furnishings from *la belle époque*. This is his personal "sacred zone," his enchanted grotto and refuge, which he needs as an antidote for his mother's rejection.

In the course of the novel, Fuentes analyzes the thralldom exercised by film images upon spectators and the actors themselves. For example, Guillermo pathetically tries to possess his mother by immersing himself in her old films. In this regard, *Holy Place* deftly captures the hypnotic attraction of films as they create a personal fantasy world for Guillermo, provide an escape from chronological time for him, and indelibly preserve his hallucinatory fantasies in a mythological space.

THE DEATH OF ARTEMIO CRUZ

Perhaps the most striking example of cinema's influence on Fuentes's work, however, is *The Death of Artemio Cruz*. Written early in his career, it is one of his most successful novels from a technical and thematic standpoint and is widely regarded as a seminal work of modern Spanish American literature. The novel owes some of its fragmented temporal structure and much of its theme of the deterioration of modern life to Orson Welles's landmark film *Citizen Kane* (1941). Through the use of such techniques as closeup, flashback, deep focus (a technique which *Citizen Kane* pioneered), crosscutting, and recurrent symbolic motifs, Fuentes's novel matches the visual appeal of Welles's cinematographic masterpiece, and it should be read and understood as a motion picture in prose.

Fuentes has discussed his indebtedness to films in general and to Welles in particular in an interview published in *Paris Review* (volume 23, number 82, Winter, 1981). "I'm a great moviegoer. The greatest day in my life as a child was when I was ten and my father took me to New York City to see the World's Fair and *Citizen Kane*. And that struck me in the middle of my imagination and never left me. Since that moment, I've always lived with the ghost of *Citizen Kane*. There are few other great movies which I am conscious of when I write." Welles's influence on Fuentes can be seen throughout *The Death of Artemio Cruz*, in characterization, themes, and filmic techniques. Artemio Cruz is a Mexican Citizen Kane in several basic respects. Fuentes chronicles his rise from an impoverished childhood on the periphery of Mexican society to the heights of power in Mexico City. The mature Artemio becomes the prime mover of a financial empire with holdings in publishing, real estate, banking, and mining. Similarly, Kane, a New York power broker with interests in mining, publishing, real estate, and manufacturing, traces his origins to a simple family in Colorado. During the course of their lives, both men reverse their beliefs from a proletarian admiration for the common person to an authoritarianism which ultimately destroys their relationships with family and friends. Furthermore, their opportunism and cynicism mirror the moral decay of their times. The degeneration of moral values finds its greatest manifestation in the failure of their respective newspapers to print the truth. In this regard, the most salient feature of their resemblance is their manipulation of the press. Both men, thinly veiled replicas of William Randolph Hearst, are publishers who resort to slander for personal gain and to yellow journalism to support their right-wing political causes.

In addition to the characterization of his protagonist, Fuentes borrows various film techniques from *Citizen Kane*. This adaptation of material from the film adds to the novel's complexity and visual richness. For example, one of the most successful reflections of the film is the novel's tightly knit fabric of fragmentary reminiscences. In *Citizen Kane*, Welles breaks up the linear narrative into overlapping vignettes. Here, newsreel footage and interviews with the people who knew Kane best flesh out the portrait of the vulnerable man behind the image of grandeur. Kane's dying word, "rosebud," forces the editors of the newsreel to discover some unifying quality in Kane's life, and it is the quest for the meaning of "rosebud" that serves as the focus of the film. Artemio's conscious and unconscious alternations between past, present, and future tenses and his strange obsession with his son Lorenzo offer a fragmentary record of his life. By deciphering the mysterious relationship between these fragments, deftly scattered throughout the novel, the reader reconstructs the world of Artemio Cruz.

A particularly striking counterpart to Welles's rosebud motif is the recurrent reference to Lorenzo, Artemio's only son. Artemio repeatedly recalls the scene when he and Lorenzo rode on horseback through the hacienda in Vera Cruz near his birthplace. Lorenzo confesses that he must leave Mexico to fight for the Republican cause in Spain. This is their last time together because, as the reader learns in another fragment, Lorenzo dies in the Civil War. Although the significance of this scene becomes clear only gradually, references to Artemio's last meeting with Lorenzo symbolize a tragic defeat, in the same way as "rosebud" signified Kane's disillusionment and his exile from his family. In Lorenzo, Artemio might have been able to combine his own instinct for survival with his son's idealism to produce a morally correct life; with Lorenzo's death, this opportunity is forever lost. Both Kane and Artemio immerse themselves in painful memories which they masochistically cultivate to the end of their lives.

The novel captures the visual starkness of the film in passages that depict characters and situations through a camera's eye, highlighting grotesque detail and situations through closeups and other pictorial techniques. For example, Welles's stumbling, bloated Charles Foster Kane is mirrored in Artemio Cruz, described as a walking mummy at his last New Year's Eve party. Cruz's fall from greatness—a counterpart to Kane's collapse during the opening scenes of the film—is captured in a clinical description of his decaying body in closeup: ". . . he must sense this odor of dead scales, of vomit and blood; he must look at this caved-in chest, this matted gray beard, these waxy ears, this fluid oozing from his nose, this dry spit on his lips and chin, these wandering eyes that must attempt another glance. . . ."

Fuentes reasserts the cinematographic closeup throughout the novel by means of a tight focus on Cruz in direct descriptions reflected in mirrors. Mirrors and reflections are useful for the narrator to witness his own physical deterioration and for the author to practice his virtuosity in manipulating "camera angles" for special effects. Early in the novel, the prosperous Artemio glances in a storefront window to straighten his tie. What he sees is his reflection, "a man identical to himself but so distant, he also was adjusting his tie, with the same fingers stained with nicotine, the same suit, but colorless." Cruz contemplates his image at a distance, as though he were watching a film of himself. In the reflection—as distant as images on a film screen—he sees himself sur-

rounded by beggars and vendors whom he ignores. Through this cinematographic technique, Fuentes projects the image of a solitary Artemio Cruz, cast in the mold of Charles Kane, divorced from the common folk and insensitive to their suffering.

Other mirror images in the novel emphasize the theme of alienation and disintegration of the protagonist, particularly in the hospital scenes where Cruz stares at his twin image in the fragmented mirrors of his wife's and daughter's purses. The doubling of Artemio in mirror images has its source in one of the most important scenes in *Citizen Kane*, a scene which associates the multiple images of the protagonist with a corresponding fragmentation of his personality. At the end of the film, after his second wife leaves him, Kane breaks up her bedroom, smashing pictures and china and yanking down her curtains. From the rubble of her belongings he picks up a small glass ball which, when shaken, produces a miniature snowstorm around a white rose. He utters the word "rosebud" and then strolls leisurely from the room, his face empty of turmoil. Kane then passes between two facing mirrors which reflect his image in infinite series. This scene indicates the extent of Kane's deterioration as he seems to put on a mask of indifference and serenity while he feels his inner self tossed about by failure.

Cruz similarly stands between such facing mirrors in a key scene following the longest fragment of the novel, which deals with Artemio's imprisonment during the Mexican Revolution. Captured by Villa's forces, Cruz, Gonzalo Bernal (the brother of the woman Cruz will later marry), and his friend Tobias, a Yaqui Indian, face execution by a firing squad. Cruz alone survives by giving false information to his captors. The mirror scene following this episode sums up Artemio's instinct for survival, the aspect of his personality that has won out over whatever charitable impulses he may have had earlier in his life. Artemio now wears the impassible mask of indifference to others, Kane's frozen persona in the mirrors:

. . . to recognize yourself; to recognize the rest and let them recognize you: and to know that you oppose each individual, because each individual is yet another obstacle to reach your goal: you will choose, in order to survive you will choose, you will choose from among the infinite mirrors one alone, one alone which will reflect you irrevocably, that will cast a black shadow on the other mirrors, you will shatter them rather than surrender. . . .

Fuentes offsets the tight focus in these mirror closeups with long shots or general establishing shots elsewhere in the novel. His technique of capturing several planes of action occurring simultaneously has its origin in the deep focus of *Citizen Kane*, where this technique is used to juxtapose several characters and situations which impinge upon one another. Perhaps the most remarkable example of deep focus shows Charles Kane's parents arranging for their son's enrollment in a boarding school. Framed by the window in the center of the screen, the young Charles plays outside in the snow with his Rosebud sled, oblivious to events indoors before the camera. In a tight shot, with Charles still in focus, his mother signs the power of attorney which establishes a trust fund for him and which symbolizes his entry into high society. Juxtaposed here are the innocent boy and his parents, who prepare his ticket to the good life. The two planes of action make a harsh visual statement about power. Charles, seen from a distance, is surrounded and overwhelmed by his elders and their financial dealings. Later in the film, in another example of deep focus, a gigantic Kane, in the foreground, dwarfs all the other characters in the scene, emblematic of his monumental power.

Fuentes's equivalent of deep focus can be found throughout the novel in fragments which juxtapose characters and situations. One of these fragments depicts Artemio's arrival at the hacienda of Gamaliel Bernal. A masterful juxtaposition of narrative planes focuses on Artemio—the survivor—telling the family of Gonzalo Bernal how their loved one perished in the Villista execution. Crosscutting from Artemio's explanation at the dinner table to his arrival in town and then to his meeting Gamaliel and Catalina Bernal, Fuentes superimposes several moments in time and space in a single scene. Thus, the reader sees the conniving Artemio in the foreground as he ingratiates himself with the Bernal family; in the background, his arrival in Puebla and the rooting out of information about the Bernals; and in the middle ground, the sumptuous furnishings which Artemio will soon possess.

Here, Fuentes achieves effects of simultaneity that compel the reader/spectator to superimpose the planes of action and modify each event in the light of what precedes and what follows it. Such is the effect of other fragments in the novel which depict Artemio's rise to power after marrying Catalina and after taking over the hacienda after Gamaliel's death. In a scene that depicts Artemio's campaign for political office, he and Catalina ride their buggy through the dusty countryside. They come upon a procession of religious zealots, *penitentes*, who impede their passage. As the narrator describes the grotesque physical deformities of the *penitentes* and their mortification of themselves, he juxtaposes their bloody parade to the religious sanctuary with Artemio's exalted and indifferent ride through their seething masses. The various planes of action appear linked for ironic purposes. In the background, the dust of the arid fields mixes with the clouds of dust raised by the buggy and that of the *penitentes*. The cinematic impact of this scene rivals that of similar settings in Mariano Azuela's photographic *Los de Abajo* (1916; *The Underdogs*, 1929). In the middle ground, the sincerity of the zealots, symbolized by their bloody footprints, is counterbalanced by the cynicism of Artemio's political campaign, which is motivated by hunger for power alone.

Fuentes has said that in all of his works, he offers Mexicans "a mirror in which they can see how they look, how they act, in a country which is a masked country. . . ." Fuentes offers Mexicans more than a mirror, however, for his fiction cinematically projects the spectacle of Mexican life and history on a broad screen in order to preserve and highlight the past.

Howard Fraser, updated by Daniel Altamiranda

OTHER MAJOR WORKS

SHORT FICTION: *Los días enmascarados*, 1954; *Cantar de ciegos*, 1964 (previous two collections published as *Días enmascarados*, 1990); *Poemas de amor: Cuentos del alma*, 1971; *Chac Mool y otros cuentos*, 1973; *Agua quemada*, 1980 (*Burnt Water*, 1980); *Constancia y otras novelas para vírgenes*, 1989 (*Constancia and Other Stories for Virgins*, 1990); *El naranjo: O, Los círculos del tiempo*, 1993 (*The Orange Tree*, 1994); *La frontera de cristal: Una novela en nueve cuentos*, 1995 (*The Crystal Frontier: A Novel in Nine Stories*, 1997).

PLAYS: *Todos los gatos son pardos*, pb. 1970; *El tuerto es rey*, pb. 1970; *Orquídeas a la luz de la luna*, pb. 1982 (*Orchids in the Moonlight*, 1982); *Ceremonias del alba*, rev. ed. pb. 1991.

SCREENPLAYS: *El acoso*, 1958 (with Luis Buñuel; adaptation of Alejo Carpentier's novel); *Children of Sanchez*, 1961 (with Abbey Mann; adaptation of Oscar Lewis's work); *Pedro Páramo*, 1966; *Tiempo de morir*, 1966; *Los caifanes*, 1967.

NONFICTION: *The Argument of Latin America, Words for North Americans*, 1963; *Paris: La revolución de mayo*, 1968; *La nueva novela hispano-americana*, 1969; *El mundo de José Luis Cuevas*, 1969; *Casa con dos puertas*, 1970; *Tiempo mexicano*, 1971; *Los reinos originarios: Teatro hispano-mexicano*, 1971; *Cervantes: O, La crítica de la lectura*, 1976 (*Cervantes: Or, The Critique of Reading*, 1976); *Myself with Others: Selected Essays*, 1988; *Valiente mundo nuevo: Épica, utopía y mito en la novela*, 1990; *El espejo enterrado*, 1992 (*The Buried Mirror: Reflections on Spain and the New World*, 1992); *Geografía de la novela*, 1993; *Tres discursos para dos aldeas*, 1993; *Nuevo tiempo mexicano*, 1994.

BIBLIOGRAPHY

Brody, Robert, and Charles Rossman, eds. *Carlos Fuentes: A Critical View*. Austin: University of Texas Press, 1982. A collection of essays by well-known scholars and critics, covering Fuentes's literary production from various critical standpoints.

Delden, Maarten van. *Carlos Fuentes, México, and Modernity*. Nashville, Tenn.: Vanderbilt University Press, 1998. Analyzes the ongoing tension in Fuentes's works between nationalism and cosmopolitanism, which stands in a complex relationship to the problem of Latin American modernization.

Durán, Gloria. *The Archetypes of Carlos Fuentes: From Witch to Androgyne*. Hamden, Conn.: Shoestring, 1980. Originally published in 1976, this study addresses the character of the witch, central to Fuentes's narrative, from a Jungian point of view. The English version includes a section devoted to the analysis of *Terra Nostra*.

Faris, Wendy B. *Carlos Fuentes*. New York: Frederick Ungar, 1983. An excellent survey, emphasizing two novels, *Where the Air Is Clear* and *The Death of Artemio Cruz*. Includes chronology, biographical introduction, and selected bibliography. The book is divided into five chapters: Early Novels, Short Fiction and Theater, The Essays, Later Novels, and Conclusion.

Helmuth, Chalene. *The Postmodern Fuentes*. Lewisburg, Penn.: Bucknell University Press, 1997. Studies the postmodern features in Fuentes's novelistic production, particularly since 1975. According to Helmuth, the postmodern novels hold a nonmimetic view of the textual representation of reality, which becomes evident when considering the continual reminders of the artificial nature of the written word that Fuentes scattered in his later narratives.

Ibsen, Kristine. *Author, Text, and Reader in the Novels of Carlos Fuentes*. New York: Peter Lang, 1993. A reader-oriented analysis of four major novels: *A Change of Skin, Terra Nostra, Distant Relations*, and *Christopher Unborn*.

Williams, Raymond Leslie. *The Writings of Carlos Fuentes*. Austin: University of Texas Press, 1996. Considering *Terra Nostra* a keystone in Fuentes's narrative production, the author maintains that the early novels contained all major themes and topics later developed by the writer and, by the same token, that the later novels are reworkings and expansion of many of the motifs found in Fuentes's masterpiece.

G

WILLIAM GADDIS

Born: New York, New York; December 29, 1922
Died: East Hampton, New York; December 16, 1998

PRINCIPAL LONG FICTION
The Recognitions, 1955
JR, 1975
Carpenter's Gothic, 1985
A Frolic of His Own, 1994

OTHER LITERARY FORMS

William Gaddis's literary reputation is based upon his novels; he also contributed a number of essays and short stories to major magazines.

ACHIEVEMENTS

Gaddis's work is convoluted, confusing, and difficult, qualities that have led some readers to criticize it. His work is also sophisticated, multilayered, and technically innovative, qualities that have led other readers to consider Gaddis one of the most important writers after World War II, and certainly one of the least appreciated and understood.

Gaddis's accomplishments began to receive greater attention in the late 1960's and early 1970's, during which time he was at work on his second monumental novel, *JR*. Between 1955 and 1970, only a single article on him appeared in the United States, but in the 1970's momentum started to build. The first doctoral dissertation on Gaddis was published in 1971, providing valuable information on *The Recognitions* and basic facts about Gaddis's life. The year 1982 saw the publication of new essays in a special issue of the *Review of Contemporary Fiction*, as well as a full-length guide by Steven Moore to *The Recognitions* and a prestigious MacArthur Prize fellowship.

Gaddis's winning the 1976 National Book Award in fiction for *JR* confirmed his success. Indeed, Gad-

dis responded by publishing his third novel only a decade later, down from the twenty years between his first two efforts. *Carpenter's Gothic* was widely hailed for its bitter yet readable satire of ethical vanity in American business, politics, and popular religion. The novel broadened the readership for a novelist accustomed to a comparatively small audience, and it confirmed him as one of the most gifted and serious writers of contemporary American fiction.

Gaddis's fourth novel, *A Frolic of His Own*, was published in 1994 to a mixed response similar to that given his earlier works. It won for him his second National Book Award and was praised for its savage wit. However, some reviewers raised the old complaints that it was difficult, long-winded, and all too faithful in its representation of the tedium of everyday conversation and legal minutiae.

Along with the National Book Awards, Gaddis was given a National Institute of Arts and Letters Award (1963), two National Endowment for the Arts grants (1963 and 1974), a MacArthur Foundation fellowship (1982), and a Lannan Foundation lifetime achievement award (1993).

BIOGRAPHY

After spending his early childhood in New York City and on Long Island, William Gaddis attended a private boarding school in Connecticut for nine years. He then returned to Long Island to attend public school from grade eight through high school. He was accepted by Harvard in 1941 and stayed there until 1945, when he took a job as reader for *The New Yorker*. Gaddis left this position after one year in order to travel. In the years that followed, he visited Central America, the Caribbean, North Africa, and parts of Europe, all of which became settings in his first novel. He continued to write after returning to the United States, and in 1955, with ten years of effort behind him, he published *The Recognitions*.

Within these broad outlines a few additional details are known despite Gaddis's extreme reluctance to discuss his life. Although he was sometimes seen at writers' conferences and occasionally did some teaching, he guarded his privacy extremely well. David Koenig and Steven Moore have made a number of important inferences about Gaddis's life. For example, the protagonist of *The Recognitions*, Wyatt, has a lonely and isolated childhood. His mother dies on an ocean voyage when he is very young, and his father gradually loses his sanity. When Wyatt is twelve, he suffers from a mysterious ailment that the doctors label *erythema grave*. They mutilate Wyatt's wasted body and send him home to die because they can find neither a cause nor a cure for his illness; unexpectedly, though, Wyatt recovers. Parallels to Gaddis's own childhood emerge. Apparently he was separated from his parents, at least while he attended a boarding school in Connecticut. He also contracted an illness that the doctors could not identify and therefore called *erythema grave*. Serious effects of the illness recurred in later years to cause further problems and to prevent the young Gaddis from being accepted into the Army during World War II. Forced to remain in college, he began to write pieces for the Harvard *Lampoon* that anticipated the satirical, humorous, and critical tone of his novels. He soon became president of the *Lampoon*.

Gaddis was involved in an incident during his final year at Harvard that required the intervention of local police. Although it was hardly a serious affair, the local newspapers covered it and created embarrassing publicity for the administration. Gaddis was asked to resign and did so. The end of traditional academic success did not prevent him from acquiring knowledge. Through his travels—and more so through many years of research—Gaddis constructed impressive works of fiction from a vast store of knowledge.

After the publication of *The Recognitions*, Gaddis supported himself by teaching and writing nonfiction. He spent four years working in public relations for the Pfizer Pharmaceutical Company. He was the father of two children. His daughter, Sarah Gaddis, is a novelist whose first book, *Swallow Hard* (1991), takes its title from a phrase in *JR* and features as protagonist an author of difficult, unpopular fiction. Gaddis's son, Matthew Hough Gaddis, is a filmmaker.

Gaddis died, of prostate cancer, in late 1998 at his home. It was reported at his death that he left behind the completed manuscript of a book called *Agape Agape*, dealing with the history of the player piano.

That was the title and description of the book on which Jack Gibbs, in *JR*, was working. Perhaps appropriately, sources do not agree as to whether the book was fiction or nonfiction.

ANALYSIS

Critics have placed William Gaddis in the tradition of experimental fiction, linking him closely to James Joyce and comparing him to contemporaries such as Thomas Pynchon. Gaddis himself also indicated the influence of T. S. Eliot on his work, and indeed his books contain both novelistic and poetic structures. The novels employ only vestiges of traditional plots, which go in and out of focus as they are blurred by endless conversations, overpowered by erudite allusions and a multitude of characters, conflicts, and ambiguities. Like Joyce and Eliot, Gaddis uses myth to create a sense of timelessness—myths of Odysseus, the Grail Knight, the Fisher King, and Christ, along with parallels to the tales of Saint Clement, Faust, and Peer Gynt. Using devices of both modern poetic sequences and modern antirealistic

(Marion Ettlinger)

fiction, Gaddis unifies the diversity of parts through recurring images, phrases, and locations; a common tone; historical and literary echoes; and other non-chronological and nonsequential modes of organization. In *The Recognitions*, point of view is alternated to create tension between the first-person and third-person voices, and there are complicated jokes and symbolism deriving from the unexpected use of "I," "you," "he," and "she." In *JR*, the first-person perspective dominates through incessant talk, with very little relief or explanation in traditional third-person passages. As one reviewer wrote: "[Gaddis] wires his characters for sound and sends his story out on a continuous wave of noise—truncated dialogue, distracted monologue, the racket of TV sets, radios, telephones—from which chaos action, of a sort, eventually emerges."

All of Gaddis's work is about cacophony and euphony, fragmentation and integration, art and business, chaos and order. To a casual reader, *Carpenter's Gothic*, *JR*, and *The Recognitions* may appear only cacophonous, fragmented, and chaotic, for their formal experimentation is so dominant. To the reader prepared for the challenge of brilliant fiction, these novels illustrate how very accurate Henry James was in predicting the "elasticity" of the novel and its changing nature in the hands of great writers.

The Recognitions

Considering the complexities of Gaddis's fiction, it is not surprising that the earliest reviews of *The Recognitions* were unenthusiastic. Although they gave Gaddis credit for his extensive knowledge of religion and aesthetics, of art, myth, and philosophy, they criticized the absence of clear chronology, the diffuseness of so many intersecting subplots and characters, the large number of references, and the supposed formlessness. In the decade following the publication of *The Recognitions*, very little was written about this allusive novel or its elusive author. Readers had difficulties with the book, and Gaddis did nothing to explain it. Few copies of the original edition were ever sold and the novel went out of print. In 1962, Meridian published a paperback edition under its policy to make available neglected but important literary works. Gradually, *The Recogni-*

tions became an underground classic, although it again went out of circulation. Not until 1970 did another paperback edition appear. Throughout the precarious life of this novel, Gaddis was probably the person least surprised by its uncertain reception and reader resistance. During a party scene in *The Recognitions*, a poet questions a literary critic about a book he is carrying: "You reading that?" The critic answers, "No, I'm just reviewing it . . . all I need is the jacket blurb."

At its most fundamental level, *The Recognitions* is about every possible kind of recognition. The ultimate recognition is stated in the epigraph by Irenaeus, which translates as "Nothing empty nor without significance with God," but this ultimate recognition is nearly impossible to experience in a secular world where spiritual messages boom forth from the radio and television to become indistinguishable from commercials for soap powder and cereal.

The characters, major and minor, move toward, from, and around various recognitions. Some search for knowledge of how to perform their jobs, others search for knowledge of fraud, of ancestors, of love, self, truth, and sin. Wyatt, settling in New York City, moves sequentially through time and according to place to find his own recognition in Spain. His traditional path is crossed by the paths of many other characters who serve as his foils and reflections. Wyatt paints while Stanley composes music, Otto writes, and Esme loves. Wyatt, though, does more than paint; he forges the masterpieces of Fra Angelico and of Old Flemish painters such as Hugo van der Goes and Dirck Bouts. Thus, his fraudulent activity is reflected in others' fraudulent schemes. Frank Sinisterra, posing as a physician, is forced to operate on Wyatt's mother and inadvertently murders her. Frank is also a counterfeiter; Otto is a plagiarist; Benny is a liar; Big Anna masquerades as a woman, and Agnes Deigh, at a party, is unable to convince people that she is really a woman, not a man in drag; Herschel has no idea who he is (a "negative positivist," a "positive negativist," a "latent homosexual," or a "latent heterosexual"). In similar confusion, Wyatt is addressed as Stephen Asche, Estaban, the Reverend Gilbert Sullivan, and Christ arriving for the Second Coming.

As Wyatt matures from childhood to adulthood, his notions of emptiness and significance, of fraud and authenticity, undergo change. While his mother Camilla and his father are on an ocean voyage across the Atlantic, his mother has an appendicitis attack, is operated on by Sinisterra, and dies. Wyatt is reared by his father but essentially by his Aunt May. She is a fanatical Calvinist who teaches the talented boy that original sketches blaspheme God's original creation, so Wyatt eventually turns to copying from illustrated books. The distinctions between original work and forgery break down. When he is a young man, Wyatt becomes a partner with Recktall Brown, a shrewd art dealer who finds unsuspecting buyers for the forgeries that Wyatt produces. Wyatt is so convinced that "perfect" forgery has nothing to do with sinning, much less with breaking the law, that he has only scorn for the nineteenth century Romantics who prized originality above all else, often, he thinks, at the expense of quality. It takes many years of disappointments and betrayals for Wyatt to recognize that perfection of line and execution are empty and without significance. The first and crucial step of any great work of art must be the conceptualization behind it, the idea from which the painting derives; there is otherwise no meaningful distinction between the work of the artist and that of the craftsman. Wyatt's abnegation of any original conception implies abnegation of self, which in turn affects his efforts to communicate and to share with his wife Esther and his model Esme. Wyatt's many failures are reflected—in bits and pieces—in the subplots of *The Recognitions*. Characters miss one another as their paths crisscross and they lose track of their appointments. They talk but no one listens, they make love but their partners do not remember, and finally, they are trapped within their useless and pretentious self-illusions.

The need for love, forgiveness, purification, and renewal emerges from this frantic activity motivated by greed and selfishness. Thus, Gaddis includes in the novel archetypal questers, priests, mourning women, arid settings, burials, dying and reviving figures, cathedrals, and keepers of the keys. These motifs bring to mind many mythic parallels, though it is hard not

to think of specific parallels with Johann Wolfgang von Goethe's *Faust* (1808, 1833) and Eliot's *The Waste Land* (1922) and *Four Quartets* (1943). Toward the end of his pilgrimage, as well as the end of the novel, Wyatt achieves his recognition of love and authenticity, yet Gaddis does not succumb to the temptation to finish with a conventional denouement but keeps the novel going. In this way, the form of *The Recognitions* reflects its theme, that truth is immutable but exceptionally well hidden. After Wyatt's success follow chapters of others' failures. Anselm castrates himself and Esme dies; Sinisterra is killed by an assassin and Stanley, while playing his music in a cathedral, is killed as the walls collapse.

Just as *The Recognitions* is rich in meaning, so it is rich in form. The forward movement through chronological time is poised against other combinations of time, primarily the juxtaposition of past and present. The immediate effect of juxtaposition is to interrupt and suspend time while the ultimate effect is to make all time seem simultaneous. For example, in chapter 2, part 2, Wyatt looks out the window at the evening sky as Recktall Brown talks. Brown begins speaking about ancient Greece and Rome but is interrupted by a description of the constellation Orion, by an advertisement for phoney gems, by instructions for passengers riding a bus, by a passage about Alexander the Great, by a quotation from an English travel book of the fourteenth century. The result is that the reader temporarily loses his or her orientation, but the reader need not lose orientation completely. Unity for these disparate time periods is provided by a quality that is part of each passage—glittering beauty marred by a flaw or spurious detail. Thus, organization is based on concept, not on chronology.

Other nonchronological modes of organization include recurring patterns. Specific words become guides for the reader through difficult sections and also repeat the essential concepts of the novel. For example, "recognitions," "origin," "fished for," "design," "originality," and "fragment" can be found frequently. Larger anecdotes may also be repeated by different speakers, and opinions or metaphysical arguments may be repeated unknowingly or even stolen. The recurring images, words, and stories constitute an internal frame of reference that creates a unity apart from the plot.

In *The Recognitions*, it is possible, though not easy, to discover what activities Gaddis believes to be of enduring value. Deception and fraud are everywhere, but they cannot destroy the truth which is hidden beneath these layers of deception. A first-time reader of this novel will probably have an experience similar to that of first-time readers of Joyce's *Ulysses* (1922) in the years soon after its publication—before full-length guides extolled its merits and explained its obscurities. Like those readers of Joyce's masterpiece, readers of *The Recognitions* will be amply rewarded.

JR

Although *JR* may be even more difficult than Gaddis's first novel, it met with a more positive reception. Critics pointed to its imposing length, diffuse form, and lack of traditional narrative devices, but they believed that it was a novel which could not be ignored by people seriously interested in the future of literature. Reviewers included John Gardner, George Steiner, Earl Miner, and George Stade, further evidence of Gaddis's growing reputation.

Like *The Recognitions*, *JR* is concerned with distinguishing between significant and insignificant activities, all of which take place in a more circumscribed landscape than that of *The Recognitions*. There are no transatlantic crossings and no trips to Central America, only the alternating between a suburb on Long Island and the city of Manhattan. Gaddis shifts his satirical eye to contemporary education through the experience of his protagonist, JR, who attends sixth grade in a school on Long Island. Amy Joubert, JR's social studies teacher, takes the class to visit the stock exchange, and JR is sufficiently impressed by it to interpret the lesson literally. He is fascinated by money and uses the investment of his class in one share of stock to build a corporate empire. Although his immense profits are only on paper, the effects of his transactions on countless others are both concrete and devastating.

Despite the centrality of this obnoxious child, JR remains a shadowy figure. The events he triggers and the people he sucks into his moneymaking whirlwind are more visible. Edward Bast, JR's music teacher and composer, Jack Gibbs, Thomas Eigen, and Shepperman are all artists of some kind, and their realm of activity is quite different from JR's. Bast is forever trying to finish his piece of music, even as he works reluctantly for JR in the Manhattan office that is broken down, cluttered, and chaotic. Thomas Eigen has been writing a play, and Gibbs has tried for most of his life to write an ambitious book, but he is always losing pages he has written. While some of Shepperman's paintings have been finished, they remain hidden from sight. The world of art is, however, at odds with the world of business. Bast wants nothing to do with his student's megalomania but proves to be no match for JR. The creative people cannot convince others to leave them alone to their paper, oil paints, and canvases, and as a result they are used and manipulated by those who serve as their liaisons to others who buy, maintain, or publish their efforts.

The primary device for communication is not art but rather the telephone. The world that technology has created is efficient and mechanical since its purpose is to finish jobs so that money can be paid, at least symbolically on paper, and then be reinvested, again on paper. The artist is replaced by the businessman, and it is not even a flesh-and-blood businessman, but only his disembodied voice issuing orders out of a piece of plastic (JR disguises his voice so that he sounds older). The central "authority" is invisible, ubiquitous, and, at least while the conglomerate lasts, omniscient. The triumph of the telephone affords Gaddis endless opportunities for humor and irony, and the failure of art is accompanied by the failure of other means of communication—notably of love. As in *The Recognitions*, lovers miss each other, do not understand each other, and end their affairs or marriages unhappily.

The real tour de force of *JR* is its language. There is almost no third-person description to establish location and speaker and few authorial links or transitions between conversations or monologues. Originally, Gaddis did not even use quotation marks to set off one speaker from the next. *JR* is nearly one thousand pages of talk. The jargon, speech rhythms, and style of those in the educational establishment and in the stock market are perfectly re-created, but their language is a self-perpetuating system; regardless of their outpouring, the expressive power of words is obliterated by the sheer noise and verbiage. One early reviewer said of *JR* that "everything is insanely jammed together in this novel's closed atmosphere—there's no causality, no progression; and the frantic farcical momentum overlies the entropic unravelling of all `systems.' " The words pile up as the structures of the culture collapse; the reader is faced with a formidable challenge in making his or her way through it all.

There can be no doubt that *JR*, probably even more than *The Recognitions*, poses serious difficulties for the reader. Despite them, and even perhaps because of them, *JR* is an extraordinary novel. Gaddis captures the dizzying pace, the language, and the absurdities of contemporary culture and mercilessly throws them back to his readers in a crazy, nonlinear kind of verisimilitude. The novel operates without causality, chronology, and the logical narrative devices upon which many readers depend. The cacophony of the characters and the lack of clarity are certainly meant to be disturbing.

CARPENTER'S GOTHIC

In *Carpenter's Gothic*, this cultural cacophony runs headlong toward a global apocalypse. Again, there is the confused eruption of voices into the narrative and the forward spinning blur of events common to Gaddis's earlier fictions. Gaddis's third novel, however, is not only more focused and brief, at 262 pages, but therefore the most readable of his works. Its story centers on Elizabeth Vorakers Booth and her husband Paul, renters of the ramshackle "Carpenter's Gothic" house, in which all of the action unfolds. Daughter of a minerals tycoon who committed suicide when his illegal business practices were exposed, Elizabeth married Paul Booth, a Vietnam veteran and carrier of Vorakers's bribes, after Paul lied in testifying before Congress.

All the novel's complexities unfold from these tangled business dealings. The Vorakerses' estate is hopelessly ensnarled in lawsuits, manipulated by swarms of self-serving lawyers. Paul is suing or countersuing everyone in sight (including an airline,

for an alleged loss of Liz's "marital services" after she was a passenger during a minor crash). Meanwhile, Paul's earlier testimony before Congress has landed him a job as "media consultant" for a Reverend Ude. Ude's fundamentalist television ministry, based in South Carolina, has mushroomed into an important political interest group, and Paul's meager pay from this group is the only thing keeping him and Liz from bankruptcy. Paul drunkenly schemes and rages at Liz, or at his morning newspaper; as in *JR*, the telephone intrudes with maddeningly insistent threats, deals, wrong numbers, and ads.

Events are intensified with the entry of McCandless, owner of the Carpenter's Gothic house. A sometime geologist, teacher, and writer, McCandless happens to have surveyed the same southeast African mineral fields on which the Vorakers company had built its fortunes. It also happens to be the same African territory in which Reverend Ude is now building his missions for a great "harvest of souls" expected during "the Rapture" or anticipated Second Coming of Christ. McCandless is being pursued by U.S. government agents for back taxes and for information about those African territories. He appears at the door one morning, a shambling and wary man, an incessant smoker and an alcoholic, but nevertheless an embodiment of romantic adventure to Liz, who promptly takes him to bed.

Events spin rapidly toward violence. During an unexpected visit, Liz's younger brother, Billy, hears McCandless's tirades against American foreign policy and promptly flies off to Africa—where he is killed when his airplane is gunned down by terrorists. The U.S. Congress has launched an investigation of Ude for bribing a senator to grant his ministry a coveted television license, a bribe that Paul carried. Ude has also managed to drown a young boy during baptismal rites in South Carolina's Pee Dee River. All of Liz and Paul's stored belongings, comprising her last links to family and tradition, have been auctioned off by a storage company in compensation for unpaid bills. Liz's behavior becomes increasingly erratic.

The apocalypse comes when all these events and forces collide. McCandless takes a payoff from the Central Intelligence Agency for his African papers and simply exits the novel, after Liz has refused to accompany him. She dies of a heart attack, the warning signs of which have been planted from the first chapter. Paul immediately files a claim to any of the Vorakerses' inheritance that might have been paid to Billy and Liz, and he too simply exits the novel—notably, after using the same seduction ploy on Liz's best friend as he had originally used on Liz herself. In Africa, though, events truly explode: U.S. forces mobilize to guard various "national interests," and a real apocalypse looms as newspapers proclaim the upcoming use of a "10 K 'DEMO' BOMB OFF AFRICA COAST."

Liz Booth's heart attack symbolizes the absolute loss of empathy and love in such a cynical and careless world. Indeed, her death is further ironized when it is misinterpreted, and also proclaimed in the newspapers, as having taken place during a burglary. As with his earlier works, Gaddis's message involves this seemingly total loss of charitable and compassionate love in a civilization obsessed by success, as well as by the technologies for realizing it. Once more his satire targets the counterfeiting of values in American life, and the explosive force of mass society on feeling individuals.

The explosion of words that Gaddis re-creates is also a warning. As the efforts of painters, writers, musicians, and other artists are increasingly blocked, unappreciated, and exploited, those urges will be acknowledged by fewer and fewer people. Without an audience of listeners or viewers and without a segment of artists, there will be no possibilities for redemption from the chaos and mechanization. There will be neither sufficient introspection nor a medium through which any introspection can take concrete form. Gaddis's novels are humorous, clever, satiric, and innovative. They are also memorable and frightening reflections of contemporary culture and its values.

A FROLIC OF HIS OWN

A Frolic of His Own could be seen as the culmination of Gaddis's career, applying to the world of law the same combination of acute detailed observation and merciless satirical invention that he gave the business world in *JR* and that of art in *The Recognitions*.

The protagonist, middle-aged college professor Oscar Crease, is suing film producer Constantine Kiester for theft of intellectual property, claiming that Kiester's film *The Blood in the Red, White and Blue* was plagiarized from Crease's unpublished and unproduced play, *Once at Antietam*. He is also suing himself (actually his insurance company) because he was run over by his own car while he was attempting to jump-start it.

Meanwhile Oscar's father, ninety-seven-year-old judge Thomas Crease, is deciding two even more bizarre cases, a wrongful-death suit against an evangelist (Reverend Ude from *Carpenter's Gothic*) for the drowning of an infant he was attempting to baptize, and a case in which a dog has become trapped in a large nonrepresentational sculpture whose creator, R. Szyrk, is demanding an injunction to forestall any attempt to damage his work in order to free the dog.

Gaddis uses these cases to spotlight the increasingly Byzantine nature of the legal process, as well as some of the artistic issues dear to his heart. The intellectual property suit focuses attention on issues of plagiarism with the same thoroughness with which *The Recognitions* looked at counterfeiting. The heirs of American dramatist Eugene O'Neill, seeing similarities between *Once at Antietam* and O'Neill's *Mourning Becomes Electra* (1931), sue Oscar in turn, and elements of both are traced back to Plato, reminding us of the complexity of determining just what constitutes an original idea. The Szyrk case opposes artistic freedom to animal rights, among other issues, and both Szyrk and Oscar can be seen as somewhat ironic versions of that recurrent Gaddis character, the unappreciated "difficult" artist. In the end, as in most of Gaddis's work, the characters are ground down by the chaos and complexity of the modern world, granted only a few Pyrrhic victories. Oscar's winnings in the plagiarism suit are sharply reduced on appeal, and the father of the baptism victim is awarded less than twenty dollars.

With *A Frolic of His Own*, the creator of Recktall Brown now gives us the law firm of Swyne & Dour and the Japanese car brands Isuyu and Sosumi. The reader's already strained suspension of disbelief may stop altogether at a suit by the Episcopal Church against the makers of Pepsi-Cola for using a brand name that is an anagram of theirs. Again the dialogue is sparsely annotated and often as vague and garrulous as actual conversation. Trial transcripts and depositions are presented in all their verbosity and redundancy. At least enough of *Once at Antietam* is presented to convince us that it is a tedious play. Those who accused Gaddis's previous works of difficulty and tedium can make the same charges against this one. Even more than his previous works, *A Frolic of His Own* displays the wit, inventiveness, and complexity of Gaddis at his best, but also the qualities to which readers have objected.

Miriam Fuchs, updated by Arthur D. Hlavaty

BIBLIOGRAPHY

Gaddis, William. "The Art of Fiction, CI: William Gaddis." Interview by Zoltan Abadi-Nagy. *Paris Review* 105 (Winter, 1987): 54-89. An extensive interview with Gaddis, conducted during a 1986 visit to Budapest, Hungary. The author talks in detail about his sources, reputation, principal themes, and work in progress. He dispels a number of misconceptions, especially those linking his work to sources in Joyce, and discusses how the writer must ignore pressures of the literary marketplace.

Green, Jack. *Fire the Bastards!* Normal, Ill.: Dalkey Archive Press, 1992. A series of three essays originally published by the author in the magazine newspaper in 1962. The pseudonymous author indignantly attacked the reviewers of *The Recognitions* for failing to appreciate its greatness. Green cites numerous factual errors in the reviews and excoriates the reviewers for being unwilling to make the effort to understand the book. In contrast to the academic tone of later studies, this book is written in tones of rage with eccentric syntax and capitalization.

Karl, Frederick R. *American Fictions, 1940-1980.* New York: Harper & Row, 1983. An important essay on Gaddis's place among contemporary writers such as Donald Barthelme and Thomas Pynchon, focusing in particular on Gaddis's satires of counterfeit art, fake sensibility, and empty values in American civilization. Includes useful discussions of Gaddis's narrative techniques, especially his development of scenes and characters in his first two novels.

Keuhl, John, and Steven Moore, eds. *In Recognition of William Gaddis.* Syracuse, N.Y.: Syracuse University Press, 1984. Gathers six previously published essays alongside seven new ones, altogether providing incisive disclosures of Gaddis's principal sources and his place among modernist and postmodernist writers. Particularly useful is David Koenig's discussion of Gaddis's early career and his sources for *The Recognitions*, and other essays on Gaddis's satire of the monetization of art and love in contemporary culture.

Knight, Christopher J. *Hints and Guesses: William Gaddis's Fiction of Longing.* Madison: University of Wisconsin Press, 1997. A good study of Gaddis's oeuvre. Includes bibliographical references and an index.

LeClair, Thomas. "William Gaddis, *JR*, and the Art of Excess." *Modern Fiction Studies* 27 (Winter, 1981/1982): 587-600. An essay that links Gaddis's narrative practice, especially his excesses of dialogue and allusion, to the main thrust of his satire: the excesses of American culture.

Moore, Steven. *A Reader's Guide to William Gaddis's "The Recognitions."* Lincoln: University of Nebraska Press, 1982. An indispensable, line-by-line guidebook to Gaddis's difficult first novel, providing concise annotations of his extratextual allusions and quotations, as well as the novel's intratextual developments of character and events. Also includes a useful introductory essay and reprints three previously published but rare early pieces by Gaddis.

_____. *William Gaddis.* Boston: Twayne, 1989. The first full-length study of the writer's career and principal works, from *The Recognitions* through *Carpenter's Gothic.* An opening biographical chapter provides extensive information about his childhood, his education, his work, and his affiliations leading up to the first novel. A readable and critically incisive overview of Gaddis's satirical preoccupation with themes of failure, fraudulence, and ethical vanity in American life.

Review of Contemporary Fiction 2 (Summer, 1982). A special issue, one-half of which is devoted to Gaddis's work. Contains a rare though brief interview with the author, as well as seven original essays on *The Recognitions* and *JR*. Most of the essays concentrate on the bases of form in novels still regarded, in 1982, as too formless and sprawling.

Wolfe, Peter. *A Vision of His Own.* Cranbury, N.J.: Fairleigh Dickinson University Press, 1997. A thoroughgoing study of all four of Gaddis's novels, emphasizing such themes as the role of the artist, particularly the difficult and unappreciated artist; language and law as efforts to assert meaning and order in the face of entropy; and the soul-destroying aspects of twentieth century American culture.

ERNEST J. GAINES

Born: Oscar, Louisiana; January 15, 1933

PRINCIPAL LONG FICTION
Catherine Carmier, 1964
Of Love and Dust, 1967
The Autobiography of Miss Jane Pittman, 1971
In My Father's House, 1978
A Gathering of Old Men, 1983
A Lesson Before Dying, 1993

OTHER LITERARY FORMS

Ernest J. Gaines published a collection of short stories, *Bloodline,* in 1968. One story from that collection, *A Long Day in November,* was published separately in a children's edition in 1971.

ACHIEVEMENTS

For more than thirty years, Gaines has been a serious and committed writer of fiction. He has always worked slowly, frustratingly slowly to his admirers, but that is because of his great devotion to and respect for the craft of fiction. The six novels he had written through 1999 are all set in rural Louisiana, north of Baton Rouge: Gaines, like William Faulkner, has created a single world in which his works are centered. Even though Gaines has written during a time of great racial turmoil and unrest, he has resisted becoming involved in political movements, feeling that he can best serve the cause of art and humanity by devoting himself to perfecting his craft. This does not mean that he has remained detached from political realities. Taken together, his novels cover the period of 1865 to 1980, reflecting the social movements that have affected black Americans during that time. Gaines has said again and again, however, that he is primarily interested in people; certainly it is in his depiction of people that his greatest strength lies. His focus is on the universals of life: love, pride, pity, hatred. He aspires thus not to have an immediate political impact with his writing but to move people emotionally. His supreme achievement in this regard is *The Autobiography of Miss Jane Pittman.* With its publication—and with the highly acclaimed television movie based on the novel—Gaines achieved the recognition he had long deserved.

BIOGRAPHY

From birth until age fifteen, Ernest J. Gaines lived in rural Louisiana with his parents. As a boy, he often worked in the plantation fields and spent much of his spare time with his aunt, Miss Augusteen Jefferson. He moved to Vallejo, California, in 1948 to live with his mother and stepfather, and he attended high school and junior college there before serving in the army. After his military service, he earned a B.A. degree at San Francisco State College. On the basis of some stories written while he was a student there, he was awarded the Wallace Stegner Creative Writing Fellowship in 1958 for graduate study at Stanford University.

He was a Guggenheim Fellow in 1971 and won an award from the Black Academy of Arts and Letters in 1972. In 1987 Gaines received a literary award from the American Academy and Institute of Arts and Letters, and in 1993 he was awarded a John D.

and Catherine T. MacArthur Foundation fellowship. Also in that year, *A Lesson Before Dying* won the National Book Critics Circle Award.

Since 1958 Gaines has lived, impermanently, by his own testimony, in or near San Francisco, feeling that living elsewhere enables him to gain a perspective on his southern material that would be unavailable were he to live in the South full-time. By making yearly trips back to Louisiana, where he holds a visiting professorship in creative writing at the University of Southwestern Louisiana in Lafayette, he retains contact with his native region.

ANALYSIS

Before it became fashionable, Ernest J. Gaines was one southern black writer who wrote about his native area. Although he has lived much of his life in California, he has never been able to write adequately about that region. He has tried to write two novels about the West but has failed to finish either of them. Thus, while he has physically left the South, he has never left emotionally. His ties remain with the South, and his works remain rooted there. When he first began reading seriously, Gaines gravitated toward those writers who wrote about the soil and the people who lived close to it, among them William Faulkner, John Steinbeck, Willa Cather, and Ivan Turgenev. He was disappointed to discover that few black writers had dealt with the black rural southern experience. (Richard Wright had begun his career by doing so, and his work weakened as he moved further from the South.) Thus, Gaines began his career with the conscious desire to fill a void. He felt that no one had written fiction about his people.

This fact helps explain why his novels always concentrate on rural settings and on the "folk" who inhabit them. One of the great strengths of his work is voice; the sound of the voice telling the story is central to its meaning. Among his works, *Of Love and Dust*, *The Autobiography of Miss Jane Pittman*, and all the stories in *Bloodline* are told in the first person by rural black characters. The voices of the storytellers, especially Miss Jane's, express the perspective not only of the individual speakers but also in some sense of the entire black community, and it is

(Jerry Bauer)

the community on which Gaines most often focuses his attention.

Louisiana society, especially from a racial perspective, is complicated. Not only blacks and whites live there, but also Creoles and Cajuns. Thus there are competing communities, and some of Gaines's more interesting characters find themselves caught between groups, forced to weigh competing demands in order to devise a course of action.

Several themes recur in the Gaines canon, and together they create the total effect of his work. Generally, he deals with the relationship between past and present and the possibility of change, both individual and social. Using a broad historical canvas in his works, especially in *The Autobiography of Miss Jane Pittman*, Gaines treats the changes in race relations over time, but he is most interested in people, in whether and how they change as individuals. The issue of determinism and free will is therefore a central question in his work. Gaines has been very interested in and influenced by Greek tragedy, and in his fiction, a strain of environmental determinism is evident. In his works prior to and including *The Autobiography of Miss Jane Pittman*, a growing freedom on the part of his black characters can be seen, but the tension between fate and free will always underlies his works.

Some of Gaines's most admirable characters—for example, Marcus in *Of Love and Dust*, and Ned, Joe, and Jimmy in *The Autobiography of Miss Jane Pittman*—have the courage, pride, and dignity to fight for change. At the same time, however, Gaines reveres the old, who, while often resistant to change, embody the strength of the black people. In his work, one frequently finds tension between generations, a conflict between old and young which is reconciled only in the character of Miss Jane Pittman, who even in extreme old age retains the courage to fight for change.

Other recurring tensions and dichotomies are evident in Gaines's novels. Conflict often exists between men and women. Because of slavery, which denied them their manhood, black men feel forced to take extreme actions to attain or assert it, a theme most evident in *Of Love and Dust*, *The Autobiography of Miss Jane Pittman*, *A Gathering of Old Men* and the stories in *Bloodline*. Women, on the other hand, are often presented in Gaines's fiction as preservers and conservers. Each group embodies a strength, but Gaines suggests that wholeness comes about only when the peculiar strengths of the two sexes are united, again most clearly exemplified in Miss Jane and her relationship with the men in her life.

Among the male characters, a tension exists between fathers and sons. Treated explicitly in Gaines's fourth novel, *In My Father's House*, this theme is implicit throughout the canon. Though young men look to the older generation for models, there are few reliable examples for them to follow, and they find it difficult to take responsibility for their lives and for the lives of their loved ones.

Gaines's characters at their best seek freedom and dignity: Some succeed, and some fail in their attempts to overcome both outer and inner obstacles. Viewed in sequence, Gaines's first three novels move from the almost total bleakness and determinism of *Catherine Carmier* to the triumph of *The Autobiography of Miss Jane Pittman*. In *My Father's House*, however, reflects a falling away of hope in both individual and social terms, perhaps corresponding to the diminution of expectations experienced in America during the late 1970's and early 1980's.

CATHERINE CARMIER

Gaines's first novel, *Catherine Carmier*, based on a work he wrote while an adolescent in Vallejo, has many of the characteristic weaknesses of a first novel and is more interesting for what it anticipates in Gaines's later career than for its intrinsic merits. Though it caused barely a ripple of interest when it was first published, the novel introduces many of the themes which Gaines treats more effectively in his mature fiction. The book is set in the country, near Bayonne, Louisiana, an area depicted as virtually a wasteland. Ownership of much of this region has devolved to the Cajuns, who appear throughout Gaines's novels as Snopes-like vermin, interested in owning the land only to exploit it. Like Faulkner, Gaines sees this kind of person as particularly modern, and the growing power of the Cajuns indicates a weakening of values and a loss of determination to live in right relationship to the land.

Onto the scene comes Jackson Bradley, a young black man born and reared in the area but (like Gaines himself) educated in California. Bradley is a hollow, rootless man, a man who does not know where he belongs. He has found the North and the West empty, with people living hurried, pointless lives, but he sees the South as equally empty. Feeling no link to a meaningful past and no hope for a productive future, Bradley is a deracinated modern man. He has returned to Louisiana to bid final farewell to his Aunt Charlotte, a representative of the older generation, and to her way of life.

While there and while trying to find a meaningful path for himself, Bradley meets and falls in love with Catherine Carmier. She, too, is living a blocked life, and he feels that if they can leave the area, they will be able to make a fulfilling life together. Catherine is the daughter of Raoul Carmier, in many ways the most interesting character in the novel. A Creole, he is caught between the races. Because of his black blood, he is not treated as the equal of whites, but because of his white blood, he considers blacks to be beneath him. He has a near incestuous relationship with Catherine, since after her birth his wife was unfaithful to him and he considers none of their subsequent children his. Feeling close only to Catherine, he forbids her to associate with any men, but especially with black men. A man of great pride and love of the land, Raoul is virtually the only man in the region to resist the encroachment of the Cajuns. His attitude isolates him all the more, which in turn makes him fanatically determined to hold to Catherine.

Despite her love for and loyalty to her father, Catherine senses the dead end her life has become and returns Bradley's love. Though she wants to leave with him, she is paralyzed by her love of her father and by her knowledge of what her leaving would do to him. This conflict climaxes with a brutal fight between Raoul and Bradley over Catherine, a fight that Bradley wins. Catherine, however, returns home to nurse her father. The novel ends ambiguously, with at least a hint that Catherine will return to Bradley, although the thrust of the book militates against that eventuality. Gaines implies that history and caste are a prison, a tomb. No change is possible for the characters because they cannot break out of the cages their lives have become. Love is the final victim. Catherine will continue living her narrow, unhealthy life, and Jackson Bradley will continue wandering the earth, searching for something to fill his inner void.

OF LOVE AND DUST

Gaines's second novel, *Of Love and Dust*, was received much more enthusiastically than was *Catherine Carmier*; with it, he began to win the largely positive, respectful reviews which have continued to the present time. Like *Catherine Carmier*, *Of Love and Dust* is a story of frustrated love. The setting is the same: rural Louisiana, where the Cajuns are gradually assuming ownership and control of the land. *Of Love and Dust* is a substantial improvement over *Catherine Carmier*, however, in part because it is told in the first person by Jim Kelly, an observer of the central story. In this novel, one can see Gaines working toward the folk voice which became such an integral part of the achievement of *The Autobiography of Miss Jane Pittman*.

The plot of the novel concerns Marcus Payne, a young black man sentenced to prison for murder and then bonded out by a white plantation owner who wants him to work in his fields. Recognizing Marcus's rebelliousness and pride, the owner and his Cajun overseer, Sidney Bonbon, brutally attempt to break his spirit. This only makes Marcus more determined, and in revenge, he decides to seduce Louise, Bonbon's neglected wife. What begins, however, as simply a selfish and egocentric act of revenge on Marcus's part grows into a genuine though grotesque love. When he and Louise decide to run away together, Bonbon discovers them and kills Marcus. Even though he dies, Marcus, by resisting brutalizing circumstances, retains his pride and attempts to prove his manhood and dignity. His attempts begin in a self-centered way, but as his love for Louise grows, he grows in stature in the reader's eyes until he becomes a figure of heroic dimensions.

Through his use of a first-person narrator, Gaines creates a double perspective in the novel, including on the one hand the exploits of Marcus and on the other the black community's reactions to them. The narrator, Jim Kelly, is the straw boss at the plantation, a member of the black community but also accepted and trusted by the whites because of his dependability and his unwillingness to cause any problems. His initial reaction to Marcus—resentment and dislike of him as a troublemaker—represents the reaction of the community at large. The older members of the community never move beyond that attitude because they are committed to the old ways, to submission and accommodation. To his credit, however, Jim's attitude undergoes a transformation. As he observes Marcus, his resentment changes to sympathy and respect, for he comes to see Marcus as an example of black manhood which others would do well to emulate.

Marcus's death gives evidence of the strain of fate and determinism in this novel as well, yet because he dies with his pride and dignity intact, *Of Love and Dust* is more hopeful than *Catherine Carmier*. Gaines indicates that resistance is possible and, through the character of Jim Kelly, that change can occur. Kelly leaves the plantation at the end of the novel, no longer passively accepting what fate brings him but believing that he can act and shape his own life. Though Marcus is an apolitical character, like Jackson Bradley, it is suggested that others will later build on his actions to force social change on the South. *Of Love and Dust* is a major step forward beyond *Catherine Carmier* both artistically and thematically. Through his use of the folk voice, Gaines vivifies his story, and the novel suggests the real possibility of free action by his characters.

The Autobiography of Miss Jane Pittman

Without a doubt, *The Autobiography of Miss Jane Pittman* is Gaines's major contribution to American literature. Except for an introduction written by "the editor," it is told entirely in the first person by Miss Jane and covers approximately one hundred years, from the Civil War to the Civil Rights movement of the 1960's. Basing the novel on stories he heard while a child around his aunt, Augusteen Jefferson, and using the format of oral history made popular in recent decades, Gaines created a "folk autobiography" which tells the story of people who are not in the history books. While the work is the story of Miss Jane, she is merely an observer for a substantial portion of its length, and the story becomes that of black Americans from slavery to the present. Gaines's mastery of voice is especially important here, for Miss Jane's voice is the voice of her people.

From the very beginning of the novel, when Miss Jane is determined, even in the face of physical beatings, to keep the name a Union soldier gave her and refuses to be called Ticey, her slave name, to the end of the novel, when she leads her people to Bayonne in a demonstration against segregated facilities, she is courageous and in the best sense of the word "enduring," like Faulkner's Dilsey. In her character and story, many of the dichotomies that run through Gaines's work are unified. The differing roles of men and women are important elements in the book. Women preserve and sustain—a role symbolized by Miss Jane's longevity. Men, on the other hand, feel the need to assert their manhood in an active way. Three black men are especially important in Miss Jane's life, beginning with Ned, whom she rears from childhood after his mother is killed and who becomes in effect a "son" to her. Like Marcus Payne, Ned is a rebel, but his rebellion is concentrated in the political arena. Returning to Louisiana after the turn of the century, he attempts to lead his people to freedom. Though he is murdered by whites, his legacy and memory are carried on by Miss Jane and the people in the community. Later, in the 1960's, Jimmy Aaron, another young man who tries to encourage his people to effective political action, appears. Again the members of the older generation hang back, fearful of change and danger, but after Jimmy is killed, Jane unites old and young, past and present by her determination to go to Bayonne and carry on Jimmy's work. Thus Marcus's apolitical rebellion in *Of Love and Dust* has been transformed into political action. The third man in Jane's life is Joe Pittman, her husband. A horse-breaker, he is committed to asserting and proving his manhood through his work. Although he too dies, killed by a wild horse he was determined to break, Jane in her understanding and love of him, as well as in her affection for all her men, bridges the gap between man and woman. In her character, the opposites of old and young, past and present, and man and woman are reconciled.

Miss Jane's strength is finally the strength of the past, but it is directed toward the future. When Jimmy returns, he tells the people that he is nothing without their strength, referring not only to their physical numbers but also to the strength of their character as it has been forged by all the hardships they have undergone through history. Even though the people seem weak and fearful, the example of Miss Jane shows that they need not be. They can shake off the chains of bondage and determinism, assert their free spirit through direct action, and effect change. The change has only begun by the conclusion of *The Autobiography of Miss Jane Pittman*, but the pride and dignity of Miss Jane and all those she represents suggest that ultimately they will prevail.

In My Father's House

Gaines's fourth novel, *In My Father's House*, was the first he had written in the third person since *Catherine Carmier*; the effect of its point of view is to distance the reader from the action and characters, creating an ironic perspective. Set during a dreary winter in 1970, in the period of disillusionment following the assassination of Martin Luther King, Jr., the novel suggests that the progress which was implicit in the ending of *The Autobiography of Miss Jane Pittman* was temporary at best, if not downright illusory. The atmosphere of the novel is one of frustration and stagnation.

Both the setting and the protagonist of *In My Father's House* are uncharacteristic for Gaines. Instead of using the rural settings so familiar from his other works, he sets his story in a small town. Rather than focusing on the common people, Gaines chooses as his protagonist Philip Martin, one of the leaders of the black community, a public figure, a minister who is considering running for Congress. A success by practically any measure and pridefully considering himself a *man*, Martin is brought low in the course of the novel. His illegitimate son, Robert X, a ghostlike man, appears and wordlessly accuses him. Robert is evidence that, by abandoning him, his siblings, and their mother many years previously, Martin in effect destroyed their lives. Having been a drinker and gambler, irresponsible, he tries to explain to his son that his earlier weakness was a legacy of slavery. Even though he seems to have surmounted that crippling legacy, his past rises up to haunt him and forces him to face his weakness. Martin wants to effect a reconciliation with his son and thus with his past, but Robert's suicide precludes that. *In My Father's House* makes explicit a concern which was only implicit in Gaines's earlier novels, the relationship between fathers and sons. No communication is possible here, and the failure is illustrative of a more general barrier between the generations. While in the earlier novels the young people led in the struggle for change and the older characters held back, here the situation is reversed. Martin and members of his generation are the leaders, while the young are for the most part sunk in cynicism, apathy, and hopelessness, or devoted to anarchic violence. If the hope of a people is in the young, or in a reconciliation of old and young, hope does not exist in this novel.

A GATHERING OF OLD MEN

Hope does exist, however, in Gaines's *A Gathering of Old Men*, for which Gaines returns to his more characteristic rural setting. Here he returns as well to the optimism with which *The Autobiography of Miss Jane Pittman* ended. This time, as at the end of that novel and in *In My Father's House*, it is up to the old among the black community to lead the struggle for change, this time primarily because there are no young men left to lead. All of them have escaped to towns and cities that promise more of a future than does rural Louisiana.

In this small corner of Louisiana, however, as elsewhere in Gaines's fiction, Cajuns are encroaching on the land, replacing men with machines and even threatening to plow up the old graveyard where generations of blacks have been buried. When Beau Boutan, son of the powerful Cajun Fix Boutan, is shot to death in the quarters of Marshall plantation, where Marshall blacks have worked the land since the days of slavery, the old black men who have lived there all of their lives are faced with one last chance to stand up and be men. They stand up for the sake of Matthu, the only one of them who ever stood up before and thus the most logical suspect in the murder. They also stand up because of all the times in their past when they should have stood up but did not. They prove one last time that free action is possible when eighteen or more of them, all in their seventies and eighties, arm themselves with rifles of the same guage used in the shooting and face down the white sheriff, Mapes, each in his turn claiming to be the killer.

As shut off as the quarters are from the rest of the world, it is easy to forget that the events of the novel take place as recently as the late 1970's. Beau Boutan's brother Gil, however, represents the change that has been taking place in the world outside Marshall. He has achieved gridiron fame at Louisiana State University by working side by side with Cal, a young black man. Youth confronts age when Gil returns home and tries to persuade his father not to ride in revenge against Beau's murderer, as everyone expects him to do. Gil represents the possibility of change from the white perspective. He convinces his father to let the law find and punish Beau's murderer, but he pays a heavy price when his father disowns him. He cannot stop other young Cajuns, led by Luke

Will, who are not willing to change but would rather cling to the vigilantism of the old South.

In spite of their dignity and pride, the old men at Marshall risk looking rather silly because after all these years they stand ready for a battle that seems destined never to take place once Fix Boutan decides not to ride on Marshall. Sheriff Mapes taunts them with the knowledge that they have waited too late to take a stand. Ironically, they are ultimately able to maintain their dignity and reveal their growth in freedom by standing up to the one person who has been most valiant in her efforts to help them: Candy Marshall, niece of the landowner. In her effort to protect Matthu, who was largely responsible for rearing her after her parents died, Candy has gone so far as to try to take credit for the murder herself. What she fails to realize is that the days are long past when black men need the protection of a white woman. She is stunned to realize that she too has been living in the past and has been guilty of treating grown black men like children.

The novel does eventually end with a gunfight, because Luke Will and his men refuse to let the murder of a white man by a black one go unavenged. It is fitting that the two men who fall in the battle are Luke Will, the one who was most resistant to change, and Charlie Biggs, the real murderer, who, at fifty, finally proves his manhood by refusing to be beaten by Beau Boutan and then by returning to take the blame for the murder that he has committed. Charlie's body is treated like a sacred relic as each member of the black community, from the oldest to the youngest, touches it, hoping that some of the courage that Charlie found late in life will rub off. Apparently it already has.

With *A Gathering of Old Men*, Gaines returns to first-person narration, but this time the history is told one chapter at a time by various characters involved in or witnessing the action. His original plan was to have the narrator be the white newspaperman Lou Dimes, Candy's boyfriend. He found, however, that there was still much that a black man in Louisiana would not confide to a white man, even a sympathetic one, so he let the people tell their own story, with Dimes narrating an occasional chapter.

A LESSON BEFORE DYING

A Lesson Before Dying, set in Gaines's fictional Bayonne during six months of 1948, reveals the horrors of Jim Crowism in the story of twenty-one-year-old Jefferson, a scarcely literate man-child who works the cane fields of Pichot Plantation. Jefferson hooks up with two criminals who are killed during the robbery of a liquor store, along with the store's white proprietor. Jefferson is left to stand trial before a jury of twelve white men who overlook his naivete despite his lawyer's argument that he is a dumb animal, a "thing" that acts on command, no more deserving of the electric chair than a hog. When this description causes Jefferson to become practically catatonic, his grandmother enlists the local schoolteacher, Grant Wiggins, to help Jefferson gain his manhood before he is put to death. Thus, like *A Gathering of Old Men*, this novel questions the traditional devaluing of black males in the south.

Reluctantly, Wiggins agrees to help Jefferson by encouraging him to speak and to write, visiting him often and giving him a journal in which to record his thoughts. Finally, right before his execution, Jefferson has a breakthrough when he tells Wiggins to thank his students for the pecans they sent him in jail. Wiggins himself becomes the central character as he learns the real lesson of the novel, that all people are connected and responsible for each other. Wiggins comes to terms with his own role in the system that victimizes Jefferson, and the entire community learns from how Jefferson faces his execution. The novel pays a tribute to those who persevere in the face of injustice, and it also puts forward hope for better racial relationships, especially in the character of Paul, the young white jailer who is sympathetic to Jefferson and to Grant Wiggins's attempts to bring forth his humanity.

If *In My Father's House* represents a falling away of hope for human progress and perhaps also a falling away in artistry, one finds once again in *A Gathering of Old Men* and *A Lesson Before Dying* evidence of the same genuine strengths that Gaines exhibited in *The Autobiography of Miss Jane Pittman*: a mastery of the folk voice, a concern for common people, a reverence for the everyday, a love of the land, and a powerful evocation of the strength, pride, and dignity people can develop by working on and living close to the soil.

Frank W. Shelton, updated by Rebecca G. Smith

OTHER MAJOR WORKS

SHORT FICTION: *Bloodline*, 1968; *A Long Day in November*, 1971.

BIBLIOGRAPHY

Auger, Philip. "A Lesson About Manhood: Appropriating `The Word' in Ernest Gaines's *A Lesson Before Dying*." *Southern Literary Journal* 27 (Spring, 1995): 74-85. Auger explains the novel as a biblical allegory, focusing on Grant Wiggins's subversion of the white Christian mythos as a rhetorical act that helps Jefferson transform himself into a New Testament God-figure as he gains control over language.

Babb, Valerie Melissa. *Ernest Gaines*. Boston: Twayne, 1991. This volume in Twayne's United States Authors series offers a chapter on each of Gaines's books through *A Gathering of Old Men*. Its insightful final chapter places Gaines in the larger context of African American literature, explaining how Gaines balances politics and his vision of the artist.

Beavers, Herman. *Wrestling Angels into Song: The Fictions of Ernest J. Gaines and James Alan McPherson*. Philadelphia: University of Pennsylvania Press, 1995. This thoughtful analysis of the literary kinship of Gaines and McPherson with their precursor Ralph Ellison focuses on all three writers' characters' sense of community, storytelling, and self-recovery. While beginning with a look at their southernness, Beavers examines all three as American writers and discusses all Gaines's work through *A Lesson Before Dying*.

Estes, David E., ed. *Critical Reflections on the Fiction of Ernest J Gaines*. Athens, Ga.: University of Georgia Press, 1994. Fourteen essays that cover all six novels to 1994 and *Bloodline* as well as film adaptations of Gaines's work, offering detailed explications in addition to broad analyses of pastoralism, humor, race, and gender. An excellent introduction highlights important biographical facts, secondary sources, and literary themes in Gaines's work.

Gaines, Ernest J. "A Very Big Order: Reconstructing Identity." *Southern Review* 26 (Spring, 1990): 245-253. In this memoir, Gaines recalls his move from Louisiana to Vallejo, California, where he first had access to a public library but did not find there books about the South that he knew. He traces the movement in his writing back into his southern past as he attempted to write for the African American youth of the South the works that did not exist for him.

Gaudet, Marcia, and Carl Wooton. "Talking with Ernest J. Gaines." *Callaloo* 11 (Spring, 1988): 229-243. In this interview, Gaines provides useful information about how his background influenced his art. He discusses his training as a writer, including the early lack of African American models and the effects of his small-town upbringing. He also analyzes his use of point of view and his treatment of black men and women.

Lowe, John, ed. *Conversations with Ernest Gaines*. Jackson, Miss.: University Press of Mississippi, 1995. This collection offers twenty-five interviews conducted from 1969 to 1994, all but the last previously published. Arranged chronologically, the interviews explore Gaines's thoughts on key aspects of all his work through *A Lesson Before Dying*, especially African American males' search for identity. Includes a useful topical index.

Shelton, Frank W. "*In My Father's House*: Ernest Gaines After Jane Pittman." *Southern Review* 17 (Spring, 1981): 340-345. In his detailed analysis of *In My Father's House*, Shelton explores the relative neglect of the novel by reviewers, attributing their less than enthusiastic response in part to the distance achieved through a third-person narrator. Where Miss Jane Pittman symbolizes human survival, the later novel's Philip Martin symbolizes human failing and provides a vehicle for Gaines to explore two earlier themes: the nature of African American manhood and the relationship between fathers and sons.

JOHN GALSWORTHY

Born: Kingston Hill, England; August 14, 1867
Died: London, England; January 31, 1933

PRINCIPAL LONG FICTION

Jocelyn, 1898 (as John Sinjohn)
Villa Rubein, 1900 (as Sinjohn)
The Island Pharisees, 1904
The Man of Property, 1906
The Country House, 1907
Fraternity, 1909
The Patrician, 1911
The Dark Flower, 1913
The Freelands, 1915
Beyond, 1917
The Burning Spear, 1919
Saint's Progress, 1919
In Chancery, 1920
To Let, 1921
The Forsyte Saga, 1922 (includes *The Man of Property*, "Indian Summer of a Forsyte," "Awakening," *In Chancery*, and *To Let*)
The White Monkey, 1924
The Silver Spoon, 1926
Swan Song, 1928
A Modern Comedy, 1929 (includes *The White Monkey*, *The Silver Spoon*, *Two Forsyte Interludes*, and *Swan Song*)
Maid in Waiting, 1931
Flowering Wilderness, 1932
Over the River, 1933
End of the Chapter, 1934 (includes *Maid in Waiting*, *Flowering Wilderness*, and *Over the River*)

OTHER LITERARY FORMS

John Galsworthy attempted and succeeded at writing in all major literary forms. His earlier short fiction is collected in *Caravan: The Assembled Tales of John Galsworthy* (1925); among the individual collections, some of the best known are *A Man of Devon* (1901), published under the pseudonym "John Sinjohn," *Five Tales* (1918), *Two Forsyte Inter-* *ludes* (1927), and *On Forsyte 'Change* (1930). His plays made him, along with George Bernard Shaw, James M. Barrie, and Harley Granville-Barker, a leading figure in British drama during the early decades of the twentieth century. Galsworthy's most enduring plays include *The Silver Box* (1906), *Justice* (1910), *The Skin Game* (1920), and *Loyalties* (1922). Collections of Galsworthy's literary sketches and essays include *A Motley* (1910), *The Inn of Tranquility* (1912), and *Tatterdemalion* (1920). Galsworthy wrote poetry throughout his life, and the *Collected Poems of John Galsworthy* were published in 1934.

ACHIEVEMENTS

Galsworthy was a writer who reaped the rewards of literary acclaim in his own time—and suffered the pangs that attend artists who prove truer to the tastes of the public than to an inner vision of personal potential. Galsworthy won the esteem of his countrymen with a play, *The Silver Box*, and a novel, *The Man of Property*, published in his *annus mirabilis*, 1906. From that time on, he was a major figure in the British literary establishment, even winning the Nobel Prize in Literature in 1932. Idealist, optimist, and activist, Galsworthy was a perennial champion of the underprivileged in his works. Women (especially unhappily married ones), children, prisoners, aliens, and animals (especially horses and dogs) engaged Galsworthy's sympathies. His literary indictments of the injustices forced upon these victims by an unfeeling society helped to arouse public support for his causes and frequently resulted in elimination of the abuses. After World War I, Galsworthy's crusading spirit was somewhat dampened. Despite his disillusionment, though, Galsworthy's conscience remained sensitive to inequities of all sorts.

Although popular as a writer of fiction and influential as a spokesman for humane, enlightened personal behavior and public policy, Galsworthy was not the sort of writer who changes the course of literature. His early works contain some powerful satire and some interesting experiments in probing and expressing his internal conflicts. By upbringing and inclination, however, Galsworthy was too "gentlemanly" to be comfortable with self-revelation or even with introspection. Thus, while the English novel was becoming increasingly psychological because of Joseph Conrad, Virginia Woolf, and D. H. Lawrence, Galsworthy continued in the nineteenth century tradition of Ivan Turgenev and Guy de Maupassant, carefully describing social phenomena and assessing their impact on private lives. Most of his characters are individualized representatives of particular social classes, whether the rural gentry, the aristocracy, the intelligentsia, or the London professional elite. He excelled at presenting the fashions, politics, manners, and phrases peculiar to certain milieus at certain times. In creating the Forsytes—and most notably Soames, "the man of property"—Galsworthy's talent transcended that of the memorialist or mere novelist of manners and provided England with a quintessential expression of the shrewd, rich, upright middle class of Victorian London, a group whose qualities subsequent generations found easy to mock, possible to admire, but difficult to love.

BIOGRAPHY

John Galsworthy, son and namesake of a solicitor, company director, and descendant of the Devonshire yeomanry, was born into the rich Victorian middle class he so accurately describes in *The Forsyte Saga*. His early years followed the prescribed pattern of that class. Having spent his childhood at a series of large, grand, ugly country houses outside of London, Galsworthy was graduated from Harrow School and New College, Oxford. Called to the bar in 1890, he commenced a languid practice of maritime law and traveled widely—to Canada, Australia, and the Far East. On returning to England, he committed an unpardonable breach of middle-class manners and morals: He openly became the lover, or more accurately husband *manqué*, of Ada, the unhappy wife of his cousin Major Galsworthy.

Having placed themselves beyond the pale, the lovers traveled abroad and in England and, with Ada's encouragement and assistance, Galsworthy began his literary career by writing books under the pen name "John Sinjohn." In 1905, after Ada's divorce, the Galsworthys were able to regularize their relationship, and, in 1906, public acclamation of *The*

Man of Property and *The Silver Box* gave Galsworthy a secure place in the British literary establishment. Substantial resources permitted the Galsworthys to maintain London and country residences and to continue what was to be their lifelong habit of extensive traveling.

A kindly, courtly, almost hypersensitive person concerned throughout his life with altruistic ventures large and small, Galsworthy was distressed that his age and physical condition precluded active service in World War I. During these years, Galsworthy donated half or more of his large income to the war effort, wrote patriotic pieces, and for some time served as a masseur for the wounded at a hospital in France.

Friends observed that neither John nor Ada Galsworthy ever truly recovered from the war, and the last decade or so of Galsworthy's life was, beneath a smooth surface, not particularly happy. He

(The Nobel Foundation)

had achieved all the trappings of success. Born rich, married to a woman he adored, he owned an elegant town house at Hampstead and an imposing country place at Bury, in Sussex. He was president of the International Association of Poets, Playwrights, Editors, Essayists and Novelists (PEN). The public honored him as a humanist and philanthropist, acknowledged him as one of the foremost British men of letters, and even—thanks to the nostalgic novels written during the 1920's which, along with *The Man of Property*, constitute *The Forsyte Saga* and its sequel *A Modern Comedy*—made him a best-selling author. Nevertheless, Galsworthy keenly felt that he had never made the most of his talent or fulfilled the promise of his early works.

Furthermore, though he was the sort of gentleman who found complaints and even unarticulated resentment "bad form," Galsworthy must have felt some unconscious hostility toward his wife, who, for all her devotion, was superficial, hypochondriacal, demanding, and possessive in the Forsyte way that Galsworthy found deplorable (at least in people other than Ada) and who, by obliging him to live life on her terms, was perhaps the principal force in the circumspection of his talents. He also felt anxious realizing that the intense, even claustrophobic bond of love that had joined him and Ada would eventually be severed by the death of one or the other. Ironically, in 1932, it became evident that the "stronger" of the two would not survive his "frail" companion. Galsworthy was stricken with an initially vague malaise that, though never satisfactorily diagnosed, was very likely a brain tumor. Galsworthy died at home in London on January 31, 1933, two months after having been awarded in absentia the Nobel Prize in Literature.

ANALYSIS

John Galsworthy is one of those authors whose works are valued most highly by their contemporaries. Once placed in the first rank by such discriminating readers as Joseph Conrad, Edward Garnett, Gilbert Murray, and E. V. Lucas (though Virginia Woolf despised him as a mere "materialist"), Galsworthy is now remembered as the workmanlike

chronicler of the Forsyte family. Most of his other works are ignored. Changing fashions in literature do not suffice to explain this shift in critical esteem. Rather, the way Galsworthy chose to employ his talents—or the way his upbringing and personal situation obliged him to use them—guaranteed him the esteem of his peers but in large measure lost him the attention of posterity.

Galsworthy's literary strengths are impressive. His works are acutely observant and intensely sympathetic. In his novels, one finds carefully detailed presentations of the manners, codes, pastimes, and material surroundings of England's ruling classes as well as enlightened consideration of the diverse injustices these classes deliberately and inadvertently inflicted on those below them. Temperamentally inclined to support the "underdog"—whether an unhappily married woman, a poor workingman less honest than those in happier circumstances would like him to be, an ostracized German-born Londoner in wartime, or a badly treated horse—Galsworthy does not treat his characters as stereotypes of good or evil. Even when he is a partisan in one of the ethical dilemmas he presents (such as Soames Forsyte's sincerely enamored but brutally proprietary attitude toward Irene, the woman who passively marries him but actively repents of that decision), he strives to show the mixture of good and bad, commendable and culpable, in all parties.

Galsworthy writes best when he deals with characters or situations from his own experience (for example, the various loves in *The Dark Flower*), comments on his own background or family history (as in the satirical group portrait of the Forsytes), or attempts to externalize the intricate course of motivations and ambivalences in his own mind (as does his study of Hilary Dallison, a prosperous writer suffering under the curse of "over-refinement," in *Fraternity*). Nevertheless, Galsworthy's reserve and stoicism, innate qualities further cultivated by his gentlemanly upbringing, made him increasingly unwilling to look within himself and write. His peripatetic existence and desire to grind out work for good causes must have made concentration on truly ambitious projects difficult. His wife's wishes and values, closer than he ever acknowledged to the more blighting aspects of Forsyteism, cut him off from many of the experiences and relationships that writers tend to find enriching. As a result, most of his carefully crafted literary works remain topical productions: He fails to confer suggestions of universality or living particularity on the social types and situations he describes, and thus, as novels of manners tend to do, his works seemed more profound and interesting to the age and society whose likenesses they reflect than they have to succeeding generations.

The first of the Forsyte novels, *The Man of Property*, is generally agreed to be Galsworthy's finest work, and the excellence of this book in great measure guaranteed that its less skillfully realized sequels and the peripheral Forsyte collections such as *Two Forsyte Interludes* and *On Forsyte 'Change* would attract and interest readers. If these social novels typify Galsworthy's achievement, two other works deserve mention, not for their continued popularity or complete artistic success but because they indicate the other avenues Galsworthy might have explored had he not directed his talent as he chose to do. *The Dark Flower*, one of Galsworthy's favorites among his works, displays his ability to handle emotional relationships; *Fraternity*, which he termed "more intimate than anything I've done . . . less *machinery* of story, less history, more life," is his most complex psychological study, a flawed but ambitious attempt at writing a "modern" novel.

FRATERNITY

In the spring of 1909, ensconced in the Devonshire countryside he loved, Galsworthy worked on the study of London life that would be *Fraternity*. The book's first title, however, was *Shadows*, a word that gives perhaps a clearer indication of the novel's ruling concern. In *Fraternity*, Galsworthy presents two adjacent but contrasting neighborhoods, elegant Campden Hill (where he and Ada then had their town residence) and disreputable Notting Hill Gate, and two sets of characters, the genteel, prosperous, enlightened Dallisons and their "shadows," the impoverished Hughs family.

Aware of the existence of their less fortunate brothers (Mrs. Hughs does household chores for Cecelia, wife of Stephen Dallison, and the Hughses' tenant models for Bianca, the artist wife of Hilary Dallison) and rationally convinced of the unity of humankind and the falseness of the divisions fostered by the class system, the Dallisons would like to take positive actions to help their "shadows" but find themselves unable to succeed at putting their theories into practice. Hilary in particular—like his creator Galsworthy a fortyish writer with a comfortable income and an uncomfortably sensitive conscience—is willing but unable to do some good. Discovering in one of many episodes of self-scrutiny that his benevolent intentions toward his wife's "little model" are far from disinterested and, worse yet, learning that the poor girl loves him, Hilary suffers a fit of repulsion. He is, as Catherine Dupre observes in *John Galsworthy: A Biography* (1976), "horrified by the prospect of any sort of union with someone whose difference of class and outlook would doom from the start their relationship." For Hilary and all the Dallisons, the common bond of shared humanity is ultimately less significant than the web of social life that separates the privileged from their "shadows," that permits observation without true empathy.

Galsworthy's friend Joseph Conrad was not alone in appraising *Fraternity* as "the book of a moralist." The great danger and difficulty of such a novel, Conrad argued to Galsworthy, is that its "negative method" of stressing a moral problem without prescribing a remedy leaves the reader dissatisfied: "It is impossible to read a book like that without asking oneself—what then?" In that sentence, Conrad characterizes a recurrent quality of Galsworthy's writing. Except in specific cases (and there were many of these—among them women's suffrage, slaughterhouse reform, docking of horses' tails, vivisection, slum clearance, the condition of prisons, the state of zoos), Galsworthy tended to be a moralist without a gospel. His scrutiny of human behavior and social conditions detracted from the artistic success of his novels without providing anything but a sense of unease. Still, as Galsworthy explained to another critic of *Fraternity*, cultivating this awareness of moral problems is a step, albeit an oblique one, toward "sympathy between man and man."

THE DARK FLOWER

The Dark Flower was one of Galsworthy's partic-ular favorites among his novels. His professed inten-tion in writing the book was to offer "a study [I hoped a true and a deep one] of Passion—that blind force which sweeps upon us out of the dark and turns us pretty well as it will." The book was taken by vari-ous readers, the most articulate among them being Sir Arthur Quiller-Couch, who reviewed it in *The Daily Mail*, as a case for free love, an assertion that commitment to a marriage should end when love ends. Interestingly, as Catherine Dupre suggests, the gist of *The Dark Flower* is something less general than either the authorial statement of purpose or the critical view would have it be: It is an emotionally faithful representation of Galsworthy's own loves—most immediately, of his 1912 infatuation with a young actress and dancer named Margaret Morris.

The Dark Flower is divided into three parts, "Spring," "Summer," and "Autumn," each depicting a romantic experience in the life of the protagonist, Mark Lennan. Attracted to his tutor's wife in "Spring," the youthful Lennan is rejected and advised to find a woman of his own age. In "Summer," he meets and comes to love a beautiful, charming mar-ried woman, Olive Cramier, whose unyielding antip-athy for the man to whom she has unwisely yoked herself obviously parallels Ada's revulsion for Major Galsworthy. Olive, the great love of Lennan's life, drowns; in "Autumn" he is happily but not passion-ately married to a wife of fifteen years, Sylvia, and infatuated with a lovely young girl, Nell. The middle-aged lover fondly hopes that he can retain Sylvia without giving up Nell. Like Ada in real life, Sylvia says she can be broad-minded but clearly demon-strates that she cannot. Lennan, like Galsworthy, ac-cordingly sacrifices the more intense love for the long-standing one—in fact, his speeches and Nell's are, as Margaret Morris recalls in *My Galsworthy Story* (1967), accurate quotations of real-life dia-logue. It is not surprising that having laid out his emotional autobiography, discreetly veiled though it may have been, and having been charged with pro-moting the sentimental and irresponsible sort of spir-itual polygamy advocated by the very young Percy

Bysshe Shelley, the reserved and dutiful Galsworthy was afterward reluctant to commit his deepest feel-ings to print.

THE MAN OF PROPERTY

The trilogy for which Galsworthy is principally known was launched with the publication of *The Man of Property* in 1906. Although Galsworthy thought at the time of continuing his satirical work and mentioned various possibilities in his letters to Conrad, not until 1917, when he returned to England from his stint of hospital service in France and began writing "Indian Summer of a Forsyte," did Gals-worthy resume the work that would be his magnum opus.

The Man of Property, the finest and fiercest of the Forsyte novels, combines portraiture of a whole gal-lery of Galsworthy's Victorian relations with a par-ticular focus on one example of the tenacious Forsyte instinct for possession: Soames Forsyte's refusal to free his beautiful and intensely unhappy wife Irene from a marriage she sees as dead; Irene's affair with a "bohemian" (June Forsyte's fiancé Bosinney); and the grim but temporary victory of Soames over Irene, of Victorian convention over love. The triangular ro-mance can be seen as symbolic or schematic—the two men, representing the possessive spirit and the creative temperament, both aspire in their different ways for Beauty—but it is also Galsworthy's thinly disguised account of Ada's tragic marriage with his cousin. The personal involvement results in what is least satisfactory about a fine book: Galsworthy's in-ability, despite an attempt to be philosophical, to moderate his extreme sympathy for Irene and his emotional if not rational assignment of total guilt to Soames, a man both sinned against and sinning.

The Man of Property begins with an "At Home" at the house of Old Jolyon, eldest of the Forsyte broth-ers and head of the family. At this gathering on June 15, 1886, a party honoring the engagement of old Jolyon's granddaughter June to the architect Philip Bosinney, the reader is privileged to observe "the highest efflorescence of the Forsytes." In the senior generation, the sons and daughters of "Superior Dosset" Forsyte, who had come from the country and founded the family's fortunes, are a variety of Victorian types, among them Aunt Ann, an ancient sybil tenaciously holding onto the life that remains to her; Jolyon, imperious and philosophical; Soames's father James, milder than Jolyon but even more single-minded in his devotion to the Forsyte principles of property and family; James's twin Swithin, an old pouter-pigeon of a bachelor whose hereditary prudence is tinged with antiquated dandyism; and Timothy, the youngest of the ten brothers and sisters and perhaps the Forsyte's Forsyte. He is a man whose caution and whose saving nature are so highly developed that he has retired early and placed all his resources in gilt-edged "Consols," retreating so successfully from the world's demands that even at his own house, the "Exchange," where Forsytes meet and gossip, his presence is felt more often than seen or heard.

The common bond that unites these superficially variegated characters and makes them representative of their whole class is described by young Jolyon, Galsworthy's mouthpiece in the novel: "A Forsyte takes a practical—one might say a common-sense—view of things, and a practical view of things is based fundamentally on a sense of property." The Forsytes, who know good things when they see them, who never give themselves or their possessions away, are the "better half" of England—the "cornerstones of convention."

The novel's principal demonstration of the Forsyte "sense of property" centers on the marriage of Soames, a prospering young solicitor, and the mysterious and lovely Irene. Troubled by his wife's chilly indifference to his strong and genuine love for her and the fine possessions which are his way of showing that feeling, Soames engages June's fiancé Bosinney to design and erect an impressive country house for him and Irene at Robin Hill, in the Surrey countryside outside of London. While building this house, a process which posits Bosinney's aesthetic scorn for base monetary matters against Soames's financial precision and passion for a bargain, the architect falls in love with Irene. She, seeing him as an emblem of all that her detested husband is not, reciprocates. The two of them betray their respective Forsytes and enter into a clandestine relationship.

These complicated circumstances pit Soames, determined to retain his property, against Irene, equally determined in her stubbornly passive way to be free of her enslaver. The outcome is tragedy. Bosinney, bankrupt because Soames has justly but vengefully sued him for overspending on the house, and crazed with jealousy and sorrow because Soames has forcibly exercised his conjugal rights, falls under a cab's wheels in a fog and is killed. As the novel ends, the errant Irene has returned to her prison-home, not out of inclination but because like a "bird that is shot and dying" she has nowhere else to fall. Young Jolyon, arriving with a message from his father, has one glimpse into the well-furnished hell that is Soames and Irene's abode before Soames slams the door shut in his face.

Galsworthy's friends and literary advisers Edward and Constance Garnett felt that this ending was unsuitable and wished for the telling defeat of Forsyteism that would be afforded by Irene and Bosinney succeeding in an elopement. Galsworthy, with better instincts, stuck to his "negative method" as a stronger means of arousing public feeling against the possessive passion he attacked. Still, if the crushing forces of property were allowed a victory, albeit a comfortless one, at the novel's end, Soames's triumph was to prove short-lived, though contemporary readers would have to wait eleven years to make the discovery. In "Indian Summer of a Forsyte," Old Jolyon, who has bought Robin Hill from Soames and lives there with his son and grandchildren, encounters Irene, now living on her own, and makes her a bequest that enables her to enjoy a comfortable independence.

In Chancery

In Chancery continues the conflict between the two hostile branches of the Forsyte clan. Soames, who feels the need for a child and heir to his property, is still in love with Irene and hopeful of regaining her. Young Jolyon, made Irene's trustee by his father's will, opposes Soames in his efforts and finds himself attracted by more than sympathy for the lovely, lonely woman. At length, Soames's persistent importunities drive Irene to elope with Jolyon. The infidelity gives Soames grounds for a divorce. Freed at last from any connection with the man she loathes, Irene marries Jolyon. Soames in his turn makes a convenient match with a pretty young Frenchwoman, Annette. The novel ends with the birth of children to both couples.

To Let

To Let, the final volume of the trilogy, brings the family feud to a new generation. Fleur, daughter of Annette and Soames, and Jon, son of Irene and Jolyon, meet first by chance, then, mutually infatuated, by strategy. The cousins intend to marry but are dramatically separated by the dead hand of the past enmity. Jon goes off to America, where after some years he marries a Southern girl. Fleur, as passionately proprietary in her feeling for Jon as her father was toward Irene, believes that she has lost her bid for love and settles for a milder sort of happiness. She accepts the proposal of Michael Mont, the amiable, humorous, eminently civilized heir to a baronetcy.

A Modern Comedy

The second Forsyte series, *A Modern Comedy* (consisting of *The White Monkey*, *The Silver Spoon*, *Two Forsyte Interludes*, and *Swan Song*) centers on the adventures of the fashionable young Monts—Michael's stints in publishing and politics, Fleur's career as society hostess, femme fatale to a promising poet, canteen-keeper during the General Strike, mother, and most of all spoiled daughter to a fond yet wise father. In his love for his child, old Soames proves as selfless and giving as young Soames was possessive in his passion for Irene. Some twenty years after introducing Soames to the world, Galsworthy had come to admire, and at moments even to like, aspects of this gruff, practical, scrupulous incarnation of the possessive instinct, a character who as the years passed had usurped the place of Irene in the artist's imagination. Soames's death at the end of *Swan Song*—he succumbs to a blow on the head inflicted by a falling painting from which he saves Fleur—is at once an ironically appropriate end to the career of a man of property and a noble gesture of self-sacrifice.

When Galsworthy chose to terminate the life of Soames Forsyte, he symbolically presented the close of an age but also implicitly acknowledged the end of what was finest in his own literary career. However wide-ranging his talent might have been if possessed by another man, his personal temperament, training, and circumstances constrained it to a certain limited excellence. Galsworthy the artist was at his best depicting conflicts typical of the Victorian period, that consummate age of property, and relevant to his own life: the contradictory urges of artistic integrity and worldly wisdom, the foolish desire to possess beauty at war with the wise inclination to contemplate and appreciate it, the altruistic motto "do good" contending with the sanely middle-class imperative "be comfortable." Because he knew the overfurnished Victorian and post-Victorian world of the Forsytes and their kind from the inside, Galsworthy's best moral fables are credibly human as well, but when the old order he comprehended if never endorsed gave way to a new and unfathomable one, the novelist of principle dwindled to a kind of literary curator.

Peter W. Graham

Other major works

SHORT FICTION: *From the Four Winds*, 1897 (as John Sinjohn); *A Man of Devon*, 1901 (as Sinjohn); *Five Tales*, 1918; *Captures*, 1923; *Caravan: The Assembled Tales of John Galsworthy*, 1925; *Two Forsyte Interludes*, 1927; *On Forsyte 'Change*, 1930; *Soames and the Flag*, 1930; *Forsytes, Pendyces, and Others*, 1935.

PLAYS: *The Silver Box*, pr. 1906; *Joy*, pr. 1907; *Strife*, pr., pb. 1909; *Justice*, pr., pb. 1910; *The Little Dream*, pr., pb. 1911; *The Eldest Son*, pr., pb. 1912; *The Pigeon*, pr., pb. 1912; *The Fugitive*, pr., pb. 1913; *The Mob*, pr., pb. 1915; *A Bit o' Love*, pr., pb. 1915; *The Little Man*, pr., pb. 1915; *The Foundations*, pr. 1917; *Defeat*, pr. 1920; *The Skin Game*, pr., pb. 1920; *A Family Man*, pr. 1921; *The First and the Last*, pr., pb. 1921; *Hall-marked*, pb. 1921; *Punch and Go*, pb. 1921; *The Sun*, pb. 1921; *Loyalties*, pr., pb. 1922; *Windows*, pr., pb. 1922; *The Forest*, pr., pb. 1924; *Old English*, pr., pb. 1924; *The Show*, pr., pb. 1925; *Escape*, pr., pb. 1926; *Exiled*, pr., pb. 1929; *The Roof*, pr., pb. 1929.

POETRY: *The Collected Poems of John Galsworthy*, 1934 (Ada Galsworthy, editor).

NONFICTION: *A Commentary*, 1908; *A Motley*, 1910; *The Inn of Tranquility*, 1912; *A Sheaf*, 1916; *Another Sheaf*, 1919; *Tatterdemalion*, 1920; *Castles in Spain*, 1927; *Candelabra: Selected Essays and Addresses*, 1932; *Letters from John Galsworthy, 1900-1932*, 1934 (Edward Garnett, editor).

MISCELLANEOUS: *The Works of John Galsworthy*, 1922-1936 (30 volumes).

BIBLIOGRAPHY

Batchelor, John. *The Edwardian Novelists*. New York: St. Martin's Press, 1982. Begins by defining "Edwardian" literature and discusses Galsworthy in terms of his surprising similarities to D. H. Lawrence. *The Man of Property* and *Fraternity* are analyzed in detail, and the overall attitude toward Galsworthy is very positive. Contains an excellent bibliography of Edwardian fiction.

Dupre, Catherine. *John Galsworthy: A Biography*. New York: Coward, McCann & Geoghegan, 1976. A well-written and well-researched account of Galsworthy's life, relying heavily on letters and other primary sources. Also contains information about the writing of his literary works. Provides an excellent index, bibliographic notes, and several photographs.

Gindin, James. *John Galsworthy's Life and Art*. Ann Arbor: University of Michigan Press, 1987. Utilizing new sources, Gindin has written a masterful literary biography, particularly appropriate since Galsworthy's fiction is itself so closely tied to his personal life, social criticism, and historic times. Galsworthy moved from apprenticeship to "public edifice," but that image was tarnished and he became a "private edifice." This well-researched biography succeeds in relating Galsworthy's literary work to his life.

Mottram, Ralph H. *For Some We Loved: An Intimate Portrait of Ada and John Galsworthy*. London: Hutchinson University Library, 1956. This informal, undocumented account of Galsworthy's life, written by a personal friend of his, is anecdotal and laudatory. Mottram's focus is biographical, not critical, and he devotes little attention to Galsworthy's literary work. Contains a serviceable index.

Rønning, Anne Holden. *Hidden and Visible Suffrage: Emancipation and the Edwardian Woman in Galsworthy, Wells, and Forster*. New York: Peter Lang, 1995. See chapter 1, "The Social Context of Edwardian Literature," chapter 4, "Marriage in Galsworthy, Wells, and Forster," and chapter 6, "Galsworthy's View on Suffragism." Includes notes and bibliography.

Ru, Yi-ling. *The Family Novel: Toward a Generic Definition*. New York: Peter Lang, 1992. Examines Galsworthy's Forsyte saga as an example of the family novel. Other authors, including Roger Martin du Gard and Chin Pa, are examined as well.

Sternlicht, Sanford. *John Galsworthy*. Boston: Twayne, 1987. The most helpful critical volume on Galsworthy's literary and dramatic works despite being relatively brief. Four chapters are devoted to his novels, some of which, notably *A Modern Comedy*, are analyzed in some depth. His short stories, plays, and literary criticism are the subjects of three additional chapters. Provides a chronology, a biographical chapter, an excellent bibliography, including annotated secondary sources, and a helpful index.

GABRIEL GARCÍA MÁRQUEZ

Born: Aracataca, Colombia; March 6, 1928

PRINCIPAL LONG FICTION

La hojarasca, 1955 (novella; *Leaf Storm and Other Stories*, 1972)

El coronel no tiene quien le escriba, 1961 (novella; *No One Writes to the Colonel and Other Stories*, 1968)

La mala hora, 1962, rev. 1966 (*In Evil Hour*, 1979)

Cien años de soledad, 1967 (*One Hundred Years of Solitude*, 1970)

El otoño del patriarca, 1975 (*The Autumn of the Patriarch*, 1975)

Crónica de una muerte anunciada, 1981 (*Chronicle of a Death Foretold*, 1982)

(The Nobel Foundation)

El amor en los tiempos del cólera, 1985 (*Love in the Time of Cholera*, 1988)
El general en su laberinto, 1989 (*The General in His Labyrinth*, 1990)
Collected Novellas, 1990
Del amor y otros demonios, 1994 (*Of Love and Other Demons*, 1995)

OTHER LITERARY FORMS

In addition to his novels, Gabriel García Márquez has also written short stories, books of conversations, essays on cultural and political subjects, and screenplays. Many of his short stories were published originally in newspapers and all have been collected in volumes in Spanish. His stories have also appeared in *The Atlantic Monthly*, *Esquire*, and *The New Yorker*. Almost all of his stories are available in English.

ACHIEVEMENTS

After the publication of *One Hundred Years of Solitude* in 1967, García Márquez enjoyed increasing

international appeal in the Hispanic world and beyond. The initial reaction to the Spanish edition, which was first issued in Buenos Aires, was overwhelming: New editions were published at the amazing rate of one per week, as the public and critics alike applauded the Colombian masterpiece. The reaction was similar as translations were published: In France, the novel was proclaimed the best foreign book of 1969; in Italy, it was awarded the Chianchiano Prize (1969); and in the United States, it was named one of the twelve best books of the year (1970). *One Hundred Years of Solitude* has been translated into more than twenty-seven languages.

The worldwide appeal of García Márquez's masterpiece is widely acknowledged to have been the single most important factor in the extraordinary growth of interest in the Latin American novel. No novelist of the postwar era has had an international influence greater than that of García Márquez; his Magical Realism has given rise to one of the dominant trends in world fiction in the 1970's and the 1980's. The winner of numerous literary honors, including the Neustadt International Prize for Literature in 1972, García Márquez was awarded the world's highest literary accolade, the Nobel Prize, in 1982.

BIOGRAPHY

Gabriel García Márquez was born in Aracataca, near the Caribbean coast of Colombia, on March 6, 1928. His parents were less important to his upbringing than his grandparents, with whom he lived for the first eight years of his life. García Márquez emphasized their significance by claiming that nothing interesting happened to him after his grandfather's death, when he was eight years old. These early years included a heavy dose of history, myth, legend, and traditional oral storytelling. The Aracataca region, which recently had experienced the economic boom of "banana fever," could no longer rely upon American funding, financially or ideologically; therefore myths and nostalgia became essential in forming young García Márquez's reality. His grandparents' home nurtured these interests: His grandmother told the most incredible tales with naturalness and nonchalance. García Márquez claimed that these were the same qualities that were key to controlling the narrative voice in *One Hundred Years of Solitude*. His grandfather's influence was equally important; it was from him that García Márquez first heard stories of the wars and fables of Colombia, including tales from the War of a Thousand Days, which so profoundly influenced Colombia, including Aracataca, at the turn of the century.

García Márquez's parents sent him from the tropical, vibrant coast to the cool and dismal highlands of Bogotá for his secondary education in a private Jesuit school, the National College of Zipaquirá. Neither the frigidity of the Andes nor Bogotá's natives were to his liking, but he was graduated in 1946. He began law studies the following year at the National University in Bogotá. Two key events, coupled with his disinterest in law, made 1947 a more important year for literature than jurisprudence. First, he met Plinio Apuleyo Mendoza, a friend and supporter in the early stages of García Márquez's writing career, and a colleague and collaborator later; in the same year, he published his first story, "La tercera resignación" ("The Third Resignation"), in one of Bogotá's major newspapers, *El Espectador*. Within the next five years, García Márquez published fifteen short stories in Colombian newspapers. Years later, traces of the journalistic style would emerge in García Márquez's straightforward retelling of seemingly incredible events.

In April, 1948, an event occurred which would affect García Márquez's life immediately and, in the course of time, mark an important direction of Colombia's history and fiction for the next twenty years. A liberal populist candidate for the presidency, Jorge Eliécer Gaitán, was assassinated on April 9. This act served as a catalyst for mass violence in Bogotá, civil unrest in much of the country, and civil war in rural areas of Colombia during the next ten years. García Márquez moved back to the coast, taking up residence in Cartagena in May. By then, he had published three stories in *El Espectador*. He began writing as a journalist for Cartagena's newspaper *El Universal* and pursued both his true interest—reading and writing fiction—and the study of law. He was enrolled in the National University of Cartagena

from June, 1948, until he finished his third year in 1949.

The period from 1949 to the mid-1950's was important primarily for the modern novels that García Márquez read for the first time and the literary friends he established in Barranquilla, a nearby coastal city to which he moved in 1950; the influence of such writers as William Faulkner, Virginia Woolf, and Franz Kafka was significant, particularly that of Faulkner. Through his journalism and from statements of his close friends of this period, scholars documented that García Márquez also read works by James Joyce, John Dos Passos, Ernest Hemingway, John Steinbeck, and William Saroyan, among others. In 1950, García Márquez began to write for the newspaper *El Heraldo* and to take advantage of the surprisingly cosmopolitan literary life available to him while meeting regularly with the literati of the Happy Bar and La Cueva bar in Barranquilla. The literary father figure of the group was Ramón Vinyes, a Catalonian who stimulated the reading of contemporary world fiction among the young future writers. García Márquez wrote a regular column, "La jirafa," in Barranquilla's newspaper *El Heraldo*. In addition to the short stories he published during this period, García Márquez completed the manuscript for a novel entitled *La casa*, an early version of what would become the novella *Leaf Storm*; the prestigious publishing firm Losada of Buenos Aires rejected the novel. In early 1954, García Márquez's friend Alvaro Mutis convinced him to return to Bogotá to write in *El Espectador*.

The year 1955 was a turning point in García Márquez's career for several reasons: He published *Leaf Storm*, his first work of long fiction; he gained official recognition as a writer when the Association of Artists and Writers of Bogotá awarded him a prize for his story "Un día después del sábado" ("One Day After Saturday"); in July of that year, *El Espectador* sent him to Geneva on a journalistic mission; the closing of *El Espectador* resulted in a change of the original plans for a short stay in Europe and eventually led to his residence in Paris until 1958.

After moving to Caracas in 1958 and New York in 1961 to work as a correspondent for Cuba's *Prensa latina*, García Márquez lived in Mexico for several years of literary silence. In 1965, the pieces of his culminating work—that is, his previous stories—began to fall into place for the creation of *One Hundred Years of Solitude*. García Márquez had found the key to the creation of the magical reality of Macondo, which had been portrayed only partially in his previous fiction. García Márquez tells of the enthusiasm and excitement involved in the culmination of the novel he had been writing for some twenty years. After its completion and resulting success, García Márquez has enjoyed economic security that enables him to live comfortably in Spain, Mexico, and Colombia, to travel extensively, and to continue writing.

ANALYSIS

Gabriel García Márquez denies that the fictional world which he describes in his novels is a world of fantasy. He concludes an article about fantasy and artistic creation in Latin America with the following statement: "Reality is a better writer than we are. Our destiny, and perhaps our glory, is to try to imitate it with humility, and the best that is possible for us." Perhaps because García Márquez began writing as a journalist, this attitude permeates much of his writing, and this version of reality is reflected in his fiction. A deep-seated strain of antirationality underlies all of his fiction, which deals with Latin American "reality" in broad terms, rejecting the narrow regionalism of his literary fathers. The result is a type of fiction that transcends its regional base, a Faulknerian fiction that one critic of Spanish American literature, John S. Brushwood, called "transcendent regionalism." A self-proclaimed admirer of Faulkner, García Márquez would strive toward a transcendent regionalism in nearly all his works, with varying degrees of success. Finally, García Márquez's redefinition of realism implies a faithfulness to a higher truth, a mythical level of reality that a more pedestrian realism cannot comprehend. These three factors—antirationality, transcendent regionalism, and myth—are integral to the aesthetics of García Márquez's fiction, aesthetics that balance journalistic depictions of historical events with fantastic stories and cultural myths.

LEAF STORM

García Márquez's first published work of long fiction was the novella *Leaf Storm*. Asked in 1982 to judge how the young García Márquez wrote this tale, the mature writer had the following response:

> With passion, because he wrote it quickly, thinking he wouldn't write anything else in his lifetime, that that one was his only opportunity, and so he tried to put in everything he had learned up to then. Especially literary techniques and tricks taken from American and English writers he was reading.

As anyone who reads *Leaf Storm* recognizes immediately, the apprentice writer used techniques from Faulkner. The parallel between *Leaf Storm* and *As I Lay Dying* (1930) in structure and narrative point of view is blatant. The setting is Macondo during approximately the first quarter of the twentieth century, and the action centers on an unnamed doctor, believed to be from France, who had lived in Macondo during this twenty-five-year period and who ultimately committed suicide. All of this is revealed through three narrators who attend the doctor's wake, a nine-year-old boy, his mother, and his grandfather; the multiple points of view involve the reader in a process of discovery. The content of the boy's narration tends to be limited to his immediate situation, revealing primarily what he sees at the wake and how he feels at the moment. The mother's scope is broader; she relates information and anecdotes beyond the immediate circumstance, although limited primarily to her own friends. The grandfather's narration provides a historical account of the doctor's life and Macondo. The effect of this structure is a deeper penetration into the reality of Macondo than either a strictly personal or a strictly historical version would have allowed.

Leaf Storm is a point of departure in establishing elements basic to all García Márquez's fiction. The underlying antirationality of this structure lies in the fact that effects are often apparent before causes or, in some cases, causes never surface. The reader can never rationally explain, for example, why the town's priest reads from the Bristol Almanac or why the doctor eats grass for dinner. The novel has the formal elements of transcendent regionalism: García Márquez constructs a story of universal thematic scope—death, solitude—on a clearly defined regional base. One reason the novel does not have the universal appeal of his later fiction is the relative ineffectiveness in creating a mythical level of reality. The portrayals of both the doctor and the grandfather make them characters with mythic potential, but neither their characterization nor any other aspect of the novel creates a true sense of myth in *Leaf Storm*. Consequently, *Leaf Storm* is an important, but not totally successful, step in the creation of the Macondo that later will blossom in *One Hundred Years of Solitude*.

The next steps in García Márquez's apprenticeship for the creation of *One Hundred Years of Solitude* were the novella *No One Writes to the Colonel* and the novella or short novel *In Evil Hour*. Both are more firmly based on Colombia's historical reality than most of the writer's later work. This reality is *la violencia*, the period of civil war during the 1950's. *No One Writes to the Colonel* is the story of a stoic retired colonel who waits fifteen years for a pension check that never arrives. Besides the psychological portrayal of this colonel, the characterization and actions of other characters reveal a town suffering from corruption and repression. This backdrop is García Márquez's subtle means of incorporating the social and political realities of life in Colombia during this period. For example, the colonel's son is killed because of his political activism, but this matter never takes the form of direct political denunciation on the part of the author. A traditional omniscient narrator tells this story in a linear fashion.

IN EVIL HOUR

In Evil Hour also features a controlling omniscient narrator and basically linear development of the story, but here García Márquez employs a juxtaposition of scenes to create a montage effect. Someone puts up placards that undermine the town's stability. These anonymous notes contain personal accusations that lead to conflicts: fights, people moving from the town, and even deaths. The mayor, who had been proud of the control he had established in the town before the appearance of the placards, is forced to repress the town's inhabitants in order to maintain order. García Márquez captures the essence of the fear and distrust that pervaded the national consciousness in Colombia at the time.

The antirationality of these stories functions as the catalyst of the anecdotes. In *No One Writes to the Colonel*, it is the inexplicable hope that the colonel has that he will receive the important letter he awaits. The antirational element in *In Evil Hour* is the presence and effect of the placards. Neither of these phenomena is fully explainable in rational terms, although the reader's speculation is invited. Both works transcend their regional base by capturing universal essences: the hope of the colonel and the fear of the town's inhabitants in *In Evil Hour*. The only element that approaches mythic dimensions is the characterization of the colonel in the first of these two books.

"Many years later, as he faced the firing squad, Colonel Aureliano Buendía was to remember that distant afternoon when his father took him to discover ice." These are the opening words of García Márquez's masterpiece, *One Hundred Years of Solitude*. Most readers have found themselves swept from these lines through the discovery of ice, to the firing squad and beyond, unable to forget the enchantment of Macondo and the attractiveness of the novel. As a matter of fact, few critics have passed the opportunity to comment on the possible sources of this very attractiveness. Many have pointed to the author's masterful synthesis of various literary traditions, from the individual biography to the epic. Other critics seem to contradict one another by attributing the novel's attractiveness, on the one hand, to its purely invented reality and, on the other, to its truthful depiction of Colombian history. Many readers are clearly attracted by the humor. In addition, the novel has other interesting characteristics: its people, its fantasy, its plot suspense, its craftsmanship, and its sense of wholeness. It is a novel that is difficult to capture—describe appropriately or analyze—because of the intangible quality of much of the reader's experience. Some critics have found the term Magical Realism useful. The term can be helpful in dealing with a novel in which a narrator describes with perfect naturalness a scene in which a character ascends to Heaven or in which no one seems to notice the massacre of thousands of striking workers. Paradoxically, despite the numerous difficulties such a novel presents for the critic, it is not at all difficult to read.

ONE HUNDRED YEARS OF SOLITUDE

One Hundred Years of Solitude is a family saga which tells the story of five generations of Buendias. It begins with the foundation of Macondo by José Arcadio Buendia and his wife Ursula. Despite their fear that the consummation of their marriage will result in the birth of a child with a pig's tail (there is a family precedent for such an event), José Arcadio Buendia decides to challenge fate to protect his image as a man. A second Macondo is established after José Arcadio Buendia kills a man in the original town. The early years of life in Macondo are primitive, albeit a kind of paradise. Macondo's only contact with the outside world is provided by gypsies who bring items such as the ice and magnets that the inhabitants find amazing. They suffer an insomnia plague that results in the loss of both sleep and memory. Modern civilization finally reaches Macondo, along with its numerous institutions; with the arrival of the national political parties come civil wars caused by their conflicts. The Americans bring economic prosperity and exploitation of the workers on the banana plantations. These intrusions of foreigners and modernity are eliminated by a flood that washes them away and returns Macondo to a state similar to its original paradise. In the end, Macondo is not a paradise, however, but a fiction: a member of the Buendia family deciphers a parchment written in Sanskrit which foretold the entire story of the family and Macondo from beginning to the end—that is, the story of *One Hundred Years of Solitude*. History is the completion of a fiction.

Part of the playfulness in the development of the plot involves following the intricate Buendia family line. The original José Arcadio Buendia engenders two sons, José Arcadio and Aureliano. The latter becomes identified as Colonel Aureliano. All their offspring also carry similar names—Arcadio, Aureliano José, Jose Arcadio Segundo, and so on—making following the Buendia family line an exercise in futility or a challenging game of identities. The English

translation, unlike the original Spanish edition, carries a genealogical chart.

One Hundred Years of Solitude is ostensibly a traditional novel which tells a story in a basically linear fashion. It is also a product of technical mastery by a superb craftsman of fiction. The novel's structure is cyclical, from the internal cycles of events that repeat within the novel to the broader cycle completed with the deciphering of the parchments.

García Márquez's handling of narrative point of view is enormously subtle, although it is managed with deceptive simplicity. On the one hand, the omniscient narrator tells the story with a perspective similar to a child's view of the world. Consequently, this childlike narrator views and describes the world with freshness and innocence, taking for granted the incredible events of Macondo. Conversely, the narrator is surprised and amazed about things that are normally considered ordinary, such as ice or magnets. García Márquez's style is based on a use of hyperbole, a constant source of humor. One of the most hilarious hyperbolic characterizations is of Colonel Aureliano Buendia, whose machismo is the target of García Márquez's superb satire.

The antirationality of *One Hundred Years of Solitude* is not only a characteristic, but also a fundamental principle of the entire narrative system. Entrance into the magical world of Macondo is an acceptance of the negation of rationality. It is soon apparent that everything is possible in Macondo. The work's transcendent regionalism can be visualized as a series of concentric circles emanating from Macondo. The circles near the center inscribe a reality of the Caribbean coast and Colombia—both its historical reality and myths. Larger circles contain patterns associated with all of Latin America, such as the tradition of machismo. Finally, the novel's connotations are universal; on this level one reads the work as a contemporary novelization of the biblical Creation and other universal patterns, such as the fear of incest that pervades the story.

Perhaps the most important achievement of this novel, however, is its expression of a mythic reality. One aspect of this is mythic time that negates linear time. The repetition of numerous cycles, such as the names of the members of the Buendia family, create this sense of an eternal present. The characterization of Colonel Aureliano Buendia and Ursula makes them characters who function at a mythic level beyond the limits of everyday reality and the capabilities of persons in our everyday world. There is also a biblical level of reading that develops myth from Creation and Original Sin to the apocalyptic ending. García Márquez's creation of a traditional yet fascinating story, his mastery of narrative technique, and his creation of myth make *One Hundred Years of Solitude* not only one of the most important novels from Latin America of the twentieth century but also a work appreciated by an international readership.

THE AUTUMN OF THE PATRIARCH

Some critics were disappointed with the appearance of *The Autumn of the Patriarch*. They found neither the accessibility nor the magical world of *One Hundred Years of Solitude*. Judged on its own artistic merit, however, *The Autumn of the Patriarch* is an outstanding novel, marked by the superb craftsmanship and humor characteristic of almost all García Márquez's work.

Several of the major Latin American writers published novels about dictators in the 1970's. García Márquez's novel deals with a dictator in an unnamed Caribbean nation. The dictator figure is a synthesis of many dictators, historical and fictional. García Márquez had spent many years researching these tyrants. The novel begins with the image of a dictator's corpse rotting in his presidential palace. From the discovery of the corpse by an unidentified narrator within the story, the narrative moves away from the immediate situation to relating events from the dictator's past. His life is bizarre and fantastic, as he is willing to take any measure—including serving one of his generals roasted on a platter—to intimidate others and maintain his power.

Structure and style can present a challenge for readers of *The Autumn of the Patriarch*; its consistently long sentences have caused some readers to question if García Márquez bothered with punctuation at all. In reality, even the length of sentences was carefully controlled in this prose poem. In each chapter, García Márquez uses progressively longer sentences, culminating in the last chapter, which is one sentence. The use of multiple narrative voices within these extensive sentences creates a full portrayal of the pitiful dictator and is a source of much of the novel's humor.

CHRONICLE OF A DEATH FORETOLD

Although it is a relatively minor work in García Márquez's oeuvre, the short novel or novella *Chronicle of a Death Foretold* is an interesting tour de force. The story centers on the assassination of its central character, Santiago Nassar. A pair of brothers kill him to save the honor of their sister, Angela Vicario.

Fascinating occurrences abound in *Chronicle of a Death Foretold*, but perhaps the most incredible of all is the series of events surrounding the assassination itself: Everyone in the town, including Nassar himself, knows that he is going to die. Nevertheless, nothing is done to obstruct the seemingly inevitable series of events leading to his death. The novel consists of five chapters which relate the story in a generally chronological fashion. The time span is quite limited: The first chapter tells the events of the morning of the assassination; the second chapter relates the courtship of Angela Vicario by Nassar up to the evening of the marriage; the third chapter covers that evening. In the fourth chapter, the narrator moves ahead in time, telling of events after the assassination, such as the autopsy. The last chapter returns to the original chronology, providing the graphic details of the killing the morning after the wedding. García Márquez's major accomplishment in this work is having written a story that maintains the reader's interest despite the fact that its denouement is announced in the first sentence.

LOVE IN THE TIME OF CHOLERA

In *Love in the Time of Cholera*, García Márquez accomplishes quite a different objective, exploring the various facets of romantic love, including both those that are readily observable and those that exist solely in the imaginations of those involved. This novel begins with the death of Dr. Juvenal Urbina, husband to Fermina Daza. Daza, in turn, is the long-standing love interest of Florentino Ariza, whose reappearance shortly after the death of Urbina prompts a reexamination of Daza's romantic history. Rather than the guiltily quixotic recollection one might expect under such circumstances, what follows is an examination of the incredible range of passion and tedium that occur during the course of a long marriage. Although criticized for being overly sentimental, this book continues García Márquez's tradition of mixing the real and the imaginary, the extraordinary and the commonplace, this time in the domestic sphere rather than a broader historical or political context, but with similarly effective dramatic results. By focusing such intense attention on what would be insignificant events from an outsider's perspective, García Márquez effectively portrays the self-referential world of love, in which each couple exists as the center of their own universe.

THE GENERAL IN HIS LABYRINTH

In his next novel, García Márquez returns to the overtly rather than the personally political. In this book, *The General in His Labyrinth*, García Márquez tells about the final days of General Simón Bolívar, who, having wrested his people from Spanish rule, subsequently struggled (and failed) to save them from themselves and each other. Unlike *Love in the Time of Cholera*, in which the intricacies of romantic relationships are the focus of the story, *The General in His Labyrinth* centers around political intrigue and malfeasance, with romantic dalliances playing a subordinate (though discomfiting) role. More disturbing, however, is the notion that because this novel treats Latin American history in greater depth than any of García Márquez's previous works, it is less susceptible to embellishment because of the inflammatory nature of the events on which the novel is based. In this story, the facts themselves are the stuff of myth, blurring the line between factual, journalistic telling and García Márquez's trademark Magical Realism.

OF LOVE AND OTHER DEMONS

The contrast reemerges in García Márquez's next novel, *Of Love and Other Demons*. This story has its roots in an event that García Márquez witnessed when he was a reporter, in which the coffin of a young woman was exhumed from a grave in which it had lain for two hundred years. When the casket was opened, it was found to contain not only the body of the woman, long dead, but also yards and yards of

her hair, still attached to her skull and as vibrant as that of a living person. From this factual event, and select details of a story his grandparents had told him of a girl who was killed after having contracted rabies, García Márquez contrives the story of Sierva Maria, a character who, like her real life counterparts, seems to be defined by the circumstances of her death rather than those of her life. In this story, as in *The General in His Labyrinth*, the most notable dangers are not from the supernatural or fantastic, but rather from ordinary human passions channeled toward violent (but human) ends.

Each of García Márquez's novels highlights the conflicts that define Latin America in the twentieth century—the tension between centuries-old myth and modern rationalism, between authentic and imagined dangers, between the fantastic and the ordinary. These negotiations take place in all arenas, from the domestic sphere to the upper echelons of government. In each case, the relationship between the real and the fantastic must be constantly redefined in relationship to the circumstances of the characters through whom the tale is told. It is this ability to capture the perceptual chaos that arises from such ideological clashes that makes García Márquez one of the greatest authors of all time.

Raymond L. Williams, updated by T. A. Fishman

OTHER MAJOR WORKS

SHORT FICTION: *Los funerales de la Mamá Grande*, 1962 (*Big Mama's Funeral*, stories included in *No One Writes to the Colonel and Other Stories*, 1968); *Isabel viendo llover en Macondo*, 1967 (*Monologue of Isabel Watching It Rain in Macondo*, 1972); *No One Writes to the Colonel and Other Stories*, 1968; *Relato de un náufrago: Que estuvo diez días a la deriva en una balsa sin comer ni beber, que fue proclamado héroe de la patria, besado por las reinas de la belleza y hecho rico por la publicidad, y luego aborrecido por el gobierno y olvidado para siempre*, 1970 (*The Story of a Shipwrecked Sailor: Who Drifted on a Liferaft for Ten Days Without Food or Water, Was Proclaimed a National Hero, Kissed by Beauty Queens, Made Rich Through Publicity, and Then Spurned by the Govern-*

ment and Forgotten for All Time, 1986); *La increíble y triste historia de la Cándida Eréndira y de su abuela desalmada*, 1972 (*Innocent Eréndira and Other Stories*, 1978); *El negro que hizo esperar a los ángeles*, 1972; *Ojos de perro azul*, 1972; *Todos los cuentos de Gabriel García Márquez*, 1975; *Collected Stories*, 1984; *Doce cuentos peregrinos*, 1992 (*Strange Pilgrims: Twelve Stories*, 1993).

NONFICTION: *La novela en América Latina: Diálogo*, 1968 (with Mario Vargas Llosa); *Cuando era feliz e indocumentado*, 1973; *Chile, el golpe y los gringos*, 1974; *Crónicas y reportajes*, 1976; *Operación Carlota*, 1977; *Periodismo militante*, 1978; *De viaje por los países socialistas*, 1978; *Obra periodística*, 1981-1983 (4 volumes; includes *Textos costeños*, 1981; *Entre cachacos I*, 1982; *Entre cachacos II*, 1982; *De Europa y América, 1955-1960*, 1983); *El olor de la guayaba: Conversaciones con Plinio Apuleyo Mendoza*, 1982 (*The Fragrance of the Guava: Plinio Apuleyo Mendoza in Conversation with Gabriel García Márquez*, 1983; also known as *The Smell of Guava*, 1984); *La aventura de Miguel Littín, clandestino en Chile*, 1986 (*Clandestine in Chile: The Adventures of Miguel Littín*, 1987); *Notas de prensa 1980-1984*, 1991; *Por un país al alcance de los niños*, 1996 (*For the Sake of a Country Within Reach of the Children*, 1998); *Noticia de un secuestro*, 1996 (*News of a Kidnapping*, 1997).

BIBLIOGRAPHY

Bell, Michael. *Gabriel García Márquez: Solitude and Solidarity*. New York: St. Martin's Press, 1993. This book explores García Márquez's works from a number of different perspectives, ranging from comparative literary criticism to political and social critiques. Aso included are commentaries on García Márquez's styles, including journalism and Magical Realism.

Bell-Villada, Gene H. *García Márquez: The Man and His Work*. Chapel Hill: University of North Carolina Press, 1990. Includes biographical information on García Márquez, an index, and a bibliography.

Bloom, Harold, ed. *Gabriel García Márquez*. New York: Chelsea House, 1989. Comprises eighteen critical essays on García Márquez, arranged in order of their original publication. Also features an index and a bibliography.

González, Nelly Sfeir de. *Bibliographic Guide to Gabriel García Márquez, 1986-1992*. Westport, Conn.: Greenwood Press, 1994. An annotated bibliography that includes works by García Márquez, criticism and sources for him, and an index of audio and visual materials related to the author and his works.

Williams, Raymond L. *Gabriel García Márquez*. Boston: Twayne, 1984. A good introduction to García Márquez's works for the beginning student.

Wood, Michael. *Gabriel García Márquez: "One Hundred Years of Solitude."* Cambridge, N.Y.: Cambridge University Press, 1990. This book provides much of the background information necessary to understand the history and cultural traditions that inform García Márquez's writings, including insight into the sociopolitical history of Latin America and biographical information about García Márquez himself.

JOHN GARDNER

Born: Batavia, New York; July 21, 1933
Died: Susquehanna, Pennsylvania; September 14, 1982

PRINCIPAL LONG FICTION
The Resurrection, 1966
The Wreckage of Agathon, 1970
Grendel, 1971
The Sunlight Dialogues, 1972
Nickel Mountain: A Pastoral Novel, 1973
October Light, 1976
In the Suicide Mountains, 1977
Freddy's Book, 1980
Mickelsson's Ghosts, 1982
"Stillness" and "Shadows," 1986 (with Nicholas Delbanco)

(Joel Gardner)

OTHER LITERARY FORMS

As a writer, John Gardner was as versatile as he was prolific. In addition to his novels, he published an epic poem (*Jason and Medeia*, 1973), two collections of short stories, four books for children, poetry, and reviews. During the early 1960's, when Gardner was a struggling assistant professor with a growing backlog of unpublished fiction and rejection slips, he turned to more academic pursuits. While some of this work is distinctly scholarly in nature, much of it is directed at a less specialized audience and is designed to make the literature more accessible and more understandable to the general reader or undergraduate student: thus Gardner's translations, or modernized versions, of medieval poetry, a textbook-anthology of fiction, a popular biography of Geoffrey Chaucer, his controversial attack on the contemporary arts and criticism, *On Moral Fiction* (published in 1978 but, like his Chaucer books, begun more than ten years

earlier), and a book of advice for young writers, *The Art of Fiction* (1984). Gardner also wrote a number of plays for National Public Radio's "Earplay" series and several opera librettos (one of which, *Rumpelstiltskin*, 1979, was professionally staged by the Opera Company of Philadelphia).

ACHIEVEMENTS

At a time when the line between popular and innovative fiction was often considered, in critic Raymond Federman's word, "uncrossable," Gardner managed to make his mark in both camps. Although his first novel, *The Resurrection*, was indifferently received, his second, *The Wreckage of Agathon*, which deals with law and order in ancient Sparta, gained a small following as a result of its relevance to Vietnam and the Nixon administration. *Grendel*, a parodic retelling of *Beowulf* (c. 1000) from the monster's point of view, was widely praised and in its paperback edition became as popular as *The Catcher in the Rye* (J. D. Salinger, 1951) was in the 1950's. Its success established Gardner's reputation as both an entertaining storyteller and an innovative parodist, a view that was confirmed by the publication of *The King's Indian: Stories and Tales* in 1974. His next three novels all became best-sellers: *The Sunlight Dialogues*, *Nickel Mountain*, and *October Light*, which won the 1977 National Book Critics Circle Award for fiction. Among his other awards and honors were a Woodrow Wilson Fellowship (1955), a Danforth Fellowship (1970-1973), an award from the National Endowment for the Arts (1972), a Guggenheim Fellowship (1973-1974), an American Academy of Arts and Letters prize for fiction (1975), the Armstrong Prize for his radio play, *The Temptation Game* (1977), and the 1978 Lamport Foundation award for his essay "Moral Fiction."

Upon the publication of the full text of *On Moral Fiction* in 1978, Gardner became a center of literary attention. His plainspoken criticism of fashionable pessimism in the contemporary arts and his generally negative remarks concerning individual writers led to an appearance on *The Dick Cavett Show* in May, 1978, a cover story in *The New York Times Magazine* in August, 1979, a special issue of the journal *Fiction*

International devoted to the question of "moral" art, as well as the censure of those who saw Gardner as a reactionary and the praise of others who quickly adopted him as a spokesman for a more traditional approach to fiction.

BIOGRAPHY

John Champlin Gardner, Jr., was born on July 21, 1933, in the western New York community of Batavia, the setting of *The Resurrection*, *The Sunlight Dialogues*, and a number of short stories. Strongly influenced by his father, a farmer and lay preacher, and his mother, an English teacher, Gardner, nicknamed Bud (Welsh for poet), began writing stories when he was eight years old and reading his work aloud to the family in the evening. The death of his younger brother, Gilbert, in a farm accident on April 4, 1945, seems to have been the most formative event in Gardner's life. He felt responsible for his brother's death, which he fictionalized in the story "Redemption" (1977), and as a result became deeply introspective. His mother suggested that Gilbert's death may also account for her son's remarkable energy and productivity, as if he wished to live both his own life and his brother's. During his high school years, Gardner commuted to the Eastman School of Music in nearby Rochester where he took French horn lessons. He attended DePauw University for two years, majoring in chemistry, and then, following his marriage to Joan Patterson, a cousin, on June 6, 1953, transferred to Washington University where, under the tutelage of Jarvis Thurston, he began writing *Nickel Mountain*. From 1955 to 1958 Gardner attended the University of Iowa; at first he studied at the Writers Workshop (his M.A. thesis and Ph.D. dissertation were both creative rather than scholarly: one a collection of stories, the other a novel, *The Old Men*) but later switched to the study of Anglo-Saxon and medieval literature under the guidance of John C. McGalliard.

Following his study at Iowa, Gardner held faculty appointments at various colleges and universities: Oberlin College (1958-1959); Chico State (1959-1962), where he coedited *MSS* and the student literary review *Selection*; San Francisco State University,

where he translated the alliterative *Morte d'Arthure* and the works of the Gawain-poet and began writing *The Resurrection*, *The Sunlight Dialogues*, and a study of Chaucer; Southern Illinois University (1965-1976), including visiting professorships at the University of Detroit (1970), Northwestern University (1973), and Bennington College (1975-1976), a sabbatical in England (1971), and a month-long tour of Japan for the United States Information Service (September-October, 1974); Skidmore and Williams Colleges (1977); George Mason University (1977-1978); and, from 1978 until his death, the State University of New York at Binghamton, where he directed the writing program. Especially significant in Gardner's biography is the period from 1976 through 1978, when *October Light* won popular and critical acclaim. During that time, Gardner lectured on moral fiction at campuses across the country, and his opera *Rumpelstiltskin* premiered in Lexington, Kentucky. Then Gardner's life took a darker turn: the breakup of his first marriage; a plagiarism charge leveled against him for his Chaucer biography, a charge that for some reason made its way into the pages of *Newsweek* magazine; a successful operation for intestinal cancer; and the uproar over *On Moral Fiction*, as well as the often hostile reviews of *Freddy's Book* and *Mickelsson's Ghosts*. Until their amicable divorce in 1982, Gardner lived with his second wife, the poet L. M. (Liz) Rosenberg, in Susquehanna, Pennsylvania, where he became active in the Laurel Street Theatre both as an actor and as a writer. He died in a motorcycle accident on September 14, 1982, a few days before he was to marry Susan Thornton of Rochester, New York. At the time of his death, Gardner had been working (as was his habit) on a variety of projects: operas, radio plays, a revival of his literary journal *MSS*, a television talk show on the arts, a book of advice for young writers (*The Art of Fiction*), a translation of *Gilgamesh* (a poem which figures prominently in *The Sunlight Dialogues*), and the novel *Shadows*.

ANALYSIS

John Gardner is a difficult writer to classify. He was alternately a realist and a fabulist, a novelist of ideas and a writer who maintained that characters and human situations are always more important than philosophy. He was, as well, an academically inclined New Novelist whose work is formally innovative, stylistically extravagant, openly parodic, and highly allusive; yet, at the same time, he was an accessible, popular storyteller, one who some critics, in the wake of *On Moral Fiction*, have labeled a reactionary traditionalist. It is perhaps best to think of Gardner not as a writer who belongs to any one school but instead as a writer who, in terms of style, subject, and moral vision, mediates between the various extremes of innovation and tradition, freedom and order, individual and society. He employed the metafictionist's narrative tricks, for example, not to show that fiction—and, by extension, life—is mere artifice, meaningless play, but to put those tricks to some higher purpose. His fiction raises a familiar but still urgent question: How is humankind to act in a seemingly inhospitable world where chance and uncertainty appear to have rendered all traditional values worthless?

As different as his characters are in most outward aspects, they are similar in one important way: They are idealists who feel betrayed when their inherited vision of harmony and purpose crumbles beneath the weight of modern incoherence. Once betrayed, they abandon their childlike ideals and embrace the existentialist position that Gardner deplores for its rationalist assumptions and pessimistic moral relativism. His antidote to the modern malaise in general and Jean-Paul Sartre's "nausea" in particular is a twentieth century version of the heroic ideal: common heroes—fathers and husbands, farmers and professors, for example—who intuitively understand that whatever the odds against them, they must act as if they can protect those whom they love. Instead of pure and powerful knights dedicated to a holy quest, Gardner's heroes are confused, sometimes ridiculous figures who learn to overcome their feelings of betrayal and find their strength in love, memory, and forgiveness. Choosing to act responsibly, they achieve a certain measure of human dignity. In effect, the choice these characters face is a simple one: either to affirm "the buzzing blooming confusion" of life, as Gardner, quoting William James, calls it, or to

deny it. Whereas the existentialist finds in that confusion meaningless abundance and historical discontinuity, Gardner posits meaningful variety and an interconnectedness that assumes value and makes the individual a part of, not apart from, the human and natural worlds in which he or she lives.

To find, or imagine, these connections is the role Gardner assigns to the artist. This view, propounded at length in *On Moral Fiction*, clearly puts Gardner at odds with other contemporary writers of innovative fiction who, he claims, too readily and uncritically accept the views of Sartre, Sigmund Freud, Ludwig Wittgenstein, and other twentieth century pessimists. Art, Gardner maintains, ought not merely to reflect life as it is but also should portray life as it should be. This does not mean that Gardner approves of simpleminded affirmations, for he carefully distinguishes "true" artists from those who simplify complex moral issues, as well as from those who, like William Gass, sidestep such issues entirely by creating "linguistic sculpture" in which only the "surface texture" is important.

Believing that art does indeed affect life and accepting Percy Bysshe Shelley's conception of the artist as legislator for all humankind, Gardner calls for a moral fiction that provides "valid models for imitation, eternal verities worth keeping in mind, and a benevolent vision of the possible" which will cause the reader to feel uneasy about his of her failings and limitations and stimulate him or her to act virtuously. Moral fiction, however, is not didactic; rather, it involves a search for truth. The author "gropes" for meaning in the act of writing and revising his story; then, by creating suspense, he devises for the reader a parallel experience. The meaning that author and reader discover in Gardner's work emphasizes the importance of rejecting existential isolation and accepting one's place in the human community, the "common herd" as Gardner calls it in one story. This meaning is not so much rational and intellectual as intuitive and emotional, less a specific message than a feeling—as is entirely appropriate in the case of a writer who defines fiction as "an enormously complex language."

Despite their very different settings—modern Batavia, New York, and ancient Sparta—Gardner's first two published novels, *The Resurrection* and *The Wreckage of Agathon*, share a number of common features—main characters who are professional philosophers, for example—and also share one common fault: Both are overrich in the sense that they include too many undeveloped points which seem to lead nowhere and only tend to clutter the narrative.

THE RESURRECTION

The Resurrection is a fairly straightforward, realistic novel about the ways in which its main character, James Chandler, confronts the fact of death. His disease, leukemia, involves the mindless proliferation of lymph cells and so reflects the universe itself, which may be, as Chandler speculates, similarly chaotic and purposeless. Philosophy does not at first provide Chandler with a Boethian consolation because he, as a distinctly modern man, suspects that philosophy may be nothing more than a meaningless technique, a self-enclosed game. The novel thus raises the question of the purpose of philosophy, art, literature, and even medicine. Chandler's mother knows that the job of philosophers is to help people like her understand what their experiences and their world mean. Meaning, however, is precisely what contemporary philosophy generally denies and what Chandler wisely struggles to find. His breakthrough occurs when he realizes Immanuel Kant's fundamental error, the failure to see that moral and aesthetic affirmations are interconnected and need not—or should not—necessitate that the individual who makes the affirmation be entirely disinterested; that is, the affirmation may have—or should have—some practical application, some usefulness.

Sharing this knowledge becomes rather difficult for Chandler. His sympathetic and loving wife Marie is too practical-minded to understand him. Nineteen-year-old Viola Stacey, who, torn between cynicism and her childlike "hunger for absolute goodness," falls in love with Chandler, misinterprets his writing as an escape from reality precipitated by his intense physical suffering. More interesting is John Horne, who, like Chandler, is a terminal patient. According to Horne, a believer in legal technique, love is illusion and humanity is composed of clowns who act

with no reason for their behavior. Like Viola, he assumes that art is an escape from life, or an "atonement" for one's failures and mistakes. Although he is interested in philosophy and acquainted with Chandler's published works, his endless prattling precludes Chandler's sharing the discovery with him. Yet Chandler does finally, if indirectly, communicate his vision. By putting it to some practical use (he dies trying to help Viola), Chandler finds what Horne never does: something or someone worth dying for, some vision worth affirming. "It was not the beauty of the world one must affirm," he suddenly understands, "but *the world*, the buzzing blooming confusion itself." Understanding that life is what drives humanity to art and philosophy, to fashion a life for oneself and others that is ennobling and useful (realistically idealistic, Gardner seems to suggest), Chandler fights down his physical and philosophical nausea. His vision worth perpetuating, he lives on—is resurrected—in the memories of those whom he loved, and thus for whom he died.

THE WRECKAGE OF AGATHON

Early in *The Resurrection*, Gardner quotes the British philosopher R. G. Collingwood: "History is a process . . . in which the things that are destroyed are brought into existence. Only it is easier to see their destruction than to see their construction, because it does not take long." Like Gardner, James Chandler in *The Resurrection* affirms Collingwood's optimistic position, a position which the title character of *The Wreckage of Agathon* unwisely rejects. Insofar as he stands in opposition to the law-and-order society established in Sparta by the tyrant Lykourgus, the seer Agathon is an appealing figure. No system built solely upon reason, least of all one as inflexible as Sparta's, is adequate to the variety and complexity of life, Gardner implies, but this does not mean that the only alternative is the nihilism espoused by Agathon, who had "spent so much time seeing through men's lies he'd forgotten what plain truth looked like." Having once been a lover of truth and beauty, Agathon ("the good") now mocks them; choosing to embody "the absolute idea of *No*," he is the one who sees the wreckage that was, is, and will be, the one who dismisses all art and ideals as mere illusions.

Whereas Chandler learns to put his philosophy to some use, Agathon comes to value his ideas more highly than people. Unlike Chandler, who eventually accepts death, mutability, and human limitations and in this way transcends them, Agathon refuses to see wreckage as being part of life; for him it is the ultimate fact. The cause of Agathon's pessimism is not cosmic but personal; it is the result of his repeated betrayals of his friends, his wife, and his lover. This is the knowledge that haunts Agathon, however much he tries to hide it behind his leering clown's mask, leading him to believe that to be alive is necessarily to be a threat to others. Although he dies of the plague, Agathon's real sickness is of the soul: the inability to believe in love and human dignity as actual possibilities. That they are real is clearly shown in the characters of his friend Dorkis, leader of the Helot revolt, and his young disciple Demodokos, whose prison journal alternates with Agathon's (together they make up Gardner's novel). Demodokos, the "Peeker" to Agathon's "Seer," represents that childlike faith and goodness of heart which the disillusioned Seer has renounced. Patient, understanding (if not completely comprehending), and above all committed to others, the Peeker is the one who, for all his naïveté, or perhaps because of it, serves as Gardner's hero.

GRENDEL

Agathon reappears in Gardner's next novel as the perversely likable narrator of *Grendel*, a retelling of *Beowulf* from the monster's distinctly modern point of view. In his 1970 essay, "Fulgentius's *Expositio Vergiliana Continentia*," Gardner argues that the *Beowulf* poet used his three monsters as perversions of those virtues affirmed by Vergil in the *Aeneid* (c. 29-19 B.C.E.): valor, wisdom, and goodness (the proper use of things). Specifically, Grendel represents perverted wisdom; in Gardner's novel, he is the one who mistakenly chooses to believe in what he rationally knows and to reject what he intuitively feels. In both the epic and the novel, Grendel is an isolate, a cosmic outlaw, but Gardner's monster is less a hulking beast than a shaggy Holden Caulfield (*The Catcher in the Rye*), a disillusioned and therefore cynical adolescent. Not simply a creature cursed by

God, he is a detached Sartrean observer, a relativist for whom "balance" can be both "everything" and "nothing," and a comic ironist trapped within his own mocking point of view. For him the world is a meaningless accident, "wreckage." Although he finds the indignity of the men he observes humorous, he is less tolerant of the factitious patterns they use to make sense of their existence.

Grendel makes his chief mistake when, having become dissatisfied with what is, he goes to the Dragon for advice and guidance. The Dragon is a bored and weary existentialist who espouses the philosophy of Sartre's *Being and Nothingness* (1943). He tells the confused and terrified Grendel that values are merely things, all of which are worthless, and counsels fatalistic passivity in the face of a fragmented, purposeless world. Although Grendel becomes infected by the Dragon's nihilism, he still feels attracted to King Hrothgar's court poet, the Shaper, whose songs he believes are lies. Unlike the Dragon, who is the ultimate realist and materialist, the Shaper is a visionary who sings of the "projected possible" and an alchemist who transforms the base ore of barbarism into the gold of civilization. His songs bespeak hopefulness and, by means of what the Dragon scornfully terms the "gluey whine of connectedness," a dream of order. Moreover, his singing works: The Shaper's words first envision Hrothgar's splendid meadhall and then inspire the men to build it.

Grendel's ambivalence toward the Shaper also marks his attitude toward Wealtheow, the wife bestowed on Hrothgar by her brother in order to save his tribe from the king's army. Whereas Grendel gloats over man's indignity, Wealtheow, whose name means "holy servant of the common good," has the power to absolve it. She brings to Hrothgar's kingdom the illusion of timeless peace, an illusion that, like the Shaper's words, works. Although her "monstrous trick against reason" enrages Grendel, he too is affected by it, temporarily discontinuing his attacks and choosing not to commit "the ultimate act of nihilism," murdering the queen.

The Shaper (art), the queen (peace and love), and the hero Beowulf represent those values "beyond what's possible" that make human existence worthwhile. Interestingly, Gardner's Beowulf is, like Grendel, an isolate, and, in his fight with the monster, appears as a dragon—not Grendel's adviser but the celestial dragon that figures chiefly in Eastern religions. Where Grendel sees accident and waste, the hero finds purpose and regeneration. During their struggle, Beowulf forces Grendel to "sing walls," that is, to forgo his mocking cynicism and to take on the role of Shaper, the one who by his art shapes reality (what is) into an illusion or vision of what can or should be. Thus, Grendel is not simply defeated; he is transformed—his death a ritual dismemberment, a symbolic initiation and rebirth.

Although the novel affirms the heroic ideal, it nevertheless acknowledges the tragic view that informs its Anglo-Saxon source. The meadhall the Shaper sings into existence, to which the queen brings peace, and that Beowulf saves, is a symbol of what virtuous man can achieve, but it is also tangible evidence that art, love, and heroic action can defeat chaos for a limited time only and that, finally, the Dragon is right: "Things fade." Against this tragic awareness, to which the Dragon and Grendel passively acquiesce, Gardner posits the creative possibilities of human endeavor, especially art. It is, after all, as much the action (plot) of *Beowulf* as Beowulf's heroic act that defeats Gardner's Grendel and the monstrous values he represents. Gardner's alternative to Grendel's mindless universe and brute mechanics is implied in the novel's very structure. Its twelve chapters suggest not only Grendel's twelve-year war against Hrothgar and the twelve books of literary epics but also the symbol of universal harmony, the zodiac (each chapter of the novel is keyed to an astrological sign). *Grendel*, therefore, is not a postmodern parody of *Beowulf*; rather, it is a work in which parody is used to test the values presented in *Beowulf* (and its other sources: William Shakespeare, William Blake, John Milton, Samuel Beckett, Georges-Eugène Sorel, Sartre, and others) to discover their usefulness in the modern world.

THE SUNLIGHT DIALOGUES

Like *Grendel*, *The Sunlight Dialogues* (which was written earlier) depends in part on Gardner's skillful interlacing of his literary sources: *Gilgamesh*, Sir

Thomas Malory's *Le Morte d'Arthur* (1485), Dante, Herman Melville's *Moby Dick* (1851), William Faulkner, and A. Leo Oppenheim's *Ancient Mesopotamia: Portrait of a Dead Civilization* (1977). It appears to be, at first glance, part family chronicle, part mystery story, but beneath the surface realism, the reader finds elements of fantasy and myth. By an elaborate system of plots and subplots, each echoing the others, Gardner weaves together his eighty-odd characters into a densely textured whole that contrasts with his characters' sense of social and spiritual fragmentation. The main characters appear as isolates—the marked children of Cain—and as prisoners trapped in cells of their own making. Some blindly strike out for absolute personal freedom (Millie Hodge, for example), while others passively accept the small measure of freedom to be had in the cage of their limitations (Millie's ex-husband, Will Hodge, Sr.). As adults living in a world "decayed to ambiguity," they are like one character's young daughter whose toys frustrate her "to tears of wrath." Their frustration leads not to tantrums but to cynical denial of all hope, all ideals, and all connections between self and other.

The modern condition is illustrated in the fate of the Hodge clan. Just as their farm, Stony Hill, is said to symbolize "virtues no longer found," the late congressman represents the unity and sense of idealistic purpose missing in the Batavia of 1966. His qualities now appear in fragmented and diluted form in his five children: Will, Sr., a lawyer and toggler who can repair but not build; Ben, the weak-willed visionary; Art, Jr., the tinkerer; Ruth, the organizer; and Taggert, who inherits his father's genius, purity of heart, and pride, but not his luck. The failure of the congressman's harmonious vision leads to the moral relativism of the Sunlight Man on one hand and the reductive law-and-order morality of Batavia's chief of police, Fred Clumly, on the other.

The Sunlight Man is the congressman's youngest child, the angelic Tag, transmogrified by misfortune into a forty-year-old devil. Badly disfigured by the fire that kills his two sons, he returns to his hometown in the shape of a Melvillean monomaniac. Having searched for love and truth but having found only betrayal and illusion, he claims that love and truth do not exist; having failed to heal his psychotic wife or protect his sons, he proclaims all actions absurd. His magic tricks are cynical jokes intended to expose all meanings as self-delusions. His four dialogues with the police chief serve the same purpose: to disillusion Clumly, representative of the Judeo-Christian culture. Taking the Babylonian position, the Sunlight Man propounds the complete separation of spirit and matter, the feebleness and inconsequentiality of the individual human life, and the futility of the desire for fame and immortality. Personal responsibility, he says, means nothing more than remaining free to act out one's fated part. Although his dialogues are in fact monologues, it is significant that the Sunlight Man feels it necessary to make any gesture at all toward Clumly and that he finds some relief once he has made it. Similarly, his magic not only evidences his nihilism, but also serves to mask the fact that despite his monstrous appearance and philosophy, he is still human enough—vulnerable enough—to feel the need for fellowship and love.

It is this need that Clumly eventually comes to understand. Powerless to stop either the local or the national epidemic of senseless crimes and bewildered by a world that appears to be changing for the worse, the sixty-four-year-old police chief at first seizes upon the Sunlight Man as the embodiment of evil in the modern world. Slowly the molelike, ever-hungry Clumly abandons this Manichaean notion and begins to search for the complicated truth. Clumly strikes through the pasteboard mask and, unlike Melville's Ahab, or the Sunlight Man who is made in his image, finds not the abyss but Taggert Hodge.

Throughout the novel, Clumly feels a strong sense of personal responsibility for his town and all its citizens, but, at the same time, he finds no clear answer to his repeated question, "What's a man to do?" He understands that there is something wrong with the Sunlight Man's philosophy but is not able to articulate what it is; he realizes that in separating the world into actual and ideal, the Sunlight Man has limited the choices too narrowly, but he has no idea what the other choices might be. The conflict between head and heart affects Clumly profoundly and eventually

costs him his job. Only at this point can he meet Taggert Hodge as "Fred Clumly, merely mortal." In the novel's final chapter, Clumly, speaking before a local audience, abandons the text of his hackneyed speech on "Law and Order" and delivers instead an impromptu and inspired sermon, or eulogy (Taggert having been killed by a policeman) that transforms the Sunlight Man into "one of our number." Ascending to a healing vision of pure sunlight, Clumly, "shocked to wisdom," spreads the gospel according to Gardner: Man must try to do the best he possibly can; "that's the whole thing."

NICKEL MOUNTAIN

Although not published until 1973, *Nickel Mountain* was begun nearly twenty years earlier while Gardner was an undergraduate at Washington University. That parts of the novel originally appeared as self-contained short stories is evident in the work's episodic structure and unnecessary repetition of background material. Still, *Nickel Mountain* is one of Gardner's finest achievements, especially in the handling of characters and setting.

The novel's chief figure is the enormously fat, middle-aged bachelor Henry Soames, owner of a diner somewhere in the Catskill Mountains. Alternately sentimental and violent, Henry is a kind of inarticulate poet or priest whose hunger is not for the food he eats but for the love he has never experienced. Similarly, his Stop Off is less a run-down diner than a communal meeting place, a church where the light ("altar lamp") is always on and misfits are always welcome. Willard Freund and Callie Wells, for example, see in Henry the loving father neither has had. Longing to escape their loveless families and fulfill their adolescent dreams, they find shelter at the diner. Willard, however, chooses to follow his father's advice rather than act responsibly toward Callie, whom he has impregnated—a choice that, perversely, confirms Willard in his cynicism and colors his view of human nature. Betrayal comes early to sixteen-year-old Callie (Calliope: the muse of epic poetry) and, as with Willard, leaves its mark. When Henry fumblingly proposes marriage, she interprets her acceptance as an entirely selfish choice. Gardner's description of the wedding, however, shows that, whatever Callie's motivation, the ceremony serves as a communal celebration of those values she and Henry unconsciously affirm and Willard mistakenly denies.

Henry's charity looms as large in the novel as his bulk and seems to extend to everyone but himself. When Simon Bale, a belligerently self-righteous Jehovah's Witness, loses his wife and his home, Henry naturally takes him in, but when Henry accidentally causes Bale to fall to his death, he turns suicidal. Henry's suicide attempt takes a rather comical form—overeating—but his predicament is nevertheless serious. To accept Simon Bale's death as an accident, Henry believes, would be to admit that chance governs the universe and to forfeit all possibility of human dignity. This either/or approach precludes Henry's understanding of one fundamental point: that man is neither hero nor clown, savior nor devil, but a mixture of both; the best he can do is to hope and to act on the strength of that hope.

Henry's friend George Loomis understands Henry's predicament and understands too the flaw in his reasoning, but George is unable to act on this knowledge when he accidentally kills the Goat Lady. As foul-smelling as her goats and even more comically grotesque in appearance than Henry Soames, the Goat Lady passes through the area on her pilgrim's progress in search of her son, Buddy Blatt. Because the drought-stricken farmers turn this mindless creature into a symbol of hopefulness, George's lie—that he knows she is still alive and searching—keeps their illusion and hopes alive; in a sense, he saves his friends from despair, or so Callie believes. From Gardner's perspective, however, George's failure to explain what actually happened and to confess his guilt signals his having lost his place in the human community. That George has always been in danger of losing his humanity, and thus becoming a Grendel, is evident in the way he is described: an ankle smashed during the Korean War, a heart broken by a sixteen-year-old prostitute, an arm torn off by a corn binder, and his lonely existence in a house much too large for one man up on Crow Mountain.

In a key scene, George leaves the Soameses and returns to his house, where, having heard about a recent murder on nearby Nickel Mountain, he becomes terrified, expecting to find murderous thieves looting his "things." Only after he has crawled through the mud, searched the house, and put his rifle down, does he realize his absurdity. More shocking is the knowledge that had Henry Soames acted in precisely the same way, there would have been nothing absurd about it for Henry would have been acting for Callie and their son Jimmie.

It is true that Henry does appear ridiculous throughout much of *Nickel Mountain*; Gardner's purpose here is not to deny his dignity but to qualify it, to make human dignity a realizable ideal in a fictional world where the prevailing mood is one of comic reconciliation rather than existential despair. Against George Loomis's isolation and love of things, the novel counsels responsibility and charitable love. It is, as its subtitle attests, *A Pastoral Novel*, in which the rural setting is used to affirm the value of community in the face of fragmentation and indifference. Gardner's pastoral simplifies the plight of modern humankind without becoming either simplistic or sentimental. Henry's Nickel Mountain represents freedom and clarity, but it also serves as a reminder of humanity's limitations and mortality. If the Christian virtues of faith, hope, and charity constitute one part of Gardner's approach to life, the other is, as one stoic character puts it, having the nerve to ride life down.

OCTOBER LIGHT

Gardner has called *Nickel Mountain* his "simplest" novel; *October Light*, also a pastoral of sorts, is a much more complex work—more varied in style and characters, at once funnier and yet more serious than *Nickel Mountain*. Most of *October Light* takes place on Prospect Mountain in Vermont, where seventy-two-year-old James L. Page and his eighty-year-old sister Sally Abbott are locked in "a battle of the bowels." James, the taciturn New England farmer, suffers from constipation as a result of having to eat his own cooking. A bigot, he simplifies right and wrong and rages against the valuelessness of modern life to the point of shotgunning Sally's television and locking her in her bedroom. James, however, is more than merely a comic buffoon; he is also a man burdened with guilt and oppressed by mortality—not only his own approaching end but also the accidental death of a young son, the suicides of his son Richard and his uncle Ira, and the passing away of his wife Ariah in bitter silence. Self-reliant in the worst sense, James is outwardly unemotional (except for his anger), distant from those around him and from his innermost feelings. Only when he realizes the degree to which he is responsible for Richard's death and the part Richard played in accidentally frightening his Uncle Horace (Sally's husband) to death, does James once again take his place in the natural world and the human community.

Sally, meanwhile, a self-appointed spokeswoman for all oppressed minorities, remains locked in her room where, having nothing to eat but apples, she suffers from loose bowels. A liberal in name if not in fact, she thinks of her stubborn refusal to leave her room as a protest against her tyrannical brother. She is encouraged in her "strike" by the paperback book she reads, *The Smugglers of Lost Souls' Rock*. Comprising nearly 40 percent of the text of *October Light*, this novel-within-a-novel parodies the two kinds of fashionable literature assailed by Gardner in *On Moral Fiction*: the reflexive and the cynically didactic. Although Sally is not an especially discriminating reader, she does understand that *The Smugglers of Lost Souls' Rock* is trash—entertaining perhaps, but certainly not true. As she continues to read, however, the book, which she begins to see as a reflection of her situation, starts to exert its pernicious influence. Slowly Sally adopts its values and point of view as her own: its moral relativism, nihilistic violence, the acceptance of an accidental and therefore purposeless universe, and a casually superficial and irresponsible attitude toward human relationships. The subjects that are so weightlessly and artlessly handled in her paperback novel (suicide, for one) are substantive matters of concern in the "real" lives of James and Sally; but this is a point that Sally, caring less for the Pages to whom she is related than for the pages of her novel, does not understand.

In effect, *October Light* successfully dramatizes the argument of *On Moral Fiction*, that art provides its audience with models and therefore affects human behavior. Reading *The Smugglers of Lost Souls'*

Rock leads Sally to devise and implement a plan to kill James; when the plan misfires and nearly results in the death of her niece, Sally, like the characters in her book, feels neither responsibility nor remorse. James is similarly affected by the violence he sees on television and, more particularly, by his Uncle Ira, who appears to have been more a monster than a man and certainly a poor model for James to pattern his own life after. The more James and Sally become like characters in what Gardner calls trivial or immoral fiction, playing out their inflexible parts as victimized woman locked in a tower or rugged New England farmer, the greater the danger that they will lose their humanity and become either caricatures or monsters. One such caricature in *The Smugglers of Lost Souls' Rock* dismisses all fiction, claiming that the trashiest "is all true" and "the noblest is all illusion." In their wiser moments, Sally and James know better; they understand that art is humanity's chief weapon in the battle against chaos and death (what James calls "gravity") and that the true artist is the one who paints "as if his pictures might check the decay—decay that . . . people hadn't yet glimpsed."

As in *Nickel Mountain*, Gardner's affirmation avoids sentimentality. Acknowledging the fact of death, acknowledging how easily the agreements that bind people together can be broken, he exposes the fragility of human existence. What makes his characters' lives even more difficult is the way in which their knowledge is, except for brief flashes of understanding, severely limited. Instead of the easy generalizations of trivial fiction, Gardner offers the complex and interrelated mysteries of Horace's death and Richard's suicide. Memory plays an especially important part in the novel; implying wordless connections between people and times, it is one effective antidote to Sally's "reasonable anger" and James's having stubbornly locked his heart against those he once loved. Another binding force is forgiveness—the willingness to forgive and to be forgiven—which absolves the individual of the intolerable burden of guilt without freeing him or her of all responsibility. James's son-in-law, Lewis Hicks, for example, can see all sides of an issue and so takes the one course open to humankind (as opposed to monsters): forgiving everyone. Lewis is the dutiful, ever-present handyman who stands ready to shore up everyone else's ruins, understanding them to be his own as well. Significantly, it is Lewis who first sees the October light that, while a sign of winter and therefore a reminder of death, has the power to transform the everyday world into a vision of radiant, magical beauty, a reminder of that life that is yet to be lived.

FREDDY'S BOOK

Many reviewers regarded *Freddy's Book* as one of the least satisfying of Gardner's novels; certainly it is the most perplexing. Like *October Light*, it comprises two distinct stories, but in *Freddy's Book* the two are not interwoven (Gardner thought *October Light* was flawed for just that reason). The first part of *Freddy's Book* is sixty-four pages long and concerns Professor Jack Winesap's visit to Madison, Wisconsin, where he delivers a lecture on "The Psycho-Politics of the Late Welsh Fairy Tale: Fee, Fie, Foe—Revolution." Winesap, a psychohistorian, is a gregarious and sympathetic fellow who appears to accept the relativism and triviality of his age until his meeting with the Agaards makes plain to him the limitations of his easygoing rationalism.

Professor Sven Agaard is a self-righteous dogmatist; his son Freddy, the victim of a genetic disorder, is another in Gardner's long line of misfits: a sickly looking eight-foot monster dripping baby fat. The manuscript Freddy delivers to Winesap at midnight (*Freddy's Book*) comprises the 180-page second part of Gardner's novel. Freddy's tale of sixteenth century Sweden, entitled "King Gustav & the Devil," is a dreadful bore—at least at first. Then the story begins to improve; the style becomes more controlled, the plot more compelling and more complex as Freddy begins to use his fiction writing to explore the possibilities inherent in his story and, analogously, to explore alternatives to his own various confinements.

Many reviewers were puzzled by Gardner's decision to use the ending of Freddy's tale to conclude the larger novel, which, they felt, seemed broken in two. This narrative strategy is both understandable and effective once it is considered in the context of Gardner's "debate on fiction" with his friend, the novelist and critic William Gass. Gass contends that

fiction is a self-enclosed and self-referential art object that does not point outside itself toward the world of men but back into "the world within the word." Gardner, on the other hand, maintains that fiction does extend beyond the page into the reader's real world, affecting the reader in various and usually indirect ways. In *Freddy's Book*, Gardner makes the reader think about what effect Freddy's manuscript has had on its midnight reader, Winesap.

Freddy's Book shares with *Grendel*, *The Sunlight Dialogues*, *Nickel Mountain*, and *October Light* the qualities that have made Gardner a significant as well as a popular contemporary American novelist: the blend of realism and fantasy, narrative game-playing and serious purpose, and the interest in character which implies Gardner's interest in humankind. The reader finds characters such as Winesap and Freddy compelling because Gardner draws them honestly, and he draws them honestly because, in part, each represents a side of his own personality. He is as much Grendel as he is the Shaper, as much the anarchic Sunlight Man as the law-and-order police chief Clumly. Gardner sympathizes with those who show the world as it is, but ultimately he rejects their realism in favor of those heroes—poets, farmers, and others—who choose to do what they can to transform the world into their vision of what it should be, those who, like Gardner, affirm the Shaper's "as if."

MICKELSSON'S GHOSTS

In the case of Peter J. Mickelsson, protagonist of Gardner's ninth and last novel, *Mickelsson's Ghosts*, the similarity between author and character is especially close: Both are middle-aged, teach at the State University of New York at Binghamton, own farmhouses in Susquehanna, Pennsylvania, have two college-age children, marriages that end badly, difficulties with the Internal Revenue Service, and both find that their careers, like the rest of their lives, are in a state of decline. The very texture of the novel's 103-word opening sentence makes clear that "something, somewhere had gone wrong with (Mickelsson's) fix on reality." According to several influential reviewers, it was not only Mickelsson who had lost his fix; in the pages of *Esquire* and *Saturday Review*, for example, Gardner was venomously attacked for his carelessness, boring and pretentious pedantry, im-plausible language, and failure to resolve or even make sense of his numerous plots: love, ghost, mur-der, academic life, philosophy, marital stress, sex, en-vironmental issues, and Mormonism. Whether these attacks were directed more against the author of *On Moral Fiction* than the author of *Mickelsson's Ghosts*, as Gardner believed, can only be conjec-tured. What is certain is that these reviews disturbed Gardner so deeply that for a time he considered giv-ing up novel-writing altogether. Moreover, the hostil-ity shown by reviewers James Wolcott, Robert K. Harris, and others is out of proportion to the novel's actual defects (in particular, the unconvincing last scene and Gardner's ill-advised attempts to deal openly with sex). Rather than being a "whopping piece of academic bull slinging" (Wolcott), *Mickels-son's Ghosts* is clearly Gardner's most ambitious work since *The Sunlight Dialogues*, the novel it most resembles both in scope and narrative power.

Mickelsson (who Gardner says is based on his friend, the poet James Dickey) is in most respects a familiar Gardner protagonist. Just as the novel fol-lows no single course but instead branches out in many seemingly unrelated directions, so too is Mickelsson a man torn apart by his own inner con-flicts. He fondly recalls the certainties and ideals of his past, yet at the same time he finds it easier to live in the present by adopting the cynical, existentially free position he abhors. Finding himself in a world that is at best trivial and at worst self-destructive, Mickelsson recoils from all sense of responsibility and from all human relationships (except the most sordid with a teenage prostitute). Having been be-trayed by his wife, he himself becomes a betrayer. Mickelsson is, however, too much the good man, the man desirous of goodness and truth, unwilling to ac-cept any rift between mind and body, thought and deed, to rest easy in his fallen state. Thus Mickels-son's many ghosts: those of the former owners of his farmhouse, the murderous Spragues; those from his past (wife, children, psychiatrist); the philosophical ghosts of Martin Luther, Friedrich Wilhelm Nietz-sche, Wittgenstein, and others; and most important, the ghost of his better self.

By restoring his farmhouse, Mickelsson is in ef-fect attempting his own moral restoration project. Before he can be freed of his ghosts, however, Mic-kelsson must first feel the need to confess his guilt (he is, among other things, responsible for a man's death)—to confess his guilt rather than to internalize it out of shame (as George Loomis does in *Nickel Mountain*) or to wallow in it as if values did not exist. Only then, through forgiveness, can he enjoy the sav-ing grace of human community. Within the novel's murder-mystery plot, Mickelsson escapes from the murderous design of a fanatical colleague, Professor Lawler, a self-appointed avenging angel, only after making his act of faith in the form of a wholly irra-tional "psychic cry for help." Acknowledging his de-pendency on others and, later, accepting his place within the human community, Mickelsson becomes whole again. More than a novel about one man's re-demption, *Mickelsson's Ghosts* is an exploration of the way in which the modern-world individual can truly find himself—the self that he longs to be—and that discovery can only occur, Gardner believes, in the context of the individual's commitment to others and of their commitment to him.

"STILLNESS" AND "SHADOWS"

The posthumously published book *"Stillness" and "Shadows"* was drawn from the University of Rochester's extensive collection of the author's pa-pers. *Stillness* appears as Gardner wrote it in the mid-1970's, in the form of a complete but unrevised draft which Gardner apparently never intended for publi-cation, though he did mine it for two of his finest short stories, "Stillness" and "Redemption." Written as psychotherapy in an effort to save his failing first marriage, it is Gardner's most intimate and autobio-graphically revealing work. The main characters ap-pear as thinly disguised versions of John and Joan Gardner. Martin Orrick, like Gardner nicknamed Buddy, is professor and novelist; he is stubborn, opinionated, unfaithful, and often drunk. Joan, his wife and cousin, is a musician who has given up her career in order to allow her husband to pursue his. Although she has reason to complain, she, too, has faults and must share responsibility for their marital difficulties. Both are, however, redeemed, in a sense, in that, as critical as they may be of each other outwardly, each is inwardly critical of himself or herself. The breakup of their marriage is handled with an intensity and sensitivity unusual in Gardner's fiction but not without the typically Gardnerian concern for seeing an isolated fact of domestic life as a sign of the universal decay which the novel's improbable happy ending serves only, ironically, to underscore.

Stillness evidences considerable promise; *Shadows*, on the other hand, suggests a certain pretentiousness on Gardner's part, given his remarks to interviewers on this work in progress. The published novel is nothing more than a patchwork toggled together by fellow novelist Nicholas Delbanco from the author's voluminous notes and drafts. Set in Carbondale, Illinois, the novel concerns Gardner's seriocomic, hard-boiled detective Gerald Craine, as he tries to find a murderer and protect a young Jewish student, Ellen Glass, who has come to him for help. Craine's search for the murderer becomes a search for truth. Delbanco's text makes clear what was to have been the novel's thematic center, Craine's discovery that he cannot protect Ellen, whom he has come to love. The published work, however, does not support Gardner's claim that *Shadows* would be his most experimental work in terms of technique as well as his most conservative in terms of values. That claim is nevertheless important, for much of Gardner's greatness as a novelist derives from the unresolved dialogue between the values he sought to affirm and the often postmodern ways he employed to test and often undermine those values.

Robert A. Morace

OTHER MAJOR WORKS

SHORT FICTION: *The King's Indian: Stories and Tales*, 1974; *The Art of Living and Other Stories*, 1981.

PLAYS: *The Temptation Game*, pr. 1977 (radio play); *Death and the Maiden*, pb. 1979; *Frankenstein*, pb. 1979 (libretto); *Rumpelstiltskin*, pb. 1979 (libretto); *William Wilson*, pb. 1979 (libretto).

POETRY: *Jason and Medeia*, 1973; *Poems*, 1978.

NONFICTION: *The Construction of the Wakefield Cycle*, 1974; *The Construction of Christian Poetry in*

Old English, 1975; *The Poetry of Chaucer*, 1977; *The Life and Times of Chaucer*, 1977; *On Moral Fiction*, 1978; *The Art of Fiction: Notes on Craft for Young Writers*, 1984.

CHILDREN'S LITERATURE: *Dragon, Dragon and Other Tales*, 1975; *Gudgekin the Thistle Girl and Other Tales*, 1976; *A Child's Bestiary*, 1977; *The King of the Hummingbirds and Other Tales*, 1977.

TRANSLATION: *Gilgamesh*, 1984 (with John Maier).

EDITED TEXTS: *The Forms of Fiction*, 1962 (with Lennis Dunlap); *The Complete Works of the Gawain-Poet*, 1965; *Papers on the Art and Age of Geoffrey Chaucer*, 1967 (with Nicholas Joost); *The Alliterative "Morte d'Arthure," "The Owl and the Nightingale," and Five Other Middle English Poems*, 1971.

BIBLIOGRAPHY

Butts, Leonard. *The Novels of John Gardner: Making Life Art as a Moral Process*. Baton Rouge: Louisiana State University Press, 1988. Butts draws his argument from Gardner himself, specifically *On Moral Fiction* (that art is a moral process) and discusses the ten novels in pairs, focusing on the main characters as either artists or artist figures who to varying degrees succeed or fail in transforming themselves into Gardner's "true artist." As Butts defines it, moral fiction is not didactic but instead a matter of aesthetic wholeness.

Chavkin, Allan, ed. *Conversations with John Gardner*. Jackson: University Press of Mississippi, 1990. Reprints nineteen of the most important interviews (the majority from the crucial *On Moral Fiction* period) and adds one never before published interview. Chavkin's introduction, which focuses on Gardner as he appears in these and his other numerous interviews, is especially noteworthy. The chronology updates the one in Howell (below).

Cowart, David. *Arches and Light: The Fiction of John Gardner*. Carbondale: Southern Illinois University Press, 1983. Discusses the published novels through *Mickelsson's Ghosts*, the two story collections, and the tales for children. As good as Cowart's intelligent and certainly readable chapters are, they suffer (as does so much Gardner criticism) insofar as they are concerned with validating Gardner's position on moral fiction as a valid alternative to existential despair.

Henderson, Jeff. *John Gardner: A Study of the Short Fiction.* Boston: Twayne, 1990. Part 1 concentrates on Gardner's short fiction, including his stories for children; part 2 contains excerpts from essays and letters in which Gardner defines his role as a writer; part 3 provides excerpts from important Gardner critics. Includes chronology and bibliography.

_____, ed. *Thor's Hammer: Essays on John Gardner.* Conway: University of Central Arkansas Press, 1985. Presents fifteen original essays of varying quality, including three on *Grendel.* The most important are John M. Howell's biographical essay, Robert A. Morace's on Gardner and his reviewers, Gregory Morris's discussion of Gardner and "plagiarism," Samuel Coale's on dreams, Leonard Butts's on *Mickelsson's Ghosts,* and Charles Johnson's "A Phenomenology of *On Moral Fiction.*"

Howell, John M. *John Gardner: A Bibliographical Profile.* Carbondale: Southern Illinois University Press, 1980. Howell's detailed chronology and enumerative listing of works by Gardner (down to separate editions, printings, issues, and translations), as well as the afterword written by Gardner, make this an indispensable work for any Gardner student.

McWilliams, Dean. *John Gardner.* Boston: Twayne, 1990. McWilliams includes little biographical material, does not try to be at all comprehensive, yet has an interesting and certainly original thesis: that Gardner's fiction may be more fruitfully approached via Mikhail Bakhtin's theory of dialogism than via *On Moral Fiction.* Unfortunately, the chapters (on the novels and *Jason and Medeia*) tend to be rather introductory in approach and only rarely dialogical in focus.

Morace, Robert A. *John Gardner: An Annotated Secondary Bibliography.* New York: Garland, 1984. An especially thorough annotated listing of all known items (reviews, articles, significant men-

tions) about Gardner through 1983. The annotations of speeches and interviews are especially full (a particularly useful fact given the number of interviews and speeches the loquacious as well as prolific Gardner gave). A concluding section updates Howell's *John Gardner: A Bibliographical Profile.*

Morace, Robert A., and Kathryn VanSpanckeren, eds. *John Gardner: Critical Perspectives.* Carbondale: Southern Illinois University Press, 1982. This first critical book on Gardner's work covers the full range of his literary endeavors, from his dissertation-novel "The Old Men" through his then most recent fictions, "Vlemk, The Box Painter" and *Freddy's Book,* with separate essays on his "epic poem" *Jason and Medeia; The King's Indian: Stories and Tales*; his children's stories; libretti; pastoral novels; use of sources, parody, and embedding; and theory of moral fiction. The volume concludes with Gardner's afterword.

Morris, Gregory L. *A World of Order and Light: The Fiction of John Gardner.* Athens: University of Georgia Press, 1984. Like Butts and Cowart, Morris works well within the moral fiction framework which Gardner himself established. Unlike Cowart, however, Morris emphasizes moral art as a process by which order is discovered rather than (as Cowart contends) made. More specifically the novels (including Gardner's dissertation novel "The Old Men") and two collections of short fiction are discussed in terms of Gardner's "luminous vision" and "magical landscapes."

Hamlin Garland

Born: West Salem, Wisconsin; September 14, 1860
Died: Hollywood, California; March 4, 1940

PRINCIPAL LONG FICTION
A Member of the Third House, 1892
Jason Edwards: An Average Man, 1892
A Little Norsk, 1892

A Spoil of Office, 1892

Rose of Dutcher's Coolly, 1895

The Spirit of Sweetwater, 1898 (reissued as *Witch's Gold*, 1906)

Boy Life on the Prairie, 1899

The Eagle's Heart, 1900

Her Mountain Lover, 1901

The Captain of the Gray-Horse Troop, 1902

Hesper, 1903

The Light of the Star, 1904

The Tyranny of the Dark, 1905

The Long Trail, 1907

Money Magic, 1907 (reissued as *Mart Haney's Mate*, 1922)

The Moccasin Ranch, 1909

Cavanagh, Forest Ranger, 1910

Victor Ollnee's Discipline, 1911

The Forester's Daughter, 1914

(Library of Congress)

OTHER LITERARY FORMS

Hamlin Garland published in nearly every literary form—short stories, biography, autobiography, essays, plays, and poems. Several of his short stories, such as "Under the Lion's Paw," "A Soldier's Return," and "A Branch Road," were much anthologized. His autobiographical quartet, *A Son of the Middle Border* (1917), *A Daughter of the Middle Border* (1921), *Trail-Makers of the Middle Border* (1926), and *Back-Trailers from the Middle Border* (1928), is a valuable recounting of life during the latter part of the nineteenth century through the early twentieth century. Garland also wrote about psychic phenomena in such books as *Forty Years of Psychic Research: A Plain Narrative of Fact* (1936).

ACHIEVEMENTS

Garland was a pioneer in moving American literature from Romanticism to realism. His early works of frontier life on the Middle Border (the midwestern prairie states of Wisconsin, Iowa, Minnesota, Nebraska, and the Dakotas) made his reputation, and even today he is best known for his strongly regional, unpretentious pictures of the brutalizing life on the farms and in the isolated communities of the monotonous prairie lands.

Even though his reception as a writer did not afford him the financial rewards he sought, he was an active participant in the literary scene in Chicago and New York. He traveled widely in the United States and made the obligatory trip to Europe. He counted among his friends and acquaintances such literary giants as William Dean Howells, Mark Twain, George Bernard Shaw, and Rudyard Kipling, and such lesser lights as Bliss Carmen, Kate Wiggins, George Washington Cable, and Frank Norris (whom he regarded as a promising young writer).

While he published stories in magazines such as *The Arena, Circle*, and *Century*, he augmented his income by lecturing, often at the University of Chicago. He was instrumental in organizing and perpetuating literary clubs and organizations such as the National Institute of Arts and Letters, The MacDowell Club, The Players, and the Cliff Dwellers Club.

When his fiction-writing skills began to abate in his late middle age, Garland wrote plays, articles about psychic phenomena in magazines such as *Everybody's*, and his memoirs. The popular reception of his autobiographical quartet on the Middle Border region revived his confidence in his writing ability, and he won the Pulitzer Prize for the second of the quartet, *A Daughter of the Middle Border*.

Though he wrote several novels after his critically noteworthy Middle Border novel *Rose of Dutcher's Coolly*, they were mostly set in the Far West and dealt with cowboys, Indians, and Rangers; compared to his earlier work, they can be considered strictly commercial potboilers.

Primarily a gifted short-story writer, Garland had difficulty sustaining a narrative for the length of a novel. With the exception of *Rose of Dutcher's Coolly*, Garland is to be remembered more for what he accomplished as a writer of short stories and autobiography than for what he produced as a novelist. He was elected to the board of directors of the American Academy of Arts and Letters in 1918, and, in 1922, he won the Pulitzer Prize for Biography and Autobiography.

BIOGRAPHY

Hannibal Hamlin Garland's early years were spent on an Iowa farm. As soon as he was big enough to walk behind a plow, he spent long hours helping to plow the acres of land on his father's farm. After twelve years of springs, summers, and early falls working at the ceaseless toil of farming, Garland came to realize that education was the way out of a life of farm drudgery. He attended and was graduated from Cedar Valley Seminary. He next held a land claim in North Dakota for a year but mortgaged it to finance a trip to Boston, where he intended to enroll in Boston University. Once in Boston, he was unable to attend the University but continued his education by reading voraciously in the Boston Public Library. He also began to write at that time.

His instincts for reform were ignited in Boston, where he joined the Anti-Poverty Society and, introduced to the work of Henry George, came to believe that the Single Tax Theory was a solution to many contemporary social problems. He eventually returned to North Dakota and began to see some of his stories,

sketches, and propagandistic novels published. By 1894, he had formulated in a series of essays his theory of realism, which he called "veritism."

He married Zulime Taft in 1899 and fathered two daughters (in 1904 and 1907). He continued to write, but by 1898 he had begun to feel that he had exhausted "the field in which [he] found *Main-Travelled Roads* and *Rose of Dutcher's Coolly*." He believed that he had "lost perspective" on the life and characters of the Middle Border and had found new "creative strength" in the Colorado Hills, where he visited frequently.

By 1911, he believed that he had "done many things but nothing which now seems important." His various literary and cultural activities seemed to him to have been "time killers, diversions [adding] nothing to [his] reputation." At age fifty-two, he knew he had "but a slender and uncertain income." His home was mortgaged, his ranch unproductive, his health not particularly good, and he had "no confident expectation of increasing [his] fortune."

Then, after rejections from six editors, he finally sold *Son of the Middle Border* to *Collier's* magazine. His reputation was firmly established by 1918 with his election to the board of directors of the American Academy of Arts and Letters and then later with the Pulitzer Prize. In 1930, he built a home in Laughlin Park, Los Angeles, probably to be near his two married daughters. He died in 1940 of a cerebral hemorrhage.

ANALYSIS

Hamlin Garland's theory of literature, detailed in his book *Crumbling Idols: Twelve Essays on Art* (1894), grew out of two concepts formulated early in his writing career: "that truth has a higher quality than beauty, and that to spread the reign of justice should everywhere be the design and intent of the artist." This theory of "veritism" obligated him to write stories early in his career that he said were "not always pleasant, but . . . [were] generally true, and always provoke thought."

Garland wrote about "truth" that, for the most part, he had himself experienced. The "justice" he sought to perpetuate was simplified by a reformer's zeal. As a result, he produced a series of didactic early novels which often retell his life experiences in thin disguise. Later on, when he began to view writing as a business, churning out books and shorter pieces that were intentionally "commercial," he wrote a series of safely inoffensive novels that were more romantic than realistic and that are consequently of little importance today.

A SPOIL OF OFFICE

In his first novel, *A Spoil of Office*, Garland set out to write propaganda, or social protest. In it, he achieved greater continuity of plot than in many subsequent books, he included fewer digressions, and he realized his indisputable though not lofty aim. *A Spoil of Office* is one of his better novels.

It is the story of a hired man, Bradley Talcott, who, inspired by political activist Ida Wilbur, decides to make something of himself, to become more than he is. He goes back to school, then on to law school, and becomes in succession a lawyer, an Iowa state legislator, and ultimately a congressman in Washington, D.C. He falls in love with and marries Ida, and together they work in the crusade for equal rights for everyone.

Garland showed in *A Spoil of Office* that corruption and inequality prevail in the legislative process. Prejudiced against the moneyed classes, Garland laid much of the injustice against the poor and average folk at the door of the well-to-do: Brad implies that the financially poorer legislators are the more honorable ones; that while living in a hovel is no more a guarantee of honesty than living in a brownstone is a "sure sign of a robber," it is a "tolerably safe inference."

Garland's own experiences and interests are reflected in Brad's fondness for oratory and Ida's alliances with various reform movements and organizations (the Grange, women's rights, the Farmers Alliance). In his youth, Garland had entertained the notion of an oratorical career; his reform activities under the influence of Benjamin O. Flowers, editor of the radical *The Arena* magazine, are well documented.

A LITTLE NORSK

The "truth" of prairie living, its harshness and its prejudices, is seen in Garland's short novel of realis-

tic incident, *A Little Norsk*. The story is about a Norwegian girl, Flaxen, adopted and reared by two bachelors. She grows up, well-loved by her adopted "father" and "uncle." When the two men find their paternal feelings changing to more romantic love, they wisely send her off to school. Flaxen, called so because of her blonde hair, meets and marries an irresponsible young man and soon bears him a child. The young man, hounded by gambling debts, flees them and his family; a drowning accident removes him permanently from Flaxen's life. She moves back with the older, fatherly bachelor, taking her baby daughter with her. The novel ends with the strong implication that she will marry the younger bachelor.

In spite of a contrived plot, the novel is a realistic portrayal of the harshness of life on the prairie. Garland desribes the blizzard that kills Flaxen's parents, conveying the terror which uncontrollable natural phenomena brought to the hapless prairie settlers. Although often romanticized for the benefit of those who had never experienced it, a blizzard on the isolated prairie was the harbinger of possible death. When a death occurs, as it does in *A Little Norsk*, there is the gruesome prospect of the dead bodies being attacked by hungry mice and even wolves—a prospect which Garland does not fail to dramatize.

Garland shows how Scandinavian women were treated by "native-born" American men when Flaxen occasionally encounters the village men who wink at her and pinch her. The two bachelors are aware that "the treatment that the Scandinavians' women git from the Yankees" is not nearly as respectful as that which Yankee women can expect. Ironically, Garland himself was probably guilty of such prejudices, because many of his fictional and autobiographical works reveal a condescending, patronizing attitude toward blacks, a disregard for hired hands (unless they are main characters, such as Brad Talcott), and an apparent dislike for aliens such as Germans, Scandinavians, and Jews. (In *Rose of Dutcher's Coolly*, a character says of another, "'he's a Jew, but he's not too much of a Jew.'") *A Little Norsk* thus documents both the harsh physical realities and the purely human harshness and prejudice of prairie life.

ROSE OF DUTCHER'S COOLLY

Garland's most sustained novel is *Rose of Dutcher's Coolly*. At the time of its publication in 1895, it was a most daring book, primarily because it treats rather openly the sexual misdemeanors of adolescents. To a modern reader, however, Garland's treatment of this subject will appear markedly restrained and even genteel, hardly in keeping with his resolve to tell the truth without evasion or prettification.

Rose, a motherless child, spends her infancy and early childhood with her father on their farm. She grows up hearing and seeing things that many children are never confronted with: the "mysterious processes of generation and birth" with a "terrifying power to stir and develop passions prematurely"; obscene words among the farm hands; "vulgar cackling of old women"; courtship, birth, and death. She goes to her father with all her questions and he, with sometimes blundering answers, manages to keep her from becoming too curious too soon. When the time comes in her teenage years when she can no longer hold her feelings in check, she, like other youngsters, experiments with sex. She tells her father, and he, by appealing to her love for him and his wish that she be a good girl, staves off further episodes.

Rose is interested in reading and writing, and a Doctor Thatcher who visits her school is so impressed by her that he promises to try to help her get into a college preparatory school. Though her father is reluctant, she is finally allowed to go. Once there, she—now a beautiful young woman—has many suitors but is not interested in them beyond friendship. She wishes for a life of intellectual activity and creative writing. Finishing the seminary, she goes to Chicago, again with her father's reluctant approval. There she meets and falls in love with Mason. After overcoming his disinclination to marry, Mason finally proposes to Rose.

Rose of Dutcher's Coolly has been called Garland's best novel. He dared to speak frankly about natural, common occurrences in a sincere, sensible way. This blunt approach was perhaps what shocked his first readers; apparently they were unprepared to face in print those things about which they hardly talked and never in mixed company. Libraries ruled out the book, calling it "unsafe reading." Yet, even with these "realistic" elements, the book does not live up to its promise because Garland, as usual, romanticizes his "beautiful" heroine. Rose is nevertheless, a heroine fit to share the stage with Stephen Crane's Maggie and Theodore Dreiser's Sister Carrie.

THE CAPTAIN OF THE GRAY-HORSE TROOP

One of Garland's most successful novels is a romanticized story of the Far West, *The Captain of the Gray-Horse Troop*. Captain George Curtis, surveying the mountainous land he has come to love, sums up the novel's plot elements when he says to his sister Jennie: "Yes, it's all here, Jennie . . . the wild country, the Indian, the gallant scout, and the tender maiden." Add the noble captain and the villainous ranchers, and the mix that makes the story is complete.

Unlike his earlier novels set in the Middle Border, *The Captain of the Gray-Horse Troop* is realistic primarily in the sense that it deals with a genuine problem (the encroachment on Native American lands and rights by avaricious Caucasians). Intentionally or not, it also reveals the white's attitude of superiority in regard to the American Indian. Curtis is a good and honorable man, yet he can say, having learned of a barbaric execution of an Indian: "It's a little difficult to eliminate violence from an inferior race when such cruelty is manifested in those we call their teachers." Earlier he remarks of the Indians that "these people have no inner resources. They lop down when their accustomed props are removed. They come from defective stock."

This "superiority" is reflected elsewhere throughout the novel: in the unintentionally ironic comment describing "a range of hills which separate the white man's country from the Tetong reservation," and in comments such as "A Mexican can't cook no more'n an Injun." Yet Garland has Captain Curtis, unaware of his own prejudice, remark about another character who is blatantly anti-Native American that she is "well-schooled in race hatred." Written in the stilted style more reminiscent of the genteel tradition than of the veritism Garland espoused in his earlier years, *The Captain of the Gray-Horse Troop* truthfully depicts relations between American Indians and Caucasians in the 1800's. Interestingly enough, all the white characters, even those who, like Curtis, want to help the Indians and thwart their persecutors, seem to believe that the Indians are at best very low on the social scale.

The significance of this novel today may well lie not in the story of one white man's attempt to secure justice for the oppressed Indians but rather in its revelation of the bigoted attitudes of whites toward nonwhites. In its time, the book sold very well, going into several editions. It ultimately sold nearly 100,000 copies, Garland's largest sale. (Thirty years after publication it was still selling.) It received better reviews than Garland had hoped for, even from critics who had condemned his earlier books.

Apparently it was the success of this book (which had been considered during the height of its popularity for a motion-picture production) that convinced Garland his earlier Middle Border stories would never bring him financial success. It is not difficult to understand why the remainder of his novels were like *The Captain of the Gray-Horse Troop*, though less successful.

Garland's subsequent literary output offers little that is memorable. His reputation in American literature rests primarily on his work as a short-story writer and autobiographer. An early realist, he also had a naturalistic bent. His earlier works, up to and including *Rose of Dutcher's Coolly*, show that man is controlled by the "outer constraints of environment and circumstance" as well as by the "inner constraints of instinct and passion." Garland used local color, not to caricature or make fun of his characters but to make his work more realistic and true to nature. The social elements he included helped provide the "significance" he felt all literature must have to survive. Certain impressionistic tendencies, seen in certain very subjective descriptions, indicate a concern for "individualism as the coloring element of a literature." His minor lapses into romantic sentimentality and genteel restraint (typified by his habit of referring to "legs" as "limbs") were in themselves evidence of this same individualism; his restraint demonstrated his personal reluctance to be unneces-

sarily graphic in describing certain aspects of life. Still he was forthright in delineating most of his subjects. Garland's early novels are, for the most part, fine examples of his veritistic theory.

American literature is indebted to Garland for the stronger realism and the wealth of social history he contributed. It is not difficult to applaud Garland's early novels. He set out to show truth in time, place, people, and incident. He sought to bring social significance to his work. He succeeded in several novels before succumbing to commercialism and the desire or need to be not only a good writer but also a financially successful one.

Jane L. Ball

OTHER MAJOR WORKS

SHORT FICTION: *Main-Travelled Roads: Six Mississippi Valley Stories*, 1891; *Prairie Folks*, 1893; *Wayside Courtships*, 1897; *Other Main-Travelled Roads*, 1910; *They of the High Trails*, 1916; *The Book of the American Indian*, 1923.

PLAY: *Under the Wheel: A Modern Play in Six Scenes*, pb. 1890.

POETRY: *Prairie Songs*, 1893.

NONFICTION: *Crumbling Idols: Twelve Essays on Art*, 1894; *Ulysses S. Grant: His Life and Character*, 1898; *Out-of-Door Americans*, 1901; *A Son of the Middle Border*, 1917; *A Daughter of the Middle Border*, 1921; *Trail-Makers of the Middle Border*, 1926; *The Westward March of American Settlement*, 1927; *Back-Trailers from the Middle Border*, 1928; *Roadside Meetings*, 1930; *Companions on the Trail: A Literary Chronicle*, 1931; *My Friendly Contemporaries: A Literary Log*, 1932; *Afternoon Neighbors*, 1934; *Joys of the Trail*, 1935; *Forty Years of Psychic Research: A Plain Narrative of Fact*, 1936.

BIBLIOGRAPHY

Folsom, James K. *The American Western Novel*. New Haven, Conn.: College and University Press, 1966. Garland wrote from the point of view of a white man moving west to settle on what had been Native American lands. This book provides a provocative criticism of Garland's treatment of Native Americans.

Garland, Hamlin. *Selected Letters of Hamlin Garland*. Edited by Keith Newlin and Joseph B. McCullough. Lincoln: University of Nebraska Press, 1998. The volume's introduction serves as a good entry into Hamlin's biography.

Gish, Robert. *Hamlin Garland: The Far West*. Boise, Idaho: Boise State University, 1976. Garland wrote his best fiction before 1895, when he wrote stories concerning life on farms in the West. This book, designed for undergraduates, examines Garland's place among Western writers.

Holloway, Jean. *Hamlin Garland: A Biography*. Austin: University of Texas Press, 1960. A standard biography, good for all students. Contains numerous photographs of Garland throughout his life and a chronology of his works.

McCullough, Joseph B. *Hamlin Garland*. Boston: Twayne, 1978. McCullough weaves analysis of Garland's major works with the story of his life. Provides an extensive bibliography of Garland's works, which consist mainly of short stories. Also lists a secondary bibliography with short annotations.

Newlin, Keith, ed. *Hamlin Garland: A Bibliography, with a Checklist of Unpublished Letters*. Troy, N.Y.: Whitston Publishing, 1998. Basically a primary bibliography, with one section listing articles that addressed Garland extensively. The introduction surveys the availability of primary and secondary sources. Newlin includes a chronology and title index.

Pizer, Donald. *Hamlin Garland's Early Work and Career*. Berkeley: University of California Press, 1960. The best book available on Garland's life and work between 1884 and 1895. Suitable for all students.

ELIZABETH GASKELL

Born: Chelsea, London, England; September 29, 1810

Died: Holybourne, England; November 12, 1865

PRINCIPAL LONG FICTION

Mary Barton, 1848
Cranford, 1851-1853
Ruth, 1853
North and South, 1854-1855
Sylvia's Lovers, 1863
Cousin Phillis, 1863-1864
Wives and Daughters, 1864-1866

OTHER LITERARY FORMS

The novels of Mrs. Elizabeth Gaskell appeared in serial form in journals such as *Household Words* and *All the Year Round* edited by Charles Dickens and *Cornhill Magazine* edited by William Makepeace Thackeray. During the years of novel-writing, she also published travel sketches, essays, and short stories. Her collections of stories which appeared in serial as well as hardcover form were *Lizzie Leigh and Other Tales* (1855); *Round the Sofa* (1859), containing also the separate tales inset in "My Lady Ludlow"; *Right at Last and Other Tales* (1860); *Lois the Witch and Other Tales* (1861); and *Cousin Phillis and Other Tales* (1865). Sketches of Manchester life appeared as *Life in Manchester* (1847) under the pseudonym "Cotton Mather Mills, Esq." A biography of Charlotte Brontë, still regarded as a standard source, appeared in 1857. The standard edition of Gaskell's work is the Knutsford edition (1906), which includes both fiction and nonfiction. *The Letters of Mrs. Gaskell* (1966) was edited by Arthur Pollard and J. A. V. Chapple.

ACHIEVEMENTS

The reputation of Gaskell sank in the modernist reaction to Victorian literature in the post-World War I period, and she was relegated to the status of a second- or third-rate novelist, markedly inferior to Dickens, Thackeray, George Eliot, George Meredith, and Anthony Trollope, and even placed below Charles Kingsley and Wilkie Collins. With the reassessment of Victorian writers that has gone on since World War II, her reputation has risen, and the concerns of the feminist movement in the 1970's have led to such a revaluation that the scholar Patricia M. Spacks refers to her as "seriously underrated" in the twentieth century. Other writers about the women's movement, including Elaine Showalter, Jenni Calder, and Ellen Moers, have praised Gaskell for detailing faithfully in her fiction the relation between women and marriage, the struggle for self-achievement, and the intermixture of women's careers and public history. The sense in her work of women of all classes as victims of economic and social restrictions has caused scholars to study her work and life more closely in the last decade. She has been elevated to the ranks of the major Victorian novelists.

BIOGRAPHY

Elizabeth Gaskell's life was divided between the industrial Midlands of the north and London and rural Hampshire in the south of England, as was that of her heroine, Margaret Hale, in *North and South*. Her mother's family, the Hollands, substantial landowners, were established near Knutsford, Cheshire, which became the "Cranford" of her best-known work. Elizabeth Cleghorn Stevenson was born on September 29, 1810, in Chelsea, then just outside London, where the family had settled after a period in Scotland. Because of her mother's death, Elizabeth was taken to Knutsford, where she spent the next thirteen years in the care of her aunt, Mrs. Hannah Lumb. The years at Knutsford were very happy ones, and her affection for the town is indicated by the tales in *Cranford* about its inhabitants. Her brother, John, twelve years older, went into the merchant navy but simply disappeared on a voyage to the Far East in 1823, an event marked in Gaskell's fiction by various lost and recovered brothers.

Her father remarried, having two more children, and at fourteen Elizabeth was sent to Avonbank School in Stratford, which was kept by the Byerley sisters, her stepmother's aunts. It was a progressive school by Victorian standards of feminine education, serving Unitarian and other liberal religious groups. She left school at seventeen to tend her paralyzed father, the relationship between the two having been somewhat strained in the preceding years. From 1827 until his death in 1829, she faithfully nursed him, her dedication to the task bringing forth a grateful testimony from her stepmother. The experience furnished

(Library of Congress)

the basis for Margaret Hale's nursing of her critically ill mother.

The experience of Margaret in the fashionable home of her London relations appears to parallel the months spent by Elizabeth with her uncle, Swinton Holland, a banker, and her cousin, Henry Holland, a London physician. Following the fashion for educated and leisured Victorian women, she visited various places during the next few years: in and out of Knutsford (like her narrator, Mary Smith, in *Cranford*), two winters in Newcastle with a minister, William Turner (the model for the kindly Unitarian minister, Thurstan Benson, in *Ruth*), and his daughter, Anne, a visit to Manchester to Anne's sister, Mary, and a winter in Edinburgh with the intellectual and artistic company there. At Manchester, she met William Gaskell, assistant minister of Cross Street Unitarian Chapel, and their warm relationship eventuated in marriage at Knutsford in August, 1832. At her various residences in Manchester, to whose busy industrial life and brusque manners she had to adjust,

Gaskell became the mother of four daughters and a son: Marianne, Margaret Emily, Florence, Julia, and William, whose death at the age of ten months caused her great sorrow and resulted in the writing of an idealized portrait of a boy, found in her novel *Ruth*.

Gaskell's husband, who became senior minister in 1854, had a solid reputation as a public speaker, teacher of English history and literature, editor of church publications, and preacher. Despite the uncomfortable weather and atmosphere of Manchester, it was a gathering place for well-educated Unitarians and other non-Anglicans, Cross Street Chapel being a center of lively discussion and numbering many self-made mill-owners among its members. It was also true, however, that class divisions between owners and mill-workers were strongly evident to Gaskell, whose character, Margaret Hale, wonders why two groups dependent upon each other regard their interests as opposed.

To understand Gaskell's preoccupation with social problems in her fiction, one must note her constant involvement in social welfare with Sunday and weekday schools for children of workers, her visits to working-class homes in the course of parish duties, and her concern for victims of the social system such as unwed mothers. The depression of 1839 to 1840, the Chartist movement aimed at gaining more political power for workers, the Factory Act of 1832 opposed by industrialists and widely evaded in its purpose of restricting hours of labor for women and children—all these conditions provided Gaskell with subject matter.

Gaskell's immediate impulse to write came from grief over her son's death, a decision which her husband hoped to channel constructively by encouraging her in her efforts. Her first attempt at a diary and further encouragement from publisher friends resulted in sketches about *Life in Manchester*, but this was a prelude to her first success as a novelist, *Mary Barton*. This novel presented the sufferings of the workers during labor unrest, the resistance of the mill-owners, the failure of parliament to respond to labor grievances, and the need for reconciliation. The book was praised by Friedrich Engels and Karl Marx and condemned as unfair by the wealthy parishioners of Cross Street Chapel, a denouncement which led Gaskell to present what she considered an account more favorable to the industrialists in *North and South*.

The acclaim and damnation of *Mary Barton* made Gaskell rather visible among British intellectuals such as Thomas Carlyle, the social critic; Walter Savage Landor, the poet; Benjamin Jowett, the classicist; John Ruskin, the reformer of industrial ugliness; Charles Kingsley, author of *Alton Locke* (1850) and *Yeast* (1851) and a founder of Christian socialism; Antony Cooper, Earl of Shaftesbury, the prime mover of legislative reform in mid-Victorian England; and Dickens. Thus, Gaskell joined the reforming group bent on altering the unsatisfactory living and working conditions among the laboring class in Britain.

Gaskell's friendship with Dickens inspired her to produce a story about an unmarried mother, "Lizzie Leigh," for Dickens's journal *Household Words* and created a writer-editor relationship that lasted more than a dozen years. Having become interested in the fate of the "fallen woman," she used, as the basis for her novel *Ruth* (first serialized and then published in 1853), the actual case of a sixteen-year-old female dressmaking apprentice who had been seduced, abandoned, and then imprisoned for theft in trying to keep herself alive. In the novel, a similar young girl is saved from a parallel disgrace by the intervention of a kindly minister and his sister and brought back to respectability and social usefulness by their tender concern. The presentation of Ruth's case, mild by modern standards, became almost instantly controversial, various prudish fathers refused to allow their wives and daughters to read it, and even Gaskell kept the book from her own daughters. Gaskell had already interested herself in promoting immigration by unwed mothers to the colonies as a practical way of restoring their reputations and building new futures; the book was an outcome of her own concern, though Ruth is rehabilitated within the community rather than leaving it and must still suffer unfair stigmatization, precisely the kind which the novel itself received.

While visiting another reformer, James Kay-Shuttleworth, who promoted educational advancements for the workers, Gaskell met Charlotte Brontë, who had recently risen to prominence with *Jane Eyre*

(1847); a strong friendship developed from this meeting and continued until Brontë's death in 1855. In fact, the riot of the working-men against their employer in *North and South* has similarities to a scene in Brontë's *Shirley*, which appeared six years before Gaskell's novel.

While *Ruth* was exciting controversy, *Cranford*, the work which for a long time overshadowed Gaskell's reputation as a social critic, created a nostalgic and melancholic mood. Yet even in this novel, Gaskell expresses a concern for lives that are close to poverty, genteel survivors of once lively and secure families. To please Dickens, in 1863 Gaskell added one more story to the collection for *All the Year Round*, his second magazine. Gaskell had by then established the parameters of her work: the creation of moving depictions of life under an industrializing social order; the alertness to social injustice; the longings for a more rural, innocent, and organic world of natural feelings and associations; and the melancholy strain of hopes unrealized because of social or financial constraints.

In *North and South*, completed two years after *Cranford*, Gaskell made a determined effort to present the mill-owner, Thornton, as a man with integrity, initiative, and humanitarian concern for his workers, a sort of Samuel Greg who weathers the financial crisis both with the support of his wife, Margaret Hale, newly rich, and that of his workers, drawn to him by his philanthropy. Northern energy, brusque efficiency, and the rough democracy of industrialists sprung from the humble origins of their own workers are set against the arduous toil and isolation of Southern farm laborers and the class-consciousness of Southern workers, town-dwellers, and professional people. In the same year, Gaskell drew upon memories of Avonbank School for stories, which she inset in a frame story narrated by an aristocrat, Lady Ludlow. These appeared as "My Lady Ludlow," later added to and published as *Round the Sofa*. During these years, Gaskell also wrote various sketches, such as "Cumberland Sheep Shearers" with its Wordsworthian setting of rough toil among natural beauties, and Christmas stories, some with ghostly apparitions in the style of Dickens's own stories,

which appeared in *Household Words*. Dickens's *Hard Times* (1854) provoked some anxiety in Gaskell since it dealt in part with union agitation and industrial unrest, as did *North and South*. What strained the relationship with Dickens, however, was the leisurely description and extended characterization in *North and South* together with difficulties of episodic compression for weekly publication in his journal. Though Dickens eventually came to appreciate the virtues of *North and South*, the editorial struggle over it induced Gaskell to look for publication elsewhere in more prestigious journals run on a monthly basis.

Upon the death of Charlotte Brontë in March, 1855, Gaskell undertook to write the authorized biography, using Brontë's words where possible but interpreting the facts somewhat freely. The biography, published in March, 1857, led to a continuing friendship with her new publisher, George Smith, Jr., whose firm, Smith, Elder, and Company, had been Brontë's publishers. Smith's support proved most helpful when questions of libelous statements in the biography necessitated apologies and vexatious changes in the third edition. Despite the partisanship evident in certain passages, the feeling for its subject and the general fairness in its presentation make it a good study of a writer by another writer.

Gaskell's work from 1858 to 1863 was uneven. She desired sales apparently to pay for increasing amounts of travel with her daughters, expenses of weddings for two of them, and new property. In Rome, in 1857, a new friend and major correspondent appeared, an American, Charles Eliot Norton, future president of Harvard University, who probably gave her information on Puritan New England to add to her lore of witchcraft and demonism on which she drew for the stories found in *Lois the Witch and Other Tales*. A trip to Heidelberg, Germany, provided legendary matter for *Right at Last and Other Tales*. At this time, there was much interest in Great Britain in folklore materials and romantic wonders derived from ghostly and spiritual legends, and Gaskell, among others, was willing to fictionalize this type of literature.

Writing in another contrary strain, Gaskell employed rural settings in her next two novels, *Sylvia's*

Lovers and *Cousin Phillis*; the novel or novella following these two was *A Dark Day's Night*, intended to capture part of the market for intriguing mystery-and-suspense stories. As *Cousin Phillis* was winding up its serial publication in August, 1864, Gaskell started what some critics consider her major work, *Wives and Daughters*, an exploration of the role of women in Victorian intellectual and social life. It was never completed. Gaskell's unceasing activity, including essays for the *Sunday School Magazine*, was taking its physical toll. She had already had fainting spells. Hoping to retire to Holybourne, Hampshire, which she had used a decade earlier as Margaret Hale's beloved home community, she had purchased a home there as a surprise for her husband. While spending a trial weekend with family and guests there, she suffered a sudden and fatal stroke on November 12, 1865. She was buried at Brook Street Chapel, Knutsford, where her husband was also buried in June, 1884.

ANALYSIS

Despite her own creativity, which certainly had the support of her husband, Elizabeth Gaskell, when questioned by a young writer, insisted that a woman's first duty was to husband and family. Friends recollected her carrying out her early career in the midst of household activities. Later, however, she often went traveling alone or with her daughters but—except for jaunts to a beloved vacation spot near Manchester—never with her husband. The traveling periods gave her isolation for writing, suggesting that her own practice ran counter to her advice.

Enid L. Duthie has found in Gaskell's fiction a strong interest in natural scenery, in country customs, crafts, and tales; a sympathy for conservative small towns, yet equally a concern for working men and women; a desire for practical knowledge to enhance living; a focus upon the family as the stable social unit where affections are close but able, on occasion, to extend to others in need; and an insistence that violence is futile, the human condition precarious, faith necessary. John McVeagh sees Gaskell as insisting that absolute judgments become meaningless when related to concrete human situations re-

quiring compromise. In Gaskell's treatment of the laboring element, Jenni Calder sees her as avoiding the duality of other portrayers of working-class families—sympathetic yet condescending—and refers to Gaskell as one of the few major Victorian writers showing marriage from a woman's viewpoint and not simply as an escape, a bid for social status, or a profitable contract. Gaskell has been praised for her concrete presentation of social milieus, in the spirit of seventeenth century Dutch genre painters, and her gift for recording the relationship between work and home and between husbands and wives is a special one. Patricia M. Spacks refers to a "steady integrity of observation" and "penetrating accuracy," especially as Gaskell draws, tacitly, the analogy between the plight of women in their dependency and that of workers in relation to their employers.

Gaskell's dilemma for a feminist such as Elaine Showalter lies in Victorian expectations of feminine domesticity and marriage as an end to intellectual creativity. Gaskell herself surmounted the problem, but her characters find it a difficult challenge. Spacks points out that Margaret Hale, Gaskell's greatest heroine, from *North and South*, tries to mediate between an impoverished working class which really does respect its own labor and an enlightened upper-class self-interest which enjoys emotional and cultural richness. In the end, however, Margaret must inherit property as a defense for her own introspective feeling and the diminution of her former social vitality. It is her way of surviving in a materialistic world.

MARY BARTON

The titular heroine of *Mary Barton* has a true lover, Jem Wilson, and a potential seducer, Henry Carson, son of a textile mill-owner. The love interest is established as the background for a social problem which Gaskell treats with historical accuracy. John Barton, Mary's father, aware of the sufferings of his fellow mill-workers during a lockout by the employers, is enraged by the death of the wife of his friend, Davenport, while the masters enjoy leisure, modernize their mills, and keep up profits by using scabs and decreasing wages when they reopen. Barton is hopeful that the workers will find redress for their grievances from a sympathetic parliament, to which the unionists will present the Chartist Petition. The charter is rejected, however, and the embittered workers are further incensed by Henry Carson's casual caricature of the striking workers, which he passes around at a meeting of employers. He is selected as the target of assassination, Barton being chosen to murder him. Jem is accused of the murder, and Mary faces a conflict, since she can clear Jem only by exposing her father. Though Jem's acquittal makes this step unnecessary, the other workers shun him (a situation Gaskell borrowed from the true story of a former convict ostracized by those in the workplace), and he and Mary are forced to emigrate. Her father, still publicly innocent, confesses, somewhat implausibly, to Carson, Sr., and gains forgiveness. The solution to class conflict comes through mutual goodwill, recognition of wrongdoing, and restitution.

RUTH

The heroine of *Ruth*, which takes issue with Victorian hostility toward the unmarried mother, is seduced among the romantic clouds and mountains of Wales. The idyllic moment turns to desperation when she is abandoned by her lover, Bellingham. A kindly, crippled Unitarian minister, Thurstan Benson, and his sister, Faith, take Ruth into their home and community, modeled on Knutsford, and deceive people about her condition to protect her reputation. The lie is the price of social respectability. Ruth's discreet conduct from this point on gains her admittance to the mill-owning Bradshaw family as companion to their daughter, Jemima. The electoral reforms of 1832 give Bellingham a chance to stand for political office, his reappearance in Ruth's life leading to a renewal of his interest in her and a new temptation for her to forgo her independence by accepting an offer of marriage. Her pride in her child, Leonard, makes Ruth reject Bellingham. Unfortunately, Bradshaw learns the truth about Ruth, and his self-righteous indignation leads him to repel Ruth and denounce his friend, Thurstan. Denied the opportunity for further cultural development in the Bradshaw family, Ruth must turn to nursing to establish her social usefulness. As a visiting nurse, her conscientious assistance during a typhoid epidemic brings the praise of the community.

Critics have said that Gaskell, having made her point that unmarried mothers should be treated humanely so that their talents can be made productive, should have ended her novel. Unfortunately, three-volume publication, extended serialization, and a tendency toward melodrama fostered by Charles Dickens, led Gaskell to have Bradshaw's son forge a signature on some stocks entrusted to him by Thurstan. Bradshaw denounces his son, comes back ignominiously to the chapel worship he has furiously abandoned, and eventually breaks down and is reconciled to Thurstan, having repented of his harshness toward Ruth. Ruth, however, is not permitted to live since Gaskell apparently felt that her rehabilitation was not enough to gain sympathy. Wearied by constant care of the sick, Ruth falls sick while somewhat improbably tending her former lover, Bellingham. She dies possessing an aura of sanctity, and perhaps it was this martyrdom which Victorian critics found too much to accept.

NORTH AND SOUTH

In *North and South*, the protagonist Margaret Hale must adjust to life in industrial Darkshire (Derbyshire) after living in rural Hampshire, and, through her perceptions, Margaret guides the reader to a major issue: the way in which a money-oriented competitive society challenges a more leisured, socially stratified one. The abrasive confrontations of Margaret and John Thornton, a mill-owner being tutored in classics by Margaret's father, define the mutual incomprehension of North and South in England. Thornton wants to have a "wise despotism" over his workers; Margaret contends for understanding based upon common destiny in the mills. The question of authority is raised in another dimension in the Hale family's personal travail over the enforced exile of Margaret's brother, Frederick, because of charges, unwarranted, of inciting the crew of his naval vessel to mutiny. Through friendship with Bessy Higgins, a mill girl dying of a disease fostered by textile manufacturing, Margaret, the central consciousness of the novel, is able to observe the sufferings of the working class during a strike caused by union efforts to prevent wage cuts, which the mill-owners justify because of American competition. The owners them-

　　　　　　　　　　　　　　　　Critical Survey of Long Fiction

selves, while cooperating in opposition to workers, fight one another for economic survival, according to Thornton, who sees an analogy with the theory of survival of the fittest. Though Margaret can see the closeness of working men and women in their common suffering, a riot, instigated without union approval by Nicholas Boucher, a weak agitator, against Irish scab labor, seriously compromises the position of the union in terms of its own self-discipline. The issue is posed whether coercive tactics to enlist worker support of unions can be justified when a weak leader can jeopardize legitimate demands. Margaret terminates the riot, in fact, by heroically intervening between Thornton and the rioters. She quite literally mediates between the two sides.

The difficulty of reconciliation is made evident, however, when Bessy's father, Nicholas Higgins, a unionist, argues that Christian forbearance will not answer the industrialists, though he admits that workers and employers might compromise if they could understand one another. The blacklisting of Nicholas by other employers leads to Margaret's intervention, encouraging Thornton to rehire him, his own persistence equally helping to regain a job. Thornton realizes that employer responsibility must be broadened. The turmoil of the riot, in which Margaret must confront social disruption, has its counterpart in her own turmoil over the approaching death of her mother and the secret reappearance of her brother to be with their mother. Unfortunately, Frederick's departure from town involves a scuffle with a drunken informer which later requires that Margaret lie to protect Frederick. This lie, like that in *Ruth*, produces its painful outcome when Thornton, who has observed the scuffle, thinks that she is lying to protect a lover, thus causing further altercations. Margaret realizes, however, that her moral condemnation of manufacturers has been too harsh. Indeed, to an Oxford don, an old family friend who comes to her mother's funeral, she suggests that it would be well if intellectuals associated with manufacturers.

Margaret's opinions about the South as a preferable society also undergo change. She counsels Nicholas that his going to the South, when he is blacklisted, would lead to deadening toil, no real

companionship, and intellectual decay because of the rural isolation. Visiting Helstone, her old home, Margaret encounters an old native superstition when a live cat is boiled to avert a curse. A meeting with her former lover, Lennox, confirms that Thornton is the more vital man. A fortunate inheritance from the Oxford don, Mr. Bell, enables Margaret to save Thornton, who is faced with mounting debts because of competition. He, too, has faced a moral dilemma: whether it is right to borrow money to keep himself afloat knowing that the lenders are at a strong risk. Thornton wishes to start again, seeking an opportunity for social interchange with his workers beyond the cash nexus. Margaret, now an heiress, helps Thornton stay afloat and marries him. Higgins, providentially having witnessed the scuffle, knows who Frederick really is. Thus, North and South are united, and Thornton becomes a philanthropist.

WIVES AND DAUGHTERS

In *Wives and Daughters*, Gaskell explores the question of the middle-class woman seeking to define herself and her goals in an atmosphere uncongenial to intellectual independence. Molly Gibson, whose mother has died, must cope in her teens with the remarriage of her father, who has sought a wife as much to guide Molly as out of real love. Her father's new wife, Hyacinthe Kirkpatrick, is the epitome of the parasitical woman, a former governess previously married out of necessity and then forced back into supporting herself and her daughter, Cynthia, upon her husband's death. She has become a companion to the newly aristocratic Cumnor family, but, wanting comfort, she can achieve it only by marrying Gibson. Molly receives her moral education, in part, by seeing through her stepmother's artificial pretenses. Cynthia, shuffled off while her mother has pursued Gibson, comes to reside in the household and establishes a close friendship with Molly despite her moral skepticism and social opportunism. Thus, the daughters are contrasted, not in black and white, but as possible responses to the dependency of women.

Cynthia's mother tries to marry her to Osborne Hamley, eldest son of an old family, not knowing that he is already married, and that the child of the marriage has been kept secret for some time. The event has caused Hamley to fail in attaining his degree, and he returns home to mope, thus arousing the antagonism of his father, to whom he cannot acknowledge his liaison. Hamley finally dies, causing Mrs. Kirkpatrick to shift her sights for Cynthia to the second son, Roger. Molly meanwhile has naïvely pledged herself at sixteen to the odious Preston, a situation from which she is rescued by the more forthright Cynthia, who is in love with Roger but also the object of the affections of Walter Henderson, Gaskell's ideal of the practical, creative scientist, a new social type. Cynthia, socially ambitious, realizes that the Hamley family enjoys ancient honor but is materially threatened, and she transfers her affections to a superficial, weak, but socially prominent young man. Molly is left to marry Roger, but the problem remains as to whether she can forge for herself a free life with her husband's support. The lifestyles of the two older women, Lady Harriet Cumnor and Mrs. Hamley, provide alternatives for her development. Lady Harriet is a realist about feminine hypocrisy as the price of dependency and wishes to challenge it, but Mrs. Hamley, despite her efforts to mother Molly, is emotionally sterile. Her death leaves Squire Hamley bereft and helplessly alienated from his infant grandson. The other, older men in the novel fare no better; Mr. Gibson suppresses his feelings about his wife to the point of emotional numbness, Lord Cumnor takes refuge in foolish snobbery, and even the younger Osborne painfully learns the price of romantic impulsiveness. The novel's probing analysis of the dilemma of femininity in a world guided by material values and restricted social consciousness, a world in which men too are caught by the inhibitions of social position and frozen into immobility, gives it peculiar power. It is an indication of what Gaskell could have accomplished if she had lived longer, and it shows her continuing effort to link broader social issues to very specific circumstances with careful attention to detail.

Roger E. Wiehe

OTHER MAJOR WORKS

SHORT FICTION: *The Moorland Cottage*, 1850; *Lizzie Leigh and Other Tales*, 1855; *The Manchester Marriage*, 1858; *Round the Sofa*, 1859; *Right at Last and Other Tales*, 1860; *Lois the Witch and Other Tales*, 1861; *The Cage at Cranford*, 1863; *Cousin Phillis and Other Tales*, 1865.

NONFICTION: *Life in Manchester*, 1847 (as "Cotton Mather Mills, Esq."); *The Life of Charlotte Brontë*, 1857; *The Letters of Mrs. Gaskell*, 1966 (Arthur Pollard and J. A. V. Chapple, editors).

BIBLIOGRAPHY

Chapple, J. A. V. *Elizabeth Gaskell: The Early Years.* Manchester, England: Manchester University Press, 1997. A good biography of Gaskell, focusing on her beginning years as a writer.

Craik, W. A. *Elizabeth Gaskell and the English Provincial Novel.* New York: Harper & Row, 1975. A major rehabilitation of Gaskell as an important novelist, comparing her with her contemporaries. Sets her five long fictions within the provincial novel tradition and demonstrates how she expanded the possibilities and universality of that tradition. A short bibliography and a chronology of major nineteenth century provincial novels are included.

Duthie, Enid. *The Themes of Elizabeth Gaskell.* Basingstoke, England: Macmillan, 1980. Despite their contrasting settings and plots, there is a unity of themes in all Gaskell's fiction. Her entire work and letters are drawn upon to reconstruct her imaginative world and the themes central to it. Contains a select bibliography and an index.

Easson, Angus. *Elizabeth Gaskell.* London: Routledge & Kegan Paul, 1979. Examines the relationship of all Gaskell's writings to her life and times, tracing the source of her fiction to her culture. A select bibliography and index are included.

Gerin, Winifred. *Elizabeth Gaskell.* New York: Oxford University Press, 1976. The first biography able to make use of the publication in 1966 of *The Letters of Mrs. Gaskell*, and still one of the best. Contains a select bibliography and an index.

Hughes, Linda K., and Michael Lund. *Victorian Publishing and Mrs. Gaskell's Work.* Charlottesville: University Press of Virginia, 1999. Part of the Victorian Literature and Culture series, this volume puts Gaskell's writing in the context of the Victorian era. Includes bibliographical references.

Spencer, Jane. *Elizabeth Gaskell*. New York: St. Martin's Press, 1993. Chapters on Gaskell's career, *Mary Barton*, her biography of Charlotte Brontë, *Cranford* and *North and South*, *Sylvia's Lovers*, and *Wives and Daughters*. Includes notes and bibliography.

Stoneman, Patsy. *Elizabeth Gaskell*. Brighton, England: Harvester Press, 1987. This feminist reading claims that previous accounts of Gaskell have seriously misread her and that the interaction of class and gender must be made central in any interpretation of her. A select bibliography and index are provided.

Uglow, Jenny. *Elizabeth Gaskell: A Habit of Stories*. New York: Farrar, Straus & Giroux, 1993. A major critical biography, exploring in detail both Gaskell's life and work. Paying close attention to primary source material, especially letters, Uglow has produced a definitive life. Includes illustrations and notes but no bibliography.

WILLIAM H. GASS

Born: Fargo, North Dakota; July 30, 1924

PRINCIPAL LONG FICTION

Omensetter's Luck, 1966
Willie Masters' Lonesome Wife, 1968
The Tunnel, 1995

OTHER LITERARY FORMS

Chiefly a writer of novels, William H. Gass is also the author of a book of short stories entitled *In the Heart of the Heart of the Country and Other Stories* (1968) and four volumes of essays about literature. In the chief of these, the collections entitled *Fiction and the Figures of Life* (1970) and *The World Within the Word: Essays* (1978), Gass illuminates his own work as a writer of fiction. He prefers novels, as his essay

"Imaginary Borges and His Books" suggests, which render fictional worlds which are highly contrived metaphors for the real world. He values the kind of verbal experimentation, and the implications about human consciousness which lie behind it, characteristic of the fiction of Jorge Luis Borges, Gertrude Stein, and Robert Coover. Ultimately, Gass sees the fictional text as less a reflection of objective reality than an artifact created out of the consciousness of the author.

ACHIEVEMENTS

While Gass is a highly individual writer, one whose work does not reflect the influence of his contemporaries, his fiction shares with work by authors such as John Barth, Donald Barthelme, and Thomas Pynchon an emphasis on the text as verbal construct. As his *On Being Blue: A Philosophical Inquiry* (1976) indicates, Gass believes that the words used to talk about a thing reveal the essence of the thing being talked about. His prose itself is highly rhythmic and reflexive, filled with images and allusions. The novels Gass has written are as much meditations on the art of writing fiction as narratives about their title characters. His essays, often published in literary journals before their appearance in book form, are cogent statements of Gass's own thematic and technical preoccupations. They influence both other writers and general readers, not only in the way they read Gass's work but also in the way they read the fiction of his contemporaries. In recognition of his contributions to literature, in 1998 Gass was honored with a star on the St. Louis Walk of Fame.

BIOGRAPHY

While born in Fargo, North Dakota, on July 30, 1924, William Howard Gass was reared in Warren, Ohio. He attended Kenyon College and Ohio Wesleyan, served in the United States Navy during World War II, and returned to receive a degree from Kenyon in 1947. Gass came into contact with John Crowe Ransom there, but his chief interest as a student was philosophy. He went on to do graduate work at Cornell University, and after writing a dissertation entitled "A Philosophical Investigation of Metaphor," he received his Ph.D. in 1954. He taught at a number of colleges, beginning to publish fiction while teaching philosophy at Purdue University. Beginning in 1969, Gass was at Washington University in St. Louis, Missouri, first as Distinguished University Professor in Humanities, then, beginning in 1990, as Director of the International Writers Center. He received grants from the Rockefeller and Guggenheim Foundations. In addition to his magnum opus, *The Tunnel* in 1995, Gass published his fourth collection of literary and philosophic essays, *Finding a Form*, in 1996 and a collection of novellas, *The Cartesian Sonata and Other Novellas*, in 1998. In the essays, he censures the Pulitzer Prize in fiction, the minimalists for lacking depth, and multicultural critics for ignoring the importance of form. In the stories, he continues to fly in the face of late twentieth century realism with stories that explore fictional figures caught in the web of language and thought.

ANALYSIS

Examination of the stories collected in *In the Heart of the Heart of the Country and Other Stories* reveals the degree to which Gass's fiction reflects his emphasis as a critic on creation of an autonomous verbal construction. In the title story of the volume, for example, he uses recurring images, syntactic patterns, and subject matter to depict a rural community as perceived by a poet who has come to a small Indiana town to recover from a failed love affair. "In the Midwest, around the lower Lakes," the first-person narrator comments, "the sky in the winter is heavy and close, and it is a rare day, a day to remark on, when the sky lifts and allows the heart up. I am keeping count, and as I write this page, it is eleven days since I have seen the sun."

IN THE HEART OF THE HEART OF THE COUNTRY AND OTHER STORIES

As is typical of all of Gass's work, the first-person narrator of "In the Heart of the Heart of the Country" controls the development of the narrative structure of the story. It is his story, and Gass works through him to reveal its meaning. The narrator's eye for detail is sharp: Nevertheless, he interprets it in terms of his own isolation and despair. "Lost in the corn rows, I

remember feeling just another stalk, and thus this country takes me over in the way I occupy myself when I am well . . . completely—to the edge of both my house and body." This metaphor is central to the point of the story, for Gass demonstrates that his protagonist so fuses the data of his sensory experience and his subjective response to it that the two cannot be separated.

OMENSETTER'S LUCK

In this respect, he is typical of characters in Gass's longer fiction. In the novels, however, the narrative strategy is more complex than in the stories. Gass uses four different narrators in *Omensetter's Luck*, circling about the meaning of the life of Brackett Omensetter without ever entering into his consciousness. According to Henry Pimber, Omensetter's friend and landlord, he

> was a wide and happy man. . . . He knew the earth. He put his hands in water. He smelled the clean fir smell. He listened to the bees. And he laughed his deep, loud, wide and happy laugh whenever he could—which was often, long, and joyfully.

To the citizens of Gilean, a town on the Ohio River to which he comes around 1890, Brackett Omensetter is a mythic figure who is magically in touch with the natural world. That perception precipitates the emotional responses they have to him. It also precipitates a series of human tragedies.

Israbestis Tott, the first narrator Gass uses in *Omensetter's Luck*, functions like the narrator of "In the Heart of the Heart of the Country," in that he chronicles the history of a town. "Imagine growing up in a world," Tott comments at the start of the book, "where only generals and geniuses, empires and companies, had histories, not your own town or grandfather, house . . . none of the things you'd loved." Tott comes at the conflict at the center of Omensetter's story indirectly, not needing to explain to himself as he muses about the past that actually took place. He speaks from the perspective of old age. His Gilean is that of the reader's present, and he refers to Omensetter's life from the perspective of a survivor of the central action of the novel, which took place before the turn of the century.

Gass's use of Tott as his initial focus, and the placement of the action of the first section of *Omensetter's Luck* at an auction of the property of the late Lucy Pimber, enables him to suggest that the lack of vitality in Gilean derives from the community's inability to accept Brackett Omensetter. One of the items at auction is the cradle Omensetter and his wife used for their infant son Amos, and Tott wonders why Mrs. Pimber had it. She never had any children of her own. Her husband, Henry, the character Gass uses to narrate the second section of the novel, is ambivalent about Omensetter's strength and vitality. Both drawn to him and jealous of him, Pimber commits suicide by hanging himself from a tree deep in the woods. This death is the central element in the plot of the novel. Unsure of what has happened to Henry Pimber, the townspeople search for his body and speculate about the role Omensetter has played in his death.

Pimber is convinced that Omensetter is lucky beyond all deserving. On the rainy day on which he brings his family and household goods to Gilean in an open wagon, Omensetter miraculously escapes the rain. The house he rents from Pimber is subject to flooding, but the Ohio River avoids it while Omensetter's family lives there. Even when a fox falls into the well at the house, he is inclined to let nature take its course in confidence that things will work out. Angered by this attitude, Pimber shoots the fox in the well and wounds himself with a refracted shotgun pellet. Neither Dr. Orcutt's drugs nor Reverend Furber's prayers seem to affect the lockjaw Pimber develops, but Omensetter's beet poultice turns the trick. The experience becomes fraught with spiritual significance for Pimber. "It lay somewhere in the chance of being new . . . of living lucky, and of losing Henry Pimber." He sees Omensetter as a sign, as a secret indication of how he himself should live; unable to see that Omensetter is no more than a man, like himself, Pimber hangs himself in despair about ever becoming the kind of person he believes Omensetter to be.

While Henry Pimber sees Omensetter as emblematic of positive elements, the Reverend Jethro Furber, the third of Gass's narrators in *Omensetter's Luck*, sees him as the embodiment of moral evil. Furber is the most difficult to understand of the men Gass uses to narrate the story. His account comes so entirely from within his own consciousness that only the previous evidence of Tott and Pimber serves to put it in perspective. Furber sees Omensetter as a threat to his moral authority. Having coerced him into attending church one Sunday morning, Furber finds himself unable to preach effectively. Speaking to Matthew Watson, the blacksmith in Gilean, he suggests that Omensetter is an agent of Satan. "Listen Matthew, he was in the young corn walking and I said leave us Omensetter, leave us all. Oh I accursed him. I did. Yes, I said, you are of the dark ways, Omensetter, leave us all." When Henry Pimber disappears and foul play is suggested, Furber encourages the townspeople to suspect Omensetter of killing his landlord.

Obsessed by the sight of Omensetter and his pregnant wife Lucy bathing in a stream, Furber makes of the scene an icon of his own lust. He is gored by sexual fantasies, conceding to himself that there is more pleasure in dirty words than real experience, yet the unconstrained relationship of Brackett and Lucy Omensetter excites his jealousy. He titillates himself with words, those drawn from scripture as well as those describing sexual acts, and eventually produces a blasphemous mixture of elements suggesting a parallel between Omensetter, his wife, Lucy, and Furber himself and Adam, Eve, and Satan.

> Now there was in heaven, as you know, an angel, prince among them, Prince of Darkness. And he felt his wife drawn painfully from him, out of his holy body, fully half of himself, and given a place of dazzling splendor. How he hated it, and suffered his loss loudly.

Furber sees himself simultaneously as Adam and Satan; he both displaces Omensetter as the husband of Lucy/Eve and reveals the guilt he feels at this idea. Furber imagines that the sex act reunites the parts that God separated, reintegrating the masculine and feminine halves of His own personality, and he thereby suggests the roots of his own jealousy of Omensetter.

Gass provides the last chapters of *Omensetter's Luck* with an anonymous third-person narrator, one who stays largely outside the consciousness of Furber. The action of the plot develops with absolute clarity at this point. Omensetter comes to the minister with the news that he has located Henry Pimber's body deep in the snowy winter forest. He knows that Furber is trying to persuade others that he murdered Pimber, and he needs to clear his name. "A friend. I've spent my life spreading lies about you," Furber tells Omensetter tauntingly. Yet he does tell the search party the truth when they find Pimber's corpse. By this time, Furber is caught up in his own dark spiritual vision. "God was coming true, coming slowly to light like a message in lemon. And, what was the message? in yet another lingo? Truth is the father of lies; nothing survives; only the wicked can afford to be wise." Since his arrival in Gilean, Furber had tended a shady, walled garden attached to his church. With the graves of his predecessors in its four corners, the garden is an emblem straight from the fiction of Nathaniel Hawthorne or Herman Melville. Furber's dark vision has the same traditional literary source, but the people of Gilean see his words only as the ramblings of a madman. The Reverend Jethro Furber spends his final years in a mental institution.

Omensetter himself does not handle well the roles in which the people of Gilean have cast him. He is essentially a careless, happy man who is not deeply reflective about life. Cast as the embodiment of natural good by Henry Pimber and spiritual evil by Jethro Furber, he himself is unsure of his identity. For Omensetter, his arrival in Gilean was filled with the promise of a new life. "The trees were bare, I remember, and as we came down the hill we could see the tracks of the wagons glistening. You could see what your life would be." He is eager to prove that this promise was not a lie, and so he gambles on the life of his sick son Amos to see if the luck imputed to him by others will hold. "The infant lingered on alive, an outcome altogether outside science, Doctor Orcutt said, and Israbestis swore that Omensetter's luck would be a legend on the river—quite a while, he claimed—perhaps forever." Omensetter and his family leave Gilean, however, suggesting that his self-confidence has been permanently shaken by his experiences. With them, Gass suggests, goes all hope for vitality in the community.

WILLIE MASTERS' LONESOME WIFE

In a fundamental sense, Omensetter, Furber, Pimber, and Tott are aspects of a single personality. They are the voices of human impulses competing for control. The multiple narrators of *Willie Masters' Lonesome Wife* are less clearly fragments of a single character, but they are equally strong symbol-making voices. Divided into four sections, each printed on paper of a different color, this novella is more overtly an experiment in narrative construction than *Omensetter's Luck*. It has little coherent plot at all, but there is plenty of action. The central character is Willie Masters's wife, a lonesome woman named Barbara who consoles herself with sexual encounters. "Well, I'm busty, passive, hairy, and will serve," she comments in the first, and blue-colored, section of the book. "Departure is my name. I travel, dream. I feel sometimes as if I *were* imagination (that spider goddess and thread-spinning muse)—imagination imagining itself imagine." While engaged in sexual intercourse with a bald man named Gelvin, "Busty Babs"—as her father called her—thinks about differences in the ways men and women think about sexuality. This is a topic to which Gass has returned time and again in his fiction; it fuels the speculations of the narrator of "In the Heart of the Heart of the Country" and the nearly pornographic fantasies of Furber in *Omensetter's Luck*.

Barbara Masters is a former stripper who danced professionally in a blue light. This explains, in part, the blue paper on which her thoughts are printed. She allows her mind to wander while Gelvin works out his fantasies on her body, and she imagines herself the author of a Russian play—printed in Gass's text on yellow paper to suggest its lurid nature—about a Russian named Ivan and his wife. Barbara casts herself in the role of the wife. The subject of the play is Ivan's reaction to evidence of his wife's infidelity, but the play soon gets overwhelmed by the footnotes providing a running commentary at the foot of each yellow page. The notes get longer, they are at times addressed to the reader of *Willie Masters' Lonesome Wife*, and eventually they swallow up the play. The text and notes do not match up, so the reader must choose whether to read the pages as printed or to work actively to construct a more coherent text.

Gass refers openly to the proposition that the reader is a collaborator in the section of *Willie Masters' Lonesome Wife* which is printed on red paper. The narrator here, perhaps still Barbara Masters, remarks,

The muddy circle you see just before you and below you represents the ring left on a leaf of the manuscript by my coffee cup. Represents, I say, because, as you must surely realize, this book is many removes from anything I've set pen, hand, or cup to.

Like the play on yellow pages, this section contains simultaneous narratives. There is a dialogue about poetry and sexuality among characters named Leonora, Carlos, Angela, and Philippe; there is a running commentary on the art of writing—containing references to works by Henry David Thoreau, Henry James, and Thomas Hardy; and there is an interior monologue composed of random memories, supposedly events in the life of the narrator. In one sense, this technique re-creates the effect of a single human mind thinking simultaneously about several different subjects. In another, it is simply an elaborate parody of the method Gass uses in *Omensetter's Luck*. In a fictional text such as this one, all interpretations of significance are equally valid (or invalid), and there is ultimately nothing but a subjective reaction to be made out of the materials.

Gass addresses this fact in the final pages of the red section of the book. "You've been had," says the narrator, "haven't you, jocko? you sad sour stew-face sonofabitch. Really, did you read this far?" As Gass has made clear in his essays about literature, the essential nature of a literary text is the fact that it is made up of words. In the fourth section of *Willie Masters' Lonesome Wife*, printed on white paper and without the typographical variation to be found in the other sections of the book, the narrator identifies herself as a verbal construct.

I am that lady language chose to make her playhouse of, and if you do not like me, if you find me dewlapped, scabby, wrinkled, old (and I've admitted as many pages as my age), well sir, I'm not like you, a loud rude noise and fart upon the town.

She is a new incarnation of the most traditional of muses, just as Willie Masters is a mask for the author William Gass himself.

THE TUNNEL

After twenty-five years of work, Gass published his long-awaited novel *The Tunnel* in 1995. The central figure and nonstop voice of the book is William Frederick Kohler, a history professor at a midwestern university, who studied in Germany during the 1930's and was a consultant during the Nuremberg Trials. Trying to write a simple, self-congratulatory preface to his magnum opus, *Guilt and Innocence in Hitler's Germany*, he writes about his own life instead. The result is *The Tunnel*, a sprawling personal exploration filled with bitterness, hatred, lies, self-pity, and self-indulgence.

In *The Tunnel*, everything that has happened to Kohler, everyone that he has encountered, is converted into the stuff of his mind. Kohler's mind is not one that many would find hospitable; rather, it is the closed-in, claustrophobic world of the narrow-minded bigot. Long passages reveal his resentment of his unforgiving, hard-fisted father and his self-pitying, alcoholic mother, as well as his loathing for his fat, slothful wife, his contempt for his nondescript adolescent sons, and his scorn for his pedantic colleagues and his superficial lovers.

However, it is not this rambling referential subject matter that makes *The Tunnel* Gass's most ambitious effort, but rather the highly polished prose, wonderfully sustained for more than six hundred pages, and the philosophic exploration of the relationship between historical fascism and domestic solipsism. Gass continually breaks up the naïve realist illusion that the subject of a novel—the territory it depicts—is identical to its maplike pattern or language. Filled with references to the great works of history, philosophy, and literature that Kohler both honors and debunks, the work seems on the surface to be a rambling free association; it is actually such a carefully controlled aesthetic pattern that readers cannot for a moment lose sight of the fact that it is language they are experiencing, not physical life.

The Tunnel is a narcissistic novel in which the only real person is the narrator; all others are merely grist for his mental mill. What it means to be human, the novel suggests, is to confront the hard truth that the self is the only consciousness one can grasp. Kohler knows that if one does not become pure subjective consciousness one runs the risk of being transformed into the consciousness of someone else. *The Tunnel* is an escape route out of the prison of the self as well as a gold mine in which the way to the treasure is the treasure. It is the entrance to the womb, the removal of all human restraints, and the reduction of the self to its most elemental.

Robert C. Petersen, updated by Charles E. May

OTHER MAJOR WORKS

SHORT FICTION: *In the Heart of the Heart of the Country and Other Stories*, 1968; *The Cartesian Sonata and Other Novellas*, 1998.

NONFICTION: *Fiction and the Figures of Life*, 1970; *On Being Blue: A Philosophical Inquiry*, 1976; *The World Within the Word: Essays*, 1978; *The Habitations of the Word: Essays*, 1985; *Finding a Form*, 1996; *Reading Rilke; Reflections on the Problems of Translation*, 1999.

BIBLIOGRAPHY

Bradbury, Malcolm. *The Modern American Novel.* New York: Oxford University Press, 1983. Places Gass in the company of postmodern writers of the 1960's and 1970's. In discussing Gass's fiction and critical writing, Bradbury notes Gass's background in philosophy and that he is conscious of the "discrepancy between language and reality."

Hadella, Charlotte Byrd. "The Winter Wasteland of William Gass's *In the Heart of the Heart of the Country.*" *Critique: Studies in Modern Fiction* 30 (Fall, 1988): 49-57. Explores the connection between Gass's rejection of models as stiflers of imagination and his use of models in this work. Analyzes the narrator who is obsessed with models yet devoid of love. This essay stays with the content of this short-story collection but does little to relate this work to Gass's other fiction.

Holloway, Watson L. *William Gass.* Boston: G. K. Hall, 1990. A formal study in which Holloway pays close attention to Gass's texts to "catch the music and intricacy of his work." Contains a valuable piece of criticism on *Omensetter's Luck.*

Kaufman, Michael. *Textual Bodies: Modernism, Postmodernism, and Print.* Lewisburg, Pa.: Bucknell University Press, 1994. Discusses *Willie Masters' Lonesome Wife* as a "metatextual" work that comments physically on its material existence by exposing its print conventions and making the printed form of the work part of the narrative itself.

Kellman, Steven G., and Irving Malin, eds. *Into the Tunnel.* Newark: University of Delaware Press, 1998. A collection of twelve "readings" of *The Tunnel* by such critics as Arthur Saltzman, Marcus Klein, Irving Malin, Steven Kellman, and Jerome Klinkowitz. Includes an interview with Gass about the novel.

Saltzman, Arthur M. *The Fiction of William Gass: The Consolation of Language.* Carbondale: Southern Illinois University Press, 1986. A solid introduction to Gass's major works. Includes an interview with Gass.

JEAN GENET

Born: Paris, France; December 19, 1910
Died: Paris, France; April 15, 1986

PRINCIPAL LONG FICTION

Notre-Dame des Fleurs, 1944, 1951 (*Our Lady of the Flowers*, 1949)
Miracle de la rose, 1946, 1951 (*Miracle of the Rose*, 1966)
Pompes funèbres, 1947, 1953 (*Funeral Rites*, 1968)
Querelle de Brest, 1947, 1953 (*Querelle of Brest*, 1966)

OTHER LITERARY FORMS

Jean Genet opened his literary career with a small group of highly personal lyric poems, beginning with "Le Condamné à mort" ("The Man Condemned to Death"). His poems are collected in *Poèmes* (1948).

Genet published several plays, including *Les Bonnes* (1947, rev. pr., pb. 1954; *The Maids*, 1954), *Haute Surveillance* (1949, definitive edition pb. 1963; *Deathwatch*, 1954), *Le Balcon* (1956, rev. pb. 1962; *The Balcony*, 1957), *Les Nègres* (1958; *The Blacks*, 1960), and *Les Paravents* (1961; *The Screens*, 1962). A so-called autobiography, *Journal du voleur* (1948, 1949; *The Thief's Journal*, 1954), contains probably more allegory than fact, but it remains the only source available covering the early years of Genet's life. Genet's nonfiction includes essays on the philosophy of art, such as "L'Atelier d'Alberto Giacometti" ("Giacometti's Studio") of 1957 and "Le Funambule" ("The Funambulists") of 1958, and essays dealing with dramatic theory, of which the most important by far is the "Lettre à Pauvert sur les bonnes," an open letter to the publisher Jean-Jacques Pauvert written in 1954 including letters to Roger Blin (collected as *Letters to Roger Blin*, 1969) and various prefaces to his own plays. Genet also wrote a series of sociopolitical broadsheets, beginning with "L'Enfant criminel" ("The Child-Criminal") of 1949 and leading to a sequence of pamphlets in defense of the Black Panthers (perhaps epitomized in his "May-Day Speech" of 1968) and of the Palestinian liberation movement.

ACHIEVEMENTS

In any attempt to assess Genet's achievement as a novelist, it is essential to separate his qualities as a writer from what might be termed the "sociological" aspect of his subject matter. Though the two interact, in the critical period between 1945 and 1965 it was the nonliterary import of his work that predominated. Genet's name came to be synonymous with the growing demand of the post-World War II generation to read what it wanted to read and to learn the truth about the less palatable aspects of the human condition, regardless of what a paternalistic censorship might decide was good for it.

In this attempt to break through the barriers of what now seems like an antiquated obscurantism but what until the late twentieth century was a powerful and deeply rooted social attitude, Genet did not stand alone. In this respect, he trod in the footsteps of James Joyce and D. H. Lawrence, of Marcel Proust and Jean Cocteau; among his contemporaries, Norman Mailer, Henry Miller, and Vladimir Nabokov were inspired by similar aims. The battle over Lawrence's *Lady Chatterley's Lover* (1928) was fought and won in 1961; behind the writers stood a small group of publishers (Grove Press in New York, Gallimard in Paris, Rowohlt-Verlag in Hamburg, Anthony Blond in London) who were prepared to fight their cases through the courts. In comparison with many of his contemporaries, Genet had one distinct advantage: He wrote in French. French censorship allowed greater latitude to "clandestine" publications (usually in the form of "limited editions," available to subscribers only) than did that of other countries. This same censorship turned a blind eye to books which, although published in France, were in languages other than French (hence the fact that Genet's earliest translator, Bernard Frechtman, lived and worked in Paris). The French magistrates presiding at censorship trials had always at the back of their minds the specter of that guffaw of disbelieving ridicule which still echoes over their predecessors, who,

(Library of Congress)

within the space of half a dozen years, had condemned as "immoral" both Gustave Flaubert's *Madame Bovary* (1857) and Charles Baudelaire's *Les Fleurs du mal* (1857, 1861, 1868).

As a result, Genet, who never once resorted to anonymity or sought to disguise who or what he was, was able to appear in print with material whose publication would have been inconceivable at that time in other societies or under other conditions. It was at this point that the quality, both of his writing and of his thought, became significant, for it won over to his cause a group of eminent figures who would scarcely have bothered to jeopardize their own reputations by championing a mere "pornographer." Thus, in 1950, when the prestigious firm Gallimard decided to risk publishing Genet's four novels (expurgated remarkably lightly) together with a selection of the early poems, the editors were able to call upon Jean-Paul Sartre, the leading intellectual of his generation, to write an introduction. This introduction, moreover, which appeared in 1952, constitutes what is one of the most significant treatises on ethics that have been written in the present century: *Saint-Genet: Comédien et martyr.*

French literature from the eighteenth century onward can boast of a long tradition of writers—from Jean-Jacques Rousseau and the Marquis de Sade, by way of Guillaume Apollinaire, to Jean Paulhan, Georges Bataille, and Monique Wittig—who have used the "pornographic" novel (that is, the novel whose principal material resides in the detailed description of extreme and violent forms of sexual experience) not merely to titillate the reader's imagination but for positive and serious purposes of their own. These purposes vary: The intention may be one of self-analysis or of "confession," it may be a concern with the absolutes of realism, or it may be a matter of denouncing the hypocrisies and the false assumptions by which the majority of "right-thinking people" choose to live. Mystics have been fascinated by the "surreal" quality of erotic experience, but so have anthropologists. The violence of sexual intensity constitutes one of the most readily accessible means of intuiting a dimension of irrational transcendentality; progressively, as European thought has moved toward a climate of materialist rationalism, the attraction of the irrational has grown more powerful. It is perhaps Genet's most significant achievement, in this quasi-sociological domain, to have brought for the first time into the full light of intellectual consciousness the role that "inadmissible" dimensions of experience may play in man's objective assessment of himself. To describe this, in Freudian terms, merely as "beneath the ego lies the id" is to bury it under the colorless abstractions of a Viennese-based scientific observer trained by Jean-Martin Charcot. Genet, in the characters of Divine and Mignon, of Bulkaen and Harcamone, of Jean Decarnin and of the Brothers Querelle, clothes these aspects of the human psyche in flesh and blood, illuminates them with the brilliant and torturous recall of his own experiences, and gives them an unforgettable reality.

BIOGRAPHY

The career of Jean Genet has often been compared to that of his late-medieval predecessor, the thief and poet François Villon. That Genet was a thief is undeniable; the interest lies in how he was transformed into a poet.

The solid facts concerning Genet's early life are few, because, for reasons that are both literary and personal, he has been at great pains to transmute them into his "legend." Born on December 19, 1910, in a public maternity ward on the Rue d'Assas in Paris, the child of a prostitute and an unknown father, Genet was adopted by the Assistance Publique (the national foundling society) and, as soon as he could crawl, was sent off to foster parents in the hill country of Le Morvan, between Dijon and Nevers. There, growing up with a classic sense of insecurity, he took to petty thieving and, by the age of ten, was branded irrevocably as a thief. Many years later, probably under the influence of Sartre's philosophy of existential choice, he attributed to this critical period of his life a positive significance: His "self" was that which he was for "others"; because, for others, he was a "thief," a thief was what he must necessarily be. How much of this persona is fact and how much is legend is impossible to determine. At all events, by his early teens, Genet found himself confined to a reformatory for juvenile criminals at Mettray, a few miles north of Tours; there, he was subjected to all the most brutal forms of assault and seduction common to establishments of that type. How and when he was released, or escaped, is unknown, as is most of his career during the next ten years or more. He appears, on the one hand, to have developed as a classic layabout—a male prostitute, a skilled pickpocket, a semiskilled shoplifter, and a remarkably unskilled burglar (burglary, considered as an exercise in poetic ecstasy, would not lead to the best results). His vagabond existence took him to Spain and then to North Africa, where he developed a feeling of kinship with the Arab victims of colonization that was later to emerge in *The Screens*. On the other hand, and less ostentatiously, he pursued a career as an assiduous autodidact who, on an occasion when he was arrested for stealing a volume of poems by Paul Verlaine, was more concerned with the quality of the poetry than with the commercial value of the book itself.

These two strains—criminality and poetry—would seem to have run together in not uncomfortable harness for a dozen years or more. According to one source, when Genet was sixteen, he worked as guide and companion to a blind poet, René de Buxeuil, from whom he learned at least the rudiments of French prosody, if not also the principles of Charles Maurras's fascism. Some years later, in 1936 or 1937, he deserted from the Bataillons d'Afrique (the notorious "Bat' d'Af"—the punitive division of the French army in North Africa), after having struck an officer and stolen his suitcases, illegally crossing frontiers in Central Europe and running a racket involving fake or clandestine currency. Yet, in the same period, he taught French literature to the daughter of a leading gynecologist in Brno, Moravia, writing her long letters in which explications of Arthur Rimbaud's "Le Bâteau ivre" (1883, "The Drunken Boat") alternate with laments for the fall of Léon Blum's Front Populaire in June, 1937. His next arrest, in or about 1938, was, according to some authorities, for stealing a car; according to others, it was for forging documents to save republican refugees from the Spanish Civil War.

Which crime led him to the prison at Fresnes in 1942 is again unknown. What is certain is that it was during this period of detention that Genet wrote his first published poem, "The Man Condemned to Death," and also drafted his first novel, *Our Lady of the Flowers*—according to the legend, on stolen brown paper; when the first draft was discovered and confiscated by a warder, Genet simply began all over again.

During this period there was a visitor to the prison at Fresnes named Olga Barbezat. Her husband, Marc Barbezat, owned a small press, L'Arbalète, in Lyons, and his friends included Jean Cocteau, while she herself had for some years been acquainted with Simone de Beauvoir. Genet's manuscripts began to circulate, and it was Cocteau who first acclaimed them as works of genius. When Genet had been released and arrested yet again (the "volume of Verlaine" thievery), Cocteau himself appeared among the witnesses in court for the defense, declaring publicly that he considered Genet to be "the greatest writer in France." The outcome is again unknown, but Genet nevertheless continued his dual career as a brilliant writer and an incompetent burglar. Between 1942 and 1946, he appears to have written all four of his novels, as well as *The Thief's Journal* and the plays *Deathwatch* and *The Maids*. *Our Lady of the Flowers* was published in September, 1944, and the other novels appeared in rapid succession over the next four years. Genet's name was becoming known; in 1948, however, he was arrested again, and on that occasion was sentenced to "perpetual preventive detention."

The circumstances of this final appearance of Genet-as-criminal are, as usual, obscure. According to his supporters, he had quixotically taken upon himself the crimes of one of his lovers, Jean de Carnin (the Jean Decarnin of *Funeral Rites*), who had died heroically fighting the Germans during the liberation of Paris some three years earlier. At all events, Genet had powerful backers. On July 16, 1948, the influential newspaper *Combat* addressed an open letter (signed by Sartre, Cocteau, and the literary editors of the paper, Maurice Nadeau and Maurice Saillet) to the president of the Republic, "imploring his clemency on behalf of a very great poet." The president, Vincent Auriol, was convinced, and a free pardon was granted. From that point on, Genet was merely a writer. "I don't steal the way I used to," he told an interviewer from *Playboy* (April, 1964) nearly two decades later. "But I continue to steal, in the sense that I continue to be dishonest with regard to society, which pretends that I am not."

Genet's later work, apart from the three plays *The Balcony*, *The Blacks*, and *The Screens*, all written during the 1950's, is comparatively slight; he never repeated the great outburst of creativity that took hold of him between 1942 and 1948. His later works include a scattering of film scripts and critical essays in the 1960's, and a series of short but searingly controversial articles in defense of the Black Panthers and of the Palestinian terrorists. It is as though, having employed literature to effect his own escape from degradation, he then had little further use for it. In the main, until his death in 1986, he seemed content simply to be alive.

ANALYSIS

The elements out of which Jean Genet contrived his vision of that haunting and monstrous "other" world, which lies carefully concealed beneath the controlled and rational surface of everydayness, all belong to previously accredited literary traditions; nevertheless, the balance, and consequently the overall impact, is new. The components can be analyzed as follows.

The confession: Both *Our Lady of the Flowers* and *Miracle of the Rose*, at least as much as the *The Thief's Journal*, are basically autobiographical and, in their original (perhaps subconscious) intention, would seem to have been inspired by a desire to *escape*—to escape from the intolerable degradations of existence as a petty criminal, convict, and male prostitute by externalizing these experiences through the rigorous and formal disciplines of prose and poetry, by projecting the self through words into the minds of others, thus making acceptable to them that which, without their connivance and acknowledgment, could not be acceptable to *him*. In one memorable phrase, Genet describes his pilgrimage through literature as "une marche vers l'homme": a progress

toward virility—or, perhaps, simply away from dehumanization.

The "normalization" of homosexuality: To the nineteenth century mind, the homosexual was the ultimate social and moral outlaw, the criminal for whom there could exist no forgiveness. Progressively, the second half of the twentieth century saw the weakening of these strictures: The homosexual, in his emotional relationships, could be as "normal" as the heterosexual lover, perhaps even more so; because of his previous persecution, he became almost a "hero of the time." If this attitude is not the most original feature of Genet's work, it nevertheless constitutes a powerful motivation: the concern to portray his own emotions as something as intense and as moving as those of "normal" human beings.

The existential formation of the self: The intellectual relationship between Sartre and Genet is complex and awaits analysis; what is clear is that if Genet was not only influenced by Sartre's *Being and Nothingness* (1943) but also, according to his own confession, reduced for years to silence by the devastating accuracy of Sartre's psychophilosophical analysis of Genet's creative processes in *Saint Genet: Actor and Martyr*, Sartre, likewise, at least in *The Devil and the Good Lord* (1951), acknowledges his debt to Genet. Genet, in fact, takes the Sartrean ontology toward conclusions that Sartre himself hardly dared to explore. If the essence of the self is a void (*un néant*), then it can only "be," either what it *thinks* itself to be (according to Sartre) or what others think it to be (according to Genet). In either case, it can *know* itself to be what it is only in terms of the effectiveness of its actions (Sartre) or by looking at itself in the mirror (Genet). Yet, if a man (a negative) looks at himself and sees his reflection (a positive) in the mirror, then that which is perceived (the inanimate-positive image) is more "real" than the perceiver (the animate-negative). Thus, the image is more "real" than the subject, the fake more "authentic" than the genuine. For Genet, "to be" (this is also a Beckettian theme) is "to be perceived"—especially in the mirror. Hence, Genet's fiction is pervaded by the image of the mirror and of the double—from the early ballet, *'Adame miroir*, to the last of the novels, *Querelle of Brest*, in which the identical twin brothers, Querelle and Robert, constitute an identity only by their absolute reflection of each other.

The reversal of moral values: If the fake is more authentic than the genuine, then, in moral terms also, the evil is more authentic than the good. Genet, brought up as a Catholic believer and profoundly influenced by another Christian believer, Dostoevski, argues as follows: Christ stated that the Kingdom of Heaven is for the humble; no man can *will* himself to be humble, any more than he can will himself to be a saint, without a degree of hypocrisy that destroys both humility and sanctity (this is, in fact, the theme of the play *Deathwatch*). Humility, the supreme virtue of the true Christian, can be achieved only involuntarily: One can be truly humble only by being *humiliated*. Consequently, the most truly meritorious acts are those that result in a total rejection or humiliation by the community—for example, murder or treason. The murderer, therefore, or the traitor (or, on a lesser level, the sneak thief) comes closer to achieving "sanctity" than the parson or the social worker. This argument is well summed up in Lawrence's vitriolic parody:

And the Dostoyevsky lot:
'Let me sin my way to Jesus!'—
And so they sinned themselves off the face of the earth.

Divine of *Our Lady of the Flowers* would agree wholeheartedly.

The attack on the establishment: Genet's existential-Dostoevskian reversal of accepted moral values is basically a rationalization of his rejection of *all* values accepted by the French establishment of his time. That does not mean, in any political sense, that he is a "revolutionary," because "the revolution" (as in *The Balcony*) implies the acceptance of a code of values as rigid as, and perhaps even more intolerant than, those which it claims to replace. In political terms, Genet is an anarchist in the most literal sense: The conformism of the Left is as repugnant to him as the conformism of the Right. Jews, blacks, criminals, Algerians, pimps, prostitutes—these are "his" people, the social outcasts, the "submerged tenth," as un-

welcome to one regime as to another. From this point of view, *Funeral Rites*, while one of the weakest of Genet's novels, is at the same time one of his most significant. Ostensibly, its hero is one Jean Decarnin, a stalwart of the Resistance, Genet's lover. Yet no sooner is Decarnin dead than Genet embarks on a paean to all that is Nazi, for Hitler and for the jackbooted SS batallions that had trampled over the fair land of France. If the new establishment is to be the victorious Resistance, then Genet is as emphatic in his rejection of it as he had been in his rejection of the *grande bourgeoisie* that had preceded it. Michel Leiris once argued that the so-called committed writer can justify his calling only if, like a bullfighter, he *genuinely* exposes himself to danger. Genet accepted the challenge, in a way that Leiris himself, for all of his intelligence, seems scarcely to have envisaged. If Genet rejected the bourgeoisie, it was not so much by writing as by *being* that which no establishment can accept. Therefore, with deliberate delight, Genet, even when he was an acknowledged poet, continued to be an inefficient burglar: the last of his protests against a society which stole "in a different way."

One of the most intriguing features of the Parisian underworld of criminals, pimps, and prostitutes is its tradition of bestowing upon this unlovely riffraff the most elaborate and frequently the most haunting of poetic nicknames. It is as though the highest form of human aspiration stood guard over the most debased of its activities. This is the paradox which Genet, with his passion for masks and symbols, for those moments of "mystic" revelation in which an object is perceived simultaneously to be itself and not itself, takes as the starting point of his first and, in the opinion of many critics, his best novel. The "magical" name Our Lady of the Flowers (which is also the designation of Filippo Brunelleschi's noble Florence cathedral) conceals beneath its high sonorities the sordid reality of a moronic adolescent thug, one Adrien Baillon, a former butcher boy and author of a particularly brutal and senseless murder; "Darling" (Mignon-les-Petits-Pieds) turns out to be a stereotypical muscleman, pimp, and shoplifter; and "Divine," the hero (or rather, the heroine, for that is how "she" would prefer it), is a transvestite male streetwalker, as are "her" companions of the sidewalk, "Mimosa II" (René Hirsch), "First-Communion" (Antoine Berthollet), and "Lady-Apple" ("Pomme d'Api," or Eugène Marceau), among others: "A host, a long litany of beings who *are* the bright explosion of their names." Half or more of these names have religious connotations, notably that of Divine herself, for surely the most beautiful of masks is that of the Son of God, even if it serves to hide a Dantesque inferno.

OUR LADY OF THE FLOWERS

There is no conventional "plot" to *Our Lady of the Flowers*, any more than there is to its successor, *Miracle of the Rose*. Because both of Genet's first two novels are, in part at least, autobiographical (the actual process of writing them was, for their author, a means of liberation, of escape from anonymous degradation, sexual abjection, and possible madness), their structure is as complex as life itself. How Louis Culafroy *became* Divine, how Divine *became* Genet-in-prison, is not told; few things interest Genet less than a coherent narrative in time. The episodes are superimposed on one another, absorbed into one another, so that the beginning is the funeral of Divine and the end is the death of Divine, and both are interwoven with the voice of Genet, who "is" Divine and who is dead and yet alive. The central figure is always Divine, who, in "her" precious dialect of a painted and decaying transvestite, pursues the unending *via dolorosa* laid down for her by her quest for the Absolute.

Divine's most terrifying characteristic is her purity, for hers is a demoniac chastity, born where good and evil meet, the purity of that hell which lies beyond Hell and which consequently drags all those who cannot follow her as far down into the depths as she herself has plunged, toward death and perdition. Her lovers are caught, one by one, in the toils of her "sanctity" and annihilated. Even Our Lady, the "sublime" adolescent strangler, becomes possessed (almost in the biblical sense) with the spirit, or rather with the gestures, of Divine, and confesses to his crime, gratuitously and needlessly—needlessly, in terms of everyday values, but *necessarily* in the context of Divine's world, where the figure has no reality

without the image, nor the criminal without his punishment, and where damnation is essential to justify the ways of God to man. Confession is not repentance but defiance without repentance. If God is infinitely high above man exactly to the extent that man is infinitely far below God, then the supreme exaltation and glorification of God lies in *willing* the opposite of God, which is evil, and, with evil, its punishment. Then, and then only, are the two halves joined and the cycle completed.

In place of plot, then, *Our Lady of the Flowers* interweaves variations on a theme; this theme is the relationship between God and his most ignominious creation, man. The vision of God, for that contemporary mystic Genet, owes much to Dostoevski, something to village-church Catholicism, and most of all to post-Freudian anthropology. From Dostoevski comes Genet's obsession with the figure of the *humiliated* Christ—the Christ who, through His humiliation, bears away the sins of the world—and of the saint who achieves his sanctity through his very degradation. From village Catholicism (albeit oddly distorted) come the cherubim and the archangels, the crude plaster statuettes of the Blessèd Virgin working fake miracles. From the anthropologists comes the notion of transgression: the sophisticated equivalent of the taboo. What transforms Genet's antiheroes from subjects of psychiatric case histories, or instances in a criminologist's notebook, into symbols of a metaphysical reality is the fact that they violate not laws, but taboos.

Hence, in *Our Lady of the Flowers*, Genet is interested in crime and in criminals only insofar as they perpetrate a sacrilege, that is, insofar as they violate the laws, not of society, but of that "Other Dimension," which is God. In one of his allegories, or "parables," Genet sees himself thwarting God. Here lies the key to Genet's attitudes and, furthermore, to the significance of Divine and Darling and Our Lady. They are at death grips with God, because God offers them sanctity and salvation on *His* terms. They are tempted, but they will not be bullied. They are human beings, and they have one inalienable right: to be what they are. God would take away from them this right, so they defy God. If they are destined for sanctity, they are resolved to achieve it in their own way, not God's. They will plunge headfirst into the mire; their abjection is their dignity; their degradation is their ultimate authenticity. God has sided with society; therefore, God has betrayed them. Not for that, though, will they renounce God's kingdom, but they will get there by diving headforemost into the ditch which reflects the stars—the mirror image of Heaven.

MIRACLE OF THE ROSE

Genet's second novel, *Miracle of the Rose*, contains at least as much, if not more, autobiographical material than the first. In *Our Lady of the Flowers*, both Divine and the child, Culafroy, are semimythical figures, all immediate reality being concealed beneath a golden mask of signs and symbols. In *Miracle of the Rose*, by contrast, Genet speaks in his own name. The "I" who endures (and endows with "magic") the sordid and stultifying brutality of the great prison-fortress of Fontevrault—now redeemed from that function and restored to its former status as a minor château of the Loire Valley—is the same "I" who earlier had been subjected to the vicious cruelty of the reformatory at Mettray, a few miles to the northeast. In neither novel is the material, in any usual sense, "romanticized." The misery and horror, the nightmarish ugliness of the life that Genet describes, is never glossed over. On the contrary, it is portrayed lingeringly in all of its nauseating detail, and the ingenious sadism by which a vengeful society deliberately sets out to reduce its victims to a level considerably below that of animals is, if anything, exaggerated. The signs and the symbols are still present and still serve to transmute prison latrines and punishment blocks into miracles and roses, but the symbolism is rather more self-conscious and therefore more self-revealing. In consequence, the reality underlying these symbols is not concealed as much as it is heightened, given a spiritual or aesthetic significance without ever losing sight of its grim and ugly materiality.

The Central Prison (Lan Centrale) of Fontevrault is an isolated community cut off from the rest of the world, cruel, intense, superstitious, hierarchical, and ascetic—not very different from the medieval abbey, with its dependent monasteries and convents, that had originally occupied the same site. The convicts of the present are simultaneously the monks and lay brothers of the long-dead past, an identification that destroys the intervening barrier of time, thus giving the whole prison a dreamlike and "sacred" quality which Genet discreetly emphasizes by setting the time of his own arrival there late on Christmas Eve: "The prison lived like a cathedral at midnight. . . . We belonged to the Middle Ages." Thus Genet establishes the basic structure of *Miracle of the Rose*, which consists in eliminating the "profane" dimension of time by superimposing different fragments of experience in time, identifying them and allowing them to interpenetrate so that the reality that survives is outside time altogether.

Undoubtedly, *Miracle of the Rose* owes something to Proust's *Remembrance of Things Past* (1913-1927); it is understandable that Genet, comparing his own childhood with that of the wealthy, spoiled hypochondriacal young Marcel, must have felt a definite sense of alienation. *Miracle of the Rose*, however, differs from the Proustian narrative in its superimposition of a third plane of experience over and above Proust's levels of time past and time present.

That plane is the plane of the sacred, of existence which is still technically *in* life but, in fact, outside life, space, and time alike—the level of experience that is symbolized by Harcamone. Harcamone, from the mystic solitude of his condemned cell, is already "beyond life"; he lives a "dead life," experiencing the "heartbreaking sweetness of being out of the world before death." Harcamone has, in fact, through his transgression and later through his condemnation, attained that level of sanctity, isolation, and total detachment from profane reality to which Divine aspired yet which he failed to reach—the level at which all miracles are possible. Genet and his convict-lovers, Bulkaen and Divers, exist simultaneously on two planes, in time and space; Harcamone, on three. Consequently, it is Harcamone who dominates the rest—and not only dominates but, being himself a symbol, gives meaning to all the other symbols which compose the worlds of Fontevrault and of Mettray.

As in *Our Lady of the Flowers*, there is no plot in *Miracle of the Rose*. It is a closely woven, glittering tapestry of memories and of symbols. It is not, however, a Symbolist novel; it is rather, a novel wherein the obsessions of memory fuse into the totality of a significant experience through the multiplicity of symbols with which they are illuminated. Frogs become princes while still remaining frogs. Murderers are changed into roses (Genet, incidentally, dislikes flowers) while still remaining murderers. Harcamone, the murderer, is the Rose of Death, yet the warden he killed was known as "Bois de Rose," recalling the rosewood used for coffins. The rose is head and heart; cut off from its stem, it falls as heavily to the ground as the head beneath the knife of the guillotine; it is mourning, it is mystery, it is passion. It is beauty that symbolizes its mirror-opposite, evil and ugliness; it is paradox, blossoming simultaneously in the profane and sacred worlds. It is the Head of Christ and the Crown of Thorns. It is the Miracle and the symbol of the Miracle; it is profanation, transgression, and ultimately—in Genet's special sense—sanctity.

Once Genet began to outgrow his basically autobiographical inspiration, his novels became less impressive; after *Miracle of the Rose*, it was the drama that was destined to become his true medium of expression. *Funeral Rites*, although it contains many interesting ideas in embryo, is the weakest of his full-length published works. Its technique is uncertain: Deprived of the electrifying impulse given by the memory of his own humiliations, Genet descends to the level of the commonplace novelist struggling with the exigencies of a conventional plot.

QUERELLE OF BREST

By contrast, *Querelle of Brest* is the most technically sophisticated of Genet's novels. It is less lyric, less subjective, less poetic, and perhaps less haunting than *Our Lady of the Flowers*; on the other hand, it has a far more substantial structure, it develops its themes with a persistence in logic (or antilogic) which was missing from the earlier works; it creates a whole new range of characters, symbols, and images to replace the purely personal obsessions of *Our Lady of the Flowers*; finally, in the character of Madame Lysiane, it introduces for the first time a woman who plays an essential part in the development of the plot.

From the outset, Genet's metaphysic was based on the symbol of the mirror. The self had reality only as observed by the other (as image and reflection), but this dual self could be granted authenticity only if apprehended simultaneously by a third source of awareness. Claire and Solange in *The Maids* are reflections of each other; their "reality" depends upon Madame, whose consciousness alone can embrace both. In *Querelle of Brest*, this theme of the double is worked out in greater complexity and is pushed toward its inevitable and logical conclusion. What previously was a mirror image is now literally incarnated in the double (Georges Querelle and his identical-twin brother Robert), while the "observers" are equally duplicated (Madame Lysiane and Lieutenant Seblon). To complicate the pattern, both Georges Querelle and Lieutenant Seblon—respectively a seaman and an officer in the French navy—are "doubled" by being both "themselves as they are" and the image or reflection of themselves presented to the world by the uniforms they wear. The double, with all its intricacies of significance in Genet's aesthetic, is the central theme of *Querelle of Brest*.

Genet, to begin, presents a double murder. In the everlasting fogs and granite-veiling mists of the traditional French naval base of Brest, Querelle murders Vic, his messmate, who was his accomplice in smuggling opium past the watchful eyes of the customs officers; perhaps in the same instant, Gil Turko, a young stonemason employed as a construction worker in the dockyard, goaded beyond endurance by the taunting contempt of Théo, a middle-aged fellow construction worker, fills himself with brandy to fire his courage and slashes his enemy's throat with the butt end of a broken bottle. From this moment onward, the two alien destinies begin to coincide—with this difference: Whereas Gil, terrified and hiding from the police in the ruined shell of the ancient galley slaves' prison by the Vieux Port, is the victim, Querelle is the master of his fate, or at least as near master as any mortal can hope to be. Querelle sees in Gil his own reflection, his imitator, his young apprentice who might one day grow up to be the equivalent of himself. He takes care of Gil, feeds him, argues with him, encourages him, secretly exploits him, and finally, for good measure, betrays him to the police. The relationship between Georges Querelle and Gil Turko is, however, only the central relationship in a series of doubles; not only is Georges Querelle doubled by his twin brother Robert, but Madame Lysiane, who loves Robert, also loves Querelle and at most times is unable to distinguish between them. Mario, the Chief of Police in Brest, finds his double in Norbert ("Nono"), the proprietor of the most favored brothel in the dock area, La Féria, and the husband of Madame Lysiane. Even in the absence of character pairs there are mirrors: the great wall mirrors of La Féria, against which a man can lean, propping himself against his own reflection so that he "appears to be propped up against himself."

The arguments of *Querelle of Brest*, both moral and metaphysical, are ingenious, intricate, and awkwardly paradoxical; as usual, they owe much to Dostoevski and something to the Marquis de Sade. Thomas De Quincey, writing "On Murder Considered as One of the Fine Arts," might have learned something from Querelle, just as Querelle might have learned something from Oscar Wilde's "Pen, Pencil and Poison." The outstanding achievement of the novel, however, lies in the way in which structure, plot, argument, and symbols are integrated, forming an imaginative pattern in which every element serves to reinforce the others. The symbol of Querelle's dangerous virility is the granitic, the vertical. Querelle, on the other hand, is flexible and smiling. His symbol is transferred outside himself: It is the ramparts of Brest where he murders Vic; it is the dockyard wall over which the packet of opium must be passed; it is the walls of La Rochelle in Querelle's childhood memories. In the place of roses and angels, Genet is now using a much more abstract, sophisticated, and, in the end, powerful type of symbol. There is a geometrical precision, both of imagery and of argument, in *Querelle of Brest*, which contrasts significantly with the comparative formlessness, the viscosity, and the self-indulgent subjectivity of *Our Lady of the Flowers* or of *Miracle of the Rose*.

In his autobiographical *The Thief's Journal*, Genet refers at one point to his "decision to write pornographic books." As a statement, this is categorical; in any context (not only in that of the 1940's), Genet's novels are unquestionably and deliberately pornographic. There are passages which, even now, are difficult to read without a sickening feeling of disgust: The animality of man is unspeakable, so why speak of it?

In earlier generations, Puritans spoke with similar disgust of the "beastliness" of human appetites. The only difference, compared with Genet, is that they spoke in generalities, allegories, or abstractions. When John Milton's Comus appeared (in *Comus*, 1634), it was in the company of a "rout of monsters, headed like sundry sorts of beasts, but otherwise like men and women, their apparel glistening." The rest of *Comus*, however, is pure poetry; the "rout of monsters" is forgotten. Genet parades before us a similar rout of monsters, but he does not forget about them. Nor, in the last analysis, is he less puritanical than Milton. The exquisite ecstasy of disgust with human sexuality is something that he has known from personal experience; if he chooses to speak of it, it is at least with an authority greater than Milton's. Pushed to its ultimate indignities, pornography becomes puritanism, and puritanical pornography is instinct with poetry. Every word that Genet uses is selected with rigorous and elaborate precision. Divine and her transvestite companions are "the bright explosion [*l'éclaté*] of their names." *L'éclaté* is a rare and precious seventeenth century word, not listed in modern dictionaries, dragged by Genet out of its antique obscurity because it alone possessed the jewel-like precision of the poetic nuance he wished to convey. Genet's pornography is poetry of the highest, most rigorous, and most uncompromising order.

Richard N. Coe

OTHER MAJOR WORKS

PLAYS: *Les Bonnes*, pr. 1947, rev. pr., pb. 1954 (*The Maids*, 1954); *Haute Surveillance*, pr., pb. 1949 (definitive edition pb. 1963; English translation, *Deathwatch*, 1954); *Le Balcon*, pb. 1956, rev. pb. 1962 (*The Balcony*, 1957); *Les Nègres*, pb. 1958 (*The*

Blacks, 1960); *Les Paravents*, pr., pb. 1961 (*The Screens*, 1962).

POETRY: *Poèmes*, 1948; *Treasures of the Night: The Collected Poems of Jean Genet*, 1980.

NONFICTION: *Journal du voleur*, 1948, 1949 (*The Thief's Journal*, 1954); *Lettres à Roger Blin*, 1966 (*Letters to Roger Blin*, 1969).

MISCELLANEOUS: *Œuvres complètes*, 1952 (4 volumes).

BIBLIOGRAPHY

Brooks, Peter, and Joseph Halpern, eds. *Genet: A Collection of Critical Essays*. Englewood Cliffs, N.J.: Prentice-Hall, 1979. Devoted primarily to Genet's plays, but there are two essays on his novels, and the introduction provides a good overview of his life and career. Includes chronology, bibliography, and an interview with Genet.

Knapp, Bettina L. *Jean Genet*. Rev. ed. Boston: Twayne, 1989. Excellent revision of a valuable introductory study. See part 1 for chapters on Genet's life and on his individual novels. Contains chronology, notes, and annotated bibliography.

McMahon, Joseph H. *The Imagination of Jean Genet*. New Haven, Conn.: Yale University Press, 1963. Reprint. Westport, Conn.: Greenwood Press, 1980. See especially the introduction and chapter 1, "The Birth of an Imagination." Provides brief bibliography.

Read, Barbara, and Ian Birchall, eds. *Flowers and Revolution: A Collection of Writings on Jean Genet*. London: Middlesex University Press, 1997. Insightful essays on the author. Includes bibliographical references and an index.

Sartre, Jean-Paul. *Saint Genet: Actor and Martyr*. New York: George Braziller, 1963. The classic biography, which made of Genet a kind of dark saint of modernism. No notes or bibliography.

Stewart, Harry E., and Rob Roy McGregor. *Jean Genet: From Fascism to Nihilism*. New York: Peter Lang, 1993. Examines Genet's political and literary leanings. Bibliographical references and an index are provided.

Thody, Philip. *Jean Genet: A Study of His Novels and Plays*. New York: Stein and Day, 1968. Especially valuable are part 1, exploring both Genet's biography and his major themes (evil, homosexuality, sainthood, and language). Part 2 is devoted exclusively to discussions of his novels. Includes bibliography and detailed notes.

White, Edmund. *Genet*. New York: Knopf, 1993. Novelist and critic White has contributed a worthy successor to Sartre's influential biography. White is more scholarly than Sartre, but he writes clearly and with flair. Provides very detailed notes and an extremely thorough chronology.

ANDRÉ GIDE

Born: Paris, France; November 22, 1869
Died: Paris, France; February 19, 1951

PRINCIPAL LONG FICTION

L'Immoraliste, 1902 (*The Immoralist*, 1930)
La Porte étroite, 1909 (*Strait Is the Gate*, 1924)
Les Caves du Vatican, 1914 (*The Vatican Swindle*, 1925 better known as *Lafcadio's Adventures*, 1927)
La Symphonie pastorale, 1919 (*The Pastoral Symphony*, 1931)
Les Faux-monnayeurs, 1925 (*The Counterfeiters*, 1927)
Thésée, 1946 (*Theseus*, 1950)

OTHER LITERARY FORMS

André Gide began his literary career with a number of prose works that defy conventional classification; among them are poetic works in prose, such as *Les Cahiers d'André Walter* (1891; *The Notebooks of André Walter*, 1968) and *Les Nourritures terrestres* (1897; *Fruits of the Earth*, 1949), and the stories *Paludes* (1895; *Marshlands*, 1953) and *Le Prométhée mal enchaîné* (1899; *Prometheus Misbound*, 1953). Although closely related to his development as a novelist, such works are perhaps best described as lyric essays discussing the nature and limits of human freedom. Gide is known also for his *Journal* (1939-

1950, 1954; *The Journals of André Gide, 1889-1949,* 1947-1951); several autobiographical volumes, including *Si le grain ne meurt* (1926; *If It Die . . .,* 1935) and *Et nunc manet in te* (1947, 1951; *Madeleine,* 1952); and the travelogues *Voyage au Congo* (1927; *Travels in the Congo,* 1929) and *Retour de l'U.R.S.S.* (1936; *Return from the U.S.S.R.,* 1937). As early as 1899, Gide also applied his talents to the writing of plays; the products of these efforts are rarely performed but were published in English in the collection *My Theater* (1952), one year after the author's death at the age of eighty-one.

ACHIEVEMENTS

Despite the relatively small portion of his output that can be classified legitimately as prose fiction, Gide ranks among the most internationally influential French novelists of his time. With the notable exception of Marcel Proust (1871-1922), Gide was the preeminent French novelist of the period between 1900 and 1950, even though he refused to apply the term "novel" to all but one of his extended prose narratives. Although his reputation declined somewhat during the two decades immediately following his death, he would later be regarded among the major figures, both as theoretician and as practitioner, in the history of modern prose fiction.

Belonging, along with Proust and the somewhat younger François Mauriac (1885-1970), to the last generation of French writers whose private means released them from the need to earn a living, Gide wrote at first in order to discover and define himself, initially supplying the costs of publication out of his own pocket. Influenced at the beginning of his career by the Decadent and Symbolist movements, Gide's work soon assumed a personal stamp and direction, acquiring universality even as the author sought primarily to find the best possible expression for his own particular concerns. *Fruits of the Earth,* a lyric meditation published in 1897, established Gide's promise as an original writer and a rising literary figure, although it was not until some twenty years later, during and after World War I, that the book would render its author famous (or infamous) for his inspiration (or corruption) of an entire generation of Euro-

(CORBIS/Bettmann)

pean youth. By that time, Gide's audacious speculations on the nature of freedom and identity had found expression also in the form of extended narratives for which the author adamantly denied the appelation "novel," preferring such recondite (and attention-getting) alternatives as *récit* (tale) or *sotie,* the latter a term for a satiric improvisation performed by French law students during the late Middle Ages.

Such early *récits* as *The Immoralist* and *Strait Is the Gate* established Gide as a master of psychological narrative; *Lafcadio's Adventures,* published in 1914 as a *sotie,* demonstrated Gide's mastery of social satire, with multiple narratives and viewpoints. In *The Pastoral Symphony,* published in 1919, perhaps the most widely read of Gide's prose narratives, he skillfully combined the psychological and satiric strains. It was not, however, until 1925 that Gide saw fit, with *The Counterfeiters,* to publish a book plainly labeled as a "novel" (*roman*). The result was one of the most widely read and influential novels of the decade—indeed, of the entire period between the two world wars and afterward, in view of its considerable effect upon such later developments as the New Novel of the 1950's.

After *The Counterfeiters*, Gide wrote extensively in a variety of genres, although among his later major efforts only *Theseus* might reasonably be considered as extended fiction. Among the first (and oldest) of literary celebrities to be extensively photographed and interviewed, the otherwise reticent Gide spent his later years as an internationally famous literary figure, receiving the Nobel Prize in Literature in 1947, not long after the publication of *Theseus*.

Perhaps correctly identified as a precursor of many significant developments in modern and postmodern fiction, Gide was among the first writers, along with Hermann Hesse (1877-1962), to explore the changing relationships between the individual and society, raising serious epistemological questions with regard to the nature of human identity. He is respected also as a master of prose style in his native language, having perfected a spare, neoclassical sentence that is almost instantly recognizable yet difficult to imitate.

BIOGRAPHY

André Paul Guillaume Gide was born in Paris on November 22, 1869, the only child of Paul Gide (a law professor) and the former Juliette Rondeaux. A shy, introspective boy, inevitably influenced by his parents' severe Protestantism, Gide soon perceived in himself an avid sexuality that would tend toward inversion; as early as the age of seven, he was expelled from school for masturbation and would remain haunted for life by a nagging guilt that he kept trying to neutralize through his various writings. The death of his father in 1880, at the age of forty-seven, added further complication to an already troubled childhood, and Gide would soon undergo treatment for a variety of nervous disorders. Around the age of thirteen, Gide developed a strong, lifelong attachment to his first cousin Madeleine Rondeaux, two years his senior, who became his wife soon after the death of his mother in 1895. Their marriage, although never consummated, was the dominant emotional relationship of Gide's life and ended only with Madeleine's death in 1938 at the age of seventy-one.

Even before his marriage, Gide had begun to emerge as a potential literary figure, thanks in part to a curious work that was written initially with Madeleine in mind. *The Notebooks of André Walter*, privately published in 1891 at the young author's expense, purports to be the diary of a young man, by then deceased, describing his love for one Emmanuèle, under which name Madeleine Rondeaux appears in thin disguise. Although the book failed to sell, it was disseminated within Parisian artistic circles, and Gide continued writing, producing such documents as the Symbolist parable *Le Traité du Narcisse* (1891; "Narcissus," in *The Return of the Prodigal Son*, 1953), the protonovel *Le Voyage d'Urien* (1893; *Urien's Voyage*, 1964), and the experimental *Paludes*, about a young man who is planning a novel to be called *Paludes*. In 1893, Gide at long last came to terms with his latent homosexuality during the course of a trip to North Africa, the details of which would receive chaste (but, for that time, explicit) fictional treatment in *The Immoralist*. Having for all practical purposes discontinued his formal education after belatedly passing the *baccalauréat* on his second attempt, in 1889, Gide nevertheless continued to develop as a self-taught intellectual, reading widely and participating fully in the vigorous cultural activity then centered in Paris. His first truly significant publication, *Fruits of the Earth*, begun as early as the trip to North Africa, was finished shortly after his marriage to Madeleine but was not published until 1897.

Gide's marriage, discussed at considerable length by numerous commentators as well as by Gide himself, remained a dominant feature of both his life and his work. There is little doubt that his love for Madeleine was as deep and intense as it was otherworldly, firmly rooted in the oddly protective emotion that had overwhelmed him when Madeleine was fifteen and he was two years younger. Like her fictional counterpart, Alissa, in *Strait Is the Gate*, Madeleine had recently discovered her own mother's marital infidelity and was quite undone by what she had learned; André, although little more than a child (and a disturbed child at that), instinctively sought to comfort his cousin. There was thus at the base of their affective relationship a denial of the physical that would never really change. Commentator Thomas Cordle, inspired in part by Denis de Rougemont's landmark essay *L'Amour et l'occident* (1939; *Love in the Western World*, 1983), sees in Gide's love for Madeleine a personification of heretical Catharist doctrine as perpetuated in the Tristan legend; in any case, the nature of Gide's love was such that the prospect of consummation might well have threatened to corrupt its "purity."

Madeleine, for her part, was surely not unaware of her cousin's sexual ambiguities by the time she consented to marry him, after several prior refusals; it is likely, too, that she shared his instinctive horror of the physical, although she appears at one time to have contemplated the possibility of pregnancy and childbirth. In either event, the union appears to have proceeded with relative mutual satisfaction until 1918, when Madeleine, bitter over Gide's apparent homosexual "elopement" with the future film director Marc Allégret (1900-1973), burned all the letters that André had written to her since their adolescence. Gide, claiming those letters to have been the only true record of his life and an irreplaceable personal treasure, decided that Madeleine's spiteful gesture had ruined his career; most of Gide's commentators agree that his career, although not in fact ruined, developed thereafter in a different direction from that it might otherwise have taken. The author's marriage, although not ruined either, remained seriously flawed for the remainder of Madeleine's life. Gide's only child, duly christened Catherine Gide, was born in 1923 to Elizabeth van Rysselberghe, daughter of Gide's close friends Théo and Maria van Rysselberghe. Although Gide claimed both Catherine and his eventual grandchildren, he left no written record of his feelings (if any) toward the mother of his only child.

In 1909, already famous as the author of *The Immoralist* and the well-circulated parable *Le Retour de l'enfant prodigue* (1907; *The Return of the Prodigal Son*, 1953), Gide assumed an active part in the founding of the influential periodical *La Nouvelle Revue française*, along with such other literary figures as Jean Schlumberger (1877-1968) and Henri

Ghéon (1875-1944). Soon thereafter, he began work (along with numerous other projects) on the controversial *Corydon* (English translation, 1950), a quasi-Socratic dialogue in defense of homosexuality that would be released privately in 1911, against the advice of Gide's closest friends, and eventually published commercially in 1924. In retrospect, it appears that Gide rather enjoyed controversy, having long (and vociferously) resisted the efforts of several fellow writers to bring him "back into the fold" of the Roman Catholic Church. Because Gide had been reared as a Protestant, there was in fact no question of bringing him "back," as he had never been there; his collected correspondence nevertheless contains a voluminous and vigorous exchange of letters, many of which appeared in print at the time, involving such noted literary contemporaries as the poet Francis Jammes (1868-1938) and the playwright-poet Paul Claudel (1868-1955). Although Gide had abjured his Protestant faith, his writings continued to give evidence of a strong religious sensibility that Claudel and others thought might still be "salvageable." The story is told that Claudel, less than a week after Gide's death in 1951, received a telegram purportedly signed by Gide and claiming, "There is no Hell."

During the 1920's, Gide's penchant for controversy began to acquire political overtones as well, albeit in sporadic and idiosyncratic ways. Ordinarily among the least political of writers, virtually oblivious to the two world wars through which he lived and wrote, Gide nevertheless aroused considerable attention with two well-publicized (and recorded) voyages, the first to colonial Africa and the second, in the mid-1930's, to the Soviet Union. For all of his intelligence, Gide on both occasions appears to have been quite naïve in his expectations; in Chad and the Congo, for example, he was as surprised as he was appalled by the frequent (and flagrant) violation of human rights by the colonial "oppressors." Partly as a result of such observations, Gide in the 1930's began flirting openly with international communism and was duly courted by the Russians in return; he repeatedly refused, however, to become a Party member, and while touring the Soviet Union as a guest of the Soviet government, he became every bit as disillusioned with the Soviet experiment as he had been by French colonialism a decade earlier in Africa. Still cherishing an ideal of communism, Gide wrote bitterly of its "failure" in the Soviet Union.

Following his visit to the Soviet Union and the death of Madeleine Gide not long thereafter, Gide effectively retreated from the political scene. Much as he personally deplored the onset of another war and the subsequent collaborationist regime at Vichy, Gide found little place for the war in his writings, preferring instead the sort of inner reflection that had characterized his work from the start. From 1942 until the end of the war, he resided in North Africa, refusing offered passage to London even after North Africa was liberated. It was there, after all, that he had experienced his first great liberations both as person and as writer, and it was there that he would produce his last great *récit*, a reflection on the life and career of Theseus. Honored in 1947 with the Nobel Prize in Literature, Gide remained active with the writing of essays, memoirs, and translations until his death in February, 1951.

ANALYSIS

Although André Gide's career as a published author spanned nearly sixty years, his position in literary history depends primarily on five prose narratives published in the first quarter of the twentieth century. As Gide's reputation rose to prominence, roughly between 1910 and 1920, critics and commentators were quick to discover the author's earlier writings and, in them, the clear annunciation of Gide's mature output. It is likely, however, that without the merited success of *The Immoralist, Strait Is the Gate, Lafcadio's Adventures, The Pastoral Symphony,* and *The Counterfeiters*, Gide's earliest writings might well have remained mere literary curiosities of the late Symbolist period. A notable exception might well be *Fruits of the Earth*, a transitional work, which in the years following World War I enjoyed a belated success quite unrelated to that of Gide's other writings. In any case, *The Immoralist* and its successors bear witness to a controlled, mature talent that has few peers in the subsequent history of French fiction.

With *The Immoralist*, a slim volume of deceptive

simplicity, Gide reclaimed for the French tradition a strong foothold in the psychological novel. Skillful psychological narrative had been associated with France as early as the seventeenth century, thanks to Madame de La Fayette and her *The Princess of Clèves* (1678), but had recently been pushed aside by the seemingly more urgent claims of realism and naturalism; it was not until the 1920's and early 1930's that the Belgian Georges Simenon, hailed and admired by Gide, would combine psychological narrative with the strongest legacies of naturalism. In the meantime, Gide further established his claim with *Strait Is the Gate*, another economical tale, which, although quite different, is in several respects a mirror image of *The Immoralist*. Particularly remarkable in both short novels is the emergence of Gide's mature style—a clear, concise form of expression far removed from his early verbosity yet not without certain affective mannerisms, particularly noticeable in his frequent inversion of adverb and verb; it is quite likely that the proverbial aspect of Gide's style derives at least in part from his frequent reading of the Bible.

Common to Gide's first two *récits* is his skillful use of a somewhat unreliable first-person narrator whose impressions are "corrected" by other narrative or correspondence that is used to frame the text. In both cases, however, Gide is careful not to point to a moral or to intrude himself as narrator within the working of the text. The canvas remains small, perhaps justifying Gide's use of the description *récit* in place of the more ambitious *roman:* In each tale, only two characters are singled out for close attention, with fewer than ten more appearing in the background. *The Immoralist* is the story of the process by which Michel, at once thoughtful and thoughtless, discovers himself, at the cost of his marriage and the life of his wife, Marceline; *Strait Is the Gate*, told mainly by the ineffectual Jérôme, presents the story of Alissa, whose renunciation and sacrifice seem hardly less selfish, in retrospect, than the deliberate indulgence of Michel in *The Immoralist*. More than once during his career, Gide pointed out that the two tales were in fact twins, having formed in his mind at the same time.

LAFCADIO'S ADVENTURES

With *Lafcadio's Adventures*, Gide broadened his narrative canvas considerably, involving a large cast of frequently outrageous characters in a broad social satire that leaves few sacred cows unmilked. For the first time in his fiction, Gide gives evidence of a perceptive, pervasive sense of humor, which, with some effort and the wisdom of hindsight, has been detected by some critics between the lines of his earlier works. If here, as elsewhere, Gide's stated aim is to disturb the reader, he manages also to entertain, and lavishly so. In his lively evocation of a criminal scheme to extort funds from the faithful in order to "ransom" a Pope who has not in fact been kidnapped, Gide expresses his familiar concerns in a most unfamiliar way; if his main preoccupation remains with the individual, Gide nevertheless gains considerable appeal by placing those individuals against the background of society. Characteristically, however, Gide eschewed the description "novel" even for this effort, preferring the archaic (and exotic) term *sotie*, in part to underscore the *sottise* (stupidity) of most of the characters involved. His true novel, *The Counterfeiters*, moreover, was already in the planning stage, although not to be published until after *The Pastoral Symphony*.

THE PASTORAL SYMPHONY

Serving clear notice of the author's ironic intentions as early as its title, *The Pastoral Symphony*, both broadens and deepens the *récit* as Gide had earlier conceived it, presenting the voice of a most unreliable narrator, who nevertheless is presented with sufficient skill not to strain the reader's credulity. Recalling the legend of Oedipus along with that of Pygmalion, The Pastoral Symphony presents the testimony of a Protestant pastor who hypocritically overlooks his own motivations as he ministers to the blind foundling Gertrude. Although the sustained images of sight and blindness are likely to appear too obvious in summary, they are extremely well-managed within the story itself, a minor masterpiece of "unreliable" first-person narrative. Here, as in *Strait Is the Gate*, and, later, in *The Counterfeiters*, Gide presents a scathing satire of the Protestant milieu from which he sprang, demonstrating the ill effects of that particular doctrine upon the human spirit. Toward the end of Gide's life, *The Pastoral Symphony* was successfully filmed, with Michéle Morgan in the role of Gertrude.

THE COUNTERFEITERS

Late in 1925, already in his middle fifties, Gide at last presented the "novel" that had long occupied his time and energy. Similar in scope to *Lafcadio's Adventures*, its satire softened somewhat by deeper reflection, *The Counterfeiters* proved well worth waiting for, assuring a receptive audience also for Gide's logbook, *Le Journal des faux-monnayeurs* (1926; *Journal of the Counterfeiters*, 1951). Like that of *The Pastoral Symphony*, the title is intended to be understood on several levels; although a band of counterfeiters does, in fact, appear in the novel, the title applies also to nearly all of the adult characters presented in the book, who assume all manner of disguises in order to serve as role models for their understandably disoriented children. It is with the children and adolescents that Gide the novelist is primarily concerned, and they receive his mature sympathy: The adults have all "sold out," in one way or another, leaving the children to fend for themselves. Particularly biting is Gide's satiric portrayal of the Pension Azaïs-Vedel, a seedy Protestant boarding school whose pastor-proprietors, a father and son-in-law, have long since lost the attention and respect of their truly inquiring charges. Through the person of one Édouard, an aspiring novelist approaching middle age, Gide explores the various levels of truth and falsehood not only in life but also in the novel; Édouard, for his part, is planning a volume to be called *Les Faux-monnayeurs*, but one that doubtless will never be written. To his credit, however, Gide in *The Counterfeiters* managed to avoid most of the pitfalls that have awaited his followers in the dubious art of writing a novel about a novelist who is writing a novel. In so doing, moreover, he brought to full expression most of the themes and concerns that preoccupied or haunted him throughout his career. *The Counterfeiters* remains both Gide's masterwork and a landmark in the development of the modern novel.

THE IMMORALIST

Gide, in his earliest attempts at writing—intended mainly for himself, his school friends, and his cousin

Madeleine—tried to discover and define the nature of a freedom that was felt but not yet experienced. Gide's initial voyage to Africa, in 1893, resulted in an awakening that was psychological and spiritual as well as sexual, inspiring the young would-be author to shake off the bonds imposed by his austere French Protestant upbringing. One of the first concepts to emerge in his quest was that of *disponibilité* (availability). As expressed primarily in *Fruits of the Earth*, Gide's idea of *disponibilité* holds that the individual should keep himself "available" to the full range of potential human experience, for only then can he discover all of himself and conduct himself in a truly sincere and authentic manner. Clearly, Gide as early as 1902 had perceived the possible dangers and advisable limits of such an attitude, for *The Immoralist* is at least in part a cautionary tale about personal freedom pushed thoughtlessly to its extreme. Still, the physical and spiritual flowering of the formerly frail and bookish Michel is not without a certain intentional appeal. Between extremes, Gide appears to be suggesting, even advocating, a self-liberation that stops short of incurring such disastrous consequences as the early death of one's wife. For the purposes of fiction, however, *The Immoralist* is extremely well structured and memorable, involving the decline and failure of Marceline's health in inverse proportion to that of her husband.

Like most of his work published both before and since, *The Immoralist* draws heavily upon the established data of Gide's life; here as elsewhere, however, it would be erroneous to see in the work of fiction a direct transposition of the author's experience. Michel's awakening under the hot sun of North Africa, complete with his sexual initiation by young Arabs, obviously owes much to Gide's own experience; Gide, however, initially discovered Africa before his marriage and not while on his honeymoon. Michel's most important discoveries, however, appear to be not sexual but psychological, as in the memorable scene of the Arab boy Moktir stealing Marceline's scissors. Michel, initially shocked, observes the theft with growing fascination and invents a false tale to tell his wife; only later does he learn from his mysterious friend Ménalque, who hands

him the worn and battered scissors, that Moktir, in turn, was aware of being watched. Michel's growing sense of complicity in the reversal of conventional morality constitutes no small part of his newfound freedom; later, upon his return to France, he will conspire with poachers to steal from his own land. Throughout the tale, recounted mainly in the first person by Michel, Gide equates Michel's growing health and strength with his increasing fondness for the wild and elemental; later, when Marceline miscarries and falls ill, the erstwhile near-invalid Michel will prove strangely insensitive to her suffering, claiming that he "got well" all by himself and wondering why she cannot do the same. Still, Michel remains sufficiently attached to Marceline that he will dismiss his "experiment in liberation" as a failure when she ultimately dies.

In *The Immoralist*, as in his later narratives, Gide is particularly concerned to show the negative effects of conventional morality upon the individual; here, however, little mention is made of religion per se, and Gide's concerns are implied rather than directly stated. Clearly, the circumstances of Michel's comfortable bourgeois background are to be seen as stifling, confining, and detrimental to his health; it is not until he breaks away from the security of a precocious academic career (as an archaeologist) that Michel begins to "get well," discovering at the same time what Gide portrays as his authentic self. As in Gide's own case, however, the ties of love remain strong and are less easily dismissed than the constraints of traditional morality.

STRAIT IS THE GATE

In *Strait Is the Gate*, conceived around the same time as *The Immoralist*, Gide presents what he sees as the other side of the same coin. Quite unlike Michel, yet with equal intransigence, Jérôme's cousin Alissa chooses the path of renunciation and self-abnegation, causing some early readers to see in *Strait Is the Gate* a religious or devotional work—indeed, a rebuttal of *The Immoralist*. As in the earlier work, however, ambiguities abound on every page, and it is soon clear that Alissa's "experiment" is hardly more successful or "exemplary" than that of her counterpart Michel; like Michel, indeed, she thoughtlessly contributes to needless human suffering.

Narrated mainly by the callow and ineffectual Jérôme, Alissa's first cousin and sometime fiancé, *Strait Is the Gate* exemplifies and partially satirizes what Cordle has identified as the Catharist dimension of Gide's thought and art. No doubt indebted to the author's life and marriage in certain details, including the age difference and Alissa's discovery of her mother's extramarital affairs, the portrayal of Alissa through Jérôme's love-struck eyes demonstrates a mastery of ironic technique that is all but lacking in *The Immoralist* and finds its strongest expression in *The Pastoral Symphony*. If Alissa indeed suffers from a variety of moral blindness in her adherence to Scripture at the expense of humanity, Jérôme, in turn, suffers from a literal-minded imperceptivity only partially explained by his scholarly training and plans. Perhaps most tellingly, he remains quite unaware of his sensual appeal to Alissa even as he records the effects of that attraction for his potential readers. The latent irony of *Strait Is the Gate* is further enhanced by the inclusion of Alissa's diaries, discovered only posthumously, recording not only her intense feelings toward Jérôme but also her "selfless," determined, and ultimately unsuccessful effort to "marry him off" to her sister Juliette.

Like the love of Gide and Madeleine, the emotion that binds Jérôme and Alissa is clearly "too good for this world," incapable in any case of satisfaction. Although some readers continue to feel that Alissa has given ample proof of sainthood, it is somewhat more likely that she, like Michel of *The Immoralist*, has pushed her inclination to extremes. The reader, although invited to share the excruciating pain of two passionate individuals so hopelessly unable to communicate, might also find occasion to question Alissa's taste in fastening her affections upon a creature as spineless as Jérôme. A stronger Jérôme would render the tale quite implausible, if not impossible, but his limitations spread outward to encompass *Strait Is the Gate* as well, perhaps adding an unintentional note of irony to the book's biblical title.

LAFCADIO'S ADVENTURES

In *Lafcadio's Adventures*, Gide at last gave free rein to the strong ironic bent that is little more than latent in his earlier efforts; in addition, he added a strong portion of humor that is generally lacking elsewhere in his work, with keen observation that often crosses over into broad caricature. Based presumably upon a true incident recorded in European newspapers during the 1890's, *Lafcadio's Adventures* is nevertheless peopled exclusively with characters that could have sprung only from Gide's increasingly active imagination. Even the names are strange, from the novelist Julius de Baraglioul and his brother-in-law Amédée Fleurissoire to Julius's illegitimate half brother Lafcadio Wluiki; there is also the prostitute Carola, whose surname, Venitequa, means "come here" in Latin. Believers and freethinkers alike are treated with irreverence, portrayed as "crustaceans" whose institutionalized beliefs have stunted and distorted what might have been their true personalities. Here, as in *The Counterfeiters*, Gide clearly adumbrates the same demand for authentic behavior that would later dominate the work of Jean-Paul Sartre (1905-1980); unlike Sartre, however, he is not quite ready to accept the implications of total human freedom. To be sure, he offers a tantalizing portrayal of freedom in the person of the nineteen-year-old Lafcadio, whose illegitimacy purportedly exempts him from the bondage of polite society, yet it is hard even for Gide to condone the now-famous *acte gratuit*, or unmotivated deed, in which Lafcadio, more or less from sheer boredom, pushes the unsuspecting Fleurissoire out the door of a moving train. As in *The Immoralist*, freedom still has its limits, and Lafcadio will find that he has thus murdered the brother of his own sister-in-law. By apparent chance, however, he will go unpunished.

Particularly effective in *Lafcadio's Adventures* is Gide's satiric portrayal of the bourgeois "crustaceans": Julius, unlike Gide, is among the most complacent (and presumably boring) of novelists; Anthime Armand-Dubois, a scientist cast in the mold of Gustave Flaubert's pharmacist Homais of *Madame Bovary* (1857), undergoes a sudden conversion to Catholicism that is no less hilarious for being totally sincere. Fleurissoire, the most amiable (if also the most apparently ridiculous) of the three, conserves his goodwill through a harrowing sequence of tortures, only to meet senseless death at the idle hands of Lafcadio; several of Gide's commentators argue with some justice that Fleurissoire may well be the true hero of the book, exhibiting the patience of Job when subjected to similar ordeals. In any event, the fundamental weakness of all three men is their gullibility, reflected in the book's resonant French title, *Les Caves du Vatican*; in French, the word *cave* can refer to the victim of a hoax, similar to the word "mark" in English.

Throughout *Lafcadio's Adventures*, Gide, despite a certain fascination, is careful not to side too closely with the hoaxers, led by the ubiquitous, many-visaged, truly protean Protos. After all, Gide suggests, such parasites can flourish only as long as they find willing victims, and who in his right mind would hand over money to ransom a captive Pope? Only a "crustacean," which further proves the need for increasingly authentic conduct of one's life. Paradoxically, even Lafcadio can exist as he does only in relation to the society he professes to despise; for all of his vaunted freedom, he functions only as the inverted mirror image of respectability, and were respectability to vanish he would vanish too—or change, as do the three "crustaceans" once they have been gulled.

THE PASTORAL SYMPHONY

With *The Pastoral Symphony*, Gide returns to the *récit*, investing the form with deeper resonance and insight than are to be found in either *Strait Is the Gate* or *The Immoralist*. As heavily ironic as *Lafcadio's Adventures*, yet tightly controlled within the first-person narrative viewpoint, *The Pastoral Symphony* continues Gide's inquiry into the potentially negative effects, both psychological and social, of organized religion. Significantly, the narrator-protagonist is a Protestant minister, subspecies Calvinist, whose Swiss enclave is hemmed in on all sides by Roman Catholicism. In apparent reaction against Roman Catholic tradition, he has developed a strong personal faith and doctrine based primarily upon the Gospels. In time, however, he has allowed his faith to harden into a crustacean shell that protects him from true introspection as well as from outside influences; thus does he remain hypocritically blind to his true

feelings toward Gertrude and insensitive to the needs of his own wife and family.

A dozen years earlier, in 1907, Gide had written the oft-reprinted *The Return of the Prodigal Son*, an extended parable or prose poem retelling the tale of the prodigal son. In Gide's version, the prodigal son returns only because he is hungry; although he decides to stay, he inspires his younger brother (a Gidean invention) to leave on the same kind of pagan pilgrimage from which the prodigal has just returned. Intended at least in part as an explanation to his Catholic friends of why he could not join their church, Gide's brief text is interpreted also by some commentators as a concise overview of Catholicism, Protestantism, Judaism, and Muhammadanism. It remains a remarkable text, foreshadowing many of the tensions that were later to animate the action of *The Pastoral Symphony*.

The pastor, like the prodigal son, instinctively recoils from the restrictions and prohibitions brought to Christianity by the epistles of Saint Paul, preferring instead the good news of love propounded by the Gospels. Unfortunately, he manages to misread the Gospels as shelter for his own hypocrisy, retreating into the shell of his faith when in fact it is his illicit love for Gertrude, and not his Calvinism, that is making his family uneasy. The conflict reaches crisis proportions when the pastor's son, Jacques, who has been preparing to follow his father into the ministry, finds himself simultaneously attracted to Gertrude and to the Roman Catholic Church; in several telling passages, the wily pastor attempts to dissuade his son from both attractions by berating his son with Protestant theology; he also attempts to forestall an operation that would restore young Gertrude's eyesight. Gertrude, meanwhile, has become increasingly sensitive to the tensions at work in the pastor's household and perceives, even before the successful operation, that she poses a threat to the pastor's marriage, even as she truly loves Jacques. Her *de facto* suicide, presented as a selfless gesture, occurs only after she and Jacques have both been baptized as Roman Catholics; thus does the pastor conclude that he has "lost" them both.

Given the time of its composition, a number of

Gide's commentators have seen in *The Pastoral Symphony* an artistic transposition of the author's own homosexual affair with the young Marc Allégret (whom he later adopted) and his subsequent rupture with Madeleine after she burned his letters. To be sure, the pastor's marriage is portrayed as dry and loveless, based more on habit than on affection; at one point, the pastor observes that the only way he can please Amélie is to avoid displeasing her. Still, *The Pastoral Symphony* might also be seen as the least autobiographical of Gide's published novels, relating less to his life than to his sustained preoccupation with religion and its potential pitfalls. In *The Counterfeiters*, albeit on a larger canvas, he continued his inquiry into what he saw as the "inevitable" hypocrisy engendered by Protestant belief.

THE COUNTERFEITERS

Reared in the austere and defensive minority environment that was and is French Protestantism, Gide experienced Calvinist guilt at an early age and never really liberated himself from its pervasive clutches. Still, he knew too much, had seen too much, ever to return to the small fold. It is hardly surprising, therefore, that in his first and only "novel" Gide should equate Christianity with Protestantism of a most narrow and unappealing kind. Almost without exception, the troubled adolescents of *The Counterfeiters* are somehow involved with the Pension Azaïs-Vedel, a marginal Protestant boarding school whose precepts are more often honored in the breach than in the observance. Earlier in life, the writer Édouard, in his late thirties at the time of the novel, was both shocked and amazed by the ease with which old Azaïs' solemn pronouncements were shrugged off by his young charges; it was not long, however, before Édouard, hired as a teacher, recognized the students' response as the only reasonable one. Like the pastor of *The Pastoral Symphony*, both Azaïs and his son-in-law Vedel are steeped in smug hypocrisy, having long since made their private, unrecognized concessions to the demands of human nature. The pupils therefore have little choice but to listen politely, then go and do as they please.

Armand Vedel, grandson of Azaïs, may well be the most potentially corrupt of all the adolescents surveyed in the novel; he is at all events the most jaded. Still seeking further corruption and "adventure," Armand refuses to consult a physician about his possible throat cancer—an affliction that symbolizes the state of his mind. His sisters, meanwhile, have fared hardly better: Rachel, the eldest, has never married and bears upon her shoulders the day-to-day administration of the school, including frequent financial shortfalls; her father, meanwhile, could not care less, blindly believing that "the Lord will provide." Her younger sister Laura, formerly in love with Édouard, who would not marry her although he returned her love, has abandoned her teacher-husband for an affair with the dissolute medical student Vincent Molinier, brother of two pension students who figure prominently in the novel. Now abandoned in turn by Vincent and carrying his child, Laura will eventually be invited to rejoin her husband with promise of forgiveness. Ironically, however, it is Édouard whom she still loves.

Perhaps because of the multiplicity of characters and necessary subplots deemed appropriate to the "novel" as opposed to the more restricted *récit,* *The Counterfeiters* often appears confused in its organization, its disparate parts frequently linked by implausible coincidence or by cumbersome (and uncharacteristic) intervention on the part of the author. In order to allow the reader access to Édouard's unpublished journal, for example, Gide arranges for Édouard to have his suitcase stolen by the runaway Bernard Profitendieu, a friend of Édouard's nephew Olivier Molinier; the reader thus reads the journal, as it were, over the shoulder of Bernard, who is reading it himself and will act upon what he has learned. The journal, meanwhile, intersperses facts with frequent ruminations on the theory of the novel.

As in *Lafcadio's Adventures*, and as befits the title of his "novel," Gide in *The Counterfeiters* appears primarily concerned with the nature of authentic thought and behavior, making fun of middle-aged "crustaceans" or "counterfeiters," whose essence has retreated behind mere form. Édouard's brother-in-law Oscar Molinier, for example, is a veteran womanizer who believes his wife, Pauline, to be quite unaware of his philandering; when a packet of letters from his mistress disappears, he concludes that Pauline has discovered him at last. Pauline, no stranger to her husband's secret life, is even more appalled by the disappearance of the letters, correctly guessing that their youngest son, Georges, has stolen them to use as a form of blackmail. Édouard, Pauline's brother, is thus drawn into several levels of intrigue within the story, and it is his rather inept effort to make sense of his own observations that provides the backbone of the novel within a novel, while Gide himself remains in control. As in his earlier efforts, Gide proves especially skillful at unreliable first-person narration, for Édouard is in his own way every bit as much a counterfeiter as the rest of his contemporaries.

Throughout *The Counterfeiters*, partly because of a more liberal literary climate than obtained at the turn of the century, Gide for the first time in his creative prose speaks freely of homosexual love and attraction, as well as of the autoeroticism that had plagued his own childhood and youth. Édouard, although apparently bisexual, is strongly attracted to boys and men, including his nephew Olivier, who, with Pauline's tacit permission, becomes Édouard's lover after Édouard saves Olivier from an attempted suicide. This sexual ambiguity in Édouard prevents him from providing Laura Douviers-Vedel with the love and affection that she both wants and needs. Nor is Édouard the only practicing homosexual in *The Counterfeiters*; several rungs below him on the moral level stands Count Robert de Passavant, also a writer, who openly seeks to corrupt the young (Olivier Molinier as well as Armand Vedel) and maintains a sporadic sybaritic relationship with the cold, frankly amoral Lilian, also known as Lady Griffith.

Bernard Profitendieu, whose flight from his home opens the action of the novel, remains a pivotal if minor figure throughout all that follows. The reason for his flight is that he has discovered his own illegitimacy, learning that his mother bore him out of wedlock. The discovery provides him with all the ammunition that he seems to need for revolt against the authoritarian figure of Judge Albéric Profitendieu, and for a while Bernard tests and tries to enjoy the

"bastardly freedom" of the author's earlier creation Lafcadio (who, according to Gide, was initially supposed to appear in *The Counterfeiters* as well). In time, however, with the approach of true spiritual maturity (symbolized by a rather bizarre supernatural experience), Bernard will return to the Profitendieu household, having grown, developed, and learned more than most of the other characters.

In the person of the diabolic counterfeiter Strouvilhou, aided by his nephew Ghéridanisol and their occasional associate Robert de Passavant, Gide invests the shadowy underworld with an even more sinister presence than that of Protos in *Lafcadio's Adventures*. Strouvilhou, himself a former student at the Pension Azaïs-Vedel, is less a confidence man than a true anarchist, for whom crime serves merely as one possible means to the eventual end of total chaos. Not content with mere counterfeiting, he inspires his young victims to blackmail their parents and consciously engineers the gratuitous suicide of the troubled young Boris, who has enrolled in the pension to be near his grandfather, Édouard's longtime friend, the elderly musician La Pérouse. As in *Lafcadio's Adventures*, however, Gide takes pains to show that the criminal element, however motivated, can exist only at the expense of a polite society that is its complaisant, if less than willing, host. If the novelist Édouard emerges at the end of the novel with the grudging respect of author and reader alike, it is because he fares better than most at the difficult task of being honest with himself. Of all the characters, however, it is doubtless Bernard whose attitude most closely approaches the exemplary.

With the publication of his "novel," Gide doubtless concluded that his exploration of the novel form was complete. An early commentator, Albert Guérard, observed that Gide was in fact less a "novelist" than a traditional French "man of letters" who happened, occasionally, to write novels. Such an assertion appears to be borne out by subsequent developments in Gide's career; although unflaggingly active as a writer well into his eighties, Gide would return only once to the prose narrative form, and then to the *récit* that he had helped to perfect nearly half a century earlier. *Theseus*, which might be read as a philosophical tale or meditation in the manner of Voltaire, provides a fitting capstone to Gide's distinguished if sporadic career as a writer of narrative prose, restating his habitual concerns about human freedom with a wisdom that only age could provide. In all likelihood, however, *The Pastoral Symphony* and *The Counterfeiters* will continue to be regarded as his true masterpieces.

David B. Parsell

OTHER MAJOR WORKS

SHORT FICTION: *Paludes*, 1895 (*Marshlands*, 1953); *Le Prométhée mal enchaîné*, 1899 (*Prometheus Misbound*, 1953).

PLAYS: *Philoctète*, pb. 1899 (*Philoctetes*, 1952); *Le Roi Candaule*, pr., pb. 1901 (*King Candaules*, 1952); *Saül*, pb. 1903 (English translation, 1952); *Bethsabé*, pb. 1903 (*Bathsheba*, 1952); *My Theater*, pb. 1952.

NONFICTION: *Amyntas*, 1906 (English translation, 1958); *Corydon*, 1911, 1924 (English translation, 1950); *Le Journal des faux-monnayeurs*, 1926 (*Journal of the Counterfeiters*, 1951); *Si le grain ne meurt*, 1926 (*If It Die . . .* , 1935); *Voyage au Congo*, 1927 (*Travels in the Congo*, 1929); *Retour de l'U.R.S.S.*, 1936 (*Return from the U.S.S.R.*, 1937); *Retouches à mon "Retour de l'U.R.S.S.,"* 1937 (*Afterthoughts on the U.S.S.R.*, 1938); *Journal*, 1939-1950, 1954 (*The Journals of André Gide, 1889-1949*, 1947-1951); *Et nunc manet in te*, 1947, 1951 (*Madeleine*, 1952); *Ainsi soit-il: Ou, Les Jeux sont faits*, 1952 (*So Be It: Or, The Chips Are Down*, 1959).

MISCELLANEOUS: *Les Cahiers d'André Walter*, 1891 (*The Notebooks of André Walter*, 1968); *Le Traité du Narcisse*, 1891 ("Narcissus," in *The Return of the Prodigal Son*, 1953); *Le Voyage d'Urien*, 1893 (*Urien's Voyage*, 1964); *Les Nourritures terrestres*, 1897 (*Fruits of the Earth*, 1949); *Le Retour de l'enfant prodigue*, 1907 (*The Return of the Prodigal Son*, 1953); *Les Nouvelles Nourritures*, 1935 (*New Fruits of the Earth*, 1949).

BIBLIOGRAPHY

Bettinson, Christopher. *Gide: A Study.* London: Heinemann, 1977. The first chapter provides a succinct biography of Gide, and subsequent chapters concentrate on the major novels, with a final chapter on his social and political activities and writings. Includes a short bibliography. A good introductory study.

Brée, Germaine. *Gide.* New Brunswick, N.J.: Rutgers University Press, 1963. A study by one of the great scholars of modern French literature, with chapters on the Gide of fact and legend, the man of letters, and on his major novels. Includes detailed notes and bibliography.

Cordle, Thomas. *André Gide.* New York: Twayne, 1969. An introductory study, with chapters on "The Gidean Personality," "Decadence and Symbolism," "Romantic Resurgence," and "Social Realism." Includes notes and bibliography.

Driskill, Richard T. *Madonnas and Maidens: Sexual Confusion in Lawrence and Gide.* New York: Peter Lang, 1999. Examines the issues of sexuality, Christianity, and psychology in Gide and D. H. Lawrence.

Fowlie, Wallace. *André Gide: His Life and Art.* New York: Macmillan, 1965. One of the enduring, standard works on Gide, with chapters on his childhood and adolescence, early career, major novels, journals and autobiography, relationship to Catholicism, and his vocation as a writer.

Littlejohn, David, ed. *Gide: A Collection of Critical Essays.* Englewood Cliffs, N.J.: Prentice-Hall, 1970. Essays by distinguished critics on Gide's fiction, including Germaine Brée on *The Counterfeiters* and Jean-Paul Sartre on Gide's career. The introduction, chronology, and bibliography provide a comprehensive overview of his life and career.

Lucey, Michael. *Gide's Bent: Sexuality, Politics, Writing.* New York: Oxford University Press, 1995. A specialized study for advanced students of Gide. Lucey discusses both his fiction and nonfiction.

Walker, David H., ed. *André Gide.* New York: Longman, 1996. Criticism and interpretation of Gide's oeuvre. Includes bibliographical references and an index.

JEAN GIONO

Born: Manosque, France; March 30, 1895
Died: Manosque, France; October 8, 1970

PRINCIPAL LONG FICTION

Colline, 1929 (*Hill of Destiny*, 1929)
Un de Baumugnes, 1929 (*Lovers Are Never Losers*, 1931)
Regain, 1930 (*Harvest*, 1939; the three previous novels are known collectively as Trilogy of Pan)
Naissance de l'"Odyssée," 1930
Le Grand Troupeau, 1931 (*To the Slaughterhouse*, 1969)
Solitude de la pitié, 1931
Jean le bleu, 1932 (*Blue Boy*, 1946)
Le Serpent d'étoiles, 1933
Le Chant du monde, 1934 (*The Song of the World*, 1937)
Que ma joie demeure, 1935 (*Joy of Man's Desiring*, 1940)
Batailles dans la montagne, 1937
Pour saluer Melville, 1943
Un Roi sans divertissement, 1947
Noé, 1947
Les Âmes fortes, 1949
Mort d'un personnage, 1949
Les Grands Chemins, 1951
Le Hussard sur le toit, 1951 (*The Hussar on the Roof*, 1953; also known as *The Horseman on the Roof*)
Le Moulin de Pologne, 1952 (*The Malediction*, 1955)
Le Bonheur Fou, 1957 (*The Straw Man*, 1959)
Angélo, 1958 (English translation, 1960)
Deux Cavaliers de l'orage, 1965 (*Two Riders of the Storm*, 1967)

OTHER LITERARY FORMS

Jean Giono is remembered chiefly for his novels. During the 1930's, however, he surfaced briefly as a social theorist with such volumes as *Les Vraies Richesses* (1936; true riches) and *Le Poids du ciel* (1938; the weight of the sky). He also wrote several performed plays, of which the most noteworthy is *La Femme du boulanger* (1942), expanded from an episode in his autobiographical novel *Blue Boy* and filmed by Marcel Pagnol in 1938.

ACHIEVEMENTS

Championed early in his career by André Gide and other prominent writers of the time, Jean Giono is the preeminent "regional," or rural, French novelist of the twentieth century; his novels have been compared to those of Thomas Hardy in England and William Faulkner in the United States. In the mid-1930's, Giono acquired a considerable following as a "poet and prophet of the soil," emerging as leader of the agrarian Contadour movement that flourished during the years preceding World War II. Briefly imprisoned both in 1939 and in 1945 for the unshakable pacifist convictions he had developed during his years of service in World War I, Giono fell from favor as a writer, only to rebound spectacularly during the late 1940's and early 1950's with a new docu-

(Archive Photos)

mentary style quite different from his earlier modes. In 1953, he received the Prix Monégasque, awarded by the Prince of Monaco for the finest ensemble of works in the French language; the following year, he was elected to the prestigious Académie Goncourt.

BIOGRAPHY

Jean Giono was born in 1895 at Manosque, a rural village in southern France where, except for extended military service during World War I, he would spend his entire life. His father, a cobbler, and his mother, a laundress, had married when they were no longer young, and Jean was their only child. His childhood, recalled in *Blue Boy* and elsewhere, appears to have been a reasonably happy one, although lived close to the poverty line and in close touch with the forces of nature. In 1911, faced with the declining health of his father, Jean cut short his formal education to take a job in the local branch of a national bank; with time out for military service, he would remain with the bank until 1930, when he at last believed himself capable of earning a living from his writings; it was in that year that he bought the house in which he would spend the remaining forty years of his life, and in which he would receive visitors attracted from throughout the world by the increased success of his writings. In 1920, soon after the death of his father, he married Élise Maurin, who bore him two daughters, Aline in 1926 and Sylvie in 1934.

As early as 1931, with *To the Slaughterhouse*, Giono began to express in his writings the deep and obdurate pacifism that was the result of nearly five years of enlisted service during World War I. With the publication of his "rural epics," notably *The Song of the World* and *Joy of Man's Desiring*, Giono's pacifism gradually fused with his glorification of rustic life to produce the phenomenon of Contadour, a back-to-the-soil movement that anticipated by some thirty years many similar communal experiments in the United States and Western Europe. According to critic and Giono expert Maxwell Smith, the Contadour experience arose more or less by accident when, in the fall of 1935, the number of youthful "pilgrims" to Giono's home in Manosque exceeded the Gionos' capacity for hospitality, and Élise suggested to her husband that he take some of their uninvited guests "for a walk." Knapsacks on backs, Giono and some three dozen of the faithful set off soon thereafter on an extended hike through areas that Giono especially loved or about which he had written. When, after several days, the leader happened to sprain his ankle near the tiny town of Contadour, the group decided that they had found what they had been seeking. Housed at first in a barn, the group later bought land for sheep farming and a permanent residence.

As Smith points out, the true function of the Contadour "pilgrimages," several of which would occur annually until the onset of World War II, was to test the mettle and adaptability of disillusioned urbanites in search of an alternative lifestyle; in time, the Contadour movement became associated with that of the International Youth Hostels, which completed the task of "resettling" many former city dwellers throughout rural France. During the late 1930's, the Contadour movement published its own quarterly, *Cahiers*, and helped to inspire Giono's social essays of the same period.

With the outbreak of war in 1939, Giono came under severe public censure for his pacifist sentiments and activism and spent two months in prison at Marseilles, from which he was released upon the combined intervention of Gide and the Queen Mother of Belgium. Erroneously suspected of being a Fascist sympathizer, Giono remained purely and simply a pacifist, who saw in all wars the denial and destruction of his strongest personal values. Returning to Manosque, he was again imprisoned at the end of the war, largely for his own protection against reprisals from the far Left, whose sympathizers had gained control of the region following cessation of hostilities; he was also censured and blacklisted for a time by the increasingly Left-leaning Comité National des Écrivains.

Between prison sentences, Giono appears to have spent most of his time and energy on the French translation of Herman Melville's *Moby Dick* (1851), a project begun in the mid-1930's with his longtime friend Lucien Jacques and their British acquaintance Joan Smith. Jacques, a writer, artist, and sometime editor, had helped to publish and publicize some of

Giono's earliest writings; the two men were further bound by shared pacifist convictions resulting from service in the previous war, and Jacques had assumed an active part in the Contadour experiment. An unexpected side effect of the translation was the writing and publication of *Pour saluer Melville*, Giono's tribute, in the form of a novel to a writer he had long admired. Bordering closely upon a literary hoax, although intended in utter good faith, *Pour saluer Melville* inserts totally invented characters and incidents between the recorded lines of Melville's life— so convincingly, in fact, that at least one of Melville's descendants would accept the story as authentic.

Once cleared of suspicion after World War II, Giono, by then in his early fifties, returned to the literary scene in full vigor, but in a new and different mode that he himself called *chroniques* (chronicles). As different from his spare early style as from his rural epics of the 1930's, the *chroniques* won for him new admirers while disappointing certain older ones. Historical in context, drawing heavily upon the lives and exploits of Giono's paternal Italian ancestors, the *chroniques* are perhaps as epic in scope as *The Song of the World*, but with new attention paid to the delineation of character, sometimes at the expense of plot. The so-called Hussar Cycle, inaugurated by *The Horseman on the Roof* in 1951, demonstrated Giono's eventual mastery of the new form and brought him honors that only a short time earlier might have been considered unthinkable. Although somewhat disillusioned by the failure of his social thought, dismissing the Contadour movement as a youthful mistake, Giono remained personally optimistic, vigorous, and active as a writer well into his seventies, continuing to welcome the visitors who came from far and wide to see him. Jean Giono died at his home in Manosque in 1970.

ANALYSIS

Almost without exception, Jean Giono's commentators trace the emergence of his early styles to his voracious reading of the Greek classics in translation, a program of self-education and entertainment begun in childhood, to be continued after-hours at the bank. While in school, Giono, like his contemporary Antoine de Saint-Exupéry (1900-1944), had performed poorly in French composition, showing little promise for his eventual career. As Henri Peyre has pointed out, however, Giono had the distinct advantage of acquiring the classics on his own, outside the classroom in a rustic Mediterranean environment not utterly different from that of ancient Greece; in all likelihood, the sights, sounds, and smells were much the same, as were man's perennial contact and struggle with the soil. Indeed, Giono's first attempt at long fiction, not published until subsequent works had made him a better risk to publishers, was *Naissance de l'"Odyssée,"* a vigorous, ironic work written "within the margins" of Homer's *Odyssey* (c. 800 B.C.).

TRILOGY OF PAN

Giono first rose to prominence in the late 1920's and early 1930's with the so-called Trilogy of Pan, comprising *Hill of Destiny, Lovers Are Never Losers,* and *Harvest*. Giono, later to be succeeded by the Spanish-born dramatist Fernando Arrabal (born 1932), evokes the spirit of Pan to symbolize the forces of nature, with which man often coexists in an uneasy truce. In *Hill of Destiny*, nature quite literally goes "on strike" against human "improvements" wrought upon the land; the elderly Janet is unjustly accused of witchcraft, having acquired the odd gift of communication with nature and having warned his fellow villagers to mend their ways before it is too late. *Lovers Are Never Losers*, by contrast, presents the lyric aspect of Pan, singing the lost-and-found love of Albin for Angèle through the voice of the old peasant Amédée. *Harvest*, later successfully filmed, unites humanity with nature in the marriage of the near-giant Panturle and the itinerant Arsule, who has saved him from drowning; love, although present, is here subordinated to the cycle of the seasons.

As Maxwell Smith observes, Giono in his Trilogy of Pan delighted readers with his seemingly effortless gift for striking, apt, and memorable metaphor, particularly in his descriptions of nature or of the forest fire in *Hill of Destiny*. In *Lovers Are Never Losers*, description is equally vivid, although style and vocabulary are pared down somewhat, to suit the speech patterns of the uneducated peasant narrator. The style of *Harvest* remains restrained if colorful, with seemingly authentic rustic speech. Only in the middle volume, *Lovers Are Never Losers*, does Giono see fit to delineate or "humanize" his characters in a way that makes them memorable; in *Hill of Destiny* and *Harvest*, it is nature itself that dominates, often attaining the stature of a character through the author's vivid descriptions.

LOVERS ARE NEVER LOSERS

Perhaps the most successful of Giono's novels in his earliest mode, *Lovers Are Never Losers* combines his rare evocative power with a sure gift for storytelling. The narrative, although limited in voice and viewpoint to the uneducated old peasant Amédée, is both sensitive and credible in its portrayal of young Albin and his pining love for Angèle, who has been "carried away by a city slicker." Within the context of the tale, Baumugnes is a village whose Huguenot inhabitants, their tongues cut out by religious persecutors, learned to communicate with one another by playing the harmonica; understandably, their descendants, including the unfortunate Albin, have supposedly inherited an uncanny gift for playing that instrument, and Albin's talent stands him in good stead in the rescue of Angèle, long since abandoned by her lover and held captive on her father's farm. Unlikely though the story may sound in summary, *Lovers Are Never Losers* remains a remarkable and memorable narrative, as notable for the deftness of its characterizations as for the economy of its style. Only the city-bred seducer Louis seems closer to caricature than to character, but even that lapse can be seen as credible within the story's rural context.

In 1930, the year that he resigned from the bank and purchased his house, Giono managed also to publish his first-written novel, *Naissance de l' "Odyssée,"* which would enjoy an even larger printing eight years later, with another publisher. He also began for the first time to put "himself" into his books, with such semiautobiographical novels as *To the Slaughterhouse* and *Blue Boy*. His style in these volumes is increasingly confident and frankly lyric, tending toward exuberance; perhaps his most masterful scene, also a metaphor (as reflected in the original title *Le Grand Troupeau*), shows two old men stampeding sheep through a provincial village; the young shep-

herds who would normally have done the job have themselves been "stampeded"—to war. Giono's descriptions, worthy of the Greek poets whom he so admired, anticipate the "epic" style that would soon burst forth, full-blown, in *The Song of the World* and *Joy of Man's Desiring*. The style of the meandering, episodic *Blue Boy* is more restrained, although amply supplied with deft similes and metaphors. Representative of the book's tone and content is the doubt of old Franchesc Odripano, on hearing of the Wright brothers' flight, "that anything will really change."

With his epic novels of the middle 1930's, Giono began increasingly to assert the claims of the soil against, and above, those of modern technology. Indeed, the modern world is conspicuous primarily by its absence from his impassioned, vivid storytelling, set in modern times but showing man eternally involved with nature.

THE SONG OF THE WORLD

In *The Song of the World*, the first, as well as the best-remembered and most durable, of his epic novels, Giono depicts the primordial, archetypal struggle between the peasants Antonio and Matelot, on one side, and the seemingly malevolent mountain tyrant Maudru, on the other; storms and the river, meanwhile, pose at least as powerful a threat to both sides as the opposing sides do to each other. Credible though the incidents may be, little effort is made toward verisimilitude; the author instead aspires to the monumental. Here, both man and nature are writ large, with much of the action taking place at night, in the false shelter of ominous shadows. Giono's choice of title is seconded by Henri Peyre, who observes that Antonio, Matelot, and even the menacing Maudru are "epic heroes not because they accumulate feats in violent battle but because they are the very forces of nature embodied in simple, strong creatures; they echo the song of the world." Reduced to simple plot, the action of *The Song of the World* might well be seen as little more than a feud among peasants. In Giono's capable hands, however, the narrative assumes truly monumental as well as highly memorable proportions, enriched by the author's vivid, resonant vocabulary and a country dweller's homage to the cycle of the seasons.

JOY OF MAN'S DESIRING

Joy of Man's Desiring, despite a proliferation of unhappy characters, waxes so lyric in its paean to the rustic life as to have inspired in some critics an unflattering recollection of Jean-Jacques Rousseau and of Voltaire's observation that his notorious contemporary was inviting humankind "to walk upon all fours." Significantly, it was soon after the publication of *Joy of Man's Desiring* that the Contadour movement arose as if spontaneously, although Giono's novels had begun to attract a following as early as 1931, before his epic phase.

BATAILLES DANS LA MONTAGNE

Batailles dans la montagne, published between the two propaganda volumes *Les Vraies Richesses* and *Le Poids du ciel*, is perhaps the most effective of the three "epics" in portraying man's struggle with nature; a small mountain village is doubly threatened with destruction by flood, both from a melting glacier and from a river accidentally dammed by a landslide. Particularly memorable, and epic, is Giono's description of the hero Saint-Jean's anguished quest for dynamite to blow up the dam, in the course of which he is pitted against an enraged bull. Here as elsewhere, Giono excels in his deft, if verbose, evocation of nature, whose phenomena are as beautiful as they are terrifying.

Thanks in part to his enviable mastery of the French language and its vocabulary—a mastery exceeding that of many more sophisticated writers—Giono managed throughout most of his career to avoid accusations of false primitivism as well as of condescension to his characters or audience. Giono was, in fact, a true provincial, a committed son of the soil who was ready and more than willing to meet the rest of the world on its own terms; many another writer, transplanted urbanite as well as native rustic, has tried and failed to achieve the artistic position that Giono was to assume as if by birthright. Despite Giono's occasional vulnerability to charges of being a latter-day Rousseau, the integrity and vigor of his thought and prose quite naturally protected him from the danger of becoming a literary counterpart to "Grandma" Moses or even Norman Rockwell. At worst, the social propaganda of his Contadour period

reflects a certain shallowness; happily, though, such weaknesses are absent from the novels written around the same time.

UN ROI SANS DIVERTISSEMENT

In his postwar novels, collectively known as *chroniques*, Giono moved on to a new, quasi-documentary style of narrative exposition that he claimed to have developed contemporaneously with his epic novels, although the results would not be seen until the late 1940's. The first published novel in the new mode, which appeared in 1947, was *Un Roi sans divertissement*, seen by some observers as a glorified detective story. Consisting of first-person testimony from a variety of participants and witnesses, *Un Roi sans divertissement* deliberately leaves unresolved many of the ambiguities that would be reconciled in a more conventional mystery. Reviewers, although somewhat nonplussed by Giono's seemingly abrupt change of manner, found much to praise in his delineation of character, especially in the case of the protagonist Langlois.

NOÉ

Noé, published later in the same year, appears to have been the author's favorite among his many novels and was reissued at his own request in 1961; described by Smith and others as a "novelist's novel," *Noé* builds upon the autobiographical foundation of the earlier *Blue Boy* to provide fresh insight into the author's art and craft as characters from his work in progress begin to appear in his mind, much in the manner of persons encountered in "real life." In style and content, however, *Noé* is closely related to the *chroniques*, with which it is usually classified.

Between 1949 and 1952, Giono added three major volumes to his series of *chroniques*. *Les Âmes fortes*, consisting entirely of conversation among three old ladies at a wake, reconstructs in often hair-raising, apparently "realistic" detail a curious tale of envy, fraud, and murder covering the preceding sixty years. *Les Grands Chemins*, likewise dealing with murder and fraud, has generally been deemed less successful. *The Malediction* recalls in grim detail the "family curse" hanging over the head of a certain Julie Coste. The novel was well received, but Giono, in the meantime, had attracted even more critical attention with

The Horseman on the Roof, published in 1951 and inaugurating what would come to be known as his Hussar Cycle.

A subgrouping of the *chroniques*, Giono's Hussar novels are set against the background of nineteenth century Europe, before the unification of Germany and Italy. Drawing heavily upon his own Italian origins, Giono presents in the Hussar cycle a colorful fresco of tribulation and adventure featuring the carbonaro Angelo Pardi, a character modeled, at least in part, on Giono's own paternal grandfather. In *The Horseman on the Roof*, Giono involves Angelo and other recurring characters in the cholera epidemic of 1838, portraying man's struggle against disease in a chronicle that has been favorably compared to Albert Camus's *La Peste* (1947; *The Plague*, 1948). *The Straw Man* shows Angelo cast as a scapegoat or "straw man" by conspirators during the Italian campaign against Austrian rule in 1848; dismissed by some commentators as an unsuccessful imitation of Stendhal's *La Chartreuse de Parme* (1839; *The Charterhouse of Parma*, 1895), *The Straw Man* was correctly recognized by others as a step in the direction of postmodern fiction; like Alain Robbe-Grillet, Michel Butor, and other New Novelists of the 1950's, Giono, in *The Straw Man*, was clearly experimenting with modes of perception and presentation in the novel, questioning established concepts of time and character even as he sought to present a rousing, well-told tale against a historical background.

THE HORSEMAN ON THE ROOF

Different though it may be from Giono's nature epics of the 1930's, the documentary style of the *chroniques*, including the Hussar Cycle, remains strongly rooted in the soil. As in his earliest novels, the landscape in *The Horseman on the Roof* is never far removed from view, even as increasing attention is paid to the delineation and development of character. Although nature is cast in a relatively minor role, Giono's characters are still very much at the mercy of the elements—the cholera epidemic, for example, is similar to the floods, storms, and savage beasts that figure prominently in the earlier novels—which in turn help define both personality and be-

havior. In the view of some critics, *The Horseman on the Roof* is the finest of Giono's novels.

Set largely in Giono's home town of Manosque as it must have been some sixty years before his birth, the novel takes its rather unusual title from the fact that Angelo Pardi, fleeing for his life after killing an Austrian spy in a duel, is eventually driven to the rooftops in his search for sanctuary; the people of Manosque, superstitious by nature and further maddened by the presence of the plague in their midst, wrongly suspect the fugitive Angelo of having poisoned the town's water supply. Told in a sober, matter-of-fact style somewhat different from Giono's earlier mode, *The Horseman on the Roof* excels also in its portrayal of man's inhumanity to man, as Angelo witnesses innumerable scenes of brutality and violence from the relative sanctuary of his elevated hiding place. As in Camus's *The Plague*, however, the narrative is saved from gloominess by the exemplary behavior of the featured characters. The character of Angelo Pardi, together with that of the Marquise Pauline de Théus, reappeared throughout Giono's subsequent novels, although here they are perhaps at their most memorable. Significantly, it is *The Horseman on the Roof* that appears to have brought to Giono's work, at long last, the double honor of the Prix Monégasque and election to the Académie Goncourt.

Although Giono's reputation declined somewhat in the years following his death, he is still recognized for a singular talent of rare scope and evocative power, perhaps impossible to imitate. As a pacifist inalienably committed to the land and its values, he may also be seen as presaging by some thirty years the counterculture of the 1960's, which in turn exerted considerable influence upon the values of the present day.

David B. Parsell

OTHER MAJOR WORKS

PLAYS: *Lanceurs de graines*, pr. 1932; *Le Bout de la route*, pr. 1937; *La Femme du boulanger*, pr. 1942; *Théâtre*, pb. 1943 (collection); *Voyage en calèche*, pb. 1946.

NONFICTION: *Les Vraies Richesses*, 1936; *Le*

Poids du ciel, 1938; *Triomphe de la vie*, 1942; *Voyage en Italie*, 1953; *Notes sur l'affaire Dominici*, 1955; *Le Désastre de Pavie*, 1963 (*The Battle of Pavia*, 1966).

TRANSLATION: *Moby Dick*, 1939, 1943 (with Lucien Jacques and Joan Smith; of Herman Melville's novel).

BIBLIOGRAPHY

Badr, Ibrahim H. *Jean Giono: L'Esthétique de la violence*. New York: Peter Lang, 1998. An examination of violence in Giono's work. In English.

Clayton, Alan J. "Giono's *Colline:* Pantheism or Humanism?" *Forum for Modern Language Studies* 7 (1971): 109-120. Complements the approach taken by Brian Nelson in his edition of the novel.

Goodrich, Norma L. *Giono: Master of Fictional Modes*. Princeton, N.J.: Princeton University Press, 1973. Chapters on Giono's major work, divided into studies of "The Apocalyptic Mode," "The Surrealist Mode," "The Symbolic Mode," "The Epic Mode," "The Tragic Mode," and "The Autobiographical Mode." Includes detailed bibliography and index.

Peyre, Henri. *The Contemporary French Novel*. New York: Oxford University Press, 1955. Contains one of the finest analyses of Giono's fiction by a distinguished critic.

Redfern, W. D. *Jean Giono: Le Hussard sur le toit*. Glasgow, Scotland: University of Glasgow French and German Publications, 1997. An introduction to *The Horseman on the Roof* for beginning students.

_____. *The Private World of Jean Giono*. Oxford, England: Basil Blackwell, 1967. Begins with a biographical note, introduction, and then chapters on uses of imagination, the inner life, the modern world, the apocalypse, a world of words, and a postwar world. Includes notes and bibliography.

Smith, Maxwell A. *Jean Giono*. New York: Twayne, 1966. Smith devotes two chapters to Giono's family background, early childhood, and youth and follows with Giono's debut in literature and his major fiction. Provides chronology, notes, and annotated bibliography.

GEORGE GISSING

Born: Wakefield, England; November 22, 1857
Died: St. Jean-Pied-de-Port, France; December 28, 1903

PRINCIPAL LONG FICTION

Workers in the Dawn, 1880
The Unclassed, 1884
Isabel Clarendon, 1886
Demos, 1886
Thyrza, 1887
A Life's Morning, 1888
The Nether World, 1889
The Emancipated, 1890
New Grub Street, 1891
Denzil Quarrier, 1892
Born in Exile, 1892
The Odd Women, 1893
In the Year of Jubilee, 1894
Eve's Ransom, 1895
The Paying Guest, 1895
Sleeping Fires, 1895
The Whirlpool, 1897
The Town Traveller, 1898
The Crown of Life, 1899
Our Friend the Charlatan, 1901
The Private Papers of Henry Ryecroft, 1903
Veranilda, 1904
Will Warburton, 1905

OTHER LITERARY FORMS

Though George Gissing will be remembered primarily as a novelist, he tried his hand at a variety of literary projects. In the 1890's especially, he found it profitable to write short stories; these were generally published in periodicals, but one volume—*Human Odds and Ends* (1897)—was published during his lifetime. Many of his other short stories, some from his early contributions to Chicago newspapers, have since been collected: *The House of Cobwebs* (1906), *Sins of the Fathers* (1924), *A Victim of Circumstances* (1927), and *Brownie* (1931). Gissing also wrote essays for a number of periodicals. *Notes on Social De-*

mocracy (1968, with an introduction by Jacob Korg), reprints three articles he wrote for the *Pall Mall Gazette* in 1880. *George Gissing: Essays and Fiction* (1970) prints nine prose works published for the first time. Late in his life, Gissing published *Charles Dickens: A Critical Study* (1898) and *By the Ionian Sea* (1901), his "notes of a ramble in southern Italy."

ACHIEVEMENTS

During his lifetime, Gissing achieved neither the fame nor the fortune that he would have liked. His reputation, though it grew steadily, especially in the 1890's, was always overshadowed by the powerhouse writers of the late Victorian era. Gissing was nevertheless seriously reviewed and often applauded by the critics for his objective treatment of social conditions in England. After his death, his reputation was eclipsed for many years, and it was only in the late twentieth century that Gissing began to receive the reevaluation needed to determine his place in English literary history. The renewed academic attention, manifested by numerous new editions of his novels, critical biographies, full-length studies of his novels, and several volumes of his correspondence, suggested that Gissing's niche would become more firmly established.

BIOGRAPHY

Born on November 22, 1857, in Wakefield, Yorkshire, George Robert Gissing was the eldest of five children of Thomas Waller and Margaret Bedford Gissing. Thomas Gissing was a chemist in Wakefield and something of a religious skeptic whose extensive library provided the young George with convenient access to a variety of reading material. The early years of financial security and familial harmony were disrupted when Thomas Gissing died in December, 1870. George, only thirteen, and his two brothers were sent to Lindow Grove School at Alderley Edge, Cheshire. There, the young Gissing's studious habits gained for him the first of many academic accolades. His performance on the Oxford Local Examination in 1872 was especially encouraging, but financial circumstances made it necessary for him to attend Owens College in Manchester, where he had won

free tuition for three sessions and where he continued with his academic success.

Gissing was not, however, enjoying the same success in his personal life. Living a lonely and studious life in Manchester, he fell in love with a young prostitute named Marianne Helen Harrison ("Nell"). With the zeal of the reformer, Gissing tried to save her from her profession and her penury, apparently not realizing at first that she was an alcoholic as well. Exhausting his own funds, the young Gissing stole miscellaneous property from his fellow students at Owens College. He was soon caught and the course of his life was radically altered, for he was forced to abandon all thoughts of an academic life. With the aid of friends, he sailed for the United States in the fall of 1876 and worked briefly as a high school teacher in Waltham, Massachusetts. Why he left Waltham, where he apparently enjoyed a reasonably good life, is not known, but in the spring of 1877 he moved to Chicago, where he tried to eke out an existence as a writer. Though he did publish his first work (a short story called "The Sins of the Fathers," in the Chicago *Tribune*, March 10, 1877), he was not well paid for his endeavors and left after only four months. He worked at odd jobs in New England and elsewhere, and then in the fall of 1877 he made his way back to England. In London, he lived in near-poverty, working sporadically as a tutor and drafting his first novels. Nell came to live with him, and in October, 1879, they were married. Despite Gissing's noble intention to reform her apparently self-destructive character, the marriage was not successful. A vivid fictionalized account of the sordidness of their married life is given in *Workers in the Dawn*, Gissing's first published novel. He lived a turbulent life with Nell until he put her in an invalids' home in January, 1882. Even after that, she gave him trouble, both financial and emotional, until she died in 1888.

The direction of Gissing's writings in the 1880's was influenced not only by his failed marriage but also by a number of other lifelong interests which were well established by the end of the decade: his friendship with the budding German writer Eduard Bertz, his reading of Auguste Comte, his unfailing compassion for the poverty of late Victorian England, his friendship with Frederic Harrison, who read his first novel and provided much-needed encouragement, and his friendship with Morley Roberts, who later became Gissing's first biographer with the thinly disguised *The Private Life of Henry Maitland* (1912). Not until 1886, with the publication of *Demos*, did Gissing gain moderate success with his writing. Buoyed by more favorable circumstances, especially the sense of freedom once Nell died, Gissing left for an extended tour of Europe in September, 1888. He also shifted the emphasis of his novels from the working class to the middle class, beginning in 1890 with *The Emancipated.*

The 1890's began auspiciously for Gissing's literary career, particularly with the publication of *New Grub Street* and *Born in Exile.* His personal life, however, was following a different course. On a trip to Italy in 1890, he noticed the first signs of the respiratory illness which would plague him the rest of his life. On February 25, 1891, he married Edith Underwood, a "work-girl," as he described her, with whom he was not in love. The marriage was a complete failure, despite the birth of two sons (Walter Leonard, born 1891, and Alfred Charles, born 1895). Gissing's literary success in the 1890's, as moderate as it was, was achieved in spite of his loveless marriage and domestic unrest. He persevered until September, 1897, when he permanently separated from his wife and went to Italy. In the summer of 1898, he met Gabrielle Fleury, a Frenchwoman who was the complete opposite of his two wives in her refined and cultured manner. Gissing was immediately attracted to her and would have legally married her had a divorce from Edith been possible. Instead, the two sanctified their relationship with each other in a private ceremony on May 7, 1899, in Rouen. Living in France under the most favorable circumstances of his entire life, Gissing continued to write, and in 1903 he saw *The Private Papers of Henry Ryecroft*, his most popular work, go through three editions. His health, however, had been growing steadily worse, and his short-lived happiness came to an end when he died on December 28, 1903, of myocarditis at St. Jean-Pied-de-Port in France.

ANALYSIS

In his personal life, George Gissing was a man of divided mind, and the biographical antitheses were paralleled by the literary and philosophical influences on his work. In private life, he gravitated toward Frederic Harrison's circle of intellectuals and sophisticated people; at the same time, he was drawn into marriages with psychologically, intellectually, and socially unsuitable women. He was attracted, on the one hand, to a scholarly career as a historian, philosopher, and classicist; on the other, he was drawn to journalism, hackwork, and lectures to workingmen's associations with an emphasis on social reform. Like many writers at the end of the nineteenth century, he was caught between the sociological realists with reform instincts and the adherents of an aesthetic movement with their emphasis on the attainment of ideal beauty. His sensuousness conflicted with his intellectual idealism; his desire for popularity and material success with his austere integrity as an artist.

Gissing's career as a novelist, at least until the late twentieth century, has been assessed in the context of nineteenth century realism and naturalism. Certainly, the techniques employed in his novels, especially the early ones, owe much to the Victorian conventions that had become well established by the time of Gissing's first published novel. He was thoroughly acquainted with the work of Charles Dickens; his own novels are often sentimental, cautiously admonitory, and riddled with subplots. Gissing, however, never treated his subject matter as humorously as did Dickens in his early novels. Dickens's treatment of poverty, for example, is sometimes used for picturesque effects; Gissing saw poverty in a solemn manner, finding it both lamentable and execrable.

For other literary precedents, Gissing turned to the French and Russian writers, discovering in the French naturalists such as Émile Zola the pervasive effects of physical and social environments and finding in the Russian naturalistic psychologists the precise and complete analysis of character. Like Zola, he described the squalor of poverty, probed the psychology of sex (though with more reserve), and generally ended his novels in dismal defeat. Yet, unlike the naturalists, Gissing was not so much concerned with the particular details of the workshop, with conflicts between capital and labor, but with the whole atmosphere of poverty, especially the resultant loss of integrity on the part of those who struggle to rise beyond and above it.

To divide Gissing's career into neat stages is not an easy task. For the purposes of an overview, however, it is convenient to look at three large, if not always distinct, groups of his novels. In the 1880's, beginning with *Workers in the Dawn* and ending with *The Nether World*, Gissing was most often concerned with the lower class and social reform. In the first half of the 1890's, beginning with *The Emancipated*, Gissing turned to the middle class, examining the whole middle-class ethic and ranging his focal point from the tradesman to the "new woman." In the last half of the 1890's and until his death in 1903, Gissing's work was more varied, ranging from a historical romance to a travel book to reworkings of his early themes. In those last years, his works were not always successful, either commercially or critically, but that was the period of his most popular work, the semiautobiographical *The Private Papers of Henry Ryecroft*.

In an early and important reassessment of Gissing's career, Jacob Korg ("Division of Purpose in George Gissing," in *PMLA*, June, 1955) points out that the dichotomy between Gissing's artistic principles and his anger over Victorian England's social problems is evident in five of his novels published in the 1880's: *Workers in the Dawn, The Unclassed, Demos, Thyrza,* and *The Nether World*. In each of these novels, Gissing the reformer contends with Gissing the artist; in none of them is the tension resolved satisfactorily.

WORKERS IN THE DAWN

Most of the material Gissing used in *Workers in the Dawn* can be found repeatedly in the other novels of the 1880's, and most of that material springs from his own experiences. Clearly, his early marriage to a girl from the slums underlined his interest in social themes throughout his life. In the late 1870's and 1880's, he had also become enthusiastic about the radical party, read Comte, promoted positivist doctrines, and spoke at various radicalist meetings. Between 1879 and 1880, Gissing began writing *Workers in the Dawn*, a novel of avowed social protest in which he serves, as he says in a letter of June 8, 1880, as "a mouthpiece of the advanced Radical party." Equally obvious in the novel, however, is the fact that Gissing is perturbed about placing art in service to political and moral dogma. Arthur Goldring, the hero of the novel, is both a painter and a social reformer, but he is clearly upset with this duality in his life. Convinced that the aims of his two avocations are antithetical, he looks for consolation from Helen Norman, the woman he loves. Through the mouth of Helen, George Gissing propounds the ideas that he had gleaned from Percy Bysshe Shelley's *A Defence of Poetry* (1840)—most specifically that art is the true legislator of the moral order. Gissing, however, found it difficult to practice what he held to be intellectually valid; thus, the early Gissing, like Goldring, constantly found difficulty in accepting the tenet that art should not attempt to teach morality directly.

THE UNCLASSED

In *The Unclassed*, Gissing continued to struggle with the intricacies of the artist's world. The result, unfortunately, was a novel in which the fall of the two artist-figures is in one case oversimplified and in the other, muddled. Confused and worried about his own failings, Gissing attempted to analyze the artistic temperament and the forces operating against such a temperament by segmenting the artist into Julian Casti and Osmond Waymark. Casti's story is Gissing's attempt to depict an artist undone by an overriding sense of moral obligation to a shrewish and possessive woman, Harriet Smales, a character with clear similarities to Gissing's own wife Nell. Not until the last chapter is the physically debilitated and intellectually frustrated Casti convinced that his moral obligation to Harriet is futile. He leaves for the Isle of Wight, where he quietly spends his last days plaintively talking of the epic he will never write.

The portrait of Waymark is Gissing's attempt to counterbalance the oversimplified Casti. Waymark is a more complex figure, and his role as an artist is more thoroughly scrutinized by Gissing. Waymark is thwarted in his pursuit of art by a variety of causes: his aborted social consciousness, his vaguely defined ideological tenets, his relationship with women, and his pecuniary predicament. By the end of the novel, after a plethora of complications, Waymark is neither a complete success nor a complete failure. His one published novel receives mediocre reviews, and Waymark himself shows little concern either for its intrinsic value or for its critical reception. By placing his artist-hero in the grips of consuming personal, political, and economic woes, Gissing tries to suggest that art cannot flourish with integrity or purity. The portrait of Waymark, however, is finally very muddled, for it is not clear to which forces Waymark the artist succumbs. Questions about the role of art in the political and moral order continued to dominate Gissing's thinking in much the same way throughout the 1880's, and he entered the 1890's very much in the middle of the two main currents of literary thought, drawn both to the angry didacticism of the realists and naturalists and to the ivory towers of the aesthetes.

In the 1890's, Gissing broadened the range of his novels and produced his best work. At the beginning of the decade, he published *The Emancipated*, the story of a young middle-class widow restricted by religious scruples until she finds release in art. In *Denzil Quarrier*, Gissing tried his hand at a political novel and produced one of his more popular works. In *Eve's Ransom*, a short novel that was first serialized, he focused on the pangs of unrequited love. In *Born in Exile*, Gissing examined the life of one born in the lower classes who has the opportunity to rise to a higher socioeconomic level. In *The Odd Women*, Gissing focused his attention on early feminists, making a careful study of women who never marry but who must support themselves in a male-dominated society.

NEW GRUB STREET

The novel on which Gissing's reputation has most depended is *New Grub Street*, his full-length study of the artist's role in society. From Jasper Milvain to Whelpdale to Alfred Yule to Edwin Reardon to Harold Biffin, Gissing offers a finely graduated hierarchy of the late nineteenth century artist. He is particularly interested in characterizing the artist *manqué* and the forces which have contributed to his failure. Unlike the earlier novels, however, *New Grub Street* presents a wider-ranging understanding of the artist's dilemma. It is no longer a simple case of idealized social reform versus an even more idealized artistic purity. In keeping with his social interests of the early 1890's, Gissing sees the factors operating against the artist arising more from without than from within. He concentrates on two particularly potent forces which militate against the artist and ultimately ensure his downfall.

The first force is the woman, and her influence on the artist is subtle, pervasive, and lasting. Often sensitive and frequently lonely, the nascent artists of Gissing's Grub Street are prime targets for the love of a good woman. She appeals particularly to the psychologically insecure artist, promising a lifetime of emotional stability. At the outset, she is a source of inspiration, yet time and disillusionment reveal more distressing realities. It is the age-old femme fatale who lures the artist away from his art into an emotionally draining existence, thwarting his inclination and energy for production. It is "the other woman" who instigates a complicated triangle with like results. It is the husband-hunting woman who tantalizes the frustrated artist with the attraction of domestic security, but soon she either stifles that inexplicable drive to write for the sake of writing or provides a marriage so socially disadvantageous that advancement is precluded.

Economics is the second, equally potent, force militating against the three failed artists (Reardon, Biffen, Yule) of *New Grub Street*. While the force of woman is chiefly felt on a psychological level, her destructive influence within the economic sphere is evident. After all, the necessity of supporting a wife and children increases the financial difficulties the artist must face. Monetary matters also prove a problem in and of themselves. An artist such as Biffen easily falls victim to the myth of so many struggling artists, convinced that poverty and hardship are essential in the experience of any would-be writer. In the portrait of Reardon, however, one quickly sees the artist at odds with real poverty, rarely an inspiration and usually a deterrent to his work.

Edwin Reardon is the novel's central character, and it is Reardon who is subjected to the greatest number of debilitating forces. When he is introduced, it is immediately clear that his marriage to Amy has entangled him in the finely woven web of woman. At the outset, Reardon is thirty-two, has been married two years, and has a ten-month-old child. None of his decisions, artistic or otherwise, can be wholly unaffected by this domestic responsibility. Gissing makes his viewpoint clear in the very first scene with Reardon and Amy. In this scene, largely a heated discussion over Reardon's approach to writing, Amy chides her husband for not compromising his artistic integrity and forcibly reminds him that "art must be practised as a trade, at all events in our time. This is the age of trade." Thus, in this one early scene, the two powerful influences of woman and commerce come together, and there is little doubt that they will take a heavy toll on Reardon the artist. Reardon's failure as an artist, both aesthetically and materially, runs in direct proportion to the failure of his marriage and the decline of his economic status.

Obviously lending itself to autobiographical interpretation, the artist-novel is the means by which the real-life writer works out—or fails to—his own aesthetic and personal conflicts. *New Grub Street*, like Gissing's earlier novels, has its share of autobiographical elements, but his analysis of his emotional and intellectual condition is far more perceptive. He has gained tighter control on the raw materials of the artist's world which are treated ambiguously in the early novels. The eleven years between *Workers in the Dawn* and *New Grub Street* were the training ground for an increased self-insight and a more encompassing, objective portraiture of the artist-figure and the gray areas with which he must cope.

The work Gissing produced in the last half of the 1890's has not generally contributed to his critical reputation. Part of his later years he spent on a variety of projects that are not especially characteristic of his overall career. In 1898, he published *Charles Dickens: A Critical Study*. In 1901, he published *By the Ionian Sea*, a travel book about his experiences in Italy. He also worked on a historical novel which was never completed but published posthumously as *Veranilda* in 1904. The novels that Gissing published in his last years are for the most part undistinguished

and often are reworkings of his earlier themes. *The Whirlpool* is a study of marriage in the "whirlpool" of modern life. *The Crown of Life* is his paean to the perfect marriage, significantly begun shortly after he met Gabrielle Fleury in 1898.

THE PRIVATE PAPERS OF HENRY RYECROFT

In 1900, Gissing did most of the writing of *The Private Papers of Henry Ryecroft*, though it was not published until 1903. The book is not really a novel. Pretending to be merely the book's editor, Gissing provides a short preface saying that he has come across the papers of his friend Ryecroft and has ordered them in an arbitrary way. There are four main sections, each labeled with one of the seasons, beginning with spring and ending with winter. The book is a mixture of autobiography and reverie, providing the author a platform on which he can discuss sundry subjects. Thus, there are memories of childhood, of poverty in London, of peaceful trips to Italy. There are descriptive sketches of rural scenes in England. There are short essays on philosophical ideas and terse confessions of various preferences, ranging from food to countries. The book provides delightful if not exciting reading and gives a memorable portrait of the aging author who has retired to the calmness of Exeter to ruminate.

When Gissing died in 1903, he left behind an impressive corpus, but the reputation he had at the time of his death did not continue to grow. By some, he was criticized as being too ponderous and undramatic, inclined to publish an analytical study rather than a dramatized story. By others, he was accused of being melodramatic, relying too exclusively on the contrivances of the Victorian "triple-decker." In the second half of the twentieth century, however, especially during the last two decades, Gissing attracted more attention in academic circles. His seriousness as a novelist has slowly been recognized, both for his historic role in the heyday of English realism and for his integrity as an individual novelist.

David B. Eakin

OTHER MAJOR WORKS

SHORT FICTION: *Human Odds and Ends*, 1897; *The House of Cobwebs*, 1906; *Sins of the Fathers,*

1924; *A Victim of Circumstances*, 1927; *Brownie*, 1931.

NONFICTION: *Charles Dickens: A Critical Study*, 1898; *By the Ionian Sea*, 1901; *The Immortal Dickens*, 1925; *Letters of George Gissing to Members of His Family*, 1927; *George Gissing and H. G. Wells: Their Friendship and Correspondence*, 1961; *The Letters of George Gissing to Eduard Bertz*, 1961; *George Gissing's Commonplace Book*, 1962; *The Letters of George Gissing to Gabrielle Fleury*, 1964; *George Gissing: Essays and Fiction*, 1970; *The Diary of George Gissing, Novelist*, 1978.

BIBLIOGRAPHY

Connelly, Mark. *Orwell and Gissing*. New York: Peter Lang, 1997. Compares *New Grub Street* to George Orwell's *Keep the Aspidistra Flying* (1936). Also, a chapter on "Doomed Utopias: *Animal Farm* and *Demos*."

Coustillas, Pierre, and Colin Partridge, eds. *Gissing: The Critical Heritage*. London: Routledge & Kegan Paul, 1972. A very important research tool for the study of Gissing, containing a large selection of reviews dating from his own time to the late 1960's. Among the notable essays is a notice by the great Victorian critic George Saintsbury, who claimed that Gissing had an obsessional interest in attacking the social order, but who nevertheless liked Gissing because his writing was difficult to forget. Paul Elmer More argued that Gissing overcame the undue realism of his first novels. Gissing's study of the classics and philosophy tempered his overblown portrayal of society.

Grylls, David. *The Paradox of Gissing*. London: Allen & Unwin, 1986. Maintains that paradox is the key to reading Gissing properly. He was attracted to conflicting points of view on various topics, including women, social reform, poverty, and art. His novels express these contradictions, often by a sharp break in the middle. In *New Grub Street*, Gissing achieved an integration of diverse opinions.

Halperin, John. *Gissing: A Life in Books*. Oxford, England: Oxford University Press, 1982. The most comprehensive life of Gissing. Its dominant theme is that he wrote about his own life in his novels, and much of the book discusses Gissing's fiction from this point of view. Halperin does not confine himself to Gissing's life, devoting considerable attention to the critical reaction to Gissing after his death. Maintains that H. G. Wells launched a campaign of vilification against Gissing. Also includes a section that offers acidulous remarks of writers about Gissing.

Michaux, Jean-Pierre, ed. *George Gissing: Critical Essays*. New York: Barnes & Noble Books, 1981. This valuable anthology gives a good selection of twentieth century critics' discussions of Gissing. Includes an influential essay by Q. D. Leavis, who praised Gissing's portrayal of the misery of the Victorian world. His careful and realistic observations achieved their culmination in *New Grub Street*, which Leavis places among the outstanding English novels. An essay by George Orwell lauds Gissing's attack on respectability.

Selig, Robert L. *George Gissing*. Rev. ed. New York: Twayne, 1995. An excellent introduction, with chapters on Gissing's major works, his career as a man of letters, and his biography. Includes chronology, notes, and annotated bibliography.

Sloan, John. *George Gissing: The Cultural Challenge*. New York: St. Martin's Press, 1989. Chapters on Gissing's "Hogarthian beginnings," his working-class novels, his career from *The Emancipated* to *New Grub Street*, and *The Odd Women*. Includes detailed notes and bibliography.

ELLEN GLASGOW

Born: Richmond, Virginia; April 22, 1873
Died: Richmond, Virginia; November 21, 1945

PRINCIPAL LONG FICTION
The Descendant, 1897
Phases of an Inferior Planet, 1898
The Voice of the People, 1900

The Battle-Ground, 1902
The Deliverance, 1904
The Wheel of Life, 1906
The Ancient Law, 1908
The Romance of a Plain Man, 1909
The Miller of Old Church, 1911
Virginia, 1913
Life and Gabriella, 1916
The Builders, 1919
One Man in His Time, 1922
Barren Ground, 1925
The Romantic Comedians, 1926
They Stooped to Folly, 1929
The Sheltered Life, 1932
Vein of Iron, 1935
In This Our Life, 1941

OTHER LITERARY FORMS

In addition to nineteen novels, Ellen Glasgow wrote a book of short stories, *The Shadowy Third and Other Stories* (1923); a book of poems, *The Freeman and Other Poems* (1902); a book on her views of fiction-writing (concerned primarily with her own

(Library of Congress)

works), *A Certain Measure: An Interpretation of Prose Fiction* (1943); and an autobiography, *The Woman Within* (1954). She also wrote a number of articles on fiction for various periodicals and magazines. Her letters were published in 1958.

ACHIEVEMENTS

Although Glasgow never felt that she had received the critical acclaim she deserved, or at least desired, she nevertheless played an important part in the development of southern letters. A significant figure in the so-called southern Renascence, she provided in her novels a new picture of the South, a region reluctantly ushered into the modern world. Against a sentimentalized view of the Old South, Glasgow advocated an acceptance of the inevitability of change.

Prior to 1925, Glasgow's critical reception was mixed—more positive than negative, but nothing that would mark her as a writer of the first rank. With *Barren Ground*, however, Glasgow's reputation began to grow with both critics and readers. That novel made the 1925 *Review of Review*'s list of twenty-five outstanding novels of the year. Represented also on the list for 1925 were Sinclair Lewis's *Arrowsmith*, Edith Wharton's *The Mother's Recompense*, Willa Cather's *The Professor's House*, and Sherwood Anderson's *Dark Laughter*. Glasgow's *The Sheltered Life* was a best-seller and greatly enhanced her reputation. *Vein of Iron* and *In This Our Life*, which received the Pulitzer Prize in 1942, helped to ensure her position as a writer of major significance.

> "The chief end of the novel, as indeed of all literature," Glasgow wrote, is "to increase our understanding of life and heighten our consciousness." To this end she directed her artistic skills, writing with care and precision, for, as she also said, "The true novel . . . is, like poetry, an act of birth, not a device or invention."

BIOGRAPHY

Born in Richmond, Virginia, in 1873, Ellen Glasgow came from a combination of stern Scotch-Irish pioneers on her father's side and Tidewater, Virginia, aristocratic stock on her mother's side. Francis Glasgow was an ironworks executive, an occupation well suited to his Puritan temperament and character. Ellen Glasgow had little positive to say about her father. Her mother, on the other hand, was a cultivated, gracious, and humane woman. These divergent influences provided the crucible from which Glasgow's writings were to emerge.

The next to the youngest in a family of four sons and six daughters, Glasgow experienced a more-or-less lonely childhood, with Rebe, her younger sister, and Mammy Lizzie Jones, her black nurse, providing her only companionship. Because of fragile health and a nervous temperament that precluded adjustment to formal schooling, her isolation was increased, and most of her education came from her father's extensive library.

As a child, Glasgow admired the novels of Charles Dickens, Henry Fielding, and Jane Austen. From Dickens, she gained reinforcement for her already strong aversion to cruelty, and from the latter two, she learned that only honest writing can endure. Lesser novelists, she felt, lacked "the creative passion and the courage to offend, which is the essential note of great fiction."

Glasgow grew up in that period following the Civil War when, as she described it, the "prosperous and pleasure-loving" agrarians of the antebellum years were struggling for existence amid "the dark furies of Reconstruction." It was a conservative, even reactionary, time when, according to Glasgow, "being a rebel, even an intellectual one, was less exciting and more uncomfortable than it is nowadays." Rejecting the harsh Calvinism of her father and the bloodless social graces of Richmond society, she retreated even further into a life of the mind. Glasgow's growing sense of alienation and rebelliousness has been seen by critics as the wellspring of her literary vision.

By 1890, just one year after her hearing had begun to fade, Glasgow had produced some four hundred pages of a novel, *Sharp Realities* (unpublished). Putting that effort aside, she began writing *The Descendant* in 1891. Two years later, however, upon the death of her mother, with whom she had great affinity, she destroyed a good part of what she had written. Another two years passed before she returned to

the novel and completed it. The following year, she made the first of numerous trips to Europe.

With the publication (anonymously) of *The Descendant* in 1897, Glasgow was launched on her prolific career, a career that saw novels appearing every two years or so. Writing became and remained her role in life, and she was ever mindful of the growth of her literary reputation, changing publishers when she felt it to her advantage and making sure that critics were fully aware of her books.

Presumably while on a trip to Europe in 1899, Glasgow fell in love with a married man, to whom she refers in her autobiography *The Woman Within* as Gerald B_____. A mystery man, Gerald B_____ was described by Glasgow as an older man with a wife and children, a Wall Street man. There is some evidence, however, indicating that Gerald B_____ was a physician. Another serious love affair was with Henry Watkins Anderson, a Richmond lawyer. He and Glasgow met in 1915 and were engaged in 1917. In July of the next year, Glasgow attempted suicide when she learned that Anderson, who was working with the Red Cross in the Balkan States, was attracted to Queen Marie of Romania. This turbulent love affair between Glasgow and Anderson was tacitly broken about 1920. In two novels, *The Builders* and *One Man in His Time*, Glasgow incorporated aspects of her relationship with Anderson.

As Glasgow began receiving the critical recognition for which she longed, her health began to fail. A heart condition worsened, and she died on November 21, 1945, in Richmond, Virginia.

ANALYSIS

Turning away from a romanticized view of her own Virginia, Ellen Glasgow became a part of the revolt against the elegiac tradition of southern letters. Although she rejected romance, she did not turn to realism; rather, she saw herself as a "verist": "The whole truth," she said, "must embrace the interior world as well as external appearances." In this sense, she strove for what she called "blood and irony"—blood because the South had grown thin and pale and was existing on borrowed ideas, copying rather than creating; and irony because it is the surest antidote to sentimental decay. Certain that life in the South was not as it had been pictured by previous writers, she produced a series of novels that recorded the social history of Virginia through three generations, picturing sympathetically the social and industrial revolution that was transforming the romantic South.

A central theme in this record is that of change—change brought about by the conflict between the declining agrarian regime and the rising industrial system. Arguing that such change must be accepted and even welcomed, Glasgow observed,

> For thirty years I have had a part in the American literary scene, either as a laborer in the vineyard or as a raven croaking on a bust of Pallas. In all these years I have found that the only permanent law in art, as in the social order, is the law of change.

In pursuing the theme of change, however, Glasgow was careful not to go to the extreme in her presentation of deterioration, feeling that "the literature that crawls too long in the mire will lose at last the power of standing erect." In this respect, her works, unlike those of William Faulkner or Erskine Caldwell, lack shocking or sensational detail and maintain an almost Victorian sense of decorum. For example, when Dorinda in *Barren Ground* goes to the city, she is first approached by a fascinating lady clad in black who wants her to enter into a disreputable house. She is then rescued by a kindly doctor who gives her money to go back to Virginia and establish a dairy farm. This tendency toward propriety found in Glasgow's writing is explained in her plea to the novelist of the southern gothic school:

> All I ask him to do is to deal as honestly with living tissues as he now deals with decay, to remind himself that the colors of putrescence have no greater validity for our age, or for any age, than . . . the cardinal virtues.

The theme of change gives a mythic quality to Glasgow's work. It is that quality that Henry Canby refers to when he says that Glasgow sees her world as always a departing and a becoming. Her instrument for this cutting away is her sense for tender and ironic tragedy, a tragedy that is, in the words of Canby, "a

tragedy of frustration—the waste of life through maladjustment of man to his environment and environment to its men."

Often, too, Glasgow's works picture nobility cramped by prejudice, or beauty gone wrong through an inability to adjust to the real, or a good philosophy without premises in existing experience. A good example of the latter theme can be found in the character of John Fincastle in *Vein of Iron*. A man of deep thought, he is considered "as a dangerous skeptic, or as a man of simple faith, who believed that God is essence, not energy, and that blessedness, or the life of the spirit, is the only reality." Fincastle is a part of the constant change in the world, but he himself does not fully realize the implications of the dynamic society in which he lives. He sees nothing of any potential value in the machine age and is unable to reconcile his own philosophy to the reality of the times.

Although all of Glasgow's works contain a note of pessimism, there is also present a note of optimism. More often than not, this hope comes after a protagonist's contact with city life. Dorinda, for example, returns to Pedlar's Mill after her stay in the city, to start a successful farm and gain revenge from Jason. Then, too, there is Ada in *Vein of Iron*, who, with her cynical husband, returns to the manse that was once her home and, strengthened by the recovery of "that lost certainty of a continuing tradition," looks forward to a new beginning.

Perhaps, when compared with Faulkner or Thomas Wolfe, the theme of change, as treated by Glasgow, may seem somewhat sentimental; there is, however, a refreshing and heartening chord in her work that lends credence to the idea that the world is not destined to be one great naturalistic garbage can, but may perhaps be fertile enough for an occasional bed of flowers. At any rate, as Glasgow phrased it, "the true revolution may end in a ditch or in the shambles, but it must begin in the stars."

VIRGINIA

In *Virginia*, her first acknowledged masterpiece, Glasgow focuses on the southern woman. "As an emblem," she writes of the southern woman in *The Deliverance*, "she followed closely the mid-Victorian ideal, and though her sort was found everywhere in the Western world, it was in Virginia that she seemed to attain her finest and latest flowering." It would follow, then, that if southern women attained their "finest and latest flowering" in Virginia, that also is where they would be most affected by the winds of social change that were sweeping over the South in the late nineteenth and early twentieth centuries. Bred and reared to tradition, they faced a new order that was both challenging and perplexing. While some held firmly to the pedestal on which they had been placed, others leaped from it and immersed themselves in the new world.

Virginia Pendleton, the heroine of *Virginia*, is, like her mother, the ideal southern woman, the image of propriety and gentility. "Whenever I attempt to recall the actual writing of *Virginia*," Glasgow says in *A Certain Measure*,

> and to recapture the mold in which the book was conceived, I find myself moving again in an imaginary world which was then more real to me than the world which I inhabited. I could not separate Virginia from her background, because she was an integral part of it, and it shared her validity. What she was, that background and atmosphere had helped to make her, and she, in turn, had intensified the life of the picture.

In Dinwiddie, Virginia, during the 1800's, Virginia has been reared as "the perfect flower of the Victorian ideal" and "logical result of an inordinate sense of duty, the crowning achievement of the code of beautiful behavior and the Episcopal Church." She has been taught that duty, devotion, and sacrifice are the lot of women and that husband and family must come before all else.

Virginia, educated at Miss Priscilla Battle's finishing school, the Dinwiddie Academy for Young Ladies, is indeed "finished," at least as far as any real purpose in life is concerned. The basis of her education was simply that "the less a girl knew about life, the better prepared she would be to contend with it." Thinking him an excellent choice for a husband, she marries Oliver Treadwell, son of an industrialist, and, bearing him three children, settles down to family life. Oliver, like his father, who had dominated Oliver's mother, exercises this same control over Virginia. A would-be dramatist, Oliver is unsuccessful as a serious playwright, but he does receive some financial return by writing claptrap for the New York stage. Although Virginia has become middle-aged and worn, Oliver has maintained the look of youth. Finding no understanding from Virginia, who is not equipped to give him any, he deserts her for Margaret Oldcastle, an actress. Not knowing how to fight for her husband's love, Virginia is left with her two daughters, whose independence and aggressiveness she cannot understand, and her devoted son, Harry. The purpose in life for which she and so many other southern women had been prepared is gone. "Nothing but constancy was left to her," says Glasgow, "and constancy, when it has outlived its usefulness, is as barren as fortitude."

Virginia, in her minor tragedy, represents the ideal woman as victim of change, a change for which she has not been prepared and for which there is no effective antidote. One detects at least a small tear shed by Glasgow for the Virginias of the world. Once seen as ornaments of civilization and as restraints upon the more coarse natures of men, they now must replace self-sacrifice with an assertiveness that will be more in keeping with the changing social order. In that sense, Virginia points forward to *Barren Ground*.

BARREN GROUND

Barren Ground marks Glasgow's emergence not only from a period of despondency regarding her social life, but also as a novelist who has moved without question from apprentice to master. Certainly her finest work to that time, *Barren Ground* was to Glasgow the best of all her novels. One of her country novels, it deals with that class of people often referred to as "poor whites." Glasgow herself refutes this appelation, preferring instead to call them "good people," a label that distinguishes them from the aristocratic "good families." Lineal descendants of the English yeoman farmer, these people were the ones who pushed the frontier westward. In this novel, they stand as a "buffer class between the opulent gentry and the hired labourers."

Dorinda Oakley, the heroine, is the offspring of a union of opposites: her father, Joshua, a landless man whose industry and good nature do not compensate for his ineffectuality; and her mother, Eudora, the daughter of a Presbyterian minister, with a religious mania of her own. This background, says Glasgow, has kept Dorinda's heart "in arms against life." More important, however, she has also inherited a kinship with the earth. This kinship enables her to make something positive out of "barren ground."

Dorinda falls in love with Jason Greylock, a young doctor, seeing in him the promise of something more than the grinding poverty she has known. They plan to marry, but Jason cannot go against his father's wishes, and he marries Geneva Ellgood instead. Pregnant by Jason, Dorinda flees to New York, where, after being struck by a taxi, she loses the baby. She works as a nurse for a Dr. Faraday until she learns that her father is dying. She returns home with enough money borrowed from Faraday to start a dairy farm. Back on the land, she becomes a tough-minded spinster and makes a success of the farm. Although she marries Nathan Pedlar, a storekeeper, she remains the head of the family. After his death in a train wreck, she is again alone, but happy, rearing Nathan's child by a previous marriage and managing the farm. Jason, in the meantime, has lost his wife by suicide and is forced to sell his farm to Dorinda. Because he is ill and an alcoholic, she unwillingly provides him with food and shelter. After a few months, he dies, and once more she is alone. When a local farmer asks Dorinda to marry him, she responds, "I am thankful to have finished with all that."

A tragic figure of sorts, Dorinda sees herself trapped by fate, "a straw in the wind, a leaf on a stream." Even so, she is not content to be simply a passive victim of that fate. Unlike Jason, who through his inherited weakness, succumbs to the forces that beset him, Dorinda looks upon the land as a symbol of that fate against which she must struggle. Hardened by adversity and with a deep instinct for survival, she refuses to surrender.

Although Dorinda's life may be compared to barren ground because it has been emotionally unfulfilled, it nevertheless is a successful life in that she does master herself and in turn masters the land. Just as the broom sedge must be burned off the land, so must romantic emotions be purged from Dorinda's

soul. In giving her life to the land, she, in a sense, gains it back—and is thus, ironically, both victim and victor.

THE ROMANTIC COMEDIANS

Following *Barren Ground*, Glasgow turned to the novel of manners with *The Romantic Comedians*. The first of a trilogy—the subsequent works being *They Stooped to Folly* and *The Sheltered Life*—this novel has been regarded by some critics as Glasgow's finest. After *Barren Ground*, Glasgow comments, a novel "which for three years had steeped my mind in the tragic life, the comic spirit, always restless when it is confined, began struggling against the bars of its cage." Because she never before had turned her hand to comedy of manners, *The Romantic Comedians* was written in the nature of an experiment.

The novel exhibits a high spirit of comedy with tragic overtones. "Tragedy and comedy were blood brothers" in Glasgow's image-making faculty, she writes, "but they were at war with each other, and had steadily refused to be reconciled." In *The Romantic Comedians*, says Blair Rouse, "we see people and their actions as participants in the follies of the comic genre; but we see, too, that a very slight shift of emphasis may reveal a tragic mask upon the actors."

Judge Gamaliel Bland Honeywell, the protagonist, "is a collective portrait of several Virginians of an older school," says Glasgow, "who are still unafraid to call themselves gentlemen." Living in Queenborough (Richmond, Virginia), he seeks female companionship after his wife of thirty-six years dies. At age sixty-five, he is expected to marry a former sweetheart, Amanda Lightfoot. Disdaining such expected decorum, however, he falls in love with and marries Annabelle Upchurch, a young cousin of his wife. Annabelle marries him not so much for love, but rather, to heal the pain of being jilted by Angus Blount. As one might suspect in such a marriage, Annabelle is soon looking for greener pastures, finding them in Delaney Birdsong, with whom she goes to New York. Unable to win her back, the Judge, ill and disillusioned, believes that life holds nothing more for him. With the coming of spring, however, he looks upon his attractive young nurse and muses,

"Spring is here, and I am feeling almost as young as I felt last year."

Judge Honeywell, like many of Glasgow's women, is of another tradition. More than age separates him from Annabelle. While he is the target of some satiric jibes in the book and one finds it difficult to find much sincerity in him, he is, nevertheless, a victim of the same kind of romantic claptrap that dooms other Glasgow characters.

A refreshing book when contrasted with Glasgow's previous efforts, *The Romantic Comedians* displays the author's humanity as well as her humor. While she makes the reader laugh at the actions of the Judge and the other characters of the novel, she never lets them become completely ridiculous. Whatever else the Judge is, for example, he is a human being—and no one recognizes that more than Glasgow.

THE SHELTERED LIFE

In *The Sheltered Life*, the last novel of her trilogy on manners, Glasgow employs two points of view— that of youth and that of age, in this case a young girl and an old man. Against the background of a "shallow and aimless society of happiness hunters," she presents more characters of Queenborough as they are revealed through the mind and emotions of Jenny Blair and her grandfather, General David Archbald.

Glasgow intended General Archbald as the central character in the novel—a character who "represents the tragedy, wherever it appears, of the civilized man in a world that is not civilized." General Archbald sees before him a changing world, a world that is passing him by. Thus, he holds to the social traditions of the nineteenth century, which have provided little shelter for him. He was never a man for his time. A sensitive person who had wanted to be a poet, he was ridiculed in his earlier years. Poetry had been his one love in life; it was lost before it could be realized. He married his wife only because of an accidental, overnight sleigh ride that, in tradition-bound Queenborough, demanded marriage to save appearances. A compassionate man, he gives up his desire to marry again after his wife dies in order not to disrupt the lives of his son's widow and her daughter Jenny.

Jenny, too, unknowingly is caught in the patterned existence of the Archbald heritage. A willful girl, she has been sheltered from the real world by culture and tradition and can see things only in terms of her own desires. At eighteen, she falls in love with an older married man, George Birdsong. George's wife, Eva, eventually finds them in each other's arms. Jenny flees the scene, only to learn later that Eva has killed George.

Eva Birdsong is another perfect image of southern womanhood, beautiful and protected all her life. A celebrated belle prior to her marriage to George, she has striven to achieve a perfect marriage. Without children, she and George are thrown upon each other. Over the years, George has been a bit of a *roué* seeking pleasure where he could find it. In the end, Eva is left with the realization that what women "value most is something that doesn't exist."

When Jenny realizes what she has done, she flies to the General's understanding and sheltering arms, crying, "Oh, Grandfather, I didn't mean anything. . . . I didn't mean anything in the world." Ironically enough, she is right: She did not mean anything.

The Sheltered Life is more a tragicomedy than simply a comedy of manners. It is also, perhaps, Glasgow's best work, the novel toward which its predecessors were pointed. Symbol, style, characterization, and rhythm all combine to make *The Sheltered Life* a poignant and penetrating illustration of the futility of clinging to a tradition that has lost its essential meaning.

Glasgow's goal in all of her writing is perhaps stated best in *A Certain Measure*, when she says in reference to her last novel, *In This Our Life*, that she was trying to show "the tragedy of a social system which lives, grows, and prospers by material standards alone." One can sense in such a statement a conservative regard for tradition; even though Glasgow and many of her characters struggled against a shallow romanticism, a yearning for a genuine tradition was never far from her own artistic vision. The land seems to be the single sustaining factor in all of Glasgow's novels—it was the land that gave rise to and nourished the so-called southern tradition and that provides the "living pulse of endurance" to so many of her characters.

Wilton Eckley

OTHER MAJOR WORKS

SHORT FICTION: *The Shadowy Third and Other Stories*, 1923; *The Collected Stories of Ellen Glasgow*, 1963.

POETRY: *The Freeman and Other Poems*, 1902.

NONFICTION: *A Certain Measure: An Interpretation of Prose Fiction*, 1943; *The Woman Within*, 1954; *Letters of Ellen Glasgow*, 1958.

BIBLIOGRAPHY

Goodman, Susan. *Ellen Glasgow: A Biography*. Baltimore: The Johns Hopkins University Press, 1998. Supersedes the only previous biography, both in terms of providing new and more reliable information on Glasgow's life and conveying sensitive intepretations of her fiction. Includes notes and bibliography.

Inge, M. Thomas, ed. *Ellen Glasgow: Centennial Essays*. Charlottesville: University Press of Virginia, 1976. Offers ten essays about Glasgow and her work. Six of these were read at the Centennial Symposium honoring Glasgow at Mary Baldwin College and the Richmond Public Library in Virginia in 1973.

McDowell, Frederick P. W. *Ellen Glasgow and the Ironic Art of Fiction*. Madison: University of Wisconsin Press, 1960. The first book analyzing Glasgow's writing. Still useful, offering insights into her writing within the context of her life story.

Matthews, Pamela R. *Ellen Glasgow and a Woman's Traditions*. Charlottesville: University Press of Virginia, 1994. Discusses Glasgow's feminism and her place as a twentieth century Southern female author. Includes bibliographical references and an index.

Raper, Julius Rowan. *From the Sunken Garden: The Fiction of Ellen Glasgow, 1916-1945*. Baton Rouge: Louisiana University Press, 1980. Raper offers criticism of ten of Glasgow's novels, including *One Man in His Time* and *Vein of Iron*, as well as an analysis of some of her short fiction. Also provides a bibliography and an index.

Scura, Dorothy M., ed. *Ellen Glasgow: New Perspectives*. Knoxville: University of Tennessee Press, 1995. Detailed essays on Glasgow's major novels and themes, two essays on her autobiographies, and two essays on her poetry and short stories. Includes a helpful overview in the introduction and a bibliography.

Thiébaux, Marcelle. *Ellen Glasgow*. New York: Frederick Ungar, 1982. Thiébaux offers extensive discussions of Glasgow's works but provides only a short biography which stresses Glasgow's divided personality and the pain that this caused her. Includes a good bibliography.

GAIL GODWIN

Born: Birmingham, Alabama; June 18, 1937

PRINCIPAL LONG FICTION

The Perfectionists, 1970
Glass People, 1972
The Odd Woman, 1974
Violet Clay, 1978
A Mother and Two Daughters, 1982
The Finishing School, 1985
A Southern Family, 1987
Father Melancholy's Daughter, 1991
The Good Husband, 1994
Evensong, 1999

OTHER LITERARY FORMS

In addition to her novels, Gail Godwin has published collections of short fiction, including *Dream Children* (1976) and *Mr. Bedford and the Muses* (1983). In the second collection, "Mr. Bedford" is a novella rather than a short story. Godwin is also a frequent reviewer of contemporary fiction for *The New York Times Book Review* and other publications. In 1985, she served as editor for *The Best American Short Stories*.

ACHIEVEMENTS

Godwin has done much to broaden the scope of the contemporary woman's novel. While the struggles of women who seek both an independent life and

(Jerry Bauer)

a productive connection to others are central to her work, she strives in her novels and short fiction to place those efforts within a larger context, especially within the framework of modern theories of art and psychology. In 1971-1972, Godwin was a fellow of the Center for Advanced Studies, University of Illinois at Urbana-Champaign. Her other awards include a grant from the National Endowment for the Arts in 1974, a Guggenheim Fellowship in 1975, and an Award in Literature from the American Institute and Academy of Arts and Letters in 1981. Her story "Amanuensis" was included in the *Prize Stories, 1980: O. Henry Awards* collection.

BIOGRAPHY

Reared by her mother and her widowed grandmother in Asheville, North Carolina, Gail Godwin attended Peace Junior College in Raleigh, North Carolina, and graduated in 1959 from the University of North Carolina at Chapel Hill (the alma mater of Asheville's other great native writer, Thomas Wolfe). Her B.A. was in journalism. After working as a reporter for the *Miami Herald*, she lived in London and worked with the United States Travel Service at the American Embassy. After returning to the United States, she took an M.A. (1968) and a Ph.D. (1971) in English at the University of Iowa, where she later served on the faculty of the Writers Workshop. She has been married twice, to *Miami Herald* photographer Douglas Kennedy and to British psychotherapist Ian Marshall. Her one-year marriage to Marshall is the basis for her first novel, *The Perfectionists*, as her early years with her mother and grandmother are for parts of *Glass People* and *The Odd Woman*. Her relationships with her father and her stepfather are also used in her fiction, especially in *Violet Clay* and *The Odd Woman*, respectively.

Godwin has achieved success as a librettist of Robert Starer's musical works, including *Remembering Felix*, recorded in 1989. She was a lecturer in English and creative writing at Vassar College in the spring of 1977 and has taught English and creative writing at Columbia University.

ANALYSIS

Gail Godwin's novels (and her short fiction as well) all deal with several easily identifiable themes. First, and most often cited perhaps, is the theme of the modern woman, her dilemma in defining self and others in an era when the old frameworks and definitions have broken down, at least for the sort of women about whom Godwin writes. The conflict most often arises between the woman's work, usually an artistic pursuit of some kind, and her desire for security, love, and connection, most often through a relationship with a man. Thus, the theme of the woman struggling for identity divides into two separate thematic strands: her identity as artist and her identity as lover.

Another recurring theme in Godwin's work is, in many ways, the reverse of this quest for self-identity.

Often, her characters long to penetrate the identities of the people around them; that is, they consciously seek to violate the human heart's sanctity, to use Nathaniel Hawthorne's description of such activity. Again, however, Godwin's perspective is definitively modern. These characters are all aware of the impossibility of coming to such knowledge in the almost mystical way that Hawthorne describes in "The Custom House" section of *The Scarlet Letter* (1850), and they are also conscious of the questionable morality of such invasions. Therefore, they seek lesser but more concrete knowledge and understanding by prying, by scrutinizing the objects the others possess or the words they write or say, words that the seeker will examine with total (or what he or she assumes to be total) awareness of the ironies and ambiguities involved in both the saying and their interpretation.

These divergent pursuits are most easily forged into a manageable aesthetic form through an artist figure; the role of the artist in relation to self, other, and art itself is, finally, Godwin's most important theme. Her main characters tend to be so self-consciously "artists," even when they are lawyers or psychiatrists or unemployed, that they make life itself into an art, which is to say that they view their own lives as artists view the canvas or the sheet of paper before them.

What makes Godwin an interesting and important figure in the world of contemporary fiction is the narrative technique by which she manages to develop and retell this essentially unchanging story. The noticeable and impressive growth in Godwin herself as an artist can be traced by examining the structural and technical variations in her telling of her stories. In the earlier novels, the distance between narrator and protagonist is less clearly defined. The overblown and romanticized version of the character sometimes seems to be an accurate representation of the narrator's perspective as well. Beginning with *The Odd Woman*, however, and culminating in *A Southern Family*, Godwin makes that distance itself a matter of chief concern. Her narrators seem acutely aware of the responsibility involved in entering into the lives and souls of "others." The characters seem to move from being primarily concerned with personal happiness and security to doing true and con-

structive work that recognizes the dignity in whatever lives the artist consumes for the sake of the work and that acknowledges the limitations and fallibilities of the artist himself. These later characters, by having real and constructive work to do, manage to be less obsessed with their personal lives as objects of art; they also manage to find satisfaction in the art and the work itself, whether their personal lives are or are not so satisfying at any given moment.

THE PERFECTIONISTS and GLASS PEOPLE

The protagonists of *The Perfectionists* and *Glass People*, Dane Empson and Francesca Bolt, are both self-absorbed and frustrated in their relationships with their spouses. They are also the last of Godwin's protagonists to be married and unemployed. Not only are they unemployed, but also neither of them shows any desire for doing constructive, creative work. When these novels are read in the context of Godwin's later work, the conclusion that their shared lack of ambition and motivation is crucial to their discontent is inevitable.

Dane Empson has been married to John Empson, a psychologist, for ten months when they go on vacation with John's illegitimate son, Robin, and one of John's female patients, Penelope MacMahon. Although she worked as a journalist prior to her marriage—in fact, she met John when she covered a meeting at which he was the speaker—she no longer pursues her career. Her primary concerns are her relationship with John, in which she has begun to lose interest, and her efforts to become a mother to his son.

Thus, what Godwin does with this character, although it is done in a most unconventional way, is to have her confront the traditional roles and conflicts of the wife and mother. Dane fails in these roles, however, and she is most aware of that failure. She feels nothing, absolutely nothing, of the satisfaction and joy that the mythic versions of those roles provide.

The overt source of conflict in the story is Robin's total refusal to acknowledge Dane. He will not speak in her presence; he will not respond to her displays of affection; he will not compromise in any way in the small, daily struggles between parent and child.

He does, however, make demands on Dane, in both practical and emotional matters. She is expected to feed, clothe, and entertain him. She is also expected to nurture and soothe him while his father is thinking and writing in his journal. Because Godwin sets up the child as a double for the father, a point that John frequently reinforces by comparing himself to the child, the narrator suggests that Dane's real problem is John's refusal to acknowledge her.

Yet, Dane is guilty of expecting her husband to provide her with an identity to be acknowledged. She surreptitiously searches through his journal entries for clues as to what he sees when he looks at her, what he thinks when he thinks of her. When she does rebel, venturing outside the prescribed role that she has accepted with apparent willingness, she takes up with another frustrated wife, Polly Heykoop, who devotes herself to spying on her husband with his lovers, photographing their sexual encounters and compiling a scrapbook of the photos to present to him in their old age.

Dane's act in defiance of this utter decadence of domestic life is to beat the child, almost to kill him, in order to reassert her personal identity. Symbolically, she is also beating John, who, in her imagination, responds to her confession by ruining it. He points out that the action she takes in order to feel a powerful and private emotion is of necessity shared with the child and, by extension, with him. Because she cannot deny the truth of that observation and because she has available to her no other means of self-expression, she remains as self-absorbed and frustrated as she is at the novel's beginning.

Dane's counterpart in *Glass People*, Francesca Bolt, is even less involved in life. Wife to a successful attorney and politician who requires absolutely nothing of her except that she be beautiful for him, Francesca has retreated from all human activity. She languishes in her bedroom, living for the alternate days when she tweezes the hairs from her legs one by one. At the instigation of Cameron, her husband, she undertakes a quest to discover a life for herself, a quest more dramatic and independent than that of Dane.

After a disappointing visit to her newly remarried and pregnant mother fails to allow Francesca to retreat into a former identity, she embarks upon a series of adventures, each eventually as unsuccessful as her visit home. She has an affair, a one-weekend liaison with a man she meets in the airport, but she romanticizes the encounter into much more than it is. When he does not reappear, she bravely tries to follow the plan the two of them laid to free her from Cameron's worshipful but manipulative grasp.

She rents a room in a cheap New York hotel and briefly takes a job as amanuensis to a bizarre woman named M. She even finds herself buoyed by the successful completion of the tasks she performs for her employer, the basic cleaning, shopping, and cooking chores she could not bring herself to do at home in California. After less than a week of being actively engaged in the world with nothing more than her own identity to define her, she collapses in a complete and devastating illness. She fears that all the fluids within her will leave her body and she will disappear.

Cameron appears, however, a *deus ex machina* in the best romantic tradition—the heroic man come to save the fallen beauty. The problem, as Francesca knows, is that he will save her for his own purposes, and her identity will be defined by those purposes. Still, despite this awareness, she cannot resist the comfort and ease of his salvation. That she is pregnant with the child of her lover seems only to increase Cameron's worshipful desire to hold and control her. As she moves around their beautiful apartment, decorated and maintained by Cameron, and eats plentifully of the food he prepares for her, secure in her knowledge that her husband will never let her get fat, Francesca thinks of the power she holds and of the possibilities for manipulating her husband with that power. She is the last of Godwin's protagonists to accept this traditional sort of power struggle as the best solution for her life.

Narratively, the problem with these novels is a matter of point of view. Because both are dominated by the perspectives of the protagonists, who have so constrained their lives as to have no outside viewpoints against which to test their own (except those of their spouses, whom they can only undermine as valid reference points), Godwin finds herself telling her stories without a reliable observer. Even in *Glass*

People, where brief passages are given over to Cameron's point of view, the reader already so distrusts Cameron, from having seen him through his wife's eyes, that the narrator cannot give his view much credence.

The narrative voice, although it is a third-person voice, does not maintain enough distance between itself and the protagonists to convince the reader that the values of that character are not, in fact, the values being espoused by the novel. At the same time, however, the violent impotence of Dane Empson and the luxurious laziness of Francesca Bolt both carry a faintly distasteful flavor for most readers.

The Odd Woman

The perspective of Jane Clifford, the protagonist of *The Odd Woman*, marks a significant step forward for Godwin as a storyteller. First, her perspective is a much broader one than that of either of her predecessors. Jane works as a teacher of literature, and her work as a graduate student writing her dissertation on George Eliot, in addition to her current work—grading the exams for her just-finished course in visionary literature and preparing to teach a course on women in literature—is an integral part of the narrative.

Furthermore, Jane Clifford has a family, a background, that is richly developed and explored across several generations. Unlike Francesca's fruitless journey back home, Jane's similar trip, to the funeral of her grandmother, produces extended encounters with her memories of the grandmother, her mother, stepfather, sister, and brothers. Kate, mother of Francesca, spends most of her daughter's visit behind the closed door of her bedroom. Jane is involved in talks, reminiscences, and arguments that test her perspective constantly.

Jane also has friends, male and female, to whom she talks, in whom she confides. There is the male colleague with whom she trades confidences about sex and bathroom regularity; there is her old college friend Gerda, the editor of a feminist newspaper in Chicago; and there is Sonia Marx, her colleague at the university where she teaches and the woman who serves as the role model for what Jane wants to be— someone with a career, husband, and family, manag-

ing it all with every sign of ease and brilliance. Again, although Jane's point of view is the point of view of the novel, her constant encounters with these others broadens and modifies her view throughout.

Jane also has a lover, a married man, Gabriel Weeks, an art historian. In him, Jane finds an alternative to the cynical and jaded perspective she finds pervasive in the academic world. She gradually comes to realize, however, that the Gabriel she has found is a creature of her own making. She has imagined him and orchestrated their relationship in such a way as to provide herself with a view of the world that must come from within, must be made from oneself, it it is to have true value.

Here, Godwin begins to develop the ironic awareness of self as artist that is crucial to the success of her subject matter. Jane Clifford is painfully aware of her life as an object of art, with herself as the artist. She sees the scenes of her life as just that, scenes, and she manipulates both her own part and the parts of others. The problem is that such a life will never reach the state of natural grace and spontaneity that is Jane's primary goal.

Thus, she is more like Dane and Francesca than she would like to be. She does not find a way to overcome her frustrations with her need to rewrite the role she has been given or has voluntarily taken on. Unlike those predecessors, however, she does not capitulate. She takes actions that give her a chance for progress. She ends her affair; she takes an extension on her temporary appointment at the university, meaning that she will have productive work for another year; she confronts the demons of her past as represented by the family, Greta, and the actor who has been for half a century the arch villain of the family history.

Through these actions and confrontations, she learns that all truths may be artificial and self-imposed, but she also comes to believe in some purer, more absolute version of her own life that will be possible for her, if she acts to pursue it. Thus, despite Jane's own limitations, because Godwin equips her with such an acute sense of irony about herself as well as others, Jane is the first step toward a successful Godwin protagonist.

VIOLET CLAY

Interestingly enough, the promise of a truly successful Godwin woman made with Jane is realized in *Violet Clay*, whose story is the first that Godwin told from a first-person point of view. Although it might seem that first-person narration would lead to even greater self-absorption, this does not happen. Using the same principles that make *The Odd Woman* such a step forward, Godwin generated a plot in *Violet Clay* with a death. Jane keeps her job and her lover through most of her story, however, while, in addition to losing her uncle—her only living relative—Violet loses what Jane has been able to keep.

She is forced by these events of plot to confront the essentials of her character, to test the view of herself that she has created. While she probes into her uncle's past to make sense of his suicide, Violet learns much about herself as well and about how the artist manufactures both life and art, each feeding off the other. When she finally paints the painting that will set her on the road she has long aspired to travel, Violet uses some of the same material that her uncle failed to transform into the novel that he had struggled for decades to write.

Violet's success comes because she learns the limits of both life and art, partly through her uncle's example, his legacy to her, and partly through her own increasing ability to forget about "poor little me" and to enter into and learn from the struggles of those around her with compassion and respect. She learns that the artist must not and finally cannot both live and work successfully if she violates the integrity of the other, of the lives out of which her art and her own life are to be constructed.

A MOTHER AND TWO DAUGHTERS

If *Violet Clay* states an aesthetic credo, *A Mother and Two Daughters* puts that credo into action. In this novel, for the first time, Godwin is able to render a world of multiple viewpoints throughout the story; not coincidentally, it is her longest book to date as well as her most accomplished.

Nell Strickland and her two daughters, Lydia and Cate, are very different women. They, too, find themselves propelled into a plot generated by a death, in this case that of their husband and father. Each also finds herself continuing in the plot of her own life. Nell finds that she relishes the independence and privacy of her widowhood, and she also finds herself in love again before the novel concludes. Lydia, who is recently separated and eventually divorced from her husband and is mother to two teenage sons, returns to school, acquires a lover, and develops a career. Cate struggles with her own love life and the roller coaster of her career as a teacher of drama.

These women are the least self-conscious of all of Godwin's heroines, and their stories are the most straightforward and least manipulated among her works. Even so, the reader is always aware that each of the three women is shaping, in an increasingly conscious way, her life, constructing it so that it gives her the most satisfaction possible within the limitations of a "realistic" environment.

All three of these women also engage in a sustained relationship with a man during the course of the story. For Nell, it is the traditional relationship of marriage, but in her second marriage she is a different woman from the one she was in her first because of the time she spends alone and the things she learns about herself during that time. She is able to bring about a merging of the independent self and the attached self. Lydia and Cate also reach such an integration of these strands of their lives, but for them, traditional marriage is not the form that integration takes. Lydia and her lover, Stanley, live in a hard-won but precarious balance, together but unmarried, separate but irrevocably joined. He thinks at the novel's end, "You can still be independent and mine, at the same time. You are these two things now."

Cate, always more independent and free-spirited than her sister or her mother, has an even more unusual arrangement. She has designed a job to suit her, packaging classes and traveling to the places people want to have them taught, a sort of academic entrepreneur. She has also reached a stability in her relationship with Roger Jernigan after years of tension about how their feelings for each other could be formed into a pattern acceptable to them both. They are good visitors to each other.

The possibilities for marriage are not closed off for either sister, but the necessity of marriage does not exert its terrifying influence over them either. As Godwin goes into and out of the consciousnesses of these women and sometimes briefly into the points of view of the people who make up their worlds, she approaches a compassionate and respectful omniscience that would be unthinkable for the narrators of the earlier work.

THE FINISHING SCHOOL

In *The Finishing School*, the narrator is again a first-person voice, this time Justin Stokes, a forty-year-old actress remembering the summer she turned fourteen. Justin's preoccupations during that summer are typical of all of Godwin's characters' preoccupations. She has experienced loss: Her father and her beloved grandparents have died, and she, her mother, and her younger brother, Jem, have had to leave their Virginia home and move north to a newly created subdivision in Clove, New York. She develops a special relationship with an older woman, Ursula DeVane, who instructs her in the art of making one's life an artistic creation, lessons that feed into Justin's predisposition for the dramatic and her aspirations to the stage. Most important, however, Justin shares, with the characters from Jane Clifford onward in Godwin's work, a deep desire to come to terms with her own use of others' lives to construct her own, to make it what she needs it to be. In addition, Justin writes to thank Ursula for her contribution to the process of Justin's becoming the adult woman she wanted to be. Despite the fact that their relationship ends badly, Justin cannot overlook the crucial role that the relationship played in helping her through the most difficult summer of her childhood.

Godwin dedicates this sixth novel to "the Ursulas of this world, whoever they were—or weren't"; that dedication seems echoed by Justin's sentiments after remembering and making a story from her summer with Ursula. Justin says:

> I was able to be charmed and possessed by that woman. Such possessions are rare now. I mean by another person. The only thing I can rely on to possess me continually with that degree of ardor is my work. Most of the time I consider this a victory. Sometimes, however, it makes me a little sad. So here I am, in the middle of my own life. . . . And it has taken me this

long to understand that I lose nothing by acknowledging her influence on me. . . . I know something of life's betrayals and stupidities myself. . . . I even know the necessity for making constant adjustments to your life story, so you can go on living in it. . . . But I also know something else that I didn't know then. As long as you can go on creating new roles for yourself, you are not vanquished.

A SOUTHERN FAMILY

In many ways Godwin's seventh novel, *A Southern Family*, is the aesthetic fruit of a challenge similar to the one her fictional alter ego raises at the end of *The Finishing School*. In *A Southern Family* Godwin creates for herself a new role as author/narrator, using for the first time in her novels the narrative strategy of multiple limited perspectives. She also appears to be moving toward a new role for the "typical" Godwin woman within her fictional world. The Godwin woman in *A Southern Family* is Clare Campion, the author's first novel protagonist to share her profession. In fact, Clare is a writer whose career, as rendered in this fiction, closely parallels Godwin's own. The "new" role Godwin carves out for Clare is that of secondary, rather than primary, character; thus, her challenge is to accept this new (and inevitably "lesser") status without losing the power to make art (stories) from her experience.

The plot of *A Southern Family* is generated by the death of Clare Campion's half brother Theo Quick in an incident that the police rule a murder-suicide. The story is presented from the perspectives of Clare, her best friend Julia Richardson, Clare's mother and her stepfather, her surviving half brother, Theo's ex-wife, and Sister Patrick, a beloved nun who has taught Clare and her brothers. (That Godwin's half brother Tommy Cole died in circumstances similar to those described in the novel further suggests the strongly autobiographical nature of *A Southern Family*.)

Perhaps the most significant achievement of the novel is Godwin's broadening of her narrative spectrum to include male characters, characters from a variety of social classes, characters with varying degrees of connection to the central action. There is no pretense of the omniscience that marks *A Mother and Two Daughters* here; the narrative in each section of the book is strictly limited to one or sometimes two perspectives.

A Southern Family opens up new narrative directions and a new approach to her "typical" protagonist for Godwin, but the novel also provides a clear culmination of other strands that are woven throughout the body of her fiction. The title makes clear that this is a family story, a southern story—themes that have always been among the author's central concerns. The greater emphasis here on the family as a group, a unit, rather than on an individual's struggles reinforces the narrative decision Godwin makes.

A Southern Family also continues Godwin's exploration of people, particularly women, who tend to see their lives as performances, themselves as actors in a drama partly of their own making, partly a byproduct of their environment and conditioning. Theo's action causes everyone in his family to reexamine his or her role in the Quick family drama, causes each individual whose consciousness the novel explores to evaluate the role he or she plays in the unfolding events before and after the momentary act that calls the foundations of family life into question. In addition to generating the story this novel tells, this profound examination of self-as-actor that takes place in *A Southern Family*, read with full knowledge of the work that precedes it, is, in a sense, a reexamination of the author's body of work as well.

FATHER MELANCHOLY'S DAUGHTER

Father Melancholy's Daughter is a first-person narrative following Margaret Gower's search for self. The daughter of an Episcopal clergyman given to bouts of depression, Margaret finds herself becoming his primary caregiver at age six when her mother, Ruth, leaves with Madelyn Farley, an artist and teacher from her college days, and is killed in a car accident a short time later. The narrative switches from present to past as twenty-two-year-old Margaret seeks to understand her mother's leaving, her father's flaws, and her own spirituality and identity.

While the narrative centers on Margaret and her close relationship with her father, it also paints a portrait of small town Romulus, Virginia, where the congregation of Margaret's father's church speculates on the reasons for Ruth's leaving. Margaret learns to

play the role of her father's accomplice in dealing with the expectations of these secondary characters. Putting her father's needs before her own becomes second nature for Margaret; by the time she goes to college to major in English, she has become almost obsessed with her father's well-being. His sudden death from a stroke, near the novel's end, leaves her free to find her own direction. Surprisingly, Margaret chooses to travel to England with Madelyn Farley, the woman whom she has practically hated all her life, to see the spot where her mother died. As the narrative ends, Margaret is applying to colleges to seek a master of divinity degree, having finally come to terms with her needs as a woman and a full human being.

Father Melancholy's Daughter portrays Margaret Gower as a modern woman who can combine the nurturing of the traditional female life with the satisfaction of a traditional male career. She, like the typical Godwin heroine, is a smart, literate woman who takes responsibility for her own life. The novel is very much a novel of ideas, not just of character. Beneath its plot lie questions about despair, self-determination, and the honorable life, but the most important issue of the novel may be the importance of understanding parents' influence. Margaret works consciously to understand the people her parents were, and then she can go forward to discover who she is and what her place in the human drama will be.

THE GOOD HUSBAND

The Good Husband returns to a multiple-perspective narrative structure, moving among the four major characters (two married couples) for its limited omniscient points of view. The central character of the four is Magda Danvers, an academic made famous by her one book on the visionary poets, *The Book of Hell*. Facing death from cancer, she imagines herself taking her "Final Examination" as her devoted younger husband, Francis Lake, attends to her every need. Less analytical than Magda, Francis, who left seminary to marry her, is unable to engage in the introspection that Magda encourages until her death frees him of her towering intellect.

Balancing this unlikely couple as the novel's protagonists are Alice Henry, an editor who as a teen-ager lost her entire family in a car accident, and her husband Hugo Henry, a brooding southern novelist who must face not only his waning literary inspiration and his son's homosexuality but also the fact that his marriage to the much younger Alice is crumbling after their child dies at birth. These characters' lives become intertwined when Alice begins to visit the dying Magda, finding herself drawn to Magda's keen understanding and to the "good husband" Francis, who thrives on nurturing the love of his life. While *The Good Husband* continues Godwin's exploration of the difficulty the modern woman has in defining her self and her art, it broadens her scope by focusing equally on the male characters' relation to self, art, and other people. All the characters face conflict in balancing the public life with the private, and all show the human need for security and love as well as for self-understanding.

Gail Godwin the author has grown in much the same direction as her characters and narrators. The movement has been in the life-affirming direction of compromise, recognition of others, acceptance of responsibility for the self, and productive creativity. The life that gets affirmed is the well-made life, the one shaped out of the complexities and ambiguities of human experience. Godwin's novels speak clearly of the enormous difficulty of being a sensitive and thoughtful woman in today's world. They speak just as eloquently of what such women can make from those difficulties.

Jane Hill, updated by Rebecca G. Smith

OTHER MAJOR WORKS

SHORT FICTION: *Dream Children*, 1976; *Mr. Bedford and the Muses*, 1983.

PLAYS: *The Last Lover*, pr. 1975; *Journals of a Songmaker*, pr. 1976; *Apollonia*, pr. 1979.

EDITED TEXT: *The Best American Short Stories*, 1985.

BIBLIOGRAPHY

Cheney, Anne. "Gail Godwin and Her Novels." In *Southern Women Writers: The New Generation*, edited by Tonette Bond Inge. Tuscaloosa: University of Alabama Press, 1990. The most comprehensive overview of Godwin's career through *A Southern Family*. Emphasizes the autobiographical elements of the works, the contemporary love-hate relationship with the traditional South, and the evolving maturity of the author's vision. Factually interesting, the article's argumentative conclusions are less reliable and significant.

Frye, Joanna S. "Narrating the Self: The Autonomous Heroine in Gail Godwin's *Violet Clay*." *Contemporary Literature* 24 (Spring, 1983): 66-85. A strong and important article dealing with narrative technique in Godwin's fourth novel which has significant implications for her later works as well.

Hill, Jane. *Gail Godwin*. New York: Twayne, 1992. An extensive analysis of all Godwin's work through *A Southern Family*, this book attempts to free Godwin from the pigeonholes of woman and southern writer. Hill analyzes autobiographical elements in the novels, examines character, plot, and narrative strategies, and connects Godwin's work to the larger literary traditions of the American and European novel.

Mickelson, Anne A. "Gail Godwin: Order and Accommodation." In *Reaching Out: Sensitivity and Order in Recent Fiction by Women*. Metuchen, N.J.: Scarecrow Press, 1979. Mickelson identifies with some accuracy the attitudes toward order in Godwin's work, primarily *The Odd Woman*, but then indicts those attitudes as inappropriate to contemporary women.

Shands, Kerstin W. "Four-telling, Foretold: Storytelling in Gail Godwin's *The Good Husband*." *Southern Quarterly* 35 (Winter, 1997): 77-86. Explores the controlling metaphor of matrimony by examining alliances among and within characters, focusing on the way the characters order their lives. Explains allusions to Carl Jung and William Blake and explores the multiple four-fold patterns in the book as well as its complex blending of oppositions such as death and birth, stasis and development, endings and beginnings.

Smith, Marilyn J. "The Role of the South in the Novels of Gail Godwin." *Critique* 26 (1980): 103-

110. Deals with the conflict in Godwin's protagonists between their impulse to flee the South and their need to hold onto certain southern ideals. Smith argues that this conflict remains unresolved through *Violet Clay*.

Wimsatt, Mary Ann. "Gail Godwin, the South, and the Canons." *Southern Literary Journal* 27 (Spring, 1995): 86-95. Presents Godwin's bestseller status and her feminism as reasons she is excluded from the southern literary canon. Argues for her inclusion in this canon based on her strong portrayals of characters' struggles with difficulties caused by family, race, and class in the changing twentieth century South even as she infuses her novels with a keen sense of Western and American civilization.

Xie-Lihong. *The Evolving Self in the Novels of Gail Godwin*. Baton Rouge: Louisiana State University Press, 1995. Explores Godwin's eight novels through *Father Melancholy's Daughter* as contemporary *Bildungsromane* in which the heroines' search for self probes the process of female development and women's complex psychological struggle for identity in a fragmented world. Uses feminist literary criticism and Mikhail Bakhtin's dialogic concept of language to analyze the multitude of voices, languages, and consciousnesses in Godwin's fiction.

JOHANN WOLFGANG VON GOETHE

Born: Frankfurt am Main, Germany; August 28, 1749
Died: Weimar, Germany; March 22, 1832

PRINCIPAL LONG FICTION

Die Leiden des jungen Werthers, 1774 (*The Sorrows of Young Werther*, 1779)
Wilhelm Meisters Lehrjahre, 1795-1796 (4 volumes *Wilhelm Meister's Apprenticeship*, 1825)
Die Wahlverwandtschaften, 1809 (*Elective Affinities*, 1849)

(Library of Congress)

Wilhelm Meisters Wanderjahre: Oder, Die Entsagenden, 1821, 1829 (2 volumes *Wilhelm Meister's Travels*, 1827)

OTHER LITERARY FORMS

Johann Wolfgang von Goethe was a master in every major literary genre. He published his first book of poetry, *Neue Lieder (New Poems*, 1853) in 1770. Most of his well-known poems appeared individually in journals and were later collected in his *Works* (1848-1890). Collections of poetry that were published separately include *Epigramme: Venedig 1790* (1796; *Venetian Epigrams*, 1853), Römische Elegien, 1793 *(Roman Elegies*, 1876), Xenien (1796, with Friedrich Schiller; *Epigrams*, 1853), Balladen (1798, with Friedrich Schiller; *Ballads*, 1853), Sonnette (1819; *Sonnets*, 1853), and *Westöstlicher Divan* (1819; *West-Eastern Divan*, 1877), the translations of which are to be found in *Works*. Many well-known poems appeared in his novels; others were published in his posthumous works.

Goethe's first play, *Die Laune des Verliebten* (The Wayward Lover, 1879), was written in 1767 and produced in 1779. Many tragedies, comedies, and operettas (or *Singspiele*) followed, the most famous of which are *Clavigo* (1774; English translation, 1798, 1897), *Stella* (1776, 1806; English translation, 1798), *Iphigenie auf Tauris* (1779, 1787; *Iphigenia in Tauris*, 1793), *Egmont* (1788; English translation, 1837), *Torquato Tasso* (1790; English translation, 1827), *Faust: Ein Fragment* (1790; *Faust: A Fragment*, 1980), *Die natürliche Tochter* (1803; *The Natural Daughter*, 1885), and *Faust: Eine Tragödie* (1808; *The Tragedy of Faust*, 1823) and *Faust: Eine Tragödie, zweiter Teil* (1833; *The Tragedy of Faust, Part Two*, 1838).

Goethe also wrote a collection of short fiction, *Unterhaltungen deutscher Ausgewanderten* (1795; *Conversations of German Emigrants*, in *1854*), and a paradigm of the short prose form entitled simply *Novelle* (1826; *Novel*, 1837). Other short stories appeared in his later novels, and he also wrote two verse epics, *Reinecke Fuchs* (1794; *Reynard the Fox*, 1855) and *Hermann und Dorothea* (1797; *Herman and Dorothea*, 1801); an autobiography, *Aus meinem Leben: Dichtung und Wahrheit* (1811-1814; *The Autobiography of Goethe*, 1824); and essays on literature, art, and science. His letters and diaries in dozens of volumes reveal insights into his life, work, and times.

ACHIEVEMENTS

Goethe has been called the last Renaissance man. Not only was he a writer whose work in every literary genre was startlingly new and exemplary for later generations of writers, but he also took great interest in painting, music, botany, geology, physiology, optics, and government, and many of his ideas in these fields of endeavor were novel and seminal.

Goethe belongs to that select group of men, including Homer, Dante, Leonardo da Vinci, Michelangelo, Miguel de Cervantes, and William Shakespeare, who were able to encompass all aspects of the human condition in their creativity. Goethe's work is universal; it reflects man's sufferings and joys, successes and failures. From his earliest work, Goethe had a concept of what he thought man should be: an active, striving individual not afraid to make errors but dedicated to discovering his capabilities and to perfecting them to the best of his ability. His tragedy, *Faust*, on which he worked for more than fifty years, can be viewed as a summation of his thought, and it belongs among the masterpieces of world literature.

Goethe's influence, like that of Shakespeare, can hardly be measured. He has become a part of German and world culture. Every generation has poets, philosophers, artists, and general readers who look to Goethe as a model, and the volumes that make up the Goethe bibliography attest that influence.

BIOGRAPHY

Johann Wolfgang von Goethe was born August 28, 1749, in Frankfurt am Main. His father, Johann Kaspar Goethe, was a well-to-do nonpracticing lawyer holding the title of Imperial Councilor. His learning and many-sided interests were passed on to the young Goethe. The father was strict, often overbearing, and Goethe was never close to him. Goethe's mother, Katharina Elisabeth (née Textor), the daughter of the mayor, received more of his affection. In Frankfurt, Goethe first made contact with the theater via puppet plays and French troupes. He recorded these impressions vividly in his autobiography, *Poetry and Truth*. From 1765 to 1768, he attended the university in Leipzig, famous for its Enlightenment and Rococo writers, and studied law. There he also studied painting and had the first of his many famous love affairs (this one with Kätchen Schönkopf), which always resulted in beautiful poetry. His not atypical student life was interrupted by a lung hemorrhage, which compelled him to return to Frankfurt. Home again, and sickly, he came under the influence of the Pietist and mystic Susanna von Klettenberg, whose teachings can be found in "Bekenntnisse einer schönen Selle" ("Confessions of a Fair Saint"), which constitutes the sixth book of *Wilhelm Meister's Apprenticeship*. Goethe returned to the university in 1770, this time to Strasbourg, where he received his degree in 1771. While in this French-German border city, he met Johann Gottfried Herder, the theologian and critic who, at this time was singing the praises of Shakespeare, Ossian, primitive poetry, and the need for a German literature freed from

French influence. Herder's great influence on Goethe is unmistakable and can be seen especially in Goethe's drama *Goetz of Berlichingen* and in a speech commemorating Shakespeare. This university period produced famous poems to Friederike Brion in *Sesenheimer Liederbuch* (1775-1789, 1854; *Sesenheim Songs*). After receiving his degree, Goethe returned to Frankfurt and somewhat grudgingly set up a law practice. The years 1771 to 1775 mark Goethe's Sturm und Drang period, years of feverish literary activity. His best-known works from these years are the play *Götz von Berlichingen with the Iron Hand*, the novel *The Sorrows of Young Werther*, and his Sturm und Drang lyrics.

In 1775, Duke Karl August invited Goethe to Weimar, and, feeling the need to begin a new "epoch" in his life, Goethe decided to stay in the Thuringian city. Except for numerous trips, he spent the rest of his life in Weimar. This transitional period from the tempestuousness of the Sturm und Drang to the restraint of his classical period was marked by an intensive study of nature and the sciences and by numerous court activities. Goethe wrote many minor works in the following decade, and he started or continued several major works which for various reasons he left unfinished. A need for a rebirth, a rejuvenation, drove Goethe to Italy, where he stayed from 1786 to 1788. There he experienced the "noble simplicity and quiet grandeur" (in Adam Oeser and Johann Winckelmann's words) of Roman and Greek art and gained new impetus for his work, completing *Iphigenia in Tauris* and *Egmont*. He chronicled these travels in his *Italienische Reise* (1816, 1817; *Travels in Italy*, 1883), which makes up part of his autobiography. In the decade after his return to Weimar, he took up new scientific endeavors and wrote numerous works, including *Torquato Tasso, Venetian Epigrams, Roman Elegies*, and *Wilhelm Meister's Apprenticeship*.

The year 1794 marked the beginning of Goethe's friendship with Friedrich Schiller, which proved fruitful for both men. Their shared interests can be seen in *Epigrams*, a collection of satiric distiches, in *Ballads*, and in their insightful two-volume correspondence. The last thirty years of Goethe's life re-

veal an unflagging productivity. Besides his increasing scientific interests, he wrote his autobiography, the novels *Elective Affinities* and *Wilhelm Meister's Travels*, and the lyric cycle *West-Eastern Divan*, and he succeeded in finishing his lifework, *Faust*. He died at the age of eighty-two on March 22, 1832, and was buried in Weimar, next to Schiller.

ANALYSIS

Johann Wolfgang von Goethe's first novel, *The Sorrows of Young Werther*, did for the German novel what his early play *Götz von Berlichingen with the Iron Hand* did for German drama—it revolutionized prose writing in German and rescued German literature from a deadening provincialism. The people and places in *The Sorrows of Young Werther* have been so well documented, to a great extent by Goethe himself in his autobiography, that the reader with biographical knowledge of Goethe has difficulty separating the author from the titular hero Werther. The autobiographical content of the novel has often led to one-sided interpretations that have ignored other important aspects of the work, yet the genesis of the story in Goethe's own experience is impossible to ignore.

After Goethe had finished his law studies in Strasbourg, he returned to his parental home in Frankfurt to pursue, somewhat halfheartedly, a law career. At the behest of his father, Goethe went in May, 1772, to Wetzlar, which still claimed fame as the seat of the Reichskammergericht (supreme court) of the Holy Roman Empire. At a ball in the small town (which becomes one of the central episodes in the novel), Goethe met Lotte Buff, who was unofficially engaged to Johann Christian Kestner, a secretary to the Hanoverian legation. Goethe often visited her at the home of her father, a widower with many children, and he, like Werther, eventually fell in love with her; but Goethe fell in love often and easily, and the intensity of his relationship with Buff has been overemphasized. Goethe's letters to her do not read like Werther's; the identification of Goethe with Werther should not be carried too far. This is not to say that Goethe's emotions for Buff were shallow—his hasty retreat from Wetzlar without even a farewell speaks against this—but Goethe was attracted to married or "taken" women, a not unimportant psychological phenomenon.

After leaving Wetzlar, Goethe visited the popular writer of sentimental novels, Sophie von La Roche, at Ehrenbreitenstein. Here, he fell in love with the author's daughter, Maximiliane, who, like Buff, was engaged to be married. This sensitive situation continued even after Maximiliane's marriage, until her husband, Brentano, put an end to it, nearly a year and a half after Goethe had left Wetzlar. Shortly after leaving Wetzlar, Kestner, who carried on a correspondence with Goethe for many years, wrote to Goethe, describing in great detail the suicide of a young man two years Goethe's senior, Karl Wilhelm Jerusalem, whom Goethe had met. Jerusalem had killed himself over unrequited love for a married woman. Although in his autobiography Goethe claims that the Jerusalem incident was the catalyst for *The Sorrows of Young Werther* (a catalyst that took nearly two years to bring about an effect), later scholarship would indicate that it was not until Goethe's affair with Maximiliane that he began to get the idea for the novel. By the time Goethe wrote *The Sorrows of Young Werther*, he was naturally no longer the same man he was two years earlier. He had essentially already left behind many of his Sturm und Drang traits, those rebellious Romantic characteristics that modern man so fondly cherishes in his struggle against society and technology. Like his contemporary, Friedrich Maximilian Klinger, Goethe saw the dangers of Romantic excess, and *The Sorrows of Young Werther* can claim to be Goethe's reckoning with his not-too-distant past.

THE SORROWS OF YOUNG WERTHER

The Sorrows of Young Werther begins (as does Jean-Jacques Rousseau's epistolary novel *Julie: Ou, La Nouvelle Héloïse*, 1761) and ends (as does Samuel Richardson's epistolary novel *Pamela*, 1740-1741) with comments by the editor, who has collected Werther's letters to provide "consolation" for those who fell like Werther. The first letter is dated May 4, 1771, and serves as exposition. Werther has been sent by his mother to find out about an inheritance. He has left behind "the poor Leonore," whom he has abandoned after being attracted to her sister.

This often overlooked fact reveals much about Werther's character and does not present Werther in a favorable light at the beginning of the novel.

Werther is an artist, or at least he claims to be, but he deludes himself. In his second letter (May 10), he writes: "I am so happy, dear friend, so completely immersed in the feeling of a tranquil existence that my art suffers from it. I couldn't draw now, not a line, and have never been a greater painter than at this moment." Werther allows himself to be overwhelmed by his feelings for nature, and he uses these feelings to rationalize his dilettantism.

Werther loses himself in nature, in reveries about an old love, in the patriarchal atmosphere of Homer, and essentially withdraws from society into himself. The letter of June 16, the longest in the novel, describes the ball where Werther meets Lotte. He has been warned that Lotte is engaged to Albert, but that is of little concern to him. His letter is replete with broken thoughts, effusions, and dashes that portray his inner turmoil, and the fact that this letter comes seventeen days after the previous one shows how enthralled he is with his "new" love. Werther imagines the idyllic scene at the end of Oliver Goldsmith's *The Vicar of Wakefield* (1766), a scene which for him must remain unrealized. Lotte serves as a new cathexis; Werther completely loses himself in thoughts of her and does not know "either that it's day or night." His search, his yearning for an idyllic, harmonious life contrasts with his romantic longing for independence.

Werther often compares himself to a child and is very fond of children. He mentions his mother only briefly and his father not at all. He often longs for the innocence of childhood and subconsciously seems to wish that he could be among children for whom Lotte cuts the daily bread. His search for security, for protection, is very childlike, and he looks to Lotte as much for maternal as for sexual affection.

His passing comment about the local preacher's daughter ("I must say I found her not unpleasing"), who again is "taken," underlines his emotional instability. At times, however, Werther is capable of profound thoughts and of analyzing his own problems: "If we once have the power to pull ourselves together, our work will pass briskly through our hands, and we shall find a true pleasure in our activity" (July 1). "Activity" is a key word for Goethe and serves as a means of interpreting the novel. Wilhelm, the recipient of Werther's letters, and Werther's mother admonish him to find some kind of productive activity, which he only ridicules: "Am I not now active, and isn't it basically one and the same whether I count peas or lentils?" (July 20).

Later in the novel, Werther begins to read James Macpherson's skillful forgery, *The Works of Ossian* (1765), in whose stormy and turbulent descriptions of nature he finds his own feelings mirrored. Goethe commented later (August 2, 1829) that Werther read Homer while sane and Ossian after he went mad. The changing style of Werther's letters reflects his inner turmoil. Absent now are the pithy statements; subjectivism has taken over. Again, his friend Wilhelm admonishes him "to get rid of the miserable feeling that must consume all of your powers," but Werther notes in his diary that there is no "apperance of improvement."

Werther's second-longest letter deals with his argument with Albert about suicide (August 12). Werther justifies it, while Albert ridicules it as a tool of a spineless man, and the reader has a presentiment. Only ten days later, Werther writes that he is incapable of doing anything: "I have no imaginative powders, no feeling for nature, and books make me sick." He hopes that a new position will cure him (another important theme in Goethe's works), but the first book closes with his statement: "I see no end to this misery but the grave."

The second book begins one month and ten days after the last letter of book 1 and more than five months after the first letter of the novel. Werther now has the position of secretary to an ambassador, a position that he cannot endure for long. The position does, however, bring about a kind of recovery that enables Werther to see his problem: "Nothing is more dangerous than solitude" (October 20). There are now longer intervals between the letters, in which he often vacillates between recognizing his problems and putting the blame on others for them: "And you are all to blame whose twaddle placed this yoke on me and who have prated so much about activity. Activity!" (December 24).

Three months after his arrival, Werther writes Lotte for the first time, and his vocabulary once again is marked by such words as "isolation," "loneliness," and "limitation." Goethe interjects the parallel story of a farmhand, whom Werther had met earlier, whose unrequited love will later lead to murder. Werther identifies so much with this man's fate that he later makes an attempt to save him. This and the parallel motif of a man who worked for Lotte's father, fell in love with Lotte, was driven from the household, and became insane as a result of his unrequited love skillfully mark Werther's decline.

On December 6, about nineteen months after the first letter of the novel, Werther's correspondence ends, and the editor tells how he gathered the material that covers Werther's last days. The editor's longer, analytical sentences contrast sharply with Werther's rhapsodic prose. Like Wilhelm, he speaks of Werther's inactivity: "He seemed to himself justified in his inactivity by all this . . . ," but he also presents material (the very informed source is not given) which shows that Lotte was not totally without blame, that she spurred Werther on somewhat until it was too late. When Werther, at the end of the novel, sends his servant to borrow Albert's pistols for a supposed trip, Lotte reacts in horror; she knows that Werther wants the pistols to shoot himself, yet she does nothing about it, because Werther had visited her against Albert's wishes and she now fears Albert's remonstrations.

The end of the novel is masterful in its succinct style: "At twelve noon he died. . . . At night toward eleven [the steward] had him buried at the spot Werther had chosen. The steward followed the body, and his sons, but Albert found it impossible. People feared for Lotte's life. Workmen carried him. No clergyman escorted him."

Goethe intended to depict in *The Sorrows of Young Werther* the problems of an excessively sensitive soul, showing how unbridled emotions and inactivity could lead to death. He drew from his own life, but he also saw many Werthers around him, as in the figure of the gifted contemporary poet and dramatist

Jakob Michael Reinhold Lenz. The influence of the novel was great, but Goethe's intent was widely misunderstood. Young men with romantic hearts saw in the book a justification for excessive emotion and suicide, and they emulated Werther by dressing in the blue coat and yellow vest that he wears in the novel. "Werther fever" was on the rise, and there was even a spate of suicides à la Werther. For this and other reasons, Goethe revised the novel in 1787. Still, Werther became a model for Romantic writers throughout the world, and to this day, his story is the best known among Goethe's works.

WILHELM MEISTER'S APPRENTICESHIP

Like most of Goethe's mature works, *Wilhelm Meister's Apprenticeship* had a long genesis. Goethe made first mention of this, his second novel, in an entry in his diary dated February 16, 1777, although he probably was working on the novel as early as 1776; it took him nearly twenty years to complete it. To be sure, he had finished a large portion of the novel by 1785, through book 6 and part of book 7, but work on the novel, as with the plays *Iphigenia in Tauris, Egmont*, and *Torquato Tasso*, was interrupted by his trip to Italy from 1786 to 1788. Not until his friendship with Friedrich Schiller, who supplied insightful criticism and suggestions, many of which Goethe adopted, did Goethe regain interest and finish the work. The novel Goethe published in 1795 and 1796 was essentially a thorough revision of the earlier version entitled *Wilhelm Meisters Theatralische Sendung* (1911; *Wilhelm Meister's Theatrical Mission*, 1913), the manuscript of which was not discovered until 1910.

Wilhelm Meister's Theatrical Mission is a *Bildungsroman* in both the literal and the figurative sense. The fragment opens with Wilhelm as a boy, and the interesting psychological development of the child, which closely follows Goethe's autobiography, is to a great extent sacrificed in *Wilhelm Meister's Apprenticeship*, which begins with Wilhelm as a young man about to leave the parental home (the few childhood scenes are told in retrospect). In *Wilhelm Meister's Apprenticeship*, the theater loses in importance: *Wilhelm Meister's Theatrical Mission* reflects the ambitions and concerns of a budding dramatist; *Wilhelm Meister's Apprenticeship*, Goethe's ideas on

culture and human development. The former follows the pattern woven by Goethe in many of his early poems and dramas about the artist; the latter can no longer be termed "a portrait of the artist as a young man." The theater represents only one step on Wilhelm's path of self-development. The language of the former reads much like Goethe's Sturm und Drang prose and is quite different from the stylized, sculptured prose in the latter, which is characteristic of Goethe's prose style after his years in Italy. Many of the ideas and most of the characters, however, were transferred from the early fragment to the novel and merely reshaped to represent the thinking of the mature Goethe.

Thematically, *Wilhelm Meister's Apprenticeship* consists of five parts: home (book 1 and book 2, chapters 1 and 2), Wilhelm's travels as a businessman and his first theatrical encounter (book 2, chapter 3, to book 3, chapter 12), the theatre of Serlo (book 3, chapter 13, to book 5, and book 7, chapter 8), "Confessions of a Fair Saint" (book 6), and the "Society of the Tower" episodes (book 7, chapters 1-7 and 9, and book 8). The linear construction enables the reader to follow the development of Wilhelm from a somewhat naïve, eager young man through his many trials and tribulations to his reception into the Society of the Tower, where he is given an indenture that will guide him in his journeyman years.

At the beginning of the novel, Wilhelm, like many young people, disdains his family's supposed avarice and bourgeois life and views the theater as a means of escape. His mother curses the day she gave him a puppet theater, for she believes his calling to the theater will ruin him physically and morally. Goethe's description of theater life mirrors quite accurately the circumstances and plight of theater groups in Germany in the 1760's and 1770's.

A series of coincidences and misunderstandings involving Wilhelm's lover, Marianne—an actress who, unbeknown to him, is pregnant—causes him to abandon her and resign himself to his father's business. Years pass; Wilhelm despairs over his ability as a writer, which he still believes to be his calling, burns his manuscripts, and seems to dedicate himself diligently to his father's merchant profession. Following the advice of his father and his friend Werner, Wilhelm sets out on a trip to collect some debts owed to his father. As soon as he hears of a theatrical troupe performing in the vicinity where his travels have taken him, the old flame smouldering inside flares up and he is consumed by the idea of the theater. He encounters a motley group of actors and takes up with them.

The two theater episodes help Wilhelm gain insights into himself. At first enthusiastic about pursuing his dream of belonging to an acting troupe, he dedicates body and soul to the theater, which he serves as actor, writer, and director. (These activities reflect Goethe's involvement as writer, actor, and, after 1791, director of the Weimar Theatre.) While at a castle with the troupe, Wilhelm is introduced to the theater of Shakespeare by Jarno, a mysterious figure and a member of the Society of the Tower whose function becomes clear only later. Shakespeare has a profound effect on Wilhelm, as he did on all the German dramatists of the 1770's; Wilhelm's conversations about Shakespeare and *Hamlet* (c. 1600-1601) with Serlo, the director of a troupe in a large city of commerce (probably modeled on Hamburg), and with his sister Aurelie, and their subsequent successful performance of the play, form the nucleus of the fourth book. The sections on *Hamlet* do not, however, represent the thinking of the older Goethe, but rather the subjective sentimentality of the Sturm und Drang writers. Wilhelm's dissatisfaction with the members of the troupe and the bustle of the city causes him to reflect on the direction he has taken in his life; for the first time, he admires the order and activity of the world of commerce (book 4, chapter 20). Wilhelm still views the theater as a goal, however, writing to his friend Werner, "to develop myself exactly as I am, that was vaguely my wish and my intention from the days of my youth." The German word *(aus)bilden* (to develop, to educate, to cultivate), whose variant is found in *Bildungsroman* is a key word in the novel and appears more than one hundred times. At this point in the novel, Wilhelm knows he must develop himself, but he still falsely views the theater as an end and not as a means.

Toward the end of the fifth book, Wilhelm be-

comes more and more disillusioned with the theater, and his criticism of it culminates in the declaration in book 7, chapter 8: "I am leaving the theatre to join up with men whose association has to lead me in every sense to a pure and certain activity." The word "activity" (*Tätigkeit*), as in *The Sorrows of Young Werther*, is a key word in Goethe's novels, and it is toward an active, constructive life that Wilhelm must move.

The Society of the Tower makes up most of book 7 and all of book 8. Wilhelm discovers that many of the people who have crossed his path throughout the novel (Jarno, the Abbé, Natalie "the beautiful amazon," the Countess, Friedrich, and others) are connected with the Society and have monitored and guided his development. Wilhelm is now initiated into the secrets of the Society, and the Abbé says: "Your apprenticeship is over, nature has released you" (book 7, chapter 9). Wilhelm discovers that the boy Felix, who has been with him since his days with Serlo, is his son by Marianne, who died in childbirth. He also learns that Mignon and the harp player, those Romantic spirits whom he met while with the first acting troupe, are father and daughter from an incestuous affair. Symbolically, they must die, for they represent an aberrant side of life not compatible with Wilhelm's active, healthy endeavors. (Significantly, and ironically, German Romantic writers and musicians of the early nineteenth century were enraptured with the figures of Mignon and the harp player.)

Wilhelm falls in love with Natalie, who, like the other members of the Society, will play a significant role in the continuation of the novel, *Wilhelm Meister's Travels*. Wilhelm's development, however, is not yet over; the Society will direct him on his next journey, which he will make with his son Felix.

Wilhelm Meister's Apprenticeship is a milestone in the development of the novel as a genre. Not until Charles Dickens did a novelist again weave such an intricate plot. Goethe had literary debts to such writers as Samuel Richardon, Jean-Jacques Rousseau, and Oliver Goldsmith, but he paid them back with interest. His use of different genres within the novel—of letters, songs, and stories within the story—was to have a great influence on the next generation of novelists in England, France, and Russia. In Germany,

Goethe made the novel into an art form, a form which, unlike poetry or drama, was able to encompass the breadth of the human condition.

ELECTIVE AFFINITIES

Goethe's third novel, *Elective Affinities*, was first conceived as a novella to be placed in what was later to become his fourth novel, *Wilhelm Meister's Travels*, but the idea became so important to Goethe that he expanded the novella into a novel in what was for him a relatively short period of time; of his novels, *The Sorrows of Young Werther* was written more quickly. Goethe himself said that *Elective Affinities* should be read three times to comprehend its ramifications, and in his diary, he noted that the idea behind the novel was to portray "social relationships and their conflicts in a symbolic way."

Elective Affinities differs from Goethe's other novels in that it focuses attention on a group of people rather than on an individual, as in *The Sorrows of Young Werther* and *Wilhelm Meister's Apprenticeship*. In *Elective Affinities*, Goethe, somewhat like his contemporary, Jane Austen, uses a small group of people as a microcosm to represent the problems of contemporary society.

Elective Affinities begins with what seems to be an idyll. Edward and Charlotte live on a large estate and are arranging it to their tastes. They are both in their second marriage. Having been lovers in their youth who were forced into marriages of convenience, they were able to marry after the deaths of their spouses. Soon, however, flaws begin to appear in the idyllic setting. Edward and Charlotte are designing a new house, a pleasure pavilion (*Lustgebäude*), and, as with most actions in the novel, this one is symbolic: The old house, representing their marriage, is no longer adequate, and the building of the new one is an unconscious admission that their marriage itself is no longer adequate to one or to both of them. Apart from *Faust, Elective Affinities* is Goethe's most symbolic work, and attention must be paid to every object—the plane trees, the church, water, the paths, headaches, and so on—for symbolic meaning blended into the novel in a masterful way.

The stagnation of the marriage becomes clear when Edward wants to invite his old friend, the Cap-

tain, who has fallen on hard times, to come live with them. Charlotte, who is by far more perceptive than Edward, fears this move. She knows that a third person will change their lives, but whereas she is completely happy and satisfied in her activity (*Tätigkeit*), Edward is a dilettante who needs the "active" Captain to stimulate him. The narrator, whose function in *Elective Affinities* is generally to analyze the characters and their relationships objectively rather than to admonish, as in *The Sorrows of Young Werther*, comments that before the arrival of the Captain, Edward and Charlotte had had less conversation than usual, because they had disagreed over the building of the park: "Thus daily Charlotte felt lonelier."

The Captain arrives, and Charlotte decides to have Ottilie, the orphaned daughter of an old friend, brought from the boarding school which she attends with Luciane, Charlotte's daughter from her first marriage; thus, the tragic constellation is complete. One day, the four of them are together when the Captain begins speaking of elective affinities, the tendency in chemistry for particles to break up and form new combinations. Edward, who misconstrues nearly everything, comments that these relationships become interesting only when they cause separations (*Scheidungen*—in German, also meaning "divorces"), and he makes the analogy (quite unaware, consciously at least, of its implications) that Charlotte represents A, he himself B, the Captain C, and Ottilie D: When A and B break up, and C and D likewise, they form the new unions of AC and BD. Edward's casual talk disturbs Charlotte, who recognizes in it his subconscious yearning.

The new pairs are indeed gradually formed. Charlotte finds with the Captain new "activity" which she no longer shares with Edward, and Edward delights in being with Ottilie, with whom he shares a childlike nature. The names of the characters are themselves significant: Edward's real name, "Otto" (which is also the Captain's first name), "Charlotte," and "Ottilie" all have the same root, showing symbolically the close affinity among them. The action of the first part pinnacles in a scene of psychological adultery. Edward visits Charlotte's bedroom one night after "a strange mix-up took place in his soul," and during intercourse, he thinks of Ottilie while Charlotte thinks of the Captain. Upon waking, Edward has a presentiment and considers what he has done a crime. Thereafter the thought of Ottilie consumes him, just as Lotte's image consumed Werther.

Elective Affinities, like most of Goethe's later works, contains the theme of renunciation (*Entsagung*), and it could, in fact, justifiably carry the subtitle of *Wilhelm Meister's Travels: Oder, Die Entsagenden* (or those who renounce). Charlotte learns to renounce the Captain; Edward does not renounce, nor does Ottilie at this point in the novel. The Captain leaves, and when Edward learns that Charlotte is pregnant, he flees to seek his end in a war of which he has no real understanding, just as he does not understand most things in his life.

The first half of the second part deals with how Charlotte and Ottilie lead their lives during the absence of Edward and the Captain. Ottilie, even though she still longs for Edward, matures, and this maturation process can be followed in her diary, excerpts from which occasionally break the narrative flow of the novel. At times, it is hard to believe that Ottilie, who had difficulties in school, can actually understand the pithy statements she copies into her diary. Readers of Goethe are inclined to view Ottilie as an authorial mouthpiece in these passages, just as the aphorisms in "Makarien's Archive," at the end of *Wilhelm Meister's Travels*, serve to represent Goethe's thinking. Ottilie's diary also prepares the reader for her renunciation of Edward and for her belief that it is wrong to break up the marriage of Edward and Charlotte. When the baby, which has Ottilie's eyes and the Captain's facial features, is born (conceived on the night of psychological adultery), Ottilie begins to sublimate her love for Edward into a pseudo-mother-love for the child.

In *Elective Affinities*, Goethe assimilates, as in his other novels, a variety of literary genres. Ottilie's diary has already been mentioned; particularly striking is the function of the novella, "The Strange Neighbor Children," which is integrated into the novel. The children in the novella parallel to a certain degree the characters in the novel, but the novella, based on events in the Captain's past, has a happy ending (de-

spite the parallel symbols of water and drowning), unlike the novel.

One day, Ottilie takes the baby to the lake, where she is suddenly surprised by Edward. Edward has returned from the war ever more intent on having Ottilie. He has met with the Captain (who is now a major, perhaps through advancement in the same war in which Edward fought) and has convinced him, even though the Captain hesitated at first, that Charlotte and he should divorce and that the Major should marry Charlotte and raise the baby. Ottilie resists Edward's proposal that they marry, saying that Charlotte must decide their fate. In her confusion, she hurries, after parting from Edward, to a skiff, loses her balance, and drops the baby into the lake. By the time she retrieves it, it is dead.

Despite the tragic loss, Charlotte agrees to a divorce. Ottilie, however, has learned to "renounce." She resolves to be a teacher and to return to the boarding school, where she can be "active." Edward surprises her on her journey back to the school and gets her to return to the estate. During their brief meeting at an inn, however, Ottilie does not say a word; she refuses to express her love for Edward, realizing that the only escape for her is in death. Her maturation and new convictions become apparent when they return to the estate and she places Charlotte's and Edward's hands together. She continues not to speak and resolves to starve herself to death. Edward soon follows her in death, and the two are buried side by side.

WILHELM MEISTER'S TRAVELS

Wilhelm Meister's Travels belongs to that group of Goethe's later works (in poetry, *West-Eastern Divan*, and in drama, *Faust*) which are characteristic of his *Altersstil* (mature style) and which are not easily accessible. Goethe himself recognized the difficulty of his last novel; he admitted (February 17, 1827) that it could not have been written earlier. In a conversation six years before this admission (June 8, 1821), he cited the problem which readers would have with the novel: "Everything is really to be taken symbolically, and everywhere there is something else hidden behind it. Every solution to a problem is a new problem." The absence of plot; the interspersed novellas, poems, letters, aphorisms, dramatic dialogue, and technical discussions of various trades; and the often obscure wisdom of the aged Goethe make for difficult reading, but when the novel is read in the context of Goethe's later works and his worldview, its seemingly vague symbols become clearer.

Goethe formed the conception of *Wilhelm Meister's Travels* as soon as he finished its companion piece, *Wilhelm Meister's Apprenticeship*, but actual work on the novel did not begin until 1807, and it was not completed for more than twenty years. The novel fuses materials of two kinds: the novellas, written mostly between 1807 and 1818, which in style and content differ from the framework, and the framework itself, most of which was completed later. A first version appeared in 1821 and was then thoroughly revised for the second version in 1829. The novellas present vignettes of the human condition and the vicissitudes of human existence, and they are moralistic in that they reinforce the teachings implicit in the novel's framework; almost all of them deal with the problem of passion. The title of the novel itself is bipartite: *Wilhelm Meister's Travels* indicates a continuation, however loosely, of *Wilhelm Meister's Apprenticeship*; the subtitle, *Die Entsagenden* (those who renounce), mirrors the philosophy of the Society which directs the protagonist.

The Society of the Tower has given Wilhelm rules which dictate his travels: He cannot stay longer than three days under one roof; when he leaves a place, he must travel at least one German mile (approximately five miles); and he cannot return to the same place for more than a year. The novel begins with Wilhelm and his son Felix journeying through the mountains. Goethe immediately introduces the symbolic figures of Joseph, a carpenter, and Maria, his wife, who live in an abandoned monastery and offer Wilhelm shelter. Goethe's ideas on religion are encapsulated in this segment, both symbolically (the ruins of the monastery and Joseph's work on it) and explicitly (in conversations between Wilhelm and Joseph). The theme of the family recurs throughout the novel, and this "first family" serves as a model.

Continuing on his wanderings, Wilhelm meets Montan, the Jarno of *Wilhelm Meister's Apprenticeship*. Like many of the characters in the novel, Montan/Jarno is one who has "renounced," and he later fulfills a utilitarian function in the new society; his métier is geology, hence his name. The characters in the novel who will later make up the Society have professions that represent the vast and varied interests of Goethe: astronomy, weaving, geology, botany, and so on.

Wilhelm and Felix come to the house of the "Uncle" (*der Oheim*), where they meet Hersilie, with whom Felix falls in love. Felix's love for Hersilie depicts the impetuous and immature side of love. His handling of the situation parallels to a great extent Wilhelm's amorous adventures in *Wilhelm Meister's Apprenticeship* and is juxtaposed to the maturity of the now older and wiser Wilhelm. Wilhelm also meets at the Uncle's house Juliette and Leonardo. Leonardo has been away to educate himself, has overcome the many obstacles of impetuous youth, and is now returning to his Uncle's to take up new activities. The Uncle owns vast tracts of land in America, which Leonardo will inherit. The Society also possesses large landholdings in America, and Leonardo plans to join them to found colonies in the new land for those people of the mountain regions whose skills are being replaced by the machines of the Industrial Revolution. (This utopian vision of America runs throughout German literature and would remain present in the novels of several young Austrian writers and German filmmakers in the late twentieth century.)

Wilhelm visits the castle of Aunt Makarie, whose nebulous figure seems to shed guiding light over the Society's proceedings. Her pithy advice and aphorisms allow Goethe to express his wisdom on every subject of interest to him. Makarie is the example *par excellence* of one who has renounced. She is confined to a chair, but her wisdom and guidance are sought by everyone. Wilhelm then comes to the Pedagogical Province, where he leaves Felix to be educated while he continues his journey. The Pedagogical Province is a strict, almost totalitarian educational system (with overtones from Plato, Rousseau, and Johann Heinrich Pestalozzi) where young people are rigorously trained to serve a function in society. Every aspect of the student's life is dictated, and at first, Felix, again as a figure of youth whose passions must be controlled, is hesitant, but he does conform. The idea behind the Province is that man can attain the highest that he is capable of reaching. Some of the Province's pupils will immigrate to America with the Society.

Wilhelm later comes to that mountainous region whose inhabitants are threatened by the Industrial Revolution. There he meets a group planning to immigrate to America, and he begins practicing the profession he has chosen in order to be a useful member of society, namely, that of a doctor. Book 3 contains long passages on technical aspects of spinning and weaving, the society's plans for colonies in America and in Europe, and finally a meeting of the immigrants at Markarie's castle. Here some of the principal characters from *Wilhelm Meister's Apprenticeship* come together; they now all have a useful profession, a function in the new society: Friedrich, because of his good memory, is a copyist; the frivolous Philine has become, somewhat incredulously, an expert, selfless seamstress; and the Abbé is a teacher.

The novel ends as it began, symbolically. As Wilhelm travels upriver to join Felix, who is now several years older, a horse with rider plunges into the river. It is Felix, who has recently visited Hersilie on a mission of love, was rejected, and was riding grief-stricken when his horse fell into the river. Wilhelm saves his son by opening a vein—he has now completed his education; several years before, a similar incident had occurred in Wilhelm's life, but he was untrained and had to watch a fisher-boy die. Wilhelm will now join Natalie and the Society.

Wilhelm Meister's Travels is not a psychological study of man and society such as *Elective Affinities*; rather, it is a receptacle into which Goethe poured the wisdom gathered over a long life. It contains some of his most profound thoughts on man, society, literature, art, music, and the sciences. It also contains the vision of *Faust:* The central themes of activity and renunciation help define man's purpose on earth and his function in society—an unusual optimism for a writer in his eightieth year.

Kim Vivian

OTHER MAJOR WORKS

PLAYS: *Die Laune des Verliebten*, wr. 1767, pr. 1779 (*The Wayward Lover*, 1879); *Die Mitschuldigen*, first version wr. 1768, pr. 1780, second version wr. 1769, pr. 1777 (*The Fellow-Culprits*, 1879); *Götz von Berlichingen mit der eisernen Hand*, pb. 1773 (*Götz von Berlichingen with the Iron Hand*, 1799); *Götter, Helden und Wieland*, pb. 1774; *Clavigo*, pr., pb. 1774 (English translation, 1798, 1897); *Erwin und Elmire*, pr., pb. 1775 (libretto; music by Duchess Anna Amalia of Saxe-Weimar); *Stella*, first version pr., pb. 1776, second version pr. 1806 (English translation, 1798); *Claudine von Villa Bella*, first version pb. 1776, pr. 1779, second version pb. 1788 (libretto); *Die Geschwister*, pr. 1776; *Iphigenie auf Tauris*, first version pr. 1779, second version pb. 1787 (*Iphigenia in Tauris*, 1793); *Jery und Bätely*, pr. 1780 (libretto); *Die Fischerin*, pr., pb. 1782 (libretto; music by Corona Schröter; *The Fisherwoman*, 1899); *Scherz, List und Rache*, pr. 1784 (libretto); *Der Triumph der Empfindsamkeit*, pb. 1787; *Egmont*, pb. 1788 (English translation, 1837); *Torquato Tasso*, pb. 1790 (English translation, 1827); *Faust: Ein Fragment*, pb. 1790 (*Faust: A Fragment*, 1980); *Der Gross-Cophta*, pr., pb. 1792; *Der Bürgergeneral*, pr., pb. 1793; *Was wir bringen*, pr., pb. 1802; *Die natürliche Tochter*, pr. 1803 (*The Natural Daughter*, 1885); *Faust: Eine Tragödie*, pb. 1808 (*The Tragedy of Faust*, 1823); *Pandora*, pb. 1808; *Die Wette*, wr. 1812, pb. 1837; *Des Epimenides Erwachen*, pb. 1814; *Faust: Eine Tragödie, zweiter Teil*, pb. 1833 (*The Tragedy of Faust, Part Two*, 1838).

SHORT FICTION: *Unterhaltungen deutscher Ausgewanderten*, 1795 (*Conversations of German Emigrants*, 1854); *Novelle*, 1826 (*Novel*, 1837).

POETRY: *Neue Lieder*, 1770 (*New Poems*, 1853); *Sesenheimer Liederbuch*, 1775-1789, 1854 (*Sesenheim Songs*, 1853); *Römische Elegien*, 1793 (*Roman Elegies*, 1876); *Reinecke Fuchs*, 1794 (*Reynard the Fox*, 1855); *Epigramme: Venedig 1790*, 1796 (*Venetian Epigrams*, 1853); *Xenien*, 1796 (with Friedrich Schiller; *Epigrams*, 1853); *Hermann und Dorothea*, 1797 (*Herman and Dorothea*, 1801); *Balladen*, 1798 (with Schiller; *Ballads*, 1853); *Neueste Gedichte*, 1800 (*Newest Poems*, 1853); *Gedichte*, 1812, 1815 (2 volumes; *The Poems of Goethe*, 1853); *Sonette*, 1819 (*Sonnets*, 1853); *Westöstlicher Divan*, 1819 (*West-Eastern Divan*, 1877).

NONFICTION: *Von deutscher Baukunst*, 1773 (*On German Architecture*, 1921); *Versuch die Metamorphose der Pflanzen zu erklären*, 1790 (*Essays on the Metamorphosis of Plants*, 1863); *Beyträge zur Optik*, 1791, 1792 (2 volumes); *Winckelmann und sein Jahrhundert*, 1805; *Zur Farbenlehre*, 1810 (*Theory of Colors*, 1840); *Aus meinem Leben: Dichtung und Wahrheit*, 1811-1814 (6 volumes; *The Autobiography of Goethe*, 1824; better known as *Poetry and Truth from My Own Life*); *Italienische Reise*, 1816, 1817 (2 volumes; *Travels in Italy*, 1883); *Zur Naturwissenschaft überhaupt, besonders zur Morphologie*, 1817, 1824 (2 volumes); *Campagne in Frankreich, 1792*, 1822 (*Campaign in France in the Year 1792*, 1849); *Die Belagerung von Mainz, 1793*, 1822 (*The Siege of Mainz in the Year 1793*, 1849); *Essays on Art*, 1845; *Goethe's Literary Essays*, 1921; *Goethe on Art*, 1980.

MISCELLANEOUS: *Works*, 1848-1890 (14 volumes); *Goethes Werke*, 1887-1919 (133 volumes).

BIBLIOGRAPHY

Atkins, Stuart. *Essays on Goethe*. Columbia, S.C.: Camden House, 1995. See essays on the apprentice novelist and on *The Sorrows of Young Werther* and the Wilhelm Meister novels, by the preeminent Goethe scholar.

Blackall, Eric A. *Goethe and the Novel*. Ithaca, N.Y.: Cornell University Press, 1976. A standard study exploring all aspects of Goethe's novels and his approach to novel writing, including his sense of irony, of poetry, of the subjective and the tragic; the epic and symbolic modes; and his use of letters. Includes detailed notes and bibliography.

Boyle, Nicholas. *Goethe: The Poet and the Age, Volume I: The Poetry of Desire (1749-1790)*. Oxford, England: Clarendon Press, 1991. A monumental scholarly biography. See the index of Goethe's works for Boyle's extended discussion of *Wilhelm Meister.*

Gray, Ronald. *Goethe: A Critical Introduction*. Cambridge, England: Cambridge University Press, 1967. See the discussion of *Wilhelm Meister* in part 3. Includes a chronological table of Goethe's life and works and a well-organized bibliography broken down by categories: reference works, periodicals, life and times, general studies, Goethe and the English-speaking world, special topics, and translations.

Lange, Victor, ed. *Goethe: A Collection of Critical Essays*. Englewood Cliffs, N.J.: Prentice-Hall, 1968. Essays on Goethe's craft of fiction, on *Wilhelm Meister*, and on other themes in his work. Contains introduction, chronology, and bibliography.

Swales, Martin. *Goethe: The Sorrows of Werther*. Cambridge, England: Cambridge University Press, 1987. A comprehensive study of the novel situating it in its cultural context and discussing critical issues, including Werther as writer, Werther and society, Werther and tragedy, and the novel's reception. There is also an extremely useful annotated guide to further reading.

Wagner, Irmgard. *Goethe*. New York: Twayne, 1999. An excellent, updated introduction to the author and his works. Includes bibliographical references and an index.

NIKOLAI GOGOL

Born: Sorochintsy, Ukraine, Russian Empire (now Ukraine); March 31, 1809
Died: Moscow, Russia; March 4, 1852

PRINCIPAL LONG FICTION

Taras Bulba, 1835 (as short story), 1842 (revised as a novel; English translation, 1886)
Myortvye dushi, part 1, 1842, part 2, 1855 (*Dead Souls*, 1887)

OTHER LITERARY FORMS

Nikolai Gogol was the author of many short stories, most of which belong to two cycles: the "Ukrainian cycle" and the later "Petersburg cycle." He wrote many plays, including *Revizor* (1836; *The In-*

spector General*, 1890) and *Zhenit'ba* (1842; *Marriage: A Quite Incredible Incident*, 1926), as well as a great deal of nonfiction, much of it collected in *Arabeski* (1835; *Arabesques*, 1982) and *Vybrannye mesta iz perepiski s druzyami* (1847; *Selected Passages from Correspondence with Friends*, 1969). Gogol's *Polnoe sobranie sochinenii* (1940-1952; collected works), which includes unfinished works and drafts, as well as his voluminous correspondence, fills fourteen volumes. All of Gogol's finished works, but not his drafts or correspondence, are available in English translation.

ACHIEVEMENTS

Gogol's first collection of short stories, *Vechera na khutore bliz Dikanki*, (1831, 1832; *Evenings on a Farm near Dikanka*, 1926), made him famous, and his second collection, *Mirgorod* (1835; English translation, 1928), highlighted by *Taras Bulba*, established his reputation as Russia's leading prose writer. While Gogol's early stories, set in the Ukraine, are for the most part conventionally Romantic, his later Petersburg cycle of short stories, among which "Zapiski sumasshedshego" ("Diary of a Madman") and "Shinel" ("The Overcoat") are among the best known, marks the beginning of Russian critical realism. Gogol's two comedies are both classics and are as popular on the stage (and screen) today as they were in Gogol's lifetime. His novel *Dead Souls* is rivaled only by Leo Tolstoy's *War and Peace* (1865-1869) as the greatest prose work of Russian literature. Russian prose fiction is routinely divided into two schools: the Pushkinian, which is objective, matter-of-fact, and sparing in its use of verbal devices; and the Gogolian, which is artful, ornamental, and exuberant in its use of ambiguity, irony, pathos, and a variety of figures and tropes usually associated with poetry. Tolstoy and Ivan Turgenev belong to the Pushkinian school, Fyodor Dostoevski to the Gogolian. In his historical, critical, and moral essays, but especially in *Selected Passages from Correspondence with Friends*, Gogol established many of the principles of Russian conservative thought, anticipating the ideas of such writers as Dostoevski and Apollon Grigoriev.

BIOGRAPHY

Nikolai Vasilyevich Gogol, the son of a country squire, was born and educated in the Ukraine. Russian was to him a foreign language which he mastered while attending secondary school in Nezhin, also in the Ukraine. After his graduation in 1828, Gogol went to Saint Petersburg, where he joined the civil service. His first literary effort, "Hans Küchelgarten" (1829), a sentimental idyll in blank verse, was a failure, but his prose fiction immediately attracted attention. After the success of *Evenings on a Farm near Dikanka*, Gogol decided to devote himself entirely to his literary career. He briefly taught medieval history at Saint Petersburg University (1834-1835) and thereafter lived the life of a freelance writer and journalist, frequently supported by wealthy patrons. The first night of *The Inspector General* at the Aleksandrinsky Theater in Saint Petersburg on April 19, 1836, attended and applauded by Czar Nicholas I, was a huge success, but it also elicited vehement attacks by the reactionary press, enraged by

Gogol's spirited satire of corruption and stupidity in the provincial administration, and Gogol decided to go abroad to escape the controversy.

From 1836 to 1848, Gogol lived abroad, mostly in Rome, returning to Russia for brief periods only. The year 1842 marked the high point of Gogol's career with the appearance of part 1 of *Dead Souls* and the publication of a four-volume set of collected works, which contained some new work, in particular the great short story "The Overcoat." After 1842, Gogol continued to work on part 2 of *Dead Souls*, but he was now increasingly preoccupied with questions of religion and morality. His book, *Selected Passages from Correspondence with Friends*, actually a collection of essays in which Gogol defended traditional religious and moral values as well as the social status quo (including the institution of serfdom), caused a storm of protest, as liberals felt that it was flagrantly and evilly reactionary, while even many conservatives considered it to be unctuous and self-righteous.

Sorely hurt by the unfavorable reception of his book, Gogol almost entirely withdrew from literature. He returned to Russia for good in 1848 and spent the rest of his life in religious exercise and meditation. Shortly before his death, caused by excessive fasting and utter exhaustion, Gogol burned the final version of part 2 of *Dead Souls*. An earlier version was later discovered and published in 1855.

ANALYSIS

The cover of the first edition of *Dead Souls*, designed by Nikolai Gogol himself, reads: "*The Adventures of Chichikov or Dead Souls. A Poem by N. Gogol. 1842.*" "The Adventures of Chichikov" is in the smallest print, "Dead Souls" is better than twice that size, and "A Poem" is twice again the size of "Dead Souls." The word "or" is barely legible. The fact that "The Adventures of Chichikov" was inserted at the insistence of the censor, who felt that "Dead Souls" alone smacked of blasphemy, accounts for one-half of this typographical irregularity. The fact that "A Poem" (Russian *poema*, which usually designates an epic poem in verse) dominates the cover of a prose work which at first glance is anything but "poetic" also had its reasons, as will be seen.

DEAD SOULS

The plot structure of *Dead Souls* is simple. Chichikov, a middle-aged gentleman of decent appearance and pleasing manners, travels through the Russian provinces on what seems a mysterious quest: He buys up "dead souls," meaning serfs who have died since the last census but are still listed on the tax rolls until the next census. Along the way, he meets various types of Russian land- and serf-owners: the sugary and insipid Manilov; the widow Korobochka, ignorant and superstitious but an efficient manager of her farm; the dashing Nozdryov, a braggart, liar, and cardsharp; the brutish but shrewd Sobakevich; and the sordid miser Plyushkin. Having returned to the nearby provincial capital to obtain legal title to his four-hundred-odd "souls," Chichikov soon comes under a cloud of suspicion and quickly leaves town. Only at this stage does the reader learn about Chichikov's past and the secret of the dead souls. A civil-service official, Chichikov had twice reached the threshold of prosperity through cleverly devised depredations of the state treasury, but each time he had been foiled at the last moment. After his second fiasco, he had been allowed to resign with only a small sum saved from the clutches of his auditors. Undaunted, he had conceived yet another scheme: He would buy up a substantial number of "dead souls," mortgage them at the highest rate available, and disappear with the cash.

The plot of part 1 takes the story only this far. In what is extant of part 2, Chichikov is seen not only trying to buy more dead souls but also getting involved in other nefarious schemes. It also develops, however, that Chichikov is not happy with his sordid and insecure existence and that he dreams of an honest and virtuous life. He would be willing to mend his ways if he could only find a proper mentor who would give him the right start. There is reason to believe that Gogol planned to describe Chichikov's regeneration and return to the path of righteousness in part 3. The whole plot thus follows the pattern of a picaresque novel, and many details of *Dead Souls* are, in fact, compatible with this genre, which was well established in Russian literature even before Gogol's day.

Actually, part 1 of *Dead Souls* is many other things besides a picaresque novel: a humorous novel after the fashion of Charles Dickens's *Pickwick Papers* (1836-1837), with which it was immediately compared by the critics; a social satire attacking the corruption and inefficiency of the imperial administration and the crudity and mental torpor of the landed gentry; a moral sermon in the form of grotesque character sketches; and, above all, an epic of Russia's abjection and hoped-for redemption. The characters of part 2, while copies, in a way, of those encountered in part 1, have redeeming traits and strike the reader as human beings rather than as caricatures. The landowner Tentetnikov, in particular, is clearly a prototype of Oblomov, the hero of Ivan Goncharov's immortal novel of that title (1859), and, altogether, part 2 of *Dead Souls* is a big step in the direction of the Russian realist novel of the 1850's and 1860's. The following observations apply to part 1, unless otherwise indicated.

The structure of *Dead Souls* is dominated by the road, as the work begins with a description of Chichikov's arrival at an inn of an unidentified provincial capital and ends with him back on the road, with several intervening episodes in which the hero is seen on his way to his next encounter with a potential purveyor of dead souls. Chichikov's tippling coachman, Selifan, and his three-horse carriage (Russian, *troika*) are often foregrounded in Gogol's narrative, and one of the three horses, the lazy and stubborn piebald, has become one of the best-known "characters" in all Russian fiction. The celebrated *troika* passage concludes part 1. Some critics, such as Vladimir Nabokov, have seen "the whole first volume of *Dead Souls* as a closed circle whirling on its axle and blurring the spokes, with the theme of the wheel cropping up at each new revolution on round Chichikov's part."

When Chichikov is not on the road, the narrative becomes a mirror, as each new character is reflected in Chichikov's mind, with the assistance of the omniscient narrator's observations and elucidations. One contemporary critic said that reading *Dead Souls* was like walking down a hotel corridor, opening one door after another—and staring at another human monster each time.

The road and the mirror by no means exhaust Gogol's narrative attitudes. *Dead Souls* features some philosophical discussions on a variety of topics; many short narrative vignettes, such as when Chichikov dreamily imagines what some of his freshly acquired dead souls may have been like in life; an inserted novella, "The Tale of Captain Kopeikin," told by the local postmaster, who suspects that Chichikov is in fact the legendary outlaw Captain Kopeikin; repeated apostrophes to the reader, discussing the work itself and the course to be taken in continuing it; and last but not least, Gogol's much debated lyric digressions. Altogether, while there is some dialogue in *Dead Souls*, the narrator's voice dominates throughout. In fact, the narrative may be described as the free flow of the narrator's stream of consciousness, drifting from observation to observation, image to image, and thought to thought. It is often propelled by purely verbal associations. A common instance of the latter is the so-called realized metaphor, such as when a vendor of hot mead, whose large red face is likened to a copper samovar, is referred to as "the samovar"; when Chichikov, threatened with bodily harm by an enraged Nozdryov and likened to a fortress under siege, suddenly becomes "the fortress"; or when the bearlike Sobakevich is casually identified as a "fair sized bear" in the role of landowner. It is also verbal legerdemain which eventually turns Sobakevich's whole estate into an extension of its owner: "Every object, every chair in Sobakevich's house seemed to proclaim: 'I, too, am Sobakevich!'"

Hyperbole is another device characteristic of Gogol's style. Throughout *Dead Souls*, grotesque distortions and exaggerations are presented as a matter of course—for example, when the scratching of the clerks' pens at the office where Chichikov seals his purchase of dead souls is likened to "the sound of several carts loaded with brushweed and driven through a forest piled with dead leaves a yard deep." Often the hyperbole is ironic, such as when the attire of local ladies is reported to be "of such fashionable pastel shades that one could not even give their names, to such a degree had the refinement of taste attained!"

A sure sign of the author's own point of view surfaces in frequent literary allusions and several passages in which Gogol digresses to discuss the theory of fiction—for example, the famous disquisition, introducing chapter 7, on the distinction between the writer who idealizes life and the writer who chooses to deal with real life. Gogol, who fancies himself to be a realist, wryly observes that "the judgment of his time does not recognize that much spiritual depth is required to throw light upon a picture taken from a despised stratum of life, and to exalt it into a pearl of creative art" but feels "destined by some wondrous power to go hand in hand with his heroes, to contemplate life in its entirety, life rushing past in all its enormity, amid laughter perceptible to the world and through tears that are unperceived by and unknown to it!" The phrases "to exalt it into a pearl of creative art" and "amid laughter perceptible to the world and through tears that are unperceived by and unknown to it" have become common Russian usage, along with many others in *Dead Souls*.

Dead Souls is studded with many outright digressions. It must be kept in mind, though, that the mid-nineteenth century novel was routinely used as a catchall for miscellaneous didactic, philosophical, critical, scholarly, and lyric pieces which were often only superficially, if at all, integrated into the texture of the novel. Still, the number and nature of digressions in *Dead Souls* are exceptional even by the standards of a *roman feuilleton* of the 1840's. According to Victor Erlich, there are two basic types of digressions in *Dead Souls:* "the lateral darts and the upward flights." The former are excursions into a great variety of aspects of Russian life, keenly observed, sharply focused, and always lively and colorful. For example, having observed that Sobakevich's head looks quite like a pumpkin, Gogol, in one of his many "Homeric similes," veers off into a village idyll about a peasant lad strumming a balalaika made from a pumpkin, to win the heart of a "snowy-breasted and snowy-necked Maiden."

Gogol's upward flights are of a quite different order. They permit his imagination to escape the prosaic reality of Chichikov's experience and allow him to become a poet who takes a lofty view of Russia and her destiny. In several of these passages, Gogol's imagination becomes quite literally airborne. One of them, at the conclusion of chapter 5, begins with a lofty aerial panorama: "Even as an incomputable host of churches, of monasteries, with cupolas, bulbous domes, and crosses, is scattered all over holy and devout Russia, so does an incomputable multitude of tribes, generations, peoples swarm, flaunt their motley and scurry across the face of the earth." It ends in a rousing paean to "the Russian word which, like no other in the world, would burst out so, from out the very heart, which would seethe so and quiver and flutter so much like a living thing."

Early in chapter 11, Gogol produces another marvelous panoramic vision of Russia, apostrophized in the famous passage, "Russia, Russia! I behold thee—from my alien, beautiful, far-off vantage point I behold thee." (Gogol wrote most of *Dead Souls* while living in Italy.) The conclusion of this, the final chapter of part 1 then brings the most famous lines of prose in all of Russian literature, the *troika* passage in which a speeding three-horse carriage is elevated to a symbol of Russia's historical destiny. The intensity and plenitude of life and emotion in these and other airborne lyric passages stand in stark contrast to the drab pygmy world which is otherwise dominant in *Dead Souls*. These lyric digressions were challenged as incongruous and unnecessary even by some contemporary critics who, as do many critics today, failed to realize that Gogol's is a dual vision of manic-depressive intensity.

As a *poema* (epic poem), *Dead Souls* is a work which Gogol perceived as the poetic expression of an important religious-philosophical conception, that is, something of the order of Dante's *The Divine Comedy* (c. 1320) or John Milton's *Paradise Lost* (1667, 1674). Incidentally, there is one rather inconsequential allusion to Dante in chapter 7, where one reads that a Collegiate Registrar "served our friends even as Virgil at one time had served Dante, and guided them to the Presence." Immediately after the appearance of *Dead Souls*, critics were split into two camps: those who, like Konstantin Aksakov, greeted the work as the Russian national epopee, found numerous Homeric traits in it, and perceived it as a true incarnation of the Russian spirit in all of its depth and plenitude, and those who, like Nikolai Polevoi and Osip Senkovsky, saw it as merely an entertaining, though rather banal and in places pretentious, humorous novel. The latter group—which included even the great critic Vissarion Belinsky, who otherwise felt that *Dead Souls* was a perfect quintessence of Russian life—found Gogol's attempts at philosophizing and solemn pathos merely pompous and false. There has never been agreement in this matter. Nevertheless, several passages in part 1, the whole drift of part 2, and a number of quite unequivocal statements made by Gogol in his correspondence (in *Selected Passages from Correspondence with Friends* and in his posthumous "Author's Confession") all suggest that Gogol did indeed perceive *Dead Souls* as a *Divine Comedy* of the Russian soul, with part 1 its *Inferno*, part 2 its *Purgatory*, and part 3 its *Paradise*.

How, then, is part 1 in fact an *Inferno*, a Russian Hell? It is set in a Hades of dead souls, of humans who lead a shadowy phantom existence bereft of any real meaning or direction. Thus, it must be understood that in the Romantic philosophy of Gogol's time, the "normal" existence of a European philistine was routinely called "illusory," "unreal," and even "ghostly," while the ideal quest of the artist or philosopher was considered "substantial," "real," and "truly alive." As Andrey Bely demonstrated most convincingly, all of part 1 is dominated by what he calls "the figure of fiction." Whatever is said or believed to be true is from beginning to end a fiction, as unreal as Chichikov's financial transactions. For example, when the good people of N. begin to suspect that something is wrong with Chichikov, some of them believe that he plans to abduct the Governor's daughter, others conjecture that he is really Captain Kopeikin, a highway robber of legendary fame, and some actually suspect that he is Napoleon escaped from his island exile, but nobody investigates his motive for buying dead souls. As Bely also demonstrated, even time and space in *Dead Souls* are fictitious: The text will not even allow one to determine the season of the year; Chichikov's itinerary, if methodically checked, is physically impossible, and so on. Behind the figure of fiction, there looms large the message that all earthly experience and wisdom are in fact illusory, as Gogol makes explicit in a philosophical digression found in chapter 10.

In this shadowy world of fiction there exist two kinds of dead souls. There are the dead serfs who are sold and mortgaged and who, in the process, acquire a real semblance of life. Mrs. Korobochka, as soon as she has understood that Chichikov is willing to pay her some money for her dead serfs, is afraid that he may underpay her and somewhat timidly suggests that "maybe I'll find some use for them in my own household." Sobakevich, who haggles about the price of each dead soul, insists on eloquently describing their skills and virtues, as though it really mattered. Chichikov himself firmly rejects an offer by the local authorities to provide him with a police escort for the souls he has purchased, asserting that "his peasants are all of eminently quiet disposition." The same night, however, when he returns home from a party thrown by the local police chief to honor the new owner of four hundred souls, he actually orders Selifan "to gather all the resettled peasants, so he can personally make a roll call of them." Selifan and Petrushka, Chichikov's lackey, barely manage to get their master to bed.

The humanitarian message behind all of this is obvious: How could a person who finds the buying and selling of dead souls "fantastic" and "absurd" have the effrontery to find the same business transactions involving living souls perfectly normal? This message applies not only to Russia in the age of serfdom (which ended only in 1861—that is, at about the same time formal slavery ended in the United States) but also to any situation in which human beings are reduced to their social or economic function.

The other dead souls are the landowners and government officials whom we meet in *Dead Souls*. As the critic Vasily Rozanov observed, the peculiar thing about Gogolian characters is that they have no souls; they have habits and appetites but no deeper human emotions or ideal strivings. This inevitably deprives them of their humanity and renders them two-dimensional personifications of their vices—caricatures. Sobakevich is a very shrewd talking bear. Nozdryov is so utterly worthless that he appears to be a mere appendage of his extraordinarily handsome, thick, and pitch-black sideburns, thinned out a bit from time to time, when their owner is caught cheating at cards and suffers a whisker pulling. Plyushkin's stony miserliness has deprived him of all feeling and has turned him, a rich landowner, into a beggar and an outcast of society. *Dead Souls* has many such caricatures, which have been likened to Brueghelian grotesque paintings. This analogy applies to the following passage in chapter 11, for example: "The clerks in the Treasury were especially distinguished for their unprepossessing and unsightly appearance. Some had faces for all the world like badly baked bread: one cheek would be all puffed out to one side, the chin slanting off to the other, the upper lip blown up into a big blister that, to top it all off, had burst."

As early as 1842, the critic Stepan Shevyrev suggested that *Dead Souls* represented a mad world, thus following an ancient literary and cultural tradition (which today is often referred to as that of the "carnival"). The massive absurdities, *non sequiturs*, and simply plain foolishness throughout the whole text could, for Gogol and for many of his readers, have only one message: That which poses for "real life" is in fact nothing but a ludicrous farce. The basic course of Gogol's imagination is that of a descent into a world of ridiculous, banal, and vile "nonbeing," from which it will from time to time rise to the heights of noble and inspired "being."

Taras Bulba

While *Dead Souls* is unquestionably Gogol's masterpiece, his only other work of long fiction, *Taras Bulba*, is not without interest. The 1835 version of *Taras Bulba* is a historical novella; the 1842 version, almost twice as long and thus novel-sized, has many digressions and is at once more realistic and more gothic, but also more patriotic, moralizing, and bigoted. The plot is essentially the same in both versions.

Taras Bulba is a Ukrainian Cossack leader, so proud of his two fine sons recently back from school in Kiev that he foments war against the hated Poles, so that Ostap and Andriy can prove their manhood in battle. The Cossacks are initially successful, and the Poles are driven back to the fortress city of Dubno.

The Cossacks lay siege to it, and the city seems ready to fall when Andriy is lured to the city by a messenger from a beautiful Polish maiden with whom he had fallen in love as a student in Kiev. Blinded by her promises of love, Andriy turns traitor. The Cossacks' fortunes now take a turn for the worse. They are hard-pressed by a Polish relief force. On the battlefield, Taras meets Andriy (now a Polish officer), orders him to dismount, and shoots him. The Cossacks, however, are defeated, and Ostap is taken prisoner. Old Taras makes his way to Warsaw, hoping to save him, but can only witness his son's execution. Having returned to the Ukraine, Bulba becomes one of the leaders of yet another Cossack uprising against the King of Poland. When peace is made, Bulba alone refuses to honor it. He continues to wreak havoc on the Poles all over the Ukraine but is finally captured by superior Polish forces. He dies at the stake, prophesying the coming of a Russian czar against whom no power on earth will stand.

There is little historical verity in *Taras Bulba*. Different details found in the text point to the fifteenth, sixteenth, and seventeenth centuries as the time of its action. It is thus an epic synthesis of the struggle of the Orthodox Ukraine to retain its independence from Catholic Poland. The battle scenes are patterned after Vergil and Homer, and there are many conventional epic traits throughout, such as scores of brief scenes of single combat, catalogs of warriors' names, extended Homeric similes, orations, and, of course, Bulba's solemn prophecy. Taras Bulba is a tragic hero who expiates his hubris with the loss of his sons and his own terrible death.

The earlier version of *Taras Bulba* serves mostly the glorification of the wild, carefree life at the Cossack army camp. In the later version, this truly inspired hymn to male freedom is obscured by a message of Russian nationalism, Orthodox bigotry, and nostalgia for a glorious past that never was. The novel features almost incessant baiting of Poles and Jews. Gogol's view of the war is a wholly unrealistic and romantic one: We are told of "the enchanting music of bullets and swords" and so on. From a literary viewpoint, *Taras Bulba* is a peculiar mixture of the historical novel in the manner of Sir Walter Scott and the gothic tale. The narrator stations himself above his hero, gently faulting him on some of his uncivilized traits, such as the excessive stock Bulba puts in his drinking prowess or his maltreatment of his long-suffering wife. Rather often, however, the narrator descends to the manner of the folktale. His language swings wildly from coarse humor and naturalistic grotesque to solemn oratory and lyric digressions. There are scenes of unspeakable atrocities, reported with relish, but also some wonderful poems in prose, such as the well-known description of the Ukrainian steppe in the second chapter.

Altogether, *Taras Bulba* contains some brilliant writing but also some glaring faults. It immediately became a classic, and soon enough a school text, inasmuch as its jingoism met with the approval of the Czar—and eventually of Soviet school administrators. Several film versions, Russian as well as Western, exist.

Although Gogol's production of fiction was quite small by nineteenth century standards, both his novels and his short stories have had an extraordinary influence on the development of Russian prose—an influence that is still potent in the late twentieth century, as witnessed by the works of Andrei Sinyavsky and other writers of the Third Emigration.

Victor Terras

OTHER MAJOR WORKS

SHORT FICTION: *Vechera na khutore bliz Dikanki*, volume 1, 1831, volume 2, 1832 (*Evenings on a Farm Near Dikanka*, 1926); *Mirgorod*, 1835 (English translation, 1928); *Arabeski*, 1835 (includes stories and essays; *Arabesques*, 1982).

PLAYS: *Vladimir tretey stepeni*, wr. 1832, pb. 1842; *Zhenit'ba*, wr. 1835, pr., pb. 1842 (*Marriage: A Quite Incredible Incident*, 1926); *Revizor*, pr., pb. 1836 (*The Inspector General*, 1890); *Utro delovogo cheloveka*, pb. 1836 (revision of *Vladimir tretey stepeni*; *An Official's Morning*, 1926); *Lakeyskaya*, pb. 1842 (revision of *Vladimir tretey stepeni*; *The Servants' Hall*, 1926); *Tyazhba*, pb. 1842 (revision of *Vladimir tretey stepeni*; *The Lawsuit*, 1926); *Otryvok*, pb. 1842 (revision of *Vladimir tretey stepeni*; *A Fragment*, 1926); *Igroki*, pb. 1842 (*The Gamblers*, 1926);

The Government Inspector and Other Plays, pb. 1926.

POETRY: *Hanz Kuechelgarten*, 1829.

NONFICTION: *Vybrannye mesta iz perepiski s druzyami*, 1847 (*Selected Passages from Correspondence with Friends*, 1969); *Letters of Nikolai Gogol*, 1967.

MISCELLANEOUS: *The Collected Works*, 1922-1927 (6 volumes); *Polnoe sobranie sochinenii*, 1940-1952 (14 volumes); *The Collected Tales and Plays of Nikolai Gogol*, 1964.

BIBLIOGRAPHY

Fanger, Donald. *The Creation of Nikolai Gogol*. Cambridge, Mass.: Harvard University Press, 1979. Part 1 puts forth problems to explore in Gogol's life and career; part 2 develops a sense of his earliest writing; part 3 concentrates on the period leading up to *Dead Souls*; part 4 assesses Gogol's vision of the world. Provides very detailed notes but no bibliography.

Lindstrom, Thais. *Nikolay Gogol*. New York: Twayne, 1974. A fine introductory study, beginning with Gogol's establishment of an identity and culminating in a discussion of *Dead Souls*. Includes chronology, notes, and an annotated bibliography.

Luckyj, George Stephen Nestor. *The Anguish of Mykola Hohol a.k.a. Nikolai Gogol*. Toronto: Canadian Scholars' Press, 1998. Explores Gogol's life and how it affected his work. Includes bibliographical references and an index.

Magarshack, David. *Gogol: A Life*. New York: Grove Press, 1957. A compact, introductory biography. Provides a bibliography.

Maguire, Robert A. *Exploring Gogol*. Stanford, Calif.: Stanford University Press, 1994. The most comprehensive study in English of Gogol's entire writing career. Incorporates a chronology, detailed notes, and an extensive bibliography.

_____, ed. *Gogol from the Twentieth Century*. Princeton, N.J.: Princeton University Press, 1974. Essays on all of Gogol's major works. See especially the introduction, "The Legacy of Criticism." Contains a bibliography and indexes of names and titles.

Peace, Richard. *The Enigma of Gogol: An Examination of the Writings of N. V. Gogol and Their Place in the Russian Literary Tradition.* Cambridge, England: Cambridge University Press, 1981. Includes detailed notes and a "biographical table."

Woodward, James B. *The Symbolic Art of Gogol: Essays on His Short Fiction.* Columbus, Ohio: Slavica, 1981. See especially the first chapter on Gogol's use of symbolism. Presents a bibliography.

WILLIAM GOLDING

Born: St. Columb Minor, Cornwall, England; September 19, 1911

Died: Perranarworthal, Cornwall, England; June 19, 1993

PRINCIPAL LONG FICTION

Lord of the Flies, 1954
The Inheritors, 1955
Pincher Martin, 1956 (also known as *The Two Deaths of Christopher Martin*)
Free Fall, 1959
The Spire, 1964
The Pyramid, 1967
Darkness Visible, 1979
Rites of Passage, 1980
The Paper Men, 1984
Close Quarters, 1987
Fire Down Below, 1989
The Double Tongue, 1995

OTHER LITERARY FORMS

William Golding's first and only book of poetry, entitled simply *Poems*, was published in 1934. "Envoy Extraordinary," a 1956 novella, was recast in 1958 in the form of a play, *The Brass Butterfly*; set in Roman times, *The Brass Butterfly* uses irony to examine the value of "modern" inventions. "Envoy Extraordinary" was published along with two other novellas, "The Scorpion God" and "Clonk Clonk," in a 1971 collection bearing the title *The Scorpion God*.

Golding also produced nonfiction; his book reviews in *The Spectator* between 1960 and 1962 frequently took the form of personal essays. Many of his essays and autobiographical pieces were collected in *The Hot Gates and Other Occasional Pieces* (1965). *A Moving Target* (1982) is another set of essays; *An Egyptian Journal* (1985) is a travelogue. Golding also gave numerous interviews explaining his work; these have appeared in a variety of journals and magazines.

ACHIEVEMENTS

Sir William Gerald Golding is without doubt one of the major British novelists of the post-World War II era. He depicted in many different ways the anguish of modern humanity as it gropes for meaning and redemption in a world where the spiritual has been all but crushed by the material. His themes deal with guilt, responsibility, and salvation. He depicts the tension between individual fallenness and social advance, or, to put it differently, the cost of progress to the individual.

Golding's work portrays a period in which the last vestiges of an optimistic belief in evolutionary progress collapsed under the threat of nuclear destruction. In doing this, he moved the classic British novel tradition forward both in stylistic and formal technique and in the opening up of a new, contemporary social and theological dialectic.

Golding was a Fellow of the Royal Society of Literature (elected in 1955), and in 1983 he received the Nobel Prize in Literature. He won the James Tait Black Memorial Prize in 1979 for *Darkness Visible* and the Booker Prize in 1980 for *Rites of Passage*. He was knighted in 1989.

BIOGRAPHY

Born in the county of Cornwall in the southwest corner of England, the son of a rationalistic schoolmaster, William Golding had a relatively isolated childhood. Eventually his family moved to Marlborough, in Wiltshire, where his father was a science teacher. There Golding received his high school education, while revisiting Cornwall frequently. He graduated from Brasenose College, Oxford, in science and literature. The choice of arts over science was made at the university, but scientific interests and approaches can be easily discerned in his literary work. Each novel is, in a way, a new experiment set up to test a central hypothesis.

After the unsuccessful publication of a book of poetry in 1934, Golding moved to London and participated in fringe theater without achieving anything of significance. In 1939 he married Ann Brookfield and accepted a teaching post at Bishop Wordsworth's School, Salisbury, also in Wiltshire. Soon after the outbreak of war, he joined the Royal Navy, seeing extensive action against German warships, being adrift for three days in the English Channel, and participating in the Normandy landings.

After the war, he resumed teaching and tried writing novels. His first four were highly imitative and met only by editorial refusals. He then decided to write as he wanted, not as how he thought he ought. This shift in approach led to the immediate publication of *Lord of the Flies* in 1954; this work became almost at once a landmark on the British literary scene. Golding was able to follow this achievement with three more novels in the space of only five years, by which time paperback versions were being issued on both sides of the Atlantic. In 1961 he retired from teaching, becoming for two years a book reviewer with *The Spectator*, one of the leading British weekly cultural reviews. In *The Paper Men*, Golding depicts a novelist whose first novel turned out to be a gold mine for him—an autobiographical echo, no doubt.

After the publication of *The Pyramid* in 1967, when Golding was fifty-six years old, there came rather a long silence, and many people assumed that he had brought his career to a close. With the publication of *Darkness Visible* twelve years later, however, a steady stream of new novels emerged, including a trilogy. This second phase also marked the reception of various prizes, including the Nobel Prize in Literature, and his being knighted, a comparatively rare honor for a novelist in Britain.

Golding had one son and one daughter. He and his wife returned to Cornwall to live in 1984. Two years after his death in 1993, a nearly completed novel, *The Double Tongue*, was published.

ANALYSIS

William Golding, like his older British contemporary Graham Greene, is a theological novelist: That is to say, his main thematic material focuses on particular theological concerns, in particular sin and guilt, innocence and its loss, individual responsibility and the possibility of atonement for mistakes made, and the need for spiritual revelation. Unlike Greene, however, he does not write out of a particular Christian, or even religious, belief system; the dialectic he sets up is neither specifically Catholic (like Greene's) nor Protestant. In fact, Golding's dialectic is set up in specific literary terms, in that it is with other works of literature that he argues, rather than with theological or philosophical positions per se. The texts with which he argues do represent such positions or

(AP/Wide World Photos)

make certain cultural assumptions of such positions; however, it is through literary technique that he argues—paralleling, echoing, deconstructing—rather than through narratorial didacticism.

Golding's achievement is a literary tour de force. The British novel has never contained theological dialectic easily, except at a superficial level, let alone a depiction of transcendence. Golding has accepted the nineteenth century novel tradition but has modified it extensively. Each novel represents a fresh attempt for him to refashion the language and the central consciousness of that tradition. Sometimes he has pushed it beyond the limits of orthodox mimetic realism, and hence some of his novels have been called fables, allegories, or myths. In general, however, his central thrust is to restate the conflict between individuals and their society in contemporary terms, and in doing this, to question at a fundamental level many cultural assumptions, and to point up the loss of moral and spiritual values in twentieth century Western civilization—an enterprise in which most nineteenth century novelists were similarly involved for their own time.

LORD OF THE FLIES

Golding's first and most famous novel, *Lord of the Flies*, illustrates this thesis well. Although there is a whole tradition of island-castaway narratives, starting with one of the earliest novels in English literature, Daniel Defoe's *Robinson Crusoe* (1719), the text with which Golding clearly had in mind to argue was R. M. Ballantyne's *The Coral Island* (1858), written almost exactly one hundred years before Golding's. The names of Ballantyne's three schoolboy heroes (Ralph, Jack, and Peterkin) are taken over, with Peterkin becoming Simon (the biblical reversion being significant) and various episodes in Ballantyne being parodied by Golding—for example, the pig-sticking.

Ballantyne's yarn relied on the English public-school ethos that boys educated within a British Christian discipline would survive anything and in fact would be able to control their environment—in miniature, the whole British imperialistic enterprise of the nineteenth century. Most desert-island narratives do make the assumption that Western men can

control their environment, assuming that they are moral, purposeful, and religious. Golding subverts all these suppositions: Except for a very few among them, the abandoned schoolboys, significantly younger than Ballantyne's and more numerous (making a herd instinct possible), soon lose the veneer of the civilization they have acquired. Under Jack's leadership, they paint their faces, hunt pigs, and then start killing one another. They ritually murder Simon, the mystic, whose transcendental vision of the Lord of the Flies (a pig's head on a pole) is of the evil within. They also kill Piggy, the rationalist. The novel ends with the pack pursuing Ralph, the leader democratically elected at the beginning; the boys are prepared to burn the whole island to kill him.

Ironically, the final conflagration serves as a powerful signal for rescue (earlier watchfires having been pathetically inadequate), and, in a sudden reversal, an uncomprehending British naval officer lands on the beach, amazed at the mud-covered, dirty boys before him. Allegorically it might be thought that as this world ends in fire, a final divine intervention will come. Ironically, however, the adult world that the officer represents is also destroying itself as effectively, in a nuclear war. Salvation remains problematic and ambiguous.

What lifts the novel away from simple allegory is not only the ambiguities but also the dense poetic texture of its language. The description of Simon's death is often quoted as brilliantly heightened prose—the beauty of the imagery standing in stark contrast to the brutality of his slaying. Yet almost any passage yields its own metaphorical textures and suggestive symbolism. Golding's rich narrative descriptions serve to point up the poverty of the boys' language, which can only dwell on basics—food, defecation, fears and night terrors, killings. Golding's depiction of the children is immediately convincing. The adult intervention (the dead airman, the naval officer) is perhaps not quite so, being too clearly fabular. In general, however, the power of the novel derives from the tensions set up between the book's novelistic realism and its fabular and allegorical qualities. The theological dialectic of humanity's fallenness (not only the boys') and the paper-thin veneer of civilization emerges inexorably out of this genre tension.

THE INHERITORS

The thinness of civilization forms the central thesis of Golding's second novel, *The Inheritors*. The immediate literary dialectic is set up with H. G. Wells's *The Outline of History: Being a Plain History of Life and Mankind* (1920), which propounds the typical social evolutionism common from the 1850's onward. At a more general level, Golding's novel might also be seen as an evolutionary version of John Milton's *Paradise Lost* (1667): Satan's temptation to Eve is a temptation to progress; the result is the fall. Just as Adam and Eve degrade themselves with drunken behavior, so do Golding's Neanderthal protagonists, Lok and Fa, when they stumble over the remains of *Homo sapiens*' cannibalistic "festivities."

Golding has subverted the Wellsian thesis that Neanderthals were totally inferior by depicting them as innocent, gentle, intuitive, playful, and loving. They stand in ironic contrast to the group of *Homo sapiens* who eventually annihilate them, except for a small baby whom they kidnap (again reversing a short story by Wells, where it is Neanderthals who kidnap a human baby). The humans experience terror, lust, rage, drunkenness, and murder, and their religion is propitiatory only. By contrast, the Neanderthals have a taboo against killing anything, and their reverence for Oa, the Earth Mother, is gentle and numinous in quality.

As in *Lord of the Flies*, the conclusion is formed by an ironic reversal—the reader suddenly sees from the humans' perspective. The last line reads, "He could not see if the line of darkness had an ending." It is a question Golding is posing: Has the darkness of the human heart an end?

Golding's technique is remarkable in the novel: He succeeds in convincing the reader that primitive consciousness could have looked like this. He has had to choose language that conveys that consciousness, yet is articulate enough to engage one imaginatively so that one respects the Neanderthals. He explores the transition from intuition and pictorial thinking to analogous and metaphoric thought. The ironic treatment of *Homo sapiens* is done also through the limits of Neanderthal perceptions and consciousness. Unfortunately, humans, as fallen creatures, can supply all too easily the language for the evil that the Neanderthals lack.

PINCHER MARTIN

Golding's third novel, *Pincher Martin* (first published in the United States as *The Two Deaths of Christopher Martin*), returns to the desert-island tradition. The immediate dialectic is perhaps with Robinson Crusoe, the sailor who single-handedly carves out an island home by the strength of his will aided by his faith. Pincher Martin is here the faithless antihero, although this is not immediately apparent. He, like Crusoe, appears to survive a wreck (Martin's destroyer is torpedoed during the war); he kicks off seaboots and swims to a lonely island-rock in the Atlantic. With tremendous strength of will, he appears to survive by eating raw shellfish, making rescue signals, forcing an enema into himself, and keeping sane and purposeful.

In the end, however, his sanity appears to disintegrate. Almost to the end it is quite possible to believe that Christopher Martin finally succumbs to madness and death only after a heroic, indeed Promethean, struggle against Fate and the elements. The last chapter, however, presents an even greater reversal than those in the first two novels, dispelling all of this as a false reading: Martin's drowned body is found washed up on a Scottish island with his seaboots still on his feet. In other words, the episode on the rock never actually took place. The reading of *Pincher Martin* thus becomes deliberately problematic in a theological sense. The rock must be an illusion, an effort of the will indeed, but an effort after physical death. Yet it is not that all of one's life flashes in front of one while one drowns, though that does happen with Martin's sordid memories of his lust, greed, and terror. It is more that the text is formed by Martin's ongoing dialectic with, or rather against, his destiny, which he sees as annihilation. An unnameable god is identified with the terror and darkness of the cellar of his childhood memories. His will, in its Promethean pride, is creating its own alternative. Theologically, this alternative can only be Purgatory or Hell, since it is clearly not heaven. Satan in *Paradise Lost* says,

"Myself am Hell": Strictly, this is Martin's position, since he refuses the purgatorial possibilities in the final revelation of God, with his mouthless cry of "I shit on your heaven!" God, in his compassion, strikes Martin into annihilation with his "black lightning."

Free Fall

Golding's first three novels hardly suggested that he was writing from within any central tradition of the British novel. All three are highly original in plot, for all of their dialectic with existing texts, and in style and technique. In his next novel, *Free Fall*, Golding writes much more recognizably within the tradition of both the *Bildungsroman* (the novel of character formation) and the *Künstlerroman* (the novel of artistic development). Sammy Mountjoy, a famous artist, is investigating his past life, but with the question in mind, "When did I lose my freedom?" The question is not in itself necessarily theological, but Sammy's search is conducted in specifically theological categories.

It has been suggested that the literary dialectic is with Albert Camus's *La Chute* (1956; *The Fall*, 1957), a novella published some three years earlier. Camus's existentialism sees no possibility of redemption or regeneration once the question has been answered; his protagonist uses the question, in fact, to gain power over others by exploiting their guilt, so the whole search would seem inauthentic. Golding sees such a search as vital: His position seems to be that no person is born in sin, or fallen, but inevitably at some stage, each person chooses knowingly to sin. At that moment he falls and loses his freedom to choose. The only possibility of redemption is to recognize that moment, to turn from it, and to cry out, "Help me!"

This is Sammy's cry when he is locked in a German prisoner-of-war camp and interrogated. His physical release from his cell is also a spiritual release, a moment of revelation described in Pentecostal terms of renewal and a new artistic vision. His moment of fall, which he discovers only near the end of the book (which is here culmination rather than reversal), was when he chose to seduce Beatrice (the name of Dante's beloved inspiration also), whatever the cost and despite a warning that "sooner or later the sacrifice is always regretted."

Other theological perspectives are introduced. Two of Sammy's teachers form an opposition: the rational, humanistic, likable Nick Shales and the religious, intense, but arrogant Miss Pringle. Sammy is caught in the middle, wanting to affirm the spiritual but drawn to the materialist. The dilemma goes back in the English novel to George Eliot. Though Golding cannot accept Eliot's moral agnosticism, he has to accept her inexorable moral law of cause and effect: Sammy's seduction of Beatrice has left her witless and insane. The scene in the prison cell is balanced by the scene in the mental institution. Redemption costs; the past remains. The fall may be arrested and even reversed, but only through self-knowledge and full confession.

In *Free Fall*, Golding chose for the first time to use first-person narrative. Before that he had adopted a third-person narrative technique that stayed very close to the consciousness of the protagonists. In *The Spire*, Golding could be said to have perfected this latter technique. Events are seen not only through the eyes of Dean Jocelin but also in his language and thought processes. As in Henrik Ibsen's *Bygmester Solness* (1892; *The Master Builder*, 1893), Golding's protagonist has an obsessive drive to construct a church tower, or rather a spire on a tower, for his cathedral lacks both. (Inevitably one takes the cathedral to be Salisbury, whose medieval history is almost identical, although it is not named.) Ibsen's play deals with the motivation for such an obsession, the price to be paid, and the spiritual conflicts. Golding, however, is not so much in a dialectic situation with the Ibsen play as using it as his base, agreeing with Ibsen when the latter talks of "the power of ideals to kill." At the end of the novel, the spire has been built in the face of tremendous technical difficulties, but Jocelin lies dying, the caretaker and his wife have been killed, the master builder, Roger, is a broken man, and the whole life of the cathedral has been disrupted.

Thus Golding raises the question of cost again: What is the cost of progress? Is it progress? The power of the book is that these questions can be answered in many different ways, and each way searches out new richness from the text. The patterning of moral and theological structures allows for almost endless combinations. The novel can also be read in terms of the cost of art—the permanence of art witnessing to humanity's spirituality and vision, as against the Freudian view of art as sublimation and neurotic outlet, the price of civilization.

By staying very close to Jocelin's consciousness, the reader perceives only slowly, as he does, that much of his motivation and drive is not quite as visionary and spiritual as he first thinks. Freudian symbolism and imagery increasingly suggest sexual sublimation, especially centered on Goody Pangall, whom he calls "his daughter in God." In fact, much later one learns that he received his appointment only because his aunt was the king's mistress for a while. Jocelin manipulates people more and more consciously to get the building done and chooses, perhaps unconsciously at first, to ignore the damage to people, especially the four people he regards as his "pillars" to the spire. Ironically, he too is a pillar, and he damages himself, physically, emotionally, and spiritually (he is almost unable to pray by the end, and has no confessor). Yet despite all the false motives, the novel suggests powerfully that there really has been a true vision that has been effected, even if marred by humanity's fallenness and "total depravity," every part affected by the fall.

THE SPIRE

The language of *The Spire* is the most poetic that Golding attempted. The density of imagery, recurring motifs, and symbolism both psychological and theological blend into marvelous rhythms of ecstasy and horror. The interweaving of inner monologue, dialogue, and narrative dissolves the traditional tight bounds of time and space of the novel form, to create an impassioned intensity where the theological dialectic takes place, not with another text, but within the levels of the moral, spiritual, and metaphoric consciousness of the text itself.

THE PYRAMID

After the verbal pyrotechnics of *The Spire*, Golding's next novel, *The Pyramid*, seems very flat, despite its title. It returns to *Free Fall* in its use of first-person narrative, to a modified form of its structure (flashbacks and memories to provide a personal

pattern), and to contemporary social comedy, strongly echoing Anthony Trollope. The language is spare and unadorned, as perhaps befits the protagonist, Olly, who, unlike Sammy Mountjoy, has turned away from art and spirit to become *un homme moyen sensual*. His life has become a defense against love, but as a petit bourgeois he has been protected against Sammy's traumatic upbringing, and so one feels little sympathy for him. Theological and moral dialectic is muted, and the social commentary and comedy have been better done by other novelists, although a few critics have made out a case for a rather more complex structuring than is at first evident.

DARKNESS VISIBLE

Perhaps the flatness of the book suggests that Golding had for the time being run out of impetus. Only two novellas were published in the next twelve years, and then, quite unexpectedly, *Darkness Visible* appeared. In some ways it echoes Charles Williams, the writer of a number of religious allegorical novels in the 1930's and 1940's. The reality of spiritual realms of light and darkness is made by Golding as explicitly as by Williams, especially in Matty, the "holy fool." Yet Golding never quite steps into allegory, any more than he did in his first novel. His awareness of good and evil takes on a concreteness that owes much to Joseph Conrad. Much of the feel of the novel is Dickensian, if not its structure: The grotesque serves to demonstrate the "foolishness of the wise," as with Charles Dickens.

The book divides into three parts centering on Matty, orphaned and hideously burned in the bombing of London during the war. At times he keeps a journal and thus moves the narrative into the first person. The second part, by contrast, focuses on Sophy, the sophisticated twin daughter of a professional chess-player (the rationalist), and overwhelmingly exposes the rootlessness and anomie of both contemporary youth culture and the post-1960's bourgeoisie (the children of Olly's generation). The third part concerns a bizarre kidnapping plot where Matty and Sophy nearly meet as adversaries; this is the "darkness visible" (the title coming from the hell of *Paradise Lost*). The end remains ambiguous. Golding attempts a reversal again: The kidnap has been partially successful. Matty has not been able to protect the victims, nor Sophy to complete her scheme, but still children are kidnapped.

Central themes emerge: childhood and innocence corrupted; singleness of purpose, which can be either for good or for evil (contrast also Milton's single and double darkness in *Comus*, 1634); and the foolishness of the world's wisdom. Entropy is a key word, and Golding, much more strongly than hitherto, comments on the decline of Great Britain. Above all, however, Golding's role as a novelist of transcendence is reemphasized: Moments of revelation are the significant moments of knowledge. Unfortunately, revelation can come from dark powers as well as from those of the light. Ultimately, Golding's vision is Miltonic, as has been suggested. The theological dialectic is revealed as that between the children of light and the children of darkness.

RITES OF PASSAGE

When *Rites of Passage* followed *Darkness Visible* one year later, Golding had no intention of writing a trilogy (now generally called *To the Ends of the Earth: A Sea Trilogy*). It was only later he realized that he had "left all those poor sods in the middle of the sea and needed to get them to Australia." The trilogy was well received, perhaps because the plot and themes are relatively straightforward and unambiguous, and the social comedy is more obvious than the theological dialectic. The trilogy fits well into the *Bildungsroman* tradition of Dickens's *Great Expectations* (1860-1861), in that it follows the education of a snob, Edmund Talbot, who, under the patronage of an aristocratic and influential godfather, is embarking on a political career by taking up an appointment in the new colony of New South Wales, Australia, in 1810. It is also enlivened by Golding's wide knowledge of sailing ships and life at sea; the trilogy is the fullest literary expression of this interest he has allowed himself.

The narrative proceeds leisurely in the first person as Edmund decides to keep a diary. In *Rites of Passage*, the plot focuses on the death of one of the passengers, a ridiculous young clergyman, the Reverend Robert James Colley. He is made the butt of everyone's fun, including that of the ordinary sailors. As

the result of the shame of a joke, where he is made drunk and then engages in homosexual activities, he more or less wills himself to die. Captain Anderson covers up the incident—at which Edmund, for the first time, feels moral outrage and vows to expose the captain to his godfather when he can. The moral protest is vitiated, however, by Edmund's use of power and privilege.

CLOSE QUARTERS

In *Close Quarters*, Edmund's education continues. As conditions on board ship deteriorate, he increases in stature, losing his aristocratic bearing and becoming willing to mix socially. His relationship with Summers, the most morally aware of the ship's lieutenants, is good for him in particular. He also shows himself sensitive: He weeps at a woman's song, he falls in love (as opposed to the lust in *Rites of Passage*), and he admires Colley's written style (Colley, too, has left behind a journal). He suffers physically and shows courage. His falling in love is delightfully described, quite unselfconsciously. He learns, too, the limits of his power: The elements control everything. The speed of the ship runs down as weeds grow on its underside, reintroducing the entropy motif of *Darkness Visible*. He cannot prevent suicide or death. As the novel proceeds, the "ship of fools" motif of late medieval literature becomes very strong. Edmund is no more and no less a fool than the others.

FIRE DOWN BELOW

Fire Down Below closes the trilogy as the ship docks in Sidney Cove, and Edmund is reunited happily with the young lady he met. The ending seems to be social comedy, until one realizes that Summers's fear, that a fire lit below decks to forge a metal band around a broken mast is still smoldering, is proved true. The anchored ship bursts into flame, and Summers is killed, having just been given promotion, partly through Edmund's efforts. Despite this tragedy, the ending is Dickensian, for the voyage has turned into a quest for love for Edmund, and love has helped mark his way with moral landmarks. Edmund has learned much, although at the end he has still far to go. The ending is perhaps the most mellow of all Golding's endings: If Australia is not "the new Jerusalem," it is not hell either, and if Edmund lacks spirituality, he is yet more than *un homme moyen sensual*.

THE PAPER MEN

The Paper Men is, like *Free Fall*, a *Künstlerroman*. The style is much more akin to that of twentieth century American confessional literature, especially Saul Bellow's. Golding's Wilfred Barclay could easily be a Henderson or a Herzog, with the same energetic, somewhat zany style, and with the themes of flight and pursuit in a frantic search for identity. Unusually for Golding, the novel seems to be repeating themes and structures, if not style, and perhaps for that reason has not made the same impact as his other novels. Wilfred's revelation of the transcendent in an ambiguous spiritual experience of Christ (or Pluto) marks the high point of the novel.

THE DOUBLE TONGUE

Golding's final novel, *The Double Tongue*, was still in its third draft at the time of his death. For the first time he uses a female first-person voice; also for the first time, there is a classical Greek setting. Arieka is the prophetess, or "Pythia," of the renowned Delphic oracle, but during a period of its decline after the Roman occupation. She tells of her own calling, her first experience of the prophetic, and of the continuing marginalization of the oracle. The male presence is represented by Ionides, the high priest of Zeus and master in charge of the sacred complex of Delphi and its wider network. The only other full character is the slave-librarian, Perseus.

The style of the novel is sparer and more relaxed than that of Golding's earlier novels, with few characters and minimal plot. Its interest lies, as in *The Paper Men*, with the nature of epiphany and with whether the experience of transcendence actualizes anything of significance in an increasingly secular world. The political genius of Rome, and even the literary legacy of the Ancient Greek writers, seem much more powerful influences. The sacred is reduced almost to superstition: The questions posed to the oracle become more and more trivial.

Ionides, while institutionally having to acknowledge the sacred, behaves as if the human spirit is the ultimate source of the prophetic. Arieka, having been siezed, or "raped," by Dionysos, the god of prophecy, knows the truth to be otherwise, but even she increasingly feels that her prophetic gift has ceased to be supernatural and has become a natural expression of her human wisdom. In a way, this concern with the prophetic can be traced back to Simon in *The Lord of the Flies*, and then to the form of the *Künstlerroman*. Unlike the latter, however, the context here is specifically sacred, and it would be a mistake to deconstruct the novel in terms of the nature of artistic inspiration. Nevertheless, the problematic nature of inspiration, whether divine or poetic, is as real to Golding in his last novel as in, say, *The Spire*.

The setting of a declining Greece continues the concern with entropy so powerfully expressed in *Darkness Visible*. Signs of cultural entropy include the growth of "copying" manuscripts rather than creating texts, the marginalization of the transcendent, and the *trahison des clercs*—Ionides is found to be plotting a pathetic revolt against Roman hegemony. Politics has undermined any integrity he had.

There would not appear to be a specific subtext with which Golding is arguing. *The Double Tongue* bears remarkable similarities to C. S. Lewis's final, and most literary, novel, *Till We Have Faces* (1956), also set in classical Greek times. In both, a female consciousness aware of its own physical ugliness, yet possessing real power, undergoes a spiritual journey with multifarious symbolic levels. Lewis's novel, however, ends with epiphany as closure; Golding's begins with it, and the rest of the novel seeks ambiguously to give it meaning. Golding's epiphany here is the god's laughter, at least that laughter of which Arieka is aware.

Although each Golding novel, with a few exceptions, is a new "raid on the inarticulate," certain thematic and technical features remain constant over the years. Golding's moral and didactic concerns consistently sought theological grounding out of which to construct a critique of the lostness and fallenness of humankind, and specifically of contemporary Western civilization, with its spiritual bankruptcy. In this quest there is a line of continuity back to George Eliot and Charles Dickens in the English novel tradition. In his affirmation of the primacy of the spiritual over the material he echoes not only them but also, in different ways, Thomas Hardy and D. H. Lawrence. In his vision of the darkness of the human soul, unenlightened by any transcendent revelation, he follows Joseph Conrad.

He also seeks, as did E. M. Forster and Lawrence, to find a style that escapes the materiality of prose and attains to the revelatory transcendence of poetry. The result is usually dramatic, incarnational metaphors and motifs. The mode is usually confessional, almost Augustinian at times, coming from a single consciousness, though often with a sudden reversal at the end to sustain an ambiguous dialectic.

There is in Golding no articulated framework of beliefs: Transcendence lies ultimately beyond the articulate. God is there, and revelation is not only possible but indeed necessary and salvific. Yet the revelation remains ambiguous, fleeting, and numinous, rather than normative. In the end, this often means that Golding's social critique, of the moral entropy of Britain in particular, comes over more powerfully than the darkness that is the refusal of the terror of believing in God.

David Barratt

OTHER MAJOR WORKS

SHORT FICTION: *The Scorpion God*, 1971.

PLAY: *The Brass Butterfly*, pr., pb. 1958.

RADIO PLAYS: *Miss Pulkinhorn*, 1960; *Break My Heart*, 1962.

POETRY: *Poems*, 1934.

NONFICTION: *The Hot Gates and Other Occasional Pieces*, 1965; *A Moving Target*, 1982; *An Egyptian Journal*, 1985.

BIBLIOGRAPHY

Baker, James R., ed. *Critical Essays on William Golding*. Boston: G. K. Hall, 1988. A collection of the best essays on Golding's novels through *The Paper Men*. It also includes Golding's Nobel Lecture and an essay on trends in Golding criticism.

Bloom, Harold, ed. *Lord of the Flies*. Broomall, Pa.: Chelsea House, 1998. Of the many collections of essays on Golding's best-known novel, this is probably the best.

Boyd, S. J. *The Novels of William Golding*. New York: St. Martin's Press, 1988. Provides a chapter on each of Golding's novels through *The Paper Men*. Includes a full bibliography.

Dick, Bernard F. *William Golding*. Boston: Twayne, 1987. Excellent introduction to Golding's life and works.

Dickson, L. L. *The Modern Allegories of William Golding*. Tampa: University of Southern Florida Press, 1990. Renewed theoretical interest in fantasy and allegory have produced this reading of Golding's novels, suggesting a useful balance to earlier studies that looked to psychological realism.

Gindin, James. *William Golding*. Basingstoke, England: Macmillan, 1988. Golding's novels are paired in essays that compare them. Additional chapters examine themes in Golding's work and its critical reception.

Kinkead-Weekes, Mark, and Ian Gregor. *William Golding: A Critical Study*. New York: Harcourt, Brace & World, 1967. Still one of the standard critical accounts of Golding. A full analysis of the first five novels, showing imaginative development and interconnection. An added chapter deals with three later novels.

McCarron, Kevin. *The Coincidence of Opposites: William Golding's Later Fiction*. Sheffield, England: Sheffield Academic Press, 1995. Analyzes Golding's late works, from *Darkness Visible* to *Fire Down Below*.

Page, Norman, ed. *William Golding: Novels, 1954-1967*. New York: Macmillan, 1985. Part of the excellent Casebook series, this volume consists of an introductory survey, several general essays on Golding's earlier work, and eight pieces on specific novels through *The Pyramid*.

Redpath, Philip. *William Golding: A Structural Reading of His Fiction*. Totowa, N.J.: Barnes & Noble, 1986. Redpath explores the way the novels create meaning, especially through their structures. The novels are treated thematically, not chronologically as in most studies. The final chapter offers suggestions for the future of Golding criticism.

OLIVER GOLDSMITH

Born: Pallas, County Longford(?), Ireland; November 10, 1728 or 1730
Died: London, England; April 4, 1774

PRINCIPAL LONG FICTION

The Citizen of the World, 1762 (collection of essays first published in *The Public Ledger*, 1760-1761)
The Vicar of Wakefield, 1766

OTHER LITERARY FORMS

Oliver Goldsmith contributed significantly to several literary genres. His works of poetry include *The Traveller: Or, A Prospect of Society* (1764) and *The Deserted Village* (1770), a classic elegiac poem of rural life. He wrote the biographies *Memoirs of M. de Voltaire* (1761), particularly interesting for its anecdotes, and *The Life of Richard Nash of Bath* (1762), especially valuable as a study in the social history of the period. Goldsmith developed principles of literary criticism in *An Enquiry into the Present State of Polite Learning in Europe* (1759), a history of literature in which he laments the decline of letters and morals in his own day. Specimens of his literary journalism are found in *Essays. By Mr Goldsmith* (1765), which includes well-written humorous studies of London society. He wrote two comic plays, *The Good-Natured-Man* (1768) and *She Stoops to Conquer: Or, The Mistakes of a Night* (1773), a rollicking lampoon of the sentimental comedy then in vogue, which is still performed today. In addition, Goldsmith published translations, histories, and even a natural history, *An History of the Earth, and Animated Nature* (1774), containing some quaint descriptions of animals.

ACHIEVEMENTS

Goldsmith's contemporaries and posterity have been somewhat ambivalent about his literary stature, which is epitomized in English writer Samuel Johnson's estimate of him: "Goldsmith was a man who, whatever he wrote, did it better than any other man

could do." However, Johnson demurred on Goldsmith's *The Vicar of Wakefield*, judging it "very faulty." Yet there can be little dispute over critic A. Lytton Sells's judgment that Goldsmith's "versatility was the most remarkable of his gifts."

Although the novel *The Vicar of Wakefield* has usually been considered his best work, Goldsmith despised the novelist's art and regarded himself principally as a poet. His most famous poem is the reflective and melancholic *The Deserted Village*, a serious piece in heroic couplets; however, perhaps his real poetic gift was for humorous verse, such as *The Haunch of Venison* (1776) and *Retaliation* (1774). Indeed, humor and wit are conspicuous in all his major works: There is the gentle irony of *The Vicar of Wakefield*, the comic portraits and satirical observations in *The Citizen of the World*, and the outright farce of *She Stoops to Conquer*.

Goldsmith was not a Romantic but a classicist by temperament, whose taste was molded by the Latin classics, the Augustan poetry of John Dryden and Alexander Pope, and seventeenth century French literature, and for whom the canons of criticism laid down by Nicolas Boileau and Voltaire were au-

(Library of Congress)

thoritative. Reflecting that background, Goldsmith's style is, in Johnson's words, "noble, elegant, and graceful."

BIOGRAPHY

Oliver Goldsmith was born of English stock to Ann Jones and the Reverend Charles Goldsmith, an Anglican curate. He first attended the village school of Lissoy and was taught by Thomas Byrne, a veteran of the War of the Spanish Sucession. Byrne, a versifier who regaled his pupils with stories and legends of old Irish heroes, perhaps inspired Goldsmith with his love of poetry, imaginative romance, and adventure. In 1747, Goldsmith attended Patrick Hughes's school at Edgeworthstown, where he received a thorough grounding in the Latin classics. While there he probably first heard Turlogh O'Carolan, "the last of the bards," whose minstrelsy left a lasting impression on him. In 1745, he entered Trinity College, Dublin, as a sizar, a position which required him to do menial work in exchange for room, board, and tuition. Goldsmith earned his B.A. degree in either 1749 or 1750. In 1752, he journeyed to Edinburgh to study medicine, pursuing his medical studies in Leyden in 1754. The next year he set out on a grand tour of the Continent. In February, 1756, he arrived in London, where he briefly taught in Dr. Milner's school for nonconformists and eked out a living doing hack writing.

A reversal of his fortune occurred in 1759, with the publication of his first substantial work, *An Enquiry into the Present State of Polite Learning in Europe*. Goldsmith subsequently befriended such luminaries as the great critic and writer Johnson, the Scottish novelist Tobias Smollett, the actor David Garrick, the writer and statesman Sir Edmund Burke, and the aesthetician and portraitist Sir Joshua Reynolds. In 1763, they formed themselves into the famous Literary Club, which is memorialized in James Boswell's great biography of Johnson. Goldsmith died in 1774, possibly of Bright's disease exacerbated by worry over debts, and was buried in Temple Churchyard. Two years later, the Club erected a monument to him in Poet's Corner of Westminster Abbey, for which Johnson wrote an inscription.

ANALYSIS

Themes that run through Goldsmith's long fiction are his philosophical inquiries into human nature, the problem of evil, the vying of the good and the bad within the human breast, and the conflict between "reason and appetite." His fiction addresses at its deepest level the perennial problem of theodicy, or why God allows the innocent to suffer so grievously. Lien Chi in *The Citizen of the World* exclaims, "Oh, for the reason of our creation; or why we were created to be thus unhappy!" Dr. Primrose in *The Vicar of Wakefield* ruminates, "When I reflect on the distribution of good and evil here below, I find that much has been given man to enjoy, yet still more to suffer." Both come to terms with the conundrum of evil practically, by resolving, in Lien Chi's words, "not to stand unmoved at distress, but endeavour to turn every disaster to our own advantage."

THE CITIZEN OF THE WORLD

The ninety-eight essays comprising *The Citizen of the World* were originally published as the "Chinese Letters" in various issues of *The Public Ledger* from January 24, 1760, to August 14, 1761. They were subsequently collated and published in book form in 1762. These essays purport to be letters from Lien Chi Altangi, a Mandarin philosopher from Peking who is visiting London, to his son Hingpo and to Fum Hoam, first President of the Ceremonial Academy of Peking. What qualifies this work as long fiction are the well-delineated characters it creates and the interwoven stories it relates The principal character is Lien Chi, a type made familiar in the eighteenth century by Charles de Montesquieu's *Lettres persanes* (1721; *Persian Letters*, 1722). Lien Chi represents the man who, through travel, has overcome provincialism and prejudice and has achieved a cosmopolitan outlook. More specifically, perhaps, he represents the sociable, sanguine, and rational side of Goldsmith, who himself had traveled extensively in Europe.

To reinforce the notion that these are the letters of a Chinese man, Goldsmith studs them with Chinese idioms and makes references throughout to Asian beliefs, manners, and customs. Lien Chi cites the philosopher Confucius, and he compares the enlightenment of the East with the ignorance and folly of the West. *The Citizen of the World* capitalizes on the enthusiasm in eighteenth century England for anything Eastern—particularly Chinese—in the way of literature, fashion, design, and art, a vogue which Goldsmith satirizes through the bemused observations of Lien Chi.

Through the character of Lien Chi, a naïve but philosophically astute observer of the human scene, Goldsmith presents a full-blown satire of English society (reminiscent of his compatriot Jonathan Swift's *Gulliver's Travels* [1726], but not so savage). In his letters, Lien Chi gives his impressions of the English, particularly of London society—their institutions, traditions, customs, habits, manners, foibles, and follies. He describes for readers a series of charming and funny pictures of London life in the eighteenth century, the literary equivalent of a William Hogarth painting. He shows us the coffeehouses, literary clubs, theaters, parks and pleasure gardens, churches, and private homes. Two scenes are particularly memorable: In one, Lien Chi describes a church service at St. Paul's Cathedral, where he mistakes the organ for an idol and its music for an oracle. In another scene, he attends a dinner for some clergy of the Church of England and is shocked to find that their sole topic of conversation is nothing more spiritual than the merits of the victuals they are intent on devouring. Aside from the entertainment and edification they afford, these letters are a document in social history, much like Samuel Pepys's diary.

While touring Westminster Abbey, Lien Chi meets and befriends the Man in Black, who represents the "melancholy man," a stock character of the Renaissance. He more particularly can be seen to represent Goldsmith's introverted and melancholy side. Through the Man in Black, Lien Chi meets Beau Tibbs, "an important little trifler" who is a rather shabby, snobbish, and pathetic fop who lives by flattering the rich and the famous. A particularly comic scene describes the visit of Lien Chi, the Man in Black, the pawnbroker's widow, Beau Tibbs, and his wife to Vauxhall Gardens. The Tibbses insist upon having supper in "a genteel box" where they can both see and be seen. The pawnbroker's widow,

the Man in Black's companion, heartily enjoys the meal, but Mrs. Tibbs detests it, comparing it unfavorably to a supper she and her husband lately had with a nobleman. Mrs. Tibbs is asked to sing but coyly declines; however, with repeated entreaties she obliges. During her song, an official announces that the waterworks are about to begin, which the widow is especially bent on seeing. Mrs. Tibbs, however, continues her song, oblivious to the discomfort she is causing, right through to the end of the waterworks. Goldsmith here anticipates Charles Dickens in his comic portrayal of character. In addition to the stories featuring the above characters, there are Asian fables interspersed throughout the book, inspired no doubt by English translations of the *The Arabian Nights' Entertainments* (fifteenth century).

The *British Magazine* aptly described *The Citizen of the World* as "light, agreeable summer reading, partly original, partly borrowed." Sells regards the work as fundamentally a parody of the genre of satiric letters, to which Montesquieu and Jean-Baptiste de Boyer had earlier contributed. It reveals Goldsmith at the top of his form as a humorist, satirist, and ironist.

THE VICAR OF WAKEFIELD

The Vicar of Wakefield, Goldsmith's only true novel, was published in 1766. It is a first-person narrative set in eighteenth century Yorkshire. It is largely autobiographical, with Dr. Primrose modeled on Goldsmith's father and brother, and George modeled on Goldsmith himself. It was likely intended to satirize the then-fashionable sentimental novel, particularly Laurence Sterne's *Tristram Shandy* (1759-1767). Its style and conventions, such as the digressions, charming pastoral scenes, and mistaken identities, are those of the eighteenth century English novel.

Dr. Charles Primrose, the vicar, narrates the story of his family's misfortunes. In addition to his wife, there are six children, among whom George, Olivia, and Sophia figure most prominently in the story. The vicar loses most of his inherited wealth to an unscrupulous banker, necessitating the removal of him and his family to a humbler abode. Their new landlord is Squire Thornhill, a notorious rake, whose uncle is

Sir William Thornhill, a legendary benefactor. There they are befriended by a Mr. Burchell and cheated by an Ephraim Jenkinson.

Olivia is then abducted. After a search, her father finds her in an inn, where she informs him that the squire had arranged her abduction and married her, as he had other women, in a false ceremony. The squire visits and invites Olivia to his wedding with a Miss Wilmot, assuring Olivia that he will find her a suitable husband. Dr. Primrose is outraged, insisting that he would sanction only the squire's marriage to Olivia. He is subsequently informed of Olivia's death and of Sophia's abduction. Presently Mr. Burchell enters with Sophia, whom he had rescued from her abductor. It is now that Mr. Burchell reveals his true identity as Sir William Thornhill. Witnesses testify that the squire had falsely married Olivia and was complicit in Sophia's abduction. However, on the occasion of the squire's marriage to Olivia, the squire was tricked by Jenkinson with a real priest and marriage license. Jenkinson produces both the valid license and Olivia, having told Dr. Primrose that Olivia was dead in order to induce him to submit to the squire's terms and gain his release from prison.

The Vicar of Wakefield can be read on many levels. First, it is a charming idyll depicting the joys of country life. Second, it dramatizes the practical working-out of virtues such as benevolence and vices such as imprudence. Third, it severely tests seventeenth century German philosopher Gottfried Wilhelm Leibniz's dictum that we live in the best of all possible worlds where all things ultimately work for good. Thus, *The Vicar of Wakefield* is a philosophical romance, like Voltaire's *Candide* (1759) and Johnson's *Rasselas* (1759), which challenges the shallow optimism of the Enlightenment.

The *Vicar of Wakefield* has been criticized for its overly sentimentalized and idealized picture of English country life, its virtuous characters whose displays of courage in the face of adversity strain credulity, and its villains bereft of any redeeming virtue. However, some commentators see these apparent faults as being integral to Goldsmith's ironic intention. E. A. Baker was the first to recognize that the work is ironic and comic. Robert Hopkins went fur-

ther by claiming that Goldsmith intended Dr. Primrose "to satirise the complacency and materialism of a type of clergy."

Richard A. Spurgeon Hall

OTHER MAJOR WORKS

PLAYS: *The Good Natured-Man*, pr., pb. 1768; *She Stoops to Conquer: Or, The Mistakes of a Night*, pr., pb. 1773.

POETRY: "An Elegy on the Glory of Her Sex: Mrs. Mary Blaize," 1759; "The Logicians Refuted," 1759; *The Traveller: Or, A Prospect of Society*, 1764; "Edwin and Angelina," 1765; "An Elegy on the Death of a Mad Dog," 1766; *The Deserted Village*, 1770; "Threnodia Augustalis," 1772; "Retaliation," 1774; *The Haunch of Venison: A Poetical Epistle to Lord Clare*, 1776; "The Captivity: An Oratoria," 1820 (wr. 1764).

NONFICTION: *An Enquiry into the Present State of Polite Learning in Europe*, 1759; *The Bee*, 1759 (essays); *Memoirs of M. de Voltaire*, 1761; *The Life of Richard Nash of Bath*, 1762; *A History of England in a Series of Letters from a Nobleman to His Son*, 1764 (2 volumes); *Essays. By Mr. Goldsmith*, 1765; *Life of Bolingbroke*, 1770; *Life of Parnell*, 1770; *An History of the Earth, and Animated Nature*, 1774 (8 volumes; unfinished).

MISCELLANEOUS: *The Collected Works of Oliver Goldsmith*, 1966 (5 volumes; Arthur Friedman, editor).

BIBLIOGRAPHY

Dixon, Peter. *Oliver Goldsmith Revisited*. Boston: Twayne, 1991. An updated introduction to the life and works of Goldsmith.

Ginger, John. *The Notable Man: The Life and Times of Oliver Goldsmith*. London: Hamilton, 1977. Possibly the most engrossing of the modern biographies of Goldsmith.

Irving, Washington. *Oliver Goldsmith: A Biography*. New York: Putnam, 1849. A biography of one distinguished man of letters by another. Goldsmith and Irving were kindred spirits.

Mikhail, E. H., ed. *Goldsmith: Interviews and Recollections*. New York: St. Martin's Press, 1993.

Contains interviews with Goldsmith's friends and associates. Includes bibliographical references and index.

Sells, A. Lytton. *Oliver Goldsmith: His Life and Works.* New York: Barnes & Noble Books, 1974. The author sets out to remedy the defects in many of the earlier biographies of Goldsmith that omit facts or tend to overlook or diminish his faults. Sells particularly criticizes Goldsmith for plagiarism.

Wardle, Ralph Martin. *Oliver Goldsmith.* Lawrence: University of Kansas Press, 1957. A scholarly and thorough study by one who is sympathetic to Goldsmith.

WITOLD GOMBROWICZ

Born: Małoszyce, Poland; August 4, 1904
Died: Vence, France; July 24, 1969

PRINCIPAL LONG FICTION

Ferdydurke, 1937 (English translation, 1961)
Opetani, 1939 (unfinished; *Possessed: Or, The Secret of Myslotch,* 1980)
Trans-Atlantyk, 1953
Pornografia, 1960 (English translation, 1966)
Kosmos, 1965 (*Cosmos,* 1966)
Three Novels by Witold Gombrowicz, 1978 (includes *Ferdydurke, Pornografia,* and *Cosmos*)

OTHER LITERARY FORMS

In addition to his four principal novels, Witold Gombrowicz was the author of three equally important plays and the monumental three-volume *Dziennik* (1957, 1962, 1967; diary), which represents a unique blend of intimate diary, fiction, and literary or philosophical essay. His literary debut was a 1933 collection of short stories (reedited in an enlarged version in 1957); the genre of the short story, however, appears as marginal in his output. The same is true of literary criticism, which he cultivated most intensely in the 1930's, returning to it only occasion-

ally in the later decades. Throughout his life, he was characteristically preoccupied with commenting upon and explaining his own work; in addition to *Dziennik,* such a self-explanatory purpose is served, more or less directly, by a book-length interview conducted by Dominique de Roux, *Rozmowy z Gombrowiczem* (conversations with Gombrowicz; actually, the writer's own confession published in guise of an interview, 1969; translated as *A Kind of Testament,* 1973) and by an autobiographical book *Wspomnienia polskie: Wędrówki po Argentynie* (Polish reminiscences: wanderings through Argentina), published posthumously in 1977.

ACHIEVEMENTS

The story of Gombrowicz's literary career presents a striking contrast between his nearly lifelong isolation as a writer and the international fame enjoyed by his works after the 1960's. He is universally considered one of the major European novelists and playwrights of the twentieth century, a towering figure in modern Polish literature; his works have been translated into many foreign languages and have occasioned numerous critical analyses. All of this, however, including the coveted Formentor Prize in 1967, came only toward the end of his life, after the sixty-year-old Gombrowicz moved back to Europe from his Argentinian retreat, where he had spent twenty-four years, known only to a handful of his Argentinian admirers and to his enthusiasts in Poland.

The Polish reception of Gombrowicz appears as another paradox. Although his work, as that of an émigré writer, was steadfastly banned by the Communist regime (with the exception of a brief interval in 1957-1958), it was always known in Poland's intellectual circles thanks to the wide circulation of émigré editions. Oddly enough, after the writer's death, it became possible in Poland to stage his plays and publish critical monographs on his work, although his books were still banned until the fall of the Communist regime. This bizarre situation resulted from the fact that Polish authorities apparently had political objections to certain passages of Gombrowicz's diary; the writer specified in his last will that his work not be reprinted in Poland unless in its entirety. In spite of the difficulties that Polish readers faced in obtaining copies of his books, Gombrowicz's reputation in his homeland grew as steadily as it did abroad; his work has exerted a particularly strong influence on the development of recent Polish fiction, drama, and criticism.

BIOGRAPHY

Witold Gombrowicz's life falls into two main phases, separated by his decision in September, 1939, to stay in Argentina, where he was caught by the outbreak of World War II in Europe. He was born in 1904 into the family of a landed proprietor-turned-industrialist; in 1911, his family moved from a country manor in southern Poland to Warsaw. The most rebellious and whimsical child in his family, Gombrowicz nevertheless was graduated from high school and, in 1922, acceding to his father's wish, began to study law at Warsaw University. After he was graduated in 1927, he continued his studies in Paris but soon returned to Poland, where his unorthodox views made it impossible for him to find a job as a lawyer. In all probability, this professional failure hastened his decision to devote himself entirely to writing. In 1933, his first book, a collection of short stories under the provocative title *Pamiętnik z okresu dojrzewania* (a memoir written in puberty), was published to rather skeptical reviews that generally dismissed the book as "immature." Nevertheless, Gombrowicz quickly won recognition in the circles of young writers. By the mid-1930's, he was already enjoying a moderate fame as a colorful personality and fascinating *causeur* as well as an insightful literary critic. It was, however, his first novel, *Ferdydurke*, that became a genuine event of Polish literary life; published in 1937, it provoked a heated critical debate on avant-garde tendencies in modern Polish prose. Before the war, Gombrowicz managed to publish in magazines and journals three more short stories, his first play, *Iwona, księżniczka Burgunda* (1938; *Princess Iwona*, 1969), and an unfinished novel, *Possessed: Or, The Secret of Myslotch*, a Gothic parody that was published pseudonymously as a newspaper series in 1939.

By a strange twist of fortune, only a few weeks before the German invasion of Poland, Gombrowicz took part in a trip of a group of young writers to Argentina. While in Buenos Aires, he learned about the outbreak of war and decided not to return. The first Argentinian years, while offering him inner freedom by cutting off all of his ties and obligations, were also extremely difficult, marked by isolation and financial hardship. To make his living, he took a poorly paid job as a clerk in a Polish bank in Buenos Aires. At the same time, he stubbornly continued his writing and after some time gained recognition—not so much among Polish émigrés, though, as among young Argentinian writers. He returned to the literary scene in 1953 with the novel *Trans-Atlantyk* and the play *Ślub* (*The Marriage*, 1969), issued jointly in a single volume by the émigré publishing house Institut Littéraire in Paris. Also in 1953, he began to publish fragments of his diary in the Institut Littéraire's monthly, *Kultura*. The publication of *Trans-Atlantyk*, a novel dealing satirically with the notion of traditional Polish patriotism, was met with vitriolic attacks from the conservative segment of the émigré community. On the other hand, after 1957-1958, when four books by Gombrowicz had been published in Poland during the short-lived political "thaw," he became almost a cult object for many young writers and critics, who enthusiastically welcomed everything avant-garde and unorthodox after the years of Socialist Realist boredom.

Between 1957 and 1966, Gombrowicz published, through the Institut Littéraire, the rest of his most important books written in exile: two novels, *Pornografia* and *Cosmos*, and the diary in three volumes, the last of which also included his third play, *Operekta* (1966; *Operetta*, 1971). Meanwhile, in 1963, he received a grant from the Rockefeller Foundation and left for Europe. After some time spent in West Berlin (this stay as well as some of Gombrowicz's public statements made him a victim of vicious attacks in the official media in Poland), he moved to Paris and finally settled with his young French wife in the small town of Vence in southern France. The last years of his life were marked by his rapidly growing international fame as well as by his deteriorating health. He died in Vence in 1969, after a long struggle with illness.

ANALYSIS

Seemingly nonsensical and capricious, Witold Gombrowicz's work is revealed, on a closer look, to be based on an amazingly consistent and complex philosophical system, as original as it is profound. Regardless of genre, the writer explores throughout his works the fundamental notions and antinomies which underlie his vision of the human world; in a sense, his novels are modern versions of the philosophical parable, although they are far from being didactic.

What can be called the basic existential experience of Gombrowicz is his awareness of man's solitude and helplessness in confrontation with the powerful pressure of culture—if "culture" is understood in a Freudian sense, as a collective superego that stifles the authentic impulses of the human self. Accordingly, the chief antinomy of Gombrowicz's philosophical system is the omnipresent conflict between the solitary individual and the rest of the human world; the individual's natural need is to remain free, independent, spontaneous, unique, whereas the outside world crams him into the schematic frames of that which is socially and culturally acceptable.

This conviction would appear as not particularly original (in fact, it would seem a mere continuation of the argument of Jean-Jacques Rousseau and the Romantics) were it not for the fact that Gombrowicz immediately counterpoises it with its exact opposite. He is equally aware that, contrary to his need to remain free and unique, the individual also feels constantly the fear of isolation and desires to affirm himself through contacts with other people, through his reflection in the eyes of others. This contradiction is particularly dominant in the case of an artist or writer: He wishes to reveal his individual uniqueness to the audience, but in order to reach the latter and be understood, he has to resort to a "language" of approved convention, which, in turn, destroys his uniqueness. In other words, each manifestation of the artist's freedom-seeking self means his imprisonment in a rigid scheme of finished shapes—and thus, it means his death as an artist.

The situation of an artist, however, is considered by Gombrowicz as only one particularly dramatic version of a more universal paradox of human existence as such. In his view, every individual lives his life in constant suspension between two ideals: "Divinity" and "Youth." Divinity can be understood as Fullness, Completeness, Perfection; Youth is synonymous with Unfulfillment, Spontaneity, Freedom. In yet other terms, the opposition of Divinity versus Youth equals that of Form versus Chaos. The main characters in Gombrowicz's fiction (more often than not, fictional impersonations of himself and his own neurotic obsessions) are always torn between their striving for Form on the one hand and Chaos on the other; or the plot consists of a clash between characters symbolizing Form and those symbolizing Chaos (significantly, the motif of a duel or fight is frequently used in crucial scenes).

This basic opposition takes on many specific shapes. The struggle between Form and Chaos may reveal itself, for example, in its sociological version, in which Aristocracy (or higher classes in general) represents the complete, perfect Form, while Peasantry (or lower classes in general) stands for spontaneous, chaotic Youth. It may also be illustrated by the inequality of civilizations—Western civilization is, in this respect, a symbol of Form, while the "second-rate," "immature" civilizations of countries such as Poland represent Chaos. Finally, the tension between the extremes of Form and Chaos can also be demonstrated on the level of individuals; here, the already shaped personality of an adult is another version of Form, while the still-developing personality of a child or teenager is a symbolic image of Chaos. It is evident that all possible embodiments of the opposition between Form and Chaos have a common denominator in the concept of inequality; each opposed pair can be interpreted as a case of Superiority confronted with Inferiority. According to Gombrowicz, the essence of human existence lies in the fact that the individual strives all of his or her life for Superiority and Form but in fact is not really attracted by these values, since their ultimate attainment would be tantamount to death. Therefore, the individual secretly desires Inferiority and Chaos, because only these extremes offer a chance of freedom. Yet, on the other hand, the ultimate attainment of this other goal would mean isolation, lack of communication, impossibility of affirming one's self-image through its reflection in the eyes of others. In the final analysis, the conflict is insoluble.

It can be, however, partly overcome and contained, if not fully resolved, by artistic creativity. Gombrowicz, as noted above, views the artist as someone who experiences the existential antinomy in a particularly acute way, but the artist has, at the same time, a certain advantage that nobody else has. Even though he cannot avoid the use of Form—if he did, he would not be understood—he can at least be aware of the artificial nature of Form and, as a consequence, he can be free to *play* with it. To play with Form means, in practice, to use it consciously and to make it "visible" instead of concealing it. Accordingly, Gombrowicz's own works are filled with deliberately introduced literary conventions which the reader can recognize instantly—the conventions of the mystery novel, operetta, family chronicle, traditional oral tale, Shakespearean historical drama, or novel of the life of the upper classes. At the same time, the personality of the narrator is usually multilayered: He exists within the world presented by his narration, but he can also at any given moment rise above that reality and his own narration to comment on them, or rise even higher to comment on his own comment, and so forth; in other words, he plays not merely with the conventions of literary genres and styles but also with the very convention of literary discourse.

All of his ambiguity considered, the narrator's point of view in Gombrowicz's novels is, however, stable in one specific sense: As a rule, he represents the author, if not fully identifying himself with Gombrowicz (even to the point of assuming the latter's name). Likewise, the time of the novel's action is always, or at least seems to be, historically specified, and it usually coincides with various phases of Gombrowicz's own life. What is particularly meaningful is the place of the novel's action, usually a single and rather limited setting; the narration more often than not begins with the moment of the narrator's arrival

in a certain place new to him, which he must then explore and comprehend. In the course of such exploration, the narrator is usually confronted with a problem that he is supposed to solve, and thus the next phases of action develop conspicuously along the lines of the traditional detective story or novel of adventure.

What seems to be particularly characteristic of Gombrowicz is that his narrator's relationship with the reality presented is twofold. On the one hand, it is a reality that oppresses him, poses problems to solve, forces him to assume a certain stance or adopt a certain behavior. On the other hand, it is, simultaneously, the narrator himself who attempts to shape reality, to stage and direct events, to manipulate other characters, to impose some sense upon the world that surrounds him. Accordingly, two basic models of fictional plot coexist with each other in Gombrowicz's novels—the model of an *investigation* (in which reality appears to the narrator as a problem to solve) and the model of a *stage-setting* (in which the narrator becomes an active manipulator of reality).

All of this is additionally complicated by the fact that the world presented in Gombrowicz's fiction consists not only of facts, persons, objects, and their mutual relations, but also of *words*, their sounds and their meanings. Words not only serve here as a means to tell the story but also assume, as it were, an independent existence. This particular aspect of Gombrowicz's artistic play has for its object the tension between the order of facts and the order of words, between the meaning of a related situation and the meaning of specific words or expressions in which the situation is related; one can never be sure whether the action will follow the former or the latter semantic line. Sometimes, for example, a word that is central to a specific situation is foregrounded by constant repetition and other stylistic devices to such an extent that it, so to speak, proliferates and begins to function as an independent Form imposed on the Chaos of reality.

FERDYDURKE

This is particularly noticeable in Gombrowicz's first and most famous work of long fiction, *Ferdydurke*, which has been perhaps artistically surpassed by his later novels, yet still remains the most exemplary illustration of his philosophy, his vision of society, his idea of narration, and his use of language. The attacks against this novel from both the Right and the Left in the late 1930's seem, in a sense, understandable, since the novel ridicules all ideologies or, more generally, all socially sanctified attitudes, conventions, or Forms. *Ferdydurke* falls into three sharply divided parts, each of which is preceded by a brief essay or parable. At the outset of the story, the reader meets the narrator (and, at the same time, the main character of the whole novel), a man in his thirties who, like Gombrowicz himself, has published his first book and has been massacred by the critics as an immature and irresponsible youngster. The narrator is torn between his desire to achieve maturity and social acceptance (that is, any Form) and his dislike for various specific Forms which have been imposed on him by others and which he cannot accept as his authentic self. What, actually, is his "authentic" Form? To find an answer, he embarks upon writing another book. Here, however, something unexpected occurs: A certain Professor Pimko, an old-fashioned high school teacher, arrives and literally kidnaps the narrator to put him back in school, as if he were still a teenager.

The subsequent three parts of the novel put the narrator-turned-teenager into three different locales, each of which represents a different kind of petrified, inauthentic Form. After the school sequence, the narrator is placed by Pimko as a subtenant in the house of Mr. and Mrs. Youthful, a middle-aged couple imprisoned, as it were, within their own idea of what is "modern" and "progressive"; finally, he finds himself in a countryside manor where the conservative social distinctions between the upper class and the "boors" are still very much alive. In none of these three places—the school, the "modern" household, the traditional manor—can the narrator feel fully identified with the Form that prevails there, nor can he find an authentic Form of his own. Each of the three plots sooner or later develops into the narrator's attempts to manipulate the people who surround him, which in turn leads each time to a conflict culminating in a grotesque brawl and the narrator's escape. The conflict between Form and Chaos, shown simultaneously in its cultural, social, civilizational, generational, and

sexual dimensions, cannot possibly be resolved—escape is the only solution. Even that, however, proves futile: In the final scene, the escaping narrator winds up in the company of his hosts' young daughter and thus unwillingly contributes to the triumph of yet another hollow Form—the romantic stereotype of lovers' elopement.

TRANS-ATLANTYK

In his subsequent novels, Gombrowicz continued to explore the fundamental problem of Form versus Chaos, illustrating it with even more intricate fictional plots. *Trans-Atlantyk*, a novel ostensibly based on the author's 1939 Argentinian defection, dissects Form in its specific version of patriotic stereotype, while the extreme of Chaos, Freedom, and Youth is identified with a refusal to conform to such a stereotype. There is, perhaps, no other work by Gombrowicz in which language, style, and literary convention would play such a crucial role: A twentieth century story is told here in the masterfully parodied style of an oral tale spoken by a seventeenth century old Polish nobleman.

PORNOGRAFIA and COSMOS

In *Pornografia*, the relationship between Form and Chaos, Divinity and Youth, takes on the shape of a perverse story of a young couple whose love is "stage-set" and "directed" by a pair of older men—all of this against the social and political background of Nazi-occupied Poland. Gombrowicz's last novel, *Cosmos*, is his most metaphysical, although, like everything he wrote, it also reveals his powerful *vis comica* and penchant for the grotesque. The central problem here is nothing less than the nature of external reality as reflected in human consciousness. Is meaning immanent, or is it merely imposed on reality by the human mind? Gombrowicz asks this question by structuring his novel once again upon the model of an investigation and by parodistically referring in its style and construction to the conventions of the mystery story. Like the rest of Gombrowicz's work, *Cosmos* can be read as a mad piece of nonsensical tomfoolery—but it can also be read as a profound philosophical treatise on the most excruciating conflicts of human existence.

Stanisław Barańczak

OTHER MAJOR WORKS

SHORT FICTION: *Pamiętnik z okresu dojrzewania*, 1933; *Bakakaj*, 1957 (includes *Pamiętnik z okresu dojrzewania* and other stories).

PLAYS: *Iwona, księżniczka Burgunda*, pr. 1938, rev. pb. 1958 (*Princess Iwona*, 1969; best known as *Ivona, Princess of Burgundia*); *Ślub*, pb. 1948, rev. pb. 1957 (*The Marriage*, 1969); *Historia*, wr. 1951, pb. 1975; *Operekta*, pb. 1966 (*Operetta*, 1971).

NONFICTION: *Dziennik, 1953-1956*, 1957 (*Diary: Volume 1*, 1988); *Dziennik, 1957-1961*, 1962; *Dziennik, 1961-1966*, 1967; *Sur Dante: Glose*, 1968; *Rozmowy z Gombrowiczem*, 1969 (*A Kind of Testament*, 1973); *Varia*, 1973; *Wspomnienia polskie: Wòdrówki po Argentynie*, 1977.

MISCELLANEOUS: *Dzieła zebrane*, 1969-1977 (11 volumes).

BIBLIOGRAPHY

Barańczak, Stanisław. *Breathing Under Water and Other East European Essays*. Cambridge, Mass.: Harvard University Press, 1990. Contains an essay on Gombrowicz (concentrating on his diaries) by one of the world's foremost scholars of Polish literature.

Boyers, Robert. "Aspects of the Perversion in Gombrowicz's *Pornografia*." *Salmagundi* 17 (Fall, 1971): 19-46. An excellent treatment of sexuality and envy, comparing Gombrowicz to Jean-Paul Sartre and his biographies of Charles Baudelaire and Jean Genet.

_____. "Gombrowicz and *Ferdydurke*: The Tyranny of Form." *Centennial Review* 14 (1970): 284-312. A solid thematic study.

Fletcher, John. *New Directions in Literature: Critical Approaches to a Contemporary Phenomenon*. London: Calder and Boyars, 1968. A brief but informative introduction to *Ferdydurke* and *Pornografia*.

Jelenski, Constantin. "Witold Gombrowicz." *Tri-Quarterly*, Spring, 1967, 37-42. An excellent overview of Gombrowicz's fiction.

Kurczaba, Alex. *Gombrowicz and Frisch: Aspects of a Literary Diary*. Bonn, West Germany: Bouvier Verlag Herbert Grundmann, 1980. This book ex-plores various aspect of Gombrowicz's famous diary. The discussion of his sensibility and literary background make this a valuable work for students of Gombrowicz's fiction. Includes extensive notes and bibliography.

Miłosz, Czesław. *The History of Polish Literature*. London: Macmillan, 1969. An authoritative discussion of Gombrowicz's place in Polish literature by a great poet, critic, and Nobel laureate.

Thompson, Ewa M. *Witold Gombrowicz*. Boston: Twayne, 1979. A solid introductory study, with chapters on Gombrowicz's biography and his short stories, plays, novels, and journals. Additional chapters examine his use of language, his treatment of women, his relationship with other writers, and his vision of the world. Contains a chronology, notes, and an annotated bibliography.

Ziarek, Ewa Plonowska, ed. *Gombrowicz's Grimaces: Modernism, Gender, Nationality*. Albany: State University of New York Press, 1998. Examines all aspects of Gombrowicz's oeuvre. Includes bibliographical references and an index.

N. V. M. GONZALEZ

Born: Romblon, Philippines; September 8, 1915

PRINCIPAL LONG FICTION

The Winds of April, 1940
A Season of Grace, 1956
The Bamboo Dancers, 1959

OTHER LITERARY FORMS

Although N. V. M. Gonzalez traveled widely and taught the craft of writing on several continents, his principal rapport has always been with the farmers and fishermen of his homeland. For such folk, social change over the centuries has been minimal, and their daily lives are attached to unvarying natural cycles. In each of his collections of short stories, Gonzalez found a deceptively simple style appropriate to the tempo of frontier life and the peasant mind set.

Many of his first stories in *Seven Hills Away* (1947) seem more like sketches, reproducing the quiet, sometimes desperate, static lifestyle of the Philippine *kainginero*. On the small islands of Romblon and Mindoro, south of Manila, the landless frontiersman regularly leaves the village barrio in search of land. The wilderness is his if he will clear it by slash-and-burn techniques; yet it can never be cultivated well enough, by these primitive means, to support a large population. The first and last stories in the collection establish an outward movement from a growing settlement by pioneers anxious to find one more uninhabited horizon. Even as the stress falls on small-scale self-reliance, however, the fulfillment of ancestral patterns in the process of pioneering becomes dramatically evident. The animistic minds of the *kaingineros* tell them that nature is unfriendly, but they meet each setback with a stoic lack of surprise and complaint. The style of these stories is stark.

In Gonzalez's next collection, *Children of the Ash-Covered Loam* (1954), the potential for melodrama and self-pity is further undercut by reliance on children and plain women as narrators or central characters. The women are long-suffering and resilient; their own bodies' rhythms have made them knowledgeable about the mysteries of nature. As for the children, they are in the midst of experiencing at first hand the wonders of birth and death, the depletion of innocence, which slowly drains away, and the gentle pace of experience. Contrasted with the enduring virtues of these ordinary people is the sophisticated lack of feeling in Mrs. Bilbao, failed wife and mother, in "Where's My Baby Now?" Too busy with city social obligations, she neglects her family.

A more elaborate contrast controls the 1963 collection, *Look, Stranger, on This Island Now*, as the restless peasants' new horizon becomes the town of Buenavista, in Romblon, and later the commercial centers of the principal Philippine island, Luzon. Disconnected from nature, the townspeople suffer from loneliness and the tensions between their competing needs for companionship and privacy. At best, they achieve momentary consolations. Stories in the second half of the volume express the sense of exile among city-dwellers who have left the rural lifestyle

behind but who have no traditions to guide them in their new life. In *Mindoro and Beyond* (1979), the five stories added to sixteen selected from previous volumes still waver between these poles: integrity, sustained with difficulty among the peasant poor, and the insecurity and corruption which befalls those who desert the land. Especially early in his career, Gonzalez wrote poetry. Though comparatively few and short, the poems found prestigious publications such as *Poetry* magazine and the anthologies *Heart of the Island* (1947), *Philippine Writing: An Anthology* (1953), and *Returning a Borrowed Tongue* (1995).

ACHIEVEMENTS

The paradox of Gonzales is that he gained an international reputation for himself at a variety of intellectual centers, while identifying constantly with the uneducated but folk-wise peasant in the Philippines. His humor is far more subtle than that of Carlos Bulosan, for example, and his social criticism, though very real, is never doctrinaire, never polemical. For the pure portrait of the Filipino as frontier farmer—the dream of every landless tenant during centuries of oppression from Spanish overlords and now from estate holders who are his own countrymen—readers turn to the deceptively simple fiction of Gonzalez. Recognition of the honesty of these peasant images has made both the author and his work required presences in many lands. A 1949 Rockefeller Fellowship led to publication of his stories in a number of distinguished American "little magazines": *Sewanee Review*, *Literature East and West*, *Hopkins Review*, *Pacific Spectator*, *Literary Review*, and *Short Story International*. Gonzalez's work also appeared in such anthologies as *Stories from Many Lands* (1955), *Mentor Book of Modern Asian Literature* (1969), *Asian PEN Anthology* (1966), and *Asian-American Authors* (1972), and, in translation, in anthologies in Malaysia and West Germany.

His tight control of form, contrary to florid Malayan-Spanish traditions, his reliance on a narrative's ability to convey its own meaning without intrusion by the author, and especially his ability to find English constructions which, to the Filipino ear, retain resemblances to the native vernaculars of his characters: All these qualities have influenced numbers of younger writers, who occasionally refer to him as the Anton Chekhov or Ernest Hemingway of the Philippines. For his influence as a writer of fiction, as an essayist, and as a workshop director, he received the Republic Award of Merit (1954), the Republic Cultural Heritage Award (1960), and the Rizal Pro Patria Award (1961), thus fulfilling the earlier promise shown when, in 1940, his first novel won honorable mention in the Commonwealth Literary Awards contest, and, in 1941, his collection of stories, then called *Far Horizons*, shared first prize in the same annual contest.

BIOGRAPHY

Born in 1915 on one of the smaller mid-archipelago Philippine islands, Nestor Vicente Madali Gonzalez was taken as a child to the larger neighboring island of Mindoro by his father, who was a teacher. There, he spent his youth among farmers and fishermen, figures which have dominated his fiction ever since. After being graduated from the University of the Philippines, then in Manila, he turned to writing a newspaper column, as well as a novel and short tales about the people of Mindoro. He was one of the Veronicans, a group of young writers striving for stark and striking imagery. The authenticity of his fiction won him national attention just before Japanese Occupation forces landed on Luzon. When English was practically forbidden by the invaders, Gonzalez and others wrote in Tagalog but brought to the native language new techniques, themes, and theories as an alternative to formulas in conventional literature.

His chance for prominence came in 1947, when the Swallow Press in Denver published his prizewinning stories, *Seven Hills Away*. In 1949, a Rockefeller grant allowed him to visit several writing centers in the United States and to attend both Stanford and Bread Loaf workshops. On his return, he was appointed to the faculty of the state university, which had just been constructed in the temporary capital, Quezon City; there, he taught creative writing and comparative literature for eighteen years. During Carlos P. Romulo's presidency of the university, Gonzalez served as public relations assistant and speech writer to the former ambassador to the United Nations. Although he held no graduate degree, he was tenured on the basis of his distinguished contributions to the national culture as a novelist and short-story writer, as well as editor of the eclectic *Diliman Review* and consultant to Benipayo Press and to Bookmark, which risked nonprofit publication of Philippine literature in order to bring recognition and rewards to young writers. In 1964, he wrote in Rome and the Italian Alps on a second Rockefeller grant. In 1968, he held visiting professorships at both the University of Hong Kong and the University of California at Santa Barbara.

Beginning in 1969, Gonzalez was Professor of English, particularly Third World literature, at California State University in Hayward. In 1977, he served as visiting professor of Asian-American literature at the University of Washington, and in the summer of 1978, after a long absence, he briefly returned to the University of the Philippines as writer-in-residence. One result of that visit was the publication of *Mindoro and Beyond*, a retrospective volume drawn from four decades of his stories, which initiated the Philippine Writers' Series for the University of the Philippines Creative Writing Center. Gonzalez retired from university teaching in 1989.

ANALYSIS

The superiority of N. V. M. Gonzalez's novels lies principally in their ability to provide social realism without submitting to sentimentality, at one extreme, or to any doctrinaire program of violent reform at the other. This same authenticity of character and situation acquits him of the charge of being a mere imitator, even though age-old struggles between peasant and proprietor, between barrio and city values, recur in his work. They do so not because of slavish adherence to literary formulas but because basic social patterns have persisted in Philippine culture for hundreds of years: It is to these patterns that Gonzalez is true, and in response to them that his vision has remained constant.

THE WINDS OF APRIL

Even in his autobiographical first novel, *The Winds of April*, written in his youth, Gonzalez presents attitudes that reappear in his short stories and later novels: an attachment to the array of creatures on land and sea; a respect for the men and women whose lives depend on nature's whims and their own unflagging efforts; and a dream of surmounting these hazards without forgetting them, by moving to cities where opportunities for education and for writing about one's discoveries and their implications abound. At the same time that *The Winds of April* describes the aspirations of the author from birth to young manhood, it captures the hopes of a whole people on the verge of independence from the United States. Virtually all the copies of that novel, along with hopes for a smooth transition to national sovereignty, were destroyed during World War II.

A SEASON OF GRACE

What emerges in *A Season of Grace*, during postwar reconstruction, is a view less naïve but still based on the courage and determination of a people who find in hardship the same promise of life's renewal that the rich volcanic ash of their soil offers their labor. They do not arise abruptly, miraculously, like the phoenix from those ashes, but their right to stand erect is wholly and undeniably earned, if only gradually, painstakingly. The young married couple, Sabel and Doro, who leave the overworked plots of Tara-Poro and the fishing barrio at Alag to claim interior *kaingins* of their own on Mindoro, are in many ways like adult children. The cadences of Gonzalez's prose resemble rituals of survival, marked by seasons of seedtime, caretaking, and harvest. The action encompasses slightly more than one year's cycle in this couple's efforts to restore a wilderness to its garden state, although Gonzalez knows well that slash-and-burn techniques can destroy more than they cultivate. Petty officials requisition several intricately and meticulously woven mats from them. Their merchant landlord Epe Ruda maintains the rule that debts double if they are not repaid in time. Yet after the year covered in the novel, Sabel and Doro are not quite so impoverished as before and they have two male children; they are likely to endure and prevail.

The year has not been one completely filled with favors. Their friend Blas Marte, once debt-free, has become a sharecropper for a usurious rice merchant.

Their own rice sack hangs empty for months, and there are nightmares, premonitions of death and disaster. Multitudes of rats attack their harvest, as greedily bent on taking what is not theirs as are the landlord, the treasurer, and his deputy. Even Sabel and her husband Doro come to blows occasionally, as a result of misunderstanding and exhaustion. She is the more resilient, gentle, contemplative, and naturally good-hearted. Doro is sometimes consumed by his own unending chores. When his wife is seriously ill, he is most concerned with how he will survive without her. He can be impatient, jealous without cause, more erratic than Sabel in growth toward maturity. Yet a contrast clearly is established between these two and their materialistic, childless landlord. The implied emphasis on their compliance rather than on bitter complaint is a sign, from the author, of a resignation nearly religious, an elemental act of faith. At the beginning of a new year, Sabel and Doro begin still another clearing; their infant lies nearby like a seedling, very much part of the stream of the life-force. What seemed a relentless cycle of trial, progress, and frustration has become a slow and painful spiral upward, a combination of change and continuity, of improvement gradual but sure.

THE BAMBOO DANCERS

The true polar opposite to the simple, instinctual peasant such as Doro is not his middle-class landlord but the *ilustrado*, the elitist intellectual portrayed in Gonzalez's *The Bamboo Dancers*. If the wilderness dominates *A Season of Grace*, wasteland imagery permeates the later novel. Ernie Rama is a sculptor who tries to conceal his lack of creativity by wandering through the world. Such is his nature that, wherever he goes on his study grant in the United States, he keeps a distance between himself and others, in order to avoid facing and confessing his own self-alienation. The stargazer at the Vermont writers' conference waves a message which Ernie avoids; the lonely United States Information Service girl in Kyoto whom he planned to meet, disappears; en route to Hiroshima, he is with an interpreter who stays mute; the Japanese switchboard operator and he are mutually unintelligible. Everyone remains a stranger, so quick is Ernie's passage among them, like someone running from an atomic cloud-burst. Despite its scenes in Hiroshima, the novel is less about the unspeakable horror of nuclear war than it is about this deliberate detachment, this maintained silence which aggravates differences and helps cause war.

In his travels, Ernie avoids even his own countrymen, especially the elderly, lest they place some claim on his social conscience. He resembles the barren Fisher King from T. S. Eliot's *The Waste Land* (1922), who is doomed to sterility because of his lack of love, his inability to share. What Ernie fathers in an old acquaintance, Helen Reyes, who has turned to him for emotional warmth, is only a miscarriage. He is at best sexually ambivalent, actually preferring no intimacy under any circumstances with anyone. While Helen's American fiancé, Herb Lane, is involved in the accidental death of a Chinese girl in Taipeh, Ernie is characteristically removed from the scene by sickness. When Herb is murdered as a result of that death, Ernie can only offer abstract sympathy. Persuading Helen to escape to Macao, where perhaps she can purchase rare cosmetics, he contaminates her with his own self-indulgence. Even at the moment of near-drowning, while fishing back in the Philippines, when he cries out to be rescued, it is unclear whether he has learned the importance of others except to satisfy his own impulsive needs. To some extent, the people of Hiroshima, who think exclusively of their own suffering but not of those who were their victims in war, represent this same egocentrism, so opposed to the traditional sense of brotherhood among Filipinos.

The great subtlety of this novel lies in the author's strict dependence on a defective narrator, whose self-deception, contradictions, and confusions become evident through a recurring pattern of nonencounters, as well as through certain symbols. The principal symbol employed by Gonzalez is the national dance, the *tinikling*, in which the object is to maintain a rhythm of rapid movement that prevents the feet from ever being touched by the clash of poles. In the Philippines, the caste of "untouchables" is not the impoverished peasant but the elite leadership, on which society depends so much for patronage, but from which

the masses more commonly have received indifference, cruelty, and betrayal of purpose.

In *The Bamboo Dancers*, as in his short stories and other novels, Gonzalez's characters are discovered rather than explained. They present themselves without comment from the author. Such subtlety and disciplined self-restraint keep Gonzalez's fiction far from the ordinary "literature of protest," which often disregards credibility or complexity of character in order to engage in extensive polemics. Perhaps Gonzalez's constant attentiveness to the manner of speech and even to silence owes much to his culture's reliance, for unobtrusive communication, on courteous consideration of others and on wordless body language. Gonzalez's craft is perfectly expressive of these Asian aspects of Philippine folkways.

Leonard Casper, updated by L. M. Grow

OTHER MAJOR WORKS

SHORT FICTION: *Seven Hills Away*, 1947; *Children of the Ash-Covered Loam*, 1954; *Look, Stranger, on This Island Now*, 1963; *Mindoro and Beyond*, 1979; *The Bread of Salt and Other Stories*, 1993; *A Grammar of Dreams and Other Stories*, 1997.

NONFICTION: *The Father and the Maid: Essays on Filipino Life and Letters*, 1990; *Kalutang: A Filipino in the World*, 1990; *Work on the Mountain*, 1995; *The Novel of Justice: Selected Essays, 1968-1994*, 1996.

BIBLIOGRAPHY

Bernad, Miguel. *Bamboo and the Greenwood Tree.* Manila: Bookmark, 1961. Contrasts the simple nobility of Gonzalez's slash-and-burn farmers in *A Season of Grace* with the directionless elite in *The Bamboo Dancers*. Presents seven pages of the author's own comments on the latter novel.

Casper, Leonard. *New Writing from the Philippines: A Critique and Anthology.* Syracuse, N.Y.: Syracuse University Press, 1966. The chapter on Gonzalez defines the folk quality of pioneers south of Manila, conveyed through the language's severe formal restraint and the slow seasonal growth of these simple farmers. The city-bred central character in *The Bamboo Dancers*, however, is self-centered and unproductive.

De Jesus, Edilberto, Jr. "On This Soil, in This Climate: Growth in the Novels of N. V. M. Gonzalez." In *Brown Heritage*, edited by Antonio G. Manuud. Quezon City: Ateneo de Manila, 1967. Presents a historian's perspective, demonstrating parallels between Philippine society and Gonzalez's novels as subsistence farming has become industrialized.

Gonzalez, N. V. M. *Kalutang: A Filipino in the World*. Manila: Kalikasan, 1990. A brief memoir of the author's development, comparable with the Hanunoo tribesman's beating two sticks together as he journeys to assure himself that body and soul have not separated.

_____. *The Father and the Maid*. Quezon City: University of the Philippines, 1990. These lectures delivered on the author's return from years of teaching in California connect much of Philippine culture with Gonzalez's attempts to re-create that culture through fiction in Philippine English.

Tiempo, Edilberto K. "The Fiction of N. V. M. Gonzalez." In *Literary Criticism in the Philippines and Other Essays*. Manila: De La Salle University Press, 1995. An expansion of a critique first published in 1955, Tiempo's meticulous examination of Gonzalez's prose works looks at Gonzalez's diction, characterization, plot structure, symbolism, and prose style in general.

Zuraek, Maria Elnora C. "N. V. M. Gonzalez' *A Season of Grace*." In *Essays on the Philippine Novel in English*, edited by Joseph A. Galdon. Quezon City: Ateneo de Manila, 1979. Comments on the two meanings of grace: a period of postponement or second chance and regeneration through sanctification by natural forces.

PAUL GOODMAN

Born: New York, New York; September 9, 1911
Died: North Stratford, New Hampshire; August 2, 1972

(Archive Photos)

PRINCIPAL LONG FICTION

The Grand Piano: Or, The Almanac of Alienation, 1942
The State of Nature, 1946
The Dead of Spring, 1950
Parents' Day, 1951
The Empire City, 1959 (includes *The Grand Piano*, *The State of Nature*, *The Dead of Spring*, *The Holy Terror*)
Making Do, 1963

OTHER LITERARY FORMS

By any standards, Goodman was a prolific writer. In addition to his novels, he wrote collections of poetry, several of which were privately printed. The most noteworthy are *The Lordly Hudson: Collected Poems* (1962); *Homespun of Oatmeal Gray* (1970); and the *Collected Poems* (1973). He also published ten plays between 1941 and 1970 and three books of literary criticism: *Kafka's Prayer* (1947); *The Structure of Literature* (1954); and *Speaking and Lan-*

guage: Defense of Poetry (1971). Goodman also wrote a partial autobiography: *Five Years: Thoughts During a Useless Time* (1966). This list, however, represents only a fraction of his oeuvre, which includes more than thirty titles. In addition, he contributed regularly to and served as film-review editor of the *Partisan Review* and as a television critic for *The New Republic*.

ACHIEVEMENTS

Goodman more closely approximates the Renaissance man than does perhaps any other twentieth century American man of letters. A prolific writer in many genres—novels, poems, essays, dramas, short stories, literary criticism, education, sociology, and community planning—and the author of studies in psychotherapy, Goodman has entries under twenty-one different categories in the catalogs of the New York Public Library. He was not discovered by the reading public until 1960 as a result of his book *Growing Up Absurd* (1960), a spirited attack on the values of mid-century America. Because Goodman wrote in such diverse forms, he is not easily categorized. He shares with many of his colleagues such as Saul Bellow, Philip Roth, and Bernard Malamud a perspective that is distinctly Jewish: a feeling for alienation, a skeptical nature that is allied with visionary tendencies, and a penchant for social justice. As a novelist, he is best remembered for *The Empire City*.

BIOGRAPHY

Paul Goodman was born in Greenwich Village, New York City, on September 9, 1911, to a family in financial straits so serious that his father deserted them soon after Paul's birth. Not surprisingly, many of Goodman's books deal with fatherless boys struggling to establish some sort of alliance both with adult males and with the society that surrounds them. The lonely boy excelled in school ("he made it difficult for us ordinary geniuses," one classmate remarked). The years he spent at the College of the City of New York between 1927 and 1931 were formative ones in his intellectual growth. Here he came in contact with the legendary teacher/philosopher

Morris Cohen, who found Goodman to be a willing student with an inquiring and skeptical mind. Thereafter, Goodman found outlets for his omnivorous interests, publishing pieces on philosophy, short stories, cinema criticism, and poetry. Though considered a promising writer while still in his twenties, Goodman did not attract a wide audience. During the 1950's, in fact, he grew despondent over his lack of recognition; it was not until shortly before his fiftieth birthday that this reputation burgeoned.

"Too long a sacrifice makes a stone of the heart," remarked William Butler Yeats in a line that is appropriate to Goodman, who was often viewed by contemporaries as arrogant, distant, and hard, yet to his credit was courageous, committed to social good, and helpful to other writers. Complicating his life was his bisexuality, which he explored at length in his fiction. At a time when others were circumspect about such things, Goodman made little effort to conceal his sexual activities, being dismissed as a graduate student from the University of Chicago and later from other teaching positions. Very likely, his novel *Parents' Day* chronicles the difficulties his sexual activities created for him.

In 1942, Goodman's first novel, *The Grand Piano*, was published. This novel (Goodman referred to this book as an educational romance) focuses on the spiritual growth of a parentless eleven-year-old boy named Horatio Alger, who roams the streets of Manhattan, surviving by his wits and defying all institutions, most notably the educational establishment. He is an "artful dodger" like Goodman himself, who also took pride in his street smarts. Goodman's fascination with psychotherapy—he became a lay analyst for the Gestalt Institute of New York—permeates the later segments of his tetralogy, *The Empire City*. Despite his prolific output, Goodman was for most of his life as unsuccessful financially as his father had been, though he was a good deal more responsible. By his own contention, he lived below the poverty line—until 1960, he both boasted and lamented that he was as poor as any sharecropper.

Goodman's most difficult period occurred during the 1950's, at the height of his creative powers. His marriage was faltering, his daughter was ill, and his submissions were regularly rejected. Very likely, his outspoken views were considered alarming during the McCarthy era. In 1960, the shift in the country's mood coincided with the publication of *Growing Up Absurd*, the book which earned Goodman recognition. His success, however, did little to reconcile him to those aspects of American culture he had been deploring; the Vietnam War, so destructive to American morale, ironically established his credentials as a prophet to the young.

Success did not appreciably alter Goodman's lifestyle, though it did make him a sought-after lecturer. The reader who wishes to gain some appreciation of what that lifestyle was like is advised to read *Making Do*, as well as the now nearly unobtainable *Parents' Day* and the poetry. In 1967, Goodman's son Matthew was killed in a climbing accident, a grievous event that Goodman dealt with extensively in his poetry. Goodman died on August 2, 1972, at the age of sixty, leaving a wife and two daughters.

ANALYSIS

"I have only one subject," wrote Paul Goodman, "the human beings I know in their man-made environments." All of Goodman's novels explore human beings in relation to the institutions that both reflect and shape their values. In Goodman's view, rather than abetting human development, institutions thwart aptitude and foster stupidity. From this base, Goodman argues passionately for a more humane society—one that would offer worthwhile goals, meaningful work, honest public speech, patriotism, and at the same time encourage healthy animal desire. Goodman indicts American culture for being unequal to all these aspirations.

In Goodman's works, society's failure leads individuals to attempt to create their own community—one that is scaled down and decentralized. The author is absorbed with the individual's wresting from the larger social order a more workable and personalized one—a community. In this endeavor, Goodman is not alone: In fact, he is engaged in a quintessentially American occupation, that of creating "a city upon a hill," however different from John Winthrop's ideal.

Indeed, Nathaniel Hawthorne manifested a similar interest when he participated in the Brook Farm experiment. In fiction, Mark Twain's Huck Finn flees the larger society to find communion with Jim on the Mississippi. Both Jay Gatsby and Dick Diver among F. Scott Fitzgerald's characters create a community but are ultimately defeated by corrosive contact with the worst aspects of American materialism and illusion. A similar concern for community informs Goodman's writing, though his novels are typically urban; the sole exception, *Parents' Day*, is set in upstate New York. In all of his novels, the protagonist and his friends strive to establish a workable, nourishing community but find themselves in constant danger of engulfment by the debased larger society.

As evidenced by the diversity of his interests, Goodman was an intellectual, keenly aware of his debt to Western traditions. His thought was shaped by Aristotle, Immanuel Kant, Thomas Hobbes, Franz Kafka, Martin Buber, and Wilhelm Reich. From Hobbes and Kant, Goodman derived material for his speculations on the social contract, by means of which people relinquished certain freedoms in order to achieve civilization. In Kafka, Goodman perceived a surrealist and comic spirit as well as the notion that writing was a form of prayer. One critic, Theodore Roszak, has identified a "coarse-grained Hasidic magic" about Goodman's work, presumably a reference to the author's search for transcendence in the mundane. Goodman may well have found Buber's idealized notion of human relations congenial—the effort to transform "I-It" relationships into "I-Thou" ones. Goodman's work as a lay therapist with the Gestalt Institute of New York no doubt reflected his interest in the psychosexual theories of Wilhelm Reich, which inform all of his writings. One detects this influence in the "therapy" sections of *The Empire City* (especially those in which Horatio woos Rosalind); in *Parents' Day*, where the teacher/narrator uses physical intimacy as an educational tool; and in *Making Do*, where Harold and Terry suffer from sexual deprivation. In all his novels, Goodman argues that personal contact should be communal and psychosexual. It may be disconcerting to the reader to discover that the narrator of *Making Do* is bisexual and that the narrator/teacher of *Parents' Day* is engaged in homosexual liaisons with his adolescent students, but Goodman does not flinch from offering such revelations. Rather, he flaunts his protagonists' (and his own) sexuality—not always to good effect. The reader may well feel distracted when an author insists on toleration for his or her sexual preferences, may feel annoyed when asked to respond not to the event the artist is rendering but to the artist's challenge.

Though one must be cautious in identifying the narrator with the author, Goodman does not make much effort to conceal the autobiographical nature of much of his fiction. On the contrary, Goodman often addresses the reader in asides which prevent the normal suspension of disbelief. "This is no book/Who touches this touches a man," boasted Walt Whitman as he artfully concealed himself, yet Goodman does not trouble to disguise himself. The narrators of *Making Do* and *Parents' Day* are interchangeable—both closely resembling the sort of intellectual Goodman was: a man of letters who was also a man of the streets.

At his best, Goodman is imaginative, profound, and witty. *The Empire City*, though uneven, is a neglected masterpiece. At his worst, Goodman becomes hortatory and shrill, as in *The Dead of Spring*, the third work in the tetralogy, or careless in his prose, as in *Making Do*.

THE EMPIRE CITY

The Empire City, Goodman's ambitious tetralogy, follows a cluster of characters who have become alienated not only from society but also from themselves. The first novel in the tetralogy, *The Grand Piano*, is subtitled "The Almanac of Alienation"; thus, Goodman announces that he will be exploring what Robert Frost called "inner weather"; he will be attempting a chronicle of the spirit as it unfolds in life. Given this aim, it should not be surprising if some of the book's passages do not yield themselves readily to analysis. Goodman, like his literary forebears, Kafka, André Gide, William Blake, and Rainer Maria Rilke, seems to be charting the ineffable and bidding his reader to follow.

THE GRAND PIANO

The narrator of *The Grand Piano*, hardly distinguishable from Goodman himself, is often obtrusive in the manner of Henry Fielding. By mediating between character and reader, the narrator encourages the reader to regard the protagonists as friends, members of a community of which he or she is a part. These new friends are vital, larger than life, multitalented, heroic. Witness the name of the hero—Horatio Alger—based on the American writer who encouraged boys to lead virtuous lives full of heroic deeds.

The Alger tales dealt with the self-made man who succeeded in that great mecca of success, New York City. Goodman's Alger, however, is a street-smart guttersnipe who, having destroyed all records of his existence, revels in his outcast status. Untouched by social institutions, such as school, he is truly a self-made eleven-year-old youth. In the opening episode, he meets Mynheer Duyck Colijn. The critic Sherman Paul has observed that Mynheer is an exemplar of the cultured man. Like his Dutch forebears, Mynheer is a model of tolerance and civic virtue. If Horatio is alienated, Mynheer is the opposite. In their initial meeting, the cunning, sneering, artful dodger is pitted against the sophisticated, virtuous adult. Reading the latter's name as "Dick Collegian," however, suggests another aspect of his character: his innocence. His rationality and civic pride will be sorely tested by the outbreak of war.

Horatio has no parents, but is being reared, as Goodman was, by a brother and sister and, again like Goodman, is searching for a father. He settles on Eliphaz, a sort of Yiddish Daddy Warbucks, but one who combines patriarchal wisdom with financial acumen. In Eliphaz, Goodman achieves the sort of fantastic realism that readers customarily associate with Charles Dickens. Eliphaz's presence creates some of the best scenes in the novel. This merchant prince represents the idealized spirit of early capitalism: He keeps a mysterious ledger containing only an accumulating number of zeros; he practices detachment by selling his own furniture, often while his family is still sitting on it; he idly places a price tag on his own son ("$84.95. $75 cash? Good!

Sold!"). He is a man of culture who can spout Johann Wolfgang Goethe and Spinoza. Opposed to the anarchistic spirit of the Algers, who subsist on welfare, he impulsively sends them a grand piano, one that is so large that they are forced to sleep under it. Gnomically, he explains his gesture, which proceeds from mixed motives: "It's always worthwhile to hurl large gifts toward your adversary. Where is she going to put such an animal? How is she going to explain it to the relief investigator I'll send around tomorrow?" So wonderful a comic creation is Eliphaz that the reader can only regret his death at the opening of the second novel of the tetralogy. His place in literature has been usurped by the more impersonal Milo Minderbinder of Joseph Heller's *Catch-22* (1961), a similarly restless but more mindless spirit of capitalism.

Other members of the community include Horatio's family, Lothario/Lothair and Laura. Lothair, a follower of the anarchist Prince Petr Kropotkin, is a reformer who is vilified and persecuted by the state. As Sherman Paul comments, he is yet another side of Goodman himself—a reformer and educator. In this respect, he is also reminiscent of the protagonists of *Making Do* and *Parents' Day. The Grand Piano* proceeds toward a communal reconciliation which is partial at best; as in Richard Wagner's music, resolution is never far away but never quite arrives. Indeed, the climax of the novel has the characters attending a performance of Wagner's *Die Meistersinger*, which promises "an exulting community spirit," but as Horatio shrewdly observes, "It's all to be paid for at [Beckmesser's] expense. . . ." The survival of the larger society, as it does in fairy tales, hinges on the scapegoating of one of its members, hinges on projecting the dark side of the psyche onto a villain who can then be defeated by a hero.

The novel ends with another musical contest, one involving the grand piano. Embedded in this section are hints of the Arthurian contest to secure the sword Excalibur. Lothair, who is a composer, performs beautifully and by rights should be declared the winner, but he is arrested and transported to jail—presumably a victim of scapegoating by a society preparing itself for war.

THE STATE OF NATURE

The second novel in the tetralogy, *The State of Nature*, pursues Goodman's interest in the contact point between the organism and its environment. The setting is now 1944. Horatio has grown to young manhood; his adopted father has, like Alfred Tennyson's King Arthur, died, leaving behind a world that has grown incomprehensible to him. In this book, the narrator discourses tirelessly (and, at times, tiresomely) on the subject of war, not only as a social reality but also as a spiritual phenomenon. Goodman viewed war as a debased form of the spiritual life which requires putting oneself in jeopardy. This novel is weaker than its predecessor, first because Goodman exhorts his reader rather than rendering his material into narrative, second because the author uses the war as a symbol but does not acknowledge the moral imperatives that made World War II a necessity.

The State of Nature explores the themes of putting oneself in danger and engaging in "a long drawn out losing fight"—both activities in which the social activist Goodman was experienced. In this book, the central figures pass from dissent to alienation. Horatio is shot at by overwrought National Guardsmen. Lothair broods in jail about the paradox that his ardent desire to serve society is unappreciated unless that service takes the form of fighting. Laura, the community planner and wife of Mynheer, has been ordered to undo her work: By means of camouflage, she is to transform a community of her design, a land of milk and honey, back into a desert. Lothair escapes, but, driven mad by social rejection (his name Lothario indicates he is a lover, but of humanity), he executes a plan to release the animals from the zoo. In the pandemonium created, little Gus, incestuous offspring of Arthur and his sister Emily (both children of Eliphaz), is killed. The zoo's curator happens to be Mynheer, who in contrast to Lothair is permitted to serve humanity but is fated to do so without conviction. He and his wife Laura, the reader is told, are "alienated from their natures." In his case, the result is that the connection between his intellect and his emotions is severed, rendering him impotent. In a scene reminiscent of Blake's prophetic books, Mynheer (intellect) is paralyzed by Emily's anguished cry (heart) concerning the sight of the tiger destroying little Gus. Lothair then leads Mynheer into the cage vacated by the tiger.

In this chapter, Goodman shifts emphasis from social concerns to psychological ones. Community needs must wait while individuals attempt to restore their shattered equilibrium. Emily, for example, is unable to save her son from the tiger; she is "frozen into action by her 'mixed desire.' " The death of her son, however, leads her to a primal cry that enables her to function once again. Her therapeutic experience (this section was conceived at the time of Goodman's developing interest in Gestalt therapy) becomes a paradigmatic model for others who also are experiencing their alienation from self. Social conditions only serve to enforce this alienation, as is revealed in the prophecy of Eliphaz which concludes the novel. In it, the dying capitalist foresees the advent of a consumer economy, mass conformity, and mass education, all resulting in "Asphyxiation"—a state in which the individual is unable to breathe freely or to experience his or her own vital desires. What has replaced human community he scornfully terms "Sociolatry."

THE DEAD OF SPRING

The third novel in the tetralogy is *The Dead of Spring*. All must come to grips with the aftermath of war, must fight the long-drawn-out losing fight of the duration, as Eliphaz predicted. Lothair turns inward to his own pain, away from social concerns; Mynheer delivers a valediction on human beings combining elements of Prince Hamlet and Fritz Perls; the marriage between Emily and Lothair proves barren; the community spirit languishes. There is a brief interlude when Horatio meets Laura, but generally this is a gloomy period. Horatio discovers himself to be impotent, but is redeemed and taught to love by a young lad, whom Sherman Paul identifies as an aspect of Horatio's own submerged self—the youthful street urchin Horatio had been in the opening novel. As is typical in a romance, the lovers overcome their vicissitudes—though here the impediments are largely of their own devising—and fall in love. As Horatio is about to become a father, however, he is arrested—

forced, as it were, by parenthood into recognition of the social contract. Horatio is indicted, not for resisting the state as Lothair had been at the conclusion of *The Grand Piano*, but for refusing to adopt a stand, much like the lost souls in Hell's anteroom of Dante's *Divine Comedy* (c. 1320). Horatio admits to his error but counters it with the information that he is in love; in comic fashion, the conflict is resolved, the charge is dropped.

This lighthearted respite provides comic relief from the chapters that precede it and the event which follows—the suicide of Laura. Her death serves as a sacrificial act, one that will redeem the community. Testaments to its effectiveness are the regenerations of Mynheer, Minetta (the social worker), and Horatio— each of whom begins finding ways to cope with the dilemma that results when one must choose between living within a mad society or the madness of living outside society. The dilemma is expressed, too, in the baseball game that follows, built as it is on a paradox: The participants "played in order to keep the ball alive, nevertheless desperately destroyed the play by bringing nearer the end of the game." Each copes with this paradox in his or her own fashion; each participates as an individual and as a teammate, but nothing can enjoin the game's end. To their common cry "Creator spirit, come," a combination of entreaty and sexual joke, a reply comes in the birth of St. Wayward. He is a restorer, a conservator of humanity's spirit, which has been abused by advancing civilization.

THE HOLY TERROR

In the fourth and final novel of the series, *The Holy Terror*, Goodman promises a "register of reconciliation," and indeed, the principals move toward a harmony, what Blake would call experiencing their "joys and desires." Such chapter titles as "conversing," "dancing," "eating," "relaxing," and "wakening" reflect the social nature of their existence. Horatio and Rosalind dance in sexual joy, while Lothair finds fulfillment in his music. They undergo a kind of Gestalt therapy, a form of body mysticism. Each pursues self-awareness: Mynheer experiences primal consciousness by means of the Tao Te Ching; Lothair, the public man, discovers his repressed rage.

In a poignant episode, Lothair, overcome by feelings of rage, hope, and love, is slain by his son Wayward in a scene rife with Oedipal implications. In killing his father, Wayward achieves manhood, and his exploits in Ireland, which later cap the book, offer an affirmative ending.

After Lothair's death, Horatio undergoes a form of madness which involves accepting the reality of the world as it is expressed by the now-defunct newspaper *The New York Herald Tribune*. The time is 1952. One symptom of Horatio's insanity is that he wishes to vote for General Eisenhower. Although this section is at times amusing, it seems inappropriate, more a symptom of the author's political outrage than a stage in the development of Horatio's personality. No effort is made by the author to imply that Horatio is seriously exploring conservative values; instead, Goodman sacrifices his character's credibility to parody topical theories of politics and education. Indeed, much of the final book reveals Goodman's flagging imagination. Events are related to one another only thematically rather than as the outgrowth of character. One such example involves the youthful cardplayers who appear as a foil for St. Wayward. The latter transcends and redeems the sordid world of boys, performing miracles in a way that suggests events in the Gospels. The boys, however, are only a convenience for the author, and they disappear from the novel. The Gospel parallel is reinforced in the next chapter, however, which is called "Good News" and deals with the discovery by Lefty Duyvendak, son of Mynheer and Laura, of an Edenic community where life is reasonable, joy permissible. As the novel nears its conclusion, the principals meet to reaffirm their sense of community, each announcing the "work that is at hand." The novel ends with a lyrical fantasy of St. Wayward freeing Ireland of its sexual repression. Horatio has the tetralogy's final word, entreating God for more life.

After its publication in 1959, *The Empire City* achieved a kind of cult status. Though at times obscure, it represents Goodman's most ambitious novelistic effort and clearly his best. His reputation as a novelist rests on this often impressive and imaginative work.

MAKING DO

In *Making Do*, Goodman develops and amplifies themes he had earlier explored in *The Empire City*. "My only literary theme has been the community," he remarked in his journal *Five Years*. Once more, he returns to familiar themes: psychology, education, radical reform, and the efforts of the individual to satisfy natural desire in a repressive environment. *Making Do* is a less hopeful and exuberant novel than its predecessor: As *Communitatis* glosses *The Empire City*, so *Growing Up Absurd* clarifies *Making Do*. The titles of these latter works suggest the more circumscribed possibilities for achievement Goodman perceived in American life. Entitling his earlier work with New York's sobriquet the "Empire City" does suggest Goodman's hope: his vision of heroism and transcendence that has the capacity to stimulate the protagonists. "Making do," on the other hand, is far less optimistic, a diminished variation of the American credo—"making it"—that spurred an earlier generation of Jewish immigrants (among them Goodman's own father, perhaps). "Making do" implies less a remaking of the environment to render it worthy of its best citizens than an attempt to adjust and find comfort in a framework of truncated possibilities.

Unlike its predecessor, *Making Do* is not a fantasy imbued with the energy and spirit that such a form implies, but is a tale conceived in a realistic-naturalistic vein. As before, the novelist has a dual role as both narrator ("the tired man") and participant (Goodman appears by name in a cameo role). Once again, Goodman presents his characters as special friends, members of a community of which his persona is the guiding spirit. Other members include the saintly Harold, spiritual father to a gang of delinquent Puerto Ricans, and Jason, a graduate student in English with passionate convictions on education. Jason is writing a dissertation on Theodore Dreiser, an author who explored the tragic implications of the American Dream. Another member of the group, Meg, has a generous sexual spirit and guilelessness which render her attractive, however undirected she appears. The narrator's friend, Roger, shares his commitment to their surroundings, as displayed in his eagerness to establish Vanderzee as a haven for artists. Finally, there is Terry, an inarticulate youth full of a kind of puppylike devotion to the community of friends.

The very qualities that make these individuals attractive also prove their undoing. Harold is mocked and abused by his hustler/lover Ramon, who eventually betrays his protector to the police. Jason expresses his rage (and probably Goodman's own) concerning educational textbooks by the impotent gesture of punching a textbook salesman. His dissertation is probably doomed for reasons that make a mockery of the notion of academia as a community of scholars. Meg's tolerant and nurturing sexual practices provide the police with a pretext for attacking the group; her innocence even permits her to cooperate with her persecutors. Terry, like Horatio, though lacking the street smarts and mental discipline to provide him with equilibrium, desperately embraces the notion of community. He is inarticulate, however, a primitive who relies on insight to the exclusion of cognitive thought; hence, he is unable to negotiate in a fallen world and is ultimately institutionalized. Unhappy though he is, the narrator, "the tired man," does cope successfully with the world— in large measure because he is sufficiently detached to achieve at least a modest success, satisfying his needs for love, work, and self-expression. As noted earlier, a character named Paul Goodman appears briefly in the novel, but the lineaments of the author's own life appear most fully in the character of the narrator.

The vicissitudes experienced by the community do not simply result from the larger society's victimization of the group (though that does exist); as in *The Empire City*, they result in large measure from weaknesses within the community. Harold has lost contact with his animal nature, as symbolized both by his impotence with Ramon and by his self-lacerating behavior at the race track, where he bets against his own selections. Meg is jealous of others' sexual pleasures; Jason is unwilling to act the responsible father; Terry is inarticulate unless he can be physically intimate. Presumably, for Goodman, Terry is the end product of all that is distorted about American cul-

ture. The reader, however, may find that Joanna's attraction to him is rather implausible. "She did not see about her any other young man who was worthwhile," the narrator remarks. Hardly a very satisfactory explanation to justify her love affair with a promiscuous, bisexual, drug-addicted dropout on the verge of being institutionalized for schizophrenia. Even the founder of the community, Meg's former husband, Amos, is "insane," and threatens to kill his wife.

The setting of this novel is Vanderzee, a community directly across the river from New York City. For Goodman, everything Dutch has positive connotations (recall Mynheer of *The Empire City* or the collection of poems *The Lordly Hudson*). Vanderzee, however, having betrayed its origins, does not actualize its potential for community; the town is controlled by a venal police force and a narrow-minded mayor, both of whom endorse "community" but mean by it a life-denying, mind-numbing conformity. There is little difference in Goodman's eyes between the self-serving values of the Puerto Rican hustlers and those of the police force (a point Goodman had already made in *Growing Up Absurd*), so that when Ramon is arrested, Judas-like, he betrays the smaller community in order to gain entrance into the larger.

The novel ends on a mixed note. The narrator, "the tired man," has a glimmering vision of a transcendent love of country—an outgrowth, he explains, of erotic love. Harold and Meg find comfort in each other's arms, but Terry is institutionalized, the Puerto Rican youths are arrested, and Amos is left free but homeless.

As a novel, *Making Do* has occasional strengths and glaring weaknesses. Goodman, as ever, is a compelling writer, with trenchant insights into American culture and social life, but this book lacks the exuberant spirit and incandescent invention of *The Empire City*. A serious drawback of the book, as Richard Poirier observes, is that "its actions never [accumulate] the necessity that brings on subsequent actions. . . . The links between the events are largely external." *Making Do* is an interesting book, but not a good novel.

Goodman's novels have had a mixed reception. *Parents' Day* is largely forgotten, out of print and unavailable even in research libraries. *Making Do*, the most popular of his novels, is marred by serious flaws; it is best remembered for its vivid scenes of communal life in the 1960's. Goodman's reputation as a novelist rests on his tetralogy *The Empire City*, a work that will no doubt endure as a minor classic.

Stan Sulkes

OTHER MAJOR WORKS

SHORT FICTION: *The Facts of Life*, 1945; *The Break-up of Our Camp and Other Stories*, 1949; *Our Visit to Niagara*, 1960; *Adam and His Works*, 1968.

POETRY: *The Lordly Hudson: Collected Poems*, 1962; *Hawkweed*, 1967; *Homespun of Oatmeal Gray*, 1970; *Collected Poems*, 1973.

PLAYS: *Stop-light: 5 Dance Poems*, pb. 1941; *Jonah*, pb. 1945; *Faustina*, pr. 1949, pb. 1961; *The Young Disciple*, pr. 1955, pb. 1965; *Tragedy and Comedy: Four Cubist Plays*, pb. 1970.

NONFICTION: *Kafka's Prayer*, 1947; *Communitas*, 1947 (with Percival Goodman); *Gestalt Therapy: Excitement and Growth in the Human Personality*, 1951 (with Frederick S. Perls and Ralph Hefferline); *The Structure of Literature*, 1954; *Growing Up Absurd*, 1960; *The Community of Scholars*, 1962; *Utopian Essays and Practical Proposals*, 1962; *Compulsory Mis-Education*, 1964; *People or Personnel: Decentralizing and the Mixed System*, 1965; *Five Years: Thoughts During a Useless Time*, 1966; *Speaking and Language: Defense of Poetry*, 1971.

CHILDREN'S LITERATURE: *Childish Jokes: Crying Backstage*, 1951.

BIBLIOGRAPHY

Fried, Lewis F. *Makers of the City*. Amherst: University of Massachusetts Press, 1990. Fried demonstrates that Goodman's exploration of the ideas of community and of urban culture unites his fiction and nonfiction. Includes detailed notes and bibliographical essay.

Gilman, Richard. Review of *The Empire City*, by Paul Goodman. *Commonweal* 70 (July 31, 1959): 401-402. This short article examines *The Empire City* as a part of the comic tradition of J. D. Salinger and Saul Bellow. Also cites Goodman's debt to Franz Kafka for his sense of the bizarre. Objects to the sermonizing quality of Goodman's fiction but notes that his characters are intended to teach us how to live.

Harrington, Michael. "On Paul Goodman." *Atlantic* 216 (August, 1965): 88-91. This short article is a general review of Goodman's work and a more intensive examination of his essays *People or Personnel*. Looks at Goodman as an existentialist critic of American life and as a philosopher of the student revolts of the 1960's, finding his belief in the goodness of human nature naïve.

Ostriker, Alicia. "Paul Goodman." *Partisan Review* 43, no. 2 (1976): 286-295. Offers a good introduction to Goodman's poetry as part of the general tradition first of Walt Whitman, then of the Black Mountain poets and the Beat generation. Notes the vigor and explicitness of his political and sexual poetry but points out that his lack of metaphoric imagination and decorum makes his poetry "unpoetic" to some readers.

Paul, Sherman. "Paul Goodman's Mourning Labor: *The Empire City*." Review of *The Empire City*, by Paul Goodman. *The Southern Review* 4, no. 4 (1968): 894-926. This meaty review is a book-by-book analysis of *The Empire City*. Examines its major themes of the education of a young man, looking especially at its themes dealing with war and at its position in the tradition of the philosophical novel.

Sontag, Susan. *Under the Sign of Saturn*. New York: Farrar, Straus & Giroux, 1980. Contains one of the most sensitive essays on Goodman, treating his fiction seriously and suggesting his reputation has suffered because he wrote in so many different genres rather than concentrating on a single form of literature.

Stoehr, Taylor, ed. *Decentralizing Power: Paul Goodman's Social Criticism*. New York: Black Rose Books, 1994. Explores Goodman's indictments of human society, and how this theme is incorporated into his books.

NADINE GORDIMER

Born: Springs, South Africa; November 20, 1923

PRINCIPAL LONG FICTION

The Lying Days, 1953
A World of Strangers, 1958
Occasion for Loving, 1963
The Late Bourgeois World, 1966
A Guest of Honour, 1970
The Conservationist, 1974
Burger's Daughter, 1979
July's People, 1981
A Sport of Nature, 1987
My Son's Story, 1990
None to Accompany Me, 1994
The House Gun, 1998

(AP/Wide World Photos)

OTHER LITERARY FORMS

Nadine Gordimer is a prolific writer and is one of the twentieth century's greatest writers of short stories. Her first collection of stories, *Face to Face: Short Stories* (1949), was published in Johannesburg by Silver Leaf Books. Her first story published in *The New Yorker*, where most of her stories first appeared, was "A Watcher of the Dead" (June 9, 1951). Gordimer's first collection of stories to be published in the United States was *The Soft Voice of the Serpent and Other Stories* (1952). This collection was followed by eight other major collections of short stories (as of 1999). She wrote the screenplays for three of her stories filmed for television ("Country Lovers," "A Chip of Glass Ruby," and "Praise"). With Lionel Abrahams she edited *South African Writing Today* (1967). Gordimer has published numerous literary reviews and other essays and short pieces, usually dealing with literature or with the culture or politics of South Africa. She also has collections of essays: *The Black Interpreters* (1973), *The Essential Gesture: Writing, Politics and Places*, edited by Stephen Clingman (1988), and *Writing and Being* (1995).

ACHIEVEMENTS

Gordimer won the W. H. Smith Literary Award in 1961 for *Friday's Footprint and Other Stories*. In 1972, she won the James Tait Black Memorial Prize for *A Guest of Honour. The Conservationist* was cowinner of the Booker Prize (1974). Gordimer also has received the French international literary prize the Grand Aigle d'Or (1975), the Italian Malaparte Prize (1985), and the Nelly Sachs Prize from Germany (1986). She was awarded the Officier de l'Ordre des Arts et des Lettres (1986) and the highest French art and literature decoration, the Commandeur dans l'Ordre des Arts et Lettres (1991). She has been awarded honorary degrees from such American universities as Harvard and Yale (both in 1986) and the New School for Social Research (1987). In the fall of 1994, Gordimer delivered the Charles Eliot Norton Lectures series at Harvard. In 1991, she was honored with the Nobel Prize in Literature.

BIOGRAPHY

Nadine Gordimer spent her childhood in a gold-mining town near Johannesburg, South Africa. Her father, Isidore Gordimer, was a watchmaker, a Jew who had immigrated from a Baltic town to Africa when he was thirteen; her mother was born in England. In writing about her childhood, Gordimer refers to herself as "a bolter." She did not care for the convent school to which she was sent as a day student, and she frequently played hooky. When she did attend, she would sometimes walk out. The pressures of uniformity produced revulsion and rebellion in young Nadine. At eleven, Gordimer was kept home from school by her mother on the pretense of a heart ailment, and she received no formal schooling for about a year; for the next three to four years, she was tutored a few hours a day.

Within Gordimer's environment, a white middle-class girl typically left school at about age fifteen and worked for a few years at a clerical job. Ideally, by her early twenties she would be found by the son of a family like her own and would then be ushered through her season of glory—the engagement party, the linen shower, the marriage, and the birth of the first child. There was no point in reading books; that would only impede the inevitable process by which the daughter was readied to fit the mold.

Gordimer, however, was an early reader and an early writer. By the age of nine, she was already writing; at fourteen, she won her first writing prize. She read the stories of Guy de Maupassant, Anton Chekhov, Somerset Maugham, D. H. Lawrence, and the Americans O. Henry, Katherine Anne Porter, and Eudora Welty. Reading these great artists of the short story refined her own story writing, making her work more sophisticated. She found herself becoming increasingly interested in politics and the plight of black South Africans. Unlike other whites who rejected the white South African way of life, Gordimer did not launch into her writing career as a way to bring change. Already a writer, she could not help "falling, falling through the surface" of white South African life.

In her early twenties, Gordimer was greatly influenced by a young male friend. She has written that he did her the service of telling her how ignorant she was. He jeered at the way she was acquiring knowledge and at her "clumsy battle to chip my way out of shell after shell of readymade concepts." Further, she says, "It was through him, too, that I roused myself sufficiently to insist on going to the university." Since she was twenty-two at the time and still being supported by her father, her family did not appreciate her desire to attend the university.

Continuing to live at home, Gordimer commuted to Johannesburg and the University of the Witwatersrand. While at the university, she met the Afrikaans poet Uys Krige, a man who had broken free of his Afrikaans heritage, lived in France and Spain, and served with the International Brigade in the Spanish Civil War. He had a profound effect upon Gordimer. She had bolted from school; she was in the process of bolting from family, class, and the superficial values and culture of white South Africa. Uys Krige gave her a final push. She was free to be committed to honesty alone. When she began sending stories to England and the United States, they were well received. Her course was set.

Despite her contempt for the social system and the economic exploitation that prevailed in South Africa, Gordimer continued to make Johannesburg her home. She gave birth to and reared her children there. She married Reinhold Cassirer, a German-born art dealer, who moved to South Africa in the late 1930's. She and her husband would frequently go abroad, to Europe, to North America, to other African countries. She lectured at leading American universities such as Columbia, Harvard, and Michigan State, but she always returned to Johannesburg. For many years some of her writing was censored or prohibited in South Africa. Gordimer is active in promoting South African culture, particularly writing. A member of Southern African PEN (International Association of Poets, Playwrights, Editors, Essayists, and Novelists) in Johannesburg, she also served as vice president for PEN International. She is a founder and an executive member of the Congress of South African Writers (COSAW), a political and cultural organization. She is a board member working under the African National Congress's Department of Arts and Culture for cultural reconstruction in South Africa. In 1990, when the African National Congress (ANC) again became legal, Gordimer joined and supported the new democracy in South Africa.

ANALYSIS

Until 1991, when the last of the apartheid laws was repealed, to be personally liberated and to be South African was to be doomed to a continuing struggle between the desire for further freedom and development for oneself and the desire for the liberation of the country's oppressed masses. The question was whether both could be pursued effectually. South Africa was a nation in which a white legislature promulgated laws that made it impossible for the overwhelming majority of nonwhite persons to advance themselves. Apartheid, which in Afrikaans means "apartness," was the law of the land. It became codified after the Nationalists came to power in 1948.

In her novels, Nadine Gordimer is engaged in an ongoing examination of the possible combinations of the private life and the public life. She has created a gallery of characters ranging from pure hedonists concerned only with their own pleasure to those who have committed their lives to bringing liberty, equality, and solidarity to South Africa. Her most interesting characters are those who are wracked and torn by the struggle, those who both want to be themselves and yet find it impossible to take personal goals seriously in a society built on the exploitation of blacks.

Some great writers—writers such as James Joyce and Thomas Mann—have felt that in order to write freely they must live in a free country. During the 1920's, numerous American writers disgusted with American values chose to become expatriates. Other writers, such as the great Russians Fyodor Dostoevski, Leo Tolstoy, and Aleksandr Solzhenitsyn, have felt that nothing could be more oppressive to them than to be separated from their fellow citizens, however oppressive the government of their country might be. With some of her books banned, with some charge or other always dangling over her head, with her passport liable to be lifted at any time, Gordimer undoubtedly was tempted to go into exile and live in a free country. She always, however, returned to Jo-

hannesburg from abroad. To her, the accident of being born in a particular place imposed obligations, and having become a writer with an international reputation imposed special obligations. At the cost of the personal freedom and the very air of freedom that could be hers elsewhere, she remained in South Africa during the apartheid years, living with frustration and danger, a witness to the power of compassion and hope.

THE LYING DAYS

A first novel is often a thinly veiled autobiography of the writer's childhood, adolescence, and coming of age. Gordimer's *The Lying Days* is of the type, but is nevertheless special. Full of innocence, tenderness, courage, and joy, it is an unusually mature celebration of a woman's coming of age. It is the story of Helen Shaw's growing up in a mining town not far from Johannesburg, the intoxication of her first love affairs, her days at the university, her immersion in the city's bohemian and radical circles, and finally her drawing back to protect herself from being swamped by values, attitudes, and goals that are not her own.

In her life at home, Helen Shaw is under the thumb of a mother who commands and dominates in the name of all that is conventional and trivial. The motivating force in the mother's life is her desire to guide her family through all the planned stops on the middle-class timetable: tea parties and dances, husband's promotions, the big vacation to Europe, and, most important, the molding of offspring to fit the community's notion of success. To celebrate these achievements and in all else to maintain an unruffled surface—such are the goals of Mrs. Shaw and the placid Mr. Shaw, who, important as he may be to the success of the gold-mining company, is completely submissive at home. As Helen comes to realize, both mother and father, their circle of acquaintances, and those in other similar circles are "insensitive to the real flow of life."

The whites of the mining town have blacks in their midst as servants and are surrounded by "locations" where the black mine workers and their families are housed. Helen Shaw chooses a lover, Paul Clark, who has committed his professional and personal life to ameliorating the misery of blacks in the townships on the periphery of Johannesburg, on weekdays through his position in the government office dealing with native housing, on weekends through work for the black African National Congress.

Paul meets with frustration at every turn. His inability to get anything done that will have a lasting impact affects the quality of his relationship with Helen. He torments her in small ways, and she reciprocates. He feels ashamed and she feels ashamed, and they become aware of "a burned-out loneliness in the very center of one's love for the other." Helen, who had come to believe that the only way for a man to fulfill himself in South Africa was "to pit himself against the oppression of the Africans" and who had wanted to live with Paul "in the greatest possible intimacy" is compelled to leave him. His political commitments, which made him so attractive to Helen in the first place, have damaged their love irretrievably.

Helen decides to go to Europe. During the few days she spends at the port city, she meets Joel Aron, with whom she had become good friends in Atherton, the town where they grew up. Joel is off to try to make a life for himself in Israel. At first, Helen is envious of Joel; he's headed for a new life in a new country. She feels homeless. South Africa is like a battleground; she cannot join the whites, and the blacks do not want her. She does not want to end up like Paul, "with a leg and arm nailed to each side." In the course of her conversations with Joel, however, she succeeds in coming to a better understanding of her situation. She is not going to be tempted by exile and a new beginning. She accepts South Africa as home and the place to which she must return.

A WORLD OF STRANGERS

Toby Hood, the protagonist of *A World of Strangers*, has grown up in England in a family quite different from Helen Shaw's. Had Toby been a bolter from school and a rebel against bourgeois values, his parents would have loved him all the more. His parents do not care about what other members of the upper-middle class think about them; they care about justice. Through his home there is a constant procession of victims of injustice who have come for aid

from the Hoods. Thus, there have been bred into Toby "a horror of the freedom that is freedom only to be free" and a consciousness of the need to make every activity in which one engages an act of conscience. Toby, however, is not persuaded. His parents have not been successful in making him into a reformer and protester like themselves. Abstractions such as justice and socialism do not thrill him. Toby wants to live a life oblivious to the suffering in the world; what he feels most inclined to do is enjoy whatever is left of privilege.

Toby is sent to take over the management temporarily of the South African branch of the family-owned publishing company. Arriving in Johannesburg, he is determined to find his own interests and amusements, and not be channeled by the reformers back in England or distracted by the examples of humanity's cruelty to others that will occur before his eyes. Indeed, it seems to Toby that those who would live private lives have become a hunted species, and he resents being hunted. Toby is confirmed in his desire to avoid being a do-gooder by his discovery of a talented black man who also insists upon living his own life, regardless of the condition of his people and his country. Toby marvels at the spirit and vitality of Steven Sitole. Steven refuses to allow the chaos and filth of the black townships and the hovels in which he sleeps either to deaden his spirit or inflame it to rage. He does what he does, seeking pleasure, satisfaction, or quick delight. He has no time for sorrow, pity, guilt, or even anger. He makes his money running an insurance racket, he gets into debt, he gets drunk, he laughs. He fleeces his own people and outwits whites. He is a new kind of man in the black townships; he is of them and not of them. The blacks who know him love him, and Toby Hood loves him as well.

Toby sees in Steven a brother. Drawn to him as if by a magnet at their first meeting, Toby goes into the townships with Steven, meets Steven's friends, gets drunk with him, and sleeps in the same hovels with him. What Steven can do with his life is so severely limited by white authority that he must live without hope or dignity; his life can only be a succession of gestures. That recognition by Toby illumines his own predicament. Steven was born into a South Africa that would not permit him "to come into his own; and what I believed should have been my own was destroyed before I was born heir to it."

Toby undergoes a transformation in the course of the novel. He has had the unusual experience of being able to enter alternately both black township life and the life of upper-crust Johannesburg. As much as he had thought that the privileged life was his natural base, he finds that life—for all its varied forms of recreation, luxury, freedom, and the outward good health of the rich—an empty, superficial existence. The rich, like Helen Shaw's middle-class mining-town family, are out of touch with "the real flow of life." Toby attempts a love affair with the most beautiful available woman among his circle of rich acquaintances. Primarily because the woman, Cecil Rowe, is incapable of expanding her concerns beyond herself, the affair comes to nothing more than a few perfunctory sexual encounters. On the other hand, Toby's relationship with Anna Louw, who is so different, is no more satisfying. She is a lawyer who is a former Communist and whose professional life is devoted to aiding blacks. Hers is anything but the self-centered life of Steven Sitole or Cecil Rowe; always sober, without embarrassment, she is unresponsive to the lure of euphoria. At the end of the novel, Cecil has accepted the marriage proposal of a wealthy businessman. Anna, too, is to begin a new phase. She has been arrested and is to be tried for treason. Anna is a prototype of the committed woman, the full development of whom in Gordimer's fiction does not occur until twenty years later, in *Burger's Daughter*.

Toby decides to stay in South Africa for a second year. His experiences with Cecil and the rich have made him reassess his conception of himself. As different as they are in character and personality, Toby has been greatly affected by both Steven and Anna, and the effect has been to make him care about the people of the townships. One of Gordimer's great accomplishments in this novel, as it is in her later work, is her rendering of township life. Toby also undergoes his transformation because Gordimer has made him think about what he has seen of township life on his sojourns with Steven. Life in the townships is more real than life among whites. There, the demands of life cannot be evaded through distractions; reality is right on the surface as well as below: "There is nothing for the frustrated man to do but grumble in the street; there was nothing for the deserted girl to do but sit on the step and wait for her bastard to be born; there was nothing to be done with the drunk but let him lie in the yard until he'd got over it." Among the whites, it is different. Frustrations can be forgotten through golf or horse racing, and trips to Europe take away the pain of broken love affairs.

In *A World of Strangers*, Gordimer has attempted to show a young man wholly bent on pursuing private concerns who, in the very process of pursuing those concerns, is changed into someone who cannot remain oblivious to South African injustice and unreason. To the extent that the reader can accept the change in Toby, the novel is successful.

OCCASION FOR LOVING

Jessie Stilwell, the protagonist of *Occasion for Loving*, is a well-educated, freethinking socialist of the most enlightened, undogmatic kind. She might well have been arrested and tried for treason, but that would be in a different life from the one that fate has bestowed upon her. Her reality is her life as the mother of four children and a helpmate to Tom, a liberal history professor. She could be Helen Shaw fifteen years later, domesticated.

Jessie is content. Her husband, children, and home give continuity to her life; she is in touch with her past, and the future, in five-year blocks at least, seems predictable. She has room to develop; she can pick and choose goals for herself and pursue them to their conclusion. She is a total realist; she knows what is possible and what is not. She is at a point in her life when she will do nothing that is "wild and counter to herself." When someone else in the family causes discord, she will deal with it. Jessie has a son by a previous marriage who, in his adolescence, has become mildly disruptive. The task she wishes to devote herself to is repairing her relationship with him.

Jessie, however, cannot become absorbed in this duty because there are two new presences in her home. Against her better judgment, she has allowed her husband to invite to live with them a colleague and his young wife, Boaz and Ann Cohen. Boaz is a musicologist and is frequently away from Johannesburg to study the music and instruments of tribes. Ann is free to occupy her time as she wishes. What comes to dominate Ann's life is a love affair with a married black man, Gideon Shibalo. The difficulties and dangers of an interracial love affair are such that the lovers necessarily need the help of others. Thus, the affair between Ann and Gideon, whom Jessie and Tom like, intrudes upon the life of the Stilwells, and Jessie resents it.

Even when Jessie goes off with three of her children for a vacation by the sea, she must deal with Ann and Gideon, for they turn up at the remote cottage. Boaz has learned about his wife's affair, and Ann and Gideon decide to be with each other day and night; given South Africa's race laws, that means they must live an underground life. They appeal to Jessie to let them stay. Again, she resents the intrusion, but she yields to their need.

Boaz will not disavow Ann. His freedom to act in response to his wife's adultery is limited by his unwillingness to do anything that would harm a black man. Indeed, the affair itself may owe its birth to its interracial difficulties: "The basis of an exciting sympathy between two people is often some obstacle that lies long submerged in the life of one." After leading Gideon to believe that she was ready to go to Europe or some other African country with him, Ann leaves him, returns to Boaz, and the two, reunited, quickly leave South Africa. This action plunges Gideon into alcoholism.

Jessie's meditation on the affair makes clear the meaning Gordimer wants to convey. Race is a force even between lovers; personal lives are affected by society and politics. In South Africa, white privilege is a ubiquitous force; it provides Ann the freedom to go, denying Gideon the same freedom. White privilege is "a silver spoon clamped between your jaws and you might choke on it for all the chance there was of dislodging it." So long as there is no change in South Africa, "nothing could bring integrity to personal relationships." Had Jessie been more involved

in the plot of the novel or even at the heart of its interest, the novel would have been more satisfying. Jessie, however, remains an objective observer and commentator. It is she with whom the reader identifies, yet not much happens to her; the events belong to Ann and Gideon.

THE LATE BOURGEOIS WORLD

Gordimer's fourth novel, *The Late Bourgeois World*, is her least successful. Brief and unconvincing, it is something of a parable, but it does not hit with the impact of the well-told parable. Too much has to be deduced. Without a knowledge of Gordimer's interests from her other works, the reader is hard pressed to see the meaning and coherence in this work. *The Late Bourgeois World* tells the story, with a great deal of indirection, of a Johannesburg woman whose marriage has broken up and who must take responsibility for a teenage son. Elizabeth Van Den Sandt, like Jessie Stilwell, does not have much feeling for the son of an ended marriage. Elizabeth's son, like Jessie's, is in a boarding school. Elizabeth's having to bring her son the news that his father is dead by suicide is what gives the plot its impetus.

Max Van Den Sandt is the scion of one of Johannesburg's best families, but he rejects his heritage and white privilege. He marries Elizabeth, the medical-lab technician whom he has made pregnant. He joins the Communist Party, he participates in marches against the government, and, in the climax to his rebellion, he is arrested on a charge of sabotage. How much of what Max has done is gesture, though, and how much is the result of conviction? After serving fifteen months in prison, Max turns state's evidence and betrays his former colleagues. In return, he is released from prison. Then comes the suicide, which for Elizabeth provides the final answer; her former husband was a hollow man. It is possible to be a revolutionary without real conviction.

While allowing herself to indulge her contempt for Max, Elizabeth herself turns out to be unwilling to risk very much for the cause. She has the opportunity to respond positively to the plea of a young, handsome black activist for money to help pay for the defense of some of his friends who have been arrested, but Elizabeth equivocates and puts him off. The participation of whites from the middle class in the black revolution, Gordimer seems to suggest, is very unreliable. No matter how strong their sympathies appear to be, for whites the political struggle is not the imperative it is for blacks. The novel's title suggests another, complementary theme. Despite its staunch defense of its own privileges, the bourgeois world is falling apart. Families rupture too easily, children are shunted off for custodial care, commitments do not count. Elizabeth and Max are case histories.

A GUEST OF HONOUR

Set in an invented nation in central Africa for which she has provided a detailed history and geography, *A Guest of Honour* is Gordimer's only novel that does not deal with South Africa. Still, the kinds of events depicted in this novel could very well occur in South Africa at some future time. With independence gained and a native government functioning in the place of the former British colonial administration, there are expectations of dramatic changes: Civil rights will be respected, greater care will be taken in administering justice, natural resources will be used for the benefit of the people, the standard of living of the masses will improve. President Mweta believes that these legitimate expectations are being fulfilled in an orderly way and at a satisfactory rate. Edward Shinza, without whom independence might not yet have come, is dissatisfied. He believes that the country is no better off than it would have been under colonial rule. He is seeking a way to have an impact on the course of events. He may even be conspiring with the nation across the border. To Mweta, his former comrade Shinza is "a cobra in the house."

The novel's protagonist is Colonel James Bray, an Englishman who has been a district officer in the colonial administration. Bray is likable and loyal, a wholly sympathetic character. During the struggle for independence, he was of significant assistance to Mweta and Shinza. Now Mweta has invited Bray back to be an honored guest at Independence Day celebrations. Much to his chagrin, Bray discovers that while Mweta is covered with glory as the new nation's leader, Shinza, every bit Mweta's equal if not his better, has no role in governing the country and has not been invited to the celebrations; indeed, Shinza is living in obscurity in the bush. To Bray, this is an ominous sign.

President Mweta sends Colonel Bray on a mission to Gala, the district Bray formerly administered. He is to survey the district's educational needs. With Gala, Gordimer gives the first demonstration of her formidable knowledge of the life and people of rural Africa, of which she was to give further demonstrations in *July's People* and to a lesser extent in *The Conservationist*. With Gala, she has the opportunity to do a canvas of a whole province. She makes Bray pleased to be back in Gala and curious about what has happened in his absence. He knows the language, he likes the people, and he resonates sympathetically with the daily round of life. While in Gala, Bray will track down Shinza and get his viewpoint on the progress of the nation.

Shinza believes Mweta's principal concern is to consolidate his own power. He has no tolerance for dissent and is quite willing to use the police and torture to stifle it. Mweta allows foreign corporations to extract raw materials and export them rather than finding opportunities to make use of the country's natural wealth at home. Mweta will not allow any changes in the country that might give pause to these foreign interests. Shinza believes that Mweta's actions, taken together, make up a pattern of betrayal. While Shinza is trying to reassert himself by becoming a force within the trade-union movement, he also may be gathering a counterrevolutionary army, but his present intention is to attack Mweta through the unions and strikes.

Shinza comes onto center stage for the length of his impassioned speech on the ideals of the revolution at the congress of the People's Independent Party (P.I.P.), which has its factions but is still the only political party. Bray, who attends, cannot help but prefer the ideals of Shinza to the charisma and policies of accommodation of Mweta. In presenting the milieu of the party congress and in revealing the subtleties of motivations, alliances, and positions, Gordimer demonstrates a first-rate political intelligence. She has Shinza make use of his union support as the first phase in his scheme to dislodge Mweta; she has Mweta in turn capitalizing on the nationalistic fervor of the youth group within the P.I.P. to get them to attack strongholds of union supporters. Violence breaks out in Gala, and Bray is an accidental victim.

Bray, Shinza, and Mweta are new characters in Gordimer's gallery. She knows them and their social and political contexts exceedingly well. *A Guest of Honour* shows a prescience and knowledge that carry it to the top rank of political novels.

THE CONSERVATIONIST

With *The Conservationist*, Gordimer turned back to South Africa. Again, she chose a male protagonist, Mehring, who bears no resemblance to anyone in her previous novels. Although this novel is of far larger scope, it is perhaps most similar to *The Late Bourgeois World*, for in both novels Gordimer attempts to delineate the lifestyle of a particular rung of white Johannesburg society. Mehring is a forty-nine-year-old industrialist and financier; he serves on several boards of directors. Given no other name, Mehring is admired and respected by everyone in his business and social circles, but it is clear that his life is essentially without meaning. He is deeply committed to nothing, not to ideology, country, or class, not to a sport, not to a single human being. He is quite the opposite of Colonel Bray.

Mehring has much more money than he needs. On impulse, he decides to buy a farm, very conveniently located only twenty-five miles from the city. Owning a farm will give him a feeling of being in contact with the land; it is something that is expected of a man of his station and wealth. The farm, however, complicates Mehring's life. He is unable to enjoy simple ownership; he must try to make the farm productive. He will practice conservation; he will see to it that buildings are repaired, fences mended, firebreaks cleared. The farm comes to occupy much more of his time and thought than he had intended. Nothing about the land, the weather, or the black people who live and work on the farm can be taken for granted. Something unexpected and unwanted is always occurring. A dead man is found on the property.

The dead man is black, and so the white police are not particularly concerned. Mehring expects them to remove the body and conduct an investigation, but they do neither. The unidentified body remains in a shallow, unmarked grave on Mehring's property. The presence of that body in the third pasture is troubling both to Mehring and to his black workers, although Mehring is never moved to do anything about it.

Much of the novel consists of Mehring's stream of consciousness. Along with the black man's body, another frequent presence in Mehring's consciousness is the woman with whom he has been having an affair. An attractive white liberal whose husband is away doing linguistic research in Australia, she has been drawn to Mehring because of his power; she is daring enough to taunt him and make light of that power. She is convinced that the reign of the whites in South Africa is nearing its end, yet she is a dilettante. When she gets into trouble with the authorities because of her associations with blacks, she wants to flee the country. She is humbled into asking Mehring to use his connections so that she can leave, and she sets herself up in London. Mehring, though, continues to think about her long after she has gone.

Mehring's relationship with this woman has been entirely superficial; when she is gone he thinks about her but does not really long for her. His relationships with his colleagues and their families are also superficial. These connections are so meaningless to him that he reaches a point where he does not want either their invitations or their concern. On the few occasions each year when he has the company of his son, he has no real interest in overcoming the barriers between them. His son, like his lover, does not believe that apartheid and white privilege can survive for long. The son is contemptuous of what his father represents. He leaves South Africa to join his mother in New York rather than serve his term in the army. In his self-willed isolation, Mehring spends more of his time at the farm. Despite himself, as he discusses routine farm business with his black foreman, Jacobus, and as they deal with the emergencies caused by drought, fire, and flooding, Mehring finds himself feeling more and more respect for Jacobus.

Mehring spends New Year's Eve alone at the farm. As the new year approaches, he wanders across his moonlit field and settles with his bottle against the wall of a roofless, stone storehouse. He carries on a convivial conversation with old Jacobus. They talk about their children, the farm, cattle. They laugh a lot. They get along well. Jacobus, however, is not there. For Mehring, such easy, honest talk with a black can take place only in fantasy.

In the final chapter of the novel, the unidentified body in the third pasture is brought to the surface by flooding. The black workers, under Jacobus's direction, make a coffin, at last giving the man a proper burial. Mehring, in the meantime, is engaged in another of his faceless sexual encounters. He could be killed. If he is killed, where will he be buried? Who are the real owners of the land to which he has title? Gordimer is suggesting that the unknown black man has more of a claim to the land than Mehring has. Mehring and his kind are going to meet ignoble ends. Their claim to the land of South Africa is so tenuous that their bodies will not even deserve burial.

There is little that is sympathetic about Mehring, which leaves Gordimer with the difficult task of keeping the reader interested in his activities. Once he begins to spend more time on the farm, his activities inevitably involve his black workers. Gordimer seizes the opportunity to render in some detail the life of their community. A few of them become minor characters of substance. Gordimer juxtaposes the flow of vital life in the black community with Mehring's isolation and decadence and thereby saves the novel from being utterly unappealing.

BURGER'S DAUGHTER

Burger's Daughter is Gordimer's best novel. It is set between 1975 and 1977, as important changes are taking place in southern Africa but not yet in South Africa. The independence movements in Angola and Mozambique have succeeded. The Portuguese are in retreat, their colonial rule to be replaced by native governments. South Africa, however, remains firmly in the grip of the white minority. The white South African government will relinquish nothing.

Rosa Burger, the protagonist, is Gordimer's most fully achieved character. The hero of the novel, however, is Rosa's father, Lionel Burger. Just before he is to be sentenced to life imprisonment, Lionel Burger

has the opportunity to address the court. He speaks for almost two hours. He explains why he and the Communist Party, of which he is a leader, have been driven to engage in the acts of sabotage for which he has been on trial. For thirty years, to no avail, he and South African Communists had struggled without resort to violence to gain civil rights and the franchise for the country's black majority. The great mass movement that is the African National Congress has been outlawed. In desperation, selected symbolic targets have been sabotaged. If such symbolic actions fail to move the white ruling class, there will be no further careful consideration of tactics. The only way to a new society will be through massive, cataclysmic violence.

Lionel Burger, in his childhood, was already sensitive to the unjust treatment of blacks. Later, as a medical student and doctor, he found it easier to accustom himself to the physical suffering of patients than to the subjection and humiliation forced upon blacks. He could not be silent and simply accept. He joined the Communist Party because he saw white and black members working side by side; there were people who practiced what they preached; there were white South Africans who did not deny the humanity of black South Africans. As a Communist, Lionel Burger came to accept the Marxist view of the dominance of economic relationships; thus, he perceived the oppression of blacks to be rooted in white South Africans' desire to maintain their economic advantages. Burger made a covenant with the victims.

Rosa Burger is very different from her father. She is also different from her mother, who was familiar with prison and who from young womanhood was known as a "real revolutionary." Both her father and her mother regard the family as totally united in their dedication to the struggle. Rosa, named in tribute to Rosa Luxemburg, the German revolutionary Marxist, knows that the family is not united. While her parents are free and active, she has no choice but to be an extension of them. Her mother has died, however, and, after three years of his life term, her father dies. When they are gone, Rosa does not take up their work. She is twenty-seven and has been in her parents' revolutionary circle since childhood. She has carried out numerous secret missions. Recently, she has pretended to be the fiancée of a prisoner in order to bring him messages. With the death of her father, she cannot deny that she is tired of such a life. She does not want to have anything more to do with the endangered and the maimed, with conspiracies and fugitives, with courts and prisons. Much more pointedly, *Burger's Daughter* deals with questions first considered in *A World of Strangers* and *Occasion for Loving:* To what extent must individual lives be governed by the dictates of time and place and circumstances not of the individual's choosing? Can a person ignore the facts and conditions that circumscribe his or her life and still live fully, or must a meaningful life necessarily be one that is integrated with the "real flow of life"? Despite his wealth and station, Mehring led a dismal life, because there was no such integration. Rosa Burger, though, is not devoid of redeeming qualities. She already has given much of herself.

Rosa chooses to escape. At first she escapes within the city of Johannesburg, in the tiny cottage of a rootless young white man, a graduate student of Italian literature who survives by working as a clerk to a bookmaker. Rosa and Conrad start out as lovers; after a while they are more like siblings. Conrad, too, is struggling to be free, not of a revolutionary heritage but of his bourgeois heritage. Even after she is no longer with him, Rosa continues to talk to Conrad, silently.

Rosa decides to leave South Africa, but she cannot get a passport because she is the daughter of Lionel Burger. Brandt Vermeulen is a cosmopolitan Boer, a new Afrikaner of a distinguished old Afrikaner family. He has studied politics at Leyden and Princeton and has spent time in Paris and New York. Vermeulen resembles Mehring, but he is rooted, more cultured, and more committed to the status quo. His solution for South Africa is to create separate nations for whites and blacks. Rosa goes to see him because he has friends in the Ministry of the Interior, which issues passports. Playing on the fact that he and Lionel Burger emerged from very similar backgrounds, Rosa succeeds in persuading him to use his influence to get her a passport.

The second part of this three-part novel takes place in Europe. Rosa goes to the French Riviera and looks up the woman who had been Lionel Burger's wife before he met Rosa's mother. The woman, who used to be known as Katya and who now is known as Madame Bagnelli, is delighted that Burger's daughter has come to stay with her. Rosa is welcomed by Madame Bagnelli's circle, consisting of unmarried couples, émigrés, homosexuals, persons formerly prominent in Paris, rootless persons for the most part. On the Riviera, life is easy, difference is distinction. Survival is not an issue. Politics seems a waste of time, revolution a form of craziness.

There is great empathy between Rosa and Madame Bagnelli. As Katya, the latter, years before, found it a relief to give up the role of revolutionary that was required of her as Burger's wife. She had not always been able to put private concerns aside; she had been considered a bourgeoise or even a traitor and was subjected to Party discipline. She has no regrets about leaving that part of her life. Rosa is encouraged about her own course. She allows herself the luxury of a love affair.

After a summer of love, Rosa and Bernard Chabalier make plans to live together in Paris, where he is a teacher at a lycée. Rosa visits London while Bernard makes arrangements in Paris. She attends a party for South African exiles and is filled with joy at meeting her black "brother," Baasie, who as a child had been taken into the Burger home but whom Rosa has not seen for twenty years. Rosa is shocked by Baasie's attitude; he is hostile and sullen.

That night in London, Rosa's sleep is broken by a phone call from Baasie. He is angry. He wants her to know that he did not have the life Burger's daughter had. He had been pushed back to the mud huts and tin shanties. His father was a revolutionary who also died in prison, driven to hang himself. No one knows of Isaac Vulindlela, but everyone talks about Lionel Burger. He hates hearing about Burger, the great man who suffered for the blacks. He knows plenty of blacks who have done as much as Burger, but they go unknown. He does not want to be her black brother, he tells Rosa.

Rosa goes back to South Africa. She does not

want the soft life Bernard will provide for her in Paris. Defection is not possible. Suffering cannot be evaded. Back in Johannesburg, Rosa takes up the occupation for which she trained, physiotherapy. She also works for the revolution. As the novel ends late in 1977, Rosa is in prison. The authorities have solid evidence of unlawful acts.

JULY'S PEOPLE

In the brief *July's People* the end has come. Civil war rages; blacks are fighting whites. The whites have discipline, organization, knowledge, equipment. The blacks have will and numbers. They have the support of the rest of the continent, and the Russians and their Cuban allies are close at hand. Thousands of lives will be lost, but there can be no doubt about the eventual outcome. The artificial society based on apartheid is finished.

Bamford Smales is an architect, an upper-middle-class professional. His wife, Maureen, is, like Jessie Stilwell, an excellent helpmate, a strong, compassionate, intelligent woman. Before the uprisings, Bam and Maureen knew that unless whites, of their own volition, made significant reforms, a conflagration was inevitable. They tried to show the way among their friends and neighbors, treating their male servant, July, with the utmost consideration. They did not, however, go so far as to break the ties with their community. They lived their lives within the pattern they found for their race and their class. Their liberal attitudes had no impact.

When the uprisings begin, the Smaleses flee their Johannesburg suburb. With their three young children, they drive six hundred kilometers in their recreational pickup truck to July's home village. Even though black-white relations are being turned upside down, July is still willing to oblige them; for fifteen years obliging the Smales family has been his life's purpose. Even after their dependence on him is clear, July continues to address Bam Smales as "master." He even moves his mother from her own hut so the Smales family can settle in it.

When they arrive in the village, the Smaleses are July's people. Over the course of a few weeks, relations change. July has been reunited with his wife and children, whom for fifteen years he has seen only

on his vacations every other year. July becomes a presence among the people of his village. *They* become July's people, and his loyalty to the white family is eroded. That erosion occurs slowly through a number of ambiguous situations, for July has no political sensibility. As the relationship between the black servant and the white family loses its structure, July becomes less and less the servant and more and more the master of the family's fate.

When the Smales vehicle, the yellow "bakkie," first pulls into the village, there is no doubt concerning its ownership, but as July runs errands to the locked bakkie, he comes to be the possessor of the keys to the vehicle. He does not know how to drive, but his young protégé Daniel does. July turns the keys over to Daniel, and they drive off to a store. After this, it is difficult for Bam Smales to claim sole ownership; and it is even more difficult once Daniel has taught July how to drive. Bam Smales has a shotgun. Although he tries to keep its hiding place a secret, the whole village seems to know where the gun is kept. When Bam discovers that the gun is gone, he is beside himself. The loss of the gun emasculates him. On his way to join the freedom fighters, Daniel has helped himself to the gun.

The family's future is completely uncertain. As the villagers begin to break the habit of deference to white skins, the Smaleses become nervous about their safety. They would leave, but they have nowhere to go. The predicament proves too much for Maureen. Sensing an opportunity to save herself, she runs off, frantically, leaving her husband and children. The Smaleses are victims of apartheid. When the tables are turned, as they surely must be, only a miracle will save whites from suffering what they made others suffer.

A SPORT OF NATURE

A Sport of Nature combines elements from several of Gordimer's earlier works. Like Helen in *The Lying Days*, Hillela Capran is a bolter, though not out of obvious rebelliousness. Rather, she is moved by the spirit of the moment in a more unthinking way. The family with whom she lives during her adolescence—her aunt Pauline, uncle Joe, and cousins Sasha and Carole—are similar to the Hoods of *A*

World of Strangers, for they also are white liberals, trying ever to be ruled by acts of conscience rather than convenience, as Hillela's Aunt Olga and Uncle Arthur are.

Gordimer's early habit of distancing the reader from her characters is echoed in her treatment of Hillela. The first half of the book has Hillela spoken of mostly in the third person; she does not really come alive until after she meets Whaila Kgomani, a black revolutionary who becomes her first husband and the father of her child. His assassination changes the course of Hillela's life as she inherits his revolution.

Hillela's character has been regarded by many of Gordimer's readers as amoral and shocking, and even Gordimer has admitted that this creation fascinates her probably as much as anyone else. Yet, she does not back down from her portrayal of a revolutionary who accomplishes most of her goals through the use of her feminine wiles. *A Sport of Nature* may not be Gordimer's best book, but it is as thought-provoking as any of her earlier works. Its portrayal of the future, which includes a black African state installed in place of South Africa, has caused some critics to label the work weak and unbelievable.

MY SON'S STORY

Gordimer's novels of the 1990's cover the years from the closing days of apartheid to the new democracy in South Africa. In *My Son's Story* the struggle for freedom is ongoing. Gordimer's recurrent theme of the balance between public and private life is again central. In this novel, the private is sacrificed to the political. Sonny initially seems destined to live under the restrictions of apartheid, but changes and sacrifices his teaching career to align his life with, and help, those he thinks of as the "real blacks." Sonny moves his family illegally to a white suburb of Johannesburg, one poor enough to ignore the settling of a family of mixed ancestry.

The movement claims first Sonny, then his daughter Baby, and finally his wife Aila. Will, the son named for Shakespeare, remains aloof from political involvement but chronicles the struggle by narrating the disintegration of his family. Before detention and exile claim the three family members and a bomb de-

stroys their home, the family is already disintegrating from Sonny's liaison with Hannah Plowman, a white human rights worker who visits Sonny the first time he is jailed.

Although Gordimer has used such narrators in her short stories, this is her first novel narrated by a young male character from one of the disenfranchised groups in South Africa. The novel fluctuates between the first-person narration by Will and a seemingly third-person account of information the young Will could not possibly know, such as Sonny's thoughts and the details of his intimacy with Hannah. The last chapter of the novel unites the dual point of view, with Will claiming authorship of the whole. He has created—out of his own frustration, experience, and knowledge of the participants—the scenes and thoughts he could not know firsthand. Thrust by the times and by his family into the role of a writer, Will plans to hone his writing skills by chronicling the struggle for freedom in South Africa.

NONE TO ACCOMPANY ME

None to Accompany Me reveals the life of Vera Stark, a lawyer who heads a foundation that during apartheid works to minimize the removal of blacks to crowded, inferior land and after apartheid works to reclaim for them the land they have lost. With some reluctance, she leaves the foundation temporarily to join a commission drafting the new constitution for South Africa. The novel emphasizes how all aspects of her personal life—her home, children, and husband—become secondary to her work. True to her name, Vera Stark whittles all excess from her life, striving to find through social responsibility her true center.

THE HOUSE GUN

In *The House Gun*, Claudia and Harald Lindgard, privileged South Africans who neither supported nor demonstrated against apartheid, are thrust out of their private lives into the public. Their twenty-seven-year-old son Duncan killed a man. The parents keep their pledge, made to Duncan in childhood, that no matter the difficulty, he can always come to them for support. Reconciling themselves to his action is no easy matter, however, and dealing with that truth causes them to question their own attitudes about justice. Suddenly, whether the new constitution outlaws capital punishment is a vital personal issue. Duncan's is a personal, not a political, crime, but the novel connects his crime to the violence the country has known and still knows. Both the easy access to a gun and the climate of violence Duncan grew up with play a part in an appeal for a lenient sentence. Even though the novel makes no overt mention of the country's Truth and Reconciliation Commission, after facing the truth, the Lindgards must search for reconciliation just as the South Africans are doing the same under the new democracy. Time must determine whether any of the three Lindgards become reconciled to the brutal truth of the murder.

From her first, somewhat autobiographical novel *The Lying Days*, Gordimer has probed moral and political questions with honesty and unfailing courage, never being dogmatic or predetermining outcomes, allowing vividly imagined characters and communities lives of their own. Her work does more than shed light on the predicament of South Africa; it deals in depth with the problems of individual identity, commitment and obligation, and justice. Gordimer is a novelist who clearly has a place in the great tradition of George Eliot, Dostoevski, Joseph Conrad, and Thomas Mann.

Paul Marx, updated by Marion Petrillo

OTHER MAJOR WORKS

SHORT FICTION: *Face to Face: Short Stories*, 1949; *The Soft Voice of the Serpent and Other Stories*, 1952; *Six Feet of the Country*, 1956; *Friday's Footprint and Other Stories*, 1960; *Not for Publication and Other Stories*, 1965; *Livingstone's Companions: Stories*, 1971; *Selected Stories*, 1975; *A Soldier's Embrace*, 1980; *Something Out There*, 1984; *Jump and Other Stories*, 1991; *Why Haven't You Written?: Selected Stories, 1950-1972*, 1992.

NONFICTION: *On the Mines*, 1973 (with David Goldblatt); *The Black Interpreters*, 1973; *Lifetimes Under Apartheid*, 1986 (with Goldblatt); *The Essential Gesture: Writing, Politics, and Places*, 1988; *Writing and Being*, 1995; *Living in Hope and History: Note from Our Century*, 1999.

TELEPLAYS: *A Chip of Glass Ruby*, 1985; *Country*

Lovers, 1985; *Oral History*, 1985; *Praise*, 1985.

EDITED TEXT: *South African Writing Today*, 1967 (with Lionel Abrahams).

BIBLIOGRAPHY

Bazin, Nancy Topping, and Marilyn Dallman Seymour, eds. *Conversations with Nadine Gordimer.* Jackson: University Press of Mississippi, 1990. Thirty-four interviews from 1958 to 1989 are chronologically arranged and include biographical material, Gordimer's views on South African politics, and discussion of her literature and of other South African writers and literature. Indexed. Includes a chronology of Gordimer's career to 1990.

Clingman, Stephen. *The Novels of Nadine Gordimer: History from the Inside.* 2d ed. London: Allen & Unwin, 1992. Interprets Gordimer's work within the context of history in general and the history of South Africa and African literature in particular. Included are annotations to references within the chapters as well as a detailed bibliography divided into works by Gordimer, works about Gordimer, and works on South African history. The second edition includes a new prologue, which notes the dismantling of apartheid and Gordimer's Nobel Prize; also adds a discussion of *A Sport of Nature* and *My Son's Story.* Indexed.

Cooke, John. *The Novels of Nadine Gordimer: Private Lives/Public Landscapes.* Baton Rouge: Louisiana State University Press, 1985. Cooke concentrates on developing the common themes that run throughout Gordimer's fiction. His bibliography includes "Primary Sources" (lists of Gordimer's canon by genre) and "Secondary Sources" (books and articles about Gordimer). Indexed.

Driver, Dorothy, Ann Dry, Craig MacKenzie, and John Read, comps. *Nadine Gordimer: A Bibliography of Primary and Secondary Sources, 1937-1992.* London: Hans Zell, 1994. More than three thousand entries listed chronologically. Each critical book or article entry indicates which Gordimer works are covered. Includes a chronology of Gordimer's career to 1993. Several helpful indexes.

Ettin, Andrew Vogel. *Betrayals of the Body Politic: The Literary Commitments of Nadine Gordimer.*

Charlottesville: University Press of Virginia, 1993. An introduction and six chapters discuss Gordimer and her literature thematically. Dealing with her short stories, essays, interviews, and novels through 1991, the book covers themes such as deceptions, family tensions, and the conflict of the private and the public. The book includes plot descriptions and analysis. Indexed.

Head, Dominic. *Nadine Gordimer*. Cambridge, England: Cambridge University Press, 1994. Head interprets Gordimer's first ten novels. Indexed. Select bibliography of works by and about Gordimer. Chronology of Gordimer's career and major South African political events to 1991.

Heywood, Christopher. *Nadine Gordimer*. Windsor, England: Profile Books, 1983. Provides literary criticism rather than biographical background. Heywood highlights Gordimer's place among African authors. A detailed bibliographical section lists Gordimer's works as well as works (such as bibliographies and critical essays) about Gordimer and about Africa and African literature.

King, Bruce, ed. *The Later Fiction of Nadine Gordimer*. New York: St. Martin's Press, 1993. The introduction, surveying the variety in Gordimer's novels from *The Late Bourgeois World* (1966) to *My Son's Story* (1990), is followed by five general essays dealing thematically or stylistically with multiple novels, seven essays dealing with one or two novels in depth, and three essays dealing with short stories. Indexed. Notes on contributors.

Smith, Roland, ed. *Critical Essays on Nadine Gordimer*. Boston: G. K. Hall, 1990. Smith's introduction details positive and negative criticism of Gordimer's works. The sixteen essays, originally published between 1954 and 1988, show the development of Gordimer criticism and deal with her short stories and first nine novels. Indexed.

Wagner, Kathrin. *Rereading Nadine Gordimer*. Bloomington, Indiana: Indiana University Press, 1994. Writing the book while teaching in South Africa, Wagner brings a view from inside Gordimer's own country. The seven chapters provide a chronological rereading of Gordimer's first ten novels. Indexed. Chronological bibliography includes Gordimer's novels, short story collections, nonfiction, and interviews.

CAROLINE GORDON

Born: Todd County, Kentucky; October 6, 1895
Died: San Cristóbal de las Casas, Mexico; April 11, 1981

PRINCIPAL LONG FICTION
Penhally, 1931
Aleck Maury, Sportsman, 1934
None Shall Look Back, 1937
The Garden of Adonis, 1937
Green Centuries, 1941
The Women on the Porch, 1944
The Strange Children, 1951
The Malefactors, 1956
The Glory of Hera, 1972

OTHER LITERARY FORMS

Although Caroline Gordon was primarily a novelist, she wrote a number of superb short stories, several of which have been reprinted in anthologies for use in the classroom; "Old Red" is perhaps the best known, though "The Captive" and "The Last Day in the Field" have also received wide circulation. These and other of Gordon's stories were published originally in quality journals such as *Scribner's Review, Harper's, Sewanee Review*, and *Southern Review*, and they have been reprinted in three collections, *The Forest of the South* (1945), *Old Red and Other Stories* (1963), and *The Collected Stories of Caroline Gordon* (1981), with an introduction by Robert Penn Warren. Gordon lectured and published commentaries on the fiction of others, but she was not a literary critic in the usual sense; her interest was in setting forth and illustrating her theories about a method of writing fiction. These are contained in two works: *The House of Fiction: An Anthology of the Short Story* (1950, edited with Allen Tate) and *How to Read a Novel* (1957).

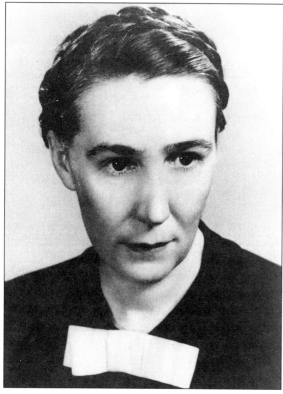

(Library of Congress)

ACHIEVEMENTS

Gordon's reputation was firmly established by the publication of her first novel, *Penhally*, particularly after it was reviewed by the English writer Ford Madox Ford in *Bookman*. Ford hailed Gordon as one of the important contemporary novelists writing in America. The succession of novels and stories that followed *Penhally*, her marriage to the poet Allen Tate and her association with the Vanderbilt Agrarians, her lectures, and the short-story textbook *The House of Fiction* are all a measure of her significant contribution to the Southern Renaissance.

Gordon has been particularly admired for her craftsmanship, for the skill with which—in the tradition of Henry James, Joseph Conrad, and Ernest Hemingway—she is able to create impressions of life that are at once realistic and symbolic. Following her chief master, James, Gordon was a scholar of the novel, and her fiction emphasizes technique above plot and character, so much so, in fact, that with few

exceptions, her books have never had popular appeal. *Aleck Maury, Sportsman* attracted an audience of hunters and fishermen, partly because of its subject, but also because the hero of the book is an appealing character. *None Shall Look Back* also attracted readers, particularly in the South, because of its evocation of the tragic heroism of the Civil War. *Green Centuries* dealt with material very popular in the 1930's, hardship on the frontier and conflicts between American Indians and white settlers, though it lacks both the sentimentality and moralizing that often made such fiction popular. The remainder of Gordon's novels are demanding books that require of the reader alertness to symbolic meanings and close attention to the implications of technique. As a consequence of its special kind of excellence, Gordon's fiction appeals primarily to other writers and scholars of narrative craft. Many novelists and short-story writers, including Flannery O'Connor and Walker Percy, have acknowledged a debt to Caroline Gordon.

BIOGRAPHY

Caroline Gordon was born on a farm in Todd County, Kentucky, on October 6, 1895. Her mother, Nancy Meriwether, was a Kentuckian; her father, James Morris Gordon, was born in Louisa County, Virginia. In the 1880's, he moved west to Kentucky and became tutor to the Meriwether family. Later, he established a classical school for boys in Clarksville, Tennessee, to which his daughter was sent. This was the beginning of her lifelong interest in classical literature, an interest that was deepened during her college years when she studied Greek literature at Bethany College (earning a B.A. in 1916). After teaching high school for three years, Gordon took a job as reporter in Chattanooga from 1920 to 1924, an experience she said was of no help to her in learning to write fiction.

In 1924, Gordon married Allen Tate, poet, essayist, and author of an important novel, *The Fathers* (1938). She had met Tate through Robert Penn Warren, who lived on a neighboring farm in Kentucky, and her marriage signaled the beginning of an important change not only in her personal life but also in her career as a novelist, for despite the fact that Tate was primarily a poet, he was also a perceptive critic of the novel and proved to be one of Gordon's most important early teachers. The Tates moved to New York the year of their marriage, and then, in 1928, went to France on money from Tate's Guggenheim Fellowship. There, a friendship with Ford Madox Ford that had begun in New York was reestablished, and Gordon offered her services to Ford as typist-secretary. The relationship with Ford was most fortunate for Gordon, because it was with Ford's help that she was able to complete her first novel, which later, through his review in *Bookman*, was called to the attention of important readers.

After *Penhally*'s critical success in 1931, Gordon was awarded a Guggenheim Fellowship, and the Tates spent the next year in France. On their return, they settled near Clarksville, Tennessee, and it was there—in a house the Tates called Benfolly—that Gordon wrote her next four novels and a number of short stories. In 1939, the Tates moved to Princeton, New Jersey, and although there were to be protracted stays in other places—Sewanee, Tennessee, and Minneapolis—Princeton was to be Gordon's permanent home for many years. The Tates were divorced in 1959, and thereafter Gordon served as visiting writer at universities in different parts of the United States. In the early 1970's, she founded her own school of writing at the University of Dallas and taught there until shortly before her death. She died in Mexico on April 11, 1981, where she had gone to be near her daughter, Nancy.

One other event in Gordon's life deserves special mention: her conversion in 1947 to Roman Catholicism. That conversion was a significant factor in her artistic as well as her personal life, for not only did it influence her subsequent fiction, but also it could be seen in retrospect as the logical culmination of a lifelong quest for models of moral perfection.

ANALYSIS

Caroline Gordon's theories of fiction and her debts to the writers who influenced her were spelled out in lectures that she gave at the University of Kansas and later published as *How to Read a Novel*, and in commentaries and appendices to *The House of Fiction*, an anthology of short stories she edited with

Tate. In her theory and in her practice, she combined ideas from Aristotle and Dante, Gustave Flaubert, Henry James, Ford Madox Ford, and James Joyce. From the modern masters came the technique of closely rendered scenes, the disappearance of the author from her fiction by means of an impersonal style, and the use of what Gordon called natural symbolism. From Aristotle came certain "constants," particularly his definition of tragedy as an "action of a certain magnitude" and the division of the novel's action into two parts, complication and resolution, with the resolution embedded in the complication. By "action," Gordon understood Aristotle to mean overt action; the hero of a novel, properly understood, was a person who acted, and Gordon went on to add that traditionally the hero always faced the same task: the overcoming of evil so that good might flourish. This is a limited view of the novelistic hero, but for understanding Gordon's fiction it is a useful definition; the heroes of all her novels, from *Penhally* to *The Glory of Hera*, can be understood in this light. The action of her novels invariably involves the facing of evil and an attempt by the hero to overcome it.

PENHALLY

In her first novel, *Penhally*, evil is defined from an agrarian perspective, and here one sees Gordon's kinship with the Vanderbilt group, who published Peter Smith's *I'll Take My Stand* in 1930. "Penhally" is the name of a plantation house in Tennessee, built in 1826 and passed down through the Llewellyn family into modern times. The current master, however—Nicholas Llewellyn—regards the Penhally lands not as a trust to be handed down but as a commodity to be exploited for his own gain. Nicholas's younger brother, Chance, loves the land but is excluded from ownership and is deeply grieved when Nicholas sells it to a Northern woman who turns it into a hunt club for rich strangers. At the opening ceremony of the new club, Chance, taunted by Nicholas for his old-fashioned attitudes, shoots his brother to death. Although this final action is presented in the detached manner of an impartial observer, the irony bitterly underscores the point, as one brother must kill another in a vain attempt to destroy what is evil: the misuse and perversion of the land.

ALECK MAURY, SPORTSMAN

Gordon's second novel, influenced to some extent by Siegfried Sassoon's *The Memoirs of a Fox-Hunting Man* (1928), also drew on her memories of her father, the prototype of the novel's hero, Aleck Maury, Gordon's most engaging character. Maury is a hunter and fisherman of remarkable skill and devotion to his sport. Unlike Gordon's other novels, which are written in the third person and in a somewhat detached manner, *Aleck Maury, Sportsman* is told in the first person by Maury himself as he recounts his attempts to escape from the demands of his wife, his teaching duties, and, later, his daughter, so that he can devote himself to the delights of his beloved pastimes. Andrew Lytle has referred to Maury as a man "dislocated" by the economic and cultural ruin of the South after the Civil War, which takes a more solemn view than the novel itself warrants, for Maury is a comic version of the hero: a man who overcomes evil (that is, duty) in order that good (fishing and hunting) might flourish. In this, he is eminently and delightfully successful.

NONE SHALL LOOK BACK

It is not surprising that *Aleck Maury, Sportsman* has been Gordon's most popular novel, for most of her novels present a tragic view of the human condition. Like F. Scott Fitzgerald, Gordon was at heart a traditional moralist, too intelligent to moralize and therefore in search of ways to establish moral values indirectly. Writing in the 1930's and 1940's, periods of disillusionment and rejection of traditional moral and religious beliefs—and herself, at the time, a nonbeliever—she had found in contrasting attitudes toward the land a way of dramatizing the conflict between good and evil. In her next novel, *None Shall Look Back*, Gordon located her moral ground on the Civil War battlefields and used actual historical personages, particularly Nathan Bedford Forrest, as exemplars of moral conduct and heroic action in the conflict between good and evil. Forrest, it might be said, represented a model or paradigm of heroic conduct, and by including him (an actual man who did act decisively and selflessly for a cause in which he believed) as a character in *None Shall Look Back*, Gordon could introduce into the novel a standard by which readers could judge the protagonist, Rives Allard, who fights and dies under Forrest's command, and his wife Lucy, who acts as the point-of-view character through whom one experiences the tragic death not only of Rives but also of the whole Southern cause. The distinguished historian of the novel, Walter Allen, complained in *The Modern Novel in Britain and the United States* (1964) that in *None Shall Look Back* Gordon failed to deal with the injustices of slavery. Such criticism misses the point. The novel is meant to be a tragic action, not a tract against slavery or racial prejudice. The Civil War happened, and people gave their lives for a cause in which they believed, a cause that they knew to be doomed. It is this quality of doom and sacrifice that *None Shall Look Back* movingly evokes.

THE GARDEN OF ADONIS

Since Gordon was neither a rebel against nor a defender of the status quo, but, like William Faulkner, a traditionalist in the modern world, she needed a way of giving authority to traditional values. Agrarianism, as a way of life as well as a philosophy, commanded respect in Nashville and in other pockets of the country, but not in New York or London. What was needed was the kind of mythological underpinning that T. S. Eliot had given his traditional moral vision in *The Waste Land* (1922). In Gordon's next novel, *The Garden of Adonis*, she was able to provide—and from one of Eliot's sources—that mythological underpinning. The title as well as the general structure of the book came from Sir James G. Frazer's *The Golden Bough* (1922); to be certain that the reader made the connection, Gordon used in an epigraph Frazer's account of how women of ancient Adonis cults would grow and tend newly sprouted plants in baskets (that is, Gardens of Adonis) that, together with images of the dead god, would then be flung into the sea or into springs. Gordon omitted Frazer's description of the more violent practice of sacrificing a living victim in a newly planted field in the belief that his or her death would propitiate the corn spirit and his or her blood would fatten the ears of corn. This omission was probably deliberate, for such descriptions standing at the head of the novel would have revealed too much too soon about the resolution of the action.

In Gordon's handling of the Adonis ritual, the sacrificial victim is a Tennessee planter named Ben Allard. With a young tenant, Allard has planted "on shares" a field of clover that becomes especially valuable when a severe drought ruins Allard's tobacco crop, for the clover survives the drought. The tenant, Ote Mortimer, becomes obsessed with winning the favors of a young woman and in order to get money to marry her, attempts to harvest the immature clover. Allard plants himself in the way of Ote's team, and Ote strikes him down and kills him. Although Ote is the instrument of Allard's death, it is clear that he is only acting symbolically for the commercial society which hems in and destroys the way of life Allard represents. This is made clear by the contrast between Allard's sense of honor and strict moral code and the promiscuity of his children and their attraction to purely material values. This moral laxness and lust for money, seen not only in Allard's family but also in the woman that Ote wants to marry, is responsible for raising Ote's hand against Allard. Allard's death, viewed in the limited perspective of naturalism, would seem a pointless and ironic sacrifice, but by giving her hero a mythological precursor, Gordon invites the reader to see him not as a hapless victim but rather as the embodiment of timeless values; for whether the world realizes it, Allard is a hero who stands up for what he believes, even gives his life in a heroic, if unprofitable, action.

GREEN CENTURIES

Four years elapsed between the publication of *The Garden of Adonis* and *Green Centuries*, Gordon's next novel, and the reason for the delay is quite clear. *The Garden of Adonis* had been written quickly and published the same year as *None Shall Look Back*; it was a novel that came out of the author's direct experience of life in Kentucky and Tennessee in the 1930's. *Green Centuries* is a carefully researched historical novel about Southern colonials pushing their way west into the vast new territory of Kentucky and is filled with the kind of detail expected of the best historical fiction: authentic accounts of daily life, travel, husbandry, courting, hunting, and quaint speech ways. One's first impression might be that in electing to write what appears to be another account

of hardihood on the frontier, Gordon has abandoned her usual subject in favor of a themeless historical romance. An exciting book about war and Indian raids and authentic historical characters such as Daniel Boone, the great hunter, and famous Cherokee Indian chiefs Atta Kulla Kulla and Dragging Canoe, the work fully deserved the Pulitzer Prize for which it was considered but which it did not win. *Green Centuries* also reflects Gordon's abiding concern for the glory and tragic splendor of heroic action. There are two main heroes in this novel: a white hunter, Rion Outlaw, a fictional creation of the author who embodies the qualities to be found in the historical Daniel Boone, and a character based on the Cherokee chief Dragging Canoe. Rion Outlaw, like his namesake Orion, the mythical hunter, leaves the Virginia colony after he participates in a raid on a government powder train and pushes into the west, where eventually he joins forces with settlers who have been attacked by the Cherokee Indians led by Dragging Canoe. When the stockade is attacked by Indians and Rion's beloved wife is killed, he is suddenly made aware both of his loss and of his irrepressible drive to continue westward, losing himself in the turning like the mythical Orion in the heavens.

Dragging Canoe, who led the attack against the settlers, is also heroic, for he has determined against the advice of older and wiser chiefs to fight the settlers rather than give up more Indian lands. Though his cause is doomed—Atta Kulla Kulla has been to London and knows the Indians are no match for the white man's "medicine"—Dragging Canoe dies fighting to preserve his nation and his way of life. Rion Outlaw and Dragging Canoe, though on opposite sides in the struggle over the Kentucky lands, are both presented sympathetically because Gordon is not interested in taking sides in the historical conflict; her interest, as usual, is in the exemplification of heroic virtue wherever it may be found.

THE WOMEN ON THE PORCH

There is a sense in which Gordon's return to an earlier and simpler time in American history can be seen as a retreat, for in order to make her case for heroism, she had to abandon the world of the present which other writers, such as Eliot, Fitzgerald, and

Hemingway, seemed to find more conducive to failure and despair than to heroic action. Gordon's next novel, *The Women on the Porch*, is set in the contemporary world, where disillusionment is rife and atrophy of the will is a mark of virtue. Her hero is Jim Chapman, a deracinated intellectual and professor of history at a New York university, whose affair with his assistant, Edith Ross, drives his wife Catherine away from the city and back to her ancestral home in Tennessee. For a time, Chapman wallows in uncertainty and moral confusion, but then he follows Catherine west, and after a strange vision in the woods of Swan Quarter, in which Catherine's pioneer forebear appears, Chapman is reunited with his wife. This action, though small when measured against the heroic deeds of the past, is for him deeply meaningful, since it signifies a return to action and a breaking out of the locked-in sensibility that has paralyzed his will.

Between the writing of *The Women on the Porch* and her next novel, *The Strange Children*, Gordon's personal life underwent a profound change: she became a convert to Catholicism. Looking backward from the perspective of this new novel, it is possible to see, if not the inevitability of that conversion, at least the logic of it. For Gordon, the commitment to art and the religious impulse were closely connected; both are, in their different ways, quests for perfection. Prior to her conversion, perfection meant not only perfection of form and style but of moral action as well, but action conceived in secular terms. In *The Strange Children* and in her next two novels, *The Malefactors* and *The Glory of Hera*, heroic action becomes not merely brave and selfless action that ends in an otherwise pointless death, but also moral action so that evil might be overcome and good might flourish.

THE STRANGE CHILDREN

The protagonist of *The Strange Children* is a girl, Lucy Lewis, whose parents, Stephen and Sarah Lewis, are cultivated intellectuals living at Benfolly, a farm in Tennessee. Stephen Lewis is writing a book about the Civil War, and on the weekend during which the action of the novel takes place, the Lewises are visited by a curious group of people: Kevin Reardon, a very rich, recent convert to Catholicism who has undergone a dramatic religious experience;

his pale, beautiful, but mad wife; and a friend, "Uncle" Tubby, who has been having an affair with Reardon's wife. The intrigue between the lovers, a moral crisis in Lucy's life (over a valuable crucifix she took from Reardon's room), and a spiritual crisis through which Lucy's parents are passing, are brought together at the end of the novel when the lovers elope, Lucy returns the crucifix, and Stephen Lewis is forced to recognize the desert in which those without religious faith are forced to wander. Reardon knew of Tubby's affair with his wife and had tried to warn him of her madness, but Tubby had only laughed. The good man had acted with the aid of a divine presence, while evil flourished in the elopement of the mad lovers; yet the seeds of understanding are planted in the mind of Stephen Lewis, who at the end of the novel is given to see the barrenness of his past and the terrors of a future devoid of faith.

THE MALEFACTORS

Thomas Claiborne, the protagonist of *The Malefactors*, Gordon's second "Catholic" novel, is in much the same state as Lewis at the end of *The Strange Children*, except that Claiborne is unaware of his spiritual emptiness. Like Isabelle Reardon, Claiborne is a poet who is also somewhat mad. He has periods during which he cannot write and hears a voice inside his head that makes critical comments about his conduct and state of mind. Claiborne lives on his wife's farm in Buck's County, Pennsylvania, and Vera Claiborne, a very rich woman, raises prize cattle. Like Tom Chapman of *The Women on the Porch*, Claiborne is a morally paralyzed intellectual, and like "Uncle" Tubby of *The Strange Children*, he becomes enamored of a woman poet, pursues her, and becomes involved in a sordid love affair that eventually drives him to seek guidance from a nun and, later, from a Catholic lay sister who operates a farm for Bowery derelicts. After a spiritual crisis in which he has frightening dreams and a drunken realization that only his wife truly loves him and that his mistress is interested only in furthering her own career, Claiborne, who had quarreled with his wife, is reunited with her at the upstate farm where she has gone to assist in the work with derelicts. The means by which Claiborne is brought to the threshold of what appears to be a religious conversion is a complicated series of actions involving insights, visions, accounts of miraculous conversions, and revelations about Vera's own early baptism into the Catholic faith. One can see how fully Gordon's own religious conversion made it possible to handle the tangled web of marital infidelity with much more complexity than she had in *The Women on the Porch*. The Church had given her the means to represent the triumph of goodness in a fallen world.

THE GLORY OF HERA

Some time after the publication of *The Malefactors*, Gordon began an ambitious project which she tentatively entitled *A Narrow Heart: The Portrait of a Woman*, a title which seemed to echo those of two works of which she was very fond: *A Simple Heart* (1877) by Flaubert and *The Portrait of a Lady* (1880-1881) by James. As originally planned, the book was to have had a higher and a lower action, the higher one consisting of tales from Greek mythology, the lower one, the author's fictionalized autobiography. The plan eventually was abandoned, however, and only the higher action of *A Narrow Heart* was published, under the title *The Glory of Hera*.

In the manner of a realistic novel, *The Glory of Hera* retells the labors of Heracles, which may seem curious in a novelist for whom Christ became the greatest hero and Christian virtue a guide to virtuous living. For Gordon, however, Heracles was a great precursor of Christ, and in retelling the story of his labors—one might say, his miracles—she paid homage to her early and abiding love of Greek mythology by suggesting the Christlike quality of its greatest hero.

When she died in 1981, Gordon was at work on another novel, the fictionalized autobiography that was to have made up the "lower action" of *A Narrow Heart*. It is not known how close that work was to completion or how it might contribute to her future reputation. Currently, there is no doubt about her historical importance; her name always appears in lists of important writers of the Southern Renaissance. As to the literary quality of her fiction, that is a matter to be decided as such matters always are, by the winnowing process of time. Her earliest works—

Penhally; Aleck Maury, Sportsman; None Shall Look Back; and *Green Centuries*—seem the best candidates for survival; her later novels, though technically more complex, demand imaginative participation in religious beliefs to which few readers are able or willing to respond. Gordon wrote against the grain of her time; while the major writers of the period, poets as well as novelists, depicted or implied the collapse of Western civilization and the invalidity of traditional values, she never lost faith in the possibility of redemption by heroic action. To some critics, this was a sign of her attachment to a vanished past and a refusal to confront contemporary realities. Gordon denied that she believed that the Southern past, or any past, was superior to the present; what she did believe, though, was that the present was nourished by the best of the past, not because of its pastness, but because it made life richer and more meaningful. Gordon was aware of the misconceptions about her fiction and of the growing indifference of readers to her later work, but she never veered from her belief in the importance of what she was doing. It was her conviction that, if she wrote well, her work would endure and that it would continue to find its own appreciative audience.

W. J. Stuckey

OTHER MAJOR WORKS

SHORT FICTION: *The Forest of the South*, 1945; *Old Red and Other Stories*, 1963; *The Collected Stories of Caroline Gordon*, 1981.

NONFICTION: *How to Read a Novel*, 1957; *A Good Soldier: A Key to the Novels of Ford Madox Ford*, 1963.

EDITED TEXT: *The House of Fiction: An Anthology of the Short Story*, 1950 (with Allen Tate).

BIBLIOGRAPHY

Fraistat, Rose A. *Caroline Gordon as Novelist and Woman of Letters*. Baton Rouge: Louisiana State University Press, 1984. Fraistat examines Gordon's life in terms of her work and places her in a historical context. A study by a modern Southern woman of letters looking at one from a previous generation.

Jonza, Nancylee Novell. *The Underground Stream: The Life and Art of Caroline Gordon.* Athens: University of Georgia Press, 1995. A good, updated biography of Gordon. Includes bibliographical references and an index.

Lindberg-Seyersted, Brita, ed. *A Literary Friendship: Correspondence Between Caroline Gordon and Ford Madox Ford.* Knoxville: University of Tennessee Press, 1999. Letters between two acclaimed authors. Provides an index.

McDowell, Frederick P. W. *Caroline Gordon.* Minneapolis: University of Minnesota Press, 1966. A short pamphlet that briefly describes Gordon's life and work. Useful for a quick overview that puts her work into its context. Contains a selected bibliography for further study.

Makowsky, Veronica A. *Caroline Gordon: A Biography.* New York: Oxford University Press, 1989. An excellent biography of Gordon, about whom little has been written. Good for all students.

Stuckey, William Joseph. *Caroline Gordon.* New York: Twayne, 1972. A very useful book for all students of Gordon. Stuckey offers a moderately detailed biography, along with analysis of Gordon's major works. Includes a primary and secondary bibliography.

Waldron, Ann. *Close Connections: Caroline Gordon and the Southern Renaissance.* New York: Putnam, 1987. The most lively book produced on Gordon. Especially helpful for exploring her connections with other Southern writers and with the Southern milieu that is so important to Gordon's fiction. Written by a Southerner steeped in Gordon's background.

MARY GORDON

Born: Far Rockaway, New York; December 8, 1949

PRINCIPAL LONG FICTION

Final Payments, 1978
The Company of Women, 1980
Men and Angels, 1985
The Other Side, 1989
Spending: A Utopian Divertimento, 1998

OTHER LITERARY FORMS

Although Gordon has built her reputation as a novelist, she has published numerous short stories in such periodicals as *The Atlantic Monthly, Harper's, The Virginia Quarterly Review,* and *Redbook. Temporary Shelter* (1987) is a collection of short stories, some of which were published previously. *Good Boys and Dead Girls: And Other Essays* (1991) is a collection of essays on topics of literature, personal history, and social commentary. Her periodical publications include "More Catholic Than the Pope: Archbishop Lefebvre and the Rome of the One True Church" (*Harper's,* 1978) and "Coming to Terms with Mary" (*Commonweal,* 1982). She has written introductions to the 1990 edition of Edith Wharton's *The House of Mirth* (1905) and the 1992 edition of Zelda Fitzgerald's *The Collected Writings* (1991) and contributed to *Spiritual Quests: The Art and Craft of Religious Writing* (1988). Perhaps her most important piece of nonfiction, *The Shadow Man* (1996), chronicles Gordon's search for her father's past. Gordon frequently contributes book reviews to such periodicals as *The Nation* and *The New York Times Book Review.*

ACHIEVEMENTS

Mary Gordon's early work, especially *Final Payments,* received good reviews, with critics hailing her as one of the first important Catholic writers in the United States. She has been compared to her literary idols, Jane Austen and Virginia Woolf, in her precision of perception and her depiction of the reflective and emotional lives of her characters. In 1979 for *Final Payments* and again in 1981 for *The Company of Women,* Gordon won the Janet Heidinger Kafka Prize for Fiction. She also received the Lila Acheson Wallace Reader's Digest Award and a Guggenheim Fellowship.

BIOGRAPHY

Mary Catherine Gordon was born on December 8, 1949, to David and Anna Gagliano Gordon. As

(AP/Wide World Photos)

tended neither Harvard nor Oxford Universities, but also he had not even attended college. He never returned to Europe and had worked for the railroad. Although she had known that David Gordon had written and published *Hot Dog*, a semipornographic periodical, before his religious conversion and later had published poetry and critical analyses of other writers in publications such as *The New Republic*, Gordon did not realize how rabidly anti-Semitic he was until she began her research. In discovering who her father really was, Gordon was in many ways able finally to come to terms with his loss, and she reburied him in a new cemetery plot away from her mother's family, the Gaglianos, who had despised him. She also discovered that her love for him transcended his political views.

Although Gordon attributes her vocation as a writer to the example and encouragement of her father, she also credits her mother's side of the family for supplying the rhythms and inflections of her style and the concerns that shape her work. Anna Gordon, a polio victim since the age of three, who had to support herself and her daughter by working as a legal secretary after David Gordon's death, was, as Gordon said, quite an excellent letter writer. Anna's Irish Sicilian family also served as models for many of the characters in Gordon's novels, often to the family's great displeasure.

Almost as influential on Mary Gordon's life as the death of her father was her decision not to accept a scholarship to Fordham University but to attend Barnard College instead. In an interview conducted by Patrick H. Samway in *America* (1994), Gordon claimed that her reasons for wanting to attend Barnard were totally shallow; she had read novelist J. D. Salinger, and she wanted to meet a Seymour Glass. Once enrolled in Barnard, where she was taught by essayist Elizabeth Hardwick, her life changed. Gordon received her B.A. from Barnard in 1971 and her M.A. from Syracuse University in 1973. A brief marriage in 1974 ended in divorce. From 1974 until 1978 Gordon taught at Dutchess Community College in Poughkeepsie, New York. In

Gordon says in *The Shadow Man*, one of the most important events of her life was the death of her father on January 14, 1957, when she was seven years old. A convert to an extreme right-wing Catholicism from Judaism, David Gordon had idolized, and been idolized by, his young daughter. "I love you more than God," he told her once, frightening the child with the ambiguity and the cosmic implications of that statement. Regaling her with tales of his days at Harvard and his experiences in Oxford and in Paris with the expatriates, and teaching her to read at the age of three, and then instructing her in French, German and Latin, Gordon left his daughter with a paradoxical legacy of lies and a deep intellectual curiosity. Only as an adult in researching *The Shadow Man* did Gordon learn the truth about her father: that he was a naturalized American citizen born in Vilna, Russia, not Lorain, Ohio, that not only had he at-

1979 she taught at Amherst College. In that same year, she married Arthur Cash, professor of English in the State University of New York (SUNY) system and biographer of eighteenth century British novelist Laurence Sterne. They have two children, Anna and David. In 1999, Gordon was acting as McIntosh Professor of Writing at Barnard College in New York City.

Literary influences on Gordon's writing are varied and many. She names, aside from Austen and Woolf, Ford Madox Ford, Charlotte Brontë, Thomas Hardy, and George Eliot as her literary forebears. Critics have noted that her writing has something of the pulse of D. H. Lawrence, the ethical concerns of Doris Lessing, and the polish of Flannery O'Connor.

ANALYSIS

Fathers, whether biological, spiritual, or heavenly, figure strongly in Gordon's fiction. Deeply affected by the death of her own father when she was a small child, as well as the patriarchal Catholic Church prior to Vatican II (1961-1963), Gordon's novels are reflective, character-driven studies which examine such contrasting topics as sacrifice and self-centeredness, sex and asceticism, art and gaudiness, legalism and spirituality. Praised for her piercing insight and finely patterned writing, Gordon admitted in an interview with Diana Cooper-Clark in *Commonweal* (1980) that what she likes most about her own writing is that occasionally she writes "really smashing sentences." As critics have compared her to both Austen and Woolf, that claim does not seem immodest. Over the years Gordon's range of characters and themes widened and her style of writing, if anything, has matured.

FINAL PAYMENTS

Her first novel, *Final Payments*, garnered Gordon respect and received glowing reviews, perhaps because it addressed topics, such as sacrifice and religious devotion, that were not fashionable. The novel opens with thirty-year-old Isabel Moore reflecting on the funeral of her father. As she thinks about the people who attended the funeral, she settles primarily on four people in particular—her two best friends, Eleanor and Liz, her favorite priest, Father Mulcahy, and

her former housekeeper, Margaret Casey. Isabel, the reader soon learns, has spent the last eleven years of her life caring for her invalid father, who had a series of debilitating strokes after discovering her in bed with his protégé, David Lowe. In reparation for her sins, she has given over her life to her father. Now free of the influence of her father, a college professor and extreme right-wing Catholic, Isabel turns to her friends Eleanor and Liz for solace and for help in beginning a new life, a new life which begins with a trip to the gynecologist for the insertion of an intrauterine device. Already, the reader sees that Isabel's sacrificing her life to her father has been superficial, for once his presence is gone, she embarks on a course similar to the one that got her into trouble in the first place.

On a visit to the home of Liz and John Ryan, Isabel obtains a job from Ryan, a handsome politician who, despite the fact that he does a lot of good for people, is totally amoral. Isabel soon falls victim to Ryan's masculinity and sleeps with him, even though she despises him as a person. She does not, however, feel terribly guilty about this act, for she had previously learned that Liz has a lesbian lover. Only when she falls in love with Hugh Slade, a local veterinarian and another married man, does Isabel suffer any real qualms about her physical relationship with Ryan. In order to keep her job with Ryan, though, she continues both affairs, until she sees the hurt it is causing Hugh.

Although she has told herself from the beginning of the affair with Hugh that he would never leave his wife, whom he detests, and his children for her, Isabel eventually breaks off her affair with Ryan, risking his anger. True to form, Ryan finds the most appropriate way to hurt her. When he sets Hugh Slade's angry wife on her, Isabel is stricken and decides she must, once again, sacrifice her life in order to pay for her sins. To do so, she goes to live with former housekeeper Margaret Casey, who had been turned out of the house when Isabel was thirteen and discovered Margaret had designs on her father. With Margaret, whom Isabel has always despised, she finds, or so she thinks, the perfect sacrifice—to love the unlovable. Isabel tries her best to deal with Margaret until Father Mulcahy visits and shows her that her sacrifice is one in name only and that she is slowly killing herself. Recognizing the truth in what he says, Isabel "pays" Margaret the twenty thousand dollars she received for the sale of her father's house and returns to her friends Eleanor and Liz to begin her real life once again.

MEN AND ANGELS

Although Gordon's second novel, *The Company of Women*, deals with many of the Catholic topics present in *Final Payments*, it was not as well received. Written as a series of monologues by Father Cyprian and his female disciples, it is nonetheless primarily the story of the youth and maturing of Felicitas Taylor, which tackles such issues as abortion and social activism. In her third novel, *Men and Angels*, however, Gordon moves away from Catholicism to a more general look at moral and religious questions. Given the opportunity to write a catalog for an exhibition by the dead artist Caroline Watson (loosely based on several female artists), Anne Foster, mother with a Harvard Ph.D., struggles with the idea of giving up a year with her husband, who has gone to France to teach, and leaving her children in the care of another person while she works. With much misgiving and also much passion, Anne begins her work. Although she dislikes Laura Post, whom she has hired to take care of the children, she can find no fault with her, and, as she desperately needs her help, continues to employ her. Through the course of the year, Anne meets Caroline Watson's daughter-in-law, Jane, for whom Caroline had been a wonderful surrogate mother, despite the fact that she had neglected her own son. Jane, childless herself, takes to Anne from the first and becomes the mother that Anne herself has needed. At the same time, Laura, who turned into a religious fanatic upon her realization that her own mother did not love her, has sought to "save" Anne from her life of the flesh and in the process has fallen in love with her as the perfect mother. When Anne discovers Laura reading while allowing her children to play on thin ice, however, Anne dismisses Laura, who then slits her wrists in Anne's bathtub. The novel focuses on the idea of mothering, the impact work has on the mother, the extremely tenuous relationship between how one mothers and the effects of that mothering, and the realization that the right mother for one person is often wrong for someone else. Though the issues the novel deals with are significant, its most memorable passages deal with Caroline Watson's life and art.

SPENDING

Gordon's fourth novel, *The Other Side*, did not receive much critical scrutiny. In many ways her most interesting novel, it tells the story of a day in the life of aged Irish immigrants, Vincent and Ellen MacNamara, through their own interior monologues and those of their family. Artist Monica Szabo's fantasy of sex and money, *Spending*, as its subtitle, *A Utopian Divertimento*, implies, seems at first to be a real departure from Gordon's more overtly moral novels. Upon closer examination, however, in its pulsing first-person narrative, its interiority, and its concern with art and life and how women combine the two, it may more accurately reflect a maturing art which no longer has to apologize for its own being. A rather successful artist, fifty-something Monica is delivering a lecture at a gallery owned by a friend, when she half-jokingly notes that male artists have always had the benefit of a Muse, the model-inspiration-housekeeper-cook-secretary who also paid the rent. Somewhat wistfully she wonders where all the male Muses are and is shocked when a gentleman in the audience announces, "Right here." This longtime admirer of Monica's work, whom she refers to only as B, also tells her he is very wealthy and offers to become her patron to enable her to take a sabbatical from her job as a college professor to paint full time. Although she wonders if she is mad, Monica readily agrees.

B becomes everything and more that Monica fantasized about. A wealthy and, of course, handsome commodities trader, his "spent" (the wordplay is intentional) condition after sex reminds her of the paintings by the old masters of the dead Christ. He thus provides the means, the inspiration, and the model for the series of paintings, "Spent Men," that brings Monica her greatest acclaim. In his complete sacrifice of himself and his goods to Monica's needs and desires, B, quite appropriately Jewish, becomes a Christ figure.

Along the way their relationship undergoes metamorphoses as their individual fortunes change. On the heels of Monica's successful show, B loses everything in risky chocolate futures. Luckily, by this time Monica has been befriended by eighty-year-old Peggy Riordan, who had inherited a fortune from her lover of forty years. Peggy becomes Monica's second Muse as well as the more appropriate mother to one of Monica's twins, the conservative Sara. Wanting to divest herself of her assets before she and her current lover have to move into a retirement home, Peggy transfers the bulk of her fortune to Monica. Peggy's resources, along with the savvy of Monica's daughter Rachel (whose Brazilian boyfriend has a genius grandfather who predicts the fate of the coffee crop by the bark of the tree), save B's business. The novel ends with Monica's celebration of B's (Bernard's) return to fortune and with her eagerness to begin her next project, "After Ingres," a series inspired by a trip to the Russian baths, her birthday present to Peggy. It ends, more philosophically, with Monica's full realization of the joys of love and work.

Jaquelyn W. Walsh

OTHER MAJOR WORKS

SHORT FICTION: *Temporary Shelter*, 1987; *The Rest of Life: Three Novellas*, 1993.

NONFICTION: *Good Boys and Dead Girls: And Other Essays*, 1991; *The Shadow Man*, 1996; *Seeing Through Places: Reflections on Geography and Identity*, 2000.

BIBLIOGRAPHY

Johnston, Eileen Tess. "The Biblical Matrix of Mary Gordon's *Final Payments*." *Christianity and Literature* 44 (Winter, 1995): 145-167. According to Johnston, the house operates as the dominant symbol in *Final Payments*.

Neary, John M. "Mary Gordon's *Final Payments*: A Romance of the One True Language." *Essays in Literature* 17 (Spring, 1990): 94-110. Neary feels Isabel Moore's epiphany occurs when she recognizes that words have meaning but that their signification is shifting and contextual rather than absolute.

Newman, Judie. "Telling a Woman's Story: Fiction as Biography and Biography as Fiction in Mary Gordon's *Men and Angels* and Alison Lurie's *The Truth About Lorin Jones*." In *Neo-Realism in Contemporary American Fiction*, edited by Kristiaan Versluys. Amsterdam: Rodopi, 1992. Newman compares the dilemmas confronting Anne Foster in *Men and Angels* and Lurie's heroine as each explores how best to tell the story of a dead artist, a dead woman. Newman's examination of foremothering, mirroring, and the degree to which women do or do not agree with male fantasies as depicted in Gordon's novel is of particular interest.

Perry, Ruth. "Mary Gordon's Mothers." In *Narrating Mothers: Theorizing Maternal Subjectivities*, edited by Brenda O. Daly and Maureen T. Reddy. Knoxville: University of Tennessee Press, 1991. Perry reads *Men and Angels* as an allegory of the dual life of the mother, who is also an intellectual being. Although the work imperils the children, Gordon finds it a necessity to the mother not only for her own intellectual health but for its regenerative powers in the intense task of child rearing.

Smiley, Pamela. "The Unspeakable: Mary Gordon and the Angry Mother's Voices." In *Violence, Silence, and Anger: Women's Writing as Transgression*, edited by Deirdre Lashgari. Charlottesville: University Press of Virginia, 1995. Smiley looks at ideal and flawed mothers in *Men and Angels*, who often exist within the same being in response to different children and environments.

Suleiman, Susan R. "On Maternal Splitting: A Propos of Mary Gordon's *Men and Angels*." *Signs* 14 (Autumn, 1988): 25-41. An important essay which was the first to examine the good-bad mother dichotomy in the novel.

Ward, Susan. "In Search of 'Ordinary Human Happiness': Rebellion and Affirmation in Mary Gordon's Novels." In *Faith of a Woman Writer*, edited by Alice Kessler-Harris and William McBrien. New York: Greenwood Press, 1988. Ward explores Gordon's theme of rebellion against the patriarchy and the accompanying need for women to establish a new feminine value system based on nature, flexibility, and instinct in order to achieve happiness.

MAXIM GORKY
Aleksey Maksimovich Peshkov

Born: Nizhny-Novgorod, Russia; March 28, 1868
Died: Gorki, U.S.S.R.; June 18, 1936

PRINCIPAL LONG FICTION

Goremyka Pavel, 1894 (novella; *Orphan Paul*,
    1946)
Foma Gordeyev, 1899 (English translation, 1901)
Troye, 1901 (*Three of Them*, 1902)
Mat, 1906 (*Mother*, 1906)
Ispoved, 1908 (*A Confession*, 1909)
Zhizn Matveya Kozhemyakina, 1910 (*The Life of
    Matvei Kozhemyakin*, 1959)
Delo Artomonovykh, 1925 (*Decadence*, 1927; also
    known as *The Artomonov Business*, 1948)
Zhizn Klima Samgina, 1927-1936 (*The Life of Klim
    Samgin*, 1930-1938; includes *The Bystander*,
    1930, *The Magnet*, 1931, *Other Fires*, 1933, and
    The Specter, 1938)

OTHER LITERARY FORMS

Maxim Gorky wrote a total of fifteen plays, only
three of which were staged during his lifetime: *Na
dne* (1902; *The Lower Depths*, 1912), *Vassa Zheleznova* (1910; English translation, 1945), and *Yegor
Bulychov i drugiye* (1932; *Yegor Bulychov and Others*, 1937). His other plays include *Meshchane* (1902;
Smug Citizen, 1906), *Dachniki* (1904; *Summer Folk*,
1905), *Deti solntsa* (1905; *Children of the Sun*,
1906), *Varvary* (1906; *Barbarians*, 1906), *Vragi*
(1906; *Enemies*, 1945), *Chudaki* (1910; *Queer People*, 1945), *Falshivaya moneta* (wr. 1913, pr., pb.
1927; the counterfeit coin), *Zykovy* (1914; *The
Zykovs*, 1945), *Starik* (wr. 1915, pr. 1919; *Old Man*,
1924), and *Dostigayev i drugiye* (1933; *Dostigayev
and Others*, 1937). All are available in Russian in the
thirty-volume *Polnoe sobranie sochinenii* (1949-
1955; complete works) and in English in *Seven Plays*
(1945), *Five Plays* (1956), and *Plays* (1975).

Gorky wrote about three hundred short stories.
Among the most important are "Makar Chudra"
(1892), "Chelkash" (1895; "Tchelkash"), "Starukha

Izergil" (1895; "The Old Woman Izergil"), "Malva"
(1897; English translation), "V stepi" (1897; "In the
Steppe"), "Dvadtsat' shest' i odna" (1899; "Twenty-
six Men and a Girl"), "Pesnya o burevestnike" (1901;
"Song of the Stormy Petrel"), "Pesnya o sokole"
(1908; "Song of the Falcon"), and the collections
Po Rusi (1915; *Through Russia*, 1921) and *Skazki ob
Italii* (1911-1913; *Tales of Italy*, 195?). A two-
volume collection of his stories, *Ocherki i rasskazy*,
was first published in Russian in 1898. The short stories are available in the collected works; some of the
best of them are available in English in *Selected
Short Stories* (1959), introduced by Stefan Zweig.

Among Gorky's numerous essays, articles, and
nonfiction books, the most important are "O Karama-
zovshchine" (1913; "On Karamazovism"), "Revol-
yutsia i kultura" (1917; "Revolution and Culture"),
Vladimir Ilich Lenin (1924; *V. I. Lenin*, 1931), and "O
meshchanstve" (1929; "On the Petty Bourgeois Mentality"). The collection *Untimely Thoughts: Essays on
Revolution, Culture, and the Bolsheviks* (1968) includes many of these essays in English translation.

ACHIEVEMENTS

Hailed by Soviet critics as a true proletarian
writer and the model of Socialist Realism, Gorky is
one of the few authors to see his native town renamed
for him. Many schools, institutes, universities, and
theaters bear his name, as does one of the main
streets in Moscow. These honors, says Helen
Muchnic, result from the fact that Gorky, along with
Vladimir Ilich Lenin and Joseph Stalin, "shaped and
disseminated the country's official philosophy." Stalin admired Gorky greatly, awarding him the coveted
Order of Lenin. As chairman of the All-Union Congress of Soviet Writers in 1934, Gorky delivered an
address in which he defined Socialist Realism, a doctrine that unfortunately was to be interpreted in a
manner different from what he intended or practiced;
the *Soviet Encyclopedia* (1949-1958) calls him "the
father of Soviet literature . . . the founder of the literature of Socialist Realism."

Although Gorky's novels are not among the best
in Russian literature, they did inaugurate a new type
of writing, revealing to the world a new Russia. In

contrast to the countless *fin de siècle* evocations of the tormented Russian soul, with their gallery of superfluous men, Gorky offered a new hero, the proletarian, the revolutionary, such as Pavel Vlassov and his mother Pelagea Nilovna in the poorly constructed but ever-popular *Mother*. Indeed, Richard Hare argues that even today *Mother* is the prototype for the socially tendentious novel in the Soviet Union, with its crude but determined effort to look into the dynamism of social change in Russia.

Gorky's highest artistic achievements, however, are his literary portraits; the best, says Muchnic, are those which he drew from life, especially of Leo Tolstoy and Anton Chekhov. Also notable is Gorky's affectionate portrait of his grandmother. Gorky had a strong visual sense, the gift of astute observation, and the ability to translate these insights into sparkling dialogue. He created an entire portrait gallery of vignettes, most of which can be traced to people he met in his endless wanderings through Russia and abroad.

The child of a lower-middle-class family that faced rapid impoverishment, a self-taught student, a young

(Library of Congress)

man whose universities were the towns along the Volga and the steamers that made their way along its mighty waters, Gorky was nevertheless sympathetic to culture. He devoured books voraciously and indiscriminately and encouraged others to study. From 1918 to 1921, not wholly in favor with the new regime, he worked tirelessly to save writers and intellectuals from starvation and from censorship. He befriended the Serapion Brothers (a group of young Russian writers formed in 1921) and later Mikhail Sholokhov, always encouraging solid scholarship.

Estimates of Gorky even now depend on political ideology, for he is closely associated with the Russian Revolution. His vision, however, is broader than that of any political movement. He repeats often in his autobiographical works his dismay at the ignorance of people and their lack of desire for a better life, and he felt keenly the injustice done to the innocent. His writing is permeated by the desire to bring people from slavery to freedom, to build a good life; he believed in the power of human beings to change their world. Courageous, generous, and devoted to the public good, Gorky was timid, lacking in self-confidence, and infinitely modest. His commitment to social justice is unquestionable. These qualities may be what Chekhov had in mind when he said that Gorky's works might be forgotten, but that Gorky the man would never be.

BIOGRAPHY

Maxim Gorky, champion of the poor and the downtrodden, was born Aleksey Maksimovich Peshkov in Nizhny-Novgorod (a town that would bear the name Gorki after 1932), on March 28, 1868. His father, who died three years later from cholera, was a joiner-upholsterer and later a shipping agent; his mother's family, the Kashirins, were owners of a dyeing establishment. After his father's death, Gorky's mother left young Gorky to be reared by her parents, with whom he lived until the age of eleven, when his recently remarried mother died. Gorky recounts his childhood experiences in brilliant anecdotes and dialogue in his autobiographical *Detstvo* (1913; *My Childhood*, 1915). The influence of his grandparents was great: His grandfather was a brutal, narrowly religious man, while his grandmother was gentle and pious; her own peculiar version of a benevolent God, sharply in contrast to the harsh religiosity of her husband, marked the impressionable child.

The frequent wanderers in Gorky's works are a reflection of his own experience. In 1879, his grandfather sent him "into the world." He went first to the family of his grandmother's sister's son, Valentin Sergeyev, to whom he was apprenticed as a draftsman. Gorky hated the snobbishness and avarice of this bourgeois family, which became the prototype of the Gordeyevs and the Artomonovs in his fiction. For the next ten years, he filled many other minor posts, from messboy on a Volga steamer to icon painter, reading when and where he could. Other than an idealistic admiration for a neighbor whom he named "Queen Margot," there were few bright spots in this period, which he describes in *V lyudyakh* (1916; *In the World*, 1917).

In 1889, after an unsuccessful suicide attempt which left him with a permanently weakened lung, Gorky met the Populist revolutionary Mikhail Romas, who helped him to clarify his confused ideas. At the same time, his acquaintance with the writer Vladimir Korolenko aided his literary development, as Tolstoy and Chekhov were to do in later years. In 1892, Gorky published his first story, "Makar Chudra," assuming at that time the pen name Maxim Gorky, meaning "the bitter one," a reflection of his painful childhood. Gorky wandered through Russia, wrote, and began a series of unsuccessful romantic involvements, first with Olga Kaminskaya, an older woman of some sophistication with whom he lived from 1892 to 1894, and then with Ekaterina Pavlovna Volzhina, a proofreader on the newspaper for which he was working. Gorky married Volzhina in 1896, and she became the mother of his two children, Maxim and Ekaterina. Imprisoned several times, Gorky was seldom free of police surveillance. In 1899, he became literary editor of the Marxist newspaper *Zhizn* and directed his attention to the problems of social injustice.

In 1905, Gorky's violent protests of government brutality in suppressing the workers' demonstrations on Bloody Sunday once again brought him imprisonment, this time in the Peter-Paul Fortress. By then, however, Gorky was famous, and celebrities all over Europe and America protested the sentence. Upon his release, he once again began to travel, both for political reasons and for his health. He visited New York, which he called "the city of the yellow devil," in 1906, where he attacked America for its inequalities and America attacked him for the immorality of his relationship with Maria Fyodorovna Andreyeva, an actress of the celebrated Moscow Art Theater. After six months in the United States, he spent seven years in Italy, settling in Capri, where his Villa Serafina became a center of pilgrimage for all revolutionaries, including Lenin.

Gorky returned to Russia in 1913. When the Revolution broke out in 1917, he was not at first among its wholehearted supporters, although he served on many committees, working especially to safeguard culture. In 1921, for reasons of health, he went to Sorrento, Italy, where he spent his time writing. Although he made periodic visits to his homeland beginning in 1928, it was not until 1932 that he returned to the Soviet Union for good; in that same year, Stalin awarded him the Order of Lenin. In 1934, he was elected chairman of the All-Union Congress of Soviet Writers; during this period, he became increasingly active in cultural policy making. Although he continued to write, he produced nothing noteworthy; his four-novel cycle *The Life of Klim Samgin*, the last volume of which he did not live to complete, is an artistic failure. Gorky's death in 1936 was surrounded by mysterious circumstances, although official autopsy reports attribute it to tuberculosis and influenza.

ANALYSIS

Although Soviet critics tend to exalt the realism of Maxim Gorky's works, D. S. Mirsky said that Gorky never wrote a good novel or a good play, while Tolstoy remarked that Gorky's novels are inferior to his stories and that his plays are even worse than his novels. Maintaining that Gorky's "tremendous heroic emotions ring false," Tolstoy criticized Gorky's lack of a sense of proportion, as Chekhov had noted Gorky's lack of restraint. It is obvious that Gorky did not know how to limit his stories, that he piles up details along with extraneous dialogue. His narrative technique consists in recounting the life story of a single protagonist or the saga of a family. His narratives are always linear, often proceeding from birth to death; the main character yearns for a new life and struggles with a stagnant environment, sometimes experiencing flashes of light. Thus, the typical Gorky novel is a tireless and often tiresome documentary on a single theme.

Gorky's weak narrative technique is counterbalanced by excellent characterization. True, he is guilty of oversimplification—his characters are types rather than individuals, figures from a modern morality play—but he introduced into Russian fiction a wide range of figures from many different walks of life rarely or never treated by earlier novelists. Though not highly individualized, Gorky's characterizations are vivid and convincing, imbued with his own energy.

Gorky sees people as social organisms, and therefore he is especially conscious of their role in society. He was particularly familiar with the merchant class or the *meshchane*, because he grew up among them, in the Kashirin and Sergeev households. They form some of his most successful portraits, representing not only the petty bourgeoisie but also the barge owners, grain dealers, mill owners, and textile manufacturers, the Gordeyevs, Artomonovs, and Kozhemyakins. Gorky represents them as self-centered individualists, characterized by envy, malice, self-righteousness, avarice, and intellectual and spiritual torpor. Their decadence is symbolic of the malady that ravages prerevolutionary Russia.

In contrast to the merchants are the lonely and downtrodden, not always idealized as in the novels of Fyodor Dostoevski but presented, rather, as the ignorant victims of society and its lethargic sycophants. The corrupt and indifferent town of Okurov in *The Life of Matvei Kozhemyakin* symbolizes Russia's decadence, as do the thieves and vagabonds of Kazan, the flophouse of *The Lower Depths*, and the orgies of the theology students in the houses of prostitution. More Dostoevskian are the *bosyaki*, the barefoot tramps, such as Chelkash and Makar Chudra, who are the heralds of the future. Along with them, yet very different in spirit, is the revolutionary intelligentsia, the new heroes created by Gorky. They

are Pelagea Nilovna, the "mother," her son Pavel and his friends, Mansurova in *The Life of Matvei Kozhemyakin*, and Derenkov and Romas in Gorky's own life; it is for such characters that Gorky is exalted by the Soviets, though to foreign readers they are usually the least attractive.

Gorky's best characters are presented without excessive ideological trappings. They range from his saintly grandmother, Akulina Kashirina, perhaps his most unforgettable character, to Queen Margot, the idol with clay feet. They include Smoury, the cook on the steamer, who first encouraged Gorky to read, and many other simple people whom Gorky was to meet, "kind, solitary, and broken off from life." They also take the form of figures such as the merchant Ignat Gordeyev, the image of the Volga, vital, seething, creative, generous, and resolute.

Most of Gorky's women are victims of violence, beaten by their husbands and unappreciated by their families, such as Natasha Artomonova and Saveli Kozhemyakin's wife, whom he beats to death. Love in Gorky's novels is either accompanied by violence and brutality or idealized, as in Queen Margot or Tanya in the story "Twenty-six Men and a Girl." It ranges from tender devotion in *Mother* to drunken orgies on Foma Gordeyev's Volga steamer. Gorky's own experience of love was unhappy, and he was ill at ease when portraying sexual scenes. Even his coarsely erotic scenes seem to be tinged with a moralizing intent.

Against a background of resplendent nature, the Volga, the sea, or the steppe, Gorky depicts the eruptions of violence and brutality, the orgies and the squalor, the pain and the harshness which, says Muchnic, are at the heart of his work. One has only to read the opening pages of *My Childhood* to feel its force. His own weight of harsh experience impelled him to force others to look at the bestiality which he saw rampant in Russia and to urge them to exterminate it. Ever the champion of social justice, Gorky felt the need to fight ignorance, cruelty, and exploitation.

FOMA GORDEYEV

Gorky's first and best novel, *Foma Gordeyev*, is set along the banks of the Volga, a region well known to the author. It is the story of the Volga merchants, represented here by the Gordeyev and Mayakin families. Rich, greedy, and passionate, both families represent the iron will and the domination of the merchant class. Gorky's merchants are of peasant origin, unsophisticated and uneducated. In Foma's revolt, Gorky shows the decay of society at the turn of the century and the impending Revolution, as yet only dimly anticipated.

Foma, the only son of Ignat Gordeyev, a self-made barge owner and one of Gorky's richest character sketches, is brought up by his godfather and his father's business colleague, Yakov Mayakin, whose family has owned the local rope works for generations. Foma shows no talent for or interest in business and, after his father's death, wastes his money on debauchery, drink, and wanton destruction. At first dimly attracted to Lyubov Mayakina, he is unable to conform to her educated tastes, and she, in obedience to her father's wishes, marries the respectable and highly Europeanized Afrikan Smolin. Foma continues his wild rebellion, actually a search for self and meaning, not unlike that of Mikhail Lermontov's Pechorin. Finally institutionalized for apparent insanity, Foma becomes an enlightened vagabond.

Foma Gordeyev follows the story line generally adopted by Gorky: the life story of the hero from birth to a crisis. Although it is weak in plot and characterization, it is readable, especially powerful in its evocation of the Volga, the elemental force that intoxicated the wealthy Ignat. Ignat is a finished portrait of the boisterous, dynamic businessman Gorky knew so well—vital, creative, and resolute. He is one of Gorky's most sympathetic portraits, along with Yakov Mayakin, who shows the characteristic traits of the Russian merchant that go back to the sixteenth century *Domostroy* (a book on social conduct). Foma, though not so well drawn, represents the rift in generations and the universally disturbed mood that pervaded Russia on the eve of the abortive Revolution of 1905. The whole novel attempts to assess the flaws in the capitalistic system and thus is very modern in spirit.

MOTHER

Mother, written while Gorky was in America after the 1905 Revolution, reflects his disillusionment with both czarist and capitalistic social structures and his desire "to sustain the failing spirit of opposition to the dark and threatening forces of life." It was published first in English, in 1906, by *Appleton's Magazine* in New York, and then in Russian in Berlin. It became the symbol of the revolutionary cause and was widely read and acclaimed, even after the Revolution, as a model of the socialist novel. Translated into many languages, it became the basis for other novels and plays, such as Bertolt Brecht's *Mutter Courage und ihre Kinder* (1941; *Mother Courage and Her Children*, 1941). As a novel, it is one of Gorky's weakest in characterization and plot, yet its optimistic message and accessible style have assured its continuing popularity.

Written in the third person, through the eyes of the courageous mother, Pelagea Nilovna Vlassova, the novel relates her encounter with the Social Democratic Party, inspired by her son Pavel. Pelagea suffered mistreatment from her husband and seems destined to continue in the same path with her son until his "conversion" to socialism. Pavel becomes a champion of the proletarian cause, the acknowledged leader of a small group of fellow revolutionaries who study forbidden books and distribute literature among the factory workers in their village. After Pavel's arrest, the illiterate Pelagea continues Pavel's work, stealthily distributing pamphlets and becoming a mother to the other members of the group: Sasha, who is secretly in love with Pavel; the "God-builder" Rybin; Andrei, the charming and humorous *khokhol*; the misanthropic Vesovshchikov; and the open-hearted urban intellectual Nikolai. Pavel's release from prison is immediately followed by his bold leadership in the May Day demonstration, for which he is again imprisoned. The mother's work becomes more daring and widespread as she passes to other villages like the holy wanderers so common in Gorky's early work. After Pavel's condemnation to exile in Siberia, Pelagea herself is arrested as she prepares to distribute the speech her son made prior to his sentence.

The best portrait in this weak novel is that of the mother, the only character to show psychological development. Yet Pelagea passes from one type of religious fervor to another, and her socialist convictions are simply the transferral of her Orthodox beliefs to the kingdom of this world. Even the revolutionaries invoke Christ and compare their work to his. The austere Pavel remains remote and unconvincing, while maternal love is the dominant force in the affectionate and almost mystical Pelagea.

THE ARTOMONOV BUSINESS

Written in 1924 and 1925 while Gorky was living abroad in Sorrento, Italy, *The Artomonov Business* is a retrospective novel on the causes of the 1917 Revolution. Encompassing three generations and covering the period from 1863 to 1917, it has a much broader base than most of Gorky's works. Although here, as elsewhere, Gorky fills his narrative with extraneous detail, he draws many convincing portraits of the demoralized merchant class at the turn of the century. Frank M. Borras singles out Gorky's interweaving of the historical theme with the characters' personal destinies as one of the merits of the novel.

Ilya Artomonov is the patriarch of the family, a passionate and dynamic freed serf who establishes a linen factory in the sleepy town of Dryomov. His son Pyotr inherits his father's sensuality but not his business skill, and the narrative of his debauchery and indifference to his workers occupies the greater part of the novel. The Artomonov family also includes the more businesslike and adaptable Aleksei and the hunchback Nikita, who becomes a monk though he has lost his faith in God. The women in the novel occupy a secondary and passive role, existing mainly for the sensual gratification of the men, both attracting and repelling them.

Pyotr has two sons and two daughters. The eldest son, Ilya, leaves home to study and, as in Chekhov's stories, becomes an unseen presence, presumably joining the revolutionary Social Democratic Party. Yakov, the second son, is a sensualist, indifferent to business, and is killed by revolutionaries as he escapes in fear of them. Miron, Aleksei's son, though physically weak, shows, like his father, an aptitude for commerce. Yet none is strong enough to save the family's ailing business, weakened by the corruption and indifference of its managers.

Gorky's symbolism is evident in his characterization of Tikhon Vialov (the quiet one), an enigmatic ditchdigger, gardener, and ubiquitous servant of the Artomonov family. It is Tikhon who at the very end of the story proclaims the Revolution, calling for revenge for the injustices that he has suffered at the hands of the Artomonovs. Quite obviously he symbolizes the proletariat, victim of the bourgeoisie. Aside from Tikhon, Gorky emphasizes much less the oppression of the workers than the empty, selfish, and superfluous lives of the factory owners.

Alternating wild episodes of debauchery, cruelty, and murder with scenes of boredom and superfluous dialogue, *The Artomonov Business* is both a modern novel and a return to Dostoevskian melodrama. Gorky had planned to write the novel as early as 1909 but was advised by Lenin to wait for the Revolution, which would be its logical conclusion. This story of the progressive deterioration of a family is also a profound study in the consequences of the failure of human relationships.

Gorky was less a man of ideas and reason than one of instinct and emotion. His best works are based upon intuition and observation. His truth and reality are humanistic, not metaphysical; they deal with the useful and the practical. Unlike Honoré de Balzac, whom he admired, Gorky did not succeed in investing the sordid with mystery or the petty with grandeur. He wrote a literature of the moment, "loud but not intense," as Muchnic describes it. It is, however, a literature of the people and for the people, accessible and genuine. Although some of his works are monotonous to today's Western reader, and no doubt to the Soviet reader as well, at their best they are honest portrayals of people, inspiring confidence in humanity's power to change the world.

Irma M. Kashuba

OTHER MAJOR WORKS

SHORT FICTION: "Chelkash," 1895 (English translation, 1901); *Ocherki i rasskazy*, 1898-1899 (3 volumes); *Rasskazy i p'esy*, 1901-1910 (9 volumes); *Orloff and His Wife: Tales of the Barefoot Brigade*, 1901; *Skazki ob Italii*, 1911-1913 (*Tales of Italy*, 195?); *Tales of Two Countries*, 1914; *Po Rusi*, 1915 (*Through Russia*, 1921); *Chelkash and Other Stories*, 1915; *Stories of the Steppe*, 1918; *Zametki iz dnevnika: Vospominaniia*, 1924 (*Fragments from My*

Diary, 1924); *Rasskazy 1922-1924 godov*, 1925; *Selected Short Stories*, 1959; *A Sky-Blue Life and Selected Stories*, 1964; *The Collected Short Stories of Maxim Gorky*, 1988.

PLAYS: *Meshchane*, pr., pb. 1902 (*Smug Citizen*, 1906); *Na dne*, pr., pb. 1902 (*The Lower Depths*, 1912); *Dachniki*, pr., pb. 1904 (*Summer Folk*, 1905); *Deti solntsa*, pr., pb. 1905 (*Children of the Sun*, 1906); *Varvary*, pr., pb. 1906 (*Barbarians*, 1906); *Vragi*, pb. 1906 (*Enemies*, 1945); *Posledniye*, pr., pb. 1908; *Chudaki*, pr., pb. 1910 (*Queer People*, 1945); *Vassa Zheleznova* (first version), pb. 1910 (English translation, 1945); *Falshivaya moneta*, wr. 1913, pr., pb. 1927; *Zykovy*, pb. 1914 (*The Zykovs*, 1945); *Starik*, wr. 1915, pr. 1919 (*Old Man*, 1924); *Yegor Bulychov i drugiye*, pr., pb. 1932 (*Yegor Bulychov and Others*, 1937); *Dostigayev i drugiye*, pr., pb. 1933 (*Dostigayev and Others*, 1937); *Vassa Zheleznova* (second version), pr., pb. 1935 (English translation, 1975); *Seven Plays*, pb. 1945; *Five Plays*, pb. 1956; *Plays*, pb. 1975.

NONFICTION: *Detstvo*, 1913 (*My Childhood*, 1915); *V lyudyakh*, 1916 (*In the World*, 1917); *Vospominaniya o Lve Nikolayeviche Tolstom*, 1919 (*Reminiscences of Leo Nikolaevich Tolstoy*, 1920); *Moi universitety*, 1923 (*My Universities*, 1923); *Vladimir Ilich Lenin*, 1924 (*V. I. Lenin*, 1931); *Reminiscences of Tolstoy, Chekhov and Andreyev*, 1949; *Untimely Thoughts: Essays on Revolution, Culture, and the Bolsheviks*, 1968.

MISCELLANEOUS: *Polnoe sobranie sochinenii*, 1949-1955 (30 volumes); *Polnoe sobranie sochinenii*, 1968-1976 (25 volumes); *Collected Works of Maxim Gorky*, 1979-1981 (8 volumes).

BIBLIOGRAPHY

Barratt, Andrew. *The Early Fiction of Maksim Gorky: Six Essays in Interpretation*. Nottingham, England: Astra Press, 1993. Excellent essays on Gorky's early works. Includes bibliographical references and an index.

Borras, F. M. *Maxim Gorky: The Writer: An Interpretation*. Oxford, England: Oxford University Press, 1967. A standard study, with chapters on Gorky's ideas and outlook, short stories, novels, memoirs, and plays. Includes a bibliography.

Habermann, Gerhard. *Maksim Gorki*. New York: Ungar, 1971. A compact, introductory study, with chapters on the writer's childhood, apprenticeship, and major works. Includes chronology and bibliography.

Hare, Richard. *Maxim Gorky: Romantic Realist and Conservative Revolutionary*. New York: Oxford University Press, 1962. Reprint. Westport, Conn.: Greenwood Press, 1978. Informative chapters on Gorky legend and fact, his travels and exile, his view of revolution, and his place in the Soviet Union. No bibliography.

Kaun, Alexander. *Maxim Gorky and His Russia*. London: Jonathan Cape, 1931. A biography that has valuable information about his early years as well as his later place in the Soviet Union.

Levin, Dan. *Stormy Petrel: The Life and Work of Maxim Gorky*. New York: Schocken Books, 1985. This reprint of Levin's 1965 work contains the detailed notes he excised from the original edition. An engrossing biographical and literary interpretation.

Scherr, Barry P. *Maxim Gorky*. Boston: Twayne, 1988. Chapters on the writer and revolutionary, his literary beginnings in the short story, his career as a young novelist, his plays, his memoirs, and his final achievements. Includes a chronology, detailed notes, and annotated bibliography. The best introductory study.

Terry, Garth M., comp. *Maxim Gorky in English: A Bibliography*. 2d rev. ed. Nottingham: Astra Press, 1992. An indispensable aid for any student of Gorky.

GÜNTER GRASS

Born: Danzig (now Gdańsk, Poland); October 16, 1927

PRINCIPAL LONG FICTION

Die Blechtrommel, 1959 (*The Tin Drum*, 1961)

Katz und Maus, 1961 (*Cat and Mouse*, 1963)

Hundejahre, 1963 (*Dog Years*, 1965)

Örtlich betäubt, 1969 (*Local Anesthetic*, 1969)

Aus dem Tagebuch einer Schnecke, 1972 (*From the Diary of a Snail*, 1973)

Der Butt, 1977 (*The Flounder*, 1978)

Das Treffen in Telgte, 1979 (*The Meeting at Telgte*, 1981)

Danziger Trilogie, 1980 (*Danzig Trilogy*, 1987; includes *The Tin Drum*, *Cat and Mouse*, and *Dog Years*)

Kopfgeburten: Oder, Die Deutschen sterben aus, 1980 (*Headbirths: Or, The Germans Are Dying Out*, 1982)

Die Rättin, 1986 (*The Rat*, 1987)

Unkenrufe, 1992 (*The Call of the Toad*, 1992)

Ein weites Feld, 1995

Mein Jahrhundert, 1999 (*My Century*, 1999)

OTHER LITERARY FORMS

Although Günter Grass achieved fame and critical acclaim as a novelist, he by no means limited his literary creativity to that genre. In fact, the author first attracted attention—albeit of a limited nature—as a playwright and a poet. In 1954, his one-act play in the absurdist vein, *Noch zehn Minuten bis Buffalo* (*Only Ten Minutes to Buffalo*, 1967), was staged, and in 1956, Grass's first collection of poetry, *Die Vorzüge der Windhühner* (the advantages of windfowl), was published. There is no exact correspondence between the German editions of Grass's plays and those in English translation. Six plays were collected in *Theaterspiele* (1970; pieces for the theater), including *Only Ten Minutes to Buffalo*, *Hochwasser* (1957, rev. 1963; *Flood*, 1967), *Onkel, Onkel* (1958; *Mister, Mister*, 1967), and *Die bösen Köche* (1961; *The Wicked Cooks*, 1967); the English versions of these plays were published in *Four Plays* (1967), whereas *Die Plebejer proben den Aufstand* (1966; *The Plebeians Rehearse the Uprising*, 1966) and *Davor* (1970; *Max*, 1972) were published independently in English translations.

Grass's collected poems in *Gesammelte Gedichte* (1971) include the previously published volumes *Die Vorzüge der Windhühner*, *Gleisdreieck* (1960; rail interchange), and *Ausgefragt* (1967; *New Poems*, 1968). Selections from the first two collections are available in translation in *Selected Poems* (1966); the small collection *Poems of Günter Grass* (1969) incorporates both *Selected Poems* and *New Poems*. *Poems of Günter Grass* is also available as a bilingual edition under the title *In the Egg and Other Poems* (1977); *Mariazuehren, Hommageàmarie, Inmarypraise* (1973) was published as a trilingual edition, as the title indicates. The collection entitled *Liebe geprüft* (1974; *Love Tested*, 1975) is a bibliophile edition. *Novemberland: Selected Poems, 1956-1993* (1996) is a bilingual collection of Grass's best poetry.

As in Grass's plays, one may discern in his poems a gradual departure from his early playfulness and an increasing concern with political and social problems. Poetry would continue to be a vital aspect of the author's creativity; this fact is clearly evidenced by the numerous poems that were integrated into the voluminous novel *The Flounder*.

There is also a considerable body of writings that originated as a result of Grass's political involvement and, to a lesser extent, his commitment to his craft. These speeches, essays, open letters, and other comments were printed in the following major collections: *Über das Selbstverständliche* (1968; partially translated in *Speak Out!*, 1969), *Über meinen Lehrer Döblin und andere Vorträge* (1968; about my teacher Döblin and other essays), *Der Bürger und seine Stimme* (1974; the citizen and his voice), *Denkzettel* (1978; lessons to remember), *Aufsätze zur Literatur* (1980; essays on literature), and *Widerstand lernen: Politische Gegenreden, 1980-1983* (1984; learning how to resist: political rebuttals). *Deutscher Lastenausgleich: Wider das dumpfe Einheitsgebot* (1990; *Two States—One Nation?*, 1990) and *Rede vom Verlust* (1992; *The Future of German Democracy*, 1993) contain Grass's controversial essays and speeches, in which he states his fierce opposition to the reunification of Germany and his subsequent deep animosity toward the politics of the first government of the reunified country. Many of the concerns that Grass voiced in his political writing are also reflected in his fiction.

ACHIEVEMENTS

Günter Grass has long been acknowledged as a novelist of international stature—a rank he achieved with the publication of *The Tin Drum*, his first novel, whose English version appeared in 1961 in Great Britain and two years later in the United States. Although Grass continued to publish at a fairly steady pace and to produce works of challenging complexity—notably *The Flounder—The Tin Drum* is his most widely acclaimed work. In 1980, the film version of *The Tin Drum*, based on the screenplay by Grass and director Volker Schlöndorff, was nominated for an Academy Award in the foreign film category; the film also received several international prizes.

Grass is generally acknowledged as the "author who put postwar German literature back in the world market" (*Newsweek*, May 24, 1965). His fiction displays a virtuosity of language practically unparalleled in contemporary letters, and he has received numerous domestic as well as foreign literary awards, among them the prestigious prize of Gruppe 47 (in 1958). Grass's impressive string of major European literary prizes also includes France's Foreign Book Prize (1962), Italy's Mondello Prize (1977), and the Viareggio-Versilia Prize (1978). Beginning in 1955, Grass won more than ten important German awards, including the Carl von Ossiersky Medal in 1977, the Majkowski Medal in 1978, and the Leonhard Frank Ring, a prestigious German award bestowed upon him in 1988. In addition, Grass was awarded three honorary doctorates, including one from Harvard University in 1976. Grass's crowning achievement was the Nobel Prize in Literature, which he earned in 1999.

Even though Grass's novels after the mid-1980's were faulted by many literary critics for their increasingly political polemics, apparent antifeminism, and flat characters, his earlier fiction is generally held in high esteem. In addition, Grass's formidable literary stature is acknowledged, if grudgingly, by most serious students of literature. There are several reasons that Grass became the center of public attention. To begin with, Grass aroused topical interest by his chronicling of Germany's Nazi past—if from an idio-syncratic narrative point of view. The surface realism of *The Tin Drum*, for example, is mingled with elements of the fantastic, grotesque, and comical that require readers to reexamine their preconceived notions not only about the period in question but also about the very nature of reality itself. Second, despite Grass's underlying view of history as ultimately meaningless and his perception of human existence as bordering on the absurd, his major works do convey a sense of commitment and responsibility that challenge the reader. Third, Grass never confined himself to the proverbial ivory tower of the artist—quite the opposite. He repeatedly stated that his responsibility as both a citizen and a writer demands his active involvement in politics, and he acted according to his professed belief. Critics claim to have discerned a diminishing of Grass's creativity as a result of his participation in left-wing political campaigns, but after each spate of intense political activity, he inevitably returned to literary pursuits.

(Mottke Weissman/Courtesy D.C. Public Library)

BIOGRAPHY

Günter Wilhelm Grass was born October 16, 1927, in the city of Gdańsk (called Danzig in German), then a Free State. Both the social milieu of the lower middle class in which he grew up—Grass's father was a grocer—and the ethnically mixed marriage of his parents (his father was a German; his mother was of Cassubian or Kashubian—that is, Slavic—origin) proved to be lasting influences. After attending school in Danzig, which in 1939 had been annexed by the Third Reich, Grass, then still a teenager, was drafted into the army during the final phase of World War II. In 1945, he was wounded and subsequently taken captive by the American forces. After a brief period of imprisonment, he began to work in a potash mine and then became a stonemason's apprentice in Düsseldorf in the Rhineland. From this period of 1946 to 1947 dates Grass's beginning awareness of Nazi atrocities as well as his first exposure to postwar politics. He was attracted to the pragmatism of the Social Democrats, who tended to prefer the achievement of tangible results in the social realm to blind adherence to ideology.

Although Grass, a self-professed autodidact, eschewed the continuation of his formal education, which had been interrupted by the war, he did enroll at the Düsseldorf and Berlin academies of art (1948-1951 and 1953-1956) to study sculpture under various teachers. In 1954, he married Anna Schwarz, a ballet student from Switzerland, with whom he had three sons and one daughter. The marriage eventually ended in divorce, and Grass was remarried, to Ute Grunert, in 1979.

During the middle and late 1950's, Grass gradually began to attract attention as a writer. In his first phase of literary activity, from approximately 1955 to 1959, he wrote primarily short prose pieces, poetry, and absurdist or poetic plays. In 1955, he was awarded a prize for his lyrics by the Süddeutsche Rundfunk (South German radio network); in the same year, he established contact with Gruppe 47, the most influential association of writers, publishers, and critics in postwar Germany, and in 1958, he was awarded that group's coveted prize. Grass's first collection of poetry, *Die Vorzüge der Windhühner*, was published in 1956; meanwhile, he had gone to live in Paris, where he worked on his novel *The Tin Drum*; its publication in 1959 propelled him to instant fame—or, owing to allegedly obscene and blasphemous passages in the novel, infamy.

Thus, the year 1959 marks the beginning of the second phase in Grass's career, which was characterized by an outburst of creative energy that the author never duplicated. In two-year intervals, from 1959 to 1963, the works of *Danzig Trilogy* were published; this trilogy was responsible for establishing Grass as one of the leading contemporary writers of fiction.

Grass's involvement in politics began as early as 1961. In that year, he provided material for the speeches of Social Democrat Willy Brandt, then mayor of West Berlin, who ran for chancellor of the Federal Republic. Only in 1965, however, did Grass actively campaign on behalf of the Social Democrats by delivering speeches in more than fifty cities. During this third phase of his career, Grass became a public figure whose celebrity, or notoriety, extended far beyond the literary scene. Grass's works from this period reflect his political commitment. The play *The Plebeians Rehearse the Uprising* takes issue with Bertolt Brecht's alleged preference for the aesthetic experience of revolutionary theater when faced with a potential revolutionary situation in East Germany. The novel *Local Anesthetic* and the play *Max* explore the alternatives for political action available to those younger Germans of the postwar generation who opposed the Vietnam War.

The year 1972 marks the beginning of a fourth phase in Grass's development as a writer. *From the Diary of a Snail*, an account of the author's participation in the 1969 election campaign that ended in Willy Brandt's election as chancellor, harks back to the themes of *Danzig Trilogy* but employs a new narrative perspective. During the early and middle 1970's, Grass refrained from extensive political involvement and devoted his energies to the completion of his great historical novel *The Flounder*, which was followed by two shorter narratives, *The Meeting at Telgte* and *Headbirths: Or, The Germans Are Dying Out*.

Grass's unequivocal and vociferous engagement

in the peace movement since 1979, the year of the North Atlantic Treaty Organization (NATO) decision to deploy medium-range nuclear missiles in Western Europe, marks a fifth stage in his development. The author was no longer content to confine himself to grassroots politics in the Federal Republic; on the contrary, owing to his exposure to problems of a global nature—particularly those of Third World countries—during his extensive travels, Grass felt compelled to speak out on a host of issues, from the nuclear arms race to the environment. Consequently, Grass's next novel, *The Rat*, envisions a surreal postnuclear future devoid of humans, where rats inherit the earth.

In Germany, the fall of the Berlin Wall in 1989 marks the sixth stage in Günter Grass's career. Almost alone among German writers, Grass fiercely opposed Germany's reunification in many polemical essays, which have been collected in *Two States— One Nation?* This deeply unpopular political stance greatly alienated his German and European readers and critics, surprised many of his former friends, and singled him out in the literary world.

Furiously stating his opposition to reunification and expressing his disgust with the German government of Chancellor Helmut Kohl, Grass's political essays continued to absorb much of his creative energies. The pieces in his 1993 collection, *The Future of German Democracy*, haunt the reader with Grass's deep disaffection with the new Germany.

Grass's two novels of the 1990's, *The Call of the Toad* and *Ein weites Feld* (a vast field), met with broad popular rejection and near-universal critical dismissal, with the occasional solitary voice of praise. Most critics, including writer Ian Buruma, objected to the novels' political sermonizing; the contrived, stereotypical plots; and the flat characters. Among friends, Grass often expressed his hurt at the intensity of his rejection. Yet Grass continued to devote himself to unpopular political causes. In 1997, at the age of seventy, he stunned his audience when he presented the Peace Prize of the German Book Trade to the Kurdish writer Yashar Kemal and accused Germany of a variety of crimes against humanity.

Often rejected for his savage style of criticism, Günter Grass nevertheless continued to draw admiration for his earlier literary work. From 1987 to 1995, Grass's literary reputation suffered in America, where many graduate students faulted Grass in their dissertations for his perceived antifeminism. A literary symposium on the subject, held in 1995, failed to fully resolve the issue. Grass did earn some grudging public respect as an intense septuagenarian who refused to give up what he considered an ongoing, uphill battle against injustice and the ghosts of Germany's Nazi past.

ANALYSIS

Although Günter Grass's novel *The Tin Drum* forms the first part of the *Danzig Trilogy* and shares some characters, events, and themes with *Cat and Mouse* and *Dog Years*, the novel was conceived independently and can be discussed without explicit reference to the other two works. Nevertheless, it should be noted that the title of the trilogy reflects the extraordinary significance of Günter Grass's birthplace for his fiction. In fact, this significance has been compared to that of Dublin for James Joyce or Yoknapatawpha County for William Faulkner. Owing to political developments after World War II, Grass was forced to sever his ties with his place of birth forever: Danzig became the Polish Gdańsk, a city that the author was able to visit repeatedly but that was no longer the predominantly German-speaking Danzig.

Hence, the very act of narration is an evocation of the past, a resurrection from oblivion. Grass, however, is concerned neither with nostalgic memories nor with mourning the lost city; rather, he wants to keep alive in the collective memory the reasons for the loss of Danzig. These reasons are to be sought in history—more specifically, in the Nazi period. In *The Tin Drum*, Grass sets out to elucidate these reasons— albeit from a highly unconventional narrative perspective.

THE TIN DRUM

Oskar, the narrator of *The Tin Drum*, is the inmate of an insane asylum in postwar West Germany—a fact that he freely admits in the very first sentence of the novel. Instead of endeavoring to offer his readers an explanation for his confinement—the reason, his implication in a murder, is only gradually revealed in the course of the novel—Oskar reverses the normal order of things by declaring his hospital bed to be his sanctuary and refuge that protects him from the outside world. Oskar's position as an unapologetic outsider tends to disorient the reader and force him or her to assume a critical attitude.

Oskar's memoirs, written during his confinement, are a record both of his family's history, which began in Danzig around the turn of the century, and of political history. Thus, the three books of the novel depict the prewar period, the war itself, and the postwar period through 1954—the year in which Oskar turns thirty and completes his narration. As aids in his efforts to evoke the past and make history come alive, the narrator uses his tin drum—the instrument that gave the novel its name—and the family photograph album.

Although the novel is realistic in the sense that it provides exact details relating to the topography of Danzig, the speech patterns of various social groups, the milieu of the lower middle class, the chronology of historical events, and so on, fantastic and supernatural elements are by no means absent. In fact, they are introduced, somewhat in the manner of Franz Kafka's *Die Verwandlung* (1915; *The Metamorphosis*, 1936), almost casually. Thus, Oskar's mental faculties are said to be fully developed at birth. Confronted with the unpleasant realization that a return to the safety of the womb is impossible, on his third birthday Oskar opts for the second-best solution— that is, to stop growing. He camouflages this willful act by injuring himself in a way that provides a medical explanation for his retarded physical development.

Without a doubt, Oskar's refusal to grow up is a protest against the world of adults in general and the narrow petit bourgeois sphere of his parents in particular. His diminutive size affords Oskar the possibility of observing the adults in their intimate moments— hence the sexually explicit passages that aroused controversy when the novel was published. Oskar, however, is not a mere voyeur. True, he has a keen eye for the triangular relationship that exists between his mother and his two "presumable" fathers, Matzerath, the German, and Bronski, the Pole, but the outsider Oskar also recognizes clearly the drift toward Nazism in Danzig with its attendant evils, such as the beginning persecution of the Jews.

Even though Oskar is an opponent of Nazism, he rarely uses his supernatural faculties—his evocative, spellbinding drumming and his ability to shatter glass with his voice—for acts of outright opposition. Admittedly, he does disrupt a Nazi rally by magically transforming the martial music of the drums and fifes into waltzes and the Charleston; conversely, Oskar employs his artistic abilities to contribute to the war effort by entertaining the German troops in France. Moreover, in some instances, Oskar's shattering of glass seems to be inspired by a desire for wanton destruction rather than by an aroused conscience.

Ultimately, Oskar's role remains somewhat ambivalent. His professed complicity in the deaths of Bronski and Matzerath, for example, appears less serious when these deaths are viewed as an inevitable consequence of his presumable fathers' actions. When the amorous but cowardly Bronski deserts the defenders of the Polish post office in Danzig at the outbreak of World War II, Oskar leads him back to the besieged building; as a consequence, Bronski is executed by the Germans. Amiable Matzerath, who has become a member of the Nazi Party, is killed at the end of World War II by the Soviets, who have invaded Danzig; Oskar contributes to his demise by handing him the Party badge that Matzerath is desperately trying to get rid of.

The fates of Bronski and Matzerath demonstrate that Grass poses the question of the individual's responsibility for his or her actions, regardless of his or her station in life. This question also applies to Oskar himself—who, in fact, seriously ponders it at a decisive juncture in his life that coincides with the historical juncture constituted by the end of World War II. At Matzerath's funeral, Oskar, who in 1945 has turned twenty-one and attained maturity, decides to grow and to assume his proper place in the adult world. Neither Maria, Matzerath's second wife, nor her son Kurth accept Oskar very enthusiastically as a husband and father substitute, however, and despite his belated growth, Oskar does not develop into a physically normal adult; he never achieves normal height and is disfigured by a hunchback. Thus, he remains a conspicuous outsider in postwar West German society; his attempts to start afresh and to assume responsibility have essentially failed. Oskar's failure is shared by an entire society that is only too eager to forget the past and savor the blessings of the economic miracle. Although Oskar, who has resumed his artistic drumming, keeps the past alive in the face of the general tendency to suppress it, he must acknowledge his complicity in the evil of the times, his standing aside while others acted. Its parodistic, comical, grotesque, picaresque, and mythical dimensions notwithstanding, in the final analysis, the telling of the story, which results in the novel, is the artist Oskar's way of atoning for his failure to conduct himself as a responsible citizen.

CAT AND MOUSE

The first-person narrator of *Cat and Mouse*, Pilenz, resembles Oskar in that he is compelled by guilt to tell the story of his ambivalent relationship with "the great Mahlke," a youth in wartime Danzig whom he both admires and envies. Mahlke seeks to divert attention from his excessively protuberant Adam's apple by accomplishing uncommon feats—among them an extended masturbation scene—that cannot be matched by his classmates. When Mahlke has become a highly decorated war hero, he gradually begins to realize that his youthful idealism has been misused. As an AWOL, he endeavors to hide on a sunken Polish navy vessel, but he perishes in the attempt as a result of Pilenz's lack of support, amounting to a betrayal. Somewhat in the manner of Oskar, Pilenz survives the war in order to be able to tell of his own failure and the martyrdom of Mahlke.

DOG YEARS

In the complex novel *Dog Years*, Matern, one of the three narrators, is induced by the chief of the "authors' collective" to revive the Danzig Nazi past in writing—although Matern is endeavoring to suppress it and even engages in acts of revenge against those people who were implicated in unsavory acts that he himself committed. One may note in concluding discussion of *Danzig Trilogy* that Grass uses in these

novels a retrospective narrative approach which draws attention to the time of World War II as well as the prewar period in order to trace their remnants in postwar society. Grass's adoption of such a perspective rested on the assumption that history was of vital significance in the consciousness of the reading public of the 1950's and early 1960's. Even if Grass interpreted history in a remarkably idiosyncratic fashion, he did not tamper with historical facts and events. After the transitional novel *From the Diary of a Snail*, however, Grass wrote three narratives—for all practical purposes, a second trilogy—in which history assumes a new dimension.

In *The Flounder*, *The Meeting at Telgte*, and *Headbirths: Or, The Germans Are Dying Out*, there is a closer correspondence between author and narrator than in *Danzig Trilogy*. This close correspondence enables Grass to transcend the chronological and spatial boundaries imposed upon a fictional first-person narrator and to give free rein to his exuberant and whimsical imagination. Here, history becomes raw material to be reshaped and reinvented by the author, who provides alternative versions that challenge presumably established facts. Such imaginative reinterpretation of history is designed to counteract the reader's tendency to regard history as an inevitable and ultimately meaningless process that absolves him or her from the responsibility of participating in it.

THE FLOUNDER

Grass's new approach can be most clearly seen in *The Flounder*, a novel set in Danzig but employing a vastly expanded time frame. Amassing information from the most diverse fields of extant knowledge, Grass uses this encyclopedic material to buttress his plausible account of the antagonistic relationship of the sexes from the Neolithic Age to the 1970's. In particular, Grass follows literary history fairly closely in developing his central conceit—the alleged former existence of a second version of the fairy tale "The Fisherman and His Wife," by the Brothers Grimm. The narrator, who closely resembles the present-day author Grass but who has also assumed the identity of male figures in past centuries, avers that in contrast to the version printed by the Brothers Grimm, the lost second version showed an overweening, prideful male instead of a female falling prey to hubris. Because the predominantly male fairy-tale collectors of the Romantic age, foremost among them the Grimms, perceived the second version to be a potential threat to the patriarchal order, they burned it. Although the narrator was not a participant in the burning, his pervasive guilt as a male who has contributed to the exploitation of women throughout the centuries impels him to reconstruct the alternative version, which depicts the woman in a favorable light.

While mindful of and sympathetic toward women in general (they are chiefly represented in their vital function as food-providing cooks), the narrator/author warns of the excesses in which the extreme fringe of the women's liberation movement is wont to indulge. On the one hand, the women's tribunal puts the mythical, omniscient Flounder of fairy-tale renown, after whom the novel is named, on trial as the embodiment of the male principle; on the other hand, the radical feminists accept the Flounder's help in their efforts to establish their domination over men. In view of the continuing antagonism of the sexes, the novel suggests a synthesis that does not seek to derive the ideological justification for the male or female cause from one version of the fairy tale only; rather, as an old woman had told one of the fairy-tale collectors who had inquired about the "correct" version, both versions taken together would yield a viable solution.

THE MEETING AT TELGTE

The Meeting at Telgte offers another instance of Grass's imaginative recreation of history and his exploration of alternative possibilities. In this narrative, a fictitious meeting of famous and lesser-known writers takes place in 1647, at the end of the Thirty Years' War. The writers' conference proceeds according to the rituals of Gruppe 47; like their twentieth century colleagues, the seventeenth century poets try to resurrect literature from the rubble caused by a devastating war—thereby demonstrating that literature will continue to flourish even in perilous times.

HEADBIRTHS

In a similar vein, *Headbirths*, Grass's literary contribution to the election campaign of 1980, is con-

cerned with the place of literature in society, the relationship of art and politics, and the function of the writer. Grass addresses a wide variety of topics; as the title suggests, he also playfully speculates on the possibility of the Germans dying out on account of their low birthrate—thus projecting history into the future. His central theme, however, is of a literary nature—that is, how to ensure the survival of literature and, for that matter, life itself, in a world that is threatened by the nuclear arms race and other undesirable results of rampant technological progress. To characterize the magnitude of the task ahead, Grass discards the metaphor of the snail, symbol of slow progress, that he had used in *From the Diary of a Snail*; instead, he employs the myth of Sisyphus as derived from Albert Camus. Only Sisyphean labors, Grass avers, will be able to prevent the advent of the Orwellian state in the 1980's.

THE RAT

Grass's next novel, the occasionally hilarious dystopian science-fiction novel *The Rat*, has its intellectual roots in the author's involvement in the German antinuclear and environmentalist protest movement of the mid-1980's. Typical of Grass's increasing pessimism and his penchant for literary experimentation, *The Rat* is a surrealistic tale of the nonfuture of humanity. As the narrator begins to converse with an extremely intelligent and witty female rat, the feisty rodent convinces him that humanity's pollution and devastation of its environment will soon lead to the demise of all people. The rats, she tells him, will inherit the earth. Even a new hybrid race of half-humans, half-rats cannot survive the destruction brought on by the humans and will eventually disappear from the face of the earth.

Told in the style of a postmodernist fairy tale, *The Rat* also showcases the reappearance of some of Grass's previous characters from *The Tin Drum* and other novels, who weave in and out of the convoluted narrative. Just as humans and rats converse easily within the novel and even interbreed, so it becomes clear that the rats of the future bear a striking resemblance to the humans of the present. Yet for all its imagination and occasionally heavy-handed allusions to topical political events and circumstances, *The Rat* ultimately lacks the brilliant genius of George Orwell's *Animal Farm* (1945), which is generally considered the best animal fable of the twentieth century.

THE CALL OF THE TOAD

To Grass's deep surprise, *The Call of the Toad* met with a generally negative, if not outright hostile, critical reception. Two of Germany's leading literary critics, Marcel Reich-Ranicki and Frank Schirrmacher, condemned the book. Calling into question its very nature as a novel, they considered it a mere platform for the author's venting of his political rage at German reunification. Critics such as Ian Buruma agreed that the book contained many stereotypes, clichés, and flat characters.

Ostensibly a tale of West German capitalist aggression and Polish helplessness, *The Call of the Toad* tells the story of two elderly lovers, a German man and a Polish woman. The two devise a plan for a German cemetery in the former city of Danzig, which became the Polish town of Gdańsk after World War II. Their idea is to allow Germans who were expelled from Danzig/Gdańsk after the war to lay their bodies to rest in the soil of the city of their birth. The well-meaning project soon runs into difficulties, however, which are stylized to serve as symbols for all that can go wrong in contemporary German-Polish relationships. The title of the novel alludes to a German folk saying in which the call of toads warns of impending doom, much as Cassandra's calls warned her fellow Trojans about the Greek invasion in Homer's *Iliad* (c. 800 B.C.E.).

EIN WEITES FELD

Negative critical reception continued to plague Grass's next novel, *Ein weites Feld* (a vast field). Set in Berlin shortly before and just after reunification, the novel reiterates Grass's misgivings about the process. When a leading German newsmagazine showed critic Marcel Reich-Ranicki ripping the book in two on its front cover, an angry Günter Grass wrote that the Nazis, too, had destroyed books. Yet the critics charged that the book was dull and full of political sermons. Too many critics felt that the novel had failed to bring Berlin to life as radiantly as *The Tin Drum* had re-created the lost city of prewar Danzig.

Siegfried Mews, updated by R. C. Lutz

OTHER MAJOR WORKS

PLAYS: *Noch zehn Minuten bis Buffalo*, pr. 1954 (*Only Ten Minutes to Buffalo*, 1967); *Hochwasser*, pr. 1957, rev. 1963 (*Flood*, 1967); *Onkel, Onkel*, pr. 1958 (*Mister, Mister*, 1967); *Die bösen Köche*, pr. 1961 (*The Wicked Cooks*, 1967); *Die Plebejer proben den Aufstand*, pr., pb. 1966 (*The Plebeians Rehearse the Uprising*, 1966); *Four Plays*, pb. 1967 (includes *Only Ten Minutes to Buffalo*, *The Wicked Cooks*, *Flood*, and *Mister, Mister*); *Theaterspiele*, pb. 1970 (includes *Noch zehn Minuten bis Buffalo*, *Hochwasser*, *Onkel, Onkel*, and *Die bösen Köche*); *Davor*, pb. 1970 (*Max*, 1972).

POETRY: *Die Vorzüge der Windhühner*, 1956; *Gleisdreieck*, 1960; *Selected Poems*, 1966 (includes poems from *Die Vorzüge der Windhühner* and *Gleisdreieck*); *Ausgefragt*, 1967 (*New Poems*, 1968); *Poems of Günter Grass*, 1969 (includes *Selected Poems* and *New Poems*; also in a bilingual edition as *In the Egg and Other Poems*, 1977); *Gesammelte Gedichte*, 1971 (includes *Die Vorzüge der Windhühner* and *Gleisdreieck*); *Mariazuehren, Hommageàmarie, Inmarypraise*, 1973 (trilingual edition); *Liebe geprüft*, 1974 (*Love Tested*, 1975); *Die Gedichte 1955-1986*, 1988; *Novemberland: Selected Poems, 1956-1993*, 1996 (bilingual edition).

NONFICTION: *Über das Selbstverständliche*, 1968 (partial trans. *Speak Out!*, 1969); *Über meinen Lehrer Döblin und andere Vorträge*, 1968; *Der Bürger und seine Stimme*, 1974; *Denkzettel: Politische Reden und Aufsätze 1965-76*, 1978; *Aufsätze zur Literatur*, 1980; *Widerstand lernen: Politische Gegenreden, 1980-1983*, 1984; *Zunge Zeigen*, 1988 (*Show Your Tongue*, 1989); *Skizzenbuch*, 1989; *Deutscher Lastenausgleich: Wider das dumpfe Einheitsgebot*, 1990 (*Two States—One Nation?*, 1990); *Ein Schnappchen namens DDR: Letzte Reden vorm Glockengelaut*, 1990; *Schreiben nach Auschwitz: Frankfurter Poetik-Vorlesung*, 1990; *Totes Holz: Ein Nachruf*, 1990; *Gegen die verstreichende Zeit: Reden, Aufsätze und Gespräche, 1989-1991*, 1991; *Günter Grass, vier Jahrzehnte*, 1991; *Rede vom Verlust: Über den Niedergang der politischen Kultur im geeinten Deutschland*, 1992 (*The Future of German Democracy*, 1993); *Angestiftet, Partei zu ergrei-*

fen, 1994; *Die Deutschen und ihre Dichter*, 1995; *Gestern, vor 50 Jahren: Ein deutsch-japanischer Briefwechsel*, 1995.

MISCELLANEOUS: *Cat and Mouse and Other Writings*, 1994.

BIBLIOGRAPHY

Brady, Philip, et al., eds. *Günter Grass's "Der Butt": Sexual Politics and the Male Myth of History*. Oxford, England: Clarendon Press, 1990. Extremely useful collection of critical essays which focus on the representation of sexuality, male-female conflicts, and Grass's use of history in his controversial novel *The Flounder*. Individual essays represent a wide range of critical approaches and viewpoints. Some authors discuss the question of Grass's presentation of women characters, which has caused great controversy in American criticism of the author.

Hollington, Michael. *Günter Grass*. Boston: Marion Boyars, 1980. Hollington's primary focus is on the novels of the *Danzig Trilogy*, with some discussion of other works. Also looks at Grass's work as poet, playwright, and political essayist.

Lawson, Richard H. *Günter Grass*. New York: Frederick Ungar, 1985. The detailed presentations of Grass's novels and poems up to the date of the book's publication provide useful information. Occasionally Lawson offers more plot information than in-depth critical analysis, but this helps readers to quickly become familiar with Grass's texts.

Mews, Siegfried, ed. *"The Fisherman and His Wife": Günter Grass's "The Flounder" in Critical Perspective*. New York: AMS Press, 1983. An excellent collection of initial critical responses to Grass's novel; very useful in connection with Philip Brady's anthology (above) about the same novel. Ruth Angress's "Der Butt: A Feminist Perspective" anticipates much of the ensuing American controversy over Grass's treatment of his women characters.

O'Neill, Patrick, ed. *Critical Essays on Günter Grass*. Boston: G. K. Hall, 1987. A useful collection of previously published work on Grass. Provides a useful biographical introduction by O'Neill and reprints reviews of Grass's novels before moving to its rich collection of critical articles.

Taberner, Stuart. *Distorted Reflections*. Amsterdam, The Netherlands: Rodopi, 1998. Analyzes the importance and function of Grass's political engagement in his fiction. Also compares Grass's use of autobiographical elements to the narrative strategies employed by his fellow German-language writers Uwe Johnson and Martin Walser.

Weber, Alexander. *Günter Grass's Use of Baroque Literature*. London: Maney, 1995. Convincingly argues that Grass's novels *The Flounder* and *The Meeting at Telgte* utilize sources from Germany's Baroque era, ranging from 1550 to 1700. Focuses on Hans Jakob Christoffel von Grimmelshausen's Baroque novel *Der abenteuerliche Simplicissimus* (1669; *The Adventurous Simplicissimus*, 1912) as a rich quarry for Grass's two novels, which take place in part during the Baroque age. Grimmelshausen's original mix of realistic description, satire, social criticism, and rough language is seen as mirrored by Grass's two texts.

SHIRLEY ANN GRAU

Born: New Orleans, Louisiana; July 8, 1929

PRINCIPAL LONG FICTION

The Hard Blue Sky, 1958
The House on Coliseum Street, 1961
The Keepers of the House, 1964
The Condor Passes, 1971
Evidence of Love, 1977
Roadwalkers, 1994

OTHER LITERARY FORMS

Although Shirley Ann Grau has written introductions and an occasional essay for magazines, two forms, the novel and the short story, have dominated her literary career. The enthusiastic reception that

(CORBIS/Bettmann)

greeted her first collection of short stories, *The Black Prince and Other Stories* (1955), has assured her reputation in the genre. Scarcely any anthology of American short fiction excludes her work. In spite of her initial success critically, her second collection of stories, *The Wind Shifting West* (1973), was not so warmly received as the first. *Nine Women*, which appeared in 1985, restored Grau's critical acclaim as a short-story writer. Grau also contributed a chapter to *Haunter of the Ruins* (1997), a book on America's foremost surrealist photographer, fellow Louisianian Clarence John Laughlin.

ACHIEVEMENTS

The most obvious testimony to Grau's success is the Pulitzer Prize for Fiction that she received in 1965 for *The Keepers of the House*. Significantly enough, the same novel appeared in condensed form in *Ladies' Home Journal*. Thus, one sees evidence of one of the distinguishing characteristics of much of Grau's fiction: the ability to appeal simultaneously to two often opposed audiences, the person looking for the "good read" and the literary sophisticate. Not many contemporary writers have published stories in both *McCall's* and *The New Yorker*. In *Evidence of Love*, Grau seems to have made an attempt to shed any vestige of her image as a "housewife writer" or yet another southern regionalist. While *Evidence of Love* is rather straightforward, even in its effective use of three overlapping narratives, it nevertheless makes few concessions to a reader looking for the conventional melodramatic staples of sex or violence. *Evidence of Love* also silences the critics who, after the disappointment of *The Condor Passes*, sought to dismiss Grau as a one-novel writer. The one recurring criticism of Grau's later work—that her characters seem bloodless—seems less relevant after the success of other novelists with similar ironic visions—Joan Didion, for example.

As is true of all but a handful of contemporary writers, Grau's achievement cannot yet be fully measured. *Evidence of Love* suggests that she has shifted her emphasis away from the engaging plot to the creation of a cool, ironic vision of psychological intensity. While *Roadwalkers* contains all the ironic vision of Grau's earlier novels and emphasizes the psychological, it represents another technical feat for Grau in a reemphasis on and experimentation with plot. Here Grau interweaves the impressionistic tale of Mary Woods with the separate histories of Charles Tucker and Rita Landry but ends the novel with the rather straightforward narrative of Nanda Woods. In the process, she has kept those elements of style—the brilliant sensory images, the directness of language, the complex heroines—that have given vitality to all her work.

BIOGRAPHY

At the age of forty-five, Katherine Grau presented her dentist husband, Adolphe, with a baby girl. Although Shirley Ann Grau's parents were well into middle age, she has described her childhood as free of unhappiness or social alienation. Her Protestant family, with roots both in New England and the South, moved back and forth from Montgomery, Alabama, to New Orleans. Shirley Ann attended a girls' finishing school in the Alabama capital until her senior year, when she transferred to an accredited high school in New Orleans, the Ursuline Academy—the institution that one of her heroines remembers as a place to knit, chant, and crochet.

Grau's first experiences with writing came while attending Sophie Newcomb College in New Orleans. Her stories appeared in the campus literary magazine, *Carnival*. After she was graduated Phi Beta Kappa, Grau lived in New Orleans' French Quarter and abandoned her graduate studies for a writing career. Success came quickly. In 1955, her volume of short stories, *The Black Prince and Other Stories*, received exceptionally fine reviews, and her work was compared favorably with that of other southern writers such as Eudora Welty, Flannery O'Connor, and Carson McCullers.

In the same year, Grau married James K. Feibleman, a remarkable professor of philosophy at Tulane University. Many years her senior, Feibleman had risen to the chairmanship of his department even though he himself had attended college for only two months. He had published numerous books and was acquainted with such luminaries as William Faulkner. Grau successfully combined her roles as wife, mother of two sons and two daughters, and writer. She has described her life as a "conventional upper middle class" one, divided between summers on Martha's Vineyard and school years in New Orleans.

As she reared her children, Grau continued to write. Novels appeared in 1958 (*The Hard Blue Sky*) and 1961 (*The House on Coliseum Street*). While both works received considerable notice, it seemed as if Grau might be categorized as a regionalist who had mastered "local color." Her selection as the Pulitzer Prize winner for fiction in 1965, however, did much to squelch such categorization. *The Keepers of the House*, a novel that attracted attention for its candid treatment of racial themes, brought her national attention; in fact, President Lyndon Johnson appointed her to the Commission on Presidential Scholars in

the same year. In spite of this recognition, the rhythm of Grau's life remained largely unchanged, and she did not rush to bring out her next novel. Instead, she taught creative writing at the University of New Orleans, wrote an occasional story, and gave birth to her fourth child. When her next novel, *The Condor Passes*, appeared in 1971, its sales surpassed the combined total of all her previous works. Its critical reception, however, was at best mixed. After that, Grau published only a few more works.

In many ways validating her comment in an interview with John Canfield that writers are "just very inefficient computers," Grau returned to the novel form with *Roadwalkers* in 1994 after an absence of seventeen years. Despite the span of time separating it from Grau's previous novel, *Roadwalkers* received much critical attention, garnering mixed reviews in a rather unique way. Most critics have been extremely favorable to the first half of the novel, which deals primarily with the "feral" child Mary Woods. They have been puzzled by the second half, which centers around her daughter Nanda, whom they see as bloodless and arrogant, a criticism that has followed Grau's heroines off and on throughout her career.

Grau worked on a piece of nonfiction, *Haunter of the Ruins*, in 1997. Her interest in and perhaps unjustified identification with the southern grotesque made Grau the perfect writer to include in a collection of essays which accompany the photographs of Clarence John Laughlin, one of America's earliest surrealist photographers. Rather than dealing specifically with Laughlin's photographs, Grau's essay is a set piece which evokes the haunting imagery that pervades his work.

ANALYSIS

Shirley Ann Grau shares a fate common to many contemporary writers not yet admitted to the pantheon. They are the object of a handful of critical studies, often short and incomplete, that make only a slight effort to detect what vision, if any, gives continuity to the writers' works. At first glance, Grau's novels do seem to defy any attempt to find even a connecting thread. Until the publication of *Evidence of Love*, the label of "southern regionalist" gave some of Grau's reviewers comfort. Readers familiar only with her last three novels could not avoid the recurrence of semilegendary patriarchs in possession of great wealth. Revenge at one time or another consumes such heroines as Joan Mitchell in *The House on Coliseum Street* and Abigail Mason Tolliver in *The Keepers of the House*, but an equally strong woman such as Lucy Henley in *Evidence of Love* possesses no such motive. Alwyn Berland (in his essay "The Fiction of Shirley Ann Grau") suggests that Grau's heroines favor the hallucinatory over the real, tend to be passive, and have ambivalent responses to sex. Berland's observation is helpful, but the title of Grau's 1977 novel, *Evidence of Love*, gives the clearest clue to the sometimes elusive vision that informs her fictional world. While most of her male characters mechanically pursue money, sex, power, or iron-clad order, the heroines seek some evidence of love. Their failure to find it renders both sexes solitary, and their subsequent sense of futility and despair makes their money and power meaningless. What saves the novels from an almost Jamesian pessimism is the possibility of redemption and rebirth. Both Joan Mitchell and Abigail Tolliver are last seen in literal fetal positions, as if awaiting resurrection. Their possibly temporary withdrawal resembles that of the wives of the fishermen in *The Hard Blue Sky*, who passively await the passing of the hurricane that may or may not destroy them.

In the development of her vision, Grau reveals considerable technical skill. Her sense of place is compelling. Equally convincing are such dissimilar scenes as William Howland's atavistic incursion into Honey Island Swamp and Harold Evans's drift into suicide in his meager and bare house in Princeton. As Paul Schlueter (*Shirley Ann Grau*, 1981) points out, few novelists are as successful as Grau in manipulating sensory images, particularly the olfactory. Most satisfying technically is her ability to treat the melodramatic with a cool, analytical detachment. The embattled house that Abigail defends and keeps is above all else a house, not Tara or Sutpen's Hundred. While Edward Milton Henley in *Evidence of Love* is capable of grandiose, operatic gestures and appetites, Grau's sardonic humor and sense of irony keeps him

in the orbit of the real. Grau steadfastly refuses to sentimentalize.

Grau's occasional limitations are perhaps most noticeable in characterization. At times her characters lack emotional depth; the rich are not inherently interesting. In spite of lurid, exotic pasts, characters such as the Old Man in *The Condor Passes* lack the complex humanity necessary to be convincing. Further, her characters' motivations are not always clear. Even the sympathetic reader is not entirely sure, for example, why it is that Abigail so intensely dislikes Margaret's children.

THE HARD BLUE SKY

Prior to 1964, Grau published two novels that anticipated her technique and vision in *The Keepers of the House*. The first, *The Hard Blue Sky*, revealed her ability to capture the world of southern Louisiana in stunning detail. Her plot consists of two different but connected stories that take place on islands along the Gulf Coast. The first story concerns the youthful Annie Landry's affair with Inky D'Alfonso. When she ultimately marries Inky, Annie is able to leave the islands for what may be a better life in New Orleans. Annie bears little resemblance to Abigail Tolliver: She has neither the wealth, the sense of family tradition, nor the consuming desire for revenge that drives Abigail. It is the second story that contains the violence and the revenge motif that will appear in *The Keepers of the House*. Rival groups on two different islands attempt to burn one another out after the disappearance of young lovers from the opposing families. Neither story ends with a clear resolution. It is not clear whether Annie's marriage will be a success, nor does one know if the feud will end, especially since both factions are threatened by a hurricane. Thus, in her first novel, Grau struck what became a crucial and familiar note in her fiction: Her characters are left in a state of uncertainty as they face potential harm or destruction.

THE HOUSE ON COLISEUM STREET

Grau's second novel, *The House on Coliseum Street*, has a much sharper focus than does her first. Joan Mitchell, the protagonist, anticipates Abigail Tolliver in several significant ways. Her relationship with men is disastrous. She is engaged to a businessman named Fred Aleman, whose rather passionless demeanor leaves her vulnerable to a young college professor, Michael Kern; their passionate lovemaking leaves Joan pregnant. After an abortion and Michael's abandonment, a guilt-ridden Joan becomes obsessed with destroying him. She does so by exposing him to his college dean. Like Abigail, Joan brings down her antagonist, but more significantly, she may have destroyed herself emotionally in doing so. That, however, is only a possibility: *The House on Coliseum Street* ends with Joan, having forgotten her key, unable to enter her family house. She is last seen in a fetal position, just as one sees Abigail at the end of *The Keepers of the House*. The possibility of rebirth and redemption is not excluded. Thus, *The House on Coliseum Street*, like *The Hard Blue Sky*, served as a preparation for the greater achievement in *The Keepers of the House*. In both, Grau was able to find sensory images that render the physical world immediate. More important, these early novels introduced Grau's evolving vision of a world with little clear evidence of love or community.

THE KEEPERS OF THE HOUSE

Nearly twenty years after its publication, the reader can see more clearly the truth of Grau's own commentary on *The Keepers of the House*: "The novel is about the whole human plight of how do you cope with evil? Do you fight back? The people are living in the South but they're just people facing the eternal human problem. I wanted to show the alternation of love and evil, which has always fascinated me. And if there is a moral, it is the self-destructiveness of hatred." If Grau sees the novel's significance in general moral terms, its popularity nevertheless was rooted in its then explosive characterization of southern racial attitudes. The novel's narrator, Abigail Tolliver, granddaughter of William Howland, who himself is one of the "keepers of the house," finds herself in almost complete isolation. She and her husband are getting a divorce, two of her children have been forced to go away to school for safety's sake, and she has alienated the citizenry of her hometown, Madison City. Her desolation, mythic in intensity, is tragically linked to the discovery that her grandfather had married his black housekeeper, Mar-

garet Carmichael. While the white community could cavalierly accept a mere sexual liaison, even one that has produced three children, marriage gives legitimacy. Thus, the men of Madison City attempt to burn the Howland estate in retaliation. The discovery of her grandfather's clandestine marriage destroys Abigail's marriage with her amoral, politically ambitious husband. The novel's evil is therefore easy to locate, as is Abigail's vengeful, Medea-like response. She not only burns the cars of the men who come to destroy her house; she also exercises her option to destroy the entire community financially. Yet difficult questions remain when one recalls Grau's own assessment of her work. How convincingly is the love that alternates with evil portrayed? How strongly felt is her "moral"—the self-destructiveness of hate?

Grau will never be accused of sentimentalizing love. Characters rarely, for example, confuse love with sex. When Abigail loses her virginity, she says, "I found that it wasn't so hard . . . nor painful either. . . . There's only one night like that—ever—where you're filled with wonder and excitement for no other reason but the earth is beautiful and mysterious and your body is young and strong." Her courtship by and marriage to John Tolliver is presented just as dispassionately. Tolliver, like Stephen Henley in *Evidence of Love* and the Old Man in *The Condor Passes*, subordinates love to ambition. Grau's sexes mate; they rarely love. Neither does there seem to be affection between generations. Abigail bears four children, but they remain abstractions. More mysterious, more horrific is the relation between the black woman, Margaret, and the children she bears William Howland. Half-white herself, Margaret sends each child off at the age of eleven to be educated in the North. She refuses to see them thereafter. She is particularly hostile and unyielding toward her oldest daughter, Nina, who returns to the South with her black husband. A certain curiosity exists between these racially mixed children and their mother, but there is no evidence of love.

The possible exception to this bleak vision of human existence is the thirty-year relationship between William Howland and Margaret. After the death of his first wife and the marriage of his daughter,

Howland discovers the eighteen-year-old Margaret Carmichael washing clothes at a spring. She comes to him as a housekeeper and ultimately marries him. Both William and Margaret are characterized by Grau in terms larger than life. Howland is heir to the frontier tradition, in which men wrenched a living, indeed an immense fortune, from a hostile environment. Prior to meeting Margaret, he makes a solitary journey into the mystery and danger of Honey Island Swamp, where he at one point strips himself naked and submerges himself into the primordial slime. When he returns to find Margaret at the spring, she appears to him as if she "had folded herself into the earth." Her stride is "a primitive walk, effortless, unassuming, unconscious, old as the earth under her feet." Like gods, apparently, William and Margaret possess the strength, the indifference to violate the most sacrosanct of southern codes. Yet their love, if it exists, is concealed. The only evidence Abigail ever sees of their love is a single embrace.

Until Abigail's epiphany at the novel's end, Margaret is the character most cognizant of evil, particularly the evil inherent in racism. Her own white father abandoned her black mother, who in turn leaves Margaret to search for her missing lover. Margaret further realizes that it is necessary to send her white-appearing children out of the South, a tragic gesture that Abigail alone understands. It is a sacrifice that ends in alienation between parent and child, between white and black.

Grau states that the moral of the novel is the self-destructiveness of hatred. Is she suggesting that the South is destroying itself with its racial hostility? The attack on the Howland farm clearly does not go without destructive retribution. The local bigots have cut their own throats, because Abigail Tolliver owns almost every business in town. Yet her revenge, just as it may be, seems miniscule compared with the sure election of a staunch segregationist as the next governor—the most far-reaching consequence of the exposure of William Howland's marriage. Of more visceral concern to the reader, though, is the effect of hatred on Abigail. Not only has she decided to destroy Madison City, but she also has chosen to terrorize Margaret's vengeful son, Robert, by threatening

to reveal his black origins to his white California wife. Stripped of compassion, devoid of love, Abigail at the conclusion of the novel has not yet taken the step that transcends hate. Her fetal position as she lies weeping in her office offers a possibility of rebirth, but the overriding vision of the novel is one of utter alienation and despair.

THE CONDOR PASSES

In the thirteen years between the publication of Grau's novels *The Keepers of the House* and *Evidence of Love*, one other novel appeared. Ironically, *The Condor Passes* received the worst reviews while posting the highest sales of any of Grau's works. The novel, a family chronicle, depicts the ninety-five years of Thomas Henry Oliver, who during his long life has amassed a huge fortune through such nefarious enterprises as prostitution and bootlegging. The novel bears only superficial resemblance to *The Keepers of the House*. As Grau herself has suggested, it is not concerned with the primitive. Survival is no longer a question. Instead, the characters seek to find a sense of identity in the presence of vast wealth. The novel, however, is wedded thematically to Grau's other works in its despairing vision. One senses that the male figures may have gained the whole world but lost their own souls. The Old Man's daughters are more complex, but their attempts to find enduring love are frustrated. They each have one son, but one dies and the other becomes a priest. The family therefore awaits little more than its own extinction.

EVIDENCE OF LOVE

By contrast, *Evidence of Love* is one of Grau's most successful novels. It too is a family chronicle, but its construction is still tight and sharply focused. Again the wealthy patriarch appears, but Edward Milton Henley possesses a sense of irony and self-awareness denied to earlier Grau patriarchs. Set outside the South, *Evidence of Love* frees Grau from often invidious comparisons with William Faulkner and allows her to concentrate on what has been one of the central concerns of all her novels, the need for some sign of love.

While the novel traces the lives of four generations of the Henley family, the voices of Edward Henley, his son Stephen, and his daughter-in-law

Lucy dominate the narrative. Paul Schlueter maintains that "no where is there any 'evidence of love.'" He sees each character "seeking his own form of satisfaction to the exclusion of others." What in fact gives focus to each of the three stories is the pursuit of some apparently reasonable alternative to love. Because he chooses to relate his story in a satirical, ironic mode, it is not always easy to locate in an exact way Edward's feelings. The evidence of paternal love, he tells the reader, is the wealth his father gave him. If his mother, who is both literally and figuratively distant, did not love him, she at least imparted to him a sense of propriety and morality—which Edward chooses to ignore. These parents were, he says, happy. Himself physically and emotionally transient, Edward rather cavalierly dispenses with wives and male lovers. Yet he never indulges in self-pity. "I prefer to see my life as a pageant. Or a processional. Like that wonderful march in *Aida*." Through the elder Henley, Grau presents her paradox. About this old man, who still dreams of recapturing the drug-induced paradise he once experienced in Mexico, there is a considerable vitality. Edward's audacity, his iconoclasm, his rather mordant humor do not diminish life. His suicide is neither cowardly nor tragic. His life has been long and in its way full—even without the presence of love.

Edward says of his son, "Stephen was quiet and totally self-contained." Stephen is a Gatsby stripped of illusion and romance. As a young man, he makes a detailed plan of his life, a schedule that he unflinchingly follows. His marriage to Lucy Evans is as rational, as free of either anguish or passion as is his commitment to the ministry without believing in God. Here is a potential monster, but Grau does not ask the reader to see him as such. He does at least have some awareness of his own condition. For Lucy, he says, "I felt a sudden flood of feeling . . . not lust, not love. Something deeper, something older, something asexually human. The sympathy of blood for blood, of aching chalky bone for aching chalky bone. . . . The visceral sympathy of acquired identity." If what Stephen feels for Lucy is only kinship, it perhaps explains why he is confused by the passionate intensity of his youngest son, Paul. Quite by chance, Paul dis-

covers, he believes, the identity of Stephen's mother, the young Irish woman Edward had paid to bear him a son sixty years earlier. Stephen wonders, "Was the presence of blood so important to him? What strange evidence of love was this?" The inability of yet another generation of Henleys to understand—or love—another is thus assured. Given Stephen's emotional isolation, one senses the inevitability of Stephen dying alone. Even death cannot shake his detachment. There has been no exhilarating pageant. Knowing he is dying, Stephen thinks, "I hardly cared. It didn't matter. Nothing did."

Although they seek refuge in quite opposing activities, both Stephen and his father rather straightforwardly eschew love. With Lucy, Stephen's wife, the case is more ambiguous, more complex. As in her earlier novels, Grau gives her female character a roundness that her males often lack. When Lucy recalls the sexual pleasure and pain she experienced with her first husband, she remarks that "All that was evidence of love." Because Lucy does not indulge in irony, the reader accepts her assessment. Her openness to physical love is reinforced by her enthusiasm for the lushness of Florida, although Lucy has reservations: When Harold makes love to her, she thinks, "I don't like this. . . . I don't like having feelings I can't control." Perhaps the fear of feeling paradoxically allows her to live comfortably for thirty years with Stephen. After his death, she states that "Old women are supposed to quake with an excess of emotion—perhaps love—and start talking to animals and birds and flowers on the windowsill. I didn't." At times, she seems even more alienated than either her husband or her father-in-law. When her worried son Paul phones her, she thinks to herself that "Love between the generations was a burdensome chore." She hopes to be saved from such love. In her way, Lucy proves as evasive to the reader as she does to her son. Ironically, her last appearance in the novel proves in a perverse way to be evidence of love. She hands Edward Henley the Seconal he wants to end a life grown exceedingly tiresome. Lucy's ambiguous complicity in his death is an appropriate action to close Grau's best work. As Edward's voice dies out, it says, "The taste of paradise, the perfect union. It must be here,

Here." Grau teases the reader into thought. Paradoxes abound. Indeed, the novel has presented little if any conventional evidence of love, but one senses the value of the lives presented. In its own characteristically ironic way, *Evidence of Love* is just that. The vision is bleak, but here is her most affirmative work.

ROADWALKERS

Roadwalkers once again chronicles a family, but the family here is very nontraditional and certainly not wealthy, at least not until the end of the novel. Mary Woods and her daughter Nanda, women of color—Mary is black and Nanda's father was from India—exhibit what Susan S. Kissel calls an "inner strength" unknown to Grau's white heroines, a strength which "empowers and enriches their lives." This strength ironically stems in many ways from Mary's early years as a "roadwalker," a child abandoned by her parents and left to roam the countryside of the South during the Depression years, accompanied first by her sister and brother, then by her brother, and finally, alone. In the description of the early years of Mary, or Baby, as she is then called, Grau produces some of her most poetic writing as she recounts the myriad sensations that make up the small child's life: "Her days were like a hoard of bright-colored beads, their connecting thread broken, lying loose, single, jumbled." The early part of the novel is impressionistic, organically written to mimic the experience that Baby is going through where day follows day unconsciously, and growth is measured only by the alternating cycle of heat and cold and the gradual accumulation of life-sustaining skills.

The progress of the novel itself can be gauged in terms of a symbol that many critics previously have noted to be central to Grau's fiction, the house. From homelessness to a shack built of license plates and Coca-Cola signs to a convent and, finally, to a mansion purchased with the profits of her own talent, Mary Woods's story parallels the rise of displaced African Americans to places of eminence in American society. In her movement from "feral" child to haute-couture designer, Mary encounters hatred, racism, and paternalism, yet somehow comes out of the experience self-assured and happy. Married at the end of the novel to an alderman who is thinking of running for state representative, Mary spends her days working in her garden, in her own soil, at her own home. The first pages of the novel claim that "[s]he knew the surface of the earth. Head down, hour after hour, she studied it as she walked. She knew all its forms: dry and blowing with each of her steps; wet and oozing through her toes with a sucking sound. And the grains of the earth: sand fine as sugar; soil black and oily." At the end, Nanda says of her, "she seems to love the feel of dirt. I've seen her rub light friable soil into dust between her palms and then toss it into the air, solemnly, like a priest dispensing incense." In the meantime the novel recounts the struggle that Mary undergoes to make the world her own from the moment she is ripped from her license-plate shack by the well-meaning Charles Tucker and delivered to the Sister Servants of Mary Home for Children and then focuses on the similarly painful but more typical battle of her own child to excel in a racially charged atmosphere.

Nanda's life resembles her mother's in its struggles. Her struggles are not as much for survival as for acceptance, and they, too, are symbolically mirrored in her places of abode. Unlike the disconnected days of her mother's early life, Nanda recalls her mother's "light high whisper threaded through all my days, linking them tightly together," and her moves are from apartment to apartment and apartment to house rather than on the dusty roads and byways of the roadwalker. "We had passed through a series of lodgings," Nanda says when they move into their first house, "but we had finally gained our castle, the one we had been searching for." She trades this safe haven, however, for a scholarship to the mostly white St. Catherine's and then to college, where she must forge the way for other African Americans. As she returns to her mother's in the summer, she notices "a change in my mother's world. Black and white were reversing themselves," and she realizes that Mary, a successful clothing designer having "conquered the black kingdom," is now entering "new and dangerous territory on voyages of conquest and discovery." Mary's rise to the top of the fashion world is capped by an article in *Newsweek*, an article which procures their acceptance into the social world.

By the end of the novel the conquest is complete for both Mary and Nanda. Nanda and her husband Mike, in a happy, if somewhat open, marriage, are free to travel the world at will. Only in the final pages of the book is Nanda settled in a home of her own. Throwing away the basket of toys that had accompanied her through her own nomadic childhood, she says triumphantly, "alone I came into my kingdom. My portion, neither more nor less." The love sought by Grau's previous heroines is found here in mother-child love, in mature husband-wife love, and most significantly and victoriously in Nanda's ability to love herself, thus making *Roadwalkers* the first of Grau's novels to end on an obvious note of triumph and true affirmation.

John K. Saunders, updated by Jaquelyn W. Walsh

OTHER MAJOR WORKS

SHORT FICTION: *The Black Prince and Other Stories*, 1955; *The Wind Shifting West*, 1973; *Nine Women*, 1985.

BIBLIOGRAPHY

Bukoski, Anthony. "The Burden of Home: Shirley Ann Grau's Fiction." *Critique: Studies in Modern Fiction* 28 (Summer, 1987): 181-193. Bukoski finds the house to be the symbolic center of Grau's fiction, from her first collection of short stories through *Nine Women*.

Grau, Shirley Ann. "A Conversation with Shirley Ann Grau." Interview by John Canfield. *Southern Quarterly* 25 (Winter, 1987): 39-52. In this important interview, Grau speaks thoughtfully about her relationship to the southern literary tradition. She also explains her concern with technique and concludes by defining the most important criterion for good writing: the power of the writer's thought.

Kissel, Susan S. *Moving On: The Heroines of Shirley Ann Grau, Anne Tyler, and Gail Godwin*. Bowling Green, Ohio: Bowling Green State University Popular Press, 1996. Focusing on *Keepers of the House* as Grau's "most important" and paradoxically "most neglected" work, Kissel explores the way Grau mutilates and examines the romantic view of southern patriarchy with its avaricious males and passive, paralyzed females.

Oleksy, Elzbieta. "The Keepers of the House: Scarlett O'Hara and Abigail Howland." In *Louisiana Women Writers: New Essays and a Comprehensive Bibliography*, edited by Dorothy H. Brown and Barbara C. Ewell. Baton Rouge: Louisiana State University Press, 1992. Centering on their heroines, Oleksy nonetheless makes a rather complete comparison of Margaret Mitchell's *Gone with the Wind* (1936) and *The Keepers of the House*. Most significantly, she finds that both heroines undergo a Jungian "individuation," that both Mitchell and Grau appear "ambivalent" about their protagonists, and that the moments of epiphany for Scarlett and Abigail are "remarkably similar" as both occur with the character moving through a literal fog to a safe haven in the family home.

O'Neal, Susan Hines. "Cultural Catholicism in Shirley Ann Grau's *The Hard Blue Sky*." *Louisiana Folklore Miscellany* 10 (1995): 24-36. O'Neal sees the islanders' attitude in the novel not as an example of their indifference to the mutability of life but rather as a ritual acceptance stemming from their Catholicism and its melding with folk philosophy and worldly truths.

Rohrberger, Mary. "Shirley Ann Grau and the Short Story." In *Women Writers of the Contemporary South*, edited by Peggy Whitman Prenshaw. Jackson: University Press of Mississippi, 1984. Beginning with Grau's earliest work, published when the writer was only nineteen, Rohrberger painstakingly traces the changes in Grau's work and art as seen in over three decades of short fiction. Rohrberger believes that Grau is given too little credit for subtlety and proves her point with numerous examples.

Schlueter, Paul. *Shirley Ann Grau*. Boston: Twayne, 1981. Although admitting that the quality of Grau's work varies greatly, Schlueter insists that hostile critics, dismissing her as a regional writer, have failed to appreciate Grau's achievements, particularly her evocation of a sense of place, her creation of vivid characters, and her mastery of language. Includes full treatment of all Grau's works up to 1981, extensive notes, and an annotated bibliography.

Wagner-Martin, Linda. "Shirley Ann Grau's Wise Fictions." In *Southern Women Writers: The New Generation*, edited by Tonette Bond Inge. Tuscaloosa: University of Alabama Press, 1990. This essay is based on the assumption that a writer's "southernness" can contribute either to superficiality and triviality or to the greatness which arises from a sense of the presence of the past. For Grau, Wagner-Martin argues, it has been a source of strength. Also devotes some space to the consideration of Grau as a woman writer, in comparison to other women writers, particularly those from the South.

ROBERT GRAVES

Born: Wimbledon, England; July 24, 1895
Died: Deyá, Majorca, Spain; December 7, 1985

PRINCIPAL LONG FICTION

My Head! My Head!, 1925
No Decency Left, 1932 (as Barbara Rich, with Laura Riding)
I, Claudius, 1934
Claudius the God and His Wife Messalina, 1934
"Antigua, Penny, Puce," 1936 (also known as *The Antigua Stamp*, 1937)
Count Belisarius, 1938
Sergeant Lamb of the Ninth, 1940 (also known as *Sergeant Lamb's America*)
Proceed, Sergeant Lamb, 1941
The Story of Marie Powell, Wife to Mr. Milton, 1943 (also known as *Wife to Mr. Milton, the Story of Marie Powell*)
The Golden Fleece, 1944 (also known as *Hercules, My Shipmate*, 1945)
King Jesus, 1946
Watch the North Wind Rise, 1949 (also known as *Seven Days in New Crete*)

The Islands of Unwisdom, 1949 (also known as *The Isles of Unwisdom*)
Homer's Daughter, 1955
They Hanged My Saintly Billy, 1957

OTHER LITERARY FORMS

Robert Graves considered himself primarily a poet. Beginning with *Over the Brazier* (1916) and ending with *New Collected Poems* (1977), he published more than fifty books of poetry. His poems during and for some years after World War I explored themes of fear and guilt, expressive of his experience of trench warfare in France. He later became more objective and philosophical. Since he developed his theory of the White Goddess in the 1940's, he wrote love poetry almost exclusively.

Graves also had more than fifty publications in the nonfiction category, including literary criticism, books about writing and language, an autobiography (*Goodbye to All That*, 1929), a biography of T. E. Lawrence (*Lawrence and the Arabs*, 1927), social commentaries, and studies in Greek and Hebrew myths. In addition, he translated such writers as Suetonius, Homer, Hesiod, Lucius Apuleius, and Lucan. He had one volume of *Collected Short Stories* (1964).

ACHIEVEMENTS

Graves was one of the most versatile writers of the twentieth century, known not only as an excellent poet but also as a mythologist, novelist, translator, lecturer, and persistent intellectual maverick. He has perhaps the clearest claim among twentieth century poets as the inheritor of the Romantic tradition, although he purified his poetry of the kind of flowery elaboration that is often associated with Romanticism. He avoided fads and schools in poetry, perfecting a delicate craftsmanship generally outside the modern trends inspired by T. S. Eliot and Ezra Pound.

For the novel *I, Claudius*, Graves received the Hawthornden Prize, oldest of the famous British literary prizes, and the James Tait Black Memorial Prize, administered through the University of Edinburgh for the year's best novel. Collections of his poetry brought the Loines Award for Poetry (1958), the William Foyle Poetry Prize (1960), the Arts Council Poetry Award (1962), and the Queen's Gold Medal for Poetry (1968).

The White Goddess: A Historical Grammar of Poetic Myth (1948) and Graves's other studies in mythology, particularly *The Greek Myths* (1955, 2 volumes), *Hebrew Myths: The Book of Genesis* (1964, with Raphael Patai), and *The Nazarene Gospel Restored* (1953, with Joshua Podro), together with his novels based on myth, have undoubtedly had a subtle and pervasive influence on modern literature. He was a prominent spokesperson for the view that women and matriarchal values were much more prominent in the ancient world than once realized and that civilization has suffered from the overthrow of women as social and spiritual leaders. The demotion of women from their former prominence, Graves said, is recorded and rationalized in Hebrew texts and classical Greek mythology.

(© Washington Post; reprinted by permission of the D.C. Public Library)

BIOGRAPHY

Robert Graves was born in Wimbledon (outside of London) on July 24, 1895, to Alfred Percival Graves and Amalie von Ranke Graves. His father was an inspector of schools, a Gaelic scholar, and a writer of poetry of a conventional sort. His mother was German, descended from Leopold von Ranke, whom Graves has called the first modern historian. Graves had a conventional Victorian home and upbringing, with summer visits to German relatives. These included an aunt, Baronin von Aufsess, who lived in an imposing medieval castle in the Bavarian Alps.

Because his name was listed as R. von R. Graves, his obvious German connections became an embarrassment during his years at Charterhouse, a private boarding school for boys, during the period before World War I when anti-German sentiment was on the rise. He finally earned his classmates' respect, however, by becoming a good boxer. He also became friends with George Mallory, a famous mountaineer who later died on Everest. Mallory interested Edward Marsh, patron of the contemporary Georgian school of poetry, in the poetry Graves was writing. Marsh encouraged Graves in his writing but advised him to modernize his diction, which was forty years behind the time.

When World War I began, Graves joined the Royal Welsh Fusiliers and soon went to France as a nineteen-year-old officer. In his autobiography, written when he was thirty-five, he provides one of the best descriptions of trench warfare to come out of the war—a gritty, objective account of a soldier's daily life. He was badly wounded, however, both physically and mentally, by his war experiences. The autobiography, which followed a long siege of war neurasthenia during which his poetry was haunted by images of horror and guilt, was a conscious attempt to put that part of his life behind him forever. Graves continued to use his gift for narrating war experiences, however, in subsequent novels, such as *Count Belisarius*, the Sergeant Lamb novels, and the Claudius novels.

During the war, Graves married Nancy Nicholson, a young painter, socialist, and vehement feminist. They were in essential agreement about the ruinous effect of male domination in modern society. Graves, along with his wartime friend, the famous war poet Siegfried Sassoon, was already thoroughly disillusioned with war and the leaders of society who supported it.

Graves and his wife parted company in 1929 after a shattering domestic crisis involving the American poet Laura Riding. Riding was Graves's companion for the next thirteen years. They established themselves in Deyá, Majorca, Spain, published the critical magazine *Epilogue* on their own Seizin Press, and devoted themselves to writing both poetry and prose. Graves wrote his best historical novels during that period—the Claudius novels and *Count Belisarius*.

After Riding met and married the American poet Schuyler Jackson, Graves—during the Spanish Civil War, when British nationals were evacuated from Majorca—married Beryl Hodge. Graves returned to Majorca with his new wife, where he stayed until his death in 1985. Graves had eight children, four by Nancy Nicholson, four by his second wife.

During the 1940's, Graves became fascinated with mythology. While he was doing research for his novel about Jason and the Golden Fleece, he became engrossed in the ubiquitous presence of a great goddess associated with the moon, the earth, and the underworld. She was not only the source of life and intuitive wisdom, but also, as Muse, the patron of the poets and musicians. She bound humans both to the seasons of nature and the demands of the spirit.

When Graves discovered a similar pattern in Celtic folklore and literature and correlated the findings of such anthropologists as Robert Briffault, J. J. Bachofen, James Frazer, Jane Harrison, and Margaret Murray and some of the recent discoveries in archaeology, he was convinced that the goddess cult once permeated the whole Western world. In this pattern of myth, as explained in *The White Goddess*, Graves found the unified vision he needed to animate his poetry and much of his subsequent prose for the rest of his life. It not only inspired some of the best love poetry of his time, but also led to some lively treatments of Greek and Hebrew myth in both fiction and nonfiction.

ANALYSIS

The novels of Robert Graves are usually a curious combination of detective work in history, legend, or myth and a considerable gift for narration. He never claimed any particular ability to invent plots, but he could flesh out imaginatively the skeletal remains of adventures he discovered in the past. Thus, the Emperor Claudius lives again as the gossipy information in Suetonius and other Roman chroniclers passes through Graves's shaping imagination. Sometimes, as in *King Jesus*, a traditional tale takes on a startling new dimension through an unconventional combination with other legendary material.

MY HEAD! MY HEAD!

Graves's first attempt at converting ancient history or myth into fiction was a short novel about Elisha and Moses, somewhat inauspiciously entitled *My Head! My Head!* It was begun, as most of Graves's subsequent novels were, because the original accounts were somewhat mysterious, leaving much unsaid about what really happened and why. The novel elaborates on the biblical story of Elisha and the Shunamite woman (2 Kings, Chapters 8-37) and, secondarily, through Elisha's narration, on the career of Moses.

The novel demonstrates both Graves's tendency to explain miracles in naturalistic terms and his contrary fascination with a certain suprarational possibility for special persons. The writer's curious views on magic are not entirely consistent with his debunking of miracles. The inconsistency is quite noticeable here because of the omniscient point of view. In most later novels, Graves wisely used a first-person narrator, which makes seeming inconsistencies the peculiar bias of a persona, rather than of the author. Thus, *King Jesus* is told by a first century narrator who is neither Jewish nor Christian. In such a person, rational skepticism about specific miracles such as the virgin birth might well coexist with a general acceptance of magic.

In spite of its technical shortcomings, *My Head! My Head!* shows Graves's interest in a number of themes which would continue to concern him for the rest of his life: the changing relationships between men and women, the nature of the gods, and the way in which knowledge of the past and of the future must depend upon an understanding of the present.

NO DECENCY LEFT

On those two occasions when Graves did not depend on mythological or historical sources for his fiction, the results were strange, satirical compositions, lucidly told, but somehow disquieting. The first of these, a collaboration with Laura Riding, appeared under a pseudonym as *No Decency Left* by "Barbara Rich." It is a satirical potpourri of events, drawing on such discordant elements as the rise of dictators, the man in the iron mask, the miraculous feeding of the multitude in the Bible, and comic-opera romance. The ideas in his fantasy may be attributable more to Riding than to Graves, though the attitudes displayed are quite consistent with Graves's views on the follies of men and the hidden strengths of women. The action occurs in one day, the twenty-first birthday of Barbara Rich, who decides that on this special day she is going to get everything she wants. She forthwith crashes high society, becomes incredibly rich, marries the heir to the throne, feeds a multitude of hungry unemployed people by invading the zoo and arranging for the slaughter and cooking of zoo animals, captures the Communists who try to take over the country when the old king dies, and becomes a dictator in her own almost-bloodless revolution.

If the tone of this outrageous fable were lighter and its protagonist more lovable, it could be converted into Hollywood farce or Gilbert and Sullivan operetta, but everyone in it is disagreeable. People are either uniformly stupid and cowardly or utterly unscrupulous. The book was probably written primarily to make money when Riding and Graves were short of cash. (Graves has always claimed that he wrote novels primarily to support himself while he wrote poetry.) It is obviously accidental that the novel, written in 1932, might seem to satirize the blanket powers given to Adolf Hitler by the Reichstag in 1933, or the famous love affair of King Edward with the commoner, Wallis Simpson, in 1936.

THE ANTIGUA STAMP

The view of the human animal, male or female, as vicious, with superior cleverness and ingenuity the mark of the female, also dominates Graves's novel *The Antigua Stamp*. The everlasting battle of the sexes is dramatized here as sibling rivalry that is never outgrown—a controversy over the ownership of an exceedingly valuable stamp. A long-standing, sour feud between brother and sister ends with the latter's victory because she is by far the more clever and conniving of the two. *The Antigua Stamp* and *No Decency Left* are potboilers, though interesting for the eccentric attitudes they exhibit toward human character and social affairs. These biases concerning the essential stupidity and greed of men and the intelligence and ruthlessness of women emerge in a somewhat softened form in Graves's better novels.

Eight of Graves's novels are based, at least in part, upon historical characters and events. The first of these is still the best—*I, Claudius*, which is probably also the best known because of the sensitive portrayal of Claudius by Derek Jacoby in the British Broadcasting Corporation (BBC) television series based on the Claudius novels. *Count Belisarius*, about the brilliant general to the Byzantine Emperor Justinian, is also a fascinating excursion into an exciting time, even though the character of Belisarius is not so clearly drawn as that of the stuttering Claudius.

THEY HANGED MY SAINTLY BILLY

Although *Count Belisarius* deserves more attention than it has received, the other historical novels appeal to a rather limited audience. The exception is the last, *They Hanged My Saintly Billy*, which Graves facetiously described in lurid terms: "My novel is full of sex, drink, incest, suicides, dope, horse racing, murder, scandalous legal procedure, cross-examinations, inquests and ends with a good public hanging—attended by 30,000. . . . Nobody can now call me a specialized writer."

The novel is hardly as shocking as this dust-jacket rhetoric implies. The case of Dr. William Palmer, convicted of poisoning his friend, John Parsons Cook, and executed in 1856, instigated a popular protest against capital punishment in Britain. The notorious case was rife with vague, unsubstantiated suspicions about Dr. Palmer's past and irrelevant disapproval of his taste for gambling and race horses. Moreover, supposed medical experts could never agree about the actual cause of Cook's death.

The novel's best feature is the technique by which Graves preserves the confusion and ambiguity of the case. Most of the novel consists of personal testimony from persons who had known Palmer. Thus, each speaker talks from his or her own biases and limited contact, some insisting that "he never had it in him to hurt a fly." Others reveal an incredibly callous schemer who takes out insurance on his brother's life, knowing him to be an alcoholic, then arranges that he drink himself to death. No sure conclusion is ever reached about the justice of the case.

As a member of the Royal Welsh Fusiliers during World War I, Graves became interested in the history of his regiment and discovered the makings of two novels in the career of Roger Lamb, who served in the Ninth Regiment during the American Revolution but joined the Fusiliers after the surrender of General Burgoyne and the incarceration of the Ninth.

SERGEANT LAMB'S AMERICA

Graves is more chronicler than novelist in the two books about Roger Lamb, much of which are devoted to details of military life, curious anecdotes about the colonists, the Indians, the French Canadians, the fiascos and triumph of generals. Graves explains in his foreword to *Sergeant Lamb's America* that this story is not "straight history," though he has invented no main characters. The reader has no way of knowing exactly how accurately he conveys the texture of life in the colonies. "All that readers of an historical novel can fairly ask from the author," Graves writes, "is an assurance that he has nowhere willfully falsified geography, chronology, or character, and that information contained in it is accurate enough to add without discount to their general stock of history." This is a statement to remember, perhaps, in connection with any of Graves's historical novels. Although Graves seemed to have no particular rancor against Americans, the books do reveal a very iconoclastic attitude toward the Founding Fathers. His view of such notables as Benedict Arnold, Major André, and George Washington at least challenges the American reader's preconceptions.

Sergeant Lamb, like Count Belisarius, seems a bit wooden for all his military ingenuity. The protago-

nist's on-and-off love affair with Kate Harlowe provides only a tenuous thread on which to hang the semblance of a plot. The novels seem to be a scholar's compilation of interesting anecdotes and factual data about the time. Of course, this unimpassioned tone could be defended as exactly appropriate, since the novels are ostensibly the memoirs of a much older Roger Lamb, written when he is a schoolmaster in Dublin. This cool, dispassionate tone is often typical of Graves's style, however, even when he is describing his own experience in warfare in his autobiography, *Goodbye to All That*.

THE ISLANDS OF UNWISDOM

The Islands of Unwisdom celebrates, or rather exposes in its pettiness and greed, an abortive sixteenth century Spanish expedition to colonize the Solomon Islands. The leader of the expedition, Don Alvaro de Mendaña y Castro, had discovered the islands many years before. He called them the Isles of Solomon, thinking perhaps they were the location of the famous gold mines of the biblical King Solomon. The natives adorned themselves with gold. When the King of Spain finally gave permission for the expedition, therefore, a great many avaricious participants joined in the venture ostensibly devoted to Christianizing the heathen.

Though a few devout persons, such as the three priests and the chief pilot, tried to maintain the Christian charity of their mission, their feeble efforts were in vain. Practically all the islanders greeted the Spaniards with affection and open hospitality, but sooner or later, the senseless slaughter of innocents converted friends into enemies. The combined stupidity and violence of the military and of the three Barretos, Don Alvaro's brothers-in-law, insured disaster wherever they went. Moreover, Doña Ysabel Barreto, Don Alvaro's beautiful wife, was as proud and cruel as her arrogant brothers. Don Alvaro was devout but indecisive and unable to control the stubborn wills that surrounded him.

Graves uses the narrator, Don Andrés Serrano, an undersecretary to the general, to propose a theory to account for the superiority of the English over the Spanish in such situations. The English soldier could and often did do a sailor's work when help was needed on shipboard. The more rigid class structure of the Spanish, however, prevented a Spanish soldier from doing anything but fighting. During long and hazardous voyages, the Spanish soldier was idle and bored, while the Spanish sailor was overworked and resentful. When a new land was reached, the Spanish soldier felt impelled to demonstrate his function by killing enemies. If none existed, he soon created them.

Graves was particularly drawn to this sordid bit of history not so much because of the too often repeated folly of bringing civilization to the heathen by murdering them, but because of a truly unique feature of this historical event. After the death of her husband, Doña Ysabel achieved the command of a naval vessel—surely an unusual event in any age, and unprecedented in the sixteenth century. Doña Ysabel is not the conventional kind of heroine, to be sure, but a kind that Graves finds most fascinating—beautiful, cruel, and ruthless. This novel was published in the year following *The White Goddess*, and the reader who is familiar with that study may see an uncanny resemblance between Doña Ysabel and the moon goddess in her most sinister phase.

THE STORY OF MARIE POWELL, WIFE TO MR. MILTON

The Story of Marie Powell, Wife to Mr. Milton is also rooted in history, yet it echoes Graves's own views of feminine nature, as well as his antipathy to John Milton, both as a poet and as a man. That Milton did, indeed, have some marital problems is clear; they were the inspiration for his pamphlet arguing that incompatibility should be sufficient grounds for divorce, which was followed by his brilliant "Areopagitica" against censorship of the press. (Graves notes that in spite of the admitted wisdom of the latter, Milton himself became an official censor under Cromwell.)

In Graves's treatment, Milton is the epitome of the self-righteous, dominating male, drawn to the poetic, half-pagan rural England from which his young wife emerges but determined in his arid Calvinism to squelch these poetic yearnings in himself and his bride. Milton chooses head over heart, always a mistake in a poet, from Graves's point of view. Though

Milton desires love, like any man, he has a preconceived set of rules that would define and coerce love, which can only be freely given. He resolutely divorces sexuality from pleasure, for example, knowing his wife only when trying to impregnate her—in compliance, presumably, with God's orders.

Marie is the weakest of Graves's fictional women, a kind of dethroned queen, a person of independent mind doomed to mental and emotional starvation in Milton's household. T. S. Matthews, in his autobiography *Jacks or Better* (1977), makes the provocative suggestion that Graves poured his frustration and resentment about the marriage of Laura Riding to Schuyler Jackson into the book. It was written immediately after Graves fled to England, bereft of his longtime companion. Matthews has considerable background for this opinion, since he and his wife were living in America with the group (including Riding, Graves, Alan and Beryl Hodge, Schuyler and Kit Jackson) when the fruit basket was upset. Even though Graves and Riding were not lovers at that time, according to James McKinley in his introduction to Graves's last book, Graves was profoundly shocked at what he may have perceived as Riding's abdication from her proper role. Whether this explanation is valid or not, this novel seems to touch a more personal vein of frustration, resentment, and sadness than his other historical novels.

Moreover, Graves indulges in a bit of romantic mysticism in this novel, more characteristic of his poetic than his prose style. Marie Milton falls into a three-day swoon during her third pregnancy, at the precise moment that her secret "true love" is killed in Ireland. According to her own account, she spends those three days with her beloved. When she awakens she knows that her cousin, with whom she had fallen in love at the age of eleven, is dead. The child she bears thereafter, her first son, looks like her cousin, not Milton, and Marie is more peaceful than she has ever been. Perhaps this touch of fantasy expresses more about Graves than about Marie Powell Milton, but the author is careful to note in the epilogue that when Marie died giving birth to a third daughter, the one son followed her to the grave shortly after.

Readers may find the style of this novel somewhat ponderous, but Graves tries to adjust his diction to the times about which he writes. He has deliberately used some archaic, seventeenth century terms, for which he provides a glossary at the end; most of these words are easily understood in context.

COUNT BELISARIUS

If the pathetic Marie Milton shows the White Goddess in her pitiable decline, one need only return to the powerful women in *Count Belisarius* to see her in her glory. This is true, despite the fact that Graves had not yet formulated his theory of the monomyth which he expressed in *The White Goddess*. In retrospect, his fictional women suggest that the goddess haunted his psyche before he knew her name. In *Count Belisarius*, not one but two striking women demonstrate the strength of the female. These are the Empress Theodora, wife to Justinian, and Antonina, Belisarius's wife. Both had been carefully educated, pagan courtesans, but they acquired Christianity when it became possible to marry prominent Christians. They inevitably display more good sense than most of the men around them. More than once, Theodora saves Belisarius from the vindictive jealousy of Justinian or convinces the negligent monarch that he should send some relief in troops or supplies to his champion on the frontier. When Belisarius's situation becomes desperate because he is almost always vastly outnumbered on the battlefield and short of supplies as well, Antonina sends a private letter to Empress Theodora, who manages, by flattery or guile, to cajole Justinian into at least some action not altogether disastrous.

Of the two prominent men in the novel, Justinian is the more carefully characterized, even though he is invariably presented in a negative light. After Theodora dies and Belisarius throws out Antonina, because of the emperor's campaign to discredit her virtue, nothing remains to protect Belisarius from Justinian's jealousy and fear. Like Samson shorn of his hair, Belisarius is imprisoned and blinded.

Belisarius, the central figure, is the least understandable in psychological terms. Though his exploits against the Persians and against the many tribes that threatened early Christendom are truly re-markable and well told, he himself seems larger than life in moral terms as well as in his undoubted military genius. He is seemingly incorruptible in a world riddled with intrigue and deception, and as such, almost too good to be true. The jealousy of Justinian is more understandable than Belisarius's unswerving loyalty, devotion, and piety. The reader never knows what preserves Belisarius from the corrupting influence of power and popular adulation.

Ultimately, the effect of the novel is ironic, in spite of the total absence of ambiguity in Belisarius's character. The irony rests in the observation that for all the lifelong efforts of one of history's military geniuses, his accomplishments mattered little, since they were so soon negated by Justinian's bad judgment after the death of his greatest general. All the drama and the pageantry of war cannot compensate for its futility and incredible waste and its glorification of destruction in the name of true religion.

For his portrait of Claudius, grandchild of Mark Antony and grandnephew of Octavius Augustus, Graves had rich sources of information on which to draw; perhaps that accounts for the greater depth and complexity Claudius seems to exhibit in comparison to Belisarius. Both *The Annals of Tacitus* (c. 119) and Suetonius's *Lives of the Caesars* (c. 120, a book that Graves translated from the Latin in 1957) contain much of the gossipy, possibly slanted history that fills Graves's *I, Claudius* and *Claudius the God*.

I, CLAUDIUS

I, Claudius is a more successful novel than its sequel. It builds to a natural climax as the protagonist, who calls himself "the cripple, the stammerer, the fool of the family," is proclaimed emperor by riotous Roman soldiers after the assassination of Caligula. Claudius captures the sympathy of the reader in this novel as a survivor of a fifty-year reign of terror in which all the more likely prospects for promotion to emperor are eliminated by Livia, Augustus's wife, to assure the elevation of her son Tiberius to the throne. Claudius owes his survival mostly to his physical defects, which seemingly preclude his being considered for high office, and to a ready intelligence and wit which protect him somewhat from the cruelties of Caligula, who is the first to give him any role at all in government. The caprice of the troops in choosing the "fool of the family" as emperor is as great a surprise to Claudius as to anyone else. Presumably the terrified Claudius acquiesces to the whim of the military because the only other alternative is assassination along with the rest of Caligula's close relatives.

Claudius the God and His Wife Messalina

With *Claudius the God and His Wife Messalina*, the reader can no longer cheer the innocent victim of the vicious intrigues of court life. Claudius now has power and, in some respects, wields it effectively and humanely. He acquires, however, many of the tastes and faults of his class. The man who, as a boy, fainted at bloodshed now has a taste for violent entertainment. The scholar who despised ostentatious show now invades Britain so he may have a glorious triumph on his return. Worse yet, the unassuming person who knew how to survive the formidable machinations of Livia now foolishly succumbs to younger women, as ruthless as Livia but without her intelligence and executive ability. He dies of poison administered by a faithless wife.

Graves seems to be making a case for the older Claudius as a kind of tragic hero, who has come to a realization of his own shortcomings as well as those of his contemporaries. He had once idealistically hoped for the return of the Republic, but in his later years he understands that he has actually made self-government less attractive, simply because his rule has been more benevolent than that of his predecessors, Tiberius and Caligula. He decides that the Rupublican dream will not arise until the country again suffers under an evil emperor. The government must be worse before it can be better.

Graves attributes to Claudius a rather improbable scheme of secluding his son from the temptations of court life by sending him to Britain, then letting his ambitious second wife secure the throne for her own son, Nero, whose cruelty and decadence Claudius foresees. In the debacle that will occur in the reign of Nero, Claudius hopes his own son can come back as a conquering hero and reestablish the Republic.

This rather fanciful scheme misfires because Claudius's son refuses to cooperate, confident that he can deal with his foster brother, Nero, himself. Ac-

tually, Claudius's son was assassinated after his father's death, presumably at Nero's orders.

This attempted explanation of Claudius's seeming gullibility in his last days is probably intended to lend dignity to his unfortunate decline into a rather foolish old age. Part of the problem with the second novel is simply the intractability of historical facts, which do not necessarily make the most effective plots. One of the usual requirements of tragic heroes is that they attain some measure of self-knowledge and that they are at least partially responsible for their own fall from greatness. Graves has tried to retain empathy for a well-intentioned, thoughtful man who foresaw and accepted his fate, to be murdered by his wife, as a means to a greater good. This attempt to salvage a fading protagonist is understandable, but not wholly successful.

Hercules, My Shipmate

As Graves's historical novels depend partially upon the intrinsic interest of a historical period, so do his novels based on myth depend upon an intrinsic interest in myth interpretation. Quite aside from the familiar story of Jason and the Argonauts, for example, *Hercules, My Shipmate* offers sometimes believable explanations of some of the common ideas found in myth. The centaurs, for example, were not half-horse, half-men, but a barbaric tribe whose totem animal was the horse. They wore horses' manes and worshiped a mare-headed mother goddess. Many of Jason's shipmates were demigods; that is, one parent was a deity. This convention has a nonsupernatural explanation as well: Their births were traceable to the ancient custom of temple prostitutes or priests whose offspring were attributed to the god or goddess under whose auspices they were conceived.

This does not mean that all supernaturalism is rooted out of Graves's treatment of mythic material. Hercules has exaggerated powers analogous to those of Paul Bunyan, a parody of the Greek ideal of the hero, a man so strong he is dangerous to foe and friend as well. Nor does Graves eliminate all supernaturalism from his *King Jesus*, the most controversial of his novels, which fuses biblical myth with his own ideas about the ancient goddess cult.

KING JESUS

King Jesus creates a new myth about Jesus—a Jesus who is literally the King of the Jews, or at least the proper inheritor of that title. He is inheritor as the grandson of King Herod (through a secret marriage between Mary and Antipater, Herod's son), but also because he is annointed by God's prophet, John the Baptist, which was the traditional Hebrew way of choosing a king. In the latter sense, Herod had less right to the throne than Jesus, since Herod derived his authority from the Romans, not from ancient Hebrew custom. Moreover, Jesus fulfills other expectations built into what Graves presents as ancient Hebrew ritual, such as a marriage to the inheritor of the land. Graves claims that ownership of the land was matrilinear and that in order to become a king, a man had to marry the youngest daughter of the hereditary line, in this case Mary, the sister of Martha and Lazarus. (Graves points out that this matrilinear descent accounts for Egyptian pharaohs marrying their sisters and King David marrying a woman from each of the tribes of Israel in order to unify the tribes.)

Jesus is an ascetic, however, and refuses to cohabit with Mary. Moreover, one of his chief adversaries in the novel is the cult of the goddess, whose chief priestess is yet another Mary, called the Hairdresser—the character known in the bible as Mary Magdalene. It is no accident that the three vital women who attend Jesus in his crucifixion conveniently represent the Triple Goddess—Mary the mother, Mary the wife, and Mary the crone, who lays out the mythic hero in death. The irony of the situation is that in spite of consciously choosing the pattern of the Suffering Servant, described in Isaiah, and trying his best to overthrow the cult of the fertility goddess, Jesus nevertheless fulfills the role of the sacrificial hero in the goddess mythology. Though some may be offended by the liberties Graves has taken with a sacred story, those who are fascinated by the whole of the mythic heritage from the ancient world will appreciate this imaginative retelling.

WATCH THE NORTH WIND RISE

If *King Jesus* is the most serious of Graves's treatments of the goddess mythology, the most lighthearted is *Watch the North Wind Rise*, a futuristic utopian novel in which the great goddess cult has been revived in Crete (its stronghold in the ancient world) as a social experiment. The protagonist is a time traveler, conjured into the future by a witch, in obedience to the goddess. He also serves a Pandora-like function, bringing unrest into a land made dull by continuous peace. Great art, after all, demands conflict, which this ideal land has left behind. The novel is entertaining as a satire of utopian ideas, but also provides an interesting exploration of the relationship between an artist (the protagonist) and his muse (the goddess).

HOMER'S DAUGHTER

Graves's last novel on a mythic theme, *Homer's Daughter*, borrows heavily from Homer's *Odyssey* (c. 800 B.C.) and from Samuel Butler's *The Authoress of the "Odyssey"* (1897), which argues that the *Odyssey* must have been written by a woman. Graves's protagonist is the princess Nausicaa, who in the *Odyssey* befriended the shipwrecked Odysseus. In the novel, it is Nausicaa who endures many rude and insistent suitors as Penelope does in Homer's epic. A shipwrecked stranger rescues her in a manner attributed to Odysseus, by shooting the unwanted suitors and winning the fair lady for himself. She is the one who composes the *Odyssey*, incorporating her experience into the story.

In spite of the fact that Graves himself dismissed his fiction as a means of providing support for his writing of poetry, his best novels deserve to live on as imaginative treatments of history and myth. While he may not always have captured the "real" past, he helped to make the past important in a time when many people considered it irrelevant. He showed how ancient symbol-systems may still capture the imagination of one of the most versatile writers of our time. He also helped to overthrow the stereotype of women as weak in intelligence and will. This does not mean that Graves was particularly accurate in his perception of women, but his biases do offer a welcome antidote to the more insipid variety of fictional women. He must be partially responsible for the contemporary interest in mythology and the beginnings of civilization. Part of this is the result of his nonfiction works, such as *The White Goddess, The Greek*

Myths, and *Hebrew Myths*, but his use of myth in popular novels has probably reached an even wider audience.

Katherine Snipes

OTHER MAJOR WORKS

SHORT FICTION: *The Shout*, 1929; *¡Catacrok! Mostly Stories, Mostly Funny*, 1956; *Collected Short Stories*, 1964.

POETRY: *Over the Brazier*, 1916; *Goliath and David*, 1916; *Fairies and Fusiliers*, 1917; *Treasure Box*, 1919; *Country Sentiment*, 1920; *The Pier-Glass*, 1921; *The Feather Bed*, 1923; *Whipperginny*, 1923; *Mock Beggar Hall*, 1924; *The Marmosite's Miscellany*, 1925 (as John Doyle); *Welchman's Hose*, 1925; *Poems: 1914-1926*, 1927; *Poems: 1914-1927*, 1927; *Poems: 1929*, 1929; *Ten Poems More*, 1930; *Poems: 1926-1930*, 1931; *To Whom Else?*, 1931; *Poems: 1930-1933*, 1933; *Collected Poems*, 1938; *No More Ghosts: Selected Poems*, 1940; *Work in Hand*, 1942 (with others); *Poems: 1938-1945*, 1946; *Collected Poems: 1914-1947*, 1948; *Poems and Satires: 1951*, 1951; *Poems: 1953*, 1953; *Collected Poems: 1955*, 1955; *Poems Selected by Himself*, 1957; *The Poems of Robert Graves Chosen by Himself*, 1958; *Collected Poems: 1959*, 1959; *The Penny Fiddle: Poems for Children*, 1960; *Collected Poems*, 1961; *More Poems: 1961*, 1961; *The More Deserving Cases: Eighteen Old Poems for Reconsideration*, 1962; *New Poems: 1962*, 1962; *Ann at Highwood Hall: Poems for Children*, 1964; *Man Does, Woman Is*, 1964; *Love Respelt*, 1965; *Collected Poems: 1965*, 1965; *Seventeen Poems Missing from "Love Respelt,"* 1966; *Colophon to "Love Respelt,"* 1967; *Poems: 1965-1968*, 1968; *The Crane Bag*, 1969; *Love Respelt Again*, 1969; *Beyond Giving: Poems*, 1969; *Poems About Love*, 1969; *Advice from a Mother*, 1970; *Queen-Mother to New Queen*, 1970; *Poems: 1969-1970*, 1970; *The Green-Sailed Vessel*, 1971; *Poems: Abridged for Dolls and Princes*, 1971; *Poems: 1968-1970*, 1971; *Poems: 1970-1972*, 1972; *Poems: Selected by Himself*, 1972; *Deyá*, 1972 (with Paul Hogarth); *Timeless Meetings: Poems*, 1973; *At the Gate*, 1974; *Collected Poems: 1975*, 1975 (2 volumes); *New Collected Poems*, 1977.

NONFICTION: *On English Poetry*, 1922; *The Meaning of Dreams*, 1924; *Poetic Unreason and Other Studies*, 1925; *Contemporary Techniques of Poetry: A Political Analogy*, 1925; *Another Future of Poetry*, 1926; *Impenetrability: Or, The Proper Habit of English*, 1926; *The English Ballad: A Short Critical Survey*, 1927; *Lars Porsena: Or, The Future of Swearing and Improper Language*, 1927; *A Survey of Modernist Poetry*, 1927 (with Laura Riding); *Lawrence and the Arabs*, 1927 (also known as *Lawrence and the Arabian Adventure*, 1928); *A Pamphlet Against Anthologies*, 1928 (with Riding, also known as *Against Anthologies*); *Mrs. Fisher: Or, The Future of Humour*, 1928; *Goodbye to All That: An Autobiography*, 1929; *T. E. Lawrence to His Biographer Robert Graves*, 1938; *The Long Week-End: A Social History of Great Britain, 1918-1938*, 1940 (with Alan Hodge); *The Reader over Your Shoulders: A Handbook for Writers of English Prose*, 1943 (with Hodge); *The White Goddess: A Historical Grammar of Poetic Myth*, 1948; *The Common Asphodel: Collected Essays on Poetry, 1922-1949*, 1949; *Occupation: Writer*, 1950; *The Nazarene Gospel Restored*, 1953 (with Joshua Podro); *The Crowning Privilege: The Clark Lectures, 1954-1955*, 1955; *Adam's Rib and Other Anomalous Elements in the Hebrew Creation Myth: A New View*, 1955; *The Greek Myths*, 1955 (2 volumes); *Jesus in Rome: A Historical Conjecture*, 1957 (with Podro); *Five Pens in Hand*, 1958; *Greek Gods and Heroes*, 1960; *Oxford Addresses on Poetry*, 1962; *Nine Hundred Iron Chariots: The Twelfth Arthur Dehon Little Memorial Lecture*, 1963; *Hebrew Myths: The Book of Genesis*, 1964 (with Raphael Patai); *Majorca Observed*, 1965 (with Paul Hogarty); *Mammon and the Black Goddess*, 1965; *Poetic Craft and Principle*, 1967; *The Crane Bag and Other Disputed Subjects*, 1969; *On Poetry: Collected Talks and Essays*, 1969; *Difficult Questions, Easy Answers*, 1972.

CHILDREN'S LITERATURE: *The Big Green Book*, 1962; *The Siege and Fall of Troy*, 1962; *Two Wise Children*, 1966; *The Poor Boy Who Followed His Star*, 1968.

TRANSLATIONS: *Almost Forgotten Germany*, 1936 (Georg Schwarz; trans. with Laura Riding); *The*

Transformation of Lucius, Otherwise Known as "The Golden Ass," 1950 (Lucius Apuleius); *The Cross and the Sword*, 1954 (Manuel de Jesús Galván); *Pharsalia: Dramatic Episodes of the Civil Wars*, 1956 (Lucan); *Winter in Majorca*, 1956 (George Sand); *The Twelve Caesars*, 1957 (Suetonius); *The Anger of Achilles: Homer's "Iliad,"* 1959; *The Rubáiyát of Omar Khayyám*, 1967 (with Omar Ali-Shah).

EDITED TEXTS: *Oxford Poetry: 1921*, 1921 (with Alan Porter and Richard Hughes); *John Skelton: Laureate*, 1927; *The Less Familiar Nursery Rhymes*, 1927; *The Comedies of Terence*, 1962; *English and Scottish Ballads*, 1975.

MISCELLANEOUS: *Steps: Stories, Talks, Essays, Poems, Studies in History*, 1958; *Food for Centaurs: Stories, Talks, Critical Studies, Poems*, 1960; *Selected Poetry and Prose*, 1961.

BIBLIOGRAPHY

Bloom, Harold, ed. *Robert Graves*. New York: Chelsea House, 1987. Essays on Graves's historical novels, autobiography, and major themes. Includes chronology and bibliography.

Canary, Robert H. *Robert Graves*. Boston: Twayne, 1980. A good general introduction to Graves's work. Emphasizes Graves the poet, but also contains helpful information on his novels and literary criticism. Includes a chronology, notes, a selected bibliography, and an index.

Day, Douglas. *Swifter than Reason: The Poetry and Criticism of Robert Graves*. Chapel Hill: University of North Carolina Press, 1963. The first full-length study of Graves's poetry and criticism. Graves's work is examined chronologically in four major phases, concluding with his emerging concept of the "White Goddess." Includes a bibliography, secondary reading materials, and an index.

Quinn, Patrick J., ed. *New Perspectives on Robert Graves*. Selinsgrove, Pa.: Susquehanna University Press, 1999. A thoughtful, updated volume on the works of Graves. Includes bibliographical references and an index.

Seymour-Smith, Martin. *Robert Graves: His Life and Works*. New York: Paragon House, 1988. Inti- mate, fascinating glimpse of Graves the man. Seymour-Smith had known Graves since 1943 and has written extensively on him since 1956. An excellent introduction to Graves's remarkable life and literary career.

HENRY GREEN
Henry Vincent Yorke

Born: Forthampton Court, England; October 29, 1905

Died: London, England; December 13, 1973

PRINCIPAL LONG FICTION

Blindness, 1926
Living, 1929
Party Going, 1939
Caught, 1943
Loving, 1945
Back, 1946
Concluding, 1948
Nothing, 1950
Doting, 1952

OTHER LITERARY FORMS

In addition to his novels, Henry Green published an autobiographical book, *Pack My Bag: A Self-Portrait* (1940), and several accounts of his World War II firefighting experiences: "A Rescue," "Mr. Jonas," and "Firefighting." Green's theories regarding writing are expressed in *Pack My Bag* and in his essays "The English Novel of the Future" and "A Novelist to His Readers," which can be found in *Contact* (1950) and *The Listener* (1950, 1951). From time to time, Green wrote book reviews on topics which interested him and personal essays ranging in subject from his friend and editor Edward Garnett to public-school life in 1914.

ACHIEVEMENTS

For a man who managed both business and literary careers, Green's achievements are remarkable.

Blindness, published in 1926 when Green was twenty-one, announced the arrival of a novelist whose artistic poise was illustrated through narrative daring and an unusual sense of characterization. Successive novels continued to impress critics and reviewers, though some either misunderstood or disliked Green's highly individual technique. "Prose," Green stated in *Pack My Bag*, "should be a long intimacy between strangers with no direct appeal to what both may have known." He continued by writing that this intimacy should build slowly and encompass unexpressed feelings which "are not bounded by the associations common to place names or to persons with whom the reader is unexpectedly familiar." Friends and fellow writers such as Edward Garnett, V. S. Pritchett, W. H. Auden, Evelyn Waugh, Christopher Isherwood, and John Lehman recognized Green's talent. Several have published articles on his work. Although Green is less widely known in the United States, Terry Southern, Eudora Welty, and John Updike have paid homage to him in interviews and articles. As critical theory has developed to encompass precisely those narrative strategies articulated by Green in 1939, it seems likely that his literary stature, already assured, will increase.

BIOGRAPHY

Henry Green was born Henry Vincent Yorke at Forthampton Court, near Tewkesbury, Gloucestershire, England, on October 29, 1905. He was the third son of a wealthy Midlands industrialist whose business concern, H. Pontifex and Sons, Green was later to manage. Like others of his social class, Green was sent away to school when he was quite young, in his case before he was seven. At twelve, he went to Eton and from there to Oxford, where he studied with C. S. Lewis.

While at Eton, Green began writing *Blindness*, whose self-conscious, awkward, dilettantish, yet introspective protagonist, John Haye, is a self-portrait. Like Haye, Green was a member of an art society, an avid reader, a self-styled aesthete. By the time he arrived at Oxford, however, already somewhat of a celebrity because *Blindness* was about to be published, Green was beginning to question his privileged posi-

tion and his right to an inherited fortune. This dilemma led him to leave Oxford at the end of his second year without taking a degree. As he reports in *Pack My Bag*, he went to Birmingham "to work in a factory with my wet podgy hands." Far from feeling superior to the laboring class, Green found these working people full of life and humor. His experiences among them inspired *Living*, published in 1929.

That same year, Green married Mary Adelaide Biddulph, with whom he had a son, Sebastian, born in 1934. From 1931 to 1938, Green continued to build his business career and wrote *Party Going*, a reflection of his London social circle. War rumblings in 1939 moved Green to join the Auxiliary Fire Service, in which he served during World War II. The war years proved to be productive for Green; not only did he write *Pack My Bag*, a sort of autobiography published in 1940, but also three unique war novels: *Caught, Loving*, and *Back*.

The war's conclusion returned Green to the directorship of his business and a busy decade of writing (during his lunch hour and after dinner every night). In the 1950's, Green began refining his theories of communication and art, which he published in essay form, delivered in a series of British Broadcasting Corporation (BBC) broadcasts, and restated in three interviews. While on a cruise to South Africa in 1958, Green decided to retire from business.

No one has been able to account for Green's almost total silence for the remainder of his life. Until his death on December 13, 1973, he published only "An Unfinished Novel" and "Firefighting." His sequel to *Pack My Bag* was unfinished. With increasing deafness, Green withdrew more and more into the privacy of his home and family, leaving behind a literary legacy rich in its suggestiveness.

ANALYSIS

The ambiguous nature of Henry Green's fiction has long piqued and captivated the attention of readers and critics alike, for his individual departures from conventional narrative technique separate him from the literary mainstream. A successful businessman independent of popular success, Green felt free to experiment with the form and theory of the novel. His novels speak directly to the reader with minimal interruption or interpretation; taking on lives of their own, they maintain their own shifting realities and sustain an uncanny sense of the present.

Evident in his novels as early as *Blindness* are characteristics that Green was to polish throughout his writing career: close attention to balance and symmetry, objectivity in character presentation, action developed through juxtaposed scenes, and remarkable re-creation of spoken English interspersed with lyrical descriptive passages. His singular treatment was given to classical themes. Fascinated by language and the human capacity to interpret, Green dramatized the problems of communication by having his characters misunderstand one another. He further complicated these problems of understanding by creating intentional verbal ambiguity, so that the reader might also be uncertain of the speaker's intent. Often talking at cross purposes, Green's characters, prompted by loneliness, search for love. Although their love objects may at times seem strange, ranging as they do from peacocks and a pig to houses and fantasies, they nevertheless reflect the range of human passion. In an atmosphere suggestive of social dissolution, Green's characters pursue the relative stability of love, which they often discover in unsuspected places.

Most of Green's solipsistic characters are neither intelligent, gifted, nor particularly beautiful. Often vain and fanciful, they reveal themselves to be profoundly human as they engage in conversations revelatory of their own preoccupations. Fascinated by what people communicate through both speech and evasion, Green sought to make dialogue the vehicle for his novels, refining his conversation and decreasing his descriptive passages until, in his last two novels, dialogue carries almost the entire weight. To avoid the static quality of conversation, he created brief scenes, shifting his reader's attention from one group of characters to another. His technique also produces an acute sense of the present, a sense emphasized by the "ing" ending of his novels' titles.

That Green's novels create their own sense of the present is only one of several important factors to be considered when reading his fiction. Above all, Green wanted his work to assume a life of its own, a life differing according to the reader, providing each one with a sense of connection until he or she is drawn into a "community of people." Green accomplishes this primarily by suggesting rather than stating. Time and place, motivation and reaction, action and resolution are often evoked rather than delineated. Behind the slight plots and often silly activities is an unstated social context which tacitly influences action. Green's characters are also created through indirection. By allowing them to inarticulately express their obsessions, fears, anxieties, or confusion, by having them avoid direct responses, by refusing to make authorial judgments, Green populates his novels with lifelike creations. Their humanness is mutely expressed in their search for love. Examining *Blindness, Loving*, and *Nothing* with these ideas in mind, the reader can begin to understand Henry Green's elusive art.

BLINDNESS

When Green had a family friend read the manuscript of *Blindness*, he did not receive much praise. He was, however, encouraged to show his work to Edward Garnett, then a publisher's reader, who gave Green sound advice concerning narrative technique and character development. The result is a first novel remarkable primarily for its close attention to structure and its multidimensional characters. While taking a usual avenue for a first novel, Green proceeded to treat his subject with daring. His protagonist, John Haye, a sensitive upper-middle-class schoolboy who aspires to be a writer, is blinded in a freak accident. During the course of the novel, John comes to new terms with himself and his world, awakening in the end to a fresh appreciation of life.

With the theme of growth in mind, Green divided *Blindness* into three sections—"Caterpillar," "Chrysalis," and "Butterfly"—suggesting John's psychological metamorphosis. "Caterpillar," presented as John's diary, reflects his physical response to natural beauty, his passion for literature, and his concentrated ambition to write. Because he derives intense pleasure from visual stimuli, John's blindness seems especially cruel. In "Chrysalis," he reconsiders himself. Lying dormant in layers of a protective cocoon—his bandages, his blindness, his fantasies and self-pity, his stepmother's pity and worry, the physical safety of his inherited estate—John's creative life is threatened until he determines to break free of this smothering safety. He emerges in "Butterfly" scarred but acutely aware of the value of life.

The narrative passages of *Blindness* are lush, as exuberant as John's imagination, as soaring as his emotions. Echoing with poetic resonance, Green's descriptive passages in *Blindness* far outweigh the oblique dialogue. Nevertheless, there are signs of Green's later mastery of dialogue: Speech patterns are distinct for each character. The language is spare, with internal monologues reflective of individual character. John's thoughts are full of wonder and pain, his stepmother's are busy with seemingly dissociated concerns. Both characters' thoughts, however, circuitously return to one subject: blindness. Where Green introduces rich visual images through John's eyes in the first portion of the novel, he later confines John's responses to those of touch and sound. Indeed, the novel ends in a cacophony of bells and traffic noises, affirming John's rebirth.

Green seems precocious in his handling of the symbolic value of blindness. This he does by indirectly comparing John's blindness with various metaphorical failures of vision. Mrs. Haye, John's horsey stepmother, is "blind" in a number of respects, lacking all aesthetic response and being completely unintellectual. Two other figures are also introduced to indicate forms of moral blindness: Joan Entwhistle and her father, an unfrocked minister. They epitomize the destructiveness of self-deception, a potential trap awaiting John. Joan, a dirty, dreamy girl who vacillates between romanticizing her situation and luxuriating in its squalor, becomes an unlikely love interest for John, who re-creates her in his imagination and renames her June. Worse still is Joan's father, who wallows in gin and self-pity. Like John, he thinks of himself as a writer, but his only creation is his disastrous life. Ultimately, Reverend Entwhistle has entered a darkness far more profound than John's.

While blindness carries much of the novel's symbolic weight, other images are also alluded to by Green, images that continue to reappear throughout his career, often assuming symbolic value. References to birds, birds' songs, and patterns of birds' flights recur throughout his novels. In *Blindness*, birds provide an oblique comment on human situations. Flowers, particularly roses, are also recurring images in Green's fiction. Their value varying according to the novel, they generally connote love.

While the language and images of *Blindness* are vivid and memorable, it is the characters who are the novel's main strength. Green's impressive talent has created four main characters whose distinct speech and thought patterns and conflicting desires he has woven into a narrative tapestry with perspective, texture, density, and dimension. Arranged in contrasting couples—John and Mrs. Haye, Joan and Reverend Entwhistle—Green plays his characters against one another, in pairs and individually, using this arrangement to illustrate mutual misunderstandings. John and Joan, who have much in common, are first drawn together and then move apart. For purely selfish reasons, each tries to impose a fantasy on the other. John imaginatively re-creates Joan, raising her from a lowly social position. Joan, in turn, sees John as a means of escape, though in the end she prefers her fantasy to reality.

Mrs. Haye and the Reverend Entwhistle are also contrasting figures. The minister, capable of the kind of aesthetic response that John admires, has, however, succumbed to self-delusion. Significantly, the Reverend Entwhistle has scarred Joan. Mrs. Haye, on the other hand, wants to protect John. As guardian of his estate (Barwood), she sees it as her duty to manage his inheritance. When John rejects Barwood, indicating a changing social order, Mrs. Haye reluctantly supports the decision although this means abandoning a comfortable home and secure social role. Rough and tweedy, Mrs. Haye is a triumph of characterization as she awkwardly assumes a maternal role for which she is unfit. She is spared from caricature by Green's ability to portray her confused, rambling feelings through indirection.

LOVING

Through three successive novels, Green continued to experiment with narrative technique and character development. In *Loving*, he achieved a balance that has continued to impress readers and critics. Skillfully arranging themes, images, symbols, and characters in the form of a fairy tale and placing them in neutral Ireland during the London Blitz, Green created what is considered to be his finest novel.

His setting, "the most celebrated eighteenth-century folly in Eire that had still to be burned down," is ideal for bringing together upper and lower classes and for elaborating favorite themes. Social dissolution, the search for love, and the inability to communicate are intensified by the distant war, which threatens and thus influences all of the characters. Most discomforting is the fact that the social order seems to have collapsed. From Raunce the footman's bold takeover of the butler's position to the mingling of the cook's nephew with the owner's granddaughters, the reader is presented with evidence of accelerating social change. Indeed, real power has gravitated to the servants, whose departure would mean disaster for the house and its owners, significantly named Tennant. Far from thinking of leaving, however, most of the servants are intent on pursuing their respective passions, all of which are forms of loving.

Green pays careful attention to balance, transition, and symbol in *Loving* as he encircles the lives of his characters. Beginning and ending with a love moan, having as its center a lost ring, and moving its main characters, Edith and Raunce, in a circular direction, this novel revolves around various love relationships. Thus, *Loving* is rich in extravagant description; only in *Concluding* does Green's language achieve *Loving*'s visual opulence. The color and detail that Green accords his gilded setting underscores its anachronistic existence and lends a sense of high comedy to the human activities taking place. Suggestive images recur throughout the novel, serving as transitional devices and assuming symbolic power. This is especially true of the peacocks and doves which stride and flutter through the action, symbolizing pride and love.

Dialogue in *Loving* is as important as narrative description, with Green seeming at times to be showing off his celebrated ability to create colloquial language. Each of the servants has a particular speech pattern, so peculiar that understanding can be a problem between them. Paddy, the single Irishman employed by the Tennants, speaks so unintelligibly that only Kate, who loves him, can understand what he says. Raunce, who acts as mediator between the servants and the Tennants, uses two different languages. Of course, the Tennants speak in the cultured tones of their class. Not surprisingly, Mrs. Tennant cannot understand what her servants are saying. Indeed, one of the high comic scenes of the novel occurs when she attempts to converse with her cook, who carries on about drains while Mrs. Tennant interrogates her about a ring.

The characters of *Loving* are to a large extent created by their language. Raunce is finely drawn, a complex of contradictory, even mysterious habits. He is a transparent manipulator who rudely asserts his authority over the other servants, and he is, apparently, a dutiful son who faithfully writes to his mother and sends money. A petty thief and would-be blackmailer, Raunce eventually becomes a father figure for a young servant and Edith's trembling lover. While Edith lacks the many facets of Raunce, she is fully realized as the most loving and beloved character in this novel. A dreamy girl believing in the power of love potions, she sheds her fantasies in favor of practical possibilities. Even minor characters achieve distinction in this novel; through wonderfully individualized conversations, Green dramatizes the manifold nature of loving.

Although he had consistently accorded dialogue a prominent role in all of his novels, Green came to believe that pure dialogue, with minimal authorial direction, would constitute the novel of the future. Accordingly, he wrote *Nothing* and *Doting*, which, while bearing familiar Green themes and characters, progress almost entirely through conversation. Again, the unelaborated social background is an important influence. In fact, it may have as much significance in *Nothing* as any other narrative component.

NOTHING

While *Nothing* seems to be about very little, involving as it does a love chase among selfish people, it nevertheless implies a great deal. To ignore the subtext of this novel is to miss Green's point, for although he might not have used the term, *Nothing* can be seen as a phenomenological novel, with subjective judgments excluded in order to show reality as it is. Revealed is a protean shield of manners concealing a moral vacuum, the ultimate hollowness of polite society. Green, however, withholds judgment even as he lends a comic ambience to his characters. Thus, whatever judgment is accorded to the themes and characters of this novel will be imposed only by the reader.

The themes of *Nothing* are on a continuum with those of *Blindness*. The social erosion marked by John Haye's departure from his estate is now complete in the almost classless society of the welfare state. Little remains of the upper-middle-class characters' inheritance except memory, and the children of this once privileged class consider themselves lucky to have dull civil service jobs. Aware of the passing of time, Green's characters turn to one another. The result is a comedy of manners involving six characters—John Pomfret and his daughter Mary; Jane Weatherby and her son Philip; Liz Jennings, John's mistress; and Dick Abbot, Jane's escort—which provides an opportunity for Green to demonstrate his ability to write ambiguously frothy conversation which reveals the intellectual and emotional shallowness of his characters and the absurdity of their lives.

At the heart of this novel is Jane Weatherby, one of Green's most effective creations, who, having determined to marry John Pomfret, skillfully arranges the lives of other people in order to achieve her ends. A study in calculating graciousness, Jane manages to retain the admiration of friends and verbally dispatch her enemies in the same breath. Though her methods are suspect, they remain undetectable, her intent double-edged. Consequently, Jane wins her man, a prize of dubious value and yet one wholly satisfying to her. The ironic justice of these two characters winding up with each other is not lost on the reader.

While *Nothing* was not Green's last novel, it can be read as a final statement, for he extends his theory of the novel to its logical conclusion. This work exemplifies what Green called the "nonrepresentational novel," a novel "which can live in people who are alive" and "which can die." More than its predecessors, *Nothing* demands the conscious collaboration of its readers. Even with active participation in the novel's present, ambiguities abound. This is just as Green would have wished, because he wanted his novels to evoke a sense of life's texture, a texture he felt was fluctuating constantly. *Nothing*'s moral ambiguity, often cited as its principal flaw, is a significant part of this texture. Creating as it does a palpable sense of life's mutability, *Nothing* perfectly embodies Henry Green's oblique, distinctive approach to the art of fiction.

Karen Carmean

OTHER MAJOR WORK

NONFICTION: *Pack My Bag: A Self-Portrait*, 1940.

BIBLIOGRAPHY

Bassoff, Bruce. *Toward Loving: The Poetics of the Novel and the Practice of Henry Green*. Columbia: University of South Carolina Press, 1975. This lengthy study offers a complex, important discussion of Green's theory of "nonrepresentational fiction." His sparse prose, reaching its epitome in *Loving*, requires a reader to participate imaginatively in the creation of the fiction. Green's novels show how a postmodernist fiction writer avoids the evaluative, determining narrator at the center of realistic fiction.

Gorra, Michael Edward. *The English Novel at Midcentury: From the Leaning Tower*. New York: St. Martin's Press, 1990. Examines the twentieth century novel, with discussions of Green, Anthony Powell, Graham Greene, and Evelyn Waugh. Includes bibliographical references and an index.

Holmesland, Oddvar. *A Critical Introduction to Henry Green's Novels*. New York: St. Martin's Press, 1985. Defines Green's originality by stressing the similarity of his "dynamic visualization and the effect of film." The author studies the novels individually and chronologically to show Green's creation of verbal montages that reveal life's multiplicity and complexity. The "living vision" is Green's pastoral ideal of a spiritually aware person living in simple communion with the natural environment.

Mengham, Rod. *The Idiom of Time: The Writings of Henry Green*. New York: Cambridge University Press, 1982. Studies Green's novelistic development from his first novel in 1926, heavily influenced by Gertrude Stein, through his unfinished novel in 1959, which made him stop writing in fear that he was repeating himself. The author finds that Green's sparse, evocative style marks him as a writer of the 1930's and 1940's but that universal themes of life and death link him to timeless writers such as Sophocles and William Shakespeare.

North, Michael. *Henry Green and the Writing of His Generation*. Charlottesville: University of Virginia Press, 1984. Explores the personal and thematic links between Green and his major literary contemporaries: Evelyn Waugh, Anthony Powell, Stephen Spender, and Christopher Isherwood. The most important tie is a sense of alienation engendered by strong political ideologies such as Fascism and Communism. These writers explore the problem of asserting the identity of the individual self in a hostile social environment.

Odom, Keith C. *Henry Green*. Boston: Twayne, 1978. Provides a useful biographical-critical study for the beginning student. After introductions to Green's life, fictional theory, and characteristic style, offers a leisurely, insightful reading of each novel, concluding with an unpretentious estimate of his importance and influence.

Russell, John. *Henry Green: Nine Novels and an Unpacked Bag*. New Brunswick, N.J.: Rutgers University Press, 1960. An enthusiastic study of Green. Offers numerous examples of Green's stylistic puzzles, poetry, enigmas, and sleights-of-hand, paying special attention to his autobiography as a source of Green's philosophy of art and life. Though Green's vision is essentially pessimistic, Russell argues that his literary artistry offers the compensating pleasure of intellectual challenge.

Ryf, Robert. *Henry Green*. New York: Columbia University Press, 1967. This brief, energetic introduction to Green's novels reads them in chronological order to trace out his diagnosis of modern society's spiritual and moral ills. His characters continually find life an enigma, a walk along fog-shrouded paths where premonitions must suffice. The novels' techniques of ambiguity (elusive plotting, shifting narrative voice, impressionistic language) reflect the characters' plight of searching for meaning without a map to guide them.

Stokes, Edward. *The Novels of Henry Green*. New York: Macmillan, 1959. Makes a case that Green is an important twentieth century novelist whose works offer a transcendent yet objective view of life and whose prose increasingly displays a poet's attention to language. Concludes with high praise: Green's prose is as original, effective, and influential among British writers as William Faulkner's prose is among American writers. Organized by topics rather than by novels.

GRAHAM GREENE

Born: Berkhamsted, England; October 2, 1904
Died: Vevey, Switzerland; April 3, 1991

PRINCIPAL LONG FICTION

The Man Within, 1929
The Name of Action, 1930
Rumour at Nightfall, 1931
Stamboul Train: An Entertainment, 1932 (pb. in U.S. as *Orient Express: An Entertainment*, 1933)
It's a Battlefield, 1934
England Made Me, 1935
A Gun for Sale: An Entertainment, 1936 (pb. in U.S. as *This Gun for Hire: An Entertainment*)
Brighton Rock, 1938
The Confidential Agent, 1939
The Power and the Glory, 1940 (reissued as *The Labyrinthine Ways*)
The Ministry of Fear: An Entertainment, 1943

The Heart of the Matter, 1948
The Third Man: An Entertainment, 1950
The Third Man and The Fallen Idol, 1950
The End of the Affair, 1951
Loser Takes All: An Entertainment, 1955
The Quiet American, 1955
Our Man in Havana: An Entertainment, 1958
A Burnt-Out Case, 1961
The Comedians, 1966
Travels with My Aunt, 1969
The Honorary Consul, 1973
The Human Factor, 1978
Dr. Fischer of Geneva: Or, The Bomb Party, 1980
Monsignor Quixote, 1982
The Tenth Man, 1985

OTHER LITERARY FORMS

In addition to his novels, Graham Greene published many collections of short stories, including *The Basement Room and Other Stories* (1935); *Nineteen Stories* (1947); *Twenty-one Stories* (1954), in which two stories from the previous collection were dropped and four added; *A Sense of Reality* (1963); *May We Borrow Your Husband? and Other Comedies of the Sexual Life* (1967); and *Collected Stories* (1972). He also wrote plays, including *The Living Room* (1953), *The Potting Shed* (1957), *The Complaisant Lover* (1959), *Carving a Statue* (1964), and *Yes and No* (1980). With the exception of his first published book, *Babbling April: Poems* (1925), he did not publish poetry except in two private printings, *After Two Years* (1949) and *For Christmas* (1950). He wrote some interesting travel books, two focusing on Africa, *Journey Without Maps: A Travel Book* (1936) and *In Search of a Character: Two African Journals* (1961), and one set in Mexico, *The Lawless Roads: A Mexican Journal* (1939). He published several books of essays and criticism, including *British Dramatists* (1942); *The Lost Childhood and Other Essays* (1951); *Essais Catholiques* (1953); *Collected Essays* (1969); and *The Pleasure Dome: The Collected Film Criticism, 1935-40, of Graham Greene* (1972), edited by John Russell-Taylor. He also wrote a biography, *Lord Rochester's Monkey: Being the Life of John Wilmot, Second Earl of Rochester* (1974),

and two autobiographical works, *A Sort of Life* (1971), carrying the reader up to Greene's first novel, and *Ways of Escape* (1980), bringing the reader up to the time of its writing. A biographical-autobiographical work, *Getting to Know the General* (1984), spotlights Greene's relationship with General Omar Torrijos Herrera of Panama. Finally, he also wrote four children's books: *The Little Train* (1946), *The Little Fire Engine* (1950), *The Little Horse Bus* (1952), and *The Little Steam Roller: A Story of Mystery and Detection* (1953).

ACHIEVEMENTS

Greene's style has often been singled out for praise. He learned economy and precision while with *The Times* in London. More than anything else, he struggled for precision, "truth" as he called it, in form as well as in substance. *The Power and the Glory* won the Hawthornden Prize in 1941. Additionally, his experience as a film reviewer seems to have given him a feel for cinematic technique.

What Greene's reputation will be a century hence is difficult to predict. Readers will certainly find in him more than a religious writer, more—at least—than a Catholic writer. They will find in him a writer who used for his thematic vehicles all the pressing issues of his era: the Vietnam War, Papa Doc Duvalier's tyranny over Haiti, the struggle between communism and capitalism, apartheid in South Africa, poverty and oppression in Latin America. Will these issues seem too topical for posterity, or will they prove again that only by localizing one's story in the specifics of a time and place can one appeal to readers of another time, another place?

BIOGRAPHY

Graham Greene was born on October 2, 1904, in the town of Berkhamsted, England. The fourth of six children, he was not especially close to his father, perhaps because of his father's position as headmaster of Berkhamsted School, which Greene attended. Some of the boys took sadistic delight in his ambiguous position, and two in particular caused him such humiliation that they created in him an excessive desire to prove himself. Without them, he claimed, he might never have written a book.

Greene made several attempts at suicide during these unhappy years; he later insisted these were efforts to avoid boredom rather than to kill himself. At Oxford, he tried for a while to avoid boredom by getting intoxicated each day of an entire semester.

During these Oxford days, Greene met Vivien Dayrell-Browning, a young Catholic woman who had written to him of his error in a film review in referring to Catholic "worship" of the Virgin Mary. He inquired into the "subtle" and "unbelievable theology" out of interest in Vivien and concluded by becoming a Catholic in 1926. Greene married Vivien, and the couple had two children, a boy and a girl. He separated from his parents' family after the wedding and was scrupulous about guarding his own family's privacy.

In 1926, Greene moved from his first, unsalaried, position writing for the Nottingham *Journal* to the position of subeditor for *The Times* in London. There, he learned writing technique, pruning the clichés of reporters and condensing their stories without loss of meaning or effect. Moreover, he had mornings free to do his own writing. When, in 1928, Heinemann accepted Greene's first novel, *The Man Within*, for publication, Greene rashly quit *The Times* to make his living as a writer.

Greene's next two novels, *The Name of Action* and *Rumour at Nightfall*, failed, and he later suppressed them. Still, in trying to understand what went wrong with these works, he discovered that he had tried to omit the autobiographical entirely; as a result, the novels lacked life and truth. He would not make that mistake again.

In 1934, Greene took the first of a seemingly endless series of trips to other parts of the world. With his cousin Barbara, he walked without maps across the heart of Liberia. Recorded in his *Journey Without Maps*, this hazardous venture became a turning point in his life. He had once thought death desirable; in the desert, he became a passionate lover of life. He came even to accept the rats in his hut as part of life. Perhaps more important for his writing, he discovered in Liberia the archetypal basis for his earliest

(AP/Wide World Photos)

nightmares. The frightening creatures of those dreams were not originally evil beings but rather devils in the African sense of beings who control power. Humankind, Greene came to believe, has corrupted these primitive realities and denied its inherited sense of supernatural evil, reducing it to the level of merely human evil. To do so is to forget "the finer taste, the finer pleasure, the finer terror on which we might have built." Greene had found the basis for themes that persistently made their way into his novels.

Greene began his great fiction with *Brighton Rock*, the publication of which, in 1938, followed a trip to Mexico that delighted him much less than the one to Africa. Nevertheless, his observations in Mexico provided the substance of what many consider his finest achievement, *The Power and the Glory*. For the reader interested in a genuine insight into the way Greene moves from fact to fiction, the travel book that emerged from the Mexican journey, *The Lawless Roads*, is very rewarding, showing for example how his fictional whiskey priest was an amalgam of four real-life priests.

With the outbreak of World War II, Greene was assigned to the Secret Intelligence Service, or MI6, as it was then called. The experience—including his work for the notorious spy Kim Philby—gave him the material for several later works, including *Our Man in Havana* and *The Human Factor*, and nurtured in him that "virtue of disloyalty" which informs his novels.

Greene ceased his writing of explicitly religious novels with *The End of the Affair* in 1951, when people began to treat him as a guru. Although his novels continued to treat religious concerns, none—with the possible exception of *A Burnt-Out Case* in 1961—was a religious problem novel. Increasingly, Greene turned to political concern in novels such as *The Quiet American* and *The Comedians*, but these political concerns transcend the topical and speak more enduringly of human involvement.

In his later years, Greene slowed his production somewhat. He continued, however, to write two hundred words every morning, then corrected in great detail in the evening. His practice was to dictate his corrected manuscript into a tape recorder and send the tapes from his home in Antibes, on the French Riviera, to England, where they were typed and then returned. Greene also continued to indulge his taste for travel: He visited dictator Fidel Castro in Cuba, General Omar Torrijos Herrera in Panama, and President Ho Chi Minh in Vietnam. A full catalog of his travels would be virtually endless. Despite the reductive label critics have applied to his settings—"Greeneland"—Greene's novels have more varied settings than those of almost any other novelist, and his settings are authentic. Greene died on April 3, 1991, at the age of eighty-six.

ANALYSIS

In an address he called the "Virtue of Disloyalty," which he delivered at the University of Hamburg in 1969, Graham Greene contended that a writer is driven "to be a protestant in a Catholic society, a catholic in a Protestant one," or to be a communist in a capitalist society and a capitalist in a communist one. While loyalty confines one to accepted opinions, "disloyalty gives the novelist an extra dimension of understanding."

Whatever the reader may think of Greene's theory, it is helpful in explaining most of his own novels. From *The Man Within* in 1929, which justified a suicide in the face of Catholic morality's abhorrence for such an act, to *The Human Factor*, forty-nine years

later, which comes close to justifying treason, Greene practiced this "virtue of disloyalty."

Most of Greene's obsessions originated in his childhood. Where did the desire to be "disloyal," to play devil's advocate, arise? Certainly his serving in MI6 under the authority of Kim Philby was a factor. Greene admired the man in every way except for what appeared to be a personal drive for power. It was this characteristic of Philby that caused Greene finally to resign rather than accept a promotion and become part of Philby's intrigue. Yet Greene later came to see that the man served not himself but a cause, and all his former admiration of Philby returned. Greene continued his friendship even after Philby's treason. As he saw it, Philby had found a faith in Communism, and he would not discard it because it had been abused by Joseph Stalin any more than Catholics would discard a faith that had been abused by the Inquisitors or the Roman Curia.

Clearly, however, Greene's "disloyalty" or sympathy for the rebel did not originate here. It too must be traced to his childhood, to his isolation at school, where neither the students nor his headmaster father could treat him unambiguously; it can be traced also to his love of poet Robert Browning, who very early instilled in him an interest in the "dangerous edge of things," in "the honest thief, the tender murderer." It was an influence more lasting, Greene said, than any religious teaching. Religiously, though, Greene's fierce independence manifested itself when, upon conversion to Catholicism, he took the name Thomas, not after the angelic doctor but after the doubter.

Though Greene wrote in so many genres, the novel is the form upon which his reputation will rest. His strengths in the genre are many. Like all novelists who are more than journeymen, he returns throughout his oeuvre to certain recurring themes. Another strength is his gift for playing the devil's advocate, the dynamics that occur when his character finds himself divided between loyalties. In Greene's first novel, *The Man Within*, that division was handled crudely, externalized in a boy's attraction to two different women; in later novels, the struggle is internalized. Sarah Miles of *The End of the Affair* is torn between her loyalty to God and her loyalty to her lover.

Fowler of *The Quiet American* cannot decide whether he wants to eliminate Pyle for the good of Vietnam or to get his woman back from a rival. The characters are shaded in, rendered complex by internal division.

BRIGHTON ROCK

Because he was a remarkable self-critic, Greene overcame most of his early weaknesses. He corrected an early tendency to distrust autobiographical material, and he seemed to overcome his difficulty in portraying credible women. In his first twenty-four years as a novelist, he depicted perhaps only two or three complex women: Kate Farrant of *England Made Me*, Sarah Miles of *The End of the Affair*, and possibly Ida Arnold of *Brighton Rock*. His later novels and plays, however, feature a host of well-drawn women, certainly the best of whom is Aunt Augusta of *Travels with My Aunt*. If there is one weakness that mars some of Graham Greene's later novels, it is their prolixity. Too often in his late fiction, characters are merely mouthpieces for ideas.

Brighton Rock was the first of Greene's novels to treat an explicitly religious theme. Moreover, in attempting to play devil's advocate for *Brighton Rock*'s protagonist, Pinkie, the author had chosen one of his most challenging tasks. He made this Catholic protagonist more vicious than he was to make any character in his entire canon, yet Greene demonstrated that Catholic moral law could not condemn Pinkie, could not finally know "the appalling strangeness of the mercy of God."

Pinkie takes over a protection-racket gang from his predecessor, Kite, and must immediately avenge Kite's murder by killing Fred Hale. This murder inspires him to commit a series of other murders necessary to cover his tracks. It also leads to Pinkie's marrying Rose, a potential witness against him, and finally to his attempt to induce Rose to commit suicide. When the police intervene, Pinkie takes his own life.

Vicious as he is, with his sadistic razor slashings, his murders to cover murders, and his cruelty to Rose, Pinkie's guilt is nevertheless extenuated, his amorality rendered somewhat understandable. Pinkie's conscience had not awakened because his imag-

ination had not awakened: "The word 'murder' conveyed no more to him than the word 'box,' 'collar,' 'giraffe'. . . . The imagination hadn't awoken. That was his strength. He couldn't see through other people's eyes, or feel with their nerves."

As with so many of Greene's characters, the explanation for Pinkie's self-destructive character lies in his lost childhood: "In the lost boyhood of Judas, Christ was betrayed." In a parody of William Wordsworth's "Ode: Intimations of Immortality" (1807), Greene said that Pinkie came into the world trailing something other than heavenly clouds of his own glory after him: "Hell lay about him in his infancy." Though Wordsworth might write of the archetypal child that "heaven lay about him in his infancy," Greene saw Pinkie in quite different terms: "Heaven was a word: hell was something he could trust." Pinkie's vivid memory of his father and mother having sexual intercourse in his presence has turned him from all pleasures of the flesh, tempting him for a while with thoughts of the celibate priesthood.

When Pinkie is seventeen, Kite becomes a surrogate father to him. Pinkie's lack of conscience, his unconcern for himself, his sadomasochistic tendencies, which early showed themselves as a substitute for thwarted sexual impulses, stand the youth in good stead for a new vocation that requires unflinching loyalty, razor slashings, and, if necessary, murder. His corruption is almost guaranteed. To say this is not to reduce the novel from a theological level to a sociological one on which environment has determined the boy's character. Rose survives somewhat the same circumstances. Pinkie's guilt is extenuated, never excused.

Pinkie, however, is not the only character in the novel on whose behalf Greene invoked his "virtue of disloyalty." Rose is a prefiguration of the unorthodox "saint" that Greene developed more subtly in his later novels, in the Mexican priest of *The Power and the Glory*, in Sarah Miles of *The End of the Affair*, and to some extent in Scobie of *The Heart of the Matter*. Like Scobie, Rose wills her damnation out of love. She is not so well drawn as Scobie, at times making her naïve goodness less credible than his, but she is motivated by selfless concern for another. When she refuses to reject Pinkie and when she chooses to commit suicide, Rose wants an afterlife with Pinkie. She would rather be damned with him than see him damned alone: Rose will show "them they couldn't pick and choose." This seems unconvincing, until one hears the old priest cite the actual case of Charles Peguy, who would rather have died in a state of sin than have believed that a single soul was damned. In her confession to the old priest, Rose learns of God's mercy and also of the "saintly" Peguy, who, like Rose, preferred to be damned rather than believe that another person had been.

One is asked, then, to be sympathetic both to a character who has willed her own damnation and to one who leads a life of thorough viciousness, to believe that the salvation of both is a real possibility. In asking for this sympathy, for this possibility, Greene is not doctrinaire. As an effective problem novelist, Greene makes no assertions but merely asks questions that enlarge one's understanding. Greene does not equate the Church with Rose's official moral teaching, suggesting that the old priest in this novel and Father Rank in *The Heart of the Matter* are as representative as the teachers of Rose and Pinkie. Still, the moral doctrine provided Greene with the material that he liked to stretch beyond its customary shape.

THE HEART OF THE MATTER

In *The Heart of the Matter*, Greene achieved the genuine tragedy that he came close to writing in many of his other novels. His protagonist, Major Scobie, is a virtuous man whose hamartia lies in an excess of pity. In Scobie, pity exceeds all bounds and becomes as vicious as Macbeth's ambition. His pity wrecks a marriage he had wanted to save, ruins a lover he had hoped to help, kills his closest friend—his "boy," Ali—and brings about his own moral corruption. Compared to Aristides the Just by one character and to the Old Testament's Daniel by another, Scobie becomes guilty of adultery, smuggling, treason, lies, sacrilege, and murder before he kills himself.

A late edition of the novel restores to the story an early scene between the government spy, Wilson, and Louise Scobie. Greene had written it for the original, then withdrew it since he believed that, told as it was

from Wilson's point of view, it broke Scobie's point of view prematurely. When this scene is restored, Louise is seen in a more sympathetic light, and one can no longer see Scobie as hunted to his death by Louise. Though the reader still likes Scobie and is tempted to exonerate him, it is difficult to read the restored text without seeing Scobie's excess of pity for what it is.

The novel's three final, anticlimactic scenes effectively serve to reduce the grandeur of Scobie's act of self-sacrifice, showing the utter waste of his suicide and the fearful pride contained in his act. It is not that the final scenes make Scobie seem a lesser person. On the contrary, his wife and Helen are made to appear more unworthy of him: Louise with her unkind judgments about Scobie's taking money from Yusef when that very money was borrowed to send her to South Africa as she wanted, and Helen giving her body to Bagster immediately after Scobie's death. Nevertheless, the very criticism of these women makes Scobie's suicide more meaningless and even more effectively shows the arrogance of his action.

Scobie's suicide, then, is not meant to be seen as praiseworthy but rather as the result of a tragic flaw—pity. In this respect, it differs from Elizabeth's suicide in *The Man Within*. Still, though his suicide is presented as wrong, the final fault in a good man disintegrating spiritually, the reader is compelled to feel sympathy for Scobie. Louise's insistence on the Church's teaching that he has cut himself off from mercy annoys the reader. One is made to see Scobie through the eyes of Father Rank, who angrily responds to Louise that "the Church knows all the rules. But it doesn't know what goes on in a single human heart." In this novel's complex treatment of suicide, then, Greene does not use the "virtue of disloyalty" to justify Scobie's act, but rather "to comprehend sympathetically [a] dissident fellow."

THE HUMAN FACTOR

The epigraph for *The Human Factor* is taken from Joseph Conrad: "I only know that he who forms a tie is lost. The germ of corruption has entered into his soul." Maurice Castle's soul is corrupted because a tie of gratitude exists between him and a Communist friend.

The Human Factor may, in part, have been suggested by Greene's friend and former superior in British Secret Intelligence, Kim Philby, although Greene had written twenty-five thousand words of the novel before Philby's defection. When Philby wrote his story, *My Silent War* (1968), Greene put the novel aside for ten years. In any case, Greene anticipated the novel long before the Philby case in his 1930 story, "I Spy," in which a young boy watches his father being whisked off to Russia after the British have detected his spying.

The Human Factor was Greene's first espionage novel since *Our Man in Havana* in 1958. Greene's protagonist, Maurice Castle, works for the British Secret Service in London and has, the reader learns halfway through the novel, become a double agent. He has agreed to leak information to the Russians to help thwart "Uncle Remus," a plan devised by England, the United States, and South Africa to preserve apartheid, even to use nuclear weapons for the purpose if necessary. Castle has not become a Communist and will not support them in Europe, but he owes a Communist friend a favor for helping his black wife, Sarah, escape from South Africa. Also, he owes his wife's people something better than apartheid.

Castle's spying is eventually discovered, and the Russians remove him from England. They try to make good their promise to have his wife and child follow, but the British Secret Service makes it impossible for Sarah to take the boy when it learns that Sam is not Castle's boy, but the boy of an African who is still alive. The novel ends in bleak fashion when Maurice is permitted to phone from Moscow and learns that his family cannot come. He has escaped into a private prison.

The Human Factor exemplifies again the "virtue of disloyalty," but even more, it demonstrates that Greene does not merely flesh out a story to embody that disloyalty. Though he does everything to enlist the reader's sympathies for Castle, demonstrating his superiority to those for whom he works, Greene ultimately condemns his actions as he condemned Scobie's. As Scobie had been a victim of pity, Castle is a victim of gratitude. In chatting with his wife, Sa-

rah, before she learns that he has been spying, Castle defends his gratitude, and his wife agrees it is a good thing "if it doesn't take you too far." Moreover, as Scobie had an excessive pity even as a boy, Maurice Castle had an exaggerated gratitude. At one point, he asks his mother whether he was a nervous child, and she tells him he always had an "exaggerated sense of gratitude for the least kindness." Once, she tells him, he gave away an expensive pen to a boy who had given him a chocolate bun. At novel's end, when Castle is isolated in Russia, Sarah asks him in a phone conversation how he is, and he recalls his mother's words about the fountain pen: "My mother wasn't far wrong." Like Scobie as well, Castle is the most appealing character in the book, and many a reader will think his defection justified.

THE POWER AND THE GLORY

The novels considered above are perhaps extreme examples of Greene's "virtue of disloyalty," but the same quality can be found in most of his novels. In his well-known *The Power and the Glory*, for example, Greene sets up a metaphorical conflict between the powers of God and the powers of atheism, yet it is his "disloyalty" that prevents the allegory from turning into a medieval morality play. The forces of good and the forces of evil are not so easily separated. Although his unnamed priest acquires a real holiness through suffering, the author depicts him as a much weaker man than his counterpart, the atheistic lieutenant. The latter is not only a strong man, but also a good man, who is selflessly devoted to the people. His anti-Catholicism has its origin in his boyhood memory of a Church that did not show a similar concern for its people. Perhaps Greene's fairness to Mexico's dusty rationalism, which he actually despised, can be seen by contrasting the novel with its film version. In John Ford's 1947 film, renamed *The Fugitive*, the viewer is given a hero, the priest, played by Henry Fonda, opposed by a corrupt lieutenant.

THE QUIET AMERICAN

That writer's judgment, so firmly founded on "disloyalty," also helped Greene to overcome his tendency to anti-Americanism in *The Quiet American*. While Greene is critical of the naïve and destructive innocence of the young American, Pyle, he is even more critical of the English narrator, Fowler, who is cynically aloof. In the end, Greene's "disloyalty" permits him to show Vietnam suffering at the hands of any and all representatives of the Western world.

Greene's painstaking attempt to see the other side, and to be as "disloyal" as possible to his own, animated his fictional worlds and gave both him and his readers that "extra dimension of understanding."

Henry J. Donaghy

OTHER MAJOR WORKS

SHORT FICTION: *The Basement Room and Other Stories*, 1935; *The Bear Fell Free*, 1935; *Twenty-four Stories*, 1939 (with James Laver and Sylvia Townsend Warner); *Nineteen Stories*, 1947; *Twenty-one Stories*, 1954; *A Visit to Morin*, 1959; *A Sense of Reality*, 1963; *May We Borrow Your Husband? and Other Comedies of the Sexual Life*, 1967; *Collected Stories*, 1972.

PLAYS: *The Heart of the Matter*, pr. 1950 (adaptation of his novel; with Basil Dean); *The Living Room*, pr., pb. 1953; *The Potting Shed*, pr., pb. 1957; *The Complaisant Lover*, pr., pb. 1959; *Carving a Statue*, pr., pb. 1964; *The Return of A. J. Raffles: An Edwardian Comedy in Three Acts Based Somewhat Loosely on E. W. Hornung's Characters in "The Amateur Cracksman,"* pr., pb. 1975; *For Whom the Bell Chimes*, pr. 1980; *Yes and No*, pr. 1980; *The Collected Plays of Graham Greene*, pb. 1985.

SCREENPLAYS: *Twenty-one Days*, 1937; *The New Britain*, 1940; *Brighton Rock*, 1947 (adaptation of his novel; with Terence Rattigan); *The Fallen Idol*, 1948 (adaptation of his novel; with Lesley Storm and William Templeton); *The Third Man*, 1949 (adaptation of his novel; with Carol Reed); *The Stranger's Hand*, 1954 (with Guy Elmes and Giorgino Bassani); *Loser Takes All*, 1956 (adaptation of his novel); *Saint Joan*, 1957 (adaptation of George Bernard Shaw's play); *Our Man in Havana*, 1959 (adaptation of his novel); *The Comedians*, 1967 (adaptation of his novel).

TELEPLAY: *Alas, Poor Maling*, 1975.

RADIO PLAY: *The Great Jowett*, 1939.

POETRY: *Babbling April: Poems*, 1925; *After Two Years*, 1949; *For Christmas*, 1950.

NONFICTION: *Journey Without Maps: A Travel Book*, 1936; *The Lawless Roads: A Mexican Journal*, 1939 (reissued as *Another Mexico*); *British Dramatists*, 1942; *Why Do I Write?: An Exchange of Views Between Elizabeth Bowen, Graham Greene and V. S. Pritchett*, 1948; *The Lost Childhood and Other Essays*, 1951; *Essais Catholiques*, 1953 (Marcelle Sibon, translator); *In Search of a Character: Two African Journals*, 1961; *The Revenge: An Autobiographical Fragment*, 1963; *Victorian Detective Fiction*, 1966; *Collected Essays*, 1969; *A Sort of Life*, 1971; *The Pleasure Dome: The Collected Film Criticism, 1935-40, of Graham Greene*, 1972 (John Russell-Taylor, editor); *Lord Rochester's Monkey: Being the Life of John Wilmot, Second Earl of Rochester*, 1974; *Ways of Escape*, 1980; *Getting to Know the General*, 1984.

CHILDREN'S LITERATURE: *The Little Train*, 1946; *The Little Fire Engine*, 1950 (also as *The Little Red Fire Engine*); *The Little Horse Bus*, 1952; *The Little Steam Roller: A Story of Mystery and Detection*, 1953.

EDITED TEXTS: *The Old School: Essays by Divers Hands*, 1934; *The Best of Saki*, 1950; *The Spy's Bedside Book: An Anthology*, 1957 (with Hugh Greene); *The Bodley Head Ford Madox Ford*, 1962, 1963 (4 volumes); *An Impossible Woman: The Memories of Dottoressa Moor of Capri*, 1975.

MISCELLANEOUS: *The Portable Graham Greene*, 1973 (Philip Stout Ford, editor).

BIBLIOGRAPHY

De Vitis, A. A. *Graham Greene*. Rev. ed. Boston: Twayne, 1986. This readable, well-organized treatment evaluates the different ways Greene seeks to embody his religious belief in his fiction. Establishes both the intellectual and the social setting in which he developed as a writer and includes detailed discussions of his novels, plays, and short stories. Places particular emphasis on publications after 1938 in which religious themes become clearly apparent. Includes a chronology, a selected bibliography, and an index.

Evans, Robert O., ed. *Graham Greene: Some Critical Considerations*. Lexington: University Press of Kentucky, 1963. This lively collection of fourteen critical essays offers a variety of approaches to Greene's novels along with frequent references to the "entertainments" and travel books. Topics include Greene's Catholicism, his similarities as a writer to François Mauriac, his intellectual background, and his accomplishments as a dramatist, short-story writer, and motion-picture critic. Includes a comprehensive bibliography of his works and the criticism of them published by 1963.

Hill, William Thomas. *Graham Greene's Wanderers: The Search for Dwelling—Journeying and Wandering in the Novels of Graham Greene*. San Francisco: International Scholars Publications, 1999. Examines the motif of the dwelling in Greene's fiction. Deals with the mother, the father, the nation, and the Church as the "ground" of dwelling.

Hoskins, Robert. *Graham Greene: An Approach to the Novels*. New York: Garland, 1999. An updated look at Greene's oeuvre. Includes bibliographical references and an index.

Sheldon, Michael. *Graham Greene: The Enemy Within*. New York: Random House, 1994. In this unauthorized biography, Sheldon takes a much more critical view of Greene's life, especially of his politics, than does Norman Sherry, the authorized biographer. A lively, opinionated narrative. Notes and bibliography included.

Sherry, Norman. *The Life of Graham Greene*. New York: Viking Press, 1989. This is the first part of what is certainly the most comprehensive, most authoritative account of Greene's life yet published, written with complete access to his papers and the full cooperation of family, friends, and the novelist himself. Leads the reader to 1939 to offer a rich account of the novelist's formative years, struggles, and experiences as a journalist. Includes a generous collection of photographs, a bibliography, and an index.

_____. *The Life of Graham Greene. Volume II: 1939- 1955*. New York: Viking, 1995. Sherry continues his superb exploration of Greene's life and the sources of his fiction.

Turnell, Martin. *Graham Greene: A Critical Essay*. Grand Rapids, Mich.: Wm. B. Eerdmans, 1967. This brief study explores the factors which determine the quality of the religion in Greene's work from a Christian perspective. Discusses his novels and dramas, includes biographical background, and considers Greene's dilemma as a Christian writer along with François Mauriac and Jean Cayrol. A selected primary/secondary bibliography is included.

Wolfe, Peter. *Graham Greene the Entertainer*. Carbondale: Southern Illinois University Press, 1972. The first book-length treatment of Greene's "entertainments." Opens by discussing the varying critical approaches that his novels have received and then offers a readable, book-by-book analysis of each novel's characterization, plot, setting, themes, and style. Includes a selected primary/secondary bibliography and an index.

JOHN GRISHAM

Born: Jonesboro, Arkansas; February 8, 1955

PRINCIPAL LONG FICTION
A Time to Kill, 1989
The Firm, 1991
The Pelican Brief, 1992
The Client, 1993
The Chamber, 1994
The Rainmaker, 1995
The Runaway Jury, 1996
The Partner, 1997
The Street Lawyer, 1998
The Testament, 1999
The Brethren, 2000

OTHER LITERARY FORMS
    John Grisham is known only for his novels.

ACHIEVEMENTS
    John Grisham joined novelist-lawyer Scott F. Turow in establishing and popularizing the genre of legal fiction. Grisham is one of a small group of American novelists whose books are termed "block-

buster" novels; so popular is his fiction that his books are almost guaranteed to lead the best-seller lists from the moment they are published. *Publishers Weekly* called Grisham the "best-selling novelist of the 1990's." Most of his novels have been made into films, from *The Firm* in 1993 to *The Rainmaker* in 1997.

BIOGRAPHY

John Grisham, the second of five children, was born and raised in the South. His father was a construction worker, and the family moved frequently during Grisham's childhood. He lived in Arkansas, Louisiana, and Mississippi while he was growing up. Whenever his family moved to a new town, his mother saw that the children received library cards as soon as possible, because, as Grisham said, his mother encouraged reading over watching television. He attended high school in Southaven, Mississippi, a small town outside Memphis. He has said that his writing ability grew out of his involvement in a family of readers and storytellers.

Grisham wanted to play professional baseball, and he spent his early college years largely ignoring his studies and concentrating on sports. When he determined that a baseball career was not likely to happen, he turned to accounting as a major, graduating from Mississippi State University in 1977 with a bachelor's degree. He attended law school at the University of Mississippi, where he received his law degree in 1981. That year he married Renee Jones, with whom he would have two children. They would reside in Charlottesville, Virginia, with Grisham writing six months of the year and coaching his son's Little League baseball team the other six months.

From 1981 to 1991, Grisham practiced law in Southaven. He also served in the Mississippi House of Representatives from 1984 to 1990. Although Grisham was a moderately successful lawyer, he said that he found himself becoming rather cynical toward the legal profession, and thus he became increasingly interested in literature and in writing. He wrote his first novel, *A Time to Kill*, in longhand, rising every morning at 5:00 A.M. and writing for one to two hours each day; he took three years to write his first book.

Eventually it was published by a small press, and Grisham personally visited bookstores in numerous locales to try to augment its sales. In spite of his efforts, the book initially sold only about five thousand copies.

The phenomenal success of his writing began with his second novel, *The Firm. The Firm* was a major best-seller, and it was made into a film, the first of many of Grisham's novels to become motion pictures. All of Grisham's novels since *The Firm* have also reached the top of the best-seller lists.

ANALYSIS

Grisham writes legal thrillers, a type of novel that has virtually become a genre of its own in recent years. Grisham credits writer Scott F. Turow's *Presumed Innocent* (1987) for beginning the trend, but his own novels have served to define that trend. If, as conventional wisdom holds, Americans do not like lawyers, they have shown that they certainly do like books about lawyers. The reading public has purchased vast numbers of Grisham's books and those of other writers of fiction dealing with the legal profession.

With *The Firm*, Grisham began a pattern (some critics call it a formula) that he used, with variations, in most of his succeeding books. His plots usually center around protagonists who are young and in some way vulnerable, who are placed in extraordinary circumstances. They find themselves fighting against overwhelming odds in situations in which they should not be able to prevail. Ultimately they may win out over antagonists of apparently superior strength: the U.S. government, the Mafia, giant insurance companies. However, Grisham cannot be counted on to give his readers a standard happy ending.

Some critics have faulted Grisham for shallow character development and for implausible plots; other critics point out, however, that popular fiction is virtually defined by such plots. Grisham himself said that he writes "to grab readers. This isn't serious literature." Still, some of Grisham's books are set apart from other action thrillers by his genuine interest in, and engrossing presentation of, social concerns affecting modern readers.

Grisham's books are based in the legal profession that he pursued for many years and are usually set in the South, where he grew up and with which he is deeply familiar. Readers curious about the internal functioning of the legal world undoubtedly find his books satisfying in their detailed outlining of the way the law works in actual practice. Readers familiar with southern settings find few false notes in Grisham's descriptions of his settings in Mississippi, Louisiana, and Tennessee.

A TIME TO KILL

A Time to Kill, set in Mississippi, begins with the brutal rape of a young black girl by two white men. The child survives, and the men are arrested, but before they can be tried the girl's father shoots them both. The question of his guilt is not at issue; he has committed the killings in public, in full view of numerous witnesses. The plot centers on whether the jury can be convinced to release a man who has acted to avenge a terrible crime inflicted on his family. Because the killer is black and the victims white, the racial implications are obvious. The book considers the uneasy nature of race relations in modern Mississippi, and it spares neither black nor white southerners in its look at the manipulations for position and media attention related to a highly publicized trial. Some critics have said that the character development in this novel is richer than in Grisham's subsequent works. The book suffers from faults common to first novels, however; Grisham fails to tie up some of his plot lines in ways that more experienced writers might. Once finished with a character or situation, he tends simply to abandon the person or issue without resolution. Nonetheless, Grisham and some critics consider this his best book.

THE FIRM

In *The Firm*, Grisham debuted the formula that would propel his books to the top of the best-seller lists. Protagonist Mitch McDeere is graduating third in his Harvard Law School class. He has several job offers, but the best is from a firm in Memphis, which offers an outstanding salary, an expensive car, an accessible purchase of an expensive home—all sounding too good to be true. Mitch begins to have questions about the firm almost at once: Why has no one ever quit? What about the two people who died a few years back? The law firm has a dirty secret, which would be deadly for Mitch to find out: The firm works for the Mafia. Once Mitch learns this, he must also learn enough to bargain for his life. The plot of *The Firm* is fast-paced and fairly straightforward. It has been called simplistic, but in some ways—concerns of popular fiction aside—it also seems more realistic than some of Grisham's later novels. That is, one might actually imagine the events of this book happening; in some subsequent Grisham books, one would be hard put to believe the occurrence of the events.

THE PELICAN BRIEF

Grisham said that he wrote *The Pelican Brief* and *The Client* to prove to his wife that he could create credible female protagonists. Both books are examples of the compelling, if improbable, popular novel. In *The Pelican Brief*, a law student named Darby Shaw writes a legal brief outlining a probable cause for the recent murders of two Supreme Court justices. After she writes the brief, Darby decides it is essentially worthless, but it is picked up and handed to the Justice Department by a law professor, who is also her lover. In fact, Darby has inadvertently discovered the truth of the situation, and from that point on, her life is in jeopardy. The book is exciting and readable but rather hard to believe, qualities shared with his fourth novel, *The Client*. Neither of these books received particularly strong reviews, though they both sold many copies and were made into films.

THE CHAMBER

The Chamber represents a departure from Grisham's two preceding novels. Dealing as it does with the imposition of the death penalty, the book is the first of Grisham's novels to take on a social issue. Sam Cayhall is scheduled to be executed for murder by the state of Mississippi. He has been convicted of planting a bomb that resulted in the deaths of two Jewish children, and his guilt is not in question. Cayhall has few redeeming qualities: He is an unrepentant racist and a member of the Ku Klux Klan.

His case is taken in the final stage of appeals by young lawyer Adam Hall. He is the grandson of the prisoner, although Cayhall is unaware of this at the beginning of their involvement. Hall realizes that he is facing an uphill fight, but he struggles with the case as if he has a chance to win. The strength of this book lies in the picture it offers the reader of the reality of the death penalty. Grisham does not rail against capital punishment; he simply shows the reader the unattractive truth of it. Even given the horror of Cayhall's crime, one is led to question whether the inhumanity of the death penalty is an appropriate response. The book is flawed by some annoying lapses in editing, but at the time it was published, it received some of Grisham's strongest critical reviews.

THE RUNAWAY JURY

This book is based on an initial premise that may be difficult for some readers to accept: By skillful positioning and design, one might arrange to become a member of a given jury. This book offers a fascinating look at the inside functions of a jury and at the incredible resources wealthy corporations can offer to secure verdicts.

In this case, the juror is Nicholas Easter, and the jury is trying a lawsuit against a major tobacco company. When the story begins, the tobacco companies have never lost a lawsuit brought because a smoker died of cancer, and they have no intention of losing this one. The lawyers for the tobacco companies have volumes of information on everyone called for jury selection, billions of dollars for defense, and no scruples. What they do not know, however, is that they are up against a person almost as skillful and knowledgeable as they are. Grisham's inside views of the law are, as always, interesting, and the inside views of the jury as it takes shape and reaches its conclusions are particularly fascinating in this novel.

THE STREET LAWYER

The Street Lawyer represents an interesting departure for Grisham. The book is set in Washington, D.C., rather than in his usual locations further south. Moreover, the story is less a novel than an attempt to raise social consciousness about the plight of the homeless. Grisham has dealt with issues of social interest before, but always in the context of a protagonist fighting large corporations for particular clients: *The Runaway Jury* took on big tobacco companies,

and *The Rainmaker* was scathing in its condemnation of practices used by unscrupulous insurance companies. *The Street Lawyer*, however, has a slim plot, with the bulk of the book devoted to the condition of being homeless in America.

In the novel, Michael Brock is a successful young attorney with a large, powerful firm. When a homeless man enters the offices one morning to seek satisfaction for a grievance inflicted by the firm, Michael's life is changed drastically. His search for answers to the man's situation leads him into the world of the homeless and those who fight their battles. It also causes him to steal a file that has the potential to cause problems for his firm.

The firm fights to have Michael arrested for theft; still, Michael has the damning file. The parties are at something of a standoff. The resolution to the conflict gives the book something of a feel-good ending, but Grisham achieves his purpose: The book is bound to make readers think twice about the ways in which government and society in the modern United States deal with the poor.

June Harris

BIBLIOGRAPHY

Bearden, Michelle. "John Grisham: In Six Years He's Gone from Rejection Slips to Mega-Sales." *Publishers Weekly* 240 (February, 1993): 70-71. The author discusses Grisham's early career and his rise to best-selling writer.

Cauthen, Cramer R., and Donald G. Alpin III. "The Gift Refused: The Southern Lawyer in *To Kill a Mockingbird*, *The Client*, and *Cape Fear*." *Studies in Popular Culture* 19, no. 2 (October, 1996): 257-275. A comparative study of the treatment of the southern lawyer in modern popular fiction.

Harris, June. "John Grisham." In *Contemporary Novelists*, edited by Susan Brown. Detroit: St. James Press, 1996. Focuses on Grisham's work and its place in contemporary fiction.

Mote, Dave. "John Grisham." In *Contemporary Popular Writers*, edited by Dave Mote. Detroit: St. James Press, 1997. A critical look at Grisham's place among popular writers. Looks at comparative merits of several books.

H

DASHIELL HAMMETT

Born: St. Mary's County, Maryland; May 27, 1894
Died: New York, New York; January 10, 1961

PRINCIPAL LONG FICTION

Red Harvest, 1927-1928 (serial), 1929 (book)
The Dain Curse, 1928-1929 (serial), 1929 (book)
The Maltese Falcon, 1929-1930 (serial), 1930 (book)
The Glass Key, 1930 (serial), 1931 (book)
The Thin Man, 1934

OTHER LITERARY FORMS

Dashiell Hammett first attracted critical attention as the author of short detective fiction published in *Smart Set* and *Black Mask* magazines as early as 1923. The best of his stories were narratives told in the first person by the nameless "Continental Op," a fat, balding operative working out of the San Francisco office of the Continental Detective Agency. The Continental Op is also the narrator and principal character of Hammett's first two novels, both of which were published in magazines before their appearance in book form. A number of his short stories were anthologized in *The Continental Op* (1945) and, after Hammett's death in 1961, *The Big Knockover* (1966).

ACHIEVEMENTS

Together with his contemporary Raymond Chandler (1888-1959), Hammett is credited with defining the form, scope, and tone of the modern detective novel, a distinctly American genre that departs considerably from the earlier tradition inspired by the British. Chandler, although some six years Hammett's senior, did not in fact begin publishing detective fiction until 1933 and readily acknowledged the younger writer's prior claim. Together, both authors have exerted considerable influence upon later exponents of the detective genre, notably on Ross Macdonald, their most distinguished successor. Hammett's work in particular has served also as a stylistic model for many novelists working outside the detective genre, among them Ernest Hemingway and John O'Hara.

Unlike his predecessors in the mystery genre, Hammett adopted a starkly realistic, tough-minded tone in his works, sustaining an atmosphere in which questions outnumber answers and no one is to be trusted. Hammett's reputation ultimately rests on his creation of two characters who embody the moral ambiguities of the modern world: Sam Spade (*The Maltese Falcon*) and Nick Charles (*The Thin Man*). Widely popularized through film adaptations of the novels in which they appear, Spade and Charles are among the most famous American detectives, known even to those with little more than marginal interest in the mystery genre. Tough-minded if occasionally softhearted, both characters may be seen as particularized refinements of Hammett's Continental Op, professional detectives who remain true to their personal code of honor and skeptical with regard to everything and everyone else.

Partially because of declining health, Hammett wrote no novels after the age of forty. His reputation, however, was by that time secure; even in the following century, his five novels would remain landmarks of the genre, a model for future novelists and a formidable standard of comparison.

BIOGRAPHY

Samuel Dashiell Hammett was born in St. Mary's County, Maryland, on May 27, 1894, of an old but modest Roman Catholic family. Leaving high school at fourteen after less than a year of attendance, Hammett worked indifferently at a variety of odd jobs before signing on with the Pinkerton Detective Agency around the age of twenty. At last, it seemed he had found work that he enjoyed and could do well, with a dedication later reflected in the character and behavior of the Continental Op. With time out for service in World War I, from which he was demobilized as a sergeant, Hammett continued to serve Pinkerton with distinction until failing health caused him to consider other options. In 1921, he married Josephine Dolan, a nurse whom he had met during one of his recurring bouts with tuberculosis. The couple moved west to San Francisco, where Hammett returned to work for Pinkerton, only to resign in frustration and disgust after an ironic incident in which his detective talents proved too great for his own good: Assigned by Pinkerton to ship out on an Australian freighter in search of stolen gold believed to be hidden aboard, Hammett managed to find the missing gold in a smokestack during a cursory search just prior to departure and was thus denied the anticipated voyage to Australia.

During such spare time as he could find, Hammett had been trying to prepare himself as a writer; upon leaving Pinkerton, he devoted himself increasingly to writing, eventually leaving his family (which by then included two daughters) and moving to a cheap furnished room where he could live and write. Fearing that he had little time left to live, he wrote at a determined pace; encouraged by his first successes, he gradually developed and refined the writing style that was to make him famous. His first story featuring the Continental Op appeared in October, 1923. Increasingly successful, Hammett soon progressed to the writing of longer stories that were in fact independent sections of novels, eventually published as *Red Harvest* and *The Dain Curse*. Both appeared as hardbound editions in 1929. The following year, Hammett achieved both critical recognition and financial independence with the publication of *The Maltese Falcon*, an unquestionably mature and groundbreaking work that sold at once to the film industry; John Huston's landmark 1941 version of *The Maltese Falcon* was the third Hollywood film to be drawn from Hammett's original novel.

In the year 1930, Hammett made the acquaintance of dramatist Lillian Hellman, eleven years his junior, who was to become the most important and influential woman in his life. Although they never married (each was unhappily married to someone else at the time of their first meeting), Hellman and Hammett remained together in an intense, often turbulent, but intellectually rewarding relationship until Hammett's

(Library of Congress)

death some thirty years later at the age of sixty-six. *The Thin Man*, Hammett's next and last published novel (*The Glass Key* having already been written by the time he met Hellman), reflects the author's relationship with Hellman in the portrayal of Nick and Nora Charles, represented in the screen version and its sequels by William Powell and Myrna Loy.

Following the success of *The Thin Man* both as book and as film, Hammett moved to Hollywood, where he worked as a writer and script doctor on a variety of screen projects. He became increasingly involved in leftist politics and toward the end of the Depression became a member of the Communist Party. Hammett did not, however, consider his politics an impediment to patriotism; soon after the United States went to war, he was back in a sergeant's uniform, despite his advanced age and obviously declining health. Attached to the Signal Corps, he served three years in the Aleutian Islands, where his duties included editing a daily newspaper for his fellow servicemen. By the end of the war, however, his health was more precarious than ever, undermined by years of recurrent tuberculosis and heavy drinking. After an alcoholic crisis in 1948, Hammett forswore drinking for the remainder of his life. At the same time, his political past was coming back to haunt him; like his fictional characters, however, he remained loyal to his convictions and his friends, declining to testify against his fellow associates in the Communist Party and other political organizations. In 1951, Hammett spent five months in various prisons for contempt of court as a result of his refusal to testify; around the same time, government authorities determined that he was several years behind in the payment of his income tax. Unable to find work in Hollywood because of his political views, Hammett was further impoverished by the attachment of his remaining income for the payment of back taxes. Increasingly infirm, Hammett spent his last years in the care and company of Hellman. He died at Lenox Hill Hospital in New York City on January 10, 1961.

ANALYSIS

Unlike most of their predecessors in the genre, Dashiell Hammett's detectives live and work, as did Hammett himself, in a world populated with actual criminals who violate the law for tangible personal gain. Significantly, Hammett did all of his creative writing during the years of Prohibition, when lawlessness was rampant and organized crime was rapidly gaining a foothold in the American social structure. Prohibition indeed functions prominently in all of Hammett's published work as background, as atmosphere, and frequently as subject. In *Red Harvest*, Hammett's first novel, a loose confederacy of bootleggers, thieves, and hired killers has set up what appears to be a substitute government, replacing law and order with values of their own; the resulting Hobbesian chaos clearly reflects, however indirectly, Hammett's own developing political consciousness. There is little place in such a world for genteel detectives cast in the mold of Dorothy Sayers's Lord Peter Wimsey; accordingly, Hammett presents in the Continental Op and his successors the kind of detective who can deal routinely and effectively with hardened criminals. As Raymond Chandler observed, "Hammett gave murder back to the kind of people who commit it for reasons."

Within such an evil environment, the sleuth often becomes as devious and mendacious as those whom he is pursuing, remaining faithful nevertheless to a highly personal code of honor and justice. Sam Spade, perhaps the most intriguing of Hammett's literary creations, is so well attuned to the criminal mind that he often appears to be a criminal himself; he is known to have been involved romantically with his partner's wife and is thus a likely suspect after the man is murdered. Still, at the end of *The Maltese Falcon*, he persists in turning over to the authorities the thief and murderess Brigid O'Shaughnessy, despite an acknowledged mutual attraction. Ned Beaumont, the protagonist of *The Glass Key*, remains similarly incorruptible despite outward appearances to the contrary: A detective by temperament, if not by trade, Ned serves as friend and aide to the rising local politician Paul Madvig, involving himself deeply in political deals and trades; still, he persists in revealing a United States senator as the murderer of his own son and insists that the senator stand trial rather than commit suicide. The law of the land, however tarnished, remains a strong value in Hammett's novels, suggesting an abiding need for structure against the threat of anarchy.

With *The Thin Man*, Hammett moved in a new direction. For the first time, humor became a significant element in Hammett's fiction, infusing the novel with a lightness of tone that sets it quite apart from the almost documentary seriousness of *Red Harvest* and *The Glass Key*. Its protagonist, Nick Charles, has retired from the detective trade after his marriage to the rich and pretty Nora, some fifteen years his junior. Released from the need to work, he clearly prefers the carefree life of parties, travel, hotels, and round-the-clock drinking, all the while trading jokes and friendly banter with his attractive wife and other boon companions. Still, some habits die hard, and unpredicted events soon bring Nick's well-honed detective instincts back into operation. Moving back and forth between speakeasies and his lavish hotel suite, getting shot at by enraged gangsters, Nick urbanely unravels the mystery until, to no one's real surprise, one of his many casual friends stands revealed as the culprit. It is no secret that Hammett, in his portrayal of the witty Nora and her relationship with Nick, was more than a little influenced by his own developing relationship with Lillian Hellman, who returned the favor in her several volumes of memoirs. Like Nick, Hammett at the time of *The Thin Man* was approaching middle age without the need to work, free at last to indulge his taste for parties and other carefree pursuits. *The Thin Man*, although certainly not planned as Hammett's final novel, is in a sense a fitting valedictory, an exuberant tour de force in which, ironically, the tensions contained in the earlier novels are finally released and perhaps dissipated. An additional irony exists within the book: Nick and Nora Charles may well be Hammett's best-known literary creations, perpetuated by the film version of the novel as well as by several sequels scripted in Hollywood by Hammett himself.

RED HARVEST

Hammett's first published novel, *Red Harvest*, originally serialized in *Black Mask*, delivers in ample portion the harsh realism promised in its title. Indeed, the high body count of *Red Harvest* may well have set a kind of record to be met or broken by later efforts in the detective genre. Hammett's intention, however, is not merely to shock the reader; seen in retrospect, *Red Harvest* emerges as a parable of civilization and its possible mutations.

Nowhere in *Red Harvest* are Hammett's intentions more evident than in his choice of location, a mythical western community called Personville, better known as Poisonville. Some fifty years after the lawless days of the Wild West, Personville/Poisonville has yet to be tamed, even as outlaws have been replaced by gangsters with East Coast accents wearing snap-brim hats instead of Stetsons. The Op, sent to Personville at the request of one Donald Willsson, makes an appointment with him only to discover that he has been murdered before the planned meeting can take place. Undaunted, the Op proceeds to investigate Donald Willsson's murder, plunging deeper and deeper into the town's menacing and malevolent atmosphere. Among the more likely

suspects is Willsson's father Elihu, the town boss, who may well have tried to put a stop to his son's muckraking activities as publisher of the local newspaper. Other suspects, however, are present in abundance, at least until they begin to kill off one another during internecine combat partially masterminded by the Op. The Op, it seems, is particularly skillful in setting the various criminal elements loose upon one another, paving the way for eventual martial law and relative peace, "a sweet-smelling and thornless bed of roses." In the process, however, he frequently faces criminal charges himself; at the same time, the authorities who are pressing the charges may well be as corrupt as the more obvious criminals. In such an environment, the closest thing to a moral imperative is the Op's own case-hardened sense of justice.

The major weakness of *Red Harvest* is a bewildering multiplicity of characters and actions; often, a new character will be introduced and established, only to be killed on the following page. The acts of violence, although symptomatic of social ills and not included for their own sake (as in the work of later hard-boiled mystery writers such as Mickey Spillane), are so numerous as to weary even the least squeamish of readers, although a number of scenes are especially effective; in one, the Op, watching a boxing match that he has helped to "unfix," stands helpless as the unexpected winner falls dead in the ring with a knife at the base of his neck.

THE DAIN CURSE

Later in the same year, 1929, Hammett published *The Dain Curse*, another formerly serialized novel featuring the Op as narrator and main character. Less sophisticated in its presentation than *Red Harvest*, *The Dain Curse* is more severely hampered by a multiplicity of characters and plot twists, all turning around the possibility of a family "curse" brought on by incest. Despite some rather skillful and memorable characterizations, *The Dain Curse* is generally agreed to be Hammett's weakest and least effective novel. Significantly, it is the last of Hammett's novels to feature the Op and the last (until *The Thin Man*, a different sort of novel) to be narrated in the first person.

THE MALTESE FALCON

Hammett's third novel, *The Maltese Falcon*, narrated dispassionately in the third person, combines the narrative strengths of his earlier works with a far more developed sense of characterization. Its protagonist, Sam Spade, although enough like the Op to be his slightly younger brother, is a more fully realized character caught and portrayed in all his ambiguity. Clearly the "brains" of the Spade and Archer Agency, he is careful to turn over to Miles Archer the case of a young woman client in whose presence he senses trouble. When Archer, blinded by the woman's flattery, goes forth to his death, Spade is hardly surprised, nor does he take many pains to hide his recent affair with the woman who is now Archer's widow. Spade, meanwhile, has grown tired of Iva Archer and her advances. Himself under suspicion for Archer's murder, Spade delves deeper into the case, learning that the young woman has given a number of aliases and cover stories. Her real name, it appears, is Brigid O'Shaughnessy, and it is not long before Spade connects her to a ring of international thieves, each of whom seems to be competing with the others for possession of an ancient and priceless treasure known as the Maltese Falcon. Supposedly, the football-sized sculpted bird, encrusted with precious stones, has been stolen and repossessed numerous times in the four hundred years of its existence, having surfaced most recently in the hands of a Russian general.

Spade's quest eventually brings him in contact with most of the larcenous principals except for the general himself (who at the end of the novel is found to have substituted a worthless leaden counterfeit for the genuine article). Among the thieves are two particularly memorable characters, interpreted in the John Huston film by Sydney Greenstreet and Peter Lorre, respectively: Casper Gutman, an eloquent, grossly fat manipulator and adventurer, keeps trying to maneuver Spade into his confidence; meanwhile, the other, Joel Cairo, a blatant homosexual and member of the international underworld, repeatedly (and most unsuccessfully) tries to intimidate Spade with a handgun that Spade keeps taking away from him. In 1930, Hammett's frank portrayal of a homosexual was considered daring in the extreme; by 1941, it was possible for Huston to apply such a characterization to Gutman as well, whose homosexuality in the novel is little more than latent. The book, for example, mentions that Gutman is traveling with a grown daughter, but the daughter is never mentioned in the Huston film.

In both novel and film, Spade's character develops considerably as he attempts to deal simultaneously with the matters at hand and with his growing affection for the obviously perfidious Brigid O'Shaughnessy. In Brigid, it seems, Spade has at last met his proper match, a woman whose deviousness and native intelligence compare favorably with his own. In her presence, it is all too easy for Spade to forget the cloying advances of Iva Archer or even the tomboyish charms of his secretary Effie Perine; it is less easy, however, for him to forget the tightening web of circumstantial evidence in which he finds Brigid strongly enmeshed. After the coveted falcon has been revealed as a forgery, Spade confronts Brigid with evidence that she, and not her deceased cohort Floyd Thursby, fired the bullet that killed Miles Archer. For all Archer's weaknesses and Spade's personal contempt for the man, Spade remains true to the code that dictates arrest and prosecution for his partner's murderer. Explaining to an incredulous Brigid that he still thinks he loves her but cannot bring himself to trust her, he declares that he is sending her to jail and may or may not be waiting when she is freed. They are locked in an embrace when the police arrive to take her away.

Considerably more thoughtful and resonant than Hammett's earlier novels, *The Maltese Falcon* is his unquestioned masterpiece. The falcon itself, a contested piece of plunder that, in the novel, has occasioned theft and murder throughout recent history and which in its present form turns out to be a fake, is without doubt one of the strongest and best developed images in contemporary American fiction. Another equally effective device, absent from the Huston film, is the Flitcraft parable that Spade tells to Brigid early in their relationship as a way of explaining his behavior. Early in his career, he recalls, he was hired to find a Seattle resident named Flitcraft who had disappeared mysteriously one day during the lunch hour, leaving behind a wife and two children. Spade later learned that, during the lunch break, Flitcraft had glimpsed his own mortality after a narrow escape from a falling beam. "He felt like somebody had taken the lid off his life and let him look at the works." That same day, he abandoned his family, wandering for two years, after which he fashioned for himself in Spokane a professional and family life very much like the one he had left behind in Seattle. "But that's the part of it I always liked," Spade tells Brigid. "He adjusted himself to beams falling, and then no more of them fell, and he adjusted himself to them not falling." Predictably, Spade's narrative has little effect on Brigid; for the reader, however, it does much to explain Hammett's approach to Spade as character and his own developing sense of the novelist's art. During that stage of his career, Hammett moved from "looking at the works" (*Red Harvest*) to a mature sense of contingency in which one's own deeply held convictions are all that matter.

THE GLASS KEY

Acknowledged to have been Hammett's personal favorite among his five published novels, *The Glass Key* is the only one not to feature a trained detective as protagonist. A rather unlikely hero at first glance, Ned Beaumont is tubercular, an avid gambler without a regular job. His principal occupation is that of friend, conscience, and unofficial assistant to Paul Madvig, an amiable politician of forty-five who, one suspects, without Beaumont's help would have made even more mistakes than he already has. Himself the father of a grown daughter, Madvig is currently unmarried and in love with Janet Henry, daughter of an aristocratic and powerful United States senator. Janet has done little to encourage Madvig's attentions, and Beaumont, for his part, is determined to prevent his friend from making a fool of himself. Complications arise with the brutal murder of Taylor Henry, Janet's brother, who may or may not have been in love with Madvig's daughter Opal. As usual in Hammett's novels, there is an underworld connection; Taylor, it seems, was deeply in debt to a professional gambler at the time of his death.

As Madvig's loyal friend and aide, Beaumont sets out to discover the truth behind Taylor Henry's murder, displaying detective instincts worthy of Sam Spade or the Continental Op. Amid serious encounters with angry gangsters and corrupt police, Ned perseveres in his efforts to clear Madvig's name of suspicion in the murder, fully aware that he may well be a suspect himself. Meanwhile, to both Madvig's and Beaumont's consternation, Janet Henry appears to be falling in love with Beaumont, if only because he seems to be proof against her charms. As the action proceeds, it becomes increasingly clear to Beaumont that Taylor Henry could only have been killed by the senator, who has somehow prevailed upon Madvig to accept the burden of suspicion. When Beaumont finally confronts the senator with his suspicions, Henry admits to killing his son in a fit of anger and tampering with evidence at the scene of the crime; he asks only that Beaumont give him five minutes alone with his loaded revolver. Predictably, Beaumont refuses: "You'll take what's coming to you." Beaumont decides to leave town permanently, and, in a surprise twist at the end, he agrees to take Janet with him; the relationship awaiting them can only be surmised.

Like *The Maltese Falcon*, *The Glass Key* is a thoughtful and resonant novel, rich in memorable scenes and images. The glass key itself occurs in a dream that Janet has shortly after the start of her problematical relationship with Ned: She dreams that they arrive at a locked house piled high with food that they can see through the windows, yet when they open the door with a key found under the mat the house turns out to be filled with snakes as well. At the end of the novel, Janet reveals that she has not told Ned all of her dream: "The key was glass and shattered in our hands just as we got the door open, because the lock was stiff and we had to force it." Just as the Maltese Falcon dominates the book bearing its name, the glass key comes to symbolize the dangerous fragility of Janet's life and especially of her relationships with men—Paul Madvig, her father, and finally Ned Beaumont. Born to wealth and privilege, Janet is potentially dangerous to herself and others for reasons that Hammett suggests are outside her control; she does not share in her father's venality and is quite possibly a decent person beneath the veneer of her upbringing.

Not easily deceived, Ned Beaumont has been skeptical about the Henrys from the beginning; early in the book, he warns Paul against deeper involvement with either Janet or her father:

> Read about it in the *Post*—one of the few aristocrats left in American politics. And his daughter's an aristocrat. That's why I'm warning you to sew your shirt on when you go to see them, or you'll come away without it, because to them you're a form of lower animal life and none of the rules apply.

To Beaumont, the Henrys are thoughtless and dangerous, much like Tom and Daisy Buchanan as seen by Nick Carraway in F. Scott Fitzgerald's *The Great Gatsby* (1925). Janet, however, develops considerably during the course of the novel, and at the end there is just the barest chance that a change of scenery will allow her to work out a decent life in Ned Beaumont's company.

THE THIN MAN

Fifth and last of Hammett's novels, *The Thin Man* is the only one to have been written during his acquaintance with Lillian Hellman, whose witty presence is reflected throughout the novel. Thanks to the successful film version and various sequels, *The Thin Man* is, next to *The Maltese Falcon*, the most famous of Hammett's novels; it is also the least typical.

The narrator and protagonist of *The Thin Man* is Nick Charles (born Charalambides and proud of his Greek extraction), a former detective in his early forties who has married the rich and beautiful Nora, nearly young enough to be his daughter. Contrary to popular belief, the novel's title refers not to Charles himself but to one Clyde Miller Wynant, suspected of various crimes throughout the novel until the end, when he is revealed to have been the real killer's first victim: Wynant, an inventor, is described as being tall and painfully thin; at the end of the novel, his bones are found buried with clothes cut to fit a much larger man. In the filmed sequel, however, the title presumably refers to the dapper detective himself.

Peopled with a cast of café-society characters in addition to the usual underworld types, *The Thin Man* is considerably lighter in tone and texture than Hammett's earlier novels. Nick Charles, although clearly descended from Beaumont, Spade, and the Op, is nearly a playboy by comparison, trading light-hearted jokes and double entendres with his wife and boon companions. Close parallels may be drawn between Charles and the author himself, who by the time of *The Thin Man* had achieved sufficient material success to obviate his need to work. Lillian Hellman observes, however, that the actual writing of *The Thin Man* took place during a period of abstemious, almost monastic seclusion that differed sharply from Hammett's usual pattern of behavior during those years, as well as from the carefree life ascribed to Nick and Nora in the novel.

Most of the action of *The Thin Man* turns upon the certifiably eccentric personality of the title character, Clyde Wynant, a former client of Nick during his latter years as a detective. Among the featured characters are Wynant's former wife, son, and daughter, as well as his lawyer, Herbert Macaulay. In particular, the Wynants are memorable, deftly drawn characters, nearly as eccentric in their own ways as the missing *paterfamilias*. Wynant's son, Gilbert, about eighteen, is notable for his voracious reading and morbid curiosity concerning such matters as murder, cannibalism, and abnormal psychology. Dorothy Wynant, a year or two older than Gilbert, keeps trying to parlay a former girlhood crush on Nick Charles into something more serious. Their mother, known as Mimi Jorgensen, is a vain, treacherous woman cut from the same cloth as Brigid O'Shaughnessy of *The Maltese Falcon*; she too makes repeated claims upon Nick's reluctant attentions.

Throughout the novel, Mimi and her children co-exist uneasily in a state of armed truce that occasionally erupts into open warfare, providing scenes of conflict between parent and child considered rather daring at the time. Among the featured characters, only Macaulay appears sane or even remotely sympathetic, yet it is he who ultimately stands accused of the financial double-dealing and multiple murders originally attributed to Wynant, not to mention the murder of Wynant himself.

Like Hammett's earlier novels, *The Thin Man* is

realistic in its portrayal of urban life during Prohibition, when the criminal element was even more visible and overt in its actions than in later times. Despite the witty urbanity of his characters, Hammett harbors few illusions concerning human nature. When Nora asks Nick at the end of the novel what will become of Mimi and her children, he replies, "Nothing new. They'll go on being Mimi and Dorothy and Gilbert just as you and I will go on being us and the Quinns will go on being the Quinns." The novel ends with Nora telling Nick that his explanation is "pretty unsatisfactory." Perhaps it is, Hammett implies, but that is the nature of life.

Partly because of failing health and the pressures of work in Hollywood, Hammett published no fiction after *The Thin Man*. His reputation thus rests on a small and somewhat uneven body of work, redeemed by frequent flashes of brilliance. Notable for their influence upon the work of Raymond Chandler, Ross Macdonald, and a host of lesser writers in the mystery genre, Hammett's novels have also exercised an immeasurable influence on novelists and filmmakers outside the genre.

David B. Parsell

OTHER MAJOR WORKS

SHORT FICTION: *Secret Agent X-9*, 1934 (with Alex Raymond); *The Continental Op*, 1945; *The Return of the Continental Op*, 1945; *The Adventures of Sam Spade, and Other Stories*, 1945; *Hammett Homicides*, 1946; *Dead Yellow Women*, 1947; *Nightmare Town*, 1948; *The Creeping Siamese*, 1950; *Woman in the Dark*, 1951; *A Man Named Thin and Other Stories*, 1962; *The Big Knockover*, 1966.

BIBLIOGRAPHY

Dooley, Dennis. *Dashiell Hammett*. New York: Frederick Ungar, 1984. A particularly useful study for those interested in Hammett's short fiction, which makes up half of this book. His major novels are also discussed in the context of his life and his works considered in the context of their times. Contains notes, a bibliography, and an index.

Gregory, Sinda. *Private Investigations: The Novels of Dashiell Hammett*. Carbondale: Southern Illinois University Press, 1985. The first chapter discusses Hammett, his Pinkerton experiences, and the hard-boiled detective genre. Subsequent chapters focus on each of his five major novels. Foreword by Francis M. Nevins, Jr. Includes a preface and a conclusion, notes, a bibliography, and an index.

Johnson, Diane. *Dashiell Hammett: A Life*. New York: Fawcett Columbine, 1985. This paperback edition of the 1983 biography was very well received critically and is an excellent source for personal information about Hammett's life. Organized chronologically. Includes illustrations, a bibliography, notes, and an index.

Mellen, Joan. *Hellman and Hammett: The Legendary Passion of Lillian Hellman and Dashiell Hammett*. New York: HarperCollins, 1996. Although primarily a biographical study, this scrupulously researched work provides insight into the backgrounds of Hammett's fiction. Includes very detailed notes and bibliography.

Metress, Christopher, ed. *The Critical Response to Dashiell Hammett*. Westport, Conn.: Greenwood Press, 1994. A generous compilation of reviews and general studies, with a comprehensive introduction, chronology, and bibliography.

Nolan, William F. *Hammett: A Life at the Edge*. New York: Congdon & Weed, 1983. This biography draws on Hammett's letters, interviews, memoirs, and public statements and attempts to organize a thematic discussion of Hammett the man. Contains illustrations, a bibliography, notes, and an index.

Nyman, Jopi. *Hard-boiled Fiction and Dark Romanticism*. New York: Peter Lang, 1998. Studies the fiction of Hammett, James M. Cain, and Ernest Hemingway. Includes bibliographical references

Symons, Julian. *Dashiell Hammett*. San Diego: Harcourt Brace Jovanovich, 1985. A good critical introduction to Hammett, his life and works. Many illustrations enliven this discussion of Hammett's short stories and major novels. Includes notes, a bibliography, and an index.

KNUT HAMSUN
Knut Pedersen

Born: Lom, Norway; August 4, 1859
Died: Nørholm, Norway; February 19, 1952

PRINCIPAL LONG FICTION

Den gådefulde, 1877
Bjørger, 1878
Sult, 1890 (*Hunger*, 1899)
Mysterier, 1892 (*Mysteries*, 1927)
Ny jord, 1893 (*Shallow Soil*, 1914)
Redaktør Lynge, 1893
Pan, 1894 (English translation, 1920)
Victoria, 1898 (English translation, 1929)
Sværmere, 1904 (*Dreamers*, 1921)
Under høststjærnen, 1906 (*Under the Autumn Star*,
    1922)
Benoni, 1908 (English translation, 1925)
Rosa, 1908 (English translation, 1926)
En vandrer spiller med sordin, 1909 (*A Wanderer
    Plays on Muted Strings*, 1922)
Den siste glæde, 1912 (*Look Back on Happiness*,
    1940)
Børn av tiden, 1913 (*Children of the Age*, 1924)
Segelfoss by, 1915 (*Segelfoss Town*, 1925)
Markens grøde, 1917 (*Growth of the Soil*, 1920)
Konerne ved vandposten, 1920 (*The Women at the
    Pump*, 1928)
Wanderers, 1922 (includes *Under the Autumn Star*
    and *A Wanderer Plays on Muted Strings*)
Siste kapitel, 1923 (*Chapter the Last*, 1929)
Landstrykere, 1927 (*Vagabonds*, 1930; also known
    as *Wayfarers*)
August, 1930 (English translation, 1931)
Men livet lever, 1933 (*The Road Leads On*, 1934)
Ringen sluttet, 1936 (*The Ring Is Closed*, 1937)

OTHER LITERARY FORMS

Although he always considered the novel his strongest genre, Knut Hamsun also wrote plays, poetry, and expository prose. *Fra det moderne Amerikas aandsliv* (1889; *The Spiritual Life of Modern America*, 1969) is an impudent but witty survey of social and cultural conditions in the United States; Hamsun later repudiated it and would not allow it to be reprinted. Some of the poems in *Det vilde kor* (1904; the wild chorus) are among the best written in Norway during the period. Hamsun was a rather weak dramatist, although his trilogy, comprising *Vid rigets port* (1895; at the gate of the kingdom), *Livets spil* (1896; the game of life), and *Aftenrøde* (1898; the red of evening), is interesting as a drama of ideas. His memoir *På gjengrodde stier* (1949; *On Overgrown Paths*, 1967), written when he was nearly ninety years old, is one of his finest books.

ACHIEVEMENTS

During his long career as a writer, Knut Hamsun was well known and highly regarded not only in his native Norway but also in the rest of Scandinavia, Continental Europe, and the English-speaking world. He was one of the first to introduce the modern psychological novel into Scandinavian literature; his *Hunger* is a classic example of the genre. Later, he created works in which analysis of the development of society played an equally important role; one of them, a celebration of agrarian values entitled *Growth of the Soil*, earned for him the Nobel Prize in Literature in 1920.

Because he was accused of collaborating with the Germans during World War II, Hamsun suffered a period of neglect in the postwar years. This is no longer the case; both Norwegian and foreign critics now consider him his country's greatest novelist. He appeals both to a general audience and to academic critics; a number of his novels have been reissued in new English translations, and his works are frequently taught in literature courses in both Scandinavia and America.

BIOGRAPHY

Knut Hamsun was born Knut Pedersen on August 4, 1859, at the farm Garmotræet in the district of Lom, Norway. His father, Peder Pedersen, was a tailor and small farmer, and Hamsun's mother, Tora, was also of peasant stock. In 1863, Pedersen moved with his family to Hamarøy in Nordland, Norway, where he settled on his brother-in-law's farm, Hamsund, from which Hamsun later took the name by which he is known.

Hamsun's earliest childhood years were happy ones. The happiness came to an end, however, when at the age of nine he was sent to live with his maternal uncle, a wealthy landowner and merchant. Hamsun's parents were not happy with this arrangement either; it was only when heavy financial pressure was brought to bear on them that they would agree to it. The uncle needed Hamsun's labor, and the boy had many experiences which later were of use to him in his art, although he was harshly treated.

Hamsun was released in 1873 and began a long career of odd jobs. He first clerked in several country stores, after which he became an itinerant peddler, then a shoemaker's apprentice, and even a sheriff's deputy. He also worked as a country schoolmaster, for which he was qualified by his native intelligence and masterful penmanship.

Hamsun did not read widely during this period of his life, but he had become familiar with the peasant tales of his countryman, Bjørnstjerne Bjørnson, and in 1877, when Hamsun was only eighteen years old, he published his first book, a naïve love story entitled *Den gådefulde* (the riddle). This youthful work is significant only as the first version of what was to become one of Hamsun's most persistent motifs—namely, a relationship between a lower-class man and an upper-class woman. In the beautiful and lyric novel *Victoria*, this motif became the main theme.

The year 1878 saw the publication of another youthful tale, *Bjørger*. Hamsun's early writings enabled him to obtain the support of a wealthy merchant, and he was able to concentrate fully on the task of becoming a poet of note. To this end, he produced a manuscript and traveled to Copenhagen, where he offered it to Scandinavia's best-known publisher, Hegel of Gyldendal. To his dismay, his manuscript was rejected, and he spent a difficult winter in the city of Kristiania, Norway. The experiences of this winter, as well as later, similar ones, provided him with the material for his novel *Hunger*, which in 1890 gave him his breakthrough as a writer.

Prior to the publication of *Hunger*, however, Hamsun spent several years in America. During two separate stays, he again worked at a variety of jobs, but in addition he read widely in both European and American literature. He also lectured to Norwegian immigrants on literary and cultural topics. In 1888, after his final return from America, he lived in Copenhagen, where he anonymously published the first chapter of *Hunger* in a periodical. This made him a talked-about figure in literary circles even though his identity was known by but a few. The following year, he gave a series of lectures about America in Copenhagen's Student Society; these lectures were published as *The Spiritual Life of Modern America* later in the same year.

After the publication of *Hunger*, a groundbreaking psychological novel, Hamsun wrote an article in 1890 in which he outlined the basic principles employed in its composition. This article, entitled "Fra det ubevidste sjæleliv" ("From the Unconscious Life

(Library of Congress)

of the Mind"), became the genesis of a series of lectures held in a number of Norwegian cities and towns during the year 1891. Hamsun attacked earlier Norwegian literature for being concerned with social conditions rather than with the mental life of the exceptional individual; he maintained that this made it dull.

The 1890's were very productive years for Hamsun, during which he wrote such significant novels as *Mysteries, Pan,* and *Victoria*. He enjoyed his growing reputation and traveled much, in both Scandinavia and Europe. He longed for more stability in his life, however, and hoped that that would be the result of his marriage to Bergljot Bech, whom he met in 1897 and married in 1898. The experience of meeting her lies behind the beautiful love story told in his novel *Victoria,* published in the same year. The couple's expectations were not fulfilled, however, and the marriage was dissolved in 1906.

During the years following the divorce, Hamsun wrote a number of works in which the protagonist is a middle-aged wanderer whose experiences and musings on existence constitute the subject of the books. Such novels as *Under the Autumn Star* and *A Wanderer Plays on Muted Strings* are not regarded as among Hamsun's best, but they are important for what they tell about his artistic development. After the author's marriage to the young actress Marie Andersen in 1909, however, his books took a different turn.

In his lectures on literature delivered in 1891, Hamsun had distanced himself from what he considered the dull social literature of his contemporaries, opting for a kind of fiction that would explore the exceptional consciousness. After his second marriage, however, he began to write books which, in a sense, mediate between these opposing standpoints, emphasizing unusual men in their social setting. *Children of the Age* and its sequel, *Segelfoss Town,* are such books; the protagonists are exceptional men, yet at the same time, Hamsun analyzes the workings of society. In *Segelfoss Town,* for example, the values embodied in the aristocratic Willatz Holmsen give way to those of the modern entrepreneur Tobias Holmengraa, and Hamsun appears to place himself in opposi-

tion to all that is new in both intellectual and material culture.

In 1911, Hamsun bought the farm Skogheim in Hamarøy in northern Norway, where he lived as a farmer and writer. In 1917, he sold this farm and moved to the southern part of the country; the farm had, however, fulfilled its mission: The year 1917 also saw the publication of Hamsun's best-known book, the novel *Growth of the Soil,* for which he received the Nobel Prize in 1920. The book tells the story of a man who goes into the northern Norwegian wilderness, clears land for a farm, and rears a family in close contact with nature. It has been regarded as a hymn both to agrarian life and to the traditional values that Hamsun had espoused in *Children of the Age* and *Segelfoss Town*.

After the publication of *Growth of the Soil,* Hamsun began searching for a new and permanent home. Eventually, he settled at the farm Nørholm, where he lived for the rest of his life. He continued as a combination of writer and farmer, and he improved the farm greatly. During this period, he also published two more novels, *The Women at the Pump* and *Chapter the Last*.

The mid-1920's was a difficult time for Hamsun. He worked hard but feared that his creative powers had begun to fail him. During the winter of 1926, he availed himself of the services of a psychiatrist, and in the fall, he began one of his finest works, the novel *Vagabonds,* which was published the following year. The book is the first volume of a trilogy; the other two volumes are entitled *August* and *The Road Leads On*. The trilogy tells about the adventures of a certain August, a dreamer and eccentric, and how his actions influence the lives of people who, were it not for him, could have possessed the stability that he is lacking. The novels continue that investigation of modern society which is so prominent in *Children of the Age* and *Segelfoss Town*. The connection between these earlier books and the trilogy has been made obvious by the fact that the action in *The Road Leads On* moves from Polden, the isolated north Norwegian community, which is the setting of the trilogy's first two volumes, to Segelfoss, where characters from *Children of the Age* and *Segelfoss Town* are again encountered. *The Road Leads On* can thus be viewed as the concluding volume of two separate trilogies, both of which treat social conditions during a period of transition.

At the time of the conclusion of his August trilogy, Hamsun was a man well into his seventies. His hearing was failing, and his energies had suffered that decline which normally comes with age. He produced only one more novel, *The Ring Is Closed*, and would probably have remained relatively silent were it not for political developments in both Europe and Norway. Hamsun had always been an admirer of Germany and German culture at the same time that he detested the British. After the German invasion of Norway and the flight to England of King Haakon and his cabinet, Hamsun supported the collaborationist government headed by Vidkun Quisling and encouraged Norwegian soldiers not to fight against the invaders. After the war, he was arrested and tried. In the course of the trial, his mental condition was examined, and he was found not to be senile, but to have permanently impaired mental faculties. He was nevertheless convicted of treason and heavily fined, the result of which was that he was left a financially ruined man. After the trial, he published the poignant memoir *On Overgrown Paths*, which abundantly demonstrated that his mental faculties were anything but impaired.

Hamsun's final years were quiet ones. By tacit agreement, no critical attention was paid to his work, and he had nothing further to say. The author died on his farm on February 19, 1952.

ANALYSIS

Knut Hamsun the novelist can be viewed as an outsider who writes about outsiders. Originating in a family that by any standard must be considered poor, Hamsun was keenly aware of the difference between himself and those who possessed power and prestige in society. Power and its opposite, powerlessness, are therefore important themes in his work.

Several of Hamsun's early novels, such as *Hunger* and *Pan*, are narrated in the first person, and their first-person protagonists have character traits and experiences that appear to have been modeled on Hamsun's own. The later novels are without exception narrated in the third person, but that does not mean that the autobiographical content is less. In addition, one can always trust the narrators in the later works to represent Hamsun's own views, while unreliability is a feature of some of the early narrators.

The author's interest in the character of the outsider manifests itself in the careful attention that is paid to individual psychology in the early novels, as well as in the interest in the exceptional individual's relation to society and social forces, especially those of social change, which is found in the later works. The early Hamsun hero, who is often an artist or an artistlike figure, attempts to overcome his powerlessness either through his ability to inspire love in a woman of higher social standing or through his art or both. The typical hero of the later works is either the victim of social change or an embodiment of that which is new in modern social and economic life. In the latter case, he is either somewhat of a charlatan, like Tobias Holmengraa in *Segelfoss Town*, or a dreamer and maker of a multitude of stillborn projects, like August of *Vagabonds* and the other two volumes of the August trilogy. Common to all of Hamsun's protagonists is their essential difference from the average person. This difference can be positive or negative, but it always makes for a character whom the reader will find interesting.

Hamsun's earliest novel of significance, *Hunger*, has as its setting Kristiania (now Oslo), a city where Hamsun had many unhappy experiences. The greater number of his later novels are set in northern Norway, where the author had lived most of his childhood and youth and where he spent a significant part of his manhood. Most of the action in these novels also takes place in the period of Hamsun's youth, the 1870's and the early 1880's. There is therefore good reason to regard his fiction as fundamentally autobiographical. He never tired of writing about the experiences of his youth, on which he reflected throughout his long career as a novelist.

HUNGER

Hunger, Hamsun's first novel of any importance, was also the first modern psychological novel in Norwegian literature. It is the story of a young writer of exceptional sensibility who, stripped of all of his property and without any secure means of support, is about to succumb to starvation in Norway's capital city of Kristiania. This first-person novel is highly autobiographical; Hamsun had experienced the same degree of destitution on several occasions, most notably in the winter of 1886. Such experiences were surely not unusual among artists at the time; the importance of *Hunger* lies not in its subject matter but rather in the manner in which the author deals with it.

The total narrated time of the novel is two months. The narration is, however, concentrated on four periods during which the narrator suffers greatly from hunger; the author does not appear to be interested in the three periods of time between them when the protagonist seems to live a relatively normal life. The narrator is clearly an individual who earlier was somewhat better off economically, but no reasons for the decline of his fortune are given. Only a few details concerning his identity are mentioned, and these details do not even include his name.

The novel also has but little action in the traditional sense. With the exception of the story of a few attempts made by the narrator to secure employment, as well as the tale of a brief encounter with a lady of the middle class, the text is almost exclusively made up of reports of the narrator's mental life during periods of extreme hunger.

The stream-of-consciousness technique employed by Hamsun is effective in portraying the strange workings of the mind while in an altered state resulting from a lack of nourishment. The reader is given access both to the perceptions, moods, and strange ideas of the narrator and to his reflections on his own state of consciousness. The narrator perceives himself as an artist, and his chief concern is twofold: on one hand, to prevent his hunger from negatively affecting those sensibilities which make him capable of producing art and, on the other hand, to utilize his unpleasant experiences in his art. The narrator's strong tendency toward self-observation can be viewed both as a means of making sure that the demands of his body do not conquer his mental or artistic needs and as part of his artistic project, the gathering of material for the novel which the reader has before him.

Hamsun is interested not in the physical effects of starvation per se, but only in its consequences for the mind. This attitude stands in direct opposition to the prevailing trends in Scandinavian literature at the time. A case in point is Arne Garborg's novel *Bondestudentar* (1883; students from the country), in which the protagonist, like the narrator in *Hunger*, suffers from starvation in the city of Kristiania. The difference is that, unlike Hamsun, Garborg portrays only the physical and social consequences of hunger. In contrast, the attitude of Hamsun's narrator toward his hunger could indeed be termed one of experimentation.

It is a question, however, whether Hamsun the artist was as exclusively concerned with the mental side of life as he claimed to be in his 1891 lectures. The narrator's attention to a mysterious young woman of the middle class does not seem to originate in any specific interest in art, but rather in a concern with the social position that can be won by a successful artist or by a young man who has success in any endeavor. The narrator-protagonist in *Hunger*, like his creator Hamsun, can also be regarded as a practical man for whom art is a means of social advancement at least as much as an end in itself.

PAN

In *Hunger*, Hamsun's autobiographical tendencies manifest themselves both in his choice of subject matter and in the location of the action. In *Pan*, the story occurs at a fictional place in northern Norway called Sirilund, but the social milieu is the same as that which Hamsun had known so well in his youth. In this novel, the theme of art is subservient to that of love, but the social function of love in *Pan* is similar to that of art in *Hunger*.

Unlike the narrative situation of *Hunger*, that of *Pan* is quite complex. The novel consists of two parts, the main text and a brief epilogue entitled "Glahn's Death." Both the text proper and the epilogue are narrated in the first person, but while the main part of the book is narrated by its protagonist, a lieutenant named Thomas Glahn, the epilogue is narrated by his hunting companion and killer, a man whose name is not given.

The main story takes place during the summer

months of the year 1855. Lieutenant Glahn is an outsider who has obtained leave from his commission and who is now leading a rather primitive life as a hunter and fisherman in a cabin near the trading post Sirilund. Tired of urban life and incapable of getting along well according to the norms of cultured society, he has immersed himself in nature, attempting to live as part of it. His intermediary position between nature and culture is symbolized by the fact that his cabin is located where the forest meets the fields surrounding Sirilund. In narrating the story, Glahn tells both about the external events of his life in nature and about his reflections on his existence, and from his story, it would appear that he is entirely successful in his attempts to live as an integral part of the natural world. It is clear, however, that he is far too reflective to lay claim to a natural existence entirely unmediated by culture. This and other signs of unreliability are of great significance to any interpretation of the book.

During visits to the trading post at Sirilund, Glahn meets the young Edvarda, the daughter of the post's owner, the trader Mack. Glahn falls in love with Edvarda, who—because of her father's wealth—is his social superior. A love-hate relationship develops between the two, and each tortures the other in turn.

Glahn's love for Edvarda is not an end in itself, however, but rather a means to social advancement. Glahn would simply like to inherit Mack's position of wealth, power, and prestige by marrying his only daughter. Edvarda, on her part, sees in Glahn an opportunity to get away from Sirilund. Glahn's true intentions are revealed by the fact that he has an affair with a young woman named Eva, the wife of a local blacksmith, as soon as he discovers that Mack uses her to satisfy his erotic needs. For Glahn, the affair is little more than a way symbolically to assume Mack's social position, but when the trader discovers it, he punishes them by having Eva killed and by forcing Glahn to leave the place.

Glahn tells the story two years later. The outward reason for his telling the story at this time is that he has just received a message from Edvarda, who is now married to another man. That Glahn writes down the story establishes as a fact, however, something

that is at best implied in the text, namely that Glahn must also be regarded as an artist. It is necessary to be aware of that when the epilogue, "Glahn's Death," is considered.

The epilogue bears the date 1861, which places its narration four years after the telling of the main part of the story. There is, however, no indication of how much time has passed between the events themselves and the telling of them.

The story in the epilogue is about how Glahn causes the unnamed narrator to take his life by making him jealous and taunting him. Glahn apparently wants to die, and this desire has at least in part been brought about by another letter from Edvarda, who cannot forget him. Glahn's killer writes down the story ostensibly in order to make it clear to the dead man's family that there is no longer any need to inquire about his whereabouts through newspaper advertisements. He seems to be unaware that by so doing, he incriminates himself.

The signs of unreliability that can be found in the main portion of the novel, however, together with the curious narrative situation in the epilogue, make it reasonable to suspect that the narrator of the epilogue is indeed Glahn himself, who has simply made up the story of his death as a final attempt to inflict pain on Edvarda. This interpretation is quite reasonable in view of the fact that when Edvarda learns of Glahn's supposed death, as it is told in Hamsun's later novel *Rosa*, it indeed causes her much grief.

Pan is one of Hamsun's most complex novels. Many critics regard it as his finest work from the 1890's, and some claim that it is his masterpiece. It clearly sets forth Hamsun's view of the relationship between power, love, and the artistic temperament.

SEGELFOSS TOWN

Published in 1915, *Segelfoss Town* stands in the middle of Hamsun's oeuvre. A continuation of *Children of the Age*, which appeared two years earlier, it is also composed in such a manner that it can be read as a separate work. If its criticism of contemporary society is to be evaluated, however, it is helpful to have some familiarity with the earlier work.

Segelfoss is a small community in northern Norway, consisting mainly of a flour mill and the large estate from which the community has derived its name. For generations, the farm and the mill have been owned by the Holmsen family, which by its inherited wealth and benevolent aristocracy has lent order and stability to the community. In *Children of the Age*, however, it is learned that business has been going poorly for the Holmsens, and when an opportunity to sell the flour mill arises, its owner eagerly accepts.

The new owner is Tobias Holmengraa, a local boy of peasant stock who has accumulated a fortune by means of rather mysterious dealings while abroad. Holmengraa is, within Hamsun's artistic universe, a relation of both the protagonist of *Hunger* and Thomas Glahn, the chief difference being that Holmengraa has both the imagination and the financial wherewithal to attempt to realize his social daydream. Once in the possession of the flour mill, he creates a new age for Segelfoss, which may now rightfully refer to itself as a town. There is an abundance of employment and, consequently, money to be had; a trader, a distant relative of Holmengraa, is asked to come and set up a store; a telegraph station is established; and both a lawyer and a doctor arrive.

Thus, new centers of power are created. The most obvious one is Holmengraa's business, but the store also becomes a means to the accumulation of wealth, especially when Theodor, the son of the original owner, takes over after his father. Through his portrayal of social and economic change, Hamsun analyzes the process by which the old and semifeudal social order vanishes and is replaced by a twentieth century social reality. He strongly voices his distrust of the new, mainly through the character Baardsen, the telegraphist, who is also a musician, something of a philosopher, and a drunkard. A character who is split and divided, he is by far the most interesting figure in the book; in the end, he takes his own life, unable to bear the tension in his existence.

The third-person narrator also allows his voice to be heard directly. What he finds most objectionable in modern life is the absence of respect for authority, especially that of the employer, the new money-based economy, and the fact that talented young people leave the class into which they have been born and

through education degenerate into clergymen, doctors, and lawyers. The view that is advanced by the author is thus a totally reactionary one, one that Hamsun later, unfortunately, did not distinguish from the ideology of the Nazi Party and that eventually caused his treason during World War II.

Segelfoss Town, however, is much more than a reactionary tract. If justice is to be done to it as a work of art, it must also be read as a novel about life in all of its variety. In the end, Holmengraa goes bankrupt as a result of his emphasis on the outward show of wealth and his lack of sound business practices, the flour mill is shut down, and the future becomes uncertain for the many workers who have depended on this entrepreneur and charlatan. The disaster is not a victory for Hamsun's reactionary views, however, but rather one for the inhabitants of Segelfoss, who despite economic misfortune find a way to get by. Life itself continues independent of the fates of individuals.

GROWTH OF THE SOIL

Hamsun had used *Segelfoss Town* as a means of voicing his distrust of the development of modern society. In *Growth of the Soil*, he expressed the same norms, but he attempted to prescribe a positive remedy for social ills by giving his public an example worthy of emulation. His rhetorical success is perhaps most clearly indicated by the fact that the novel earned for him the Nobel Prize in 1920.

The protagonist of *Growth of the Soil* is Isak Sellanraa, a man without a past but also without any of the cultural baggage of contemporary life. One day, he is walking through the wilderness somewhere in northern Norway, searching for a place to settle down and make a home for himself, his situation not unlike that of many Norwegian immigrants to America. The American immigrant pioneer was a well-known figure in Norway; Hamsun used the comparison in order to point out that breaking new soil in one's own land is better than emigrating.

The first part of the book details the growth of Isak's farm as he clears the land, builds shelter, and acquires both farm animals and a wife, Inger. The qualitative difference between the man and his wife is indicated by the fact that he has been given the name of an Old Testament patriarch, while her name, Inger, is a common one. Inger is an entirely ordinary person; she casts her lot with the antisocial Isak only because she has a harelip and is therefore unable to find a husband in any other way. Inger is possessed by fear that one of her children will inherit her defect, which indeed happens to her third baby, a girl. Knowing the suffering that is in store for the infant, Inger kills her, later confesses her crime, and is sent to prison for five years.

During this time, she has an operation on her lip, is educated in modern life, and, in Hamsun's view, is spoiled by civilization. When she returns, she is no longer satisfied with the simple life of the farm. This division in Isak's family is then extended to the children; one of his two sons remains a solid young man, while the other is sent to town and is finally fit for nothing but immigration to America.

While Isak is struggling to maintain his (and Hamsun's) values in his home, civilization closes in on the farm, both through the arrival of more settlers and through the discovery of copper ore in a nearby mountain, which leads to the establishment of a mine. The catalyst in this development is a curious character named Geissler, who is a carrier of both Hamsun's values and their opposites. Geissler makes *Growth of the Soil* a complex novel whose value system is perhaps not as clear as it has traditionally been thought to be, and this lack of univocality is indicated by his referring to himself as "the fog" in an important monologue at the end of the book.

Growth of the Soil is undoubtedly Hamsun's most widely read novel. Seductive in both rhetoric and style, the novel makes it difficult for the reader to maintain a proper distance from the author's norms. As a work of art, it is splendid; its values, however, like those of *Segelfoss Town*, are some of those which later led Hamsun to embrace the Nazi ideology.

VAGABONDS

The first volume of a trilogy and the most significant novel from Hamsun's later years, *Vagabonds* is set mainly in northern Norway. It is centered on a community named Polden, similar to Segelfoss but much smaller. There is, for example, no social or economic leader on the order of a Holmsen or even a Holmengraa. In the novel, the Polden environment is significant as a laboratory for the social change that Hamsun so thoroughly despises, but it is also important as the background for one of Hamsun's most tragic characters and for one of his most comical ones.

The tragic character is Edevart, who as a young boy has one of his decisive experiences in the first few pages of the book. During the wintertime, when all the adult males in the community are away at the Lofoten fisheries, Polden is visited by two foreign-looking confidence men who, by appealing to the inhabitants' need for adventure, succeed in tricking them out of whatever small amounts of money they have. Edevart, who at first is taken in by them but then sees through their sham, thus receives his initiation into the deceit and hollowness of the world. As a result, he loses both some of his innocence and much of that innate faith which, if shielded from the attacks of the world, would have aided him in living a life of happiness and satisfaction. This episode is an important one, for it presents Hamsun's thesis that modern civilization is essentially a similar kind of confidence game, albeit on a grander scale, and that its effects on people are similar to those of the strangers on Edevart.

Edevart has another important experience a few years later, when as a young man he encounters a woman named Lovise Magrete Doppen, with whom he falls deeply in love and who initiates him sexually. Shortly thereafter, Lovise Magrete accompanies her husband, an ex-convict who was in jail when Edevart met her, to America. This man, like one of Isak's sons in *Growth of the Soil*, is so depraved that he is fit for nothing but emigration. This experience causes Edevart to lose his trust in the power of love, much as his experience with the confidence men had caused him to lose faith in people. As a result, Edevart becomes a "vagabond in love."

These and similar experiences lead to Edevart's complete demoralization. Dishonesty takes the place of his original honesty, restlessness replaces his sense of belonging in Polden, and dissatisfaction takes the place of his ability to be happy in limited circumstances. The fundamental cause of Edevart's moral decline, however, is not a defect in his personality but the changes that society is undergoing. They include the capitalization of agriculture, the process of industrialization, and the change to a monetary economy, all of which Hamsun opposes. Edevart's development parallels that of society at large.

Hamsun's views, however, are somewhat equivocal. The ambiguity is expressed mainly through the character August, who is one of only two important figures in *Vagabonds* but the clear protagonist of the trilogy of which the novel is the first volume. August has no close relatives; like Tobias Holmengraa in *Segelfoss Town*, he has spent a number of years abroad, and, like Tobias, August is a dreamer. In both *Vagabonds* and the trilogy as a whole, he is an embodiment of the social forces to which Hamsun is opposed. One would, therefore, expect that August should be portrayed as a villain of the highest order, but that is not the case. The author is charmed by him, admires him, and causes the reader to share that admiration. At the same time, Hamsun is critical of what August represents. August therefore expresses Hamsun's ambivalent attitude toward those forces in society that he so soundly condemns. This might be taken as an indication that the author's values are confused, but it could also simply mean that Hamsun, in the final analysis, views life as more complex than any theory or ideology. His tendency to cling to an ideology is, however, present in *Vagabonds* as well as in *Growth of the Soil* and *Segelfoss Town*.

To many present-day readers, Hamsun will seem like a reactionary writer whose values are out of touch with the modern world. There is a fundamental irony in this, as the charge is similar to that which he, in his youth, leveled against his immediate predecessors in Norwegian literature. Even though today's critics thus will find little to admire in Hamsun's value system, his books nevertheless have the power to charm new generations of readers. Hamsun is a master of his craft, of rhetoric, and of style, and he is therefore a true artist whose books attract readers not because of but in spite of some of the values they express.

Jan Sjåvik

OTHER MAJOR WORKS

SHORT FICTION: *Siesta*, 1897; *Kratskog*, 1903; *Stridende liv*, 1905.

PLAYS: *Vid rigets port*, pb. 1895; *Livets spil*, pb. 1896; *Aftenrøde*, pb. 1898; *Munken Vendt*, pb. 1902; *Dronning Tamara*, pb. 1903; *Livet i vold*, pb. 1910 (*In the Grip of Life*, 1924).

POETRY: *Det vilde kor*, 1904.

NONFICTION: *Fra det moderne Amerikas aandsliv*, 1889 (*The Spiritual Life of Modern America*, 1969); *I æventyrland*, 1903; *På gjengrodde stier*, 1949 (memoir; *On Overgrown Paths*, 1967).

BIBLIOGRAPHY

Brown, Berit I., ed. *Nordic Experiences: Exploration of Scandinavian Cultures*. Westport, Conn.: Greenwood Press, 1997. See essay 21, "The Ocean of Consciousness Novel I: *Hunger* by Knut Hamsun—Progenitor of Modernism." Also see essay 22, "Knut Hamsun in His Letters."

Buttry, Dolores. "Knut Hamsun and the Rousseaunian Soul." *Scandinavica* 19 (1980): 121-138. Useful as a different approach, emphasizing the Romantic as well as the realistic elements in Hamsun's fiction.

Ferguson, Robert. *Enigma: The Life of Knut Hamsun*. New York: Farrar, Straus & Giroux, 1987. The best available biography in English, with a comprehensive bibliography.

McFarlane, J. W. "The Whisper of the Blood: A Study of Knut Hamsun's Early Novels." *PMLA* 71 (1956): 563-575. A frequently cited article; especially fruitful when read in conjunction with Buttry.

Mazor, Yair. *The Triple Cord: Agnon, Hamsun, Strindberg: Where Scandinavian and Hebrew Literature Meet*. Tel Aviv, Israel: Papyrus, 1987. Six chapters exploring Hamsun's influence on Hebrew literature, with extensive notes but no bibliography. This work is more wide-ranging than its title suggests. It draws on the best scholarship in both literatures, exploring the fundamental problems of representation in literature and the development of modern fiction.

Naess, Harald. *Knut Hamsun*. Boston: Twayne, 1984.

A good introductory study, with chapters on Hamsun's life and on all of his major novels. Includes chronology, detailed notes, and an annotated bibliography.

Pepperwell, Ronald G. "Interrelatedness in Hamsun's *Mysteries*." *Scandinavian Studies* 38 (1966): 295-301. A good study of character relationships and imagery.

PETER HANDKE

Born: Griffen, Austria; December 6, 1942

PRINCIPAL LONG FICTION

Die Hornissen, 1966

Der Hausierer, 1967

Die Angst des Tormanns beim Elfmeter, 1970 (*The Goalie's Anxiety at the Penalty Kick*, 1972)

Der kurze Brief zum langen Abschied, 1972 (*Short Letter, Long Farewell*, 1974)

Wunschloses Unglück, 1972 (*A Sorrow Beyond Dreams*, 1975)

Die Stunde der wahren Empfindung, 1975 (*A Moment of True Feeling*, 1977)

Die linkshändige Frau, 1976 (*The Left-Handed Woman*, 1978)

Langsame Heimkehr, 1979 (*The Long Way Around*, 1985)

Die Lehre der Sainte-Victoire, 1980 (*The Lesson of Mont Sainte-Victoire*, 1985)

Kindergeschichte, 1981 (*Child Story*, 1985)

Der Chinese des Schmerzes, 1983 (*Across*, 1986)

Slow Homecoming, 1985 (includes *The Long Way Around*, *The Lesson of Mont Sainte-Victoire*, and *Child Story*)

Die Wiederholung, 1986 (*Repetition*, 1988)

Die Abwesenheit: Ein Märchen, 1987 (*Absence*, 1990)

Nachmittag eines Schriftstellers, 1987 (*The Afternoon of a Writer*, 1989)

Mein Jahr in der Niemandsbucht: Ein Märchen aus den neuen Zeiten, 1994 (*My Year in the No-Man's-Bay*, 1998)

In einer dunklen Nacht ging ich aus meinem stillen Haus, 1997

OTHER LITERARY FORMS

Peter Handke made his debut on the German stage with the drama *Publikumsbeschimpfung* (1966; *Offending the Audience*, 1969). His subsequent dramatic works include *Hilferufe* (1967; *Calling for Help*, 1970), *Kaspar* (1968; English translation, 1969), *Das Mündel will Vormund sein* (1969; *My Foot My Tutor*, 1970), *Quodlibet* (1970; English translation, 1976), *Der Ritt über den Bodensee*, 1971 (*The Ride Across Lake Constance*, 1972), *Die Unvernünftigen sterben aus* (1973; *They Are Dying Out*, 1975), *Über die Dörfer* (1982; *Among the Villages*, 1984), *Das Spiel vom Fragen: Oder die reise zum sonoren Land* (1989; *Voyage to the Sonorous Land: Or, The Art of Asking*, 1996); and *Die Stunde da wir nichts voneinander wussten* (1992; *The Hour We Knew Nothing of Each Other*, 1996).

After publishing several radio plays in the early

(Jerry Bauer)

1970's, Handke wrote a film script, *Chronik der laufenden Ereignisse* (1971; chronicle of occurring events), which he also produced, and a television script, *Falsche Bewegung* (1975; wrong move). He has collaborated frequently with film producer/director Wim Wenders and was the screenwriter (with Wenders) for Wenders's 1987 film, *Der Himmel über Berlin* (*Wings of Desire*). An early collection of short stories, *Begrüssung des Aufsichtsrats* (1967; saluting the trustees), should also be noted. Handke's collection of poetry *Die Innenwelt der Aussenwelt der Innen welt* (1969; *The Innerworld of the Outerworld of the Innerworld*, 1974) gives poetic expression to his recurring concern with language as its phrases, in their description of the outer world, simultaneously reflect the inner world or consciousness of the author and vice versa. These concerns have also been raised in several of Handke's critical essays, notably *Ich bin ein Bewohner des Elfenbeinturms* (1972; I am an inhabitant of the ivory tower).

ACHIEVEMENTS

With the sudden and unprecedented advent of Handke on the German literary scene in 1966, the era of postwar German literature, which had tried to come to terms with World War II and the Nazi past, reached its conclusion. Handke is the representative of a new generation of German writers for whom the Federal Republic of Germany constitutes the societal reality that furnishes the material and the conflicts that inform their works. Born in Austria, then reared in East Berlin for some years before returning to Austria, Handke regards the new Germany with the eyes of an outsider who nevertheless possesses an insider's intimate knowledge of his subject. Handke's stance as an outsider is reflected in his disregard for social problems, unless they reflect his primary concern for language: In the midst of the student revolts of the late 1960's, he became one of the first writers in West Germany to emphasize that changes in the political realities of the new republic would not come about through protest resolutions or political manifestos but rather through the exact use of the word, the honesty of literary expression, and the truth of fiction (as Manfred Durzak notes). The majority of

Handke's West German fellow writers recognized the validity of his claim only after the fall of Willy Brandt as chancellor in 1974.

Handke's outsider's attempts at registering German societal developments and their effects upon the individual are in some ways mirrored on a larger and certainly less intellectual scale by frequent media attempts in Germany today in which the social and economic ills of that society are blamed on America, from which they have supposedly been imported. In contrast, Handke traces the ills that afflict his characters to the larger ills of German society. Under these circumstances, it becomes noteworthy that in two of his novels, *Short Letter, Long Farewell* and *The Long Way Around*, Handke has depicted America's untouched nature as regenerative, offering the possibility of spiritual rebirth for his protagonists. Such a special relationship with America is perhaps connected to the fact that Handke's own birth as an author of prominence took place in the United States rather than in Germany.

In Princeton in early 1966, at the conference of the West German writers' group, Gruppe 47, Handke was suddenly pushed into the limelight not so much for his literary production—which was just getting under way—as for his attacks upon the production of the German literary establishment at that time. The young outsider Handke had recently had his first novel, *Die Hornissen* (the hornets), accepted by the renowned German publishers Suhrkamp Verlag, under whose auspices he was more or less incidentally invited to participate at the conference. There, he immediately affronted the German literary establishment, proclaiming that their writings were characterized by a sterile descriptive tedium and a total disregard for the dimension most essential to literary realization—namely, language itself. During the next few years, Handke wrote in almost every genre imaginable, while his theme remained always the same. In his prose, his drama, and his poetry, his mission was to question the value of life in a modern age of directed mass communication, whose net of linguistic standards had entangled the individual, leaving him no room for self-expression. Literature should, therefore, make the individual conscious of himself again.

Handke perceived a metareality beyond the barriers of language, and only the perception of this reality would render the material character of language obvious.

The intensity of Handke's metaphysical search led to his second creative phase, in the early 1970's, when the author's private life began to play an ever-increasing role in his prose. Several critics have termed this "autobiographical" phase Handke's most fruitful and accomplished period; during these years, he wrote his best-known novels, *The Goalie's Anxiety at the Penalty Kick*, *Short Letter, Long Farewell*, and *A Sorrow Beyond Dreams*.

In his later prose and drama, written after the late 1970's, Handke's ego seems to have attained a somewhat inflated stature of "well-practiced narcissism," as one critic has observed. Handke exhibits the visionary zeal of a religious prophet in such novels as *The Long Way Around* and *The Lesson of Mont Sainte-Victoire*. Similar tendencies are obvious in his diary, *Das Gewicht der Welt* (1977; *The Weight of the World*, 1984). Handke is quoted as having uttered in this context, "I don't aspire to being a star, but a figure with certain mystical intentions . . . I would not mind that at all." It should be noted that Handke has won most of the prestigious literary awards available to German-language writers.

BIOGRAPHY

Peter Handke's early literary revolt against all repressive systems of rules and social customs and against the experience of daily dependency and dull coercive repetition is certainly linked to his birth and upbringing in a poor working-class environment. His birthplace, Griffen, in the province of Carinthia, Austria, lies about twenty-five miles northeast of Klagenfurt, the only sizable city in the region, and only a few miles from the border with Yugoslavia. Handke's maternal grandfather, of Slovak descent, was a peasant and carpenter; his mother, the fourth of five children, worked as a dishwasher, maid, and cook during the war and became pregnant with Handke by a German soldier, a bank clerk in civilian life, who was already married. Before Handke's birth, his mother married another German soldier,

Bruno Handke, in civilian life a streetcar conductor in Berlin. In 1944, Maria Handke moved to Berlin with her son to await her husband's return from the war. For some time after 1945, Handke's stepfather continued to work as a streetcar conductor in Berlin, until in 1948 he moved his family to Griffen, where he found employment with Maria's father. The stepfather's alcoholism, the cramped quarters—the family, by then numbering six, shared two attic rooms—and the backwardness of the region became increasingly oppressive for the young Handke. After attending the local elementary school, he finally escaped from his hated stepfather and the confines of home by entering a parochial boarding school near Klagenfurt.

At the parochial school, the quiet and serious-minded Handke remained isolated from his fellow pupils. His superior intelligence allowed him to catch up on a year's work in Latin within a short time, and to become the best student in class. His German teacher recognized his writing talent and encouraged him to publish his first short stories in the school newspaper. Through this teacher, Handke became acquainted with the works of Thomas Wolfe and William Faulkner, among others. Handke, however, soon felt the pressure of conformity at this school, with its expressed purpose of preparing young men for the priesthood, and he changed schools once more, to attend the *gymnasium* in Klagenfurt, from which he graduated in 1961. Apparently his former teacher advised Handke upon graduation to enter law school so that the young man might have enough time to pursue his love of writing and reflection. He entered the University of Graz, where he soon came into contact with an avant-garde group of young writers. He was able to publish in their literary magazine, and in 1963 a short story by Handke was broadcast over a regional radio station.

In Graz, Handke met the actress Libgart Schwarz, whom he married soon afterward. Their daughter, Amina, was born in 1969, and in 1972 Handke and his wife separated; Amina continued to live with him. Handke's marriage and divorce and his daughter Amina respectively form the autobiographical cores of the novels *Short Letter, Long Farewell* and *Child*

Story. In November, 1971, Handke's mother committed suicide. Handke was deeply shaken by her death; it rekindled long-suppressed memories of his own childhood and of his mother's life of constant stricture and monotony, from which she freed herself through voluntary death. Within a few months, Handke wrote *A Sorrow Beyond Dreams,* which several critics consider to be his best work.

Repeated moves and frequent travel characterized Handke's life in the decade after 1965. His spectacular appearance at the 1966 conference of Gruppe 47 had launched his career as a serious and financially independent writer, and he quit law school after having passed several preliminary examinations with distinction. His travels led him to Romania, to Yugoslavia, and, in 1971, on a second trip through the United States. During that decade, he moved several times: In 1966, he left Graz for Düsseldorf; in 1968, he moved to Berlin; in 1969, to Paris; in 1971, to Cologne; in 1972, to Kronberg (outside Frankfurt). In 1975, Handke moved back to Paris, thereafter living in Salzburg, the setting for *Across.*

In 1978-1979 Handke was in United States, and in the late 1980's he went on extended trips and hiking tours in Europe, Alaska, and Japan. His main residence from 1979 to 1991 was in Salzburg, which honored him in 1986 with the City of Salzburg Prize for Literature. In 1987 he received the Great Austrian State Prize.

Handke is a versatile writer; he is not only a novelist, poet, and playwright but also a literary translator, screenwriter, and film director. He and German director and producer Wim Wenders have collaborated on a number of films, including three films of Handke's novels: *The Goalie's Anxiety at the Penalty Kick* (1971), *The Left-Handed Woman* (1978), and *The Absence* (1993). Handke was the screenwriter for Wender's successful film *Wings of Desire* (1987). In 1991 Handke moved close to Paris in Chaville, France, where a second daughter was born.

Handke chose to take a winter honeymoon trip through war-torn Serbia in November of 1995. His account of the trip, *Eine winterliche Reise zu den Flüssen Donau, Save, Morawa and Drina: Oder, Gerechtigkeit für Serbien* (1996; *A Journey to the Rivers: Justice for Serbia,* 1997), unleashed a storm of protest in the German press. Handke's observations are personal and geographical and portray the Serbians as ordinary human beings. By ignoring the political situation and not prejudging the Serbians on the basis of press reports, Handke reinforced his reputation as a polemicist. More important, he and his publisher, Suhrkamp, strongly defended the right of authors to think for themselves.

ANALYSIS

"Every story distracts me from my real story. Through its fiction it makes me forget myself and my situation. It makes me forget the world." With this statement from his artistic credo, *Ich bin ein Bewohner des Elfenbeinturms* (I am an inhabitant of the ivory tower), Peter Handke demonstrated not only the intent of his writing but also his relationship to the art of fiction. For the author Handke and for his reader, the familiar fictional methods of describing the world are no longer valid, since their familiarity is evidence that they are not descriptions of the world itself, but rather copies of other descriptions. Such copies cannot render any new insights; it is the primary function of genuine literature to break open all seemingly finite concepts of the world. The familiarity with and acceptance of the customary methods of description render society incapable of sensing that it is not the world which is being described but rather the method of description, which finally becomes completely automated in a "trivial realism," in advertising and modern mass communication.

Handke's purpose in writing is to gain clarity about himself, to get to know himself, to learn what he does wrong, what he says without thinking, what he says automatically. His goal is to become more attentive and to make other people so—to become more sensitive, more exact in his communication with other people. Improved communication becomes possible through a close investigation of the vehicle of communication itself—namely, language. Handke's method in his investigation is to observe how he, as an individual, continually grows into a linguistic "adulthood" through an increasing awareness of his encounters with the everyday world, with its commonplaces, its extraordinary situations, its images, and particularly its words.

As the objects of the outside world become in the true sense of the word "literal" in the mind, they can be expressed only through the words assigned to them. Their power as signature diminishes, however, as soon as the true reality behind the words is forgotten. Handke's argumentation is indebted to the philosophy of Ludwig Wittgenstein, who postulated that language can never be employed as an instrument in the search for truth, since reality itself is obstructed by the tautological fiction of language.

For Handke it therefore becomes essential to transcend the signature character to reach the real object. This can be accomplished by making the reader conscious of the mere signature character of the word and thereby emphasizing the actual reality behind it. Handke renders the signature character of a given word, phrase, or even story obvious through the conscious—perhaps self-conscious—use of language, syntax, and plot structure. These become the "material" through which the individual gains access to the "real reality" beyond. This "real reality" no longer requires the invention of a fable in the traditional sense; as a matter of fact, such fiction obviously hampers access to it. Handke is concerned with the transmission of experiences, linguistic and nonlinguistic, and for this purpose a conventional story is no longer needed. He concedes that literature might lose some of its "entertainment value" through this method, but through it, the reader gains the "real" aspect of each individual sentence, and the individual word in a sentence, once the obstructive fable is stripped away.

DIE HORNISSEN

Handke's first two novels, *Die Hornissen* and *Der Hausierer* (the peddler), illustrate his theoretical position. They are novels without plots, becoming—in the case of *Die Hornissen*—linguistic exercises which bore the reader to the level of exhaustion, as one critic remarked. *Die Hornissen* represents the creative process of writing a novel rather than the end result of that process. The narrator acts out the perennial dilemma of the writer, who must make choices at all times and who does not—as the reader might imagine from the finished product—have firm control over the action and the characters of the story which he unfolds. Thus, there is no continuity of plot in *Die Hornissen*; instead, there is continuous vacillation between descriptions and explanations, fantasies and dreams. This novel is a writer's confession about the difficulties encountered during his work. Such difficulties can be illustrated only through a plot which the narrator is attempting more or less successfully to construct; thus, there is the trace of a conventional story in *Die Hornissen*. The novel is about two brothers, or perhaps three. One of them has become blind while searching for the second one. A war may have had some influence upon his blindness. On a Sunday, much later, the blind brother awakens and is reminded of his absent brother by something that remains rather vague in his mind. The periodic arrival of the local commuter bus seems to be important for the blind man, who shares a house with his father and his second wife. The Sunday events are reminiscent of events during the war. Shortly before the end of the novel, there is a hint at a possible connection among all these disjointed elements. The blind narrator thinks of a book, possibly with the title *Die Hornissen*, which he once read. He vaguely remembers some of the events in the book, while he has forgotten particulars. The events still remembered begin to change and become superimposed on events from the present.

DER HAUSIERER

Handke had observed that a method of description can be used only once before its repetition becomes the description of the method rather than that of the world, and his second novel, *Der Hausierer*, was an attempt to salvage and revivify a method made moribund by repetition. In it, Handke begins with the perception that the detective story has a plot structure which is always the same, with the same descriptive clichés of murder, death, fear and fright, pursuit and torture. By making his readers conscious of the signature character of these clichés, he wanted to show the true human emotions of fear and pain behind them. *Der Hausierer*, with its barren attempt at making "real reality" perceptible behind a huge inventory of detective-story clichés, has been deemed a monumental failure in novel writing.

THE GOALIE'S ANXIETY AT THE PENALTY KICK

Some early critics thought that this failure, as well as possible difficulties in discovering constantly new descriptive methods, might have forced Handke back into a more conventional narrative stance in his third novel, *The Goalie's Anxiety at the Penalty Kick*. The novel indeed possesses a continuously unfolding plot, clearly defined characters, and a recognizable setting and time frame. Nevertheless, Handke did not abandon his original intention of discovering metaperspectives for himself and his readers. Rather than focusing on language, his investigation this time concentrates on the reliability of psychological causality as it is conventionally depicted in literature. The leitmotif of the novel is the false interpretation of a gesture by the protagonist, Josef Bloch—an "insignificant" event that sets in motion everything which happens thereafter. By describing Bloch's reaction, Handke again questions the validity of a "signature."

A construction worker who was once a well-known soccer goalie, Josef Bloch thinks that he has been fired from his job. Nothing has been said to him to indicate his termination; Bloch has interpreted as a sign of his dismissal the fact that only the foreman looked up from his lunch when Bloch entered the workers' shack, while the other workers continued eating. Out of work, Bloch roams the streets and frequents cheap restaurants and motion-picture houses. He sleeps with a film usherette, Gerda, whom he chokes to death the following morning. He flees to a small border village to hide out with a former acquaintance, Herta, an innkeeper. The police have no leads in the murder case, yet Bloch's reactions and observations of his surroundings are those of a hunted man. He interprets every event in the village—a missing child who accidentally drowned, inquisitive policemen, customs officials on guard—as connected to him alone. The novel's last scene shows a soccer field, where Bloch asks a bystander to observe the game from the perspective of the goalie, for a change, rather than from that of the players. Bloch's whole life by now has assumed the typical reactive attitude of a goalie defending against a penalty kick, who must try to anticipate the direction in which the opposing player will kick the ball. A comparison to Franz Kafka's *Die Verwandlung* (1915; *Metamorphosis*, 1936) seems to offer itself, as Bloch also undergoes an inner metamorphosis and loses contact with his environment. Handke has stated that it was his intention to portray a protagonist for whom the environment proceeded to turn into a "signature" as a consequence of a single event—namely, the murder: "A schizophrenic interprets every event as alluding to himself. This is the principle behind the story, yet the process is not applied to a schizophrenic, but rather to a 'normal' protagonist." *The Goalie's Anxiety at the Penalty Kick* became a best-seller in Germany shortly after its publication, and it established Handke's reputation in the United States as one of the foremost modern German-language writers.

SHORT LETTER, LONG FAREWELL

In 1972, Handke published two well-received novels, *Short Letter, Long Farewell* and *A Sorrow Beyond Dreams*. The detective-story cliché of the pursuit, which Handke had used in *The Goalie's Anxiety at the Penalty Kick*, is varied once more in *Short Letter, Long Farewell*. The narrator is at once the victim and the detective-observer of the pursuit. The adoption of first-person narrative in this novel as well as in *A Sorrow Beyond Dreams* is significant. Handke's earlier linguistic experimentation, which he had largely overcome in *The Goalie's Anxiety at the Penalty Kick*, was abandoned altogether to make room for the author-narrator's ego and its relationship to the surrounding world. Destabilizing events in Handke's personal life contributed to this new perspective; in an interview, he stated that these events had led to an expansion of his definition of himself. His mother's death, the birth of his daughter, and the protracted proceedings surrounding his divorce from his wife brought on the realization that the automatisms of life itself were as unreliable as the linguistic ones had been found to be. The autobiographical component would be overstated, however, if one were to assume that these events triggered the writing of the two novels in order simply to free the author from his emotional distress. Handke asserted that he had planned the writing of a *Bildungsroman*, a label frequently applied to *Short Letter, Long Farewell*, for almost ten years prior to its date of publication. Also, the novel does remain a typical Handke product, because, in contrast to the traditional novel of education, it educates its author rather than the protagonist.

The author-narrator, no longer merely Handke's abstract alter ego sifting through possible literary methods and models, has become a concrete and discernible individual in his appeal to himself to know and experience more of the world per se in order to reach his goal of cognition. Handke's former protest against stagnant literary conventions has thus given way to his attempt to find the communicative possibilities inherent in his own earlier models. In *Short Letter, Long Farewell*, Handke has gone forward another step in his quest for truth, now seeking the moral veracity of his own writing. The narrator asserts at the end that "all this has really happened," which is, of course, not true in a factual sense, since Handke never really met the filmmaker John Ford, as depicted in the last scene of the novel. The "real happening" has taken place inside the author-narrator. Repeated statements in the work indicate that Handke had by then separated himself completely from his earlier linguistic experiments as purely evasive maneuvers, in order to come to terms with his literary environment.

The assessment of a nonliterary and very real environment, which Bloch had attempted unsuccessfully in *The Goalie's Anxiety at the Penalty Kick*, is taken up by the narrator-author of *Short Letter, Long Farewell*, who has traveled to America in search of a new self. The firm ground of his prior existence has begun to sway during the separation from his wife. The fears of his childhood as well as present anxieties and threats must be raised from the subconscious to the level of consciousness. Only then can the narrator, at long last, free himself from them, bid them good-bye, and achieve a new sense of life without fear. The stations of his journey through America become the symbolic backdrop for his gradual liberation. Time and space form a curious congruity in the novel, as the narrator travels from east to west. America's geographic east-west progression in time from infancy to maturity becomes the larger reflection upon the narrator's development, as in St. Louis he separates from his traveling companion Claire and

her daughter Benedictine. (Their names are certainly symbolic as well.) The child, through her sudden outbreaks of fright, has helped him to comprehend his own childhood fears. A happily married couple in St. Louis serves as a foil in the narrator's assessment of his ended marriage. After these events, he can embark upon his journey to the new frontiers of America and his own life.

The novel is divided into two parts, entitled "Short Letter" and "Long Farewell," both of which are prefaced by a quotation from a *Bildungsroman*. The first part is prefaced by a passage from *Anton Reiser* (1785-1790), by Karl Philipp Moritz, an eighteenth century writer and companion of Johann Wolfgang von Goethe. The book, written in the form of an autobiographical account, was of great historical importance to the development of psychological fiction, as it entered the innermost depths of the soul and at the same time attempted to be an objective sociocritical and pedagogical account of the age, thereby combining the two prominent currents of Pietism and Enlightenment thought. The relevance of *Anton Reiser* for Handke becomes obvious in its protagonist's disrupted relationship to his environment. He— like Handke's unnamed narrator—draws his sole understanding of his environment from the books which he reads during his journey. The loneliness, estrangement, and fear of Anton Reiser are shared by Handke's traveler in the first part. The second part, "Long Farewell," is prefaced by a quotation from the Swiss writer Gottfried Keller's *Der grüne Heinrich* (1854-1855; *Green Henry*, 1960), in which the protagonist does finally achieve the elusive union between himself and his environment, between the inner world and the outer world.

Short Letter, Long Farewell is the story of an unnamed Austrian first-person narrator who is being pursued by his estranged wife, Judith. He has arrived in America, endowed with sufficient financial means to undertake what might be referred to ironically as the customary nineteenth century *Bildungsreise* (educational journey)—with the typical Handke twist that it is a *Bildungsreise* in reverse, from Europe to America. In Providence, Rhode Island, he receives a letter from Judith advising him not to look for her, as it "would not be nice" to find her. He travels back to New York, on to Washington, and then to a small town in Pennsylvania, where he is joined by Claire and Benedictine, with whom he continues to the Midwest. From St. Louis, he sets off by himself to Arizona and finally to Oregon: Pursuer and pursued meet at Oregon's Hay Stack Rock. Its enormous granite form, standing alone in the midst of the ocean but at the same time in harmonious union with its natural environment, becomes the backdrop for their encounter, as the narrator faces Judith's pointed gun. Together, Judith and the narrator travel on to California to meet John Ford. Ford's film *Young Mr. Lincoln* (1939) had touched the narrator's inner sense of reality, as the people on the screen prefigured those he would soon meet. Like them, he desires to be fully present in body and mind, an equal moving among equals, carried along by their motion yet free to be himself.

A SORROW BEYOND DREAMS

A Sorrow Beyond Dreams replaces the utopian hopefulness of America with a provincial Austrian remembrance of the past, dictated by the finality of death. Handke's mother, who, at the age of fifty-one, lay down to swallow a whole prescription of sleeping pills, bore little resemblance to the young and spirited woman of thirty years earlier. Again, quotations preface the novel, this time by Bob Dylan ("He not busy being born is busy dying") and mystery writer Patricia Highsmith ("Dusk was falling quickly. It was just after 7 P.M., and the month was October"). The quotation of Highsmith is meant to evoke the tone of her novels, which are not tied to spectacular events or extraordinary characters and seem to eschew judgmental statements. Handke's often expressed aversion for characterizing, and thereby judging and degrading, the individual prevails in the *Erzählung* (short narrative). Nevertheless, the author seems to reach far beyond the customary emotional detachment from his earlier and also his later protagonists. *A Sorrow Beyond Dreams* may be considered Handke's first work to strike an emotional chord. In it, as June Schlueter has observed, "the intellectual coldness of the earlier novels gives way to a deeply personal retelling of his mother's life and death."

The metalevel of the narrative, as in *Short Letter, Long Farewell*, remains the differentiated investigation of the author-narrator's ability to perceive his environment as well as an analysis of these perceptions themselves. Thus, the narrator is again the focal point. He explicitly notes the dangerous tendency among abstractions and formulations to grow independent of the person for whose characterization they were created. Consequently, a chain reaction of phrases and sentences sets itself in motion, "as in a dream, a literary ritual in which the life of the individual functions merely as the triggering occasion. Two dangers—the mere realistic retelling of events on the one hand, and the painless disappearance of a person in poetic sentences on the other—these retard my writing." As in his early revolutionary statement at Princeton, Handke thus cautions himself in *A Sorrow Beyond Dreams* against the sterile descriptive tedium of simply retailing a plot, in which he would either permit life itself to tell the story, thereby rendering it without interest to anyone outside his immediate family, or bury the story under an overpowering aesthetic superstructure that would choke it in meaningless poetic formalism.

Handke first had to overcome the stunned perplexity which he felt at reading the obituary notice in the *Kärntner Volkszeitung*. The notice turned his mother's death into a statistic without any further human implication whatsoever. His narration takes its departure from this printed notice: "In the village of A. (G. township), a housewife, aged 51, committed suicide on Friday night by taking an overdose of sleeping pills." Even beyond her death, this woman has thus been denied her existence as an individual. The author-narrator becomes the "remembering and formulating machine" which will restore to his mother what is rightfully hers, at the same time departing, as in *Short Letter, Long Farewell*, on a voyage into his own childhood, which he begins to see in a different light through the description of his mother's life. Two continuous impediments seem to have stifled his mother's attempts at individuation: the socially conditioned, material limitations during her youth, exemplified in the description of the grandfather, and her individually motivated depressions, which she felt as a result of the growing automatisms of her particular life as a woman, for whom a palm reading at the county fair, which was to reveal the future, was nothing but a cruel joke. Handke quotes a rhyme which the girls in her village chanted about the stations in a woman's life: "Tired/ Exhausted/ Sick/ Dying/ Dead."

As the son begins to study at the university, he introduces her to literature: "She read every book as a description of her own life, felt revitalized, learned to speak about herself . . . and so I gradually found out details about her life." Different from those in *Short Letter, Long Farewell*, Maria Handke's visions gleaned from books are only those of the past, making obvious to her the fact that she has no future. Having led his mother to the Tree of Knowledge, the son has become the tempter in the Garden of Eden and therefore is, at least in part, responsible for her death.

A Sorrow Beyond Dreams was Handke's second attempt to "describe the political circumstances as part of an individual story, to connect the individual with the general events." At the same time, the author could reach into himself within a concrete and historically verifiable context instead of his usual private method. This has made *A Sorrow Beyond Dreams* arguably his most lucid and most successful work.

A MOMENT OF TRUE FEELING and THE LEFT-HANDED WOMAN

In *A Moment of True Feeling* and *The Left-Handed Woman*, Handke made two renewed attempts at reaching a higher level of feeling beyond the usual literary clichés. Yet in the same measure in which he strove to depict these truer feelings, he seems to have missed his mark because of an increasing abandonment of a concretely discernible narrative. *A Moment of True Feeling* has been labeled "an angry act of regression," and *The Left-Handed Woman* "as closed as an oyster, a sign- and signal-labyrinth similar to the universe of a schizophrenic, in which language no longer serves the purpose of communicating, but rather to encode communication."

THE WEIGHT OF THE WORLD

The diary *The Weight of the World* is the harbinger of Handke's new perception of the world during the

1980's. German critics have been divided in their response to this work; some have seen it as an "inventory of [Handke's] delusions of grandeur," a "trite game of hide-and-go-seek with notes arbitrarily strung together," while others have regarded it as an expansion of Handke's earlier efforts to overcome the shortfalls and deficiencies of language on a higher and more sophisticated level. Peter Pütz states that *The Weight of the World* is Handke's most radical attempt "to note, catalogue and thus preserve all appearances, experiences and acts of consciousness" in a preselective state, when their value has not yet been conditioned by human judgments. Everything should be freed from the superfluous value which humans attach to it, permitting a fresh assessment of the world's net weight.

THE LONG WAY AROUND

Handke widens the focus from singular things, perceptions, and feelings and the intended preservation of their individual weight in his next novel, *The Long Way Around*. There, he strives to uncover the connection between all things as well as their salutary harmony. During his slow homecoming to Europe from the snowy loneliness of Alaska via California and New York, Valentin Sorger, the protagonist of the novel, rediscovers nature as the new essence of reality. In California, Sorger had lost his sense of space under the impact of his return to civilization; in a New York coffee shop, he regains the consciousness of his "earthen form" and subsequently regards his return to Europe as the beginning of a prophetic revelation. There exists an immediate connection between natural things, which fantasy must uncover or—more skeptically—to which Sorger "must apply his own lie." Glimpses of such nature revelations can be found in Handke's earlier novels—for example, in the heaving cypress tree in *Short Letter, Long Farewell* and in the chestnut-tree leaf in *A Moment of True Feeling*. In *The Long Way Around* and *The Lesson of Mont Sainte-Victoire*, these revelations of nature become the essence of reality altogether.

THE LESSON OF MONT SAINTE-VICTOIRE

In *The Lesson of Mont Sainte-Victoire*, a narrative situated somewhere between a short story and an essay, the protagonist of the trilogy has returned to Europe. The narrative perspective has changed from the third to the first person to allow Handke to supply the theoretical supplement for the trilogy that comprises *The Long Way Around*, *The Lesson of Mont Sainte-Victoire*, and the dramatic poem *Über die Dörfer*. Biblical allusions abound, as well as references to Goethe's *Zur Farbenlehre* (1810; *Theory of Colors*, 1840), in which artistic endeavor overcomes the boundaries between writing and painting, poetry and philosophy, and also between present and past, fact and fantasy. Nature, as revealed in art, becomes the author's weapon against the "calcified Federal Republic which has grown more and more evil" and against the raw brutality of a madly barking dog along the narrator's path. Mont Sainte-Victoire, near the southern French city of Aix-en-Provence, was painted repeatedly by Paul Cézanne during his most creative years after 1870. In these paintings, the narrator perceives the perfect synthesis between the eternal and the transitory, between nature and human endeavor. As the narrator climbs the mountain for a second time, "the realm of the words" lies suddenly open before him, "with the Great Spirit of The Form." He senses the structure of all things in himself as the ready substance of the works which he will write. His future works will be devoted to the metamorphosis of nature into art and the salvation of those things threatened by the human world.

CHILD STORY

Handke's attempt in *Child Story* to repeat the delicate balance of the inner with the outer world, which he had achieved in *A Sorrow Beyond Dreams*, met with mixed reactions from the critics. The narrator's daughter begins to loosen her bonds with him at the age of ten or eleven, and he reflects on her influence on him and his writing during the decade of their lives together. In the spirit of *The Lesson of Mont Sainte-Victoire*, the novel is Handke's attempt at saving the endangered daughter and eternalizing her. Some critics have noted the "insurmountable ego-stylization" in the novel and have criticized Handke for turning his daughter into a marketable commodity; others interpret the book as Handke's successful redemption from the "almost choking solipsism" that

he had displayed in *The Lesson of Mont Sainte-Victoire* and *The Long Way Around*.

ACROSS

His *Across* seems to indicate Handke's return to the messianic stance of those two novels, in this case filtered through the classical restraint of a first-person narrator who is a teacher of Greek and Latin; his name, Loser, might be translated as "the listener." Loser goes further than the protagonists of Handke's earlier novels in his attempts to preserve that which is in danger. He removes language from nature by destroying election posters and slogans which have been attached to trees, and in the second part of the novel, he intervenes decisively by hurling a stone and thereby killing a swastika painter who has desecrated a mountain. "The mountain must remain empty," he triumphs over the murdered man. A circle in Handke's work seems to close with Andreas Loser, a teacher of classical languages and an etymologist whose favorite work is Vergil's *Georgics* (c. 37-29 B.C.E.).

Throughout Handke's novels, the unusually close bond between author and work seems to have been both a source of strength and a liability. Handke's early questioning of the automatisms of postwar German literature—and consequently the automatisms of life altogether—required the undetached participation of the author in his works, for Handke, like the schizophrenic whom he mentions in his discussion of *The Goalie's Anxiety at the Penalty Kick*, needed to interpret every event as alluding to him and him alone. Such a schizophrenic stance made Handke the outsider from the start, and it has led almost automatically to some narcissistic excesses in his novels, in which he has begun to regard himself as an isolated seer who can save himself and the world from the forces of these automatisms through an intense, more direct, and somewhat mystical kinship with nature, as it had already been advocated by his nineteenth century compatriot, the Austrian novelist Adalbert Stifter. Such prophetic visions have naturally antagonized some of Handke's critics, who see him as having moved dangerously close to a Nazi *Blut und Boden Romantik* (blood and earth romanticism).

My Year in the No-Man's-Bay

Handke wrote *My Year in the No-Man's-Bay* in 1993. It is set ahead in 1997–a technique designed to keep vague any references to world events. The main character, Gregor Keuschnig, is soon to be fifty-six. Like Handke, he studied law before becoming a writer, and like Handke, he found himself a single parent after his wife left him. Keuschnig is self-absorbed and goes into great detail about his writing and the landscape in which he feels at home, a place near Paris that he calls the No-Man's-Bay.

As indicated by the subtitle, *A Fairytale from the New Times*, the focus is not on factual events, but on personal perceptions. Keuschnig's goal is "to find the way back to the dreamlike, to keep that basic tone and be clear as sunlight." People interest him most as silhouettes. The less he knows about them, the better they fit into his fantasies. For example, he imagines a singer who feels something healing in him that he did not want healed, a painter who loses his relationship to distance, and a priest who has not yet given up the priesthood, but may.

There are strong undercurrents of emotion as Keuschnig acknowledges the importance of others in establishing his own identity. In his solitude he senses the presence of ancestors who dream on in him. Ana, the wife who left him (twice), is present in his thoughts, interrupting his concentration, and appearing to him in others as her double. A midlife situation that could be seen as sad is instead made to seem unconventional by Keuschnig's eccentricities. Handke's subtle use of language and wry humor sustain the sunlight through a long book.

In einer dunklen Nacht ging ich aus meinem stillen Haus

Handke wrote the novel *In einer dunklen Nacht ging ich aus meinem stillen Haus* in the summer and fall of 1996. The main character, the pharmacist in the small city of Taxham outside Salzburg, likes to read medieval epics, and Handke has worked medieval motifs into the story. Like the knights who set out to seek adventure, the pharmacist leaves his house from July to October to work out his problems on a long trip. During that time he is unable to speak and traverses a landscape that bears no resemblance to present-day Europe. In fact, he wonders at one point if he has ever left the environs of Salzburg.

The trip changes him both outwardly and inwardly for the better. People had previously overlooked him or failed to recognize him outside his pharmacy. On his return, he seems to have more presence. A neighbor's child says: "I know you. You live here. That is your house. You are the pharmacist of Taxham." The pharmacist has come to accept two aspects of his family situation that had previously preyed on his mind. Seeing his son with the gypsies, the pharmacist no longer "disowns" him, but realizes that the boy must go his own way. Second, he understands that he is not the only man whose wife chooses to live separately from him in other parts of the house. This complex, well-crafted novel supports many levels of interpretation.

Klaus Hanson, updated by Jean M. Snook

Other major works

SHORT FICTION: *Begrüssung des Aufsichtsrats*, 1967.

PLAYS: *Publikumsbeschimpfung und andere Sprechstücke*, pr., pb. 1966 (*Offending the Audience*, 1969); *Selbstbezichtigung*, pr., pb. 1966 (*Self-Accusation*, 1969); *Weissagung*, pr., pb. 1966 (*Prophecy*, 1976); *Hilferufe*, pr. 1967 (*Calling for Help*, 1970); *Kaspar*, pr., pb. 1968 (English translation, 1969); *Kaspar and Other Plays*, pb. 1969; *Das Mündel will Vormund sein*, pr., pb. 1969 (*My Foot My Tutor*, 1970); *Quodlibet*, pr. 1970 (English translation, 1976); *Der Ritt über den Bodensee*, pr., pb. 1971 (*The Ride Across Lake Constance*, 1972); *Die Unvernünftigen sterben aus*, pb. 1973 (*They Are Dying Out*, 1975); *The Ride Across Lake Constance and Other Plays*, pb. 1976; *Über die Dörfer*, pr., pb. 1982 (*Among the Villages*, 1984); *Das Spiel vom Fragen: Oder die reise zum sonoren Land*, pb. 1989 (*Voyage to the Sonorous Land: Or, The Art of Asking*, 1996); *Die Stunde da wir nichts voneinander wussten*, pr., pb. 1992 (*The Hour We Knew Nothing of Each Other*, 1996).

SCREENPLAYS: *Chronik der laufenden Ereignisse*, 1971; *Der Himmel über Berlin* (*Wings of Desire*, with Wim Wenders), 1987.

TELEPLAY: *Falsche Bewegung*, 1975.

POETRY: *Die Innenwelt der Aussenwelt der Innenwelt*, 1969 (*The Innerworld of the Outerworld of the Innerworld*, 1974); *Gedicht an die Dauer*, 1986.

NONFICTION: *Ich bin ein Bewohner des Elfenbeinturms*, 1972; *Als das Wünschen noch geholfen hat*, 1974; *Das Gewicht der Welt*, 1977 (journal; *The Weight of the World*, 1984); *Das Ende des Flanierens*, 1980; *Die Geschichte des Bleistifts*, 1982 (journal); *Phantasien der Wiederholung*, 1983 (journal); *Aber ich lebe nur von den Zwischenräumen*, 1987; *Versuch über die Müdigkeit*, 1989; *Versuch über die Jukebox*, 1990; *Versuch über den geglückten Tag*, 1991; *The Jukebox and Other Essays on Storytelling*, 1994 (translation of *Versuch über die Müdigkeit*, *Versuch über die Jukebox*, and *Versuch über den geglückten Tag*); *Eine winterliche Reise zu den Flüssen Donau, Save, Morawa and Drina: Oder, Gerechtigkeit für Serbien*, 1996 (*A Journey to the Rivers: Justice for Serbia*, 1997); *Am Felsfenster morgens: Und andere Ortszeiten 1982-1987*, 1998 (journal).

BIBLIOGRAPHY

Firda, Richard Arthur. *Peter Handke*. New York: Twayne, 1993. An excellent overview of Handke's life and work up to 1987, with interpretations of the major works. A useful chronology, index, and annotated bibliography.

Klinkowitz, Jerome, and James Knowlton. *Peter Handke and the Postmodern Transformation: The Goalie's Journey Home*. Columbia: University of Missouri Press, 1983. A well-organized, appreciative study of Handke's works. Terminology is lucidly defined and illustrated with examples. Convincing refutation of negative criticism.

Linstead, Michael. "Peter Handke." In *The Modern German Novel*, edited by Keith Bullivant. Leamington Spa: Berg, 1987. A good essay that explains Handke's ideas about forms of description and examines their application in the novels. Finds the content lacking.

Perram, Garvin H. C. *Peter Handke: The Dynamics of the Poetics and the Early Narrative Prose*. New York: Peter Lang, 1992. Examines Handke's early works. Includes bibliographical references.

Ran-Moseley, Faye. *The Tragicomic Passion: A History and Analysis of Tragicomedy and Tragicomic Characterization in Drama, Film, and Literature*. New York: Peter Lang, 1994. Explores the tragicomic genre in Handke and Isaac Bashevis Singer.

Rorrison, Hugh. "The 'Grazer Gruppe,' Peter Handke, and Wolfgang Bauer." In *Modern Austrian Writing: Literature and Society After 1945*, edited by Alan Best and Hans Wolfschütz. London: Oswald Wolff, 1980. All quotations are translated into English. Deals succinctly with Handke. Presents the Graz Group as an alternative to the Group of 47 (Gruppe 47).

Schlueter, June. *The Plays and Novels of Peter Handke*. Pittsburgh, Pa.: University of Pittsburgh Press, 1981. Chapters on individual works up to 1979. Includes an interview with Handke. Extensive selected bibliography.

Sharp, Francis Michael. "Peter Handke." In *Major Figures of Contemporary Austrian Literature*, edited by Donald G. Daviau. New York: Peter Lang, 1987. Good overview of the drama, then the prose up to 1983. Places Handke in the context of contemporary German literature.

BARRY HANNAH

Born: Clinton, Mississippi; April 23, 1942

PRINCIPAL LONG FICTION

Geronimo Rex, 1972

Nightwatchmen, 1973

Ray, 1980

The Tennis Handsome, 1983

Hey Jack!, 1987

Boomerang, 1989

Never Die, 1991

OTHER LITERARY FORMS

Barry Hannah has published short stories in *Es-

quire magazine; some of his short fiction has been collected in *Airships* (1978), *Captain Maximus* (1985), *Bats out of Hell*, 1993, and *High Lonesome*, 1996.

ACHIEVEMENTS

Because his fiction is often set in the contemporary South and is characterized by violence and gothic humor, Barry Hannah has most often been compared to William Faulkner, Flannery O'Connor, and Carson McCullers, other southern writers who have explored violent and eccentric human behavior in southern settings. Yet Hannah has a style and an energy that set him apart from others as a highly original American writer. His much-acclaimed first novel, *Geronimo Rex*, was awarded the William Faulkner Prize for Fiction and was nominated for a National Book Award, while *Airships*, his first book of short stories, received the Arnold Gingrich Short Fiction Award (Gingrich was founder and editor of *Esquire* magazine). Hannah has also received a Bellaman Foundation Award in Fiction (1970) and a Bread Loaf Fellowship (1971), and has been honored by the American Academy of Arts and Letters.

BIOGRAPHY

Barry Hannah was born on April 23, 1942, in Clinton, Mississippi, but grew up primarily in Meridian. He attended the public schools in Clinton, playing trumpet in the school band, and went on to Mississippi College, where he received his A.B. degree. He continued his education at the University of Arkansas, where he received both an M.A. and an M.F.A. in creative writing. Hannah began writing his first novel, *Geronimo Rex*, while he was working toward his creative writing degree, and an early version of a chapter from that novel appeared in the first issue of *Intro*, a journal that presented the best work from the nation's university writing programs. Much like Hannah, the protagonist of *Geronimo Rex*, Harry Monroe, is a young man searching for identity in a socially troubled South, and his name, Harry (Barry) Monroe, suggests that the author drew heavily from his own experience. Other fictional work, such as *Boomerang*, also seems to draw upon Hannah's per-

(AP/Wide World Photos)

sonal life: The narrator of *Boomerang* is named Barry, and the novel is set in Clinton and Oxford, where Hannah resides.

Much of Hannah's early fiction was published in *Esquire* magazine, where it received critical acclaim and wide readership. Nine of these stories were among the twenty collected in *Airships*, his finest and best-known collection of short fiction. Hannah is often at his best in short works, and sometimes his novels seem more collections of vignettes and short pieces than expanded unified narratives. Following *Airships* came four novels: *Ray*, *The Tennis Handsome*, *Hey Jack!*, and *Boomerang*. Hannah has also written three other volumes of short stories including *Captain Maximus*, *Bats out of Hell*, and *High Lonesome*, which received excellent reviews and was nominated for the Pulitzer Prize in Fiction.

Except for a brief period in California, where he

worked on film scripts for director Robert Altman, Hannah has for the most part remained in the South, teaching creative writing and literature at Clemson University in South Carolina, at the University of Alabama, and at the University of Mississippi. He has also taught creative writing at the University of Iowa and the University of Montana, and was a writer-in-residence at Middlebury College in Vermont. He is the father of three children, two sons, Barry, Jr., and Ted, and one daughter, Lee, and as of the late 1990's he lived with his third wife, Susan, in Oxford, Mississippi.

Hannah's life and writing have been shaped by many influences, from teachers and musicians to other writers. Music has always been a significant part of Hannah's life (he is often called a "jazz" writer); *Geromimo Rex*, one critic claims, has the best description of marching band music ever written. In interview after interview Hannah notes the impact his high school band director had on his life and writing. At the other end of the musical spectrum, rock and roll legend Jimi Hendrix has had a great impact on Hannah, both for the fury and vision of his music and for the paradoxes of his life and his love of motorcycles. In a more conventional strain, Hannah mentions the influence the poets and professors J. Edgar Simmons and James Whitehead exerted on him during his years at Mississippi College and the University of Arkansas, respectively. Although his style of writing is unique, Hannah cites William Faulkner, James Joyce, and Ernest Hemingway as his literary idols, but he also invokes the names of Henry Miller and John Berryman as kindred spirits. Another spirit, alcohol, however, may have had the most direct bearing on Hannah's writing until he became sober in the early 1990's.

ANALYSIS

Barry Hannah's fiction is populated with the Confederate soldiers, redneck idlers, gifted liars, failed intellectuals, desperate women, and violent men that readers of American literature have come to expect from southern writers, but Hannah's comic inventiveness, dazzling prose, and lopsided view of life make them highly original portraits. Hannah writes like a juiced-up Faulkner, and the reader is often swept along by the sheer manic energy of his narratives. While his fiction is often short on plot, it is full of loopy twists and turns, imaginative surprises, and hilarious nonsense.

GERONIMO REX

Hannah's highly acclaimed first novel, *Geronimo Rex*, is a good example. Owing much to the *Bildungsroman*, the novel of experience that chronicles a young person's rise to maturity, and to picaresque tales of adventurous rogues, *Geronimo Rex* is Hannah's portrait of the artist as a young punk. Growing up in a southern mill town during the 1950's, Harry Monroe, Hannah's principal character, is a complexity of self-hatred and egotism, sensitivity and self-righteousness, artistry and violence. He sees himself in an old photograph of Apache chieftain Geronimo as a rebel warrior in a wild and savage country; he even starts wearing an American Indian kerchief, boots, and a snake-skin jacket, does war dances on top of parked cars, and carries a gun. What he likes about Geronimo, he muses at one point, is that the Native American had "cheated, lied, stolen, usurped, killed, burned, raped, pillaged, razed, trapped, ripped, mashed," and Harry decides that he "would like to go into that line of work." Unlike other fictional depictions of youth in the 1950's—J. D. Salinger's Holden Caulfield in *The Catcher in the Rye* (1951), for example—Harry is no idealist surrounded by hypocritical adults. Harry *is* the world around him—hypocritical, violent, self-centered, and cynical.

In college, Harry becomes involved with mad racist Peter Lepoyster, whose hatred and sexual obsessions have driven him in and out of Whitfield, the local insane asylum. Harry's college roommate, Bobby Dove Fleece, has stolen from Lepoyster a bundle of erotic love letters written to a woman named Catherine, and Harry and Fleece become as obsessed with Lepoyster as he was with his woman. Lepoyster stalks the streets, spouting racial and anti-Semitic filth, breaking up civil rights demonstrations, and even becoming incensed when a black marching band shows up in a local parade. Harry and Fleece, equally obsessed, stalk Lepoyster and even sneak up on his house one night to take a shot at him, wounding him in the knee. Lepoyster is clearly what Harry himself could become, a comically frightening racist driven out of his mind by sexual desire and hatred, a mad pervert who has succumbed to the irrational drives of death, violence, and despair.

Opposed to Lepoyster, however, is Harley Butte, a black man who once worked in the mattress factory owned by Harry's father. Butte, who worships John Philip Sousa and writes march music of his own, is the director of a high school band modeled on the incredible Dream of Pines Colored High School Band, the best band in the state. If Lepoyster represents southern racial hatred, Butte clearly represents racial harmony, the desire to see both blacks and whites marching to the same music. A musician like Butte, Harry plays the trumpet, but he likes blues and jazz, not Sousa. Harry, it is clear, improvises his own tunes and marches to his own drummer.

Yet it is the pathetic Lepoyster, not Harry, who is the true Geronimo, the savage killer in a country not his own. Lepoyster dies violently, shot to death in a gunfight with Fleece, a gentle soul who has never before even fired a gun. By the end of the novel, Harry has married Prissy Lombardo, a young girl who looks like a "pubescent Arab," writes poetry as well as plays the trumpet, and pursues an academic career as an English teacher. Although he is a poet and musician, Harry is still partly Geronimo Rex, the rebel with a streak of violence. Still, the novel, which begins and ends with brilliant descriptions of marching bands (Hannah writes about marching bands better than any other American writer), ends with harmony and hope.

While *Geronimo Rex* may not be a great American novel, it is a very good one, and an exceptional first novel for a beginning author. The story is told with a memorably comic and exuberant first-person narrative voice that Hannah skillfully employs in all of his later novels, and it is full of memorable scenes and characters: the death of an old dog and mule that wander into the Monroe yard when Harry is a boy; the rambling, sexually obsessed monologues of Bobby Dove Fleece, Harry's college roommate; and the comic and pathetic Mother Rooney, who runs a boardinghouse where Harry stays.

NIGHTWATCHMEN

Hannah's second novel, *Nightwatchmen*, continues the exploits of Harry Monroe, but he is not the central character. That distinction goes to Thorpe Trove, a striking figure who wears purple prescription glasses perched on his long nose beneath a wild shock of orange hair. In this novel of many voices, Trove is the central narrative voice, and it is he who tape-records the others for the reader. The central plot of *Nightwatchmen*, a kind of surreal mystery thriller, takes place at mythical Southwestern Mississippi University, where an unknown assailant called The Knocker is clubbing graduate students and faculty as they work in their offices late at night. When Conrad, a nightwatchman, and Spell, a janitor, are not only knocked but also beheaded, it becomes apparent that The Knocker may also be The Killer. Trove becomes obsessed with finding this mysterious figure (actually, two mysterious figures, as it turns out) and begins tape-recording anyone who might have clues—such as graduate student Harry Monroe. Harry and fellow graduate student Lawrence Head theorize that The Knocker intends only to conk pedants and bores, but when Didi Sweet, a fellow graduate student and an attractive divorcée, is knocked, that theory falls into doubt. The murders of Conrad and Spell, and the later murder of graduate student William Tell, dispel it entirely. Other clues come from part-time plumber Frank Theron Knockre and Douglas David "Dougie" Lotrieux, a film projectionist in a local theater.

Independently wealthy, Trove hires aging private detective Howard Hunter, and together they track down and destroy The Killer during the onslaught of Hurricane Camille. All of this takes place during some memorable scenes of storm and destruction: Dougie being swept along the countryside by 150-mile-per-hour winds, Head's landlady being decapitated by the tin roof of her house, and the dead being blown by the hurricane from a local graveyard and found hanging in the trees.

Deciding upon corporal punishment for Dougie Lotrieux, who has known all along the identity of The Killer and now wants to die, Trove and his associates bring in Harry Monroe as executioner. Harry is by now completing his Ph.D. in English at Clemson and is about to bring out a second volume of poetry, but he still carries his gun and has wanted throughout the novel to kill something. Harry, who shoots Dougie through the head and buries his body on the beach, remains the divided Harry Monroe of the first novel: a sensitive artist, a judgmental observer of life, and a violent man.

Exactly what issue *Nightwatchmen* is trying to address is unclear. "A nightwatchman," Lawrence Head meditates at one point, "ought to be rather hungry for conversation. He ought to be dying to flood you with talk." The novel is, above all, a flood of talk from lonely and tormented people. Nightwatchmen keep lonely vigils, like these isolated and lonely night people, and Hurricane Camille seems an appropriate metaphor for the swirling turbulence of emotions within the characters, whose lives also cause death and destruction.

RAY

Hannah's third novel, *Ray*, is a departure from his first two. Condensed from a manuscript that was originally four hundred pages, *Ray* is a book of little more than a hundred pages and sixty-two short sections, some of them consisting of only a sentence or two. Furthermore, the novel is more upbeat than the previous two, for the title is a hearty cheer for life ("Hoo! Ray") as well as the narrator's name. Ray is an Alabama doctor and a former Vietnam fighter pilot whose fantasies of the Civil War, in which heat-seekers and phosphorus bombs battle sabers and horsemen, equate one war with another. An alcoholic, Ray administers drugs to addicted patients and practices selective euthanasia on the hurtful and depraved. The divorced father of three children, Ray seeks comfort from Sister, the daughter of the poor and hopeless Hooch family. Sister leaves home to become a prostitute and model for pornographic photographs and is eventually shot to death by Baptist preacher Maynard Castro, while her father is almost killed when his propane lantern explodes.

Ray confronts these tragedies, ministers to the needy, and meets a woman with whom he falls in love and marries. The victim of life's suffering—"I am infected with every disease I ever tried to cure,"

he says—Ray survives war, the poverty-ridden South, the loss of friends and lovers, and his own self-pity to become a heroic figure. By the end of the novel, he is plunging forward, saber raised, like the Confederate officers of his Civil War fantasies. A Christ-figure—he is thirty-three and, as he states in the opening sentence, "born of religious parents"—Ray suffers so that others may live (old man Hooch survives to become, under Ray's guidance, a gifted poet) and is himself resurrected.

Ray is Hannah's most concise novel, a carryover perhaps from the volume of short stories that constituted his previously published book, and in it Hannah comes to grips with the historical past of the Civil War and the grinding poverty of southern families like the Hooches. Ray is in many ways a personification of the United States itself during the 1970's: haunted by war, divided by violent emotions and yearnings for peace, and searching for historical roots. Like his country, Ray lives through the worst of times and survives, perhaps even stronger than ever.

THE TENNIS HANDSOME

The Tennis Handsome, Hannah's fourth novel, first appeared in *Esquire* magazine and was later collected in *Airships*. The wildly improbable tale of a charismatic but brain-damaged tennis professional, his companion, and his high school tennis coach, the novel is a return to Hannah's comic exuberance and expansive style. French Edward, the "tennis handsome" of the title, is a kind of idiot savant, a brilliant tennis player but a vegetable off the court, having survived a plunge from a bridge with only part of his faculties intact. While in high school, French comes home one afternoon to find his mother in bed with his tennis coach, Jimmy Word, who, previously gay, has apparently rediscovered the joys of heterosexuality. Riddled with Freudian hatred, French gets even with Word by challenging the older man to a tennis match; hoping for a heart attack, French succeeds in giving the coach only a stroke, but it is enough to make Word partially blind and to give him a frightful voice ("like that of a man in a cave of wasps"). Such is French's charisma that Word loves him all the more, following him from tournament to tournament, his voice bleating above the crowd and—"crazed with partisanship"—pinching French with pride after each victory. Even worse, French's mother still loves Word, a fact that drives French to desperation. Grappling with Word above a river, French drops off the bridge with the old man. Word is no worse for the experience, but French is brain-damaged.

Now cared for by Dr. Baby Levaster, a former high school tennis teammate and another admirer of tennis handsomes, French wanders the tennis circuit in search of the ineffable. During a match in Boston, lightning strikes his metal racket, turning French "radiant as a silver-plated statue" and somewhat psychic and, for a time, clearing his damaged brain. He even begins to write poetry, though only bawdy doggerel. French continues to seek these crystalline moments. Meanwhile, separated from his wife Cecelia, French finds comfort with a crippled woman named Inez, a Cuban polio victim who becomes pregnant with his child. In spite of being in a wheelchair, Inez also comforts Levaster. In fact, Levaster finds carnal comfort with practically anyone he can, including French's mother, Olive, and a woman named Beth Battrick, who has been having an affair with her nephew, Bobby Smith, a Vietnam veteran haunted by his past.

Smith's story, previously published in both *Esquire* and *Airships* as "Midnight and I'm Not Famous Yet," recounts his capture and subsequent killing of Li Dap, a North Vietnamese general, and the loss of Smith's friend Tubby Wooten. Returned from the war and in love with his aunt, Smith has become entwined in the lives of French and Levaster. The aunt, after nearly being raped by a walrus, runs off with a southern senator. Inez dies in childbirth. Word dies of natural causes in Smith's car, and Smith dumps him off a bridge near Vicksburg. French, looking for the ultimate fix, almost electrocutes himself by clamping onto battery cables. Cecelia, angered at Levaster's refusal to give up French's baby (which has passed from Inez to Smith to Levaster), murders Levaster with a crossbow. Smith, having seen senseless devastation before, somehow survives along with French.

The zaniness of Hannah's narrative—Carson McCullers rewritten by Groucho Marx, as one reviewer put it—is entertainment enough, but there may even be message in his madness. The American reverence for athletic prowess, Hannah suggests, is a kind of misplaced religious awe with a dose of sexual longing, as slightly off-center as Bobby Smith's passion for his own aunt. French Edward, a Christ-figure in shorts and sneakers, is both saintly and visionary, capable of arousing desire in both sexes, and tennis, like war, is a field of combat where courage, victory, and defeat are exhibited. Like all athletes, French helps the spectator to define himself through the athlete's continual Christlike struggles.

HEY JACK!

Between *The Tennis Handsome* and Hannah's next two novels came his second volume of short stories, *Captain Maximus*. In some of those stories he pays homage to Ernest Hemingway and Richard Hugo, two American authors who confront personal experience directly and write about it with honest sentiment. Hannah attempts to do the same in *Hey Jack!* and *Boomerang*, and both novels are a radical departure from his earlier work. Hannah abandons the wildly exuberant comic style of the earlier works for a more measured and direct prose, his narrator seems closer to Hannah himself (the narrator of *Boomerang* is called Barry), and his characters seem drawn more directly from experience than from the imagination.

The Jack of *Hey Jack!* is a seventy-seven-year-old café owner, a former war correspondent, Kentucky sheriff, college professor of criminal science, and Mississippi cattleman. The plot of the novel involves Jack's daughter, a forty-year-old schoolteacher named Alice, who is seeing rock star Ronnie Foot against her father's wishes. Foot, a kind of Elvis Presley from Hell, is a cocaine-snorting egotist who lives in a large mansion with Gramps, an alcoholic redneck who likes to shoot his .22 rifle at the chickens and people outside. Foot, who has a history of using and destroying women, abuses and humiliates Alice, turns her into a drug addict, and kills her with Gramps's .22 while trying to shoot a Coca-Cola bottle off her head. On trial for murder, Foot hangs himself in his cell. The novel is a tribute to men such as Jack and the narrator, Homer, who are like the First Marine Division at Chosin, site of the great Korean War battle in which Homer fought thirty years earlier and which still haunts his dreams:

They dig in, attack when they can, bury their dead, and learn to survive.

BOOMERANG

Boomerang, another novel of survival, again attempts to deal with life's past and present pains. Like the actual boomerang that the narrator finds and learns how to control, past experiences that one has tried to cast away come back to strengthen and instruct the narrator, whose name by this sixth novel has become "Barry." From Harry to Barry, Hannah's voice has been at the center of his narratives, connecting past with present, viewing life's experiences with black humor and irreverence, and involving the reader in his hatreds, loves, failures, and many moods. By this sixth novel, that voice is hard to distinguish from that of the author, for it confronts the reader directly with shared experiences in straightforward, unadorned prose. While Hannah's writing gains strength from the realistic characters and situations, *Boomerang* as a whole lacks the unpredictability and lyric humor of his earlier writings, and the sentiment often teeters into the maudlin.

NEVER DIE

Set in the West in 1910-1913, Hannah's seventh novel, *Never Die*, received mixed reviews. Some critics claimed that although Hannah's characters are usually intentionally undeveloped—although not simple—the characters in *Never Die* are caricatures. Hannah's omnipresent violence was also targeted in this novel as too sweeping, too parodic.

The novel opens with a flashback to the Civil War as young Kyle Nitburg turns his mother over to the authorities for spying. It then proceeds to relate events involving the characters who live in the town that bears his name. Aside from Judge Nitburg, who in the past sold one wife into Comanche slavery and then wed a blind dowager, the town is peopled with a wild assortment of characters. Thirty-eight-year-old college-educated gunslinger Fernando Mure, bankrupt and semi-suicidal, has two goals: to burn down the town he has always hated but now detests (it has been overrun by the Chinese) and to build a magnificent coffin factory.

In love with a tubercular whore, Stella, Fernando has his knees broken by Judge Nitburg's thug, the dwarf Smoot, who imagines that he has underground roots and who lusts after the monkey owned by wealthy Navy Remington. Nitburg's daughter is Nandina, a nymphomaniacal schoolteacher with a passion for automobiles. Other characters include homosexual Dr. Fingo, supplier of morphine to kill mental or physical pain; Reverend McCorkindale, who believes himself hated by God because of his hairy body and perpetual erection; and Hermit Nermer. Nermer is a one-time gunslinger who once killed an Apache child simply because Nermer had a new gun; now he is a penitent mountain man awaiting the judgment of fire that Fernando has promised to inflict on Nitburg.

After Fernando finally sets fire to the courthouse, Nitburg hires assassins to kill him. Forewarned, Fernando goes to his uncle, Navy Remington, for money and ammunition. Events come to a head on the day Fernando returns to Nitburg to await his fate and marry Stella, who, standing in the church door, is mortally wounded by Smoot. Hit man Luther Nix and his assassins storm the town, killing anyone who comes within their sights, including Nandina. Entering the church to face Fernando, Nix decapitates and undresses the corpse of Stella so that he can clothe himself in her rose dress. Even greater chaos erupts; Nix and his band, faced down only momentarily by a lesbian named Tall Jane, seem ready to claim victory when Reverend McCorkindale swoops down in his Sopwith Camel and drops nitroglycerin onto the church. Nix goes into the fire to find Fernando, who shoots him in the stomach. When the smoke clears, there are twelve bodies. Two years later, photographer and voyeur Philip Hine assures Fernando that history will relieve them of their self-hatred. Assured instead of his own villainy, Fernando is buoyed only by the thought that he has another, and better, chance to "make a high mark for good."

Barry Hannah remains one of America's most original talents, a southern regionalist whose hilarious, weird, and very human characters shock readers into recognition of themselves, a lover of the English language who, as he has said, is always trying to get as much as he can out of words.

Kenneth Seib, updated by Jaquelyn W. Walsh

OTHER MAJOR WORKS

SHORT FICTION: *Airships*, 1978; *Captain Maximus*, 1985; *Bats out of Hell*, 1993; *High Lonesome*, 1996.

BIBLIOGRAPHY

Cawelti, Scott. "An Interview with Barry Hannah." *Short Story* 3 (Spring, 1995): 105-116. This intriguing interview contains Hannah's avowal that he himself has never carried a gun along with the assertion that "it's the absolute act, the act of firing a gun randomly into a crowd—it's the absolute act of art."

Hannah, Barry. "The Spirits Will Win Through." Interview by R. Vanarsdall. *The Southern Review* 19 (Spring, 1983): 317-341. A fine interview conducted in 1982. Hannah talks of his influences—Walker Percy, Ernest Hemingway, William Faulkner, James Joyce, Thomas Wolfe—and his friendships with Jimmy Buffett, Thomas McGuane, Richard Brautigan, and others, as well as voicing his thoughts on writing and life.

Hill, Robert. "Barry Hannah." *South Carolina Review* 9 (November, 1976): 25-29. Hill finds that, in the midst of "some of the most baroque plots this side of *Titus Andronicus*," Hannah is one of the United States' best stylists, a writer whose works are filled with memorable characters and meaningful, though random, experiences.

Kennedy, Randy. "At Home with: Barry Hannah; Mellowing Out but Unbowed." *The New York Times*, July 9, 1998, F1:1. An interesting interview with Hannah at his home in Oxford, Mississippi, after his return from a stint at the Iowa Writers' Workshop. He mentions that he is almost finished with his twelfth book, a novel tentatively titled "Yonder Stands Your Orphan with His Gun." Among other things, Hannah discusses alcohol, his recently deceased father who had attended the University of Mississippi when William Faulkner was postmaster there, the "homogenization" of American fiction, and his status as a cult figure in France.

Madden, David. "Barry Hannah's *Geronimo Rex* in Retrospect." *The Southern Review* 19 (Spring, 1983): 309-316. Madden once found *Geronimo Rex* "the best first novel I've ever reviewed." Considering it again ten years later, he agrees with his original assessment but now finds it lacking an intellectual framework and a "conceptualizing imagination."

Noble, Donald R. "'Tragic and Meaningful to an Insane Degree': Barry Hannah." *Southern Literary Journal* 15 (Fall, 1982): 37-44. Noble finds Hannah's vision split: While he believes that the world is chaotic and disconnected, Hannah still seems to have an abundant comic spirit and love of life. Hannah holds his readers not by his vision but by the power of his voice, that of a "jazz speaker" who plays with words the way a musician plays with notes.

Updike, John. "From Dyna Domes to Turkey-Pressing." *The New Yorker*, September 9, 1972, 121-124. Updike, one of the United States' best novelists in the late twentieth century, places Hannah's *Geronimo Rex* in the 1950's tradition of "the whining adolescent novel." Nevertheless, he admires Hannah's energy, style, and "morbid zest."

Weston, Ruth. *Barry Hannah: Postmodern Romantic*. Baton Rouge: Louisiana State University Press, 1998. The first important book-length study of Hannah to examine his work as a unified whole in terms of thematic concerns as well as narrative techniques and to place it in the context of American literature. Weston explores such issues as violence and the American "man-child," the search of southerners for an identity even a century and a half after defeat in the Civil War (a defeat echoed in the Vietnam conflict), characteristics of surfiction in Hannah's work, and Hannah's use of humor.

THOMAS HARDY

Born: Higher Bockhampton, England; June 2, 1840
Died: Dorchester, England; January 11, 1928

PRINCIPAL LONG FICTION

Desperate Remedies, 1871
Under the Greenwood Tree, 1872
A Pair of Blue Eyes, 1872-1873
Far from the Madding Crowd, 1874
The Hand of Ethelberta, 1875-1876
The Return of the Native, 1878
The Trumpet-Major, 1880
A Laodicean, 1880-1881
Two on a Tower, 1882
The Mayor of Casterbridge, 1886
The Woodlanders, 1886-1887
Tess of the D'Urbervilles, 1891
Jude the Obscure, 1895
The Well-Beloved, 1897

OTHER LITERARY FORMS

In addition to his novels, Thomas Hardy published four collections of short stories, *Wessex Tales*

(Library of Congress)

(1888), *A Group of Noble Dames* (1891), *Life's Little Ironies* (1894), and *A Changed Man, The Waiting Supper and Other Tales* (1913). In the latter part of his life, after he had stopped writing novels altogether, he published approximately one thousand poems in eight separate volumes, which have since been collected in one volume by his publisher, Macmillan & Company. In addition to this staggering body of work, Hardy also published an epic-drama of the Napoleonic wars in three parts between 1903 and 1908 entitled *The Dynasts*, a one-act play entitled *The Famous Tragedy of the Queen of Cornwall* (1923), and a series of essays on fiction and other topics, which have been collected in individual volumes. All the novels and stories are available in a uniform library edition in eighteen volumes, published in the early 1960's by Macmillan & Company. Finally, *The Early Life of Hardy* (1928) and *The Later Years of Thomas Hardy* (1930), although ostensibly a two-volume biography of Hardy by his second wife, Florence Hardy, is generally recognized to be Hardy's own autobiography compiled from his notes in his last few years.

ACHIEVEMENTS

Hardy is second only to Charles Dickens as the most written-about and discussed writer of the Victorian era. At least one new book and dozens of articles appear on his work every year. Certainly in terms of volume and diversity alone, Hardy is a towering literary figure with two admirable careers—one as novelist and one as poet—to justify his position.

Interest in Hardy's work has followed two basic patterns. The first was philosophical, with many critics creating metaphysical structures that supposedly underlay his fiction. In the late twentieth century, however, interest shifted to that aspect of Hardy's work most scorned before—his technical facility and generic experimentation. One hundred years after his heyday, what once was termed fictional clumsiness was reevaluated in terms of poetic technique.

Furthermore, Hardy's career as a poet, which has always been under the shadow of his fiction, has been reevaluated. Hardy was a curious blend of the old-fashioned and the modern. With a career that began in the Victorian era and did not end until after World War I, Hardy was contemporary both with Matthew Arnold and with T. S. Eliot. Critics such as Babette Deutsch and Vivian De Sola Pinto claim that Hardy bridged the gulf between the Victorian sensibility and the modern era. In his unflinching confrontation with meaninglessness in the universe, Hardy embodied Albert Camus's description of the absurd creator in *The Myth of Sisyphus* (1942); he rebelled against the chaos of the world by asserting his own freedom to persist in spite of that meaninglessness.

Hardy was a great existential humanist. His hope for humanity was that people would realize that creeds and conventions which presupposed a god-oriented center of value were baseless. He hoped that humans would loosen themselves from those foolish hopes and creeds and become aware of their freedom to create their own value. If human beings would only realize, Hardy felt, that all people were equally alone and without hope for divine help, then perhaps they would realize also that it was the height of absurdity for such lost and isolated creatures to fight among themselves.

BIOGRAPHY

Thomas Hardy was born in the small hamlet of Higher Bockhampton in Stinsford parish on June 2, 1840. His father was a master mason, content with his low social status and at home in his rural surroundings. His mother, however, whom Hardy once called "a born bookworm," made Hardy aware of his low social status and encouraged his education. John Hicks, a friend of Hardy's father and a Dorchester architect, took the boy on as a pupil at the age of sixteen. The well-known poet William Barnes had a school next door to Hicks's office, and Hardy developed an influential friendship with the older man that remained with him. Another early influence on the young Hardy was Horace Moule, a classical scholar with a Cambridge education who was an essayist and reviewer. Moule introduced Hardy to intellectual conversation about Greek literature as well as contemporary issues; it was at Moule's suggestion that Hardy read John Stuart Mill as well as the infamous *Essays and Reviews* (1860, Reverend Henry Bristow

Wilson, editor), both of which contributed to the undermining of Hardy's simple religious faith.

Hardy was twenty-two when he went to London to pursue his architectural training. By that time he also entertained literary ambitions and had begun writing poetry. The publication of A. C. Swinburne's *Poems and Ballads* in 1866 so influenced Hardy that he began a two-year period of intensive study and experimentation in writing poetry; none of the many poems he sent out was accepted, however, and he returned to Bockhampton in 1867. It was at this point that Hardy decided to turn to writing fiction. In his old age, he wrote in a letter that he never wanted to write novels at all, but that circumstances compelled him to turn them out.

Hardy's first fictional effort, *The Poor Man and the Lady*, based on the contrast between London and rural life, received some favorable responses from publishers, but after a discussion with George Meredith, Hardy decided not to publish it and instead, on Meredith's advice, wrote *Desperate Remedies* in imitation of the detective style of Wilkie Collins. Later, eager to publish works that would establish his career as a writer, Hardy took the advice of a reader who liked the rural scenes in his unpublished novel and wrote the pastoral idyll *Under the Greenwood Tree*. The book was well received by the critics, but sales were poor. One editor advised him to begin writing serials for periodical publication. With the beginning of *A Pair of Blue Eyes*, Hardy said good-bye to architecture as a profession and devoted the rest of his life to writing.

In 1874, Hardy married Emma Lavinia Gifford, a dynamic and socially ambitious young woman who shared his interests in books. In the meantime, *Far from the Madding Crowd* had appeared to many favorable reviews, and editors began asking for Hardy's work. While living with his wife in a cottage at Sturminster Newton, Hardy composed *The Return of the Native* and enjoyed what he later called the happiest years of his life. Hardy and his wife began a social life in London until he became ill and they decided to return to Dorset, where, while writing *The Mayor of Casterbridge*, he had his home, "Max Gate," built. For the next several years, Hardy continued his writing, traveled with his wife, and read German philosophy.

His enthusiasm for *Tess of the D'Urbervilles* was dampened when it was turned down by two editors before being accepted for serial publication by a third. The publication of the work brought hostile reaction and notoriety—a notoriety that increased after the publication of *Jude the Obscure*. Hardy was both puzzled and cynical about these reactions, but he was by then financially secure and decided to return to his first love: After 1897 he wrote no more fiction but concentrated solely on poetry. His volumes of poetry were well received, and his experiment with metaphysics in the epic-drama, *The Dynasts*, brought him even more respect, honor, and fame. These final years of Hardy's life appear to have been spoiled only by the death of his wife in 1912. Within four years, however, he married Florence Dugdale, who had been a friend of the family and had done secretarial work for him. She cared for him for the remainder of his life. Hardy continued to write poetry regularly. His final volume of poems, *Winter Words*, was ready to be published when he died on January 11, 1928. His ashes were placed in Westminster Abbey.

ANALYSIS

In *The Courage to Be* (1952), Paul Tillich has said that "the decisive event which underlies the search for meaning and the despair of it in the twentieth century is the loss of God in the nineteenth century." Most critics of the literature of the nineteenth century have accepted this notion and have established a new perspective for studying the period by demonstrating that what is now referred to as the "modern situation" or the "modern artistic dilemma" actually began with the breakup of a value-ordered universe in the Romantic period. Thomas Hardy, in both philosophical attitude and artistic technique, firmly belongs in this modern tradition.

It is a critical commonplace that at the beginning of his literary career Hardy experienced a loss of belief in a divinely ordered universe. The impact of this loss on Hardy cannot be overestimated. In his childhood recollections he appears as an extremely sensitive boy who attended church so regularly that he knew the service by heart, and who firmly believed in a personal and just God who ruled the universe and took cognizance of the situation of humanity. Consequently, when he came to London in his twenties and was exposed to the concept of a demythologized religion in the *Essays and Reviews* and the valueless nonteleological world of Charles Darwin's *On the Origin of Species by Means of Natural Selection* (1859), the loss of his childhood god was a traumatic experience.

What is often called Hardy's philosophy can be summed up in one of his earliest notebook entries in 1865: "The world does not despise us; it only neglects us." An interpretation of any of Hardy's novels must begin with this assumption. The difference between Hardy and other nineteenth century artists who experienced a similar loss of belief is that while others were able to achieve a measure of faith—William Wordsworth reaffirmed an organic concept of nature and of the creative mind which can penetrate it, and Thomas Carlyle finally entered the Everlasting Year with a similar affirmation of nature as alive and progressive—Hardy never made such an affirmative leap to transcendent value. Hardy was more akin to another romantic figure, Samuel Taylor Coleridge's Ancient Mariner, who, having experienced the nightmarish chaos of a world without meaning or value, can never fully get back into an ordered world again.

Hardy was constantly trying to find a way out of his isolated dilemma, constantly trying to find a value to which he could cling in a world of accident, chance, and meaningless indifference. Since he refused to give in to hope for an external value, however, he refused to submit to illusions of transcendence; the only possibility for him was to find some kind of value in the emptiness itself. Like the Ancient Mariner, all Hardy had was his story of loss and despair, chaos and meaninglessness. If value were to be found at all, it lay in the complete commitment to this story—"facing the worst," and playing it back over and over again, exploring its implications, making others aware of its truth. Consequently, Hardy's art can be seen as a series of variations in form on this one barren theme of loss and chaos—"questionings in the exploration of reality."

While Hardy could imitate popular forms and create popular novels such as *Desperate Remedies*, an imitation of Wilkie Collins's detective novel, or *The Hand of Ethelberta*, an imitation of the social comedy popular at the time, when he wished to write a serious novel, one that would truly express his vision of humanity's situation in the universe, he could find no adequate model in the novels of his contemporaries. He solved this first basic problem in his search for form by returning to the tragic drama of the Greek and Elizabethan ages—a mode with which he was familiar through extensive early reading. Another Greek and Elizabethan mode he used, although he was less conscious of its literary tradition, was the pastoral narrative—a natural choice because of its surface similarity to his own subject matter of isolated country settings and innocent country people.

Hardy's second problem in the search for form arose from the incompatibility between the classical tragic vision and his own uniquely modern view. The classical writers saw humanity within a stable and ordered religious and social context, while Hardy saw humanity isolated, alone, searching for meaning in a world that offered none. Because Hardy denied the static and ordered worldview of the past, he was in turn denied the broad context of myth, symbol, and ritual which stemmed from that view. Lost without a God-ordered mythos, Hardy had to create a modern myth that presupposed the absence of God; he needed a pattern. Hardy's use of the traditional patterns of tragedy and pastoral, combined with his rejection of the old mythos that formerly gave meaning to these patterns, resulted in a peculiar distortion as his novels transcended their original patterns.

Nature in Hardy's "pastoral" novels, *The Woodlanders* and *Far from the Madding Crowd*, is neither benevolent nor divinely ordered. Similarly, the human dilemma in his "tragic" novels, *The Return of the Native* and *The Mayor of Casterbridge*, is completely antithetical to what it was for the dramatists of the past. The Greek hero was tragic because he violated a cosmic order; Hardy's heroes are tragic precisely because there is no such order. For the Greek hero there is a final reconciliation which persuades him to submit to the world. For Hardy's hero there is

only the never-ending dialectic between people's nostalgia for value and the empty, indifferent world.

In *Tess of the D'Urbervilles* and *Jude the Obscure*, Hardy rejected the traditional tragic and pastoral patterns and allowed the intrinsic problem of his two protagonists to order the chaotic elements of the works. The structure of these novels can be compared to that of the epic journey of Wordsworth in *The Prelude* (1850) and Coleridge in *The Rime of the Ancient Mariner* (1798). As critic Morse Peckham has said in *Beyond the Tragic Vision: The Quest for Identity in the Nineteenth Century* (1962), the task of the nineteenth century artist was no longer to find an external controlling form, but to "symbolize the orientative drive itself, the power of the individual to maintain his identity by creating order which would maintain his gaze at the world as it is, at things as they are." The loss of order is reflected in the structure of *Tess of the D'Urbervilles*, as the young heroine is literally evicted from the familiarity of her world and must endure the nightmarish wandering process of trying to get back inside. The structuring drive of *Jude the Obscure* is Jude's search for an external order that will rid him of the anguish of his own gratuitousness.

FAR FROM THE MADDING CROWD

Hardy's first important novel, *Far from the Madding Crowd*, was the first in which he successfully adapted a traditional form, the pastoral, to his own purposes, greatly altering it in the process. In *Elizabethan Poetry: A Study in Conventions, Meaning and Expression* (1952), Hallet Smith has described the pastoral as constituting the ideal of the good life: In the pastoral world, nature is the true home of man; the gods take an active concern in man's welfare; the inhabitants of this world are content and self-sufficient. The plot complications of the pastoral usually arise by the intrusion of an aspiring mind from the outside, an antipastoral force which seeks to overthrow the idyllic established order. On the surface, *Far from the Madding Crowd* conforms perfectly to this definition of the pastoral. The story is set in an agricultural community, the main character is a shepherd, and the bulk of the inhabitants are content with their lives. The plot complications arise from the intrusion of the antipastoral Sergeant Troy and the love of three different men for the pastoral maid, Bathsheba. To see the novel as a true pastoral, however, is to ignore living form in order to see a preestablished pattern. The pastoral ideal cannot be the vision of this novel because Hardy was struggling with the active tension between human hopes and the world's indifference.

Far from the Madding Crowd begins in a light-hearted mood with the comic situation of Gabriel Oak's unsuccessful attempts to woo the fickle maid Bathsheba, but Oak, often called the stabilizing force in the novel, is an ambiguous figure. Although he is described as both a biblical and a classical shepherd, he is unequivocally neither. Moreover, the first section of the novel hovers between tragedy and comedy. Even the "pastoral tragedy," the "murder" of all of Gabriel's sheep by the foolish young dog, is equivocal; the dog is not so much destroyed for his crime as he is executed. Gabriel's character, as well as the entire tone of the novel, shifts after this short prologue. When he next appears he is no longer the contented shepherd with modest ambitions; rather, he has developed the indifference to fate and fortune which, Hardy says, "though it often makes a villain of a man, is the basis of his sublimity when it does not."

The change that takes place in Gabriel is caused by his loss and is more significant than the change in Bathsheba because of her gain of an inheritance. Bathsheba, a typical pastoral coquette in the prologue of the novel, makes an ostensible shift when she inherits a farm of her own, but she is still coquettish and vain enough to be piqued by Farmer William Boldwood's indifference to her charms and to send him the valentine saying "Marry Me." Boldwood, "the nearest approach to aristocracy that this remote quarter of the parish could boast of," is a serious, self-sufficient man who sees "no absurd side to the follies of life." The change the valentine causes in him is so extreme as to be comic.

The Bathsheba-Gabriel relationship is complicated by this new wooer. In this section of the novel, until the appearance of Sergeant Troy, there appears a series of scenes in which Gabriel, Boldwood, and Bathsheba are frozen into a tableau with the ever present sheep in the background. The death and physical suffering of the sheep take on a sinister, grotesque imagery to make an ironic commentary on the absurdity of humanity's ephemeral passions in a world dominated by cruelty and death. The irrationality of physical passion is more evident when Bathsheba is overwhelmed by Troy. Their relationship begins with the feminine frill of her dress being caught in his masculine spur and blossoms with her submission to his dazzling sword exercises. After Boldwood's complete demoralization and the marriage of Bathsheba and Troy, the antipastoral Troy corrupts the innocent harvest festival until it becomes a wild frenzy and then a drunken stupor. The pastoral world of the "good life" is turned upside down as the approaching storm transforms the landscape into something sinister. It is significant that the rustics are asleep during the storm, for they are truly unaware of the sickness of the world and its sinister aspect. Troy, too, is unaware of the storm, as he is always unaware of an incongruity between humanity and the indifferent world. Only Gabriel, Bathsheba, and Boldwood, the involved and suffering characters of the novel, react to this symbolic storm.

Just as the death of the sheep formed the ever present background to the first two parts of the novel, the death of Fanny Robin dominates the third section. From the time her body begins its journey in Joseph Poorgrass's wagon until the "Gurgoyle" washes Troy's flowers off her grave, death becomes the most important element in the book. By far the most important effect of Fanny Robin's death is on Bathsheba. When she opens the coffin to find out that Fanny was pregnant with Troy's child, the scene is "like an illusion raised by some fiendish incantation." Her running away to seclude herself in the wood is called by many critics her reconciliation with the natural world of the pastoral, but this view is wholly untenable: Her retreat is on the edge of a swamp of which the "general aspect was malignant." There is no pastoral goodness about the hollow in which she hides. It is a "nursery of pestilences. . . . From its moist and poisonous coat seemed to be exhaled the essences of evil things in the earth." This is one of those grotesque situations in which people become aware of their isolated state, when their need for solace in the natural world is met with only indifference, when they become aware of the absurdity of their demands on a barren and empty world. Bathsheba changes after her experience in this "boundary situation"; she gains the awareness which has characterized Gabriel all along.

After this climactic scene of confrontation with the indifferent world, the book loses its focus. In a diffuse and overlong denouement, Boldwood presses his advantage with Bathsheba until the night of the party, when she is on the point of giving in. Troy's return at this moment and his murder by Boldwood seems forced and melodramatic. Bathsheba's return to marry Gabriel is a concession to the reading public as much as it is to the pastoral pattern of the novel itself. *Far from the Madding Crowd*, a fable of the barrenness and death of the pastoral world and the tragic results of wrong choice through the irrationality of sexual attraction, truly ends with Bathsheba's isolation and painful new awareness in the pestilent swamp.

THE WOODLANDERS

The Woodlanders, although more explicit in its imagistic presentation of the unhealthy natural world and more complex in its conflicts of irrational sexual attraction, manifests much of the same kind of formal distortion as is found in *Far from the Madding Crowd*. The world of Little Hintock, far from being the ideal pastoral world, is even more valueless, more inimical a world than Weatherbury. Instead of the grotesque death of sheep, trees become the symbolic representation of humanity's absurd situation in an empty world. Little Hintock is a wasteland, a world of darkness, isolation, guilt, and human cross-purposes. One's nostrils are always filled with the odor of dead leaves, fermenting cider, and heavy, blossomy perfume. One cannot breathe or stretch out one's arms in this world. The so-called "natural" inhabitants of the Wood are dissatisfied with the nature of the world around them. Grace's father, Mr. Melbury, cramped and crippled by his lifetime struggle to make his living from the trees, wants his daughter to be able to escape such a world by marrying an outsider. A conflict is created, though, by the

guilt he feels for a wrong he did to Giles Winterborne's father; he tries to atone for it by promising Grace to Giles. John South, Marty's father, on whose life the landholdings of Giles depend, is neurotically afraid of the huge tree in his yard. The tree takes on a symbolic aura as representative of the uncontrollable force of the natural world.

Furthermore, the sophisticated outsiders in the novel are cut off from the world they inhabit and are imaged as "unnatural." Strange unnatural lights can be seen from the house of the young Dr. Fitzpiers, who is said to be in league with the devil. The bored Felice Charmond is so unnatural that she must splice on the luxuriance of natural beauty by having a wig made of Marty South's hair. The isolated and cramped Hintock environment creates a boredom and ennui in these two characters that serve to further the narrative drive of the novel.

Grace, the most equivocal character in the novel, is the active center of its animating conflicts. Her wavering back and forth between the natural world and the antinatural is the central tension that crystallizes the tentative and uncomfortable attitude of all the characters. It is her dilemma of choice that constitutes the major action, just as it was Bathsheba's choice that dominated *Far from the Madding Crowd*. The choices that the characters make to relieve themselves of tension are made through the most irrational emotion, love, in a basically irrational world. Grace marries Fitzpiers in an effort to commit herself to a solid world of value. Fitzpiers sees in Grace the answer to a Shelleyan search for a soul mate. To commit oneself to a line of action that assumes the world is ordered and full of value, to choose a course of action that hopes to lessen the tentativeness of life, to deceive oneself into thinking that there is solidarity—these are the tragic errors that Hardy's characters repeatedly make.

The marriage begins to break up when Fitzpiers, aware that Grace is not the ideal he desired, goes to the lethargic Mrs. Charmond, and when Grace, aware that her hope for solidarity was misdirected, tries to go back to the natural world through the love of Giles. Social conventions, however, which Hardy says are holdovers from outworn creeds, interfere.

Grace is unable to obtain a divorce, for the law makes her irrational first choice inflexible. Despairing of the injustice of natural law as well as of social law, she runs away to Giles, who, too self-effacing to rebel against either code, lets her have his house while he spends the night in an ill-sheltered hut. At this point, confused and in anguish about what possibility there is left for her, uncertain of the value of any action, Grace confronts the true nature of the world and the absurdity of her past hopes for value in it. The storm that catches Grace alone in the house is a climactic representation for her of the inimical natural world, just as the pestilent swamp was for Bathsheba. "She had never before been so struck with the devilry of a gusty night in the wood, because she had never been so entirely alone in spirit as she was now. She seemed almost to be apart from herself—a vacuous duplicate only." Grace's indecision and absurd hopes have been leading to this bitter moment of realization in which she is made aware of the ephemeral nature of human existence and the absurdity of human hopes in a world without intrinsic value.

Just as in *Far from the Madding Crowd*, the tension of the action collapses after this confrontation. Giles dies and Fitzpiers returns after having ended his affair with Mrs. Charmond. After a short period of indifference, Grace, still his wife by law, returns to him. In his customary ironic way, however, Hardy does not allow this reconciliation to be completely satisfying, for it is physical only. Grace, having narrowly missed being caught in a mantrap set for Fitzpiers, is enticingly undressed when Fitzpiers rushes to her and asks to be taken back. This physical attraction is the only reason that Fitzpiers desires a reconciliation. Grace is still indifferent to him, but it is now this very indifference that makes their reunion possible. Seeing no one reaction as more valuable than another, she takes the path of least resistance. The rural chorus ends the novel by commenting that they think the union will not last.

THE RETURN OF THE NATIVE

Although many critics have pointed out the formal framework of *The Return of the Native*—the classical five-act division; the unity of time, place, and line of action; and the character similarities to Oedipus and Prometheus—other studies have struggled with the book's ambiguities and the difficulties involved in seeing it as a classical tragedy. Certainly, the pattern is classical, but the distortion of the pattern becomes the more significant structuring principle. Egdon Heath is the landscape from which God has departed. People in such an empty world will naturally begin to feel an affinity with the wasteland, such as islands, moors, and dunes. Little more needs to be said here about the part the Heath plays in the action, for critics have called it the principal actor in the drama. Indeed, it does dominate the scene, for the actions of all the characters are reactions in some way to the indifference the Heath represents.

As in *Far from the Madding Crowd*, there is a chorus of rustics in *The Return of the Native*. They belong on the Heath because of their ignorance of the incongruity between human longing for meaning and the intractable indifference of the world. They still maintain a mythical, superstitious belief in a pagan animism and fatalistically accept the nature of things. The Druidical rites of the opening fires, the unimportance of Christian religion, the black mass and Voodoo doll of Susan Nonesuch: All these characterize the pagan fatalism of the rustics.

The main characters, however, do not belong with the rustics. They make something other than a fatalistic response to the Heath and are characterized by their various reactions to its indifference. Mrs. Yeobright is described as having the very solitude exhaled from the Heath concentrated in her face. Having lived with its desolation longer than any of the others, she can no longer escape, but she is desperate to see that Clym does. Damon Wildeve does not belong to the Heath but has taken over a patch of land a former tenant died in trying to reclaim. Although he is dissatisfied, he is not heroic; he is involved in no search, no vital interaction with the indifferent world. Tomasin Yeobright is characterized in a single image, as she is in the house loft, selecting apples: "The sun shone in a bright yellow patch upon the figure of the maiden as she knelt and plunged her naked arms into the soft brown fern." She aligns herself with the natural world through her innocence and consequently perceives no incongruity. Diggory Venn, the most puzzling figure in the novel, is an outcast. The most typical image of him is by his campfire alone, the red glow reflecting off his own red skin. He simply wanders on the open Heath, minding other people's business, and waiting for his chance to marry Tomasin.

These characters, regardless of their conflicts with the irrationality of human choice or the indifference of the Heath, are minor in comparison with the two antithetical attitudes of Eustacia Vye and Clym Yeobright. The most concrete image of Eustacia is of her wandering on the Heath, carrying an hourglass in her hand, gazing aimlessly out over the vast wasteland. Her search for value, her hope for escape from the oppressive indifference of the Heath, lies in being "loved to madness." Clym, however, sees friendliness and geniality written on the Heath. He is the disillusioned intellectual trying to make a return to the mythic simplicity of the natural world. Clym would prefer not to think, not to grapple with the incongruities he has seen. The very disease of thought that forces him to see the "coil of things" makes him desire to teach rather than to think. He is indeed blind, as his mother tells him, in thinking he can instill into the peasants the view that "life is a thing to be put up with," for they have always known it and fatalistically accepted it. Furthermore, he shows his blindness by marrying Eustacia, thinking she will remain with him on the Heath, while Eustacia reveals that she is as misdirected as he is by idealizing him and thinking that he will take her away from the Heath. Both characters search for a meaning and basis for value, but both are trapped by the irrationality of love and vain hopes in an irrational world.

At the beginning of book 4, Clym literally goes blind because of his studying and must actually look at the world through smoked glasses. He welcomes the opportunity to ignore the incongruities of the world by subsuming himself in the Heath and effacing himself in his furze-cutting. In his selfish attempt to "not think" about it, he ignores what this means to Eustacia. She can find no meaning at all in such self-effacing indifference; it is the very thing against which she is rebelling. She returns again to her old pagan ways at the village dance and considers the possibility of Wildeve once more.

Mrs. Yeobright's journey across the Heath, a trip colored by grotesque images of the natural world—the tepid, stringy water of nearly dried pools where "maggoty" shapes cavort; the battered, rude, and wild trees whose limbs are splintered, lopped, and distorted by the weather—is a turning point in the action of the book. In a concatenation of chance events and human misunderstanding, Eustacia turns Mrs. Yeobright away from the door, and the old woman dies as a result. At this point, Eustacia blames some "colossal Prince of the world for framing her situation and ruling her lot."

Clym, still selfish, ignores the problems of the living Eustacia and concentrates on the "riddle of death" of his mother. Had he been able to practice what he professed—human solidarity—he might have saved Eustacia and himself, but instead he bitterly blames her for his mother's death and is the immediate cause of Eustacia's flight. Eustacia's trip across the Heath to her death is similar to Mrs. Yeobright's in that the very natural world seems antagonistic to her. She stumbles over "twisted furze roots, tufts of rushes, or oozing lumps of fleshly fungi, which at this season lay scattered about the Heath like the rotten liver and lungs of some colossal animal." Her leap into the pool is a noble suicide. It is more a rebellion against the indifference of the world around her than it is a submission to its oppressiveness. It is the admission of the absurdity of human hopes by a romantic temperament that refuses to live by such absurdity.

THE MAYOR OF CASTERBRIDGE

The tragic pattern of *The Mayor of Casterbridge* has been said by most critics to be more explicit than that of *The Return of the Native*; in the late twentieth century, however, critics were quick to point out that there are serious difficulties involved in seeing *The Mayor of Casterbridge* as an archetypal tragic ritual. Although Henchard is Oedipus-like in his opposition to the rational, Creon-like Farfrae, the plot of the novel, like that of *The Return of the Native*, involves the reactions of a set of characters to the timeless indifference of the world. In this case, the mute and intractable world is imaged in the dead myths and classical legends of Casterbridge. Secluded as much as

Little Hintock, the world of *The Woodlanders*, Casterbridge is "huddled all together, shut in by a square wall of trees like a plot of garden by a box-edging." The town is saturated with the old superstitions and myths of the past. The primary image of the desolate world of the town and its dead and valueless past is the Casterbridge Ring, a relic of an ancient Roman amphitheater. The Ring is a central symbol which embodies the desolation of the old myths of human value. It formerly had been the gallows site, but now it is a place for illicit meetings of all kinds, except, Hardy notes, those of happy lovers. A place of man's inhumanity to man is no place for the celebration of love.

The inhumanity of one person to another and the human need for love play an important part in the action of the novel. While the classical Oedipus is guilty of breaking a cosmic law, Henchard is guilty of breaking a purely human one. By selling his wife, he treats her as a thing, not a human being. He rejects human relationships and violates human interdependence and solidarity. This is the sin that begins to find objectification years later when the blight of the bread agitates the townspeople and when his wife, Susan, returns.

It is not this sin alone that means tragedy for Henchard, just as it is not Oedipus's violation alone that brings his downfall. Henchard's character—his irrational behavior, his perverse clinging to the old order and methods, his rash and impulsive nature—also contributes to his defeat. Henchard is an adherent of the old ways. Though he is ostensibly the mayor, an important man, he is actually closer to the rustic, folk characters than the hero of any other Hardy novel. He is not a rebel against the indifference of the world so much as he is a simple hay-stacker, trying desperately to maintain a sense of value in the worn-out codes and superstitions of the past. In the oft-quoted "Character is Fate" passage in the novel, Hardy makes explicit Henchard's problem. He calls him a Faust-like character, "a vehement, gloomy being who had quitted the ways of vulgar men without light to guide him on a better way." Thus, Henchard is caught between two worlds, one of them dead and valueless, the other not worthy enough to be a positive replacement. The levelheaded business sense of Farfrae, the social climbing and superficiality of Lucetta, the too-strict rationality of Elizabeth-Jane—all who represent the new order of human attitudes—appear anemic and self-deceived in the face of Henchard's dynamic energy.

It often seems that the nature of things is against Henchard, but the nature of things is that events occur that cannot be predicted, and that they often occur just at the time when one does not want them to. Many such unpredicted and ill-timed events accumulate to cause Henchard's tragedy. For example, just when he decides to marry Lucetta, his wife Susan returns; just at the time of Susan's death, he is once more reminded of his obligation to Lucetta; just at the time when he tells Elizabeth-Jane that she is his daughter, he discovers that she is not; and just at the time when he calls on Lucetta to discuss marriage, she has already met and found a better mate in Farfrae.

Many of the events that contribute to his own downfall are a combination of this "unholy brew" and his impulsive nature. That the weather turned bad during his planned entertainment he could not prevent, but he could have been more prepared for the rain had he not been in such a hurry to best Farfrae. The unpredictable nature of the weather at harvest time was also beyond his control, but again had he not been so intent on ruining Farfrae he might have survived. He begins to wonder if someone is roasting a waxen image of him or stirring an "unholy brew" to confound him. Moreover, the attitudes of other characters accumulate to contribute to Henchard's downfall. Farfrae, as exacting as a machine, rejects Henchard's fatherly love and makes few truly human responses at all. Lucetta, once dependent on Henchard, becomes so infatuated with her new wealth that she no longer needs him. At the beginning of the novel, Susan's simple nature is incapable of realizing that Newsom's purchase of her is not valid, and at the end, her daughter, Elizabeth-Jane, is so coldly rational that she can cast Henchard off without possibility of reconciliation. None of these characters faces the anguish of being human as Henchard does.

The ambiguity that arises from the combination of all these forces makes it difficult to attribute Henchard's tragedy to any one of them. His death in the end marks the inevitable disappearance of the old order, but it is also the only conclusion possible for the man who has broken the only possible existing order when a cosmic order is no longer tenable—the human order of man himself. The reader is perhaps made to feel that Henchard has suffered more than he deserved. As a representative of the old order, his fall must be lamented even as the search is carried on for a new foundation of value and order. At the death of the old values in *The Mayor of Casterbridge*, a new order is not available.

TESS OF THE D'URBERVILLES

The form and meaning of *Tess of the D'Urbervilles* springs from Tess's relation to the natural world. At the beginning of the novel she is a true child of nature who, although sensitive to painful incongruities in her experience, is confident that the natural world will provide her with a basis of value and will protect and sustain her. When nature fails her, her perplexity throws her out of the comfortable world of innocence and natural rapport. Tess then begins a journey both inward and outward in search of a stable orientation and a reintegration into a relationship with the natural world.

Tess first appears in her "natural home" in the small hamlet of Marlott, where her innocence is dramatized as she takes part in the May Day dance. There is a sensitivity in Tess that sets her apart from the other inhabitants. Shame for her father's drunken condition makes her volunteer to take the beehives to market, and despair for the laziness of her parents makes her dreamily watch the passing landscape and ignore where she is going. When, as a result, the horse Prince is killed, Tess's sense of duty to her family, now in economic difficulties, overcomes her pride, and she agrees to go to her aristocratic relatives for help. It is her first journey outside the little world of Marlott and her first real encounter with corruption. Alec, her cousin, is a stock figure of the sophisticated, antinatural world. Their first scene together is formalized into an archetypal image of innocence in the grasp of the corrupt.

Just as it is Tess's natural luxuriance and innocence that attracts Alec, it is also her innocence that leads to her fall. When he takes her into the woods, strangely enough she is not afraid of him as before. She feels that she is in her natural element. She so trusts the natural world to protect her that she innocently falls asleep and is seduced by Alec. The antinatural force that began with her father's alleged nobility, coupled with Tess's own innocence and sensitivity and her naïve trust in the world, all work together to make her an outcast. When her illegitimate child dies and the church refuses it a Christian burial, Tess unequivocally denies the validity of organized religion. She probes within herself to try to find some meaning in her despair. Suddenly she becomes quite consciously aware of the abstract reality of death: "Almost at a leap Tess thus changed from simple girl to complex woman." The facing of the idea of death without a firm hope for transcendence is the conclusion of Tess's inward search in this second phase of her experience, when, still maintaining a will to live and enjoy, she has hopes of submerging herself into the natural world again.

The Valley of the Great Dairies where Tess goes next is the natural world magnified, distorted, thrown out of proportion. It is so lush and fertile as to become a symbolic world. As Tess enters the valley, she feels hope for a new reintegration. For the time being, she dismisses the disturbing thought of her doubt in her childhood God and is satisfied to immerse herself within the purely physical world of the farm's lushness. She manages to ignore her moral plight until she meets the morally ambiguous Angel Clare. In contrast to Tess, Angel's moral perplexity arises from intellectual questioning rather than from natural disillusionment. Intellectually convinced that he has lost faith, Angel rebels against the conventions of society and the church and goes to the Valley of the Great Dairies where he believes innocence and uncontaminated purity and goodness prevail. For Angel, Tess represents the idealistic goal of natural innocence, but the natural world no more affirms this relationship than it did condemn the former one. On the first night of their marriage, Tess confesses to Angel her relationship with Alec. Angel, the idealist, has desired to see a natural perfection in Tess. Doubting that perfection, he rejects her as antinatural. Angel cannot accept the reality of what nature is truly like; he is tied to a conventional orientation more than he realizes.

After Angel leaves her, Tess wanders about the countryside doing farm work at various places until one morning on the road she awakes to find dead pheasants around her. At this point, Tess becomes aware that in a Darwinistic universe, without teleological possibility and without inherent goodness, violation, injury, even death are innate realities. Tess realizes that she is not guilty by the laws of such a world. After this realization she can go to the barren world of Chalk-Newton and not feel so much the incongruity of the place. With its "white vacuity of countenance with the lineaments gone," Chalk-Newton represents the wasteland situation of a world without order or value. Tess can remain indifferent to it because of her new realization of its indifference to her.

Cold indifference, however, offers no escape from her moral conflict. Alec D'Urberville comes back into her life, proclaiming that he has accepted Christianity and exorting her not to "tempt" him again. Ironically, by trying to convince him of her own realization of a world without God and by propounding Angel's uncommitted humanism to him, she only succeeds in reconverting Alec back to his old demonic nature and thus creates another threat to herself. When her father dies and the family loses its precarious freehold, Tess gives in to Alec's persistent urging once more. When Angel, in the rugged South American mountains, comes to the same realization that Tess experienced on the road, he returns to find that Tess has renounced life and self completely, allowing her body to drift, "like a corpse upon the current, in a direction dissociated from the living will." After the return of Angel, when Tess finds her last hopes dashed, she sees in Alec all the deception and meaninglessness of a world she trusted. When she kills him, she is transformed by her rebellion. Like Percy Bysshe Shelley's Beatrice Cenci, she is aware of no guilt; she transcends any kind of moral judgment. She acknowledges her absolute freedom, and

in that fearful moment, she is willing to accept the human penalties for such freedom.

In the last part of the novel, when Angel and Tess wander without any real hope of escape, Tess is already condemned to die. Isolated in the awareness of her own ephemerality in a valueless world, Tess vows she is "not going to think of anything outside of now." The final scene at Stonehenge is a triumph of symbolic realization of place; the silent, enigmatic stones, mysterious and implacable, resist any attempt at explanation. Tess, in saying that she likes to be there, accepts the indifferent universe. Lying on the altar of a heathen temple, she is the archetypal sacrifice of human rebellion against an empty world. When the carriers of the law of nature and society arrive, Tess, having rebelled against these laws and rejected them, can easily say, "I am ready."

Tess's real tragedy springs from her insistent hope throughout the novel to find external meaning and justification for her life. Only at the end of the novel, when she rebels by killing Alec, does she achieve true awareness. Unlike the classical tragic hero, she is not reconciled to the world through an acceptance of universal justice. Her very salvation, the only kind of salvation in Hardy's world, lies in her denial of such a concept.

JUDE THE OBSCURE

With some significant differences, *Jude the Obscure* is concerned with the same problem that animates *Tess of the D'Urbervilles*—the absurdity and tragedy of human hopes for value in an indifferent universe. As a literary creation, it is a "process" through which Hardy tries to structure the symbolic journey of every person who searches for a foundation, a basis for meaning and value. The problem, however, is that all the symbols that represent meaning to Jude—the colleges, the church, the ethereal freedom of Sue Bridehead, and even the physical beauty of his wife Arabella—are illusory. By contrast, those things that have real symbolic value in the world are the forbidding, sacrosanct walls of the college complex, which Jude cannot enter; the decaying materiality of the churches which he tries to restore; the neurotic irrationality of Sue, which he fails to understand; and his own body, to which he is inextricably tied. It is precisely Jude's "obscurity," his loss of "at-homeness" in the world, with which the novel is concerned. He is obscure because he is without light, because he tries in every way possible to find an illumination of his relation to the world, but without success.

It is significant that the novel opens with the departure of the schoolmaster Phillotson, for to Jude, orphaned and unwanted by his aunt, the teacher has been the center of the world. His leaving marks the necessity of Jude's finding a new center and a new hope to relieve his loneliness. The first projection of his hopes to find value is naturally toward Christminster, the destination of his teacher. In the first part of the book his dream is seen only as an indefinable glow in the distance that offers all possibilities by its very unknown nature. Although he consciously devotes himself to the Christian framework, one night after having read a classical poem, he kneels and prays to Diana, the goddess of the moon. Both of these value systems—Christian faith and Greek reason—are projected on his vision of Christminster, but both of them are temporarily forgotten when he meets Arabella, "a substantial female animal." Later, when she tells him that she is pregnant, although it destroys all his former plans, he idealizes the marriage state, calls his hopes for Christminster "dreams about books, and degrees and impossible fellowships," and dedicates himself to home, family, and the pedestrian values of Marygreen. His discovery that Arabella has deceived him is only the first reversal in his search for unity and value.

In the second phase of Jude's development, the long-planned journey to Christminster is prompted by the immediacy of seeing a picture of Sue Bridehead; she becomes a concrete symbol of his vision. His first glimpse of Sue has the quality of idealistic wish fulfillment. His growing desire for her expresses a need for an "anchorage" to his thoughts. He goes to the church she attends, and this church, associated with his vision of Sue, temporarily becomes that anchorage. Sue is not, however, representative of Christian values; she is rather the classical pagan. This dichotomy of values creates a recurring tension in Jude's search throughout the book.

Jude's first major disillusionment at Christminster comes when he is turned down by all five colleges to which he has applied. After this disappointment, he shifts his hopes from the reason and knowledge of the schools to the faith of the Church. This religious impulse dominates Jude's hopes in the third phase of his development. He practices the rituals of the Church in the hope that he can find a meaning for himself, but Sue, who laughed at his idealistic notions of the intellectual life, tells him that the Church is not the way either. Sue, who changes in Jude's eyes as his goals change, is always important to him as a symbol of his aspirations and ideals. When he loses her to Phillotson, he is struck even more by the "scorn of Nature for man's finer emotions and her lack of interest in his aspirations."

Phase four of Jude's search is a transition section presenting the decay of the values of the past. Jude, studying theology and church ritual with a last weakening hope, is only vaguely aware of the decay and aridity around him. His need for Sue, an ambiguous mixture of desire for the ideal and the physical, begins to take on more importance for him until he decides that he is unfit "to fill the part of a propounder of accredited dogma" and burns all his theology books. Sue, a spiritual creature, cannot live with Phillotson any longer. She goes to Jude, who, having rejected everything else, is ready to project his desires for meaning entirely on an ambiguous union with her as both physical wife and Shelleyan soul mate.

The fifth part of the novel is a phase of movement as Jude and Sue wander from town to town, living as man and wife in all respects except the sexual. Not until Arabella returns and Sue fears she will lose Jude does she give in to him, but with infinite regret. In the final phase of Jude's development, after the birth of his children, including the mysterious child named "Father Time," the family moves back to Christminster. Instead of being optimistic, Jude is merely indifferent. He recognizes himself as an outsider, a stranger to the universe of ideals and hopes of other men. He has undergone a process that has slowly stripped him of such hopes for meaning. He sees the human desire for meaning as absurd in a world that has no concern for humanity, a universe that cannot fulfill dreams of unity or meaning.

The tragedy of Father Time causes Sue to alter her belief that she can live by instinct, abjuring the laws of society. She makes an extreme shift, accepting a supreme deity against whose laws she feels she has transgressed; her self-imposed penance for her "sin" of living with Jude is to go back to Phillotson. After Sue leaves, Jude goes to "a dreary, strange flat scene, where boughs dripped, and coughs and consumption lurked, and where he had never been before." This is a typical Hardy technique for moments of realization: The natural world becomes an inimical reflection of the character's awareness of the absurd. After this, Jude's reaction to the world around him is indifference: He allows himself to be seduced by Arabella again and marries her. Jude's final journey to see Sue is a journey to death and a final rejection of the indifferent universe of which his experiences have made him aware.

In his relentless vision of a world stripped of transcendence, Hardy is a distinctly modern novelist. As Nathan A. Scott has said of him, "not only does he lead us back to that trauma in the nineteenth century out of which the modern existentialist imagination was born, but he also brings us forward to our own time."

Charles E. May

OTHER MAJOR WORKS

SHORT FICTION: *Wessex Tales*, 1888; *A Group of Noble Dames*, 1891; *Life's Little Ironies*, 1894; *A Changed Man, The Waiting Supper and Other Tales*, 1913; *The Complete Short Stories*, 1989 (Desmond Hawkins, editor).

PLAYS: *The Dynasts: A Drama of the Napoleonic Wars*, pb. 1903, 1906, 1908, 1910 (verse drama), pr. 1914 (abridged by Harley Granville-Barker); *The Famous Tragedy of the Queen of Cornwall*, pr., pb. 1923 (one act).

POETRY: *Wessex Poems and Other Verses*, 1898; *Poems of the Past and Present*, 1901; *Time's Laughingstocks and Other Verses*, 1909; *Satires of Circumstance*, 1914; *Moments of Vision and Miscellaneous Verses*, 1917; *Late Lyrics and Earlier*, 1922; *Human

Shows, Far Phantasies: Songs and Trifles*, 1925; *Winter Words*, 1928; *Collected Poems*, 1931; *The Complete Poetical Works*, 1982-1985 (3 volumes; Samuel Hynes, editor).

NONFICTION: *Life and Art*, 1925 (E. Brennecke, editor); *The Early Life of Hardy*, 1928; *The Later Years of Thomas Hardy*, 1930; *Personal Writings*, 1966 (Harold Orel, editor); *The Collected Letters of Thomas Hardy*, 1978, 1980 (2 volumes; Richard Little Purdy and Michael Millgate, editors).

BIBLIOGRAPHY

Bayley, John. *An Essay on Hardy.* Cambridge, England: Cambridge University Press, 1978. Gives a close reading of most of Hardy's major novels, stressing the instability in his style. Hardy's writing was often ambiguous and, by arousing uncertain expectations in the reader, he was able to enhance suspense. His later novels, culminating in *Jude the Obscure*, were more tightly organized, a feature not to Bayley's liking, who prefers the adventitious and unplanned. Also notes that Hardy's attitude toward his male heroes is often determined by their relations with the novel's central female personality.

Campbell, Matthew. *Rhythm and Will in Victorian Poetry.* Cambridge, England: Cambridge University Press, 1999. Examines the literature and poetry of Victorian greats Hardy, Robert Browning, Alfred, Lord Tennyson, and Gerard Manley Hopkins.

Kramer, Dale, ed. *The Cambridge Companion to Thomas Hardy.* Cambridge, England: Cambridge University Press, 1999. An indispensable tool for students of Hardy. Includes bibliographical references and an index.

_____. *Critical Essays on Thomas Hardy: The Novels.* Boston: G. K. Hall, 1990. Divided into a section of overviews and a section on individual novels: *Far from the Madding Crowd, The Return of the Native, The Mayor of Casterbridge, The Woodlanders, Tess of the D'Urbervilles*, and *Jude the Obscure*. Includes an introduction but no bibliography.

Millgate, Michael. *Thomas Hardy: A Biography.*

New York: Random House, 1982. The most
scholarly biography by one of Hardy's best critics. Includes detailed notes and bibliography.

Seymour-Smith, Martin. *Hardy*. New York: St. Martin's Press, 1994. An opinionated major biography, taking issue with but not superseding Michael Millgate's important work. No notes, brief
bibliography.

Southerington, F. R. *Hardy's Vision of Man*. London:
Chatto & Windus, 1971. Defends at considerable
length a revolutionary account of Hardy. Most authorities see Hardy as a pessimist: His "President
of the Immortals" is indifferent to human concerns. However, for Southerington, he is an optimist; his novels show that given appropriate attitudes, one need not be overcome by adversity. The
novels also contain many autobiographical passages, which the book traces in detail.

WILSON HARRIS
Kona Waruk

Born: New Amsterdam, British Guiana; March 24,
1921

PRINCIPAL LONG FICTION

Palace of the Peacock, 1960
The Far Journey of Oudin, 1961
The Whole Armour, 1962
The Secret Ladder, 1963
Heartland, 1964
The Eye of the Scarecrow, 1965
The Waiting Room, 1967
Tumatumari, 1968
Ascent to Omai, 1970
Black Marsden, 1972
Companions of the Day and Night, 1975
*Da Silva da Silva's Cultivated Wilderness and
Genesis of the Clowns*, 1977
The Three of the Sun, 1978
The Angel at the Gate, 1982
Carnival, 1985

The Guyana Quartet, 1985 (includes *Palace of the
Peacock*, *The Far Journey of Oudin*, *The Whole
Armour*, and *The Secret Ladder*)
The Infinite Rehearsal, 1987
The Four Banks of the River of Space, 1990
The Carnival Trilogy, 1993 (includes *Carnival*, *The
Infinite Rehearsal*, and *The Four Banks of the
River of Space*)
Resurrection at Sorrow Hill, 1993
Jonestown, 1996

OTHER LITERARY FORMS

Wilson Harris's first published novel appeared in
1960, when he was thirty-nine. Before this, his creative efforts were mainly in poetry, which, given the
poetic-prose of his novels, is not surprising. He published a few volumes of poems, including *Fetish*
(1951), issued under the pseudonym Kona Waruk,
and *Eternity to Season* (1954). While the first collection is perceived as apprenticeship material, the second is generally praised and seen as complementary
to his early novels; it anticipates the novels' symbolic
use of the Guyanese landscape to explore the various
antinomies that shape the artist and his community.
Harris published volumes of short stories, *The
Sleepers of Roraima* (1970), with three stories, and
The Age of the Rainmakers (1971), with four. These
stories are drawn from the myths and legends of the
aborigines of the Guyanese hinterland. Harris does
not simply relate these myths and legends; as in his
novels, he imbues them with symbolic and allegorical significance. Harris, conscious of how unconventional and difficult are his novels, attempted to elucidate his theories of literature in several critical
works. His language here, however, is as densely
metaphorical as in his novels. Harris's ideas are outlined in *Tradition, the Writer, and Society* (1967), a
group of short exploratory essays on the West Indian
novel, and *History, Fable, and Myth in the Caribbean
and Guianas* (1970), a series of three lectures. These
ideas are developed in his later volumes of essays,
Explorations: A Selection of Tales and Articles
(1981) and *The Womb of Space: The Cross-Cultural
Imagination* (1983), in which Harris analyzes the
works of a wide range of writers, including Ralph

Ellison, William Faulkner, Paule Marshall, Christopher Okigbo, Edgar Allan Poe, Raja Rao, Jean Rhys, Derek Walcott, and Patrick White.

Harris's introduction to the 1993 Faber and Faber edition of *The Carnival Trilogy* is a major statement of his principles of concept and technique. Originally an article for the British spiritual journal *Temenos*, the introduction discusses Harris's various debts to Dante, the Faust legend, and modern science. The introduction is valuable not only for explicating the trilogy but also for exposing Harris's pulling together of myth, storytelling, and symbol. *The Radical Imagination*, a book of interviews with Harris, was published in 1992; *The Selected Essays of Wilson Harris* appeared in 1999. Aside from providing expositions of his own fiction, Harris addressed issues of conquest and hegemony often assayed by "postcolonial critics" who desired to revise the cultural arrogance of Western imperialism. Harris, though, draws more or less equally from European and non-European culture and (as in his essay "Quetzalcoatl and the Smoking Mirror") is more interested in using myth to advance beyond worldly aggression than he is in addressing specific acts of colonial aggression as such.

ACHIEVEMENTS

From the publication of his very first novel, Harris's work attracted much attention. Though many readers are puzzled by his innovative techniques and his mystical ideas, his works have received lavish praise. While firmly established as a major Caribbean novelist, Harris is not seen as simply a regional writer. Critics outside the Caribbean perceive him as one of the most original and significant writers of the second half of the twentieth century, and, in trying to come to grips with his ideas and techniques, have compared him with William Blake, Joseph Conrad, William Faulkner, Herman Melville, and W. B. Yeats. As would be expected of one who eschews the conventional realistic novel, Harris is not without his detractors. Some readers have pounced on his work for being idiosyncratic, obscure, and farraginous. Those who defend him indicate that Harris's novels demand more of the reader than the conventional work and that what initially appears to be merely ob-

scure and confused is intended to shock the reader and force him or her to deconstruct habitual perceptions and responses. His importance has been acknowledged by the many awards he has received from cultural and academic institutions: He received the English Arts Council Award twice (in 1968 and in 1970) and a Guggenheim Fellowship (in 1972), and held many visiting professorships and fellowships at such institutions as Aarhus University (Denmark), Mysore University (India), Newcastle University (Australia), the University of Toronto, the University of the West Indies, the University of Texas, and Yale University. In 1984, he received an honorary doctorate from the University of the West Indies, and subsequently he was awarded the 1985-1987 Guyana Prize for Fiction. In 1992 he won Italy's Mondello Prize for fiction.

BIOGRAPHY

Theodore Wilson Harris was born in New Amsterdam, British Guiana (now known as Guyana), on March 24, 1921. He attended Queen's College, a prestigious high school staffed by English expatriates, from 1934 to 1939. He went on to study land surveying and geomorphology, and in 1942 became an assistant government surveyor and made the first of many expeditions into the interior of Guyana. Between 1944 and 1953, he led several expeditions into other interior and coastal areas. The interior, with its dense tropical jungles, vast savannahs, and treacherous rivers, and the coastal region, with its mighty estuaries and extensive irrigation system, had a strong effect on Harris, later reflected in his novels. These expeditions also made Harris aware of the life of the American Indians and of the various peoples of Guyana of African, Asian, and European ancestry, who came to populate his novels. While working as a surveyor, he nurtured his artistic talents by writing numerous poems, stories, and short essays for the little magazine *Kyk-over-al*, edited by the poet A. J. Seymour. In 1950, he visited Europe for the first time, touring England and the Continent, and in 1959 he emigrated to Great Britain. That year, he married Margaret Burns, a Scottish writer. (He was married in 1945 to Cecily Carew, but the marriage ended in divorce.) With the publication of his first novel in 1960, Harris became a full-time writer. He settled in London but constantly traveled to take up fellowships and professorships in Europe, Australia, India, the Caribbean, Canada, and the United States. Harris stated that these travels assisted him in providing some of the global, almost cosmic backdrops of his later fictions. His trip to Mexico in 1972 seems to have been especially influential on his use of the Quetzalcoatl legend in *The Carnival Trilogy*.

ANALYSIS

Wilson Harris's novels are variations on one theme. He believes that polarization in any community is destructive in any form it takes, whether it is between the imperial and the colonial, the human and the natural, the physical and the spiritual, the historical and the contemporary, the mythic and the scientific, or even the living and the dead. The healthy community should be in a constant state of evolution or metamorphosis, striving to reconcile these static opposites. The artist must aspire to such a unifying perception if he or she is to be truly creative, and his or her art must reflect a complementary, reconciling vision. The artist should reject, for example, the rigid conventional demarcation between past and present, corporeal and incorporeal, literal and allegorical. Time past, present, and future should be interlaced. The dead should exist side by side with the living. The literal should be indistinguishable from the metaphorical. In adhering to such ideas of fictional form, Harris produced innovative novels that some see as complex and challenging, others as obscure and idiosyncratic.

This perception of society and the artist and of the form fiction should take informs all of Harris's novels, with gradations in emphasis, scope, and complexity. Some novels, for example, emphasize the polarization rather than the integration of a community. Some accent the allegorical rather than the realistic. Some juxtapose the living with the dead. There are shifts in setting from novel to novel. Harris's artistic psyche is embedded in Guyana, and, though he settled in Great Britain in 1959, in his fiction he constantly returns to his native land, making use of the varied landscape of coastland, estuaries, jungles, wa-

terfalls, mountains, and savannahs. In his later novels, the range of his settings expands to include the Caribbean, Great Britain, and Latin America.

The polarization in the assessment of Harris's work continues. His advocates lavish praise on him, some perceiving him as a candidate for the Nobel Prize. Though Harris has had an enormous amount of scholarly work done on his fiction, especially in the 1990's, this Guyanese novelist has not entered into the broad circle of vaguely cultured readership that has embraced his Caribbean contemporaries V. S. Naipaul of Trinidad and Gabriel García Márquez of Colombia. Naipaul and García Márquez, both outstanding journalists as well as novelists, create a clear historical context for their fiction. Though a deep level of historical awareness is present in Harris's canon, history is braided with other discourses, such as those of myth, science, and anthropology, as in his use of the Carnival motifs. Perhaps this multilayered quality has inhibited his mass reception. His upbraiders continue to complain that his novels are strange, with, as David Ormerod observes, "no discernible yardstick for meaning—just a simple bland identification, where X is symbolic of something, perhaps Y or Z, because the author has just this minute decided that such will be the case." Shirley Chew, speaking of *The Three of the Sun*, states: "Harris has failed to rise to some of the more common expectations one brings to the reading of a novel." It is possible that such criticism is indicative of an inability to respond to the demands of Harris's challenging innovations; on the other hand, it is perhaps a reminder to Harris of his own rejection of the static polarization in community and creativity, a warning to him to heed the conventional in his pursuit of the innovative.

THE GUYANA QUARTET

Palace of the Peacock, Harris's first novel, is the first of *The Guyana Quartet*, four sequential novels set in different regions of Guyana. The novel is a perfect introduction to Harris's canon: It establishes the ideas and forms that are found in subsequent works. Of all of his novels, this is the one which has received the most extensive critical scrutiny and explication. Set in the Guyanese interior, the novel recounts the journey upriver of Donne, an efficient and ruthless captain, and his multiracial crew. They are looking for a settlement where they hope to find the Amerindian laborers who earlier fled Donne's harsh treatment. The account of the journey is provided by a shadowy first-person narrator, Donne's brother, who accompanies them. After an arduous journey, Donne and his crew reach the settlement, only to find that the American Indians have left. They again set out in search of them and, as they travel further upriver, several of the crew meet their deaths—some of them accidentally, some not. Eventually, Donne and two members of the crew reach the source of the river, a waterfall, and, abandoning their boat, begin climbing the cliff, only to fall to their deaths. The narrative is quite thin and is not given in as linear and realistic a way as this outline suggests. The novel, for example, begins with Donne being shot and killed before undertaking his journey, then proceeds to tell of the entire crew drowning but coming alive just before they reach the Amerindian settlement, and concludes with Donne falling to his death but reaching the mountaintop where stands the Palace of the Peacock.

The novel clearly is allegorical. Critics agree that Harris employs Donne and his strange crew as representations of antithetical yet complementary aspects of human experience. Yet their interpretations of what precisely these characters represent are quite diverse, and the novel accommodates them all. The novel is seen as examining the brotherhood of invader and invaded, the common destiny of the diverse races of Guyana, and the complementary and interdependent relationship between the material and the spiritual, the historical and the contemporary, and the living and the dead. The novel could be interpreted also as an allegorical study of the growth of the artist in an environment inhospitable to art. Drawing from his own experience in the challenging Guyanese hinterland, where he wrote his early pieces while working as a land surveyor, Harris shows that harsh surroundings put the aspiring artist in a quandary, for he is forced to look to his physical well-being by developing a materialistic, aggressive outlook that works against his contemplative, humane, artistic nature. At the end of the novel, Harris's narrator comes to realize that as an artist he must accept that he is the sum total of all the diverse antithetical experiences and impulses that coexist tensely but creatively in his psyche.

A cursory explication of the novel as such an allegorical *Bildungsroman* will provide an insight into Harris's unconventional artistry. Harris examines his narrator-protagonist's progression toward acceptance of the polarities of his artistic psyche in four broad phases which correspond to the four books of the novel. In book 1, the narrator, aspiring toward artistic and humane goals, suppresses his assertive and dictatorial tendencies. From the opening paragraph, it is evident that the narrator and Donne are alter egos: They represent antithetical aspects of one individual, who could be termed the protagonist. Their oneness is emphasized as much as their polarities. The protagonist's rejection of his Donnean qualities is signified by Donne's death in the novel's opening section and by the awakening of the narrator in a maternity ward, suggestive of a birth. After this scene, the journey upriver begins and Donne is found aboard the boat with his crew, but it is the narrator whose voice is prominent. At the end of book 1, Donne is described as being a shadow of his former self.

In book 2, the protagonist discovers that he cannot totally suppress his Donnean qualities, for to survive as an artist in his harsh environment he must be both the humane, contemplative observer and the assertive, forceful participant. This shift is indicated by the narrator's mellowing attitude toward Donne, who reappears as his former assertive self in book 2. Donne himself, however, mellows toward the narrator, admitting that he is caught up in "material slavery" and that he hates himself for being "a violent taskmaster." Their gradual adjustment to each other is shown in the relationships among the eight members of the crew, who, described by Harris as "agents of personality," represent overlapping but distinct impulses of the divided protagonist. Their personalities tend to run the scale from Donne's to the narrator's. They have their own alter egos. In book 3, as Donne and the narrator adjust to each other—that is, as the protagonist tries to resolve the inner conflict between his contemplative and active natures—various pairs of the crew die.

In book 4, the protagonist attains a new conception of himself as an artist—a conception that accommodates his antithetical feelings and attitudes. He now perceives that though as an artist he must resist the qualities of Donne and members of the crew close to him, he cannot deny them, for the artist incorporates all of their characteristics no matter how unrelated to art they may appear to be. The artist must acquire the all-embracing vision. A host of metaphors suggests this complementary conception. The protagonist reaches the Palace of the Peacock, with its panoramic perspective of the savannah, by falling back into the savannah. The Palace of the Peacock is also El Dorado, which Harris describes as "City of Gold, City of God"; it encompasses both material and spiritual riches. The Palace, moreover, has many windows offering an encompassing view of the world below and stands in contrast to Donne's one-windowed prisonhouse of the opening chapter. Taken together with the peacock's color spectrum, the many eyes of the peacock's tail, and the harmonious singing which pervades the many palatial rooms, the Palace paradoxically suggests both oneness and multiplicity. Such a perception of the artistic vision offered in this interpretation of *Palace of the Peacock* is not unique; it is found, for example, in the works of Yeats and Blake, whom Harris quotes several times in the novel. The uniqueness of the novel is to be found in the form and setting Harris employs to explore this familiar theme.

The Guyanese hinterland is most evocatively depicted in the novel, though realistic description recedes before the symbolic and allegorical functions of the setting. Though the characters occasionally emerge as living individuals and though their conversations have the authentic ring of Guyanese dialect and speech rhythm, they do not appear primarily as human figures but as allegorical forms. As a result, the protagonist's conflicts are not dramatized in any particularly credible, realistic situation. (*The Secret Ladder*, the last novel of *The Guyana Quartet*, which describes a similar river journey and a similarly ambivalent, tormented protagonist, provides a slightly more realistic, less allegorical study.)

The Far Journey of Oudin, Harris's second novel, is set in the riverain Abary district of Guyana, which is not too far inland from the Atlantic coast. The setting is as evocatively portrayed as is the Guyanese interior in *Palace of the Peacock*. The inhabitants of this community are East Indian farmers whose forefathers came to Guyana as indentured laborers. A few of these farmers have accumulated material wealth and have established a contemporary version of the master-laborer relationship with the less fortunate. *The Far Journey of Oudin* emphasizes the community's greed. It tells of Rajah's conspiring with his cousins to murder their illegitimate half brother, to whom their father left his property. The murderers suffer for their crime: Ram, a powerful, ruthless moneylender, brings about their ruin, with the help of Oudin, a drifter, who resembles the murdered half brother. Ram orders Oudin to abduct Rajah's daughter, Beti. Oudin, however, elopes with her. Thirteen years later, when Oudin is dying, Ram seeks to make Oudin and Beti's unborn child his heir.

The narrative is slightly more substantial in this novel than in *Palace of the Peacock*, but it is similarly submerged beneath Harris's allegorical emphasis. The characters, fluctuating between allegorical and literal functions, do not really come alive. The novel begins with Oudin's death and his vision of the past, which merges with the present and the future. He exists on several levels; he appears, for example, to be the murdered half brother. The novel emphasizes the polarized relationship between Ram, the unscrupulous materialist, and the sensitive, spiritual Oudin, whose unborn child to whom Ram lays claim symbolizes the possibility in the dichotomized community of reintegration—a factor which is underscored by the novel's circular structure and the recurring images of the union of opposites, such as the reference to the marriage of the sun and moon, to the juxtaposition of fire and water, and to the natural cycle of death and rebirth. Oudin, who strives to be an integrated individual, refers to "the dreadful nature in every compassionate alliance one has to break gradually in order to emerge into one's ruling constructive self."

The Whole Armour, the third novel of *The Guyana Quartet*, examines the fragmentation and integration of another Guyanese community, that of the riverain-coastal Pomeroon region. While the society of *The Far Journey of Oudin* is disrupted by greedy materialists, whom Harris perceives as the contemporary equivalents of the exploitative colonizers, that of *The Whole Armour* is disturbed by unbridled passion which erupts into violence and murder. Harris does not want to suppress passion, but he believes that it should be counterbalanced by discipline and control. This complementary Dionysian-Apollonian relationship is suggested by a series of betrothal images and particularly by the image of the tiger (the word used for what in the novel is actually a jaguar), which connotes the antithetical but complementary aspects of Blake's tiger.

The plot is difficult to extract because of the virtual inseparability of the actual and the allegorical, the living and the dead, and because of the elusive metaphors, described by Harris as his "fantastication of imagery." The novel, in bare outline, tells of the protagonist Cristo's fleeing the law, having been accused, apparently without justification, of the murder of Sharon's sweetheart. Cristo is sheltered from the law by his mother, Magda, a prostitute, and Abram, who falsely claims to be his father. Cristo and Sharon become lovers and are fugitives together. Eventually, they are caught but view the future hopefully because of the child Sharon has conceived. Cristo, who is linked with both the tiger and Christ, and the virginal Sharon are set against the passionate older generation. The two constantly yearn for regeneration and perceive themselves as being the founders of a new social order. The explicit discussion of this need for a new order has encouraged some critics to see *The Whole Armour* as Harris's most obviously political novel.

The Secret Ladder could be considered a restatement of and a sequel to *Palace of the Peacock*; it has, however, more plausible characterization and straightforward structuring. Like Donne, the protagonist, Fenwick, is in charge of a crew of men who reflect the racial mixture of Guyana. They are on a government hydrographic expedition that is surveying a stretch of the Canje River as the first step in a planned water conservation scheme. Poseidon, the patriarchal head of a primitive community of descendants of runaway slaves, violently resents their intrusion. Fenwick tries, with the help of Bryant, one of his crew, and Catalena, Bryant's mistress, to win him over. There is much misunderstanding and confrontation. In the end, Poseidon is accidentally killed.

Fenwick, like the protagonist of *Palace of the Peacock*, is torn between "imagination and responsibility," between dominating and accommodating. His boat significantly is named *Palace of the Peacock*. Evidently, he is aware of the importance of integrating his contrary impulses. He is attempting to live in the world of men with the insight his counterpart, Donne, has gained in the Palace of the Peacock. This attempt leads to inner turmoil and disturbing ambivalence, which the novel underscores with numerous images and metaphors. Fenwick frequently mentions the need to unify the head and the heart. His inner contradiction, like Donne's, is externalized in the relationship among his crew: For example, Weng the hunter is compared with Chiung the hunted; Bryant the thoughtful is juxtaposed with Catalena the emotional. Despite the more conventional plot, characterization, and structure, the novel is clearly Harris's. Its theme is polarization and reconciliation, and it is charged with allegorical and symbolic implications.

Harris's next five novels—*Heartland*, *The Eye of the Scarecrow*, *The Waiting Room*, *Tumatumari*, and *Ascent to Omai*—are also set in Guyana and provide further explorations of community and creativity imperiled by various confrontations and polarizations. Yet he places the emphasis now on individuals and on deep probing of their consciousness. The protagonists become progressively more internalized. Subtler dichotomies are examined, such as concrete and abstract realities, scientific and mythic truths, fiction reflecting and being reality, and individual and communal aspirations. In *The Waiting Room* and *Tumatumari*, Harris examines for the first time the psyche of female protagonists. He portrays Prudence of *Tumatumari*, for example, as engaged in an imaginative reconstruction of her brutal past, which she metamorphoses into something meaningful to her present. *Ascent to Omai* similarly affirms the possibility of creativity in catastrophe. In these five novels, Harris's audacious experiments with form continue. In *The Eye of the Scarecrow*, which is perhaps the Harris novel that is structurally furthest removed from conventional form, and *The Waiting Room*, he introduces the disjointed diary form.

LATER NOVELS

In the later novels *Black Marsden, Companions of the Day and Night, Da Silva da Silva's Cultivated Wilderness and Genesis of the Clowns, The Three of the Sun*, and *The Angel at the Gate,* Harris shifts the emphasis from portraying society's fragmentation, as he did in the early novels, to its possibilities for reintegration. Rebirth and resurrection are common motifs. If the Caribbean's brutal colonial history and its multiracial population provide the ideal context for a heightened consideration of communal disintegration, its "cross-cultural imagination" is similarly suited to an exploration of communal integration. These later novels all feature cross-cultural Caribbean or South American protagonists. In so doing, they are not restrictively regional in scope; they are concerned with the human community at large. This is pointed up by their larger canvases. They are set not simply in the Caribbean and Guyana but in Great Britain, India, and Latin America as well. An increasingly common form of these novels is the employment of narrators as editors and biographers who seek to piece together the protagonists' lives and raise questions about the polarities of art and life and about the literal and representational functions of language itself.

THE CARNIVAL TRILOGY

The Carnival Trilogy is, after *The Guyana Quartet*, Harris's second great masterwork. Although the three books that compose it do not continue with the same set of characters, they possess common motifs which contribute to a structural unity. *Carnival* is set in London in 1982, though the action stretches back to the town of New Forest in Guyana decades in the past. Everyman Masters, an industrial laborer, who dies in the first chapter of the book, and Jonathan Weyl, a writer, are both Guyanese who have emigrated to Great Britain. Weyl is a generation younger than Masters. This enables Masters to be a surrogate father figure to Weyl and Weyl's guide to the spirit world, conducting him as Vergil conducted Dante in the *Divine Comedy* (c. 1320). The killing of the Carnival King by the aggressive Thomas parallels political upheavals of the twentieth century, in all their grandeur and folly. Weyl's father, Martin, is killed on the day of the Carnival, yet the enactment of the festival keeps his memory alive for his son many years later. Similarly, Amaryllis, the beloved of Weyl, is not just an individual but also an abstract prototype representing several other women in the story: Aunt Alice Bartleby, two women named Jane Fisher, and Aimée, whose name, symbolically, represents love. Masters's descent to the underworld yokes together primitive savagery and modern experience. It provides a crucial act of tutelage not only to Weyl but also to all who live in the modern world. Masters, both ordinary Everyman and Carnival king, encompasses all this experience. He achieves wholeness without self-delusion, a state also represented by the Carnival.

The second book of the *Carnival Trilogy, The Infinite Rehearsal*, concentrates memorably around one image: the drowning of a mother, son, and aunt in 1961 a short distance from a South American beach. The most lyrical of the three books, *The Infinite Rehearsal* features a fascinating protagonist, Robin Redbreast Glass. Though he drowns in the book at the age of sixteen, Glass represents all the potential of humanity. Indeed, death is welcome to him, as life is one of the many barriers he tries to transcend. Glass, born in 1945, the year the atomic bombs were dropped, tries to rescue beauty and overcome the horrors of the twentieth century. There is much that is admirable in Glass's ambition and drive to perfection. However, he also has liabilities: a naive optimism, of the sort associated with a red-breasted robin, and the fact that, like glass, his temperament is too transparent, lacking the murky depths of the truly integrated human soul. Appearances by Glass's grandfather, who had written a revisionary treatment of the Faust legend in which Robin is also a character, and the seemingly malevolent Ghost embody the oscillation between dream and reality in Glass's mind. This "infinite rehearsal," which evades any settled definition, helps overcome human aggression and authoritative reality. By the end of the book, the spirit of Robin Redbreast Glass has come to terms with the female, as represented his cousin Emma, who survives the drama and becomes an archbishop by the year 2025. He has also reconciled with the spirit of death, represented by the Ghost, who ends up redeeming Glass and helping him fulfill his voyage into the future.

The Infinite Rehearsal is a concrete and lyrical novel. *The Four Banks of the River of Space*, however, is far more abstract and discursive. Whereas *The Infinite Rehearsal* is poised on the beach where Glass drowns, in a kind of borderline state between sea and land, *The Four Banks of the River of Space* is set deep within the rain forest of the Guyanese interior. This interior, however, is far from purely physical. Indeed, it represents the totality of the cosmos itself. The main characters in this book are Anselm, an architect and engineer, and Lucius Canaima, a revenge deity. The action begins in 1988; Anselm and Canaima have not met since their youth forty years ago. Anselm's name may allude to the eleventh century Christian writer Anselm of Canterbury, who dealt with the nature of being. Canaima represents the indigenous peoples of South America as well as the entire process of conquest and savagery through history. The river of space transcends time even as it incorporates its terrible, creative beauty. Evil and good change places to a degree, in the manner of Glass and the Ghost in the previous book, as the "good" Anselm is implicated in trends that threaten to destroy the world and the "evil" Canaima is seen as a spirit of renewal. Like Harris himself, Anselm, in the 1940's, had been a government surveyor among the indigenous Macusi people. Macusi spirituality centers around the waterfall, which dominates their territory. The image of the waterfall is converted into the idea of the four banks of the river of space, which all the characters have to traverse to complete their journey toward the future. The action is complicated by a romantic triangle consisting of Penelope George, modelled after the heroine of Homer's *Odyssey* (c. 800 B.C.E.), and her two husbands, Simon and Ross. As is typical of characters in this trilogy, Simon, Ross, and Penelope are all dead in the actual

"time" of the novel. The rivalry of Simon and Ross duplicates the antagonism between Canaima and Anselm, who turn out to be complementary, as both evil and good are crucial features of the cosmos. At the end of the book, Anselm and Canaima merge into each other. Anselm becomes genuinely "good," now that he has absorbed the presence and responsibility of evil. The story of Penelope comes to a healing resolution as she brings forth a child, who promises to repair the spiritual and psychological ravages of the past.

JONESTOWN

In *Jonestown*, Harris takes the event for which Guyana is most known in the outside world, the mass suicide in November, 1978, of the People's Temple cult led by Jim Jones, and links it to a far wider set of associations. Fictionalizing Jim Jones as Jonah Jones, Harris totally invents the rest of his major characters, creating an effect that is the opposite of a journalistic account of the Jonestown massacre. His protagonist, Francisco Bone, is the only survivor of the massacre. He is also heir to the spiritual quest pursued through so many avatars in *The Carnival Trilogy*, as he journeys through past, present, and future in search of a complete understanding of the universe.

Victor J. Ramraj, updated by Nicholas Birns

OTHER MAJOR WORKS

SHORT FICTION: *The Sleepers of Roraima*, 1970; *The Age of the Rainmakers*, 1971.

POETRY: *Fetish*, 1951 (as Kona Waruk); *Eternity to Season*, 1954.

NONFICTION: *Tradition, the Writer, and Society*, 1967; *History, Fable, and Myth in the Caribbean and Guianas*, 1970; *Fossil and Psyche*, 1974; *Explorations: A Selection of Tales and Articles*, 1981; *The Womb of Space: The Cross-Cultural Imagination*, 1983; *The Radical Imagination: Lectures and Talks*, 1992; *The Selected Essays of Wilson Harris*, 1999.

BIBLIOGRAPHY

Cribb, Tim. "T. W. Harris, Sworn Surveyor." *Journal of Commonwealth Literature* 28, no. 1 (1993): 33-46. A biographically oriented essay that discusses the relevance of Harris's early experience as a surveyor in the Guyanese interior to his fictional oeuvre; especially relevant to *The Four Banks of the River of Space*.

Drake, Sandra. *Wilson Harris and the Modern Tradition: A New Architecture of the World*. Westport, Conn.: Greenwood Press, 1986. Places Harris in the modernist tradition and shows how his fiction comprises a "third-world modernism." The reading of four novels—*Palace of the Peacock, Tumatumari, Ascent to Omai*, and *Genesis of the Clowns*—in this light rounds out the discussion. The accompanying bibliographical essay provides a valuable survey of the critical response to Harris's work.

Gilkes, Michael, ed. *The Literate Imagination: Essays on the Novels of Wilson Harris*. London: Macmillan, 1989. This collection, edited by a well-known scholar of Caribbean literature, includes Harris's discussion of "Literacy and the Imagination," as well as eleven essays by international critics whose work is divided into three sections: "Phenomenal Space," "Language and Perception," and "The Dialectical Imagination."

Howard, W. J. "Wilson Harris's *Guyana Quartet*: From Personal Myth to National Identity." *Ariel* 1 (1970): 46-60. Placing the novels that compose *The Guyana Quartet*—*Palace of the Peacock, The Far Journey of Oudin, The Whole Armour*, and *The Secret Ladder*—into the symbolist tradition, the essay links Harris's work with the poetry of William Blake and W. B. Yeats. Concludes that, like these earlier poets, Harris transforms history into myth.

Maes-Jelinek, Hena. *Wilson Harris*. Boston: Twayne, 1982. An excellent introduction to a complex body of fiction, the study provides biographical materials and traces the progress of Harris's fiction through detailed analyses of theme and technique. Includes extensive primary and secondary bibliographies and a chronology. Overall, a good book for the beginning reader of Harris's work.

The Review of Contemporary Fiction 17, no. 2 (Summer, 1997). Special issued devoted to Harris, which contains essays and interviews by Harris, his literary peers such as Zulfikar Ghose and Kathleen Raine, and a selection of critical essays by international contributors, ranging from the analytical to the theoretical.

Riach, Alan, and Mark Williams. "Reading Wilson Harris." In *Wilson Harris: The Uncompromising Imagination*, edited by Hena Maes-Jelinek. Sydney: Dangaroo Press, 1991. Two New Zealand critics provide one of the most insightful practical guides to Harris's work.

Sharrad, Paul. "The Art of Memory and the Liberation of History: Wilson Harris's Witnessing of Time." *The Journal of Commonwealth Literature* 27, no. 1 (1992): 110-127. A well-known commentator reflects on whether Harris is a mythical or historical novelist.

Slemon, Stephen. "Carnival and the Canon." *Ariel* 19, no. 3 (1988): 47-56. A prominent Canadian critic and theorist situates the first part of the *Carnival* trilogy within and against the Western tradition.

JIM HARRISON

Born: Grayling, Michigan; December 11, 1937

PRINCIPAL LONG FICTION

Wolf: A False Memoir, 1971
A Good Day to Die, 1973
Farmer, 1976
Legends of the Fall, 1979
Warlock, 1981
Sundog: The Story of an American Foreman, 1984
Dalva, 1988
The Woman Lit by Fireflies, 1990
Julip, 1994
The Road Home, 1998

OTHER LITERARY FORMS

To appreciate fully the lyrical voice that dominates Jim Harrison's best novels, it is helpful to bear in mind that he began his career as a poet. His first two volumes, *Plain Song* (1965), written under the name "James Harrison," and *Locations* (1968), received very little attention, and the reviews were mixed. With the publication of *Outlyer and Ghazals* (1971), critics began to give Harrison his due, but his next two volumes, *Letters to Yesenin* (1973) and *Returning to Earth* (1977), both issued by small publishing houses, were again overlooked, even after they were reissued in a single volume in 1979. *Selected and New Poems: 1961-1981* (1982), a volume which included the best of his previous work, demonstrated Harrison's range and complexity and established his as a major voice in American poetry. His collection *The Theory and Practice of Rivers: Poems* (1986) only served to demonstrate more fully both his breadth of interests and his mastery of the poetic form. *The Shape of the Journey: New and Collected Poems* (1998) restores to print lyrics and protest poems of *Plain Song*, the effusive *Letters to Yesenin*, and the Zen-inspired *After Ikkyu and Other Poems* (1996).

In addition to novels and poetry, Harrison has published numerous essays, predominantly in *Sports Il-* *lustrated* and *Esquire*. In his essays, Harrison emerges as an amateur naturalist who denounces fish-and-game violators, sings praises to seasoned guides and to ardent canoe racers, and laments the passing of the wilderness in the face of urban development.

ACHIEVEMENTS

Harrison, a venturesome and talented writer, proved himself an able poet, novelist, and journalist by revitalizing the territories and boundaries explored by others. Both northern Michigan and Key West, the Hemingway provinces, are re-created in Harrison's work. Also present are the subterranean worlds and the connecting roads which the Beats had earmarked, the relatively unsullied outback celebrated by Edward Abbey and Theodore Roethke, and the predominantly masculine worlds explored by writers such as Harrison's friend and fellow hunter Thomas McGuane and Larry McMurtry.

By refusing to limit himself to a single genre and by attending to "audible things, things moving at noon in full raw light," Harrison appeals to a diversified audience and portrays an integrated vision that reflects the subtler nuances of the physical and natural world. While his references are often esoteric, he is a masterful storyteller who easily blends primitive and naturalistic images with arcane literary allusions. The reader is thus able to hear and feel simultaneously the meaning and motion of objects and experiences.

BIOGRAPHY

James Thomas Harrison was born December 11, 1937, in Grayling, Michigan; soon after his birth, his family moved to Reed City and then to the East Lansing area when Harrison was twelve. While he repeatedly stated that his childhood was unremarkable, he clearly assimilated the spirit of the land and people found in northern Michigan and was deeply affected by the emotional bonds which held his family together. Perhaps because so much of this land has been ravaged by development, northern Michigan has come to constitute Harrison's Yoknapatawpha County, peopled by figures drawn from his German and Swedish ancestral lines.

(Library of Congress)

Convinced that "you couldn't be an artist in Michigan," he made a number of treks to various metropolitan areas in search of the "right setting" in which to write; not surprisingly, these forays, described in *Wolf*, were unsuccessful. Tragedy struck Harrison early in life, when he lost sight in one eye after being cut with a broken bottle. Later, his fourteen-year-old niece died. It was not until after his father and sister were killed in a head-on crash that he began to write in earnest. These personal losses, all the greater because they were unexpected, inform several of his novels and poems.

As the allusions that pepper Harrison's writing make clear, he became a prodigious reader early on. Not surprisingly, his graduate work was in comparative literature, and he called himself an "internationalist" in terms of his literary tastes and influences. An outspoken and somewhat outrageous man, Harrison experienced bouts with severe depression that would drive him periodically from urban existence to the woods of Michigan, where he would write until exhausted, then play, hunt, and wander the beloved fields near his home. An avid outdoorsman, Harrison adopted fishing as a counterweight to his time devoted to writing, being committed to a code of ethics and a way of life that discourage superfluous self-indulgence and encourage husbanding of resources. This earthy, well-read man is known for shunning the literary associations so expectant of famed authors, preferring instead a simpler existence of sharing the backwoods with friends when not engaged in verse.

ANALYSIS

What is perhaps most striking about Jim Harrison's novels is the range of emotions which they encompass. While he consistently assumes a masculine point of view and revels in violence and debauchery, he is able to capture the romantic spirit which energizes his protagonists. He also avoids the bathetic trap that undermines the artistry of so many novels written from an aggressively male perspective. His central characters, though often wantonly callous in their attitudes toward women, are propelled by a youthful wanderlust and are always extremely affable.

In his novels, Harrison often routinely suspends the narrative sequence and deletes causal explanation. In this way, he constructs a seamless web and traps reader and character alike in a world inhabited by legendary figures who are attuned to primeval nuances and thrive on epic adventure. His penchant for the episodic is complemented by his metaphorical language and lyric sensibilities, which enhance his ability to shift scenes rapidly without sacrificing artistic control or obscuring the qualitative aspects of his various milieus.

Harrison is willing to tackle topics considered too pedestrian for other artists. He is willing to experiment and risk the wrath of his critics. While in terms of his allusions he is very much an artist's artist, he is also very much a people's artist—willing to confront the dilemmas of aging that confront us all and make us look ridiculous on more than one occasion. More important, Harrison is capable of conveying a sense of loss and dispossession as it relates to the wilderness. What saves this sense from overwhelming his writing is his capacity for wonder and his ability to capture the mystery resident in the land and to imagine in life legendary figures whose exploits make life bearable. If one accepts Waldo Frank's definition of a mystic as being one "who *knows* by immediate experience the organic continuity between himself and the cosmos," then Harrison is a mystic. He is a superlative storyteller who is attuned to the rhythms of the earth and a poet whose lyrical voice can be heard on every page.

WOLF

By giving *Wolf* the subtitle *A False Memoir*, Harrison properly alerts the reader to the poetic license that he has taken in reconstructing his biography. Much of what is included is factual, but he has embellished it and transformed it into art. The work is "false" in that it merges time and place in such a way as to convey a gestalt of experiences rather than a sequence of events. It is also "false" because he succumbs to his "constant urge to reorder memory" and indulges himself in "all those oblique forms of mental narcissism." What results is a compelling odyssey of Swanson's impetuous flirtation with decadence and debauchery.

In his relatively obtuse author's note, Harrison provides some biographical data to flesh out the Swanson persona. Also included is an admission that the romance he is about to unfold is somewhat of a self-indulgence which, like his desire to see a wolf in broad daylight, is central to no one but himself. Having thus offered his apologia, he proceeds to enmesh the reader in the tangles of people and places that have affected his narrator, Swanson. When Swanson is introduced, he is on a weeklong camping trip in northern Michigan's Huron Mountains. In the course of the novel, he is alternately lost in the woods and lost in his own mental mires as he reflects on the "unbearably convulsive" life he had led between 1956 and 1960.

Swanson's wilderness excursions constitute a correlative for his sallies into the mainstream. When he is in the woods, his hikes produce a configuration resembling a series of concentric circles; he is guided largely by his instincts and his familiarity with certain reference points. Similarly, his treks to Boston, New York City, and San Francisco have a cyclical cadence and his itineraries are dictated more by his primal emotions than by conscious planning. In both environments, he assumes the stance of a drifter who is searching, against the odds, to discover an ordering principle around which to unscramble his conflicting longings.

A careful reading of *Wolf* reveals that the tension between the freewheeling and nostalgic selves energizes the entire book. By coming to the woods, Swanson is attempting somehow to resolve the dualistic longings that have colored his first thirty-three years, to "weigh the mental scar tissue" acquired during his various rites of passage. While in the woods, he is constantly recalling the head-on crash which killed both his father and his sister; the pain of this memory is undisguised and serves as a counterweight to the bravado with which he depicts his adventuring.

Appropriately, the dominant chord in *Wolf*, as in most of Harrison's work, is a sense of dispossession and loss. Throughout the book, he emphasizes the ways in which greed, technology, and stupidity have led to the despoliation of the wilderness and endan-gered not only species but ways of life as well. Noting that the "continent was becoming Europe in my own lifetime," Swanson recognizes that the "merest smell of profit would lead us to gut any beauty left." It is this understanding that leads him to depict governments as "azoological beasts," to conceive of the history of the United States in terms of rapine and slaughter, and to indulge himself in fantasies of depredation which come to fruition in *A Good Day to Die*.

When one reaches the end of the novel, however, one senses that Swanson has resolved very little. During his week in the woods, he has not only failed to see the wolf but also failed to illuminate a route "out of the riddle that only leads to another"; even as he labels his urban adventures "small and brutally stupid voyages" and accepts the fact that he longs for the permanence once provided by the remote family homesteads, he acknowledges that he will continue to drift, to "live the life of an animal" and to "transmute my infancies, plural because I always repeat never conquer, a circle rather than a coil or spiral."

A GOOD DAY TO DIE

A Good Day to Die, as William Crawford Wood observes, constitutes the second part of the song begun in *Wolf*. The novel, which takes its title from a Nez Perce Indian saying regarding war, chronicles the journey of the nameless narrator (who bears a marked resemblance to Swanson) from Key West to northern Arizona and on to Orofino, Idaho. As in *Wolf*, Harrison relies heavily on flashbacks and melds the narrator's memories with ongoing events; the novel is then less a correspondence between two periods than the route by which the narrator comes to accept life's capriciousness as a matter of course.

The nascent urge to avenge nature present in *Wolf* comes to fruition in *A Good Day to Die*. While the narrator, in retreat from his domestic woes, is vacationing and fishing in Key West, he is befriended by Tim, a Vietnam veteran whose philosophy of life is fatalistic and whose lifestyle is hedonistic. In the midst of an intoxicating evening, the two formulate a vague plan to go west and save the Grand Canyon from damnation. En route, they stop in Valdosta, Georgia, to pick up Sylvia, Tim's childhood sweetheart, who is the epitome of idealized womanhood—beautiful, innocent, and vulnerable—and who, in the course of the journey, unwittingly evokes the basest emotions and reactions from both of her cohorts.

The improbability that such a threesome could long endure is mitigated by Harrison's ability to capture the conflicting urges and needs of all three. While Sylvia may be too homey to be entirely credible, she does assume a very real presence. Throughout the novel, she functions as a counterweight to her companions and serves to underscore the risks inherent in not controlling one's romanticism. While all three have a tendency to delude themselves, she seems the most incapable of grounding herself and perceiving her situation clearly.

FARMER

In *Farmer*, Harrison frees himself from his tendency to write false memoirs in lieu of novels. There are passing references to a nephew who resembles the author, but these serve to underscore Harrison's familiarity with the people and the milieu he is depicting. The portraits are especially sharp and clear in the cases of Joseph, a forty-three-year-old farmer schoolteacher, and Dr. Evans, a seventy-three-year-old country physician. Equally crystalline is Harrison's portrayal of the northern Michigan environs in which Joseph's long overdue "coming of age" occurs.

Against the advice of his twin sister, Arlice, and his best friend, Orin, Joseph has remained on the family homestead in northern Michigan "not wanting to expose himself to the possible cruelties of a new life." Crippled in a farm accident at the age of eight, he has used various pretexts to avoid travel; he has lived through books rather than opening himself to firsthand experience. While his reading has kept him abreast, it has done little to sate his hunger for a fuller existence. In fact, his preference for books dealing with the ocean, marine biology, distant wars, and the Orient has contributed to his growing dissatisfaction; he longs to visit the ocean, to partake more fully of the life about which he has only read and dreamed.

Against this backdrop Harrison develops a strain which was present in both of his previous novels: the counterpointing of characters. In this case, the restrained but steadfast Rosealee is set in contrast to the urbanized and impetuous Catherine. Rosealee and Joseph, both reared in the provincial backwaters, have been about to be married for approximately six years. Joseph, who has made love to only a few women in his lifetime, impulsively enters into an affair with Catherine, his seventeen-year-old student, who is attractive, experienced, and willing.

Structurally, the novel moves from June, 1956, back to the events which transpired between October, 1955, and the following June. The affair begins as a self-indulgence, but Joseph becomes increasingly lightheaded and childlike, revelling in a swell of sensations and previously unknown emotions; he becomes embroiled in the kind of sexual morass which he had previously associated with the fictional worlds of Henry Miller and D. H. Lawrence. Only in retrospect does he understand the risks he has taken in order to free himself from his spiritual torpor; he has nearly destroyed Rosealee's love.

In the hands of a lesser writer, the story which Harrison unfolds could quickly become melodrama, the tone maudlin. That it does not is a measure of Harrison's talent. The book, far from lacking ironic distance, as some critics have charged, constitutes a parody of the Romantic novel; throughout the book, Harrison burlesques Joseph's inability to attain "a peace that refused to arrive" and with mock-seriousness describes self-pity as "an emotion [Joseph] had never allowed himself." Using Dr. Evans as a foil, Harrison unearths Joseph's buried resentments and fears and concludes the novel in such a way as to confirm the doctor's earlier statement that Catherine "is not even a person yet" and that the dallying has simply served as a diversion for both of them. The fact that Joseph cannot come firmly to this conclusion on his own clearly distinguishes him from the protagonists in *Legends of the Fall*.

LEGENDS OF THE FALL

Legends of the Fall, a collection of three novellas, confirms Harrison's fascination with those elemental and primal emotions that defy logic, are atavistic, and propel one into the "nether reaches of human activity" despite the attendant risks. Cochran in *Re-

venge, Nordstrom in *The Man Who Gave up His Name* and Tristan in *Legends of the Fall* operate in defiance of consensual reality; each builds his own fate, guided more by inner compulsions and a taste for the quintessential mystery of existence than by rational planning.

All three of the main characters are blessed with "supernatural constitutions" and a wariness which allows them to survive against the odds and to perform feats of strength and cunning. Running like a chord through all three of these novellas is Harrison's sense of the gratuitousness of any life plan, his belief that events are "utterly wayward, owning all the design of water in the deepest and furthest reaches of the Pacific." There are countless chance meetings and abrupt turns of plot and any number of catalytic conversions. While in novels such confluences might have strained the reader's ability to suspend disbelief, in the novellas one is swept along and becomes a willing coconspirator.

Revenge is, in some respects, the weakest of the three pieces because the reader is asked to believe that Cochran, who spent twenty years in the Navy as a fighter pilot, is so transported by his affair with Miryea that he is blind to the warnings issued by her husband, whose nickname, Tibey, means shark. In the service, Cochran had earned a reputation for being "enviably crazier and bolder than anyone else," but he had also maintained the instinctual mindfulness of the Japanese samurai, insisting on understanding "as completely as possible where he was and why." Once he meets Miryea, however, his circumspection is superseded by his romanticism and his "visionary energy." He conceives of her in terms of an Amedeo Modigliani painting, the quintessence of female beauty and charm; he is plummeted into a "love trance" which "ineluctably peels back his senses." Failing to comprehend the meaning of Tibey's gift of a one-way ticket to Madrid and seven thousand dollars, Cochran sets out heedlessly on a weekend tryst to Agua Prieta, where he and Miryea are beaten unmercifully by Tibey and his henchmen.

Opening with a visage of the badly wounded Cochran lying in the desert, Harrison neatly discounts the pertinence of biographical data and sum-

marily explains how Cochran arrived at his unenviable state. The focus of *Revenge* then comes squarely to rest on Cochran's attempts to avenge himself and recover Miryea. Despite the novella's sparsity, the reader is given sufficient information to comprehend the separate agonies which Cochran, Miryea, and Tibey are experiencing and to understand the emotional flux which resulted in the die being "cast so deeply in blood that none of them would be forgiven by their memories."

The events which transpire are a mix of the comic and the deadly serious, which come to a head when Miryea, succumbing to her own agony, becomes comatose—a development which allows Cochran to discover her whereabouts. The denouement follows quickly; Cochran and Tibey journey together to perform what amounts to a death watch. The epilogue is deftly understated so as to capture the enormity of Cochran's loss—he mechanically digs a grave "with terrible energy, methodical, inevitable"—and the meaning of the Sicilian adage "Revenge is a dish better served cold" becomes clear and indisputable.

Harrison's ability to write economic and yet sufficiently comprehensive novellas is more fully realized in *The Man Who Gave up His Name*. While again Harrison provides minimal biographical data to explain how Nordstrom, once a prominent Standard Oil executive, has come to be a cook in a modest restaurant in Islamorada, Florida, he focuses the novel in such a way as to make Nordstrom's conversion convincing and compelling. Nordstrom, like Joseph in *Farmer*, gradually awakens to his lassitude and, unlike Joseph, decides to do something positive to change his life and to get back in touch with the elemental pleasures which had sustained him when he was growing up in Reinlander, Wisconsin. What enables Nordstrom to make the transition is the fact that he has retained a healthy capacity for wonder. The novella opens with the image of Nordstrom dancing alone so as to recapture the metaphysical edginess which his years of success have denied him. Harrison then provides an overview of the pivotal experiences which have left Nordstrom dissatisfied with himself "for so perfectly living out all of his mediocre assumptions about life." In the course of two short chapters, Harrison introduces Laura, Nordstrom's former wife, and their daughter Sonia who, when she was sixteen, had jolted Nordstrom out of his lethargy with the observation that he and Laura were both "cold fish." This observation prompted Nordstrom to resign his Standard Oil job and take a less demanding job as vice president of a large book wholesaler and to seek fulfillment through any number of expensive purchases and avocations.

Nordstrom's quest for the "volume and intensity" which had been lacking in his corporate existence is accelerated when his father unexpectedly passes away in October of 1977. As he is grappling with his own sense of loss and "the unthinkable fact of death," he is compelled to question why he has conformed to all the normative expectations which have so little to do with the essence of life. To the amazement and horror of friends and family, he resigns his position and tries to give his money away, even making a contribution of twenty-five thousand dollars to the National Audubon Society "though he had no special fascination for birds." At the behest of his broker and his ex-wife, he sees a psychiatrist, and it becomes clear that he has exchanged the inessential insanities fostered by the American Dream for the essential insanities which will allow him to free himself from stasis and fulfill personal desires.

The defiance of social expectations which lies at the heart of Nordstrom's transition is even more central to an understanding of Tristan, the main character in *Legends of the Fall*. Unlike Nordstrom, however, Tristan has never paid obeisance to anyone. Having abandoned any sense of cosmic justice at the age of twelve, Tristan has steadfastly made his own rules and run his life according to personal design. He emerges as a legendary voyager, propelled by a seemingly genetic compulsion to wander; spiritually he is the direct descendant of his grandfather, who at the age of eighty-four is still engaged in high seas adventuring. Like Cochran and Nordstrom, Tristan has chosen to "build his own fate with gestures so personal that no one in the family ever knew what was on his seemingly thankless mind." Accordingly, Tristan is fated to live out certain inevitabilities.

Legends of the Fall is an episodic saga with perimeters which are staggering in their breadth. In the course of eighty-one pages, Harrison manages to imagine into being a multigenerational extended family, recount several complete cycles of events, and examine the ramifications of these sequences as they affect each member. The action spans several decades and several continents and it is a measure of Harrison's mastery that he can cover this range without sacrificing context or character delineation.

The tale opens in 1914 with the departure of Tristan and his brothers, Alfred and Samuel, from the family homestead in Choteau, Montana; accompanied by One Stab, they travel to Canada to enlist in the war effort. Using several complementary techniques, Harrison economically contrasts the personalities of the three brothers; it quickly becomes clear that Tristan and Alfred are polar opposites and that Samuel, a romantic naturalist in the tradition of Jean Louis Rodolphe Agassiz, is fated to die in World War I.

Just how opposed Tristan and Alfred are becomes a central thread in the novel. After Samuel is killed, Harrison makes a point of underlining the grief and guilt experienced by Tristan and Ludlow, their father; Alfred's response is virtually nonexistent, since "as a child of consensual reality" he alone escaped feelings of guilt. Equally important for understanding the distance between the two is that Tristan's career moves him from the status of horse wrangler to outlaw, while Alfred goes through all of the "proper" channels, beginning as an officer and ending as a United States senator. Finally, the response of Susannah, who is first married to Tristan and then to Alfred, is telling; her breakdown and ultimate suicide are a response, in part, to the impossibility of ever regaining Tristan's love.

The "legends" that constitute the heart of the novella are Tristan's, but the dominating spirit is One Stab's "Cheyenne sense of fatality." Samuel's death is the first turning point, and, while Ludlow is consumed by his own powerlessness, Tristan is compelled to act. That Samuel's death was the product of the Germans' use of mustard gas serves not only to justify Tristan's revenge—scalping several German soldiers—but also to convey Harrison's antipathy for the grotesqueries justified in the name of modernization.

Tristan's legendary status is enhanced by his joining and then succeeding his grandfather as the pilot of a schooner which traffics in munitions, ivory, and drugs. Rather than dwelling on the specifics of the seven years that Tristan spends at sea, Harrison merely provides a glimpse of the first year and an outline of the next six, noting that the substance of these years is known only to Tristan and his crew. The next leg of Tristan's journey is also neatly understated. It begins when he returns home, "still sunblasted, limping, unconsoled and looking at the world with the world's coldest eye." It soon becomes evident, however, that the wounds that the sea could not assuage are virtually washed away by his marriage to Two, the half-American Indian daughter of Ludlow's foreman, Decker. The seven-year grace period that Tristan experiences is elliptically treated because "there is little to tell of happiness"; Harrison quickly shifts to the *coup de grâce* which kills Two and leaves Tristan inconsolable, "howling occasionally in a language not known on earth."

With a growing realization that he could never even the score with the world, that his losses far exceeded his ability to avenge the capriciousness of either Samuel or Two's death, Tristan nevertheless becomes embroiled in a final sequence of death-defying events. Again the denouement is quick, but it involves an unexpected turn as Ludlow assumes the active role. As in the other novellas, the epilogue adds a sense of completeness and juxtaposes the modernized ranch owned by Alfred's heirs with the family graveyard in the canyon where they once had found "the horns of the full curl ram." It comes as no surprise that, "always alone, apart, somehow solitary, Tristan is buried up in Alberta." So ends the legend.

WARLOCK

In his 1981 novel, *Warlock*, Harrison melds the tone and techniques of the "false memoir" with those associated with the genre of detective fiction; what initially appears to be a marked unevenness in the pacing of the book is a direct result of this unconventional wedding. The first part of the novel contains minimal action and is used primarily to develop the central characters; the second and third parts, on the other hand, are packed with action and abrupt turns of plot. What unifies the work is Harrison's adept use of several comic devices, including a great deal of what Sigmund Freud called "harmless" wit and humor.

When he is introduced, Warlock, at the age of forty-two, has recently lost his forty-five-thousand-dollar foundation executive position and expends much of his time in self-indulgent reverie and experiments in creative cookery. He is a Keatsian romantic who began his career as an artist "on the tracks of the great Gauguin," finds resonance in the nobility and idealism of works such as Boris Pasternak's *Doctor Zhivago* (1958) and Miguel de Cervantes' *Don Quixote de la Mancha* (1605, 1615), and spends countless hours dreaming of a new beginning. He and Diana have moved north to Michigan's Lake Leelanau Peninsula to maintain "the illusion that one lived in a fairy tale, and everything would work out," a motive which makes him an unlikely candidate for top-secret sleuthing.

Diana, on the other hand, appears to be relatively stable with a nature almost antithetical to Warlock's. Yet, it becomes clear that she is not really any more able to decode the enigmas of reality than he. Although she is repeatedly depicted as a pragmatist, this trait is counterbalanced by her affinity for Asian mysticism and her infatuation with genius. While she is an ardent feminist and an excellent surgical nurse, she is equally drawn to the charades that animate their sexual life and constitute a variant of the living theater in which Warlock later becomes the unwitting star.

It is the dynamic tension between Diana and Warlock that leads him to accept a position as a troubleshooter for Diana's associate, Dr. Rabun; while both acknowledge that Rabun is an eccentric, neither knows the extent of his idiosyncrasies. From the onset, Rabun lets it be known that he does not like to reveal all that he knows; it is his very elusive nature that energizes the last two parts of the novel. How little either Diana or Warlock knows about him becomes clear only after both have been sufficiently beguiled to prostitute themselves and do his bidding.

The initial meeting between Warlock and Rabun and its immediate aftermath resemble slapstick comedy. In addition to the absurdist context into which Harrison implants their clandestine meeting, there is the brusque repartee and the importance each attaches to the inessentials. The contents of a briefcase, which Rabun entrusts to Warlock, are telling; in addition to two folders outlining Rabun's holdings, there are copies of *Modern Investigative Techniques*, a guide to tax law regulations, and a sensationalized, paperback best-seller on business crime. Warlock is given two days and instructed to study the material and to write a brief reaction to it. Warlock's behavior is no less comic; he arrives home and promptly secretes the briefcase into the refrigerator for safe keeping and deludes himself with grandiose dreams that his life is beginning to merge "with a larger scheme of affairs," a truth which, unknown to him, constitutes a pithy double entendre.

Warlock's father, a top detective in Minneapolis, tries to warn his son away from the position and, failing at that, offers a good deal of advice and assistance. Their conversations are peppered throughout and serve to infuse the novel with a droll midwestern humor and to underline Warlock's comic naïveté. Warlock's unpreparedness and vulnerability quickly become a dominant chord; while he conceives of himself as one of the "knights of the surrealistic age," the author makes it clear that, as a knight-errant, he lacks the purity of motive which spurred Don Quixote and the equivalent of a Sancho Panza. Instead, he has only his most unfaithful dog, Hudley, as his "Rozinante though without saddle or snaffle."

Part 2 opens with an image of Warlock setting north on his first mission, completely undaunted despite the fact that he is en route to walk a two-thousand-acre area in the Upper Peninsula in search of lumber poachers. While he has the appropriate sense of adventure for the mission he undertakes, his idealism repeatedly blinds him to clues that should have been obvious to the most amateur sleuth. During the third part of the novel, Warlock abruptly discovers that reality is far more evanescent than even the most fleeting of dreams. Sent to Florida to "get the goods" on Rabun's estranged wife and his ostensibly homosexual son, who appear to be cheating Rabun out of millions of dollars, and on a society dame who has filed a seemingly outrageous suit against Rabun for injuries incurred when one of his health spa machines went wild, Warlock finds himself in a veritable house of mirrors.

The events that transpire during his Florida sally are unexpected and outrageously comedic. Again, Harrison relies on "harmless" humor and evokes compassion for the hapless hero. As a result of Warlock's adventures, Harrison abruptly turns the tables and destroys his preconceptions by unmasking Rabun as a perverted swindler and forcing Warlock to the realization that he has been "played for the fool" by almost everyone, including the charmed Diana.

After recovering a modicum of equilibrium, Warlock takes the offensive; reading only children's books "to keep his mind cruel and simple," he launches a counterattack which is simultaneously programmatic and impulsive, the former aspects resulting from the work of his father and the latter from Warlock's own primal energies. There is a good deal of mock-heroics on Warlock's part, but in the end, Rabun is brought to justice and Warlock and Diana are reunited. Like his spiritual heir who returns to La Mancha after having been bested by the Knight of the White Moon, Warlock rejects a job offer to track down a Moonie and returns to his pursuit of Pan.

While *Warlock* is not a "representative" novel, it contains many of the elements which unify Harrison's oeuvre. Warlock, like Swanson in *Wolf* and Joseph in *Farmer*, is a romantic and a dreamer; he is a man ruled by elemental desires, who repeatedly becomes embroiled in ill-conceived liaisons and who "belongs" in northern Michigan despite the fact that he has a habit of getting lost in the woods. All of Harrison's central characters seem to have a "capsulated longing for a pre-Adamic earth" and a nostalgia for the unsullied woodlands of their childhoods.

SUNDOG

With the publication of *Sundog*, Harrison returns to his technique of employing the almost all too present narrator. The novel hopscotches between revealing the life of Robert Corvus Strang and chronicling the misadventures of the narrator, who bears a strong resemblance to the persona Harrison has created in his earlier works.

The narrator meets Strang during what he describes as a "long voyage back toward Earth," a voyage that would put him in touch with the quintessential American. Strang pursued the American Dream only to be crippled in a fall down a three-hundred-foot dam. His experiences, no less than his persistent refusal to accept defeat, make Strang worth knowing. He is, as Harrison describes him, "a man totally free of the bondage of the appropriate."

It becomes clear that Strang and the narrator are kindred spirits—two sides of a single being. Both have more than average appreciation and respect for the forces of nature, even if the narrator is far less willing to plunge heart, soul, and body into its incomprehensible eddy. Both have unbounded passions and lusts, even if the narrator seems less in control of his anima or animus than Strang and more prone to succumb to melancholy, confusion, and despair. Both harbor a deep need to make sense of their own biographies and to plumb the depths of forgotten events that have unmistakably marked their personalities and approaches toward life. The hint of a biographical connection only strengthens their correspondences.

Robert Corvus Strang, as the reader comes to know him, is a man who has been involved on an international scale, building bridges, dams, and irrigation systems since his debut involvement in the construction of the Mackinac Bridge, despite the fact that he contracted epilepsy after he was struck by lightning at the age of seven. His has been a life influenced by the polar personalities of his father, who traveled the revival circuit, and his older brother, Karl, who viewed truth as largely situational. His understanding of mechanical and electrical principles is balanced by his understanding of people, most of whom suffer, in his estimation, "because they live without energy" and can accomplish nothing. Strang, on the other hand, even as he attempts to recover from the side effects of a local remedy for his epilepsy, lives with great energy and maintains his commitment to regain his health and resume his career as

a contractor on an upcoming project in New Guinea.

His self-imposed cure requires him to regress to a preadolescent state so as to "repattern his brain and body," the physical corollary to what the narrator asks him to do on a more personal and emotional level. At the novel's conclusion, Strang's attempts to begin again can be seen both as a therapeutic renewal process and as an exorcism through which he conquers the artificial barriers imposed by both modern medicine and those who profess to care for him.

Among the personal dramas of Strang's early life and his current battles, Harrison interweaves a sense of wonder that has served as a leitmotif in each of his earlier works, again claiming the Upper Peninsula as his own. Against this setting, Harrison offers counterpoints of urban violence, corporate greed and venality, and the unbridled insensitivity and martyrdom of the missionaries.

Harrison's ambiguous denouement only serves to underline his conviction that life resembled a "crèche-like tableau, a series of three-dimensional photographs of the dominant scenes, the bitterest griefs and the accomplishments." Harrison captures these images in his portrayal of Strang, whose life is keynoted by "love, work, and death . . . held together by wholeness, harmony and radiance."

DALVA

Despite its multiple plot lines, *Dalva* is also held together by a wholeness and a humanitarian spirit. The novel, in some ways, is Harrison's most ambitious undertaking. It is ambitious not only because it seeks to communicate a multigenerational family history but also because two-thirds of the novel is told from a woman's perspective.

Harrison's use of Dalva as the primary narrator, no less than his use of Clare as the major force in *The Woman Lit by Fireflies*, demonstrates his capacity to transcend the masculine point of view and enter into a world that, according to the majority of critics, he has never even conceptualized. Dalva, like her mother Naomi, emerges as a woman capable of acting and reacting with an equal amount of certitude.

From the beginning it is clear that, despite caprice and mistreatment, Dalva is not about to "accept life as a brutal approximation." Having lost her only child to adoption, and Duane, the only man she ever loved, to circumstances (and later death), Dalva is caught amid conflicting emotions—knowing what she has to do to earn her own freedom but fearing the consequences and the pain she could cause others. She is also mired in a family matrix that defies easy explanation.

Harrison structures *Dalva* as a three-part novel, centering the first book on Dalva's longings and aspirations, the second on Michael's misbegotten attempts at scholarship, and the third on the events leading up to Dalva's eventual reintegration of the various aspects of her biography. While each of the books has a completeness on a superficial level, the three are ineluctably associated with Dalva's grandfather and his allegiance to the American Indians.

Grandfather's journals allow the reader to comprehend a period of history that has long been whitewashed in history textbooks, and his sage advice allows Naomi, Dalva, Rachael, and others to make sense out of the tragedies that pepper their lives. His attitude is one born of pragmatism and necessity; having seen the less seemly side of American culture, he fully understands that "each of us must live with a full measure of loneliness that is inescapable and we must not destroy ourselves or our passion to escape this aloneness." It was this same uncanny understanding of the human condition that allowed Grandfather to coexist with the Sioux, who found his ethic toward the land and his rapport with people akin to their own.

THE WOMAN LIT BY FIREFLIES

The ongoing vulnerability of the American Indians is a theme that dominates *Brown Dog*, the first of the three novellas that constitute *The Woman Lit by Fireflies*. Harrison's tone, however, is distinctly different. Rather than delving into the historical record, Harrison highlights the insensitivity of modern Americans to Native American traditions and culture and lampoons a legal system that defends the denigrators of history. While his sympathies remain the same as in his earlier works, the approach he takes is more reminiscent of *Warlock* than of *Dalva*.

Because of the seriocomic tone of the work, the book is dominated by characters (both living and dead) who are not entirely believable and who serve, instead, to buttress an assault against the materialism and insensitivity of the modern world. That Harrison casts his story through the filtered lens of Shelly, an aspiring anthropology graduate student, tips his hand from almost the first page of the book. While it is clearly apparent that Brown Dog may well need an editor, Shelly serves as a deflector rather than an editor.

Brown Dog, as a typical Harrison protagonist, is a man trying to cope with middle age. When he finds a three-hundred-pound American Indian chief at the bottom of Lake Superior, he responds with the same degree of maturity that destined Warlock to his misadventures. Like Warlock, he stumbles through life, but unlike Warlock, he lacks an intelligent counterpart. Instead, Brown Dog is teamed with the female equivalent of Dalva's Michael. Shelly is opportunistic and insensitive to the values that make certain areas off-limits to outsiders. She is not unlike Brown Dog, however, as both are comic characters obviously unprepared to deal with the modern world. What she has over Brown Dog is that she comes from a wealthy family and can generally extract the results that she desires.

The ability to buy oneself out of trouble is also a theme which dominates *Sunset Limited*, the second novella in *The Woman Lit by Fireflies*. *Sunset Limited*, unlike *Brown Dog*, reads as a parable in which one is forced to reconsider the parable of the camel and the eye of the needle. It is an abbreviated retrospective akin to Thomas Pynchon's *Vineland* (1989), in which the reader is reacquainted with 1960's radicals and forced to deal with the ways in which their pasts have shaped their presents. Gwen, who seems like an unlikely revolutionary, is teamed with two individuals who have clearly abandoned any insurrectionary thoughts and another who has merely retreated from the fray. That their quest is to gain the freedom of a tired gadfly of a revolutionary who has been hanging on long after his time is both relevant and beside the point. Harrison rather heavy-handedly points out in the final chapter that this is a fable, and as in most fables, there is a moral that has to do with basic values and the risks of renouncing those values at the expense of the immediate community. Hence, once Billy confesses to his past complicity with the authorities, it comes as no surprise that if a life must be spared, it will be his. Riches, in the elemental world in which Harrison dwells, guarantee very little.

As if to reinforce this point, but from a very different perspective, Harrison closes his set of novellas with *The Woman Lit by Fireflies*, which leaves the reader with no illusions about the protections offered by money. *The Woman Lit by Fireflies* may silence those critics who cannot see Harrison as a universal novelist. His appreciation for the lot of women—their failed expectations, existential angst, and lack of challenge—comes through quite clearly. Clare is a woman wearied from "trying to hold the world together, tired of being the living glue for herself, as if she let go, great pieces of her life would shatter and fall off in a mockery of the apocalypse."

Clare is not an extraordinary character, yet she has the courage to abandon a marriage that has betrayed her expectations decades before. The impetuous escape, half-consciously orchestrated by Clare, constitutes a psychic rebirth, a coming to terms with her childhood, adulthood, and future. In relinquishing the creature comforts to which she had always been accustomed, she finds new sources of strength as she conquers the dangers of finding shelter, water, and mental balance in a world that is dominated by elemental urges and necessities.

Clare is not renouncing money or creature comforts, although along the way she does prove that she can live without them; instead, she is renouncing the predatory ethic of dominance. As she says at one point, "I want to evoke life and [Donald] wants to dominate it."

JULIP

Julip expands Harrison's manly image by leaping past the tradition of maleness to address tender life issues. Like *Legends of the Fall* and *The Woman Lit by Fireflies*, the book is composed of three novellas. The title story focuses on the stressful attempts by Julip to retrieve her brother Bobby from jail. Surrounded by adversity, an alcoholic father, a cold, calculating mother, a crazy brother, and a nymphoma-

niac cousin, the tough and resourceful Julip resorts to the gentleness of training dogs and reading Emily Dickinson's poetry to gain solace from the madness surrounding her. Julip attempts to convince her incarcerated sibling to plead insanity as a ploy to be released from his sentence, the result of his killing three men—Julip's past lovers. The ever-continuing conflict between her parents creates a young woman full of doubts and confusion.

In *The Seven Ounce Man*, Harrison renews themes and characters from earlier works. Brown Dog, the epitome of the American existential hero, reminisces of his love for an anthropologist who attempts to desecrate an American Indian burial ground. Somewhat like Harrison, Brown Dog prefers the quiet rhythm of nature to the roaring pace of humanity. He cannot seem to avoid trouble, haphazardly bumbling through incidents, revealing the ridiculous folly that ultimately entangles him with American Indian rights groups.

Harrison selects a fifty-year-old professor accused of having a tryst with a young student as the focus in *The Beige Dolorosa*. Satiated with accusations of impropriety and campus politics, Phillip, the professor, retreats from campus life to the relaxed cadence of the Latino Southwest, where he discovers serenity. Like Julip and Brown Dog, Phillip surrenders to nature as both a form of survival and a restoration of the soul.

THE ROAD HOME

The Road Home, a deep, complex, and spiritually oriented work, demonstrates Harrison's maturity. He offers five compelling stories, told through multigenerational characters of *Dalva*'s Northridge family. Harrison's strong narrative weaves fantasy with reality and Native American perspectives with midwestern mentality. The novel opens in the 1950's, with the half-Sioux patriarch John remorsefully recounting his youth, his attempts at art, and his final acceptance of a way of life as a horse rancher in Nebraska. Ruthless at times in business, John amasses land, status, and a legacy, but he bemoans not achieving artistic fulfillment. Nelse, Northridge's grandson and Dalva's son, given up at birth for adoption to a wealthy family, portrays himself as a loose wanderer whose passion for birding chips away at his opportunity for a "normal" existence. Nelse targets a spousally abused wife whom he learns to love—and who loves him. Dalva's mother, Naomi, who motivates Nelse into rejoining the family, and Paul, son of Naomi and John, offer rich viewpoints of the intriguing tale from their perspective. Finally, Dalva, the strong, willful one, faces a life-threatening illness and the turmoil of understanding the man who was the baby she gave away at birth.

Harrison uses death as a metaphor for the concept of home, but home also is the Nebraska lands surrounding the Niobara Valley and River, which courses through all the characters in the novel. The author's attention to detail, melding of familiar characters, and masterful storytelling make *The Road Home* a strong sequel to *Dalva*.

C. Lynn Munro, updated by Craig Gilbert

OTHER MAJOR WORKS

POETRY: *Plain Song*, 1965; *Locations*, 1968; *Outlyer and Ghazals*, 1971; *Letters to Yesenin*, 1973; *Returning to Earth*, 1977; *Selected and New Poems: 1961-1981*, 1982; *The Theory and Practice of Rivers: Poems*, 1986; *The Theory and Practice of Rivers and New Poems*, 1989; *After Ikkyu and Other Poems*, 1996; *The Shape of the Journey: New and Collected Poems*, 1998.

NONFICTION: *Just Before Dark: Collected Nonfiction*, 1991.

BIBLIOGRAPHY

Bourjaily, Vance. "Three Novellas: Violent Means." *The New York Times Book Review* (June 17, 1979): 14. With an understanding of the modus operandi needed for a successful novella, Bourjaily evaluates Harrison's craftsmanship in each of the three novellas included in *Legends of the Fall*. Most useful for the points that are raised and are equally pertinent to Harrison's later collection of novellas *The Woman Lit by Fireflies*.

Harrison, Jim. "An Interview with Jim Harrison." Interview by Kay Bonetti. *Missouri Review* 8, no. 3 (1985): 63-86. In this wide-ranging interview, Harrison discusses his impetus for writing, the

writers who have influenced him, his view of art, and his sources for ideas. He explains that building sentences and plausible explanations constitutes his defense against the outside world.

_____. "From the *Dalva* Notebooks: 1985-1987." *Antaeus* 61 (Autumn, 1988): 208-214.

_____. "Poetry as Survival." *Antaeus* 64 (Spring/Autumn, 1990): 370-380. These articles can be considered companion pieces. The first sheds insight into both *Dalva* and *The Woman Lit by Fireflies*, and the latter does much to explain Harrison's affinity with the poetic process and American Indian art. Taken together, the two pieces remind the reader that Harrison remains a reflective critic and commentator, attuned to the forces of the late twentieth century.

McClintock, James I. "*Dalva*: Jim Harrison's 'Twin Sister.'" *The Journal of Men's Studies* (Spring, 1998): 319-331. A post-Jungian perspective of *Dalva* exploring the feminine side of masculinity as influenced by psychologist James Hillman. Harrison's previous works usually portrayed men struggling with external and internal environments, but this book, and this study, reveal women's consciousness through the author's alignment as a "sister" to Dalva.

Mesic, Penelope. "Riders on the Storm." *Chicago Magazine* (January, 1995): 31-32. Interview with Harrison about his views on *Legends of the Fall* facing Hollywood attention as a subject for a feature film. Interesting comments by Harrison on his challenges to keep the film and novella cohesive and his newly found personal attraction to the story.

Morgan, Thais E. *Men Writing the Feminine: Literature, Theory, and the Question of Genders*. Albany: State University of New York Press, 1994. A collection of essays that explores questions about gender and writing from a wide range of theoretical perspectives, including psychoanalysis, semiotics, deconstruction, feminism, postmodernism, and discourse analysis. A good insight to Harrison's style.

Reilly, Edward C. *Jim Harrison*. New York: Twayne, 1996. The first book-length appraisal of the writer's life and works. Draws on an array of primary and secondary sources, including personal interviews with Harrison and his family and friends. Assessing Harrison's poetry, Reilly pinpoints common motifs and identifies links between the poetry and the fiction

Roberson, William H. "Macho Mistake: The Misrepresentation of Jim Harrison's Fiction." *Critique* 29 (Summer, 1988): 233-244. Roberson directly confronts Harrison's reputation as a "macho" fiction writer, analyzing and debunking critics' claims with pithy analyses of Harrison's first six novels. He acknowledges that figures such as Tibey in *Revenge* and Tristan in *Legends of the Fall* support the "myopic critical perception of [Harrison's] fiction" but delves deeper to unearth the "angst of the middle-aged American male" struggling to come to terms with both himself and his surroundings—subjects that have long been Harrison's forte.

Smith, Wendy. "Jim Harrison: The Poet and Novelist Considers 'This Shuddering Elevator That Is a Writer's Life.'" *Publishers Weekly*, August 3, 1990, 59-60. A practical discussion by Harrison concerning his success as a writer, both critically and financially, from his years of striving, starving poet to acclaimed author. Typical of Harrison, the no-nonsense approach to life shines through in this revealing interview.

L. P. Hartley

Born: Whittlesea, England; December 30, 1895
Died: London, England; December 13, 1972

Principal long fiction

Simonetta Perkins, 1925
The Shrimp and the Anemone, 1944
The Sixth Heaven, 1946
Eustace and Hilda, 1947
The Boat, 1949
My Fellow Devils, 1951
The Go-Between, 1953
A Perfect Woman, 1955
The Hireling, 1957
Facial Justice, 1960
The Brickfield, 1964
The Betrayal, 1966
Poor Clare, 1968
The Love-Adept, 1969
My Sisters' Keeper, 1970
The Harness Room, 1971
The Collections, 1972
The Will and the Way, 1973

Other literary forms

L. P. Hartley published, in addition to eighteen novels, six collections of short stories: *Night Fears* (1924), *The Killing Bottle* (1932), *The Traveling Grave* (1948), *The White Wand* (1954), *Two for the River* (1961), and *Mrs. Carteret Receives* (1971). Reprinted in *The Complete Short Stories of L. P. Hartley* (1973), with the exception of ten apprentice pieces from *Night Fears*, the stories reveal Hartley's reliance on the gothic mode. At their least effective, they are workmanlike tales utilizing conventional supernatural machinery. At their best, however, they exhibit a spare symbolic technique used to explore individual human personalities and to analyze the nature of moral evil. The best of Hartley's ghost and horror stories include "A Visitor from Down Under," "Feet Foremost," and "W. S.," the last dealing with an author murdered by a character of his own creation. "Up the Garden Path," "The Pampas Clump," and "The Pylon" reveal a more realistic interest in human psychology, and they deal more directly with the theme central to Hartley's major fiction: the acquisition, on the part of an innocent, even morally naïve, protagonist, of an awareness of the existence of evil.

A frequent lecturer, and a reviewer for such periodicals as *The Observer, Saturday Review*, and *Time and Tide* from the early 1920's to the middle 1940's, Hartley published a volume of essays entitled *The Novelist's Responsibility: Lectures and Essays* (1967), in which he deplored the twentieth century devaluation of a sense of individual moral responsibility. These essays explain Hartley's fictional preoc-

(CORBIS/E. O. Hoppé)

cupation with identity, moral values, and spiritual insight. His choice of subjects, particularly the works of Jane Austen, Emily Brontë, Nathaniel Hawthorne, and Henry James, suggests the origins of the realistic-symbolic technique he employs in both his short stories and his novels.

ACHIEVEMENTS

While Hartley's novels from *Simonetta Perkins* to *Facial Justice* were published in the United States, they did not enjoy the popularity there which they earned in England. *The Go-Between*, for example, continued to be in print in England since its publication in 1953, and the *Eustace and Hilda* trilogy—comprising *The Shrimp and the Anemone*, *The Sixth Heaven*, and *Eustace and Hilda*—was given a radio dramatization by the British Broadcasting Corporation (BBC). In the course of a literary career of roughly fifty years, Hartley came to be a noted public figure, and his work received favorable attention from Lord

David Cecil, Walter Allen, and John Atkins. Only in the United States, however, did his novels receive detailed critical attention. The three full-length studies of his fiction—Peter Bien's *L. P. Hartley* (1963), Anne Mulkeen's *Wild Thyme, Winter Lightning: The Symbolic Novels of L. P. Hartley* (1974), and Edward T. Jones's *L. P. Hartley* (1978)—are all American, as are the notable treatments of Hartley's work by James Hall and Harvey Curtis Webster.

BIOGRAPHY

Born on December 30, 1895, near Whittlesea in Cambridgeshire, Leslie Poles Hartley was named for Sir Leslie Stephen, the father of Virginia Woolf and himself a noted late Victorian literary man. Hartley's mother, Mary Elizabeth Thompson, according to Edward T. Jones, whose book on the novelist contains the most complete biographical account, was the daughter of a farmer named William James Thompson of Crawford House, Crowland, Lincolnshire. His father, H. B. Hartley, was a solicitor, justice of the peace, and later director of the successful brickworks founded by the novelist's paternal grandfather. This information figures as part of the background to Hartley's *The Brickfield* and *The Betrayal*.

Hartley was the second of his parents' three children; he had an older sister, Enid, and a younger, Annie Norah. None of the three ever married. Reared at Fletton Tower, near Peterborough, Hartley was educated at Harrow and Balliol College, Oxford, his stay at the latter interrupted by military service as a second lieutenant in the Norfolk Regiment during World War I. He was discharged for medical reasons and did not see action in France. In Oxford after the war, Hartley came into contact with a slightly younger generation of men, among them the future novelists Anthony Powell, Graham Greene, and Evelyn Waugh. His closest literary friend at this period, however, may have been Lord David Cecil. After leaving Balliol with a Second Honours Degree in 1921, Hartley worked as a reviewer for various periodicals, wrote the stories later collected in *Night Fears* and *The Killing Bottle*, and cultivated friendships with members of both Bohemian Bloomsbury and British society. His novella *Simonetta Perkins*, a Jamesian story of a young American woman's inconclusive passion for a Venetian gondolier, was published in 1925.

Hartley made many trips to Venice. From 1933 to 1939, he spent part of each summer and fall there, and he drew on this experience for parts of *Eustace and Hilda, The Boat*, and *My Fellow Devils*. Returning to England just before the start of World War II, Hartley started work on the series of novels which earned for him a place in the British literary establishment. Given the James Tait Black Memorial Prize for *Eustace and Hilda* in 1947 and the Heinemann Foundation Prize for *The Go-Between* in 1953, he served as head of the British Association of Poets, Playwrights, Editors, Essayists and Novelists (PEN) and on the management committee of the Society of Authors. In 1956, he was created a Commander of the British Empire by Queen Elizabeth II. In his later years, Hartley gave frequent talks, most notably the Clark Lectures delivered at Trinity College, Cambridge, in 1964. Joseph Losey won the Grand Prize at Cannes, France, in 1971 for a film version of *The Go-Between*, for which Harold Pinter wrote the script, and in 1973, Alan Bridges's film of *The Hireling*, from a script by Wolf Mankowitz, won the same prize. Hartley died in London on December 13, 1972.

ANALYSIS

Indebted to Bloomsbury, as shown by a concern with personal conduct and a highly impressionistic style, L. P. Hartley betrays affinities with D. H. Lawrence, Aldous Huxley, and George Orwell in a more fundamental concern with larger social and moral issues. His best books argue for the existence of a spiritual dimension to life and demonstrate that recognition of its motive force, even union of oneself with its will, is a moral imperative. In this emphasis on connection, his novels recall those of E. M. Forster, but unlike his predecessor, Hartley insists that the nature of the motive force is supernatural, even traditionally Christian. In his most successful books, Hartley draws upon elements of both novel and romance, as Richard Chase defines them in *The American Novel and Its Tradition* (1957), and the uniqueness of the

resulting hybridization precludes comparisons with the work of most of his contemporaries.

Hartley's moral vision, revealed by the gradual integration of realism and symbolism in his novels, is the most striking characteristic of his long fiction. In a book such as *The Go-Between*, he shows that all men are subject to the power of love, even when they deny it, and that achievement of insight into love's capabilities is a prerequisite to achieving moral responsibility. This pattern of growth at the center of Hartley's novels is conventionally Christian in its outlines. The protagonist of each book, beginning with Eustace Cherrington in the *Eustace and Hilda* trilogy, accepts his status as a "sinner" and experiences, if only briefly and incompletely, a semimystical transcendence of his fallen state. The epiphanic technique Hartley develops in the trilogy to objectify these moments of insight recurs in various forms in all of his novels, coming in time to be embodied not in symbolism but in the pattern of action in which he casts his plots. Without suggesting that Hartley's fiction is about theology, it is clear that his concern with the subject of morality cannot avoid having religious overtones. Like Nathaniel Hawthorne, he traces the process of spiritual growth in innocent, morally self-assured, and thereby flawed personalities who experience temptation, even commit sins, and eventually attain spiritual kinship with their fellow people. These encounters, in a book such as *Facial Justice*, occur in settings symbolic of traditional religious values, and so while Hartley's novels may be read from psychoanalytic or mythic points of view, they are more fully comprehended from a metaphysical vantage point.

There is a thematic unity to all of Hartley's longer fiction, but after 1960, there is a marked decline in its technical complexity. In one sense, having worked out his thematic viewpoint in the process of fusing realism and symbolism in his earlier books, Hartley no longer feels the need to dramatize the encounter of good and evil and to set it convincingly in a realistic world. His last novels are fables, and in *The Harness Room*, the most successful of them, the lack of realism intensifies his treatment of the psychological and sexual involvement of an adolescent boy and his father's slightly older chauffeur. This book brings Hartley's oeuvre full circle, back to the story of the American spinster and the Venetian gondolier he produced in *Simonetta Perkins* at the start of his career.

THE EUSTACE AND HILDA TRILOGY

The three novels constituting the *Eustace and Hilda* trilogy—*The Shrimp and the Anemone, The Sixth Heaven*, and *Eustace and Hilda*—objectify a process of moral growth and spiritual regeneration to be found in or behind all of Hartley's subsequent fiction. The process is not unlike that which he describes, in the Clark Lectures reprinted in *The Novelist's Responsibility*, as characteristic of Hawthorne's treatment of the redeeming experience of sin in *The Marble Faun* (1860). The epiphanic moments Hartley uses to dramatize his protagonist's encounters with Christ the Redeemer reveal truths which can be read on psychological, sociological, and theological levels.

In *The Shrimp and the Anemone*, Hartley depicts the abortive rebellion of Eustace Cherrington, aged nine, against the moral and psychological authority of his thirteen-year-old sister Hilda. Set in the summers of 1905 and 1906, the novel reveals young Eustace's intimations of a spiritual reality behind the surface of life. Unable to act in terms of these insights, for they are confused with his aesthetic sense, Eustace feeds his romantic inclination to construct an internal fantasy world and refuses to see the moral necessity of action. In *The Sixth Heaven*, Hartley details Eustace's second effort to achieve his freedom from Hilda, this time by engineering a socially advantageous marriage for her with Dick Staveley, a war hero and rising young member of Parliament. This novel focuses on a visit the Cherringtons make in June, 1920, to the Staveleys, acquaintances who live near their childhood home at Anchorstone. Eustace's adult epiphanic experiences are more insistent. Less tied to his childish aestheticism, they emerge in the context of the novel as hauntingly ambiguous intimations of a moral and spiritual realm which he unconsciously seeks to avoid acknowledging. In *Eustace and Hilda*, the final novel in the trilogy, Hartley brings his protagonist face to face with Christ during the Venetian Feast of the Redeemer, the

third Sunday in July, 1920. This encounter leads to Eustace's return to Anchorstone and acceptance of moral responsibility for the emotionally induced paralysis Hilda experienced at the end of her love affair with Dick Staveley. Back in his childhood home, Eustace learns the lesson of self-sacrificial love in Christ's example, and he effects a cure for Hilda by staging a mock-accident for her at the edge of Anchorstone Cliff. Because of the strain this involves, he suffers a fatal heart attack, and the novel ends. His death signals the genuineness of the moral growth and spiritual regeneration which had begun in Venice. The interpenetration of realistic narrative and symbolic subtext which occurs by the end of the *Eustace and Hilda* trilogy objectifies Hartley's vision of the world.

THE BOAT

Hartley's equivalent of Ford Madox Ford's and Evelyn Waugh's treatments of men at war, *The Boat* presents the mock-epic struggle of Timothy Casson, a forty-nine-year-old bachelor writer, to gain permission to use his rowing shell on the fishing stream that runs through Upton-on-Swirrell. Timothy, settling back in England in 1940 after an eighteen-year stay in Italy, consciously attempts to isolate himself from the effects of the war in progress in the larger world. He devotes himself to collecting china, to cultivating friends, to raising a dog, and to forcing the village magnates to allow him to row on the Swirrell. In the process, Timothy violates his own self-interest, as well as that of his nation and his class, but he is not the tragicomic figure that Eustace Cherrington becomes in the trilogy. In Hartley's hands, Timothy achieves only a degree of the self-awareness that Eustace does, and this enables the novelist to label him the "common sinner" that all people are, a figure both sinned against and sinning.

Timothy's desire to take his boat out on the river is an assertion of individuality that polarizes the community. His attachment to his boat becomes a measure of his moral and political confusion, for Timothy is torn between the influences of Vera Cross, a Communist secret agent sent to Upton-on-Swirrell to organize unrest among the masses, and Volumnia Purbright, the wife of the Anglican vicar and an unconventional, perhaps mystical, Christian. The emblematic names suggest the comic possibilities Hartley exploits in his treatment of the two, but *The Boat* is a serious novel. Vera represents a social disharmony resultant upon the advocacy of ideology, while Volumnia reflects both social harmony and personal tranquillity resulting from sacrifice of self. Indeed, when Timothy persists in his protest against the prohibition against rowing and sets forth on the flooded Swirrell with two children and his dog as passengers, Volumnia confronts Vera on the riverbank. Vera attacks the vicar's wife, and the two women tumble into the water. When Vera drowns in the Devil's Staircase, Volumnia blames herself for the younger woman's death and subsequently dies from exposure and pneumonia. When at the end of *The Boat* Timothy, who had to be rescued from the river when his boat capsized in the flooded stream, dreams he receives a telephone call from Volumnia inviting him to tea, he hears Vera's voice as well as Volumnia's, and the two women tell him that they are inseparable, as are the moral and ethical positions they represent.

Near the end of the novel, Timothy prepares to leave Upton-on-Swirrell in the company of two old friends, Esther Morwen and Tyrone MacAdam. The two discuss the prospects for Timothy's acceptance of himself as an ordinary human being. At the time of the boating accident, he had managed to rescue one of the children with him, but he needed the fortuitous help of others to rescue the second child and to reach safety himself. Timothy is clearly partially responsible for the deaths of Vera Cross and Volumnia Purbright, and the "true cross" he must bear is an acceptance of moral complexity. Whether he will achieve this insight is an open question at the end of *The Boat*, and Hartley's refusal to make the book a neat statement reinforces its thematic point.

THE GO-BETWEEN

Hartley's *The Go-Between*, arguably his finest novel, is the only one with a first-person narrator as protagonist. Leo Colston, like the focal characters of the *Eustace and Hilda* trilogy and *The Boat*, frees himself from psychological constraints and achieves a measure of moral insight. Indeed, Leo's story

amounts to a rite of passage conforming to the pattern of initiation characteristic of the *Bildungsroman*. More significantly, *The Go-Between* is a study of England on the verge of its second Elizabethan Age, and the patterns of imagery which Hartley uses to reveal the personality of Leo suggest indirectly that the Age of Aquarius will be a golden one.

These linguistic patterns, introduced into the novel by Leo himself, derive from the signs of the zodiac. On one hand, they are a pattern manufactured by Leo as a schoolboy and utilized to explain his conviction that the start of the twentieth century, which he dates incorrectly as January 1, 1900, is the dawn of a second Golden Age. On the other hand, the zodiac motifs, as associated with Leo and other characters in the novel, underscore Hartley's thematic insistence on the power of self-sacrificial love to redeem both individuals and society from error. At the start of the novel in 1951 or 1952, Leo is an elderly man engaged in sorting through the accumulated memorabilia of a lifetime. Coming upon his diary for the year 1900, inside the cover of which are printed the zodiac signs, he recalls his experiences at Southdown Hill School and his vacation visit to a schoolmate, Marcus Maudsley. In the body of the novel, the account of that nineteen-day visit to Brandham Hall, the narrative voice is split between that of the thirteen-year-old Leo of 1900 and that of the aged man with which the book begins. Used by Marcus's sister Marian to carry messages to her lover, the tenant farmer Ted Burgess, Leo finds himself faced with the dubious morality of his actions when Marcus tells him that Marian is to marry Viscount Trimingham, the owner of Brandham Hall and a scarred veteran of the Boer War.

In Leo's mind, Marian is the Virgin of the zodiac, Trimingham the Sagittarian archer, and Burgess the Aquarian water-carrier. Determined to break the bond between Marian and Ted and to restore her to Viscount Trimingham, Leo resorts to the schoolboy magic with which he had handled bullies at school. He plans a spell involving the sacrifice of an *atropa belladonna* or deadly nightshade growing in a deserted outbuilding, but the ritual goes awry and he finds himself flat on his back with the plant on top of him. The next day, his thirteenth birthday, Leo is forced to lead Marian's mother to the spot where the girl meets her lover, and they discover the pair engaged in sexual intercourse. For Leo, whose adult sexuality has just begun to develop, this is a significant shock, and he feels that he has been defeated by the beautiful but deadly lady, both the deadly nightshade and Marian herself.

In the epilogue to *The Go-Between*, the elderly Leo Colston returns to Norfolk to find out the consequences of the mutual betrayal. Encountering Marian, now the dowager Lady Trimingham, once more, he undertakes again to be a messenger. This time he goes to her grandson Edward in an effort to reconcile him to the events of the fateful year 1900, to the fact that his father was really the son of Ted Burgess. This action on Leo's part embodies the theme of all of Hartley's fiction: The only evil in life is an unloving heart. At the end of his return journey to Brandham Hall, Leo Colston is a more vital man and a more compassionate one. Having faced the evil both inside and outside himself, he is open to love, and the Age of Aquarius can begin. That it will also be the age of Elizabeth II, given the political and sociological implications of the central action, gives Hartley's *The Go-Between* its particular thematic rightness.

Robert C. Petersen

OTHER MAJOR WORKS

SHORT FICTION: *Night Fears*, 1924; *The Killing Bottle*, 1932; *The Traveling Grave*, 1948; *The White Wand*, 1954; *Two for the River*, 1961; *Mrs. Carteret Receives*, 1971; *The Complete Short Stories of L. P. Hartley*, 1973.

NONFICTION: *The Novelist's Responsibility: Lectures and Essays*, 1967.

BIBLIOGRAPHY

Bien, Peter. *L. P. Hartley*. University Park: Pennsylvania University Press, 1963. The first book on Hartley's fiction, important for its Freudian analysis of his novels; its identification of his indebtedness to Nathaniel Hawthorne, Henry James, and Emily Brontë; and its examination of Hartley's literary criticism. At its best when discussing the novels about the transition from adolescence to adulthood. Includes a brief bibliography.

Bloomfield, Paul. *L. P. Hartley*. London: Longmans, Green, 1962. An early short monograph by a personal friend of Hartley, coupled with one on Anthony Powell by Bernard Bergonzi. Focuses on character analysis and thematic concerns, providing a brief discussion of Hartley's novels. Laudatory, perceptive, and very well written.

Fane, Julian. *Best Friends*. London: Sinclair Stevenson, 1990. Contains a memoir of Hartley that helps to situate his fiction in terms of his sensibility and his time.

Hall, James. *The Tragic Comedians: Seven Modern British Novelists*. Bloomington: Indiana University Press, 1963. Claims that the Hartley protagonist possesses an inadequate emotional pattern that leads inevitably to failure. This neurotic behavior is discussed in his major fiction: *The Boat, Eustace and Hilda, My Fellow Devils*, and *The Hireling*. In these novels Hartley demonstrates that confidence is accompanied by a contradictory desire to fail.

Jones, Edward T. *L. P. Hartley*. Boston: Twayne, 1978. Provides an excellent analysis of Hartley's literary work, particularly of his novels, which are conveniently grouped. Also contains a chronology, a biographical introductory chapter, a discussion of Hartley's literary criticism, and an excellent annotated bibliography. Of special interest are Jones's definition of the "Hartleian novel" and his discussion of Hartley's short fiction.

Mulkeen, Anne. *Wild Thyme, Winter Lightning: The Symbolic Novels of L. P. Hartley*. Detroit, Mich.: Wayne State University Press, 1974. Focuses on Hartley's fiction until 1968, stressing the Hawthornian romance elements in his early novels. Particularly concerned with his adaptations of the romance and how his characters are at once themselves and archetypes or symbols. An extensive list of helpful secondary sources is provided.

Webster, Harvey Curtis. *After the Trauma: Representative British Novelists Since 1920*. Lexington: University Press of Kentucky, 1970. The chapter on Hartley, entitled "Diffident Christian," concerns his protagonists' struggles to distinguish between God's orders and society's demands. Discusses *Facial Justice, Eustace and Hilda, The Boat*, and *The Go-Between* extensively, concluding that Hartley merits more attention than he has been given.

Wright, Adrian. *Foreign Country: The Life of L. P. Hartley*. London: A. Deutsch, 1996. A good biography of Hartley for the beginning student. Includes bibliographical references and an index.

NATHANIEL HAWTHORNE

Born: Salem, Massachusetts; July 4, 1804
Died: Plymouth, New Hampshire; May 19, 1864

PRINCIPAL LONG FICTION

Fanshawe: A Tale, 1828
The Scarlet Letter, 1850
The House of the Seven Gables, 1851
The Blithedale Romance, 1852
The Marble Faun, 1860
Septimius Felton, 1872 (fragment)
The Dolliver Romance, 1876 (fragment)
The Ancestral Footstep, 1883 (fragment)
Doctor Grimshawe's Secret, 1883 (fragment)

OTHER LITERARY FORMS

Many of Nathaniel Hawthorne's short stories were originally published anonymously in such magazines as the *Token* and the *New England Magazine* between 1830 and 1837. Several collections appeared during his lifetime, including *Twice-Told Tales* (1837; expanded 1842), *Mosses from an Old Manse* (1846), and *The Snow-Image and Other Twice-Told Tales* (1851). Houghton Mifflin published the complete works in the Riverside edition (1850-1882) and the Old Manse edition (1900). Hawthorne also wrote stories for children, collected in *Grandfather's Chair* (1841), *Biographical Stories for Children* (1842), *True Stories from History and Biography* (1851), *A Wonder-Book for Boys and Girls* (1852), and *Tanglewood Tales for Boys and Girls* (1853). With the help

of his sister Elizabeth, he edited the *American Magazine of Useful and Entertaining Knowledge* (1836) and *Peter Parley's Universal History* (1837) and, as a favor to would-be president Franklin Pierce, wrote a biography for the presidential campaign. His last completed work was *Our Old Home* (1863), a series of essays about his sojourn in England. At the time of his death, he left four unfinished fragments: *Septimius Felton* (1872), *The Dolliver Romance* (1876), *The Ancestral Footstep* (1883), and *Doctor Grimshawe's Secret* (1883).

ACHIEVEMENTS

Few other American authors, with the possible exception of Henry James, have engaged in so deliberate a literary apprenticeship as Hawthorne. After an initial period of anonymity during his so-called "solitary years" from 1825 to 1837, he achieved an unfaltering reputation as an author of short stories, romances, essays, and children's books. He is remembered not only for furthering the development of the short-story form but also for distinguishing between the novel and the romance. The prefaces to his long works elucidate his theory of the "neutral ground"—the junction between the actual and the imaginary—where romance takes place. He is noted for his masterful exploration of the psychology of guilt and sin; his study of the Puritan heritage contributed to the emerging sense of historicity which characterized the American Renaissance of the mid-nineteenth century. Hawthorne is unrivaled as an allegorist, especially as one whose character typologies and symbols achieve universality through their psychological validity. While he has been faulted for sentimentality, lapses into archaic diction, and gothicism, Hawthorne's works continue to evoke the "truth of the human heart" that is the key to their continuing appeal.

BIOGRAPHY

Nathaniel Hawthorne was born in Salem, Massachusetts, on July 4, 1804. On his father's side, Hawthorne was descended from William Hathorne, who settled in Massachusetts in 1630 and whose son John was one of the judges in the 1692 Salem witchcraft trials. Hawthorne's father, a sea captain, married Elizabeth Clarke Manning in 1801. Mrs. Hathorne's English ancestors immigrated to the New World in 1679; her brother Robert, a successful businessman, assumed responsibility for her affairs after Captain Hathorne died of yellow fever in Suriname in 1808.

After his father's death, Hawthorne, his two sisters Elizabeth Manning and Maria Louisa, and his mother moved into the populous Manning household, a move that on one hand estranged him from his Hathorne relatives and on the other provided him with an attentive family life, albeit an adult one, for the eight aunts and uncles living there were unmarried at that time. Perhaps the adult company accounted in part for his literary tastes, as did his less than regular education. Although he attended a school taught by Joseph Emerson Worcester, a renowned philologist of the time, Hawthorne led a sedentary existence for almost three years after being lamed at the age of nine. During his enforced inactivity, he spent long afternoons reading Edmund Spenser, John Bunyan, and William Shakespeare, his favorite authors.

(Library of Congress)

When Hawthorne was twelve, his mother moved the family temporarily to Raymond, Maine, where the Mannings owned a tract of land. The outdoor activity occasioned by nearby Lake Sebago and the surrounding forest land proved beneficial to Hawthorne; quickly recovering his health, he became an able marksman and fisherman. During these years, interrupted by schooling with the Reverend Caleb Bradley, a stern man not to Hawthorne's liking, Hawthorne accumulated Wordsworthian memories of the wilderness and of village life that were to be evoked in his fiction. Recalled to Salem, he began in 1820 to be tutored for college by the lawyer Benjamin Lynde Oliver, working, in the meantime, as a bookkeeper for his Uncle Robert, an occupation that foreshadowed his later business ventures. He continued his reading, including such authors as Henry Fielding, Sir Walter Scott, William Godwin, Matthew "Monk" Lewis, and James Hogg, and produced a family newspaper, *The Spectator*, characterized by humorous notices and essays and parodies of sentimental verse. The first member of his family to attend college, he was sent to Bowdoin, where he was graduated eighteenth in a class of thirty-eight. Known for his quietness and gentle humor, he disliked declamations, was negligent in many academic requirements, and, indeed, was fined for playing cards. His fellow students at Bowdoin included Henry Wadsworth Longfellow and Franklin Pierce, who later was elected president of the United States.

Hawthorne had determined early on a career in letters. Returning to Salem upon graduation, he began a self-imposed apprenticeship, the so-called "solitary years." During this time, Hawthorne privately published *Fanshawe*, a work that he so thoroughly repudiated that his wife, Sophia, knew nothing of it; he published many short stories anonymously and unsuccessfully attempted to interest publishers in such collections as *Seven Tales of My Native Land*, *Provincial Tales*, and *The Storyteller*. As a means of support he edited the *American Magazine of Useful and Entertaining Knowledge* and compiled *Peter Parley's Universal History*. Not until the publication of *Twice-Told Tales* under the secret financial sponsorship of his friend Horatio Bridge did Hawthorne's name become publicly known. The label "solitary years" is somewhat of a misnomer, for, as his journals indicate, Hawthorne visited with friends, went for long walks and journeys, and, most important, met Sophia Peabody, the daughter of Dr. Nathaniel Peabody. For Hawthorne, Sophia was the key by which he was released from "a life of shadows" to the "truth of the human heart." Four years passed, however, before they could marry—four years in which Hawthorne became measurer in the Boston Custom House, which he called a "grievous thraldom," and then, although not sympathetic to the burgeoning transcendental movement, joined the utopian community Brook Farm (April, 1841), investing one thousand dollars in an attempt to establish a home for himself and Sophia.

After little more than six months, Hawthorne gave up the communal venture and, settling in the Old Manse at Concord, married Sophia on July 19, 1842. His financial difficulties were exacerbated by the birth of Una in 1844; finally, in 1846, when his son Julian was born and *Mosses from an Old Manse* was published, he was appointed Surveyor of the Salem Custom House, a post he held from 1846 to 1849, when a political upset cost him his job. With more time to write and with the pressure to support a growing family, Hawthorne began a period of intense literary activity; his friendship with Herman Melville dates from that time. *The Scarlet Letter*, whose ending sent Sophia to bed with a grievous headache, was finished in February, 1850. *The House of the Seven Gables* appeared in 1851, the year Hawthorne's daughter Rose was born; by the end of the next year, Hawthorne had completed *The Blithedale Romance*, two volumes of children's tales, *The Life of Franklin Pierce*, and a collection of stories, *The Snow-Image and Other Twice-Told Tales*.

From 1853 to 1857, Hawthorne served as United States Consul at Liverpool, England, a political appointment under President Pierce. After four years of involvement with the personal and financial problems of stranded Americans, Hawthorne resigned and lived in Rome and Florence from 1857 to 1858, where he acquired ideas for his last romance, *The Marble Faun*. After returning with his family to the United States, Hawthorne worked on four unfinished romances, *Doctor Grimshawe's Secret*, *Septimius Felton*, *The Dolliver Romance*, and *The Ancestral Footstep*, in which two themes are dominant: the search for immortality and the American attempt to establish title to English ancestry. His carefully considered essays on the paucity of American tradition, the depth of British heritage, and the contrast between democracy and entrenched class systems were first published in *The Atlantic Monthly* and then collected as *Our Old Home*. After a lingering illness, he died at Plymouth, New Hampshire, on May 19, 1864, during a trip with Franklin Pierce. He was buried at Sleepy Hollow Cemetery in Concord, Massachusetts.

ANALYSIS

Central to Nathaniel Hawthorne's romances is his idea of a "neutral territory," described in the Custom House sketch that precedes *The Scarlet Letter* as a place "somewhere between the real world and fairyland, where the Actual and the Imaginary may meet, and each imbue itself with the nature of the other." A romance, according to Hawthorne, is different from the novel, which maintains a "minute fidelity . . . to the probable and ordinary course of man's experience." In the neutral territory of romance, however, the author may make use of the "marvellous" to heighten atmospheric effects, if he or she also presents "the truth of the human heart." As long as the writer of romance creates characters whose virtues, vices, and sensibilities are distinctly human, he or she may place them in an environment that is out of the ordinary—or, that is, in fact, allegorical. Thus, for example, while certain elements—the stigma of the scarlet letter, or Donatello's faun ears—are fantastical in conception, they represent a moral stance that is true to nature. Dimmesdale's guilt at concealing his adultery with Hester Prynne is, indeed, as destructive as the wound on his breast, and Donatello's pagan nature is expressed in the shape of his ears.

A number of recurring thematic patterns and character types appear in Hawthorne's novels and tales, as Randall Stewart suggests in the introduction to *The American Notebooks by Nathaniel Hawthorne* (1932). These repetitions show Hawthorne's emphasis on the effects of events on the human heart rather than on the events themselves. One common motif is concern for the past, or, as Hawthorne says in the preface to *The House of the Seven Gables*, his "attempt to connect a bygone time with the very present that is flitting away from us." Hawthorne's interest in the Puritan past was perhaps sparked by his "discovery," as a teenager, of his Hathorne connections; it was certainly influenced by his belief that progress was impeded by inheritance, that "the wrong-doing of one generation lives into the successive ones, and . . . becomes a pure and uncontrollable mischief." For Hawthorne, then, the past must be reckoned with, and then put aside; the eventual decay of aristocratic families is not only inevitable, but desirable.

Hawthorne's understanding of tradition is illustrated in many of his works. In *The Scarlet Letter*, for example, he explores the effect of traditional Puritan social and theological expectations on three kinds of sinners: the adulteress (Hester), the hypocrite (Dimmesdale), and the avenger (Chillingworth), only to demonstrate that the punishment they inflict on themselves far outweighs the public castigation. Hester, in fact, inverts the rigidified Puritan system, represented by the scarlet letter, whose meaning she changes from "adultress" to "able." Probably the most specific treatment of the theme, however, is found in *The House of the Seven Gables*, in which the Pyncheon family house and fortune have imprisoned both Hepzibah and Clifford, one in apathy and one in insanity; only Phoebe, the country cousin who cares little for wealth, can lighten the burden, not only for her relatives, but also for Holgrave, a descendent of the Maules who invoked the original curse. In *The Marble Faun*, Hawthorne goes to Italy for his "sense of the past," although Hilda and Kenyon are both Americans. The past in this novel is represented not only in the setting but also in Donatello's pagan nature; at the end, both Miriam and the faun figure engage in a purgatorial expiation of the past.

Another recurring theme is that of isolation. Certainly Hawthorne himself felt distanced from normal social converse by his authorial calling. The firsthand descriptions of Hawthorne extant today present him more as an observer than as a participant, a stance over which he himself agonized. In writing to Longfellow about his apprenticeship years, he complained that he was "carried apart from the main current of life" and that "there is no fate in this world so horrible as to have no share in either its joys or sorrows. For the last ten years, I have not lived, but only dreamed about living." For Hawthorne, Sophia was his salvation, his link to human companionship. Perhaps that is why he wrote so evocatively of Hester Prynne's isolation; indeed, Hester's difficult task of rearing the elfin child Pearl without help from Dimmesdale is the obverse of Hawthorne's own happy domestic situation. Almost every character that Hawthorne created experiences some sense of isolation, sometimes from a consciousness of sin, sometimes from innocence itself, or sometimes from a deliberate attempt to remain aloof.

According to Hawthorne, this kind of isolation, most intense when it is self-imposed, frequently comes from a consciousness of sin or from what he calls the "violation of the sanctity of the human heart." For Hawthorne, the "unpardonable sin" is just such a violation, in which one individual becomes subjected to another's intellectual or scientific (rather than emotional) interest. Chillingworth is a good example; as Hester's unacknowledged husband, he lives with Dimmesdale, deliberately intensifying the minister's hidden guilt. In *The Blithedale Romance*, Coverdale's voyeurism (and certainly his name) suggests this kind of violation, as does Westervelt's manipulation of Priscilla and Hollingsworth's of Zenobia. Certainly, Clifford's isolation in insanity is the fault of Judge Pyncheon. There is also the implication that the mysterious model who haunts Miriam in *The Marble Faun* has committed the same sin, thereby isolating both of them. One of the few characters to refuse such violation is Holgrave, who, in *The House of the Seven Gables*, forbears to use his mesmeric powers on Phoebe.

Such a set of recurring themes is bolstered by a pervasive character typology. While literary works such as those by Edmund Spenser, John Milton, William Shakespeare, and John Bunyan form the historical context for many of Hawthorne's characters, many are further developments of his own early character types. *Fanshawe*, for example, introduced the pale, idealistic scholarly hero more fully developed in Dimmesdale. Others, personifications of abstract qualities, seem motivated by purely evil ends. Westervelt is one type; sophisticated and learned in mesmerism, he takes as his victim the innocent Priscilla. Chillingworth, whose literary ancestry can probably be traced to Miltonic devil-figures, is old and bent but possesses a compelling intellect that belies his lack of physical strength. Finally, the worldly Judge Pyncheon manifests a practical, unimaginative streak that connects him to Peter Hovenden of Hawthorne's short story "The Artist of the Beautiful." As for Hawthorne's heroines, Hilda and Phoebe embody the domesticity that Hawthorne admired in Sophia; Priscilla, like Alice Pyncheon before her, is frail and easily subjugated; and Hester, Zenobia, and Miriam exhibit an oriental beauty and intellectual pride.

FANSHAWE

Three years after Hawthorne was graduated from Bowdoin College, he anonymously published the apprenticeship novel *Fanshawe* at his own expense. While he almost immediately repudiated the work, it remains not only a revealing biographical statement but also a testing ground for themes and characters that he later developed with great success.

"No man can be a poet and a bookkeeper at the same time," Hawthorne complained in a letter he wrote while engaged in his Uncle Robert's stagecoach business before college. Just such a dichotomy is illustrated in *Fanshawe*, in which the pale scholar fails to rejoin the course of ordinary life and, in effect, consigns himself to death, while the active individual Edward Walcott wins the heroine, Ellen Langton, and so becomes, to use Hawthorne's later words, part of "The magnetic chain of humanity." To be sure, Fanshawe is an overdrawn figure, owing, as Arlin Turner points out, something to Gorham Deane, a Bowdoin schoolmate, and much to Charles Maturin's gothic novel, *Melmoth the Wanderer* (1820), from which Ellen's guardian, Dr. Melmoth, takes his name. In repudiating the book, however, Hawthorne is less repudiating the gothic form than he is an early, faulty conception of a writer's life. Certainly, Hawthorne recognized the tension between

the intellectual and the practical lives, as his letters and journals suggest, especially when he was at the Boston and Salem Custom Houses and at the consulate in Liverpool. Moreover, as Frederick Crews notes, Fanshawe and Walcott are "complimentary sides," together fulfilling Hawthorne's twin desire for "self-abnegation" and "heroism and amorous success." Nevertheless, as the pattern of his own life makes clear, Hawthorne did not retire (as did Fanshawe) to an early grave after the solitary apprenticeship years; rather, he married Sophia Peabody (fictionally prefigured in Ellen Langton) and, in becoming involved in the ordinary affairs of life, merged the figures of Fanshawe and Walcott.

The plot of the novel—the abduction of Ellen by the villainous Butler—introduces Hawthorne's later exploration of the misuse of power, while the configuration of characters foreshadows not only the scholar figure but also two other types: the dark villain, whose sexual motivation remains ambiguous, and the innocent, domestic young heroine, later developed as Phoebe and Hilda. That Fanshawe should rescue Ellen, appearing like Milton's Raphael over the thickly wooded valley where Butler has secluded her, suggests that he is able to enter the world of action; but that he should refuse her offer of marriage, saying, "I have no way to prove that I deserve your generosity, but by refusing to take advantage of it," is uncharacteristic in comparison with Hawthorne's later heroes such as Holgrave and Kenyon. It may be that after his marriage to Sophia, Hawthorne could not conceive of a triangle existing when two "soul mates" had found each other, for in similar character configurations in *The House of the Seven Gables* and *The Marble Faun*, both Holgrave and Kenyon have no rivals to fear for Phoebe and Hilda.

In setting, however, *Fanshawe* is a precursor to the later novels, as well as an unformulated precedent for Hawthorne's famous definition of romance. Probably begun while Hawthorne was enrolled at Bowdoin, the novel has as its setting Harley College, a picturesque, secluded institution. Formal classroom tutoring is not the novel's central interest, however, just as it was not in Hawthorne's own life; nor is the novel completely a *roman à clef* in which actual people and places are thinly disguised. Rather, as is the case in the later novels in which Salem itself, Brook Farm, and Rome are the existing actualities on which Hawthorne draws, so in *Fanshawe* the setting is an excuse for the psychological action. To be sure, the later, sophisticated, symbolic effects are missing, and the interpenetration of the actual by the imaginary is not as successful as in, for instance, *The Scarlet Letter*; nevertheless, although what later becomes marvelous is here simply melodramatic, the imagination plays a large, if unformulated, role in the novel's success.

THE SCARLET LETTER

Begun as a tale and completed shortly after Hawthorne's dismissal from the Salem Surveyorship, *The Scarlet Letter* is prefaced by an essay entitled "The Custom House" in which Hawthorne not only gives an imaginative account of his business experience but also presents a theory of composition. The essay is thus a distillation of the practical and the imaginative. It includes scant praise for the unimaginative William Lee, the antediluvian permanent inspector whose commonplace attitude typified for Hawthorne the Customs operation. In writing, however, Hawthorne exorcised his spleen at his political dismissal which, coupled with charges of malfeasance, was instigated by the Whigs who wanted him replaced; as Arlin Turner comments, "The decapitated surveyor, in becoming a character in a semifictional account, had all but ceased to be Hawthorne." The writer, in short, had made fiction out of his business experiences. He also had speculated about the preconceptions necessary for the creator of romances; such a man, he decided, must be able to perceive the "neutral territory" where the "actual" and the "imaginary" meet. The result of that perception was *The Scarlet Letter*.

In the prefatory essay to the book, Hawthorne establishes the literalism of the scarlet letter, which, he says, he has in his possession as an old, faded, tattered remnant of the past. Just as Hawthorne is said by Terence Martin to contemplate the letter, thus generating the novel, so the reader is forced to direct his attention to the primary symbol, not simply of Hester's adultery or of her ability, but of the way in which the restrictions of the Puritan forebears are transcended by the warmth of the human heart. Through this symbol, then, and through its living counterpart, Pearl, the daughter of Hester and Dimmesdale, Hawthorne examines the isolating effects of a sense of sin, using as his psychological setting the Puritan ethos.

With Hester's first public appearance with the infant Pearl and the heavily embroidered scarlet letter on her breast, the child—Hester's "torment" and her "joy"—and the letter become identified. Hester's guilt is a public one; Dimmesdale's is not. To admit to his share in the adultery is to relinquish his standing as the minister of the community, and so, initially too weak to commit himself, he pleads with Hester to confess her partner in the sin. She does not do so, nor does she admit that Chillingworth, the doctor who pursues Dimmesdale, is her husband. Three solitary people, then, are inexorably bound together by the results of the sin but are unable to communicate with one another.

The Puritan intention of bringing the sinner into submission has the opposite effect upon Hester, who, with a pride akin to humility, tenaciously makes a way for herself in the community. As an angel of mercy to the suffering, the sick, and the heavy of heart, she becomes a living model of charity which the townspeople, rigidly enmeshed in their Puritan theology, are unable to emulate. In addition, she exercises a talent for fine embroidery, so that even the bride has her clothing embellished with the sinner's finery. Hester's ostracization hardens her pride until, as she says to Dimmesdale in the forest, their act has a "consecration of its own." The adultery, in short, achieves a validation quite outside the letter of the Puritan law, and Hester finds no reason not to suggest that Dimmesdale run away with her in a repetition of the temptation and the original sin.

In the meantime, Dimmesdale has not had the relief of Hester's public confession. As veiled confessions, his sermons take on an ever growing intensity and apparent sincerity, gaining many converts to the church. Under Chillingworth's scrutiny, however, Dimmesdale's concealed guilt creates a physical manifestation, a scarlet letter inscribed in his flesh. While Hester's letter has yet to work its way inward to repentance, Dimmesdale's is slowly working its way outward. Chillingworth himself, initially a scholar, becomes dedicated to the cause of intensifying the minister's sufferings. Although Chillingworth eventually takes partial responsibility for Hester's sin, admitting that as a scholarly recluse he should not have taken a young wife, he inexorably causes his own spiritual death. He joins a line of scientist-experimenters who deprive their victims of intellectual curiosity, violating "the truth of the human heart" and severing themselves from "the magnetic chain of humanity." He becomes, as Harry Levin notes, the lowest in the hierarchy of sinners, for while Hester and Dimmesdale have at least joined in passion, Chillingworth is isolated in pride.

As Terence Martin suggests, the scaffold scenes are central to the work. For Dimmesdale, public abnegation is the key: Standing as a penitent on the scaffold at midnight is insufficient, for his act is illuminated only by the light of a great comet. His decision to elope with Hester is also insufficient to remove his guilt; what he considers to be the beginning of a "new life" is a reenactment of the original deed. In the end, the scaffold proves the only real escape from the torments devised by Chillingworth, for in facing the community with Hester and Pearl, the minister faces himself and removes the concealment that is a great part of his guilt. His "new life" is, in fact, death, and he offers no hope to Hester that they will meet again, for to do so would be to succumb to temptation again. Only Pearl, who marries a lord, leaves the community permanently; as the innocent victim, she in effect returns to her mother's home to expiate her mother's sin.

Like Fanshawe, then, Dimmesdale causes his own demise, but he is provided with motivation. In Pearl, Hawthorne was influenced perhaps by the antics of Una, his first child, but even her name, which is reminiscent of the medieval Pearl-Poet's "pearl of great price"—his soul—indicates that she is emblematic. Likewise, the minister's name is indicative of the valley of the shadow of death, just as Chillingworth's suggests his cold nature. The successful meshing of the literal and allegorical levels in this tale of the effects of concealed sin and the universality of its theme continues to lend interest to the work.

THE HOUSE OF THE SEVEN GABLES

As Hawthorne notes in his preface to *The House of the Seven Gables*, he intends to show the mischief that the past causes when it lives into the present, particularly when coupled with the question of an inheritance. Hawthorne's mood is similar to that of Henry David Thoreau when, in *Walden* (1854), he makes his famous plea to "simplify," evoking the image of Everyman traveling on the road of life, carrying his onerous possessions on his back. The family curse that haunts Hepzibah and Clifford Pyncheon, the hidden property deed, and even Hepzibah's dreams of an unexpected inheritance are so centered on the past that the characters are unable to function in the present. In fact, says Hawthorne, far more worrisome than the missing inheritance is the "moral disease" that is passed from one generation to the next.

This "moral disease" results from the greed of the family progenitor, Colonel Pyncheon, who coveted the small tract of land owned by one Matthew Maule. Maule's curse—"God will give him blood to drink"—comes true on the day the new Pyncheon mansion, built on the site of Maule's hut, is to be consecrated. The Colonel dies, presumably from apoplexy but possibly from foul play, and from that day, Hawthorne says, a throwback to the Colonel appears in each generation—a calculating, practical man, who, as the inheritor, commits again "the great guilt of his ancestor" in not making restoration to the Maule descendants. Clifford, falsely imprisoned for the murder of his uncle Jaffrey Pyncheon, the one Pyncheon willing to make restitution, is persecuted after his release by Judge Pyncheon, another of Jaffrey's nephews and Jaffrey's real murderer, for his presumed knowledge of the hiding place of the Indian deed giving title to their uncle's property.

In contrast to these forces from the past, Hawthorne poses Phoebe, a Pyncheon country cousin with no pretensions to wealth but with a large fund of domesticity and a warm heart. Almost certainly modeled on Sophia, Phoebe, like Hilda in *The Marble Faun*, possesses an unexpected power, a "homely witchcraft." Symbolically, as Crews suggests, she neutralizes the morbidity in the Pyncheon household and eventually stands as an "ideal parent" to

Hepzibah and Clifford. Indeed, Phoebe brings her enfeebled relatives into the circle of humanity.

If Phoebe represents the living present, Holgrave, the daguerreotypist and descendant of the Maules, represents the future. Like Clifford, however, who is saved by his imprisonment from an aesthetic version of the unpardonable sin, Holgrave runs the risk of becoming merely a cold-blooded observer. Like Hawthorne, Holgrave is a writer, boarding at the House of the Seven Gables to observe the drama created as the past spills into the present and turning Pyncheon history into fiction. He is, nevertheless, a reformer. In an echo of Hawthorne's preface, he would have buildings made of impermanent materials, ready to be built anew with each generation; likewise, he would merge old family lines into the stream of humanity. While Holgrave's progressive views become mitigated once he marries Phoebe, he is rescued from becoming a Chillingworth by his integrity, his conscience, and his reverence for the human soul. Although he unintentionally hypnotizes Phoebe by reading her his story of Matthew Maule's mesmerism of Alice Pyncheon, he eschews his power, thereby not only saving himself and her from a Dimmesdale/Chillingworth relationship but also breaking the chain of vengeance which was in his power to perpetuate. The chain of past circumstances is also broken by the death of Judge Pyncheon, who, unlike Holgrave, intended to exercise his psychological power to force Clifford to reveal where the Indian deed is hidden. Stricken by apoplexy (or Maule's curse), however, the Judge is left in solitary possession of the house as Clifford and Hepzibah flee in fear.

Holgrave's integrity and death itself thus prevent a reenactment of the original drama of power and subjection that initiated the curse. As Holgrave learns, the Judge himself murdered his bachelor uncle and destroyed a will that gave the inheritance to Clifford. Although exonerated, Clifford's intellect cannot be recalled to its former state, and so he remains a testimonial to the adverse effects of "violation of the human heart."

During Hepzibah and Clifford's flight from the scene of the Judge's death, Phoebe, representing the present, and Holgrave, the future, pledge their troth, joining the Pyncheon and Maule families. Hawthorne's happy ending, although deliberately prepared, surprised many of his critics, who objected that Holgrave's decision to "plant" a family and to build a stone house were motivated only by the dictates of the plot. F. D. Matthiessen, for example, suggests that Hawthorne's democratic streak blinded him to the implication that Holgrave was simply setting up a new dynasty. On the other hand, for Martin, the decision is foreshadowed; Holgrave's is a compromise position in which he maintains the importance of the structure of society while suggesting that the content be changed, just as a stone house might be redecorated according to its owners' tastes. In marrying Holgrave, Phoebe incorporates Pyncheon blood with the "mass of the people," for the original Maule was a poor man and his son a carpenter.

THE BLITHEDALE ROMANCE

The only one of Hawthorne's romances to be told by a first-person narrator, *The Blithedale Romance* is grounded in Hawthorne's abortive attempt to join the utopian Brook Farm. Like Hawthorne, Miles Coverdale notes the disjunction between a life of labor and a life of poetry; like Hawthorne, he never wholeheartedly participates in the community. In fact, to Crews, the work displays "an inner coherence of self-debate." Coverdale is the isolated man viewed from inside; as a self-conscious observer, he is the most Jamesian of all of Hawthorne's characters. As Martin notes, Hawthorne sacrifices certain aesthetic advantages in allowing Coverdale to tell his own story. Although his name is as evocative as, for example, Chillingworth's, Coverdale loses symbolic intensity because many of his explanations—his noting, for example, that his illness upon arriving at Blithedale is a purgatory preparing him for a new life—sound like figments of an untrustworthy narrator's imagination.

As in his other romances, Hawthorne begins with a preface. While he points out the realistic grounding of the romance, he maintains that the characters are entirely imaginary. He complains that since no convention yet exists for the American romance, the writer must suffer his characters to be compared to real models; hence, says Hawthorne, he has created the Blithedale scenario as a theatrical device to separate the reader from the ordinary course of events (just as the gothic writer did with his medieval trappings). In effect, Coverdale, isolated as he is, serves as the medium who moves between two worlds.

Coverdale's destructive egocentricism is evident throughout the work. His unwillingness to grant a favor to Old Moodie loses him an early acquaintanceship with Priscilla; he cements his position as an outsider by belittling Priscilla and by spying on Zenobia; finally, seeing the intimacy that develops between Priscilla and Hollingsworth after Zenobia's suicide, he retires to enjoy his self-pity. As a minor poet, an urban man who enjoys his cigars and fireplace, he is out of place in the utopian venture; in fact, after his purgatorial illness, he wakes up to death-in-life rather than to reinvigoration. As he moves from Blithedale to the city and back again, his most active participation in the events is his searching for Zenobia's body.

Zenobia herself harks back to Hester, another in the line of Hawthorne's exotic, intellectual women. Like Miriam in *The Marble Faun*, Zenobia has a mysterious past to conceal. She is dogged by Westervelt, her urbane companion whose mesmeric powers become evident in his attempted despoliation of Priscilla. Coverdale imagines her as an orator or an actress; indeed, she is a female reformer whose free and unexpected rhetoric seems to bypass convention. Priscilla, on the other hand, is a frail version of Phoebe and Hilda; she is pliant, domestic, and biddable—hence her susceptibility to Westervelt's powers and her brief tenure as the Veiled Lady. Like Zenobia (whose sister she is revealed to be), she believes in Hollingworth's reformism, but less as a helpmate than as a supporter. In coming to Blithedale, Priscilla really does find the life that is denied to Coverdale, but in falling in love with Hollingsworth, she finds spiritual death.

Hollingsworth is related to Hawthorne's scientist figures. With Holgrave he wants to change society, but his special interest is in criminal reformation. It is Zenobia who, at the end of the novel, realizes that Hollingsworth has identified himself so closely with his plan that he has *become* the plan. Hollingsworth

encourages Zenobia's interest in him because of her wealth; he spurns Coverdale's friendship because Coverdale objects to devoting himself entirely to the monomaniacal plan. It is, however, Hollingsworth who rescues Priscilla from Westervelt, exercising the power of affection to break mesmerism, but with him Priscilla simply enters a different kind of subjection.

Indeed, all the main characters suffer real or metaphorical death at the end of the book. Westervelt, like Chillingworth, is frustrated at his victim's escape; Zenobia's suicide has removed her from his power. Priscilla becomes a handmaiden to the ruined ideal of what Hollingsworth might have been, and Hollingsworth becomes a penitent, reforming himself—the criminal responsible for Zenobia's death. Even Coverdale relinquishes a life of feeling; his final secret, that he loves Priscilla, seems only to be fantasizing on the part of the poet who was a master of missed opportunities and who was more comfortable observing his own reactions to a lost love than in pursuing her actively himself.

THE MARBLE FAUN

In *The Marble Faun*, the product of a sojourn in Rome, Hawthorne seems to have reversed a progressively narrowing treatment of the effect of the past. In *The Scarlet Letter*, he deals with Puritan theology; in *The House of the Seven Gables*, a family curse; and in *The Blithedale Romance*, the effects of Coverdale's self-created past. In his last completed work, however, he takes the past of all Rome; in short, he copes with a length of time and complexity of events unusual in his writing experience. Hawthorne's reaction to Rome, complicated by his daughter Una's illness, was mixed. While he objected to the poverty, the dirt, and the paradoxical sensuality and spirituality of Rome, he never, as he put it, felt the city "pulling at his heartstrings" as if it were home.

Italy would seem to present to Hawthorne not only the depth of the past he deemed necessary for the flourishing of romance but also a neutral territory, this time completely divorced from his readers' experience. It can be said, however, that while *The Marble Faun* is Hawthorne's attempt to come to terms with the immense variety of the Italian scene, he was not completely successful. In his preface, he once again declares that the story is to be "fanciful" and is to convey a "thoughtful moral" rather than present a novelistic, realistic picture of Italian customs. He inveighs against the "commonplace prosperity" and lack of "antiquity" in the American scene, a lack which satisfies the kind of reforming zeal pictured in Holgrave but mitigates against the writer of romance.

Hawthorne broadens his canvas in another way as well; instead of presenting one or two main characters, he gives the reader four: Donatello, presumably the living twin of the sculptor Praxiteles' marble faun; Miriam Schaeffer, the mysterious half-Italian painter pursued by the ill-fated Brother Antonio; Kenyon, the American sculptor; and Hilda, the New England copyist. Donatello's double is not found elsewhere in the romances; in fact, he seems to be a male version of both Phoebe and Hilda. Unlike the two women, however, he comes in actual contact with evil and thereby loses his innocence, whereas Hilda's and Phoebe's experiences are vicarious. Perhaps the nearest comparison is Dimmesdale, but the minister is portrayed after he chooses to hide his guilt, not before he has sinned. In Donatello's case, Hawthorne examines the idea of the fortunate fall, demonstrating that Donatello grows in moral understanding after he murders the model, a movement that seems to validate Miriam's secular interpretation of the fall as necessary to the development of a soul more than it validates Hilda's instinctive repudiation of the idea. For some critics, such as Hyatt Waggoner and Richard Fogle, the *felix culpa* or fortunate fall is indeed the theme of *The Marble Faun*; Crews, however, emphasizes Hawthorne's unwillingness to confront the problem, noting that Kenyon is made to accept Hilda's repudiation without question. In the final analysis, Hawthorne does indeed seem reluctant to examine the ramifications of the theme.

Like Zenobia and Hester, Miriam is presented as a large-spirited, speculative woman whose talents are dimmed by a secret past, symbolized by the blood-red jewel she wears. Supposedly, Miriam (unlike Hester), has run away from a marriage with a much older man, but, Hawthorne suggests, her family lineage reveals criminal tendencies. She is followed by Brother Antonio, a wandering devil-figure whom she

meets in the catacomb of St. Calixtus and whom she employs as a model. The crime that links Miriam to Donatello is not, in this case, adultery, but rather murder. Donatello, who accompanies Miriam everywhere, throws the model from the Tarpeian Rock, the traditional death-place for traitors, saying later that he did what Miriam's eyes asked him to do. Linked in the crime and initially feeling part of the accumulated crimes of centuries, they become alienated from each other and must come separately to an understanding of their own responsibility to other human beings. During this time, Donatello retires to Monte Beni, the family seat, to meditate, and Miriam follows him, disguised.

Just as Miriam and Donatello are linked by their complicity, Kenyon and Hilda are linked by a certain hesitation to share in the other pair's secrets, thereby achieving an isolation that Hawthorne might earlier have seen as a breaking of the magnetic chain of humanity. Unnoticed as she observes the murder, Hilda nevertheless becomes a vicarious participant. She rejects Miriam's friendship, maintaining that she has been given an unspotted garment of virtue and must keep it pristine, but she does agree to deliver a packet of Miriam's letters to the Palazzo Cenci. For his part, Kenyon compensates for his earlier coldness to Miriam by effecting a reconciliation between her and Donatello. Visiting Monte Beni, he is struck by Donatello's air of sadness and maturity and believes that the pagan "faun," whose power to talk to animals was legendary, has come to an understanding of good and evil and has thereby escaped the possibility of a sensual old age to which the throwback Monte Beni eventually succumbs. Kenyon encourages his friend to work out his penitence in the sphere of human action and reunites him with Miriam under the statue of Pope Julius III in Perugia.

In the meantime, Hilda, suffering the pains of guilt for the murder as if she were the perpetrator, paradoxically gains comfort from confession in St. Peter's. Once she goes to the Palazzo Cenci to deliver Miriam's letters, however, she is incarcerated as a hostage for Miriam. Her disappearance is the novel's analogue to Donatello's self-imposed isolation; her experience in the convent, where she is detained, convinces her of her need for Kenyon. In searching for Hilda, Kenyon undergoes his own purgation, meeting the changed Donatello and Miriam in the Compagna and learning about Miriam's past. On Miriam's advice, he repairs to the Courso in the height of the carnival; it is there that he is reunited with Hilda. Her freedom means the end of Miriam and Donatello's days together, for Donatello is imprisoned for the murder of Brother Antonio.

As did Sophia for Hawthorne, Hilda becomes Kenyon's guide to "home"; she is Hawthorne's last full-length evocation of the New England girl on whose moral guidance he wished to rely.

Patricia Marks

OTHER MAJOR WORKS

SHORT FICTION: *Twice-Told Tales*, 1837, expanded 1842; *Mosses from an Old Manse*, 1846; *The Snow-Image and Other Twice-Told Tales*, 1851.

NONFICTION: *Life of Franklin Pierce*, 1852; *Our Old Home*, 1863.

CHILDREN'S LITERATURE: *Grandfather's Chair*, 1841; *Biographical Stories for Children*, 1842; *True Stories from History and Biography*, 1851; *A Wonder-Book for Boys and Girls*, 1852; *Tanglewood Tales for Boys and Girls*, 1853.

EDITED TEXT: *Peter Parley's Universal History*, 1837.

MISCELLANEOUS: *Complete Works*, 1850-1882 (13 volumes); *The Complete Writings of Nathaniel Hawthorne*, 1900 (22 volumes).

BIBLIOGRAPHY

Baym, Nina. *The Shape of Hawthorne's Career*. Ithaca, N.Y.: Cornell University Press, 1977. This mid-sized book presents a readable and challenging portrait of Hawthorne as an artist in touch with the demands of his readers and his society. Identifies three distinctive phases in Hawthorne's artistic development and successfully brings feminist sensitivities to the discussion of his work.

Bloom, Harold, ed. *Nathaniel Hawthorne*. New York: Chelsea House, 1986. This collection of fourteen concise essays by different contemporary critics is introduced by Bloom and presents a use-ful overview of topical critical methods and issues as relating to Hawthorne's work. A chronology and rich bibliography make this collection valuable for a reader interested in a contemporary discussion of Hawthorne's art.

Colacurcio, Michael J. *The Province of Piety: Moral History in Hawthorne's Early Tales*. Cambridge, Mass.: Harvard University Press, 1984. The definitive modern guide to Hawthorne's early works, this voluminous book offers a thorough and exhaustive discussion of the tales covered; individual chapters read well on their own. Colacurcio's scholarship is outstanding, his style gripping, and his critical observations compelling, with their insistence on the importance of history for Hawthorne's fiction. Notes and an index are included.

Crews, Frederick C. *The Sins of the Fathers: Hawthorne's Psychological Themes*. New York: Oxford University Press, 1966. Rejects earlier, religiously oriented criticism of Hawthorne's work and proceeds along the lines of a psychoanalytical study, but avoiding distracting jargon. Hawthorne's innovative creation of psychologically motivated characters bestows some validity on Crews's ideas, yet his insistence on the dark obsessions of the author is not undisputed.

Miller, Edward Haviland. *Salem Is My Dwelling Place: A Life of Nathaniel Hawthorne*. Iowa City: University of Iowa Press, 1991. A full-scale scholarly biography, beginning with the "contemporary portrait" and including notes and bibliography. Miller's aim is to carefully analyze Hawthorne's many different poses in life and in art.

Newman, Lea Bertani Vozar. *A Reader's Guide to the Short Stories of Nathaniel Hawthorne*. Boston: G. K. Hall, 1979. For each of the fifty-four tales discussed, provides a "Publication History," "Circumstances of Composition, Sources, and Influences," "Relationship with Other Hawthorne Works," and "Interpretation and Criticism." Extremely valuable to a reader interested in detailed information about a particular tale; the bibliography is nicely specific as well.

Scharnhorst, Gary. *The Critical Response to Hawthorne's "The Scarlet Letter."* New York: Greenwood Press, 1992. Includes chapters on the novel's background and composition history, on the contemporary American reception, on the early British reception, on the growth of Hawthorne's reputation after his death, on modern criticism, and on *The Scarlet Letter* on stage and screen. Includes bibliography.

Stoehr, Taylor. *Hawthorne's Mad Scientists*. Hamden, Conn.: Archon Books, 1978. This lucid and concise discussion of the science and pseudoscience of Hawthorne's age shows how these respective ideas were handled by him. Distinguishes two kinds of Hawthornian scientist: the utopian idealist, who functions much like an early social scientist, and the gothic "pseudoscientist," who is given evil ambitions and uncanny powers.

Von Frank, Albert J., ed. *Critical Essays on Hawthorne's Short Stories*. Boston: G. K. Hall, 1991. Divided in nineteenth and twentieth century commentary, with a section of new essays, an introduction, and a chronology of the tales. No bibliography.

JOSEPH HELLER

Born: Brooklyn, New York; May 1, 1923
Died: East Hampton, New York; December 12, 1999

PRINCIPAL LONG FICTION

Catch-22, 1961
Something Happened, 1974
Good as Gold, 1979
God Knows, 1984
Picture This, 1988
Closing Time, 1994

OTHER LITERARY FORMS

Joseph Heller's first published piece was a short story in *Story Magazine* (1945), and in the late 1940's, he placed several other stories with *Esquire* and *The Atlantic Monthly*. Heller's enthusiasm for the theater accounts for the topic of his master's thesis at

Columbia University, "The Pulitzer Prize Plays: 1917-1935," and he wrote three plays that deal directly or indirectly with the material he used in *Catch-22*. *We Bombed in New Haven*, a two-act play, was first produced by the Yale School of Drama Repertory Theater in 1967. It later reached Broadway and was published in 1968. *Catch-22: A Dramatization* (1971) was first produced at the John Drew Theater in East Hampton, Long Island, where Heller spent his summers. *Clevinger's Trial*, a dramatization of chapter 8 of *Catch-22*, was produced in London in 1974. Only *We Bombed in New Haven* enjoyed a modicum of critical and commercial success. Heller also contributed to a number of motion-picture and television scripts, the best known of which is *Sex and the Single Girl* (1964), for which he received his only screen credit.

ACHIEVEMENTS

Heller's reputation rests largely on his first novel, *Catch-22*, the publication of which vaulted Heller into the front ranks of postwar American novelists. Critics hailed it as "the great representative document of our era" and "probably the finest novel published since World War II." The phrase "catch-22" quickly entered the American lexicon; more than eight million copies of the novel have been printed; and it has been translated into more than a dozen languages. In 1970, Mike Nichols's film adaptation of Heller's tale sparked renewed interest in the novel itself and launched it onto the best-seller lists.

Catch-22 was one of the most widely read and discussed novels of the 1960's and early 1970's; its blend of humor and horror struck a responsive chord, particularly with the young, during the upheavals of the Vietnam era. The critic Josh Greenfield, writing in 1968, claimed that it had "all but become the chapbook of the sixties." Within the context of Vietnam, the novel seemed to be less about World War II than about that Asian war over which America was so furiously divided. *Catch-22*, then, remains the classic fictional statement of the antiwar sentiments of its time.

Although some have compared *Catch-22* to Norman Mailer's *The Naked and the Dead* (1948), James

(Mariana Cook)

about the life of a soldier (as in *Catch-22*), the life of a businessman (as in *Something Happened*), or the life of a would-be politician (as in *Good as Gold*) as about the threats posed to individual identity by the institutions of modern life.

BIOGRAPHY

Joseph Heller was born in Brooklyn, New York, on May 1, 1923, the son of Russian-Jewish immigrants only recently arrived in America. His mother then barely spoke English; his father drove a delivery truck for a bakery until, when Heller was only five, he died unexpectedly during a routine ulcer operation. The denial of this death in particular and the bare fact of mortality in general were to color Heller's later life and work. The youngest of three children, Heller spent his boyhood in the Coney Island section of Brooklyn, an enclave of lower- and middle-class Jewish families, in the shadow of the famed amusement park. Both his family and his teachers recognized Heller as a bright but bored student; he tinkered with writing short stories while still in high school.

In 1942, at the age of nineteen, Heller joined the Army Air Corps. He spent one of the war years flying sixty missions as a wing bombadier in a squadron of B-25's stationed on Corsica. This proved to be the crucial year of his life; it provided him with the materials, and the bitterly sardonic attitude, out of which he forged his major work—*Catch-22*—as well as his three plays. Moreover, his sixty missions, many of them brutal and bloody (including the series of raids on Bologna which form the core of *Catch-22*), profoundly affected the attitude toward death which informs all of his work.

Demobilized in 1945, having achieved the rank of first lieutenant, Heller married fellow Brooklynite Shirley Held, with whom he had two children. Heller spent the next seven years within academe. Under the G.I. Bill, he attended college, first at the University of Southern California and then at New York University, where he received his B.A. in 1948. Heller then traveled uptown to take a master's degree at Columbia University before receiving one of the first Fulbright scholarships to study at Oxford. He re-

Jones's *The Thin Red Line* (1962), and other essentially naturalistic war tales written by Heller's contemporaries, its conception of war in basically absurdist terms and its crazy-quilt structure suggest affinities rather with such works as Kurt Vonnegut, Jr.'s *Slaughterhouse-Five* (1969). Heller's fiction is frequently described as "black comedy." In the tradition of Nathanael West, Günter Grass, Ralph Ellison, and Thomas Pynchon, Heller stretches reality to the point of distortion.

In his novels, as well as in his plays, Heller displays a worldview which shares much with twentieth century existentialist thought: The world is meaningless, it simply exists; humankind by its very nature seeks meaning; the relationship between humanity and its world is thus absurd; when a person recognizes these facts, he or she experiences what Jean-Paul Sartre termed the "nausea" of modern existence. In all of his work, Heller argues for "massive resistance" to routine, regimentation, and authority in whatever form. He affirms, no matter how much that affirmation may be qualified by pain and defeat, the sanctity of the individual. He writes not so much

turned to the United States to teach English at Pennsylvania State University between 1950 and 1952.

During the remainder of the 1950's, Heller was employed in the advertising departments of *Time, Look*, and *McCall's* magazines successively. In 1954, he began writing, at night and during odd hours, the manuscript that would be published eight years later as *Catch-22*. Almost forty when *Catch-22* finally appeared, Heller ironically referred to himself as an "aging prodigy."

Heller abandoned his successful advertising career during the 1960's and returned to teaching. His position as Distinguished Professor of English at the City University of New York afforded him both the salary to support his family and the free time to devote to his writing. In these years, he began work on a second novel, wrote several motion-picture and television scripts (usually adaptations of the work of others and often using a pseudonym), and completed his first play, *We Bombed in New Haven*.

Something Happened, Heller's second novel, took thirteen years to complete before appearing in 1974. Never fully at ease with academic life, Heller resigned his chair at CUNY in 1975, and in 1979 he published his third novel, *Good as Gold*. Although he has occasionally lectured on the college circuit and has served as writer-in-residence at both Yale University and the University of Pennsylvania, Heller is basically a reclusive writer, uncomfortable at literary gatherings and suspicious of the trappings of literary success. His life and work seem guided by Ralph Waldo Emerson's dictum that "a foolish consistency is the hobgoblin of little minds."

In December, 1981, Heller was diagnosed as a victim of Guillain Barré syndrome, a sometimes fatal condition involving progressive paralysis. He was hospitalized for several months but eventually recovered. The experience resulted in a book, *No Laughing Matter* (1986), written with his friend Speed Vogel, describing Heller's condition and its resolution; the illness also led to his second marriage, to one of his nurses, Valerie Humphries, in 1987.

God Knows returns to the irreverence and defiance of logic which characterized *Catch-22*. Its narrator, the biblical King David, speaks in modern jargon and in his extended version of his life and career displays knowledge of events long after his own time. *Picture This* is a protracted meditation on the ironies of history and of human life, focusing on the Netherlands of Rembrandt's time and the Athens of Aristotle.

In 1994, more than thirty years after the release of *Catch-22*, Heller published *Closing Time*, a sequel to *Catch-22*. Set in the late 1980's, this novel revisits both the characters from Heller's first novel and the experiences of Heller's generation of New York Jews, for whom World War II was a formative experience. In *Closing Time*, both groups come face to face with their own mortality and the fate of a world governed by flawed human institutions.

Now and Then: From Coney Island to Here (1998) is an autobiographical account of Heller's life from his boyhood days in Coney Island through the period following the publication of *Catch-22*. Devotees of *Catch-22* may be disappointed to find that Heller spends only part of a chapter on his wartime experience, while much of the early sections of the memoir chart the geography of Coney Island in elaborate detail. Heller would make his home in East Hampton, Long Island. He died there on December 12, 1999.

ANALYSIS

At first glance, Joseph Heller's novels seem quite dissimilar. Heller's manipulation of time and point of view in *Catch-22* is dizzying; it is a hilariously macabre, almost surreal novel. *Something Happened*, on the other hand, is a far more muted book composed of the slow-moving, pessimistic broodings of an American business executive. *Good as Gold* is part remembrance of family life in the impoverished sections of Coney Island and part savage satire of contemporary American political life. Throughout Heller's work, however, all his characters are obsessed with death and passionately searching for some means to deny, or at least stay, their mortality. Heller's characters, like those of Saul Bellow, cry out to assert their individuality, their sense of self, which seems threatened from all sides. Yossarian, for example, in *Catch-22*, finds the world in conspiracy to blow him out of the sky. The worlds of *Catch-22, Something Happened*, and *Good as Gold* are not so much chaotic as absurdly and illogically routinized. In such an absurd world of callous cruelty, unalloyed ambition, and blithe disregard for human life, Heller maintains, the individual has the right to seek his own survival by any means possible.

CATCH-22

While *Catch-22*'s most obvious features are its antiwar theme and its wild, often madhouse humor, the novel itself is exceedingly complex in both meaning and form. In brief, the plot concerns a squadron of American airmen stationed on the fictional Mediterranean island of Pianosa during World War II. More specifically, it concerns the futile attempts of Captain John Yossarian, a Syrian-American bombardier, to be removed from flying status. Every time he approaches the number of missions necessary to complete a tour of duty, his ambitious commanding officers increase it. Yossarian tries a number of ploys to avoid combat. He malingers, feigns illness, and even poisons the squadron's food with laundry soap to abort one mission. Later, after the gunner Snowden dies in his arms during one particularly lethal mission, Yossarian refuses to fly again, goes naked, and takes to walking backward on the base, all in an attempt to have himself declared insane.

Yossarian is motivated by only one thing—the determination to stay alive. He sees his life threatened not only by the Germans who try to shoot him out of the sky but also by his superior officers, who seem just as intent to kill him off. "The enemy," he concludes at one point, "is anybody who's going to get you killed, no matter which side he's on." When Yossarian attempts to convince the camp's medical officer that his fear of death has driven him over the brink and thus made him unfit to fly, he first learns of the "catch" which will force him to keep flying: "There was only one catch and that was Catch-22, which specified that a concern for one's own safety in the face of dangers that were real and immediate was the process of a rational mind." As Doc Daneeka tells Yossarian, "Anyone who wants to get out of combat duty isn't really crazy."

Most of the large cast of characters surrounding Yossarian are, by any "reasonable" standard, quite mad. They include Colonel Cathcart, who keeps raising the number of missions his troops are required to fly not for the sake of the war effort but for his own personal glory; Major Major Major, who forges Washington Irving's name to official documents and who is pathologically terrified of command; and Milo Minderbinder, the mess officer, a black marketeer who bombs his own base under contract with the Germans. These supporting characters most often fall into one of four categories. The ranking officers—Cathcart, Dreedle, Korn, Black, Cargill, and Scheisskopf—appear more concerned with promotion, neat bombing patterns, and their own petty jealousies than with the war itself or the welfare of their men. A second group, including Doc Daneeka, Minderbinder, and Wintergreen, are also concerned with pursuing the main chance. They are predatory but also extremely comic and very much self-aware. Another group, including Nately, Chief Halfoat, McWatt, Hungry Joe, and Chaplain Tappman, are (like Yossarian himself) outsiders, good men caught within a malevolent system. The dead—Mudd, Snowden, Kraft, and "the soldier in white"—constitute a final group, one which is always present, at least in the background.

It is the military system—which promulgates such absurdly tautological rules as "Catch-22"—that is Yossarian's real enemy. He and the other "good" men of the squadron live in a world that is irrational and inexplicable. As the company's warrant officer explains, "There just doesn't seem to be any logic to their system of rewards and punishments. . . . They have the right to do anything we can't stop them from doing."

As the novel progresses, the victims, increasingly aware of the menace posed by this system, carry their gestures of rebellion to the point of open defiance. Yossarian is the most blatant in this regard: He moans loudly during the briefing for the Avignon mission; he insists that there is a dead man in his tent; he goes naked during the Avignon mission itself and then again during the medal ceremony afterward; he halts the Bologna raid by putting soap in the squadron's food and by moving the bomb-line on the squadron's map; and he requests that he be grounded and eventually refuses to fly. Finally, he deserts, hoping to reach sanctuary in neutral Sweden.

In the world of *Catch-22*, then, the reader is forced to question the very nature of sanity. Sanity is commonly defined as the ability to live within society and to act appropriately according to its rules. If those rules—such as Catch-22—are patently false, however, then adhering to them is in truth an act of insanity, for the end result may be death or the loss of freedom. The world of *Catch-22* is, to Yossarian, a spurious culture, as anthropologists would call it, one which does not meet the basic needs of its members—above all, the need to survive. Authority, duty, and patriotism are all called into question, and Heller demonstrates that when those in authority lack intelligence or respect for life, as is the case with Yossarian's commanding officers, obeying authority can only be self-defeating. Heller thus argues that in an absurd universe, the individual has the right to seek his own survival; he argues that life itself is infinitely more precious than any cause, however just. When Yossarian decides that he has done his part to defeat the Nazis (and after all, he has flown many more missions than most other airmen), his principal duty is to save himself. Yossarian's desertion, then, is a life-affirming act.

As one critic noted, *Catch-22* "speaks solidly to those who are disaffected, discontented, and disaffiliated, and yet who want to react to life positively. With its occasional affirmations couched in terms of pain and cynical laughter, it makes nihilism seem natural, ordinary, even appealing." Thus the surface farce of *Catch-22*, when peeled away, reveals a purpose which is literally deadly serious.

If the basic plot of *Catch-22* is fairly simple, its narrative technique and structure most certainly are not. The novel appears to be a chronological jumble, flashing forward and backward from the central event—the death of Snowden—which marks Yossarian's final realization of the mortal threat posed by Catch-22. Time in the novel exists not as clock time but rather as psychological time, and within Yossarian's stream-of-consciousness narrative, events in the present intermingle with cumulative repetitions and gradual clarifications of past actions. For example, in chapter 4, the bare facts of Snowden's death are revealed, that he was killed over Avignon when Dobbs,

his copilot, went berserk and grabbed the plane's controls at a crucial moment. Yossarian returns to this incident throughout the novel, but it is not until the penultimate chapter that he reconstructs the story in full. In this fashion, Heller seeks to capture the real ways in which people apprehend the world, incompletely and in fragments.

Catch-22 is intricately structured despite its seeming shapelessness. Until chapter 19, almost everything is told in retrospect while Yossarian is in the hospital; chapter 19 itself begins the movement forward in time leading to Yossarian's desertion. The gradual unfolding of the details of Snowden's death provides another organizing device. Such structural devices as parallelism, doubling, and—most important—repetition, force the reader to share Yossarian's perpetual sense of *déjà vu*, the illusion of having previously experienced something actually being encountered for the first time. The ultimate effect of such devices is to reinforce the novel's main themes: Yossarian is trapped in a static world, a world in which nothing seems to change and in which events seem to keep repeating themselves. He does not move *through* his experiences but rather seems condemned to a treadmill existence. The only way to resist this world is to escape it, to desert.

SOMETHING HAPPENED

Heller himself once revealed that he considered Bob Slocum, the protagonist-narrator of his second novel, *Something Happened*, to be "the antithesis of Yossarian—twenty years later." Indeed, the scene shifts dramatically from the dusty, littered airfields of Pianosa to the green, well-kept lawns of suburban Connecticut. In *Something Happened*, Heller details—some say monotonously details—the inner life of an outwardly successful man and, in doing so, seeks to expose the bankruptcy of contemporary middle-class American culture.

Slocum works as a middle-level marketing research manager in a large company. He is middle-aged, married, and the father of three children. Although he is by all appearances successful, Slocum's extended monologue of memories, self-analysis, and carpings at the world reveal that he is anything but happy: "I keep my own counsel and drift speechlessly with my crowd. I float. I float like algae in a colony of green scum, while my wife and I grow old." He sees his life as a series of humiliating failures of nerve, of unfulfilled expectations and missed opportunities. Slocum harks back repeatedly and with regret to his adolescent yearnings for an office girl—later a suicide—with whom he had worked shortly after finishing high school. He now wishes in vain that he could desire someone or something as desperately as he once desired her.

Slocum despises his present job and mistrusts his associates yet politics shamelessly for promotion; he feels bound to his family yet commits numerous adulteries. He is hopelessly at odds with himself and his life. For example, he loves his family in a temporizing kind of way, but he also fears that he has made them all unhappy. His wife, bored and restless, feels isolated in the suburbs and turns to alcohol. His sixteen-year-old daughter is sullen and promiscuous. One son is hopelessly brain-damaged and an insufferable burden to Slocum; the other, Slocum seems truly to want to love, but he cannot help browbeating him. The novel reaches its bleak climax when this latter son is hit by a car and lies bleeding in the street. Slocum cradles the boy in his arms and, at the moment when he feels he can express his love, inadvertently smothers him.

There is no real resolution in *Something Happened*. At novel's end, Slocum has not changed or learned anything of importance. Unlike Yossarian, who is threatened from without, Slocum is his own worst enemy. His sense of alienation, of loss, of failure, is unrelieved.

Critical opinion of *Something Happened* has been mixed. Those who admire the novel most often praise its exact and mercilessly honest replication of the banality and vacuousness of everyday life among the American middle classes, and they argue that Heller, as in *Catch-22*, nicely fuses form and meaning. Others find the novel irritatingly tedious and pessimistic and consider the character of Slocum seriously flawed, unlikable, and unheroic by any standard. Many reviewers could not resist quipping that a more appropriate title for Heller's novel would be *Nothing Happens*.

GOOD AS GOLD

Heller's third novel, *Good as Gold*, savagely satirizes the aspirations of the Jewish intellectual community in America. The comic dimension of *Catch-22*, so absent from *Something Happened*, returns. Bruce Gold is a forty-eight-year-old Brooklyn-born English professor who desperately wants to make—or at least have—money. Like Bob Slocum, Gold has problems with his family, which, he knows, considers him a failure because he is not rich. Much of the novel takes place within the Gold family itself, which Gold finds oppressive, if at times amusingly so.

Gold is in most ways a fool—albeit a cynical one—a hypocrite, and a congenital social climber. He is a 1970's version of Budd Schulberg's Sammy Glick. One evidence of this is his engagement to a wealthy WASP socialite with political connections. Gold himself harbors political ambitions. He hungers to replace his alter-ego and arch-nemesis Henry Kissinger as secretary of state, and hopes that his fiancé's tycoon-father will help him in his quest for political power. Heller savages both Gold and Kissinger, and for precisely the same reason: They represent to him those in the Jewish community who want to escape their heritage while at the same time exploiting it (to further his financial, academic, and political fortunes, Gold wants to write a "big" book about the Jewish experience in America, about which he knows next to nothing).

Gold understands his own hypocrisy but promptly dismisses it. Yet, when Gold is eventually offered Kissinger's former cabinet position, he experiences a change of heart. Prompted by the death of his older brother, Gold refuses the post and returns to New York and his family. Like Yossarian, Gold is able to restore his own integrity by deserting.

Heller's work has been compared to that of artists as varied as Eugène Ionesco and the Marx Brothers; *Good as Gold* lies closer to the latter than to the former. Until his decision to renounce his political ambitions, Gold is very much the comic intellectual, pathetically incapable of coping with the difficulties in which he finds himself. The humor of *Good as Gold* is painted with the broadest brush of Heller's career, but its target is his familiar one: the means by which institutions in the modern world coerce the individual and the way in which individuals—such as Slocum and, until his turnabout, Gold—become co-conspirators in their own demise.

GOD KNOWS

God Knows is Heller's rewriting of a major element of the Old Testament, the story of David. As in all of his fiction, Heller focuses here on the human insistence on repeating earlier mistakes and on the ironies of life. His David is a prototypical wise guy, looking back over his life from his death bed; his language veers from that of the King James version of the Bible to twentieth century slang as he presents his side of various stories, from his encounter with Goliath to his problems with King Saul to his troubles with his children and his various wives.

His first wife, Saul's daughter Michal, was a shrew to whom he refers as the first Jewish American Princess. He misses Abigail, his second wife, the only one who loved him completely; she has been dead for many years. Bathsheba, the great passion of his life, has turned into an overweight nag, bored with sex and interested only in trying to convince David to name their son, Solomon, as his successor. Solomon, in David's eyes, is an idiot, a humorless man with no original thoughts who writes down everything his father says and later pretends that they are his ideas. The old king's only solace is the young virgin Abishag the Shunnamite, who waits on him and worships him.

David complains about his present state, remembers his days of glory, and rationalizes his deeds, avoiding responsibility for any evil that has befallen others but claiming credit for benefits. His knowledge is modern. He maintains, for example, that Michelangelo's famous statue of him is a nice piece of work but it is not "him." His language is laden with quotations from William Shakespeare, Robert Browning, T. S. Eliot, and many others, and he seems to have direct knowledge of most of ancient and modern history.

God Knows is Heller's most engaging fiction since *Catch-22*. Suspense is maintained by David's reluctance to name Solomon as his successor, as he must do, and by the question of whether he will ever hear

the voice of God, which he desperately wants. Heller's David is not an admirable man, but he is a fascinating one and an interesting commentator not only on his own life but on human frailty and ambition as well. He is cynical, his faith in God and humanity having left him years before, but even as he complains about the pains of old age, his memory keeps reminding him of the enjoyments of the life he has led.

PICTURE THIS

Picture This is neither conventional fiction nor history but a kind of extended meditation on human weakness. Its inspiration is the famous painting *Aristotle Contemplating the Bust of Homer*, by the Dutch painter Rembrandt van Rijn. Heller presents many historical facts, chiefly about the Greece of the time of Aristotle, Plato, and Socrates, as well as the Netherlands of the time of Rembrandt, and he draws frequent parallels between events of those periods and those of the modern age. In discussing the Athenian wars, for example, he makes clear his conviction that the motivations, the mistakes, and the stupidities are parallel to those made by the United States in the years since World War II.

Picture This contains much authentic information, most of which is intended to demonstrate human greed and weakness. Heller seems to be fascinated by the financial aspects of Rembrandt's life, in which great success was frittered away and in which a life of luxury ended with enormous debts; he also writes at length about Rembrandt's marriage and his mistresses. In writing about Greece in the Golden Age, he focuses on the failings of government. The great leader Pericles, in his view, led Athens into self-destructive wars. Pericles was personally noble, but he did his city no good. The tyrant Creon was even worse. Much of what Plato wrote about he could not have observed.

Unlike either *Catch-22* or *God Knows*, *Picture This* fails to provide a leavening of irreverent humor to lighten Heller's dark view of human existence. The only fictional elements in the book are imaginary dialogues between some of the historical figures and the fantasy that Aristotle exists in the painting of him and can observe Rembrandt and his labors; these imaginary flights are only occasionally humorous. Otherwise, the irony in *Picture This* is unrelenting and bitter.

CLOSING TIME

Though *Closing Time* is more humorous, Heller's irony remains bitter, as a World War II generation contemplating the later years of their lives takes the whole world down with them, courtesy of an incompetent U.S. president who, at the novel's conclusion, launches a nuclear strike under the mistaken impression that he is playing a video game. Prior to that apocalyptic finale, readers are reintroduced to Yossarian, who, in the thirty years since the events of *Catch-22*, has been working as an ethics adviser for Milo Minderbinder's multinational corporation. He has been married, had four children, and divorced. As he faces retirement and realizes he is not long for the world, he worries about the future of his children, begins an affair with a younger nurse, and resolves "to live forever, or to die trying."

In terms of genre, *Closing Time* is a difficult book to characterize. As a sequel to *Catch-22*, it takes familiar characters such as Yossarian, Chaplain Tappman, and Milo Minderbinder through an absurdist parody of business, medicine, government, and the military. The addition of two World War II veteran characters (Sammy Singer and Lew Rabinowitz) with only ancillary connections to the main plot brings a nostalgic realism to the novel, more in keeping with Heller's subsequent memoir, *Now and Then*, than with the Yossarian sections of the novel. *Closing Time* also is Heller's most self-consciously postmodern novel, as real-life figures, such as author Kurt Vonnegut, Jr., are intertwined with fictional ones; references are made not only to the events of *Catch-22* but also to the novel itself and the entry of the term "catch-22" into the popular lexicon. At its best, this generic combination allows Heller to range widely in his criticism of contemporary society (as in a priceless explanation Yossarian is given of the Freedom of Information Act). However, too often these various formats seem at odds with each other, leading to a novel which moves both slowly and in too many directions.

Richard A. Fine, updated by Jim O'Loughlin

OTHER MAJOR WORKS

PLAYS: *We Bombed in New Haven*, pr. 1967; *Catch-22: A Dramatization*, pr. 1971; *Clevinger's Trial*, pb. 1973.

SCREENPLAY: *Sex and the Single Girl*, 1964 (with David R. Schwartz).

NONFICTION: *No Laughing Matter*, 1986 (with Speed Vogel); *Now and Then: From Coney Island to Here*, 1998.

BIBLIOGRAPHY

Aldridge, John W. *The American Novel and the Way We Live Now.* New York: Oxford University Press, 1983. Aldridge's overview of American fiction after World War II gives Heller's work high marks, praising his skeptical view of modern society and the imaginative qualities of his novels.

Craig, David M. *Titling at Mortality: Narrative Strategies in Joseph Heller's Fiction.* Detroit, Mich.: Wayne State University Press, 1997. An examination of the ethical dimensions of Heller's work, linking his distinctive stylistic features to his preoccupation with questions of death, meaning, and identity.

Klinkowitz, Jerome. *The American 1960's: Imaginative Acts in a Decade of Change.* Ames: Iowa State University Press, 1990. This analysis of American fiction in political terms suggests that Heller's *Catch-22* introduces a distinctively new kind of politics, that of withdrawal from impossible situations, and that in this sense the novel is one of the truly original works of its time.

LeClair, Thomas. "Joseph Heller, *Something Happened*, and the Art of Excess." *Studies in American Fiction* 9 (Autumn, 1981): 245-260. This essay focuses on Heller's second novel, defending its repetitive quality as a stylistic device, necessary to the portrayal of the dullness and mediocrity of the life of its protagonist and the other characters.

Martine, James J., ed. *American Novelists.* Detroit, Mich.: Gale Research, 1986. This extended bibliography includes Heller's work and the criticism devoted to him.

Merrill, Robert. "The Structure and Meaning of

Catch-22." Studies in American Fiction 14 (Autumn, 1986): 139-152. This offers the most detailed outline of the careful structure which underlies the apparently chaotic movement of Heller's first novel and the ways in which the novel's meaning depends on that structure.

Plimpton, George, ed. *Writers at Work*. Vol. 5. New York: Penguin Books, 1981. Contains an extended and informative interview with Heller dealing with his own conception of what his fiction is about.

Potts, Stephen W. *From Here to Absurdity: The Moral Battlefields of Joseph Heller*. 2d ed. San Bernardino, Calif.: The Borgo Press, 1995. This insightful and accessible overview of Heller's novels and plays emphasizes the continuities throughout Heller's writings, despite the various genres within which he has worked. As a moralist and political cynic, Heller creates characters whose personal crises drive them either to confront or to conform to governing orthodoxy.

MARK HELPRIN

Born: New York, New York; June 28, 1947

PRINCIPAL LONG FICTION

Refiner's Fire: The Life and Adventures of Marshall Pearl, a Foundling, 1977

Winter's Tale, 1983

A Soldier of the Great War, 1991

Memoir from Antproof Case, 1995

OTHER LITERARY FORMS

Besides his novels, Mark Helprin has published short fiction, including *A Dove of the East and Other Stories* (1975) and *Ellis Island and Other Stories* (1981). He has also published a children's book, *Swan Lake* (1989).

ACHIEVEMENTS

Mark Helprin's fiction celebrates the past. Readers who are accustomed to plot-driven fiction within the

conventional forms of realism find his work challenging. Helprin writes long novels (in excess of five hundred pages), and he creates worlds in which anything can and does happen. He received the Prix de Rome in 1982 and a Guggenheim Fellowship in 1984. In 1982, he was awarded the National Jewish Book Award for *Ellis Island and Other Stories*, his second collection of short fiction. *Publishers Weekly* selected *A Soldier of the Great War* as one of its "Best Books" of 1991.

BIOGRAPHY

Mark Helprin is the only child of Morris Helprin, a journalist who became the president of London Films in California, and Eleanor Lynn (née Lin), a Broadway actress in the 1930's and daughter of Max Lin, a Jew from Sinkiang Province in China. Born in New York City, Helprin spent his early years in Hollywood before his family settled in Ossining, a town along New York's Hudson River, mainly known for its prison, Sing-Sing. Born two months premature, Helprin suffered from problems with his spine and his lungs and was frequently ill as a child.

Helprin earned his B.A. in English from Harvard University, where in 1972 he also earned an M.A. in Middle Eastern studies. He lived in Israel in 1973 and spent the 1982-1983 academic year in Rome after he received the Prix de Rome. He traces the start of his literary career to the summer of 1964, when on a trip through Europe he wrote a description of the Hagia Sophia church in Istanbul from memory on a blotter in a hotel in Paris. Between 1965 and 1969, he wrote numerous short stories, eventually selling two simultaneously to *The New Yorker*.

In 1989, Helprin signed an unusual multibook publishing contract with the publishing firm Harcourt Brace Jovanovich, which bought the rights to three forthcoming novels and two collections of short stories. The contract was rumored to be worth at least two million dollars. The 1995 novel *Memoir from Antproof Case* was the first book published under this contract.

Helprin's personal experiences with illness, his education, and his love of mountain climbing, as well as his service in both the Israeli Air Force and the British Merchant Navy, are incorporated into his novels. His closeness to his family is also reflected in the parent-child relationships found in his books. Helprin married the New York tax lawyer and banker Linda Kennedy in 1980, and the couple had two children, Alexandra Morris and Olivia Kennedy. After a few years in Seattle in the 1980's, the Helprins settled in the Hudson River Valley, where Helprin assumed the role of contributing editor to *The Wall Street Journal*. He was former senator Robert Dole's speechwriter at the beginning of Dole's 1996 U.S. presidential campaign, and he became a senior fellow in Middle Eastern Affairs at the Hudson Institute.

ANALYSIS

Each of Mark Helprin's novels features a carefully developed, multilayered plot. Helprin pays particular attention to descriptive details and limits the use of literary devices such as symbolism and allusion, yet imagery is key. The stories are narrated in plain language with flashbacks commonly used to fill in gaps in the characters' lives. Helprin's characters live in a world in which time is told by the seasons; horses, trains, and airplanes are more common than cars; and common standards and values exist among all people. Recurring themes are those of father-son loyalty; the strengths of friendship, especially among men; the beauty of women and children; and the ability to turn weaknesses into strengths. The people in the stories endure a series of illnesses and encounters with insanity; many are orphaned or lose their parents at a young age and have to struggle to survive in an adult world. Helprin's characters are robust sorts of heroes, whose adventures and the obstacles they overcome reinforce their appreciation for society, one another, and the beauty and power of God and nature.

Helprin creates opportunities in his stories for his often-elderly characters to say that they are telling their tales to preserve them in the minds of the living, so their pasts will not "die." In 1993, Helprin told an interviewer that he writes "in the service of illumination and memory." On his manner of composing, Helprin decides first how the story will end and then develops the plot to focus on those events that will prepare the characters for their fictional fates. Like those of Henry Fielding, Charles Dickens, and An-

thony Trollope, Helprin's novels have multiple characters who find themselves in diverse, challenging situations. He is equally at home in creating male and female characters, and his methods of characterization focus on dialogue and description, not on a narrator's analysis. The characters are routinely on quests for justice, identity, or honor, and their actions cause them to intersect with people from all levels of society. Helprin often includes animals in his stories; his characters admire horses greatly for their beauty and strength, and in *Memoir from Antproof Case* two cats play central diversionary roles.

The scope and range of the novels have troubled some book reviewers, who fault Helprin for a lack of control in the complex plots, for arbitrariness in character development, and for the inclusion of extraneous historical or political information that causes unnecessary digression. In *Memoir from Antproof Case*,

(Jerry Bauer)

he pared the narrative down to involve a first-person speaker who tells a principally fictional story with no strong use of contemporary history or current events. While it is true that some of the events that befall Helprin's characters test the limits of realism, it is always clear that Helprin is writing fiction. In that genre, what readers believe to be true takes precedence over any notion of external truth.

Helprin's plots tend to follow the pattern of the drama. He uses exposition and rising action to lead to a specific climactic moment from which the action falls and concludes. As in epics, the main character descends into different sorts of underworld experiences, usually involving madness and illness, from which he or she emerges to continue fighting. Helprin uses flashbacks in the plots in different ways, but his writing is not experimental.

Helprin's eye for detail in the settings gives the novels their distinctive quality. He writes of places he has been with the eye of a landscape painter or a photographer. His characters experience the physical world as a source of both pleasure and punishment, and the power of nature is both respected and feared. His narrators concentrate on the actions in which the characters are involved more so than on their inner states of mind.

One of Helprin's chief themes is parents' love for their children. He allows the narrator of *Memoir from Antproof Case*, for example, to state the importance of parental love most succinctly, while other characters, such as Hardesty Marratta in *Winter's Tale*, show it. Helprin avoids ideologies in his fictions, presenting ideas in the debates of the times in which the stories are set. He favors treatment of such universals as the conflicts between good and evil, right and wrong, and justice and injustice. Repeatedly, his characters benefit the most from love of family and friends, and it is from this love and for these people that the characters turn their incapabilities into their capabilities. The novels are only mildly formulaic—the primary character is dead at the end in three of them, and all the characters are variously abandoned, challenged by evil, loved, or strengthened to perform good works. The works are uniformly positive, and the reliance on the past for settings enables Helprin

to focus on those characteristics which unify, not divide, people.

REFINER'S FIRE

Refiner's Fire, Helprin's first novel, was published in 1977. It is the story of Marshall Pearl, from his birth in 1947 through his late twenties, when he is wounded as an Israeli soldier in the Israel-Syrian War. The novel commences shortly before Marshall is born with the story of his mother Katrina Pearl's escape from Europe in World War II on a ship sailing for Palestine. During a sea battle with the British, who are refusing the refugee ship entry, Katrina is crushed in the hold. The baby is discovered by a child, whose mother gives him to the American captain, Paul Levy, who in turn sends Marshall to French nuns with a note explaining the circumstances of his birth. The sisters send him to a U.S. orphanage, where he is adopted by the Livingstones, a wealthy and childless upstate New York couple. During his first summer-camp experience, Marshall's prowess as a rider earns him the love of Lydia Levy. After some years in New York, Mr. Livingstone removes the family to Jamaica, where Marshall, though a boy, is involved in a territorial war between a local family and Rastafarians. Marshall proves himself an able guerilla, foreshadowing his future as a soldier.

After enrolling at Harvard, Marshall drops out before he graduates and travels west. He works in a slaughterhouse, spends time with a naturalist in the Rockies, and enlists in the navy. He is reunited with Paul Levy, who tells him who he really is, and he learns that Lydia is Paul's younger sister and an heiress. Marshall and Lydia marry and set out to find Marshall's father. This portion of the novel contains the greatest suspense, as Marshall and Lydia are separated as he climbs in the Alps and again when he is drafted into the Israeli Army, where he eventually meets his father, Arieh Ben Barak. Helprin tells the story of Marshall's parents' courtship in a flashback.

Fighting against the Syrian tanks, Marshall is severely injured, becomes comatose, and is reported missing. All the members of his family, Paul Levy, the Livingstones, and Lydia set out separately to find him, finally converging at the hospital. In the final pages, Marshall regains his consciousness before he sees anyone, muttering to his faithful nurse, "By God, I'm not down yet. By God, I'm not down yet." Helprin uses a third-person narrator and limited symbolism in the novel, with the title referring to the purifying power of fire. He also uses flashback, dialogue, suspense, and his own experiences as a soldier in the telling of his story.

WINTER'S TALE

Winter's Tale, published in 1983, is a fantasy that tells the story of New York City in the winters of the nineteenth and twentieth centuries. The parallel main characters are Peter Lake, an Irishman and a thief, and Hardesty Marratta, a San Francisco newspaper writer who moves to New York as a young man. Peter Lake's main companion is a magical white horse, Athansor, while Hardesty's is his wife, another writer, Virginia Gamely. The story is narrated by a third-person omniscient speaker, and Helprin allows both Lake and his horse to fly and to perform great feats of strength and personal endurance.

Lake's life is a series of adventures and misadventures, beginning with his orphanhood and life with the Reverend Mootfowl, who teaches him how to operate complicated nineteenth century machines. After he kills Mootfowl, he joins the Short Tails, a gang led by Pearly Soames. Lake informs on the Short Tails, and for his crime he is pursued for nearly one hundred years in New York City. On the run, he breaks into the home of Isaac Penn. There he sees, then becomes involved with, his beautiful, musical, and terminally ill daughter, Beverly Penn, who becomes his mystical protector after her death. When Lake is later injured, he becomes an amnesiac. On the street he encounters the Marratta family, with their friends, Praeger de Pinto and Jessica Penn, Isaac's granddaughter. They all work for Harry Penn's newspaper, where Lake eventually gets a job operating the old machines, which none of the new mechanics understand. The machines regulate the actions of the city.

When the Marattas' daughter Abby is dying, her father once more encounters Peter Lake, who is now living behind the clock in New York's Grand Central Station. Helprin's knowledge of the city and of the Hudson Valley region are key to the descriptions that drive this book. Lake and Marratta join forces in an effort to travel across the city to his daughter, made difficult because the city's boroughs are at war, thanks to the Short Tails and the sinister Jackson Mead. Lake is wounded by a Short Tail in the journey, and Abby dies.

Lake returns to his job in the machine room at *The Sun* newspaper, where Harry Penn is able to tell him of his identity and his past. He leaves the paper and finds Athansor, who has had a terrible parallel life without Peter, and they go off to their separate ends. In the epilogue, Helprin asks the reader if Lake's death had a purpose and if his attempt to create a city built on justice, with Marratta, was worth the costs. As critic David Rothenberg observed in his writings about the winters of this novel, the cold landscapes are used as positive sources of self-reliance and as images of containment.

A SOLDIER OF THE GREAT WAR

Alessandro Giuliani is the son of a prominent Roman banker and a soldier in Italy's war with Austria (1908). Eschewing a career in the law, Alessandro trains to be a professor of aesthetics, and it is the pursuit of beauty and truth which gives him the greatest personal strength. Once enlisted, he is not at sea but instead on land, serving in the River Guard, a unit which recaptures Italian deserters. One of the deserters kills the captain of this unit, and all the soldiers flee. Alessandro and his friend Guariglia return to Rome. Caught, they are sentenced to death, but Alessandro is saved by orders which his father's former scribe, Orfeo, keeps writing for him at the Ministry of War. Alessandro's life parallels Orfeo's, who is described as the person who is really running the war.

The unit to which Alessandro is assigned is on the front; while digging trenches he is engaged in hand-to-hand combat with Austrian soldiers, and he is seriously wounded. His beautiful nurse, with whom he falls in love, Ariane, is a French Italian, whom he actually saw once when she was a child. They become lovers and plan to marry; however, the hospital dormitory in which Ariane lives is bombed before Alessandro's eyes by Austrians pursuing an Italian cavalry unit.

As the story is told in a flashback sequence, the

reader knows that Ariane is not dead, but it is the perceived loss of her that colors all Alessandro's actions in his years remaining in the service. For instance, he is taken prisoner while retrieving the body of a college friend, Rafi Foa, to whom his sister was engaged. As a prisoner, Alessandro's adventures include riding with the enemy's hussars, stealing a Lipizzaner stallion to escape, and attempting to kill the German pilot who he thought had killed Ariane. Back in Rome, he is reunited with her and their son, Paolo, and the next chapters cover Alessandro's life between 1915 and 1921.

The story is framed by two modern-day chapters in which Alessandro is still demonstrating his sense of justice and his strong will to live. In 1964, he is seventy-four years old and on his way to see his granddaughter, when he gets into an altercation with the bus driver who fails to stop for a young passenger, Nicolò Sambucco. The busdriver puts the rather frail old man off the bus, and the two unlikely companions decide to walk to their destinations, though this will take several days. During this time, Alessandro tells the willing Nicolò about the past and provides him with an education the younger man could not have obtained in school.

Helprin said the idea for this novel grew from an experience he had in Italy in 1964. He was stranded at a train station and engaged in a staring match with an elderly, decorated Italian soldier. Helprin believed the incident was an effort on the older man's part to impress his past upon the writer's memory and imagination. Although the book is rich in historical and scenic detail, Helprin clarified that it is not heavily researched and is based mostly on his year in Rome and early travels.

Memoir from Antproof Case

This 1995 novel is a stream-of-consciousness narrative from a father to his son. The pages are kept in an antproof case, so ants cannot destroy the pages. The narrator calls himself Oscar Progresso, which is just one of several aliases he has used in his life. Now in his eighties, he tells a tale of military heroism as a pilot in the Army Air Force during World War II, of a brilliant robbery, and of his relocation to Nitéroi, Brazil. Once in Brazil, he marries a beautiful bank

teller, Marlise, and teaches English to Brazilian naval cadets. He is obsessed with the evil effects of coffee, which he hates because of how it changes the body's action and smell; Helprin humorously dedicated the book to Juan Valdez, the fictitious advertising icon of Colombian coffee.

The narrator is a violent youth who first kills a man on a commuter train in his native New York, over an incident involving coffee. He also divorces his first wife, a billionairess, Constance Lloyd, when she takes up coffee drinking. He is sent as a boy to an asylum in Switzerland, and after his release he works as a runner for the banking firm of Stillman and Chase. He attends Harvard and Oxford, serves as a flying ace in World War II, and rises to partnership as an investment banker in his firm. He offends the senior partner, Edgar B. Edgar, in an incident involving coffee and is sent to stack gold bars in the building's basement. There he sees the foolish overseer throwing out bullion because it does not shine, and he realizes he can steal the gold bars with no trouble.

With a partner who is an engineer and works for the Transit Authority, he devises a successful and elaborate plan which allows them to succeed. His partner settles with his family in luxury in Europe, while Oscar relocates to Brazil. In a flashback chapter, it is revealed that Edgar killed Oscar's parents when they refused to sell their farm for the building of a bridge across the Hudson River in 1914. Oscar kills Edgar before he flees, but on the flight to Brazil he has to urgently land in a river, losing the plane and the gold.

The witty and eccentric Oscar places family loyalty above all else in his hierarchy of values. He is even happy to raise the boy Funio, the product of Marlise's affair with another man, as his son. Among the other characters in Helprin's fiction, Oscar is the most physically fit. He is injured only a few times, and his dread of coffee and of alcohol keep him largely in good health. As a first-person narrator, he is engaging, and because he is eighty, his movements in time create variety in the tales he tells. Instead of framing the story with present-time narration at the beginning and the end, Helprin incorporates past and present into most of the chapters, effectively creating time shifts in Oscar's memory. Readers of the three previous novels will recognize the allusions to the bridge building and a discussion of *La Tempesta* by the Venetian Renaissance painter Giorgione, which was a unifying device in *A Soldier of the Great War.* *Memoir from Antproof Case* ends with Oscar recognizing it is time to end the writing when he can not buy a larger antproof case from the son of the stationer in the shop where he bought the first one in 1952. *Memoir from Antproof Case* is a humourous satire on social ideas of vice and virtue.

Beverly Schneller

OTHER MAJOR WORKS

SHORT FICTION: *A Dove of the East and Other Stories*, 1975; *Ellis Island and Other Stories*, 1981.

CHILDREN'S LITERATURE: *Swan Lake*, 1989.

(The Nobel Foundation)

BIBLIOGRAPHY

Butterfield, Isabel. "A Metaphysical Scamp?" *Encounter* 72 (January, 1989): 48-52. Reviews *Winter's Tale* and offers an analysis of the quality of Helprin's ideas and his prose style.

Helprin, Mark. Interview by James Linville. *The Paris Review* 35 (Spring, 1993): 160-199. Offers a thorough look at Helprin's ideas on writing, politics, and the reaction he has received to his fiction. The article includes holograph pages from his novels and copies of his service records.

Rothenberg, David. "The Idea of the North: An Iceberg History." In *Wild Ideas*. Minneapolis: University of Minnesota Press, 1995. Comments very briefly on Helprin's descriptions of winter as compared with the writer's own experiences and other stories set in winter.

ERNEST HEMINGWAY

Born: Oak Park, Illinois; July 21, 1899
Died: Ketchum, Idaho; July 2, 1961

PRINCIPAL LONG FICTION

The Sun Also Rises, 1926
The Torrents of Spring, 1926
A Farewell to Arms, 1929
To Have and Have Not, 1937
For Whom the Bell Tolls, 1940
Across the River and into the Trees, 1950
The Old Man and the Sea, 1952
Islands in the Stream, 1970
The Garden of Eden, 1986
True at First Light, 1999

OTHER LITERARY FORMS

Ernest Hemingway will be best remembered for his novels and short stories, though critical debate rages over whether his literary reputation rests more firmly on the former or the latter. In his own time, he was known to popular reading audiences for his newspaper dispatches and for his essays in popular magazines. He wrote, in addition, a treatise on bull-fighting (*Death in the Afternoon*, 1932), which is still considered the most authoritative treatment of the subject in English; an account of big-game hunting (*Green Hills of Africa*, 1935); two plays (*Today Is Friday*, 1926, and *The Fifth Column*, 1938); and reminiscences of his experiences in Paris during the 1920's (*A Moveable Feast*, 1964).

ACHIEVEMENTS

There is little question that Hemingway will be remembered as one of the outstanding prose stylists in American literary history, and it was for his contributions in this area that he was awarded the Nobel Prize in Literature in 1954, two years after the publication of *The Old Man and the Sea*. The general reader has often been more intrigued by Hemingway's exploits—hunting, fishing, and living dangerously—than by his virtues as an artist. Ironically, he is often thought of now primarily as the chronicler of the "lost generation" of the 1920's, a phrase which he heard from Gertrude Stein and incorporated into *The Sun Also Rises* as one of its epigraphs. The Hemingway "code," which originated as a prescription for living in the post-World War I decade, has become a catch-phrase for academicians and general readers alike.

BIOGRAPHY

Ernest Miller Hemingway was the first son of an Oak Park, Illinois, physician, Clarence Edmonds Hemingway, and Grace Hemingway, a Christian Scientist. As a student in the Oak Park public schools, Hemingway received his first journalistic experience writing for *The Trapeze*, a student newspaper. After serving as a reporter for the Kansas City *Star* for less than a year, he enlisted as an ambulance driver for the American Red Cross and was sent in 1918 to serve on the Italian front. He received a leg wound which required that he be sent to an American hospital in Milan, and there he met and fell in love with Agnes Von Kurowski, who provided the basis for his characterization of Catherine Barkley in *A Farewell to Arms*. Hemingway was married in 1921 to Hadley Richardson. They moved to the Left Bank of Paris, lived on her income from a trust fund, and became

friends of Gertrude Stein and other Left Bank literary figures. The Paris years provided Hemingway with material for the autobiographical sketches collected after his death in *A Moveable Feast*. Also in the Paris years, he met the people who would become the major characters in his *roman à clef*, *The Sun Also Rises*. Hemingway dedicated the novel to Hadley, divorced her (in retrospect, one of the saddest experiences in his life), and married Pauline Pfeiffer in 1927. During the 1930's, Hemingway became attached to the Loyalist cause in Spain, and during the years of the Spanish Civil War, he traveled to that country several times as a war correspondent. His feelings about that war are recorded in *For Whom the Bell Tolls*, which was an enormous popular success. In 1940, he divorced Pauline and married the independent, free-spirited Martha Gellhorn, whom he divorced in 1945, marrying in that same year Mary Welsh, his fourth wife. The 1952 publication of *The Old Man and the Sea* is usually regarded as evidence that the writing slump which Hemingway had suffered for nearly a decade was ended. The last years of his life were marked by medical problems, resulting to a great extent from injuries which he had sustained in accidents and from years of heavy drinking. In 1961, after being released from the Mayo Clinic, Hemingway returned with his wife Mary to their home in Ketchum, Idaho. He died there on July 2, 1961, of a self-inflicted shotgun wound.

ANALYSIS

"All stories, if continued far enough, end in death, and he is no true story teller who would keep that from you," Ernest Hemingway wrote in *Death in the Afternoon*. He might have added that most of his own stories and novels, if traced back far enough, also begin in death. In *The Sun Also Rises*, death from World War I shadows the actions of most of the main characters; specifically, death has robbed Brett Ashley of the man she loved before she met Jake, and that fact, though only alluded to in the novel, largely accounts for her membership in the lost generation. *A Farewell to Arms* begins and ends with death: Catherine Barkley's fiancé was killed before the main events of the novel begin, and her own death at the end will profoundly influence the rest of Frederic Henry's life. The Caporetta retreat scenes, often referred to as the "death chapters" of *A Farewell to Arms*, prompt Frederic Henry to give up the death of war for what he believes to be the life of love. In *For Whom the Bell Tolls*, death is nearby in every scene, a fact suggested first by the image of the bell in the novel's title and epigraph, the bell whose tolling is a death knell. Perhaps most important in *For Whom the Bell Tolls*, Robert Jordan's choice to die as he does comes from his reflections on the heroic death of his grandfather compared with what he sees as the cowardly suicide of his father. Finally, Santiago's memories of his dead wife in *The Old Man and the Sea* play in and out of his mind as he confronts the possibility of his own death in his struggle against the great marlin and the sea.

Indeed, in Hemingway's work, as Nelson Algren observes, it seems "as though a man must earn his death before he could win his life." Yet it would be a mistake to allow what may appear to be Hemingway's preoccupation—or, to some, obsession—with death to obscure the fact that he is, above all, concerned in his fiction with the quality of individual life, even though it must be granted that the quality and intensity of his characters' lives seem to increase in direct proportion to their awareness of the reality of death.

There is a danger, however, in making so general an observation as this. Hemingway's attitudes about life, about living it well and living it courageously in the face of death, changed in the course of his most productive years as a writer, those years between 1926 and 1952, which were marked by the creation of his three best novels and the Nobel Prize-winning novella *The Old Man and the Sea*. During this period, Hemingway shifted away from what many consider the hedonistic value system of Jake, Brett, Frederic, and Catherine, a system often equated with the Hemingway code, to a concern with the collective, almost spiritual value of human life reflected in the actions of Robert Jordan and Santiago. If the constant in Hemingway's works, then, is the fact that "all stories, if continued far enough, end in death," the variable is his subtly changing attitude toward the implications

of this fact, no better gauge of which can be found than in the ways his characters choose to live their lives in his major novels.

"BIG TWO-HEARTED RIVER"

The best prologue to Hemingway's novels is a long short story, "Big Two-Hearted River," which has been described as a work in which "nothing happens." By the standards of the traditional, heavily plotted story, very little does happen in "Big Two-Hearted River," but the main reason for this is that so much has happened before the story opens that Nick, Hemingway's autobiographical persona, has been rendered incapable of the kind of action one usually associates with an adventure story. Death has occurred: not literal human death, but the death of the land, and with it the death of Nick's old values. It has been brought about by the burning of once-lush vegetation that covered the soil and surrounded the water of Nick's boyhood hunting and fishing territory. Presented with this scene, Nick must find a way of living in the presence of it, which he does by granting supremacy to his senses, the only guides he can trust. He earns the right to eat his food by carrying the heavy backpack containing it to his campsite; after working with his own hands to provide shelter, he can savor the cooking and eating of the food. He can then catch grasshoppers, which have adapted to the burning of the woods by becoming brown, and use them as natural bait for fishing. Then he can catch fish, clean them, eat them, and return their inedible parts to the earth to help restore its fertility.

It is appropriate that "nothing happens" in this prologue to Hemingway's novels because the dilemma of his main characters is that "nothing" is going to happen unless a modern Perceval removes the plagues of the people and restores fertility to the land. The task for Hemingway's characters, particularly those in his early works, is to establish a code by which they can live in the meantime. Nick, like T. S. Eliot's Fisher King, who sits with his back to an arid plain at the end of *The Waste Land* (1922), is shoring up fragments against his ruins: He is developing a personal system that will enable him to cope with life in the presence of a burned-out, infertile land. Also, like Eliot and many other lost-generation writers, Hemingway suggests that the actual wasteland is a metaphor for the spiritual and psychological impotence of modern humanity, since the state of the land simply mirrors the condition of the postwar human psyche. Like the grasshoppers in "Big Two-Hearted River," who have changed color to adapt outwardly to the changing of the land, Nick must adjust internally to the altered condition of his psyche, whose illusions have been destroyed by the war, just as the land has been destroyed by fire.

THE SUN ALSO RISES

An understanding of the principles set forth in "Big Two-Hearted River" is perhaps essential to an understanding of the life-in-death/death-in-life philosophy that Hemingway presents in his major novels, particularly in *The Sun Also Rises* and *A Farewell to Arms*. Bringing these principles in advance to *The Sun Also Rises* enables a reader to see the mythical substructure that lies beneath the apparent simplicity of the story line. On the face of it, *The Sun Also Rises* tells the story of Jake Barnes, whose war wound has left him physically incapable of making love, though it has done so without robbing him of sexual desire. Jake has the misfortune to fall in love with the beautiful and, for practical purposes, nymphomaniac Lady Brett Ashley, who loves Jake but must nevertheless make love to other men. Among these men is Robert Cohn, a hopeless romantic who, alone in the novel, believes in the concept of chivalric love. Hemingway explores the frustration of the doomed love affair between Jake and Brett as they wander from Paris and its moral invalids to Pamplona, where Jake and his lost-generation friends participate in the fiesta. Jake is the only one of the group to have become an *aficionado*, one who is passionate about bullfighting. In the end, though, he betrays his *aficion* by introducing Brett to Pedro Romero, one of the few remaining bullfighters who is true to the spirit of the sport—one who fights honestly and faces death with grace—and this Jake does with full knowledge that Brett will seduce Romero, perhaps corrupting his innocence by infecting him with the jaded philosophy that makes her "lost." Predictably, she does seduce Romero, but less predictably she lets him go, refusing to be "one of these bitches that ruins children." Finally, she and Jake are left where they started, she unrealistically musing that "we could have had such a damned good time together"—presumably if he had not been wounded—and he, perhaps a little wiser, responding, "Yes. . . . Isn't it pretty to think so."

Few will miss the sense of aimless wandering from country to country and bottle to bottle in *The Sun Also Rises*. The reader who approaches Jake's condition as a logical extension, symbolically rendered, of Nick's situation in "Big Two-Hearted River," however, will more fully appreciate Hemingway's design and purpose in the novel. As is the case in "Big Two-Hearted River," the death with which *The Sun Also Rises* begins and ends is less a physical death than it is living or walking death, which, granted, is most acute in Jake's case, but which afflicts all the characters in the novel. They must establish rules for playing a kind of spiritual solitaire, and Jake is the character in the novel who most articulately expresses these rules, perhaps because he is the one who most needs them. "Enjoying living," he says, "was learning to get your money's worth and knowing when you had it." In a literal sense, Jake refers here to the practice of getting what one pays for with actual money, but in another sense, he is talking more abstractly about other kinds of economy—the economy of motion in a good bullfight, for example.

To see how thoroughly Hemingway weaves this idea of economy into the fabric of the novel, one needs only to look at his seemingly offhand joke about writing telegrams. On closer examination, the joke yields a valuable clue for understanding the Hemingway code. When Jake and Bill, his best friend, are fishing in Burguete, they receive a telegram from Cohn, addressed simply, "Barnes, Burguete": "Vengo Jueves Cohn" [I come Thursday]. "What a lousy telegram!" Jake responds. "He could send ten words for the same price." Cohn thinks that he is being clever by writing in Spanish and saving a word, an assumption as naïve as the one that leads him to shorten the name and address to "Barnes, Burguete." The address was free, and Cohn could have included full name and address, thus increasing the probability that Jake would get the message. As a response to Cohn's telegram, Jake and Bill send one equally wasteful: "Arriving to-night." The point is that the price of the telegram includes a laugh at Cohn's expense, and they are willing to pay for it.

After the Burguete scene, there is no direct discussion of the price of telegrams, but through this scene, Hemingway gives a key for understanding how each character measures up to the standards of the code. Ironically, Bill, with whom Jake has laughed over Cohn's extravagance and whom Jake admires, is as uneconomical as Cohn. From Budapest, he wires Jake, "Back on Monday"; his card from Budapest says, "Jake, Budapest is wonderful." Bill's wastefulness, however, is calculated, and he is quite conscious of his value system. In his attempt to talk Jake into buying a stuffed dog, Bill indicates that, to him, things are equally valueless: Whatever one buys, in essence, will be dead and stuffed. He is a conscious spendthrift who has no intention of conserving emotions or money. He ignores the fact that letters, cards, and telegrams are designed to accommodate messages of different lengths and that one should choose the most appropriate (conservative) form of communication available. At first, it seems strange that Jake can accept as a true friend one whose value system is so different from his, but just as Frederic Henry in *A Farewell to Arms* will accept the priest, whose code is different, so can Jake accept Bill. Both the priest and Bill are conscious of their value systems. Thus, if Bill's extravagance appears to link him with the wasteful Cohn, the similarity is a superficial one. Like Jake—and unlike Cohn, who still believes in the chivalric code—he has merely chosen extravagance as a way of coping, knowing that whatever he gets will be the equivalent of a stuffed dog. Morally, Bill is less akin to Cohn than he is to Rinaldi in *A Farewell to Arms*, who continues his indiscriminate lovemaking, even though he knows it may result in syphilis. Just as Frederic Henry remains true to Rinaldi, so Jake remains true to Bill.

Standing midway between Bill and Cohn is Brett's fiancé Michael, whose values, in terms of the code, are sloppy. Like Cohn, Mike sends bad telegrams and letters. His one telegram in the novel is four words long: "Stopped night San Sebastian." His letters are in clipped telegraphese, filled with abbreviations such as "We got here Friday, Brett passed out on the train, so brought her here for 3 days rest with old friends of ours." Michael could have gotten more for his money in the telegram by using the ten allotted words, just as he could have sent a letter without abbreviations for the same price. The telegram and the letter suggest that although he is conscious of the *principle* of economy, he simply has no idea how to be economical. Thus, when Brett says of Michael that "He writes a good letter," there is an irony in her comment which Jake acknowledges: "I know. . . . He wrote me from San Sebastian." In juxtaposing the telegram and the letter, Hemingway shows Michael to be a man without a code, a man who, when asked how he became bankrupt, responds, "Gradually and then suddenly," which is precisely how he is becoming emotionally bankrupt. He sees it coming, but he has no code that will help him deal directly with his "lostness."

Unlike Cohn, Bill, and Mike, both Brett and Jake send ten-word telegrams, thus presumably getting their money's worth. When Brett, in the last chapters of the novel, needs Jake, she wires him: "COULD YOU COME HOTEL MONTANA MADRID AM RATHER IN TROUBLE BRETT"—ten words followed by the signature. This telegram, which had been forwarded from Paris, is immediately followed by another one identical to it, forwarded from Pamplona. In turn, Jake responds with a telegram which also consists of ten words and the signature: "LADY ASHLEY HOTEL MONTANA MADRID ARRIVING SUD EXPRESS TOMORROW LOVE JAKE." Interestingly, he includes the address in the body of the telegram in order to obtain the ten-word limit. The sending of ten-word telegrams indicates that Jake and Brett are bonded by their adherence to the code; since they alone send such telegrams, the reader must see them as members of an exclusive society.

Yet ironically, to Jake and Brett, the code has become a formalized ritual, something superimposed over their emptiness. They have not learned to apply the code to every aspect of their lives, the most striking example of which is Brett's ten-word (excluding the signature) postcard at the beginning of chapter 8: "Darling. Very quiet and healthy. Love to all the chaps. Brett." The postcard has no word limit, except that dictated by the size of one's handwriting. Brett, however, in the absence of clearly labeled values, must fall back on the only form she knows: in this case, that of the ten-word telegram, which is here an empty form, a ritual detached from its meaningful context.

Jake and Brett, then, come back full circle to their initial frustration and mark time with rituals to which they cling for not-so-dear life, looking in the meantime for physical pleasures that will get them through the night. Yet if this seems a low yield for their efforts, one should remember that Hemingway makes no pretense in *The Sun Also Rises* of finding a cure for "lostness." In fact, he heightens the sense of it in his juxtaposition of two epigraphs of the novel: "You are all a lost generation" from Gertrude Stein, and the long quotation from Ecclesiastes that begins "One generation passeth away, and another generation cometh; but the earth abideth forever. . . . The sun also ariseth, and the sun goeth down. . . ." As Hemingway maintained, the hero of *The Sun Also Rises* is the abiding earth; the best one can hope for while living on that earth, isolated from one's fellows and cut off from the procreative cycle, is a survival manual. Finally, that is what *The Sun Also Rises* is, and this is the prescription that it offers: One must accept the presence of death in life and face it stoically, one must learn to exhibit grace under pressure, and one must learn to get one's money's worth. In skeleton form, this is the foundation of the Hemingway code—the part of it, at least, that remains constant through all of his novels.

A Farewell to Arms

Many of the conditions that necessitated the forming of a code for Jake and Brett in *The Sun Also Rises* are still present in *A Farewell to Arms*, and there are obvious similarities between the two novels. Like Jake, Frederic Henry is wounded in the war and falls in love with a woman, Catherine Barkley, whose first love, like Brett's, has been killed before the main events of the novel begin. Yet there has been a subtle change from *The Sun Also Rises* to *A Farewell to Arms* in Hemingway's perception of the human dilemma. The most revealing hint of this change is in the nature of the wound that Frederic receives while serving as an ambulance driver on the Italian front. Unlike Jake's phallic wound, Frederic's is a less debilitating leg wound, and, ironically, it is the thing that brings him closer to Catherine, an English nurse who treats him in the field hospital in Milan. Though their relationship begins as a casual one, viewed from the beginning by Frederic as a "chess game" whose object is sexual gratification, it evolves in the course of Catherine's nursing him into a love that is both spiritual and physical. Catherine's pregnancy affirms at least a partial healing of the maimed fisher king and the restoration of fertility to the wasteland that appeared in *The Sun Also Rises*.

With this improved condition, however, come new problems, and with them a need to amend the code practiced by Jake and Brett. Frederic's dilemma at the beginning of the novel, how to find meaning in life when he is surrounded by death, contains clear-cut alternatives: He can seek physical pleasure in the bawdy houses frequented by his fellow soldiers, including his best friend Rinaldi, or he can search for meaning through the religion practiced by the priest from the Abruzzi; he can do either while fulfilling his obligation to the war effort. His choices, simple ones at first, become limited by forces beyond his control. First, he must discard the possibility of religion, because he cannot believe in it; then, he must reject the life of the bawdy houses, both because it is not fulfilling and because it often brings syphilis. These are choices which even a code novice such as Frederic Henry can make, but his next decision is more difficult. Knowing that Catherine is pregnant and knowing that he loves her, how can he continue to fight, even for a cause to which he feels duty-bound? Catherine, who had earlier lost her fiancé to the war and who had refused to give herself to him completely because of her sense of duty to the abstract virtue of premarital sexual purity, has prepared Frederic for his decision, one forecast by the title *A Farewell to Arms*. Frederic's choice is made easier by the disordered and chaotic scenes that he witnesses during the Caporetta retreat, among them the shooting of his fellow officers by carabinieri. Partly because Catherine has initiated him into the life of love, then, and partly because he needs to escape his own death, Frederic deserts the Italian army in one of the most celebrated baptismal rites in American literature: He dives into the Tagliamento River and washes away his anger "with any obligation," making what he terms a separate peace.

If Hemingway were a different kind of storyteller, the reader could anticipate that Frederic and Catherine would regain paradise, have their child, and live happily ever after. In fact, however, no sooner have they escaped the life-in-death of war in Italy to the neutrality of Switzerland, where the reader could logically expect in a fifth and final chapter of the novel a brief, pleasant postscript, than does the double edge hidden in the title become clear. Catherine has foreseen it all along in her visions of the rain, often a symbol of life but in *A Farewell to Arms* a symbol of death: "Sometimes I see me dead in it," she says. The arms to which Frederic must finally say farewell are those of Catherine, who dies in childbirth. "And this," Frederic observes, "is the price you paid for sleeping together. . . . This was what people get for loving each other."

Some will take this ending and Frederic Henry's observations about love at face value and accuse Hemingway of stacking the odds against Frederic and Catherine, maintaining finally that Hemingway provides a legitimate exit from the wasteland with a code that could work and then barricades it capriciously. There is, however, ample warning. From the beginning of the novel, Hemingway establishes Catherine as one who knows well the dangers of loving, and from the time of her meeting with Frederic, she balances them against the emptiness of not loving. In most ways, Catherine is a model of the code hero/heroine established in *The Sun Also Rises*: She stoically accepts life's difficulties, as evidenced by her acceptance of her fiancé's death; and she exhibits grace under pressure, as shown in her calm acceptance of her own death. In giving herself to Frederic, she adds a dimension to the code by breaking through the isolation and separateness felt by Jake and Brett; finally, even though she does not complete the re-cre-

ative cycle by giving birth to a child conceived in love, she at least brings the possibility within reach. The reader must decide whether Frederic will internalize the lessons he has learned through Catherine's life and allow his own initiation into the code, which now contains the possibility of loving, to be accomplished.

There are some tenets of Hemingway's philosophy through the publication of *A Farewell to Arms* about which one is safe in generalizing. The most obvious and most important of these is his belief that the only things in life that one can know about with certainty are those things that can be verified through the senses, as Jake can confirm that he has had good food or good wine and as Frederic can verify that being next to Catherine feels good. Hemingway refuses to judge this belief in the primacy of the senses as moral or immoral, and Jake articulates this refusal with mock uncertainty during a late-night Pamplona monologue on values: "That was morality; things that made you disgusted after. No, that must be immorality." The point is that in referring observations about life to the senses, one relieves oneself of the need to think about abstractions such as love and honor, abstractions that the main characters in the first two novels carefully avoid. Frederic, for example, is "always embarrassed by the words sacred, glorious, and sacrifice and the expression in vain." With such a perspective, the value of life can be rather accurately measured and described in empirical terms. Similarly, death in such a system can be described even more easily, since there is nothing in death to perceive or measure, an idea vividly rendered in Frederic's remarks about his farewell to Catherine: "It was like saying good-by to a statue."

In looking back on Catherine's death, Frederic or the reader may conclude that it had sacrificial value, but until the 1930's, Hemingway was reluctant in his novels to identify death with an abstract virtue such as sacrifice or to write about the value of an individual life in a collective sense. By 1937, however, and the publication of what most critics regard as his weakest novel, *To Have and Have Not*, Hemingway's attitudes toward life and death had changed. Harry Morgan, the "have not" spokesman of the novel, finally with much effort is able to mutter at the end, "One man alone ain't got . . . no chance." After saying this he reflects that "it had taken him a long time to get it out and it had taken him all his life to learn it." The major works to come after *To Have and Have Not*, namely, *For Whom the Bell Tolls* and *The Old Man and the Sea*, amplify Morgan's view and show Hemingway's code characters moving toward a belief in the collective values of their own lives.

FOR WHOM THE BELL TOLLS

The epigraph of *For Whom the Bell Tolls*, which was taken from a John Donne sermon and which gives the novel its title, points clearly to Hemingway's reevaluation of the role of death in life: "No man is an *Iland*, intire of it selfe; every man is a peece of the *Continent*, a part of the *maine*. . . . And therefore never send to know for whom the bell tolls; It tolls for thee." Regardless of the route by which Hemingway came to exchange the "separate peace" idea of *The Sun Also Rises* and *A Farewell to Arms* for the "part of the *maine*" philosophy embraced by Robert Jordan in *For Whom the Bell Tolls*, one can be sure that much of the impetus for his changing came from his strong feelings about Spain's internal strife, particularly as this strife became an all-out conflict during the Spanish Civil War (1936-1939). This war provides the backdrop for the events of *For Whom the Bell Tolls*, and the novel's main character, like Hemingway, is a passionate supporter of the Loyalist cause. The thing that one immediately notices about Jordan is that he is an idealist, which sets him apart from Jake and Frederic. Also, unlike Jake, who wanders randomly throughout Europe, and unlike Frederic, whose reasons for being in Italy to participate in the war are never clearly defined, Jordan has come to the Sierra de Guadaramas with the specific purpose of blowing up a bridge that would be used to transport ammunition in attacks against the Loyalists. Thrown in with the Loyalist guerrillas of Pablo's band at the beginning of the novel, Jordan is confronted with the near-impossible task of accomplishing the demolition in three days, a task whose difficulty is compounded by Pablo's resistance to the idea and, finally, by increased Fascist activity near the bridge.

Potentially even more threatening to Jordan's mission is his meeting and falling in love with the beautiful and simple Maria, who is in the protection of Pablo's band after having been raped by the Falangists who killed her parents. Again, however, Jordan is not Frederic Henry, which is to say that he has no intention of declaring a separate peace and leaving his duty behind in pursuit of love. He sees no conflict between the two, and to the degree that Hemingway presents him as the rare individual who fulfills his obligations without losing his ability to love, Jordan represents a new version of the code hero: the whole man who respects himself, cares for others, and believes in the cause of individual freedom. Circumstances, though, conspire against Jordan. Seeing that his mission stands little hope of success and that the offensive planned by General Golz is doomed to failure by the presence of more and more Fascists, he attempts to get word through to Golz, but the message arrives too late. Although he manages successfully to demolish the bridge and almost escapes with Maria, his wounded horse falls, rolls over, and crushes Jordan's leg. He remains at the end of the novel in extreme pain, urging the others not to stay and be killed with him, and waiting to shoot the first Fascist officer who comes into range, thus giving Maria and Pablo's group more time to escape.

Jordan is perhaps Hemingway's most ambitious creation, just as *For Whom the Bell Tolls* is his most elaborately conceived novel. Its various strands reflect not only what had become the standard Hemingway subjects of personal death, love, and war, but also his growing concern with the broader social implications of individual action. Jordan's consideration of his mission in Spain clearly demonstrates this: "I have fought for what I believe in for a year now," he says. "If we win here we will win everywhere." How well Hemingway has woven together these strands remains a matter of critical debate, but individually the parts are brilliant in conception. One example of the many layers of meaning contained in the novel is the Civil War framework, which leads the reader not only to see the conflict of social forces in Spain but also to understand that its analogue is the "civil war" in Jordan's spirit: The reader is reminded periodically of the noble death of Jordan's grandfather in the American Civil War, compared to the "separate peace" suicide of Jordan's father. Jordan debates these alternatives until the last scene, when he decides to opt for an honorable death which gives others a chance to live. This, Hemingway seems finally to say, gives Jordan's life transcendent value.

THE OLD MAN AND THE SEA

F. Scott Fitzgerald theorized early in his friendship with Hemingway that Hemingway would need a new wife for each "big book." As Scott Donaldson observes, the "theory worked well for his [Hemingway's] first three wives (Hadley: *The Sun Also Rises*; Pauline: *A Farewell to Arms*; Martha: *For Whom the Bell Tolls*) but breaks down in Mary's case" because *The Old Man and the Sea* does not qualify as a "big book." It does qualify, however, as a major epilogue to the "big books," much as "Big Two-Hearted River" qualifies as their prologue. In the prologue, Hemingway outlines the dilemma of modern man and establishes the task with which he is confronted in a literal and figurative wasteland. For Nick in the story, Hemingway posits a swamp, which Nick may fish "tomorrow" and which is a symbolic representation of life with all its complexities, including male-female relationships. In the "big books," Hemingway leads the reader through the wasteland, showing first, in *The Sun Also Rises*, the risk of personal isolation and despair in a life cut off from the regenerative cycles of nature. In *A Farewell to Arms*, he dramatizes the vulnerability of the individual even in a life where there is love, and finally, in *For Whom the Bell Tolls*, he presents a "whole man" who recognizes the value of individual sacrifice for the survival of the human race. In the epilogue, *The Old Man and the Sea*, Hemingway carries this principle to its final step and issues, through Santiago, his definitive statement about the role of life in death.

It is no surprise that *The Old Man and the Sea* takes the form of a parable and that its old man takes the form of the archetypal wise man or savior common to most cultures, mythologies, and religions. While others who surround Santiago depend on gadgets to catch their fish, Santiago relies only on his own endurance and courage. He goes eighty-four

days before hooking the marlin, against whose strength he will pit his own for nearly two full days, until he is finally able to bring him to the boat and secure him there for the journey from the Gulf Stream. Numerous critics have noted the similarities between Santiago and Christ. Santiago goes farther out than most men, symbolically taking on a burden for humankind that most men could not or would not take on for themselves. When Santiago returns to land from his ordeal, secures his boat, and heads toward his shack, Hemingway describes his journey explicitly in terms of Christ's ascent to Calvary: "He started to climb again and at the top he fell and lay for some time with the mast across his shoulder." Moreover, Santiago talks with the boy Manolin about those who do not believe in him or his ways in terms that are unmistakably religious: Of the boy's father, who does not want his son to be with the old man, Santiago remarks, "He hasn't much faith." In all of this, Hemingway is leading the reader to see that some, in going out "too far," risk their lives in order to transmit to others the idea that "a man can be destroyed but not defeated." Finally, it is of little importance that sharks have reduced Santiago's great fish to a skeleton by the time he has reached land because the human spirit which has been tested in his battle with the fish has in the end prevailed; those who are genuinely interested in that spirit are rarely concerned with ocular proof of its existence. Santiago's legacy, which must stand as Hemingway's last major word on the human condition, will go to Manolin and the reader, since, as the old man tells him, "I know you did not leave me because you doubted"; he did not doubt that man's spirit can prevail.

Hemingway, then, traveled a great distance from the nihilistic philosophy and hedonistic code of *The Sun Also Rises* to the affirmative view of humankind expressed in *The Old Man and the Sea*. His four major works, if read chronologically, lead the reader on an odyssey through the seasonal cycle of the human spirit. "All stories, if continued far enough, end in death," and Hemingway never stops reminding the reader of that fact. He does add to it, though, in his later work, the hope of rebirth that waits at the end of the journey, a hope for which nature has historically provided the model. The reader of Hemingway's work may find the idea of metaphorical rebirth less a solace for the individual facing literal death than Hemingway seems to suggest it can be. Few, however, will leave Hemingway's work without feeling that he, at least, speaks in the end with the authority of one who has earned, in Carlos Baker's words, "the proud, quiet knowledge of having fought the fight, of having lasted it out, of having done a great thing to the bitter end of human strength."

Bryant Mangum

OTHER MAJOR WORKS

SHORT FICTION: *Three Stories and Ten Poems*, 1923; *In Our Time*, 1924, 1925; *Men Without Women*, 1927; *Winner Take Nothing*, 1933; *The Fifth Column and the First Forty-nine Stories*, 1938; *The Snows of Kilimanjaro and Other Stories*, 1961; *The Nick Adams Stories*, 1972.

PLAYS: *Today Is Friday*, pb. 1926; *The Fifth Column*, pb. 1938.

NONFICTION: *Death in the Afternoon*, 1932; *Green Hills of Africa*, 1935; *A Moveable Feast*, 1964; *By-Line: Ernest Hemingway, Selected Articles and Dispatches of Four Decades*, 1967; *Ernest Hemingway: Selected Letters, 1917-1961*, 1981; *The Dangerous Summer*, 1985; *Dateline, Toronto: The Complete "Toronto Star" Dispatches, 1920-1924*, 1985.

BIBLIOGRAPHY

Benson, Jackson J., ed. *New Critical Approaches to the Short Stories of Ernest Hemingway*. Durham, N.C.: Duke University Press, 1990. Section 1 covers critical approaches to Hemingway's most important long fiction, section 2 concentrates on story techniques and themes, section 3 focuses on critical interpretations of the most important stories, section 4 provides an overview of Hemingway criticism, and section 5 contains a comprehensive checklist of Hemingway short fiction criticism from 1975 to 1989.

Bloom, Harold, ed. *Ernest Hemingway: Modern Critical Views*. New York: Chelsea House, 1985. After an introduction that considers Hemingway in relation to later criticism and to earlier American writers, includes articles by a variety of critics who treat topics such as Hemingway's style, unifying devices, and visual techniques.

Lynn, Kenneth S. *Hemingway*. New York: Simon and Schuster, 1987. A shrewd, critical look at Hemingway's life and art, relying somewhat controversially on psychological theory.

Mellow, James R. *Hemingway: A Life Without Consequences*. Boston: Houghton Mifflin, 1992. A well-informed, sensitive handling of the life and work by a seasoned biographer.

Meyers, Jeffrey. *Hemingway: A Biography*. New York: Harper & Row, 1985. Meyers is especially good at explaining the biographical sources of Hemingway's fiction.

Reynolds, Michael. *The Young Hemingway*. Oxford, England: Blackwell, 1986. The first volume of a painstaking biography devoted to the evolution of Hemingway's life and writing. Includes chronology and notes.

_____. *Hemingway: The Paris Years*. Vol. 2. Oxford, England: Blackwell, 1989. Includes chronology and maps.

_____. *Hemingway: The American Homecoming*. Vol. 3. Oxford, England: Blackwell, 1992. Includes chronology, maps, and notes.

_____. *Hemingway: The 1930s*. Vol. 4. Oxford, England: Blackwell, 1997. Volume 4 of Reynolds's biography.

JOHN HERSEY

Born: Tientsin, China; June 17, 1914
Died: Key West, Florida; March 24, 1993

PRINCIPAL LONG FICTION

A Bell for Adano, 1944
The Wall, 1950
The Marmot Drive, 1953
A Single Pebble, 1956
The War Lover, 1959
The Child Buyer, 1960

White Lotus, 1965
Too Far to Walk, 1966
Under the Eye of the Storm, 1967
The Conspiracy, 1972
My Petition for More Space, 1974
The Walnut Door, 1977
The Call, 1985
Antonietta, 1991

OTHER LITERARY FORMS

John Hersey is as well known for his nonfiction as he is for his novels. As a young journalist in World War II, Hersey wrote for *Time* and *Life*, interviewing such figures as Japan's Foreign Minister Matsuoka, Ambassador Joseph Grew, and Generalissimo Chiang Kai-shek. His first book, *Men on Bataan* (1942), was written in New York from files and clippings; his second, *Into the Valley: A Skirmish of the Marines* (1943), from his own experiences. *Hiroshima* (1946), generally considered to be his most important book, was based on a series of interviews. After *Hiroshima*, he concentrated on writing novels for twenty years, though he often employed the techniques of interviewing and research to establish a factual basis for his novels. *Here to Stay: Studies in Human Tenacity* (1962) reprinted *Hiroshima* and a number of other interviews with people who had survived similar horrors, such as the Warsaw Ghetto. *The Algiers Motel Incident* (1968) was based on research and interviews concerning the Detroit police killing of three blacks during a period of riots. *Letter to the Alumni* (1970) was a portrait of Yale University during May Day demonstrations, and *The President* (1975) followed President Gerald R. Ford on a typical day. *Life Sketches* (1989) is a book of autobiographical pieces. Hersey's collections of short stories include *Fling and Other Stories* (1990). *Blues* (1987), also classified as short fiction, is an idiosyncratic book about bluefishing, cast in the form of a dialogue between a fisherman and a curious stranger and interspersed with poems by Elizabeth Bishop, James Merrill, and others. Hersey also edited *The Writer's Craft* (1974), an anthology of famous writers' comments on the aesthetics and techniques of literary creation.

ACHIEVEMENTS

Hersey's primary achievement was his mastery of the nonfiction novel. Although all the particular techniques of the nonfiction novel have been used for centuries, Hersey can be said to have anticipated the form as it was practiced during the 1960's and 1970's, the era of the New Journalism and of such novels as Gore Vidal's *Burr* (1973) and E. L. Doctorow's *Ragtime* (1975), to cite only two examples. At the beginning of his career as a writer, Hersey was a reporter and based his books on events and people he had observed. Rather than merely recounting his experiences, Hersey molded characters and events to fit a novelistic form, basing, for example, *A Bell for Adano* on what he observed of the American military government at Licata, Sicily. This attention to realistic detail and psychological insight characterizes his best writing and enriches his more imaginative novels, such as *White Lotus*, although these novels were not nearly as well received. Hersey's humanistic perspective is also an important trait of his works and provides a sense of values.

BIOGRAPHY

John Richard Hersey was born in Tientsin, China, on June 17, 1914, to Roscoe and Grace Baird Hersey. His father, a Young Men's Christian Association (YMCA) secretary, and his mother, a missionary, took him on a trip around the world when he was three years old, but most of the first decade of his life was spent in the missionary compound, where, although isolated to an extent from the community, he learned to speak Chinese before he spoke English. From the time he learned to read and write, he amused himself by playing reporter and writing his family news and daily events at the British Grammar School and the American School in Tientsin. Despite his early life abroad, Hersey considered his life there "no more exciting than the average child's."

In 1924, Hersey, who knew of the United States only from secondhand accounts and what could be gleaned from books and magazines, was enrolled in the Briarcliff Manor public schools in New York. Three years later, he entered the Hotchkiss School in Lakeville, Connecticut, and was graduated in 1932.

After receiving his B.A. from Yale in 1936, he went on to study eighteenth century English literature on a Mellon Scholarship at Clare College, Cambridge. During this time, he became determined to be a reporter for *Time*, because it seemed "the liveliest enterprise of its type." While waiting for an opening, he became the secretary and driver of Sinclair Lewis in the summer of 1937, the same summer that the Japanese invaded Manchuria. Born in China, Hersey was a natural choice for covering the Sino-Japanese War, and he served as a staff member for *Time* from the fall of 1937 until he was assigned to the Chungking bureau under Theodore White in 1939, where he began the itinerant life he would lead throughout the war.

An enthusiastic, courageous reporter, Hersey often found himself in mortal danger as he covered the war in the South Pacific in 1942, the Sicilian invasion and Mediterranean theater in 1943, and Moscow between 1944 and 1945. Twice, he went down in planes; once he crashed into the Pacific, nearly losing the notes he had taken on Guadalcanal. He was treading water when his notebooks from the sunken plane surfaced only a few feet in front of him. Among other stories which he covered was the first account of PT 109 and its young lieutenant, John F. Kennedy, an account that Kennedy would later use in his campaign for Congress. During one trip to the United States from Asia, he married Frances Ann Cannon on April 27, 1940. They had four children (Martin, John, Ann, and Baird) before being divorced in 1958, when he married Barbara Day Addams Kaufman, with whom he had a daughter, Brook.

In 1942, Hersey published his first book, *Men on Bataan*, basically a morale-builder for an America that had suffered serious setbacks at Pearl Harbor and in the Philippines. Hersey wrote the book only a month after the fall of Corregidor, when most of the men who had actually been on Bataan were imprisoned or assigned to new posts in the Pacific. In New York, he combined *Time-Life* files, letters to the servicemen's families, and a few interviews with reporters and other witnesses to write the book, which had a generally favorable if not overenthusiastic reception. In 1943, he published *Into the Valley*, based on

his own experiences with the Marines at the Matanikau River on Guadalcanal. With his experience in actual combat, *Into the Valley* had a substantially different tone from that of *Men on Bataan*, which often tended to jingoism. The extent of Hersey's closeness to combat can be measured by his receiving a letter of commendation from the Secretary of the Navy for his work removing wounded during the fighting.

A Bell for Adano, the first book Hersey published as fiction, followed in 1944, based on his observations of the American military governance of Licato, Sicily. The novel was later turned into a Broadway play and a motion picture. Hersey missed much of the praise because of his continuing assignments as a journalist. During the last year of the war, he observed the evidence of Nazi atrocities in Warsaw and Tallinn that would later lead to his novel *The Wall*. Just as V-E Day occurred, Hersey was awarded the Pulitzer Prize for *A Bell for Adano* and emerged from World War II an extremely successful writer.

During the rest of 1945 and 1946, Hersey was assigned to China and Japan, where he wrote for *Life* and *The New Yorker* and gathered material for what would be his most famous book, *Hiroshima*, the carefully understated story of six people who were in the city when the first atomic bomb was dropped. The editor of *The New Yorker*, William Shawn, had intended to run *Hiroshima* as a three-part article; he later changed his mind, however, and decided to print the entire text alone. Nothing else would share the issue with *Hiroshima* except advertising. This dramatic step was kept a secret from the regular staff as Shawn and Hersey sequestered themselves in the office from 10:00 A.M. to 2:00 P.M., Hersey rewriting while the text was fed to a harried makeup man.

Hiroshima became a phenomenon. The Book-of-the-Month Club distributed free copies to its members. It was read aloud in four hourlong radio programs. Physicist Albert Einstein ordered one thousand copies, businessman Bernard Baruch was said to have ordered five hundred, and the Mayor of Princeton sought three thousand reprints. The Belgian Chamber of Commerce ordered five hundred copies to distribute to officials in Brussels. Three

London newspapers requested serial rights. *Hiroshima*, with its concentration on ordinary people trying to cope with the horror of the first atomic blast, made Hersey known worldwide, except in Japan, where the book was banned by the American military government. Hersey donated many of his proceeds from the book to the American Red Cross. Nearly twenty years later, in 1965, when Hersey was invited to the White House Festival of the Arts by President Lyndon Johnson, *Hiroshima* was still considered Hersey's most profound work; he read sections of it at the White House gathering in a dramatic protest against the escalation of the war in Vietnam.

The year following *Hiroshima*, Hersey became one of the founders, writers, and editors of *'47—The Magazine of the Year*. It only survived one issue. Hersey became increasingly involved in politics, an involvement that would continue throughout his career. He vigorously supported the United Nations and became a member of such organizations as the Authors' League. During the 1950's, he became a speechwriter for politician Adlai Stevenson and actively campaigned for his election by serving as chairman of Connecticut Volunteers for Stevenson. Long before the Watergate affair made it fashionable to question the roles of the FBI and CIA, Hersey was a member of the Committee to End Government Secrecy. He also became interested in education, becoming a member of various educational committees and study groups, including the Westport, Connecticut, Board of Education.

Writing *The Wall* left Hersey little time for journalism in the late 1940's, though he published a few items such as a profile of Harry S Truman in *The New Yorker*. After extensive research, Hersey published *The Wall* in 1950, repeating the success of *A Bell for Adano* by winning such awards as the Anisfield-Wolf Award, the Daroff Memorial Fiction Award of the Jewish Book Council of America, and the Sidney Hillman Foundation Award. *The Wall*, like *A Bell for Adano*, was later dramatized and then made into a motion picture.

In the early 1950's, Hersey was one of America's most famous writers and was placed in the awkward position of trying to write up to the increasingly higher level expected of him. He began to rely more heavily on his imagination, which tended toward allegorical situations. *The Marmot Drive*, set in Tunxis, a rural New England town, made a political allegory of the town's attempt to rid itself of a threatening colony of woodchucks. A number of Hersey's later books, including *The Child Buyer*, *White Lotus*, *Too Far to Walk*, *Under the Eye of the Storm*, *The Conspiracy*, *My Petition for More Space*, and *The Walnut Door*, have been criticized for their reliance on an underlying allegory or parable to support the plot.

From the 1950's on, Hersey was associated with Yale University, with Berkeley College from 1950 to 1965 as a nonteaching fellow, and with Pierson College from 1965 to 1970, as master. In the latter position, Hersey served as a counselor, confidant, resident administrator, social director, and intellectual mentor for the students, among whom was his son John, Jr. His closeness to the students allowed him the perceptions he revealed in *Letter to the Alumni*, which was a factual description of the May Day demonstrations of 1969, when Yalies supported the Black Panthers.

After leaving Yale and Connecticut, Hersey lived in Key West, until his death there in 1993, involving himself in political issues of the day, especially those directly affecting writers. Although he was not a recluse, Hersey generally avoided media attention, only occasionally speaking in public and granting interviews.

ANALYSIS

Critics have generally agreed that John Hersey's greatest strengths as a novelist derive from two sources: the observational skills he developed as a journalist and his belief in the importance of individual human beings in difficult situations. Reviewers throughout his career have praised his attention to realistic detail, which rivals that of William Dean Howells. Hersey gets very close to the realistic details of the lives of his characters, so that in his most successful works (both fiction and nonfiction), the reader gets a strong sense of "being there."

When Hersey recaptured his memories of China in the novel *A Single Pebble*, in 1956, he was praised for his acute observations and simple handling of realistic detail, as he would be for nonfictional works such as *Here to Stay*, *The Algiers Motel Incident*, *Letter to the Alumni*, and *The President*. Throughout his career, however, Hersey insisted that he mentally separated and saw a clear difference between the way he wrote fiction and the way he wrote nonfiction. He saw the fiction as his chance to make more profound statements of lasting value—tending to push the works into the allegorical realm—although, ironically, most critics have seen his most profound themes in his more journalistic works, whether fiction or nonfiction, such as *Hiroshima*, *The Wall*, and *A Single Pebble*.

Sometimes, however, Hersey has been criticized for having insufficiently explored his characters in the apparent belief that documentary evidence sufficiently explains them. He has also been charged with cluttering his narratives with excessive detail. Although *A Single Pebble* was generally positively received, one of the criticisms leveled at it was its heavy use of nautical terms that the main character would readily understand but that are confusing to most readers. A similar criticism was leveled at *The War Lover* by a reviewer who asked if Hersey's accounts of twenty-three bombing raids, heavily laden with hour-by-hour details, were really necessary to develop his theme.

Ironically, in his 1949 essay for *The Atlantic Monthly*, "The Novel of Contemporary History," Hersey presented an aesthetic which established the primacy of character over realistic detail. "Palpable facts," he wrote, "are mortal. . . . The things we remember . . . are emotions and impressions and illusions and images and characters: the elements of fiction." He went on to argue that the aim of the novelist of contemporary history was not to illuminate events, but to illuminate the human beings caught up in the events. This concern with the individual gives Hersey great sensitivity to suffering, a sympathy that, combined with his liberal political views, makes his thematic intentions manifest in nearly all of his works, leading to the accusation that Hersey is too allegorical, too moralistic, and too "meaningful" to be taken seriously as a creative artist. Although some critics

hoped he would reverse the general trend of antimoralism and experimentalism in the postmodern fiction of the 1950's and 1960's, the more Hersey tried to escape the reportorial style, the less critically successful his novels became, though they continued to sell well.

A BELL FOR ADANO

The genesis of Hersey's first novel, *A Bell for Adano*, was a journalistic assignment in wartime Italy. During the Sicilian campaign, he visited the seaport of Licata, where he observed the workings of the American Military Government and filed a story for *Life* entitled "AMGOT at Work," which was printed on August 23, 1943, along with photographs. The article described a typical day in the life of an anonymous Italo-American major from New York as he tried to cope with the problems of governing the newly liberated town. Obviously impressed by the major's common sense, fairness, and accessibility to the natives, Hersey wrote *A Bell for Adano*, based upon the article, within six weeks of the *Life* publication.

A comparison of the article with the book provides an interesting insight into Hersey's work methods in those days. He retained every person in the article and expanded several of the problems. The major became Major Victor Joppolo; Licata became Adano. The central problem of the novel is Joppolo's attempt to find a bell to replace the seven-hundred-year-old bell melted down for bullets by the Nazis. Introducing the unsympathetic character of General Marvin, Hersey was clearly making reference to General George Patton, who was known among reporters for his having slapped two shell-shocked soldiers. Because Joppolo disobeys Marvin's orders, he is reassigned to North Africa after getting Adano its bell. Hersey also invented a romantic interest for Joppolo, an invention that later led to a lawsuit by the original major.

With the exception of *Hiroshima*, *A Bell for Adano* is Hersey's most widely read book. Published by Alfred A. Knopf in early 1944, it was a huge success, mostly because of its representation of the ordinary American as good-hearted, sentimental, and rigorously fair. The book reminded the reader that the war was a struggle to preserve democracy, that government was only as good as the people who govern, and that Americans were better than Fascists. Despite all the praise, Hersey understood the effect the political situation of the time was having on the evaluation of his work. In 1944, he was in the Soviet Union and wrote an article on the role of Soviet writers in the war effort, saying "Not a word is written which is not a weapon." One sees, perhaps, in Hersey's ambivalent feelings about his instantaneous success, a motivation for his continual effort to increase the literary merit of his fiction, an effort which, in the estimate of many readers, worked against his best qualities.

Not all reviewers joined the chorus of praise for Hersey's first novel. Malcolm Cowley said that *A Bell for Adano* should be read as a tract and should not be expected to meet the criteria for a novel as well. Diana Trilling ascribed the book's success to its "folk-idealisms and popular assumptions" that surfaced because of the speed of its composition; she saw "very little writing talent" in the novel. These criticisms, though not entirely without justification, did not diminish Hersey's instant reputation as an important novelist.

Shortly after his assignment to Moscow by *Time-Life* in 1945, Hersey and several other reporters were given a tour of the Eastern Front by the Red Army. He saw the ruins of the Warsaw Ghetto, interviewed the survivors of the Lodz Ghetto, and saw signs of the atrocities at Tallinn and Rodogoscz. He knew immediately that he would have to write a novel on what he had seen, though his interviews with survivors of Auschwitz convinced him he could never write about the death camps themselves. Later, he wrote, his time spent in Hiroshima "lent urgency to what had been a vague idea." Another possible source of inspiration for *The Wall* may have come from Hersey's childhood friendship with Israel Epstein, who first interested Hersey in the history of the Jews and later became a staunch supporter of the Chinese revolution, editing the English-language magazine *China Reconstructs*.

He went to the survivors in Eastern Europe and discovered a wealth of diaries, medical records, and other documentary evidence, most of which was un-

translated from the original Polish and Yiddish. He hired Mendel Norbermann and L. Danziger to translate directly from the text onto a wire recorder and did further research himself, reading *The Black Book of Polish Jewry* (1943), the works of Sholom Aleichem, the Old Testament, and the Orthodox prayer book, among other sources. Immersed in the moving experience of listening to the tapes, he began writing and soon found the number of characters, themes, and action had grown far too complicated. Four-fifths of his way through the novel, he scrapped what he had written to retell the story through the point of view of Noach Levinson, chronicler of life in the ghetto from November, 1939, to May, 1943, when the last of the buildings was leveled.

THE WALL

Hersey has observed that "Fiction is not afraid of complexity as journalism is. Fiction can deal with confusion." In *The Wall*, Hersey confronted a multiplicity of emotions, attitudes, customs, and events beyond a journalist's interest. The novel derives its power from this confrontation with the ragged edges of reality, and a number of critics consider it to be Hersey's greatest work. Although many reviewers expressed reservations about the length of the book and its numerous characters, most praised Hersey's compassion and argued that the strong feelings which emerged from the sustained reading of it more than made up for the technical faults of the book. Leslie Fiedler, however, said that *The Wall* lacked the strength of inner truth, depending too heavily on statistical, objective material, and he particularly criticized Hersey's themes as unconvincing.

Although Hersey argued in *The Atlantic Monthly* that fiction allowed the writer to deal with confusion and complexity, most of his novels after *The Wall* were criticized for their overly simplistic, message-bearing, allegorical intent. Hersey's works continued to sell very well, but he never earned the esteem of literary critics. Most critics consider Hersey's work to be without sufficient technical expertise. Some defenders of his work, however, compare it to that of John Dos Passos and argue that his humanistic themes are too valuable to ignore.

J. Madison Davis

Other major works

short fiction: *Blues*, 1987; *Fling and Other Stories*, 1990; *Key West Tales*, 1994.

nonfiction: *Men on Bataan*, 1942; *Into the Valley: A Skirmish of the Marines*, 1943; *Hiroshima*, 1946; *Here to Stay: Studies in Human Tenacity*, 1962; *The Algiers Motel Incident*, 1968; *Letter to the Alumni*, 1970; *The President*, 1975; *Aspects of the Presidency: Truman and Ford in Office*, 1980; *Life Sketches*, 1989.

edited texts: *Ralph Ellison: A Collection of Critical Essays*, 1974; *The Writer's Craft*, 1974.

Bibliography

Fiedler, Leslie. "No! in Thunder." In *The Novel: Modern Essays in Criticism*, edited by Robert Murray Davis. Englewood Cliffs, N.J.: Prentice-Hall, 1969. In discussing authors from his point of view that "art is essentially a moral activity," the controversial Fiedler accuses Hersey of being the author of "The Sentimental Liberal Protest Novel" who fights for "slots on the lists of best sellers" with his "ersatz morality." The essay makes for lively reading at best.

Huse, Nancy L. *The Survival Tales of John Hersey.* New York: Whitston, 1983. An eminently readable and informed study on Hersey which is useful in understanding the scope and development of Hersey as a writer. Explores the relationship between art and moral or political intentions. Includes extensive notes and a bibliography.

Sanders, David. "John Hersey." In *Contemporary Novelists*, edited by James Vinson. New York: St. Martin's Press, 1982. Covers Hersey's work from wartime journalist to novelist. Cites *The Wall* as his greatest novel and considers him the "least biographical of authors." A rather dense study but helpful in quickly establishing themes in Hersey's writings. A chronology and a bibliography are provided.

_____. "John Hersey: War Correspondent into Novelist." In *New Voices in American Studies*, edited by Ray B. Browne, Donald M. Winkelman, and Allen Hayman. West Lafayette, Ind.: Purdue University Press, 1966. A well-known scholar on Hersey, Sanders defends him and insists that he should not be dismissed because of his popularity. Traces Hersey's origins as a war correspondent and the writings that emerged from these experiences. Finally, Sanders settles the dispute as to whether Hersey is a novelist and hails him as a "writer."

_____. *John Hersey Revisited*. Boston: Twayne, 1991. A revised edition of Sanders's 1967 study. The first chapter introduces Hersey's career as reporter and novelist, and subsequent chapters discuss his major fiction and nonfiction, including his later stories. Includes chronology, notes, and bibliography.

Hermann Hesse

Born: Calw, Germany; July 2, 1877
Died: Montagnola, Switzerland; August 9, 1962

Principal long fiction

Peter Camenzind, 1904 (English translation, 1961)
Unterm Rad, 1906 (*The Prodigy*, 1957; also known as *Beneath the Wheel*)
Gertrud, 1910 (*Gertrude and I*, 1915; also known as *Gertrude*, 1955)
Rosshalde, 1914 (English translation, 1970)
Knulp: Drei Geschichten aus dem Leben Knulps, 1915 (*Knulp: Three Tales from the Life of Knulp*, 1971)
Demian, 1919 (English translation, 1923)
Klingsors letzter Sommer, 1920 (*Klingsor's Last Summer*, 1970; includes the three novellas *Klein und Wagner*, *Kinderseele*, and *Klingsors letzter Sommer*)
Siddhartha, 1922 (English translation, 1951)
Der Steppenwolf, 1927 (*Steppenwolf*, 1929)
Narziss und Goldmund, 1930 (*Death and the Lover*, 1932; also known as *Narcissus and Goldmund*, 1968)
Die Morgenlandfahrt, 1932 (*The Journey to the East*, 1956)

Das Glasperlenspiel: Versuch einer Lebensbeschreibung des Magister Ludi Josef Knecht samt Knechts hinterlassenen Schriften, 1943 (*Magister Ludi*, 1949; also known as *The Glass Bead Game*, 1969)

OTHER LITERARY FORMS

In 1899, Hermann Hesse published a collection of his poems under the title *Romantische Lieder* (romantic songs), and this was to be the first volume of a truly prodigious literary output. In addition to his longer prose works, Hesse wrote several volumes of poems, fairy tales, and short prose pieces. Hesse was also a prolific letter writer and reviewer: In the course of his lifetime, he reviewed more than twenty-five hundred books, and his correspondence fills many volumes. Hesse's essays, which typically express pacifist views or a humanitarian identification with all humankind, have appeared both as separate volumes and as a part of his massive collected works.

ACHIEVEMENTS

By the beginning of World War I, Hesse had become, in the German-speaking countries of Europe, a solid literary success. His poems, prose vignettes, and novels sold well, and he was tantamount to a habit with German readers by 1914. At the outbreak of the war, however, this situation soon changed in Germany, the result primarily of Hesse's outspoken disparagement of militarism and chauvinism. After the war, Hesse once again became a popular author, especially among younger readers, but this popularity lasted only until the advent of National Socialism, and in 1939, Hesse was officially placed on the list of banned authors, having long since been vilified as a "Jew lover" and unpatriotic draft dodger (from 1890 to 1924, Hesse was a German, not a Swiss, citizen). Throughout and despite this ebb and flow of critical celebration, Hesse continued to write.

After World War II, Hesse was once again sought after—personally and as a writer—as one who could offer moral guidance to a spiritually bankrupt and physically crippled Germany. He became, almost overnight, a celebrity, and was awarded a series of literary prizes, including the Goethe Prize and the No-

bel Prize in Literature, both in 1946. Although some still voiced doubts about Hesse as a writer and insisted he was not of the stature of a Thomas Mann, a Bertolt Brecht, or a Franz Kafka, Hesse's popularity in Germany lasted until about 1960, when it rapidly declined. It was at that time, paradoxically enough, that an international "Hessemania" took hold, a kind of exuberant reverence which was particularly strong among disaffected young people in countries as disparate as Sweden, Japan, and the United States. In America alone, more than ten million copies of Hesse's works were sold between 1960 and 1970 (when the Hesse wave crested), a literary phenomenon without precedent. Whatever reservations one may have about Hesse, it is a fact that he remains the most widely read German author of all time.

BIOGRAPHY

Hermann Hesse was born on July 2, 1877, in Calw, Germany, the son of Johannes Hesse, a Baltic-born Pietist missionary, and Marie Hesse (née Gundert), the oldest daughter of the missionary and scholar of Indic languages Hermann Gundert. From 1881 to 1886, Hesse lived with his parents in Basel, Switzerland, where his father taught at the Basel Mission School, but in 1886, Hesse returned to Calw to attend elementary school. During the academic year 1890-1891, Hesse was a pupil at the Göppingen Latin school, where he prepared to take the rigorous state examinations for entrance to one of Württemberg's four church schools. He passed, and in the fall of 1891 he was sent to the seminary in Maulbronn. There the young Hesse was desperately unhappy, and after seven months, he fled from the institution, resolving to be "either a writer or nothing at all." After a suicide attempt in June of 1892, Hesse was sent for a few months to a home for retarded children in Stetten. Promising better behavior, Hesse was sent in November to the *gymnasium* in Cannstatt; once again he ran away, however, and this episode concluded Hesse's formal education.

From 1895 to 1898, Hesse worked as an apprentice in a Tübingen bookstore owned by J. J. Heckenhauer, and from 1899 to 1903, he was employed as a stock clerk in a rare-book store in Basel; it was dur-

(The Nobel Foundation)

was to have a profound influence on Hesse for the rest of his life.

From the outbreak of World War I through 1919, Hesse's pacifist articles appeared in German, Swiss, and Austrian newspapers. In 1915, Hesse suffered a nervous breakdown and underwent psychotherapy with J. B. Lang, a student of psychologist Carl Jung, in Sonnmatt, near Lucerne. In 1919, he moved to Montagnola, Ticino, in part to escape the memories of Gaienhofen and his first marriage, which ended with his wife's institutionalization. He lived in Montagnola in the Casa Camuzzi until 1931. A writer's block of some eighteen months precipitated therapy once again, this time with Jung himself, in Küsnacht near Zurich. In 1924, Hesse became a Swiss citizen and married Ruth Wenger, the daughter of a writer; at her request, the unhappy union ended in divorce in 1927. In 1931, Hesse married the art historian Ninon Dolbin. The couple moved into a house on the Collina d'Oro with lifetime right of occupancy; this marriage, at last, was a happy one. From 1939 to 1945, Hesse's works were proscribed in Germany, but in 1946, publication of his works was resumed by Suhrkamp, and it was in this year that Hesse received the Goethe Prize and the Nobel Prize. In 1955, Hesse was awarded the Peace Prize of the German Booksellers' Association, and in 1956, a Hermann Hesse Prize was established by the state of Baden-Württemberg. Hesse died at Montagnola on August 9, 1962.

ANALYSIS

Despite a literary career which, if measured by quantity of literary output or by size of readership, was enormously successful, Hermann Hesse has not been numbered among the luminaries of twentieth century German literature. There are two primary reasons for this critical assessment: First, Hesse's prose is simply too readable and discursive to be considered profound; second, Hesse's limited and recurring themes remain, in their many novelistic permutations, rather juvenile and solipsistic in nature. This may well explain the fact that Hesse's readership has always been primarily a young one.

Hesse was among the first European writers to un-

ing the latter years that Hesse began to write in earnest. When his articles and reviews began to appear in the *Allgemeine schweizer Zeitung*, he achieved some measure of local success, which was a great source of encouragement to him. Volumes of poems were published in 1899 and 1902, and by the time *Peter Camenzind* was published in 1904, Hesse had "arrived" as a writer. In this same year, Hesse married his first wife, Maria Bernoulli, a member of an old Basel academic family. The couple moved to an idyllic peasant house in Gaienhofen on Lake Constance, where Hesse worked on his novels, painted, and continued his career as a freelance contributor to numerous journals and newspapers. Hesse's sons Bruno, Heiner, and Martin were all born at Gaienhofen between 1905 and 1911. By the latter year, however, Hesse was restless and felt the need to travel to India with his artist friend Hans Sturzenegger; this journey dergo psychoanalysis, and it was his fascination with the self which, from the beginning to the end of his literary career, was to remain the wellspring of his inspiration. Hesse's interior life became the stuff of his fiction, and it is this "private mythology" (Hesse's term) that is the organizing principle of his novels. It is in this sense that Hesse is a "psychological" writer, and it has often been pointed out in Hesse scholarship that, to a rare degree and perhaps in too facile a manner, the link between personal life and literary work is transparent. As Christopher Middleton has observed, Hesse can be characterized as a literary "acrobat of self-exploration," one who oscillates between self-esteem and self-disgust, often with an implicit moralizing intent. Hesse is an essentially confessional writer, an inveterate and somewhat didactic self-anatomizer.

The narrative scheme of all of Hesse's novels is essentially triadic: A protagonist's character and background are carefully presented; the disillusioned main character chooses to break with his setting and/ or former self in search of a new identity or individuation (Hesse's protagonists are invariably males); and the experiment results in a prodigal's return or in a successful forging of deeper inroads into the self, sometimes even in the adoption of an almost new personality.

Demian, published in 1919, was Hesse's sixth novel, but it can be considered his first major one. It was preceded by the following less distinguished works: *Peter Camenzind*, the story of a Swiss village lad who leaves his native surroundings in search of inner peace and who, after much meandering and a variety of experiences, returns to his ailing father and accepts a village way of life; *Beneath the Wheel*, a somewhat stock *Schulroman*, or school novel, which depicts the extreme authoritarianism, inhumanity, and pressures of a typical German secondary school of the time; *Gertrud*, a *Künstlerroman* (a genre which arose in German literature in the late eighteenth century—the term used to designate any novel with an artist as its protagonist) treating the tribulations of a physically handicapped composer; *Rosshalde*, an autobiographical novel reflecting the breakup of Hesse's marriage to Maria Bernoulli, who suffered

from a progressive mental illness; and finally *Knulp*, a novel in three parts which marks the culmination of Hesse's Romantic phase and which narrates the picaresque life and death of its central character.

DEMIAN

Demian, Hesse's first postwar novel, incorporates Hesse's reaction to World War I as well as his psychoanalysis during 1916 and 1917. Both of these experiences had led Hesse to a fundamental reassessment of his life, and this reevaluation finds expression in the *Bildungsroman*, which chronicles (in a first-person narrative) the youth of Emil Sinclair. At the outset of the novel, Sinclair becomes acutely conscious of the essential duality of life, a polarity he notes in the disparity between the safe, moral, ordered world of his home and the dynamic, cruel world outside. The latter is represented by the bully Franz Kromer, from whom Sinclair is rescued by a new boy at school, Max Demian. Demian alleviates Sinclair's moral confusion by telling him of the god Abraxas, in whom good and evil are fused and who represents the highest moral order. Demian also emphasizes the decline of European civilization, predicts its impending doom, and anticipates the advent of a regeneration of the world. With the outbreak of war in 1914, Demian's prophecy comes true. Both Demian and Sinclair are called up, and the latter is wounded. He is brought to a field hospital, where he has a final encounter with Demian, who lies dying; Sinclair is then separated from his mentor forever, but he believes himself to be the inheritor of his friend's personality.

Considered as a whole, therefore, the division of the novel is tripartite: Sinclair goes from a state of initial "light," of childhood innocence and security, to a period of "dark," of doubt and inner torment, to a final internal synthesis of the two antipodes. The novel is somewhat fraught with symbols that are intended to underscore the universality of this sequence; one of the book's central dream-images is elucidated in a manner which succinctly captures the dynamics of any process of individuation: "The bird fights its way out of the egg. The egg is the world. Who would be born must first destroy a world." Demian is Sinclair's shaman for this process of destruction (Socrates used the word *daimon* to describe the admonishing inner spirit), a process that Hesse imbues with tension by mixing Nietzschean thought, Christian terminology, and a religious, often parable-like tone. At the end of the novel, Sinclair has internalized Demian, much as the Church Fathers and later Christian authors admonished their readers to internalize Christ. Emil Sinclair is, therefore, now a missionary of the new gospel of Demian (read: Hesse)—namely, that one must be willing to suffer the progressive alienation and pain that result from shedding traditional or inherited strictures and definitions, a necessary divestiture which will ultimately make possible a rejuvenation, an authentic sense of self-identity.

SIDDHARTHA

Siddhartha, Hesse's second major novel and arguably his best-known work, took nearly four years to complete. *Siddhartha* is the product both of Hesse's trip to India in 1911 and of his lifelong fascination with that country's philosophy and religion. At the same time, however, it would be an oversimplification to state (as some critics have done) that this novel is a paean to Indic philosophy or Eastern mysticism, since the implicit admonition of the work is that one must seek one's own way in life and not simply adhere to a prescribed system or path.

The plot of *Siddhartha* exhibits the essential tripartite structure of all of Hesse's works, two-section and twelve-chapter divisions notwithstanding: The Brahman's son Siddhartha (whose name means "he who has achieved his aim") leaves his paternal home, has the requisite educative experiences of a *Bildungsroman* protagonist, and finally achieves peace. What makes *Siddhartha* such an atypical and successful "novel of education" are its Eastern setting and its complementary stylistic features, the latter signifying a level of technical originality and subtlety Hesse was never again to achieve. Feeling restless, Siddhartha forsakes his home and the teachings of Brahmanism and, with his friend Govinda, becomes a total ascetic. Still unsatisfied, he considers the teachings of Buddha but ultimately departs from him, leaving Govinda behind. As an alternative to his previous existence, Siddhartha seeks a life of the senses; the

courtesan Kamala teaches him the art of love, and he acquires a great deal of wealth. After a time, however, he comes to feel that this surfeit of sensual pleasures is robbing him of his soul, and he takes sudden leave of this life and of Kamala, unaware that she is pregnant. In despair and on the verge of suicide, he encounters the wise ferryman Vasudeva, from whom he learns "the secrets of the river," the simultaneity, unity, and timelessness of all that is:

> This stone is stone: it is also animal, it is also God, it is also Buddha. I love and venerate it not because it might someday become this or that—but because it has long been all these things and always will be.

After Siddhartha has spent twelve years at the river, Kamala unexpectedly arrives with their son, whereupon she is bitten by a snake and dies. Siddhartha's love and teaching are rejected by his son—just as Siddhartha himself rejected his father many years earlier—but the protagonist overcomes his anguish and loss with the help of the river. Vasudeva dies, Siddhartha becomes the ferryman in his place, and the narrative concludes with the reunion of Siddhartha and Govinda.

Like *Demian*, *Siddhartha* is meant to carry universal implications. The protagonists in both novels are stylized figures whose lives and personalities are only episodically sketched, since what was important to Hesse was less their individuality as literary personae than what they embodied. Both stories possess only a modicum of realistic narrative, and both central figures represent the path of individuality which, Hesse was convinced, must be chosen by all self-seekers. Demian's Abraxas and Siddhartha's river are simply narrative means to this end, symbols of the conflux of opposites, the harmony one experiences with self and all existence in a heightened state of self-awareness. As Hesse stated in his diary of 1920, "Nirvana, as I understand it, is the liberating step back behind the *principium individuationis*." Artistically, however, *Demian* and *Siddhartha* are very different. Unlike *Demian*—and indeed, unlike the several major novels of Hesse to follow—*Siddhartha* maintains a stylistic simplicity and an extraordinary harmony of form and substance which Hesse was never again to capture. The book's initial paragraph reveals, even in translation, much of the stylistic genius of *Siddhartha*:

> In the shade of the house, in the sun of the river bank by the boats, in the shade of the Sal forest, in the shade of the fig tree Siddhartha grew up, the handsome son of the Brahman, the young falcon, along with Govinda, his friend, the son of the Brahman.

The paratactic repetitions—incantatory, alliterative, and often threefold in nature—give the work an almost liturgical quality that is consonant with the novel's theme and setting and that exerts a subliminal but obviously well-calculated effect on the reader. Hesse's following work was to be a radical departure in terms of both style and narrative tack.

STEPPENWOLF

Steppenwolf, published in 1927, is certainly Hesse's most unorthodox novel, one that Mann compared to James Joyce's *Ulysses* (1922) and André Gide's *Les Faux-monnayeurs* (1925; *The Counterfeiters*, 1927) in experimental daring. Like these novels, Hesse's work met with a great deal of criticism, a fact that is easily explained in the light of the demands that these narratives place on their readers. Although it is in places essentially surrealistic and is hence somewhat difficult to recapitulate adequately, *Steppenwolf* does evidence Hesse's typical three-part structure: a preliminary or introductory segment, a somewhat realistic central section, and a final part chronicling the protagonist's experiences in a "Magic Theater."

An unnamed and self-described "bourgeois, orderly person" functions as the author of an introduction to the reflections of Harry Haller, whose first-person jottings he is editing. This editor also articulates the two poles of existence, the inner tension of Harry Haller, namely, his fundamental dichotomy as both "wolf" and "bourgeois." The schizophrenic protagonist, a scholarly aesthete and conformist by day but at night an outsider who despises society and its values, describes himself as a living dualism: "I don't know why it is, but I—the homeless Steppenwolf and lonely hater of the petty bourgeois world—I always live in proper middle-class houses." Haller's ruminations on his rootless existence are interrupted, however, by the interjection of a "Tract of the Steppenwolf," a booklet which he has mysteriously acquired while on one of his frequent nocturnal walks. This tract, prefaced by the motto "only for madmen," distinguishes between three levels of existence: that of the Bourgeois, that of the Immortals (the highest plane, which transcends all polarities), and that of the Steppenwolf, a level midway between the first two. In describing a particular Steppenwolf called Harry, the document suggests that he abandon polarity as a life-ordering principle and simply affirm all that is as good, and do so with "a sublime wisdom that can only be realized through humor." Harry Haller is unable to comply, however, and he soon takes up with several sympathizers. Hermine, an oracular prostitute, and Pablo, a drug-using saxophone player, show Haller that there are others of his ilk who choose not to conform to society and yet are happy among themselves. Finally, Harry enters into the "Magic Theater" alluded to in the "Tract" and announced earlier in the novel as well. In this penny arcade of the mind, he sheds the final vestiges of his bourgeois personality by means of a series of surreal, drug-induced experiences. The novel concludes on a note of cautious optimism, with Haller projecting that he will someday "play the game of figures better," that he will someday "learn how to laugh."

As Hesse made obvious by the choice of Harry Haller as his protagonist's name, *Steppenwolf* is a highly autobiographical work. Haller's physiognomy, habits, and tastes are Hesse's, as is his basic psychological dilemma. Hesse at the time of the novel's composition was a fifty-year-old man looking inward and outward with little satisfaction. This accounts for the self-laceration as well as the cultural pessimism of *Steppenwolf*, and such disharmony and negativity reflect an inner relapse on the part of the author of the placid *Siddhartha*. Whether Hesse himself indulged in the erotic and chemical adventures of his protagonist is not known and, ultimately, is of little consequence. Certain, however, is the fact that Hesse suffered a good deal of censure as a result of these elements of the book, a fact which distressed him greatly and which caused him to compose and publish in 1928 a poetic postlude to the novel, entitled *Krisis*, a candid personal account of his intention in writing *Steppenwolf* and an assessment of the literary realization of this intention.

Like those of many of Hesse's novels, the ending of *Steppenwolf* is abrupt and unsatisfactory. The concept of humor as a tool for rising above inner and outer tensions seems an inadequate solution for Haller's problems, and one senses that this is a very forced conclusion. This feeling is reinforced as well by the amazing formal pendulations of Hesse's novels: *Demian* employs psychological symbolism, *Siddhartha* utilizes psychological exoticism, and *Steppenwolf* uses psychological fantasy and even hallucination in order to delineate the same essential problems (How does one arrive at any true self-definition? How is one to reconcile inner polarities, the flesh and the spirit? What is the artist's place in society?) via a variety of expressive modes. If the endings are often truncated or lacking in aesthetic closure, it is because these individual "fragments of a long confession" (Hesse's phrase) represent only one phase, one segment of a process that was to continue. It is no surprise, therefore, that Hesse chose in his next novel yet another narrative format with which to allegorize his dualistic dilemmas.

NARCISSUS AND GOLDMUND

Much like *Siddhartha, Narcissus and Goldmund* can be viewed as a lull following a storm. Hesse himself described *Narcissus and Goldmund* as an essentially escapist tale, and it is the novel about which his critics are most divided. Joseph Mileck, for example, considers it Hesse's finest work, whereas Theodore Ziolkowski flatly states that it is his "most imperfect" work; many critics find the story cloying and regard the novel as a whole as highbrow kitsch.

The names of the two protagonists are symbolic: Narcissus represents the world of the spirit—in this case, the medieval monastery—and is a prototype of the introverted, reflective, self-preoccupied individual; Goldmund (golden mouth) is an artistic extrovert who personifies the world of nature, of the flesh. Hesse once again presents the reader with types rather than with flesh-and-blood characters. Narcissus is the mentor of Goldmund in a monastic school

called Mariabronn, but it soon becomes evident that the latter is rather unsuited for a celibate life. He leaves the monastery and leads a life replete with varied experiences and love affairs, all of which lead him closer to his artistic crystallization of the "pole of nature," exemplified in his mind by the image of his mother and eventually by Eve, the "primal mother."

Related to these love-thematics is the stark reality and insuperable dominance of death, which Goldmund seeks to conquer by love. Both protagonists discuss the topic of death and confront it, each in his own manner: Narcissus seeks to exist in a timeless realm of the spirit which in itself is a preparation for death, while Goldmund, hearing in his heart but dreading "the wild song of death," abandons himself to life and love. Sensing this to be an unsatisfactory *modus vivendi* in the light of the transitory nature of everything human, yet unable to accept Narcissus's way as his own, Goldmund eventually discovers in art his answer to death: "When, as artists, we create images or, as thinkers, seek laws and formulate thoughts, we do so in order to save something from the Great Dance of Death, to establish something that has a longer duration than we ourselves." Goldmund dies in peace, having returned to the monastery not as an ascetic, but as an artist.

The underlying idea or conception of art personified in Goldmund is Hesse's own, at least in that it represents his personal ideal. That this ideal is in essence a Romantic one is clear if one outlines the narrative trellis on which the Goldmund character is strung: He represents the vital vagrant who, by dint of a wealth of contacts and experiences, is impelled (if only temporarily) to recede from the din of life in order to internalize, incubate, and finally express what he has encountered in the Orphic creation of a new and timeless work of art. It is in a certain sense true, therefore, that the Hesse who published from 1898 to 1930 never went beyond Romanticism, beyond this conception of the self as the font of meaning and progenitor of all art. This explains as well why realistic fiction was of little importance to Hesse; if literary art is conceived of as an array of self-reflecting mirrors, then exterior reality can be of only secondary or even tertiary significance. It is to Hesse's credit that he came to see that such self-preoccupation was tantamount to irresponsible self-paralysis, and that this *l'art pour l'art* approach was abandoned in his final novel.

Shortly after Hesse's *Narcissus and Goldmund*, his *The Journey to the East* appeared, in 1932. The novel is another experiment in narrative technique and setting and is perhaps the most esoteric of Hesse's works. In many ways, this story of "H. H."— of his acceptance into an Order, his participation in a "journey to the East," and his defection and eventual return to the fold—prefigures the dynamics and thematics of Hesse's final novel, *The Glass Bead Game*, published in 1943. The latter took eleven years to compose and is considered by many critics to be Hesse's most substantive novel, his *magnum opus*, which recapitulates but also modifies all that preceded it.

THE GLASS BEAD GAME

The Glass Bead Game is a modified *Bildungsroman* about Josef Knecht, whose surname means "servant," and is seen by some critics as Hesse's response to the quintessential German novels of education, Johann Wolfgang von Goethe's Wilhelm Meister novels (the surname meaning "master"). Hesse's novel contains three chief divisions: an introduction describing the history of the "glass bead game," characterized as "the quintessence of intellectuality and art, the sublime cult, the *unio mystica* of all separate members of the *universitas litterarum*"; the middle section, which outlines the life of Josef Knecht; and finally an appendix, consisting of some of Knecht's supposed posthumous papers.

The novel is set in the twenty-fourth century in a "pedagogical province" called Castalia, in which, in at least quasi-monastic fashion, an elite group dedicates itself to the life of the spirit and the highly developed glass bead game. The latter has evolved in the course of time from a relatively simple game played on an abacus frame into a complex interdisciplinary exercise combining quantitative and theoretical knowledge from various disciplines with symbology and meditation. Knecht becomes a master game-player, the *magister ludi* and head of the Order.

Gradually, however, inspired partly by his conversations with a brilliant Benedictine monk by the name of Pater Jakobus and partly by his own nagging feelings of responsibility to the world at large, Knecht's reservations about Castalia and its life of utter aestheticism grow to the point that he resigns his post and leaves the rarefied realm he seemed destined from his very youth to lead. Three days after doing so, however, he drowns by accident in an icy mountain lake.

Hesse's final novel is many interesting things, not the least of which is a very clever *roman à clef* whose name-games and onomastics can occupy one inclined to puzzle over them for some time. More significantly, however, the work represents a personal breakthrough for Hesse, since in Knecht one is at last presented with a Hessean protagonist who attempts to overcome his paralytic self-enclosure and accept some notion of social responsibility. Theodore Ziolkowski has suggested that this gesture, represented clearly by Knecht's decision to leave Castalia and commit himself to something practical, was not Hesse's original intention, but that the imminent outbreak of war forced Hesse to abandon his initial literary and aesthetic ideal while writing the second section of the novel. This is more than plausible, and it would explain as well the book's narrative shift regarding the depiction of Castalia.

A stylistic comparison of *The Glass Bead Game* with Hesse's earlier works reveals that language has been given less attention in this final novel, the result in part of the work's heavy freight of theoretical and philosophical ideas (ranging from a theory of music to intellectual concerns of various kinds). Indeed, Josef Knecht is even less a flesh-and-blood persona than Hesse's customary protagonists.

As to the glass bead game itself—described in length but always in somewhat nebulous terms—it appears clear that it symbolizes the attempt on the part of some to achieve an integrated synthesis of what is good or salvageable from the fragmented debris of modern civilization. In this respect, Hesse's last novel marks a fitting conclusion to a lifelong quest for spiritual wholeness.

N. J. Meyerhofer

OTHER MAJOR WORKS

SHORT FICTION: *Eine Stunde hinter Mitternacht*, 1889; *Hinterlassene Schriften und Gedichte von Hermann Lauscher*, 1901; *Diesseits: Erzählungen*, 1907; *Nachbarn: Erzählungen*, 1908; *Umwege: Erzählungen*, 1912; *Aus Indien*, 1913; *Am Weg*, 1915; *Schön ist die Jugend*, 1916; *Märchen*, 1919 (*Strange News from Another Star and Other Tales*, 1972); *Piktors Verwandlungen: Ein Märchen*, 1925; *Die Nürnberger Reise*, 1927; *Kleine Welt: Erzählungen*, 1933; *Stunden im Garten: Eine Idylle*, 1936; *Traumfährte: Neue Erzählungen und Märchen*, 1945 (*The War Goes On*, 1971); *Späte Prosa*, 1951; *Beschwörungen*, 1955; *Gesammelte Schriften*, 1957; *Stories of Five Decades*, 1972.

POETRY: *Romantische Lieder*, 1899; *Unterwegs: Gedichte*, 1911; *Musik des Einsamen: Neue Gedichte*, 1915; *Gedichte des Malers*, 1920; *Ausgewählte Gedichte*, 1921; *Krisis*, 1928; *Trost der Nacht: Neue Gedichte*, 1929; *Vom Baum des Lebens*, 1934; *Neue Gedichte*, 1937; *Die Gedichte*, 1942; *Späte Gedichte*, 1946; *Poems*, 1970.

NONFICTION: *Boccaccio*, 1904; *Franz von Assisi*, 1904; *Zarathustras Wiederkehr: Ein Wort an die deutsche Jugend von einem Deutschen*, 1919; *Blick ins Chaos*, 1920 (*In Sight of Chaos*, 1923); *Betrachtungen*, 1928; *Kleine Betrachtungen*, 1941; *Krieg und Frieden: Betrachtungen zu Krieg und Politik seit dem Jahr 1914*, 1946, rev. ed. 1949 (*If the War Goes On . . . Reflections on War and Politics*, 1971); *Hermann Hesse: Essays*, 1970; *Autobiographical Writings*, 1972; *My Belief: Essays on Life and Art*, 1974; *Reflections*, 1974.

BIBLIOGRAPHY

Boulby, Mark. *Hermann Hesse: His Mind and Art.* Ithaca, N.Y.: Cornell University Press, 1967. A standard study of Hesse's career, with separate chapters on *Siddhartha* and *Steppenwolf*, a biographical note, and a bibliography.

Field, George Wallis. *Hermann Hesse.* New York: Twayne, 1970. Chapters on Hesse's early years, his Romanticism, his major novels, and his work as poet and critic. This introductory study includes a chronology, notes, and bibliography.

Freedman, Ralph. *Hermann Hesse: Pilgrim of Crisis.* New York: Pantheon, 1978. A well-told biography with notes but no bibliography.

Otten, Anna, ed. *Hesse Companion.* Albuquerque: University of New Mexico Press, 1977. Includes essays on Hesse's life and art, *Siddhartha*, *Steppenwolf*, and other aspects of his literary career. Provides a vocabulary and glossary section and bibliography.

Richards, David G. *Exploring the Divided Self: Hermann Hesse's "Steppenwolf" and Its Critics.* Columbia, S.C.: Camden House, 1996. An excellent study of the seminal novel. Includes bibliographical references and an index.

Rose, Ernst. *Faith from the Abyss: Herman Hesse's Way from Romanticism to Modernity.* New York: New York University Press, 1965. A compact biographical and literary study. Includes a bibliography.

Sorell, Walter. *Herman Hesse: The Man Who Sought and Found Himself.* London: Oswald Wolff, 1974. Chapters on Hesse as culture hero, the artist as a young man, his view of East and West, his humor, and the critic's meeting with Hesse. Contains a bibliography.

Stelzig, Eugene L. *Hermann Hesse's Fictions of the Self: Autobiography and the Confessional Imagination.* Princeton, N.J.: Princeton University Press, 1988. A scholarly exploration of the way Hesse incorporated his life into his fiction. Provides detailed notes but no bibliography.

Tusken, Lewis W. *Understanding Hermann Hesse: The Man, His Myth, His Metaphor.* Columbia: University of South Carolina Press, 1998. Tusken examines Hesse's major novels, including *Siddhartha*, *Narcissus and Goldmund*, and *The Glass Bead Game*.

Ziolkowski, Theodore, ed. *Hesse: A Collection of Critical Essays.* Englewood Cliffs, N.J.: Prentice-Hall, 1973. Contains essays on Hesse's major fiction as well as on his place in German literature. The introduction, chronology, and bibliography make this a particularly useful introduction to Hesse.

PATRICIA HIGHSMITH

Born: Fort Worth, Texas; January 19, 1921
Died: Locarno, Switzerland; February 4, 1995

PRINCIPAL LONG FICTION

Strangers on a Train, 1950
The Price of Salt, 1952 (as Claire Morgan; also
    published as *Carol*)
The Blunderer, 1954
The Talented Mr. Ripley, 1955
Deep Water, 1957
A Game for the Living, 1958
This Sweet Sickness, 1960
The Cry of the Owl, 1962
The Two Faces of January, 1964
The Glass Cell, 1964
The Story-Teller, 1965
Those Who Walk Away, 1967
The Tremor of Forgery, 1969
Ripley Under Ground, 1970
A Dog's Ransom, 1972
Ripley's Game, 1974
Edith's Diary, 1977
The Boy Who Followed Ripley, 1980
People Who Knock on the Door, 1983
The Mysterious Mr. Ripley, 1985 (includes *The Tal-
    ented Mr. Ripley*, *Ripley Under Ground*, and
    Ripley's Game)
Found in the Street, 1986
Ripley Under Water, 1991
Small g: A Summer Idyll, 1995

OTHER LITERARY FORMS

In addition to her novels, Patricia Highsmith wrote several collections of short stories, including *The Snail-Watcher and Other Stories* (1970), *The Animal-Lover's Book of Beastly Murder* (1975), *Slowly, Slowly in the Wind* (1979), *The Black House* (1981), *Mermaids on the Golf Course and Other Stories* (1985), and *Tales of Natural and Unnatural Catastrophes* (1987). In 1966, she published a how-to book, *Plotting and Writing Suspense Fiction*, which provides a good introduction to her work. It was re-

printed and expanded three times by the author. She also wrote one children's book in collaboration with a friend, Doris Sanders, *Miranda the Panda Is on the Veranda* (1958). Although Highsmith wrote prize-winning short stories, she is best known for her novels, especially the Ripley series.

ACHIEVEMENTS

Highsmith was honored several times. For her first published story, "The Heroine," written while she was a student at Barnard College, she was included in the *O. Henry Prize Stories of 1946*. The novel *The Talented Mr. Ripley* was awarded the Grand Prix de Littérature Policière in 1957 and the Edgar Allan Poe Scroll from the Mystery Writers of America. For *The Two Faces of January* she received the Award of the Crime Writers Association of Great Britain.

BIOGRAPHY

Patricia Highsmith's mother, father, and stepfather were all commercial artists. She was born a few months after her mother, Mary Coates, and father, Jay Bernard Plangman, were divorced, and she lived the first six years of her life with her grandmother in the house where she was born, in Fort Worth, Texas.

At six, she went to New York to join her mother and stepfather in a small apartment in Greenwich Village. She later went to high school in New York City and on to Barnard College. Life with quarreling parents made her unhappy, but she did inherit from them a love of painting, and she considered it as a vocation. She ultimately decided to be a writer because she could explore moral and intellectual questions in more depth by writing novels than by painting. Highsmith enjoyed early success with a short story she wrote in college which was later published in *Harper's Bazaar* and included in the *O. Henry Prize Stories of 1946*.

Attracted to travel early, she set out for Mexico in 1943 to write a book. With only part of it written, she ran out of money and returned to New York, where she continued living with her parents and writing comics in the day and fiction at night and on the weekends in order to save enough money to go to Eu-

(Archive Photos)

rope. She left for Europe in 1949, after finishing her first novel, *Strangers on a Train*, which was bought and made into a film by Alfred Hitchcock.

The next few years saw Highsmith traveling between Europe and New York and writing novels and short stories that found publishers in New York and throughout Europe. After several visits, she moved permanently to Europe, first to England for four years, then to France (to a small town near Fontainebleau, which became the setting for later Ripley stories), and finally to Switzerland in 1982. When she died in a hospital in Locarno in 1995, she left an estate of more than five million dollars. Highsmith was a solitary figure, shunning reporters and publicity. She lived alone with her favorite cat, Charlotte, working in her garden and painting. She revisited the United States but never returned to live.

ANALYSIS

Highsmith remains less a household name than other, more traditional crime novelists largely because she wrote about good men who turn bad and

bad men who escape punishment. A moral compass is missing in her work, and guilt is hard to assign. She is better known and more interesting to critics in Europe, especially in England and Germany, than in her own country, which she left permanently in 1963. In a final tribute at the time of her death in 1995, critic Michael Tolkin wrote that the Hitchcock adaptation of her first published novel, *Strangers on a Train*, in which only the psychopath is permitted to kill, "is a perfect example of the kind of American cultural repression that I like to imagine as one of the reasons she left."

Yet in Europe too, her heroes who "kill not without feeling," says critic Susannah Clapp in *London Review of Books*, "but without fear of reprisal" have brought cries of disapproval. In a 1965 review of *The Glass Cell*, one critic declared, "There are not many nastier fiction worlds than Patricia Highsmith's and soon they sicken." Margharita Laski wrote in *The Listener*, "I used to be the only person I knew who loathed Patricia Highsmith's work for its inhumanity to man, but our numbers are growing." On the other hand, a number of respected crime writers, including Julian Symons, consider her among the best crime writers and at least one of her novels a work of true literature. American novelist and critic Gore Vidal wrote, "She is one of our greatest modernist writers."

Her killers or near-killers are middle class and intelligent; they are usually artists or professionals, and they often have sophisticated tastes. In a 1980 interview with Diana Cooper-Clark, Highsmith explained why this is so. Since she believes that most criminals are not particularly intelligent, they do not interest her very much. She chooses middle-class characters because she thinks writers can write successfully only about their own social milieu. Since "standards of morality come from the society around," pleasant, well-mannered men often commit murder in her fictional world: "The contrast between respectability and murderous thoughts is bound to turn up in most of my books." The five novels about Tom Ripley focus on an otherwise nice young man who gets away with murder. Critics have analyzed this unlikely killer in considerable detail.

In the 1980's and 1990's there was renewed interest in Highsmith as a lesbian writer. In most of her novels women are not the active center; they do not commit murder. When asked about this, she explained that she found men more violent by nature than women. Women seemed passive to her, less likely to create action. Her women characters are among her least admirable. They often seem present only as decor or as a means of furthering the actions of the male characters. There are three novels that represent a degree of exception to this pattern. *The Price of Salt* (later published as *Carol*) is the story of two women who fall in love, and the novel—"a very up-beat, pro-lesbian book," according to its editor, Barbara Grier—has a relatively happy ending. *Edith's Diary*, the only other Highsmith novel with a woman at the center, was viewed more as a commentary of American political and social life in the 1960's than as a suspense novel. Her last book, *Small g: A Summer Idyll*, about gays, lesbians, and the human immunodeficiency virus (HIV), could not find an American publisher and was published in England to mixed reviews. Feminists find little support in Highsmith's work. Feminist critic Odette L'Henry Evans observed in a 1990 essay that the women are not loving wives and mothers, and it is often the father who loves and cares for the child.

If Highsmith has a philosophy, it could best be described as a negative one, difficult to identify except as a rebellion against the moral status quo. In spite of the disturbing and pessimistic conclusion that readers must draw from her work—that justice is seldom truly important in human affairs, that it is a "man-made conceit," in the words of critic Brooks Peters—she is recognized as a crime writer who has important things to say about human nature and who says them uncommonly well.

Russell Harrison, in the first full-length study of Highsmith, categorized most of the best known of her novels. The early novels may generally be considered stories of American domestic life: *Deep Water*, *This Sweet Sickness*, and *The Cry of the Owl*. In the 1960's, according to Harrison, Highsmith began to examine U.S. foreign relations and political and social issues in *The Tremor of Forgery*, *A Dog's Ransom*, and *Edith's Diary*. Finally, he examines the gay and lesbian novels, *The Price of Salt* and *Small g: A Summer Idyll*. Two important novels he does not discuss are *The Glass Cell* and *The Two Faces of January*, which might be grouped with the social-issue novels.

THE TALENTED MR. RIPLEY

The Talented Mr. Ripley was the author's favorite book, and Tom Ripley is her most popular character. Highsmith once said that writing fiction was a game to her and that she had to be amused to keep writing. The game here is keeping Ripley out of the hands of the police, and much of the fun lies in allowing him to live high on his ill-gotten gains. "I've always had a lurking liking for those who flout the law," Highsmith once admitted. Tolkin described Ripley aptly as "a small-time American crook who moves to Europe and kills his way to happiness." Highsmith was at odds with herself about Ripley's true value. He stands in sharp contrast to stereotypical morality, which is often hypocritical, but he also has almost no conscience and so is, in Highsmith's words, "a little bit sick in the head."

Dickie Greenleaf, a rich young man who has left home and his disapproving parents to become a painter in Italy, is Ripley's first victim. Ripley arrives on the scene, sent by the father to persuade Dickie to return. Ripley decides that he would rather stay and share Dickie's lazy expatriate life. When Dickie becomes angry about Ripley's imitation of him, Ripley decides to eliminate the real Dickie and take his place. Ripley's real talent is this imitation—he once thought of becoming an actor—and he succeeds in deceiving everyone until Freddie, an old friend of Dickie, becomes suspicious. It is necessary for Ripley to murder again in order not to be unmasked. Freddie is killed, but the police suspect Tom/Dickie of the crime. So Dickie is twice murdered, and Tom Ripley is reborn—along with a fake will in which Dickie leaves him everything. One critic finds this protean man a very contemporary type, one often found in serious literature. Ripley is indeed a classic of his kind, and while Highsmith's touch is almost playful, some readers shudder at Ripley's indifference to his own ghastly crimes. As the Ripley stories multiplied, some readers and critics alike worried that Highsmith had grown too fond of her talented but diabolical hero who is in some ways a monster.

THE GLASS CELL

The dreariness of the style of *The Glass Cell* is the dreariness of its prison atmosphere. There is very little relief from the monotony of wrongfully convicted Philip Carter's life in prison, and there are no scenes of the high life to enjoy. In *Plotting and Writing Suspense Fiction*, Highsmith provides a case history of how three versions of this novel came to be written.

The idea came from a true story, but the story changed as Philip Carter became a Highsmith protagonist. To be interesting, he had to become more active as the novel evolved, and so he kills not once but three times. The alibi he concocts for the murders is coldly calculated; prison has made a ruthless man of him. Highsmith says that she wanted Carter to go free after he commits two postprison murders because he had suffered so much in prison. He had been strung up by his thumbs by a sadistic guard, and he suffers continual physical pain in his hands. The police suspect him of murder but can prove nothing, and Carter and his wife and son are free to go on with their lives together. Highsmith delivers her own kind of justice to a once-innocent man unjustly punished by the courts.

Lucy Golsan

OTHER MAJOR WORKS

SHORT FICTION: *The Snail-Watcher and Other Stories*, 1970 (also known as *Eleven*); *Kleine Geschichten für Weiberfeinde*, 1974 (*Little Tales of Misogyny*, 1977); *The Animal-Lover's Book of Beastly Murder*, 1975; *Slowly, Slowly in the Wind*, 1979; *The Black House*, 1981; *Mermaids on the Golf Course and Other Stories*, 1985; *Tales of Natural and Unnatural Catastrophes*, 1987.

NONFICTION: *Plotting and Writing Suspense Fiction*, 1966.

CHILDREN'S LITERATURE: *Miranda the Panda Is on the Veranda*, 1958 (with Doris Sanders).

BIBLIOGRAPHY

Brophy, Brigid. *Don't Never Forget: Collected Views and Reviews*. New York: J. Cape, 1966. Brophy claims that Highsmith and Georges Simenon are the only two crime writers whose books transcend the limits of the genre while strictly obeying its rules. An interesting discussion of both writers, who have created art out of what is usually a game.

Contemporary Literary Criticism. Vol. 102. Detroit: Gale Research, 1998. Pages 166-221 of this volume contain an extensive collection of criticism. This source also contains an excellent general essay on Highsmith and her work. Bibliographical items are very helpful. See also volumes 2, 4, 14, and 48 for earlier essays and criticism.

Harrison, Russell. *Patricia Highsmith*. New York: Twayne, 1997. The only full-length scholarly study of Highsmith's work to have appeared as of the 1990's. The bibliography, which includes items in German, is generally helpful although not complete.

Reilly, John M., ed. *Twentieth Century Crime and Mystery Writers*. New York: Macmillan, 1980. On pages 765-768 Highsmith is identified as a serious fiction writer whose studies of guilt do not always end in crimes being punished. There is a discussion of the Ripley novels and the "brooding menacing atmosphere" of the more somber novels.

Summers, Claude J., ed. *Gay and Lesbian Literary Heritage*. New York: H. Holt, 1995. Includes an excellent essay by Gina Macdonald on Highsmith's life work to the time of her death in 1995.

Symons, Julian. "Patricia Highsmith: Criminals in Society." *London Magazine*, June, 1969, 37-43. A good place to begin in a study of Highsmith's work. Symons claims that Highsmith is a more serious writer than most who write about crime and that *The Two Faces of January*, one of her finest novels, is a true work of literature.

Tolkin, Michael. "In Memory of Patricia Highsmith." *Los Angeles Times Book Review*, February 12,

1995, 8. A tribute to Highsmith as "our best expatriate writer since Henry James," and an excellent analysis of why her heroes, especially Ripley, are not appreciated in America.

Vinson, James, ed. *Contemporary Novelists*. 2d ed. New York: St. Martin's Press, 1974. A statement of purpose by Highsmith is followed by assessments of Ripley, of novels involving paired men, and of innocence punished in her novels.

JAMAKE HIGHWATER

Born: Place unknown; probably early 1930's

PRINCIPAL LONG FICTION

Anpao: An American Indian Odyssey, 1977
Journey to the Sky, 1978
The Sun, He Dies, 1980
Legend Days, 1984
The Ceremony of Innocence, 1985
Eyes of Darkness, 1985
I Wear the Morning Star, 1986
Kill Hole, 1992
Dark Legend, 1994
Rama, 1994
The Ghost Horse Cycle, 1997 (includes *Legend Days*, *The Ceremony of Innocence*, and *I Wear the Morning Star*)

OTHER LITERARY FORMS

Published under the name J. Marks, the early works of Jamake (juh-MAH-kuh) Highwater include *Rock and Other Four Letter Words* (1968) and *Mick Jagger: The Singer, Not the Song* (1973). *Moonsong Lullaby* (1981), relating the importance of the moon in American Indian culture, is a tale for young children. Highwater has also published books on Native American painting, artists, and history through art as well as on Native American dance and ceremonies. Other book-length publications include five editions of *Europe Under Twenty-five: A Young Person's Guide* (1971) and *Indian America: A Cultural and Travel Guide* (1975). This latter book, the first Fodor guide on American Indians, is important not only as a guide for tourists but also as a study of the history and cultures of American Indians. Highwater has also written short fiction and magazine articles as well as scripts for television shows.

Highwater published the nonfiction work *The Language of Vision: Meditations on Myth and Metaphor* in 1994. *Songs for the Seasons* (1995) is a children's book in which Highwater tells a tale of two red-tailed hawks. Highwater interprets the lifestyle changes facing the hawks during different seasons; illustrations are by Sandra Speidel. *The Mythology of Transgression: Homosexuality as Metaphor* (1997) is a weighty essay focused on the homophobic tendencies of Western culture.

ACHIEVEMENTS

Highwater has been recognized for a variety of talents. Novelist John Gardner said of Highwater that "he is one of the purest writers at work—a clean, clear voice." In addition to writing books and articles, Highwater hosted, wrote, and narrated *Songs of the Thunderbird* (1979) for the Public Broadcasting Service. In the field of music, Highwater's interests are diverse and include rock, American Indian, and classical music; he has been a contributing editor of *Stereo Review* and classical music editor of the *Soho Weekly News*.

Highwater has been called "a writer of exceptional vision and power" by Anaïs Nin. Highwater was named a consultant to the New York State Council on the Arts, and at one time he served on the Art Task Panel of the President's Commission on Mental Health. He has also been named an Honorary Citizen of Oklahoma.

Among the honors that Highwater has received, one of the most important to him personally was awarded at the Blackfeet Reserve in Alberta, Canada. Ed Calf Robe, elder of the Blood Reserve of Blackfeet, gave Highwater the name of Piitai Sahkomaapii, which means Eagle Son. This honor, Calf Robe stated, was given because Highwater "soars highest and catches many truths which he carries to many lands." In spite of Highwater's genuine talents and achievements, since the mid-1980's he has been viewed less favorably by some critics because his long-standing claim of American Indian ancestry was found to be essentially insupportable.

BIOGRAPHY

Portions of Highwater's biography are open to question. Until the mid-1980's, Highwater had maintained that he was born in Glacier County, Montana, on February 14, 1942, and that his mother, Amana Bonneville, was of the Blackfeet nation (or was part Blackfoot and part French Canadian) and his father, Jamie, was a Cherokee. His early years, he said, were spent on the Blackfeet Indian Reservation in Montana and in Alberta, Canada, where the Blackfeet people held their summer encampments. At the age of eight, Highwater went to Hollywood with his father, a founding member of the American Indian Rodeo Association and a stunt man in Western films. Highwater said he lived in an orphanage after his father was killed in an automobile accident until his mother remarried. His stepfather, Alexander Marks, a white man, adopted him.

In the mid-1980's, this version of Highwater's life story was called into question by journalists and scholars. Highwater himself eventually intimated that he had invented some of the details. As a result, a new effort was made to construct his biography. The following represents as much of a general consensus as there is.

Highwater was probably born between 1930 and 1933. The place and date of his birth are unknown, because he was given up for adoption by his mother. He was adopted when he was about five years old and lived most of his childhood in the San Fernando Valley, just north of Los Angeles. He was known as Jay or Jack Marks, Marks being the last name of his adoptive parents. In the 1950's he was inspired to continue to pursue a writing career by a correspondence with writer Anaïs Nin. He also became interested in modern dance. He moved to San Francisco; there, with others, he formed a dance company called the San Francisco Contemporary Dancers. Highwater moved to New York in 1967.

Events such as the 1969 takeover of Alcatraz Island by American Indian activists bolstered his already strong interest in Native American issues and culture. Highwater has said that in the mid-1970's his adoptive mother and foster sister told him they believed he had at least some "Indian blood." Around 1974 he changed his name to Jamake Highwater. In the 1970's and 1980's Highwater lived primarily in the Soho section of Manhattan. He founded the Native Land Foundation to promote world folk art and its influence on the modern visual and performing arts.

In the 1980's Highwater's American Indian identity was publicly called into question, and some Indian activists and writers, among them Vine Deloria, Jr., stated their belief that he was not Native American. Highwater was undoubtedly disappointed in a lack of support from his associates regarding his claim to Indian ancestry. In 1992 he moved to Los Angeles and relocated the Native Land Foundation there. His writing generally began to move away from specifically Native American topics.

ANALYSIS

In much of his fiction and nonfiction, Highwater attempts to convey basic American Indian beliefs and presuppositions. When he emphasizes the differences between contemporary American values and those of American Indians, he stresses that there is more than one reality and that one is not necessarily more valid than another. Each reality has its own truths. By expressing the truths of various Indian cultures as he understands them, Highwater attempts to foster the understanding that must precede peaceful coexistence.

ANPAO

Anpao, a Newbery Honor book in 1978, has perhaps received less attention than it deserves. Recognition as an outstanding book for children suggests to some critics that a book is intended only for a young audience. Like Mark Twain's *The Adventures of Huckleberry Finn* (1884), however, *Anpao* may be enjoyed by those of all ages. As an odyssey of the American Indian, *Anpao* is a compilation of legends, an oral history of Indian tribes. Highwater chooses a number of versions from recorded accounts of these legends, giving credit to his sources. The book's hero, Anpao, is his own creation.

The novel begins with Anpao's falling in love with the beautiful Ko-ko-mik-e-is, who agrees to marry him if he will journey to the Sun and get the Sun's permission for her to marry. The quest begins; Anpao, also called Scarface, sets forth. On his journey, he learns that Anpao means "the Dawn" and that his father is the Sun. Anpao's mother was a human who went to the World-Above-the-World without dying. After the birth of her son, Anpao, she becomes homesick and attempts an escape with her son, but manages to get only part way to the earth because the rope that she has woven from sinew is not long enough. When the Sun is taunted by his jealous first wife, the Moon, he becomes angry. He follows the footsteps of his human wife to a hole in the sky. Seeing her dangling just above the trees on earth, he makes a hoop from the branch of a willow tree and orders the hoop to kill the woman but to spare the child. The Sun is not quick enough to snatch the rope when the root which holds the rope in the World-Above-the-World sags because of pity for the dead mother of Anpao. When the child falls onto the dead body of his mother, blood from her body causes a scar to appear on his face. The child, Anpao, lives on the earth, and his journey toward the Sun involves the learning of basic truths of American Indian culture. The legends that he learns on his travels are primarily learned through traditional storytelling, a mode of teaching used not only by Native Americans but also by ancient Greeks and Romans.

Like Homer in the *Iliad* and the *Odyssey* (both c. 800 B.C.E.), Highwater states his theme in the short opening chapter and then moves to the story *in medias res*. Anpao and his twin brother (created when Anpao disobeyed the warning of the Spider Woman, with whom he lived, not to throw his hoop into the air) are poor youths who arrive in the village where the beautiful young girl Ko-ko-mik-e-is lives. After Anpao sets forth on his journey to the Sun, he meets an old woman who tells him the story of the beginning of the world, of the death of the creator Napi, and of his own birth. Then the creation of Oapna, the contrary twin brother of Anpao, is accounted for, and his death is also told. The Clown/Contrary is a familiar figure in American Indian legends.

In another typical Indian legend, Anpao meets with a sorceress, a meeting which invites comparison with Odysseus's meeting with Circe. One of the most important obstacles that Anpao has to overcome is the intense dislike of the Moon, who, as the first wife of the Sun, despises the child born to the human responsible for the Sun's misalliance. Anpao, however, earns the love of the Moon when he saves her son, Morning Star, from death; thus, Anpao becomes the first person to have the power of the Sun, Moon, and Earth.

As a result of his journey to the Sun, Anpao has the ugly scar removed from his face, thus enabling him to prove to Ko-ko-mik-e-is that he did indeed make the journey. The marriage of Anpao (the Dawn and the son of the Sun) and Ko-ko-mik-e-is (Night-red-light, which is related to the Moon) takes place, and Anpao begs the people of Ko-ko-mik-e-is's village to follow the couple as they leave to escape the death, sickness, and greed which are coming to their world. The people will not follow; instead they laugh at Anpao. (This action suggests the lack of unity among American Indians, a lack that may have been crucial to the course of Indian history.) Undaunted, Anpao, taking his beautiful bride with him, goes to the village beneath the water. Ko-ko-mik-e-is is assured by Anpao that what is happening will not be the end, because they and their people are the rivers, the land, the prairies, the rocks—all of nature. This unity with nature is fundamental to American Indian culture.

Most of the legends in *Anpao* belong to times long ago, but Highwater has also included some more modern tales which tell of the arrival of whites with their horses, weapons, and diseases. The legends selected by Highwater are, as American Indian writer N. Scott Momaday says, "truly reflective of the oral tradition and rich heritage of Native American storytelling." The legends, old and new, are the cornerstone of Indian culture.

JOURNEY TO THE SKY

After writing *Anpao*, essentially a mythical journey, Highwater turned to recorded events for material for his next novel, *Journey to the Sky*. This journey is a fictionalized account of the actual explorations of two white men, John Lloyd Stephens, a New York attorney, and Frederick Catherwood, a British artist and architect. Stephens and Catherwood began their first trip in search of the lost cities of the Mayan kingdom in October, 1839. Although the men made two extended trips to the kingdom of the Mayan peoples, Highwater confines his tale to the first exploration, which ended late in July, 1840.

Journey to the Sky is a suspense-filled adventure story that displays Highwater's writing talents more effectively than does his first novel. Although the narrative is interrupted from time to time by Highwater's accounts of later archaeological findings, the suspense and excitement of the journey are sustained throughout. Particularly impressive is Highwater's narrative skill in selecting highlights from the historical account of the Stephens-Catherwood expedition (Stephens did the writing, while Catherwood provided illustrations). Like a number of novels that appeared in the 1970's, including E. L. Doctorow's *Ragtime* (1975) and Aleksandr Solzhenitsyn's *Lennin v Tsyurikhe* (1975; *Lenin in Zurich*, 1976), *Journey to the Sky* is a new kind of historical fiction.

Having been appointed by President Martin Van Buren as U.S. diplomatic agent to the Central American Confederacy, Stephens fulfills his public duties as a diplomat, but his true interest is in the search for ruins. He meets with leaders of various colonies in Central America, paying courtesy calls and extending greetings from the American government. Although Stephens finds the performance of his official duties pleasurable, he is in a hurry to begin explorations.

Early in the trip, while in Belize, the two explorers hire a young cutthroat, Augustin, as their servant. Although they seriously doubt that he will serve them well, by the end of the journey, they realize the rightness of their choice; he proves to be a loyal and valuable servant and friend. They also hire men to help transport their belongings, which include tools, food (including live chickens), and clothing. From time to time, and for differing reasons, new employees must be found.

The trip over Mico Mountain is extremely hazardous because of jungle, rocks, mud, and treacherous gullies. The rough terrain is only one of many natural hazards that they encounter during their explorations in Central America. Insects, climate, earthquakes, and malaria are some of the other forces of nature that they encounter. In addition, they meet such varied characters as the double-dealing Colonel Archibald MacDonald, superintendent of the English colonies in Central America, the petty tyrant Don Gregorio in Copan, good and bad padres, and hospitable and inhospitable people. The explorers are imprisoned, threatened with murder, and surrounded by an active rebellion in Central America.

Highwater captures the enthusiasm of Stephens and Catherwood as they discover the "lost city" just outside Copan. They are the first white men to see these tumbling pyramids and idols, evidence of the religion of the Mayas. Stephens and two helpers begin removing the foliage from rock piles that the people of Copan have been ignoring as piles of rubbish, and Catherwood sets to work documenting their discovery by making drawings of each of the fallen figures. To Stephens, this desolate city with its many magnificent works of art is evidence that the Mayas were master craftsmen.

Having located and documented the ruins at Copan, Stephens and Catherwood move to other sites, where they find further evidence of the Mayan culture. Even illness cannot deter them. From one site to another, the explorers continue their amazing trip. Although warned not to go to Palenque because of the danger to whites as a result of political upheaval, they go. There they find ruins that are quite different from those in Copan. After documenting the Palenque ruins, they go to Uxmal. Many times during the journey in Central America, the New York attorney and the British artist are warned about the hostile Indians, yet the Indians are often more hospitable than the white people they encounter. Stephens and Catherwood's discoveries of a Mayan civilization which rose and fell prior to the Spanish invasion corroborate a basic thesis of Highwater's—that American Indian cultures are meaningful and remarkable.

THE SUN, HE DIES

In *The Sun, He Dies*, Highwater once again turned to recorded history to provide a firm base for his story. The conquering of Montezuma II, ruler of the Aztec nation, by the Spaniard Hernando Cortés with a small contingent of men is perplexing to some historians, who sometimes credit Cortés with an unusual amount of tactical knowledge and ability. Highwater, on the other hand, looks carefully at the character of Montezuma and the religious beliefs of this powerful figure and concludes that these elements were the basic causes of his downfall.

Although the downfall of Montezuma is the backdrop for *The Sun, He Dies*, the novel is also an initiation story, a history of an important Aztec ruler, a history of the Aztec people, and an immersion into Native American culture. Highwater creates a narrator, Nanautzin, to tell the story: This narrative voice unifies the episodic material drawn from the oral traditions of American Indian peoples.

Beginning with "Call me Nanautzin," echoing the opening sentence of Herman Melville's *Moby Dick* (1851), *The Sun, He Dies* unfolds in chronological order. In the epic tradition, Nanautzin, the outcast woodcutter, despised by his people, announces his intention to sing of the great Aztec nation. Like Ishmael in *Moby Dick*, he alone is left to tell the story of all that happened.

Nanautzin briefly tells of his early life in his native village, where he is taunted by the children, cast away by his father, and loved by his mother. The ugly scars that signal the beginning of the unhappy life of the narrator are created by his fall, as a small child, into a cooking fire. The resultant deformities cause his father to abandon him and the villagers to name him the Ugly One. Unlike Oedipus, Nanautzin is not physically cast away; he is given an ax, called a woodcutter, and forgotten. He grows up lonely and friendless.

Nanautzin goes to Tenochtitlan for the installation of Montezuma II as the Great Speaker, even though the people of his village, Tlaxcala, loathe the lord of the greatest city in Mexico. Although Nanautzin feels honor for this great man, the trip does nothing to win for him honor or friends among his people. Because of his physical appearance, he remains the Ugly One, despised and rejected.

Eventually, Nanautzin wanders into a marvelous forest, where, although he knows he should not, he begins to chop firewood. Soon a man appears and questions him, demanding to know why he is cutting wood in the forest. The young man blurts out that, since Montezuma has become ruler, the people of Tlaxcala have not been permitted to cut dead wood wherever they wish and life has become very difficult for his people. Instead of being punished on the spot, Nanautzin is ordered to appear at the Palace of Tenochtitlan on the following day.

Fearing for his life, yet obedient, Nanautzin goes to the palace, where he discovers that the stranger he met in the forest is the Great Speaker himself. Instead of receiving punishment for his honest reply to Montezuma on the preceding day, Nanautzin is transformed into the Chief Orator because of his honesty. Then he is taken to the ruins at Tula, the once great city of the ancient Toltecs, where he, along with young boys, is taught by the priests and where he learns that here the greatest of all men once lived. This experience at Tula is both an initiation and a religious experience.

After his experience at Tula, Nanautzin becomes the confidant of Montezuma, who tells him the many legends of his people. Montezuma also confides that, according to his horoscope, his life is balanced between the war god, Huitzilopochtli, who fills the body of Montezuma with power, and the gentle god, Quetzalcoatl, who fills Montezuma's body with love. The Toltecs were the wise people created by the gentle Quetzalcoatl, who, like the Norse god Odin, was a benefactor to his people. Evil people loathed Quetzalcoatl, the tall, noble, holy white god who would not permit his people to be sacrificed. The evil men managed to trick this loving god with a mirror; drunk with pulque, Quetzalcoatl, who had seen his body in the mirror, became passionate and slept with a forbidden priestess. Evil came into the land and Quetzalcoatl went into exile in the land of Yucatan, but promised to return in the year One Reed, at which time he would recapture his throne and bring peace forevermore. Montezuma believes that Quetzalcoatl will return.

Although believing in the return of Quetzalcoatl, Montezuma also believes the horoscope, thus making him susceptible to doubt about himself: Is he one of the evil ones who destroyed this great god or one of the faithful who follow him? On the one hand, he demands tributes and sacrifices from the people, ruling much of the time by force, thus acceding to Huitzilopochtli and alienating many of the tribes. On the other hand, he honors the gentle Quetzalcoatl and longs for his return.

During his early years as Chief Orator, Nanautzin learns the beliefs of this mighty leader and the history of the people. He recognizes the goodness in the Great Speaker of Tenochtitlan. Even though Montezuma appears to be a ruthless ruler, he has been kind to Nanautzin, he admires honesty, and he has great faith in the prediction that Quetzalcoatl will return. Montezuma's faith in the promise of this great and good god indicates the Aztec ruler's devotion to his religion.

From the favorable signs that appear in the year One Reed, Montezuma draws great confidence, but a time comes when the signs change. Montezuma is no longer the almost divine figure that Nanautzin has observed. Instead, the Great Speaker can no longer make up his own mind, which has become so divided that one part is contrary to the other part. Montezuma, like Ahab in *Moby Dick*, becomes a man obsessed. When he learns of the white men who have arrived at Chalco, the Great Speaker concludes that Quetzalcoatl's prediction is about to come true. Although the priests, the soothsayers, the noblemen, and the warriors warn Montezuma that these mysterious men are not Quetzalcoatl and his court, the Great Speaker is not to be shaken in his belief. Because Montezuma has alienated many of the neighboring tribes, he is hated; it is, therefore, easy for Cortés and his troops to enlist the aid of the alienated tribes, including the people of Tlazcala, in the march against Tenochtitlan.

Instead of trying to defend his city, Montezuma makes offerings to Cortés, whom he believes to be the gentle god Quetzalcoatl. It becomes an easy matter for Cortés to enter the realm of Montezuma and then, with the help of the alienated tribes, wreak havoc not only on the Great Speaker but also on the people of Tenochtitlan.

The narrative structure of *The Sun, He Dies* is strong, and the development of the character of Montezuma makes believable the idea that Tenochtitlan falls not because of the tactical superiority of Cortés but because of Montezuma's religious beliefs and obsessions. In addition to the recounting of history, the novel is a collection of tales that are an integral part of the beliefs of the Aztec nation. The Ugly One who becomes the Chief Orator for Montezuma II, although he comes full circle from being a lonely figure in Tlaxcala to being the figure left alone, is far wiser than the ignorant woodcutter Nanautzin who wanders into the forest owned by the Great Speaker. Nevertheless, the once powerful Aztec nation is destroyed and Nanautzin can only sing of what has been.

"What has been" is pertinent to many of Highwater's novels. Based on oral and recorded history, *Anpao*, *Journey to the Sky*, and *The Sun, He Dies*, for example, convey truths of three important American Indian cultures. The Indian respect for and allegiance to the forces of nature determined their actions. The significance of religion in the fall of Montezuma, in the ruins of Yucatan, and in the lives of Native Americans adds another dimension to recorded history.

THE GHOST HORSE CYCLE

Using his knowledge of Native American myth and his own techniques of storytelling, Highwater applied his enthusiasm for the retelling of history to his trilogy, collectively referred to as *The Ghost Horse Cycle*. In the first book, *Legend Days*, the story begins as a mythic chronicle of the character Amana, a young girl of the Blood tribe of the northern plains, who lived in the late nineteenth century. Her people have contracted smallpox from the white traders and are dying in large numbers. Her sister, SoodaWa, sends Amana away; in a strange, dreamlike sequence, Amana is captured by the evil owls, rescued by the kindly foxes, and protected from harm by sleeping in a cave for a year. During that time, she receives a vision in which she becomes a man, a warrior, and hunts with other men. She is given a set of warrior's clothes by her spirit helper, which she must never reveal until the proper time. She returns to her village only to find two old women left, all the rest having died or fled.

Eventually Amana is reunited with her sister SoodaWa and her sister's husband, Far Away Son, who have been living with Big Belly, a chief of the Gros Ventres tribe. Amana marries Far Away Son, as is the custom among the Bloods—orphaned girls marry their sister's husbands. She tries to be a good wife, but secretly her vision makes her long to be a warrior. The story rehearses the agonizing plight of the northern plains tribes as the extensive hunting of buffalo dwindled the supply of food, disease ravaged the population, and the whites' influence, such as whiskey, paralyzed Native American culture.

Legend Days—a book written as a myth and centered in recorded history—reads very much like other Highwater narratives, but *The Ghost Horse Cycle* trilogy is more personal than most Highwater works. Continuing with *Eyes of Darkness* and then with *I Wear the Morning Star*, it becomes evident that the myth only begins the story. Amana eventually weds a French trader named Jean-Pierre Bonneville and has a daughter, Jemina Bonneville, who in turn weds Jamie Ghost Horse, a Native American working as a Hollywood stuntman. They have two children, Reno and Sitko. The focus of the novels turns from the rather hazy myth of *Legend Days* to the concrete story of one family's efforts to survive the onslaught of the modern world in their lives.

Eyes of Darkness chronicles the marriage of Amana and Jean-Pierre, as well as Amana's introduction into white society, a transition that for her is never really successful. Her daughter Jemina's stormy marriage to Jamie Ghost Horse shows Native Americans confronting newly acquired economic realities, newly acquired problems such as alcoholism, and newly acquired stigmas, such as discrimination and racism.

I Wear the Morning Star focuses on Jemina's two children, Reno, who seeks to deny his American Indian heritage, and Sitko, who listens attentively to his grandmother's stories and longs for the old ways. Jemina is forced by circumstance and poverty to place the boys in an orphanage until she remarries a white man named Alexander Miller, and the boys re-

turn to her household only to aggravate further the number of underlying problems each is having. For the grandchildren of Amana, life has become too complex; they live in a world that is neither American Indian nor white, not knowing whether to follow the ways of the whites or to listen to the compelling stories of their grandmother. The need to adopt white customs and practices is apparent, but Sitko especially learns that Grandmother Amana offers something that the whites cannot: "[F]rom Grandmother Amana I learned how to dream myself into existence." Sitko becomes an artist and begins to explore his heritage through his art.

KILL HOLE

In *Kill Hole*, Highwater leads Sitko Ghost Horse, his artist-hero, through life experiences that appear as nightmarish sequences. They bring to light the idea that imagination is the only human identity of consequence. Sitko, an adopted child who has been renamed Seymour Miller by his father, suffers the indignities of this abusive parent who erases Sitko's North American Indian identity. Sitko's grandmother inspires the youth with her tribal stories, compelling him to seek his lost culture. Discovering art as his medium of expression, Sitko makes the visionary connection between his ancestral past of harmony with nature and the present marked by environmental calamities, a plague reminiscent of acquired immunodeficiency syndrome (AIDS), and a breakdown of human connections in a society that exhibits a hatred of art and a fear of the unknown.

In a Kafkaesque desert village, Sitko is tried for being an interloper; unless he can prove that he is a bona fide Indian, he will be put to death. Imprisoned, he comes in contact with a brutish dwarf who instills his hatred of the arts on the villagers he rules. Patu, Sitko's sympathetic supporter, overcomes her fear of art to nurture her compassion for him. Sitko survives prison by recounting his past and bringing truth and art together in picture stories. Highwater concludes his complicated story by affirming the power of artistic imagination over social antagonism. A number of commentators have noted that to some extent the tale represents Highwater's response to the assertions he is not Native American.

DARK LEGEND

Dark Legend provides Highwater a forum for introducing European concepts to non-European settings. The novel is based on the story of Richard Wagner's Ring cycle (1874; *Der Ring des Nibelungen*). It adapts the operatic story to mythic pre-Columbian America. The book teems with gods, goddesses, giants, and other supernatural beings. Magical maidens bathe in a gold-blessed river that loses its precious metal to Caru, a greedy dwarf. In short duration, the thief is captured and the gold is recovered, now forged into a ring and magic crown. Lord Kuwai and his consort Amaru remain worried; the recovered treasure no longer shines. Kuwai's avarice spreads disaster. His zeal for the treasure causes his son's death and estrangement from his only daughter. The valiant warrior Washi collects the gold, falls in love with the daughter, Idera, and returns the metal to the river. The earth becomes balanced again.

Virginia A. Duck, updated by Craig Gilbert

OTHER MAJOR WORKS

NONFICTION: *Rock and Other Four Letter Words*, 1968 (as J. Marks); *Europe Under Twenty-five: A Young Person's Guide*, 1971; *Mick Jagger: The Singer, Not the Song*, 1973 (as J. Marks); *Indian America: A Cultural and Travel Guide*, 1975; *Fodor's Indian America*, 1975; *Song from the Earth: American Indian Painting*, 1976; *Ritual of the Wind: North American Indian Dances and Music*, 1977; *Many Smokes, Many Moons: A Chronology of American Indian History Through Indian Art*, 1978; *Dance: Rituals of Experience*, 1978; *The Sweet Grass Lives On: Fifty Contemporary North American Indian Artists*, 1980; *The Primal Mind: Vision and Reality in Indian America*, 1981; *Arts of the Indian Americas: Leaves from the Sacred Tree*, 1983; *Native Land: Sagas of the Indian Americas*, 1986; *Shadow Show: An Autobiographical Insinuation*, 1986; *Myth and Sexuality*, 1990; *The Language of Vision: Meditations on Myth and Metaphor*, 1994; *The Mythology of Transgression: Homosexuality as Metaphor*, 1997.

CHILDREN'S LITERATURE: *Moonsong Lullaby*, 1981; *Songs for the Seasons*, 1995 (Sandra Speidel, illustrator).

EDITED TEXT: *Words in the Blood: Contemporary Indian Literature of North and South America*, 1984.

BIBLIOGRAPHY

Adams, Phoebe-Lou. "Review of *Song of the Earth*." *The Atlantic* 240 (March, 1977): 117. Adams's short review of this book's American Indian paintings and the commentary that accompanies them is somewhat condescending toward contemporary American Indian art. She mentions several remarks by Buckbear Bosin that she says indicate a reluctance on the part of Native American artists to acknowledge white culture, an approach that Adams finds less than realistic.

Churchill, Ward. *Fantasies of the Master Race: Literature, Cinema, and the Colonization of the American Indians*. Monroe, Maine: Common Courage Press, 1992. An intriguing exposé of the business of pretending to be American Indian. Highwater receives ample attention in the book, and Churchill disputes his claim of North American Indian heritage.

Grimes, Ronald L. "To Hear the Eagles Cry: Contemporary Themes in Native American Spirituality." *The American Indian Quarterly* 20 (June 22, 1996): 433-451. This lengthy multiple-participant discussion focuses on educating American Indians in religious precepts. Highwater serves as a source for several of the concepts discussed in the debate.

Katz, Jane, ed. *This Song Remembers: Self-Portraits of Native Americans in the Arts*. Boston: Houghton Mifflin, 1980. Katz's work includes essays from many different American Indian artists who are active in the visual arts, poetry, literature, and dance. Highwater's self-portrait centers on the importance of myth and Indian culture to his life and art.

Lee, Michael. "Kill Hole." *National Catholic Reporter*, May 28, 1993, p. 38. Lee presents a perceptive critique of Highwater's 1992 novel.

Stott, Jon C. "Narrative Expectations and Textual Misreadings: Jamake Highwater's *Anpao* Analyzed and Reanalyzed." *Studies in the Literary Imagination* 18 (Fall, 1985): 93-105. Highwater's award-winning book *Anpao* is given a thorough critical analysis.